THE OXFORD COMPANION TO

FAIRY TALES

THE OXFORD COMPANION TO

FAIRY TALES

Second edition

EDITED BY JACK ZIPES

OXFORD
UNIVERSITY PRESS

OXFORD

UNIVERSITY PRESS

Great Clarendon Street, Oxford, OX2 6DP,
United Kingdom

Oxford University Press is a department of the University of Oxford.
It furthers the University's objective of excellence in research, scholarship,
and education by publishing worldwide. Oxford is a registered trade mark of
Oxford University Press in the UK and in certain other countries

First published 2000
Issued in paperback 2002
First published online 2005
Second edition 2015

Impression: 1

Published in the United States of America by Oxford University Press
198 Madison Avenue, New York, NY 10016, United States of America

British Library Cataloguing in Publication Data
Data available

Library of Congress Control Number: 2014960116

ISBN 978-0-19-968982-8

Printed in Great Britain by
Clays Ltd, St Ives plc

Contents

List of Contributors

AAR	Amelia A. Rutledge	**KNH**	Karen Nelson Hoyle
AD	Anne Duggan	**KS**	Karen Seago
AL	Alison Lurie	**LCS**	Lewis C. Seifert
ALL	Ann Lawson Lucas	**LS**	Louisa Smith
AMM	Anne-Marie Moscatelli	**MBS**	Mary Beth Stein
AR	Amy Ransom	**MF**	Marcie Fehr
AS	Anita Silvey	**MLE**	Mary Louise Ennis
AZ	Adrienne E. Zuerner	**MN**	Maria Nikolajeva
BH	Betsy Hearne	**MNP**	Maria Nicolai Paynter
BKM	Bettina Kümmerling-Meibauer	**MT**	Maria Tatar
CB	Cristina Bacchilega	**NC**	Nancy Canepa
CFR	Carolina Fernández Rodríguez	**NI**	Niels Ingwersen
CGS	Carole Silver	**NJW**	Naomi J. Wood
CLMF	Claire-Lise Malarte-Feldman	**PAOB**	Patricia Anne Odber de Baubeta
CM	Cheryl McMillan	**PFI**	Philip Furia
CS	Caroline Schatke	**PFN**	Peter F. Neumeyer
CT	Catherine Tosenberger	**PG**	Pauline Greenhill
DH	Donald Haase	**PGS**	P. G. Stanwood
DJB	David J. Buch	**RAS**	Richard A. Schindler
DMT	D. Maureen Thum	**RBB**	Ruth B. Bottigheimer
EMM	Eva-Marie Metcalf	**RD**	Robert Dunbar
EWH	Elizabeth Wanning Harries	**REF**	Robyn Elaine Floyd
GA	Gillian Avery	**RF**	Richard Flynn
GD	Giuseppe Di Scipio	**RM**	Robyn McCallum
GF	Geoffrey Fenwick	**SB**	Stephen Benson
GRB	George R. Bodmer	**SCR**	Steven C. Ridgely
HG	Harriet Goldberg	**SJ**	Shawn Jarvis
HNBC	H. Nicholls B. Clark	**SR**	Suzanne Rahn
IWA	Ian Wojcik-Andrews	**SS**	Sharon Scapple
JAS	John Stephens	**ST**	Susan Tan
JB	Jeannine Blackwell	**SW**	Shira Wolosky
JGH	Joan G. Haahr	**TAS**	Terry Staples
JMM	James M. McGlathery	**TH**	Tom Higgins
JR	Joellyn Rock	**THH**	Thomas H. Hoernigk
JS	Jan Susina	**TSH**	Thomas S. Hischak
JSN	Judith S. Neaman	**TW**	Terri Windling
JZ	Jack Zipes	**UM**	Ulrich Marzolph
KD	Klaus Doderer	**WC**	William Crisman
KMJ	Kendra Magnus-Johnston	**WM**	Wolfgang Mieder

JACK ZIPES was Professor of German and Comparative Literature at the University of Minnesota from 1989 until 2008 when he retired as Professor Emeritus. His many books on fairy tales and associated subjects include *Breaking the Magic Spell: Radical Theories of Folk and Fairy Tales* (1979), *Fairy Tales and the Art of Subversion* (1983), *The Brothers Grimm: From Enchanted Forests to the Modern World* (1988), *Fairy Tale as Myth/Myth as Fairy Tale* (1994), *When Dreams Came True: Classical Fairy Tales and their Tradition* (1999), *Hans Christian Andersen: The Misunderstood Storyteller* (2005), *Why Fairy Tales Stick: The Evolution and Relevance of a Genre* (2006), and *The Irresistible Fairy Tale: The Cultural and Social Evolution of a Genre* (2012). He also edits a book series, *Oddly Modern Fairy Tales*, at Princeton University Press and co-edits the *Palgrave Studies in Contemporary European Culture and History*.

NON-CONTRIBUTING EDITORS

RICHARD LEPPERT, Professor of Cultural Studies and Comparative Literature at the University of Minnesota, is the author of *The Sight and Sound: Music, Representation, and the History of the Body* (1993) and *Art and the Committed Eye* (1999).

CATHERINE VELAY-VALLANTIN (CV-V) is Maître de Conférence at the École des Hautes Études en Sciences Sociales in Paris, France. She is the author of *L'Histoire des contes* (1992).

CONTRIBUTING EDITORS

GILLIAN AVERY is a historian of children's literature whose books include *Childhood's Pattern* (1975) and *Behold the Child: American Children and their Books 1621–1922* (1994).

CRISTINA BACCHILEGA is Professor of English at the University of Hawai'i at Manoa, and author of *Postmodern Fairy Tales: Gender and Narrative Strategies* (1997) and *Fairy Tales Transformed? Twenty-First Century Adaptations & the Politics of Wonder* (2013). She is co-editor of *Marvels & Tales: Journal of Fairy-Tale Studies*.

JEANNINE BLACKWELL is Professor of German and Women's Studies at the University of Kentucky, and co-editor of the anthologies *Bitter Healing: German Women Writers 1700–1840* (1990) and *The Queen's Mirror: Fairy Tales by German Women, 1780–1900* (2001).

RUTH B. BOTTIGHEIMER, Adjunct Professor of Comparative Literature at the State University of New York at Stony Brook, is the editor of *Fairy Tales and Society* (1986) and the author of *Grimms' Bad Girls and Bold Boys* (1987) and *Fairy Tales: A New History* (2009).

NANCY CANEPA, Associate Professor of French and Italian at Dartmouth College, is the editor of *Out of the Woods: The Origins of the Literary Fairy Tale in Italy and France* (1997) and author of *From Court to Forest: Giambattista Basile's 'Lo cunto de li cunti' and the Birth of the Literary Fairy Tale* (1999).

PROFESSOR KLAUS DODERER is the founder and former director of the Institut für Jugendbuchforschung at the Johann-Wolfgang-Goethe-Universität in Frankfurt am Main. He has published numerous books and essays on topics dealing with children's literature and fairy tales.

HARRIET GOLDBERG, Professor of Spanish at Villanova University, is the author of *Motif-Index of Medieval Spanish Folk Narratives* (1998).

PAULINE GREENHILL, Professor of Women's and Gender Studies at the University of Winnipeg, has authored a number of articles and books on fairy tales including *Fairy Tale Film and Cinematic Folklore: Visions of Ambiguity* (2010) with Sydney Eve Matrix and *Channeling Wonder: Fairy Tales on Television* (2014) with Jill Terry Rudy.

DONALD HAASE, Professor of German Studies at Wayne State University, is the editor of *The Reception of Grimms' Fairy Tales: Responses, Reactions, Revisions* (1993), *Feminist Fairy-Tale Scholarship* (2004), and *The Greenwood Encyclopedia of Folktales and Fairy Tales* (2007). He served as editor of *Marvels & Tales: Journal of Fairy-Tale Studies* for twenty years.

NIELS INGWERSEN, Professor of Scandinavian Studies at the University of Wisconsin, Madison, was director of the Folklore Program, and has published on narrative folklore.

ALISON LURIE, Professor of Folklore and Children's Literature at Cornell University, is the author of *Don't Tell the Grownups* (1990) and three collections of folk tales for children.

KENDRA MAGNUS-JOHNSTON, PhD student in the department of English, Film & Theatre at the University of Manitoba, has published several articles on Hans Christian Andersen and the Brothers Grimm.

MARIA NIKOLAJEVA, Professor of Education at the University of Cambridge, is the author of *The Magic Code: The Use of Magical Patterns in Fantasy for Children* (1988), *Children's Literature Comes of Age: Toward a New Aesthetics* (1996), and *Power, Voice and Subjectivity in Literature for Young Readers* (2006). She has also co-edited *How Picturebooks Work* (2001).

LEWIS C. SEIFERT, Associate Professor of French Studies at Brown University, is the author of *Fairy Tales, Sexuality, and Gender in France, 1690–1715* (1996) and co-edited *French Women Writers* (2010).

MARIA TATAR, Professor of German at Harvard University, is the author of *The Hard Facts of the Grimms' Fairy Tales* (1987), *Off with their Heads! Fairy Tales and the Culture of Childhood* (1992), and *Secrets Beyond the Door: The Story of Bluebeard and his Wives* (2006).

JACK ZIPES, General Editor.

CONTRIBUTORS

STEPHEN BENSON, Senior Lecturer in Literature at East Anglia University, is the author of *Cycles of Influence: Fiction, Folklore, Theory* (2003).

GEORGE R. BODMER, Professor of English at Indiana University Northwest, has published on illustration and the American picture book.

DAVID J. BUCH, Professor of Music History at the University of Northern Iowa, has written *Magic Flutes and Enchanted Forests: Music and the Marvelous in the Eighteenth-Century Musical Theatre* (2008).

H. NICHOLS B. CLARK, an art historian, is Chief Curator at the Eric Carle Museum of Picture Book Art.

WILLIAM CRISMAN, Associate Professor of English, Comparative Literature, and German at Pennsylvania State University at Altoona, is the author of *The Crises of 'Language and Dead Signs' in Ludwig Tieck's Prose Fiction* (1997).

GIUSEPPE DI SCIPIO, Professor of Italian at City University of New York/Hunter College, is the author of works on Dante and editor of *Telling Tales: Medieval Narratives and the Folk Tradition* (1998).

ANNE DUGGAN, Professor of French at Wayne State University in Detroit and Co-Editor of *Marvels & Tales*, is the author of *Salonnières, Furies, and Fairies: The Politics of Gender and Cultural Change in Absolutist France* (2005) and *Queer Enchantments: Gender and Class in the Fairy-Tale Cinema of Jacques Demy* (2013).

ROBERT DUNBAR, lecturer in English at the Church of Ireland College of Education, Dublin, is editor of the anthologies *First Times* (1997) and *Enchanted Journeys* (1997).

MARY LOUISE ENNIS, Professor of French Literature at Wesleyan University in Connecticut, has published on gardens, clandestine literature, and fairy tales.

MARCIE FEHR, currently a graduate student at the University of Winnipeg, has published several articles on North American folklore.

GEOFFREY FENWICK, author of *Teaching Children's Literature in the Primary School* (1990), specializes in reading studies and children's literature at the Department of Education and Community Studies at John Moores University, Liverpool.

CAROLINA FERNÁNDEZ RODRÍGUEZ, Assistant Professor at the University of Oviedo, Spain, is the author of *Las nuevas hijas de Eva: re/escrituras feministas del cuento de 'Barabazul'* (1997) and *Las re/escrituras contemporáneas de 'Cenicienta'* (1997).

ROBYN FLOYD, Assistant Principal of Glen Iris Primary School in Melbourne, is writing her PhD dissertation on Australian fairy tales and Olga Ernst.

RICHARD FLYNN, Professor of English at Georgia Southern University, is the author of *Randall Jarrell and the Lost World of Childhood* (1990).

PHILIP FURIA, Chair, Department of English at the University of North Carolina at Wilmington, is the author of *The Poets of Tin Pan Alley: A History of America's Great Lyricists* (1990).

JOAN G. HAAHR, Professor of English at Yeshiva University, has published on the medieval amatory tradition, medieval historiography, and Chaucer's poetry.

ELIZABETH WANNING HARRIES, Professor of English and Comparative Literature at Smith College, is the author of *The Unfinished Manner: Essays on the Fragment in the Later Eighteenth Century* (1994) and *Twice Upon a Time: Women Writers and the History of the Fairy Tale* (2003).

BETSY HEARNE is Professor Emerita in the Graduate School of Library and Information Science at the University of Illinois, Urbana-Champaign, and is the author of *Beauty and the Beast: Visions and Revisions of an Old Tale* (1989).

TOM HIGGINS was formerly Associate Conductor of the Kingston Orpheus Society and is currently Music Director of Opera South and the Richmond Symphonic Wind Ensemble.

THOMAS S. HISCHAK, Professor of Theatre at the State University of New York College at Cortland, is the author of *Word Crazy: Broadway Lyricists from Cohan to Sondheim* (1991) and *Stage it with Music: An Encyclopedic Guide to the American Musical Theatre* (1993).

THOMAS H. HOERNIGK teaches German literature and history in Berlin and writes regularly on music for German publications.

KAREN NELSON HOYLE, Professor Emerita, was Head Curator of the Children's Literature Research Collections at the University of Minnesota Libraries, and is the author of *Wanda Gág* (1994).

SHAWN JARVIS, Professor of German at St Cloud State University, Minnesota, is the editor of two critical editions of fairy tales by Gisela von Arnim and is co-editor of *The Queen's Mirror: Fairy Tales by German Women Writers, 1780–1900* (2001).

BETTINA KÜMMERLING-MEIBAUER, Professor in German at the University of Tübingen, Germany, is the editor of *Current Trends in Comparative Children's Literature Research* (1995) and *Klassiker der Kinder- und Jugendliteratur* (1998).

ANN LAWSON LUCAS, Lecturer in Italian at the University of Hull, is the translator and editor of *The Adventures of Pinocchio* (1996) and has edited *The Presence of the Past in Children's Literature* (2003).

ROBYN MCCALLUM is Lecturer of English at Macquarie University, Australia and is the author of *Ideologies of Identity in Adolescent Fiction* (2002). She is also co-author of *Retelling Stories, Framing Culture: Traditional Story and Metanarratives in Children's Literature* (1998) and co-editor of *New World Orders in Contemporary Children's Literature: Utopian Transformations* (2008).

JAMES M. MCGLATHERY, Professor Emeritus of German and Comparative Literature at the University of Illinois at Urbana-Champaign, is the author of books on the Grimms' fairy tales, E. T. A. Hoffmann, Richard Wagner, and Heinrich von Kleist.

CHERYL MCMILLAN, Ph.D. candidate at Macquarie University, Australia, was researching postmodernism in young adult fiction until her untimely death in 2001.

CLAIRE-LISE MALARTE-FELDMAN, Professor of French at the University of New Hampshire in Durham, is the author of *Charles Perrault's Critique since 1960: An Annotated Bibliography* (1989).

ULRICH MARZOLPH, Professor of Islamic Studies at the University of Göttingen and senior member of the editorial committee of the *Enzyklopädie des Märchens*, is the author of *Arabia ridens* (1992), and editor of *Grimms Märchen International* (1995), *The Arabian Nights Encyclopedia* (2003), and *The Arabian Nights in Transnational Perspective* (2007).

EVA-MARIA METCALF, Professor of German at the University of Mississippi, is the author of *Astrid Lindgren* (1995).

WOLFGANG MIEDER, Professor of German and Folklore in the Department of German and Russian at the University of Vermont, is the author of *Grimms Märchen-modern: Prosa, Gedichte, Karikaturen* (1979), *Tradition and Innovation in Folk Literature* (1987), *Hänsel und Gretel: Das Märchen in Kunst, Musik, Literatur, Medien, und Karikaturen* (2007), and *'Proverbs Speak Louder Than Words': Folk Wisdom in Art, Culture, Folklore, History, Literature, and Mass Media* (2008).

ANNE-MARIE MOSCATELLI, Associate Professor of Languages at West Chester University, Pennsylvania, works on Rabelais, Francophone literature, and comparative studies on French and Italian fairy tales.

JUDITH S. NEAMAN, Professor of English at Yeshiva University, has written numerous articles on medieval optics, art, and literature.

PETER F. NEUMEYER has taught at universities in Europe and the United States and is a regular children's book reviewer for the *Boston Globe*.

PATRICIA ANNE ODBER DE BAUBETA is a Senior Lecturer and Director of Portuguese Studies at the University of Birmingham, and has published on medieval Portuguese literature.

MARIA NICOLAI PAYNTER, Professor of Italian at City University of New York/Hunter College, is the author of *Ignazio Silone: Beyond the Tragic Vision* (2000).

SUZANNE RAHN, Associate Professor in the English Department at Pacific Lutheran University, is the author of *Rediscoveries in Children's Literature* (1995) and *The Wizard of Oz: Shaping an Imaginary World* (1998).

AMY RANSOM, Professor of French at the University of Montevallo, is the author of *The Feminine as Fantastic in the Conte fantastique: Visions of the Other* (1995).

STEVEN C. RIDGELY, Assistant Professor of Japanese at the University of Wisconsin, Madison, is the author of *The Antiestablishment Art of Terrayama Shūji* (2010).

JOELLYN ROCK, Assistant Professor of Digital Art in the Department of Art and Design at the University of Minnesota, Duluth, has created various websites on fairy tales and also illustrated Sicilian folk and fairy tales collected by Laura Gonzenbach.

AMELIA A. RUTLEDGE, Associate Professor of English at George Mason University, has published on science fiction, Merlin, Italo Calvino, Philip Pullman, and Richard Wagner.

SHARON SCAPPLE teaches children's and adolescent literature at Minnesota State University-Moorhead and has written extensively on fairy tales.

CAROLINE SCHATKE has studied English and German Literature at the University of Hanover, Germany, and Corpus Christi College, Oxford, specializing in fairy tales, children's literature, and the Gothic novel.

RICHARD A. SCHINDLER, Associate Professor of Art at Allegheny College in Meadville, Pennsylvania, has published on Joseph Noel Paton and Victorian fairy painting, and is himself an illustrator of fantasy and science fiction.

KAREN SEAGO is Director of the MA Translating Popular Culture at City University London and has published on the reception of the Grimms' fairy tales in English translation and on Angela Carter.

CAROLE SILVER, Professor of English at Stern College, Yeshiva University, is the author of *Strange and Secret Peoples: Fairies and Victorian Consciousness* (1998).

ANITA SILVEY, editor of *Children's Books and their Creators* (1995) and author of *Children's Book-A-Day Almanac* (2012), served as Vice-President and Publisher, Children's Books, at Houghton Mifflin from 1995–2001.

LOUISA SMITH, Professor Emerita of English at Mankato State University, served as co-editor of *The Lion and the Unicorn*.

P. G. STANWOOD, Professor of English at the University of British Columbia, is co-editor of *The Selected Prose of Christina Rossetti* (1998) and the author of essays on seventeenth- and twentieth-century opera.

TERRY STAPLES is a freelance teacher and cinema researcher, author of *All Pals Together: The Story of Children's Cinema* (1997) and *Film in Victorian Britain* (1998).

MARY BETH STEIN, Associate Professor of German and International Affairs at George Washington University in Washington, DC, has written extensively on German folklore and East German culture.

JOHN STEPHENS, Professor Emeritus of English at Macquarie University, Australia, is the author of *Language and Ideology in Children's Fiction* (1992) and co-author of *Retelling Stories, Framing Culture: Traditional Story and Metanarratives in Children's Literature* (1998). He has also edited *Ways of Being Male: Representing Masculinities in Children's Literature and Film* (2002) and co-edited *New World Orders in Contemporary Children's Literature* (2008).

JAN SUSINA, Professor of English, specializing in children's and adolescent literature, at Illinois State University, is the author of *The Place of Lewis Carroll in Children's Literature* (2009).

SUSAN TAN, currently a graduate student at the University of Cambridge, has published essays on fantasy and children's literature.

MAUREEN THUM, Director of the Honors Program at the University of Michigan-Flint, has published on Wilhelm Hauff, the Brothers Grimm, and folkloric motifs in literature.

CATHERINE TOSENBERGER, Associate Professor of English at the University of Winnipeg, has written several articles on the Harry Potter series and on fandom and fanzines.

TERRI WINDLING, writer, artist, and editor with Ellen Datlow of sixteen anthologies of contemporary fiction based on fantasy, horror stories, and fairy tales, has published three fairy-tale inspired novels, *The Wood Wife* (1996), *The Moon Wife* (2012), and *Little Owl* (2012). She has also edited *The Armless Maiden* (1995), an important collection of essays dealing with fairy tales.

IAN WOJCIK-ANDREWS, Professor of English at Eastern Michigan University, is the author of *Children's Films: History, Ideology, Pedagogy, and Theory* (2000).

SHIRA WOLOSKY, Professor of English at the Hebrew University of Jerusalem, is the author of *The Riddles of Harry Potter: Secret Passages and Interpretative Quests* (2012) and *Feminist Theory Across Disciplines: Feminist Community and American Women's Poetry* (2013).

NAOMI J. WOOD, Professor of English at Kansas State University, has published on Philip Pullman, C. S. Lewis, and on nineteenth-century literary fairy tales by George Mac-Donald, Charles Kingsley, and Lucy Clifford.

ADRIENNE E. ZUERNER, Associate Professor of French at Skidmore College in New York, has published on Corneille, Mme d'Aulnoy, and Mme de Villedieu.

Introduction

𝒯HERE is no such thing as the fairy tale; however, there are hundreds of thousands of fairy tales. And these fairy tales have been defined in so many different ways that it boggles the mind to think that they can be categorized as a genre. In fact, the confusion is so great that most literary critics continually confound the oral folk tale with the literary fairy tale and vice versa. Some even argue, to the dismay of folklorists, that we might as well label any text or narrative that calls itself and is called a fairy tale as such since the average reader is not aware of the distinction between the oral and literary traditions or even cares about it. Why bother with distinctions when very few people necessarily want them? There is even a strong general tendency among many readers in the West to resist defining the fairy tale. It is as though one should not tamper with sacred material. By dissecting the fairy tale, one might destroy its magic, and it appears that this magic has something to do with the blessed realm of childhood and innocence.

On the other hand, almost every reader of fairy tales, young and old, is curious about their magic. What is it that endows fairy tales with such enchantment? Where do these tales come from? Why do they have such a grip on us? Why do we always seem to need them? We want to know more about ourselves by knowing something more about fairy tales. We want to fathom their mysterious hold on us. Perhaps this is why there are literally hundreds of scholarly books and essays about the tales, and why the more serious studies insist on making a distinction between the oral folk tale and the literary fairy tale. It is distinction that preserves the unique socio-historical nature of genres. It is distinction that exposes the magic of a genre while at the same time allowing us to preserve and cultivate it so that it will continue to flourish.

One of the first German scholars to analyse the literary fairy tale systematically in our contemporary period is Jens Tismar, who has written two important studies, *Kunstmärchen* (1977) and *Das deutsche Kunstmärchen des zwanzigsten Jahrhunderts* (1981). In his first short monograph, Tismar set down the principles for a definition of the literary fairy tale (*das Kunstmärchen*) as genre: (1) it distinguishes itself from the oral folk tale (*das Volksmärchen*) in so far as it is *written* by a single identifiable author; (2) it is thus synthetic, artificial, and elaborate in comparison to the indigenous formation of the folk tale that emanates from communities and tends to be simple and anonymous; (3) the differences between the literary fairy tale and the oral folk tale do not imply that one genre is better than the other; (4) in fact, the literary fairy tale is not an independent genre but can only be understood and defined by its relationship to the oral tales as well as to the legend, novella, novel, and other literary fairy tales that it uses, adapts, and remodels during the narrative conception of the author.

Tismar's principles are helpful when contemplating the distinguishing features of the literary fairy tale. But there are many other distinctions that must be made, and this *Companion* is one of the first major efforts in the English language to make some of these distinctions and to define the socio-historical rise of the fairy tale mainly in the nation-states of Western Europe and North America that share common literary traditions. It also seeks to provide information on all the writers, artists, musicians, film-makers, and movements that have contributed to the changing nature of the fairy tale as genre. Whenever possible, the contributions of other cultures from Eastern Europe, the Middle East, Asia, South America, and Africa have been included, but the focus of this *Companion* is essentially on the *literary* formation of the Western fairy-tale genre and its expansion into opera, theatre, painting, photography, and film, and other related cultural forms.

During its long evolution, the literary fairy tale distinguished itself as genre by 'appropriating' many motifs, signs, and drawings from folklore, embellishing them and combining them with elements from other literary genres, for it became gradually necessary in the modern world to adapt a certain kind of oral storytelling called the wonder tale to standards of literacy and make it acceptable for diffusion in the public sphere. The fairy tale is only one type of literary appropriation of a particular oral storytelling tradition related to the oral wonder tale, often called the *Zaubermärchen* or the *conte merveilleux,* which existed throughout Europe in many different forms during the medieval period. As more and more wonder tales were written down in the 14th, 15th, 16th, and 17th centuries—often in Latin—they constituted the genre of the literary fairy tale that began establishing its own conventions, motifs, topoi, characters, and plots, based to a large extent on those developed in the oral tradition but altered to address a reading public formed by the aristocracy, clergy, and middle classes. Though the peasants were marginalized and excluded in the formation of this literary tradition, their material, voices, style, and beliefs were incorporated into the new genre during this period.

What exactly is the oral wonder tale? This is a question that is almost impossible to answer because each village and community in Europe and in North America developed various modes of storytelling in thousands of dialects and different types of tales closely connected to their customs, laws, morals, and beliefs. But Vladimir Propp's now famous study, *The Morphology of the Folk Tale* (1928), can be some-what helpful here. Using 600 texts from Aleksandr Afanasyev's *Russian Folktales*

(1855–63), he outlined 31 basic functions that constitute the formation of a paradigmatic wonder tale, which was and still is common in Russia and shares many properties with wonder tales throughout the world. By functions, Propp meant the fundamental and constant components of a tale that are the acts of a character and necessary for driving the action forward. Consequently, most plots will follow a basic pattern which begins with the protagonist confronted with an interdiction or prohibition which he or she violates in some way. This leads to the banishment of the protagonist or to the assignment of a task related to the interdiction or prohibition.

His or her character will be marked by the task that becomes his or her assigned identity and destiny. Afterwards the protagonist will have encounters with all sorts of characters: a deceitful villain; a mysterious individual or creature, who gives the protagonist gifts; three different animals or creatures who are helped by the protagonist and promise to repay him or her; or three different animals or creatures who offer gifts to help the protagonist, who is in trouble. The gifts are often magical agents, which bring about miraculous change. Since the protagonist is now endowed with gifts, he or she is tested or moves on to deal with inimical forces. But then there is a sudden fall in the protagonist's fortunes that is generally only a temporary setback. A wonder or miracle is needed to reverse the wheel of fortune. The protagonist makes use of endowed gifts (and this includes magical agents and cunning) to achieve his or her goal. Often there are three battles with the villain; three impossible tasks that are miraculously completed; or the breaking of a magic spell through some counter-magical agent. The inimical forces are vanquished. The success of the protagonist usually leads to marriage and wealth. Sometimes simple survival and acquisition of important knowledge based on experience form the ending of the tale.

Propp's structural approach to the wonder tale, while useful, should be regarded with caution because there are innumerable variations in theme and plot types throughout Europe and North America. In fact, the wonder tale is based on a hybrid formation that encompassed the chronicle, myth, legend, anecdote, and other oral forms and constantly changed depending on the circumstances of the teller. If there is one 'constant' in the structure and theme of the wonder tale that was also passed on to the literary fairy tale, it is *transformation*—to be sure, miraculous transformation. Everybody and everything can be transformed in a wonder tale. In particular there is generally a change in the social status of the protagonists. For the peasants who constituted the majority of the population in the Middle Ages, the hope for change was embedded in this kind of narrative, and this hope had nothing to do with a systematic and institutionalized belief system. That is, the tales told by the peasants were secular, and the fortuitous changes and happenings that occur in the tales cannot be predicted or guaranteed.

Rarely do wonder tales end unhappily in the oral tradition. They are wish fulfilments. They are obviously connected to initiation rites that introduce listeners to the 'proper' way to become a member of a particular community. The narrative elements issue from real-life experiences and customs to form a paradigm that facilitates recall for tellers and listeners. The paradigmatic structure enables teller and listeners to recognize, store, remember, and reproduce the stories and to change them to fit their experiences and desires due to the easily identifiable characters who are associated with particular assignments and settings. For instance, many tales concern a simple fellow named Jack, Hans, Pierre, or Ivan who is so naive that he seems as if he will never do well in life. He is often the youngest son, and his brothers and other people take advantage of him or demean him. However, his goodness and naïveté eventually enable him to avoid disasters. By the end of the tale he generally rises in social status and proves himself to be more gifted and astute than he seems. Other recognizable characters in wonder tales include: the Cinderella girl who rises from the ashes to reveal herself to be more beautiful than her stepsisters; the faithful bride; the loyal sister; the vengeful discharged soldier; the boastful tailor; the cunning thief; devious robbers; ferocious ogres; the unjust king; the queen who cannot have a child; the princess who cannot laugh; a flying horse; a talking fish; a magic sack or table; a powerful club; a kind duck; a sly fox; treacherous nixies; a beast bridegroom. The forests are often enchanted, and the settings change rapidly from the sea to glass and golden mountains. There are mysterious underground realms and caves. Many tales are about the land of milk and honey where everything is turned upside down, and the peasants rule and can eat to their heart's content. The protagonist moves faster than jet planes on the backs of griffins and eagles or through the use of seven-league boots. Most important are the capes or clothes that make the hero invisible or magic objects that endow him with power. In some cases there are musical instruments with enormous captivating powers; swords and clubs capable of conquering anyone or anything; lakes, ponds, and seas that are difficult to cross and serve as the home for supernatural creatures. The characters, settings, and motifs are combined and varied according to specific functions to induce *wonder*. It is this sense of wondrous change that distinguished the wonder tales from other oral tales as the chronicle, the legend, the fable, the anecdote, and the myth; it is clearly the sense of wondrous change that distinguishes the *literary* fairy tale from the moral story, novella, sentimental tale, and other modern short literary genres. Wonder causes astonishment, and the marvellous object or phenomenon is often regarded as a supernatural occurrence and can be an omen or portent. It gives rise to admiration, fear, awe, and reverence. In the oral wonder tale, listeners are to ponder about the workings of the universe where anything can happen at any time, and these happy or fortuitous events are never to be explained. Nor do the characters demand an explanation—they are opportunistic. They are encouraged to be so, and if they do not take advantage of the opportunity that will benefit them in their relations with others, they are either stupid or mean-spirited. Only the 'good' opportunistic protagonist succeeds because he or she is open to and wants a change. In fact, most heroes need some kind of wondrous transformation to survive, and they indicate how to take advantage of the unexpected opportunities that come their way. The tales seek to awaken our regard for the marvellous *changing* condition of life and to evoke in a religious sense profound feelings of awe and respect for life as a miraculous process which can be altered and changed to compensate for the lack of power, wealth, and pleasure that most people experience. Lack, deprivation, prohibition, and interdiction motivate people to look for signs of fulfilment and emancipation. In the wonder tales, those who are naive and simple are able to succeed because they are untainted and can recognize the wondrous signs. They have retained their belief in the miraculous condition of nature and revere nature in all its aspects. They have not been spoiled by conventionalism, power, or rationalism. In contrast to the humble characters, the villains are those who use their status, weapons, and words intentionally to exploit, control, transfix, incarcerate, and destroy for their benefit. They have no respect or consideration for nature and other human beings, and they actually seek to abuse magic by preventing change and causing everything to be transfixed according to their interests. The wondrous protagonist wants to keep the process of natural change flowing and indicates possibilities for overcoming the obstacles that prevent other characters or creatures from living in a peaceful and pleasurable way.

The focus on wonder in the oral folk tale does not mean that all wonder tales, and later the literary fairy tales, served and serve a liberating purpose, though they tend to conserve a utopian spirit. Nor were they subversive, though there are strong hints that the narrators favoured the oppressed protagonists. The nature and meaning of folk tales have depended on the stage of development of a tribe, community, or society. Oral tales have served to stabilize, conserve, or challenge the common beliefs, laws, values, and norms of a group. The ideology expressed in wonder tales always stemmed from the position that the narrator assumed with regard to the developments in his or her community, and the narrative plot and changes made in it depended on the sense of wonder or awe that the narrator wanted to evoke. In other words, the sense of wonder in the tale and the intended emotion sought by the narrator is ideological. The oral tales have always played some role in the socialization and acculturation of listeners. Certainly, the narratives were intended to acquaint people with learning experiences so that they would know how to comport themselves or take advantage of unexpected opportunities. The knowledge imparted by the oral wonder tales involves a learning process through which protagonist and listener are enriched by encounters with extraordinary characters and situations.

Since these wonder tales have been with us for thousands of years and have undergone so many different changes in the oral tradition, it is difficult to determine clearly what the ideological intention of the narrator was; and if we disregard the narrator's intention, it is often difficult to reconstruct (and/or deconstruct) the ideological meaning of a tale. In the last analysis, however, even if we cannot establish whether a wonder tale is ideologically conservative, sexist, progressive, liberating, etc., it is the celebration of wondrous change and how the protagonist reacts to wondrous occurrences that account for its major appeal. In addition, these tales nurture the imagination with alternative possibilities to life at 'home', from which the protagonist is often banished to find his or her 'true' home. This pursuit of home accounts for the utopian spirit of the tales, for the miraculous transformation does not only involve the transformation of the protagonist but also the realization of a more ideal setting in which the hero/heroine can fulfil his or her potential. In fairy tales home is always a transformed home opening the way to a different future or destiny than the hero or heroine had anticipated.

Ultimately, the definition of both the wonder tale and the fairy tale, which derives from it, depends on the manner in which a narrator/author arranges known functions of a tale aesthetically and ideologically to induce wonder and then transmits the tale as a whole according to customary usage of a society in a given historical period. The first stage for the literary fairy tale involved a kind of class and perhaps even gender appropriation. The voices of the non-literate tellers were submerged. Since women in most cases were not allowed to be scribes, the tales were scripted according to male dictates or fantasies, even though many were told by women. Put crudely, one could say that the literary appropriation of the oral wonder tales served the hegemonic interests of males within the upper classes of particular communities and societies, and to a great extent this is true. However, such a crude statement must be qualified, for the writing down of the tales also preserved a great deal of the value system of those deprived of power. And the more the literary fairy tale was cultivated and developed, the more it became individualized and varied by intellectuals and artists, who often sympathized with the marginalized in society or were marginalized themselves. The literary fairy tale allowed for new possibilities of subversion in the written word and in print, and therefore it was always looked upon with misgivings by the governing authorities in the civilization process.

The literary fairy tale is a relatively young and modern genre. Though there is a great deal of historical evidence that oral wonder tales were written down in India, Persia, and Egypt thousands of years ago, and all kinds of folk motifs of magical transformation became part and parcel of national epics and myths throughout the world, the literary fairy tale did not really establish itself as a genre in Europe and later in North America until some new material and socio-cultural conditions provided fruitful ground for its formation. The most significant developments from 1450 to 1700 include: the standardization and categorization of the vernacular languages that gradually became official nation-state languages; the invention of the printing press; the growth of reading publics throughout Europe that began to develop a taste for short narratives of different kinds for their reading pleasure; the conception of new literary genres in the vernacular and their acceptance by the educated elite classes.

Literary fairy tales were not at first called fairy tales, nor can one with certainty say that they were simple appropriations of oral folk tales that were popular among the common people. Indeed, the intersection of the oral tradition of storytelling with the writing and publishing of narratives is definitely crucial for understanding the formation of the fairy tale, but the oral sources were not the only ones that provided the motifs, characters, plot devices, and topoi of the genre. The early authors of fairy tales were generally extremely well educated and well read, and drew upon both oral and literary materials when they created their fairy tales. Beginning with Apuleius' fairy tale 'Cupid and Psyche', part of *The Golden Ass*, which appeared in the 2nd century AD, we can see that the fairy tale distinguished itself from the oral tradition—as it did throughout the early medieval period— through carefully constructed plots, sophisticated references to religion, literature, and customs, embellished language that signified the high civilized status of the writer, and linguistic codes that were informed by a particular civilizing process and carried information about it.

Contained in chivalric romances, heroic sagas and epics, chronicles, sermons, poems, lais, and primers during the European Middle Ages, the fairy tale was often a story about miraculous encounters, changes, and initiations illustrating a particular didactic point that the writer wished to express in an entertaining manner. It was often written in Latin, Middle English, or in some old high form of French, Spanish, Italian, or German. For the most part, these early fairy tales were not intended for children. In fact, they were not intended for most people since most people could not read. The fairy tale was thus marked by the social class of the writers and readers, and since the clerics dominated literary production in Latin up through the late Middle Ages, the 'secular' if not hedonistic fairy tale was not fully acceptable in European courts and cities, and it was certainly not an autonomous literary genre.

In the late 13th century the anonymous collection *Novellino* (*The Hundred Old Tales*), with its fantastic themes, unusual medieval exempla, and fables, indicated along with other medieval marvellous tales and reports that new literary genres were about to flower, and in the 14th century writers like Boccaccio (*The Decameron*, 1349–50) and Chaucer (*The Canterbury Tales*, 1387) helped prepare the way for the establishment of the fairy tale as an independent genre. Although they did not write 'pure' fairy tales per se, many of their stories—and these were not the only writers who influenced the development of the fairy tale—have fairy-tale motifs and structures and borrow from oral wonder tales. Moreover, the frame narratives that they created allowed for the introduction of diverse tales told in different modes and styles, and it is the frame that became extremely important for Giovan Francesco Straparola in his *Le piacevoli notti* (*The Pleasant Nights*, 1550–53) and for Giambattista Basile in *Lo cunto de li cunti* (*The Tale of Tales*) better known as *Il Pentamerone* (1634–6), for they used their frames to produce some of the most illustrious literary fairy tales in the West that were to influence major writers of the genre in the 16th, 17th, and 18th centuries.

In many ways the tales of Straparola and Basile can be considered crucial for understanding the rise of the genre. Straparola wrote in succinct Tuscan or standard Italian, and Basile wrote in a Neapolitan dialect marked by an elaborate baroque style with striking metaphors and peculiar idioms and references that are difficult to decipher today. Though all their fairy tales have moral or didactic points, they have very little to do with official Christian doctrine. On the contrary, their tales are often bawdy, irreverent, erotic, cruel, frank, and unpredictable. The endings are not always happy. Some are even tragic; many are hilarious. Some tales are very short, but most are somewhat lengthy, and they are all clearly intended to represent and reflect upon the mores and customs of their time, to shed light on the emerging civilizing process of Italian society. From the beginning, fairy tales were symbolic commentaries on the mores and customs of a particular society and the classes and groups within these societies and how their actions and relations could lead to success and happiness.

Although other Italian writers such as Cesare Cortese and Pompeo Sarnelli created fairy tales in the 17th century, the conditions in the different reading publics in Italy were not propitious for the genre to take root. The oral tradition and the 'realistic' novellas and stories remained dominant in Italy. This was also the case in Great Britain. Although there was a strong interest in fairylore in the 1590s, as indicated by *The Faerie Queene* (1590-96) written by Sir Edmund Spenser, who was influenced by Italian epic poetry, and although Shakespeare introduced fairies and magical events in some of his best plays such as *A Midsummer Night's Dream* and *The Tempest*, the trend in English society was to ban the fairies and to make way for utilitarianism and puritanism. There were, of course, some interesting attempts in poetry by Ben Jonson, Michael Drayton, and Robert Herrick to incorporate folklore and fairy-tale motifs in their works. But the waning interest in fairy tales and the obstacles created by censorship undermined these literary attempts. Fortunately, oral storytelling provided the refuge for fairy beliefs.

It was not until the 1690s in France that the fairy tale could establish itself as a 'legitimate' genre for educated classes. It was during this time that numerous gifted female writers such as Mme d'Aulnoy, Mme d'Auneuil, Mme de Murat, Mlle Lhéritier, Mme de La Force, Mlle Bernard, and others introduced fairy tales into their literary salons and published their works, and their tales, along with those of Charles Perrault and Jean de Mailly, initiated a mode or craze that prepared the ground for the institution of the literary fairy tale as a genre. First of all, the French female writers 'baptized' their tales *contes de fées* or fairy tales, and they were the first to designate the tales as such. The designation is not simply based on the fact that there are fairies in all their tales but also on the fact that the seat of power in their tales—and also in those of Perrault and other male writers of the time—lies with omnipotent women. Similar to the tales of Straparola and Basile, whose works were somewhat known by the French, the *contes de fées* are secular and form discourses about courtly manners and power. The narratives vary in length from 10 to 60 pages, and they were not at all addressed to children. Depending on the author, they are ornate, didactic, ironic, and mocking. In the period between 1690 and 1705, the tales reflected many of the changes that were occurring at King Louis XIV's court, and Perrault wrote his tales consciously to demonstrate the validity of this 'modern' genre as opposed to the classical Greek and Roman myths. Many of the tale types can be traced to the oral folk tradition, and they also borrow from the Italian literary fairy tale and numerous other literary and art works of this period. In addition to the accomplishments of the first wave of French authors, mention should be made of Antoine Galland and his remarkable translation of Arabic narratives in *Les Mille et une nuits* (*The Thousand and One Nights*, 1704-17). Not only did Galland introduce the tradition and customs of the Middle East to Western readers, but he also imitated the oriental tales and created his own—something hundreds of authors would do in the centuries that followed up through our present times.

By 1720, at the very latest, the fairy tale was being institutionalized as genre, and the paradigmatic form and motifs were becoming known throughout Europe. This dissemination of the tales was due in large part to the dominance of French as the cultural language in Europe. But there were other ways in which the French tales became known and set a pattern for most fairy-tale writers. It was during this time that chapbooks or 'cheap' books were being produced in series such as the *Bibliothèque bleue*, and the books were carried by pedlars from village to village to be sold with other goods. The 'sophisticated' tales of the upper-class writers were abbreviated and changed a great deal to address other audiences. These tales were often read aloud and made their way into or back into the oral tradition. Interestingly, the tales were retold innumerable times and circulated throughout diverse regions of Europe, often leading to some other literary appropriation and publication. In addition, there were numerous translations into English, German, Spanish, and Italian. Another important development was the rise of the literary fairy tale for children. Already during the 1690s, Fénelon, the important theologian and Archbishop of Cambrai, who had been in charge of the Dauphin's education at King Louis XIV's court, had written several didactic fairy tales to make the Dauphin's lessons more enjoyable. But they were kept for private use and were printed only in 1730 after Fénelon's death. More important than Fénelon was Mme Leprince de Beaumont, who published *Le Magasin des enfants* (1757), which included 'Beauty and the Beast' and ten or so overtly moralistic fairy tales for girls. Leprince de Beaumont was one of the first French writers to write fairy tales explicitly for children, and the frame for her first major work was based on Sarah Fielding's *The Governess* (1749), which contained two didactic fairy tales for young girls. More artistic than Fielding, Leprince de Beaumont depicted a governess engaging several young girls between 6 and 10 in discussions about morals, manners, ethics, and gender roles that provide her with the opportunity to tell stories to illustrate her points. Mme Leprince de Beaumont's utilization of such a frame was based on her work as a governess in England, and the frame was set up to be copied by other adults to cultivate a type of storytelling and reading in homes of the upper classes that would reinforce acceptable notions of propriety, especially proper sex roles. It was only as part of the civilizing process that storytelling developed within the aristocratic and bourgeois homes in the 17th and 18th centuries, first through governesses and nannies, and later in the 18th and 19th centuries through mothers, tutors, and governesses who told stories in separate rooms designated for children and called nurseries.

Towards the end of the 18th century numerous publishers in France, England, and Germany began serious production of books for children, and the genre of the fairy tale assumed a new dimension which now included concerns about how to socialize children and indoctrinate them through literary products that were appropriate for their age, mentality, and morals. The rise of 'bourgeois' children's literature meant that publishers would make the fairy-tale genre more comprehensive, but they would also—along with parents, educators, religious leaders, and writers—pay great attention to the potential of the fantastic and miraculous in the fairy tale to disturb and/or enlighten children's minds. There were numerous debates about the value of the fantastic and the marvellous in literary form and their possible detrimental effects on the souls of readers in many European countries. They were significant and interesting, but they did not have any real impact on the publication of fairy tales. Certainly, not in France. Indeed, by 1785 Charles-Joseph Mayer could begin producing his famous 40-volume *Cabinet des fées*, which was completed in 1789 and contained the most significant of the 100-year mode of fairy tales that paved the way for the institution of the fairy tale in other countries. From this point on, most writers in the West, whether they wrote for adults or children, consciously held a dialogue with a fairy-tale discourse that had become firmly established in Europe and embraced intercourse with the oral storytelling tradition and all other kinds of folklore that existed throughout the world. For instance, the French fairy tale, which now included *The Arabian Nights*, had a profound influence on German writers of the Enlightenment and romanticism, and the development in Germany provided the continuity for the institution of the genre in the West as a whole. Like the French authors, the German middle-class writers like Johann Musäus in his collection *Volksmärchen der Deutschen* (1782-6) and Benedikte Naubert in her work *Neue Volksmährchen der Deutschen* (1789-93) employed the fairy tale to celebrate German history and customs. Musäus and Naubert both combined elements of German myth, folklore, legend, and the French fairy tale to address educated Germans. At the same time, Christoph Martin Wieland translated and adapted numerous fairy tales from the *Cabinet des fées* in *Dschinnistan* (1786-9), and he also wrote a novel and some poems that revealed his familiarity with Basile and the Italian fairy-tale tradition. Aside from these collections for upper-class readers, numerous French fairy tales became known in Germany by the turn of the century through the popular series of the *Blaue Bibliothek* and other translations from the French, and children's books began to carry more and more fairy tales.

Most important at the turn of the century was the contribution of the German romantic writers. Wilhelm Heinrich Wackenroder, Ludwig Tieck, Novalis, Joseph von Eichendorff, Clemens Brentano, Adelbert Chamisso, Friedrich de la Motte Fouqué, E. T. A. Hoffmann, and others wrote extraordinary and highly complex metaphorical tales that revealed a major shift in the function of the genre: the fairy tale began to address philosophical and practical concerns of the emerging middle classes and was written in defence of the imagination and as a critique of the worst aspects of the Enlightenment and absolutism. This viewpoint was clearly expressed in Johann Wolfgang von Goethe's classical narrative bluntly entitled 'The Fairy Tale' (1795), as though it were the fairy tale to end all fairy tales. Goethe optimistically envisioned a successful rebirth of a rejuvenated monarchy that would enjoy the support of all social classes in his answer to the violence and destruction of the French Revolution. In response, Novalis wrote a long, elaborate fairy tale in *Heinrich von Ofterdingen* (1798) called 'Klingsohrs Märchen', that celebrates the erotic and artistic impulses of revolution and emphasizes magical transformation and flexibility. Though hopeful, many of the romantics were sceptical about prospects for individual autonomy and the reform of decadent institutions in a Germany divided by the selfish interests of petty tyrants and the Napoleonic Wars. Characteristically many of the early romantic tales do not end on a happy note. The protagonists either go insane or die. The evil forces assume a social hue, for the witches and villains are no longer allegorical representations of evil in the Christian tradition but are symbolically associated with the philistine bourgeois society or the corrupt aristocracy. The romantics did not intend their fairy tales to amuse audiences in the traditional sense of *divertissement*. Instead, they sought to engage the reader in a serious discourse about art, philosophy, education, and love. The focus was on the creative individual or artist, who envisioned a life without inhibitions and social constraints. It was a theme that became popular in the romantic fairy tales throughout Europe and in North America. In contrast to most folk tales or fairy tales that have strong roots in folklore and propose the possibility of the integration of the hero into society, the fairy tales of the 19th and 20th centuries tend to pit the individual against society or to use the protagonist in a way to mirror the foibles and contradictions of society.

This conflict between the 'heroic' individual, often identified with Nature or natural forces, and society, understood as one-dimensional rationality and bureaucracy, became a major theme in British romanticism. At the same time the romantics also sought to rediscover their English, Scottish, Welsh, and Irish heritage by exploring folklore and the history of the fairies, elves, leprechauns, and other 'little people'. Here the prose (Sir Walter Scott, James Hogg, Allan Cunningham), poetry (Samuel Coleridge, Robert Southey, John Keats, Percy Bysshe Shelley, Tom Moore, Thomas Hood), and folklore and fairy-tale studies (Walter Scott,

Thomas Crofton Croker, Thomas Keightley) paved the way for an astounding production of fairy tales in the second half of the 19th century. In addition, the fairy paintings of William Blake and Henry Fuseli had an enormous impact on the later fantastic paintings of Daniel Maclise, Joseph Noel Paton, Richard Dadd, John Anster Fitzgerald, Arthur Hughes, Richard Doyle, and many others, and numerous plays and operas were also influenced by the fairy-tale vogue, as can be seen in the work of James Robinson Planché.

While the function of the fairy tale for adults underwent a major shift in the 19th century that made it an appropriate means to maintain a dialogue about social and political issues within the bourgeois public sphere—and this was clear in all nations in Europe and North America—the fairy tale for children was carefully monitored and censored until the 1820s. Although there were various collections published for upper-class children in the latter part of the 18th century and at the turn of the century along with numerous chapbooks containing classical fairy tales, they were not regarded as prime and 'proper' reading material for children. They were not considered to be 'healthy' for the development of young people's minds. For the most part, publishers, church leaders, and educators favoured other genres of stories, more realistic, sentimental, and didactic. Even the Brothers Grimm, in particular Wilhelm, began to revise their collected tales in *Kinder- und Haus-märchen* (*Children's and Household Tales*, 1812–15), making them more appropri-ate for children than they had done in the beginning and cleansing their narratives of erotic and bawdy passages. However, the fantastic and miraculous elements were kept so that they were not at first fully accepted by the middle-class reading audience, which only began to change its attitude towards the fairy tale during the course of the 1820s and 1830s throughout Europe.

The tales of the Brothers Grimm played a key role in this change. More than the collections of the French writers of the 1790s, the Grimms' work was consciously designed to address two audiences at the same time, and they carefully cultivated the form of their tales so that they could be easily grasped by children and adults. From 1812 until 1857, the Grimms published seven editions of what they called the *Grosse Ausgabe* (Large Edition), which ultimately contained 211 tales, for the household in general and for scholars as well. The Grimms thought of their book as an *Erziehungsbuch* (an educational manual), and thus they also wanted to attract children and appeal to the morals and virtues of middle-class readers. Thus they also published a so-called *Kleine Ausgabe* (Small Edition), a selection of 50 tales, in 1825 to popularize the larger work and create a more manageable best-seller. There were ten editions of this book from 1825 to 1858, and they contained the majority of the magic fairy tales such as 'Cinderella', 'Snow White', 'Sleeping Beauty', 'Little

Red Riding Hood', and 'The Frog King'. Since they all underlined morals in keeping with the Protestant ethic and a patriarchal notion of sex roles, the book was bound to be a success. When we think of the form and typical fairy tale today, we tend to think of a paradigmatic Grimms' fairy tale (quite often modified by the Disney industry). Their tales are all about three to five pages long and are constructed rationally to demonstrate the virtues of an opportunistic protagonist who learns to take advantage of gifts and magic power to succeed in life, which means marriage to a rich person and wealth. Most of the male heroes are dashing, adventurous, and courageous. Most of the female protagonists are beautiful, passive, and industrious. Their common feature is cunning: they all know how to take advantage of the rules of their society and the conventions of the fairy tale to profit. Very few of the Grimms' fairy tales end on an unhappy note, and they all comply with the phallocratic impulses and forces of the emerging middle-class societies of Western culture.

Aside from the gradual success that the Grimms' tales had as a 'children's book', the publication of Wilhelm Hauff's *Märchen Almanach* (1826), containing oriental-flavoured tales for young people, Edgar Taylor's translation of the Grimms' tales as *German Popular Stories* (1823), with illustrations by the famous George Cruikshank, and Pierre-Jules Hetzel's *Livre des enfants* (1837), which contained 40 tales from the *Cabinet des fées* edited for children, indicated that the fairy tale had become acceptable for young readers. This acceptance was largely due to the fact that adults themselves became more tolerant of fantasy literature and realized that it would not pervert the minds of their children. Indeed, the middle-class attitudes towards amusement began to change, and people understood that children needed the time and space for recreation without having morals and ethics imposed on them and without the feeling that their reading or listening had to involve indoctrination.

It is not by chance, then, that the fairy tale for children came into its own from 1830 to 1900. The most significant writer of this period was Hans Christian Andersen, who began publishing his tales in 1835, and they were almost immediately translated into many different languages and became popular throughout the Western world. Andersen combined humour, Christian sentiments, folklore, and original plots to form tales which amused and instructed old and young readers at the same time. More than any writer of the 19th century, he fulfilled what Perrault had begun: to write tales such as 'The Ugly Duckling', 'The Little Mermaid', and 'The Princess and the Pea' which could be readily grasped by children and adults alike. Of course, Andersen wrote many tales that were clearly intended for adults alone, and they are filled with self-hate, paranoia, and dreams of vengeance.

More and more the fairy tale of the 19th century became marked by the very individual desires and needs of the authors who felt that industrialization and rationalization of labour made their lives compartmentalized. As daily life became more structured and institutions more bureaucratic, there was little space left for leisure, hobbies, daydreaming, and the imagination. It was the fairy tale that provided room for amusement, nonsense, and recreation. This does not mean that it abandoned its more traditional role in the civilizing process as agent of socialization. For instance, up until the 1860s the majority of fairy-tale writers for children, including Catherine Sinclair, George Cruikshank, and Alfred Crowquill in Britain, Collodi in Italy, comtesse Sophie de Ségur in France, and Ludwig Bechstein in Germany, emphasized the lessons to be learned in keeping with the principles of the Protestant ethic—industriousness, honesty, cleanliness, diligence, virtuousness—and male supremacy. However, just as the 'conventional' fairy tale for adults had become subverted at the end of the 18th century, there was a major movement to write parodies of fairy tales, which were intended both for children and adults. In other words, the classical tales were turned upside down and inside out to question the value system upheld by the dominant socialization process and to keep wonder, curiosity, and creativity alive.

By the 1860s numerous writers continued the 'romantic' project of subverting the formal structure of the canonized tales (Perrault, Grimm, Bechstein, Andersen) and to experiment with the repertoire of motifs, characters, and topoi to defend the free imagination of the individual and to extend the discursive social commentary of the fairy tale. The best example of the type of subversion attempted during the latter part of the 19th century is Lewis Carroll's *Alice in Wonderland* (1865), which engendered numerous imitations and original works in Europe and America. Even today, unusual versions of *Alice* have been created for the theatre, television, the cinema, comic books, and other kinds of literature, demonstrating the exceptional way that the fairy-tale genre has evolved to address changing social issues and aesthetic modes.

Of course, Victorian England was an unusual time for fairylore because many people from all social classes seriously believed in the existence of fairies, elves, goblins, selkies, and dwarfs otherwise known as the little people, and their beliefs were manifested in the prodigious amount of fairy stories, paintings, operas, plays, music, and ballets from the 1820s to the turn of the century. The need to believe in other worlds and other types of living people was certainly connected to a need to escape the pressures of utilitarianism and industrialism and a rebellion against traditional Christian thinking. But it was also linked to a scientific quest to explain the historical origins of the little people, and folklorists, anthropologists, and ethnologists contributed to the flowering of the fairy tale and folk tale. The work of the Scottish scholar Andrew Lang, who published 13 coloured books of fairy tales from 1889 to 1910, still in print today, is a good example of how important the fairies and their lore had become in Britain. Influenced greatly by the anthropological school of folklore, Lang sought to further historical investigation into the origins of myths and rituals and their connection to folk tales while at the same time he collapsed distinctions between folk and fairy tales and sought to address young and adult audiences with international collections of tales and his own literary fairy tales.

By the beginning of the 20th century, the fairy tale had become fully institutionalized in Europe and North America, as indicated by the great success and popularity of L. Frank Baum's *The Wonderful Wizard of Oz* (1900) and James Barrie's *Peter Pan* (1904) and their sequels in literature, drama, and film up to the present. The full institutionalization of the genre means that a specific process of production, distribution, and reception had become regularized within the public sphere of each Western society, and it began to play and continues to play a significant role in the formation and preservation of the cultural heritage of a nation-state. Without such institutionalization in advanced industrialized and technological countries, the genre would perish, and thus any genre must be a kind of self-perpetuating institution involved in the socialization and acculturation of readers. It is the interaction of writer/publisher/audience within a given society that makes for the definition of the genre in any given epoch. This has certainly been the case with the fairy tale. The aesthetics of each literary fairy tale will depend on how and why an individual writer wants to intervene in the discourse of the genre as institution. Such interventions bring about transformations in the institution itself and its relation to other institutions so that the fairy tale today is unthinkable without taking into consideration its dialectical relationship with other genres and media as well as its actual 'absorption' of these genres and media.

The absorption is based on cross-connections to other genres as institutions and mutual influences that had been present ever since the rise of the literary fairy tale. The theatre, opera, ballet, poetry, painting, and even sermons had made use of fairy-tale material since the 17th century if not even earlier. The pageants at various European courts in the 16th and 17th centuries had actually influenced and helped further the development of the literary fairy tale which became the subject matter of great composers such as Mozart, Schumann, Delibes, Puccini, Rossini, Tchaikovsky, Wagner, Humperdinck, Offenbach, and Dvořák in the 18th and 19th centuries. What became apparent by the beginning of the 20th century was that the fairy tale had developed a canon of 'classical' fairy tales ('Cinderella', 'Sleeping

Beauty', 'Little Red Riding Hood', 'Snow White', 'Rumpelstiltskin', 'Rapunzel', 'Puss-in-Boots', 'The Princess and the Pea', 'Aladdin and the Lamp', etc.) that served as reference points for the standard structure, motifs, and topoi of a fairy tale for readers young and old throughout the Western world. Other important features of the genre as institution were: (1) schools integrated the teaching of fairy tales into the curriculum, included them in primers, and purchased them for libraries; (2) in the adaptations of the tales for children, many of the tales were 'sanitized' so that putative terrifying aspects of some tales were deleted and also the language was simplified if not made simplistic; (3) fairy tales for adults often took the form of a novella or a novel and, though the authors would rely on the formulaic form of the classical fairy tale, they would often experiment and vary the form in highly original and innovative ways; (4) clearly, the tales of Perrault and the Brothers Grimm set the pattern for what was considered the fairy tale, but there were also interesting nationalistic developments in the genre that led many authors and scholars to cultivate specific ethnic themes; (5) at the same time, the intertextuality of most literary fairy tales in the 20th century demanded that the readers transcend their nationalities and make connections between cultures in a 'universal' sense; (6) the so-called universality of the folk tales and fairy tales began to draw the interest of psychologists and other social scientists who departed from the traditional approaches of folklorists and anthropologists to analyse the impact that the tales had on individual psyches.

As the printing of illustrated books in colour became cheaper and as more children learned to read through obligatory schooling, more and more publishers produced the classical fairy tales in the hundreds of thousands if not the millions throughout the 20th century. The tales have been printed in all sorts of formats ranging from 10×10 cm tiny (4×4 in.) booklets to gigantic picture books over 30×30 cm (12×12 in.), not to mention comic books and cartoons. The illustrations have varied from hackwork to brilliant interpretations of the stories. Artists such as Walter Crane, Arthur Rackham, Charles Folkard, Harry Clarke, and Edmund Dulac made major contributions to the genre at the beginning of the century, and contemporary illustrators such as Eric Carle, Raymond Briggs, Anthony Browne, Nikolaus Heidelbach, Susanne Janssen, Maurice Sendak, Mercer Mayer, Benjamin Lacombe, Lisbeth Zwerger, Shaun Tan, Andrea Dezsö, and Natalie Frank have produced their own unique drawings that endow the tales with special personal meanings and social commentary. The tales of Perrault, Grimm, and Andersen have been translated into practically every language in the world, and together they vie with the Bible as the most widely read literature in the world.

Though the classical fairy tales soon dominated the market for children at the turn of the century, there were important endeavours to create new literary fairy tales for adults and children. For instance, numerous European writers such as Hermann Hesse, Apollinaire, Edwin Hoernle, Hermynia zur Mühlen, Béla Balázs, Naomi Mitchison, Oscar Maria Graf, Kurt Schwitters, and Bruno Schönlank sought to politicize the fairy tale; there were numerous attempts from the right and the left before and after the First World War to use fairy tales for explicit political purposes.

After the Nazis rose to power, fairy tales and folk tales were interpreted and used to spread the Aryan ideology throughout Europe, and the situation was no different in the Soviet Union, where tales had to suit communist notions of socialist realism, proletarian literature, and class struggle. Ironically, the most significant 'revolution' in the institution of the fairy tale took place in 1937, when Walt Disney produced the first animated feature fairy-tale film, *Snow White and the Seven Dwarfs*. Although fairy tales had been adapted for film as early as the 1890s by George Méliès, Disney was the first to use Technicolor, to expand on the Broadway and Hollywood formula for a musical, to print books, records, toys, and other artefacts to accompany his films, and to spice the classical tales with delightful humour and pristine fun that would be acceptable for middle-class families. The commercial success was so great that Disney used the same cinematic devices and ideological messages in his next three fairy-tale films *Pinocchio* (1940), *Cinderella* (1950), and *Sleeping Beauty* (1959). After his death, the Disney formula has not changed much, and even films such as *The Little Mermaid* (1989), *Beauty and the Beast* (1991), *Aladdin* (1992), *Mulan* (1998), *The Emperor's New Groove* (2000), *The Princess and the Frog* (2009), *Tangled* (2010), *Frozen* (2014), *Maleficent* (2014), and *Cinderella* (2015) follow a traditional pattern of a 'good' young man or woman, who finds some magical means to help himself or herself against sinister forces. In the end the 'goodness' of the hero or heroine shines through, and there is a happy end that generally culminates in marriage. The story is always predictable. What counts most in the Disney fairy tale is the repetition of the same message: happiness will always come to those who work hard and are kind and brave, and it is through the spectacular projection of this message and through music, jokes, dazzling animation, and zany characters that the Disney corporate artists have made a profitable business out of the fairy tale. Indeed, the Disney Corporation has literally commercialized the classical fairy tale as its own trademark.

This commercialization does not mean that the fairy tale has become a mere commodity, for the conventional Disney fairy tale in film and literature serves as a referential text that has challenged gifted writers and artists to create fascinating critiques of some of the blatant sexist and racist features of the Disney films and the classical canon as well. The works of these writers and artists offer alternatives to the standard formulas that stimulate readers/viewers to rethink their aesthetic and ideological notions of what a fairy tale is. In particular the period from 1960 to the present has witnessed a flowering of remarkable experiments in the institution of the fairy tale. Significantly, the fascination with fairy-tale writers began with the late 1960s counter-culture movement and its turn towards writers like J. R. R. Tolkien, Hermann Hesse, and to a certain extent C. S. Lewis. One of the slogans of the anti-war movement in Europe and America was 'power to the imagination', that is, 'empower the imagination', and thousands of students turned to fantasy literature and fairy tales as a revolt against the reality of the Vietnam War and the rationalizations of the so-called military-industrial complex that the younger generation could not trust. The turn to the fairy tale and other forms of fantasy was not so much escapism as a rejection of the compromising policies of educational and political institutions that the young regarded as corrupt. This was the period when no one above the age of 30 was to be trusted.

Though there were few specific 'political' fairy tales written during the Vietnam era, feminist fairy tales soon began to be produced by writers such as Anne Sexton, Olga Broumas, Angela Carter, and Tanith Lee, along with feminist cooperatives in Italy, Ireland, and Britain. In addition, Edith Johnston Phelps, Alison Lurie, and other feminist writers began publishing collections of feminist fairy tales or tales in which traditional sexuality was questioned, and this work has been continued in anthologies edited by Suzanne Barchers, Ellen Datlow, Terri Windling, Kathleen Ragan, and Jane Yolen. Indeed, if the Disney fairy-tale factory marked one sort of revolution in the genre, the feminist fairy-tale production that generally involves a questioning of gender roles and a recording of personal experiences in poetry and prose marked a second one by breathing new life into the genre, and it has led to exciting experiments up through Emma Donoghue's *Kissing the Witch* (1997) and Catherynne Valente's *Six-Gun Snow White* (2013).

In fact, experimentation linked to magic realism and a postmodern sensibility have become the key words in the fairy-tale genre from 1980 to the present. In Great Britain there are several notable authors who have stamped the fairy tale with their diverse perspectives and unusual discourses: Angela Carter, who edited important volumes of folk tales and fairy tales about women, produced the provocative *Bloody Chamber and Other Tales* that turns Perrault on his head; Salman Rushdie, who relies on a variety of oriental and Western folklore in his novels, wrote an important political novella, *Haroun and the Sea of Stories*, for young people that reveals the dangers of and the necessity for storytelling. A. S. Byatt produced the novel *Possession*, one of the most creative explorations of the genre in prose and poetry, not to mention her shorter fairy tales that have raised questions about social codes and narratology. The list of contemporary talented writers who have endeavoured to break with the classical tradition is great. Their styles range from oblique postmodern montage to poetic, straightforward traditional narrative styles, and they include Michel Tournier, Michael Ende, Robert Coover, Donald Bartheleme, Peter Redgrove, Michael de Larrabeiti, Janosch, Steven Millhauser, Jane Yolen, Donna Di Napoli, Gregory Maguire, John Barth, Italo Calvino, and Gianni Rodari. In addition, many film-makers such as Jim Henson, Tom Davenport, John Sayles, Hayao Miyazaki, Michel Ocelot, Catherine Breillat, and others, including numerous East European filmmakers such as Jan Svankmajer, Jirí Barta, and Garri Bardin have sought to go beyond Disney and bring about new perspectives on the fairy tale and society through cinematic experimentation.

The present *Companion* seeks to document all these recent endeavours while providing as much information about past efforts of authors who have contributed to the rise of the literary fairy tale in Europe and North America. There are separate entries on specific national developments in France, Germany, Britain, Ireland, Italy, North America, Portugal, Scandinavia, Slav and Baltic countries, and Spain. Most of the articles deal with the literary formation of the genre and the development of specific types of tales. Plays, operas, paintings, films, musicals, illustrations, paintings, and fairy-tale artefacts such as stamps and postcards are also included. Although every effort has been made to be as comprehensive and inclusive as possible, there are bound to be some regrettable gaps that will be covered in future editions of the *Companion*. The present edition has been updated to make the *Companion* more comprehensive and thorough. There are over 130 new entries and numerous additions to another 70 or so entries based on recent information. Every effort has been made to verify the data and provide reliable accounts about the writers and artists and their works. The production of different types of fairy tales continues to grow at a rapid rate each year. It is mind baffling to see how our lives are filled with fairy tales, and the *Companion* is only one drop in the bucket, but, I hope, it is a fulfilling one.

This work would not have been made possible without the dedicated efforts of my assistant Anne Duggan, who supervised all the manuscripts and helped me organize the entire project. I am deeply grateful for all the work that she put into the *Companion*. Special thanks are also due to: Terry Staples, who brilliantly reorganized the film entries and wrote wonderful entries; Rosemary Creeser, Lydia Marhoff, and Ulrike Sieglohr, who supported Terry Staples with all-round advice; Tom Higgins and Thomas Hoernigk, members of the Offenbach-Gesellschaft, who developed the opera and music entries with their expertise; Mary Lou Ennis, who repeatedly came to the rescue with new fascinating entries; Carole Silver, who went out of her way at the last moment to add important entries, as did Gillian Avery with great generosity. From the beginning I could not have done without the advice of all the contributing editors who helped conceive the lists and provided me with wise counsel. Last but not least I want to thank everyone at the Oxford University Press for their tireless efforts to assist me. Michael Cox provided the initial spark for the project. Pam Coote and Alison Jones were always helpful and patient, and they constantly gave me sound editorial advice. Wendy Tuckey made certain that there was some semblance of order as the work developed. Veronica Ions did a splendid job of copy-editing the entire book and offered useful suggestions for changes. For the present revised second edition I have been ably assisted by Rebecca Lane, Joanna Harris, Cornelia Haase, and Bethan Lee who have made invaluable contributions to the *Companion*. Altogether their work and the collaborative effort of scholars from many different countries has, I hope, borne fruit, and a touch of magic was especially necessary to harvest the results.

JACK ZIPES

Aarne, Antti *See* AARNE–THOMPSON INDEX.

Aarne–Thompson index Shorthand for *The Types of the Folktale*, the classification system for international folk tales developed and first published in 1910 by the Finnish folklorist Antti Aarne under the title *Verzeichnis der Märchentypen* (*Index of Types of Folktale*). Aarne's system, designed initially to organize and index the Scandinavian archival collections, was translated and enlarged by the American folklorist Stith Thompson in 1928, and revised again in 1961. Although its scope is limited primarily to European and European-derived tales known to have existed in oral tradition at the time of publication, the principal value of the index lies in the creation of a single classification system by which culturally distinct variants are grouped together according to a common reference number.

Together with Thompson's six-volume *Motif-Index of Folk Literature* with which it is cross-indexed, *The Types of the Folktale* constitutes the most important reference work and research tool for comparative folk-tale analysis. These two indexes, designed to aid the researcher in identifying tale types, isolating their motifs and locating cultural variants, are most closely associated with the historical-geographic (or Finnish) method, which sought to reconstruct the hypothetical original form (*Urform*) as well as the history of a given tale by plotting the distribution of different versions over time and space. Although the historical-geographic method is no longer fashionable, the reference works produced by that direction of folk-narrative research remain one of the most enduring contributions to the study of folk tales.

In *The Types of the Folktale*, tales are organized according to type (defined by Thompson as 'a traditional tale that has an independent existence') and assigned a title and number and/or letter. For

example, the Brothers *Grimms' tale of *'Sleeping Beauty' appears in the Aarne–Thompson index as 410, 'Sleeping Beauty'. Scholars citing either the Grimm or non-Grimm version could then refer to it by its tale-type number, as AT (or AaTh) 410. Each entry begins with a description of the principal traits of the tale in abbreviated narrative form, followed by a list of individual motifs in existent variants, and often concludes with bibliographic information. The bibliography contains information on the pattern of distribution by country and the number of known versions at the time of compilation, as well as the print or archival sources of the variants.

The tales are divided into the following categories: Animal Tales (Types 1–299), Ordinary Folk Tales (Types 300–1199), Jokes and Anecdotes (Types 1200–1999), Formula Tales (Types 2000–2399), and Unclassified Tales (Types 2400–2499). Most folk tales or fairy tales are classified under 'ordinary tales', which comprise roughly half of the catalogue.

In 2004 Hans-Jörg Uther published a revised edition of the Aarne/Thompson tale-type index under the title *The Types of International Folktales: A Classification and Bibliography*. In three volumes, Uther changed many of the titles and descriptions of the original index that tended to have a gender bias, and he broadened the coverage to include tale types beyond the Indo-European range. Now most scholars use the initials ATU when referring to tale types in Uther's revised classification system. MBS

Baughman, Ernest W., *Type and Motif-Index of the Folktales of England and America* (1966).

Georges, Robert, 'The Universality of the Tale-Type as Concept and Construct', *Western Folklore* 42 (1983).

Thompson, Stith, *The Folktale* (1946).

Thompson, Stith, *Motif-Index of Folk Literature* (1955).

Achebe, Chinua (1930–2013) Nigerian novelist, poet, academic, and critic. Professor at Brown University, and winner of the Man Booker International Prize (2007) among others, he received more than 30 honorary degrees. He is best known for his novels and essays which critique postcolonial Nigerian politics and society, and explore the friction between traditional African ideas and values and Western colonial cultures. Achebe's widely read and much-translated first novel, *Things Fall Apart* (1958), responds to and undermines Joseph Conrad's *Heart of Darkness*. Achebe advocated maintaining traditional culture to preserve a sense of Nigerian identity, and saw his role as writer to resurrect and popularize traditional lore. His work extensively employs Igbo folk stories, proverbs, and oratory. Somewhat paradoxically, he uses the colonizer's language—English—and literary form—the novel. However, he adapts form and content to his own purposes. He also published short stories and children's books. Linguists and folklorists seeking to understand traditional lore and proverbs in particular employ his work.   PG

Ada, Alma Flor (1938–) Cuban-American writer and professor who has been a pioneer in the development of multicultural and bilingual books for children and has written the important study *A Magical Encounter: Spanish-Language Children's Literature in the Classroom* (1990). Ada writes her own texts in Spanish and English as well as translating and adapting folk tales that emphasize the themes of cooperation, trust, and liberty. She often collaborates with F. Isabel Campoy. Among her important books in Spanish and English are *El enanito de la bared* (*The Wall's Dwarf*, 1974), *La gallinata costurera* (*The Little Hen Who Enjoyed Sewing*, 1974), *La gallinata roja* (*The Little Red Hen*, 1989), *La tataranieta de Cucarachita Martina* (*The Great-Great Granddaughter of the Little Cockroach Martina*, 1993), and *Mediopollito* (*Half-Chicken*, 1995). *Dear Peter Rabbit* (1994), a unique montage of fairy tales and fables in the form of letters, won the Parents' Choice Honor. *The Malachite Palace* (1998), one of Ada's original fairy tales, recounts the adventures of a sequestered princess who is not allowed to play with the common people until she is liberated by a tiny bird. In 2006 Ada and Campoy published an important collection of twelve folk tales, *Tales Our Abuelitas Told*, which includes stories the authors had heard in their childhood.   JZ

Adams, Richard (1920–) British novelist and writer of children's fantasy literature. His distinctive trademark is the use of animal protagonists: rabbits search for the promised land in *Watership Down* (1972), a bear is deified in *Shardik* (1972), and dogs escape from an experimental lab in *The Plague Dogs* (1977). Adams's choice of subject-matter not only demonstrates a sensitivity toward animals; it also reflects his interest in the animal tale, which suggests we should read his stories as allegories for the human condition.

In his well-known novel *Watership Down*, Adams uses the basic plot of a group of rabbits setting out to found a new warren as a pretext to explore various socio-political utopias (or dystopias). The central exodus or quest narrative is punctuated with tales about El-ahrairah ('the Prince with a Thousand Enemies'), a trickster-type folkloric hero whose exploits provide the group with exempla and mythological explanations for their rabbit-universe. Given the importance of these tales to the main narrative, it comes as no surprise that Adams later published versions of them, along with other stories from the novel, in *Tales from Watership Down* (1996).   AD

Meyer, Charles A. (ed.), 'Richard Adams' *Watership Down*', spec. issue of *Journal of the Fantastic in the Arts*, 6.1 (1993).

Petzold, Dieter, 'Fantasy out of Myth and Fable: Animal Stories in Rudyard Kipling and Richard Adams', *Children's Literature Association Quarterly*, 12.1 (spring 1987).

Addy, Sidney (1848–1933) English lawyer and folklorist who published two important pioneer works, *Folk Tales and Superstitions* (1895) and *Household Tales with Other Traditional Remains, Collected in the Counties of York, Lincoln, Derby and Nottingham* (1895). In both books he attempted to record oral tales exactly as he heard them, often in dialect, and with information about the teller.

JZ

Adventures of Pinocchio See PINOCCHIO, ADVENTURES OF.

advertising and fairy tales Verbal folklore genres such as proverbs, riddles, folk songs, nursery rhymes, legends, and of course fairy tales have long been used as attention-getting devices in advertising. While proverbs, for example, are particularly suitable to create slogans, fairy tales meet the needs of advertising agents since they create a world of desire, hope, and perfection. Anybody wishing to sell a product would want to describe it in such a way that purchasers or consumers would thank their good fortune if they could obtain it. Fairy tales have as their basis this wish for happiness and bliss, where all wishes come true, and where everybody lives happily ever after. By using traditional fairy-tale motifs and by adapting them to the modern world of consumerism and the instantaneous gratification syndrome, advertising agencies create the perfect medium with the irresistible message.

When advertising started to gain ground at the beginning of the 20th century, fairy-tale titles, certain poetic verses, and short allusions to well-known fairy tales began to be used as manipulative bait. The reader would be reminded of the happy and satisfied fairy-tale ending, thus deciding subconsciously that the advertised product must be the perfect choice. As time went on, ever more glamorous illustrations were added to the verbal messages, combining the advertisement for a necklace or a piece of clothing, for example, with a beautiful woman standing in front of the mirror asking that eternal question, 'Mirror, mirror on the wall, who is the fairest of them all?' And who would not want to be the most beautiful, especially since, in the modern world of advertising and consumerism, everything is possible. All that it takes is fairy-tale formulas and allusions together with manipulative texts and glittering illustrations. Naturally sophisticated television advertisements can create a state of enchantment which barely leaves the viewer any choice but to accept the message as the ultimate wish fulfilment.

Since advertisers want to communicate effectively with their readers and television audiences, they will choose motifs only from those fairy tales that are especially well known. Many times an advertisement is simply based on the title of a fairy tale. Thus a beauty shop was named *'Rapunzel' and on a flyer used the headline 'Rapunzel's Creative Hair Styling Salon'. A German champagne producer simply named its product 'Rotkäppchen' ('Little Red Cap'), and every bottle since the early part of this century has had a red cap on the top of the bottle. The name and this symbol bring with them the positive feeling of *Little Red Riding Hood going off to her grandmother's house with a good bottle of expensive alcohol. What is right for a fairy tale ought to be very suitable indeed for the realistic world as well. Little wonder that the Martini vermouth producers used the slogan 'Fairy tales can come true' to sell their perfect drink.

Cosmetic firms especially make use of such fairy-tale allusions. Revlon came up with the slogan '*Cinderella—nails and the Magic Wand', thereby claiming that its cosmetics will make the difference between homeliness and beauty. Of course, this beautiful person would need a gorgeous automobile, and so the Fisher Body company used the slogan 'A Coach for Cinderella' in the 1930s to help advertise such a car for General Motors. But for this the consumer would need money, and as luck would have it the Bank of America, according to an advertisement from the year 1947, is the 'Godmother to a Million Cinderellas'. There is one wish fulfilment after another, and such slogans with their coercive texts and inviting pictures make all of this look as easy as the waving of a magic wand—until the reality check sets in, of course.

The Dilder carpets company tried as well to create a special mood for its magnificent products. The headline of its advertisement very effectively coupled the perfect world of the fairy tale with monetary reality: 'A Fairy Tale for Real People with Real People Budgets'. There is no talk of a particular fairy tale here. Rather the words 'fairy tale' stand for something perfect and beautiful. A German carpet company had similar ideas, but its slogan read more precisely: 'A carpet as beautiful as *Snow White'. A bit strange perhaps, to compare a carpet with a beauty like Snow White, but the idea is to conjure up the feeling of perfection. Of course, the picture of this advertisement also shows Snow White sitting on the carpet and the seven dwarfs turning somersaults from sheer joy and excitement about this incredible carpet. Perfectly fitting seems to be the slogan which the Royal Doulton Dolls company added to a picture of one of its magnificent creations: 'Royal Doulton presents the fairest of them all'. A mere allusion to the well-known verse from the 'Snow White' fairy tale, but enough to convey the claim that Doulton dolls are absolutely beautiful products.

The Waterford Crystal company quite frequently employs fairy-tale references for its marvellous glass creations. Nobody will have any difficulty recognizing the fairy tale behind the slogan 'One of her glass slippers fell off'. And how appropriately worded was the statement 'Oh, what lovely ears you have' next to the picture of a number of pitchers whose handles brought about this variation of Little Red Riding Hood's questions to her grandmother. Such wordplay always presupposes that the reader and consumer will also juxtapose the traditional tale with it, thus creating a world where magic and reality can meet in harmony at least once in a while. One of the most elaborate uses of fairy tales for advertising purposes was AT&T's

special issue (spring 1995) of *Time* entitled 'Welcome to Cyberspace'. In numerous two-page spreads AT&T illustrates the fairy-tale-like inventions of modern electronic technology. Fairy-tale motifs of The *'Frog King', 'Little Red Riding Hood', *'Hansel and Gretel', 'Cinderella' and *'Rumpelstiltskin' appear. The fairy-tale heroes and heroines are, of course, spruced up to fit the age of cyberspace. The same is true for their modern fairy-tale-like messages, as for example: 'Rumpelstiltskin is my name. Spinning straw into gold was my game. But now I'm a new man and I have new cravings. I spin phone calls into savings.' But it does not really matter what new products and wishes will come about, the traditional fairy tales as expressions of wish fulfilment will be suitable to advertising in ever new forms and disguises.   WM

Dégh, Linda, and Vázsonyi, Andrew, 'Magic for Sale: Märchen and Legend in TV Advertising', *Fabula*, 20 (1979).

Dundes, Alan, 'Advertising and Folklore', *New York Folklore Quarterly*, 19 (1963).

Herles, Helmut, 'Sprichwort und Märchenmotiv in der Werbung', *Zeitschrift für Volkskunde*, 62 (1966).

Horn, Katalin, 'Grimmsche Märchen als Quellen für Metaphern und Vergleiche in der Sprache der Werbung, des Journalismus und der Literatur', *Muttersprache*, 91 (1981).

Mieder, Wolfgang, *Tradition and Innovation in Folk Literature* (1987).

Röhrich, Lutz, 'Folklore and Advertising', in Venetia J. Newall (ed.), *Folklore Studies in the Twentieth Century* (1978).

Afanasyev, Aleksandr (1826–71) Russian folklorist. Born in a provincial Russian town, he studied law at Moscow University, worked in state archives, and published numerous essays on Russian history and culture. From the 1850s his attention shifted towards Slavic mythology, and he started collecting and publishing Russian folklore. From 1855 to 1863 he published his world-famous collection *Russian Fairy Tales*, in eight volumes, along with *Russian Folk Legends* in 1859 and *Russian Fairy Tales for Children* in 1870. Besides fairy tales, Afanasyev collected folk songs, proverbs, and parables. His major scholarly work, *The Poetic Views of Slavic Peoples on Nature*, was published in three volumes in 1865-9.

The significance of Afanasyev's contribution to the study of folklore is primarily his systematic collection, description, and classification of material. His *Russian Fairy Tales*, including 600 texts and variants, are still today the most comprehensive work on East Slavic folk tales, widely acknowledged internationally. At the time of its publication, it was superior to any similar West European collection. Although he lacked predecessors in Russia, Afanasyev was familiar with the work of European collectors, such as the Brothers *Grimm, *Asbjørnsen and Moe, J. M. Thiele, the Czech Bozena Nemcova, the Serbian Vuk Karadzic, and took into consideration their positive results as well as evident shortcomings. His collection carries references to a number of European counterparts.

Afanasyev was very careful with variants and tried to preserve the peculiarities of oral speech and dialects and their specific grammatical and syntactic structures, avoiding variants supplied by servants and educated people. He was very critical of his colleague Ivan Khudyakov and his collection *Russian Fairy Tales* (1860), which retold folk tales in a bookish language and made no effort to disentangle the many obscure places in his oral sources. Afanasyev took the Grimms' *Kinder- und Hausmärchen* as a model, the Russian translation of which he reviewed in 1864. As a comparatist, he was especially interested in parallels between Slavic and Germanic folk tales.

Afanasyev himself collected folk tales from different sources, starting with his home town and province, but he made use too of the scarce previous publications of the archives of the Russian Geographic Society, founded in 1845, as well as amateur collectors all over Russia. He also made some careful extractions from old chapbooks. His goal was to find genuine texts, free from contaminations and fusions. Unlike the Grimm Brothers, he rejected retelling, polishing, or literary revisions. Thus, unlike the Grimms' collection, Afanasyev's was a purely scholarly publication, not addressed to a wide readership. However, further editions, selections, and adaptations have indeed reached a mass audience of adults as well as children.

After the publication of the first volume of *Russian Fairy Tales*, Afanasyev received a great deal of support from collectors and folk-tale lovers. One of his most significant informants was Vladimir Dal, the famous author of *The Dictionary of the Living Russian Language* (1863-6), who supplied Afanasyev with over a thousand transcripts of folk tales, of which Afanasyev used about 150. Texts in Afanasyev's collection originate from over 30 Russian provinces, three Ukrainian, and one Belorussian. He also proposed scholarly strategies for collecting, transcribing, editing, and publishing oral sources, as well as criteria for using reliable informants. He was criticized for his views, especially since the Russian literary establishment doubted that illiterate Russian peasants were capable of telling coherent stories. Many critics also questioned the artistic merits of Russian folk tales as compared to European. Still, the collection was widely appreciated by scholars in Russia and abroad.

Afanasyev not only collected, but studied his material. The second edition of *Russian Fairy Tales*, which appeared posthumously in 1873, was annotated and classified according to recent scholarly theories. As his foremost objective, Afanasyev envisioned the study of the mythological origins of folklore, consistent with the position of the so-called mythological school of comparative folklore studies (the Grimm Brothers, in Russia Fyodor Buslayev). He was fascinated by the scope of material which this approach offered, and in his own work he managed to widen the perspective still further, incorporating folklore genres such as the heroic epic, ritual folklore, etc.

The classification of fairy tales, which Afanasyev compiled for his collection (animal tales, magic tales, humorous tales, satirical tales, anecdotes, etc.) is, with some minor amendments, still used by folklorists. A complete collection of *Russian Fairy Tales* was reprinted six times, most recently in 1984, and many volumes of selections have been published. It has been translated into all major languages. The standard edition in English was published in New York in 1945, translated by Norbert Guterman and with an introduction by Roman Jakobson.

In his edition for young readers, *Russian Fairy Tales for Children*, Afanasyev included 29 animal tales, 16 magic tales, and 16 humorous tales from his collection, carefully adapting the language, substituting standard Russian for dialectisms, and excluding everything not suitable for children. However, even this edition was criticized because many fairy tales had trickster heroes and depicted the triumph of cunning. The collection has been reprinted over 25 times and illustrated by the most prominent Russian and Soviet artists.

Both Afanasyev's scholarly studies and his collections were subjected to severe censorship in Tsarist Russia. *Russian Folk Legends*, although passed by censors, was banned soon after it appeared; the church viewed the collection as blasphemous and obscene. The volume was reprinted by the Free Russian Publishers in London. In fact, these stories of Adam and Eve, Noah, the prophets, Jesus and his disciples contain a bizarre mixture of Christian and pagan views as well as clear social satire. The ban complicated the publication of the last two volumes of *Russian Fairy Tales* in which Afanasyev was obliged to delete the most offensive passages, according to censors' orders. The deleted material, together with other tales marked by Afanasyev as 'unprintable', was published anonymously in Switzerland, presumably in 1872, under the title *Russian Forbidden Tales* (the Russian word 'zavetny' can also mean 'sacred', which stresses the much-discussed links between the sacral and the obscene in archaic thought). It contained 77 tales and about 20 variants, mostly humorous, but also some magic and animal tales. They were omitted from the main collection not only because of their open obscenity and eroticism, but also because of their anticlerical attitude: many portrayed priests and monks in an unfavourable light. The collection was published in French as *Contes secrets russes* in 1912.   MN

Bremond, Claude, and Verrier, Jean, 'Afanassiev et Propp', *Littérature*, 45 (February 1982).

Haney, Jack V., *An Introduction to the Russian Folktale* (1999).

Pomeranceva, Erna, 'A. N. Afanas'ev und die Brüder Grimm', *Deutsches Jahrbuch für Volkskunde*, 11 (1963).

Aiken, Joan (1924–2004) British writer of novels, poetry, short stories, and plays for children and adults. The daughter of the American poet Conrad Aiken, she was born and educated in England but never attended a university. She published over 60 children's books, as well as many adult novels. Her titles for children include ghost stories, historical fiction, plays, and picture books. She also wrote several collections of brilliantly original fairy tales. They include *All You've Ever Wanted* (1953), *More Than You Bargained For* (1955), *A Necklace of Raindrops* (1968), *A Small Pinch of Weather* (1969), *A Harp of Fishbones* (1972), *Not What You Expected* (1974), *Up the Chimney Down* (1984), *The Last Slice of Rainbow* (1985), and *Past Eight o'clock* (1987).

As a teller of fairy stories, Aiken was the natural heir of Edith *Nesbit. Her vivid and amazingly inventive tales, like Nesbit's, are usually set in contemporary England, and much of their surprise and humour comes from the juxtaposition of traditional magic and modern technology. (In 'Up the Chimney Down' the wicked witch even owns a computer.)

Like Nesbit's, Aiken's tales sometimes have an undertone of social satire. In 'The Brat Who Knew Too Much', for instance, an 8-year-old girl with magical encyclopaedic knowledge disrupts first a pretentious panel of experts on the BBC and eventually a large number of international organizations.

Joan Aiken's tales feature not only standard fairy-story personages and props (kings and queens, witches and wizards, magic objects and spells), but characters and events from modern folklore, including the Tooth

Fairy and Good King Wenceslas. Her take on all of them is original and surprising. King Wenceslas's charity, for instance, is misplaced, and in the end it is the 'poor man gathering winter fuel' who offers a good meal to the king.

Many of Aiken's tales centre on the experiences of Mark and Harriet Armitage, who live in a rural English village where the existence of magic is taken for granted. Mark and Harriet go to a school run by a witch, have a temporary governess who is a ghost, and keep a pet unicorn. In one of her best stories, 'A Small Pinch of Weather', the family is visited both by a pompous ex-colonial great-uncle and the Furies, three dog-faced ladies in black who eat pins and cause everyone who comes to the house to reveal their past crimes: 'the window-cleaner . . . was now on his knees in the flowerbed, confessing to anyone who would listen that he had pinched a diamond brooch. . . . the man who came to mend the fridge . . . seemed frightfully upset about something he had done to a person called Elsie'.

Most of Joan Aiken's tales are full of fun and surprise and end happily, but some look at the world from a more contemplative and poetic perspective. A few even end with sadness and loss, like 'The Serial Garden', where lovers are separated forever when a cut-out paper panorama from the back of cereal boxes is destroyed. Clearly, Aiken not only had tremendous inventive powers, but unusual emotional range. AL

Apseloff, Marilyn, 'Joan Aiken: Literary Dramatist', *Children's Literature Association Quarterly*, 9.3 (fall 1984).

Ainsworth, Ruth (1908–84) English writer of books for children who published numerous retellings of the classical fairy tales. Her more original work consists of the fairy-tale novels *The Talking Rock* (1979) and *The Mysterious Baba and her Magic Caravan: Two Stories* (1980). In *The Talking Rock* a young boy named Jakes makes a figure in the sand who magically comes to life. This Sand Boy joins with Jakes and a mermaid to overcome the sea monster Glumper, who is oppressing all the

sea creatures. Ainsworth's two stories in *The Mysterious Baba and her Magic Caravan* take place in the Left-Over Land, a place where unsold toys make their home and where a homeless Russian doll named Baba creates excitement for the rest of the dolls. Ainsworth has also published *The Ruth Ainsworth Book* (1970) and *Mermaids' Tales* (1980), which include fairy-tale narratives.

JZ

Aladdin Protagonist of a tale named 'Aladdin and the Wonderful Lamp', which is included in most standard editions of *The Arabian Nights* (also known as *The Thousand and One Nights*). The tale takes place in the mountains of China where the boy Aladdin lives with his poor widowed mother. Aladdin is sought out by a Moroccan sorcerer, for whom he is to recover an oil lamp from a subterranean treasure grove. When he refuses to deliver the lamp while still inside the cave, the evil sorcerer deserts him. With the aid of a magic ring, Aladdin is rescued. By chance he discovers that the lamp commands a powerful demon, becomes rich, and eventually marries the princess. As the sorcerer learns about Aladdin's luck, he approaches the princess in disguise, tricks her into giving him the lamp, and has the demon kidnap her. Aladdin manages to find the sorcerer's hiding place, kills him, and recovers his wife.

The tale did not form an integral part of *The Arabian Nights* prior to their Western reception. First published in 1712, the tale originates from Antoine *Galland's autobiographically influenced reworking of an alleged oral performance in 1709 by the Christian Syrian narrator Hanna Diyab, who also contributed the tale of *'Ali Baba and the Forty Thieves' to Galland's *Arabian Nights*. Arabic manuscripts discovered later proved to be forgeries. Soon after its original publication, the tale became extremely popular in chapbooks, literary adaptations, children's literature, stage performances (above all, British Christmas pantomime), and movies. In 1992 it was further popularized by a *Disney animated film (and a number of sequels), which modified Aladdin into a cunning trickster character. By the end of the 20th century, it has come to represent the standard Western notion of the classical oriental fairy tale. Indeed, the image of the omnipotent demon hidden inside a humble lamp has become proverbial in everyday language, literature, politics, science, and commerce.   UM

Gerhardt, Mia I., *The Art of Story-Telling* (1963).
Irwin, Robert, *The Arabian Nights* (1994).
Mahdi, Muhsin, *The Thousand and One Nights (Alf Layla wa-Layla) from the Earliest Known Sources*, iii (1994).
Ranke, Kurt *et al.* (eds.), 'Alad(d)in', *Enzyklopädie des Märchens*, i (1977).

Alcott, Louisa May (1832–88) American writer of fantasy tales, best known for her classic novel *Little Women* (1868). Alcott, whose father was friends with Henry David Thoreau and Ralph Waldo Emerson, was strongly influenced by transcendentalism, particularly the idea, which permeates all her tales, that in order to change society as a whole one must begin by reforming the individual. In her *Flower Fables* (1854), initially written for Emerson's daughter Ellen, Alcott's fairy-flower protagonists learn that love can transform a cold heart ('The Frost-King; or, the Power of Love') and that selfishness leads to unhappiness ('Lily Bell and Thistledown'). In her second collection, *The Rose Family* (1864), three fairy sisters go to the good fairy Star to overcome their idleness, wilfulness, and vanity. Among other stories with fairy-tale motifs, Alcott wrote 'Fairy Pinafores', in which Cinderella's fairy godmother, looking for 'some other clever bit of work to do', gathers 100 homeless children to make magic pinafores (published in *Aunt Jo's Scrap-Bag: Cupid and Chow-Chow*, 1873); and 'The Skipping Shoes', in which Alcott rewrites 'The *Red Shoes' and has Kitty, who refuses to do what people ask, wear shoes she does not like, the magical powers of which force her to do as she is told (published in *Lulu's Library: A Christmas Dream*, 1886). Other collections of Alcott's fairy and fantasy stories include *Morning Glories, and Other Stories* (1867), and *Lulu's Library: The Frost King* (1887).   AD

Alexander, Lloyd (1924–2007) Major American author of fairy-tale novels. He studied at the Sorbonne and translated Sartre and Éluard. His best-known work, the so-called Prydain Chronicles, consists of five novels, *The Book of Three* (1964), *The Black Cauldron* (1965), *The Castle of Llyr* (1966), *Taran Wanderer* (1967), and *The High King* (1968), which received the Newbery Medal. The cycle is based on the Welsh collection *Mabinogion*. Alexander's initial intention was simply to retell the stories, but instead he created his own fairy-tale world, inhabited by wizards and dwarfs, the three wise witches Orddu, Orwen, and Ordoch, the invincible Cauldron-born, and the Huntsmen. This world is threatened by Arawn, the Death-Lord of Annuvin, assisted by the treacherous enchantress Achren. A variety of magical objects from Celtic folklore are featured, such as a cauldron, a magic sword, and a book of spells.

The central character of the cycle, Taran, is a typical folk-tale 'common hero' of unknown origin. He becomes an Assistant Pig-Keeper, and the disappearance of the sacred animal in his charge, the traditional Welsh folktale character Hen-Wen, draws Taran into a struggle between good and evil. After many trials, Taran finds his true identity and wins the love of the brave and extravagant princess Eilonwy. When all the old magic forces, the Sons and Daughters of Don, leave Prydain, Taran is left to be the High King, endowed with great power, but also bearing responsibility for the country which has been delivered from evil.

For Alexander, the fairy-tale form is a means to describe reality, and many real events, characters, and settings have been woven into Prydain stories. He makes use of European folklore heritage, overtly taking *Tolkien and C. S. *Lewis as his models. The Prydain Chronicles are also characterized by their humour and irony, uncustomary in the heroic fairy tale. Comical figures, like the ever-hungry Gurgi, and the boastful bragging bard Fflewddur Fflam with his magic harp, give the novels an unforgettable charm. Alexander has also published a collection of fairy tales and two fairy-tale picture books connected with the Prydain novels. In 1985, the Prydain cycle was made into a major *Disney movie entitled *The Black Cauldron*.

In *The First Two Lives of Lukas-Kasha* (1978) Alexander sends his hero to an alternative world which recalls the universe of *The *Arabian Nights*, where he becomes involved in a struggle against a bloodthirsty tyrant. Unlike Taran, Lukas does not win a princess and a kingdom, but returns to his own world, presumably as a spiritually better person.

Two other sequel fairy tales, the Westmark Trilogy (1981–3) and the so-called Vesper Books (1986–90), although they lack magic, follow closely the traditional narrative patterns of fairy tales. In many of his novels Alexander explored a number of ancient mythologies, always moulding them into stories of quest and maturation: Chinese in *The Remarkable Journey of Prince Jen* (1991), Greek in *The Arcadians* (1995), and Indian in *The Iron Ring* (1997). *Gypsy Rizka* (1999) and *The Rope Trick* (2002) take place in pseudo-historical settings and paint colourful panoramas of folk life, especially wandering performers. He also produced a comic version dealing with the origin myth *How the Cat Swallowed Thunder* (2002), in which Mother Holle, the witch from the Grimms' fairy tale, plays a significant role. A significant feature of these, as well as Alexander's earlier novels, is a presence of strong and independent young women, evolving from the fairy-tale tradition of the active heroine.   MN

Bagnall, Norma, 'An American Hero in Welsh Fantasy: The Mabinogion, Alan Garner and Lloyd Alexander', *New Welsh Review*, 2.4 (1990).

Kuznets, Lois, '"High Fantasy" in America', *The Lion and the Unicorn*, 9 (1985).

May, Jill P., *Lloyd Alexander* (1991).

Stott, Jon, 'Alexander's Chronicles of Prydain: The Nature of Beginnings'. In *Touchstones: Reflections on the Best in Children's Literature*, ed. Perry Nodelman, vol. 1 (1985).

Tunnell, Michael O., *The Prydain Companion: A Reference Guide to Lloyd Alexander's Prydain Chronicles* (1989).

Ali Baba Protagonist of the tale 'Ali Baba and the Forty Thieves', included in most standard editions of *The *Arabian Nights* (also known as *The Thousand and One Nights*). The poor woodcutter Ali Baba one day observes a band of 40 robbers who access their treasure grove by pronouncing a magic formula ('Open, Sesame') that makes the mountain split. After the robbers have left, Ali Baba enters the cave and takes away some bags of money. At home he secretly counts the money using a measure he borrowed from his rich brother. However, the latter's wife has prepared the measure so that a coin is left sticking to it when returned. In that way, the rich brother finds out about the treasure, has Ali Baba disclose the working mechanism of the magic opening, and enters the cave himself. Wishing to leave, he has forgotten the magic formula and is trapped. The returning robbers discover and subsequently kill him. Ali Baba later recovers his brother's body, carries him home, and has him buried. Meanwhile, the robbers have located Ali Baba's home and try to murder him. Their leader disguises himself as a travelling merchant and smuggles the robbers into the house concealed in oil casks. Ali Baba's wily slave girl Marjana (Morgiana) finds out about their plans and kills the hidden robbers by pouring hot oil on their heads. Their leader manages to escape and later returns in a different disguise. Since he refuses to salt his meal (which would compel him to form a friendship with his host), Marjana discloses his identity and stabs him.

First published in 1717 in volume xi of Antoine *Galland's *Les Mille et une nuits*, the tale does not form an integral part of *The Arabian Nights* as part of an authentic Arabic tradition. Rather, it constitutes the inspired reworking of an oral performance in 1709 by the Christian Syrian narrator Hanna Diyab, who also contributed the tale of Aladdin to Galland's *Arabian Nights*. The only extant Arabic manuscript of the tale of *Ali Baba* has been proved to constitute a forgery by the orientalist Jean Varsy. From the second half of the 18th century, the tale was published in numerous popular prints of the chapbook variety. Besides adaptations and allusions in literature, it inspired a number of operas, toy theatre plays, and stage performances (such as British Christmas pantomime), films, cartoons, and numerous versions in popular storytelling. **UM**

Gerhardt, Mia I., *The Art of Story-Telling* (1963).

Irwin, Robert, *The Arabian Nights* (1994).

Mahdi, Muhsin, *The Thousand and One Nights (Alf Layla wa-Layla) from the Earliest Known Sources*, iii (1994).

Ranke, Kurt, *et al.* (eds.), 'Ali Baba und die vierzig Räuber', *Enzyklopädie des Märchens*, (1977).

Ali Baba and the Forty Thieves (film versions)

The cinema has generally been keener on the title than it has on the original storyline from The *Arabian Nights*. In a wartime adaptation directed by Arthur Lubin (USA, 1944), Ali is a young prince rather than a woodcutter, and the thieves are swashbuckling adventurers rather than brutal murderers. Ali joins their band as a way of hiding from the invading Mongols who have killed his father, the caliph. The story is primarily a peg on which to hang an escapist Technicolor extravaganza; at the same time it nods to the contemporary situation by suggesting that Ali Baba and the thieves offer a parallel to underground resistance movements, and that the cruel, tyrannical Mongols are like Nazis.

Eleven years later (France, 1955) Jacques Becker directed a version, shot partly on location in Morocco, which retains more of the situations from the original text, but plays them for laughs. Conceived primarily as a vehicle for the leading comic actor Fernandel, this adaptation makes Ali a crafty underling, servant of a brutal master who orders Ali to go and buy him a wife. Ali chooses a beautiful dancer, Morgiane, but falls in love with her himself, and then spends a lot of time helping her evade her eager husband's sexual claims. When Ali finds out the thieves' cave and its secret password he takes some of the treasure and is able to buy Morgiane from his master, but before they can live happily together there are forty angry thieves to contend with. **TAS**

Alice in Wonderland (1865)

Classic Victorian fairy tale by Lewis *Carroll (Latinized pseudonym of Charles Lutwidge Dodgson, 1832–98). First published as *Alice's Adventures Under Ground* (1863), it was inspired by a boating party with Alice Liddell and her sisters, daughters of an Oxford don. The fictional Alice is a 7-year-old who falls down a rabbit hole, changes from microscopic to telescopic proportions, and encounters a hookah-smoking Caterpillar, Mock Turtle, and Cheshire Cat. This early version was expanded to include the Mad Tea Party, the Pig and Pepper episode with the Ugly Duchess, Alice's trial by the Queen of Hearts, and parodies such as 'Speak Roughly to Your Little Boy' and 'Twinkle, Twinkle, Little Bat'. The revised text also included illustrations by John *Tenniel, the political cartoonist for *Punch* who also worked on the sequel. *Through the Looking-Glass and What Alice Found There* (1871) has Alice participating in a Rabelaisian living chess game with Red and White Queens and a White Knight. On her way to becoming a Queen, she meets talking flowers, a battling Lion and Unicorn, Humpty Dumpty, and the twins Tweedledum and Tweedledee, who recite 'You Are Old, Father William' and 'The Walrus and the Carpenter'. 'Jabberwocky', perhaps the most celebrated English nonsense poem, and 'Upon the Lonely Moor', a parody of Wordsworth, are also included.

The fact that nonsense and literary parody coexist in these novels underscores the dual nature of their child/adult readership—and their author. Often described as a Jekyll-and-Hyde personality, C. L. Dodgson was a celebrated Victorian photographer, ordained deacon, and Oxford don who delivered dry mathematics lectures and published logic texts. As the pseudonymous Lewis Carroll, however, he wrote whimsical fiction that challenged the moralizing children's literature of the period. His Alice is in the tradition of the abandoned child heroine, but the Wonderland she explores borders on Victorian Gothic horror fiction. Carroll's originality was to combine the two genres. He tempered his allegorical portrait of socio-economic upheaval with humorous doses of thought-provoking paradox. This fresh didacticism made his 'love-gift of a fairy-tale' so popular that his books were second only to the Bible in bourgeois Victorian nurseries.

Alice's commercial value rose as she was reproduced on everything from teapots to chess sets. Marketing reached new heights with playing cards, puzzles, songs, plays, and broadcasts once the copyright expired in 1907. Alice, the Mad Hatter, and the Ugly Duchess had long entered national folklore by 1928, when Sotheby's auctioned the original manuscript for the unheard-of sum of £15,400; it was later sold to the Parke-Bernet Galleries for $50,000. In 1948, to show its appreciation of Britain's war efforts, the United States donated this national treasure to the British Museum—where it was received by no less than the Archbishop of Canterbury.

What in the *Alice* books could possibly have commanded such respect? For many, Alice is the epitome of the brave Victorian innocent in a confusing magical land. Translated into languages ranging from Swahili to Esperanto, her fairy tales are surpassed only by Shakespeare and the Bible for expressions that have entered the English language (such as 'mad as a hatter'). Given this lofty company, it is little wonder that those who wax nostalgic for these children's books find it a sin to dissect them. Psychoanalysts, for example, puncture the *Alice* books' myth of childhood innocence. Focusing on the author's sexuality, they document his fantasies about becoming a little girl and cite scores of letters to 'little-girlfriends' whom he adored kissing, sometimes photographing or drawing them in the nude. They also speculate on his attraction and rumoured marriage proposal to young Alice Liddell, and find phallic symbolism in the fictional Alice's snake-like neck and bodily distortions from large to small. Freudians feel that this may also represent a return to the womb; others posit a hallucinogenic drug experience. Literary historians, on the other hand, note that Gulliver and Micromégas underwent similar changes, and place the *Alice* books in the satiric tradition of Swift and Voltaire. Sociopolitical criticism of a fragmented bourgeois society is also noted by historians: they find parallels with the dizzying pace at which the early Industrial Revolution reacted to technological, demographic, and political changes as it embraced industrialization, laissez-faire capitalism, and a free-market economy. Still others analyse Alice's dream and parallel universe that violate spatio-temporal laws. For them, Alice exists in an eternal moment out of time, a Heideggerian space between consciousness and reality where she poses existential questions of identity and confronts problems of maturation. Moreover, she must function in a metaphorical world where everyone is 'quite mad' and relationships are paradoxical. Indeed, linguistic and physical realities rarely coincide in Wonderland, and semioticians annotate disjunctions between sign and signifier whenever smiles represent Cheshire cats or boys turn into pigs. In addition to Alice's numerous meta-referential allusions to her own fairy tale, they examine Carroll's linguistic experimentation and portmanteau words with reference to Edward Lear (a contemporary) and James Joyce (who was reared on the *Alice* books). Carroll's marvellous images are balanced by Tenniel's illustrations, which caricatured real-life politicians like Disraeli (the Unicorn) and Gladstone (the Lion). It is in this combination of text and image, of fantasy and reality, of the abstract and the concrete that Alice's dual readership finds meaning and enjoyment.

Alice's enduring influence is attested by some 200 pastiches and parodies, some reproduced in Carolyn Sigler's *Alternative Alices: Visions and Revisions of Lewis Carroll's Alice Books* (1997). Many of these texts were produced by Victorian women writers: just as the *Alice* books comment on Victorian girlhood, so these imitations construct women's cultural authority. Other texts were blatantly didactic, still others were humorously political. All were subversive. Their popularity waned during the 1920s when Alice left popular culture for high culture and was appropriated by scholars and theorists. Film-makers adopted her as well, and her representations ranging from *Disney animation (1951) to pornographic musicals (1976) underscore her mythic capacity to adapt to genres for both children and adults. Today's Alice, a bit wiser than Carroll's, is a postmodern empowered heroine in control of Wonderlands of her own (feminist) design.   MLE

Bloom, Harold (ed.), *Lewis Carroll* (1987).
Gardner, Martin, *The Annotated Alice* (1960).
Heath, Peter, *The Philosopher's Alice* (1974).
Rackin, Donald, *Alice's Adventures in Wonderland and Through the Looking-Glass: Nonsense, Sense, and Meaning* (1991).
Sigler, Carolyn (ed.), *Alternative Alices: Visions and Revisions of Lewis Carroll's Alice Books* (1997).

Alice in Wonderland (film versions) *Alice in Wonderland*, a classic Victorian fantasy, has proved more difficult than most to bring to the screen. The rambling, dreamlike structure coupled with the book's literary stature and the renown of the original John *Tenniel drawings have created problems for a range of film-makers.

Alice in Wonderland (film: USA, 1933) combined the first Alice book with its sequel, *Through the Looking Glass*. The result is a series of assorted incidents which come and go without much relation to each other. Further, the Tenniel factor influenced the director to decide that each of the actors must wear a Tenniel-style mask of the character being portrayed; thus an array of stars including Gary Cooper (the White Knight), Cary Grant (the Mock Turtle), W. C. Fields (Humpty Dumpty), and Jack Oakie (Tweedledum) are heard but not seen.

In the early 1950s, with Lewis *Carroll's book just out of copyright, two fresh attempts at making cinematic sense of the stories appeared. A British-French-American co-production of 1951 began by locating their origins in Victorian Oxford. Alice, her father the Dean, the Vice-Chancellor, and Queen Victoria all feature in a live-action prologue; then Carroll, as maths lecturer Dodgson, makes up for Alice the story which the film, with some fidelity, goes on to show. The creatures Alice meets in Wonderland, played by 128 articulated Tenniel-based puppets brought to life by stop-motion photography, are derived from the people and events of Oxford. Thus the Cheshire Cat is Alice's father, the White Rabbit is the Vice-Chancellor, and the head-chopping Queen of Hearts is Queen Victoria. This last identification, and the caricature presentation of Victoria in the prologue, led to problems which resulted in the film having to wait till the 1980s before getting a release in the UK.

Elsewhere it competed with *Disney's animated version (USA, 1951), which tried to make the story accessible by rearranging Carroll's sequence of events, omitting some characters, bringing in others from the second book, inventing a new one, and giving the narrative a logical chase structure—Alice constantly in pursuit of the White Rabbit. The surrealism of Carroll's scene in which a baby turns into a pig while Alice is holding it is one of the elements left out by Disney as being too repulsive. Also missing are the White Knight, the Duchess, Humpty Dumpty, and the Mock Turtle. They are replaced by the Jabberwock and its backing group, and by the only totally Disney invention, Doorknob, who guards the entrance to Wonderland. In the late 1960s, despite its omission of the pig-baby scene, the film acquired a reputation as a 'head-trip', and for a while had cult status.

Another 1960s fashion—sitar music played by Ravi Shankar—accompanies an adaptation directed by Jonathan Miller for the BBC in 1966. Apart from that, the film contains no contemporary references. It aims, rather, to lay bare what was in Carroll's mind. Miller would have liked to re-title the story 'Growing Pains', perceiving it to be not in any sense a fairy tale, but a Victorian child's-eye-view of a gallery of upper middle-class characters and their servants, thinly disguised by animal names and by the Tenniel drawings. This version therefore uses authentic Victorian locations but no masks, no special effects, and no animal costumes. John Gielgud (the Mock Turtle), Peter Cook (the Mad Hatter), Peter Sellers (the King of Hearts), and other actors create their characters solely through the use of voice, face, and gesture. Their caperings, ramblings, gravity, and outbursts of bad temper are all mediated by Alice's disdainful gaze and cool questioning, as she realizes with dismay that she is doomed to grow up and become like them.

Far away from Carroll's narrative line, but aiming to be close to him in spirit, is Jan Swankmajer's *Alice* (*Neco z Alenky*, Switzerland, 1988). Swankmajer, a Czech surrrealist working within the medium of three-dimensional animation, was inspired by Carroll's stories to make a film which illustrates his belief that there is no simple distinction between dreams and reality: for him, dreams are reality. With no dialogue, using a mixture of human Alice and doll Alice, real animals and puppet animals, he begins the story in the traditional way—Alice falling asleep by a stream. As soon as she dreams, however, the White Rabbit is different: stuffed with sawdust, he escapes from a glass case by smashing it from the inside with scissors; and he leads Alice into her adventures not down a rabbit hole but through the drawer of a kitchen table in the middle of a field. The subsequent incidents sometimes derive from Carroll—the 'pool of tears' scene is seized with relish—but mainly consist of variations on Carroll's themes. Alice is constantly hungry, but cannot satisfy her hunger: a scoop of jam contains tacks, a baguette sprouts nails, lumps of raw bleeding meat pass by, a sardine tin yields a key but no sardines, tarts just make her grow bigger or smaller. The Caterpillar—played by a sock, a pair of glass eyes, and a set of false teeth—darns his eyes shut with a needle and thread when he wants to retire. When Alice wakes up she is no longer by the stream; she is now where she was at the beginning of the dream—on her nursery floor. Everything she has dreamed about is around her, except that the glass case is still smashed—and the rabbit has not returned to it.

A kind of postscript to all these adaptations is offered by *Dreamchild* (UK, 1985), written by Dennis Potter, which centres on the real-life Alice Liddell, at the age of 80, visiting New York in 1932. A young American reporter charms her into talking and wins the love of her young companion, Lucy. Alice opens up, goes back in her mind to 1862, and becomes haunted by her memories of Dodgson and the characters he made up for her. Some of them—the Mad Hatter, the Caterpillar, the Gryphon, the Mock Turtle—come alive on the screen in the form of animatronic creatures designed and performed by the Jim *Henson company. At the degree ceremony which is her reason for being in New York, Alice finally comes to understand and accept Dodgson's gift, and the love for her which it expressed.

The perpetual love for Alice, real and fictional, can be seen in the many twenty-first century cinematic adaptations such as Tim Burton's *Alice in Wonderland* (2010).   TAS

Alice's Adventures in Wonderland See ALICE IN WONDERLAND.

Álvarez González, Blanca (1957–)
Spanish journalist, poet, and writer of fiction for adults, teenagers, and children. She has been awarded prestigious prizes in Spain and her works have received distinctions for their quality, as with her story *Milú, un perro en desgracia* (*Milú, An Unlucky Dog*, 2001), which was included in the White Ravens Catalogue in 2001. Her interest in fairy tales manifests itself in fiction works such as *Se busca novio principesco* (*Looking for a Princely Fiancé*, 2004) and *La princesa Shiro* (*Princess Shiro*, 2014). She has also published a number of critical essays on fairy tales in *CLIJ*, a Spanish journal devoted to children's and young adult literature, now included in a book entitled *La verdadera historia de los cuentos populares* (*The True History of Folk Tales*, 2011).   CFR

Alverdes, Paul (1897–1979) German
writer and dramatist who turned to writing for children in the late 1930s and published an adaptation of German folk tales in 1939. He is best known for his charming fairy-tale picture books such as *Das Männlein Mittenzwei* (*The Little Man Mittenzwei*, 1937), *Grimbarts Haus* (*Grimbart's House*, 1949), and *Vom dicken fetten Pfannkuchen* (*About the Thick Fat Pancake*, 1960).   JZ

Andersen, Hans Christian (1805–75) Danish writer, often regarded as the father of modern fairy tales. Son of a cobbler and a washerwoman, he rose to the position of a national poet and is the most well-known Scandinavian writer of all times.

Although Andersen considered himself a novelist and playwright, his unquestionable fame is based on his fairy tales. He published four collections: *Eventyr, fortalte for børn* (*Fairy Tales, Told for Children*, 1835–42), *Nye eventyr* (*New Fairy Tales*, 1844–8), *Historier* (*Stories*, 1852–5), and *Nye eventyr og historier* (*New Fairy Tales and Stories*, 1858–72), which already during his lifetime were translated into many languages.

The sources of his stories were mostly Danish folk tales, collected and retold by his immediate predecessors J. M. Thiele, Adam *Oehlenschläger, and Bernhard *Ingemann. Unlike the collectors, whose aim was to preserve and sometimes to classify and study fairy tales, Andersen was in the first place a writer, and his objective was to create new literary works based on folklore. As exceptions, some fairy tales have their origins in ancient poetry ('The Naughty Boy') or medieval European literature ('The Emperor's New Clothes').

There are several ways in which Andersen may be said to have created the genre of modern fairy tale. First, he gave the fairy tale a personal touch. His very first fairy tale, 'The Tinder Box', opens in a matter-of-fact way, instead of the traditional 'Once upon a time', and its characters, including the king, speak a colloquial, everyday language. This feature became the trademark of Andersen's style. Quite a number of his early fairy tales are retellings of traditional folk tales, such as 'Little Claus and Big Claus', 'The *Princess and the Pea', 'The Travelling Companion', 'The Swineherd', 'The Wild Swans'; however, in Andersen's rendering they acquire an unmistakable individuality and brilliant irony. Kings go around in battered slippers and personally open gates of their kingdoms; princesses read newspapers and roast chicken; and many supernatural creatures in later tales behave and talk like ordinary people. An explicit narrative voice, commenting on the events and addressing the listener, is another characteristic trait of Andersen's tales. It is not accidental that many fairy tales were told by Andersen to real children before he wrote them down. However, there are no conventional morals in them, possibly with the exception of 'The *Red Shoes'.

Secondly, Andersen brought the fairy tale into the everyday. His first original fairy tale, 'Little Ida's Flowers', recalls the tales of E. T. A. *Hoffmann in its elaborate combination of the ordinary and the fantastic, its nocturnal magical transformations, and its use of the child as a narrative lens. Still closer to Hoffmann is 'The *Steadfast Tin Soldier' with its animation of the realm of toys. However, in both tales Andersen's melancholic view of life is revealed: both end tragically, thus raising the question whether children's literature must depend on happy endings. These may be counterbalanced by more conventional stories of trials and reward, such as *'Thumbelina' or 'The *Snow Queen', the latter based on the popular Norse legend of the Ice Maiden.

In a group of fairy tales, Andersen went still further in animating the material world around him and introducing everyday objects as protagonists: 'The Sweethearts' (also known as 'The Top and the Ball'), 'The Shepherdess and the Chimney Sweep', 'The Shirt Collar', 'The Darning-Needle'; he is credited with being a pioneer in this respect. Also, flowers and plants are ascribed a rich spiritual life, as in 'The Daisy', or arrogance, as in 'The Fir Tree', or otherwise are depicted as having a limited petty bourgeois horizon, as in 'Five Peas from One Pod'.

Andersen's animal tales are also radically different from traditional fables. While in 'The Storks' he makes an original interpretation of the popular saying that babies are brought by storks, in several stories ('The Happy Family', 'The Sprinters', 'The Dung-Beetle') Andersen makes animals represent different perspectives on life, and the stories themselves are more like satirical sketches of human manners than fairy tales for children. 'The *Ugly Duckling', probably one of Andersen's best-known stories, is a camouflaged autobiography, echoing the writer's much-quoted statement: 'First you must endure a lot, then you get famous.' The animals, including the protagonist, possess human traits, views, and emotions, making the story indeed a poignant account of the road from humiliation through sufferings to well-deserved bliss. The message is, however, ambivalent: you have to be born a swan in order to become one.

Another programmatic fairy tale is 'The *Little Mermaid', based on a medieval ballad, eagerly exploited by romantic poets. Andersen, however, reversed the roles and, toning down the ballad's motif of the Christian versus the pagan, created a beautiful and tragic story of impossible love, which certainly also reflected his personal experience.

While most of Andersen's fairy tales are firmly anchored in his home country and often mention concrete topographical details, like the Round Tower in Copenhagen, some fairy tales have exotic settings, like China in 'The Nightingale', or unspecified 'Southern countries' in 'The Shadow'. This tale, based loosely on a story by Adelbert von *Chamisso, which it also mentions indirectly, is probably the most enigmatic and disturbing of his tales. Published in 1847, it marked a general change in Andersen tales, from being addressed to children to a wider audience, even primarily adults. In fact, his late tales, which he himself characterized as 'Stories' rather than 'Fairy Tales', are much less known and almost never published in contemporary collections for children. Among them is Andersen's tribute to modern technology, 'The Great Sea-Serpent', depicting the first transatlantic telegraph cable.

The significance of Andersen may be illustrated by the fact that the world's most prestigious prize in children's literature, the Andersen Medal, is named after him, and that his birthday, 2 April, is celebrated as the International Children's Book Day.

MN

Andersen, Jens, *Hans Christian Andersen: A New Life* (2006).

Binding, Paul, *Hans Christian Andersen: European Witness* (2014).

Bredsdorf, Elias, *Hans Christian Andersen* (1975).

Grønbech, Bo, *Hans Christian Andersen* (1980).

Rossel, Sven Hakon (ed.), *Hans Christian Andersen: Danish Writer and Citizen of the World* (1996).

Wullschlager, Jackie, *Hans Christian Andersen: The Life of a Storyteller* (2000).

Zipes, Jack, *Hans Christian Andersen: The Misunderstood Storyteller* (2005).

Andersson, Christina (1936–) Finnish-Swedish author and illustrator of children's literature that offers subversive retellings of traditional folktales, frequently imposing modern language and urban settings. Andersson's adaptations often reverse traditional gender roles and hero/villain binaries. Popular tales like *'Red Riding Hood', *'Hansel and Gretel', and *'Sleeping Beauty' present female heroines rescuing princes, wolves victimized by woodsmen, and parents falling prey to children/executioners. Andersson's stories are not just comical, but they provide a critical lens for reconsidering modern understandings of childhood and morality. Famous publications include *Jakob Dunderskägg Sitter Barnvakt* (*The Babysitter Jacob Rumblebeard*, 1969), *Sagoblunten* (*Fairy Bumble*, 1974), *Sagoluvern* (*Fairy Ruffle*, 1979), and *Glada Korven Eller Inget Har en Ande* (*The Happy Sausage or Nothing Has an Ending*, 1980). KMJ

Anstey, F. (pseudonym of **Thomas Anstey Guthrie**, 1856–1934) Author of stories of fantasy and humour. *Vice-Versa* (1882), his best-known work, was also his first, begun when he was an undergraduate at Cambridge. Subtitled 'A Lesson to Fathers', it shows the consequences of rashly wishing to be a boy again. Paul Bultitude unwittingly holds a magical talisman as he lectures his son Dick on his good fortune to be going back to school. He finds himself transformed into Dick, while Dick becomes his father. Paul has to endure the humiliating miseries of Dr Grimstone's school, but when he does escape, his son is reluctant to reverse the situation. No subsequent Anstey book had the success of *Vice-Versa*, though *The Brass Bottle* (1900) equals it in humour. Here a young architect inadvertently releases a powerful jinn from a bottle, and has to endure the jinn's misguided efforts to reward him. Anstey frequently used the device of the disastrous intrusion of magic into everyday life. *The Tinted Venus* (1885) deals with a statue of Aphrodite that comes to life and nearly wrecks a hairdresser's long-standing romantic attachment; *A Fallen Idol* (1886) is about the repercussions that ensue when the image of an ancient Indian guru who was also a practical joker is acquired by a worthy young artist in Victorian London. His last book, *In Brief Authority* (1915), about a *nouveau riche* family who get whisked off to rule Fairyland, was written when readers' taste for magic had evaporated.   GA

aphorisms and fairy tales In addition to the numerous literary adaptations of fairy tales in the form of prose works, poems, and plays, there also exists a tradition of reducing well-known tales to short aphorisms of a few lines. These aphorisms allude to fairy tales in general or to specific tales and their individual motifs. These allusions can be found not only among the aphorisms of highly intellectual authors but also among the anonymous one-liners of modern graffiti. They represent remnants of the original fairy tales and form a small sub-genre of the aphorism and might be labelled as fairy-tale aphorisms.

One of the earliest aphorisms of this type is Johann Wolfgang von *Goethe's somewhat paradoxical text 'Fairy tale: indicating to us the possibility of impossible occurrences under possible or impossible conditions'. The reactions of later authors to fairy tales in general or specific motifs reflect this ambiguity between the wishful world of the fairy tale and the reality of everyday life. The dreams, hopes, and fulfilments expressed in fairy tales appear impossible in an imperfect world, but by relating our problems and concerns to the possible solutions in fairy tales, we tend to be able to cope with our sometimes desperate conditions. Gerhart *Hauptmann expressed this thought quite similarly to Goethe's statement in his aphorism 'The teller of fairy tales gets people used to the unusual, and it is of great importance that this happens because mankind suffocates from the usual.'

How much the universal nature of fairy tales is also of relevance to people of the modern age was summarized by Elias Canetti in 1943: 'A closer study of fairy tales would teach us what we can still expect from the world.' But people are not to use fairy tales as escapist literature, as Stanislaw Jerzy Lec warns: 'Don't believe the fairy tales. They were true.' Fairy tales, after all, also express cruel aspects of the social reality of the Middle Ages, and once one looks at some of the individual scenes of cruelty and fear, fairy tales can in fact reflect the anxieties of the present day as well. Thus Lec claims that 'Some fairy tales are so bloody that they actually cannot be regarded as such.' Little wonder that Gabriel Laub concluded that 'Fairy tales definitely belong to realistic literature. They promise fortune and joy—but only in the fairy tale.'

Looking at the technological world and its seemingly insurmountable challenges and problems leads aphoristic writers to question the hope for any fairy-tale future for humanity. The Austrian author Zarko Petan thus changed the introductory formula into the future tense to state his view that 'All socialist fairy tales begin with: "Once upon a time there will be…"' And a reader of a German tabloid newspaper submitted the following saying which contains a similar ironic twist regarding the socio-economic differences between capitalism and socialism: '"Once upon a time there was", so begin the fairy tales in the West. "Once upon a time there will be", so they start in the East.' Aphorists with socio-political concerns also exploit the traditional closing formula of the fairy tale. For those people who are sick of waiting and hearing yet another promise from their leaders, the following poster parody might be an appropriate cynical remark: 'And if they haven't died, then they are still waiting today.' Such pessimism is commonplace in these modern fairy-tale aphorisms. Politicians are seen as liars by Werner Sprenger: 'Most politicians are nothing but occupational swindlers who with dignified faces tell those fairy tales which happen to be the most popular.' And very aggressive against the 'haves' of society is Nikolaus Cybinski's cynical aphorism: 'Fairy tales are the digestive medicine of those who are full and who try to completely digest their old utopias with their help.'

Those aphorisms based on individual fairy tales and their motifs usually lend an ironic twist to the well-known original formulation. Sometimes the authors of these parodies are unknown, as for example in the new American proverb 'You have to kiss a lot of toads (frogs), before you meet your handsome prince', which clearly refers to 'The *Frog King'. An anonymous graffito takes the sexual implications of this fairy tale one step further: 'Better one night with a prince than a whole life with a frog.' It should come as no surprise that quite a few anonymous graffiti and slogans based on *'Snow White' also enter the sexual sphere: 'Better once with Snow White than seven times with the dwarfs', or 'Did you know that Snow White had no rest on any day of the week?' And among German students the slogan 'Oh, how good that nobody knows that I shit independently' has become a popular take-off on the popular verse, 'Oh, how good it is that nobody knows that I am called *Rumpelstiltskin'. On the more serious level of sexual politics, there are Edith Summerskill's 'The housewife is the *Cinderella of the affluent state', Mae West's 'I used to be Snow White . . . but I drifted', and Lee Miller's 'I'm not Cinderella. I can't force my foot into the glass slipper.' Mention must also be made, of course, of Colette Dowling's 'Here it was— the Cinderella Complex' out of her bestseller *The Cinderella Complex* (1982).

The modern German author Werner Mitsch is the most prolific creator of fairy-tale aphorisms, of which a few might serve as examples here: 'The Brothers *Grimm awakened our fairy tales from their Briar Rose sleep', 'Fairy tales are called fairy tales because you only have to pass a total of three tests in fairy tales', 'There once was a young woman [*Rapunzel] who lived in a tower and who one day got a permanent. Much to the dismay of the Brothers Grimm', '*Hansel and Gretel got lost in the wolf. There Snow White played golf with Rumpelstiltskin', 'Feminism. Better blood in the shoe than a prince around the neck [referring to "Cinderella"]', 'All good things come in threes, said the wolf and took the huntsman as his dessert' [*'Little Red Riding Hood'], 'Seven hills don't make a mountain and seven dwarfs don't make a prince', and 'What good does it do a person if he/she can spin straw into gold and still remains his/her whole life long a Rumpelstiltskin?'

This last interrogative aphorism illustrates clearly that fairy-tale aphorisms for the most part question the positive nature of the traditional versions. Power, crime, violence, selfishness, greed, materialism, sex, and hedonism are the subjects of these aphorisms. This is the case because many people never quite attain their full potential as social beings. Instead they hide behind a makeshift façade of deception like the emperor in Hans Christian *Andersen's popular tale 'The Emperor's New Clothes', which the American poet Idries Shah reduced to the telling aphorism 'It is not always a question of the Emperor having no clothes on. Sometimes it is, "Is that an Emperor at all?"' The questions of identity, character, and truthfulness are all addressed in the old fairy tales, and when modern aphoristic and graffiti writers present laconic antipodes based on them, they quite often express a deep moral commitment to bringing about a change towards a more fairy-tale-like existence. To every humorous, ironic, or satirical fairy-tale aphorism belongs a seriously positive fairy tale, and it is the juxtaposition of the long tales with the short aphorisms which makes for meaningful communication of basic human needs and desires.   WM

Jones, Steven Swann, 'Joking Transformations of Popular Fairy Tales', *Western Folklore*, 44 (1985).

Mieder, Wolfgang, 'Sprichwörtliche Schwundstufen des Märchens', *Proverbium*, 3 (1986).

Mieder, Wolfgang, 'Fairy-Tale Allusions in Modern German Aphorisms', in Donald Haase (ed.), *The Reception of Grimms' Fairy Tales* (1993).

Röhrich, Lutz, *Der Witz* (1977).

Apollinaire, Guillaume (pseudonym of **Wilhelm-Apollinaris de Kostrowitzky**, 1880–1918) French poet and critic. Although he was a central figure in the Parisian avant garde prior to the First World War, the fairy tradition influenced his early literary experiments. A precursor to the surrealists, he coined the motto, 'J'émerveille' ('I marvel'), and treated marvellous themes like 'Lorelei' (in *Alcools*, 1913) and 'The Wandering Jew' ('Le Passant de Prague' in *L'Hérésiarque et cie*, 1910) in poetry and prose. Fascinated by the Arthurian cycle, Apollinaire based *L'Enchanteur pourrissant* (*The Rotting Sorcerer*, 1909), and 'Merlin et la vieille femme' ('Merlin and the Old Lady' in *Alcools*, 1913) on the figure of Merlin. The last work he ever wrote was a unique fairy tale entitled 'La Suite de Cendrillon, ou le rat et les six lézards' ('*Cinderella Continued, or The Rat and the Six Lizards'), and was published in *La Baïonette* on 16 January 1919, after his death.

AR

approaches to the literary fairy tale
The literary fairy tale has been of scholarly interest since the 19th century and it has been discussed from a range of conceptual viewpoints using a variety of methodologies. Conceptual approaches to literary texts are always underpinned and shaped by ideological assumptions about relationships between language, meaning, narrative, literature, society, and literary audiences; and, to some extent, varying approaches to the fairy tale reflect the critical, cultural, and historical contexts in which they have been formulated. No single approach or methodology is able to arrive at a 'correct' interpretation of the fairy tale; instead, different methodologies suit different critical and ideological purposes. The main conceptual approaches to the literary fairy tale to have emerged in the 20th century are: folkloricist, structuralist, literary, psychoanalytic, historicist, marxist, and feminist approaches.

1. Folkloricist approaches
The literary fairy tale as it emerged in the 17th century constitutes a literary sub-genre distinct from the oral folk tale, but the oral folk tale has had a formative influence on the fairy tale and on scholarship in both areas. The 'Finnish' (or historical-geographic) method, developed by Thompson, Krohn, and Aarne, aims at reconstructing the history of particular tale types by collecting, indexing, and analysing all of their variants. There are two key underlying assumptions informing the work of folkloricists: that folk tales have their origins in oral traditions; and that a single definitive version of a particular tale type as it may have existed in the oral tradition might be reconstructed from its variants. The Finnish method was developed in an attempt to avoid reductive trajectories of folk-tale history, but the assumption that in identifying the basic structure of a specific tale type an originary 'ur-text' might be reconstructed is grounded in a romantic ideology which conceives of the folk-tale tradition as pure and genuine, and the literary fairy tale as an impure, inauthentic derivative. Such an originary text could only ever be artificially constructed from existing known versions, and the task of collecting all variants defies completion. Furthermore, the traffic between oral and literary folk and fairy tales is not one-way: literary variants have had a formative influence on subsequent oral versions of tales.

Despite such problematic ideological assumptions, a key principle of the historical-geographic method, that a scholar must take all known versions of a story into consideration, has been enormously influential, and the folk-tale indexes compiled by Thompson, Aarne, and Krohn are invaluable resources for scholars interested in a range of approaches to the folk and fairy tale. The approach enables identification of the basic structure of specific tales and it has been combined with other approaches (see collections edited by Bottigheimer, and McGlathery).

2. Structuralism: Vladimir Propp
There are similarities between the methodologies and assumptions of folkloricist and structuralist approaches to the folk tale in that both are preoccupied with the stable underlying form of tales. However, whereas folklorists identified the basic

'story' components of particular tale types, structuralists are interested in the underlying structural components of the folk-tale genre. A key aspect of Propp's methodology is the analysis of the structure of folk tales according to character functions or spheres of action. His analysis of Russian folk tales suggests the following principles: functions are stable, constant elements in a tale, independent of how and by whom they are fulfilled, so they constitute the fundamental components of a tale; the number of functions known to fairy tale is limited; the sequence of functions is always identical; and all fairy tales are of one type in regard to their structure.

The uniformity which Propp finds in fairy-tale structure raises questions about the origins and meanings of tales. While structuralists typically evade questions of meaning and historicity, an implication of Propp's findings is that all folk tales express the same thing, opening the way for assertions of universal ahistorical meanings. However, a criticism of folkloricist and structuralist scholars alike is that they rarely interpret folk-tale content. The conception of structuralism as a 'science' of narrative dictates a methodological rigour which excludes from analysis those narrative components, such as discourse and signification, which are variable, but which also shape form and meaning. Propp acknowledges the cultural context of the folk tale, but he is more concerned with its non-variable structural elements and excludes social and historical aspects and variations of form and content from his analysis. However, in focusing exclusively on stable narrative components, structuralist analysis is frequently reduced to empirical description and observation of manifest content of tales.

Structuralist analysis, however, is not an end in itself and need not ignore either the variable narrative components or the cultural contexts of folk tale. Propp's work, like that of Stith Thompson, has had, despite its shortcomings, a formative influence on the methodologies used in fairy-tale research. His methodology enables discrimination of key structural elements and can be usefully combined with other literary approaches which seek to analyse the possible ways in which texts construct meaning, and with more ideologically oriented forms of analysis which seek to study the formative influence of social, historical, and cultural contexts on folk-tale variants and reversions (for example, see Tatar, 1987; Bottigheimer, 1986, 1987).

3. Literary approaches: Max Lüthi

Whereas structuralist and folkloricist approaches tend to disregard meaning in an attempt to examine form and structure, Lüthi combines stylistic analysis of fairy-tale texts and an interest in their significance. Using the methodologies of new criticism, he analyses the stylistic features and thematic significance of the fairy-tale genre and its historical development. A key assumption informing Lüthi's work is that fairy tales contain essential underlying meanings which, in so far as form and meaning are thought of as integral, are manifest in the basic style of the fairy tale. Thus, like his structuralist colleagues, Lüthi focuses on those formal stylistic features which characterize the genre and which, according to Lüthi, function thematically. For Lüthi, the 'common style underlying all European fairy tales' points to common significances for the genre. His assertions are supported by close textual analysis of particular tales and their variants, but he largely ignores the social and cultural contexts of particular retellings, focusing instead on those story elements and motifs which remain stable despite progressive retellings. His analyses tend to proceed from the particular to the general. Specific features are discussed in so far as they are typical of the genre and can be used to assert abstract general ideas. The methodology thus avoids imposing specific meanings on individual tales, and Lüthi is able to make assertions about the 'timeless validity' of the essential image of 'man' in fairy tales.

4. Psychoanalysis: Jungian and Freudian approaches

Psychoanalytic approaches to the fairy tale are preoccupied with their symbolism. Although Jungian and Freudian interpretations of tales differ, they share key assumptions about language, narrative, and the universality of meaning and utilize similar methodologies. For Jungians, such as Maria Luise von Franz, folk and fairy stories represent archetypal psychological phenomena and are an expression of 'collective unconscious psychic processes'. For Freudians, such as Bruno Bettelheim, they are expressions of individual psychological development, and they deal with universal human problems. Thus both make universal claims for the relevance of the fairy-tale genre for human beings which ignore differences produced by age, gender, race, social class, and education. According to Bettelheim, fairy tales communicate with the uneducated, preconscious, and unconscious minds of children and adults. He thus assumes that meaning exists independent of form and structure and can be directly apprehended, regardless of the linguistic, narrative, and cultural structures and conventions used to encode it. He also assumes a fundamental link between childhood and the fairy-tale genre, the logic of which is circular: fairy tales contain symbolic images which reflect inner psychic processes and which, in so far as these processes are common to all children, enable children to externalize and work through their psychological problems.

Bettelheim and von Franz's methodologies are also similar in so far as both proceed via content analysis of story motifs and the imposition of an, albeit different, interpretative paradigm. Von Franz acknowledges that her 'task of translating the amplified story into psychological language' might perhaps be seen as 'replac[ing] one myth with another', indicating that she is at least aware of the hermeneutic circle in which interpretation is enclosed. Bettelheim evades such methodological questions, however, by contextualizing his Freudian analyses of fairy tale within an ideology of childhood and human existence which sees the Oedipal myth as paramount. This myth functions in Bettelheim's work as a metanarrative which structures both child development and the fairy tale. However, the Oedipal myth, as it has been appropriated by modern psychoanalysis

and by Bettelheim in particular, is a patriarchal metanarrative which, when applied to theories of child development, constructs the child as disturbed and in need of therapeutic instruction, conceives of female sexuality as deviant, and imposes a universal theory of sexual and psychological maturation which ignores the historicity of notions of sexuality, subjectivity, childhood, and the family (see Tatar, 1992; Zipes, 1979, 1986).

Psychoanalytic approaches are problematic when applied to the fairy tale in so far as they often involve mechanically imposing an interpretative paradigm upon select tales without taking into account the oral and literary history which produces diverse variants, the discursive and narratological aspects of literary versions, the audiences for tales, or the cultural and social context in which tales are produced and reproduced. In adopting them scholars assume an opacity of narrative and language; that is, meaning is directly apprehensible independent of its discursive, textual, narrative, cultural, and ideological contexts. They thus assume that meanings are universal and ahistorical, hence presupposing the validity of the interpretative paradigms they utilize. However, psychoanalytic approaches have been highly influential in shaping critical discourse about fairy tale. Bettelheim's *Uses of Enchantment* has provoked fierce opposition and hostility, but few scholars since have failed to acknowledge its influence and to enter into dialogue with Bettelheim. Recent scholarship has tended to be eclectic in its use of myth and psychoanalysis (for example, see Tatar, 1987 and 1992, and essays by Dundes, in Bottigheimer, 1986, and by Grolnick, in McGlathery).

5. Historicist, sociological, and ideological approaches

Whereas psychoanalytic theorists see fairy and folk tales as mirroring collective and individual psychic development, historical and sociological theorists see such tales as reflecting social and historical conditions. Any approach which attempts to extrapolate social conditions and values from literary texts runs the risk of assuming a one-to-one relationship between literature and reality. However, contemporary historicist and sociological theorists typically avoid such conceptual problems through an eclectic, but highly theorized, combination of a range of methodologies (for example, see Zipes, 1979, 1983, 1986, and 1994, and collections edited by Bottigheimer and McGlathery).

There are two main historical approaches to the fairy tale. The first, associated with Nitschke, Kahlo, and Scherf, stresses the social and cultural purposes such narratives served within the particular communities from which they emerged. Nitschke and Kahlo trace many folk-tale motifs back to rituals, habits, customs, and laws of pre-capitalist societies and thus see the folk tales as reflecting the social order of a given historical epoch. The assumption that individual tales 'developed at specific moments and passed unchanged through subsequent eras' implicitly denies the historicity of the genre (Bottigheimer, 1986). Zipes, however, adapts Nitschke's method for defining the socio-historical context of folk tales to the study of the literary fairy tale, arguing that fairy tales 'preserve traces of vanished forms of social life' even though tales are progressively modified ideologically.

A second approach stresses the historical relativity of meaning: textual variants of tales reflect the particular cultural and historical contexts in which they are produced. Bottigheimer's work is concerned with the complex relation between the collections by the Brothers *Grimm and 19th-century German society, the role played by Jacob and Wilhelm Grimm in shaping the fairy-tale genre, and the ideological implications of the tales, especially their reflection of social constructions of gender. Zipes focuses on the relations between fairy tales and historical, cultural, and ideological change, especially how the meanings of fairy tales have been progressively re-shaped as they have been appropriated by various cultural and social institutions through history. Zipes's studies of the fairy tale seek to relocate the historical origins of folk and fairy tales in politics and class struggle and thus fill a gap in literary histories of folk and fairy

tales. His use of marxist paradigms presupposes an instrumental link between literary texts and social institutions and ideologies. Whereas psycho-analytic theorists see fairy tales as reflecting child development, Zipes sees them as having a formative socializing function. He adapts early marxist and cultural historicist approaches, which stressed emancipatory, subversive, and utopian elements in folk and fairy tales, arguing instead that, as folk tales were appropriated by and institutionalized within capitalist bourgeois societies, the emergent culture industry sought to contain, regulate, and instrumentalize such elements, but with limited success. Thus contemporary fairy tales are neither inherently subversive nor inherently conservative; instead, they have a subversive potential which the culture industry both exploits and contains in an effort to regulate social behaviour.

Socio-historicist, marxist and other culturally oriented approaches to literary texts have in part developed as a response to textualist modes of criticism which tend to ignore the impact of social and cultural contexts on significance in their almost exclusive focus on textually produced meanings. However, a common criticism of culturally oriented approaches is that in stressing the socio-historical context of texts, stylistic and formal textual features are ignored and textual analysis is thereby limited to descriptive discussions of thematic and ideological content. A key feature and strength of Zipes's approach is his utilization of a range of critical material relating to literary, social, and historical theory to elaborate on the place and function of the fairy tale within literary and social history. Both Zipes and Bottigheimer extend structuralist methods of analysis and, like other socially oriented researchers, see a link between structural components and socio-historical conditions.

6. Feminist approaches
Studies which examine the social conditions within which folk and fairy tales are produced also reveal the extent to which such tales both reflect and reproduce gender

differences and inequalities within the societies which produce them. Such studies also reveal how interpretative traditions which assume universal meanings and/or forms for fairy tale and ignore their socio-historical contexts can obscure the extent to which the genre is shaped by and reproduces patriarchal constructions of gender.

Feminist fairy-tale criticism is more explicit about its political and ideological agenda than most other approaches; it aims to raise awareness of how fairy tales function to maintain traditional gender constructions and differences and how they might be reutilized to counter the destructive tendencies of patriarchal values. However, feminist research has produced diverse interpretations of fairy tales. All theoretical approaches are selective. Feminist approaches which are critical of fairy tales tend to focus on those tales which evince 'negative' female role models; that is, heroines who are passive, submissive, and helpless. Less critical approaches tend to select tales which portray 'positive' female characters; that is, heroines who are strong, resourceful, and aggressive. Obviously, such evaluative responses also reflect contemporary social values and reveal a second methodological problem, namely a tendency to ignore the historical development of the genre in relation to social and cultural institutions. Feminist researchers also tend to focus primarily on 'story' elements, such as character traits and plot devices; as with much cultural analysis of literary forms, there is a tendency, in relying too heavily on theme and content analysis, to ignore the discursive, narratival, and ideological construction of literary texts. Finally, concerns with the socializing function of fairy tales are often informed by simplistic assumptions about the effects of literary texts, especially an assumption that tales are automatically subject to fixed interpretations.

These methodological problems are avoided by various contemporary researchers, such as *Warner (1994), Tatar (1987, 1992), and Bottigheimer (1987), through the combination of feminist concerns with the interrelation between gender and genre and other conceptual approaches and methodologies, such as psychoanalysis, structuralist analysis, and discourse and cultural analysis (see also collection edited by Zipes, 1986).

7. Conclusion

For some time now socio-historians and folkloricists have maintained that each variant of a particular story will have its own meaning, within a given cultural context. An important implication of this argument is that interpretations of texts are also determined by the cultural context in which they are formulated. As Tatar points out, 'every rewriting of a tale is an interpretation; and every interpretation is a rewriting'. Any given tale will accrue a range of interpretations, as it is interpreted and reinterpreted. The possibility of arriving at a definitive textually grounded interpretation is infinitely deferred partly because of the nature of folkloric material and the impossibility of collecting every version and variant, and partly because any interpretation is in part the product of the culture in which it is produced. Hence there are various approaches to the fairy tale and many diverse interpretations, but no single 'correct' interpretation. On the other hand, however, progressive critical and creative interpretations reveal a history of ideology as well as a history of adaptation, interpretation, and reception. RM

Bettelheim, Bruno, *The Uses of Enchantment* (1976).

Bottigheimer, Ruth (ed.), *Fairy Tales and Society: Illusion, Allusion and Paradigm* (1986).

Bottigheimer, Ruth, *Grimms' Bad Girls and Bold Boys: The Moral and Social Vision of the Tales* (1987).

Franz, Marie Luise von, *An Introduction to the Interpretation of Fairy Tales* (1970).

Lüthi, Max, *Once upon a Time: On the Nature of Fairy Tales* (1970).

McGlathery, James, *The Brothers Grimm and Folktale* (1988).

Propp, Vladimir, *Morphology of the Folktale* (1968).

Tatar, Maria, *The Hard Facts of the Grimm's Fairy Tales* (1987).

Tatar, Maria, *Off with Their Heads! Fairy Tales and the Culture of Childhood* (1992).

Warner, Marina, *From the Beast to the Blonde: On Fairy Tales and their Tellers* (1994).

Zipes, Jack, *Breaking the Magic Spell: Radical Theories of Folk and Fairy Tales* (1979).

Zipes, Jack, *Fairy Tales and the Art of Subversion: The Classical Genre for Children and the Process of Civilization* (1983).

Zipes, Jack, *Don't Bet on the Prince: Contemporary Feminist Fairy Tales in North America and England* (1986).

Zipes, Jack, *Fairy Tale as Myth/Myth as Fairy Tale* (1994).

Zipes, Jack, *Why Fairy Tales Stick: The Evolution and Relevance of a Genre* (2006).

Apuleius, Lucius (125–?) Roman rhetorician and Platonic philosopher. Born in Hippo, now Annaba, Apuleius was educated at Carthage and Athens. He travelled widely in Greece and Asia Minor and practised for a while as a lawyer in Rome. When he was about 30 years old, he returned home, where he gained a distinguished reputation as a writer and lecturer. His most famous work is *Metamorphoses*, also known as *The Golden Ass*, which includes the famous fairy tale 'Cupid and Psyche'. He also wrote *The Apology, or On Magic* (*Apologia: Pro se de magia liber*), his defence in a suit against him by his wife's relatives, who accused him of gaining her affections through magic, and three philosophical treatises, *On the God of Socrates* (*De deo Socratis*), *On the Philosophy of Plato* (*De Platone et eius dogmate*), and *On the World* (*De munde*).

The Metamorphoses concerns a young man named Lucius who sets out on a journey to Thessaly, a region in northern Greece known for its witches. While there he indulges himself in a decadent life with a servant girl named Fotis, who gives him a magic ointment that will supposedly allow him to change himself at will into a bird. When he applies the ointment on himself, he is transformed into an ass. Though he keeps his human understanding, he is mute and cannot explain his situation to anyone. Stolen by a band of robbers, he has numerous adventures and hears all sorts of stories, among them the tale of 'Cupid and Psyche'. In this version Cupid becomes enamoured of the beautiful Psyche and saves her life. He sleeps with her at night on the condition that she never look at him. However, on the urging of her jealous sisters, she turns a light on him, and he disappears. Venus makes her complete three difficult tasks before Psyche can be reunited with her lover.

The Golden Ass was very successful during the Middle Ages, and it served as a model for Boccaccio and Cervantes. In 1566 William Adlington published the first English translation, which was very popular. The plot of 'Cupid and Psyche' was also well known in 17th-century France and was transformed by La Fontaine into a long story, *Amours de Psyche et de Cupidon* (1669) and made into a tragédie-ballet, *Psyché* (1671), by Corneille and Molière. It served as the basis for numerous fairy tales by Mme d'*Aulnoy and inspired the two classic versions of *'Beauty and the Beast' by Mme de *Villeneuve and Mme *Leprince de Beaumont.   JZ

Hood, Gwyneth, 'Husbands and Gods as Shadowbrutes: "Beauty and the Beast" from Apuleius to C. S. Lewis', *Mythlore*, 15 (winter 1988).

Leinweber, David, 'Witchcraft and Lamiae in '"The Golden Ass"', *Folklore*, 105 (1994).

Relihan, Joel (ed. and trans.), *Apuleius, The Tale of Cupid and Psyche* (2009).

Scobie, Alex, 'The Influence of Apuleius' *Metamorphoses* on some French Authors, 1518–1843', *Arcadia*, 12 (1977).

Walsh, P. G. (ed. and trans.), 'Introduction', in Apuleius, *The Golden Ass* (1994).

Arabian Nights, The (also known as *The Thousand and One Nights* (Arabic: *alf laila wa-laila*)) Originally a collection of oriental tales in the Arabic language that developed into a powerful vehicle for Western imaginative prose since the early 18th century (*see* ORIENTAL FAIRY TALES). The collection has a long and convoluted history which mirrors its complex narrative structure; one amazing story evokes another, so that the reader is drawn into a narrative whirlpool. The development of the *Nights* from the oriental oral and literary traditions of the Middle Ages into a classic work for Western readers is a fascinating one. The notebook of a Jewish book dealer from Cairo around the year 1150 contains the first documentary evidence for the Arabic title. The oldest preserved manuscripts, comprising a core corpus of about 270 nights, appear to date from the 15th century. The tales in the collection can be traced to three ancient oral cultures, Indian, Persian, and Arab, and they probably circulated in the vernacular hundreds of years before they were written down some time between the 9th and 15th centuries.

The apparent model for the literary versions of the tales was a Persian book entitled *Hazar Afsaneh* (*A Thousand Tales*), translated into Arabic in the 9th century, for it provided the framework story of a caliph who, for three years, slays a new wife each night after taking her maidenhead, and who is finally diverted from this cruel custom by a vizier's daughter, assisted by her slave-girl. During the next seven centuries, various storytellers, scribes, and scholars began to record the tales from this collection and others and to shape them either independently or within the framework of the Scheherazade/Shahryar narrative. The tellers and authors of the tales were anonymous, and their styles and language differed greatly; the only common distinguishing feature was the fact that they were written in a colloquial language called Middle Arabic that had its own peculiar grammar and syntax. By the 15th century there were three distinct layers that could be detected in the collection of those tales that formed the nucleus of what became known as *The Thousand and One Nights*: (1) Persian tales that had some Indian elements and had been adapted into Arabic by the 10th century; (2) tales recorded in Baghdad between the 10th and 12th centuries; (3) stories written down in Egypt between the 11th and 14th centuries. By the 19th century, the time of Richard *Burton's unexpurgated translation, *The Book of the Thousand Nights and a Night* (1885–6), there were four 'authoritative' Arabic editions, more than a dozen manuscripts in Arabic, and Antoine *Galland's translation that one could draw from and include as part of the tradition of the *Nights*. The important Arabic editions are as follows:

Calcutta I, 1814–18, 2 vols. (also called Shirwanee edn.)
Bulak, 1835, 2 vols. (also called the Cairo Edition)
Calcutta II, 1839–42, 4 vols. (also called W. H. Macnaghten edn.)
Breslau, 1825–38, 8 vols. (ed. Maximilian Habicht)

Galland, the first European translator, published a French translation, *Les Mille et une nuits*, in twelve volumes from 1704 to 1717. He relied on a four-volume Arabic collection to which he added some stories told to him by a Maronite Christian Arab from Aleppo named Youhwnna Diab or Hanna Diab, who had also written down others in Arabic for him ('*Aladdin and the Wonderful Lamp' and '*Ali Baba and the Forty Thieves' (1703–13). He had translated 'The Voyages of Sindbad' in 1701 and placed it in *Mille Nuits* after the 'Three Ladies'. It is supposed that the Sindbad tales originated in Baghdad. Edward William Lane translated a judiciously selected compilation of the frame story into English, 30 of the long pieces, and 55 short stories (1839–41). Burton undertook the monumental task of translating ten volumes, *The Book of a Thousand Nights and a Night* (1885), followed by a six-volume *Supplemental Nights* (1886–8). The Burton edition features archaizing prose, frequent colourful coinages when translation failed, and astonishing anthropological footnotes. Enno Littmann translated and edited a scholarly German edition in six volumes, universally praised for its fidelity to the text and for its excellent notes.

The labyrinthine intertwined stories in *The Thousand and One Nights* are framed by a tale of a jaded ruler named Shahryar, whose disappointment in womankind causes him to marry a new woman every night only to kill her in the morning. The grand-vizier's clever daughter, *Scheherazade, determined to end this murderous cycle, plans an artful ruse. She tells the sultan a suspenseful tale each night promising to finish it in the morning. This narrative device of delaying unpleasant events by means of arousing the curiosity of a powerful figure is a constant feature in the stories themselves, e.g. the three *shaykhs* whose stories free the trader from the *ifrīt*, and the culprits who had disobeyed the three ladies' injunction not to question what they saw. Their curiosity compelled them to save their lives by satisfying their hosts' curiosity ('The Porter and the Three Ladies of Baghdad').

Just as Scheherazade's tales inspire wonder and astonishment in the public, they awaken the same emotions in their fictitious audience, who typically menace the storyteller with demands for yet another story. Thus the frame story of Scheherazade and the Sultan Shahryar generates a parallel series of interpolated tales told to stave off disaster. Mia Gerhardt points out that the fairy tales in *The Arabian Nights* are classifiable thematically: powerful demon stories, talisman stories where a magical object protects and guides the hero, quest stories, transformation tales, and tales of demons under restraint.

In this vast collection there is only one true fairy, in the Persian story of 'Ahmed and Perī Banū', but there are frequent appearances of *ifrīt*, variously translated as 'demon', 'genius', 'genie', or 'jinni'. Gerhardt distinguished fairy tales of Persian origin, in which a supernatural being acts independently and is in control of events, and Egyptian stories where these beings are subject to the possessor of a talisman or other magical object. In 'The Trader and the Jinni' a powerful *ifrīt* seeking revenge for the death of his son is deterred by a series of tales related by three passing *shaykhs*, who bargain for the presumed assassin's life.

A number of the tales deal with the transformation of humans into animals (frequently reversible). In 'The Trader and the Jinni', 'The First Shaykh's Tale' relates how a wife had changed her stepson into a calf and the boy's mother into a heifer. As a punishment she was transformed into the gazelle with whom he is travelling. In 'The Second Shaykh's Tale' his two black dogs had been his two unreliable brothers, before his wife, an *ifritah*, had transformed them. In 'The

Third Shaykh's Tale' his adulterous wife sprinkles him with water and casts a spell that turns him into a dog. The daughter of a stall-owner releases him from the spell and helps him transform his erring wife into a she-mule, his travelling companion. 'The Fisherman and the Jinni' concludes with the tale of 'The Ensorcelled Prince' whose angry wife cast a spell changing him into a man of half-stone, half-flesh. She also transformed his entire realm into a lake, and his subjects into fish distinguishable chromatically (Muslims, white; Christians, blue; Magians, red; Jews, yellow). Galland had added two typical quest stories of Persian provenance in which the protagonist seeks a special object, 'The Envious Sisters' and 'Ahmed and Perī Banū', and also the familiar talisman tale 'Aladdin and the Wonderful Lamp'.

In regard to the development of the fairy tale as genre in the West, *The Thousand and One Nights* played and continues to play a unique role. From the moment Galland translated and invented *Les Mille et une nuits*, the format, style, and motifs of the so-called Arabian tales had a profound effect on how other European and American writers were to define and conceive fairy tales. In some respects, the *Nights* are more important and famous in the West than they are in the Orient. Robert *Irwin discusses this point in his chapter on the European and American 'children of the nights' in his critical study, and he shows how numerous authors were clearly influenced by *The Thousand and One Nights*: in France, Anthony *Hamilton, Thomas-Simon *Gueulette, *Crébillon fils, Denis *Diderot, Jacques *Cazotte, and *Voltaire; in England, Joseph Addison, Samuel Johnson, William Beckford, Horace Walpole, Robert Southey, Samuel Coleridge, Thomas De Quincey, George Meredith, and Robert Louis *Stevenson; in Germany, Wilhelm Heinrich *Wackenroder, Friedrich *Schiller, Wilhelm *Hauff, and Hugo von *Hofmannsthal; in America, Washington *Irving, Edgar Allen Poe, and Herman Melville. In recent times such gifted writers as John *Barth, Jorge Luis *Borges, Steven *Millhauser, and Salman *Rushdie

Arabian Nights, The In the fifth voyage of 'Sindbad the Seaman and Sindbad the Landsman', Sindbad almost loses his life when he agrees to carry the Old Man of the Sea, who habitually eats the men he has tricked into bearing him. Fortunately, Sindbad escapes the Old Man, who assumes a horrific shape in Louis Rhead's illustration printed in *The Arabian Nights' Entertainments* (1916).

have given evidence of their debt to the *Nights*. In addition there have been numerous popular films based on the *Nights* such as The *Thief of Baghdad* (1924, 1939) and *Disney's *Aladdin* (1994) as well as unusual contemporary anthologies, Susan Schwartz's *Arabesques: More Tales of the Arabian Nights* (1988) and Mike Resnick and Martin Greenberg's *Aladdin, Master of the Lamp* (1992), in which some of the more gifted American and British fantasy writers have experimented with motifs and characters from the *Nights*. HG

Gerhardt, Mia A., *The Art of Story-Telling: A Literary Study of the Thousand and One Nights* (1963).

Grossman, Judith, 'Infidelity and Fiction: The Discovery of Women's Subjectivity in The *Arabian Nights'*, *Georgia Review*, 34 (1980).

Irwin, Robert, *The Arabian Nights: A Companion* (1994).

Kennedy, Philip, and Warner, Marina (eds.), *Scheherazade's Children: Global Encounters with the Arabian Nights* (2014).

Marzolph, Ulrich (ed.), *The Arabian Nights in Transnational Perspective* (2007).

Marzolph, Ulrich, and van Leeuwen, Richard (eds.), *The Arabian Nights: An Encyclopedia* (2 vols., 2004).

Nurse, Paul McMichael, *Eastern Dreams: How the Arabian Nights Came to the World* (2010).

Warner, Marina, *Stranger Magic: Charmed States and the Arabian Nights* (2011).

Ardizzone, Edward (1900–79) British author and illustrator, born in Vietnam (then Haiphong, French Indo-China) and domiciled in England from age 5 on. An acclaimed book illustrator for children as well as for the works of *Dickens, *Thackeray, Trollope, Cervantes, *Shakespeare, Bunyan, Walter *de la Mare, James Reeves, and Eleanor *Farjeon, Ardizzone is most noted for the Tim series, Little Tim's sea-going adventures which were rooted in Ardizzone's childhood days roaming the docks with his cousin at Ipswich. In 1956 he received the first Kate Greenaway Medal for *Tim All Alone*. Self-identified as a 'born illustrator', as one who does not draw from life, but who draws symbols for things yet uses his eye and his memory to 'augment and sweeten his

knowledge', Ardizzone viewed illustration as a stage designer. Richly drawn settings became the hallmark of his style. His success largely rests with his ability to integrate text and illustrations and critics have lauded his blending of text and line. Perhaps his greatest achievement as a children's book illustrator is Eleanor Farjeon's *The Little Book* (1955), which received the 1955 Carnegie Medal of the British Library Association and the 1956 Hans Andersen Medal of the International Board on Books for Young People. Among Ardizzone's most interesting illustrated fairy-tale books are *Peter Pan* (1962), *How the Moon Began* (1971), *The Gnome Factory* (1978), *Ardizzone's Hans Andersen* (1978), and *English Fairy Tales* (1980). SS

Alderson, Brian, *Edward Ardizzone* (1972).

Ardizzone, Edward, *On the Illustrating of Books* (1957; 1986).

Ardizzone, Edward, *The Young Ardizzone* (1970).

White, Gabriel, *Edward Ardizzone* (1979).

Arène, Paul (1843–96) French drama critic, author, and collaborator of Alphonse *Daudet. Arène's many short stories reflect the provincial charm of southern France. He wrote several fairy tales, including 'Les Ogresses' ('The Ogresses', 1891) and 'La Chèvre d'or' ('The Golden-Fleeced Goat', 1889), one of his best-known works. Here a conventional romance overlay the local legend of a magical goat who guards a fabulous treasure. The hero ultimately renounces the treasure for the love of the pretty young goatherd. AZ

Armando (**Herman Dirk van Dodeweerd**, 1929–) Dutch painter, musician, journalist, and writer, who was a member of the Situationist movement and is known for his abstract and experimental artworks and writings. His experiences during the Second World War had a profound effect on him, and the major themes in his art involve violence and death. However, his fairy tales, considered crossover works for young and old, are much lighter. His books, *Dirk de dwerg en zeven andere Sprookjes* (*Dirk the Dwarf and Seven Other Fairy Tales*, 1990) and *De prinses met de dikke bibs* (*The*

Princess with the Fat Butt, 1997) are light parodies of conventional fairy tales with bizarre twists. JZ

Arndt, Ernst Moritz (1769–1860) German writer and historian who wrote numerous patriotic pamphlets and books against the French occupation of German principalities during the Napoleonic Wars. Aside from his political writings, Arndt was known for his folk and religious poetry and travel diaries. In 1818 he published his first collection of fairy tales under the influence of the Brothers *Grimm, and in 1842 he revised and expanded this work under the title *Märchen und Jugenderinnerungen (Folk Tales and Memories of my Youth)*. Like the Brothers Grimm, Arndt gathered various kinds of folk tales from oral and literary sources and reproduced them in an unusual quaint and elegant style to make them appear as genuine manifestations of the German folk. JZ

Portizky, J. E., 'Der Märchendichter Arndt', in *Phantasten und Denker* (1922).
Pundt, Alfred G., *Arndt and the Nationalist Awakening in Germany* (1935).

Arnim, Achim von (1781–1831) German author of the romantic period. With Clemens *Brentano he published the classic collection of German folk song, *Des Knaben Wunderhorn: Alte deutsche Lieder (The Boy's Horn of Plenty: Old German Songs*, 1806–8), which in turn helped inspire their younger collaborators, the Brothers *Grimm, to produce their monumental world classic, the *Kinder- und Hausmärchen*. Arnim's stories and novels contain many elements from folk beliefs, a chief example being his tale 'Isabella von Ägypten, Kaiser Karls des Fünften erste Jugendliebe' ('Isabella of Egypt, Emperor Charles the Fifth's First Young Love', 1812). JMM

Arnim, Bettina von (*née* **Brentano**, 1785–1859) A German romantic and social activist, Arnim wrote one tale, 'Der Königssohn' ('The King's Son') and collected two others, 'Hans ohne Bart' ('Beardless Hans') and 'die blinde Königstochter' ('The Blind Princess'), for the projects organized by her husband, Achim von *Arnim, and stepbrother, Clemens *Brentano, around 1808. In gratitude for her friendship, the Brothers *Grimm dedicated their *Tales* to her (in editions from 1812 to 1843). She assisted her daughter Gisela in writing the fairy-tale novel *Gritta* (1843), in which twelve girls escape from a convent school to the island of Sumbona, a land of enchantment; it offers strong social criticism in a humorous, magical style. In 1845, the year of her politically critical *Armenbuch (Book of the Poor)*, she wrote the 'Erzählung vom Heckebeutel' ('Tale of the Lucky Purse'). The fairy-tale salon *Kaffeterkreis, run by her daughters, met in her Berlin home (1840s). JB

Ebert, Birgit, 'Bettina Brentano-von Arnim's "Tale of the Lucky Purse" and Clemens Brentano's "Story of Good Kasperl and Beautiful Annerl" ', trans. Patrick McGrath, in Elke P. Frederiksen and Katherine R. Goodman (eds.), *Bettina Brentano-von Arnim: Gender and Politics* (1995).
Jarvis, Shawn C., 'Spare the Rod and Spoil the Child? Bettina's *Das Leben der Hochgräfin Gritta von Rattenzuhausbeiuns*', Women in German Yearbook, 3 (1986).
Jarvis, Shawn C. (ed.), *Das Leben der Hochgräfin Gritta von Rattenzuhausbeiuns. Von Gisela and Bettina von Arnim* (1986).
Rölleke, Heinz, 'Bettinas Märchen', in Christoph Perels (ed.), *Herzhaft in die Dornen greifen . . . : Bettina von Arnim (1785–1859)* (1985).
Thielenhaus, Vera, 'Die "Göttinger Sieben" und Bettina von Arnims Eintreten für die Brüder Grimm', *Internationales Jahrbuch der Bettina-von-Arnim Gesellschaft*, 5 (1993).
Waldstein, Edith, 'Romantic Revolution and Female Collectivity: Bettina and Gisela von Arnim's *Gritta*', Women in German Yearbook, 3 (1986).

Arnim, Gisela von (1827–89) German writer of fairy tales and stage plays; daughter of the romantic writers Achim and Bettina von *Arnim. In the 1840s she co-founded a female salon, the *Kaffeterkreis, from which some of her published works issued. One of her most interesting tales is a fairy-tale novel and female Robinsonade, *Das Leben der Hochgräfin Gritta von Rattenzuhausbeiuns*

(*The Life Story of the High Countess Gritta*) which she illustrated together with Herman Grimm, Wilhelm's son and her future husband. Her works reflect her intimate reception of the work of the Brothers *Grimm and her proto-feminist revisions of their tradition.   SJ

Arpino, Giovanni (1927–87) Italian writer, poet, journalist, and playwright. He made his debut with picaresque adventure tales, but is best known as a novelist whose style evolved from neo-realism to neo-naturalism, with *La suora giovane* (*The Novice: A Novel*, 1959), and *L'ombra delle colline* (*The Shade of the Hills*, 1964). In the later period he wrote surrealistic and allegoric tales. His fairy tales, such as 'Shiff il verme' ('Shiff the Worm'), and 'I peccati di *Pinocchio' ('The Sins of Pinocchio'), explore the themes of self-identity and freedom. His complete tales are in *Un gran mare di gente* (*A Great Sea of People*, 1981) and *Raccontami una storia* (*Tell Me a Story*, 1982). He wrote the following works for children: *Rafè e micropiede* (1959), *Le mille e una Italia* (*The Thousand and One Italies*, 1960), and *L'assalto al treno* (*The Attack of the Train*, 1966).   MNP

Asbjørnsen, Peter Christen (1812–85) and **Moe, Jørgen** (1813–82) Asbjørnsen and Moe have, justifiably, earned acclaim as the major collectors of Norwegian folk tales. They met as students, and once they realized they shared an interest in folklore, they decided that, together, they would try to do for Norway what the Brothers *Grimm had done for Germany.

Their romantic initiative was, however, tempered by an inclination that would not have interested the Grimms: Asbjørnsen and Moe insisted on keeping the language as close as they could to that of their informants, and they successfully managed to give the reader of their published tales the illusion of listening to a language that retained the presence of the genuine storyteller. In that sense they are more in line with Hans Christian *Andersen, who, similarly, created the illusion that many of his tales were rendered in the vernacular.

Asbjørnsen and Moe's initial plan was to report tales told to them verbatim, but they eventually began mixing and fusing variants. Instead of inserting their own additions to the tales or adding details, however, they retained the plots of the traditional oral tales, and they retold them with a keen sense of the difference between literature and folklore.

That similitude to veracity proved to be most successful. The tales recorded and retold by Asbjørnsen and Moe have achieved a popularity exceeding that of any other Nordic collection. Perhaps the fact that 19th-century Norway was only marginally a bourgeois country may account for the fascination with the tales told in the vast countryside. Norway's historical situation increased their popularity, for it had suffered under Danish rule since the Middle Ages and had achieved semi-autonomy only after it was ceded to Sweden in 1814. That new status, coinciding with romantic notions of folk character, gave way to an urge—among both intellectuals and the bourgeoisie—to discover or create a national identity.

Today Asbjørnsen and Moe may receive less attention for contributing to a sense of national identity than do the sagas for Iceland or *Kalevala* for Finland, but there can be little doubt that the tales recorded by them are still tremendously popular in Norway. Many editions include Theodor Kittelsen's and Erik *Werenskiold's fascinating drawings (as do numerous selections translated into English). Werenskiold's drawings underscore the humour found in many tales, whereas Kittelsen manages to make the supernatural come hauntingly alive in Norwegian nature.

Asbjørnsen and Moe, traversing the Norwegian countryside, collected numerous tales from various informants. They published their first collection of tales, *Norske folkeeventyr* (*Norwegian Folktales*) in 1841, and there were three more collections to follow (1842–4). While Moe, a theologian, was the theorist—he wrote the scholarly introduction to an edition published in 1851—Asbjørnsen was a man who loved roving the countryside, and he shared little of Moe's romantic leanings, for the legends he published as *Norske huldreeventyr og folkesagn* (*Norwegian Fairy Tales and Folk Legends*, 1845-8) include tales that scarcely conform to romantic ideology. Asbjørnsen often created a frame—an old trick used in Boccaccio's *Decameron* and in Chaucer's *Canterbury Tales*—for the unrelated stories he wanted to retell, and in those frame stories the reader gains a glimpse of an eager folklorist culling tales from people who have absolutely no awareness of any romantic awakening. In one instance, the folklorist locates a glum gravedigger who, when first prodded by bribes in the form of chewing tobacco, relents to tell a series of tales about witches.

The tales collected and published by Asbjørnsen and Moe span from the marvellous magic or wonder tales to the *Schwank* (anecdote) or trickster stories, texts that may be diametrically opposed in terms of world view: the hope vested in humankind in such optimistic magic tales as 'De tre prinsesser fra Hvidtenland' ('The Three Princesses from Whittenland') or 'Prins Hvidbjørn' ('Prince White Bear') is contested by the egoism and immorality of the protagonists of 'Store Per og Vesle Per' ('Big Per and Little Per') and 'Peik'. If those texts reflect the contrastive world views of Norwegian folk tales—or of folk tales everywhere—the legend may posit a middle ground that explores existence on an *ad hoc* basis: for instance, its view of the Norwegian *huldre*—those who live in the mountains—is telling, for they vary from legend to legend, from malevolent demons to benevolent beings and even to ambivalent figures. Some of the informants obviously believed in the *huldre*, while others used them as allegorical figures representing 'otherness'. If the outcome of the magic tale and the trickster stories is fairly predictable, the listener or reader cannot know what turns the legend will take, and, consequently, the legend is the more realistic and ambivalent—and the least formulaic—of these genres.

The impact of Asbjørnsen and Moe's collections on later Norwegian literature was profound. Young Henrik Ibsen worked as a collector of folklore, and his *Peer Gynt* (1867), based on a folk tale, is suffused with folk beliefs. Many of Ibsen's later plays use such beliefs and motifs, as the title of *Fruen fra havet* (*The Lady from the Sea*, 1888) may suggest. In *Trold* (*Weird Tales from Northern Seas*, 1891-2), Jonas Lie used the plots of the folk tale to chart the irrational workings of the human mind. Beliefs from Norwegian folklore appear in Sigrid Undset's famous novel *Kristin Lavransdatter* (1920-2) and in those of numerous 20th-century authors. In America, the folk beliefs in the tales collected by Asbjørnsen and Moe echo in O. E. Rölvaag's pioneer epic *Giants in the Earth* (1927) and in Ethel Phelps Johnston's retelling of a number of tales within a feminist scenario in *Tatterhood and Other Tales* (1978). The title tale and the concluding 'Mastermaid' ('Mestermøy') are both free adaptations of well-known tales collected by those two eminent Norwegians, who knew that the illusion of the presence of a storyteller must be retained on the printed page. NI

Asbjørnsen, Peter Christen, and Moe, Jørgen, *Norwegian Folktales* (1960).

Christiansen, Reidar (ed.), *Folktales of Norway* (1964).

DesRoches, Kay Unruh, 'Asbjørnsen and Moe's Norwegian Folktales: Voice and Vision', in Perry Nodelman (ed.), *Touchstones: Reflections on the Best in Children's Literature: Fairy Tales, Fables, Myths, Legends, and Poetry* (1987).

Hult, Marte, *Framing a National Narrative: The Legend Collections of Peter Christen Asbjørnsen* (2003).

Solheim, Svale, 'Die Brüder Grimm und Asbjørnsen und Moe', *Wissenschaftliche Zeitschrift der Ernst Moritz Arndt-Universität Greifswald: Gesellschaftswissenschaftliche Reihe*, 13 (1964).

'Aschenputtel' *See* 'CINDERELLA'.

Ashton, Sir Frederic (1904-88) British dancer and choreographer who played a leading role in establishing the importance of the Royal Ballet in particular and of British dance in general. Encouraged by Marie Rambert, he commenced working as a choreographer while still a young dancer. Later in 1935 he was invited by Ninette de Valois to join her Sadler's Wells Ballet company as resident choreographer. This company eventually moved into residence at Covent Garden in 1946. Later, when the Royal Ballet was formed at Covent Garden in 1956, Ashton was one of its founders, creating many new ballets, and from 1963 to 1970 serving as the company's director.

For over five decades Ashton was a significant figure in the British ballet world, originating many new works and preserving the traditions of British classical ballet, the foundations of which he helped lay. Among his foremost ballets may be counted *Facade* (Walton, 1931), *Symphonic Variations* (Franck, 1946), and *Enigma Variations* (*Elgar, 1968).

His work in the area of ballets with fairy-tale themes include *Cinderella* (*Prokofiev, 1948) and *Undine* (1956), a collaboration between him and the outstanding German composer Hans Werner Henze. *Undine*, which is on the subject of the water nymph, was created for Margot Fonteyn and the Royal Ballet.   TH

Attwell, Mabel Lucie (1879–1964) British children's illustrator who studied at Regent Street and Heatherley's Schools of Art. Her pen-and-ink and watercolour drawings of rosy-cheeked chubby toddlers graced nurseries the world over, and were reproduced on postcards, Underground posters, china, and toys. She illustrated *Mother Goose* (1910), *Alice in Wonderland* (1911), and the fairy tales of the Brothers *Grimm and *Andersen (1910, 1914). Queen Marie of Romania and J. M. *Barrie requested her work for *Peeping Pansy* (1918) and *Peter Pan and Wendy* (1921).   MLE

Dalby, Richard, *Golden Age of Children's Book Illustration* (1991).

Doyle, Brian, *Who's Who of Children's Literature* (1968).

Peppin, Brigid, and Micklethwait, Lucy, *Dictionary of British Book Illustrators* (1983).

Atwood, Margaret (1939–) Canadian author whose works evoke and revise fairy tales. Born in Ottawa, strongly influenced by scientific and visual-arts traditions in her family, and active in freedom of speech and other political organizations, Atwood has been acclaimed critically and has to date published thirteen novels, nine collections of short stories, twenty books of poems, and several volumes of non-fiction. Harold Pinter wrote the screenplay for the 1990 film adaptation of Atwood's dystopia *The Handmaid's Tale*.

Atwood positions herself as a Canadian and feminist writer. In *Survival: A Thematic Guide to Canadian Literature* (1972), where she foregrounds the '*Rapunzel syndrome' imprisoning many heroines of Canadian novels, she argues that Canada is an 'unknown territory' for its people because of its colonial history, and that its writers can provide a creative map, 'a geography of the mind', to bring about self-knowledge and de-colonization. The same critical exploration and repudiation of a collective victim position is at the heart of Atwood's writing about and for women. Fairy tales, in which unpromising heroes and heroines explore symbolically charged unknown territory and survive thanks to their resourcefulness, are crucial to this dual project. A student of Northrop Frye, Atwood recognizes the folk tale to be, like the Bible and Greek mythology, a foundational Western narrative. Furthermore, as a careful reader of the tales collected by the Brothers *Grimm, she asserts that, counter to common beliefs, fairy-tale heroines are often central characters who overcome challenges with intelligence and wit.

Atwood reworks the symbolic and woman-centred core of a few Grimm tales throughout her work: 'The *Juniper Tree' (in the early novel *Surfacing*), 'Fichter's Bird' or *'Bluebeard' (most clearly in the title story of the 1983 collection *Bluebeard's Egg* but also in 'Alien Territory' and 'The Female Body', short pieces from the 1992 *Good Bones*, and much earlier in *Surfacing*), 'The *Robber Bridegroom' (from the 1969 *Edible Woman* to many other texts), 'The Girl Without

Hands' (in the 1981 politically charged novel *Bodily Harm*, but also in the lyrical poem 'Girl Without Hands' in the 1995 *Morning in the Burned House*), *'Little Red Riding Hood' (especially in *The Handmaid's Tale* 1986), and 'The White Snake'. Exemplary of Atwood's use of doubles and her cutting humour, her novel *The Robber Bride* (1993) amplifies women's sisterhood as a survival tool in 'Fichter's Bird' and presents a scathing gender reversal of 'The Robber Bridegroom' in the character of Zenia. Atwood also draws on Hans Christian *Andersen's stories, especially 'The *Snow Queen', and French-Canadian animal tales. In her reworkings, the fairy-tale themes of violence, cannibalism, dismemberment, and transformation become tools for critiquing the dynamics of sexual politics and urging change. In *Lady Oracle* (1976) she weaves intertextual references to folklore and fairy tales such as 'The *Ugly Duckling', 'The *Red Shoes', and *'Rapunzel'. More recently, she has reinterpreted the Homeric myth of Penelope and Odysseus in her novel, *The Penelopiad* (2005).

As the critic Sharon Rose Wilson has shown, Atwood's little-known watercolours, drawings, collages, and cartoon strips also focus on the power of fairy-tale images. Among Atwood's four books for children, *Princess Prunella and the Purple Peanut* (1995) stands out as a witty tale of transformation in which the pampered protagonist must reconsider her self-centred behaviour, while Atwood plays out an amazing range of 'p' alliterations for young and older listeners/readers. Atwood makes pointed observations about fairy tales and fellow-writer Angela *Carter in 'Running with the Tigers'. CB

Atwood, Margaret, 'Running with the Tigers', in Lorna Sage (ed.), *The Flesh and the Mirror* (1994).

Godard, Barbara, 'Tales Within Tales: Margaret Atwood's Folk Narratives', *Canadian Literature*, 109 (1986).

Manley, Kathleen, 'Atwood's Reconstruction of Folktales: *The Handmaid's Tale* and "Bluebeard's Egg" ', in Sharon R. Wilson (ed.), *Approaches to Teaching Atwood's* The Handmaid's Tale *and Other Works* (1997).

Tatar, Maria, *Secrets Beyond the Door: The Story of Bluebeard and His Wives* (2004).

Wilson, Sharon Rose, *Margaret Atwood's Fairy-Tale Sexual Politics* (1993).

Aulnoy, Marie-Catherine Le Jumel de Barneville, baronne d' (or comtesse)

(1650/51–1705) The most famous French writer of fairy tales after *Perrault, d'Aulnoy had a significant influence on the development of the genre in France and other countries (especially Germany).

Born in Normandy, Marie-Catherine Le Jumel de Barneville was married at 15 or 16 to François de la Motte, baron d'Aulnoy, who was more than 30 years her elder. The marriage, which had been arranged by her mother, Mme de Gudane, and her mother's companion, Courboyer, quickly turned sour, leading to the most turbulent phase of her life. The baron's financial difficulties and abusive behaviour created a hostile relationship between Marie-Catherine's mother and husband. In 1669, Mme de Gudane, Courboyer, and other accomplices hatched a plot to accuse M. d'Aulnoy of *lèse-majesté*, a capital offence. Although arrested, the baron quickly proved his innocence and turned the tables on his accusers: Courboyer and his accomplices were charged with calumny and executed; Mme de Gudane was forced to flee France, and Marie-Catherine was briefly imprisoned with her new-born third daughter (the first two had died in infancy). Little is known of Mme d'Aulnoy's life between her release in 1670 from the Conciergerie prison and 1690, except that she gave birth to two daughters (in 1676 and 1677) and probably travelled to Flanders, England, and Spain. However, by 1690, she had returned to Paris, had established numerous contacts at court, and began a prolific writing career, with the publication of *Histoire d'Hypolite, comte de Duglas* (*Story of Hypolitus, Count of Douglas*), which included the first published literary fairy tale in French (which later anthologies called 'L'Île de la félicité' ('The Island of Happiness'). In 1691, d'Aulnoy published her lively travel narrative *Relation du voyage d'Espagne* (*Travels in Spain*), which includes another fairy tale (about a fateful princess named Mira). In the ensuing years she published with great success novels, short stories, devotional works, and collections of historical memoirs. But she is best known for the two collections of fairy tales published in 1697 and 1698: *Les Contes des fées* (*Tales of the Fairies*, 1697–8), with 15 tales and two frame narratives (*Dom Gabriel Ponce de Léon* and *Dom Fernand de Tolède*), and *Contes nouveaux ou les fées à la mode* (*New Tales, or Fairies in Fashion*, 1698), which contains nine more tales and a frame story entitled *Le Gentilhomme bourgeois* (*The Bourgeois Gentleman*). By the time of her death a few years later (1705), d'Aulnoy's name had become synonymous with an expression she was the first to use—'conte de fées'.

D'Aulnoy's fairy tales owe much to the novels of her day. Unlike Perrault (whose prose tales were published only a few months before the first instalment of *Les Contes des fées*), d'Aulnoy regularly incorporates motifs, characters, and devices that are typical of the pastoral and heroic romances popular in the first part of the century. Hence, her protagonists are always involved in a love story, and the narration examines their emotions at great length. Indeed, this 'sentimental realism' makes d'Aulnoy's fairy tales a significant (but generally unacknowledged) transitional moment in the evolution of the 17th- and 18th-century French novel. It also explains in part the reticence many critics express about her stories, beginning especially in the 19th century, when literary fairy tales were increasingly judged in terms of their putative faithfulness to folkloric models. None the less, d'Aulnoy (like Perrault for that matter) had no intention of making her *contes* ethnographic documents, but rather literary texts suitable for the tastes of refined readers.

Even so, d'Aulnoy displays a wide knowledge of folkloric material. Of all the 17th- and 18th-century French fairy tales, only Perrault's make more frequent use of discernible folkloric tale types (10 out of 11) than d'Aulnoy's (19 out of 25). Whether she knew these in their oral form or exclusively through literary renderings, d'Aulnoy rewrote 15 different oral tale types, ranging from 'L'Oranger et l'abeille' ('The Orange-tree and the Bee') to 'Le Mouton' ('The Ram'). She seems to have been particularly fascinated by the animal spouse cycles (the most famous examples of which are *Apuleius' 'Cupid and Psyche' and Mme *Leprince de Beaumont's *'Beauty and the Beast'), for she wrote five animal groom tales ('Gracieuse et Percinet', 'Le Mouton', 'L'Oiseau bleu' ('The *Blue Bird'), 'Le Prince Marcassin' ('The Boar Prince'), 'Serpentin vert' ('The Green Serpent') and two animal bride tales ('La Chatte blanche' ('The White Cat') and 'La Biche au bois' ('The Doe in the Woods')).

Perhaps most significant are the multiple ways d'Aulnoy's *contes de fées* meld literary and folkloric traditions. Not unlike Perrault, she often employs humorous names, expressions, devices, and situations that create an ironic distance from popular oral narratives and their (reductive) association with children. This is the case of the versed morals she almost always places at the end of her tales: the *moralités* recall the formulaic endings of both the oral storyteller and the illustrious fabulist La Fontaine while often questioning the obvious 'point' of the story. D'Aulnoy is also famous for her profuse imagination, and she repeatedly incorporates rich descriptions that fuse supernatural beings or traits with historical and literary allusions from her day. Thus, the fairy characters who appear in her tales, recalling fairies in opera and the term used to honour the hostesses of the salons, play a much more prominent role than those in either oral traditions or the stories of *Straparola and *Basile. Thus she also creates numerous strong heroines, akin to those of several prominent 17th-century French female novelists (e.g. Lafayette and Villedieu) but distinct from most of their folkloric homologues. Among others, the heroine of her fascinating 'Finette-Cendron' is a resolutely active character who combines the qualities of both *Thumbelina and *Cinderella.

The popularity that met d'Aulnoy's fairy tales immediately upon publication continued well into the 18th century, during

Aulnoy, Baronne d' Laidronette meets the pygmies in Mme d'Aulnoy's 'Green Serpent', originally published in 1698. This illustration by Gordon Browne is taken from d'Aulnoy's *Fairy Tales* (1923).

which her works were often republished and many of her tales found their way into the *Bibliothèque bleue*. Beginning in the 19th century, however, several critics inaugurated a tradition of comparing d'Aulnoy unfavourably (and unfairly) to Perrault, and only a few of her tales were regularly republished, in editions specifically for children. In the past 20 years, serious scholarly attention to d'Aulnoy has finally begun to gain momentum, and critics have increasingly recognized her important place in the history of French literature and the fairy tale.   LCS

> Defrance, Anne, 'Écriture féminine et dénégation de l'autorité: les Contes de fées de Madame d'Aulnoy et leur récit-cadre', *Revue des sciences humaines*, 238 (1995).
>
> DeGraff, Amy, *The Tower and the Well: A Psychological Interpretation of the Fairy Tales of Madame d'Aulnoy* (1984).
>
> Hannon, Patricia, 'Feminine Voice and the Motivated Text: Mme d'Aulnoy and the Chevalier de Mailly', *Marvels and Tales*, 2.1 (1988).
>
> Jasmin, Nadine, *Naissance du Conte Féminin. Mots et Merveilles: Les Contes de fées de Madame d'Aulnoy (1690–1698)* (2002).
>
> Welch, Marcelle Maistre, 'Les Jeux de l'écriture dans les contes de fées de Mme d'Aulnoy', *Romanische Forschungen*, 101.1 (1989).

Auneuil, Louise de Bossigny, comtesse d' (d. 1700?) French writer of fairy tales. Virtually nothing is known of d'Auneuil's life, save that she had connections with the high society of her day and probably held a salon. Her works reflect the light-hearted social milieu for which many fairy tales were written in France at the turn of the 18th century. D'Auneuil's collection, *La Tyrannie des fées détruite* (*The Tyranny of the Fairies Destroyed*, 1701), begins with a story of the same name that depicts the end of fairies' powers; however, they reappear, their magic intact, in the subsequent tales. The cataclysmic title was doubtless a marketing ploy but none the less reflects the significant narrative and cultural role fairies play in French *contes de fées*. Three of her fairy tales are published as letters and are early examples of women's periodical literature: 'La Princesse de Pretintailles' (1702) and 'Les Colinettes' (1703), which concern decorations on early 18th-century women's clothing, and 'L'Inconstance punie' ('Inconstancy Punished', 1703), in which a sylphid punishes her unfaithful lover. D'Auneuil's final work, *Les Chevaliers errans* (*The Errant Knights*, 1709), features embedded narratives that borrow from medieval chivalric romance and orientalist writing. Several of these tales present a critical perspective on

love by rejecting the conventional happy ending.   LCS

Austin, Keith Contemporary Australian journalist and writer of stories and novels. Originally from London, England, Austin has made his home in Sidney and has published two fairy-tale novels for young adults, *Grymm* (2012) and *Snow, White* (2014). Inspired by the fairy tales of the Brothers *Grimm, *Grymm* is more a horror story than a fairy tale. It tells the story of a brother and a sister, Mina and Jacob, whose brother disappears in an eerie mining town filled with dreadful characters reminiscent of some of the weird characters in the Grimms' tales. *Snow, White*, too, has elements of both horror stories and fairy tales and concerns a young boy haunted by nightmares and intimidated by bullies at school. Though there are happy ends to these novels, the happiness is not the stereotypical fairy-tale ending.   JZ

Avery, Frederick Bean (Fred Avery, Tex Avery) (1908–80) American animator, cartoonist, and director, who was famous for producing some of the most original and provocative cartoons during the Golden Age of Hollywood animation (1930–1950). He worked for almost all the important studios, including MGM and Warner Brothers, and created the characters of Daffy Duck, Snoopy, Bugs Bunny, and Porky Pig. He caused controversy wherever he worked because of his provocative approach to fairy tales and traditional stories. Early in his career at Warner Brothers Studio, for instance, he directed two fairy–tale cartoons, *Little Red Walking Hood* (1937) and *Cinderella Meets Fella* (1938) that are filled with sexual innuendos and hilarious role reversals. It is also clear that Avery was satirizing the infantile cartoons produced by Walt *Disney. His favourite characters were *Red Riding Hood and the Wolf, and his carnivalesque Red Riding Hood cartoons are stunning and delirious. They are even 'politically correct' in their exaggerated play with sexism, depicting strong feminine characters long before the feminist movement began to gather momentum in the late 1960s. He portrayed three types of Red Riding Hoods: the sexy curvaceous singer who speaks with the voice of Katherine Hepburn in *Red Hot Riding Hood* (1945), *Swing Shift Cinderella* (1945), *The Shooting of Dan McGoo* (1945), *Uncle Tom's Cabana* (1947), and *Little Rural Riding Hood* (1945); the diminutive, blonde doll-like girl in *Little Red Walking Hood* (1937) and *The Bear's Tale* (1940); and the scraggly farm girl in *Little Rural Riding Hood* (1945). All of them delight in showing off their bodies and cunning and in avoiding the clutches of the wolves. There are, of course, different kinds of wolves: the country bumpkin wolf, the suave wolf in a tuxedo, the pool-playing sleazy wolf, the pistol-slinging bandit wolf, the Simon Legree wolf. The grandmas, who dress in sleek nightgowns and chase the wolf, are depicted as fairy godmothers who persecute the wolf, or are old without teeth and are chased by the wolf. Often the chases lead to nerdy heroes protecting Red Riding Hood such as Egghead and Droopy, who hit the wolf over the head with mallets. Avery was fond of having his characters stop the action, argue with the director of the film, speak to the audience, and change the plot of the film. For instance, in *Red Hot Riding Hood*, the country wolf, the diminutive Red Riding Hood, and sick grandma are depicted in a style similar to the Disney characters, but they are disgusted with their roles and the story, stop the film, and demand that the director modernize the story. In *Swing Shift Cinderella*, the wolf and Little Red Riding Hood realize that they are in the wrong film when the title flashes on the screen. The wolf sends the little girl packing while he changes clothes and drives to Cinderella's house to seduce her. In *Little Red Walking Hood*, the grandma stops the chase scene when the phone rings and makes the wolf wait until she places an order with the grocer. All the sight gags and word plays with literal meanings undermine the conventional plot of the classic 'Little Red Riding Hood' versions. Avery's cartoons reveal a tendency to make a mockery of male lust while celebrating a carnival spirit.   JZ

Adamson, Joe, *Tex Avery: King of Cartoons* (1987).

Brion, Patrick, *Tex Avery* (1984).

Gaines, Jane, 'The Show Girl and the Wolf', *Cinema Journal*, 20.1 (Fall 1980).

Morris, Gary, 'Goosing Mother Goose: The Fairy Tales of Tex Avery', *Bright Lights Film Journal* (1998): <http://www.brightlightsfilm.com/22/texaverytales.php>.

Place-Verghnes, Floriane, *Tex Avery: A Unique Legacy (1942–1955)* (2006).

Awa, Naoko (1943-93) Birth- and pen-name of Naoko Minegishi, award-winning Japanese fairy-tale writer. Her stories, influenced by the brothers *Grimm, Hans Christian *Andersen, Wilhelm *Hauff, and *The *Arabian Nights*, are also based in Japanese folk tales. Collected and translated by Toshiya Kamei in *The Fox's Window and Other Stories* (2009), there are 30 examples that span Awa's literary career from the 1960s on. In this collection, magical animals, witches, ogres, and traditional Japanese characters interact with humans, who ride buses and trains or more supernatural conveyances, and may live in such places as a village, the seaside, or a hospital. Trickster characters operate in a sphere mixing fantasy with contemporary settings. A turtle courts one young woman and a whale marries another; a weasel roller-skates; and animals speak, wear clothing, and turn into humans. But the line between fantasy and reality can be unclear, and everyday life is infused with magic.   SCR

Aymé, Marcel (1902–67) An eclectic French author of plays, novels, and essays best known for his short stories in which fantasy coexists with reality. He spent his childhood in his grandparents' village in the Jura, where illness later forced him to abandon engineering studies for a career in writing. In 1933 he gained international fame with *La Jument verte* (*The Green Mare*) and its risqué talking horse. He wrote several award-winning narratives about peasants, corrupted cities, and post-war France before embracing the theatre. His most celebrated play, *La Tête des autres*

(*Other Peoples' Heads*, 1952), was a vitriolic indictment of the judicial system; his last works were science-fiction satires about absolute power and man's inhumane nature.

Aymé's social satire, ludic wordplay, ribald humour, and use of the marvellous earned comparisons to Rabelais, Balzac, Voltaire, Lewis *Carroll, Queneau, and Verne. *Les Contes du chat perché* (*The Wonderful Farm*, 1934) was a popular prize-winning series of illustrated tales 'for children from 4 to 75'. Here, as with the medieval *fabliaux* and La Fontaine's *Fables*, talking animals inhabit a rural Wonderland. All of his short stories, such as 'Le Passe-muraille' ('The Walker-Through-Walls', 1943), were actually philosophical tales that used fairies, seven-league boots, parallel worlds, divided identities, or time travel to allegorize man's relation to society.   MLE

Brodin, Dorothy, *The Comic World of Marcel Aymé* (1964).

Lecureur, Michel, *La Comédie humaine de Marcel Aymé* (1985).

Lord, Graham, *The Short Stories of Marcel Aymé* (1980).

Propp, Vladimir, *Theory and History of Folklore* (1984).

Bába Yagá The witch in Slavic fairy tales. Her most common attributes are a bony leg (sign of her being dead, non-human), a hut on chicken legs (remnants of a totemic ancestor), and a mortar, which she uses for transportation. Often she is portrayed spinning, which connects her to the ancient figure of Fate. Like all witches, Bába Yagá has an ambivalent function, since she can be both the opponent and the helper of the protagonist. Usually she threatens to eat the hero (Ivan), but he coaxes her to give him a bath and share a meal with him first, thus turning her into his ally instead. She then gives him advice and provides him with a magical agent, often a horse or a ball of yarn which shows him the way to his goal. Sometimes Ivan has to obtain these things by cunning or by performing three tasks. Often Bába Yagá has a beautiful daughter who assists the hero and becomes his wife. In some fairy tales, the hero's wife gives him some object when he sets out on his trials, and when he meets Bába Yagá she recognizes her daughter's possession and is obliged to support the hero.

In other tales, notably with a female hero, Bába Yagá, like the ogre of Western fairy tales, eats small children. The heroine outsmarts her and escapes. In the famous tale 'The Magic Swan-Geese', Bába Yagá has a flock of birds to assist her in kidnapping children. MN

Forrester, Sibelan, trans., *Baba Yaga: The Wild Witch of the East in Russian Fairy Tales* (2013).
Johns, Andreas, *Baba Yaga: The Ambiguous Mother and Witch of the Russian Folktale* (2004).

Babbitt, Natalie (1932–) American writer and illustrator of children's books. Her first critically acclaimed work, *The Search for Delicious* (1969), is a fantasy story about the adolescent Gaylan, who is sent on a quest to find the best definition of the word 'delicious' in order to avert a civil war, and on his way encounters woldwellers, dwarfs, and the mermaid Ardis. Many of her stories encourage children to confront their fears, whether it be monsters, as in *Kneeknock Rise* (1970), a Newbery Honor Book, or the dark, as in *The Something* (1970). In *The Devil's Storybook* (1974) and *The Devil's Other Storybook* (1987), Babbitt draws from popular folklore and depicts the Devil as a trickster-type character who is constantly foiled by his own pranks. In her most famous novel, *Tuck Everlasting* (1975), Babbitt tackles the question of death from the perspective of the eleven-year-old Winnie Foster. Winnie comes across the Tuck family who attained everlasting life by drinking from the spring near an ash tree—probably a reference to the marvellous ash tree Yggdrasil and Urda's Well of Norse mythology—and must confront the possibility of eternal life which, as the story of the Tuck family conveys, can be more frightening than death itself. Other works by Babbitt which draw from folk or fantasy tradition include: *The Eyes of the Amaryllis* (1977), based on sea lore; *Herbert Rowbarge* (1982), which contains allusions to *Alice in Wonderland*; and *Nellie—a Cat on her Own* (1989), a story inspired by *Pinocchio*. AD

Levy, Michael M., *Natalie Babbitt* (1991).

Bail, Murray (1941–) Award-winning Australian author known primarily for his novels and short stories. He has also published criticism and travel writing and has edited a collection of essays about the artist Ian

Fairweather. He is famous for his award-winning fairy-tale themed novel *Eucalyptus* (1998). In this book, a beautiful young woman's father promises her hand in marriage to the suitor who can correctly identify over 100 species of eucalyptus trees found in the family orchard. Other works include *Homesickness* (1980) and *Holden's Performance* (1987), both of which were honoured by accolades such as the Victoria Premier's Award for Fiction. KMJ

Bain, R. Nisbet (Robert Nisbet Bain, 1854–1909) British historian, folklorist, and translator. He wrote extensively on early modern Slavic and Scandinavian history, and translated collections of folk and fairy tales from Cossack, Finnish, Hungarian, and Russian into English. His important collections include *Russian Fairy Tales* (1892), *Cossack Fairy Tales and Folk Tales* (1894), *Turkish Fairy Tales and Folk Tales* (1896), *Tales from Tolstoi* (1901), and *Tales from Gorky* (1902). AD

Bakshi, Ralph (1938–) American animator. After limbering up with *Wizards*, a fairy-tale film about the conflict between good and evil played out through magic and technology, Bakshi made his most ambitious contribution to animated film by adapting the first two books of *Tolkien's Lord of the Rings* trilogy (1978) for the screen. Seeking naturalism, rather than cartoon caricatures, he shot the whole script in live action, then set an army of illustrators to work tracing these sequences, frame by frame, with appropriate modifications, onto cels. The mixed critical and audience response to this technique and to the heavy compression of the Tolkien characters and narrative in the script led to book three of the trilogy remaining unfilmed. TAS

Balanchine, George (original name **Giorgi Balanchivadze**, 1904–83) The most important Russian-American choreographer of classical ballet in the 20th century. Born in St Petersburg, Russia, Balanchine studied at the Imperial School of Ballet, and in 1925 he left the Soviet Union to dance with Sergei

Diaghilev's Ballets Russes. He also began choreographing at this time, and when Diaghilev died in 1929, Balanchine worked for the Royal Danish Ballet and the Ballet Russe de Monte Carlo, primarily as a choreographer. In 1933 Lincoln Kirstein invited Balanchine to organize the American School of Ballet and the American Ballet Company, which developed into the famous New York Ballet in 1948.

By his death in 1983, Balanchine had created 150 works for the company, and many were fairy-tale ballets. One of his very first significant productions was *Le Baiser de la fée* (*The Fairy's Kiss*, 1937), and he also staged innovative productions of *The Nutcracker* (1954), *A Midsummer Night's Dream* (1962), *Coppélia* (1978), and **Sleeping Beauty* (1978). Beside his classical work, he choreographed numerous musical comedies and opera-ballets and did a great deal of work for television. Balanchine sought to fuse modern notions of dance with traditional ideas. He himself was a neo-classicist who de-emphasized plot in his ballets to show off the talents of his dancers and to create magical scenes. He also experimented with modern music and created original ballets that emphasized graceful precision and striking lines of movement. JZ

Gottlieb, Robert, *George Balanchine: The Ballet Maker* (2004).

Taper, Bernard, *George Balanchine: A Biography* (1996).

Balázs, Béla (pseudonym of **Herbert Bauer**, 1884–1949) Hungarian writer, film director, poet, and journalist, whose interest in fairy tales developed during his student years in Budapest. Aside from writing unusual folk and oriental fairy tales published in his collection *Seven Fairy Tales* (1917), he created the ballet *The Wooden Prince* (1917) with music by Béla Bartók, in which a princess falls in love with an enchanted wooden prince until a fairy breaks the spell of the wooden prince and enables the princess to wed a human prince. Balázs also wrote the libretto for Bartók's opera, *Duke Bluebeard's Castle* (1918), an adaptation of Charles Perrault's **'Bluebeard'*, which depicted a solipsistic duke, who collected women rather than killing them. In 1919, Balázs had to flee Hungary because of his involvement with the Communist Party and its short-lived control of the government. At first he lived in Vienna, where he began writing film reviews in German and published a remarkable collection of pseudo Chinese fairy tales, *The Cloak of Dreams* (1922). After the publication of his important study of film, *The Visible Man or the Culture of Film* (1924), he moved to Berlin, where he was active in left-wing cultural politics. As part of this involvement he published political fairy tales for children such as *The Real Sky-Blue* (1925). By far his most significant work for children was the play *Hans Urian Goes in Search of Bread* (1927), which he wrote with Lisa *Tetzner. This fairy-tale drama about a young boy's magical learning experiences during the beginning of the Great Depression was a great success in Germany and was later published as a fairy-tale novel. Before fleeing the Nazis in 1933, Balázs collaborated with Leni Riefenstahl and wrote the script for *The Blue Light* (1932), which has strong fairy-tale motifs. It concerns a young woman who is persecuted as a witch by Italian villagers. Balázs himself felt persecuted in the Soviet Union during the 1930s and 1940s. He returned to Budapest in 1946 where he spent his last years lecturing on film, writing books, and revising his fairy tales.   JZ

Balázs, Béla, *The Cloak of Dreams* (2010), ed. Jack Zipes.
Frank, Tibor, 'Béla Balázs: From the Aestheticization of Community to the Communization of the Aesthetic' *Journal of the Interdisciplinary Crossroads* (2006).
Loewy, Hanno, *Béla Balázs: Märchen, Ritual und Film* (2003).
Zsuffa, Joseph, *Béla Balázs: The Man and the Artist* (1987).

Baldini, Antonio (1889–1962) Italian poet, critic, and dramatist. The long novella *Michelaccio* (1924) recounts the life of the proverbial Michelaccio in a mixture of real and fabulous elements also used in *Rugantino* (1942), a mythical interpretation of Rome through the centuries. Rome in its giant-like transformation becomes an abstract creation, a myth, close to the heart and imagination of the author. Baldini's *La strada delle meraviglie* (*The Road of Wonders*, 1923) contains the tale of three poor sisters whose wish is to marry the king's baker, cook, and son, respectively. The youngest one, having married the prince, gives birth to two beautiful children who are hated by the queen. The tale revolves around the deeds, sorcery, and magical elements that affect the fate of the three sisters, and in the end, good is restored and the wicked queen and witch are punished. *La dolce calamità* (*The Sweet Magnet*, 1992), a book on women figures, contains the dream-like fairy tale 'Il gigante Paolone e la piccola Mabruca' ('The Giant Paolone and Little Mabruca').   GD

ballet and fairy tales The traditional association of classical ballet with the fairy tale is based not merely on the fame of such ballets as *Swan Lake*, *Cinderella*, and *The *Sleeping Beauty*, but on a fundamental affinity between the two art forms. Like fairy tales, ballets are constructed as highly formalized narratives which make extensive use of repetition and tell their stories primarily through the physical actions of their characters. Excessive complexity in plot or characterization is as inappropriate for a ballet as it is for a fairy tale. And ballet, by its very nature, contains an element of fantasy. Dancers seem to float in mid-air as easily as butterflies; opera singers, despite *Wagner's attempt to get his fleet of Valkyries off the ground, cannot. Even before the romantic period and the ascendancy of the fairy tale, ballet relied on mythological stories and characters. In ballet, moreover, as in the literary fairy tale, the supernatural is often used symbolically to express concepts, ideologies, and spiritual beliefs.

Fairy-tale ballets have drawn upon four main sources: fairy bride legends (for example, *Swan Lake* and *Giselle*), folk fairy tales (*Cinderella*, *The Sleeping Beauty*), literary fairy tales (*The Nutcracker*, *The *Red Shoes*), and stories of toys, puppets, or automata that come to life (*Coppélia, Pet-rushka*). During its romantic period—from the 1830s to the 1850s—ballet was dominated by the fairy bride motif. Towards the end of the 19th century—and again in the 1940s—folk tales, 'live toy' stories, and literary fairy tales (particularly those of *Hoffmann and *Andersen) became common sources of inspiration. A more recent development, dating from the 1980s, has been an ironic, revisionist approach to familiar fairy tales, often with psychological or strongly ideological overtones.

Filipo *Taglioni's *La Sylphide* (1832), the first romantic ballet, established the fairy bride legend as the means by which romanticism could be expressed in dance. The scenario was loosely inspired by Charles *Nodier's *Trilby, ou Le Lutin d'Argail* (1822), the story of a Scots fisherman whose wife is tempted away from him by an amorous male sprite. In the ballet, however, the genders are reversed. James, a Scottish farmer, is about to marry Effie, but as he sits dreaming by the fireplace a beautiful winged sylph appears to him; they dance together and fall in love. Although James attempts to fulfil his vows to Effie, his new passion is too strong for him; he breaks away in the midst of his own wedding dance and pursues the sylph into the forest. Here, among her own kind, she proves elusive. A treacherous witch offers James an enchanted scarf with which to capture her, but when he loops it round her the sylph's wings drop off, and she sinks dying to the ground. As her fellow sylphs carry her body into the sky, James hears in the distance the music of a wedding procession; Effie has married someone else.

La Sylphide's impact was immense. As the ballet critic Théophile *Gautier summarized it, 'After *La Sylphide*, *Les Filets de Vulcain* and *Flore et Zéphire* were no longer possible; the Opera was given over to gnomes, undines, salamanders, elves, nixes, wilis, peris—to all that strange and mysterious folk who lend themselves so marvellously to the fantasies of the *maître de ballet*. The 12 palaces in marble and gold of the Olympians were relegated to the dust of the storerooms, and the scene-painters received

orders only for romantic forests, valleys illumined by the pretty German moonlight reminiscent of Heinrich Heine's charming ballads.' The ballerina was transformed into a supernatural being, elevated *en pointe*, literally above the earth. Even her costume was revolutionized. Female dancers of the early 19th century had worn high-waisted pleated tunics that revealed every curve. Marie Taglioni's sylph dress consisted of a close-fitting, low-necked bodice and long, bell-shaped skirt of gauzy white material; this 'romantic tutu' reflected the spiritual nature of the romantic heroine. Atmospheric lighting—made possible by the invention of gaslight—and magical special effects enhanced the sense of fantasy. While Charles *Didelot, inspired by a stage production of *A Midsummer Night's Dream*, had employed the newly invented 'flying wires' to suggest the antics of the wind god in *Flore et Zéphire* (1796), Taglioni used them to launch an entire flock of sylphs into the air.

The fairy bride legend dramatized a central dilemma of romanticism—the search for the unattainable ideal, and its often tragic outcome. The sylph is James's dream, the creature of his poetic imagination, for whom he deserts his earthly love. His attempt to grasp the ideal only ends in destroying it. Yet the fairy bride of romantic ballet is more than an elusive abstraction. Mindful, perhaps, of Fouqué's sympathetic portrayal of a loving water sprite in *Undine* (1811), Taglioni gave his sprite the ability to return James's love; the story becomes as much her tragedy as his. This humanization of the fairy bride not only increased the complexity and dramatic interest of the romantic ballet, but sometimes made possible a happy ending. The motif underwent every possible variation. In Filippo Taglioni's *L'Ombre* (*The Shadow*, 1839), the ghost of a murdered woman haunts her lover. In Paul *Taglioni's *Electra* (1849), a Norwegian shepherd falls in love with one of the Pleiades; this ballet was the first to create special effects with electric lights. In Joseph Mazilier's *Le Diable amoureux* (*The Amorous Demon*, 1840), a female demon falls in love with the man she has been ordered to seduce, and thus redeems herself from Hell. In August Bournonville's *A Folk Tale* (*Et Folkesagen*, 1854), a human girl raised by trolls vies for a man's love with the troll changeling who replaced her. In his *Napoli* (*The Fisherman and his Bride*, 1842), an Italian peasant girl falls overboard from a fishing boat, is transformed into a naiad in the Blue Grotto of Capri, and must be rescued by her lover. In Jean Coralli's highly popular *La Péri* (1843), Achmet smokes a pipe of opium and dreams of an oasis inhabited by peris— Persian fairies—with whose queen he falls in love. Jules Perrot's *Ondine* (1843) and Paul Taglioni's *Coralia, or The Inconstant Knight* (1847) retell Fouqué's story.

The greatest of *La Sylphide*'s successors was Coralli's and Perrot's *Giselle, ou Les Wilis* (1841). The scenario, by Coralli and Gautier, was inspired by Heinrich *Heine's description in *De l'Allemagne* (1835) of the *wilis*—the vengeful ghosts of unmarried maidens. The peasant maiden Giselle, betrayed by Count Albrecht, goes insane, dies, and becomes a *wili*. At night, when Albrecht visits her forest grave, the *wilis* waylay him, and their queen, Myrtha, orders Giselle to kill him by dancing him to death. Instead, still loving him, she manages to protect and support him till dawn comes, when the *wilis* disappear and she returns to her grave.

By the 1870s, romanticism had faded, and the centre of creative energy in dance was shifting eastward, from France to Russia. Here, Arthur Saint-Léon became the first choreographer to draw upon the rich Russian folk tradition with *The Little Hump-backed Horse* (1864), based on the folk tale of a peasant boy and his magical steed, which carries him through the kingdoms of earth, air, fire, and water. *Coppélia* (1870), Saint-Léon's last ballet, demonstrated the potential of 'live toy' stories. In this E. T. A. *Hoffmann tale, the toymaker Dr Coppelius creates a life-size mechanical doll so realistic that the gullible Franz falls in love with her and must be rescued by his clever sweetheart. In 1877 Piotr Ilyich *Tchaikovsky consciously attempted to revive the romantic spirit with *Swan Lake* (*Le Lac des cygnes*), whose variation of the fairy bride motif was probably inspired by Russian folk tales of swan maidens. His partnership with the choreographer Marius Petipa produced two other famous fairy-tale ballets, *The Sleeping Beauty* (*La Belle au bois dormant*, 1890) and the Hoffmann-based *Nutcracker* (*Casse noisette*, 1892). The former, while paying homage to Charles *Perrault (many of whose characters arrive as guests in the final wedding scene) also takes full advantage of the fairy tale's affinity for multi-layered symbolism. The story of Princess Aurora, whose name means 'dawn', suggests the cycle of human life—birth, youth, love, marriage, even a form of death and resurrection. At the same time, the ballet's opulent Louis XIV setting hints at a parallel with the reign of Russia's Alexander III; what seems a glorification of the tsar's imperial power, however, may conceal subtle criticism in such episodes as the botched christening celebration. Petipa returned to Perrault for inspiration in *Cinderella* (1893) and an elaborated version of *Bluebeard* (*Barbe-bleue*, 1896) with a medieval setting.

The surge of nationalist feeling at the end of the century inspired a more extensive use of Russian folk traditions. Under the sponsorship of Sergei Diaghilev and his Ballets Russes, Michel *Fokine choreographed *Firebird* (*L'Oiseau de feu*, 1910), based freely on one of Russia's best-known folk tales, and *Petrushka* (1911), both to the music of Igor Stravinsky. The traditional Petrushka is the Russian Punch, an anarchic puppet character who defies the Devil himself. In Fokine's ballet, the puppet—danced originally by Vaslav Nijinsky—becomes a tragic figure, a sad-faced clown struggling to escape the role he is forced to play. 'Live dolls' are the protagonists of the Ballets Russes's more cheerful *La Boutique fantasque* (*The Fantastic Toyshop*, 1919) as well. Choreographed by Léonide Massine, the story is set in a French toyshop full of dancing dolls who come to life at night after the shop has closed. When a Russian family purchase a female Cancan Dancer and an American family her male partner, the two dolls run away together rather than face separation, and all the toys join to defend their shop from the angry customers. The ballet's internationalism and themes of rebellion and liberation are playfully suggestive of the new, post-war era. Equally forward-looking was *Le Chant du rossignol* (*The Nightingale's Song*, 1914), based on *Andersen's fairy tale of 'The Nightingale', created to Stravinsky's music by the young choreographer George *Balanchine. By the 1920s, however, the full-scale fairy-tale ballet seemed old-fashioned. Influenced by revolutionary developments in music, the visual arts, and modern dance, choreographers sought fresh sources, such as classical myth or contemporary life. Or they abandoned storytelling altogether in 'abstract' ballets inspired by works of music. Yet by the late 1930s interest in the fairy tale was already reviving. Fokine returned to well-known folk tales in *Le Coq d'or* (*The Golden Cockerel*, 1937), based on the *Rimsky-Korsakov opera, in *Cinderella* (1938), and in his comic *Bluebeard* (1940). Sergei *Prokofiev's *Peter and the Wolf* became a children's ballet in 1940. And Andersen's darker fairy tales inspired several choreographers. *The Hundred Kisses* (1935), by Bronislava Nijinska, was based on his sardonic fable 'The Swineherd'. *Le Baiser de la fée* (*The Fairy's Kiss*, 1937), another collaboration between Balanchine and Stravinsky, reconceived Andersen's 'The Ice Maiden' as a fairy-bride story in homage to Tchaikovsky. The most famous movie with a ballet theme, *The Red Shoes* (1945), translated Andersen's story of vanity and redemption into a suicidal conflict between art and love.

Fairy-tale ballets—both revivals of the classics and newly commissioned works—flourished through the 1940s and 1950s. In some respects, they represented a conscious return to tradition. When Frederick *Ashton set out to create the first full-length 20th-century English ballet for the Sadler's Wells company, he chose in *Cinderella* (1948) the subject of several previous ballets and countless English pantomimes. His *La Péri* (1956) and *Undine* (1956) recalled the fairy-bride ballets of the romantic period. But fairy-tale subjects could also reflect contemporary sensibilities. Todd Bolender's *Mother Goose Suite* (1943), set to Maurice *Ravel's music, is a fantasy for adults, in which the fairy-tale characters represent a woman's memories of her search for love. John *Cranko used the same music for his 1949 *Beauty and the Beast*, in which the secondary elements of the fairy tale have been stripped away, and the entire story is expressed as a *pas de deux*. *The Unicorn, the Gorgon and the Manticore* (1956), with music and libretto by Gian Carlo Menotti, uses its mythological monsters—the creations of a poet's youth, middle, and old age—to comment ironically on the relationship between the artist and his fickle audience, which finds each monster only briefly titillating. Even *Cinderella* (*Zolushka*), as interpreted by Prokofiev in 1945, took on marxist overtones, depicting the prince's court as decadent and corrupt. Prokofiev's *The Stone Flower* (1958) similarly reinterprets the fairy-bride motif; the stonecutter's choice between the supernatural Queen of the Copper Mountain and his peasant sweetheart is made to symbolize the choice between his search for perfection in art and the dedication of his art to the people.

A straightforward use of fairy-tale material was still possible in the 1960s, when both George Balanchine and Frederick Ashton produced versions of *A Midsummer Night's Dream*, Balanchine in 1962 and Ashton—a one-act ballet called *The Dream*—in 1964. Ashton emerged from retirement in 1971 to create the choreography for the Royal Ballet's lavish motion picture *Tales of Beatrix Potter*, and to play Mrs Tiggy-Winkle himself. Experimental choreographers of this period, however, tended to reject any type of narrative, drama, or illusion for minimalism and abstraction. It was the rising influence of postmodernism, with its interest in narrative and tradition, that made possible a new approach to narrative in dance. At the same time, studies of fairy tales based on psychoanalytical theory, feminism, and cultural history suggested new uses for fairy-tale subjects.

In her *tanztheater* (dance-theatre) version of *Bluebeard* (1977), for example, the German choreographer Pina *Bausch used the tale as a metaphor for oppressive male–female relationships. In a room whose floor is covered with dried leaves, a man and woman—sometimes multiplied into groups of men and women—torment each other until the woman is killed, while snippets of Béla *Bartók's opera *Bluebeard* (1911) are played by the man on a tape recorder. Using sections of Prokofiev's *Cinderella* score, the French choreographer Maguy Marin created a *Cinderella* (1985) in which the dancers are masked and costumed to represent clumsy wax dolls in a giant, multi-compartmented doll's house. The royal ball becomes a birthday party with a cake and candles and children's games of rope jumping and hopscotch. This version of the fairy tale seems to parody both ballet traditions and the tale itself—as though only a toddler could believe in the Cinderella story. Kinematic, the American dance group, produced a trilogy of fairy tales in the late 1980s: *The *Snow Queen* (1986), based on Andersen's story; *The Handless Maiden* (1987), based on the lesser-known Grimms' fairy tale 'The Girl without Hands'; and *Broken Hill* (1988), based on the Grimms' tale of 'The Twelve Dancing Princesses'. Dance movements were combined with the spoken texts of the fairy tales, which were broken into fragments and randomly re-ordered in a kind of postmodern narrative. In *The Handless Maiden*, for instance, phrases and sentences from the Grimms' text were interwoven with phrases from Carl Jung's *Man and his Symbols*, underlining the archetypal imagery of the tale. Emblems of childhood and of cultural tradition, fairy tales provide ideal vehicles through which choreographers may question gender roles, social and political structures, the value and meaning of tradition, the nature of narrative, and the universality of art.

Indeed, it seems likely that whatever future directions ballet may choose to travel, it will always be accompanied by its old companion, the fairy tale. SR

Banes, Sally, 'Happily Ever After?—The Postmodern Fairy Tale and the New Dance', in *New Dance: Questions and Challenges* (1987).

Canton, Katia, *The Fairy Tale Revisited* (1994).

Gautier, Théophile, ed. Ivor Guest, *Gautier on Dance* (1986).

Godden, Rumer, *The Tale of the Tales: The Beatrix Potter Ballet* (1971).

Kirstein, Lincoln, *Four Centuries of Ballet* (1984).

Wiley, Roland John, *Tchaikovsky's Ballets* (1985).

Baluschek, Hans (1870–1935) German illustrator, painter, and writer, known for his graphic depictions of the proletarian milieu and hard life in big cities. Baluschek was also a renowned illustrator of fairy tales and produced superb illustrations for five books in the series Deutsche Märchenbücherei published by the Klemm Verlag between 1878 and 1923: *Peterchens Mondfahrt* (*Little Peter's Flight to the Moon*, 1915), *Pips der Pilz. Ein Wald- und Weihnachtsmärchen* (*Pips the Mushroom: A Forest and Christmas Fairy Tale*, 1920), *Prinzessin Huschewind* (*Princess Hush Wind*, 1922), and *Ins Märchenland* (*Into Fairyland*, 1922). He employed aquarelles and oils to form unusual and bizarre characters and also used ink to create the text. In 1925 he produced ten marvellous pen-and-ink drawings for an edition of the *Grimms' fairy tales edited by Paul Samuleit. JZ

Banville, Théodore de (1823–91) French poet and playwright associated with the Parnassian movement. His vast poetic *œuvre* depicts nymphs, satyrs, and fairies walking side by side with members of the literary, artistic, and social circles of 19th-century France. In the 50 *Contes féeriques* (*Fairylike Tales*, 1882), he critiques the bourgeois values of contemporary society, but at the same time creates fantasy situations in which good fairies reward struggling young artists and poets. Banville also adapted *Perrault's 'Riquet à la houpe' (*'Riquet with the Tuft', 1884) to the stage. AR

'Barbe-bleue' *See* 'BLUEBEARD'.

Bardin, Garri (1941–) Russian animator, director, and screenwriter, who has produced fascinating, political clay animation films. *Grey Wolf and Little Red Riding Hood* (1990) mocks the old Stalinist Soviet regime by depicting it in the form of a toothless wolf unable to catch a petite *Red Riding Hood. Bardin's transformation of Charles *Perrault's *'Little Red Riding Hood' into a political film about freedom and the assumption of a new identity bursts with good humour and artful design. All the characters are made out of clay, and Bardin has developed an unusual technique so that their movements are fluent and flexible. He uses old popular songs in unusual ways with new lyrics. Aside from the wolf singing 'Mack the Knife' as his leitmotif, he also has a seductive ditty based on 'Tea for Two', Little Red Riding Hood and her mother are associated with Russian folk music, granny sings a song from her bed to the tune of 'La Vie en Rose', and the final marching song is a composition based on 'Auld Lang Syne'. Though Bardin is sceptical about the new Russian identity, his film is filled with carnivalesque hope. With the wolf levelled at the end of a hazardous journey to Paris from Russia, Little Red Riding Hood strides forward in solidarity with an eccentric group of people who believe in peace and must still be on the alert against wolves. On the other hand, *Puss in Boots* (1995) portrays an inept Russian peasant unable to adapt to modern times. Fond of depicting the fates of outsiders, Gardin's hope for Russia lies in young people born in the wrong country. In *The Ugly Duckling* (2010), his first animated feature film, he depicts present-day Russia as a dilapidated barnyard. Bardin also uses puppets effectively and has a droll sense of humor that reinvigorates classical fairy tales. Here the noble ugly duckling who turns into a handsome swan brings out the ugliness of all the fowls in the barnyard, and he flies away with white swans to liberty.   JZ

Baret, Paul (1728-95) French novelist and dramatist. He created a satirical fairy tale for adults, 'Foka, ou les métamorphoses, conte chinois' ('Foka or the Metamorphoses, a Chinese Tale', 1777), which lampoons 18th-century society and mores. The tale's ironic narrator contends that a fairy named

Frivolity is responsible for ridiculous fashions, affected language, insipid novels, and pretty female philosophers. Ultimately conservative in its social vision, this amusing tale ridicules the pretensions of those who stray beyond their designated place in society.   AZ

Baring-Gould, Sabine (1834-1924) English folklorist. His voluminous output ranging from devotional works to guide books includes many retellings and compilations of myths and legends. Early works include *The Book of Were-Wolves* (1865) and *The Silver Store* (1868), versified legends from medieval, Jewish, and Christian sources. In *A Book of Fairy Tales* (1894) he retold French and English stories, and included two of his own: 'Pretty Marushka' and 'Don't Know'. In *Old English Fairy Tales* (1895) and *The Crock of Gold* (1899) he reworked stories from ancient ballads, incorporating fragments from many different sources which 'I have taken the liberty of embroidering'.   GA

Dickinson, Bickford Holland Cohan, *Sabine Baring-Gould: Squarson, Writer and Folklorist, 1834-1924* (1970).

Purcell, William Ernest, *Onward Christian Soldier: A Life of Sabine Baring-Gould, Parson, Squire, Novelist, Antiquary, 1834-1924* (1957).

Sutton, Max Keith, 'Place, Folklore, and Hegelianism in Baring-Gould's Red Spider', *VIJ: Victorians Institute Journal*, 13 (1985).

Baroja, Pío (1872-1956) Contemporary Spanish novelist whose protagonists are usually rebellious men of action. Baroja's style has been praised for its spontaneity and vivacity, but it has also been characterized as cumbersome. Baroja preferred to write novels all his life, yet composed some short stories, a few of which could be considered novellas. Over time, Baroja's tales became more realistic, but in an early collection of short stories, *Vidas sombrías* (*Sombre Lives*, 1900), he included a few fantastic tales: 'Médium' ('Medium', 1900), 'El trasgo' ('The Goblin', 1900), and 'El reloj' ('The Clock', 1900). Among his short novels, it is worth noting 'La dama de Urtubi' ('The Lady of Urtubi', 1916), a story about witchcraft in the Basque country, Baroja's birthplace, and 'La casa del crimen' ('The House of Crime', 1920). In the latter, ghosts of dead men appear, a man is buried alive, and another character loses his mind after murdering a kinsman, making this story equal to the best of Poe.   CFR

Aubrun, Charles V., 'Baroja et le conte', *Revista Hispanica Moderna: Columbia University Hispanic Studies*, 36 (1970).

Dean-Thacker, Veronica P., *Witchcraft and the Supernatural in Six Stories by Pío Baroja* (1988–1989).

Barrie, Sir James Matthew (1860–1937) Scottish creator of *Peter Pan. He studied at the University of Edinburgh (of which he would become Chancellor in 1930) and was a journalist before freelancing in London. His first novel inspired the 'Kailyard' school with its quaint sentimentality, Scots dialect, and local colour. His material came from reminiscences of his mother, who never overcame the death of her eldest son, whom Barrie sought to replace. Critics find an intricate Oedipal relationship reflected in his novels and plays with fantasy settings, character definition, problematic marriages, and manipulative women. Sentimentality and portrayal of contemporary society especially date his theatre, which has been labelled 'childish' and inferior to the social comedies or intellectual dramas of contemporaries like *Wilde or Shaw.

It was precisely this naïve quality, however, that charmed the public. Literary success arrived with the melodramatic novel *The Little Minister* (1891); *Walker, London* (1892) was his first theatrical triumph, and featured Barrie's future wife. Unfortunately, their marriage was childless, and he looked elsewhere for a surrogate family. He found one in the five Llewelyn Davies brothers, to whom he became extraordinarily attached. He regaled them with tales later collected for *The Little White Bird* (1902), an adult story about a bachelor who tries to charm a youngster away from his parents with tales of a boy who could fly. Barrie refashioned these episodes into a fairy play—and the rest is history.

Peter Pan, or The Boy who Wouldn't Grow Up (1904), was a phenomenon and remains—with his social-caste fantasy, *The Admirable Crichton* (1903)—one of the few Barrie plays still performed. With the advent of television and improved theatrical effects, it easily outdistances rival children's plays like *The *Blue Bird* and *Toad of Toad Hall*. Peter, the fairy Tinkerbell, and Captain Hook were popularized by countless authors, and had entered modern British folklore long before Barrie received a baronetcy (1913) or the Order of Merit (1922). Although he issued an illustrated version of the *White Bird* episodes as *Peter Pan in Kensington Gardens* (1906), he did not produce the narrative *Peter and Wendy* until 1911, and only published his play's definitive version in 1928.

None of his later theatre was as popular as this paean to Eternal Youth. He did, however, re-enter fairyland with *A Kiss for Cinderella* (1916). Set in wartime London, it concerns a girl nicknamed *Cinderella who does drudge's work for a German family, runs an illegal daycare service, and dreams of accompanying the Duke of Wales to a ball. A magical pantomime recreates the ball that she hallucinates attending, all but freezing to death on her doorstep. Unlike *Andersen's Little Match Girl, though, she catches pneumonia and receives a kiss from her Prince before dying. In short, where the fantasy of *Peter Pan* is life-affirming, that of *Cinderella* is destructive.   MLE

Birkin, Andrew, *J. M. Barrie & The Lost Boys: The Love Story That Gave Birth to Peter Pan* (1979).

Dunbar, Janet, *J. M. Barrie: The Man behind the Image* (1970).

Geduld, Harry M., *James Barrie* (1971).

Rose, Jacqueline, *The Case of Peter Pan, or The Impossibility of Children's Fiction* (1984).

Wullschlager, Jackie, *Inventing Wonderland: The Lives and Fantasies of Lewis Carroll, Edward Lear, J. M. Barrie, Kenneth Grahame, and A. A. Milne* (1995).

Barta, Jiří (1948–) Czech animator, filmmaker, and director, who is known for his brilliant use of stop animation and wood puppets. Barta does not hesitate to probe the dark side of 'The Pied Piper' in his stop-motion animated film, *Krysar* (1986). Children do not appear in harrowing adaptation, nor are they abducted. They are behind the scenes, so to speak. Barta is more concerned with revealing the materialism of the entire populace of a medieval town. Rich and poor alike are absorbed by making money. They bargain bitterly with one another and fight over money, or they literally make money, that is, stamp and hoard coins. They are all wasteful and corrupt, no matter what their social class. In short, they are infected by petty greed not by rats. There is no reference to Hamelin in his film about the 'Pied Piper' as the designated town, for Barta has sought to create a universal parable about the pestilence of money. Consequently, the Piper destroys the entire town and flies away, leaving only a fisherman and a newborn baby behind him. He is more optimistic in a recent film, *Toys in the Attic* (2009), in which a pretty doll named Buttercup lives in an attic full of discarded junk. When she is kidnapped and taken to the Land of Evil, her friends, the marionette Prince Charming, lazy Teddy Bear, and the plasticine creature Schubert go on a long arduous journey to rescue her. The artwork in this film is magnificent. In all of Barta's films he reveals how strongly he has been influenced by the expressionist films of the 1920s and also by the work of his Czech compatriot Jan *Svankmajer and the Russian Yuri *Norstein.   JZ

Barth, John (1930–) American writer known for his highly innovative experiments with different genres. For instance, his two highly acclaimed novels, *The Sot-Weed Factor* (1960) and *Giles Goat-Boy, or The Revised New Syllabus* (1966), play with the picaresque novel and the fable as science fiction. Barth's interest in fairy tales is primarily focused on the tradition of *The *Arabian Nights*. In *Chimera* (1972), a collection of stories, he reintroduces *Scheherazade in 'Dunyazadiad' and enables her to make sense out of her life and survive through stories passed back in time by Barth himself. Other fairy tales such as 'Perseid' and 'Bellerophoniad' celebrate the role of the storyteller, who endows life with significance. In another collection, *The Tidewater Tales* (1987), Barth makes ample use of Scheherazade and other fantastic characters from fairy tales. In his superb fairy-tale novel *The Last Voyage of Somebody the Sailor* (1991), Scheherazade appears again but this time she takes second place to Sindbad the sailor. In this narrative, Simon William Behler, a well-known journalist, becomes lost overboard off the coast of Sri Lanka and eventually finds himself in Sindbad's house in medieval Baghdad. In order to return to the modern world, he must challenge Sindbad to a storytelling marathon with the hope that he can solve his predicament and overcome the crisis in his own life. The theme of re-creation through storytelling is also prominent in *Once Upon a Time* (1994) in which the narrative threads of the story incorporate timeslips and illusions to form an author who is called Barth. The fairy-tale genre has been particularly valuable for Barth, who uses the marvellous and intricate plots of transformation to demonstrate how crucial the imagination is for self-definition and identity as boundaries keep shifting in the postmodern world.   JZ

Kurk, Katherine C., 'Narration as Salvation: Textual Ethics of Michel Tournier and John Barth', *Comparative Literature Studies*, 25 (1988).
Vickery, John B., 'The Functions of Myth in John Barth's Chimera', *Modern Fiction Studies*, 38 (1992).
Ziegler, Heide, 'The Tale of the Author: Or, Scheherazade's Betrayal', *Review of Contemporary Fiction*, 10 (1990).

Bartók, Béla (1881–1945) Hungarian composer and ethnomusicologist. A central figure in 20th-century music, Bartók devoted a significant part of his musical life to the collection, classification, and study of folk music, most extensively that of Hungary, Romania, and Slovakia. This music had a profound influence on his own compositions, from the many didactic piano pieces based on folk melodies, to the major works, in which the forms, rhythms, and melodic patterns of specific folk-music traditions are variously, and pervasively, present.

Two of his three stage works are based on fairy tales. The one-act opera *Duke Blue-beard's Castle* (composed 1911; first performed 1918), written to a libretto by Béla Balázs (influenced by Maurice *Maeterlinck's *Ariane et Barbe-bleue*), uses the castle, with its seven locked rooms, as a physical manifestation of *Bluebeard's inner self. The gradual opening of each door by the heroine, here named Judith, culminates in the discovery of the ghostly figures of three former wives. Having urged her husband to reveal all, it only remains for Judith to take her place at their side. In contrast, the ballet *The Wooden Prince* (1917), with scenario again by Balázs, follows a more traditional fairy-tale pattern. A prince, hindered by the Fairy of the Forest from wooing a princess, resorts to carving a puppet of himself. Although the princess initially falls for the puppet (brought to life by the Fairy), she finally acknowledges the real prince.   SB

John, Nicholas (ed.), *The Stage Works of Béla Bartók* (1991).

Kroó, György, 'Duke Bluebeard's Castle', *Studia Musicologica*, 1 (1961).

Basile, Giambattista (1575–1632) Italian writer, poet, and courtier. He was born outside Naples to a middle-class family of courtiers and artists. He spent his life in military and intellectual service at courts in Italy and abroad, was active in several academies, held administrative positions in the Neapolitan provinces, and by the end of his life had received the title of count. During his lifetime he was fairly well known for his poetic works in Italian, written in the style of the baroque poet Giambattista Marino. Today, however, Basile is remembered principally for his literary corpus in Neapolitan dialect, radically different in its popular content and playful style from his more orthodox Italian works. This corpus consists principally of *Le Muse napolitane*, a series of nine satiric eclogues depicting popular culture in Naples; and the fairy-tale collection *Lo cunto de li cunti overo lo trattenemiento de peccerille* (*The Tale of Tales, or Entertainment for Little Ones*, 1634–6), also known as the *Pentamerone*. Although there is no trace of a

manuscript nor reference to the elaboration of *Lo cunto*, the tales were probably intended to be read aloud in the 'courtly conversations' that were an élite pastime of this period.

Lo cunto constituted a culmination of the interest in popular culture and folk traditions that permeated the Renaissance, when isolated fairy tales had started to be included in novella collections, most notably in Straparola's *Le *piacevoli notti* (*The Pleasant Nights*, 1550–3). Indeed, Basile did not merely transcribe the oral materials that he heard around Naples and in his travels, but transformed them into original tales distinguished by vertiginous rhetorical play, abundant references to the everyday life and popular culture of the time, and a subtext of playful critique of courtly culture and the canonical literary tradition. Besides being one of the most suggestive expressions of the search for new artistic forms and content theorized by the baroque poetics of the marvellous, *Lo cunto* is the first integral collection consisting entirely of fairy tales to appear in Europe, and thus marks the passage from the oral tradition of folk tales to the artful and sophisticated 'authored' fairy tale. As such, it exerted a notable influence on later fairy-tale writers such as *Perrault and the *Grimms.

Lo cunto comprises 49 fairy tales contained within a 50th frame story, also a fairy tale, that opens and closes the collection. In the frame tale, a slave girl deceitfully cheats Princess Zoza out of her predestined prince Tadeo (the 'false-bride' motif), and the princess reacts by using a magic doll to instil in the slave the need to hear tales. The prince summons the ten best tale-tellers of his kingdom, a motley group of hags, and they each tell one tale apiece for five days, at the end of which Zoza tells her own tale, reveals the slave's deceit, and wins back Tadeo. In many ways the structure of Basile's work mirrors, in parodic fashion, that of earlier novella collections, in particular Boccaccio's *Decameron*: there are five days of telling that contain ten tales each; the tales are told by ten grotesque and lower-class women; the tale-telling activity of each day is preceded by a banquet, games, and other entertainment; and verse eclogues that satirize the social ills of Basile's time follow each day's tales.

Lo cunto contains the earliest literary versions of many celebrated fairy-tale types— *'Cinderella', *'Sleeping Beauty', *'Rapunzel', and others—that later appeared in Perrault's and the Grimms' collections. But Basile's tales are often bawdier and crueller than their more canonical counterparts. In 'La gatta Cennerentola' ('The Cinderella Cat'), for example, the heroine is far from the epitome of feminine passivity for which she has come to be known, since she first kills off her stepmother and then astutely intervenes in the events of the story in order to attain her final triumph; she is even described during one of her outings as a whore parading her wares. Or in 'Cagliuso', Basile's version of *'Puss-in-Boots', the cat who has helped her master rise from rags to riches is thrown out of the window when he no longer needs her, to which she responds with a long-winded speech on ingratitude and an indignant departure. Indeed, the final outcome of these tales often does not quite fit into the 'happily ever after' mould. In 'La vecchia scortecata' ('The Old Woman who was Skinned'), two ancient sisters have, for purely arbitrary reasons, radically different fates: one is transformed into a beautiful young woman and marries a king, while the other, in an attempt to achieve the same, meets death when she orders a barber to shave her skin off. Other tales are explicitly autobiographical in tone, such as 'Corvetto', the story of a virtuous courtier who is forced to overcome a series of obstacles devised by his envious colleagues, but whose worth is finally recognized by his patron. Finally, Basile's tales feature a surprising number of ingenious heroines, such as the protagonist of 'La Sapia' ('The Wise Woman'), who is hired as a tutor for a hopelessly ignorant prince, finally manages to slap—quite literally—some sense into him, and then manipulates his plans for fierce revenge into a final recognition of her worth in the form of a loving marriage.

Basile does not offer easy answers to the problem of how an archaic, oral narrative genre can, or should, be re-proposed in literary form; in *Lo cunto* 'high' and 'low' cultures intersect to create a 'carnivalesque' text in which linguistic and cultural hierarchies, as well as the conventional fairy-tale hierarchies, are rearranged or made to show their weak spots. The new narrative model that emerges is one of the most complex tributes to the power of the fairy tale not only to entertain, but also to interpret the world.   NC

Basile, Giambattista, *Giambattista Basile's The Tale of Tales, or Entertainment for Little Ones* (2007) (trans.) Nancy Canepa.

Canepa, Nancy L., *From Court to Forest: Giambattista Basile's 'Lo cunto de li cunti' and the Birth of the Literary Fairy Tale* (1999).

Croce, Benedetto, Introduction to Giambattista Basile, *Il pentamerone* (1982).

Penzer, Norman (ed.), *The Pentamerone of Giambattista Basile* (2 vols., 1932).

Piccone, Michelangelo and Messerli, Alfred (eds.), *Giovan Battista Basile e l'invenzione della fiaba* (2004).

Rak, Michele, *Logica della fiaba* (2005).

Bassewitz, Gerdt von (1878-1923) German writer and playwright who is chiefly famous for his fairy-tale play *Peterchens Mondfahrt* (*Little Peter's Flight to the Moon*, 1911). Influenced by James *Barrie's play *Peter Pan*, Bassewitz depicted two children, Peter and Anneliese, who are transported to a magical dreamworld where they meet a beetle by the name of Sumsemann, who has lost one of his legs. The children decide to help the beetle find his leg and travel through the Milky Way on a rocket to the moon, where they encounter the sandman and other creatures. They learn that the man in the moon has stolen the beetle's leg, and with the help of the lightning man and the storm giant the children retrieve the beetle's leg. Bassewitz's sentimentalized portrayal of the children and their childish language contributed to making this play a classic in German children's theatre, and it was performed regularly at Christmas time up to the end of the 1960s. In recent years it has lost its popularity. Though Bassewitz wrote other plays for children such as *Pips, der Pilz* (*Pips, the Mushroom*, 1916) and *Der Wahrhaftige* (*The True One*, 1920), he never achieved the success that he scored with *Peterchens Mondfahrt*.   JZ

Schedler, Melchior, *Kindertheater: Geschichte, Modelle, Projekte* (1972).

Baum, L. Frank (Lyman Frank Baum, 1856-1919) American author of the Oz books and other fantasies for children. Born in Chittenango, New York, Baum enjoyed a sheltered and prolonged childhood on his family's country estate, Rose Lawn. Because of a heart defect, he was educated at home—except for a miserable two years at Peekskill Military Academy—and his father, a prosperous oil man and banker, willingly financed his hobbies. When Baum decided on a stage career, his father bought him an acting company, enabling him to play the lead in his own melodrama, *The Maid of Arran* (1882). After his father and older brother died, however, the family business collapsed, and Rose Lawn was sold. Baum and his wife—he had married Maud Gage, daughter of a famous woman suffragist—went west to Aberdeen, Kansas, investing first in a variety store, then in a newspaper, both of which soon failed. The family, now with four sons, moved to Chicago in 1891, where their fortunes gradually improved. Drawing on his knowledge of theatrical effects and his retail experience, Baum founded a successful journal for professional 'window trimmers'. He also published his first children's book, *Mother Goose in Prose* (1897), a collection of stories based on *Mother Goose rhymes, illustrated by the young Maxfield *Parrish. With *The *Wonderful Wizard of Oz* (1900), colourfully illustrated by W. W. *Denslow, Baum's reputation as a children's author was established, and his lifelong love of the theatre seemed vindicated when a musical adaptation of *The Wizard* became a smash hit in 1902. Throughout his life, however, he was to court financial disaster. While *The Land of Oz* (1904) was received with delight, the musical based on it was an expensive flop.

He was forced not only to begin producing an annual Oz book, but to adopt various pseudonyms for such formulaic series as 'Aunt Jane's Nieces' and 'The Boy Fortune Hunters'. In 1910 he and Maud moved to California, where they built a house in Hollywood called 'Ozcot'. Inevitably, Baum became involved in silent films, forming the short-lived Oz Film Manufacturing Company to produce his own stories. After his death, his publisher hired Ruth Plumly *Thompson, who added another 19 Oz books to Baum's original 14 stories before she retired in 1939.

Baum is considered the pivotal figure in the history of American fantasy—the first author to create a sustained work of fantasy with a distinctively American character. A lover from childhood of fairy tales, he had studied both traditional and literary tales with something like a scholar's interest. He wrote a historical introduction on Mother Goose for his own *Mother Goose in Prose*, and his 1909 article 'Modern Fairy Tales' shows his broad acquaintance with contemporary authors such as Howard *Pyle and E. *Nesbit, as well as *Andersen, *Carroll, and Frank *Stockton. His introduction to *The Wizard of Oz* reveals his awareness of attempting something new, claiming that 'the old-time fairy tale, having served for generations, may now be classed as "historical" in the children's library; for the time has come for a series of newer "wonder tales" in which the stereotyped genie, dwarf and fairy are eliminated, together with all the horrible and bloodcurdling incidents devised by their authors to point a fearsome moral to each tale.' *The Wizard*, he announced, would be 'a modernized fairy tale, in which the wonderment and joy are retained and the heartaches and nightmares are left out'. In fact, Baum's indebtedness to his predecessors and his willingness to innovate are equally apparent. *The Wizard* follows the traditional pattern of the magical quest, in which a human protagonist is helped by talking animals or other supernatural creatures, and must defeat a monster in order to attain his goal. Yet the 'modernized fairy tale' begins not 'once upon a time' but in the drought-stricken Midwest Baum had known first-hand. Its protagonist is a self-reliant American girl, her first companion a homely scarecrow, and the Wizard a con-man from Omaha. Oz itself, despite its royal rulers, is essentially democratic; its inhabitants show no trace of class-consciousness, while its economy—as described in the sixth Oz book, *The Emerald City of Oz* (1910)—is that of a socialist utopia. His cast of characters features a high proportion of original creations—the Tin Woodman, the Patchwork Girl, the Wogglebug, and many more—yet the 'stereotyped' fairies, witches, and talking animals can be found in Oz as well. Baum's singular success in reconciling through fantasy the Old World and the New surely accounts for much of the Oz books' appeal.

While Baum is best known as the 'Royal Historian of Oz', several of his other experiments with the fairy tale are also worthy of note. *Queen Zixi of Ix* (1905), a full-length story of a magic wishing cloak, proves his expertise with the more traditional fairy tale; critics consider it among his finest works. *American Fairy Tales* (1908) is an interesting (though only intermittently successful) attempt to adapt to an American setting the E. Nesbit type of fantasy, in which magical happenings erupt into the everyday world. Perhaps his boldest experiment, however, is *The Life and Adventures of Santa Claus* (1902), a unique amalgamation of myth, saint's legend, and fairy tale. In Baum's 'explanation' for the existence of Santa Claus, a human boy raised by nymphs in the mythical Forest of Burzee dedicates his life to giving children pleasure, invents the first toys, is attacked by the forces of evil and defended by the fairy immortals who have nurtured him, and finds himself finally endowed—on his deathbed—with immortality. That Baum identified with this protagonist is clear; he too had consciously dedicated himself to the happiness of children. SR

Harmetz, Aljean, *The Making of 'The Wizard of Oz'* (1977).

Hearn, Michael Patrick, *The Annotated Wizard of Oz* (1973).

Rahn, Suzanne, *The Wizard of Oz: Shaping an Imaginary World* (1998).

Vidal, Gore, 'The Wizard of the "Wizard"', *New York Review of Books* (September 1977) and 'On Rereading the Oz Books' (October 1977).

Zipes, Jack, 'Oz as American Myth', in *Fairy Tales as Myth/Myth as Fairy Tale* (1994).

Bausch, Pina (1940–2009) German dancer and choreographer who started her formal dance education at the age of 15 at the famous Folkwang school in Essen. Five years later she received a scholarship to study at the Juilliard School in New York, where she also danced at the Metropolitan Opera House. In 1962, she returned to Germany, where she danced as a soloist in the Kurt Jooss Ballet for the following six years and also started her career as a choreographer. In 1969 Bausch won first prize in the Cologne Choreographic Competition, and in 1973 she was appointed director of the Wuppertal Opera Ballet, which became famous worldwide as the Wuppertaler Tanztheater. With her multimedia theatrical dance style she defined the concept of 'tanztheater' (dance-theatre), combining dance, opera and spoken text. Fairy tales are an important source material for her work, often used to stimulate her own and the performers' reminiscences and emotional repertory, as in her first Wuppertal production, *Fritz* (1974), a one-act piece about the surreal daydreams of a child. One of her most famous works is *Blaubart* (**Bluebeard*, 1977), in which she reinterprets the *Perrault fairy tale on the basis of Béla *Bartók's opera *Duke Bluebeard's Castle*, placing it against a modern background. Bausch's Bluebeard is not a duke, but a common man, who exerts his power by physical violence and by manipulating the tape that plays Bartók's opera throughout the piece. In *Bluebeard*, Bausch explores the antagonism between men and women, a basic topic of her work. CS

Canton, Katia, *The Fairy Tale Revisited: A Survey of the Evolution of the Tales, from Classical Literary Interpretations to Innovative Contemporary Dance-Theater Productions* (1994).

Bayley, Frederick W. N. (1808–53) English writer, poet, and journalist. Aside from writing travel books, he was the author of *Comic Nursery Rhymes* (1846), which contain hilarious parodies of *'Bluebeard', *'Little Red Riding Hood', and *'Cinderella' in verse and with illustrations by gifted artists such as Alfred Crowquill. JZ

Bayley, Nicola (1949–) English illustrator of children's books. She has provided the illustrations for the pop-up book *Puss-in-Boots* (1977) and Russell *Hoban's *La Corona and the Tin Frog* (1978). In addition she has produced a Copycats series in 1984 consisting of several small books in which a cat imagines himself to be some other animal such as a parrot cat, crab cat, and elephant cat. Bayley works in watercolours and uses a stippling technique of small dots that make her illustrations lush in exquisite detail. JZ

Beagle, Peter S. (1939–) Award-winning American fantasy and non-fiction writer, screenwriter, and editor. His best-known work, the allegorical bestseller *The Last Unicorn* (1968), has been adapted for film, stage, and comic book, and translated. This quest story about a unicorn seeking others of her kind employs fairy-tale figures like the enchanted princess and wicked witch. PG

Beaumont, Jeanne-Marie Leprince de
See LEPRINCE DE BEAUMONT, JEANNE-MARIE.

'Beauty and the Beast' A fairy tale of the modern world which is related in plot to *Apuleius' 2nd-century Latin 'Cupid and Psyche' in *The Golden Ass*, and in motif to the ancient *Panchatantra* tale, 'The Girl who Married a Snake'.

1. History
Unknown during most of the medieval period, 'Cupid and Psyche' re-emerged in MS in the late Middle Ages and—of greater consequence—was printed in 1469 in an edition whose Latin text eventually spread throughout Europe. (In France alone, *The Golden Ass* was published four times between 1600 and 1648.) Subsequently translated out of Latin for larger reading publics with less education, Apuleius' text took on local coloration from the vernacular culture surrounding each new language in which it appeared. From this process emerged a family of European 'Beauty and the Beast' tales, whose plots arise from a narrative requirement that characterizes modern but not medieval stories; namely, that a beautiful woman accept and love an ugly husband.

The version of 'Beauty and the Beast' composed by Mme *Leprince de Beaumont in 1757 for her *Magasin des enfants* (translated as *The Young Misses' Magazine*) has become canonical in the modern world via print dissemination that repeated the post-1469 dissemination of 'Cupid and Psyche'. Its plot is as follows. A rich merchant who has lost his fortune wanders onto the grounds of an enchanted palace where he plucks a flower to take home to his youngest daughter. His act enrages the palace's owner, the Beast of the title, who as retribution exacts a promise that the merchant will surrender one of his daughters. The youngest willingly redeems her father's promise, and, expecting death, enters the enchanted palace. Instead, she enjoys luxury and elevated conversation with her monstrous partner, whom, however, she is unable to love. Released to visit her family, she overstays the time allotted for her absence, but when a sick and dying Beast appears in her dreams she hastily returns, declaring not only that she will marry him, but that she cannot live without him. Indeed, her tender sentiments restore the Beast to his princely appearance. The statues into which her wicked sisters are turned warn viewers against personal vanity and sisterly jealousy.

Numerous versions of 'Beauty and the Beast' predated Mme Leprince de Beaumont's tale. *Straparola's mid-16th-century 'Re Porco' ('King Pig') exhibits a swinish husband who delights in rooting in rotting filth and rolling in mud before climbing into bed with each of three successive wives. He murders the first two when they express their revulsion at his stinking habits, but makes the third his queen when she smilingly acquiesces in his muck.

Bayley, Frederick W. N. Frederick Bayley's *Comic Nursery Rhymes* (1846) are filled with hilarious scenes such as these two that mock Charles Perrault's *'Bluebeard'. While Bluebeard's young wife is puzzled by an enormous key, the murderous villain knows exactly what he wants to do with his sword.

'Beauty and the Beast'/'Cupid and Psyche' Beauty's compassion is about to lead her to save this strange monster in this anonymous illustration printed in *Beauty and the Beast* (*c*.1900).

*Basile's *Pentamerone* (1634–6) included four 'Beauty and the Beast' tale types. The first three—'The Serpent' (Day 2, Tale 5), 'The Padlock' (Day 2, Tale 9), and 'Pinto Smalto' (Day 5, Tale 3) resemble Apuleius' tale in that the husbands in each story are reputed, but not actual, monsters. However, in the fourth story, 'The Golden Root' (Day 5, Tale 4), the handsome husband simply trades his black skin for white at night.

Charles *Perrault includes a highly ethicized conclusion in his 'Beauty and the Beast' tale, *'Riquet à la Houppe' (1697), but leaves readers in doubt about whether the monstrously ugly hero Riquet actually becomes handsome, or whether he only appears so in the eyes of his besotted beloved. In 1697 Mme d'*Aulnoy also published 'Le Mouton' ('The Ram'), but with a tragic ending: her heroine's dear Ram dies in her absence. Other 'Beauty and the Beast' tale types in Mme d'Aulnoy's *œuvre* include 'La Grenouille bienfaisante' ('The Beneficent Frog'), 'Serpentin vert' ('The Green Serpent'), and 'Le Prince Marcassin'.

In 1740 Mme de *Villeneuve published a novel, *Les Contes marins, ou la jeune Américaine*, containing a 'Beauty and the Beast' tale, which details the merchant's stay in the monster's enchanted palace and has the Beast transformed into a Prince after he and the heroine spend the night together. In contrast, Mme Leprince de Beaumont presents a highly moralized conclusion, when Beauty's promise to marry the Beast restores his handsomeness. The *Grimms' tale 'Das Singende, Springende Löweneckerchen' ('The Singing, Springing Lark') offers yet another 'Beauty and the Beast' tale.

'Beauty and the Beast' tales, which all require a woman's patient tolerance of an ugly mate, have no companion tales in the modern period in which the obverse obtains, that is, a man who must love an ugly wife. In the medieval period, however, numerous companion stories circulated, the most famous of which is the Wife of Bath's story in Chaucer's *Canterbury Tales*. Another of the many now-forgotten and similar medieval tales, *Le Bel inconnu*, tells of a handsome knight who kisses a lady who has been turned into a serpent. Such stories survived into Basile's 17th-century collection, but between 1634 and the emergence of French fairy tales in print form in the 1690s, this trope largely disappeared from European storytelling.

2. Scholarship

Listings that combine 'Cupid and Psyche' with 'Beauty and the Beast' recognize plot similarities, but obscure story differences. The tale itself has been understood as a means of harnessing female sexuality, of describing female destiny, of coming to terms with sexual aspects of love, or of providing a 'philosophical allegory of the progression of the rational soul towards intellectual love' in the words of Robert Graves. Oralists maintain, though without material evidence, that 'Beauty and the Beast' tales enjoyed an independent oral existence from ancient Rome to the present; social-historical analyses see the money component of marriage arrangements reflected in Beauty's story; anthropologically oriented researchers understand 'Beauty and the Beast' as an allegory of the tension between endogamy and exogamy, as well as a verbal expression of the relationship between myth, rite, and fairy tale.

From the 17th to the 19th century, the plot of 'Beauty and the Beast' was adopted and adapted for musical drama, cantata, comedy, ballet, lyric tragedy, and fable. In the 20th century film has predominated: Jean *Cocteau's 1946 *Beauty and the Beast* began a tradition that has included a broad range of variations on the theme of female beauty vs. male ugliness.

Illustrations often concentrate on the Beast's head. Many a modern Beast is deformed by a boar's tusk, bull's horn, or goat's poll. Gorillas, scaly giants, hairy dogs, bears, wolves, and indeterminately generic prehistoric creatures complete the catalogue of illustrators' Beast incarnations.   RBB

Fehling, Detlev, *Amor und Psyche: Die Schöpfung des Apuleius und ihre Einwirkung auf das Märchen* (1977).

Hearne, Betsy, *Beauty and the Beast: Visions and Revisions of an Old Tale* (1989).

Pauly, Rebecca, 'Beauty and the Beast: From Fable to Film', *Literature/Film Quarterly*, 17.2 (1989).

Swahn, Jan-Öjvind, *The Tale of Cupid and Psyche* (1955).

Zipes, Jack, 'The Origins of the Fairy Tale for Children, or, How Script Was Used to Tame the Beast in Us', in Gillian Avery and Julia Briggs (eds.), *Children and their Books* (1989).

Beauty and the Beast A musical in two acts after the fairy tale of the same name. Premièred at the Palace Theatre, New York, in 1994, its book was by Linda Woolverton, lyrics by Howard Ashman and Tim Rice, and music by Alan Menken. The musical is based on the film made by Walt Disney Studios in 1991.   TH

Bechstein, Ludwig (1801–60) German writer. His two widely popular collections of fairy tales, the *Deutsches Märchenbuch* (*German Fairy Tale Book*, 1845) and the *Neues Deutsches Märchenbuch* (*New German Fairy Tale Book*, 1856) dominated the German fairy-tale market from their initial appearance until the 1890s, a period during which they far outsold the *Grimms' tales. Bechstein borrowed many fairy tales from the Grimm collection, but retold them, with very few exceptions, in a manner that suited the taste and norms of Germany's educated classes. In the rich German wall-poster tradition, it was usually Bechstein's editions of fairy tales from which publishers preferred to excerpt tales such as his 'Gestiefelte Kater' (*'Puss-in-Boots') and his 'Aschenbrödel' (*'Cinderella').

As a young man trained as an apothecary, Bechstein gained his prince's favour by a well-crafted volume of poetry and won a stipend to study at the university, after which he became a librarian and a *Hofrat* (court adviser) at the court of Sachsen-Meiningen. The security of his lifetime appointment allowed Bechstein to continue to write and eventually to turn to fairy tales.

Bechstein had honed a popular literary style in scores of semi-scholarly books before undertaking his best-selling *German Fairytale Book*. After only a few years his publishers changed the volume's name to *Ludwig Bechstein's Fairytale Book*, reflecting the extent to which his own name played a part in stimulating sales. Its popularity persisted abroad, where it was published numerous times for the children of German immigrants in America.

Any discussion of Bechstein's fairy tales must necessarily refer to the Grimms and their collection of fairy tales. Bechstein's tales, illustrated with delightful, often humorous pictures, and without scholarly notes, addressed an adolescent readership; the Grimms' tales, initially unillustrated but extended by copious scholarly notes, anticipated a dual audience—young children on the one hand, and the German people on the other. Bechstein, like Wilhelm Grimm, reworked his tales stylistically, introducing ever more exuberant nouns and adjectives specific to 19th-century experience: '[It was a pity that Rupert] wasn't allowed to make himself nice and neat, with either a crop-beard or a pointbeard, all blackwaxed, and that he didn't have coifed locks and slender sides and smooth fingernails or Eau-de-Cologne or any first-class Havana cigars' (from 'Rupert Bearskin'). Grimm, on the other hand, smoothed his fairy tales' vocabulary until it achieved a transcendent timelessness.

Bechstein gave his characters memorable names like Käthchen, Abraham, and Christinchen, whereas Grimm preferred generically German names like 'Hans', 'Hänsel', or 'Heinrich', 'Liesel' or 'Gretel'. Bechstein introduced irony throughout his tales, especially in connection with the intrusion of magic; his heroes and heroines, like those of *Musäus, know the 'rules' of magic and often comment on them. He also both accepted and propagated the view of his fairy tales as book-tales, whereas the Grimm

œuvre excludes irony and maintains the fiction that their tales are quintessentially oral in nature and in transmission.

Bechstein's presentation of characters is striking for its gender-egalitarianism. The numbers of wicked men equal those of evil women, and stepmothers do not form a self-evident well of iniquity, both of which depart distinctly from the gender-specific distribution of malevolence in the Grimms' fairy tales. Bechstein's mothers typically survive to the happy end of his stories, which are marked by joyously reunited families. Brothers and sisters love and help one another; and his child heroes and heroines exhibit self-reliance, imagining solutions to their problems and often implementing them independently.

In thematic terms, Bechstein treated work as an effort that would reliably lead to rewards in the here and now. He faulted anti-Semitism as a sin of community; did not ascribe danger to woods and forests in and of themselves; neither silenced nor inculpated girls and women; avoided prohibitions whose only function was to test obedience; rewarded initiative; and generally stayed clear of gruesomely violent conclusions. In the worst of cases, he had a malicious crone who tried to drown a heroine thrown into prison, her accomplice whipped out of the castle. Euphemism dealt with the rest: at the end of 'The Witch and the Royal Children', a stag hooked the witch together with her magic ring on his antlers, leapt into a pond, and emerged 'free of his burden'.

Bechstein established a jocularly familiar relationship with his readers by gently poking fun at the adult world, irreverently setting authority on its head, and forging solidarity with them through playfully satirizing language. None the less, Bechstein's tales remain socially conservative, ultimately accepting the validity of contemporary social values like demonstrating gratitude, prospering through work, and maintaining the status quo.

The overall social and moral system exemplified in Bechstein's tales was appropriate for bourgeois children who expected—generally speaking—to be in control of the course their lives took, an aspect of Bechstein's fairy-tale collection that provoked violent attack. In 1908 Franz Heyden used *Jugendschriften-Warte*, the leading teacher's journal of the day, to revise the public's perception of Bechstein's tales 'in the interest of our folk fairy-tale writing and of our children'. A generation after Prussia had instituted a broad-based welfare system for its working poor, proletarian 'folk' values collided with and vanquished a value system inherited from the Enlightenment. With a reprieve during the Weimar period when Bechstein's tales regained fleeting popularity, they gave way to the Grimm corpus almost entirely during the 20th century.

Bechstein used many published sources, including the Grimms' edition of 1840, and expanded his corpus notably by incorporating numerous animal fables. Translated into English as *The Old Storyteller* in 1856, Bechstein's tales were also published under other titles, such as *Pretty as Seven* (1872) and *The Rabbit Catcher* (translated by Randall *Jarrell, 1972).   RBB

Bottigheimer, Ruth B., 'Ludwig Bechstein's Fairy Tales: Nineteenth Century Bestsellers and Bürgerlichkeit', *Internationales Archiv für Sozialgeschichte der deutschen Literatur*, 15.2 (1990).

Fiedler, Alfred, 'Ludwig Bechstein als Sagensammler und Sagenpublizist', *Deutsches Jahrbuch für Volkskunde*, 12 (1966).

Schmidt, Klaus, *Untersuchungen zu den Märchensammlungen von Ludwig Bechstein* (1935; 1984).

Schneider, Rolf-Rüdigger, 'Bechsteins "Deutsches Märchenbuch" ' (Diss., Gesamthochschule Wuppertal, 1980).

Bécquer, Gustavo Adolfo (1836–70) Bécquer occupies a most important place among 19th-century Spanish poets, although he made his living as a journalist. He also contributed some literary prose of which *Leyendas* (*Legends*, 1871) is his best-known work. This collection is made up of 28 short narrations which are based on popular Spanish legends, folk motifs found in European and other literatures, mythological characters (especially Nordic), and typical romantic and Gothic elements. For example, in 'El *Miserere*' (1862), Bécquer employed the motif of the monks who, after being slaughtered, return to their monastery as ghosts; magical transformations of human beings into animals take place in 'La corza blanca' ('The White Doe', 1863), while the popular folk motif of the hunter who falls in love with a nymph and meets his death in the fountain she inhabits plays a major role in 'Los ojos verdes' ('The Green Eyes', 1861). The motif of the dead coming back to life recurs in several stories, such as 'Maese Pérez el organista' ('Master Peter, the Organist', 1861) or 'El Monte de las Ánimas' ('The Mountain of the Souls in Purgatory', 1861), the latter being a paradigmatic example of Bécquer's relish for horrific and mysterious elements. Underlying a good number of the stories is the leitmotif of an impossible love which is frustrated by death or some kind of supernatural intervention. There is also one story, 'La creación' ('The Creation', 1861) which is unique in the way it deals with certain aspects of Indian cosmogony.   CFR

Belasco, David (1853–1931) American playwright and producer, especially known for his melodrama *Madame Butterfly* (1900) and his frontier play *The Girl of the Golden West* (1905), both of which were made famous by Giacomo *Puccini. While these plays are not fairy tales *per se*, their basic plotlines draw from the genre. The Japanese Madame Butterfly, for instance, recalls fairies like *Mélusine and *Undine whose tragic fates are determined by the betrayal of mortal (here American) men. In fact, Belasco put together a collection of tales with Chas. A. Byrne entitled *Fairy Tales Told by the Seven Travelers at the Red Lion Inn* (1906), structured much in the tradition of *The Decameron*, in which a group of travellers, including an American, a Frenchman, an Englishman, a Swede, and a Russian, each tell a tale which is then discussed by the group. The collection includes 'The Wonderful Horse', in which an apparently useless animal brings a poor boy good fortune; and 'A Chinese Idyl', in which a Genie helps Hyson get his princess.   AD

'Belle au bois dormant, La' '*See* SLEEPING BEAUTY'.

Benavente, Jacinto (1866–1954) Spanish playwright who was awarded the Nobel Prize in 1922. He wrote a few tales with child protagonists, such as 'En la playa' ('On the Beach', 1897) and 'Juegos de niños' ('Children's Games', 1902), but owes his fame to his plays. Benavente was particularly interested in children's theatre and many of his plays are inspired by classic fairy tales. Thus *Y va de cuento...* (*And It Has to Do with Tales...*, 1919) is based on 'The Pied Piper of Hamelin', while *La Cenicienta* (*Cinderella*, 1919) is a revision of **'Cinderella'*, and *El nietecito* (*The Little Grandson*, 1910), is an adaptation of the *Grimms' 'The Old Man and his Grandson'. Other plays by Benavente influenced more generally by the fairy-tale genre include: *La princesa sin corazón* (*The Princess without a Heart*, 1907) and *El príncipe que todo lo aprendió en los libros* (*The Prince who Learnt Everything by Reading*, 1909). Finally, *La novia de nieve* (*The Bride of Snow*, 1934) is a play that revises the Russian legend of Snegurochka.   CFR

Díaz-Bernabé, José A., 'Jacinto Benavente and his Theatre' (Diss., Columbia University, 1967).
Peñuelas, Marcelino C., *Jacinto Benavente* (1968).

Bergstrom, Erik (1981–) American comedian and illustrator and author of *Grimmer Tales: A Wicked Collection of Unhappily Ever After Stories* (2009). He turns classic tales upside down and inside out in hilarious illustrations so that they become grotesque and absurd: *Rapunzel's hair is a fatal disadvantage, the frog as prince retains many reptilian traits, and *Sleeping Beauty suffers from malnourishment.   JZ

Berman, Steve (1949–) American novelist and short-story writer, considered the foremost editor of queer speculative fiction in the United States. One of his books, *So Fey: Queer Fairy Fiction* (2007), an anthology of LGBT short fiction dealing with fairies, was a finalist for the Golden Crown Literary Awards, while another anthology, *The Touch of the Sea* (2012), featured gay-themed fantastical stories based on maritime folklore. In 2014, he published *Red Caps: New Fairy Tales for Out of the Ordinary Readers*, which includes thirteen haunting hybrid fairy tales that are coming-of-age stories mainly set in contemporary America and filled with motifs from science fiction and Gothic literature.   JZ

Bernard, Catherine (1663–1712?) French novelist, playwright, and poet. Born in Rouen to a comfortable Huguenot family, she moved to Paris to pursue her literary interests. Bernard wrote four historical novels, a short story, and two plays, all of which were well received in her time and continue to be appreciated for their stylistic and psychological depth. Her novel *Inès de Cardoue* (1696) not only features two fairy tales, but also formulates what is considered to be the fundamental aesthetic principle for the 17th- and 18th-century French *conte de fées*: 'the [adventures] should always be implausible and the emotions always natural'. The first tale in this novel, 'Le Prince Rosier' ('Prince Rosebush'), is based on an episode by Ariosto and tells of a princess's love for an enchanted rosebush. After regaining his human form and marrying her, the prince admits his love for another woman, which causes the heroine to denounce her husband and the hero to be transformed once again into a rosebush. The second tale, 'Riquet à la houppe' (*'Riquet with the Tuft'), preceded *Perrault's more famous version and, like his, is not thought to be of folkloric origin. Often likened to *'Beauty and the Beast', this story relates the encounter and eventual marriage of a beautiful but feeble-minded woman with an ugly but intelligent gnome. Bernard's tale, unlike Perrault's, does not condemn the heroine's imagination but rather women's confinement in marriage. It also ends on a resolutely pessimistic note, in further contrast to Perrault's.   LCS

Berner, Rotraut Susanne (1948–) Prominent German illustrator and graphic designer who is best known for her 'Wimmel' and 'Karlchen' books. The six Wimmel books (2003–8) are filled with large detailed images of incidents in daily life that are amusing and puzzling and offer very young children who cannot read an opportunity to exercise their imaginations in visual reading. The nine 'little Karl' books (2001–12) depict the adventures of a clever boy rabbit who is always surprisingly inventive. Berner has also written and illustrated fairy tales, and her best-known work is *Märchen-Stunde* (*Fairy-Tale Hour*, 1998), which she revised, expanded, and reissued as *Märchen-Comics* (*Fairy-Tale Comics*) in 2008. She adapted eight *Grimms' fairy tales and transformed the stories into contemporary witty cartoons by altering the plots to respond to present-day conditions. Her unusual comic approach allows readers to question the traditional meanings of the tales and simultaneously to grasp how the Grimms' narratives are still relevant for exploring modern social issues.   JZ

Bernheimer, Kate (1967–) Novelist and editor who has promoted the writing of modern fairy tales. She founded the journal *Fairy Tale Review*, which publishes contemporary fairy tales and poems, and has edited three important anthologies, *Mirror, Mirror on the Wall* (2002), *Brothers and Beasts* (2007), and *My Mother She Killed Me, My Father He Ate Me: Forty New Fairy Tales* (2010). In addition, she has published three autobiographical fairy-tale novels, *The Complete Tales of Ketzia Gold* (2001), *The Complete Tales of Merry Gold* (2006), and *The Complete Tales of Lucy Gold* (2011), blending the hopes and dreams of three sisters in magical realist sequences. Her children's book, *The Girl in the Castle Inside the Museum* (2008), continues some of the themes in her novels and depicts a lonely girl dreaming of friendship inside a snow globe of a museum.   JZ

Bernis, François-Joachim de Pierres de (1715–94) French writer. Especially known for his poetry, he served in many official capacities, including minister of

foreign affairs, cardinal, and ambassador to Rome. His licentious tale *Nocrion, conte allobroge* (*Nocrion, Allobrogian Tale*, 1747) reworks a medieval fabliau in which a knight has the power to make female genitalia speak. This story is also the basis for Denis *Diderot's *Les Bijoux indiscrets* (*The Indiscreet Jewels*, 1748).   LCS

Bertall (pseudonym of **Charles Albert d'Arnoux**, 1820–93) French illustrator who worked as a caricaturist for many important Parisian magazines such as *L'Illustration*, *Journal pour Rire*, and *La Semaine*. He was particularly successful as an illustrator of fairy tales and made a name for himself with the publication of his drawings for E. T. A. *Hoffmann's 'The Nutcracker' in 1846. In addition he provided exquisite illustrations for Charles *Perrault's *Contes* (*Tales*) in 1851 and for Wilhelm *Hauff's *La Caravane* (*The Caravan*) and the *Grimms' tales in 1855. His drawings are notable for their strong lines, inventiveness, and subtle characterization.   JZ

Beskow, Elsa (1874–1953) Swedish writer and illustrator of more than 30 children's books. Many of her picture books, such as *Peter in Blueberryland* (1901), *Children of the Forest* (1910), *The Little Elves of Elf Nook* (1910), *Grandma's Quilt* (1922), and *The Sun Egg* (1932), contain fairy-tale motifs. Influenced by Walter *Crane and art nouveau of the early 20th century, Beskow is regarded as a classic writer/illustrator for children in Sweden. She stressed the importance of children's relationship with nature, and nature always tended to be filled with magical creatures.   JZ

Bettelheim, Bruno (1903–90) Austrian-born American psychologist and writer who wrote *The Uses of Enchantment: The Meaning and Importance of Fairy Tales* (1976). He argued that children need fairy tales' symbolic emotional lessons to work through repressed fears and desires, including Oedipal conflicts, sibling rivalry, negative or ambivalent feelings about parents, and oral fixations. Bettelheim's neo-Freudian perspective made the Brothers *Grimm's 1857 edition of *Kinder- und Hausmärchen* the distillate of folk wisdom which parents must read to their children word for word. He was apparently unaware that the brothers themselves heavily censored and Christianized those versions. Perhaps because he advocated for reading and telling to children fairy tales that included sex and violence, Bettelheim remains extraordinarily, unreflectively popular. Nevertheless, scholars criticize his classism, sexism, and Eurocentrism; his lack of awareness of significant scholarship on fairy tales, including psychological perspectives; and his plagiarism of Julius Heuscher's *A Psychiatric Study of Fairy Tales: Their Origin, Meaning and Usefulness* (1963). *Folklore and fairy tale scholars point out that Bettelheim's over-reliance on details of a few European versions often led him to problematic conclusions about specific tales. Despite his abhorrence of fairy-tale illustration, reinterpretation, and retelling, Bettelheim's ideas continue to influence creative artists.   PG

Dundes, Alan, 'Bruno Bettelheim's Uses of Enchantment and Abuses of Scholarship', *Journal of American Folklore*, 104 (1991).

Zipes, Jack, *Breaking the Magic Spell: Radical Theories of Folk and Fairy Tales* (2002).

Bewick, John (1760–95) English children's book illustrator who worked closely with his older brother Thomas. Their innovative work in wood engraving extended the expressive idiom of the genre and greatly improved English children's book illustration. Strictly speaking he did not illustrate fairy tales, but among his work are *Selected Fables* (with Thomas, 1784), Joseph Ritson's two-volume collection of popular tales *Robin Hood* (1795), and *The Children's Miscellany* (1804), which included Thomas Day's 'The History of Little Jack'.   KS

Biegel, Paul (1925–2006) Prominent Dutch writer of children's literature who published over 75 books during his lifetime, many with fairy-tale motifs and original plots. He also translated and adapted the Grimms' folk and fairy tales into Dutch in 1966 and 1970. Among his more unusual fairy-tale picture books and novels translated into English are *The King of the Copper Mountains* (*Het sleutelkruid*, 1964), *The Seven-Times Search* (*Ik wou dat it anders was*, 1967), *The Twelve Robbers* (*De twaalf rovers*, 1971), *The Dwarfs of Nosegay* (*De dwergjes van Tuil*, 1976), and *The Tin-Can Beast and Other Stories* (*De toverhoed*, 1979). Biegel was strongly influenced by the Brothers Grimm and Hans Christian Andersen, but he developed his own brisk, humorous style and favoured moral struggles in which good always triumphed over evil. Many of his tales concerned little protagonists who had to undergo tests and fulfil tasks to discover their true identities. For instance, in *The Seven-Times Search*, a plump little boy, clumsy at games, is bewitched and changed into a tiny Tom-Thumb figure who must battle with strange insects and birds to demonstrate his courage and integrity. Biegel was also very fond of frame novels, in which he used a major narrative that would enable him to tell a series of stories within this narrative. So, in *The King of the Copper Mountains*, a wonder doctor goes on a quest to find a magic plant which will heal a thousand-year-old king, who is dying. This plant, however, only blooms once a year. During his quest the doctor encounters many different animals and asks them to go to the Copper Castle and tell the king stories so that he will remain alive until the doctor returns. The animal's enchanting stories filled with dragons, fairies, and dwarves do, indeed, keep the king alive until the doctor safely returns with the magic plant. Biegel was honoured with over 15 different awards for his writing in the Netherlands and was also nominated for the international Hans Christian Andersen Prize in 1996. A prolific and imaginative writer, he was known for taking children and fairy tales seriously.   JZ

Biermann, Wolf (1936–) Former East German poet and singer whose outspoken critique of the Socialist Unity Party caused him to be exiled from the German Democratic Republic in 1976. His notorious use of fairy-tale material was his adaptation of Yevgeni *Schwartz's *The Dragon* (1943), which

Biermann entitled *Der Dra-Dra* in 1970. A musical parody, *Der Dra-Dra* reveals how government officials exploit the common people. Indeed, they fear for their lives because of the ruling monster Dra-Dra, who is eventually ridiculed and overcome; the play could only be performed in West Germany. His *Deutschland: Ein Wintermärchen* (*Germany: A Winter's Tale*), which appeared in 1972, borrows more from Heinrich *Heine's satirical poem of the same title than from fairy-tale tradition. In the 1970s he published several collections of children's fairy tales including *Das Märchen vom kleinen Herrn Moritz, der eine Glatze kriegte* (*The Fairy Tale of Little Mr Moritz, who was Growing Bald*) and *Das Märchen von dem Mädchen mit dem Holzbein* (*The Fairy Tale of the Girl with the Wooden Leg*). In addition to his many other records for adults, he produced a record of children's songs, *Der Friedensclown* (*The Peace Clown*).   MBS

Bignon, Jean-Paul (1662–1743) French writer, academician, and royal librarian. Inspired by the success of Antoine *Galland and Pétis de la Croix, Bignon published a collection of *oriental tales entitled *Les Aventures d'Abdalla, ou son voyage à l'isle de Borico* (*The Adventures of Abdullah, or His Voyage to the Island of Borico*, 1712). Bignon contends in his preface that he only slightly modified Abdalla's 'original' text, which he claims to have translated from Arabic, a typical authenticating ruse of the period. The frame story concerns Abdalla's quest to bring back waters from the fountain of youth at Borico, and is punctuated by tales told by those he meets on the way, including the 'Histoire de la princesse Zeineb et du roi Léopard' ('Princess Zeineb and King Leopard'), which draws from *Apuleius' 'Cupid and Psyche' and prepared the way for Mme de *Villeneuve's 'La Belle et la bête' (*'Beauty and the Beast').   AD

Bilibin, Ivan Yakovlevich (1876–1942) Russian illustrator and stage designer. Commissioned as a young artist by the Department for the Production of State Documents to illustrate a series of fairy-tale books (1899–1902), Bilibin built his entire career on the interpretation of Russian folk tales and bylinas (traditional folk epics), often depicting the same stories again and again. Frances Carpenter's *Tales of a Russian Grandmother* first brought his work to English-speaking children in 1933. Like many artists of the late 19th century, he was influenced by the Japanese print, particularly in his early illustrations, with their asymmetrical compositions and soft, bright colours outlined in black ink. His main inspiration, however, was Russian folk art. He acquired an extensive study collection, which eventually formed the basis of the ethnographic section at the Russian Museum in St Petersburg, and became famous for the authenticity of his details. Increasingly influenced by Russian icons and the popular prints of the 17th century, his later illustrations acquired a flat, stylized look, with stronger colour, a more pronounced black outline, and a proliferation of repetitive, patterned detail. Bilibin illustrated many of *Pushkin's fairy-tale poems and designed sets and costumes for several of the operas based on them, including *Glinka's *Russlan and Ludmilla* and *Rimsky-Korsakov's *The Golden Cockerel* and *The Tale of Tsar Saltan*. Although he left Russia as a refugee in 1920, he returned in 1936, dying six years later in the siege of Leningrad.   SR

Golynets, Sergei, *Ivan Bilibin* (1982).

Black, Holly (1971–) American fantasy writer and editor, whose stories generally feature American children encountering fairies and other supernatural creatures. Her best known work, the children's novel series *The Spiderwick Chronicles* (2003–9), in collaboration with artist Tony DiTerlizzi, was adapted for film in 2008, made into a video game, and translated into more than thirty languages. *Spiderwick* also participates in the extensive culture industry surrounding literature for children and young adults, including paratextual interactive works like *The Spiderwick Chronicles Notebook for Fantastical Observations* (2005), inviting readers to add stories, maps, charts, notes, lists,

Bilibin, Ivan Yakovlevich Illustration by Bilibin based on the story of 'Tsarevitch Ivan, the Fire Bird and the Grey Wolf' in *Russian Wonder Tales*, ed. Post Wheeler. The Century Co., 1919.

diagrams, and drawings. Black's young-adult writing includes her first novel *Tithe: A Modern Faerie Tale* (2002), beginning with a quotation from the fairy ballad 'Tam Lin'. Her writing includes the graphic novel series

The Good Neighbors (2008–10), short fiction, poetry, and story anthologies. PG

Black Crook, The An 1866 melodramatic musical spectacle by Charles M. Barras (libretto) that is generally considered the first American musical. The fantastic plot, loosely derived from the Faust legend, concerns the crook-backed magician Herzog, who must deliver the soul of the painter Rudolf to the devil by midnight on New Year's Eve, and the fairy queen who warns and rescues the innocent artist. The songs, by various authors, were secondary to the spectacular stagecraft, the chorus of nymphs and water sprites in pink tights, and the winning combination of song, dance, and story into one evening's performance.   TSH

Blackwood, Algernon (1869–1951) English-born author of horror and fantasy tales. Thought to be the last British master of supernatural fiction, Blackwood is also perceived as the literary heir of Sheridan LeFanu. Perhaps because of his fascination with the mystical and occult, he incorporated fairies and elemental spirits into his fiction, often depicting them as frightening. Fairies mislead or abduct mortals in 'Entrance and Exit', 'Ancient Lights', and 'May Day Eve'. They are threats to life in 'The Glamour of the Snow', while their world is the subject of *A Prisoner in Fairyland* (1913).   CGS

Blake, Quentin (1932–) British illustrator and author of children's books and educational texts. He was educated at Cambridge and the University of London Institute of Education and trained at the Chelsea School of Art. An illustrator for *Punch* and the *Spectator*, since 1978 he has taught at the Royal College of Art in London and was made an officer in the Order of the British Empire in 1988. His other numerous honours (for self-illustrated works) include the Hans Christian *Andersen honor book for illustration, Kate *Greenaway Medal, Kurt Maschler Award, and Children's Book Award.

An economical use of deft pen strokes and watercolours characterize Blake's mischievous illustrations for more than 200 books. He has illustrated Lewis *Carroll's nonsense verse (*The Hunting of the Snark*, 1976), *Kipling's tall tales (*How the Camel Got his Hump*, 1984), and Orwell's dark fantasy *Animal Farm* (1984). He particularly enjoys

collaborating with authors such as Joan *Aiken, Russell *Hoban, and John Yeoman. His fairy-tale-related work includes the *Albert the Dragon* series (by Rosemary Weir, 1961–4), *The Gentle Knight* (Richard Schickel, 1964), *Wizards are a Nuisance* (Norman Hunter, 1973), and *Mortimer and the Sword Excalibur* (Aiken, 1979). He has also re-illustrated the complete works of Roald *Dahl, of whose fan club he is the honorary president.   MLE

Lesniak, James, and Trosky, Susan M. (eds.), *Contemporary Authors*, New Revision Series, 37 (1993).

Peppin, Brigid, and Micklethwait, Lucy, *Dictionary of British Book Illustrators: The Twentieth Century* (1983).

'Blanca Nieve', 'Blanche neige' *See* 'SNOW WHITE'.

Blasco Ibáñez, Vicente (1867–1928) Novelist who has been called 'the Spanish Zola' because of his attachment to the naturalistic school. He wrote several collections of short stories as well, such as *Cuentos valencianos* (*Tales from Valencia*, 1893) and *La condenada* (*The Condemned Woman*, 1896). Many of his tales are set in his native land, Valencia. In general, his stories are very realistic, sometimes verging on naturalism. Blasco Ibáñez shows his predilection for poor and marginal characters and tends to depict the tension that exists between people from different social classes. Nevertheless, he also wrote such stories as 'El dragón del patriarca' ('The Patriarch's Dragon', 1893) and 'En la puerta del cielo' ('At Heaven's Door', 1893), which are apparently based on folk material; in any case, they have a considerable number of fantastic and supernatural elements.   CFR

'Blaubart' *See* 'BLUEBEARD'.

Block, Francesca Lia (1962–) American writer of contemporary fantasy novels. Block specializes in hip, punk-influenced fantasy tales for teenage readers, bringing magical elements into colourful stories of modern urban life. *Ectasia* (1993) is a novel in this vein in which Block retells the Orpheus myth—placing her tale in a surreal world of streetwise children and wandering souls, set to the beat of rock-and-roll. The sequel, *Primavera* (1994), is based on the Persephone myth. Other works, including *Weetzie Bat* (1989) and *The Hanged Man* (1995), contain classic tropes of folklore (witches, vampires, angels, ghosts) transplanted to Block's unique magical version of Los Angeles. Many of the characters from her *Weetzie Bat* book have been depicted in some of her other novels and stories such as *Girl Goddess 9: Nine Stories* (1996), which depict the difficult problems of teenage girls mainly in Los Angeles, and *Dangerous Angels* (1998) and *I was a Teenage Fairy* (1998), which follow the confused lives of young people often portrayed as the prey of adults. In 2005, Block re-created Weetzie Bat as a woman in her forties facing a mid-life crisis in *Necklace of Kisses*. Though she is primarily known as a writer of YA works, which contain explicit descriptions of sexual abuse faced by teenagers, she also writes for adults or produces stories considered crossover narratives. For instance, *Nymph* (2003) is a collection of nine stories about nymph-like young women that border on erotica, while *Blood Roses* (2008), also a collection of nine stories, explores the sexual transformation and maturation of young women. Perhaps her best work is *The Rose and the Beast* (2001), a collection of adapted classic fairy tales set in contemporary society. Sleeping Beauty is a heroin addict; Red Riding Hood is pursued by a lecherous stepfather; Snow White is a sex goddess. Block follows in the tradition of Anne *Sexton, Angela *Carter, and Tanith *Lee and writes feminist fairy tales that turn the classics upside down. TW

Campbell, Patricia, 'People Are Talking about Francesca Lia Block', *Horn Book Magazine* (1993).
Russell, David, 'Young Adult Fairy Tales for the New Age: Francesca Lia Block's *The Rose and the Beast*', *The Lion and the Unicorn* (2002).
Susina, Jan, 'The Rebirth of the Modern Flâneur: Notes on the Postmodern Landscape of Francesca Lia Block's *Weetzie Bat*', *Marvels & Tales* (2002).
Talley, Lee, 'Fantasies of Place and Childhood in Francesca Lia Block's *I Was a Teenage Fairy*, *Children's Literature* (2011).

'Bluebeard' ('Barbe-bleue') This fairy tale made its literary debut in Charles *Perrault's *Histoires ou contes du temps passé* (*Stories or Tales of Past Times*, 1697), a collection that placed the earthy, ribald narratives of a peasant culture between the covers of a book and turned them into bedtime reading for children. Like the other fairy tales in Perrault's collection, 'Bluebeard' has a happy ending: the heroine marries 'a worthy man who made her forget the miserable time she spent with Bluebeard'. But 'Bluebeard' also deviates from the norm of most fairy tales in its depiction of marriage as an institution haunted by murder. While canonical fairy tales like *'Cinderella' and *'Snow White' begin with unhappy situations at home, centre on a romantic quest, and culminate in visions of marital bliss, 'Bluebeard' shows us a woman leaving the safety of home and entering the risky domain of her husband's castle. As Bruno Bettelheim has argued, Perrault's story represents a troubling flip side to 'Beauty and the Beast', for it arouses disturbing anxieties about marriage, confirming a child's 'worst fears about sex' and portraying marriage as life-threatening.

Just who was Bluebeard and how did he get such a bad name? As Anatole *France reminds us in his story 'The Seven Wives of Bluebeard', Charles Perrault composed 'the first biography of this seigneur' and established his reputation as 'an accomplished villain' and 'the most perfect model of cruelty that ever trod the earth'. Perrault's 'Bluebeard' recounts the story of an aristocratic gentleman and his marriage to a young woman whose desire for opulence conquers her feelings of revulsion for blue beards. After a month of married life, Bluebeard declares his intention to undertake a journey. 'Plagued by curiosity', Bluebeard's wife opens the door to the one chamber forbidden to her and finds a pool of clotted blood in which are reflected the bodies of Bluebeard's dead wives, hanging from the wall. Horrified, she drops the key and is unable to remove a tell-tale bloodstain from it. Bluebeard returns home to discover the evidence of his wife's transgression and is about to execute her, when his wife's brothers come

'Bluebeard' Bluebeard's wife tries to forestall the vicious killer's sword with her prayers in this anonymous illustration taken from *Les Contes des fées offerts à Bébé* (*c*.1900).

to the rescue and cut him down with their swords.

'Bloody key as sign of disobedience': this is the motif that folklorists consistently read as the tale's defining moment. The blood-stained key (in some cases it is an egg or a flower) points to a double transgression, one that is at once moral and sexual. If we recall that the bloody chamber in Blue-beard's castle is strewn with corpses, this reading of the key as a marker of infidelity becomes wilfully wrong-headed in its effort to vilify Bluebeard's wife. Yet illustrators, commentators, and retellers alike seem to have fallen in line with Perrault's view, as expressed in his moral to the tale, that 'Bluebeard' is about the evils of female curiosity. A 19th-century Scottish version summarizes in its title what appears to be the collective critical wisdom on this tale: 'The Story of Bluebeard, or, The Effects of Female Curiosity'.

The French folklorist Paul Delarue has mapped the evolution of 'Bluebeard', docu-menting the liberties taken by Perrault in transforming an oral folk tale into a literary text. The folk heroines of 'Bluebeard' delay their executions by insisting on donning bri-dal clothes, and they prolong the possibility of rescue by recounting each and every item of clothing. Perrault's heroine, by contrast, asks her husband for time to say her prayers, thus becoming a model of devout piousness. Unlike folk heroines, who figure as their own agents of rescue by dispatching letter-carry-ing dogs or talking birds, Perrault's heroine sends her sister up to the castle tower to watch for her brothers. Most importantly, folk versions of the tale do not fault the heroine for her curiosity. On the contrary, when these young women stand before the forbidden chamber, they feel duty-bound to open its door. 'I have to know what is in there', one heroine reflects just before turning the key. These folkloric figures are described as courageous: curiosity and valour enable them to come to the rescue of their sisters by reconstituting them physically (putting their dismembered parts back together again) and by providing them with safe passage home.

The French versions of 'Bluebeard' that predate Perrault's story reveal a close relationship to two tales recorded by the Brothers *Grimm. The first of these, 'Fitcher's Bird', shows the youngest of three sisters using her 'cunning' to escape the snares set by a clever sorcerer and to rescue her two sisters. The heroine of '*The *Robber Bridegroom*' also engineers a rescue, mobilizing her mental resources to thwart the thieves with whom her betrothed consorts. Oddly enough, however, these two variants of 'Bluebeard' seem to have fallen into a cultural black hole, while Perrault's 'Bluebeard' and its literary cousins have been preserved and rewritten as cautionary stories warning about the hazards of disobedience and curiosity. It is telling that Margaret *Atwood turned to 'Fitcher's Bird' and 'The Robber Bridegroom' for inspiration (for her 'Bluebeard's Egg' and for *The Robber Bride*, in particular) and that a visual artist like Cindy Sherman created a picture book of the Grimms' 'Fitcher's Bird'. Along with Angela *Carter, whose 'Bloody Chamber' rewrites the Bluebeard story from the point of view of the wife, Atwood and Sherman have reinvigorated a story that lost its socially critical edge when it was appropriated for children. MT

Barzilai, Shuli, *Tales of Bluebeard and His Wives from Late Antiquity to Postmodern Times* (2009).

Hermansson, Casie, *Bluebeard: A Reader's Guide to the English Tradition* (2009).

Lewis, Philip, 'Bluebeard's Secret', in *Seeing through the Mother Goose Tales: Visual Turns in the Writings of Charles Perrault* (1996).

Tatar, Maria, *Secrets Beyond the Door: The Story of Bluebeard and His Wives* (2004).

Zipes, Jack, 'The Male Key to Bluebeard's Secret', in *Why Fairy Tales Stick: The Evolution and Relevance of a Genre* (2006).

Bluebeard's Eighth Wife (film: USA, 1938) Starring Gary Cooper as a multi-marrying American millionaire and Claudette Colbert as an impoverished aristocrat, it met with a cool reception. The famed 'Lubitsch Touch' seemed to have lost its magic, for the effort to produce screwball comedy foundered on a somewhat contrived plot that even Billy Wilder's screenwriting talents could not rescue. The rich possibilities opened by the title are explored to some extent, but Lubitsch's American tycoon lacks the aggressive edge of his folkloric counterparts and is effortlessly tamed by his eighth wife. MT

'Bluebird, The' ('L'Oiseau bleu', 1696) By Mme d'*Aulnoy, 'L'Oiseau bleu' has literary precursors in *Marie de France's 'Yonec' and *Basile's 'Verdeprato' and 'Lo Serpe'. In this animal metamorphosis fairy tale, a widow with an ugly daughter (Truitonne) marries a grieving king with a beautiful one (Florine). The wicked stepmother wants her daughter married first, locks Florine in a tower, and has an evil fairy transform her suitor (King Charming) into a bluebird. He is injured two years later when his secret visits are discovered. His enchanter rescues him, but conspires to have him marry Truitonne. A good fairy, magic eggs, and an echo chamber help Florine regain the king's love.

*Maeterlinck's 1909 allegorical fairy play, *The Blue Bird*, is about the failed search of a brother and sister for the Bluebird of Happiness—which they discover has been at their home the whole time. MLE

DeGraff, Amy Vanderlyn, *The Tower and the Well: A Psychological Interpretation of the Fairy Tales of Madame d'Aulnoy* (1984).

Mitchell, Jane Tucker, *A Thematic Analysis of Mme d'Aulnoy's Contes de fées* (1978).

Blue Bird, The (film versions) This play by the Belgian writer Maurice *Maeterlinck has reached the screen several times. It differs from his other dramas in having a fairy element, but shares their philosophical concerns and symbolist style. Two years after *The Blue Bird* was published (1909), Maeterlinck won a Nobel Prize, which brought his work wider attention in the Anglophone world and prompted various successful stage productions.

In essence, *The Blue Bird* tells the story of Tyltyl and Mytyl, discontented son and daughter of a woodcutter living in the depths of a forest, who are visited one night by the fairy Berylune. She asks for help in finding the Blue Bird, which alone can cure a little girl who is ill and unhappy. The children already have a blue bird, but it is not blue enough. To help them, Berylune provides a magic diamond which enables them to see things as they really are. Suddenly their house seems beautiful, and they can see the souls of Fire, Water, Sugar, Bread, Milk, Cat, and Dog, all of whom join the quest. These children go through the Mists of Time to the Land of Memory, where they meet their dead grandparents; in the Palace of Night they tour chambers containing all the world's ghosts, sickness, terrors, and mysteries; they ask a forest for help; they get bored in the Palace of Luxuries; they visit the Palace of the Future, full of unborn babies. Nowhere do they find the Blue Bird. Disconsolate, they return home, only to find their own blue bird much bluer than before. The girl who was ill can now run and dance.

The makers of an early film version (USA, 1918) took advantage of newly developed techniques of multiple exposure, allied to huge specially constructed sets, to create the lands and palaces the children and their new friends visit. Missing from the gathering are Bread, Milk, and Sugar, regarded then as too difficult to personify and dramatize. There is, though, an extra character, Light, who is given the job of helping the children find their way. In this version heaven is the Palace of Joys and Delights; there Tyltyl and Mytyl meet not their grandparents but their mother, who is known as the Joy of Maternal Love.

The best-known adaptation is that directed for Fox by Walter Lang (USA, 1940). It was made as a vehicle for Shirley *Temple, then near the end of her reign as child star; as a showcase for full Technicolor, only recently perfected; and as a rival to MGM's The *Wizard of Oz*. The children's companions are further reduced in number—they have only Berylune, Tylette (cat), Tylo (dog), and Light to go with them—and their travels are simplified. First they talk to their grandparents in the Land of Memory. Next they stay for a while with Mr and Mrs Luxury. As they pass through the Haunted Forest, Oak and Cypress conspire with Wind and Fire to frighten them. Finally, in the Land of Unborn Children, they meet the Studious Boy, unhappily but courageously setting sail for an earthly life.

Fox revisited the story 36 years later (USA/USSR, 1976) and made a film that took advantage of advances in film technology, of the lower shooting costs on offer in Russia, and of the availability of a gallery of female adult stars. Elizabeth Taylor appears in various roles as Maternal Love, Light, and a Witch; Jane Fonda is Night, the Princess of Darkness; Cicely Tyson plays Cat; and Ava Gardner represents Luxury. For the first time, Sugar, Milk, and Bread are included among the children's screen companions, and the Blue Bird, too, gets a personification.

None of these versions has stuck to Maeterlinck. They have selected the picturesque sequences that suited their stars and their available special effects; and they have invented new ones. Maeterlinck's philosophizing has tended to get pushed into the background, except the simple central idea that happiness is to be found in your own heart when you know how to look.   TAS

Blue Light, The (**Das blaue Licht**; film: Germany, 1932) Written and directed by Leni Riefenstahl. The Hungarian writer Béla *Bálazs also contributed to the script. Its story (not based on the Grimms' tale of the same name) was conceived by Riefenstahl as a mountain legend matching in beauty the perfection of the Dolomites, her primary inspiration. Emanating from a peak which only wild-child Junta can reach, the blue light—symbolizing in German romanticism the quest for the unattainable—lures young men to climb and fall. In a departure from folk-tale convention, the villagers discover Junta's route, plunder the crystal, and get rich. Horrified at this despoliation of her mountains, Junta plunges to her death and is commemorated as the village's benefactor.   TAS

Berg-Pan, Renata, *Leni Riefenstahl* (1980).

Blunck, Hans Friedrich (1888–1961) German writer whose novels, plays, poetry, and fairy tales articulated a folk-nationalist ideology. Blunck himself became a high-ranking cultural official during the Nazi period. However, most of his major works such as the novel *Heinz Hoyer* (1922) were produced before the National Socialists came to power. A prolific author, he produced numerous volumes of fairy tales such as *Märchen von der Niederelbe* (*Fairy Tales from the Lower Elbe*, 1923), *Kindermärchen* (*Fairy Tales for Children*, 1929), *Neues Volk auf der Heide und andere Märchen* (*New Folk on the Meadow and other Fairy Tales*, 1934), *Märchen* (*Fairy Tales*, 1942), and *Neue Märchen* (*New Fairy Tales*, 1951). Most of his tales emanate from a North German folk tradition, and they tend to celebrate regional customs and rituals written in a charming and nostalgic style. In some tales there are clear racial overtones and a tendency to embellish a patriarchal world order.   JZ

Bly, Robert (1926–) American poet, storyteller, and translator. Though he is primarily known for his poetry, Bly achieved international fame by writing two prose books that use fairy tales for social commentary. His first book, *Iron John* (1991), takes the *Grimms' *Iron Hans' as the frame to illustrate an initiation process that would heal the wounds of contemporary men and enable them to become 'inner warriors', more in touch with the earth and their desire to love, not kill. In this regard, he transforms 'Iron Hans' into a celebration of the positive aspects of the men's movement. His next book, *The Sibling Society* (1996), incorporates *'Jack and the Beanstalk', 'The Adventures of Ganesha', 'The Wild Girl and her Sister', and others to demonstrate how adults have regressed towards adolescence while adolescents refuse to assume responsibility for their lives. Both books enjoyed considerable success in the United States, but they have also been criticized for their mythopoeic distortions of the meanings of fairy tales and of social conditions in America.   JZ

Amis, Martin, 'Return of the Male', *London Review of Books*, 13 (5 December 1991).

Doubiago, Sharon, '"Enemy of the Mother": A Feminist Response to the Men's Movement', *Ms.*, 2 (March–April 1992).

Johnston, Jill, 'Why Iron John Is No Gift to Women', *New York Times Book Review*, 23 February 1992.

Zipes, Jack, 'Spreading Myths about Iron John', in *Fairy Tale as Myth/Myth as Fairy Tale* (1994).

Blyton, Enid (1897–1968) A prolific writer for children, Blyton included many fairy stories in her vast output (37 books a year in the early 1950s). Her first book, *Child Whispers* (1922), a collection of verse, contained 'witches, fairies, goblins, flowers, little folk, butterflies . . .', all subjects popular with children's writers between the wars. In 1926 she took on the editorship of a new two-penny magazine, *Sunny Stories*, entirely made up of her own work. Here *The Adventures of the Wishing Chair* (1937), perhaps inspired by Frances *Browne's *Granny's Wonderful Chair*, first appeared. As a child she had read 'every single old myth and legend I could get hold of' but found them 'rather cruel'. *Grimm she disliked as 'cruel and frightening' and *Andersen was 'too sad'. In her Faraway Tree series, based, though very remotely, on Yggdrasil, the world tree of Scandinavian mythology, she eliminated all 'rather cruel' elements, substituting her own cosy inventions. *The Enchanted Wood* (1939) is perhaps the best of her fairy books. She was, said Michael Woods in a psychiatrist's assessment, 'a person who never developed emotionally beyond the basic infantile level'. Noddy, the wooden puppet, is her most famous character. *Little Noddy Goes to Toyland* (1949) was the first of his many adventures, which she filled with 'toys, pixies, goblins, Toyland, brick-houses, dolls' houses, toadstool houses' to suit the style of Noddy's first illustrator, Harmsen Van Der Beek.   GA

Crago, Hugh, 'Faintly from Elfland: How this Column Originated', *Children's Literature Association Quarterly*, 13.3 (fall 1988).

Stoney, Barbara, *Enid Blyton* (1974).

Woods, Michael, 'Blyton Revisited', *Lines* (autumn 1969).

Böhl de Faber, Cecilia ('Fernán Caballero', 1796–1877) Spanish novelist and short-story writer. Her enthusiasm for popular stories, her knowledge of the work of the Brothers *Grimm as compilers of such narrations in Germany (she was of German origin herself), and the realization that no similar project such as theirs had been undertaken in Spain compelled her to gather a good number of tales from Andalusian peasants. She then transcribed them and adapted them to suit her literary taste, despite her claim in the Preface of one of the collections she published that she had left the language of the tales untouched and full of its popular flavour. In many cases, Fernán Caballero, the male pseudonym by which she was known, used those tales for political satire and moral lessons. Most of her stories appeared in Spanish magazines such as *Semanario Pintoresco Español* (*Spanish Picturesque Weekly*). In 1859 she published a collection entitled *Cuentos y poesías populares andaluzas* (*Popular Andalusian Tales and Poems*, 1859), in which there are a good number of fairy stories that had previously appeared in *Semanario Pintoresco Español*. One such story is 'Las ánimas' ('The Souls in Purgatory', 1853), an Andalusian version of the tale called 'The Three Spinners' in the Grimms' collection. Other fairy stories by Fernán Caballero can be found in the first part of her work *Cuentos, oraciones, adivinas y refranes populares e infantiles* (*Tales, Prayers, Riddles, and Popular Children's Proverbs*, 1877), entitled 'Cuentos de encantamiento' ('Tales of Enchantment').   CFR

Bonaviri, Giuseppe (1924–) Italian writer, playwright, and poet, born in Mineo, Sicily. The novel *Il sarto della strada lunga* (*The Tailor On Main Street*, 1954) marks his debut as a writer, followed by many successful novels such as *La divina foresta* (*The Divine Forest*, 1969), *Il dottor Bilob* (*Doctor Bilob*, 1994), and collections of tales such as: *La contrada degli ulivi* (*Where Olive Trees Grow*, 1958), *Il treno blu* (*The Blue Train*, 1978), and *Novelle saracene* (*Saracen Stories*, 1980), the characters of which are derived from the folklore of Sicily and its heritage of multicultural civilizations. Bonaviri's interest in the fabulous and fairy tales is present in all his narratives, which are imbued with the marvellous and a rich sense of oral tradition influenced by his mother's storytelling. In the volume *Fiabe regionali siciliane* (*Sicilian Fairy Tales*, 1990), which he edited and translated, he speaks of 'il futuribile' that he attributes to the fairy tale, which he defines as 'la progettazione futuribile di un mondo sognato' ('the "futurible" projection of a dream world').

Novelle saracene is a collection of oral tales dealing with the shopkeepers of Mineo, the author's quasi-mythological birthplace. The book is subdivided into 'Gesù e Giuffà', 'Novelline Profane', and 'Fiabe', all of which describe a world of myth and fairy tale. In 'Gesù e Giuffà', Gesù, son of Mary the jar-seller and perhaps of Milud, is also the nephew of Michele Gabriele in whose shoemaker's shop Gesù meets Giuffà, son of Mary Magdalene. Giuffà is the one who performs miracles, not Gesù. Both are friends of Orlando and the Paladins, whose common enemies are Frederick II and the Pope. All the characters are outside history and the legendary tradition, yet they live together without any difficulty. Their story is a sort of quilt spanning centuries of fabulous oral narrative. The characters range from the Greek philosopher Gorgias, Eumaeus the swineherd of Ulysses, to the apostle Peter and Francesco di Paola, a modern saint. The author labels these tales *matrilinear* with a Sicilian and Mediterranean matrix, and they show that 'Everything undergoes a reversal...even time and space and the way one understands the Divine.'   GD

Bonsels, Waldemar (1881–1952) Popular and widely translated German author of works for children and adults who wrote novels, novellas, travelogues, poems, and fairy tales. Stylistically, Bonsels was influenced by new romanticism and nature mysticism. His keen and sensitive observations of nature during his many travels and his desire for drama and adventure are reflected in his tales for children. Bonsels is best known for his children's book *Die Biene Maja und ihre Abenteuer* (*The Adventures of Maja, the Honeybee*, 1912), which traces the adventures of a young bee who, driven by curiosity and desire, ventures out into the world, experiencing both its beauty and its danger, and who in the end saves her entire swarm from death and destruction by hornets. This animal tale, which depicts a young person's maturation process in the home–away–home structure characteristic of the fairy tale, became a children's book classic in Germany, and also gained great popularity internationally. Whereas some other tales by Bonsels, such as *Himmelsvolk* (*Heavenly People*, 1915) and *Mario und die Tiere* (*Mario and the Animals*, 1928) did not survive changes in taste of the reading public, *Die Biene Maja* remained popular into the 1960s. In the 1970s Bonsels was criticized for delivering the wrong ideological message and for the book's sentimental and trivial language; the story about Maja the Honeybee, however, regained popularity as a cartoon series on German television in the 1980s. EMM

Müller, Lothar, 'Die Biene Maja von Waldemar Bonsels', in Marianne Weill (ed.), *Wehrwolf und Biene Maja. Der deutsche Bücherschrank zwischen den Kriegen* (1986).

Borges, Jorge Luis (1899–1986) Argentinian poet, literary critic, and short-story writer. He is reputed, together with his compatriot Julio *Cortázar, to have written some of the best short stories in the Spanish language. Furthermore, he has been considered one of the most outstanding figures in contemporary world literature. Most of Borges's stories belong to the genre of fantastic literature. He has borrowed a good number of stylistic traits from Edgar Allen Poe and Franz *Kafka, and, according to some critics, he is likewise indebted to E. T. A. *Hoffmann and Lovecraft. Nevertheless, the fantastic genre in Borges's hands underwent a drastic and unique transformation, since he used his fiction to explore philosophical ideas. As a result of this, his literature is profoundly complex and erudite. Borges's first collection

of tales was *Historia universal de la infamia* (*A Universal History of Infamy*, 1935), and his last two collections of fantastic short stories were *El libro de arena* (*The Book of Sand*, 1975) and *Veinticinco Agosto 1983 y otros cuentos* (*August 1983 and Other Stories*, 1983). Borges's world-wide reputation rests upon these works: *El jardín de senderos que se bifurcan* (*The Garden with Paths that Fork*, 1942), *Ficciones* (*Fictions*, 1944), *El aleph* (*The Aleph and Other Stories*, 1949), and *La muerte y la brújula* (*Death and the Compass*, 1951).

Among Borges's youthful readings there is one book that figures prominently: *The *Arabian Nights*. It influenced the Argentinian writer to a great extent, which is evident in the fact that, as an adult, he wrote two essays on it: 'Los traductores de *Las mil y una noches*' ('The Translators of *The Arabian Nights*', 1935) and '*Las mil y una noches*' ('*The Arabian Nights*', 1980). In particular, he was deeply interested in the problems posed by the different translations of *The Arabian Nights* into Western languages, by the dichotomy East/West that it helped to establish, and by the concept of infinitude that it so well exemplifies. Borges also wrote a poem entitled 'Metáforas de *Las mil y una noches*' ('Metaphors of *The Arabian Nights*', 1977), and, above all, he scattered dozens of references to this book throughout his fiction. In this sense his fantastic tales are no exception. Thus, many of his most emblematic stories include allusions to *The Arabian Nights*: 'El informe de Brodie' ('Doctor Brodie's Report', 1970), 'El otro' ('The Other', 1975), 'El libro de arena' ('The Book of Sand', 1975), 'Tlön, Uqbar, Orbis Tertius' (1942), and 'El aleph' ('The Aleph', 1949), to cite but a few.

'The Book of Sand' is the story of an infinite book which Borges buys from a bookseller specializing in sacred tracts; there is neither an end nor a beginning to the Book of Sand, which is also the case, Borges believes, of *The Arabian Nights*. In 'Tlön, Uqbar, Orbis Tertius' Borges talks about how a group of people gathered to create an imaginary world of a literary nature in its origins, but one which ends up being interwoven with the real world; in this manner the borders between fiction and reality are shown to be rather diffuse or simply non-existent. 'The Aleph', one of Borges's best-known stories, deals with the concepts of space and time; the main symbol in this tale is an 'aleph', a tiny spot where all acts and worldly places can be simultaneously contemplated from every single angle. Through the story of the 'aleph', Borges not only explores the notion of infinitude by locating it within the minute spot or 'aleph', but also, in the very act of relating the story, makes something which is simultaneous (the aleph) become successive (narrative description). The symbol of the aleph, as the story makes clear, is not unique in Borges, but has previously appeared in other works, *The Arabian Nights* (Night 272) being one of them. In the latter, however, the aleph takes the appearance of a mirror that reflects the seven climates of the world.   CFR

Alazraki, Jaime (ed.), *Critical Essays on Jorge Luis Borges* (1987).

Friedman, Mary L., *The Emperor's Kites: A Morphology of Borges' Tales* (1987).

Rodríguez-Luis, Julio, *The Contemporary Praxis of the Fantastic: Borges and Cortázar* (1991).

St. Armand, Barton Levi, 'Synchronistic Worlds: Lovecraft and Borges', in D. E. Schultz and S. T. Joshi (eds.), *An Epicure in the Terrible: A Centennial Anthology of Essays in Honor of H. P. Lovecraft* (1991).

Wheelock, Carter, *The Mythmaker: A Study of Motif and Symbol in the Short Stories of Jorge Luis Borges* (1969).

Bouwman, Heather M. American author of a fantasy novel for children, *The Remarkable and Very True Story of Lucy and Snowcap* (2008), which takes place in the 18th century and depicts the journey of two girls who seek to save a new-born boy on the Island of Tatenland, where all the men are mysteriously turned to stone.   JZ

Boyle, Eleanor Vere (1825–1916) Victorian fairy illustrator. Born in Scotland, 'E.V.B.' painted demure children for more than 50 years. Her fairy work includes *Andersen's Fairy Tales* (1872) and the lavish gift-book

Beauty and the Beast: An Old Tale New-Told (1875). Its engravings and lush colour plates feature a Pre-Raphaelite treatment of nature and Italianate backgrounds and costumes. Boyle's Gothic text and themes of nature, dream, and fate complement her heavily chiaroscuroed scenes, said to anticipate Jean *Cocteau's 1946 film in their treatment of light and dark, illusion and reality.   MLE

Dalby, Richard, *Golden Age of Children's Book Illustration* (1991).

Darling, Harold, and Neumeyer, Peter (eds.), *Image and Maker* (1984).

Hearne, Betsy, *Beauty and the Beast: Visions and Revisions of an Old Tale* (1989).

Boy who Went Forth to Learn What Fear Was, The *See* TALE OF A YOUTH WHO SET OUT TO LEARN WHAT FEAR WAS, THE.

'Brave Little Tailor, The' Unlikely hero who kills seven flies with one stroke and capitalizes on that feat to become king. Popularized in the 19th century by the *Grimms' 'Das tapfere Schneiderlein' ('The Brave Little Tailor', 1812), which combined Martin Montanus's literary version (*c.*1557) with oral variants, the humorous tale has been frequently adapted, notably in Walt *Disney's animated film featuring Mickey Mouse, *The Brave Little Tailor* (1938). The story's modern appeal derives from its cunning, entrepreneurial hero, who undertakes his quest not because he is oppressed or lacks something, but because he possesses immense self-confidence and a talent for self-promotion.   DH

Bray, Anna (1790–1883) British author and early female collector of folklore. When she became the wife of the Vicar of Tavistock in Cornwall through a second marriage, she began to collect accounts of the superstitions and traditions of the area. Publishing her findings in a series of letters to Robert Southey called *The Borders of the Tamar and the Tavy* (3 vols., 1836), she made the fairies of Cornwall and Devon famous. Her accounts of pixie origins, fairy midwives, and magic ointments were used a great deal by later folklorists. She also retold pixie tales in a children's book called *A Peep at the Pixies* (1854).   CGS

Breillat, Catherine (1948–) French novelist and filmmaker who has written and directed two adaptations of the classic fairy tales *Bluebeard* (2009) and *Sleeping Beauty* (2010). She is known as a provocatrice, who has explored women's sexuality and the shame that they have been compelled to feel under the male gaze. Breillat had shown no artistic interest in fairy tales until 2005, when she began work on adapting Perrault's 'Bluebeard'. Here it is important to note that Breillat is the first female filmmaker ever to adapt a fairy tale for the screen—in this case, first for television—not only in France but also in all of Europe. There have been approximately twenty films worldwide since 1945 that have been based on Charles *Perrault's *'Bluebeard'; the most important French versions were directed by Christian-Jaque, Claude Chabrol, Alexandre Bubnov, and Pierre Boutron. But none of the directors of the twenty-odd films, including Charlie Chaplin, whose *Monsieur Verdoux* (1947) is an extraordinary remake with grave political allegations, has remade the tale with such exquisite photography and with such a profound focus on a young woman's passionate desire to assert herself than Breillat. To a certain extent, it is because Breillat lives and breathes through all her stories and films that she has managed to transform Perrault's 'Bluebeard' into a film that explores a young woman's rebellion rather than her victimization. Her most recent remake film, *La Belle endormie* (*The Sleeping Beauty*, 2010), is a pastiche of Perrault's *'Sleeping Beauty' and Hans Christian *Andersen's The *'Snow Queen'. In this film there is a touch of feminism as Breillat seeks to transform Perrault's and Andersen's fairy tales into a coming of age story with Sleeping Beauty moving in and out of predictable experiences, mimicking Andersen's tale.   JZ

Keesey, Douglas, *Catherine Breillat* (2001).

'Bremen Town Musicians, The' Four animals who strike out together to become musicians in the city of Bremen. On their way they use their unusual 'musical' skills to frighten robbers from a house, which the animals then occupy and decide to make their own. In the *Grimms' telling of 'Die Bremer Stadtmusikanten' ('The Bremen Town Musicians', 1819), the travelling musicians consist of a donkey, a dog, a cat, and a rooster. In other variants, especially from Eastern Europe and Asia, the travellers include other animals or even inanimate objects, while the robbers are replaced by wolves, werewolves, or an old woman. Best known in the Grimms' version, the story charts the triumph of the weak through resolve and cooperation. Facing death at the hands of their masters, who show no gratitude for the faithful service the worn-out animals have provided, they each adopt the donkey's initial resolve to become a musician in Bremen. By developing a common plan of action and orchestrating their natural talents (braying, barking, meowing, and crowing), they empower themselves as a group, frighten the robbers who live off others, and reclaim a life for themselves. While the social themes of just deserts and solidarity have made the story popular and motivated numerous 20th-century adaptations, the story's identification with Bremen has made it a valuable commodity in that city's tourist industry.   DH

Richter, Dieter, 'Die "Bremer Stadtmusikanten" in Bremen: Zum weiterleben eines Grimmschen Märchens', in Hans-Jörg Uther (ed.), *Märchen in unserer Zeit: Zu Erscheinungsformen eines populären Erzählgenres* (1990).

Brentano, Clemens (1778–1842) German author of poems, novellas, and literary fairy tales. Brentano was the son of a Frankfurt merchant of Italian descent and the grandson of the German novelist Sophie von La Roche. With Achim von *Arnim, his brother-in-law through marriage to his sister Bettina, he published the first collection of German folk song, *Des Knaben Wunderhorn* (*The Boy's Magic Horn*, first volume in 1805, second and third in 1808). Before his public conversion to Catholicism in 1817 and subsequent dedication to predominantly religious topics, Brentano had been part of the Heidelberg circle of romantic writers, which included Jacob and Wilhelm *Grimm as well as E. T. A. *Hoffmann and Joseph von *Eichendorff, authors of romantic novellas and literary fairy tales. In contrast to the Grimms, who supplied him with some of his source material, Brentano's interest in oral tradition was fuelled largely by the desire to reproduce the style of folk songs and folk tales in his own writing. Contained in *Des Knaben Wunderhorn* are many of Brentano's own poems, which are of such simple musical quality that they are not easily distinguished from the traditional folk song. Best known is 'The Lore-Lay', his ballad of a young woman whose beauty seduced men and who threw herself from a cliff along the Rhine river.

The Rhine was also the setting for many of Brentano's fairy tales. *Fairy Tales of the Rhine* was written between 1809 and 1813, but published posthumously with other tales in 1846–7 by Guido Görres under the title *Die Märchen des Clemens Brentanos* (*The Fairy Tales of Clemens Brentano*). In the frame story of the Rhine fairy tales, Brentano combines motifs from the legends of the Pied Piper of Hamelin and the Lore-Lay, to name a few of the more recognizable sources, with stylistic artistry and yet with little regard for the integrity of individual legend traditions. Brentano's Italian heritage and familiarity with *Basile's *Pentamerone* were reflected in his collection of Italian fairy tales, which included shorter tales, such as *Das Myrthenfräulein* (*The Tale of the Myrtle Girl*) and *Witzenspitzel* (*Smart Alec*) as well as the more elaborate *Gockel and Hinkel* (*Rooster and Hen*), revised and expanded years later under the title *Gockel, Hinkel and Gackeleia* (*Rooster, Hen and Little Cluck*). His fairy tales are generally characterized by the combination and elaboration of motifs from traditional literature, intricate and complex plots, and a poetic, often ornate, style of language.

Brentano's greatest contribution to fairy-tale scholarship is arguably the preservation in his literary estate of a manuscript of early folk-tale versions and notes sent to him by Jacob Grimm in 1810 and discovered in Alsace during the 1920s. The discovery of the Ölenberg manuscript, published first in 1927 and revised in 1975, which consists of some of the earliest extant versions of tales contained in the Grimms' *Kinder- und Hausmärchen* (*Children's and Household Tales*), has offered subsequent generations of scholars invaluable insights into the editorial practices of the Brothers Grimm.   MBS

Fetzer, John F., *Clemens Brentano* (1981).
Frye, Lawrence, 'The Art of Narrating a Rooster Hero in Brentano's *Das Märchen von Gockel und Hinkel*', *Euphorion*, 72 (1978).
Riley, Helene M. K., *Clemens Brentano* (1985).
Seidlin, Oskar, 'Wirklich nur eine schöne Kunstfigur? Zu Brentanos Gockel-Märchen', in *Texte und Kontexte: Studien zur deutschen und vergleichenden Literaturwissenschaft* (1973).

Breton lai (in English, **lay**) A brief, narrative poem rooted in Arthurian material. The word *lai* is probably derived from the Irish *laid*, or song. The 12th-century Anglo-Norman chronicler Wace praised a bard famous for 'harping lais of vielles, . . . rotes, harps, and flutes', but the term *lai* also referred to the words or tales accompanied by music. The modifier 'Breton' indicates the lays' Arthurian character and motifs, now thought to have been transmitted by Welsh harpers and storytellers from Ireland, Wales, and Cornwall to Brittany, where the famous Breton *conteurs* and harpers performed them throughout the continent. Although examples of the early Breton lays are lacking, they probably contained some or all of such romance elements as aristocratic love relationship, marvellous adventures, and encounters with supernatural or magical events and beings.

The earliest known lay is considered Robert Biket's *Lai du Cor*, composed sometime between 1150 and 1175. It recounts a chastity test administered by means of a magic drinking horn made by a fay, whom the later *Prose Tristan* identifies as '*Morgan le Fay'.

Widespread use of the term 'Breton lai' should probably be attributed to *Marie de France, author of lays and fables and

St Patrick's Purgatory. Composing at the court of Henry II of England sometime between 1160 and 1199, she wrote in her lay of *Equitan* that, 'The Bretons, who lived in Brittany, were fine and noble people. In days gone by these valiant, courtly, and noble men composed lays for posterity.' She claimed that the lays she 'put into verse' had originally been composed by Bretons 'to perpetuate the memory of adventures they had heard'. Marie's lays contain numerous motifs associated with Celtic fairy lore. These include a fairy mistress, a white stag that speaks, a strange world of light, and magic potions.

Some scholars think that Breton lais may have been among the important literary conduits of the Celtic legend and fairy lore included in Arthurian romances like those of Chrétien de Troyes, probably the originator of the Arthurian romance. Versions of the Breton lai were composed well into the 14th century. In one well-known example, the Middle English *Sir Orfeo*, the King of Fairy carries off Sir Orfeo's queen to the land of the dead. Chaucer pays homage to the genre in 'The Franklin's Tale'. Later imitators often used the word 'lay', as in Sir Walter Scott's 'Lay of the Last Minstrel', to evoke a medieval mood.   JSN

Burges, Glynn S., and Busby, Keith (eds. and trans.), *The Lais of Marie de France* (1986).
Hoepffner, Ernst, 'The Breton Lai', in R. S. Loomis (ed.), *Arthurian Literature in the Middle Ages* (1959).
Maréchal, Chantal, *In Quest of Marie de France: A Twelfth Century Poet* (1992).

'Briar Rose' *See* 'SLEEPING BEAUTY'.

Brigadoon *See* LERNER, ALAN JAY.

Briggs, Katharine (**Katharine Mary Briggs**, 1898–1980) English folklorist, scholar, and children's author. Internationally famous for her encyclopaedic surveys of British folk tales, fairy traditions, and fairy folk, K. M. Briggs received her doctorate from Oxford in 1952. Her dissertation, on folklore in 17th-century literature, indicated the direction much of her future work would take,

including her two fantasies for children—tracing the connections between literature and folk belief, particularly fairy lore, during the centuries of transition between medieval and modern times. Her special interest in the many varieties of British fairy folk was evident in her first published book, *The Personnel of Fairyland: A Short Account of the Fairy People of Great Britain for Those who Tell Stories to Children* (1953), a prelude to her later, more comprehensive work in this area, which builds upon the tradition of Thomas *Keightley's *The Fairy Mythology* (1828). *The Anatomy of Puck: An Examination of Fairy Beliefs among Shakespeare's Contemporaries and Successors* (1959) was the first of a trilogy on British fairy folk traditions; *Pale Hecate's Team* (1962) examined beliefs in witchcraft and magic during the same period, while *The Fairies in English Tradition and Literature* (1967) traced fairy traditions forward to modern times. Her definitive *A Dictionary of British Folk-Tales in the English Language*, in four volumes, appeared in 1970-1, followed by a one-volume selection, *British Folktales* (1977). In 1976 she published her monumental reference work on varieties of British fairy folk, *A Dictionary of Fairies* (in America, *An Encyclopedia of Fairies*), with entries ranging from Abbey Lubbers to 'Young Tam Lin'. A useful overview of fairy traditions, *The Vanishing People*, came out in 1978, and *Nine Lives: The Folklore of Cats* in 1980, the year of her death.

Although Briggs wrote only two children's books, both are unique, drawn from the depths of her scholarship in British fairy lore. *Hobberdy Dick* (1955) is told from the point of view of a hobgoblin—the guardian spirit of a country manor—just after the English Civil War. When a Puritan family from London takes over the property, Dick must cope with their ignorance of country ways, and intolerance of the fairy traditions intertwined with them, before he can restore Widford Manor to prosperity and happiness. The alien quality of his perceptions and ways of thought is wonderfully imagined and totally convincing. Briggs incorporates many folk beliefs and customs into the story, as well as a variety of supernatural beings;

Dick and his friends are contrasted with the evil ghost that haunts the attic and the coven of witches who kidnap one of the children. *Kate Crackernuts* (1963) expands the folk tale from Joseph *Jacobs's *English Fairy Tales* into a full-length novel, setting the story in 17th-century Scotland and reducing the characters from fairy-tale royalty to a Scottish laird and his family. Briggs treats the supernatural very differently here than in *Hobberdy Dick*, raising the possibility that the evil spell cast on the laird's daughter—even Fairyland itself—may be more illusory than real.   SR

Briggs, Raymond (**Raymond Redvers Briggs**, 1934–) English illustrator and author-illustrator of picture books. *The *Mother Goose Treasury* (1966), a vigorous modern interpretation, won Briggs the Kate *Greenaway Award. His first original picture book, *Jim and the Beanstalk* (1970), radically and optimistically revised the folk tale; unlike his predecessor, Jim does not steal the old giant's possessions, but renews his vitality by procuring him a wig, spectacles, and false teeth. *Father Christmas* (1974), Briggs's startlingly fresh look at a mythical figure, and another Greenaway-winner, marked his first use of the innovative strip-cartoon format that became his stylistic trademark. In the controversial *Fungus the Bogeyman* (1977), Briggs postulated the existence of an entire race of mythical creatures, whose values comment paradoxically on our own. His most popular picture book (and an award-winning children's film), *The Snowman* (1979), was based on a concept familiar in folklore, of a creature made from snow who comes temporarily to life. A theme that runs through all these stories, expressed through creatures of fantasy, is that of the outsider, hovering on the fringes of the modern world. Briggs's later picture books, clearly adult-oriented, became increasingly satirical and pessimistic, dealing with such topics as social injustice and nuclear war.   SR

Martin, Douglas, 'Raymond Briggs', in *The Telling Line* (1989).

Moss, Geoff, 'The Film of the Picture Book: Raymond Briggs's *The Snowman* as Progressive and Regressive Texts', *Children's Literature in Education*, 22 (1991).

Rahn, Suzanne, 'Beneath the Surface with Fungus the Bogeyman', in *Rediscoveries in Children's Literature* (1995).

British and Irish fairy tales *See* p. 76.

British comics These were being published as early as 1874. It is not surprising, therefore, that during such a lengthy period a considerable number of fairy stories appeared within their pages. Comics in Great Britain, with several exceptions, tended to be short-lived, often remaining in print for little more than three years. F. Gifford's catalogue (1975) provides the best record to date of their contents, including fairy tales.

Comics can be placed in a number of categories according to the age-range for which they are intended. Nursery comics have been the most frequent source of fairy tales. Comics for juveniles and for young adolescent girls have also occasionally included them. They are not to be found in comics for older adolescents. This is probably because they are frequently regarded as being mainly suitable for young children.

Within most comics there are three main formats. There is the text story which usually has only one illustration alongside the title; there is the picture story which is made up of a series of pictures with the narrative beneath them; and there is the comic strip which contains brief dialogue in speech bubbles within a series of cartoon frames. Fairy tales have usually occurred in text and picture stories. The cartoon format does not easily lend itself to such stories because the number of words used is so limited. At the present time fairy tales are mainly confined to picture stories because text stories all but disappeared from comics with the advent of television in the 1950s.

Fairy stories in comics are usually serialized, and their contents tend to deviate from the original tales in order to sustain a variety of sub-plots. Alternatively, new, original stories are created.   GF

Gifford, Denis, *The British Comic Catalogue 1874–1974* (1975).

British and Irish fairy tales

1. THE MEDIEVAL PERIOD

English fantasy could be said to have its beginning in the Anglo-Saxon epic poem *Beowulf*, the best-known early work in English literature, generally dated in the 8th century. The eponymous hero (his name means Bear) fights and kills the monster Grendel, and then follows Grendel's avenging mother to her underwater lair, killing her too with the aid of a giant's sword, whose blade melts in the heat of her blood. As a king, 50 years later, Beowulf fights a dragon who, enraged by the theft of a golden goblet from his treasure hoard, has emerged to devastate the country. The dragon is killed, and Beowulf dies. J. R. R. *Tolkien had this episode in mind when he described the death of the dragon Smaug in *The Hobbit*.

Marvellous stories have always held a strong appeal, as shown by the long-enduring popularity of the *Gesta Romanorum*, a collection of tales compiled from many different sources, probably in the late 13th century, and frequently drawn upon by preachers to hold listeners' attention. In the opening pages of the great 14th-century poem *Sir Gawain and the Green Knight* we are shown young King Arthur celebrating the New Year with his court, but restless until he has been told the expected story 'of some perilous incident, of some great wonder'. Medieval writers often showed the natural and the supernatural side by side. Geoffrey of Monmouth in his *Historia Regum Britanniae* (*c.*1136) presents a mythic history of the kings of Britain, which begins when Brutus, great-grandson of Aeneas, collects up survivors of the Trojan War and brings them to England, then uninhabited, 'except for a few giants'. Not only does Geoffrey write of giants and ogres, but also dragons and a sea-monster who swallows up the wicked King Morvidus, and of Merlin, who first became well known in England through this work. Here Merlin is shown as a seer and a prophet, as well as a *deus ex machina*, capable of transferring the stones brought from Africa by giants, from Naas in Ireland to Stonehenge. He also brings about the begetting of King Arthur when he transforms Uther, who desires Igerna [Igraine], into the likeness of Igerna's husband. Geoffrey dealt more fully with Merlin in his poem *Vita Merlini* (*c.*1150).

Sir Thomas Malory assembled his *Le Morte d'Arthur* (printed by Caxton in 1485) from 13th-century French prose romances which he augmented with English material. Repeatedly insisting that the account is historical, he also introduces magic. The sword Excalibur is delivered to Arthur by an arm clad in white samite, and the same arm appears out of the lake to receive it before he dies. There are spells and magic potions, and enchantresses among whom is *Morgan le Fay, half-sister of Arthur. Merlin is a less dominant figure and disappears after the opening sections of the book. We see him besotted with 'one of the damosels of the Lady of the Lake that hight Nenivel'. Rashly he initiates her into the mysteries of necromancy, and 'ever passing weary of him', she imprisons him under a rock.

Sir Gawain and the Green Knight, one of the most brilliant of all medieval poems, a story of how Sir Gawain's honour and chastity are tempted with the aid of magic, blends chivalric romance with elements from old tales of Beheading Games, and also with an apparent vestige of some nature myth. A huge green man on a green horse rides into the castle hall at Camelot where Arthur's court is feasting, and offers his axe to anyone who will meet him in single combat. Sir Gawain accepts the challenge and strikes off the green man's head. The following New Year's Day, as agreed, the giant awaits him at his Green Chapel for the second part of the contest.

The Protestant Roger Ascham (1515/16–68), tutor to Princess Elizabeth and Lady Jane Grey, referred to tales of chivalry and courtly love with great disgust in *The Scholemaster* (1570) as belonging to the papist decadence of the past when 'fewe bookes were read in our tong, savyng certaine bookes of Chevalrie . . . as one, for example, Morte Arthur'. Even to Chaucer (*c.*1343–1400), who began *The Canterbury Tales* about 1387, much the same time as the *Gawain* poet was writing, they seemed in a past mode. The Wife of Bath talks about fairies as bygones, belonging to King Arthur's day, 'But now can no man see none elves mo'. Though there is enchantment in *The Canterbury Tales*, such as in the incomplete Squire's Tale in which a king of Arabia sends magic gifts to the king of Tartary and his daughter, Chaucer's own interrupted tale of Sir Thopas, who breathlessly gallops around, encountering the Fairy Queen and a three-headed giant, but accomplishing nothing, is a parody of a metrical romance, and the impatient host shouts 'No more of this, for goddes dignitee', as Chaucer catalogues 'romances of prys' such as Horn Childe, Sir Bevis [of Hampton] and Sir Guy [of Warwick]. These were popular verse romances of the fairly recent past. In all three, deeds of knightly valour mingle with accounts of invincible swords, magic rings, dragons, and giants. The story of *Huon of Bordeaux*, a French romance of the same period, done into English by Sir John Bourchier, Lord Berners, and printed by Wynkyn de Worde in 1534, did not have the same popularity, but is important because in it Oberon, king of the fairies (son of Julius Caesar and Morgan le Fay), makes his first English appearance, a 3-foot being of 'aungelyke visage'. It was one of the romances contemptuously dismissed by Thomas Nashe in *The Anatomie of Absurditie* (1589) as 'worne out impressions of fayned no where acts'.

2. THE BANISHMENT OF THE FAIRIES

Arthurian legend virtually disappears from English literature after the medieval period and was used very little by writers until the 19th century. Though there is an element of it in *The Faerie Queene* (1590–6), *Spenser was primarily influenced by Italian epic poetry. There are no native English fairies in it; the enchanters are allegorical figures, Archimago representing Hypocrisy, and Duessa—the daughter of Deceit and Shame—representing

Falsehood. The queen herself is of course Elizabeth, and the fact that Spenser addresses her as 'The greatest Glorious Queene of Faerie lond' is some indication of Elizabethan preoccupation with fairies. They appeared in poems, in plays, in masques, in practical jokes—as in the one played on Falstaff in *The Merry Wives of Windsor*, and on the credulous clerk, Dapper, in *Jonson's *The Alchemist* (1610) by the two tricksters who tell him he is going to meet the Queen of the Fairies. Though Jonson regarded his contemporaries' obsession with magic as a national mania, his position as a writer of court masques obliged him to use it in such works as *The Satyr* (also known as *The Masque of the Fairies*), presented at Althorpe in 1603 to amuse James I's queen, and *Oberon, the Fairy Prince*, given at Whitehall in 1611. Milton's *Comus*, written for a performance at Ludlow in 1634, is the richest of all the masques in terms of poetry, and a most unexpected work for a Puritan. Comus himself is an imaginary pagan god with magic powers, who waylays travellers and with his potion changes their faces 'into some brutish form'. In 'L'Allegro' Milton names more traditional fairies, including Faery Mab.

Mercutio's description of Queen Mab in *Romeo and Juliet* was to be built upon by Drayton and Herrick and subsequent poets, who presented her as the queen of fairies and the wife of Oberon, whereas originally *queen* meant no more than *woman*. But the most influential fairy play of all was *A Midsummer Night's Dream*. In this *Shakespeare created a new species of fairy, and in doing so he brought about the destruction of the fairies of English folklore. Presumably because the play was to celebrate a marriage, he softened their image. Before that the folk view was that they were malevolent spirits, associated with witchcraft. Puck or *pouke* was a term applied to a class of demons; the naïve little devil who visits London in Jonson's *The Devil is an Ass* (1616) is called Pug—another variant of the name. Shakespeare conflated Puck with Robin Goodfellow, a hobgoblin, an earthy spirit who did household tasks in return for a saucer of milk, but also played impish tricks, such as leading travellers astray, as are described in *The Mad Prankes and Merry Jests of Robin Goodfellow*. The first known printing of this prose story with verse interpolations is in 1626, though there is evidence that it had appeared at least 40 years earlier. Robin Goodfellow here is the son of Oberon, who bestows magic gifts on him, such as the ability to change his shape 'for to vex both foole and knave'. He is described as 'famozed in every old wives chronicle for his mad merrye prankes', like Shakespeare's Puck, but in capacity for magic he falls far short of the latter.

Nor was he an inhabitant of fairyland, nor a minuscule being. The fairy of English folklore seems to have been the size of a small man, and it was Shakespeare's depiction of fairies as diminutive and picturesque, with pretty garden names, employed in hanging pearls in cowslips' ears and gathering bats' wings to make elfin coats, that captured the literary imagination. Poets such as Michael Drayton (1563–1631), Robert Herrick (1591–1674), Margaret, Duchess of Newcastle (1623–72) constructed elaborate conceits about fairy revels and banquets, embellished with details of microscopic clothes and food. Drayton's *Nimphidia* (1627) is a mock-heroic poem describing the efforts of Pigwiggen, a fairy knight, to seduce Queen Mab, and the battle that then ensues between him and Oberon, but it is the descriptions of the fairy palace, costume, chariots, and armour that are the poet's chief concern. Herrick's fairy poems in *Hesperides* (1648) used the same sort of detail. All this was of course for a limited readership. The poor man's Pigwiggen was Tom Thumb, a legendary character included—along with elves and hobgoblins and such—by Reginald Scot in his *Discoverie of Witchcraft* (1584) as an object of popular superstition. His history was set down by 'R.J.', probably Richard Johnson (1573–?1659) in *The History of Tom Thumbe, the Little*. Though it may well have appeared earlier, the earliest known copy is dated 1621. Merlin (here described as 'a conjurer, an inchanter, a charmer [who] consorts with Elves and Fayries') promises a childless elderly couple a thumb-sized child. The child is delivered by the 'midnights Midwife, the Queene of Fayries' and 'in less than foure minutes [grows] to be a little man'. In episodes later bowdlerized he is eaten by his mother's cow, and snatched up by a raven and a giant; his godmother the fairy queen bestows magical gifts on him, and he becomes a valued member of King Arthur's court.

*'Little Tom Thumb' was a fairy tale singled out for particular execration by Puritan preachers, who regarded all works of imagination as lies and therefore damnably wicked—an attitude that persisted longer in America than it did in England. John Bunyan in *Sighs from Hell: or The Groans of a Damned Soul* (1658) lamented his youthful addiction to romances which drove him away from more profitable reading: 'Thought I...give me a Ballad, a News book, George on Horseback, or Bevis of Southampton...' George on Horseback is St George, one of Richard Johnson's *Seven Champions of Christendom*, a long romance published in two parts in 1596 and 1597, in which St George is instructed in magic arts by an enchantress who steals him in infancy. Like the tale of Bevis, *The Seven Champions* (albeit drastically shortened) remained popular reading for centuries, and *The Pilgrim's Progress* (1678) owes much to both of them. Not many in the 17th century spoke up for such stories. The convivial Richard Corbet (1582–1635), Bishop of Oxford and then of Norwich, and fiercely opposed to Puritanism, was one notable exception. His poem, 'Farewell, Rewards and Fairies', quoted by Kipling's Puck, lamented that Puritans had banished fairies, and 'now, alas, they all are dead; Or gone beyond the seas'.

Fairies did not flourish in the utilitarian and sceptical 18th century. So far as children were concerned, the old romantic tales of magic were held to belong to the ignorant and credulous, and conscientious parents wished their young to be well-informed, rational beings. That arbiter of correct behaviour, Philip Dormer Stanhope, fourth Earl of Chesterfield (1694–1773) in one of his letters to his (natural) son, then aged 8, was contemptuous about the old-style romances, 'stuft with enchantments, magicians, giants'. And when Sarah *Fielding introduced a d'Aulnoy-style fairy story into *The Governess* (1749) it was with warnings that 'Giants, Magic, Fairies, and all sorts of supernatural Assistances in a Story' should only be used to point a moral. A few d'*Aulnoy stories were translated in 1699, and more in 1707 and 1716, and a translation of *Perrault's *Histoires ou contes du temps passé* appeared in 1729, but for the most part fairies seemed a forgotten species, so that in 1744 when a mother, Jane Johnson, was writing a story for her small children, she used 'pretty little angels' in their place to dole out treats to the good characters. (The manuscript of this story, the earliest known juvenile fairy tale, is in the Bodleian Library, Oxford.)

Oriental magic took over in such 18th-century English fantasy writing as there was. A 'Grub-street' English version of *Galland's translation of *The *Arabian Nights* was being published in London from about 1704 and made far more impact on the literary imagination than the French fairy tales. Writers began to produce tales set in exotic eastern locations, with enchantments, genii, and magical objects such as rings and talismans. William Beckford's *Vathek* (1786), written in French when the author was only 21, is the most extravagant of these. The Caliph Vathek, whose mother is a sorceress, lured on by lust for even greater power and magnificence than he already possesses, becomes a servant of the Devil. Despite the author's hedonism and seeming pleasure in cruelty, there is an ostensible moral: the worthlessness of riches and the fearful end of tyrants. Indeed a concluding moral reflection was a feature of the oriental tale, though some writers laboured the point more than others as, for instance, James Ridley in *Tales of the Genii* (1764), a book read by the young Charles *Dickens, who was terrified by the diminutive old hag in 'The History of the Merchant Abudah'. Few oriental tales were designed for children. Horace Walpole's 'The Dice-Box', one of his *Hieroglyphic Tales* written between 1766 and 1772, is a rare exception, written for the small niece of a friend. The heroine of this brief and crudely comic extravaganza, wholly without a moral, is the 9-year-old Pissimissi from Damascus, who travels in a pistachio-nut stuffed with toys and sugarplums and drawn by an elephant and a ladybird.

3. THE RETURN OF THE FAIRIES

By the end of the century there was a marked change; from the 1780s the supernatural became fashionable. Reynolds's painting of Shakespeare's Puck as an impish, satyr-like child (1789) was much admired. It had been commissioned by Alderman John Boydell for his Shakespeare gallery, to which leading artists of the time contributed, including *Fuseli, whose

Midsummer Night's Dream paintings show an erotic dreamworld into which he introduced such folklore beings as night-hags and changelings, while Puck appears as a huge elemental figure in his painting of the fairy Cobweb (1785–6). Blake, though he stood outside all fashion, also used folklore fairies in an illustration for Milton's 'L'Allegro' in 1816. Walter Scott was a literary pioneer. His *Minstrelsy of the Scottish Border* (1801–2) includes an essay 'The Fairies of Popular Superstition', and among the ballads is the legend of Thomas the Rhymer, who followed the Queen of Elfland to her country and never came back. (Keats uses the same theme of a mortal ensnared by an elfin woman in 'La Belle Dame sans Merci' (1819), and Mrs *Craik and Andrew *Lang both built stories on it.) Christina *Rossetti's poem *Goblin Market* (1862), more dark and sinister than any of these, describes goblins trying to seduce two sisters with forbidden fruit. Scott's first important original work, *The Lay of the Last Minstrel* (1805), is based on a Border legend about a goblin, and *The Lady of the Lake* (1810) includes a fairy ballad, 'Alice Brand'. In his novel *The Monastery* (1820), set in Elizabethan times, there is a sylph, the White Lady of Avenelf, who acts as *deus ex machina*. He also started a revival of interest in Arthurian legend; there are many extracts from Malory in footnotes to *Marmion* (1808). Scott was responsible for encouraging James Hogg, the Ettrick Shepherd, in a literary career. Hogg's 'Kilmeny', the 13th tale in *The Queen's Wake* (1813), where a girl walks into 'A land of love and a land of light, Withouten sun, or moon, or night' which she cannot bear to leave, is one of the most haunting poems about fairy enchantment.

Important work was also done by the Irishman Thomas Crofton *Croker, whose *Fairy Legends and Traditions in the South of Ireland* (1825–8) Scott knew, and by Thomas *Keightley, another Irishman, whose *Fairy Mythology* (1828) covers an astonishing range of European legends, and includes a section on English fairies, a subject that had received little attention before. Material from it was frequently used by subsequent writers, including Archibald Maclaren, who drew on Scott's *Border Minstrelsy* as well for his *The Fairy Family: Ballads and Metrical Tales of the Fairy Faith of Europe* (1857).

The *Grimms' *Kinder- und Hausmärchen* were translated by Edgar *Taylor under the title *German Popular Stories* (1823), with illustrations by George *Cruikshank (which *Ruskin remembered copying when he was a boy), and translations of Hans Christian *Andersen appeared in 1846. They were enthusiastically received. Early Victorians, seeking an escape from the ugliness of industrial society, turned to chivalric ideals and fairy mythology, which seemed to belong to a lost innocent world. *Tennyson's 'Morte d'Arthur' was published in 1842, to be gradually followed over many years by the other 11 poems which make up *Idylls of the King*. Unexpected artists responded to the fashion for fairy pictures; Landseer painted Titania with

Bottom, and J. M. W. Turner *Queen Mab's Cave*. John Anster Fitzgerald (the most obsessive fairy painter of all), Daniel Maclise, Joseph Noël *Paton, and Richard *Dadd were among those who depicted fairy worlds with minute realism and sometimes erotic detail, often on huge canvases. C. L. Dodgson (Lewis *Carroll) counted 165 fairies in Paton's *The Quarrel of Oberon and Titania* (*A Midsummer Night's Dream* was a favourite subject), but there are over 200 in Richard *Doyle's watercolour *The Fairy Tree*. *In Fairyland* (1870), with 36 of his illustrations for which the Irish poet William Allingham wrote the verse, was the most lavish fairy picture book of the period.

The theatre of the time was an important influence on many artists, notably on Doyle and Fitzgerald. Stage productions were spectacular, using elaborate stage machinery and lighting, and there was a memorable production by Charles Kean of *A Midsummer Night's Dream* in 1856, and one of *The Tempest* the following year where Ariel sailed on a dolphin's back and rode on a bat, and Prospero's freed spirits flew through the air. Pantomimes were particularly rich in fairies; Richard Henry Horne in *Memoirs of a London Doll* (1846) gives a chapter to one performed at Drury Lane, with a long description of the transformation scene and its frost fairies.

Literary fantasy, especially where children were concerned, was more purposeful. The first full-length juvenile fairy story was Francis *Paget's *The Hope of the Katzekops* (1844), a vivacious comedy which becomes serious in the final pages. The prince who is the Katzekopf hope is reformed by fairy means, as Scrooge is by the ghosts of Christmases past, present, and future in Dickens's *The Christmas Carol* (1843), and variations on this theme played a large part in Victorian fantasy. It could involve savagely unpleasant punishment, as in Christina Rossetti's *Speaking Likenesses* (1874), or in Lucy Lane *Clifford's 'The New Mother' (1882), where two naughty children are abandoned by their mother and her place is taken by one with glass eyes and a wooden tail. Other improving fairy tales ranged from simplistic stories, such as those by Mary Louisa *Molesworth, about children who are cured of faults by encounters with magic, to the complex symbolism of George *MacDonald. Nearly all his fantasies, for both adults and children, describe a quest for spirituality, but the meaning is left for readers to infer— MacDonald always denied that he wrote allegory. In *Phantastes* (1858) the hero's name, Anodos, Greek for 'a spiritual ascent', is a clue to what follows.

Both this and *Lilith* (1895), his last work, describe strange encounters, often full of sexual imagery, as the central characters wander in a dream world. Neither was popular in MacDonald's lifetime, the *Athenaeum* saying of the first that it read as if the author had supped 'too plentifully on German romance, negative philosophy, and Shelley's "Alastor"'. His greatest work lies in the simpler fantasies for children. Charles *Kingsley's *The Water-Babies* (1863), though didactic on many fronts, imparting lessons in moral improvement and natural history as well as asides on topics dear to the author, was also highly original, written with an infectious verve that carries the reader through the book's chaotic organization.

Lewis Carroll's *Alice* books of 1865 and 1871 have often been cited as a watershed in the history of children's books; F. J. Harvey Darton referred to the first as a spiritual volcano. It is a mark of their originality that not only do they have no moral, but they owe nothing to any fantasy that preceded them, establishing their own species of nonsense which, once Carroll had shown the way, was palely imitated by many other authors. His attempt at conventional fairies in *Sylvie and Bruno* (1889–93) is best forgotten.

Victorian writers for children tended to draw on German and French sources rather than on native tradition. Frances *Browne and John *Ruskin both wrote stories which owe much to the Grimms. Hans Christian Andersen's bitter-sweet melancholy was often imitated; Oscar *Wilde's 'The Happy Prince' (described by John Goldthwaite as 'quasi-religious bathos') is the best-known of these pastiches. George MacDonald was influenced by German romantic writers such as *Novalis and E. T. A. *Hoffmann, and echoes of the latter can be found in Mary *De Morgan. The background of Perrault fairy stories was used in burlesque accounts of court life such as in *Thackeray's *The Rose and the Ring* (1855) and in Andrew *Lang's chronicles of Pantouflia, beginning with *Prince Prigio* (1889), a hero whose ancestors included Cinderella, the Marquis de Carabas, and the Sleeping Princess. Juliana Horatia *Ewing's *Lob Lie-by-the-Fire* (1873) is one of the few stories to draw on English folklore. There are some English tales in Andrew Lang's *Fairy Books* (1889–1910), but Joseph *Jacobs was the first to give them serious attention, in two volumes of 1890 and 1893. Neil Philip in *The Penguin Book of English Folktales* (1992) summarizes the work done by English collectors.

The Scots and Irish had always shown far more interest than the English in their folklore and native tales. For his *Fairy and Folk Tales of the Irish Peasantry* (1888), William Butler *Yeats drew on material from many collectors of the past such as Croker and Patrick *Kennedy, and expressed particular admiration for 'the pathos and tenderness' of Lady (Jane Francesca) Wilde's *Ancient Legends of Ireland* (1887). He also included fairy poems by William Allingham, and more robust material from William Carleton, author of *Tales of Ireland* (1834). Yeats was unusual among literary fantasists in that he actually claimed to believe in the superstitions he described. But he was a born syncretist, equally interested in Irish tales and oriental magic, and did not mind how incompatible his ideas were if they appealed to the imagination and helped inspire creative work. Lord *Dunsany, though associated with the Irish Revival, drew little on Celtic tradition, more on invented mythology of his own, in his mistily romantic fairy tales. Padraic *Colum, the only Irish Revival writer who was peasant-born and country-bred, used an Irish background and traditional tales in his children's books, and wove several legends into a single narrative in *The King of Ireland's Son* (1916).

4. THE 20TH-CENTURY REVIVAL

The turn of the century saw another English eruption of enthusiasm for fairies, perhaps prompted by reaction against liberal progressive late Victorian culture. On 27 December 1904 an audience of adults at a London theatre responded to *Peter Pan's appeal by enthusiastically assenting that yes, they did believe in fairies. *Barrie had been much impressed by Seymour Hicks's *Bluebell in Fairyland* (1901), and determined to write a children's play of his own. *Peter Pan* is an amalgam of magic, nostalgia, and his own complex psychological problems, but Barrie wrote other plays using more traditional elements. In *Dear Brutus* (1917) an elfin host, Lob, sends his guests into an enchanted wood to seek the second chance all of them desire; *Mary Rose* (1920) draws on the Scottish legend where a mortal can vanish for a lifetime and reappear no older, and not knowing what has passed. *Peter Pan* is still an annual Christmas event in London; its rival in popularity, *Where the Rainbow Ends* (1911) by Clifford Mills and 'John Ramsey' (Reginald Owen) with music by Roger Quilter, a heady mixture of jingoism and magic, with St George as presiding genius, did not long survive the Second World War. The Peter Pan chapters of *The Little White Bird* (1902), where Barrie represents London's Kensington Gardens as inhabited by fairies who emerge after lock-up time, were reissued as *Peter Pan in Kensington Gardens* (1906), and illustrated by Arthur *Rackham, the most distinguished fantasy artist of his generation.

In her children's books E. *Nesbit avoided sentimentality, combining her fantasy with humour, and magic is mostly used to show how *not* to use it. *The Story of the Amulet* (1906) is probably the first children's book with time travel, later to become very popular. It was used by Alison Uttley in *A Traveller in Time* (1939) and Philippa Pearce in *Tom's Midnight Garden* (1958), one of the best examples of the genre. The magic worked by *Kipling's Puck in *Puck of Pook's Hill* (1906) and *Rewards and Fairies* (1910) summons up the past for two children. Puck here is the Robin Goodfellow of tradition, as ancient as the land itself. Walter *de la Mare, though he wrote of fairies in his verse and used them more obliquely in his short stories, stands apart from any literary movement. *The Three Mulla-Mulgars* (1910) is an account of a spiritual quest, and perhaps this is at the root of his writing, which so often has death as its theme. Eleanor *Farjeon was an admirer of de la Mare, but her whimsically fanciful tales fall far short of his.

In general, fairies before the Second World War were of the gauzy, winged little buzzfly sort that Kipling's Puck had derided. Appetite for them seemed insatiable; they appeared in verse, illustrations, comic strips, advertisements;

'Practically every author begins his or her career by writing a fairy tale', stated a 1934 guide. By the 1940s the preoccupation had dwindled, though there are late instances. The title story in Naomi *Mitchison's *Five Men and a Swan* (1957), is about a West Highland trawler skipper who chances on a swan maiden, while the stories in Sylvia Townsend *Warner's *The Cat's Cradle Book* (1960) and *Kingdoms of Elfin* (1977) build ingeniously on fairy literature of the past.

The most compelling and elaborately constructed fantasy world must be that of J. R. R. *Tolkien, who had been brooding over the landscape, people, history, and legends of Middle-Earth, and formulating its language, for over 20 years before he wrote *The Hobbit* (1937), to which *The Lord of the Rings*, taking nearly 20 more years to complete, was started as a sequel. (It is perhaps not surprising that he disliked his friend C. S. *Lewis's very different Narnia fantasies (1950–6), written at great speed, using—not a coherent mythology, but any elements that caught the author's fancy.) Other writers have since tried their hand at creating imaginary worlds; Peter Carey's *The Unusual Life of Tristan Smith* (1994) is one of the more inventive. T. H. *White's *The Sword in the Stone* (1938) is a witty story about the boyhood of Arthur, later adapted to form the first part of *The Once and Future King* (1958); its touches of satire raise it above the level of ordinary comic fantasy.

Alan *Garner began a new style of fantasy for children (albeit with echoes of Tolkien) with *The Weirdstone of Brisingamen* (1960) and its successors, weaving myth with characters from the past and the present. *The Owl Service* (1967) and *Red Shift* (1973), though far more complex and sophisticated, develop the same theme. Richard *Adams's *Watership Down* (1972), where rabbits set out on an epic journey to found a new colony, became something of a cult, and there were many imitations. Mary Norton's five books about the Borrowers (1953–82), three Lilliputian people, the last of their kind, is a more poignant treatment of the same sort of quest for safety and permanence. Angela *Carter in *The Bloody Chamber and Other Stories* (1979) created new adult interest in fairy tales by reworking traditional stories and infusing them with dark and often erotic comedy. A. S. *Byatt built *Possession* (1990) round the character of a Victorian poetess obsessed with the legend of the French snake-fairy, Mélusine; the novel includes accomplished pastiches of fairy tales of the period.

5. NEW SIGNS IN THE 21ST CENTURY

A. S. Byatt has continued her prolific output in the new century with her grand fairy-tale novel, *The Children's Book* (2008), in which she deals with the decline of Victorian culture and the fairy tale. More contemporary are Sarah Maitland's collections of fairy tales, *On Becoming a Fairy Godmother* (2003) and *Far North & Other Dark Tales* (2008). To celebrate the bicentenary of the first edition of the Grimms' fairy tales, first published in 1812, she produced a collection of essays, *Gossip from the Forest: the Tangled Roots of our Forests and Fairytales* (2012), which included modern adaptations of the Grimms' tales. In addition, Philip Pullman published *Fairy Tales from the Brothers Grimm* (2012), a small selection of the Grimms' tales, which he rewrote. Finally, Neil Gaiman continues to produce fantasy and fairy-tale stories and books such as *Coraline* (2002), *Wolves in the Walls* (2003), and *Hansel and Gretel* (2014), a toon graphic, with the illustrator Lorenzo Mattotti. GA

Darton, F. J. Harvey, *Children's Books in England* (1960; 3rd edn., 1982).
Girouard, Mark, *The Return to Camelot* (1981).
Goldthwaite, John, *The Natural History of Make-Believe* (1996).
Latham, Minor White, *The Elizabethan Fairies* (1930).
Martineau, Jane (ed.), *Victorian Fairy Painting* (1997).
Talairach-Vielmas, Laurence, *Fairy Tales, Natural History and Victorian Culture* (2014).
Warner, Marina, *Once Upon a Time—A Short History of Fairy Tale* (2014).

Brlić Mažuranić, Ivana (1874–1938) Called the Croatian Hans Christian *Andersen, Brlić was a twice Nobel-prize-nominated writer whose work included children's stories inspired by and based upon fairy tales, folktales, and Slavic mythology, in particular *Čudnovate zgode šegrta Hlapića* (*The Brave Adventures of a Shoemaker's Boy* or *The Brave Adventures of Lapitch*, 1913, English version by Lorna Wood, translated by Theresa Mravintz and Branko Brusar, 1971) and *Priče iz davnine* (*Croatian Tales of Long Ago*, 1916, translated by F. S. Copeland, 1924). In 1937, she became the first woman accepted as a Corresponding Member into the Yugoslav Academy of Sciences and Arts. Brlić Mažuranić's stories have a broad international audience, and have been translated into many languages and dialects, and adapted for theatre, ballet, puppet theatre, and radio drama. The opera *Šuma Striborova* by Ivan Josip Skender is based on 'Stribor's Forest' from the *Croatian Tales*. Milan Blažeković's 1997 feature film for children, *Lapitch, The Little Shoemaker*, in production at Croatia Film from 1991 to 1997, was based on Brlić Mažuranić's book. It features anthropomorphized animal characters, and combines traditional Disney-style cel animation in the foreground with limited animation/abstraction in the background. A welcome escape from wartime, it soon became the highest-grossing Croatian animated film. PG

broadside (or Épinal) Broadsides, an early mass-cultural form—print media on single paper sheets—were posted or sold on European streets from the sixteenth to the twentieth centuries as disposable popular literature, and sometimes created as fine art in the twentieth and twenty-first centuries. Historically often illustrated with woodcuts and hand-stencilled with bright colours, they could include sensationalist content such as reports of executions or marvels, or be religious or political tracts. Precursors to and/or counterparts of newspapers, comics, and *chapbooks (pamphlets), broadsides offer informative and entertaining documents, sometimes consisting of folktale and fairy-tale texts and illustrations. As popular media, broadsides suggest a public that is at least basically literate or has access to literacy, and thus they implicate a long-term interplay between oral and written fairy tales. Read silently or aloud, broadsides were significant to the dissemination of traditional and popular folkloric texts, in particular ballads, but also legends and other narrative forms.

Épinal, named after the small French town in which they were produced by the family firm of Fabrique Pellerin from the eighteenth century, depicted popular fairy tales such as *'Donkey-Skin', *'Puss-In-Boots', *'Little Red Riding Hood', *'Rapunzel', and the *Jack tales, as well as less well-known examples. PG

Preston, Cathy Lynn, and Preston, Michael J. (eds.), *The Other Print Tradition: Essays on Chapbooks, Broadsides, and Related Ephemera* (1995).

Broumas, Olga (1949–) Greek-born American poet. Broumas's first volume, *Beginning with O* (1977) was a winner in the Yale Series of Younger Poets. Openly feminist and lesbian, her poetry explores both Greek myth and European fairy tales, further transforming some of Anne *Sexton's *Transformations* of the most familiar *Grimm tales, from *'Beauty and the Beast' and *'Cinderella' to *'Rumpelstiltskin' and *'Snow White'. In *'Sleeping Beauty', for example, the narrator is awakened by another woman's 'public kiss'; in *'Little Red Riding Hood', Broumas transforms the tale into a return to the mother, evading the obstetrician/wolf. EWH

Broun, Heywood (1888–1939) American journalist, columnist, and writer of novels and short stories, who founded the American Newspaper Guild and often wrote on social issues, especially during the 1920s. He also wrote provocative fiction. For instance, his unusual fairy tale, 'The 51st Dragon' (1919) was an ironic anti-war depiction of a naive knight trained to become a killer of dragons. His fairy-tale novel, *Gandle Follows his Nose* (1926), is a bizarre story of the education of a young man in a fantasy world. 'The 51st Dragon' was made into a significant UFA cartoon in 1954.   JZ

Kramer, Dale, *Heywood Broun* (1949).
O'Connor, Richard, *Heywood Broun* (1975).

Browne, Anthony (1946–) Internationally acclaimed British author and illustrator of children's books. Among many accolades, he was given the international Hans Christian Andersen Award in 2000 and was named Children's Laureate in 2009. Noteworthy works include *Gorilla* (1983) and *Voices in the Park* (1998). Many of Browne's stories include fairy-tale themes and imagery. Browne's first book, *Through the Magic Mirror* (1976), features a young boy who passes through a mirror into an imaginative world replete with surrealist visual humour. Browne is also responsible for a rendition of Lewis *Carroll's *Alice's Adventures in Wonderland* (1988) and *Into the Forest* (2004). Other works emphasize themes of transformation, such as *Piggybook* (1986), in which a slovenly household transforms into a literal pigsty. Other titles offer more nuanced expressions, such as in *Hansel & Gretel* (1981), in which visual cues suggest that the cruel stepmother doubles as the villainous witch.   KMJ

Browne, Frances (1816–79) Irish writer. The seventh of 12 children of a Donegal village postmaster, she lost her sight in infancy, but nevertheless all her writing is marked by a strong sense of place. She wrote poems, novels, and a few children's stories, but is only known now for *Granny's Wonderful Chair* (1857), a collection of seven tales in the *Grimm tradition within a frame story about a magical chair which can not only travel but also tell fairy tales. The book, which was not reprinted in her lifetime, was rediscovered by Frances Hodgson *Burnett in 1887 and has remained a children's classic ever since.   GA

Filmer, Kath, 'Happy Endings in *Hard Times* and *Granny's Wonderful Chair*', in *The Victorian Fantasists: Essays on Culture, Society, and Belief in the Mythopoeic Fiction of the Victorian Age* (1991).

Bruna, Dick (1927–) Dutch writer and illustrator of children's picture books. In the 1950s and 1960s Bruna wrote a series of books about the adventures of Miffy ('Nijntje' in Dutch) the rabbit, and another series about Snuffy (or 'Snuffie') the dog. In 1966 the Follett Publishing Company of Chicago issued several retellings of fairy tales by Bruna: *Dick Bruna's Cinderella*, *Dick Bruna's Little Red Riding Hood*, *Dick Bruna's Snow-White and the Seven Dwarfs*, and *Dick Bruna's Tom Thumb*.   AD

Brust, Steven (1955–) American writer of Hungarian descent known for swashbuckling novels in the spirit of Alexander Dumas. Brust retells a Hungarian fairy tale in *The Sun, the Moon and the Stars* (1987), alternating a lively traditional tale of three Gypsy brothers on a magical quest with a contemporary story concerning a studio of painters in Minneapolis. Brust returns to themes from Hungarian Gypsy lore in his dark urban fantasy novel *The Gypsy* (1992), co-written with Megan Lindholm. A CD of related songs by Brust, also titled *The Gypsy*, was released by the folk-rock band Boiled in Lead (1992).   TW

Buckley, Michael (1969–) American author and screenwriter responsible for the *New York Times* bestselling children's book series *The Sisters Grimm* (2005–12), illustrated by Peter Ferguson. *The Sisters Grimm* features two orphaned sisters who are the descendants of the brothers Grimm. While many of the characters are from *Kinder- und Hausmärchen*, many are from other books, folktales, and fairy tales. The companion, *A Very Grimm Guide* was published in 2012. Buckley's other successes include the series *N.E.R.D.S.* (2009–13) and the picture book *Kel Gilligan's Daredevil Stunt Show*. He has also developed television programming for Discovery Channel, TLC, and MTV Animation, among others.   KMJ

Burgess, Gelett (1866–1951) American poet and illustrator who achieved fame with his nonsense verse for children. In

1900 he published *Goops and How to Be Them*, tongue-in-cheek stories that poked fun at bad manners and warned children what would happen to them if they became like Goops. These figures, rubber-like ghosts with oversized heads, were also depicted in *The Burgess Nonsense Book* (1901), a collection of his verse, strongly influenced by Lewis *Carroll and Edward Lear. Burgess also published *The Lively City O'Ligg* (1899) with such droll fairy tales as 'The House who Walked in her Sleep' and 'The Terrible Train', which depicted animated objects as protagonists whose fantastic and bizarre relations reflected a world turned upside down.   JZ

Burkert, Nancy Ekholm (1933–) American author and illustrator known for her elegant art and careful research in preparing her books. Her two illustrated *Andersen fairy tales, *The Nightingale* (1965) and *The Fir Tree* (1970), are remarkable for their period settings. For the *Grimms' *Snow White and the Seven Dwarfs* (1972), Burkert drew a full-size teenage girl's face for the book jacket. In the interior illustrations, she incorporated herbs and symbols associated with witchcraft. Bats fly against the moon, a spider spins a web, and a mushroom lies on the table. While one of the wicked stepmother's hands holds the apple, evidently poisoned with the paraphernalia including mortar and pestle on the table, the other is positioned to indicate evil intent. While all her books present characters as though on a stage, the most notable book is *Valentine & Orson* (1989). She devised a unique way of presenting the story so children could better understand. Characters wear period costumes, and the story is re-created as a folk play in verse and paintings. Separated at birth, the twin brothers are raised by a king and by a bear respectively. Their meeting as costumed characters in a play is poignantly placed mid-page front and centre, lending the tale an exquisite dramatic quality. KNH

burlesque fairy-tale films These films are sometimes framed as dreams and often used as vehicles for stars, or topical satire, or

both. *Ali Baba Goes to Town* (USA, 1937) chose the Middle East as a setting for political quips about Roosevelt's New Deal. In it Al Babson (Eddie Cantor) dreams himself into Baghdad where, finding the people fed up with the Sultan, he suggests Roosevelt's policies as a cure for the country's economic ills. Believing Al to be the son of *Ali Baba, the Sultan agrees to the proposal, and abdicates in order to be able to run for the presidency. However, Al himself unintentionally becomes the people's favourite and is elected. Faced by a challenger preparing to use force against him, Al abandons the New Deal and wins the day with the help of a much older policy—a magic flying carpet.

In the same year, *Disney's *Snow White and the Seven Dwarfs* was such a success that it prompted numerous parodies. One was *Ball of Fire* (USA, 1942) which starred recent Oscar-winner Gary Cooper and transposed the story to a city. The opening titles set the tone: 'Once upon a time, in 1941 to be exact, there lived in a great tall forest—called New York—eight men who were writing an encyclopaedia.' These scholars are chastely and single-mindedly devoted to their academic labours until, in a quest to record demotic vocabulary, their leader, Professor Potts, goes out into the streets and brings back Sugarpuss O'Shea, a nightclub singer with underworld connections. Her uninhibited speech and behaviour cause the seven to fall at her feet immediately, but Potts holds out for a while before succumbing to the thrill of being kissed. Soon Sugarpuss's criminal associates want her back, and brain has to battle against brawn—with no help from magic—before Potts and Sugarpuss can be happy together. *Ball of Fire* is basically a romantic comedy; it does not depend upon 'Snow White', but it gets some fun out of the intermittent parallels.

A decade later *Jack and the Beanstalk* (USA, 1952) was a stopover for fast-moving comic duo Abbott and Costello during a series of films in which they toured the universe—Mars, Hollywood, the Foreign Legion—and met a host of famous people— Jekyll and Hyde, Frankenstein, the Invisible Man. In the black-and-white opening sequence Jack and his friend Dinkelpuss work as babysitters. Reading a bedtime story to his charge, Jack falls asleep and dreams, in colour, that he is in it, and has accepted five beans from the butcher—Dinkelpuss—in exchange for a cow. The beans grow tall overnight, and at the top of the beanstalk Jack finds a hen that lays golden eggs. This factor lures the avaricious Dinkelpuss up as well. They rescue the prince and princess and defeat the giant before Jack's moment of glory is shattered by an abrupt black-and-white awakening. The screenplay was customized to suit the two stars' proven abilities, and they gave it their standard treatment—lots of cross-talk and buffoonery—before moving on to Alaska.

Disney/*Grimm came in for attention again when one new star and three old ones needed a framework. *Snow White and the Three Stooges* (USA, 1961) brought Swiss world champion figure-skater Carol Heiss into CinemaScopic contact with Larry Fine, Moe Howard, and Joe de Rita, two of whom had been in films together since the 1930s. Spared by the queen's assassin, Snow White meets three wandering clowns and their young assistant, who turns out to be her childhood betrothed, Prince Charming. The prince rallies the people against the queen and rescues Snow White from the effects of the poisoned apple. Heiss gets opportunities to exhibit her ice-skating prowess, and to sing a little; the Stooges throw pies and engage in their customary violent knockabout routines. Heiss gave up film-making after this, but the Three Stooges went on to meet Hercules.   TAS

Burne-Jones, Edward Coley (1833–98) English painter, illustrator, and designer of stained glass and tapestries. A disciple, with his lifelong friend William *Morris, of Dante Gabriel *Rossetti, Burne-Jones belonged to the second Pre-Raphaelite generation. Idealized figures in dreamlike settings and a strong sense of rhythmic form characterize his work. His numerous subjects from classical myth and medieval literature include the stories of Pygmalion, Perseus, and Cupid and Psyche (*see* APULEIUS), 'St George

and the Dragon', 'Merlin and Vivien', *'Morgan le Fay', 'The Sleep of King Arthur in Avalon', and a magnificent series illustrating the fairy tale 'Briar Rose' (*see* 'SLEEPING BEAUTY').   SR

Burnett, Frances Hodgson (1849–1924) Anglo-American novelist and children's writer. Burnett published a number of undistinguished fairy tales, such as *Queen Silver-Bell* (1906), and these have been deservedly forgotten. An interesting exception is 'Behind the White Brick' (1879), a take-off from the *Alice books, in which Jemima's anger at her aunt is exorcized by her dream-visit to the nest of secret rooms hidden inside the chimney. Burnett uses fairy-tale elements most effectively, however, in her 'realistic' stories—particularly in *A Little Princess* (1905), one of the best *Cinderella stories ever written for children.   SR

Burton, Richard (1821–90) British scholar, translator, and explorer, famous for his ten-volume translation *The Book of the Thousand Nights and a Night: A Plain and Literal Translation of The *Arabian Nights Entertainment* (1885–6). Burton was educated in France and Italy during his youth. By the time he enrolled at Trinity College, Oxford, in 1840, he could speak French and Italian fluently along with the Béarnais and Neapolitan dialects, and he had an excellent command of Greek and Latin. In fact, he had such an extraordinary gift as linguist that he eventually learned 25 other languages and 15 dialects. Expelled from Oxford in 1842, Burton followed in his father's footsteps; he enlisted in the British army and served eight years in India as a subaltern officer. During his time there, he learned Arabic, Hindi, Marathi, Sindhi, Punjabi, Tengu, Pashto, and Miltani; this enabled him to carry out some important intelligence assignments, but he was eventually forced to resign from the army because some of his espionage work became too controversial. After a brief respite (1850–2) with his mother in Boulogne, France, during which time he published four books on India, Burton explored the Nile Valley and was the first Westerner to visit forbidden Muslim cities and shrines. In 1855 he participated in the Crimean War, then explored the Nile again (1857–8), and took a trip to Salt Lake City, Utah (1860). In 1861, after Burton's marriage to Isabel Arundell, he accepted a position as consul in Fernando Po, a Spanish island off the coast of West Africa, until 1864. Thereafter, he was British consul in Santos, Brazil (1864–8), Damascus, Syria (1868–71), and finally Trieste, Italy, until his death in 1890.

Wherever he went, Burton wrote informative anthropological and ethnological studies such as *Sindh, and the Races that Inhabit the Valley of the Indus* (1851) and *Pilgrimage to El-Medinah and Mecca* (1855–6), composed his own poetry such as *The Kasidah* (1880), translated unusual works of erotica such as *Kama Sutra of Vatsyayana* (1883), and significant collections of fairy tales such as Giambattista *Basile's *Pentamerone* (1893). Altogether he published 43 volumes about his explorations and travels, over 100 articles, and 30 volumes of translations.

Burton's *Nights* is generally recognized as one of the finest *unexpurgated* translations of William Hay Macnaghten's 'Calcutta II' edition of 1839–42 (*see* ARABIAN NIGHTS, THE). The fact is, however, that Burton plagiarized a good deal of his translation from John Payne's *The Book of the Thousand Nights and One Night* (1882–4) so that he could publish his book quickly and acquire the private subscribers to Payne's edition. Payne (1842–1916), a remarkable translator and scholar of independent means, had printed only 500 copies of his excellent unexpurgated edition, for he had not expected much of a demand for the expensive nine-volume set. However, there were 1,000 more subscribers who wanted his work, and since he was indifferent with regard to publishing a second edition, Burton received Payne's permission to offer his 'new' translation to these subscribers about a year after Payne's work had appeared. Moreover, Burton profited a great deal from Payne's spadework (apparently with Payne's knowledge). This is not to say that Burton's translation (which has copious anthropological notes

and an important 'Terminal Essay') should not be considered his work. He did most of the translation by himself, and only towards the end of his ten volumes did he apparently plagiarize, probably without even realizing what he was doing. In contrast to Payne, Burton was more meticulous in respecting word order and the exact phrasing of the original; he included the division into nights with the constant intervention of *Scheherazade and was more competent in translating the verse. Moreover, he was more insistent on emphasizing the erotic and bawdy aspects of the *Nights*. As he remarked in his Introduction, his object was 'to show what *The Thousand Nights and a Night* really is. Not, however, for reasons to be more fully stated in the Terminal Essay, by straining *verbum reddere verbo*, but by writing as the Arab would have written in English.' The result was a quaint, if not bizarre and somewhat stilted, English that makes for difficult reading today but remains as a classic of its own kind in the reception of the *Nights* in the Western world.   JZ

Brodie, Fawn M., *The Devil Drives: A Life of Sir Richard Burton* (1967).

Eckley, Grace, 'The Entertaining Nights of Burton, Stead, and Joyce's Earwicker', *Journal of Modern Literature*, 13 (1986).

Ferris, Paul, *Richard Burton* (1981).

McLynn, F. J., *Burton: Snow upon the Desert* (1990).

Rosenthal, Melinda M., 'Burton's Literary Uroburos: The Arabian Nights as Self-Reflexive Narrative', *Pacific Coast Philology*, 25 (1990).

Burton, Tim (1958–) American filmmaker, director, and artist, who studied animation at California Institute of the Arts and began his career as an animator in the Disney Studios. His earliest endeavour to create a fairy-tale cartoon was his short, *Hansel and Gretel* (1982), which made use of Japanese myth, but it was too risqué for the Disney Studios and has never been re-issued. Burton also directed *Aladdin and his Wonderful Lamp* (1982) for Shelly *Duvall's Faerie Tale Theatre and by using Hollywood stars transformed the tale into an amusing comedy. It was not until Burton became an independent filmmaker that he began creating highly unconventional films that explored the dark and grim aspects of fairy tales. In films such as *Edward Scissorhands* (1990), *Sleepy Hollow* (1999), and *Corpse Bride* (2005). Burton displayed his fondness for the Gothic arts and also his partiality for outsiders who triumph over the dark powers that haunt them and the people around them. The eccentric nature of his dark humour reveals the banality of people caught in the daily conventions of life. In the delightfully bizarre *Alice in Wonderland* (2010), a mixture of computer animation and live action, his Alice rejects conventionality and runs away from pep talks by people who want to encourage her to marry a dim-witted, pretentious aristocrat. Burton's Alice is nineteen years old and fortunately has a mind of her own as well as a great imagination, which she has clearly inherited from her father. The film begins with a six-year-old Alice talking to her merchant father, who has wild dreams of opening trade routes to the Pacific. She clearly admires him and needs his love and affection before going to bed because she has been troubled by nightmares about a weird kingdom. Her father tucks her in bed and jokingly tells her that she's bonkers and all the best people are bonkers. Unfortunately, Alice's father dies before she reaches puberty, and it is because her mother has fallen on hard times that she has arranged a marriage for Alice against the girl's will. She is obviously more interested in money than Alice's welfare. But since Alice is indeed a bit bonkers in the positive sense of the word, she runs off into the nearby forest just as her unctuous suitor is officially proposing to her at a posh garden party. As usual, she falls down a rabbit hole, but this time she arrives in 'queerland', not wonderland. Indeed, Burton queers the narrative of Alice in Wonderland by crossing genders, mixing sexual identity, and creating all sorts of bizarre animated characters who remind us that there is no such thing as normal, whether in reality or in our imaginations. Burton's film is lavish—the images of the castles and the forests are gorgeous and stunning. The

plants and characters are bombastic and exotic, and all the characters act with exaggerated mannerist gestures and hyperbole. Interestingly, Alice is never overwhelmed by anyone or anything because she has been there before. Her trip down the rabbit hole only reinforces her independent spirit, which is celebrated in a unique fairy-tale film.   JZ

Kevorkian, Martin, '"You Must Never Move the Body!" Burying Irving's Text in *Sleepy Hollow*'. *Literature/Film Quarterly* (2003).

McMahan, Alison, *The Films of Tim Burton: Animating Live Action in Contemporary Hollywood* (2005).

Ray, Brian, 'Tim Burton and the Idea of Fairy Tales', in Pauline Greenhill and Sidney Eve Matrix (eds.), *Fairy Tale Films: Visions of Ambiguity* (2010).

Busch, Wilhelm (1832–1908) German writer, painter, and poet, who is internationally famous for his *Max and Moritz* (1865) illustrated stories in verse that served as a model for the American comic strip 'The Katzenjammer Kids', which originated in 1897. Busch created other books for children that depicted their comic antics and can be considered forerunners to the 20th-century cartoon. Early in his career, from 1859 to 1871, he participated in creating many of the humorous broadsheets for the *Münchner Bilderbogen*. One of his earliest, not included in the *Münchner Bilderbogen*, was a farcical portrayal of *'Hansel and Gretel', printed in *Bilderpossen* (*Farcical Pictures*, 1864). Given his sceptical if not pessimistic outlook on life, in part due to the influence of Schopenhauer, Busch was not drawn to the optimistic fairy tale, unless he could sarcastically criticize it and re-design it to make some biting social commentary. His best work along these lines was his illustrated book *Sechs Geschichten für Neffen und Nichten* (*Six Stories for Nephews and Nieces*, 1881). These hilarious tales, told in verse, with simple coloured ink drawings, turn the traditional tales upside down. An example is 'Die beiden Schwestern' ('The Two Sisters'), which is a parody of both 'The *Frog King' and 'Mother *Holle' in which Busch portrays the sisters the industrious Kätchen and the vain Adelheid. One day Kätchen goes into the woods and meets a frog who cries out, 'Pity me and give me a kiss.' In fact, she gives him three kisses, and he turns into a prince, rewarding her with wealth and marriage. Then Adelheid goes dressed to kill into the woods and meets a prince playing a harp next to a pond. When he asks for a kiss, she consents, but he turns into a water imp and drags her into the pond, where she must spend her life serving him. The tongue-in-cheek ending is typical of most Busch stories that, similar to Heinrich *Hoffmann's *Struwwelpeter*, take delight in provocative cruel punishments.   JZ

Bohne, F., *Wilhelm Busch* (1958).

Ehrlich, J., *Wilhelm Busch, der Pessimist* (1962).

Butcher, Jim (1971–) American fantasy writer. His ongoing contemporary fantasy series *The Dresden Files* opened with *Storm Front* (2000). The novels feature Chicago wizard/private investigator Harry Dresden's struggle to contain his powers while manifesting compassion and good deeds. Generically complex, with real-life setting and supernatural characters such as fairies, demons, and vampires, these works intersect with detective fiction, comedy, and horror. *Dresden's* paratexts include audiobooks, a role-playing game, and a television series (2006–7). Butcher's six-book high-fantasy series *Codex Alera* (2004–9) is set in the imaginary world of Carna. His newest work, the steampunk *The Cinder Spires* trilogy, begins with *The Aeronaut's Windlass* (2014).   PG

Buzzati, Dino (1906–72) Italian writer, playwright, poet, painter, and journalist. Symbolic surrealism and the fantastic are the distinctive traits of Buzzati's writing, from his first work *Bernabò delle montagne* (*Bernabo of the Mountains*, 1933), to his best novel *Il deserto dei tartari* (*The Tartar Steppe*, 1990), to his countless amusing and moving tales which reveal the often absurd or banal sources of anguish, fear, doubt, and wickedness. His most popular works include *Il colombre* (1966), *Le notti difficili* (*Restless Nights: Selected Stories of Dino Buzzati*,

1971), and *I dispiaceri del re* (*The King's Regrets*, 1982). *La famosa invasione degli orsi in Sicilia* (*The Bears' Famous Invasion of Sicily*, 1945) is a tale for young readers.
MNP

Byatt, A. S. (Antonia Susan Byatt, 1936–) English novelist and critic. Before leaving academia in 1983 to concentrate full-time on writing, she had published book-length studies of Iris Murdoch—a significant influence on her work—and Wordsworth and Coleridge. Byatt's fiction combines a detailed evocation of time and place, including cultural and intellectual milieu, with an almost 19th-century concern for character and morality. It can also be densely allusive, exploring the interaction between art and life, and it is as part of this exploration that the fairy tale has come to figure in her work.

The Booker Prize-winning *Possession: A Romance* (1990), an erudite and complex novel interweaving Victorian lives with late 20th-century biographical and academic investigations into the written evidence of these lives, contains several interpolated fairy tales. Along with an epic poem concerning the Fairy *Mélusine, these include 'The Glass Coffin' (a variation on *'Sleeping Beauty'), and a bleak and elliptical oral narrative told by a Breton servant. Both of these tales were subsequently reprinted as the first two items in a collection of five fairy stories by Byatt, *The Djinn in the Nightingale's Eye* (1995). Her awareness of generic conventions, together with her adoption of a characteristically enriched fairy-tale idiom, is evident in 'The Story of the Eldest Princess', which tells of a young heroine whose perspicacity enables her to succeed against the grain of fairy-tale expectation. The title story of the collection is a novella set in 1991, involving the punningly named Gillian Perholt, a 55-year-old narratologist who comes face-to-face with a Djinn while attending a conference in Ankara devoted to 'Stories of Women's Lives'. Drawing heavily on *The *Arabian Nights*, Byatt spins a narrative web around the themes of plotting, powerlessness, and fate in the folk tale, and the meeting of cultures via storytelling.

Its length and interweaving of motifs suggests parallels with the extended salon fairy tales of Mme d'*Aulnoy and Mme *Leprince de Beaumont; indeed, Byatt herself translated Mme d'Aulnoy's 'Le Serpentin vert' ('The Great Green Worm') for Marina *Warner's collection of *Wonder Tales* (1994).

Employing the same technique as *Possession*—allowing narrator and tale to resonate within the context of the work as a whole—Byatt's novella 'Morpho Eugenia' (1992) includes the embedded fairy tale 'Things Are Not What They Seem'. Based around the themes of language and scientific classification, Byatt again explores the place of the fairy tale in the intellectual climate of the second half of the 19th century. Byatt often sets narrative frames in which she incorporates shorter fairy tales. For instance, in her most recent remarkable novel, *The Children's Book* (2008), shortlisted for the Booker Prize, she covers the period from 1890 through the First World War. Her focus is on Olive Wellwood, a successful writer of fairy tales, woven throughout the broad historical novel, and Byatt's fairy tales reflect the hopes and anxieties of the pre-First World War period in England. Olive is loosely based on Edith *Nesbit, known for her fantasy novels and fairy tales and her involvement in the Fabian movement. Byatt succeeds in providing a grand historical portrait of the times in which fairy tales were a serious part of Victorian culture. SB

Ashworth, Ann, 'Fairy Tales in A. S. Byatt's *Possession*', *Journal of Evolutionary Psychology*, 15 (1994).

Franken, Christien, *A. S. Byatt: Art, Authorship, Creativity* (2001).

Henscher, Philip, 'A. S. Byatt, The Art of Fiction No. 168', *Paris Review* (2001).

Sanchez, Victoria, 'A. S. Byatt's *Possession*: A Fairytale Romance', *Southern Folklore*, 52 (1995).

Todd, Richard, *A. S. Byatt* (1997).

Caballero, Fernán *See* BÖHL DE FABER, CECILIA.

Cabinet des fées, Le *See* MAYER, CHARLES-JOSEPH.

Cadnum, Michael (1949–) American poet and novelist who has written more than thirty books and is renowned for both his adult suspense fiction and young-adult fiction, much of which is based on myths, legends, and historical figures. The range of Cadnum's work—from Robin Hood to werewolves to Greek Gods—is best exemplified in his short fiction collection *Can't Catch Me and Other Twice-Told Tales* (2006). The collection includes folktales and fairy tales like 'The Gingerbread Man,' 'Goldilocks', *'Jack and the Beanstalk', *'Cinderella', 'The Fisherman's Wife', as well as fables about Greek gods and goddesses and 'Humpty Dumpty'. KMJ

Caldecott, Randolph (1846–86) English children's book illustrator whose drawings and illustrations are considered among the best of 19th-century art for children in England. They had a tremendous influence on contemporary artists and crucially formed the work of Walter *Crane and Kate *Greenaway. Idyllic representations of nature and rural life, his work includes many single-sheet illustrations of nursery rhymes such as 'Hey diddle diddle', 'Bye baby bunting', 'The fox jumps over the parson's gate', and 'A frog he would a-wooing go', as well as *Babes in the Wood* (1879), *Sing a Song for Sixpence* (1880), and *Aesop's Fables* (1883). KS

Calvino, Italo (1923–85) Italian writer, critic, and editor. He was born in Cuba to Italian parents, but grew up in San Remo, on the Ligurian Riviera. He was a partisan during the Second World War, and after the war embarked on his career as a writer, in which he was initially influenced by the neo-realism movement, and an editor, assuming an important role in the growth of the Turin press Einaudi, which also published his works. From 1964 to 1980 he lived in Paris.

Calvino's fame as one of the most significant literary figures of the 20th century rests primarily on his novels and short stories. He has been called a 'writer's writer' for his consummate ability to combine spectacular storytelling with self-conscious reflection on the nature of the combinatorial mechanics of narration itself. In many of his works, especially the early ones, fabulous and realistic elements are woven into an original synthesis which often adopts the familiar folkloric progression of initiation and personal transformation through the successful completion of trials. Even the most fantastic scenarios, however, seem to be a way for Calvino to offer alternative interpretations of, and give new meaning to, everyday reality. In his first novel, *Il sentiero dei nidi di ragno* (*The Path of the Nest of Spiders*, 1947), the Italian resistance is told as through the eyes of a young boy; the three works of the trilogy *I nostri antenati* (*Our Forefathers*, 1960), which include the previously published *Il visconte dimezzato* (*The Cloven Viscount*, 1952), *Il barone rampante* (*The Baron in the Trees*, 1957), and *Il cavaliere inesistente* (*The Nonexistent Knight*, 1959), are allegorical fables on modern life populated by fantastic characters; and the stories of *Marcovaldo ovvero le stagioni in città* (*Marcovaldo, or The Seasons in the City*, 1963) feature the bewildered city-dweller Marcovaldo and his family, whose encounters with urban life have the flavour of fairy tales gone awry.

In 1954 Einaudi asked Calvino to edit a collection of folk tales which could represent Italy's entire traditional heritage. Convinced that Italy lacked a 'master collection' along the lines of the *Grimms'* (to whose endeavour he compares his own), he published *Fiabe italiane* (*Italian Folktales*) two years later. The 200 tales of the collection were chosen with the criteria of offering every major tale type, of which *Folktales* includes about 50, often in multiple versions, and of representing the 20 regions of Italy. Fairy tales predominate, but there are also religious and local legends, novellas, animal fables, and anecdotes. Calvino selected his materials from 19th-century folkloric collections such as Giuseppe *Pitrè's Fiabe, novelle e racconti popolari siciliani* (*Fairy Tales, Novellas, and Popular Tales of Sicily*, 1875) and Gherardo Nerucci's *Sessanta novelle popolari montalesi* (*Sixty Popular Tales from Montale*, 1880), and by 'touching up', imposing 'stylistic unity', and often translating from Italian dialects created his own versions of the tales. This procedure has been likened to the Grimms', but Calvino is entirely self-conscious about his 'half-way scientific' method, discussing at length his techniques of recasting the tales and integrating variants so as to produce the 'most unusual, beautiful, and original texts' and often specifying his changes in the extensive notes that accompany the tales. In the words of a Tuscan proverb that he cites, 'The tale is not beautiful if nothing is added to it.'

Although in his introduction to *Folktales* Calvino claims he possesses neither the folklorist's expertise nor an 'enthusiasm for anything spontaneous and primitive', he motivates his endeavour by maintaining that folk tales are the thematic prototype of all stories, just as he finds an essential structural paradigm for all literature in the multiple narrative potentialities that folk tales offer, with their 'infinite variety and infinite repetition'. The Italian corpus that Calvino discovers is, in his eyes, comparable in richness and variety to the great Northern European collections; at the same time, it possesses a distinctly personal and 'unparalleled grace, wit, and unity of design'. He also identifies a series of more specific characteristics of the Italian tales, though critics have pointed out that they may be in part Calvino's own invention: a sense of beauty and an attraction to sensuality, an eschewal of cruelty in favour of harmony and the 'healing solution', 'a continuous quiver of love' that runs through many tales, a 'tendency to dwell on the wondrous', and a dynamic tension between the fantastic and the realistic.

Calvino offers suggestive reflections on the vital importance of his material. 'Folktales are real', he tells us, since they encompass all of human experience in the form of a 'catalogue of the potential destinies of men and women' in which we find 'the arbitrary division of humans, albeit in essence equal, into kings and poor people; the persecution of the innocent and their subsequent vindication... love unrecognized when first encountered and then no sooner experienced than lost; the common fate of subjection to spells, or having one's existence predetermined by complex and unknown forces'. From folk tales we learn, ultimately, that 'we can liberate ourselves only if we liberate other people'; that 'there must be fidelity to a goal and purity of heart, values fundamental to salvation and triumph'; that 'there must also be beauty, a sign of grace that can be masked by the humble, ugly guise of a frog'; and that 'above all, there must be present the infinite possibilities of mutation, the unifying element in everything: men, beasts, plants, things.' That a postmodern man of letters discovered a key for interpreting the world in one of the most archaic narrative genres is not the least of the wondrous surprises that Calvino's decades-long engagement with folk tales offers us. Perhaps it is only logical that in his last work, *Six Memos for the Next Millennium* (1988), a series of lectures that were to be delivered at Harvard University, the six qualities that are for Calvino the essence of literature—lightness, quickness, exactitude, visibility, multiplicity, and consistency—are all defining characteristics of the folk tale as well. NC

Adler, Sara Maria, *Calvino: The Writer as Fablemaker* (1979).

Bacchilega, Cristina, 'Calvino's Journey: Modern Transformations of Folktale, Story, and Myth', *Journal of Folklore Research*, 26 (1989).

Beckwith, Marc, 'Italo Calvino and the Nature of Italian Folktales', *Italica*, 64 (1987).

Bronzini, Giovanni Battista, 'From the Grimms to Calvino: Folk Tales in the Year Two Thousand', in Lutz Röhrich and Sabine Wienker-Piepho (eds.), *Storytelling in Contemporary Societies* (1990).

Cannon Movietales A series of feature-length films based on classic fairy tales. Produced by Menahem Golan and Yoram Globus in 1987–8, the series includes *Beauty and the Beast*, *The Emperor's New Clothes*, *The *Frog Prince*, **Hansel and Gretel*, **Puss-in-Boots*, *Red Riding Hood*, **Rumpelstiltskin*, **Sleeping Beauty*, and **Snow White*. Apparently seeking to duplicate the popular success of Shelley *Duvall's productions in *Faerie Tale Theatre* (1982–5), these live-action film adaptations are the work of various screenwriters and directors and rely on recognizable stars such as Sid Caesar, Rebecca DeMornay, Morgan Fairchild, Helen Hunt, Amy Irving, Cloris Leachman, Craig T. Nelson, and Diana Rigg. Facing the challenge of turning brief tales into feature-length movies, the screenplays modify and elaborate on the characters and plots of the tales on which they are based. The alterations, however, do not as a rule result in significant fairy-tale adaptations or innovative film-making. Heavily influenced by the Walt *Disney model of the fairy-tale film, the Cannon Movietales are produced as musicals and frequently foreground a love story.

Rumpelstiltskin, written and directed by David Irving, is a full-fledged musical that involves a love story not present in the *Grimms' tale. Despite attempts to portray the miller's daughter as a woman of some independence, the love story demands that the film make her increasingly dependent on the prince, whose greedy, materialistic father wishes to exploit her alleged talent at spinning straw into gold. *Red Riding Hood*, written by Carole Lucia Satrina and directed

by Adam Brooks, also manages to incorporate a love story. In this musical adaptation, the sexual implications involved in the wolf's desire for Red Riding Hood are displaced onto the adult level. The plot revolves around the desire of Red Riding Hood's paternal uncle and lord of the castle—her father's evil twin—to possess his brother's beautiful wife. The resolution comes when the father returns, leads a revolt to overthrow his brother, and reclaims his family. The Disney influence is clearly signalled in *Sleeping Beauty*, where the song 'Once upon a Dream' is played as the fairies bestow their gifts.

Generally considered by reviewers to be unimaginative and dull, the Cannon Movietales did not achieve the critical success or wide popularity of Duvall's *Faerie Tale Theatre*. After their unremarkable release they were targeted for the children's home video market.   DH

Haase, Donald, 'Gold into Straw: Fairy Tale Movies for Children and the Culture Industry', *The Lion and the Unicorn*, 12.2 (December 1988).

Čapek, Karel (1890–1938) Czech writer, most famous for his play *R.U.R.* (1920), in which the word 'robot' was coined, and the dystopian novel *Salamander War* (1935). His collection *Nine Fairy Tales* (1931) contains humorous and satirical fairy tales based on traditional patterns, but taking place in everyday surroundings, mostly small Czech villages. The *mundus inversus* device is the most prominent feature of these fairy tales; for instance, a robber is nice and kind, but turns into a real villain when he becomes a state tax collector ('A Robber Tale'); a beggar appears to be the most honest person in the world ('A Beggar Tale'). Fairy-tale characters behave like ordinary people: a water spirit gets rheumatic fever, a wizard chokes on a plum stone and needs a doctor ('The Great Doctor Tale'); while ordinary people, like a woodcutter or a postmaster, become heroes. Even when kings and princesses are portrayed, they have more human than traditional fairy-tale traits ('The Great Cat Tale'). Čapek's intention with his fairy tales was mostly educational, and he viewed language as the most important component in them. Therefore, his fairy tales abound in puns, enumerations, and other creative linguistic play. Following *Nine Fairy Tales*, he wrote *Dashenka: A Puppy's Life* (1932), a realistic animal story which also contains a number of short fairy tales featuring dogs.   MN

Bradbrook, Bohuslava, *Karel Čapek: In Pursuit of Truth, Tolerance, and Trust* (1998).

Makin, Michael, and Toman, Jindřich (eds.), *On Karel Čapek: A Michigan Slavic Colloquium* (1992).

Capuana, Luigi (1839–1915) Italian writer, dramatist, and journalist. He was born to a wealthy bourgeois family outside of Catania, in Sicily, and as a young man abandoned his law studies to dedicate himself to writing and journalism. He is known, together with Giovanni Verga, as one of the foremost exponents of the *verismo* literary movement. Among his many novels are *Giacinta* (1879), *Profumo* (*Perfume*, 1890), and his most famous work, *Il marchese di Roccaverdina* (*The Marquis of Roccaverdina*, 1901); he also published 19 volumes of short prose. Following Verga's example, Capuana recognized the artistic and expressive value of folkloric material, and often incorporated it into his work; indeed, the 'impersonal' style advocated by *verismo* found a natural correlate in folk and fairy tales.

Capuana also contributed significantly to the canon of children's literature that was being created during the late 19th century in Italy by Carlo *Collodi and others. His children's works include the novels *Scurpiddo* (1898), a realistic tale of an orphan, *Re Bracalone* (*King Bracalone*, 1905), an extended fairy tale, and *Cardello* (1907), the story of a marionette theatre; numerous volumes of fairy tales, among which *C'era una volta* (*Once Upon a Time*, 1882), *Il regno delle fate* (*The Kingdom of Fairies*, 1883), *La reginotta* (*The Princess*, 1883), *Il Racconta-fiabe* (*The Fairy Tale-Teller*, 1894), *Chi vuol fiabe, chi vuole?* (*Who Wants Fairy Tales, Who Wants Them?*, 1908), and *Le ultime fiabe* (*The Last Fairy Tales*, 1919); as well as

the theatrical fairy tales *Rospus* (*Toad*, 1887), *Spera di sole: Commedia per burattini* (*Sunbeam: A Comedy for Marionettes*, 1898), and *Milda* (1913). He was also editor of several children's journals, such as *Cenerentola*.

A number of critics maintain that Capuana's best prose is to be found in his fairy tales. Capuana used his familiarity with Sicilian folklore and with the work of folklorists such as Giuseppe *Pitrè to create tales that often evoked, in tone and in structure, the formulaic oral tales of tradition. But it is his elaboration of these materials through the use of irony, humour, and whimsical fantasy that gives his tales their true flavour, and that makes for the creation of a fairy-tale world that is entirely and originally his own. This world is best represented in *Once Upon a Time*, Capuana's most famous collection of fairy tales, which in its enlarged version of 1889 contained 19 tales: 'Spera di sole' ('Sunbeam'), 'Le arance d'oro' ('The Golden Oranges'), 'Ranocchino' ('Little Froggy'), 'Senza-orecchie' ('No-Ears'), Il lupo mannaro' ('The Werewolf'), 'Cecina' ('Little Chick-Pea'), 'L'albero che parla' ('The Talking Tree'), 'I tre anelli' ('The Three Rings'), 'La vecchina' ('The Little Old Woman'), 'La fontana della bellezza' ('The Fountain of Beauty'), 'Il cavallo di bronzo' ('The Bronze Horse'), 'L'uovo nero' ('The Black Egg'), 'La figlia del Re' ('The King's Daughter'), 'Serpentina' ('Little Snake-Girl'), 'Il soldo bucato' ('The Coin with a Hole in It'), 'Tì, tìriti, tì', 'Testa di rospo' ('Toad-Head'), 'Topolino' ('Little Mousy'), and 'Il racconta-fiabe' ('The Fairy Tale-Teller'). In these tales we find the typical elements of princes and princesses engaged in challenging adventures and battles with fierce antagonists, enchanted objects and magic formulas that save the day, fantastic creatures like flying horses and steel giants, and above all marvellous metamorphoses. The bipolar oppositions characteristic of the fairy tale are evident in Capuana's tales, where kings and queens rule tyrannically, and the ruled—artisans, farmers, beggars, and other members of the lower classes—are consumed by their primary needs of food, shelter, and good health. But the tales also abound in more realistic details. Sicilian landscapes and domestic scenes are lovingly depicted, and even the most fantastic characters have surprisingly earthy characteristics. In particular, magic helpers tend to be of humble and familiar appearance, seeming more like benevolent grandparents than fairies and wizards, and kings and queens are depicted in their everyday routines. Capuana's satirical humour is often directed at, if not royal figures themselves, the courtiers and ministers that attend to their needs, and in the triumph of the simple virtues of perseverance, goodness of heart, and humility that his lower-class heroes possess, we may glimpse his own allegiances. The later collections, such as *Who Wants Fairy Tales, Who Wants Them?*, are increasingly coloured by an idealistic optimism, offering the explicit message that kindness, hard work, and innocence will ultimately triumph over evil.

Capuana's most poignant reflection on fairy tales is perhaps to be found in 'The Fairy Tale-Teller', the final tale of *Once Upon a Time*. In this tale, a storyteller who is tired of the same old *Cinderellas and *Sleeping Beauties wanders into a forest in search of new material, where he meets some fairies who direct him to the wizard Tre-pi (a transparent reference to the folklorist Pitrè). But Tre-pi, although he has drawers full of fairy tales, wants to keep them all for himself, and tells the storyteller to consult an old fairy named Fairy Fantasy. She in turn gives him a number of objects (a golden orange, a black egg, and other items that are the subjects of Capuana's own tales), and from then on whenever he opens his mouth new tales magically come out. Soon, however, the children with whom he shares his tales tire of them, too, and he goes back to Tre-pi and offers to contribute them to his collection. But as the storyteller is handing them over, he discovers that he is holding a 'handful of flies'. The storyteller loses interest in his art, concluding that 'there are no more new fairy tales; we've lost the seed'. This tale neatly illuminates the nature of the polemic between Capuana and rigorous folklorists like Pitrè, who were intent on storing up traditional tales for posterity. Even more, it is a tribute to the powers of the human imagination to create new tales, guided by 'Fairy Fantasy'. Only its pessimistic ending does not ring true, for Capuana's tales are as delightful today as they were a hundred years ago, and we would be hard pressed to agree with his storyteller that since then the fairy-tale tradition has borne no new fruit.   NC

Davies, Judith, *The Realism of Luigi Capuana: Theory and Practice in the Development of Late Nineteenth-Century Italian Narrative* (1979).

Marchese, Giuseppe, *Capuana poeta della vita* (1964).

Miele, Gina, 'Luigi Capuana: Unlikely Spinner of Fairy Tales?', *Marvels & Tales* (2009).

Robuschi, Giuseppina, *Luigi Capuana, scrittore per l'infanzia* (1969).

Zangara, Mario, *Luigi Capuana* (1964).

Zipes, Jack, 'Luigi Capuana's Search for the New Fairy Tale', *Marvels & Tales* (2009).

Card, Orson Scott (1951–) American author, essayist, and columnist, who is primarily known as a science fiction writer. However, in two of his novels, *Enchantment* (1999) and *Magic Street* (2005), he incorporates numerous folkloristic motifs. *Enchantment* is adapted from an old Russian version of *'Sleeping Beauty' and other European folk tales. *Magic Street* makes full use of trickster tales in a contemporary fantasy novel about the exploits of a con man in an upscale community of Los Angeles.   JZ

Carle, Eric (1929–) American author, reteller, illustrator, and designer of children's picture books. Because his parents were German and longed for their homeland, when he was six Carle returned with them in 1935 to live in Stuttgart; he eagerly returned to New York in 1952. His Germanic education was void of emotion and, as a result, he consciously compensated by incorporating it in his book illustration. Carle's art is distinctive and easily recognizable, particularly for its artistic innovations, such as collage, die-cut pages, movable parts, cut-out shapes and accordion-folded friezes that give his texts a playful quality and toy appeal. Sales for his most acclaimed text,

The Very Hungry Caterpillar (1969), exceeded 12 million copies and the text was translated into more than 25 languages. It is a multi-laden concept book, humorously telling the metamorphosis of a caterpillar as it literally eats its way through the week to emerge after sleep as a beautiful butterfly. As a reteller of tales, Carle diverged from a conventional narrative tradition by simplifying and modernizing them, as in his delightful *Walter the Baker* (1972), about a baker who bakes the best pretzel in the world for a king. While some critics have objected to the cutting and altering of passages, others have praised his adaptations, saying that his brevity and clarity were virtues, making the stories more accessible to young readers. Their allure overall, however, rests with the full-colour, detailed illustrations, as can be seen in *Eric Carle's Storybook: Seven Tales by the Brothers Grimm* (1976), *Seven Stories by Hans Christian Andersen* (1978), *The Foolish Tortoise* (1985), *The Greedy Python* (1985), and *Eric Carle's Treasury of Classic Stories for Children* (1988).   SS

Carle, Eric, *The Art of Eric Carle* (1996).

Carmody, Isobelle (1958–) Award-winning Australian fantasy, science fiction, children's literature, and young-adult literature writer. She began the first novel of her *Obernewtyn Chronicles* in high school; it ends with *The Red Queen* (2014). Other series include *Legendsong Saga*, *Gateway Trilogy*, *The Legend of Little Fur*, and *The Kingdom of the Lost*, as well as many individual novels, collections, and short stories. Her post-apocalyptic worlds and mythic themes concern confrontation between good and evil, and deal with social and moral issues. Her fan site Obernewtyn.net includes message, writing, gallery, and theory boards encouraging reader participation.   PG

Carroll, Jonathan (1949–) American-born writer who has long resided in Vienna, the author of an interconnected cycle of magical contemporary novels which defy easy categorization—published alternately as fantasy, horror, and mainstream fiction. Although much of Carroll's work makes use of fantasy motifs common to folk tales and myth (shamanism, spirit hauntings, journeys into Otherworlds), his novel *Sleeping in Flame* (1988) is of particular interest to fairy tale aficionados: a dark, fascinating reworking of **'Rumpelstiltskin'* set in modern-day Vienna. Other magical novels by Carroll include *The Land of Laughs* (1980), *Bones of the Moon* (1987), and *From the Teeth of Angels* (1994).   TW

Carroll, Lewis (pseudonym of **Charles Lutwidge Dodgson**, 1832–98) Author of the *Alice* books. An enthusiastic photographer, his first encounters with the young Liddells, children of the dean of Christ Church, the Oxford college where Dodgson taught mathematics, were in 1856 when he went to photograph Christ Church cathedral from the deanery garden. The first Alice story was extemporized for the three eldest daughters, Lorina, Alice, and Edith, on a summer picnic in 1862. The written version that the 10-year-old Alice begged for did not materialize until Christmas 1864, when Dodgson presented her with the neatly handwritten text of *Alice's Adventures under Ground*, which he had illustrated himself. Encouraged by such friends as George *MacDonald, Dodgson decided to flesh out the story for publication. He expanded it to more than twice its original length, enhancing the comedy, adding some of his most original characters like the Duchess and the Cheshire Cat, and the entire episode of the Mad Tea-Party. Illustrated by John *Tenniel, it was published for Christmas 1865 with the new title **Alice's Adventures in Wonderland*.

The fantasy derives not from traditional fairy stories but from the violence and anarchy of English nursery rhymes—that unique corpus of verse fragments never primarily intended for children. He added sharply delineated comic characters, many of them caricatures of people known to the Liddell children, and, being a mathematician, he made much of pursuing concepts to their logical and often ludicrous ends. It is the first literary fairy tale for children with no moral purpose whatever. Alice moves in a dreamworld, remote from ordinary laws and

Carroll, Lewis Bruno seats himself on a dead mouse and prepares to sing. One of Harry *Furniss's whimsical illustrations for Carroll's *Sylvie and Bruno* (1889).

principles. At first bewildered by her size-changes, intimidated by the grotesque and often ill-mannered beings that she encounters—types of the adult world—she gradually gains confidence to argue with them, and finally triumphantly dismisses them: 'Who cares for you . . . You're nothing but a pack of cards!' she says contemptuously to the formidable Queen of Hearts who has ordered her to hold her tongue, indeed has threatened to have her beheaded.

Dodgson was completely unconscious of the nihilistic character of Wonderland. This can be seen from the way he reduced it in *The Nursery 'Alice'* (1889) to a bland mush, excluding all the humour and wordplay and adding moral comment. Indeed he was always to think of the *Alice* books as sedate and soothing, saying to a correspondent that he hoped they had given 'real and innocent pleasure . . . to sick and suffering children'. He was also unaware of the implication of his parodies of pious Sunday verse by such writers as Southey and Isaac Watts, though

in ordinary life he was morbidly scrupulous, with an exaggerated dread of irreverence.

Through the Looking-Glass and What Alice Found There appeared as a Christmas book for 1871, though with the date 1872. By this stage Dodgson was no longer friendly with the Liddells, and Alice Liddell herself was 20; Looking-Glass Alice tells Humpty-Dumpty that she is 'seven years and six months'. He retorts that it is an uncomfortable sort of age; his dispassionate view being that it would be better to 'leave off at seven'—which perhaps Dodgson wistfully regarded as the perfect age in Alice Liddell. Except in the opening poem and in the epilogue his feeling for her was not shown in *Wonderland*, but it creeps into *Looking-Glass*. The White Knight with his bizarre inventions is often taken to be a self-portrait, and there is a yearning note in the description of his parting with Alice.

Though still taking place in a dream, *Looking-Glass*, with its account of Alice's chessboard progress to queenhood, is more tightly organized than its predecessor. Many of the characters are from nursery rhymes, but the humour has a ruthless, nightmare quality, especially in the Jabberwock poem (enhanced by a powerful Tenniel illustration originally intended as a frontispiece). The Walrus and the Carpenter eat the trusting Oysters; Alice is expected to carve the leg of mutton to whom she has just been introduced. *The Hunting of the Snark* (1876), Dodgson's only other extended work of nonsense, a mock-heroic poem which he called 'an agony in eight fits' is the most nihilistic of all his works. It ends with the Baker's triumphant shout as he finds the Snark, but then

> In the midst of the word he was trying to say,
>   In the midst of his laughter and glee,
> He had softly and suddenly vanished away—
>   For the Snark was a Boojum, you see.

Much has been made of the possible symbolism of Dodgson's nonsense; there have been many attempts to discover hidden meanings and lurking cryptograms. There have also been many imitations; once the way had been shown, dreams seemed a useful device to avoid constructing a plot. Among the more popular were George Edward Farrow's *The WallyPug of Why* (1895) and its sequels, and Eleanor Gates's *The Poor Little Rich Girl* (1912), where the logic of a child's dreamworld shows up the illogicality of adults.

Dodgson wrote one work of fiction for adults, *Sylvie and Bruno* (1889, with a continuation in 1893); it was illustrated by Harry *Furniss. The nucleus of this was 'Bruno's Revenge', a short story about two fairy children which had appeared in *Aunt Judy's Magazine* in 1867. He embedded it in a rambling novel which he hoped 'would not be out of harmony with the graver cadences of life'. Of it his biographer, Morton Cohen, said: 'as a novel it is trite; as a work of philosophic speculation, hazardous', but that it was the most personally revealing of all Dodgson's works.   GA

Carpenter, Humphrey, 'Alice and the Mockery of God', *Secret Gardens* (1985).
Cohen, Morton N., *Lewis Carroll* (1995).
Goldthwaite, John, 'The Unwriting of Alice in Wonderland', in *The Natural History of Make-Believe* (1996).
Gray, Donald J. (ed.), *Alice in Wonderland*, Norton Critical Edition (2nd edn., 1992).
Jaques, Zoe, and Giddens, Eugene, *Lewis Carroll's Alice in Wonderland and Through the Looking-Glass: A Publishing History* (2013).
Sigler, Carolyn (ed.), *Alternative Alices: Visions and Revisions of Lewis Carroll's Alice Books* (1997).
Susina, Jan, *The Place of Lewis Carroll in Children's Literature* (2011).

Carter, Angela (1940–92) British fiction writer whose most acclaimed work, *The Bloody Chamber and Other Stories* (1979), rewrites classic fairy tales for adults in a woman-centred and erotically charged way.

Born in London, Carter worked as a journalist, studied medieval literature in Bristol, and in her late twenties became an award-winning novelist. After ending her first marriage, she lived in Japan, where her 1960s radicalism became informed by a strong feminist consciousness. Carter also taught in the United States and travelled to Australia, but remained rooted in a south London sensibility fortified by her grandmother's Yorkshire spirit. At the age of 51 and at the height of her creative powers, she died of lung cancer, survived by her second husband and young son. She published four collections of short stories, nine novels (*Shadow Dance* was her first in 1966 and *Wise Children* her last in 1991), and three works of non-fiction (*The Sadeian Woman* in 1979; *Nothing Sacred*, revised in 1992; and *Expletives Deleted* in 1992); she edited two collections of fairy tales and wrote two screenplays, a number of radio plays, and even an opera, *Lulu*, which was produced posthumously; she continued throughout her life to write for *New Society* and other magazines, including *Vogue*, about literature, fashion, recipes, films, and other aspects of everyday culture.

Strongly enmeshed in the English medieval and Gothic narrative traditions, Carter was also affected by experimentation with the visual imagination (from Blake to the surrealist poets and, significantly, fairy-tale and science-fiction films). She explicitly aligned herself with magic realism and post-colonial writers whose concerns necessarily involve transforming both fictional forms and political awareness. Feminist critics have given mixed reviews to her work, but she perceived herself as a socialist feminist and strongly argued for rejecting the identification of women with innocent victims, focusing instead on an effort to transform psychosexual politics by exploring the wide-ranging desires and strategies of women. A provocative, linguistically dazzling, and intellectually daring writer, she gained extraordinary fame after her death (even in the United Kingdom where the literary establishment had acknowledged her bravura but not warmed to her unsettling tricks) and her magic has been celebrated by fellow fiction-makers Margaret *Atwood, Robert *Coover, Salman *Rushdie, and Marina *Warner.

Carter's writing articulates a consistent and yet varied involvement with fairy tales. Her novels include recurring fairy-tale themes or images: the *Sleeping Beauty, especially in *The Infernal Desire Machines of Doctor Hoffman*; the two sisters in *Wise Children*; the damsel in the tower in *Heroes and Villains*; and everywhere it would seem the enchanting powers of the mirror and the large-looming figure of *Bluebeard. Building on the utopian structure and extreme vision of the fairy tale, her novel *The Magic Toyshop* (1967) is an early example of Carter's complex relationship to the fairy tale: Melanie is first lured by the mystifying image of the 'princess-to-be-married'; then, as a powerless orphan, she is oppressed by her Uncle Philip's autocratic and dehumanizing patriarchy; and finally she is transformed by the music-filled and grittily passionate embrace of her acquired Irish family. The end of the novel represents Melanie and her young lover Finn facing, as if in the garden of Eden, a world of possibilities.

But the form of the tale itself paradoxically offers Carter more room for experimenting. Her fairy tales for children, 'Miss Z, the Dark Young Lady' and 'The Donkey Prince' (both published in 1970), and her translation of *The Fairy Tales of Charles Perrault* in 1977 show some of the tongue-in-cheek and re-working-from-the-inside strategies that inform her 1979 collection. *The Bloody Chamber*'s ten stories retell well-known tales like 'Bluebeard' ('The Bloody Chamber'), *'Beauty and the Beast' ('The Courtship of Mr Lyon' and 'The Tiger's Bride' explicitly, but thematically all ten), *'Puss-in-Boots' (her homonymous exuberantly 'naughty' text), *'Snow White' ('The Snow Child'), 'Sleeping Beauty' ('The Lady of the House of Love'), and *'Little Red Riding Hood' ('The Werewolf', 'The Company of Wolves', 'Wolf-Alice'). The fifth story in the collection, 'The Erl-King', eerily explores the connection between romanticism and fairy tale more generally. Adopting a variety of narrative strategies (first-person narration, reflective self-perception of the protagonist, multiple tellings of one story, replotting to change the ending, updating and definitely dating the 'once upon a time' framework), Carter's stories conspire to transform the dreamlike imagery of fairy tales. She illustrates their misogynistic uses and exposes the dangerous appeal of their suggestiveness; and she simultaneously retraces, and gives substance to the courage and multiple desires of her heroines, who struggle in specific cultural and historical contexts. 'The Bloody Chamber', the first story in this collection and acclaimed by most critics as her richest and most provocative story, unflinchingly explores the young bride's collusion with Bluebeard's objectifying plot and also proposes a mother–daughter model of development based on conviction, search for knowledge, and integrity.

Like later tales, such as 'Peter and the Wolf' in *Black Venus* (1985) and 'Ashputtle or The Mother's Ghost' in *American Ghosts and Old World Wonders* (1993), *The Bloody Chamber* re-envisions fairy tales in a proliferation of intertextual possibilities: remembering oral versions that talk back at the authoritative Perrault or Brothers *Grimm texts; juxtaposing the pornographic with the mystic and the Gothic in an ironic mode; destabilizing interpretation by presenting versions that are to be read with and against each other; training readers in 'intersensuality', a curiosity for and awareness of all five senses; reappropriating storytelling, as the imaginative performance of options, for women; engaged in a productive dialogue with critics Jack Zipes and Marina Warner, themselves in turn tellers of the cultural history of the fairy tale.

When Carter revised the 'Little Red Riding Hood' tales into a screenplay for *The Company of Wolves* (directed by Neil *Jordan in 1984), and then the novel *The Magic Toyshop* for the homonymous film (directed by David Wheatley in 1987), she continued to transform fairy-tale images of women, historicize the genre itself, localize its images, and sensitize audiences to the limitations of 'seeing is believing', all the while exuberantly playing up to the visual possibilities of dream and magic tricks allowed by the cinematic apparatus.

The two volumes of fairy tales she edited (*The Virago Book of Fairy Tales* in 1990, retitled *Old Wives' Fairy Tale Book* in the American edition; and *The Second Virago Book of Fairy Tales* or *Strange Things Sometimes Still Happen: Fairy Tales from around the World*, published posthumously in 1993; both illustrated by her artist friend Corinna *Sargood) constituted her final contribution to a women-centred and culturally diversified approach to fairy tales. Defined as 'the perennially refreshed entertainment of the poor', fairy tales are here presented in terms of the 'domestic arts' and are exemplary of women's many different 'strategies' and 'plots', their 'hard work' and resourcefulness, never 'their passive subordination'. As the 'Brave, Bold, and Wilful' meet the 'Sillies' and hear about the 'Good Girls and Where It Gets Them' (these are some of the headings under which Carter groups her tales), today's readers participate in an invigorating women's show of romance, bawdy jokes, defiant curiosity: the mundane and the magic intertwined to a sparkle. CB

Bacchilega, Cristina, *Postmodern Fairy Tales: Gender and Narrative Strategies* (1997).
Bacchilega, Cristina, and Roemer, Danielle (eds.), 'Angela Carter and the Literary Märchen', spec. issue of *Marvels & Tales*, 12.1 (1998).
Dutheil de la Rochère, Martine Hennard, *Reading, Translating, Rewriting: Angela Carter's Translational Poetics* (2013).
Easton, Alison, *Angela Carter* (2000).
Gamble, Sarah, *The Fiction of Angela Carter* (2001).
Grossman, Michele, '"Born to Bleed": Myth, Pornography and Romance in Angela Carter's "The Bloody Chamber"', *Minnesota Review*, 30/31 (1988).
Milne, Andrew, *Angela Carter's* The Bloody Chamber: *A Reader's Guide* (2007).
Sage, Lorna (ed.), *Flesh and the Mirror: Essays on the Art of Angela Carter* (1994).
Sheets, Robin Ann, 'Pornography, Fairy Tales, and Feminism: Angela Carter's "The Bloody Chamber"', *Journal of the History of Sexuality*, 1 (1991).
Topping, Angela, *Focus on* The Bloody Chamber and Other Stories (2009).

cartoons and fairy tales The wish by artists to illustrate the *Kinder- und Hausmärchen* of the Brothers *Grimm has a long tradition, starting with their own brother Ludwig Emil *Grimm and Ludwig *Richter in the 19th century, and the fascination continues today with such well-known artists as Tomi *Ungerer and Maurice *Sendak. But while these illustrators in general recreated the world as it is described in the fairy tales, cartoonists approach specific episodes of the tales quite differently in their humorous or satirical drawings. Beginning in the second half of the 19th century and maintaining considerable popularity to this day, cartoonists have presented telling images which place the perfect world of the actual fairy tales in striking juxtaposition to harsh reality. They ignore the positive resolution of all problems at the end of the traditional tales and instead interpret certain scenes as reflections of a troubled society. The innovative drawings together with the revealing captions add up to meaningful communication in the mass media. These reinterpretations often deal with such problems as greed, insensitivity, deception, cruelty, vanity, selfishness, hate, power, irresponsibility, sexual politics, and sex.

Over the years the *New Yorker* magazine has published dozens of fairy-tale cartoons. One of them can serve as a general statement of some of the grim variations of fairy-tale motifs depicted in them. The cartoonist has simply drawn a car approaching a large road sign with the inscription: 'You are now entering [the town of] Enchantment—"Gateway of Disenchantment".' One can well imagine a somewhat archaic town crier walking through the streets of this town lying ahead calling out the following news stories of the day, as was shown by another cartoon: *'Snow White kidnapped. Prince released from spell. Tailor kills seven. These are the headlines. I'll be back in a moment with the details.' Fairy-tale violence appears to be making the big news, and thus a small boy comments quite critically to his mother reading him Grimms' tales for the umpteenth time: 'Witches poisoning princesses, giants falling off beanstalks, wolves terrorizing pigs . . . and you complain about violence on TV!' And to top things off, yet another *New Yorker* cartoon goes even so far as to accuse the Brothers Grimm of having concocted the tales without any belief in the authenticity of folk traditions: 'All right, Wilhelm, we have the child walking through the woods.' 'Please, Jacob, don't you think we've been using the woods too much?' 'Woods are always good, Wilhelm. Now, who[m] does the child meet?' 'Perhaps a dwarf or two?' 'We did that, Wilhelm.' 'How about a wolf, Jacob?'

The disbelief in fairy-tale existence goes so far as to put the formulaic beginning and end of many tales into question. Thus a schoolchild whispers impatiently to a friend as their teacher prepares to read one of the tales to them: 'If it starts with "Once upon a time" I'm leaving.' And then there is the divorced mother ending her reading of a fairy tale with the statement: 'And they lived happily ever after—she in New York, he in L.A.' The utopian world established at the end of fairy tales is questioned again and again in cartoons, especially as they comment on marriage and sex. The cartoonist Charles Addams drew a picture of a royal couple at a marriage counsellor's admitting, 'We haven't lived happily and contentedly ever after for years.' Another king is more explicit about his marriage problems, asking the counsellor, 'How can we live happily ever after if she refuses to have oral sex?' There is also the caption 'You're not even

trying to live happily ever after!' Considering the psychological meanings of fairy tales, it should not be surprising that such interpersonal interpretations are prevalent in socially aware cartoons.

There is a definite predominance of sexually oriented cartoons in the modern mass media. Some of them in such mainstream magazines as the *New Yorker*, *Better Homes and Gardens*, and *Good Housekeeping* are usually in good taste, but some cartoonists have also published quite crude illustrations in such erotic magazines as *Playboy*, *Penthouse*, and *Hustler*. There is an entire industry of sexually oriented cartoons and comic strips of fairy tales which reaches from the merely suggestive to hard-core pornography. In this regard cartoonists reflect the modern trend of a more outspoken approach to sexuality, where taboos must be broken and where the indirect language and metaphors of the fairy tales must be translated into crude reality.

This is not to say that there are not also many cartoons which react in a charmingly humorous fashion or in satirical ways to the world of fairy tales by placing them in opposition to the social and political life of the day. Such major satirical magazines as *Simplicissimus*, *Kladderadatsch*, *Fliegende Blätter*, *Eulenspiegel* (all from Germany), *Nebelspalter* (Switzerland), *Krokodil* (Russia), *Punch*, and *Mad* frequently contain fairy-tale cartoons or comic strips. Usually they use only about half a dozen of the most popular fairy tales as their basis (for example, 'The *Frog King'*, *'Little Red Riding Hood'*, 'Snow White', *'Cinderella'*, 'Briar Rose', and *'Rapunzel'*; occasionally also Hans Christian *Andersen's* 'The Emperor's New Clothes' and 'The *Princess* and the Pea'), thus assuring meaningful communication. Hans Ritz has put together 100 cartoons and caricatures relating to 'Little Red Riding Hood' alone in his book *Bilder vom Rotkäppchen* (1986), and Lutz Röhrich has done the same for 'The Frog King' in his study *Wage es, den Frosch zu küssen!* (1987). There are also entire books by individual cartoonists dealing with nothing but fairy tales, as for example Heinz Langer's

Grimmige Märchen: Cartoons (1984) and Petra Kaster's *Traumprinzen: Märchen-Cartoons* (1992). The well-known cartoonist Gary Larsen could easily put together a similar book of his many 'Far Side' illustrations, and the same is true for the creators of such long-standing cartoon and comic-strip series as 'The Family Circus', 'Dennis, the Menace', 'The Wizard of Id', 'Peanuts', 'Blondie', 'Short Ribs', and 'Garfield'. There is even a comic strip entitled 'Mother Goose & Grimm' which specializes in basing the individual frames on fairy tales, nursery rhymes, and other verbal folklore genres.

A final stomping ground for fairy tales in the mass media is found in social and political caricatures in which humour and irony are usually replaced by satire, sarcasm, and cynicism. When illustrators such as Olaf *Gulbransson, Horst Haitzinger, Tony Auth, and Patrick Oliphant add faces and shapes of known politicians or celebrities to their caricatures, the step from indirect to direct confrontation and ridicule is quickly taken. Internationally recognized people like Richard Nixon, Indira Gandhi, Prince Charles and Princess Diana, Mikhail Gorbachev, Elizabeth Taylor, Willy Brandt, Margaret Thatcher, and Ronald Reagan have all been attacked or ridiculed in fairy-tale caricatures. The most common motif is simply to place the person in question in front of a mirror and then in the caption asking that ultimate question 'Mirror, mirror on the wall' with an appropriate alteration to the traditional 'who is the fairest of them all?' of the 'Snow White' fairy tale. Whether humorous or slanderous, such cartoons and caricatures reflect a basic dissatisfaction with reality by juxtaposing it to the perfect world of fairy tales. As long as these tales still belong to the cultural literacy of modern people, this interplay of tradition and innovation in the mass media will enrich communication through effective images and captions.   WM

Flanagan, John T., 'Grim Stories: Folklore in Cartoons', *Midwestern Journal of Language and Folklore*, 1 (1975).

Horn, Katalin, 'Märchenmotive und gezeichneter Witz', *Österreichische Zeitschrift für Volkskunde*, 37 (1983).

Mieder, Wolfgang, (ed.), *Grimms Märchen—modern: Prosa, Gedichte, Karikaturen* (1979).

Mieder, Wolfgang, *Tradition and Innovation in Folk Literature* (1987).

Röhrich, Lutz, 'Wandlungen des Märchens in den modernen Bildmedien Comics und Cartoons', in Hans-Jörg Uther (ed.), *Märchen in unserer Zeit* (1990).

Smith, Grace Partridge, 'The Plight of the Folktale in the Comics', *Southern Folklore Quarterly*, 16 (1952).

Castroviejo, Concha (1915–95) Spanish novelist and writer of children's tales. She published her stories in several periodicals such as *Informaciones* (*Pieces of Information*) and *La Noche* (*The Night*). In 1961 she received the Doncel Award of Children's Literature for a book entitled *El jardín de las siete puertas* (*The Garden with Seven Doors*, 1961). This work contains a small play, from which the whole collection takes its title, and 14 tales very much influenced by the fairy-tale genre. Some of the most beautiful tales in this book are: 'La tejedora de sueños' ('The Weaver of Dreams', 1961), 'El país que no tenía pájaros' ('The Country without Birds', 1961), and 'Karlatán y las perlas del príncipe Atal' ('Karlatán and Prince Atal's Pearls', 1961).   CFR

Cavalli, Ennio (1947–) Italian poet, editor of cultural programmes for the radio, and writer of novels and short stories. In 2003 he published *Fiabe Storte* (*Twisted Fairy Tales*), an unusual collection of stories influenced by magic realism. Cavalli sets most of his tales in recognizable locations but then twists the plot and descriptions to lead readers to discover alternative perspectives on the incidents that he depicts. His tales have a subversive quality that calls for self-reflection.   JZ

Cavicchioli, Giovanni (1894–1964) Italian writer, poet, and playwright. He wrote an autobiographical novel, *Il bambino senza madre* (*The Motherless Child*, 1943), and many collections of tales, including: *Le nozze di Figaro* (*The Marriage of Figaro*, 1932), *Avventure del pagliaccio* (*The Buffoon's*

Adventures, 1935), *Favole* (*Tales*, 1951) and *Nuove favole* (*More Tales*, 1960). His story 'Il cavaliere fedele' ('The Faithful Knight') exemplifies how he blends tradition and the fantastic. Here the Arthurian quest for the Holy Grail is the background for the tale of Redibis who, after a life of searching, realizes that the Holy Grail is within him.   MNP

Caylus, Anne-Claude-Philippe de Tubières de Grimoard de Pestels de Levis, comte de (1692–1765) French fairy tale author. Caylus presents a paradox. A conservative member of an old aristocratic family (he was the son of Mme de Maintenon's niece), he was a noted archaeologist, antique connoisseur, engraver, patron of the arts, art historian, member of learned academies—and popular author of *poissard* (coarse) stories and fairy tales. He published these in the 1740s, during fairy tales' later vogue when authors were nostalgically recreating tales of their childhood. Many were presented at the irreverently witty salon of Mlle Quinault, where one was required to compose (vs. sing) for one's supper. Such entertainment often produced collaborative efforts, and early critics either hesitated to attribute some solely to Caylus, or dismissed all of his tales as trash; today's scholars are more discerning.

Caylus's tales typically begin with ironic verve and promise parody. 'Le Prince Courtebotte et la princesse Zibeline' (1741), for example, presents a brilliant *scène des dons* (gift-giving scene) in which the king valiantly tries to invite every single fairy and genie to his son's christening. The rest of his story, however, collapses into traditional exposition. This vacillation between the parodic and banal is elsewhere seen when pointed contemporary allusions and social criticism give way to gratuitous use of the marvellous.

While Caylus rarely based his fairy tales on French folklore, he carefully adapted the Koran and Muslim lore for his *Contes orientaux* (*Oriental Tales*, 1743). This collection therefore stands apart from the scores of parodic imitations of *Les Mille et une nuits, contes arabes* (*The Thousand and One Nights*, 1704–17) that deluged the public (*see* ARABIAN NIGHTS).   MLE

Robert, Raymonde, 'Le Comte de Caylus et l'orient', *Studies on Voltaire and the Eighteenth Century*, 154 (1976).

Robert, Raymonde, *Le Conte de fées littéraire en France* (1982).

Rocheblave, Samuel, *Essai sur le comte de Caylus* (1889).

Cazotte, Jacques (1719–92) French author of fairy and fantastic tales. After serving in French colonies, he pastiched *oriental fairy tales with 'La Patte du chatte, conte zinzinois' ('The Cat's Paw', 1741), whose ironic chapter titles parody *Crébillon. Likewise, the supposed publishing house of 'L'Endormy' in 'Baillons' ('The Sleeper' in 'Let's Yawn') parodically presents 'Les Mille et une fadaises, contes pour dormir debout' ('The Thousand and One Trifles, Tales to Fall Asleep by', 1742), written for an insomniac princess. Cazotte was later inspired by the fairy-tale revival of *Le Cabinet des fées* (*The Fairies' Study*, 1785) and wrote the *Continuation des mille et une nuits* (*Arabian Tales*, 1788–9). Based on genuine folklore, these stories feature good vs. evil jinns, socio-political criticism, and Cazotte's Illuminism.

He is best known for taking fairy-tale magic into the realm of the occult. Psychological portraits, the questioning of illusion vs. reality, and the spiritual importance of dreams characterize his masterpiece, *Le Diable amoureux* (*The Devil in Love*, 1772), in which the devil (a woman) loves his/her conjuror. It influenced *Hoffmann, *Gautier, *Nodier, and *Nerval, who revealed Cazotte's initiation into Martinist theosophy. In later years, the royalist Cazotte was known for his prophecies concerning the Revolution, and foretold his death by guillotine.   MLE

Castex, Pierre-Georges, *Le Conte fantastique en France de Nodier à Maupassant* (1951).

Shaw, Edward Pease, *Jacques Cazotte* (1942).

Todorov, Tzevtan, *The Fantastic: A Structuralist Approach to a Literary Genre*, trans. Richard Howard (1975).

'Cendrillon', 'Cenerentola', 'Cenicienta' *See* 'CINDERELLA'.

Chamisso, Adelbert von (1781–1838) German author, poet, and botanist. His family fled France during the French Revolution and settled in Berlin in 1796, where he became page to the Prussian queen and then an officer in the Prussian army, participating in the ill-fated campaign against Napoleon in 1806. After studying botany in Berlin, he took part in a voyage around the world (1815–18), and subsequently received an appointment at the Botanical Garden in Berlin. He was much admired for his lyric poetry and ballads, but is best remembered for his tale *Peter Schlemihls wundersame Geschichte* (*Peter Schlemihl's Amazing Story*, 1814), a minor classic of world literature widely read and translated in the 19th century. The story concerns a young man's encounters with the devil, who bargains with him first for his shadow and then, as in the Faust legend and subsequent literary versions of it, for his soul. Unlucky in love because of his missing shadow, Schlemihl in the end embraces a solitary life devoted to the study of nature. Because the story is told in the first person and Schlemihl, in recounting his experiences, addresses himself to Chamisso, we may understand that Schlemihl is the author's fanciful *alter ego*. JMM

Flores, Ralph, 'The Lost Shadow of Peter Schlemihl', *German Quarterly*, 47 (1974).
Pavlyshyn, Marko, 'Gold, Guilt, and Scholarship: Adelbert von Chamisso's "Peter Schlemihl"', *German Quarterly*, 55 (1982).
Swales, Martin, 'Mundane Magic: Some Observations on Chamisso's "Peter Schlemihl"', *Forum for Modern Languages Studies*, 12 (1976).

Chamoiseau, Patrick (1953–) Martinican novelist, playwright, and essayist. Born in Martinique and living in France, he has written extensively the language and history of creole culture. In his novels (*Chronique des sept misères* (*Chronicle of Seven Miseries*, 1986); *Solibo magnifique* (*Magnificent Solibo*, 1988); *Texaco*, 1992, among others), he frequently employs characters and motifs from Caribbean folklore. Chamoiseau's *Au temps de l'antan: contes du pays martinique* (*Creole Folktales*, 1988) features versions of well-known fairy tales, such as **Bluebeard' in 'Une affaire de mariage' ('A Little Matter of Marriage'), while highlighting the remarkable wit and irony of the storyteller. LCS

chapbook Historically (seventeenth to twentieth century) a cheaply printed pamphlet sold by pedlars and popular in America, China, Europe, and India, containing vernacular literature including folktales and fairy tales. Booklets usually of sixteen or twenty-four pages, around four by six inches in size, they incorporated humour and entertainment, practical matters such as recipes, or newsworthy topics such as crimes. But they also dealt with marvels and thus sometimes used traditional narrative forms; some publishers gathered traditional folktales and fairy tales in chapbook series such as *La Bibliothèque bleue* in France and *Die Blaue Bibliothek* in Germany. Fairy-tale texts thus disseminated include the **Jack tales, **'Sleeping Beauty', **'Little Tom Thumb', **'Little Red Riding Hood', **'Bluebeard', and *The *Arabian Nights*, but also versions and translations of literary tales. Like the *broadside, chapbooks intermediated between elite written and *oral traditions of *storytelling and fairy tales.

Chapbooks, like many current forms of popular literature, had a reputation for vulgarity and low quality, intended for a juvenile and/or a working-class audience rather than for sophisticated adult readers. A particular form of fairy-tale dissemination, chapbooks play a part in the complex social history of traditional and literary fairy tales. Chapbooks show fairy tales' malleability to different contexts; as the common people's oral stories—though they were sometimes associated with elite groups and literature—chapbook fairy tales found everyday printed forms and mass audiences. PG

Kaliambou, Maria, 'The Transformation of Folktales and Fairy Tales into Popular Booklets', *Marvels & Tales*, 21.1 (2007).
Schenda, Rudolf, 'Semiliterate and Semi-Oral Processes', *Marvels & Tales*, 21.1 (2007).

Chase, Richard (1904–88) American folklorist and storyteller. As a young schoolteacher, he was one of the first to record the traditional tales and songs of the southern Appalachian mountains. They were published as *The *Jack Tales: Told by R. M. Ward and his Kindred in the Beech Mountain Section of Western North Carolina and by Other Descendants of Council Harmon (1803–1896) Elsewhere in the Southern Mountains: With Three Tales from Wise County, Virginia* (1943), *Grandfather Tales: American-English Folk Tales* (1948), and *Hullabaloo, and Other Singing Folk Games* (1949). As Chase noted, many of the stories he collected were modernized and Americanized versions of popular European fairy tales like *'Cinderella' and 'The *Brave Little Tailor'. In 'Jack and Old Tush', for instance, the hero ends up not with a princess and half a kingdom, but with a pretty girl and 'a pretty house and some good land and a thousand dollars'.

Chase's best-known work, *American Folk Tales and Songs* (1956), includes many remarkable tales of magic, humorous tales, legends, songs, and ballads from his collections and those of other folklorists. His notes include the names of the original storytellers and singers, and discuss European parallels. The book has been criticized for sometimes combining several recorded versions of a story or song into one, but it is still in print and widely read and admired.   AL

Chatelain, Clara de (1807–76) English writer and composer who wrote numerous charming ballads and songs as well as a *Handbook of the Four Elements of Vocalisation* (1850). In addition, she produced several books of fairy tales: *The Silver Swan* (1847), *Child's Own Book of Fairy Tales* (1850), *Merry Tales for Little Folk* (1851), *Little Folks' Books* (1857), and *The Sedan-Chair: Sir Winifred's Seven Flights* (1866). Her tales for small children are retellings of classic tales such as *'Little Tom Thumb' and *'Jack and the Beanstalk', whereas her other work like *The Sedan-Chair* has a complex frame narrative reminiscent of Boccaccio, and the tales themselves depend on motifs from the French and *oriental fairy-tale tradition.   JZ

Children's and Household Tales *See* KINDER- UND HAUSMÄRCHEN.

Chiostri, Carlo (1863–1939) One of the foremost Italian illustrators of fairy-tale books in the 19th and early 20th centuries. An autodidact, he developed his own unusual style of photographic realism and psychological introspection and provided pictures for over 200 books during his lifetime. He illustrated works by most of the important Italian fairy-tale writers of his time such as Carlo *Collodi, Luigi *Capuana, Emma *Perodi, and Adriano Salani and also provided drawings for the fairy tales of the Brothers *Grimm.   JZ

Choisy, François-Timoléon, abbé de (1644–1724) French cleric, diplomat, and writer. Perhaps best known as a cross-dresser, Choisy was a prolific author of works on church history as well as memoirs and fiction. He knew other writers of fairy tales, including *Perrault and *Lhéritier, with whom he may have written the novella 'Histoire de la marquise-marquis de Banneville' ('Story of the Marquess-Marquis of Banneville'), a love story about two cross-dressers. Choisy's posthumously published 'Histoire de la princesse Aimonette' ('Story of Princess Aimonette') and 'Histoire turque' ('Turkish Story') contain chivalric and orientalist features typical of late 17th-century French fairy tales.   LCS

Chorpenning, Charlotte (1872–1955) American playwright, theorist, and teacher, who was at the forefront of school and community drama programmes across the country. Chorpenning studied playwriting at Radcliffe College, and from about 1915 to 1919 she was a playwright in residence for several Winona, Minnesota organizations, helping them write issue-based plays. From 1932 to 1951 Chorpenning wrote and directed most of the plays for the Children's Theatre at the Goodman Theatre of the Art Institute of Chicago, many of which were based on popular fairy tales like *The Emperor's New Clothes* (1932), **Jack and the Beanstalk* (1937), **Cinderella* (1940), **Little Red Riding Hood, or Grandmother Slyboots* (1943), and **Rumpelstiltskin* (1944) to name a few. In her plays, Chorpenning often complemented the fairy-tale character with an older but wiser double of her own invention (the Old Wolf in *Red Riding Hood*, Mother Hulda in *Rumpelstiltskin*), a device which draws out character motivation and encourages the audience to reflect on the action of the play.   AD

Christiansen, Reidar (1886–1971) Norwegian folklorist, professor at Oslo University 1921–51. Reidar published two significant studies on Norwegian folklore, *Norske Eventyr: En systematisk fortegnelse efter trykte og utrykte kilder* (*Norwegian Folktales: A Systematic List of Published and Unpublished Sources*, 1921) and *The Migratory Legends: A Proposed List of Types* (1958); and a comparative work *Studies in Irish and Scandinavian Folktales* (1959) in which he is somewhat sceptical about the early theories of the mutual Celtic–Nordic influence in folklore tradition.   MN

Chukovsky, Kornei (1882–1969) Outstanding Russian writer and educationalist, critic, and translator. He translated books by Daniel Defoe, Mark *Twain, Rudyard *Kipling, Oscar *Wilde, and retold nursery rhymes. In *From Two to Five* (1928) he stressed the importance of fairy tales in the development of a child's language and imagination.

Chukovsky's own versified fairy tales are humorous, often nonsensical, stimulating imagination and mastery of language. *The Crocodile* (1917) plays with the dragon-slayer motif in contemporary surroundings. *Wash 'em Clean* (1922) and *Theodora's Misery* (1926) portray animated household objects and are didactic as well as dynamic and funny. *Barmaley* (1925) is likewise a didactic story about two naughty children who run away and fall into the hands of a terrible ogre, but are saved by helpful animals. *The Cockroach* (1922), *The Telephone* (1926), and *The Stolen Sun* (1935) are tales about anthropomorphic animals, featuring a rich variation of colourful images. *Fly's Wedding* (1924) is a mock-heroic story about insects. *Dr Concocter* ('Aibolit' in Russian, literally 'Ouch, it hurts'), written both as a prose

story (1925) and a versified tale (1926), is a retelling of Hugh Lofting's *Doctor Dolittle*, where the humane mission of the kind doctor in Africa is accentuated. In all these tales, style is important, with puns, alliterations, rhythm, and rhyme, which often have their origins in folk poetry. *Bibigon* (1945), inspired by *'Little Tom Thumb', but depicting a Lilliput in a contemporary Russian setting, is a combination of prose and poetry, also involving a wicked magician and an enchanted princess. Most of Chukovsky's fairy tales were banned by the Soviet censorship between 1939 and 1955 because of their possible political connotations.   MN

Cicognani, Bruno (1879–1971) Italian playwright and critic, deeply tied to his Tuscan origins, whose realism evolves into the fantastic as in *Storielle di novo conio* (*Brand New Little Stories*, 1917) and his novel *La Velia* (*The Shrike*, 1923). A collection of short stories, *Il figurinaio e le figurine* (*The Pedlar and the Statuettes*, 1928), contains the tale 'La locanda dei tre Re' ('The Inn of the Three Kings', 1928), the magical story of Diomira's three simple daughters whose dream of marrying three kings becomes a reality, but only for one night, after which it evaporates like a bubble. The dramatic fairy tale *Bellinda e il mostro* (*Belinda and the Monster*, 1927), a version of *'Beauty and the Beast' which the author wrote between 1913 and 1918, was staged at the Teatro Argentina in Rome on 23 March 1927, under the direction of Luigi Pirandello.   GD

'Cinderella' This fairy tale belongs to a group of tales that have enjoyed both temporal and spatial stability. Although its first European literary appearances were in Bonaventure des Périers' *Les Nouvelles Recréations et joyeux devis* (*New Recreations and Joyous Games*, 1558), and in Giambattista *Basile's *Pentamerone* (1634–6), the best-known versions were in Charles *Perrault's *Histoires ou contes du temps passé* (*Stories or Tales of Times Past*, 1697) and in Wilhelm and Jacob *Grimm's *Kinder- und Hausmärchen* (*Children's and Household Tales*, 1812–15). This story has lived as a sum of all its realizations

'Cinderella' Cinderella is pleased to encounter her fairy godmother in George *Cruikshank's sanitized version entitled 'Cinderella and the Glass Slipper', published in Cruikshank's *Fairy Library* (1853–4).

without losing its integrity, despite repeated distortions. Walter Anderson's 'Law of Self-Correction' explains how some relatively stable stories persist in the popular tradition because storytellers, upon hearing a defective version, correct it in the retelling.

While the tale had circulated principally in the Indo-European world, it was comfortably accepted into the Chinese folk-tale canon because it resembled an already familiar stepchild story. The same can be said for Africa, Australia, Java, Japan, and the Indian subcontinent. Perhaps the universal appeal of a 'rags to riches' story with emphasis on sensitive family issues explains its successful diffusion through time and space.

The story of this persecuted heroine is easily segmented: Girl's mother dies; father remarries and brings to household two daughters; stepmother and stepsisters mistreat her; father is either indifferent or malevolent (threatens death in 'Cap o'Rushes' and importunes her sexually in 'Catskin'). She performs all the household's menial tasks and must live and work among the ashes on the hearth ('Cinderwench', 'Cinderella', 'Aschenputtel', 'Ashypet', 'Cendrillon', 'Cenerentola', 'Pepelluga', 'Allerleirauh').

Cinderella is aided by a magical helper (fairy godmother, magical bird, magic tree, enchanted cow, enchanted fish). In some versions the mother had been transformed into a cow (a fish). When the cow is to be killed, she tells her daughter to collect her bones and to save them. These bones turn into a magical agent like a magic wand. While her magical helper, a fairy godmother in the Perrault version, comes to her unbidden, the Grimms' Cinderella is a resourceful person who acts to improve her condition. She calls upon pigeons and turtle-doves to come to her aid to complete her stepmother's impossible tasks. Not a passive creature awaiting deliverance, she is also a resourceful person who plants the twig, waters it, tends it, and then tells the tree to shake and shower her with silver and gold.

If one aim of the story is to illustrate the ascent from low to high status, then Cinderella must meet a man in that social milieu who will free her from her miserable circumstances. Furthermore, marriage represents an effort to gain independence from the previous generation and to create a new family. In most of the versions, she will meet the man she is to marry at a social occasion, a festival, a ball, or a party. The Grimms' storyteller reported a version in which she went to the ball on three successive nights, obeying Olrik's 'law of repetition of three'. The stepmother forbids her attendance at the event and imposes impossible tasks so that the unfortunate young woman may not attend the event. She must separate lentils from ashes, beans from gravel, carry water in buckets with sieved bottoms. However, she summons animal helpers (sparrows, doves) to come to her aid.

The heroine finally attends the ball (festival, party), at which time a prince falls in love with her at first sight. In the Grimms' tale, in response to the prince's report that the beautiful maiden who had eluded him had hidden in her father's dovecote (pear tree), Cinderella's father thinks it might be his daughter and takes an axe to the dovecote (pear tree). As Max Lüthi has observed, fairy-tale motivations are often unspoken. The storyteller does not explain why the father wants to destroy his daughter. Furthermore, fairy-tale tradition frequently demands that an interdiction accompany magical gifts. She must leave the ball at midnight, accidentally leaving behind a shoe.

The shoe-test that proves her identity has fuelled an academic debate as to the material of the lost slipper (glass, fur, gold, embroidered silk). However, the test itself matters more than the material details. Once again the stepsisters fail to imitate her successfully, even mutilating their feet to make them small enough for the slipper. As is the case with many fairy tales, the ending is the least stable part. The stepsisters either suffer a cruel punishment (birds peck out their eyes), or Cinderella, in her new-found wealth and power, arranges advantageous marriages for them both.

There have been hundreds if not thousands of literary, dramatic, musical, poetic, and cinematic versions of 'Cinderella' since the early 19th century, and the 'heroine' of the story has become the icon of a rags-to-riches success story. Certainly, this is the way she is portrayed in the famous *Disney film of 1950. However, since the 1970s, many feminist and postmodern writers have questioned the passive aspects of a girl who waits for her prince, and the term 'Cinderella complex' has come to stand for a troubled woman who cannot determine her own destiny. Whatever the 'truth' may be, contemporary writers such as Anne *Sexton, Wendy *Walker, Peter *Redgrove, Jane *Yolen, Roald *Dahl, Tanith *Lee, and Angela *Carter have explored the complex of the fictional Cinderella in ways that would astound the classic writers of this tale.   HG

Cox, Marian Roalfe, *Cinderella: Three Hundred and Forty-Five Variants of Cinderella, Catskin and Cap o'Rushes* (1893).
Dundes, Alan (ed.), *Cinderella: A Folklore Casebook* (1982).
Lüthi, Max, *The Fairytale as Art Form and Portrait of Man* (1985).
Olrik, Axel, *Principles for Narrative Research* (1921).
Rooth, Birgitta, *The Cinderella Cycle* (1951).
Waley, Arthur, 'The Chinese Cinderella Story', *Folklore*, 58 (1947).

'Cinderella' (film versions) *'Cinderella', a tale which in *Perrault, *Grimm, pantomime, and modernized versions has inspired filmmakers for a hundred years, beginning with *Méliès in 1899. Over 50 of the adaptations have borne the name 'Cinderella' (or the equivalent in another language, e.g. 'Cendrillon' or 'Aschenputtel'); some of the titles offer playful variations such as *Cinderfella; a third group invoke fairy-tale iconography (*The Slipper and the Rose*) or phraseology (*Ever After*) in their names. The films that update the story normally reduce magic to the status of chance, charm, or dream and replace majesty by money.

Christmas 1914 saw Mary Pickford, well on her way to becoming 'the world's sweetheart', star as Cinderella in a sumptuous high-budget version derived from traditional pantomime, with the sisters presented as ugly and comic. Early in the 1920s, by contrast, Lotte *Reiniger produced a short and simple Grimm-based Cinderella out of scissors and cardboard.

After that, for over two decades, modernized versions held sway. From the makers of *Peter Pan came another *Barrie adaptation, *A Kiss for Cinderella* (USA, 1926). Set in London during the air raids of the First World War, it presents a lodging-house skivvy as Cinderella, a compassionate policeman as the prince, and a harsh landlady as one of the ugly sisters. Cinderella's visit to the palace takes place within a dream she has while sitting on a doorstep in a snowstorm. A year later the comedienne Colleen Moore was *Ella Cinders* (USA, 1927). This satirizes film studios through showing how the dowdy drudge Ella wins a beauty contest by mistake, wreaks havoc in Hollywood, and marries a millionaire football player. A third updating, *First Love* (USA, 1939), features the young singing star Deanna Durbin as an orphan who, by virtue of having won the hearts of the servants in her uncle's house, drives in style to the ball with a police escort, and marries into money.

In the 1950s, magic came back. *Disney's *Cinderella* (USA, 1950) exploited animation's capacity to effect a seamless pumpkin transformation. In the main it follows Perrault even though, while researching the story's sources, Disney learned that Perrault had misheard 'vair' as 'verre', which meant that Cinderella's slippers should really be made of fur, not glass. Disney, however, preferred to stick with Perrault, and put the fragility of glass to a dramatic use—the stepmother smashes the slipper into fragments before Cinderella can try it on—that the flexibility of fur would not have allowed. Overall, Disney expands seven pages into 75 minutes, with the mice in particular getting greatly enlarged roles: in Perrault they do nothing except turn into horses and pull Cinderella's coach, whereas in Disney two of them have rounded characters and interact with Cinderella throughout the film. Another change is that Disney rejects Perrault's choice of a rat as coachman and lizards as footmen, preferring to use homelier animals—a horse and a dog—for those purposes.

Most major adaptations since then have followed Disney in finding or creating situations ripe for enhancement by music. Set in

'Cinderella' (film) The clock strikes midnight in Georges Méliès's experimental film *Cendrillon* ('Cinderella'), made in France in 1899. The director himself plays Father Time. Photo: Iconothèque de la Cinémathèque française.

the early 19th century, *The Glass Slipper* (USA, 1954) contains not only songs but also sequences in which Leslie Caron, as Ella, dances with the Ballet de Paris. This version does not set out to create narrative tension; rather, it defuses it by having the Prince know all about Ella before inviting her to the ball. With similar effect, Ella's midnight flight is caused not by the imminent disappearance of her finery, but by the fact that her coachman wants to be back home with his family by one o'clock. The focus is instead on Ella's psychology, on how long her spirit can remain unbowed by oppression, on what is real and what is only in her mind. In keeping with this, nothing happens through overt glittering magic: the godmother character, a whimsical, pixilated woman named Mrs Toquet, makes dreams come true by a practical approach, using things that come to hand in the kitchen.

The same decade gave birth to a full-scale musical comedy *Cinderella* (USA, 1957), written for television by Rodgers and Hammerstein, following in the wake of such stage and movie successes as *South Pacific* and *Oklahoma!* The approach is essentially that of pantomime: the stepsisters are vain and repellent, the godmother is eccentric, the prince is charming. The whole production revolves round the songs, which explore the characters' situations. Cinderella sings about her repressed yearnings in 'In My Own Little Corner'; her stepsisters give vent to their jealousy in 'Stepsisters' Lament'; and Cinderella and the Prince together ask a question central to many fairy tales—'Do I Love You Because You're Beautiful, Or Are You Beautiful Because I Love You?'

Another screen musical, *The Slipper and the Rose* (UK, 1976), sought to inject reality into the story, without abolishing magic, by taking it out of the studio and away from pantomime. The characters are presented as capable of change. As in both Grimm and Perrault, the stepsisters are attractive in physical appearance; only in their natures are they ugly. The actors, though not professionally trained, did their own singing; and the songs arise naturally from the situations. In 'Why Can't I Be Two People?', Prince Edward rails against the restrictions imposed on him by royal obligations; in reply the Chamberlain argues the importance of hierarchical distinction—'Position and Positioning'. He fails to convince the prince, but later succeeds with Cinderella, persuading her that the prince cannot possibly marry a commoner. The fairy godmother thus has an extra problem to sort out.

In the 1990s the trend in screen Cinderellas has been towards contemporization—keeping the original setting, but injecting contemporary values. A 1997 revival of the Rodgers and Hammerstein television version, with an amended screenplay and a multiethnic cast, brings about a discussion between Cinderella and the Prince a few days before the ball. Wandering incognito through a market-place on a meet-the-people excursion, he bumps into Cinderella. They talk, and without knowing who he is she asserts that she does not want to be treated like a princess—all she wants is the respect due to anyone. In similar vein the fairy godmother (Whitney Houston) insists that the transformative magic comes not from her wand, but from deep down in Cinderella's soul.

This overhauling continued in the nonmusical cinema feature *Ever After: A Cinderella Story* (USA, 1998) which sets its face against the notion that happiness equals marrying a rich man. The background is still class and castles, but the Cinderella character (Drew Barrymore) does not even start as a sooty victim. Feisty, self-assertive, and able to carry the Prince on her back when necessary, she has no need of a spell-casting godmother or a pumpkin-turned-coach or a particularly dainty foot.

After a century of screen adaptations, 'Cinderella' seems now to be a fairy tale without fairies.   TAS

Cinderella (musical) A television version of the famous fairy tale by composer Richard Rodgers and librettist Oscar Hammerstein. First produced in 1957, starring Julie Andrews, it was remade in 1965. In between these two dates, the show was adapted for the stage, arriving at London's Coliseum for the Christmas season of 1956.   TH

Cinderfella A feature-length American movie from 1960 starring Jerry Lewis. The musical adaptation of Charles *Perrault's *'Cinderella' hinges on a reversal of gender, which puts the simpleton Lewis into the role of the oppressed hero Fella. Unlike his stepmother and her two sons, who have designs on the hidden fortune his father has bequeathed to him, Fella rejects the values of contemporary high society. He achieves his happy end not by reclaiming his identity as a 'person' of wealth and class, but by declining his fortune and opting with Princess Charmein for a life among the unpretentious 'people'.   DH

Clarke, Harry (Henry Patrick Clarke, 1889–1931) Irish stained glass artist and illustrator. Son of a church decorator, he studied at the Dublin Metropolitan School of Art and won two scholarships and three gold medals in stained glass competitions. After studying medieval cathedral windows in France, he returned to his father's stained glass studio and worked on church commissions. Because most of his work is found in churches, it is rare that secular panels come on the market—as evidenced by a recent Christie's auction that brought £331,500 for scenes depicting J. M. Synge's poem 'Queens'. The Geneva Window, his masterpiece, was commissioned by the Irish government and records scenes from 20th-century Irish literature.

Clarke also worked as an illustrator. His whimsical, linear style with textured patterns, areas of black, and morbid or sexual imagery, recalls that of Aubrey Vincent Beardsley and Gustav Klimt. Called 'the leading symbolist artist of Ireland', he illustrated special editions of fairy tales by Hans Christian *Andersen and Charles *Perrault (1916, 1922) as well as Johann Wolfgang von *Goethe's *Faust* (1925) and Edgar Allan Poe's *Tales of Mystery and Imagination* (1919).   MLE

Bowe, Nicola Gordon, *The Life and Work of Harry Clarke* (1989).

Clarke, Harry There are nothing but false compliments for the proud king in Harry Clarke's illustration for Hans Christian *Andersen's 'The Emperor's Clothes', published in *Fairy Tales by Hans Christian Andersen* (1900).

Houfe, Simon, *The Dictionary of British Book Illustrators and Caricaturists 1800–1914* (1996).
Peppin, Brigid, and Micklethwait, Lucy, *Dictionary of British Book Illustrators* (1983).
Turner, Jane (ed.), *The Dictionary of Art* (1996).

Clarke, Susanna (1959–) British writer who has published two important fairy-tale works, *Jonathan Strange and Mr. Norrell* (2004) and *The Ladies of Grace Adieu and Other Stories* (2006), which are closely connected. Though it may be misleading to refer to *Jonathan Strange and Mr. Norrell* as a fairy-tale novel, it certainly incorporates many aspects of the fairy-tale genre. The long narrative begins in 1806, when England is involved in the Napoleonic wars, and two mysterious men, Gilbert Norrell and Jonathan Strange, bring back magic to the country at a time of need. Once Norrell, a reclusive magician, demonstrates that he can resurrect a young woman from death, he inspires other magicians to restore the importance of magic to England. The younger, more experimental magician, named Strange, becomes his apprentice in 1809, and though he does not learn all of Norrell's secrets about magic, he is able to help the English defeat Napoleon and prevent King George III from becoming enchanted. He and his wife become famous in London, and then Strange begins to criticize Norrell. The split between the two magicians leads to bitter arguments, also among different groups of people in London who side with one or the other magician. In 1816, however, both of them become trapped in eternal darkness because of a fairy's curse. Throughout the novel questions about insanity and reason, what constitutes Englishness, and the purpose of historical scholarship are raised. Clarke weaves numerous romantic, Gothic, and fairy-tale motifs into this complex fantasy novel, which recalls the fairy-tale tradition of the 'magician and his apprentice'. In *The Ladies of Grace Adieu and Other Stories*, Clarke included seven fairy stories that she had previously published in magazines and anthologies, each one narrated by a different author who extols the magic power of women and touches upon certain incidents involving Norrell and Strange. Together the tales form an ironic feminist revision of the history in *Jonathan Strange and Mr. Norrell* and they reveal that there is an alternate history of magic that illuminates the extraordinary skills of women. JZ

Clément, Frédéric (1949–) French artist, designer, and illustrator, who has written and drawn over 50 picture books and held exhibits of his works throughout Europe. Among the most interesting fairy-tale books that he authored are: *The Voice of the Wood* (*Songes de la Belle au Bois Dormant*, 1994) and *The Merchant of Marvels and The Peddler of Dreams* (*Magasin Zinzin*, 1995), which won the won the Children's Literature International Prize in 1996. It concerns Frederick Knick-Knack, the peddler of dreams, who embarks on a journey to find a unique birthday gift for his friend the Merchant of Marvels, who already has everything imaginable. Clément employs all kinds of extraordinary types of illustrations as part of the text. He has also illustrated tales by important classic authors, such as Mme d'Aulnoy's *La Chatte Blanche et autres contes* (*The White Cat and Other Tales*, 1989) and *L'Oiseau Bleu et autres contes* (*The Blue Bird and Other Tales*, 1991), as well as *Les Mille et une nuits* (*The Thousand and One Nights*, 2004). JZ

Perrot, Jean, 'Les déplacements poétiques de Frédéric Clément. Mort et résurrection sous l'empire de la lune', *CEDIS/Inter CDI* (1989).

Clifford, Lucy Lane (1853?–1929) English author of *Anyhow Stories* (1882). This collection contains 'The New Mother', a remarkable fantasy about adult corruption of children which seems to anticipate Henry James's *The Turn of the Screw*. Two children meet a strange girl who offers to show them a little man and woman dancing on a musical instrument she calls a peardrum. But they have to prove first that they have been truly naughty. Though their naughtiness never satisfies her, their mother sadly tells them she will have to leave them to a new mother with glass eyes and a wooden tail.

Still yearning to see the dance, they are eventually driven out of the house in terror as the new mother smashes down the door with her wooden tail. GA

Ekstein, Rudolf, 'Childhood Autism: Its Process, as Seen in a Victorian Fairy Tale', *American Imago*, 35 (1978).

Moss, Anita, 'Mothers, Monsters, and Morals in Victorian Fairy Tales', *The Lion and the Unicorn*, 12.2 (December 1988).

Cocteau, Jean-Maurice-Eugène-Clément (1889–1963) French artist, writer, and cinematographer. Given Cocteau's loose ties to futurism, dada, and surrealism, his penchant for the fantastic, from the very beginning of his career, is not at all surprising. Hence, he explores various types and levels of 'reality' in much of his work, including his early cartoon, *Le Potomak* (1919); his plays *Oedipus Rex* (1927), *La Machine infernale* (*The Infernal Machine*, 1934), and *Les Chevaliers de la table ronde* (*The Knights of the Round Table*, 1963); and his films *L'Éternel retour* (*The Eternal Return*, 1943) and *La Belle et la bête* (*Beauty and the Beast*, 1946).

Cocteau deals most directly with the fairy tale in his cinematic version of 'Beauty and the Beast'. Although now considered a classic, at the time of its release in the aftermath of the Second World War when people were struggling to meet their most basic needs, the film was considered by many to be shockingly frivolous. Cocteau countered that he was offering a means of survival by renewing people's 'spirit'. He also deemed his reworking of this fairy tale to be an expression of his own being. Encompassing both the personal and the social, this film, like most of Cocteau's œuvre, explores different facets of reality such as dreams, daily life, and the supernatural. To evoke these, Cocteau makes a particularly effective use of lighting, including blurred shots, shadows, and contrasts between light and dark, but also many special effects, such as candelabras with human arms, bodiless hands that serve meals, doors that open mysteriously, that have lost nothing of their charm even today. The acting in this film is often praised for striking a delicate balance between archetypal and individual expression that reveals Cocteau's belief in the intersection of these aspects of reality.

Although Cocteau bases his film on Mme *Leprince de Beaumont's version of the tale, he inevitably adds his own distinctive touch. Some of the changes he makes are outright additions to the plot and list of characters. Such is the case of Avenant, the Beast's rival, whose death at the very moment of the Beast's transformation and whose identical appearance to that of the Beast-turned-prince suggest that male sexual objects are interchangeable and that Belle's desire is a matter of perception. Other changes made by Cocteau develop aspects left implicit in Leprince de Beaumont's tale. Most obvious is the sensuality conveyed by the Beast but also Belle throughout the film. So, too, is Belle's admission at the end that she, and not the Beast, was the monster. If Cocteau's version is far less overtly moralizing than Leprince de Beaumont's, it forcefully drives home the message that appearances are deceptive.

Cocteau's *Beauty and the Beast* is one of the most important 20th-century reworkings of the tale, and its influence has been considerable. In the time since its release, it has gone from being an avant-garde to a classic film that now inspires new versions. LCS

Cocteau, Jean, *Journal d'un film* (1946).

Hearne, Betsy, *Beauty and the Beast* (1989).

cognitive criticism and fairy tales Cognitive criticism examines how texts stimulate recipients' perception, attention, imagination and other cognitive activity through recognition of recurrent patterns: scripts, schemas, prototypes—and through awareness of deviation from these patterns. While the basic structures of folktales and fairy tales are universal, recipients respond to variations in setting, character gallery, the nature of tasks, and other culture-specific elements. Cognitive criticism also explores why and how we engage with fictional characters through employing the cognitive-affective concepts of theory of mind (ability to understand other people's thoughts, intentions, and beliefs) and empathy (ability to understand other people's emotions). Although fairy-tale characters are not normally associated with a rich internal life, cognitive poetics demonstrates that human brains can, through mirror neurons, respond to fictional events and characters as if they were real, and how fiction can stimulate such responses through various narrative devices. With empathy and theory of mind, it is possible to discern the implicit interiority that explains why we engage with fairy-tale characters in the first place, and how we make inferences about their motivations and judge their ethical choices. Cognitive criticism offers new ways of thinking about audience engagement, providing a persuasive explanation of fairy tales' everlasting appeal.   MN

Nikolajeva, Maria, 'Do we feel sorry for the older brothers? Exploring Empathy and Ethics in Fairy Tales through Cognitive Poetics', in Maria Tatar (ed.), *Cambridge Companion to Fairy Tales* (2015).

Cole, Babette (1949–) English author and illustrator known for her idiosyncratic books for children. Cole has written and illustrated four provocative fairy tales that are outrageously funny and question traditional fairy-tale conventions from a feminist perspective. In *Princess Smartypants* (1986), she reverses the 'taming-of-the-shrew' syndrome of King Thrushbeard by depicting a young girl in dungarees, who does not want to be married and thwarts her parents by turning her major suitor into a frog, when she kisses him. In *Prince Cinders* (1988), a revision of **'Cinderella'*, the youngest of three brothers is forced to do the housework until he is rescued by a zany fairy and a princess. *King-Change-a-lot* (1988) spoofs the **Aladdin* fairy tale by introducing a monarch who rubs a potty to produce a magic genie, who in turn helps him solve problems in the kingdom. In *Cupid* (1990) Cole sends the god of love to earth where he becomes involved in the Miss Universe contest. In all her books Cole displays an uncanny sense for explosive situations that she captures in bright, often dazzling illustrations made with dyes. Although she has been dubbed an anarchic writer and illustrator, there is always a clear provocative purpose in her fairy-tale reversals.   JZ

Cole, Sir Henry (1808–82) English civil servant and editor, under the name of 'Felix Summerly', of the Home Treasury series in which traditional stories and rhymes of childhood were reissued. Cole said in the prospectus that he aimed at cultivating 'the Affections, Fancy, Imagination, and Taste of Children', at a time when moral tales and books of instruction dominated the juvenile market. The first books, published by Joseph Cundall, appeared in 1843 and included versions of **'Beauty and the Beast'*, **'Little Red Riding-Hood'*, 'Chevy Chase', 'Reynard the Fox', and *Traditional Nursery Songs*.   GA

Colfer, Chris (1990–) American singer, writer, actor, and producer, who first made a name for himself in the popular American TV series *Glee*. Among his numerous accomplishments are two fairy-tale novels for young adults, *The Land of Stories: The Wishing Spell* (2012) and *The Land of Stories: The Enchantress Returns* (2013). In the first novel the twins Alex and Conner Bailey are given a magical fairy-tale book which transports them to a land where fairy tales are real and where they encounter many characters from traditional fairy tales such as **'Red Riding Hood'*, **'Sleeping Beauty'*, and 'The **Little Mermaid'*. In the second novel the twins return to the Land of Stories to rescue their mother, who has been kidnapped by the Evil Enchantress. They accomplish this task with the help of Queen Red Riding Hood, Goldilocks, Jack, and their friend Froggy.   JZ

Collins, Suzanne (1962–) American television writer and author of books for young adults. She is best known for *The Hunger Games* trilogy (2008–10), now a major film franchise. Collins has credited the story of Theseus and the Minotaur as a model for her dystopian series, in which sixteen-year-old Katniss Everdeen takes her sister's place in the Hunger Games, a fight-to-the-death between children from across a future United States. The novels make use of various fairy-tale tropes. Collins' lesser-known, but highly lauded *Underland Chronicles* (2003–7) consists of five books which follow eleven-year-old Gregor as he discovers a world beneath his city. In this urban high fantasy, Gregor must fulfil an ancient prophecy, bringing peace to the subterranean kingdom of Regalia. ST

Collodi, Carlo (pseudonym of **Carlo Lorenzini**, 1826–90) Italian writer, journalist, civil servant, and patriot, the author of *Le avventure di *Pinocchio* (1881–3), generally regarded as the masterpiece of Italian children's literature. *Pinocchio* is not a traditional story reworked, but is, nevertheless, a fairy tale, a principal character being 'the Fairy with indigo hair' (*not* 'the Blue Fairy', which is a *Disney distortion of the original). Collodi came to fairies and to children late and simultaneously, when he was nearly 50 in 1875. By then he had long been noted in his native Florence for his cultural activities for adults and for his political commitment. One of many siblings brought up in poverty, he knew both the historic city and the Tuscan countryside from boyhood; he was given a good education with priests, thanks to his parents' noble employer. Work in a prominent bookshop brought him into contact with the liberal Florentine intelligentsia. He became an ardent supporter of the ideals of the Risorgimento, eager to see the Italian states freed from foreign domination and from antiquated regimes, and able to unite as one nation. In 1848, the great year of European revolutions, he fought against the Austrians in the First War of Independence in Italy. Returning safely, he embarked on his life's twin professions, becoming a civil servant with the Tuscan legislature and launching a politico-satirical newspaper. Because of the censorship, his journalism soon turned towards the theatre, and he began to write plays and then novels.

At 32, Collodi enlisted for the Second War of Independence, and before long Garibaldi brought about the unification of Italy (1860). In 1865, the year that Lewis *Carroll's *Alice's Adventures in Wonderland* was published, Florence briefly became Italy's capital and saw a resurgence of dynamic political and cultural activity. Ten years later Collodi, who was a passionate theatregoer, music-lover, and journalist of mordant wit, was commissioned by the Florentine publishing house of the Paggi brothers to translate a collection of French literary fairy tales of the 17th and 18th centuries. They were Charles *Perrault's eight *Histoires ou contes du temps passé* (*Stories or Tales of Past Times*, 1697) and his 'Peau d'âne' (*'Donkey-Skin'), along with four stories by Mme d'*Aulnoy (including 'The *Blue Bird' and 'The White Cat') and two by Mme *Leprince de Beaumont (including *'Beauty and the Beast'). Among Perrault's reworkings of ancient and well-known fairy tales (*'Cinderella', *'Little Red Riding Hood') was *'Puss-in-Boots' which, through Collodi, returned to Italy from France after a circular journey of several hundred years: the earliest known versions are those of the Italian writers Giovan Francesco *Straparola (*Le *piacevoli notti*, 1550–3) and Giambattista *Basile (*Pentamerone*, 1634–6). Collodi brought a Tuscan realism to his first children's book and first fairy book, *I racconti delle fate* (*Fairy Tales*, 1875); it made possible a new direction in his writing, which, within six years, was to result in his classic work, *Pinocchio*. First, however, he was commissioned to write a modernized version of an innovative children's book of 1837; his *Giannettino* of 1877 disguised didacticism within a more natural and playful narrative than had previously been acceptable, and its huge success led to a long series of entertaining but informative stories concerning the same central character, a lively boy who was not a model of perfect behaviour. In 1880 *Giannettino* began a tour of Italy in three volumes, which again demonstrated Collodi's determination to create Italians for the new Italy.

This was a period of considerable developments in journalism for children in Italy, and in 1881 Collodi was invited to contribute a serial story to a new and distinguished children's weekly paper, *Il Giornale per i Bambini*, published in Rome. *La storia di un burattino* (*The Story of a Puppet*) began in the first issue on 7 July 1881. It came to a premature end with the hanging of

Pinocchio in October. Following clamorous requests, the serial started again in February 1882 under the definitive title, *Le avventure di Pinocchio*, and after a further interruption achieved its happy ending on 25 January 1883. It was immediately published as a volume with line illustrations by Enrico Mazzanti, who worked in close partnership with Collodi. While some of his other stories, such as 'Pipì o lo scimmiottino color di rosa' ('Pipì or the Pink Monkey', 1887), have some common ground with fairy tales, *Pinocchio* is Collodi's unique original contribution to the lore of fairies. Not surprisingly, his fairy is modelled on those of Perrault and his contemporaries, being human in scale and character and a good fairy godmother in type. Yet, despite her dark blue hair, she is modern in her ideals and tutelage, urging Pinocchio to be studious. Judged within the context of its times, Collodi's fairy tale is both illuminating and extraordinary for its social and political satire on the one hand, and on the other because of its exuberant fantasy, especially remarkable because the fairy-tale tradition generally had only a limited impact on the development of children's literature in Italy. In the late 19th century, Italy's usual response to fairies was confined to the rewriting of folk tales from the oral tradition. Luigi *Capuana's Sicilian stories for children, *C'era una volta* (*Once Upon a Time*, 1882), are a distinguished example.

Pinocchio was instantly a great popular success, the fifth edition appearing in 1890, the year of Collodi's death; the first English translation, published in 1892, heralded innumerable versions world-wide and a vast international industry of abridgements, films, plays, toys, and other products. *Pinocchio* is one of the most translated books in the world and has been interpreted according to many ideologies and philosophies.   ALL

Fedi, R. (ed.), *Carlo Collodi. Lo spazio delle meraviglie* (1990).

Perella, Nicolas, 'An Essay on *Pinocchio*', in Carlo Collodi, *The Adventures of Pinocchio, Story of a Puppet* (1986).

Traversetti, Bruno, *Introduzione a Collodi* (1993).

Wunderlich, Richard, and Morrissey, Thomas, *Pinocchio Goes Postmodern: Perils of a Puppet in the United States* (2002).

Zipes, Jack, 'Towards a Theory of Fairy-Tale Film: The Case of Pinocchio', *The Lion and the Unicorn* (1996).

Colum, Padraic (1881–1972) Irish poet, playwright, and children's author. Colum's father administered the town workhouse in Longford, Ireland; the boy grew up listening to stories, not only from the old people of the workhouse, but also from the tramps and other nomads who stopped for a night's shelter. In his twenties Colum arrived in Dublin and joined the flourishing Celtic Revival; his first plays were produced by W. B. *Yeats's Irish Theatre. He emigrated to America in 1914 and became a children's author when an Irish folk tale he had translated and expanded was published as *The King of Ireland's Son* (1916), illustrated by Willy *Pogány. He had a poetic gift for weaving traditional stories into a flowing narrative, while preserving their authentic flavour; his full-length narrative versions for children of Greek, Norse, and Welsh myths have never been surpassed. *The Girl Who Sat by the Ashes* (1919) expands the tale of *Cinderella, while *The Children who Followed the Piper* (1922) is an imaginative extrapolation of the Pied Piper legend. *The Forge in the Forest* (1925), strikingly designed and superbly illustrated by Boris Artzybasheff, creates a narrative frame for eight folk tales about horses drawn from several cultures—two tales for each of the four elements. In 1923 the Hawaiian legislature invited Colum to survey and make accessible their Polynesian heritage; this compilation was published as *Tales and Legends of Hawaii* (1924–5). His original fairy tales include *The Boy Apprenticed to an Enchanter* (1920) and *The Peep-Show Man* (1924).   SR

comic books and graphic novels Those comic books and graphic novels that employ fairy-tale themes and motifs stem from the broadsides and chapbooks of the eighteenth and nineteenth centuries as well as from the single-volume picture books that were widespread by the end of the nineteenth century. Comic books and graphic novels have also been influenced by fairy-tale cartoon strips and films. Generally speaking, comic books and graphic novels with fairy-tale contents are reproductions of well-known stories represented by drawn pictures (and sometimes by photographs). The comics, graphics, and designs are often highly experimental, and the well-known fairy tales are sometimes drastically transformed and made into pastiches.

The differences between a fairy-tale comic book and a fairy-tale graphic novel are slight. Some critics have asserted that the term graphic novel, which came into use during the 1960s, is simply a commercial term for a more expensive comic book in hardback format that is allegedly more artistic than a comic book. Implicit is the desire of publishers to make more money by sprucing up a paperback comic book. This criticism of the graphic novel may be true to a certain extent, but there are distinctions to be made. Comic books tend to address younger audiences, are issued in paperbacks, and tend to be produced as serials or compilations of traditional fairy tales. Graphic novels are slanted towards young adults and adults, undertake more experimentation in design and narrative, and make greater changes in traditional fairy tales. Moreover, graphic novels are frequently long, original fairy tales with hybrid texts and borrow from different genres such as myth, legend, the Gothic story, and so on.

Among the first significant fairy-tale comic books was *Fairy Tale Parade*, published by Dell from 1942 to 1944. There were nine issues drawn for the most part by the famous illustrator Walt Kelly, and each issue featured tales from many different countries. Part of the purpose in publishing the comics was to instill a desire in children to read the original books. This pedagogical goal was also true of the *Classics Illustrated* comics created by Albert Kanter in 1941. This series had 169 issues and lasted until 1971 and included numerous fairy tales such as *The *Arabian Nights*, *'Áladdin and his Lamp', and *Alice in Wonderland*. After 1971 the lists were revised, modernized, and amended, and a junior classics series was added and included classical fairy tales such as *'Cinderella', *'Sleeping Beauty', *'Snow White', *'Jack and the Beanstalk'. and *'Little Red Riding Hood'. Numerous comic book publishers have reproduced the traditional tales from the 1940s to the present, and the Disney Corporation transformed most of its fairy-tale films into comic books. Several important examples of early fairy-tale comics can be found in Art Spiegelman and Françoise Mouly's collection, *Folklore and Fairy Tale Comics* (2000).

The graphic novel flowered later than the comic book and is very similar to the French *bande dessinée*, which has a fine-art appeal and yet is more often pulp and sensational than fine. In English-speaking countries, Neil Gaiman and other talented British and American writers and artists set the pace with the production of *The Sandman* series (1988–96), based on the publisher DC's 1974–1976 comic book series, *The Sandman*, illustrated by Jack Kirby and Ernie Chua and written by Joe Simon and Michael Fleisher. The major protagonist of the series is a character named Dream, imprisoned for his past sins. As he recalls incidents from his life, his stories are filled with fairy-tale, mythic, biblical, and Shakespearean characters and employed in suspenseful and surrealist plots. Gaiman's *Sandman* series fostered numerous imitations and also innovative experiments by graphic artists, especially in the field of the fairy tale. One of the more significant fairy-tale graphic novels is *Scary Godmother* (1997–2006), developed by Jill Thompson, in which an odd fairy-witch befriends a young girl named Hannah and helps her in comic situations in the modern world. Linda Medley's *Castle Waiting* (1996–2006) uses the fantastic to subvert the classical fairy tales. She self-published her graphic novel with black and white ink drawings in 1996 and has intermittently produced comic book sequels and graphic novels that focus on different characters who come to inhabit the castle that Sleeping Beauty abandoned after she had been wakened by a prince. Zenescope Entertainment began publishing a horror comic book series, *Grimm Fairy Tales*, in 2005 that is still in process. It concerns a professor of literature named Dr. Sela Mathers who helps people by showing them gruesome fairy tales that provide lessons about their lives. Another series, *Nightmare and Fairy Tales* (founded in 2002) also introduces the macabre into traditional fairy tales. One of the more interesting series of comic books is Fables, which began appearing in 2002. It deals with a besieged community of refugees and now includes over 60 issues of stand-alone comics and composite graphic novels. Conceived by Bill Willingham, the series begins with the premise that numerous characters from fairy tales, legends, myths, and folklore have been compelled to leave the lands of their origins, or Homelands. They do not know their mysterious enemy called the Adversary, except that he has taken over their homelands. So they migrate to New York City and form a clandestine community called Fabletown. However, many of them have difficulty adapting to the contemporary world, and their community is dysfunctional. The first five episodes, gathered in a trade paperback titled *Legends in Exile* and illustrated by Lan Medina, Steve Leialoha, and Craig Hamilton, concern the alleged murder of Rose Red, whose body is missing from her devastated apartment, which has a warning written in blood on a wall: "No More Happy Endings." Actually, there will be a happy ending because Bigby Wolf, security officer of Fabletown, discovers that Jack the Beanstalk and Rose Red concocted a scheme to make it appear she had been murdered because they were in need of money. During the investigations we learn that King Cole is the incompetent head of the Fabletown community; Snow White is the intrepid director of operations, trying to hold the fairy-tale and legendary characters together; Prince Charming is a philanderer; Beauty and the Beast are having marital problems; Bluebeard is a wealthy baron and philanthropist; and a talking pig escapes the Farm in upstate New York where non-human characters from fables must live. Inversion and subversion of classical fairy tales are characteristic of the more prominent fairy-tale graphic novels, which are at their best when they employ irony so that they are not taken seriously.   JZ

Flanagan, John, 'Grim Stories: Folklore in Cartoons', *Midwestern Journal of Language and Folklore* (1975).

Gravett, Paul, *Graphic Novels: Stories to Change Your Life* (2005).

Sanders, Joe, 'Of Storytellers and Stories in Gaiman and Vess's "A Midsummer Night's Dream"', *Extrapolation* (2004).

Spiegelman, Art, and Mouly, Françoise (eds.), *Folklore & Fairy Tale Funnies* (2000).

Weiner, Stephen, and Couch, Chris, *Faster Than a Speeding Bullet: The Rise of the Graphic Novel* (2004).

communist folk-tale films These were produced regularly in the Grimm heartlands and nearby countries, normally inflected in a particular political direction. However, despite a common overarching ideology, there was great diversity in these films, both from one country to another, and from one decade to another.

In the late 1930s the successful release of *Disney's *Snow White and the Seven Dwarfs* prompted Alexander Rou to make *The Magic Fish* (*Po shchuhemu veleny*, USSR, 1938), which initiated more than half a century of Soviet cinematic activity in this field. Based on an old Russian tale, it tells of Yemelya who one day catches a fish which pleads to be spared, saying that in exchange it will grant any wishes. Yemelya agrees. Nearby is a Tsar with a beautiful daughter, Nesmeyana, who is always bad-tempered and rude, and never laughs. In desperation, the Tsar makes a public proclamation that he will give her hand in marriage to any man who can make her laugh. Many suitors arrive and try, but none succeeds till Yemelya uses one of his wishes. The Tsar goes back on his promise, but Nesmeyana likes Yemelya so much that she runs away with him. This story is punctuated by various magical transformations effected by the fish: winter turns into summer, a lake grows out of a puddle, houses evolve from nowhere.

So popular was *The Magic Fish* that Rou's follow-up, *Koniok gorbunok* (*The Little*

Humpback Horse, USSR, 1939), was made in colour. It features the same leading actors and tells a similar story: a peasant wins the heart of a princess. Ivan, a young shepherd, catches a little white pony, and in its mane he discovers the glowing feathers of the fire-bird which alone can lead to princess Silver Morning. After freeing the pony, Ivan finds a talking humpback horse waiting for him at home. He becomes a groom in the service of a decrepit Tsar and is sent on pain of death to find Silver Morning, whom the Tsar plans to marry. With the humpback horse, Ivan has many adventures on land, under the sea, and in the sky, before finding the princess and bringing her back. However, she refuses to marry the Tsar; instead she rescues Ivan from gaol.

Apart from their portrayal of Tsars as senile and treacherous, there is little explicitly political in these and other similar films of the period: they could be interpreted in the West as simply promoting secular humanist values. Consequently, during the war, at the height of the Western alliance with the USSR, they were brought into distribution in the UK and shown to children in some Saturday cinema clubs. However, the tenor of Russian fairy-tale films soon began to change, and so did their reception in the West. *Volshebnoye zerno* (*The Magic Seed*, USSR, 1941) is about two peasant children, Andreika and Marika, who are presented by a legendary singing blacksmith with a magic seed, one of only two in the world. If planted in good soil, it will feed the world. The other is possessed by Karamur, a wicked ogre who keeps it locked up. Hearing about the children's seed, Karamur sends an army of Longnoses to destroy it, but the children go to another planet to consult a wise scientist. With his aid, plus that of a black slave and a flute, they overpower Karamur and set about spreading food and happiness to all humankind. Within the context of an exciting narrative the story presents, by implication, contemporary political ideas about oppression, liberation, the proletariat, progress through science, and the desirability of spreading happiness/communism to other countries. It was released in the UK over

Christmas 1944, but was not shown in children's Saturday matinees.

The end of the war saw the emergence of Aleksandr Ptushko as one of the pre-eminent Russian directors of folklore on screen, and an inspiration for film-makers elsewhere. Based on a folk-tale from the Ural Mountains, Ptushko's film *Kamenni tsvetok* (*The Stone Flower*, USSR, 1946), offers spectacle, adventure, suspense, and an analysis of the satisfactions of craftsmanship. It achieved fame and distribution in several countries, including the US and the UK.

During these immediate post-war years DEFA, the state film company of the communist-controlled sector of Germany, was making no fairy-tale films at all, partly because directors and writers were uncertain how to interpret and apply to this genre the Soviet doctrine of socialist realism. However, within a year of the 1949 establishment of the German Democratic Republic (East Germany) as a separate state, director Paul Verhoeven had followed Ptushko's lead and made *Das kalte Herz* (*The Cold Heart*, GDR, 1950). Steering clear of *Grimm princesses, Verhoeven adapted a text by the 19th-century German writer Wilhelm *Hauff. The film uses an enchanted forest, scenes of banqueting, and a giant's gruesome repository of bartered, still-beating hearts as a vivid background for the story of a young man who learns that riches are worthless without a social conscience. It was well received in both Germanies; and after an eight-year delay reached selected Saturday matinees in the UK.

Back in the USSR, Ptushko was developing further his expertise in bringing myth to the screen. *Sadko* (USSR, 1952) was based on medieval Russian legends which Rimsky-Korsakov had used in the 1890s as the basis for an opera of the same name. Ptushko retained snatches of the music, but reshaped the narrative significantly to suit his medium and ideology. In the film Sadko is a wandering minstrel who, when he arrives at the port of Novgorod, is so appalled by the disparity between the poverty-stricken conditions of the working people and the well-being of the prosperous merchants that he vows to take a selected company on a voyage round the world in search of the legendary bird of happiness. Needing ships and money to make this happen, he receives unexpected help from an underwater princess, whose father is the powerful Tsar of the Ocean. In India he thinks he has found the bird of happiness, but it turns out to be a phoenix, which lulls people into forgetting their problems, rather than overcoming them. Returning home empty-handed, they encounter a great storm; Sadko is able to save his comrades only by giving up his life to the Tsar of the Ocean. However, the Ocean Princess sets him free. Back on Russian soil, Sadko realizes that his journey was misconceived: happiness is in one's native country and has to be worked for, not found. In addition to this moral, the film stresses collectivism rather than individuality and points to the iniquities of capitalism, while at the same time getting full entertainment value from its energetic dances, its phoenix, and its underwater action. The film won a prize at the Venice Film Festival and achieved distribution in the UK, the USA (where it was retitled *The Magic Voyage of Sindbad*) and other Western countries; but it was the last Russian film of this genre to do so.

In the same year, Czechoslovakia launched several decades of cinematic production of this type with its first film made especially for children. Derived from national legends collected in the 19th century by the Czech novelist Bozena Nemcova, *Pysna princezna* (*The Proud Princess*) shows how good King Miroslav humbles the overbearing pride of Princess Krasomila. Under his guidance, and with the help of a singing flower, she learns to respect the work of the common people, recognizing it as the source of all prosperity.

Still in 1952, the GDR Communist Party held a conference which resulted in a decree that socialist realism included a requirement to show optimism in facing the future. Little more than a year later, at Christmas 1953, DEFA unveiled *Die Geschichte vom kleinen Muck* (*Little Mook*), which was to revitalize DEFA by becoming the most successful film it ever produced. Mindful of the popularity

of *The Cold Heart*, the director Wolfgang Staudte stuck with Hauff and adapted a story of an unwanted, orphan hunchback boy in the Orient who hears about the legendary Merchant who Sells Happiness, and runs away to the desert to find him. This film adds a new ingredient to standard themes by putting a frame round the comedy of Mook's magic shoes: at the beginning, middle, and end of the film are scenes showing Mook as an old man relating his story to a group of young children. By the time he finishes they are roused to declare that they will look after him and will henceforth speak out loud and clear against injustice and prejudice. Mook eventually reached selected Saturday morning screens in the UK, but only as a boy having fun: the sequences showing him as a wise old man were cut out.

All three countries were now committed to the idea that tales, legends, and myths could provide the basis of films that were edifying as well as entertaining—and not only for children—but they developed such projects in their own ways, in the light of their own national culture and the prevailing interpretation of socialist realism. A comparison of three films made near the end of the 1950s, one from each country, will illustrate the range of possibilities which they perceived as being open to them. In the USSR Ptushko saw out the decade as co-director of an elemental epic; in the GDR the spirit of Bertolt Brecht encouraged audiences to keep their distance; and in Czechoslovakia a beautiful princess became mousy.

Ptushko's epic was *Sampo* (USSR/Finland, 1959), which drew on **Kalevala*, the Finnish version of a Nordic myth about the origins of the world. Against a backdrop of Finnish locations, and the colour and special effects which create a flying cloak, a woman walking on waves, and a fire-breathing snake-trampling iron horse, *Sampo* validates labour—logging, hunting, blacksmithing—and puts a higher value on the community and its culture than on any one individual. No character or relationship is depicted in any detail, or given any idiosyncrasy. When a young man is drowned, it is his mother, not his betrothed, who pleads with the sea to give him up, and with nature to give him breath again. The film ends not with the wedding, but with the wider picture—the community rejoicing that their dream of a better life may be about to come true.

By contrast the GDR film from the same period, *Die Geschichte vom armen Hassan* (*The Story of Poor Hassan*, 1958) has a restricted cast and no exterior locations. Made in response to the GDR's second film conference, which had criticized the neo-realist quasi-documentary style of some recent productions, *Hassan* adapts Brechtian distancing techniques, developed for the stage, to the screen. Their purpose is to undermine any illusion of reality that may develop in an audience's mind. The film starts with the actors introducing themselves direct to camera and talking about the characters they are going to play. The Hassan actor leafs through a book to emphasize that what the audience will see is a constructed tale. When the story is acted out, no exterior locations are used; every scene takes place in a stylized studio set with minimal decor. Till just before the end the characters are one-dimensional—Hassan, naïve; the merchant, brutal; the judge, corrupt; the slave Fatima, helpless. The director's intention, through this style of telling, was to stimulate in the viewer a gradual sharpening of awareness of the painful contradictions (workers oppressed and poor, bosses idle and wealthy) in the characters' social relations. Not all GDR critics were entirely happy with this film, but for some the obvious seriousness of its intentions made it vastly preferable not only to neo-realism but also to what they saw as the bourgeois flimflam of *The Singing Ringing Tree*, made in the same country the year before.

Such critics would not have much liked a Czech film produced a year later. *Princezna se zlatou hvezdou* (*The Princess with the Golden Star*, 1959) was again from a story by Bozena Nemcova, who had herself derived it from the Brothers *Grimm. It is similar in some ways to Jim *Henson's *Sapsorrow*, but in this version the threat of incest is omitted, leaving it as a fairly traditional type of story about a princess who escapes

from a wedding to a king she detests by dressing in a mouse-skin coat and passing as a scullery-maid. The result is a film which shows little political awareness. The princess's father, Hostivit, is lightly mocked for his senile stubbornness; and Kazisvet, the hated suitor, is scorned for his arrogance and aggressiveness. There are romantic songs, performed by the popular singer who plays the prince; and there is ballet, for which several opportunities are created. The only real moral that the film illustrates is the universal lesson that people should be judged for what they are, not for how they look; and the only ideological reference is to an uprising which asserts the liberal democratic notion that ultimate political power lies with the people, not with any individual.

In the following three decades, culminating in the collapse of communist systems all over Europe, the three countries carried on making folklore films as a significant part of their overall programme, with each of them staying, to some extent, within the pattern established in the 1950s. In the USSR, Ptushko directed more national epics, such as *Russlan and Ludmilla* (1973), based on a long narrative poem by the venerated writer Alexander Pushkin. In the GDR, where films operated within a narrower definition of what was politically acceptable, one filmmaker adapted a book derived from fantasy characters invented by Karl Marx as a way of introducing his own children to the basics of dialectical materialism—*Hans Rockle und der Teufel* (*Hans Rockle and the Devil*, 1974). And in Czechoslovakia several more Bozena Nemcova stories about princes and princesses were brought to the screen.

But there were plenty of variations from this pattern as well. Directors in the USSR sometimes went outside their own national literatures, and made, for example, a version of *Ali Baba and the Forty Thieves* (shot in Tashkent, not Moscow, 1980) and several films based on stories by Hans Christian *Andersen, including *Rousalochka* (*The Little Mermaid*). In the GDR, the tales of the Brothers Grimm gradually became politically acceptable, especially those stories which do not feature royalty, such as *Sechse* *kommen durch die Welt* (*How Six Made their Way in the World*, 1972), *Gevatter Tod* (*Godfather Death*, 1980), and *Jorinde und Joringel* (1986). Meanwhile Czechoslovakian filmmakers went outside the communist bloc not only for stories, such as Andersen's *Galose stastia* (*The Lucky Boots*, 1986), but also for stars, such as the Austrian Maria Schell, who played the Queen Mother in *Kral Drozdia brada* (*King Thrushbeard's Bride*, 1984).

Nor were such productions isolated from the major philosophical currents that influenced the rest of Europe in these decades. Ideas about female emancipation, for example, are evident in various films. A Bozena Nemcova variation on the Cinderella story—*Tri orisky pro Popelku* (*Three Hazelnuts for Cinderella*)—was turned in 1974 into a film which presents the heroine as positive and self-confident, rather than resigned and submissive (as she had been in an earlier East German version based on the Grimms' tale). And a decade later two other 19th-century women writers, Gisela and Bettina von *Arnim, provided the source material for *Gritta von Rattenzuhausbeiuns* (*Gritta of Rat Castle*, GDR, 1985). This centres on Gritta, a 13-year-old countess, whose eccentric father is so obsessed with inventing machines that he lets the family castle fall into ruin. It is, therefore, up to Gritta and her rat friends to defeat the schemes of her new stepmother, who with the help of an evil abbess plans to defraud girls of their inheritances by getting them locked up. Gritta is shown as being rebellious and independent-minded, just as happy to consort with Peter the gooseboy as with Prince Bonus. The contemporary tone of these attitudes is reinforced by the dialogue, which is peppered with 1980s German slang.

One of the catalysts of such new orientations was television, the influence of which spread outwards. In the 1970s and 1980s some German and Czech fairy-tale films were made directly for the home screen, rather than for the cinema, a change which had several effects. It allowed some films to be shorter, around an hour rather than the 90 minutes which cinema expects. Its fitness

for close-ups of facial expressions and for voice-overs encouraged directors to explore characters' interior psychological dimensions. Its preference for realism led to films being shot on location in the countryside as far as possible, rather than in studios. And sharing the screen with news and current affairs programmes sharpened film-makers' desire to find and point up contemporary relevance in the tales they were telling.

When communist government in these countries ended at the close of the 1980s, state subsidy of film production ended too. In the 1990s, fairy-tale films are still made, but on an opportunistic rather than a systematic basis. A co-production deal between Russian and Chinese film companies resulted in *Magic Portrait* (1997), which begins, in traditional fashion, with a hard-working young Russian peasant called Ivan who, in return for kindness to a fairy, is given a picture of a beautiful girl. Stepping down from the painting, she says she is only a soul without a body. The difference from any previous Russian film is that she is Chinese. On a quest to bring her body and soul together, Ivan travels to China and there confronts many dangers. Another painting plays a significant role in the Czech *The Magic of a Beautiful Girl* (1995), which introduces new elements into fairyland and dispenses with magic completely. Made for television, it features a prince so in love with the portrait of an unknown woman (who turns out to be his late mother) that he will marry no one else, thereby showing an obstinacy which enrages his power-hungry young stepmother so much that she persuades the prince's best friend to murder him by using sexual wiles. Climactically, the prince marries a young woman who looks like the portrait; and the stepmother commits suicide.

In Germany DEFA still exists but is now a commercial company, facing west as well as east. Five years after the Berlin Wall came down it produced a kind of valediction in which a famous detective, called upon to solve the mystery of the missing last pages in fairy-tale books, discovers that they have been torn out by the Black Wizard, who is intent on changing the way the stories end.

This post-modern, self-reflexive, east-meets-west way of saying goodbye to Grimmland was called *Sherlock Holmes und die sieben Zwerge* (*Sherlock Holmes and the Seven Dwarfs* (Germany 1994). TAS

Berger, Eberhard, and Giera, Joachim (eds.), *77 Märchenfilme* (1990).

Koenig, Ingelore, *et al.*, *Zwischen Marx und Muck: DEFA-Filme für Kinder* (1996).

Shen, Quinna, 'Barometers of GDR Cultural Politics: Contextualizing the DEFA Grimm Adaptations,' *Marvels & Tales* (2011).

Company of Wolves, The (film) *See* JORDAN, NEIL.

Comyns, Barbara (1907–92) English writer and artist. Her novel *The Juniper Tree* (1985), set in contemporary London, follows details of 'The *Juniper Tree', such as a juniper-berry-eating mother dying in childbirth and a stepchild killed by the lid of an apple chest. But this feminist revision sides with the stepmother. Comyn's novel *Mr. Fox* (1987) alludes to 'The *Robber Bridegroom' and is based on the author's own relationship with a black marketeer. These semi-autobiographical works echo dark fairy-tale views of tragicomic family horror. PG

Coover, Robert (1932–) Distinctive award-winning American writer, several of whose postmodern fictions for adults rewrite the folk tale as a foundational narrative of Western literature and culture. Born in Iowa, he has been teaching at Brown University for many years and has also lived in Spain, the United Kingdom, and Italy. For Coover, a passionate interpreter of Miguel de Cervantes and Samuel Beckett (see his essay 'The Last Quixote'), it is through stories that we construct the world itself; thus the writer's vocation is to furnish 'better fictions with which we can re-form our notion of things'. Disruption of expectations, parodic repetition, keen pursuit of both metaphor and mundane detail, and unflinching entanglement in and critique of the workings of sexuality and power characterize Coover's unmaking and remaking of social fictions (e.g. religious ritual in *The Origin of the Brunists*, 1966; games and sports in *The Universal Baseball Association*, 1968; political structures in *The Public Burning* 1977; master–slave dynamics in *Spanking the Maid*, 1982; image and film in *A Night at the Movies*, 1987; and family in *John's Wife*, 1996). In proposing fictions that are overtly aware of themselves, Coover places himself in the tradition of 'intransigent realists' like Franz *Kafka and Angela *Carter. His more recent work involves a dialogue with film and creative uses of hypertext.

In *Aesop's Forest* (1986) Coover questions the fable: 'Three Little Pigs' frames *Hair O' the Chine* (1979), and *A Political Fable* (1980) displaces Dr *Seuss's *Cat in the Hat* from young children's bedtime to presidential elections. Some of his other fictions intensely engage specific fairy tales. Coover's 1969 experimental collection of short stories *Pricksongs & Descants* (1969) unsettles not only worn interpretations of Old Testament narratives, urban legends, and crime stories, but also tales like *'Little Red Riding Hood' and *'Jack and the Beanstalk' (in 'The Door: A Prologue of Sorts'), and *'Hansel and Gretel' ('The Gingerbread House'). A haunting and funny tale, 'The Dead Queen' (1973) retells *'Snow White' from the perspective of the prince.

Coover's grotesque and linguistically inventive *Pinocchio in Venice* (1991) makes a puppet, and then a book, of an American art history professor in decaying and carnival-esque Venice. In his quest to finish his autobiography, Professor Pinenut pursues the Blue-Haired Fairy turned college student, and is in turn pursued by pigeons and policemen. While reflecting on the pre-Second World War politics of the *Disney *Pinocchio* film, Coover playfully retells *Collodi's 19th-century *Pinocchio* in a struggling embrace of the *mamma/Madonna*-centred Italian tradition.

Another sustained exploration of a single fairy tale, *Briar Rose* (1996) retells the versions of 'The *Sleeping Beauty' of Giambattista *Basile, Charles *Perrault, the Brothers *Grimm and others to foreground the pain that quest-driven fairy tales demand and yet overlook. Storyteller, cook, and fairy, Coover's old crone has both deadly and antidotal tricks to play over and over again to awaken us all to the horrors of the tale which, like a dream, has captured her as well as the sleeping Rose and the frustrated 'hero'. While exposing the poverty and violence of desire in this romanticized tale, *Briar Rose* also pushes the central metaphor of the tale to its limits in a powerfully generative play of perspectives and tale-spinning.

Coover's more recent works, *Stepmother* (2004) and *A Child Again* (2005), continue his droll, postmodern interrogation of fairytale stereotypes. *Stepmother* is a long novella, similar in some respects to his 'Sleeping Beauty'. Here the stepmother is a witch in an enchanted forest. She tries to free her daughter from a royal prison, and chaos ensues with no promise of a happy end. *A Child Again* is a collection of short 'mock' postmodern tales, some of which had already been published. True to his style, Coover disassembles Alice, a fisherman, the Pied Piper and other well-known tales of childhood. But the return to childhood in Coover's narratives does not leave much room for optimism.   CB

Bacchilega, Cristina, 'Folktales, Fictions and Meta-Fictions: Their Interaction in Robert Coover's *Pricksongs and Descants*', *New York Folklore*, 1980.

Bond, Barbara, 'Postmodern Mannerism: An Examination of Robert Coover's *Pinocchio in Venice*', *Critique* (2004).

Evenson, Brian, *Understanding Robert Coover* (2003).

Redies, Sünje, 'Return with New Complexities: Robert Coover's *Briar Rose*', *Marvels & Tales* (2004).

Correia, Hélia (1949–) Portuguese writer, poet, and dramatist, who draws on folk and fairy-tale motifs in her novels and novellas such as *O número dos vivos* (*The Number of the Living*, 1982) and *Montedemo* (*Devil's Mountain*, 1983). The female voice is central to her works such as *Villa Celeste* (*Celestial Village*, 1985) and *A Fenda Erótica* (*The Erotic Fissure*, 1988). Writing from a feminist perspective, she has also adapted and rewritten folk tales from the oral tradition in her collection *Fascinação* (*Fascination*, 2004) and in her

Shakespearean adaptation, *A Ilha Encantada* (*The Enchanted Island*, 2005).   KMJ/JZ

Owen, Hilary, 'Feast or Faminism? Women, Revolution and Class in Works by Hélia Correia and Olga Gonçalves', *Forum for Modern Language Studies* (1992).

Owen, Hilary, 'Fairies and Witches in Hélia Correia', in Cláudia Pazos Alonso and Glória Fernandes (eds.), *Women, Literature, and Culture in the Portuguese-Speaking World* (2004).

Cortázar, Julio (1914–84) Argentinian novelist and, like his compatriot Jorge Luis *Borges, one of the best authors of short stories in the Spanish language. His sometimes complex writing techniques and expansive use of intertextuality do not result in depoliticized stories. On the contrary, Cortázar's tales tend to carry a political message that may be more or less overt but is always present, conditioned both by his implacable rejection of bourgeois society and his wish to question anything that has been socially sanctioned. Many of Cortázar's stories are fantastic tales, presenting numerous disturbing continuities between one human being and his or her *Doppelgänger*, between humans and animals, dream and wakefulness, art and reality. 'La bruja' ('The Witch', 1944), published in the periodical *Correo Literario* (*Literary Post*), was Cortázar's first fantastic tale, and *Bestiario* (*Bestiary*, 1951) was the first of his many collections of short stories which include *Final del juego* (*End of the Game*, 1956), *Todos los fuegos el fuego* (*All Fires the Fire*, 1966), *Alguien que anda por ahí* (*A Change of Light*, 1977), and *Deshoras* (*Out of Phase*, 1983).   CFR

Blanco, Mercedes, and Flotow-Evans, Luise von, 'Topology of the Fantastic in the Work of Julio Cortázar', *Canadian Fiction Magazine*, 61–2 (1987).

Noguera, Ruben, 'The Fantastic in the Stories of Julio Cortázar', *Revista de Estudios Hispánicos*, 21 (1994).

Review of Contemporary Fiction, spec. issue on Cortázar, 3 (1983).

Costa, Nicoletta (1953–) Italian writer and illustrator of fairy-tale-like tales for young children. Born in Trieste, Costa has a degree in architecture; has received several awards, including the 1989 and the 1994 Andersen Prize; and some of her books have been translated into English, Spanish, and Japanese. Her light-hearted, tongue-in-cheek books feature the confused but well-meaning witch Teodora who tries her magic out on a young frustrated dragon (*Teodora e Draghetto*, 1991), an unconventional princess who meets her match in *La principessa dispettosa* (*The Mischievous Princess*, 1986), and several chorus-like cats. CB

Cottingley Fairies, The Two 'epoch-making' photographs—'Frances and the Dancing Fairies' and 'Elsie and the Gnome'—taken in July 1917 by girls aged 9 and 16. In 1920 copies reached Sir Arthur Conan Doyle, creator of the deductive detective Sherlock Holmes. Doyle published them, along with three new ones the girls had taken, in his book *The Coming of the Fairies* (1922), which endorsed them as proof of the existence of psychic phenomena. Many people doubted the photographs' authenticity, but no trickery could be proved. After more than 50 years, the first screen version of the story reached television. 'Fairies', a 1978 dramatization by Geoffrey Case for the BBC, treats the girls' claims sympathetically. However, in the 1980s both photographers admitted deceit: they had used hat-pins and paper cut-outs to fake the pictures. *Fairytale: A True Story* (USA, 1997) condenses the controversy into a wartime argument between Doyle the believer and pre-eminent illusionist Harry Houdini, who remains sceptical. The film hints that the girls could have been hoaxers, but leaves the question open, preferring to end with an affirmation that, whether or not they can be photographed, fairies do exist for people who believe in them. In *Photographing Fairies* (UK, 1997), based on a novel, the Cottingley pictures are ridiculed by a professional photographer, Charles Castle, when Doyle presents them in a public lecture as hard evidence. Different fairy photos do, however, convince Castle. Investigating, he discovers that what is needed in order to see fairies is not faith but

a special magic flower. When eaten, it induces a trance in which he sees fairies as sexual beings and then has a vision of making love to his late wife. Fully confident that he will be reunited with her not in death but in a different world, he happily submits to being hanged for a murder he did not commit. TAS

Cooper, Joe, *The Case of the Cottingley Fairies* (1990).

Szilagyi, Steve, *Photographing Fairies* (1995).

Cox, Palmer (1840–1924) Canadian illustrator and author of light verse for children. Drawing on Scottish legends told to him as a child, Cox began his 'Brownies' series for *St Nicholas Magazine* in 1883. Short tales in rhyming couplets chronicled the harmless and amusing exploits of a brownie band intent on imitating human activities; the brownies could be individually identified in Cox's lively illustrations by their distinctive hats. *The Brownies: Their Book* (1887) and its twelve successors were wildly popular, even inspiring a three-act entertainment, *Palmer Cox's Brownies* (1895), that ran for years; children still enjoy them today. SR

Coypel, Charles-Antoine (1694–1752) Director of the French Royal Academy and principal painter of Louis XV. He illustrated many literary works, including editions of Molière's plays, and was himself a prolific dramatist. Coypel wrote one fairy tale, 'Aglaé ou Nabotine' ('Aglaé or Little One'), published posthumously in 1779. Coypel weaves several traditional fairy-tale motifs into the story of a benevolent fairy who tests the kindness and sincerity of an ugly little girl whose virtue is eventually rewarded with beauty and the love of a handsome young man. AZ

Craik, Dinah Maria (*née* Mulock, 1818–87) English novelist. *Alice Learmont* (1852), inspired by the Scottish ballad of Thomas the Rhymer, describes how Alice, a descendant of the legendary Thomas who was seduced by the Queen of Elfland, is stolen from her cradle by the elves and grows up in their country. She is finally released from her thraldom by her mother's determined love and by the spirit of Thomas the Rhymer himself. She compiled *The Fairy Book* in 1863, and included versions of French and English tales, and a few of the *Grimms' tales including, unusually, 'The *Juniper Tree'. There was also one Norwegian rarity, 'House Island', in which elements of pagan and Christian beliefs mingle. She wrote several works for children, including two fairy tales. *The Adventures of a Brownie* (1872) is a light-hearted account of the antics of a mischievous household elf. *The Little Lame Prince and his Travelling Cloak* (1875) is one of the most original allegorical fantasies of the period, comparable, though the meaning is more carefully indicated, to those of George *MacDonald. Described by the author as a parable, it relates how the throne of the hopelessly crippled little Prince Dolor is usurped by his uncle, who imprisons the child on top of the desolate Hopeless Tower, proclaiming that he is dead. Here his fairy godmother visits him, leaving a magical cloak that will take him anywhere he wishes. Restored to the throne, but still blessed with his travelling cloak, he becomes a good and wise king and finally leaves, as mysteriously as he has come. GA

Mitchell, Sally, *Dinah Mulock Craik* (1983).
Philipose, Lily, 'The Politics of the Hearth in Victorian Children's Fantasy: Dinah Mulock Craik's *The Little Lame Prince*', *Children's Literature Association Quarterly*, 21.3 (fall 1996).
Richardson, Alan, 'Reluctant Lords and Lame Princes: Engendering the Male Child in Nineteenth-Century Juvenile Fiction', *Children's Literature*, 21 (1993).

Cranch, Christopher Pearse (1813–92) American Unitarian minister, author and illustrator of two fantasies. *The Last of the Huggermuggers* (1856) and its sequel, *Kobboltozo* (1857) are possibly the first fairy stories for children by an American author. The Huggermuggers are two kindly and affectionate giants, the last of their race. Captured by a grasping Yankee trader who wants to make his fortune exhibiting them, they sicken and die. The sequel describes the end of the malicious dwarf Kobboltozo, who had betrayed them. Highly original and written with wry humour, the stories had no lasting popularity, perhaps because of the sadness of their theme. GA

Crane, Walter (1845–1915) British illustrator, designer, teacher, and painter, whose popular toybooks for children helped to bring inexpensively coloured books to a greater mass audience. He was born in Liverpool and died in London at the age of 69. Trained in wood engraving, he knew the printing process and was able to bring his skill to take advantage of the developing technology of his day in the field of children's books. He was a politically involved artist who also changed the recognition which an artist received in the publication of his books.

Crane's father was an unsuccessful artist and portraitist who nevertheless encouraged his son's early attempts at drawing. Shortly before his father's death, Walter entered a three-year apprenticeship with a wood engraver at the age of 13. His work was in drawing for the block, and he made vignettes and sketches for advertising cuts. After attending classes at Heatherley's Art School and selling freelance work, Crane made the acquaintance of the Victorian printer Edmund Evans, who first used him for drawing cover pictures. Evans worked with Crane (also Kate *Greenaway and Randolph *Caldecott) on a series of cheap picture books known as 'toybooks', indicating they were for children and were in colour, published by George Routledge and Frederick Warne in the latter half of the 19th century. The first of these bearing Crane's name appeared around 1865 and included *Farmyard Alphabet, Cock Robin, The House that Jack Built,* and *Sing a Song of Sixpence*. Crane eventually produced about 50 volumes in this series, which specialized in nursery rhymes (*Old Mother Hubbard, 1, 2, Buckle my Shoe,* and *This Little Pig Went to Market*), fairy tales (*The *Frog Prince, *Jack and the Beanstalk,* and **Cinderella*), and educational books (*Multiplication Tables in Verse, Grammar in Rhyme,* and *Baby's Own Alphabet*). In addition, he illustrated 45 books written by

Out set Riding Hood, so obliging and sweet,
And she met a great Wolf in the wood,
Who began most politely the maiden to greet,
as tender a voice as he could.

He asked to what house she was going, and why;
Red Riding Hood answered him all:
He said, "Give my love to your Gran; I will try
"At my earliest leisure to call."

Crane, Walter The wolf greets *Little Red Riding Hood with politeness while the hunters look on in Walter Crane's adaptation of the *Grimms' version of 'Little Red Riding Hood', published in *Walter Crane's New Toybook* (1874).

others, including Nathaniel *Hawthorne's *A Wonderbook for Boys and Girls* (1892), Oscar *Wilde's *The Happy Prince and Other Tales* (1888), and 13 books for Mary *Molesworth, an extremely popular and prolific children's writer.

In his pictorial style, Crane was influenced not only by the techniques he worked in but also Japanese woodcuts, which had made their way to Europe. He used strong outline, vertical lines, and bright colours, and signed many of his pictures with a small monogram of his initials inside a circle with a drawing of a crane. His illustrations were frequently of an architectural nature, and often he would make decisions about colour once his line drawings were cut into the wood blocks and proofs returned to him. As photographic printing methods replaced the woodblocks, he quickly adapted to the new techniques. His pictures were busy and filled to the edges, with costume, floor tiling, vases, flowers, figured carpets, and decorative items which encouraged others to steal his patterns. As a result, he began to market his own fabric and wallpaper designs and promoted the Arts and Crafts movement associated with William *Morris, with whom he also campaigned for socialist political causes. He served as the first president of the Arts and Crafts Society in 1888 and joined the Fabians in 1885. When his pictures were reprinted without his permission, he took control of his art and his name appears on several titles, such as *Walter Crane's Painting Book* (1889). At the end of his life, he turned his attention to education and served in leadership positions in the Manchester School of Art and the Royal College of Art in South Kensington. In addition to a volume of verse and his autobiography *An Artist's Reminiscences* (1907), he wrote several influential books on his theories of art and design, *Of the Decorative Illustration of Books Old and New* (1896), *The Bases of Design* (1898), and *Line and Form* (1900). Although he made paintings throughout his life, he never achieved fame for this form of his work; the formality of his carefully designed compositions for children's books were thought stilted in easel paintings.

To contrast his styles, *Beauty and the Beast* (1874) portrays the beast as a tusked and monocled wart hog, decked out in elaborate and colourful costume, seated on a settee, surrounded by mandolin, gold chandelier, tea set, and leopard skin rug. Beauty's robe, murals, fans, and gloves are all ornately figured with exotic animals and scenes from mythology. *Household Stories from the Collection of the Brothers Grimm*, published eight years later in 1882 with a translation of *Kinder- und Hausmärchen* by Crane's sister Lucy, is lavishly illustrated in black-and-white wood engravings with head pieces, friezes, tail pieces, and full-page pictures with a blank sheet behind. His pictures for this volume explain, symbolize, and elaborate 52 fairy tales, emphasizing the light and dark of the stories as well as positioning them in a timeless landscape of the past. This is a respectful volume, which highlights the artist (a table of contents lists the pictures but not the stories), portrays the characters as adults, and illustrates just what pictures can add to storytelling. Drawings are enclosed in architectural frames, often with quotes and objects which symbolize the themes of the stories.

He married Mary Frances Andrews in 1871, and they had five children, two of whom died as infants. At the end of his life he was much honoured in Britain as well as several European countries. Though he felt limited by his fame as an illustrator of works for children, he brought great respect to this craft. His gift was in bringing animation to his pictures, taking the subjects, such as fairy tales, seriously, and working copiously in the mass media.   GRB

Engen, Rodney K., *Walter Crane as a Book Illustrator* (1975).
Smith, Greg, and Hyde, Sarah, *Walter Crane 1845–1915: Artist, Designer, and Socialist* (1989).
Spencer, Isobel, *Walter Crane* (1975).

Cranko, John (1927–73) Dancer and choreographer. Born in South Africa, Cranko was a student at the University of Cape Town Ballet School. In 1946 he moved to London to complete and perfect his training. He started as a dancer at the Sadler's Wells

Theatre Ballet, but it soon became clear that his true talent lay in choreography. During his time in London he produced numerous ballets, among them the fairy-tale ballets *Beauty and the Beast* (1949) and *The Prince of the Pagodas* (1957), which was set to music by Benjamin Britten. This ballet combines elements of several traditional fairy tales in the story of the beautiful and kind princess Belle Rose, whose malicious sister Belle Épine takes over their father's kingdom and imprisons her family. Belle Rose and the kingdom are rescued by an enchanted green salamander who, when she promises to marry him, changes back to the Prince of the Pagodas. In 1961 Cranko moved to Stuttgart, where he became the ballet director of the Württembergisches Staatstheater, which became famous world-wide through his work. In Stuttgart he choreographed traditional ballets like Tchaikovsky's *The Nutcracker* (1966), as well as his own, among them another fairy-tale ballet, *Quatre Images* (1967), in which a prince flees from his monotonous court and meets and falls in love with a mermaid who is his doom. Cranko died in 1973 on the return flight from a USA tour.   CS

> Canton, Katia, *The Fairy Tale Revisited: A Survey of the Evolution of the Tales, from Classical Literary Interpretations to Innovative Contemporary Dance-Theater Productions* (1994).
> Percival, John, *Theatre in My Blood: A Biography of John Cranko* (1983).

Crébillon fils, Claude-Prosper Jolyot de

(1707–77) French novelist. Son of a playwright and French academician, Crébillon fils used the parodic fairy tale to satirize political and religious issues. His *L'Écumoire* (*The Skimmer*, 1734), *Atalzaide* (1745), and *Ah! Quel conte* (*Ah! What a Tale*, 1754) use oriental settings, erotic *double-entendre*, and sophisticated narrative techniques. Of these tales, *L'Écumoire* is especially significant. Besides earning Crébillon fils a brief prison sentence, it inaugurated a series of 18th-century French libertine fairy tales and provides an innovative critique of prevailing narrative models.   LCS

Croker, Thomas Crofton (1798–1854)

Irish antiquary and one of the first systematic chroniclers of Irish folklore. His rambles in southern Ireland collecting songs and legends of the people resulted in the anonymous publication in 1826 of the first volume of *Fairy Legends and Traditions of the South of Ireland*. A second and third series under Croker's name appeared in 1828, and an edition of the whole, from which Croker excluded tales collected by his friends, was issued in 1834. Frequently reprinted throughout the rest of the century, illustrated by artists including Daniel Maclise and George *Cruikshank, *Fairy Legends* is a significant contribution to the development of British folklore studies since its materials were collected in the field. The Brothers *Grimm quickly translated the first volume into German (it was also translated into French) and offered Croker their work on Irish and Scottish fairies and their long essay 'On the Nature of the Elves' for his third volume, which concentrated on Welsh and surviving English fairy legends. Although later accused of being excessively literary and of adding humour to the Irish materials, Croker presented a large audience with authentic traditional legends. Noting that supernatural beliefs survived in Ireland, he made such figures as the Phooka, the Cluricaune (leprechaun) and the Banshee important. Croker also arranged and edited *Legends of the Lakes* (1829), tales of Killarney collected by R. Adolphus Lynch, and was an impetus behind Thomas *Keightley's *Fairy Mythology* (1828), a work which grew from Keightley's collaboration on *Fairy Legends*.   CGS

> Dorson, Richard M., *The British Folklorists: A History* (1968).
> Fitzsimons, Eileen, 'Jacob and Wilhelm Grimm's *Irische Elfenmärchen*: A Comparison of the Translation with the English Original, *Fairy Legends and Traditions of the South of Ireland* by T. Crofton Croker' (Diss., University of Chicago, 1978).
> Kamenetsky, Christa, 'The Irish Fairy Legends and the Brothers Grimm', in Priscilla Ord (ed.), *The Child and the Story: An Exploration of Narrative Forms* (1983).

Crossley-Holland, Kevin John William
(1941–) British translator, poet, and reteller
of myths, legends, and fairy tales. Apart from
The Fox and the Cat (1985), 11 animal tales
from the *Grimms, he has specialized in
retellings of British (and Irish) folk tales.
Outstanding works are *British Folk Tales:
New Versions* (1987) and two collections of
tales from East Anglia, *The Dead Moon and
Other Tales from East Anglia and the Fen
Country* (1982) and *Long Tom and the
Dead Hand* (1992). Brief notes in these volumes on sources and on strategies for retelling various tales reflect Crossley-Holland's
concern both to preserve local traditions
and to render these tales pertinent and
meaningful to the lives of a modern audience. He has a gift for reinventing folk tales
in a way that makes the characters real
people, whose thoughts and feelings are
our own. In 2007 he brought together some
of his finest short retellings of folk tales and
myths about exile and banishment, including 'The Green Children', 'Sea-Tongue', and
'The Wild Man' in *Outsiders*.   JAS

Crowley, John (1942–) American author
of *Little, Big* (1981) an ambitious, highly influential work of American fantasy. The
novel begins with a quest motif as the hero
sets off from a magical version of New York
City to the extraordinary country house
where his fiancée awaits him. The tale is set
in modern America yet has the flavour of
British Victorian fiction, moving leisurely
through an enchanted landscape filled with
secrets within secrets, stories within stories.
Crowley draws upon a dazzling breadth of
fairy lore and classic fantasy themes to create
a vivid fairy world coexisting with our own.
The book weaves numerous disparate
threads into a bright and seamless cloth—
making use of traditional folklore motifs
('changeling' tales, animal guides, fairy godmothers, 'the sleeper under the hill') as well
as imagery from *Mother Goose rhymes,
William *Shakespeare's fairy court, Lewis
*Carroll's *Alice books, the fairy poetry of
William Butler *Yeats, the *Cottingley fairy
photographs, the ideas of the theosophists,
and other magical esoterica.

The publication of *Little, Big* revitalized
the field of American fantasy fiction, proving
it was possible to write a New World fantasy
rooted in Old World themes. In subsequent
books, *Aegypt* (1987) and *Love and Sleep*
(1996), Crowley continues to develop the
'Secret History of the World' which lies just
beyond mundane perception, although he
bases these novels on alchemical philosophy
rather than the fairy tradition. In Crowley's
short fiction two stories are of particular
interest: 'The Green Child' (1981), a simple,
elegant retelling of a curious English legend,
and 'Lost and Abandoned', a contemporary
meditation on *'Hansel and Gretel' (1997).
                                                              TW

Crowquill, Alfred (pseudonym of **Alfred
Henry Forrester**, 1804–72) English illustrator and writer, brother of Charles Robert
Forrester whose books—published under
the joint name of 'Alfred Crowquill'—he illustrated. After his brother stopped writing
in the early 1840s, he took over the name.
His preferred vein was comedy and the grotesque (he did many stage designs for pantomime), but he wrote a number of fairy tales
for children featuring giants, dwarfs,
gnomes, fairy talismans, all with a strong
moral purpose, the folly of the pursuit of
gold, and the virtues of diligence and a
kind heart being favourite themes. Some
tales were issued individually, such as *Gruf-
fel Swillendrinkem; or The Reproof of the
Brutes* (1856); others came in collections,
Tales of Magic and Meaning (1856), *Fairy
Tales* (1857), *Fairy Footsteps, or Lessons
from Legends* (1860). His illustrations, like
his writing, could be vapid and unremarkable, but when he broke free from the usual
restraints imposed by convention the results
were both striking and macabre. In 'Peter
Finnigan and the Spirits' in *Fairy Footsteps*,
a facetious Irish story about the evils of
drink, drunken Peter meets 'a great, pale
face, as big as the side of a house', drawn
by Crowquill with a nightmare intensity that
he brought to other illustrations of giants
and ogres, as when Harry sets fire to the
giantess in *The Good Boy and the Black
Book* (1858).   GA

Crowquill, Alfred It is 'too late' for the hero given to drink in Alfred Crowquill's 'Peter Finnigan and the Spirits', published in *Fairy Footsteps* (1860) and illustrated by the author.

Cruikshank, George (1792–1878) Hailed as one of the most important British graphic artists of the 19th century. Born in London, Cruikshank was Scottish by blood; his father, Isaac, was a leading political caricaturist in the 1790s, alongside Rowlandson and Gilray. Unfortunately, Isaac Cruikshank died in 1811, after meeting a challenge in a drinking game.

George Cruikshank began his career as an artist when he was 13, working as his father's apprentice and assistant. By the age of 18 he had achieved notoriety as a political caricaturist. He moved 13 years later into book illustration with the successful printing of *Points of Humour* (1823). The glowing review of this book in *Blackwood's Edinburgh Magazine* in July 1823 prompted the publisher, Charles Baldwyn, to issue the *German Popular Stories* (1823), translated by Edgar Taylor. It was the first English translation of the *Grimms' tales and was reputed to be a masterpiece. In 1868, the Grimms' tales

were reissued and carried an introduction by John Ruskin, who compared the quality of Cruikshank's etchings to those of Rembrandt. In the next year Baldwyn issued *Italian Tales* (1824). Here the 16 full-page woodcuts demonstrated the refinement of Cruikshank's skills and the adeptness and vitality of his line. In 1848 he produced 12 etchings for fairy stories in an expurgated text of Giambattista *Basile's *Pentamerone*, adapted by Edgar *Taylor, the translator of the Grimms' stories.

Like Hogarth and other 19th-century artists, Cruikshank used his art to critique 18th-century mores. During the decade 1853–64, Cruikshank wrote and illustrated four stories for children, gathered under the title of *Fairy Library*, to incorporate his social criticism: 'Hop o' my Thumb and the Seven League Boots' (1853); 'History of *Jack and the Bean-Stalk' (1854); *'Cinderella and the Glass Slipper' (1854); and *'Puss-in-Boots'. Fuelled by his ardent enthusiasm for the temperance

The Pumpkin, and the Rat, and the Mice, and the Lizards, being changed by the Fairy, into a Coach, Horses, and Servants; to take Cinderella to the Ball at the Royal Palace.

Designed & Etched *George Cruikshank*

The Fairy changing Cinderella's Kitchen dress into a beautiful Ball dress !!!

Cruikshank, George The fairy godmother creates miracles in George Cruikshank's version of Perrault's **'Cinderella', published in *George Cruikshank's Fairy Library* (1853–4).

movement (his own abstinence beginning in 1847 when he wholeheartedly embraced the cause of Total Abstinence), Cruikshank altered the tales by moralizing against drinking and other licentious behaviour. Because he took such liberties with the traditional tale, Cruikshank angered Charles *Dickens who protested against the subversion of children's imagination by parodying Cruikshank's abstinence in 'Frauds on the Fairies', in *Household Words* (October 1853). The *Fairy Library* suffered for this controversy between Dickens and Cruikshank and failed commercially.

With an interest in fairy tales came a fascination with the supernatural. Outstanding among Cruikshank's book illustrations and notable for their narrative quality and rendering of light and shadow are eight etchings for a translation of Adelbert von *Chamisso's *Peter Schlemihl* (1823), the tale of a man who sold his shadow to the devil. Cruikshank illustrated another work of fantasy in 1861, *A Discovery concerning Ghosts, with a Rap at 'Spirit Rappers'*, written to poke fun at the contemporary interest in necromancy. Seven woodcuts followed in 1852 for E. G. Flight's 'The True Legend of St Dunstan and the Devil'.

Towards the end of his career, Cruikshank employed woodcuts to decorate Juliana H. *Ewing's *The Brownies and Other Tales* (1871) and three tales collected in *Lob Lie-by-the-Fire*, or the *Luck of Lingborough*

Cruikshank, George 'My how dark it was in there', says *Little Red Riding Hood as she exits from the wolf's belly in George Cruikshank's illustration for *German Popular Stories* (1823), translated by Edgar Taylor.

(1874). Cruikshank's last commission, the frontispiece for *The Lily and the Rose* by Mrs Blewitt (1877) closed his 72 years as an artist with his formidable abilities and genius intact.   SS

Altick, Richard, *Paintings from Books: Art and Literature in Britain 1760–1900* (1985).
Buchanan-Brown, John, *The Book Illustration of George Cruikshank* (1980).
Patten, Robert L. (ed.), *George Cruikshank: A Revaluation (1974; 1992).*
Patten, Robert L., *George Cruikshank's Life, Times, and Art* (1992).
Vogler, Richard, *Graphic Works of George Cruikshank* (1979).

Cummings, E. E. (Edward Estlin Cummings, 1894–1962) American poet, essayist, and artist. Known for his dramatic experiments in typography and syntax, Cummings also wrote some charming but fairly conventional fairy tales for his daughter: 'The Old Man Who Said "Why"', 'The Elephant and the Butterfly', 'The House that Ate Mosquito Pie', and 'The Little Girl Named I' (collected in 1965 with illustrations by John Eaton). His 1932 essay 'A Fairy Tale' has little to do with fairy tales, but celebrates art as detached from economics and politics and even 'life'.

EWH

Cunningham, Alan (1784–1842) Scottish writer and commentator on Border traditions. The actual author of publisher R. J. Cromek's *Remains of Nithsdale and Galloway Song* (1810), Cunningham presented his own fairy poems, including 'The Mermaid of Galloway' and 'We Were Sisters, We Were Seven', as authentic folklore materials. He also wrote several stories involving fairy abductions, 'The Haunted Ships' and 'Elphin Irving: The Fairies' Cupbearers' for his *Traditional Tales of the English and Scottish Peasantry* (1822). The valuable appendices he wrote for the *Remains* include essays on the 'Scottish Lowland Fairies' and on the mischievous brownie, Billie Blin.   CGS

'Cupid and Psyche' *See* 'BEAUTY AND THE BEAST'.

Curtin, Jeremiah (1835–1906) American folklorist, linguist, and ethnologist of Irish descent. A lover of languages, Curtin studied German, Swedish, Italian, Hebrew, and Sanskrit, to name a few. From 1864 to 1870 Curtin, a junior diplomat, lived in Russia and studied the Slavic languages and Hungarian. In 1883–91 Curtin was a field worker at the Bureau of Ethnology of the Smithsonian Institution, where he gathered information on Native American languages, religions, and mythology, the results of which were published posthumously with the exception of *Creation Myths of Primitive America, in Relation to the Religions, History, and Mental Development of Mankind* (1898). It was not until 1887 that Curtin first went to Ireland, which he believed to be the last bastion of European mythology and folklore.

Curtin greatly contributed to the collecting methods of the time. Aided by his wife and collaborator, Alma Cardell Curtin, he recorded stories verbatim, making only minor changes for an audience of readers, and indicated the name and location of his sources. He believed that language and folklore were intricately connected; the decline of certain languages like Gaelic, then, went hand in hand with the decline of that particular folklore. His drive to collect the languages and folklore of so many different cultures was fuelled in part by his belief that he could establish 'a history of the human mind . . . with a basis as firm as that which lies under geology'. His collections include *Myths and Folk-Lore of Ireland* (1890), *Myths and Folk-Tales of the Russians, Western Slavs, and Magyars* (1890), *Hero-Tales of Ireland* (1894), *Tales of the Fairies of the Ghost World, Collected from the Tradition of South-West Munster* (1895), and *Fairy Tales of Eastern Europe* (1914).   AD

Murphy, Maureen, 'Jeremiah Curtin: American Pioneer in Irish Folklore', *Eire-Ireland*, 13.2 (summer 1978).

Czarnecki, Thomas (1980–) French photographer, advertising art director, and co-creator of Mustribe artists' laboratory. His still series, 'From Enchantment to Down' (2009–12), imagines dire fates for *Disney feature-film ingénue characters, identifiable as such by their clothing and Czarnecki's inclusion of the legendary Pocahontas along with fairy-tale figures such as Jasmine from *Aladdin* (1992) and Tinkerbell from *Peter Pan* (1953). His adult Little Red Riding Hood—a child in Disney's (1922) black-and-white cartoon short—is telling, given feminist analysis of her story as a rape and/or (sexual) initiation. Czarnecki's images of women sprawled on the ground with open legs and raised skirts suggest assault and femicide, and confront a naive world view of sweet fairy tales.   PG

Dadd, Richard (1817–86) The first Victorian fairy painter to gain recognition for his genre (*see* VICTORIAN FAIRY PAINTING). He trained at London's Royal Academy, and his early works *Puck* (1841) and *Titania Sleeping* (1841), like those of other fairy painters, were inspired by Shakespeare. Unfortunately, he suffered from demonic hallucinations, murdered his father, and was incarcerated in Bethlem Hospital's criminal lunatic ward. While enlightened doctors prescribed painting as therapy, the public began to equate fairy painting and madness. Isolated from artistic movements like Impressionism, Dadd continued his esoteric, minutely detailed fairy scenes in *Contradiction: Oberon and Titania* (1854–8) and the enigmatic *Fairy-Feller's Master-Stroke* (1855–64). MLE

Allderidge, Patricia, *The Late Richard Dadd* (n.d.).

Greysmith, David, *Richard Dadd: The Rock and Castle of Seclusion* (1973).

Dadié, Bernard Binlin (1916–) West African novelist, essayist, playwright, and poet, who has served as the minister of culture in the Ivory Coast, his home country. Many of his works deal with colonial oppression and the tensions between modern changes and traditional customs. He writes in French, and while working at the Institut Français d'Afrique Noire he began collecting material from the oral heritage of the Ivory Coast that he adapted in French for the purpose of achieving widespread circulation of the tales in Africa and Europe. His work led to the publication of several important books of folk tales: *Légendes africaines* (*African Legends*, 1953), *Le Pagne noir* (*The Black Cloth: A Collection of African Folktales*, 1955), *Les Belles Histoires de Kakou Ananze, l'Araignée*, (*The Wonderful Stories of Kacou Amanzè*, 1979), and *Les contes de Koutopu-as-Samala* (*The Tales of Koutou-as-Samala*, 1982). These collections include historical legends, myths, moral fables, comic anecdotes, pourquois tales, and spider stories. Dadié has a fondness for the trickster character, Ananaze, who imparts important lessons to his readers. The diverse tales in all his collections are intended to preserve the richness of African culture and at the same time to connect with European folklore. JZ

Edebiri, Unionmwam (ed.), *Bernard Dadié: Hommages et Études* (1992).

Egonu, Iheanachor, 'The Nature and Scope of Traditional Folk Literature', *Présence Africaine* (1987).

Quillateau, Claude, *Bernard Binlin Dadié: L'homme et l'œuvre* (1967).

Wynchank, Anny, 'Transition from an Oral to a Written Literature in Francophone West Africa', *African Studies* (1985).

Dahl, Roald (1917–90) British author of macabre short stories and liberating fairy tales. Born in Wales of Norwegian parents, he always felt an affinity to Norway and its folklore. He attended British schools where, according to his first autobiography (*Boy: Tales of Childhood*, 1985), he met the nasty authority figures like children-flogging headmasters and grouchy sweet-shop owners that would figure in his books. At Repton School, where his marks were undistinguished, he volunteered as a chocolate taster for Cadbury's. He opted not to attend university, worked for Shell Oil in East Africa, and during the Second World War flew with the Royal Air Force as a fighter pilot and wing commander—events recorded in *Going Solo* (1986). Sidelined by a severe crash, he became an air attaché in the British Embassy in Washington, DC, did intelligence work, and started writing short stories about his flying experience (collected in *Over to You*, 1946). His tales became increasingly imaginative, and in 1943 he penned *The Gremlins*, a *Disney-illustrated children's fantasy about tiny beings that sabotage fighter planes. His next work for children would not come until 1961.

In the interim, Dahl distinguished himself as an 'intellectual Alfred Hitchcock' whose morbid plot twists thrice won the Edgar Award from the Mystery Writers of America (1954, 1959, 1980). These macabre tales for magazines from *Harper's Bazaar* to *Playboy* were later collected in *Kiss, Kiss* (1969), *Switch Bitch* (1974), and *Tales of the Unexpected* (1979), which prompted a television series.

He married the actress Patricia Neal in 1953, and his second career as a children's author was an outgrowth of telling stories to their children. *James and the Giant Peach* (1961) is a marvellous fairy tale about a quiet young orphan and two evil aunts. A giant peach grows when James spills some magic seeds, and within its (womb-like) interior he meets giant insects like the maternal Ladybug, paternal Old-Green-Grasshopper, bragging Centipede, and timid Earthworm. Psychoanalysts interpret them as parts of James's fragmented self that he successfully integrates when he emerges from the peach to pilot it on adventures; children delight in its sheer fantasy and cruel come-uppance when the peach squashes the aunts. Critics challenged this violence, but others said it was no worse than that of traditional fairy tales. A similar objection was raised with respect to *Charlie and the Chocolate Factory* (1964). Written after the death of the Dahl's eldest child and dedicated to their brain-damaged son, it tells how poverty-stricken Charlie Bucket wins a tour of a mysterious chocolate factory and becomes heir to its fabulous owner, Willy Wonka. Critics objected when greedy, spoiled, or media-addicted children met cruel deaths to the sardonic verses of the Oompa-Loompas (pygmy factory workers

whose racist depiction Dahl later corrected). Dahl replied that children's sense of humour was more vulgar and crude than that of adults—a fact borne out by recent studies. He also asserted that he only wrote to entertain, but scholars interpret the story as a post-industrial parable of moral lessons (anti-oral greed, anti-TV) in which poor Charlie's empty bucket is filled with excremental wonders of the underground *Inferno*-like factory.

In 1965, Patricia Neal suffered a massive stroke, and the authoritarian Dahl undertook her recovery. Hospital bills necessitated his working on screenplays (*You Only Live Twice*, 1967; *Chitty Chitty Bang Bang*, 1967; *Willy Wonka and the Chocolate Factory*, 1970), but he continued to write stories. His children's tales further exploited the marvellous, fables, and folk tales with quick-paced plots, *Dickens-like names, Joycean wordplay, nonsense rhymes à la Lewis Carroll, and delightful artwork by illustrators like Quentin *Blake. This lightness is balanced by dark humour. In Dahl's world, as in traditional fairy tales, the oppressed (usually children) triumph over the tyrants (usually adults), who are often morbidly punished. In *George's Marvellous Medicine* (1981), for example, a witch-like grandmother is killed, and a girl turns a family of hunters into hunted ducks in *The Magic Finger* (1966), which attacks the gun lobby. Situational ethics are also explored in *The Fantastic Mr Fox* (1970), where a modern-day Renard rather subversively defends poaching when familial needs supersede societal laws.

Where Dahl's Cadbury work coloured *Charlie* and his African experiences enriched *The Enormous Crocodile* (1978), the Norse legends of his youth influenced two later novels about witches and giants. *The BFG* (1982) is about the dream-giving Big Friendly Giant who helps the orphaned Sophie overthrow child-munching giants who have nightmares about *Jack (of Beanstalk fame). Likewise, the orphaned boy of the award-winning *Witches* (1983) learns from his Norwegian grandmama how to identify and overthrow these cleverly disguised hags. Both of these coming-of-age quests break taboos about bodily functions in juvenile literature: witches spit blue mucous, the gently aphasic BFG delights in 'whizzpopping' (flatulating) before the Queen. These scatological references charm children as they identify with their problem-solving heroes. Especially liberating is the genius Matilda's wish fulfilment: she uses telekinesis to punish an evil headmistress and rescue a gentle teacher (*Matilda*, 1988).

Interestingly, although critics always identified his children's stories as fairy tales, the only one Dahl labelled as such was *The Minpins* (1991), about a boy who explores the Forest of Sin and rescues a gremlin-like people. He openly lampooned fairy tales, however, in collections of verse like *Roald Dahl's Revolting Rhymes* (1982) and *Rhyme Stew* (1989). These blatantly subvert the genre by opining on the cruelty of the original versions (as in his *'Hansel and Gretel') and providing surprise twists to updated tales (for example, *Little Red Riding Hood sports a wolfskin coat, and *Snow White uses the Magic Mirror to help gambling-addicted dwarfs win at the races).   MLE

> Bosmajian, Hamida, 'Charlie and the Chocolate Factory and Other Excremental Visions,' *The Lion and the Unicorn*, 9 (1985).
> Treglown, Jeremy, *Roald Dahl: A Biography* (1994).
> West, Mark I., *Roald Dahl* (1992).

Dandy, Beano, and **Bunty** The best-known British comics by virtue of their longevity, being first published in 1937, 1938, and 1950 respectively. The first two are juvenile comics and the last is intended for young adolescent girls.

Fairy tales in the *Dandy* have tended to be robust and dominated by male characters. An early example, '*Jack the Dragon Killer', was initially a text story published in 1939, and later became a picture story with the slightly changed title of 'Jak the Dragon Killer'. Other picture stories have included 'Dick Whittington' (1943) and *'Hansel and Gretel' (1944). A parody with the title 'Joe White and the Seven Dwarfs' was published in 1943.

Consistently recognized as Britain's most popular comic, the *Beano* has made rather more use of fairy stories than the *Dandy*. Male robustness has again been the main characteristic. The earliest fairy tale to be included was *'Little Tom Thumb', which was first introduced as a text story in 1938, later becoming a picture story in 1940. There have been two examples of monster-slayers in picture-story form, these being 'Morgyn the Mighty' in 1938 and 'Strang the Terrible' in 1943. *'Cinderella' (1940) and 'Sinbad' (1950) have also been used as picture stories. A popular long-running story, 'Jimmy and his Magic Patch', was introduced in 1943. Jimmy was a small boy who had a magic patch stitched to the seat of his trousers. At his request it transported him to a past which included adventures with Sindbad and Aladdin.

Fairy stories have been absent from the pages of the *Dandy* and the *Beano* for many years, a process which started when both comics began to adopt a predominantly comic-strip format.

The *Bunty* has published very few fairy stories, probably because they do not appeal to young adolescent girls. On the rare occasions when they have appeared, they have been placed in a modern context, for example 'Myrtle the Mermaid' (1958) and 'Lydia and the Little People' (1970). In a more recent example, 'The Mermaid's Spell', a well-known theme is also given a modern background when a mermaid attempts to persuade a schoolgirl to change places with her. This story, contained in a single issue, was unusual because of its cartoon-strip format. The few fairy stories included in the *Bunty* have all been concerned with female characters.   GF

Daudet, Alphonse (1840–97) French writer known for his novels of bohemian Paris and traditional Provence. Daudet wrote *Le Roman du Chaperon-Rouge* (*Novel of Red-Riding Hood*, 1859) and 'Les sept pendues de Barbe-bleue' ('Bluebeard's Seven Hanged Wives', 1861). These and other marvellous tales like 'La Légende de l'homme à la cervelle d'or' ('The Man with the Golden Brain', 1868) twist conventional stories to fit contemporary mores. Playing on misogynistic attitudes, Daudet depicts *Little Red Riding Hood as a free spirit condemned by pedantry and provincialism while his *Bluebeard is portrayed as a victim of feminine wiles. In 'Les Fées de France' ('The Fairies of France', 1873), he deals with the Franco-Prussian War and presents the fairy *Mélusine as a Prussian war patriot.   AR

Davenport, Tom (1939–) Independent American film-maker. Besides documentaries focusing on the traditional culture of the American South, Davenport has created an innovative series of live-action fairy-tale adaptations called *From the Brothers Grimm: American Versions of Folktale Classics* (*see* FILM AND FAIRY TALES). Films in the series include *Hansel and Gretel: An Appalachian Version* (1975), *Rapunzel, Rapunzel* (1979), *The Frog King* (1980), *Bristlelip* (1982), *Bearskin, or The Man who Didn't Wash for Seven Years* (1982), *The Goose Girl* (1983), *Jack and the Dentist's Daughter* (1983), *Soldier Jack, or The Man who Caught Death in a Sack* (1988), *Ashpet: An American Cinderella* (1990), *Mutzmag: An Appalachian Folktale* (1992), and *The Step Child* (1996). The fundamental concept behind the series is the recreation of traditional tales in historical American settings, such as the Civil War, the Great Depression, and the Second World War era. Unlike most film adaptations for children, Davenport's productions do not conform to the *Disney model of fairy-tale romance. Instead, by stressing realistic historical settings and character development, Davenport has been able to cultivate a unique style and to explore themes related to American culture.

Despite their innovative qualities, the earlier films in the series are uneven and sometimes still dominated by the *Grimms' 19th-century perspective. In later films, beginning with *Jack and the Dentist's Daughter*, Davenport draws on American variants of traditional tale types found in Grimm, especially the versions collected and published by Richard Chase and Marie Campbell. These later films are seamlessly integrated with the American experience and tend to be more sophisticated, both visually and thematically. They also show a critical awareness of themes such as race and gender, particularly as these relate to recent American history. In the feature-length film *The Step Child*, based on *'Snow White' and set in the South during the 1920s, Davenport even introduces a self-reflective dimension by thematizing performance, film-making, and the creation of illusion.

In this respect Davenport's entire fairy-tale project is unique because it seeks to empower viewers—especially teachers and students—to look behind the scenes of fairy-tale performance. He provides critical contexts for further study in a newsletter, a teacher's guide, a website, and a book version of ten tales as retold by Gary Carden (*From the Brothers Grimm: A Contemporary Retelling of American Folktales and Classic Stories*, 1992). In addition, a three-part video on *Making Grimm Movies* (1993) introduces teenagers to the techniques of filming folktale adaptations. While *From the Brothers Grimm* has not achieved mainstream commercial success, it has been highly praised by educators and librarians, who constitute its primary market. The series has won numerous awards and has been shown on national Instructional Television through the Public Broadcasting Service.   DH

Haase, Donald, 'Gold into Straw: Fairy Tale Movies for Children and the Culture Industry', *The Lion and the Unicorn*, 12.2 (1988).
Manna, Anthony L., 'The Americanization of the Brothers Grimm, or Tom Davenport's Film Adaptations of German Folktales', *Children's Literature Quarterly*, 13 (fall 1988).
Zipes, Jack, 'Once Upon a Time beyond Disney: Contemporary Fairy-Tale Films for Children', in *Happily Ever After: Fairy Tales, Children, and the Culture Industry* (1997).

Davies, Peter Llewelyn (1897–1960) English publisher and godson of J. M. *Barrie, who allegedly created his famous character *Peter Pan because he was inspired by Davies as a young boy. Davies came to dislike his association with Peter Pan but was always keen about fairy tales. In 1934 he published *The Fairies Return: New Tales for Old by Several Hands*. The book contained retellings of classic tales by *Perrault, the *Grimms, and *Andersen by well-known contemporary authors such as A. E. Coppard, Lord Dunsany, Eric Linklater, Helen Simpson, and E. OE. Somerville.   JZ

Davis, Kathryn (1946–) American novelist whose writings are known for their surrealism and great psychological depth. Her novel, *The Girl Who Trod on a Loaf* (1993), is a remarkable adaptation of Hans Christian Andersen's fairy tale with the same title. Andersen's tragic story is about a vain girl named Inger, who is more concerned about her shoes than in delivering bread to her starving family. Because of her sin, she becomes trapped in a bog and is turned to stone. Moreover, she will hear all the nasty things that people say about her without being able to rectify anything. Davis's other important fairy-tale novel, *Duplex* (2013), is a work of magic realism. It concerns an ordinary schoolteacher named Miss Wicks who lives on an ordinary street. When she receives a visit from Walter, a sorcerer, her life and world are transformed in startling ways so that the real becomes surreal.
JZ

Dean, Pamela (1953–) American writer of fantasy novels for children and adults. Dean's novel *Tam Lin* (1991) is based on the Scottish ballad and folk tale of that name. Dean transplants the story from its traditional setting in Scotland's Border country to a college campus in the American Midwest during the Vietnam War. Despite the modern trappings, the traditional story remains intact in Dean's poetic retelling: a headstrong young woman falls under the spell of a mysterious lover, pitting herself against the Faery Queen to save his soul.
TW

Perry, Evelyn, 'The Ever-Vigilant Hero: Revaluing the Tale of Tam Lin', *Children's Folklore Review* (1997).

Debussy, Claude (1862–1918) French composer who was greatly influenced by literature and whose music has had an enormous impact on all successive generations of composers. Among Debussy's best-known works are songs set to poetry by *Banville, Baudelaire, Mallarmé, and Verlaine. Two of his songs are based on fairy tales, 'La Fille aux cheveux de lin' ('The Girl with the Flaxen Hair'), and 'La Belle au bois dormant' (*'Sleeping Beauty'). Debussy also had close ties to many of the writers of his time, such as Louÿs and Maeterlinck, and collaborated with them on many projects. The most famous of these, his opera *Pelléas et Mélisande* (1902), adapts a *Maeterlinck play whose vague medieval decor is reminiscent of fairy tales. He contemplated but never completed several other projects based on fairy-tale motifs, including 'Cendrelune' ('Cindermoon', with Pierre Louÿs), 'Le Chat botté' (*'Puss-in-Boots', with Gabriel Mourey), 'Huon de Bordeaux' (13th-century *chanson de geste*, Mourey), and 'Le Marchand de rêves' ('The Pedlar in Dreams', Mourey). It is likely that Debussy was drawn to fairy tales because of his conviction that the beauty of all art is ultimately mysterious.   LCS

de la Mare, Walter (1873–1956) English poet and writer. All de la Mare's short stories and longer prose works are touched with mystery, if not fantasy. The two recurrent themes are the child's vision of the world, and death; the usual setting is an unspecified candle-lit, horse-drawn age; houses are old, many-roomed and have secrets. The characters often seem to have strayed from another world, or to be in close contact with it, and many of his stories touch on ghostly visitations. Though his verse often deals with conventional fairy matters—witches on broomsticks, fairy dancers, elves, will-o'-the-wisps, he is far more oblique in his fiction. In *Memoirs of a Midget* (1921), for instance, Miss M, whose size is never specified though at a late stage we are told that she is barely taller than a book, seems more like *Andersen's *Thumbelina than a human, and the mystery of her final disappearance with an unknown visitor (death?), leaving a message 'I have been called away' is left unresolved, like much else in de la Mare's writing.

He wrote three other full-length books. His first, *Henry Brocken* (1904), is subtitled 'his travels and adventures in the rich, strange, scarce-imaginable regions of romance'. Henry Brocken, a solitary dreamer who has spent his youth in the library of a remote old house, rides out to find people he has encountered in books, since to him they have more reality than the flesh-and-blood world. *The Return* (1910) describes how Arthur Lawford, falling asleep by the grave of a Huguenot adventurer who has died by his own hand, wakes to find himself physically changed into that man. *The Three Mulla-Mullgars* (later retitled *The Three Royal Monkeys*), published in the same year, is supposedly for children, though there is very little difference in style or content from his adult writing. He had been reading Samuel Purchas's *Purchas his Pilgrimes* (1619) and many of the incantatory names, descriptions of exotic scenery, even actual adventures and the old sailor Andy Battle, have their origin in this compilation of travellers' tales. *The Three Mulla-Mullgars* is the story of a spiritual quest, from life to death. The three little monkeys set out to find the Valleys of Tishnar, the kingdom from which their father had originally come and for which he has departed. Nod, the folkloristic youngest son, who is also the leader, is entrusted with the talismanic Wonderstone. In the journey 'beyond and beyond, forest and river, forest, swamp and river, the mountains of Arakkkabao— leagues and leagues' they encounter strange and wonderful animals, among them the spirit of evil, the menacing Immanala—'she who preys across the shadows', and survive terrifying perils, including the loss of the Wonderstone, wheedled from Nod by a seductive Water Maiden. Though the last few pages are anticlimactic, even weak compared to what has gone before, it is the most magical and original of all de la Mare's stories.

Most of de la Mare's fairy stories were published in collections for children. The title story in *Broomsticks and Other Tales* (1925) is about a sinister cat owned by a sedate lady who only gradually realizes that he is a witch's familiar. In 'Alice's Godmother' Alice has been summoned to the vast old house owned by her godmother, who is also her great-grandmother to the power of eight. Aged 350, she can remember the funeral of 'poor young Edward VI'. She suggests that Alice should live with her forever and share the secret of eternal life: 'It means, my child, postponing a visit to a certain old friend of ours—whose name is Death.' But Alice, terrified, wants 'to die when I must die' and runs back to the world of ordinary mortality. 'The Three Sleeping Boys of Warwickshire' are the ill-used climbing boys of a miserly master sweep. At night in their dreams they can escape, but the miser resents even this, and asks a witch for a spell so that they can be totally his, body and soul. She cheats him as he has cheated her, and they only fall into a trance from which they cannot be woken. They sleep on for half a century, the marvel of Warwickshire, until one day a young girl kisses them in the glass case where they are displayed, and releases them to play forever as they had in their dreams. 'Miss Jemima' is the only story in this collection with a fairy, here one of those malevolent spirits who steal mortal souls, but also a manifestation of the hatred which an unhappy child feels for the unsympathetic housekeeper in charge of her; perhaps too of the woman's own malice. The child in her misery yields to its seductive calls and finally runs away in search of the enchantress's own country.

In 1927, de la Mare published *Told Again: Old Tales Told Again*, which contained 19 graceful but simple adaptations of classical fairy tales.

The stories in *The Lord Fish and Other Tales* (1933) are also straightforward, and include several like 'A Penny a Day' and 'Dick and the Beanstalk' in the traditional fairy-tale style, where magic is an everyday matter. But two at least have the haunting qualities we associate with de la Mare. In 'The Scarecrow' a small boy chances upon a fairy lurking in a scarecrow; in 'The Riddle' seven children living with their grandmother in an old house wander off while she sits dreaming of the past. As the days pass by, one by one they climb into an old oak chest and are seen no more. These four pages epitomize de la Mare's style.   GA

Atkins, John, *Walter de la Mare: An Exploration* (1947).

Bonnerot, Luce, *L'Œuvre de Walter de la Mare: une aventure spirituelle* (1969).

Hopkins, Kenneth, *Walter de la Mare* (1953).

Reid, Forrest, *Walter de la Mare: A Critical Study* (1929).

Whistler, Theresa, *Imagination of the Heart: The Life of Walter de la Mare* (1993).

De Larrabeiti, Michael (1937–2008) British writer known for his fantasy series which includes *The Borribles* (1976), *The Borribles Go for Broke* (1981), *The Borribles: Across the Dark Metropolis* (1986). He writes from the perspective of the urban lower class and seeks to subvert *Tolkien's *The Lord of the Rings* and Richard *Adams's *Watership Down* by exposing idyllic illusions. De Larrabeiti's Borribles are outcasts or runaways who value their independence more than anything else. They avoid adults, live on the run, and form their own tribes or communities, mainly in and around London. Their ears grow long and pointed, and if they are caught by the law their ears are clipped, and their will is broken. All the fairy-tale novels in the Borrible series concern racial, sexual, and political struggles that deal with contemporary social problems, the disenfranchisement of the young, and the false promises of the classical fairy tales. In De Larrabeiti's other work, *The Provencal Tales* (1988), he returned to the more traditional form of retelling fairy tales using shepherds to recall the magical lore of their region.   JZ

Delessert, Étienne (1941–) Swiss illustrator, writer, publisher, film director, and contributor of illustrations to magazines like the *Atlantic Monthly* and *Punch*, who moved to the United States in 1965. Delessert perceives his brand of illustration to be an interpretation of the general story. For instance, in his illustrations for Eugene Ionesco's children's book *Story Number One for Children under Three Years of Age* (1968), Delessert tries to highlight the story's 'social comment on conformity'. Interested in the child's perspective of natural phenomena, Delessert worked with the child psychologist Jean Piaget on *How the Mouse was Hit on the Head by a Stone and So Discovered the World* (1969). In 1973 he established Carabosse Studios, where he produced commercials and animated films for children, including pieces for *Sesame Street*. In 1977 he put together a series of children's books, 'Éditions Tournesol' ('Sunflower Editions'), in collaboration with Gallimard, and in 1982 supervised the production of a fairy-tale series which published 'unsugarcoated' versions of tales like *'Little Red Riding Hood', 'Fitcher's Bird', and *'Bluebeard'. Delessert illustrated Rudyard *Kipling's *Just So Stories* (1972), Oscar *Wilde's *The Happy Prince* (1977), and Mme de Villeneuve's *La Belle et la Bête* (*Beauty and the Beast*, 1984). Through his illustrations, Delessert aims to expose children to 'another kind of reality'.   AD

Delibes, Léo (1836–91) French composer of opera and ballet. At the Paris Conservatoire Delibes studied composition with Adolphe Adam, whose influence helped him secure the post of accompanist at the Théâtre Lyrique in 1853. In the same year he also took on the post of organist at St Pierre de Chaillot. There then followed a series of operettas, the second of which, *Deux vieilles gardes* (*The Patient*) in 1856, was much praised. The ballet *La Source* (1866) marked a turning point in his career.

Delibes's wealth of melodic invention and assured style suited him for work as a composer of ballet music, the culmination of which was his masterpiece, *Coppélia* (première Paris Opera, 1870). The work is in three scenes and is based on a fairy tale by E. T. A. Hoffmann. The toymaker, Coppelius, has produced a number of lifelike mechanical dolls which are able to dance. One, Coppélia, is especially beautiful, and for a time it causes jealously between the lovers Swanhilda and Franz. They are eventually reconciled and the story ends happily.

A later work, *Sylvia* (1876), has been styled as a grand mythological ballet and is based on a drama by the Italian poet Torquato Tasso (1544–95). Delibes's last significant work was the opera *Lakmé* (1883). Set in mid-19th-century India, it tells of a doomed love story between a British officer and the daughter of a Brahmin priest (Lakmé).   TH

De Lint, Charles (1951–) Canadian author whose work brings folklore imagery into tales of modern urban life. *Moonheart* (1984), *Memory and Dream* (1994), *Someplace to Be Flying* (1998), *The Onion Girl* (2001), and *Widdershins* (2006), and other novels combine elements of Native North American legends (tricksters, shamans, shape-shifters) with those of European folklore (faeries, trolls, magical instruments, enchanted forests). *Jack the Giant-killer* (1987) transplants an English fairy tale to the streets of modern Ottawa. *The Little Country* (1991), set in Cornwall, and *The Wild Wood* (1994), based on the fairy art of Brian Froud, are novels which make extensive use of traditional British fairy lore. A prolific author, De Lint has published over 70 books of fantasy, science fiction, and horror. In addition he has written two important young-adult fairy-tale novels, *Cats of Tanglewood Forest* (2013) and *Seven Wild Sisters: A Modern Fairy Tale* (2014), both illustrated by Charles *Vess, who has contributed illustrations to several other works written by De Lint.   TW

De Morgan, Mary (1850–1907) British writer of fairy tales. The youngest child of a professor of mathematics at London University and sister of William De Morgan, artist and author, after the death of her father in 1871 she went to live with her brother in the Chelsea house where he designed pottery and ornamental tiles. Here she met Pre-Raphaelite writers and artists such as William *Morris and Edward *Burne-Jones (to whose children she told her first stories). Her first book of fairy tales, *On a Pincushion*, illustrated by her brother, was published in 1877. The opening preamble, 'On a Pincushion', is in the style of Hans Christian *Andersen, and his influence can be detected in 'The Story of Vain Lamorna', where pride and vanity are humbled. But the magical stealing of Lamorna's reflection is a theme used by E. T. A. *Hoffmann in his 'Das

Abenteuer der Silvester-Nacht' ('A New Year's Eve Adventure'), and De Morgan's stories certainly suggest that she had read Hoffmann as well as Andersen. In 'Siegfrid and Handa' the Owl who flies away 'hooting in triumph' with one of Siegfrid's eyes reminds us of Hoffmann's Sandman in the story of that name who tears out children's eyes, and a version of the automaton Olimpia from the same tale appears in De Morgan's 'A Toy Princess'. This describes how a fairy godmother substitutes a lifelike doll for the real princess in a country where the people were 'so very polite that they hardly ever spoke to each other'. The unvarying perfection of the toy princess's manners and the civil responses which are the only words she can utter captivate the king and his courtiers, and rejecting the flesh and blood princess they choose to keep the automaton.

De Morgan's second collection of tales, *The Necklace of Princess Fiorimonde* (1880), illustrated by Walter *Crane, contains her best and most deeply felt writing. The title story is sinister and powerful. Fiorimonde is bewitchingly beautiful but a sorceress. She turns each prince who comes to court her into a bead which she wears on a golden string round her neck, until she is finally destroyed by her own jealous vanity. 'The Wanderings of Arasmon' is a poignant account of a girl turned by an evil spell into a golden harp, and carried unknowingly by the young Arasmon with him as he spends the rest of his life searching for her. The heroine of 'The Wise Princess' finds only in death the happiness she has sought.

The Windfairies (1900) was dedicated to the children of Margaret Burne-Jones who had heard the first stories. There is less enchantment and more homeliness and moral purpose in these, but 'Dumb Othmar' with Hulda's hallucinatory quest, accompanied by a glittering green snake, for her lover's lost voice has echoes of the supernatural world of Hoffmann's 'The Golden Pot'.   GA

Demy, Jacques (1931–90) French filmmaker who belonged to the 1960s New Wave of experimental cineastes including

De Morgan, Mary The prince seeks help in Mary De Morgan's 'The Wanderings of Arasmon', published in *The Necklace of Princess Fiorimonde and Other Stories* (1880) and illustrated by Walter *Crane.

Jean-Luc Godard, Alain Resnais, and François Truffaut. However, he differed from the key members of this group by focusing more on fantasy, musicals, and romance than realistic or political themes. For instance, in *Les Parapluies de Cherbourg* (*The Umbrellas of Cherbourg*, 1964), nominated for an Oscar, and *Les Demoiselles de Rochefort* (*The Young Girls of Rochefort*, 1967) he used sweet melodic tunes, songs, and dance in idyllic settings to brighten mundane daily life. In the process he sought to subvert sentimental and romantic genres and the expectations of audiences by exaggerating and embellishing banal events. Such subversion can also be detected in his adaptations of two well-known fairy tales, Charles *Perrault's 'Donkey-Skin' and Robert Browning's 'The Pied Piper'. In *Peau d'Âne* (*Donkey-Skin*, 1970) Demy was influenced by the work of Jean *Cocteau and especially by Cocteau's *Beauty and the Beast* (1946), evident first, in the casting of Jean Marais (the beast in Cocteau's film) as the incestuous father, and second, in the film's surreal aesthetics. Furthermore, he depicted the people, the castles, and palaces with pastel colours, predominantly blue and red, and filled the places with statues of other fairy tales such as 'The White Cat' by Mme d'*Aulnoy and *Puss-in-Boots by Perrault. Then, instead of critiquing the king who wants to marry and sleep with his daughter, Demy portrayed a princess who appears to be so attached to her father that she is willing to acquiesce to his offer of marriage. Demy created dream scenes of romance and lush scenes of pomposity in the prince's palace, where extravagance and elegance are prized, and eventually the incestuous father is forgiven at a grand wedding with a young prince. This controversial ending makes it difficult to say whether Demy wanted to mock or criticize a laissez-faire attitude towards incest. In contrast, Demy's *The Pied Piper* (1972) is more realistic and direct. The action takes place in northern Germany during the Black Plague of 1349, and Demy's film is a serious, straightforward critique and condemnation of the nobility and the church. Here he painted a huge canvas of corruption, pestilence, and suffering. The only hope for the children of the city is to follow the pied piper and to escape the decadent politicians who are more concerned about self-aggrandizement than saving the people from a plague. In 1979 Demy turned to Japanese manga in his film, *Lady Oscar* (1979), an adaptation of *The Rose of Versailles* (1972–73) by Riyoko Ikeda, which draws on the European and Asian maiden warrior tradition. In *Parking* (1985) he reworked the story of Orpheus. In all his films Demy deployed fairy-tale aesthetics and motifs to challenge normative forms of gender, sexuality, and class.   AED

Berthomé, Jean-Pierre. *Jacques Demy et les racines du rêve* (1982).

Duggan, Anne E, *Queer Enchantments: Gender, Sexuality, and Class in the Fairy-Tale Cinema of Jacques Demy* (2013).

Denslow, W. W. (William Wallace Denslow, 1856–1915) American illustrator of *Oz* characters. He brought American picturebook illustration into the 20th century by combining colour and design, thus raising its quality to that of the Victorian illustrators *Crane, *Greenaway, and *Caldecott. He studied art at the Cooper Institute and National Academy of Design and was a successful illustrator of theatrical posters, book covers, and mail-order catalogues when he met L. Frank *Baum. The friends first collaborated on *Father Goose: His Book* (1899), a beautifully crafted text in the William *Morris tradition whose delightful rhymes and humorous designs complemented each other. This hugely successful enterprise was surpassed by *The Wonderful *Wizard of Oz* (1900), Baum's modern American fairy tale. Denslow brought to life the Tin Woodsman, Scarecrow, and Lion in scores of drawings and 24 colour illustrations that reflect the influence of Japanese woodcuts. Unfortunately, Baum and Denslow disliked sharing credit for their collaboration and dissolved their partnership in an acrimonious copyright dispute. Denslow went on to issue his own editions of Oz characters and *Mother Goose stories, all with his poster-like manner and stylized sea-horse monogram

Denslow, W. W. The wizard as con man performs one of his illusory feats as little Dorothy gazes at the spectacle in L. Frank *Baum's *The Wizard of Oz* (1900), illustrated by W. W. Denslow.

(reminiscent of Walter Crane's trademark crane) that earned him the nickname of 'Hippocampus Den'. But his style soon became outdated and ill-suited to photo-re-production, and librarians (the new arbiters of juvenile literature) derided his work. He died in obscurity, with no obituary appearing in the newspapers for which he had worked.   MLE

Greene, David L., and Martin, Dick, *The Oz Scrapbook* (1977).
Greene, Douglas G., and Hearn, Michael Patrick, *W. W. Denslow* (1976).
Meyer, Susan E., *A Treasury of the Great Children's Book Illustrators* (1983).
Snow, Jack, *Who's Who in Oz* (1954).

dePaola, Tomie (1934–) American author and artist. He began to illustrate children's books in 1965 and created his fairy-tale-like book *The Wonderful Dragon of Timlin* in 1966. DePaola's European and American Indian folk tales and legends are among the more than 200 books he illustrated. He created the name for a grand-mother witch, 'Strega Nona', borrowing from Italian folklore. *Strega Nona: An Old Tale* (1975) recalls how an apprentice recited a magic spell that keeps a pot boiling and causes trouble that only the grand-mother can resolve. *Big Anthony and the Magic Ring* (1979), *Strega Nona's Magic Lessons* (1982), *Merry Christmas, Strega Nona* (1986), *Strega Nona Meets her Match* (1993), *Strega Nona Takes a Vacation* (2000), *Strega Nona's Harvest* (2009), and *Strega Nona's Gift* (2011) continue the adventures of Strega Nona and are purely dePaola's inventions, but told in a folklore style. While he honoured his paternal Italian ancestry for *The Prince of the Dolomites: An Old Italian Tale* (1980) and *The Legend of Old Befana: An Italian Christmas Story* (1980), he later retold *Fin M'Coul: The Giant of Knockmany Hill* (1981) from his Irish heritage. American Indian works include *The Legend of the Bluebonnet* (1996), an old tale of Texas legend, and feature children. DePaola has a distinctive recognizable style and colour scheme, positioning his characters as though they are on stage. He researches in libraries for costume and architectural backgrounds and travels extensively for authenticity, such as in the period and Italian setting for *Clown of God: An Old Story* (1978).   KNH

De Simone, Roberto (1933–) Italian composer, conductor, theatre director, and ethnomusicologist. In his theatrical version of 'La gatta Cenerentola' ('The *Cinderella Cat', 1976) he set Giambattista *Basile's 17th-century fairy tale to music, incorporating popular songs of Basile's own time with original variations on the modern folk repertoire of the Naples area. In 1994 he published *Fiabe campane: i novantanove racconti delle dieci notti* (*Fairy Tales from Campania: The Ninety-Nine Tales of the Ten Nights*), the result of 20 years spent tape-recording oral storytellers in the Campania region of Italy.   NC

Deulin, Charles (1827–77) French writer and theatre critic. Born in a small French town near the Belgian border, Deulin rose from humble origins to write three important collections of fairy tales: *Contes d'un buveur de bière* (*Beer-Drinker's Tales*, 1868), *Contes du roi Cambrinus* (*Tales of King Cambrinus*, 1874), and *Contes de petite ville* (*Village Tales*, 1875). Widely read in their day, Deulin's tales are distinguished by their strong regional flavour: Low Country settings and customs provide the backdrop for traditional fairy-tale stories and motifs. 'Cambrinus, roi de la bière' ('Cambrinus, king of beer') tells the story of a lowly glassmaker who trades his soul to the devil for the love of a wealthy young girl. With the devil's help, he garners fame and fortune by producing 'Flemish wine', that is, beer. When the

devil comes to claim Cambrinus's soul 30 years later, he finds only a beer cask. Deulin's scholarly monograph *Les Contes de ma Mère l'Oye avant Perrault* (*Mother Goose Tales before Perrault*, 1879), published posthumously, documents different versions and possible sources of *Perrault's tales. Vast in scope, surveying European, African, Asian, and American folklore traditions, this work constitutes an erudite tribute to the fairy-tale genre and reflects the pervasive fascination with folklore and fairy tales in the 19th century.   AZ

Bocquet, Léon, Introduction to Charles Deulin, *Contes d'un buveur de bière* (1943).

Dauby, Jean, Preface to Charles Deulin, *Intégrale des contes* (1992).

Dick, Philip K. (1928–82) American science fiction and fantasy writer. Born in Chicago, Dick studied briefly at the University of California in Berkeley, where he also worked for a radio station and managed a record store while publishing science fiction stories. After 1955, with the publication of his novels *Solar Lottery* and *A Handful of Darkness*, he established himself as one of the leading writers of science fiction and fantasy in America. Among his best-known works are *Eye in the Sky* (1957), *Do Androids Dream of Electric Sheep?* (1968), *The Preserving Machine and Other Stories* (1969), and *A Scanner Darkly* (1977). He introduced fairy-tale motifs into many of his works, and in some of his stories like 'The King of the Elves' (1953), he incorporated traditional fairy-tale characters into a realistic narrative about the owner of a gas station in the desert who is strangely called upon to save the Kingdom of the Elves.   JZ

Dickens, Charles (1812–70) English novelist. Dickens was a passionate supporter of fairy tales. In 'A Christmas Tree' (*Household Words*, Christmas Number, 1850) he recalled the favourite tales of his youth, above all *The Thousand and One Nights*, which he frequently invoked in his writings, and *Jack and the Beanstalk, Valentine and Orson, *Little Red Riding Hood, and Mme d'*Aulnoy's 'The *Yellow Dwarf'. *Tales of the*

Genii (1764), modelled on *The *Arabian Nights*, by 'Sir Charles Morell' (in reality the Revd James Ridley) had also made a great impression on him. He was angered by attempts to 'improve' fairy tales, and in 'Frauds on the Fairies' (*Household Words*, 1 October 1853) he mocked George Cruikshank's *Fairy Library* for its attempts to rewrite the traditional stories with a temperance message. Three of his Christmas books include supernatural happenings. In *A Christmas Carol* (1843) the miserly Scrooge is transformed into a miracle of genial generosity by the ghosts of Christmas Past, Present, and Yet to Come. *The Chimes* (1844), though in effect a political manifesto, is subtitled 'A Goblin Story', and *The Cricket on the Hearth* (1845) 'A Fairy Tale of Home'. He wrote one fairy story for children, 'The Magic Fishbone', a cheerful burlesque of no great distinction, which formed part of *Holiday Romance* (serialized in 1868 in *All the Year Round* and the American *Our Young Folk*).   GA

Briggs, Katharine M., 'The Folklore of Charles Dickens', *Journal of the Folklore Institute*, 7 (1970).

Hillard, Molly Clark, *Spellbound: The Fairy Tale and the Victorians* (2014).

Kotzin, Michael C., *Dickens and the Fairy Tale* (1972).

Stone, Harry, *Dickens and the Invisible World: Fairy Tales, Fantasy, and Novel-Making* (1979).

Tremper, Ellen, 'Commitment and Escape: The Fairy Tales of Thackeray, Dickens, and Wilde', *The Lion and the Unicorn*, 2.1 (1978).

Didelot, Charles (1767–1837) French dancer, choreographer, and influential teacher. Popular dance memoirs hold that Didelot's historical significance was assured when his ballet *Flora and Zephyr* (1796) was the first to feature dancing on toes. He spent much time in Russia between the years 1801 and 1836 where he choreographed many ballets, some based on Russian folklore. His pupil Adam Gluzkovsky based a ballet, *Russlan and Ludmilla*, on *Pushkin's poem with folklore themes.   TH

Diderot, Denis (1713–84) Pre-eminent French Enlightenment philosopher. Especially known as the editor of the *Encyclopédie*,

Diderot was a prolific writer of essays, fiction, letters, and plays. He wrote numerous short stories (*contes* in French), which, besides treating ethical problems, explore the formal limits of the genre (e.g. *Ceci n'est pas un conte* (*This is not a Tale*). His one fairy tale properly so called, *L'Oiseau blanc, conte bleu* (*White Bird, Blue Tale*), was published posthumously, although it was probably composed early in his career. The religious satire and oriental setting in this tale resemble Diderot's more famous *Les Bijoux indiscrets* (*The Indiscreet Jewels*), yet the metamorphosis of the hero into a white pigeon, his adventures in that guise, and his final de-metamorphosis and marriage more clearly recall folkloric models. Through allegory, Diderot's tale derides fundamental aspects of Christian doctrine—such as the trinity and the Virgin Mary—and this helps explain why it was never published in his lifetime. *L'Oiseau blanc* also contains allusions to the frivolity at the court of Louis XV, although this critique is more personal than political.   LCS

digital fairy tales In the 1990s, use of personal computers and the Internet reached critical mass. Over the next two decades (1990–2010), the explosion of digital tools and media formats created new ways for fairy tales to be duplicated, distributed, and disrupted. Born-digital texts exploited the potential of the computer as both creative tool and delivery system. An early web work by Blais, Frank, and Ippolito, *Fair e-Tales*, broke the rules of conventional narrative with its DHTML-based interface, enabling dynamic navigation between multiple character perspectives and destinies. Writers working in electronic literature experimented with structural, ludic, and code-based systems to generate new variants of old tales. Nick Montfort's *The Girl and The Wolf, A Variable Tale*, offered multiple text options via its ornamental grid with interactive axis instructing the reader to 'choose the amount of sex and violence you would prefer'. Emerging media formats, from CD-ROMs and websites to video-game systems and mobile devices, provided expansive options for participatory engagement in media-rich narratives. Digital artist Donna Leishman used Web animation to reinvent the visual world of *RedRidinghood*, an interactive landscape that is part toy, part game, and part story. In the digital environment, multiplicity is now more possible than ever, leading to experiments with non-linear, multimodal, and transmedia storytelling. A hybrid episodic work by Kate Pullinger and Chris Joseph, *Inanimate Alice*, is designed to introduce teen readers to multimedia fiction. Creative artists collaborate on tales that integrate text, image, sound, animation, video, and interactivity into a user-controlled experience, an evolution from the single-authored text. In the digital age, well-worn tales morph dramatically, while their motifs remain resonant and resilient. As in the past, digital fairy tales may be fractured and subverted to redress issues of gender, class, and social justice, while other digital tales work hard to maintain the status quo. JR

Blais, Joline, Frank, Keith, and Ippolito, Jon, *Fair e-Tales* (1999). <http://www.three.org/fairetales/>.
Leishman, Donna, *RedRidinghood* (2001). <http://collection.eliterature.org/1/works/leishman__redridinghood.html>.
Montfort, Nick, *The Girl and The Wolf, A Variable Tale* (2001). <http://beehive.temporalimage.com/content_apps41/app_b.html>.
Pullinger, Kate and Joseph, Chris, *Inanimate Alice* (2005). <http://www.inanimatealice.com>.

Dinesen, Isak (pseudonym of **Karen Blixen**, 1885–1962) Danish writer and storyteller. From 1934 she wrote and published mostly in English. Born Christentze Dinesen into a wealthy, aristocratic Danish family, Dinesen studied literature and fine arts in Switzerland and in Copenhagen. In 1913 she married Bror Blixen and moved to Kenya, where she owned and later managed a coffee plantation in the Ngong Hills. Dinesen had published a few poems and stories in Danish journals since 1904, but her career as a writer began relatively late in life with the publication of *Seven Gothic Tales*. Although the tales were published after Dinesen's return to Denmark, they had already existed first in oral and later in written form before her departure from Kenya in 1931. Dinesen saw herself as a storyteller much more than a writer throughout her career. With the exception of her memoirs *Out of Africa* (1937, 1984) and the thriller *Angelic Avengers* (1946), she mainly published collections of tales. Her first and most popular anthology, *Seven Gothic Tales* (1934), was an immediate success when it was published by the Book of the Month Club in 1934. This book was followed by *Winter's Tales* (1942) and *Last Tales* (1957). Dinesen's narratives are quite similar both stylistically and thematically. Indebted to the romantic grotesque tradition, they foreground storytelling in a self-consciously self-referential manner. The reader is immersed in a complex web of tales within tales that illuminate the mysteries and magic of life and lean toward the artificial, the exotic, the supernatural, and horror. EMM

Henriksen, Aage, *Isak Dinesen/Karen Blixen: The Work and the Life* (1988).
Thurman, Judith, *Isak Dinesen: The Life of a Storyteller* (1982).

Disney, Walt (1901–66) Pioneer American animator, producer, entrepreneur, and founder of a media conglomerate. Perhaps the single most influential figure in American children's literature of the 20th century, Walt Disney set his personal stamp upon almost every classic story for children, simultaneously determining what was to become a classic and the way in which that classic was to be read. In fairy tales Disney harnessed wonder through animation, using it to create visual effects notable for their ingenuity while at the same time maintaining a securely middle-American sensibility (*see* FILM AND FAIRY TALES).

Walt Disney himself embodied the fairy tale of the American Dream he so successfully marketed. He was the fourth of five children born to a struggling lower middle-class family. Disney moved frequently during his childhood, his father Elias Disney endlessly seeking the financial security that perpetually eluded his grasp. Born in

Chicago, Disney spent his formative years on a Missouri farm, where he imbibed the vision of rural America he was later to mythologize, making friends with the animals who were subsequently transformed into chief actors in his cartoons: pigs, cows, dogs, and mice. After the farm failed, in part because the two eldest Disney boys fled their exacting father's demands, the family moved to Kansas City, where Elias became a newspaper route manager, giving each of his remaining sons, Roy and Walt, a share of the labour. In Missouri Walt was first paid for a drawing—of a horse. A casual student, in part because of his heavy workload, Walt still enjoyed reading adventure and romance stories by Mark *Twain, Robert Louis *Stevenson, Horatio Alger, Sir Walter Scott, and Charles *Dickens, and watching the early silent movies of Charlie Chaplin, Mary Pickford, and others.

In 1917 Disney moved back to Chicago, began high school and enrolled in classes at the Art Institute, but soon dropped out and enlisted in the First World War as a Red Cross ambulance driver. At the war's end in 1919, Disney returned to Kansas City and took a position with a commercial art studio. The most momentous outcome of this job was his alliance with Ub Iwerks, another young artist who not only shared Disney's interest in cartoons, but had a genius for animating. Better and more efficient technically than Disney, Iwerks provided the nuts and bolts drawing while Disney generated the ideas. Over the years, this partnership would create Mickey Mouse and spawn one of the most powerful media giants in the world. Together, they began a company called 'Laugh-O-Grams Films', short animated features relying on fairy-tale characters and sight-gags for their interest. Some of Disney's best animated fairy-tale films were made during this period: *Little Red Riding Hood* (1922), *The Four Musicians of Bremen* (1922), and *Puss in Boots* (1924). Although audiences responded well to the cartoons, the company soon went broke in 1924 because of distribution problems. After the bankruptcy, Disney moved to Hollywood to be closer to the movie industry, persuading

his brother Roy, whose business acumen provided another essential link in the formation of what would become the Walt Disney Company, to invest in yet another business scheme. Iwerks had followed Disney to Hollywood and with his help, Disney concocted another fairy-tale venture. Combining live action and animation in the *Alice Comedies* (1924–7), they began to evolve the winning formulas that became the Disney-brand fairy tale. Basing this series very loosely on Lewis *Carroll's literary fairy tale—only the heroine's name and the concept of an adventure in a far-fetched place remained the same—they altered the story to admit cute animal characters, slapstick gags, and ingenious visual effects while expressing safely middle-American values and beliefs.

The late 1920s and 1930s saw the fledgling Disney company perpetually striving for increasing realism through technological innovation and artistic refinement. Disney soon gave up any attempt to draw cartoons himself; his genius lay in generating ideas and inspiring others to produce his vision. To increase efficiency, Disney divided cartoon production into hierarchized departments: from the élite cadre of animators (the Nine Old Men) who, together with Disney, created the characters, stories, and gags; to the 'in-betweeners', less adept animators who filled in the sketches between the main actions of a story; to photography, sound, and music departments; down to the low-status, mostly female, cel painters and inkers who coloured the slides and finished the product. In his devotion to efficiency and micro-division of labour in the spirit of Frederick W. Taylor, Disney was a businessman of his time, even if his factory's product was artistic instead of technological.

With each cartoon, Disney pushed his employees to press against the boundaries of their medium, by synchronizing music and movement in *Steamboat Willie* (1928), by using Technicolor in *Flowers and Trees* (1932), and in general striving to increase animation's realism through studying movement and developing new ways of creating visual depth, such as the multiplane camera, developed by William Garity and first used to make *The Old Mill* in 1937. Throughout the 1930s, the Disney Studio won Academy Awards almost as a matter of course because of the creativity and innovation of its cartoons. During this period the company also began to diversify, marketing not just cartoons, but the cartoon characters as well through books, music, and novelty items such as the Mickey Mouse watch. These marketing strategies generated cash during the expensive process of creating the cartoons that would satisfy Walt Disney's stringent vision and eventually became standard business practice for all family-oriented media marketing.

The success of 'Disney's Folly', the feature-length cartoon of *Snow White* in December 1937, paved the way for Disney's eventual domination of the children's fairy-tale industry. A labour of love and artistic commitment, *Snow White and the Seven Dwarfs* involved hundreds of Disney employees working overtime for months for little or no extra pay to create the two million images demanded by the project. Its astonishing success paved the way for further animated folk- and fairy-tale adaptations: *Pinocchio* (1940), *Fantasia* (1940), *Dumbo* (1941), *Cinderella* (1950), *Alice in Wonderland* (1951), *Peter Pan* (1953), *Sleeping Beauty* (1959), and *Mary Poppins* (1964), to name the most significant fairy-tale films produced during Disney's lifetime.

The euphoria induced by the success of *Snow White* did not, however, translate into fairy-tale labour relations at the Disney Studio. Increasing bureaucratization and division among departments, along with the expanding staff necessary to implement the many new projects the studio had undertaken, created a less egalitarian, more factory-like atmosphere than had prevailed earlier. Walt Disney's artistic autocracy and paternalism, however benevolent, was resented by some of his staff, and in May 1941 the Screen Cartoonists Guild struck in response to a series of lay-offs. The resulting confrontation between labour and management cleared the studio of many talented and independent artists and precipitated a

hiatus in the studio's fairy-tale production, particularly since during this period Disney conducted a goodwill tour in Latin America and then began to help the US government produce propaganda films for the war effort. *Dumbo* (1941) was the last feature-length animated film to issue from the studio for almost ten years. This, together with Disney's role as an alleged FBI informant about supposed communist activity in Hollywood, further expressed his political orientation—a fundamentally conservative allegiance—and cost him some of the critical support he had enjoyed in the 1930s.

In the 1950s and 1960s, Disney's considerable visionary energies were given over to other media—he embraced television and became deeply involved in the physical construction of fairylands rather than their animation through film. Disneyland, a theme park that embodied the same ideology of the Disney fairy-tale cartoons in its emphasis on cleanliness, order, and innocence, opened in Orange County, California, in 1955. Disney also oversaw the purchase of land near Orlando, Florida, in 1965 for the Experimental Prototype Community of Tomorrow (EPCOT) and what would become Walt Disney World Resort. Here Disney's utopian bent had free rein as he attempted to enlist American industry and technology in the service of bourgeois community life. From almost nothing, Disney and his team of devoted supporters had created a multi-million-dollar commercial empire based on the fairy tale.

Disney's death on 15 December 1966 halted his personal involvement in the project of creating a fairy-tale virtual reality, but the Walt Disney Studios lived on. The corporation, like many other American companies, suffered during the recession of the 1970s but was revitalized in the 1980s as it reinvented itself, under the leadership of Michael Eisner, to correspond to a new vision of the bourgeois American fairy tale. After a long pause, Disney Productions brought out a new string of popular animated versions of fairy tales, starting with *The *Little Mermaid* (1989), *Beauty and the Beast* (1991), *Aladdin* (1992), *The Lion King* (1994), *Hercules*

(1997), and *Mulan* (1998). In addition to reworking traditional fairy-tale material, the Walt Disney Company also attempted to work its magic upon history in *Pocahontas* (1995) and tragic romance in *The Hunchback of Notre Dame* (1996). Although critical response to these last was ambivalent, the strategy of reworking recalcitrant material into fairy tale was successful enough to prompt other companies, such as 20th-Century Fox, to issue their own fairy-tale version of history in *Anastasia* (1998).

Characteristic Disney fairy-tale formulas are apparent as early as *Snow White*. Because most of his sources were short and emblematic, more material needed to be added to lengthen the plot and sustain interest in the characters. For characterization Disney relied upon the formulas of early movies, which themselves drew from 19th-century melodrama: the innocent heroine, the gallant hero, the evil villain, and comic relief in the form of the clown. Although the heroine and hero were often rather wooden, the antics of cute or grotesque sub-characters, such as animals or dwarfs, fleshed out the action and created sympathy and comedy. Using familiar comic types (the Laurel-and-Hardyesque pairing of a tall, thin body with a short fat one was a frequent figure), Disney's artists gave their characters distinctive idiosyncrasies, which in turn drew out the plot enough to make a feature-length presentation. A good portion of each story session was devoted to brainstorming the 'gags' (a good new gag earned its creator a bonus of $5) which were to become one of the trademarks of a Disney fairy tale. A further development, appearing first in *Pinocchio*, of the cute, usually miniature, sidekick of the protagonist also became a standard feature of a Disney fairy tale, allowing for comic relief from the romantic business of the fairy tale as well as offering endless marketing opportunities.

If a Disney fairy tale inflated the ridiculous, it also heightened the romantic aspects of the story. In contrast with the rather matter-of-fact treatment sex and marriage receives in traditional folk tales, Disney's versions always emphasized true love, with love-at-first-sight the preferred type. Thus, in *Snow White*, *Cinderella*, and *Sleeping Beauty*, all three heroines fall in love with their princes before the identity of either is fully established, avoiding connotations of interested or self-aggrandizing love. 'Love's first kiss' is the only spell-breaker in the Disney version, in contrast to the rather clumsy awakening of Snow White, jostled out of her coffin, in the *Grimms' version, or the wakening of the princess by a complete stranger in earlier versions of 'Sleeping Beauty'. If portions of the fairy tale seemed arbitrary, inhumane, or irrational in his lights, Disney changed them; thus, in *Snow White*, the evil stepmother falls to her death in a semi-natural catastrophe rather than being forced to dance in red-hot iron shoes at her stepdaughter's wedding, and *Cinderella* leaves out any final reference to the antagonists at all, in stark contrast to the Grimms' version, in which the stepsisters' eyes are pecked out by the heroine's bird allies.

Other Americanizing aspects of the Disney version included demystifying royalty (in general they are depicted as well-meaning comic types or utterly malevolent usurpers); portraying protagonists in voice and manner as all-American teens with generation-gap problems and romantic ideals; and mechanizing magic by emphasizing laboratories, magic wands, and other machines to suggest contemporary American technology. As Disney's critics began increasingly to complain, the attempts to improve animation by studying movement and striving for realistic effects paradoxically kept the company from exploring animation's unique potential for envisioning other dimensions.

Animation provided a perfect opportunity to create convincing magical effects, a fact not lost on Disney. Whole departments were devoted to special effects of bubbles, water drops, and other miracles of delicacy; menace and evil were effectively conveyed through colour, shape, and angle without any words at all. Animation allowed animals to talk and act like humans, for detailed transformations from beautiful queen to appalling hag in *Snow White* or from pumpkin to coach in *Cinderella*, for elephants to fly using their ears as wings in *Dumbo*, for household furniture to come alive in *Beauty and the Beast*, and for the dizzying physical morphing of *Aladdin*'s Genie. Ultimately, however, the very smoothness and hard, clean finish of the Disney house style worked against the establishment of a truly magical atmosphere, and the very workers of magic became buffoons and bumblers, as in *Sleeping Beauty*'s trio Flora, Fauna, and Merryweather. The Disney style relied more upon techniques of novelistic realism than on the suggestive power of symbol found in other fantasy works.

A study of Disney heroines and heroes over the course of the 20th century reveals the extent to which Disney Americanized his tales. Each fairy-tale heroine embodies the characteristic beauty ideals of her decade: Snow White is as flat-chested as a flapper, while Cinderella and Sleeping Beauty sport Monroe-esque curves; Ariel is a Farrah Fawcett-coiffed teeny-bopper, and the heroines of the 1990s are 'multicultural' versions of Barbie. Initially oblivious embodiments of what Betty Friedan was to denounce as the Feminine Mystique, Disney's fairy-tale heroines have a great affinity for housework and care-giving. Although the Eisner-era cartoons attempt to broaden heroines' spectrum to include other races and identities, the 'good' girl is still characterized as spirited, gently rebellious, but ultimately domesticated by love. Ariel, in *The Little Mermaid*, rejects the sexual power of Ursula the seawitch and supports her father and boyfriend in frustrating Ursula's attempt to rule. Jasmine defies her father only because he is old-fashioned enough to want to arrange her marriage. Girls' attempts to create a liberated and independent role for themselves are frequently overshadowed by plots that foreground masculine struggle. After *Mermaid*, female characters, even in the 'feminist' *Beauty and the Beast*, are relegated to the sidelines of the climactic struggles, while the primary conflicts are between male combatants.

Beginning with *Pinocchio*, Disney fairy-tale heroes are not calculating so much as they are innocents in search of happiness. Pinocchio, Dumbo, Mickey Mouse as the Sorcerer's Apprentice in *Fantasia*, Peter Pan, Arthur, Mowgli, Aladdin, the Beast, Simba, even Quasimodo and Hercules possess boyish high spirits and a propensity for mischief, a dislike of hard work, and a sweet attractiveness that draws other characters to them. Mentored by complementary yet competing role models driven on one side by conscience and on the other by pleasure, as with Mowgli's Bagheera and Baloo, young heroes learn to make their own way in the world. Like Tom Sawyer, a figure close to Walt Disney's Missouri roots, these heroes love the fun of male company but bow to the heterosexual imperative: ultimately, they learn that to be 'real', to be 'a man', an 'adult', they must accept the constraints of civilization and domestication and with it, usually, the hand of the beautiful maiden. While the Eisner-era hero, notable in *Pocahontas* and *The Hunchback of Notre Dame*, might be already grown and ready to be taught lessons in love by a dynamic woman, the most popular films, such as *The Lion King*, have featured boys' coming of age as struggle over women or kingship. Reproducing movie and cartoon convention in which it is not as important for men or boys to find true (heterosexual) love as it is for girls, there are exceptions to this generalization—*Pinocchio*, *Dumbo*, *Peter Pan*, and *Hunchback* conclude by highlighting male friendship, and indeed, the sidekick trope necessitates male bonding. Consistent throughout the Walt Disney Company's *œuvre* is the privileging of innocence, the valorization of sentiment, the belief in true love, the reliance upon the shorthand of stereotype combined with anti-intellectualism, a jovial disdain for ugliness or deformity, and a luxuriant, infantilizing celebration of the cute. The combination has resulted in fairy-tale wealth and power for a major world player in the entertainment industry.   NJW

Bell, Elizabeth, Haas, Lynda, and Sells, Laura, *From Mouse to Mermaid: The Politics of Film, Gender, and Culture* (1995).

Eliot, Marc, *Walt Disney: Hollywood's Dark Prince* (1993).

Merritt, Russell, and Kaufman, J. B., *Walt in Wonderland: The Silent Films of Walt Disney* (1993).

Schickel, Richard, *The Disney Version: The Life, Times, Art, and Commerce of Walt Disney* (1968; rev. edn., 1985).

Wasko, Janet, *Understanding Disney: The Manufacture of Fantasy* (2001).

Watts, Steven, *The Magic Kingdom: Walt Disney and the American Way of Life* (1998).

Zipes, Jack, 'De-Disneyfying Disney: Notes on the Development of the Fairy-Tale Film', *The Enchanted Screen: The Unknown History of Fairy-Tale films* (2011).

Disney comics The animated cartoon film *Snow White, which first appeared in 1937, greatly influenced Disney comics. Fairy tales occur frequently in these comics, and the illustrations are very similar to those which appeared in the film. Disney comics are now available in many countries.

Disney and Me, currently available in Great Britain, is a nursery comic which is issued fortnightly. Fairy tales are almost always included. *'Cinderella', *'Aladdin', *'Peter Pan', and 'Pegasus and Hercules' have all appeared recently in picture stories. The illustrations are tastefully coloured, pleasant, and non-threatening. Even villains such as Captain Hook are not particularly frightening. The stories often include friendly birds and harmless animals such as rabbits, fawns, and chipmunks.   GF

Ditlevsen, Tove (1918–76) One of the few major Danish women writers of the 1940s. Her autobiographical works voice a longing for fulfilment, but depict experiences of sadness and disillusionment. The poems in *Den hemmelige Rude* (*The Secret Pane of Glass*, 1961) directly refer to a number of Grimms' tales. Formally, Ditlevsen is traditional and thus her poems are not as striking as Anne *Sexton's haunting invocations of well-known tales, but Ditlevsen's identification with the demons of the tales, such as the witch in *'Hansel and Gretel', reveal that she perceived that the texts were not innocent entertainment.   NI

Divakaruni, Chitra Banjerjee (1956–) Indian-American award-winning author and poet, and Professor of Writing at the University of Houston Creative Writing Program. Divakaruni authored a collection of short stories titled *Arranged Marriage* (1995), which won an American Book Award and a PEN Josephine Miles Award. She is also known for her novels *The Mistress of Spices* (1997), *Sister of My Heart* (1999), and *Queen of Dreams* (2004); screen adaptations have been made of all but the last. Divakaruni's creative works synthesize modern and traditional themes, often integrating Bengali myths and tales of the Hindu tradition, in occasionally magic realist tradition.   KMJ

Döblin, Alfred (1878–1957) German writer. From the very outset of his career he incorporated a variety of fairy-tale motifs in his work, even in his celebrated novel *Berlin Alexanderplatz* (1929). He wrote remarkable fairy tales for adults, such as 'Der Ritter Blaubart' ('The Knight *Bluebeard', 1911), 'Vom Hinzel und dem wilden Lenchen' ('About Hinzel and the Wild Lenchen', 1917), and 'Märchen von der Technik' ('Fairy Tale of Technology', 1935). In his famous 'Märchen vom Materialismus' ('Fairy Tale of Materialism', 1948) Döblin illustrated the disastrous consequences of Demokrit's materialistic nuclear theory.   BKM

Kümmerling-Meibauer, Bettina, *Die Kunstmärchen von Hofmannsthal, Musil und Döblin* (1991).

Doherty, Berlie (1943–) Irish novelist, poet, and playwright, who has written mainly for children and young adults. Aside from her novel *The Snow Queen* (1998), an adaptation of Hans Christian *Andersen's tale, she has edited an anthology of stories, *Tales of Wonder and Magic* (1997), and published her own collection, *Fairy Tales* (2000).   JZ

Dokey, Cameron (1956–) An American author of young-adult fiction with over 30 titles to her name. She has worked as a ghostwriter for books in a number of supernatural fiction series such as *The Fear Street Sagas, Buffy and Angel*, and *Charmed*. She has also written several books featured in

The Once Upon a Time series and contributed over half a dozen titles, including *The Storyteller's Daughter* (2002) and *The World Above* (2010).   KMJ

Donaldson, Julia (1948–) Popular British writer, dramatist, and performer, who was awarded the position of UK Children's Laureate from 2011 to 2013. She is famous for her unusual rhymed books for young children such as *The Gruffalo* (1999) and *Room on the Broom* (2002), illustrated by Axel Scheffler and made into films. *The Gruffalo* is based on a Chinese folk tale in which a little girl encounters a tiger in the jungle and avoids being eaten by the terrifying creature by claiming to be the courageous queen of the jungle. She demonstrates her alleged power by telling the tiger to walk behind her as they stroll through the jungle. As they meet other animals, the tiger sees that they are terrified, and he mistakenly thinks that it is because of the girl that they are frightened, not because of him. So, he flees out of fright. Donaldson adapted the tale and transformed the girl into a little mouse who imagines a terrifying creature named the Gruffalo so she can avoid being eaten by other creatures. However, the Gruffalo turns out to be real, and she must use her wits to save herself from him just as the girl in the Chinese tale did. Most of Donaldson's delightful short tales such as *The Smartest Giant in Town* (2002), *The Gruffalo's Child* (2004), *Princess Mirror-Belle* (2005), *The Princess and the Wizard* (2006), *Freddie and the Fairy* (2011), and *The Singing Mermaid* (2012) stem from the tradition of folk and fairy tales with tiny heroes who triumph in difficult situations because they are smart. Donaldson's tales of magic are all designed to be told from a child's perspective and to empower children's imaginations. As a singer, performer, and writer, Donaldson used her position as Children's Laureate to campaign actively against library cuts in the UK and to foster plays based on children's books to be performed by children in libraries.   JZ

'Donkey-Skin' ('Peau d'âne', 1694) A verse fairy tale, composed by *Perrault

when 'Donkey-Skin tales' were already synonymous with 'fairy tales'. Its rich oral heritage found literary versions in *Straparola's 'Doralice' and *Basile's 'L'Orza' ('The Bear'). A defence of women written during the 'Querelle des femmes' ('Debate about Women'), its virtuous heroine, depictions of fashion, and social commentary on hypocritical courtiers, impotent pedants, and parasitic curates appealed to the 17th-century French salon public. Jacques Demy's 1971 film starring Catherine Deneuve has likewise enchanted 20th-century audiences.

A dying queen makes her husband promise to remarry only someone as beautiful as she: he pursues their daughter. On her fairy godmother's advice, the daughter tries to repel his incestuous designs by demanding impossibly lavish gowns and the slaughter of his cherished, gold-defecating donkey. Disguised by its pelt, she flees, works as a peasant, and is reviled for her uncivilized appearance. One day, a prince spies upon a lovely maiden trying on opulent garments. He becomes dangerously lovesick, and can be cured only by one of her cakes. Her tiny ring slips into the batter, he arranges a contest to locate the damsel whose finger it fits, and—like *Cinderella—the filthy worker regains her royal status.   MLE

Lewis, Philip, *Seeing Through the Mother Goose Tales* (1996).

Morgan, Jeanne, *Perrault's Morals for Moderns* (1985).

Soriano, Marc, *Les Contes de Perrault* (1968).

Donoghue, Emma (1969–) Irish novelist, playwright, and scholar. Donoghue's *Kissing the Witch: Old Tales in New Skins* (1997) is a series of linked retellings of twelve well-known fairy tales. One character in each tale becomes the narrator of the next; for example, the fairy godmother in 'The Tale of a Shoe' (a *'Cinderella' variant) tells the next tale, 'The Tale of a Bird' (a *'Bluebeard' variant) as her own. Donoghue disrupts the usual patterns of heterosexual desire; in these tales princesses often ignore princes to fall in love with fairy godmothers, stepmothers, and even with witches—older, powerful women usually portrayed as

'Donkey-Skin' The princess is appalled by her father's incestuous advances and his willingness to kill his favourite donkey for her in Charles *Perrault's 'Donkey-Skin', reproduced from an anonymous illustration in *Les Contes des fées offerts à Bébé* (*c*.1900).

threatening or evil in the fairy-tale canon. The thirteenth story, 'The Tale of the Kiss', told by a cave-dwelling witch, is not a variant of any traditional tale; it is deliberately inconclusive, enlisting the reader in the task of narration: 'This is the story you asked for. I leave it in your mouth.'

Donoghue's tales are also linguistically inventive, particularly in 'The Tale of the Cottage' (a *'Hansel and Gretel' variant), where a limited Gretel tells her new version of the story in blunt, uninflected prose: 'I once had brother that mother say we were pair of hands one fast one slow.' In all the tales her prose is simple and sure: 'Bowls spun like snow, goblets shattered like hail.' She continues the work of writers like Anne *Sexton, Olga *Broumas, and Angela *Carter, giving new life to old stories, recasting them to question old paradigms.   EWH

Doré, Gustave (1832–83) French illustrator, painter, and sculptor, whose fame grew world-wide with the publication of his engravings in *Dante's Inferno* (1861). Doré was a skilled draughtsman (drawing directly onto woodblocks), theatrical, poetic, versatile, and incredibly prolific. He was often criticized for his fecundity and for the rapidity of his work, having produced more than 8,000 wood engravings, 1,000 lithographs, 400 oil paintings, and 30 works of sculpture. Anecdotes told frequently about Doré relate how he began to draw when about 4, that he always had a pencil in hand, and that he preferred his pencils sharpened at both ends. With little formal training, Doré began as a young comic-strip artist, a boy genius, at the age of 15 illustrating a parody of Greek mythology, *Les Travaux d'Hercule* (*Labours of Hercule*, 1847), and evolved into a literary artist illustrating the works of Rabelais, Balzac, Milton, Chateaubriand, Byron, Hugo, *Shakespeare, and *Tennyson. Doré elevated illustration/wood engraving to the level of fine art. Doré's illustrations in Balzac's *Contes Drolatiques* (*Droll Stories*, 1855) are often regarded as transitional, moving him towards a more serious or higher stage of art, to literary folios, to painting, to

Doré, Gustave 'All the better to eat you, my dear', says the wolf in Gustave Doré's illustration of Charles *Perrault's 'Little Red Riding Hood' in *Les Contes de Perrault* (1867).

sculpture, to the English, and to religious art. An immensely popular Doré folio, *Contes de fées* (*Perrault's Fairy Tales*) found its way to a first English translation (*The Fairy Realm*, 1865) in verse by Tom Hood the Younger. Nine tales were included: 'Hop-o'-my-Thumb' (*'Little Tom Thumb'*), '*Sleeping Beauty in the Wood*', *'Donkey-Skin'*, *'Puss-in-Boots'*, *'Bluebeard'*, *'Little Red Riding Hood'*, *'Cinderella'*, 'The Fair' ('The *Fairies'*), and *'Ricky of the Tuft'*. His illustrations of the *Perrault fairy tales are generally considered to be classics, and he set a standard of fairy-tale illustration that few artists have met even today. The first Doré book to be translated into English was *Le Chevalier Jaufré* (*Jaufry the Knight*, 1856), a romance of chivalry written by Jean-Bernard Lafon (pseudonym, Mary Lafon). Contemporary criticism of Doré's work was mixed; some critics denounced him for his inability to paint as a painter would; others for the horror, lewdness, and gloom they saw in his engravings. Most seemed to acknowledge that his art was powerful and highly imaginative.   SS

Doré Gallery: Illustrated Catalogue (1974).

Jerrold, Blanchard, *The Life of Gustave Doré* (1891).

Malan, Dan, *Gustave Doré: Adrift on Dreams of Splendor* (1995).

Malan, Dan, *Gustave Doré: A Biography* (1996).

Richardson, Joanna, *Gustave Doré: A Biography* (1980).

Doyle, Richard (1824–83) English humorous artist, cartoonist, and fairy illustrator, affectionately referred to as 'Dicky' Doyle. A highly skilled draughtsman, he worked from an early age for the satirical magazine *Punch* and designed its famous front cover, used for over a century and depicting a procession of tiny fairy figures. Praised for his over 500 decorative illustrations, Doyle was also criticized for being too kindly in his caricatures, and he eventually resigned from *Punch* for its anti-papal sentiments. His critically acclaimed illustrations of famous children's stories and fairy tales such as *Dickens's Christmas Books* (1845–6) and *The Cricket on the Hearth* (1846), selected *Grimms' fairy tales in *The Fairy Ring* (1846), John

*Ruskin's *The King of the Golden River* (1851), and J. R. Planché's *An Old Fairy Tale: The Sleeping Beauty* (1865) made him a household name. In his late work he concentrated on fairy paintings, drawing heavily on the Grimms' fairy tales for inspiration. Critical judgement is divided on the quality of his large watercolours such as *Snow White and Rosy Red* (1871), but *The Enchanted Fairy Tree: Or a Fantasy based on 'The Tempest' by Wm. *Shakespeare (painted 1845, exhibited 1868) is a masterwork, typical of his incredibly detailed scenes depicting the antics of wicked elves and the romance of fairy maidens and their knights. His most celebrated book is *In Fairyland* (1870), a series of 16 watercolour scenes of fairyland, which accompanied a poem by William Allingham and, in the 1884 reissue, a specially written fairy tale by Andrew *Lang, 'The Princess Nobody'.   KS

Engen, Rodney, *Richard Doyle* (1983).

Engen, Rodney, *Richard Doyle and his Family* (1984).

Hambourg, Daria, *Richard Doyle: His Life and Work* (1948).

Martineau, Jane (ed.), *Victorian Fairy Painting* (1997).

Peppin, Brigid, *Fantasy Book Illustration 1860–1920* (1975).

drama and fairy tales A fairy-tale drama is a theatrical work that uses the motifs, characters, and genre markers of the fairy tale. These plays have variously served as entertainment, socializing tools, pedagogical and didactic instruments, and critiques of the social, literary, and political order. Written for both adult and juvenile audiences, fairy-tale drama shares a great affinity with the other theatrical genres of ballet, opera, and musical theatre.

Before the advent of the *contes de fées* craze in France, works like *Shakespeare's *A Midsummer Night's Dream* (*c.*1600), Ben *Jonson's *Oberon: The Fairy Prince* (1611), and Henry *Purcell's *The Fairy Queen* (1692) featured fairies and magical events; they preceded the rise of the fairy-tale play in France with the publication of the earliest collections of fairy tales in the 1690s.

The theatre of the 17th century had been replete with magicians and sorcerers in pastoral plays, machine plays, court ballets, and operas. Plays that featured fairies—without exception comedies—were a conglomeration of music, dance, and special effects. They enjoyed great resonance among theatregoers, and their popularity often drove both what was written and what was performed. The use of fairies and demons allowed the troupe to use exotic costumes, and the exciting plots and the silly transformations the characters underwent all contributed to the audience's affection for this genre. In all probability the original audiences saw the fairies' capricious and tyrannical behaviour as a commentary on the mores of the French aristocracy.

Although the craze lasted only two decades in France, the ensuing years were formative and defining for the genre throughout Europe. In the 18th century more fairy plays and fairy-tale plays began to appear, as the genre became more established and playwrights took inspiration from their own cultural and theatre traditions and indigenous tale collections. In England John Hawkesworth's *Edgar and Emmeline: A Fairy Tale in Dramatic Entertainment for Two Acts* (1761); Michael Arne's *A Fairy Tale*, adapted from Shakespeare's *A Midsummer Night's Dream* (1763); J. Chr. Smith's *The Fairies* (1755); and Chr. Dibdin's *Queen Mab* (1769) all worked from Celtic mythology. In Italy, Carlo *Gozzi's fairy-tale plays valorized the *commedia dell'arte* and presented stories based on puppet plays, oriental stories, popular fables, fairy stories, and the works of Calderón. Two that have withstood the test of time and have been revisited over the centuries are *L'amore delle tre melarance* (*Love of the Three Oranges*, 1761) and *Turandot* (1762). The ten tales Gozzi wrote for the stage in many ways were the beginning of the fairy-tale play as a satire of literary conventions of the times; his tales criticized and lampooned the 18th-century *Zeitgeist* and the Enlightenment's cultural reformist aims. German stages initially relied heavily on translations of popular French comedies and dramatized *contes de fées*, although an indigenous tradition began with such plays as *Mägera, die fürchterliche Hexe* (*Megera, the Terrible Witch*, 1763); *Das Donauweibchen* (*The Maid of the Danube*, 1798); and *Hulda, das schöne Wasserfräulein* (*Hulda, the Beautiful Water Maiden*, 1799). Literary histories consider the real breakthrough work for the genre in Germany to be Christoph *Wieland's *Oberon* (1789).

By the 19th century, more theatres were in existence and accessible to more people, more fairy-tale books were in print, audience familiarity with the motifs and themes had increased dramatically, and new artistic tastes were developing. The fairy-tale play began to adapt to political, social, and literary sensibilities as playwrights exploited the malleability of the tales. Over the course of the century, fairy-tale dramas reflected the pervading trends within literary movements and shifted from comedy to often more serious works and even tragedies. The genre also began to differentiate more clearly into musical (opera and ballet) and non-musical versions (*see* BALLET AND FAIRY TALES; OPERA AND FAIRY TALES; OPERETTA AND FAIRY TALES).

There had already been a century and a half of works based on *Perrault, the *oriental fairy-tale collections, and the Italian medieval collections that had been received and that playwrights were adapting, but there were also new impulses spawned by the romantic interest in the genre, the rise of the literary *Kunstmärchen*, and the advent of the *Grimms' *Kinder- und Hausmärchen*. As the romantic wave swept Europe, playwrights from England to Hungary produced numerous fairy-tale plays, many engendered by the romantic interest in Shakespeare. In Scandinavia, Adam Oehlenschläger wrote the outstanding *Sanct hafsaften-spil* (*Play for Midsummer Eve*, 1802) and *Aladdin* (1805); P. D. A. Atterbom, a leader in the Swedish romantic movement, created his greatest poetic work, the fairy-tale play *Lycksalighetens ö* (*The Isle of the Blessed*, 1824–7) that explores the beguiling power of imagination in the history of poetry. In Hungary, Mihály Vörösmarty produced the great work *Csongor és Tünde*, a symbolic fairy-tale play reminiscent of Shakespeare's *Midsummer*

Night's Dream. In England Thomas Cooke further explored Celtic sources in his *Oberon, or, The Charmed Horn* (1826, based on Wieland) and his 'grand melodramatic fairy tale' *Thierna-na-oge, or, The Prince of the Lakes* (1829). In Germany, Ludwig *Tieck took up Gozzi's gauntlet and produced numerous works that were social, political, and literary critiques of his times, as *Der gestiefelte Kater* (*Puss-in-Boots*, 1804). Friedrich de la Motte Fouqué introduced the dilemma of the ill-fated love between humans and other-worldly *Undines and *Mélusine, a theme that was to re-emerge in later, neoromantic plays; his 'Undine' was put to music by E. T. A. *Hoffmann and produced as a fairy-tale play (1816); Franz Grillparzer (among many others) took up the Melusine theme (1833). As the century progressed, other writers like Georg Büchner responded to Germany's aesthetic and political nationalism by creating a deliberately senseless, chaotic and amoral universe in his anti-fairy-tale play *Leonce and Lena* (1843).

By mid-century, the tragic fairy tale coexisted with the socially satiric and light entertainment, and the commercial popularity of the fairy tale reached new heights. J. R. *Planché achieved great success in England with his extravaganzas like *The Good Woman in the Wood: A New and Original Fairy Tale* (based on Mlle de *La Force's 'La Bonne Femme' ('The Good Woman'), 1852) and Tom Taylor's *Wittikind and his Brothers, or, The Seven Swan Princes and the Fairy Melusine* (1852). In 1857, in Germany, fairy-tale plays as popular family entertainment made their debut in Hamburg with Carl August Görner's introduction of the opulently staged Christmas fairy tale, a tradition that has continued to this day. Theatres around Europe were quick to pick up the trend because Christmas plays tided more than one theatre budget over to the next season.

By the end of the century, the genre's happy-end solutions dissolved into tragedy. The fantastic, utopian world of the original tales was shown to be inadequate, unable to resolve real-life conflicts. Romantic themes were back in vogue, as playwrights like Maurice *Maeterlinck, August *Strindberg,

Gerhart *Hauptmann, Fyodor Sologub, Henrik Ibsen, Hugo von *Hofmannstal, and William Butler *Yeats all turned to fairy tales and other anti-realistic forms to bring poetry and spiritual meaning back into the theatre. They employed elements from tales of Perrault and the Grimms and from Hans Christian *Andersen. Their plays often used the pattern of enchantment and disenchantment à la *A Midsummer Night's Dream,* or took up the idea of contact with other-worldly females as an allegorical conflict between art and life, as Hauptmann's *Die versunkene Glocke* (*The Sunken Bell*, 1896), Ibsen's *Peer Gynt* (1876), and Hofmannstal's *Das Bergwerk zu Falun* (*The Mines of Falun*, 1906). The mood of these plays was decidedly gloomy. The Belgian Nobel laureate Maeterlinck's *Pelléas et Mélisande* (1892), considered the unquestioned masterpiece of symbolist drama and basis for the opera by Claude *Debussy, conveys a mood of hopeless melancholy and doom, an obsession with love and death. Following Maeterlinck, other playwrights dissolved the fairy-tale happy end into disillusionment and despair. Perhaps one of the most interesting paradigm shifts within the genre at the *fin de siècle* is apparent in Robert *Walser's 1901 dramolette *Schneewittchen* (*Snow White*). His work questions the very transmissibility of an ordered, traditional system of values as his characters possess literary self-consciousness: the queen and Snow White come to understand that their every move and thought is directed by their role as fictitious characters of two versions of a fairy tale, the Grimms' and Walser's. Walser saw his use of an unpoliticized, 'purely' poetic language as the only vehicle to imaginative transcendence.

While the symbolists and surrealists explored fairy-tale themes as meditations on the human condition and the role of literature and art, others, like their predecessors in earlier centuries, were attracted to fairy-tale themes as a reflection on the social and political climate of the historical moment. The Russian Yevgeni *Schwartz's *Drakon* (*The Dragon*, 1943), for example, presents images of the way dictatorships and revolutionary politics work, a theme the East German poet Wolf *Biermann revisited in *Der Dra-Dra. Die grosse Drachentöterschau* (*The Great Dragon Slayer's Show*, 1970). As society and culture shifted around changing sexual, gender, and family attitudes, artists also used the adaptability of the fairy tale as a vehicle for their messages. In the mid-1980s in the United States James Lapine and Stephen Sondheim's *Into the Woods* (1987) was a social parable that valorized traditional family values, monogamy, and hearth and home. By 1994, the fairy tale was used in the cause against Aids in Doug Holsclaw's *Myron: A Fairy Tale in Black and White.*

Fairy tale plays and children's theatre
In works for children some of the most essential liberating and transformational potential of the fairy tale is exploited as well as the genre's ability to reinforce gender roles and the socio-political status quo. Pedagogical and philosophical debates about childrearing, appropriate literature for juvenile audiences, and the needs of the child as audience have often informed these deliberations.

Privileged juvenile audiences enjoyed fairy-tale plays as early as Françoise de Graffigny's *Ziman et Zénise* (1748, performed privately for the children of the Emperor of Austria). But the advent of fairy-tale plays for children can be traced back more clearly to the reception and dramatization of the French *contes de fées*, Perrault, and the Grimms. Two trends of production exist: home theatre (the earliest form of participatory theatre) and commercial theatre. By the middle of the 19th century, with growing literacy and great numbers of fairy-tale books on the market, fairy-tale plays for home productions abounded throughout Europe and North America, a tradition that has continued up to the present day. Female playwrights and adapters were and are in the majority. Mostly excluded from 'serious' theatre, women turned to home productions as a vehicle to gain a kind of public voice before a limited, surely receptive audience of parents and friends. These plays and their production offered a kind of complicity between

writers and performers—the disenfranchised groups of women and children gained a voice and declaimed. Most of these plays were adaptations of well-known tales, based on the standard corpus by Perrault, the Grimms, and Hans Christian Andersen found in popular anthologies: 'Snow White', *'Sleeping Beauty', *'Hansel and Gretel', *'Little Red Riding Hood', 'The Emperor's New Clothes', and a smattering of stories from *The *Arabian Nights*, like *'Aladdin'. The French tradition of the *conteuses* was also adapted for home use, as Eliza H. Keating's *The White Cat: An Old Fairy Tale Made into a Modern Extravaganza* (1860). Anglo-American adapters also paid attention to their own children's books that gave rise to *Dickens's *The Cricket on the Hearth* (1846) or Frank L. *Baum's The *Wizard of Oz* (performed in Chicago as a musical in 1901). As reforms in schooling and pedagogy swept Europe and America, fairy-tale plays became part of these reformist and kindergarten movements and works like Lady Florence E. E. O. Bell's *Fairy Tale Plays and How to Act Them* (1896) provided guidance. Henriette Kühne-Harkort's Grimm adaptation *Schneewittchen* (1877) is a typical example of these kinds of works: played by children, the seven dwarfs bear names of minerals and elements and explain the natural world to the performers and audience. Because these plays were not staged in theatre houses, critical reception of this tradition barely exists.

With the exception of Christmas fairy-tale plays, commercial theatres rarely performed pieces deemed appropriate for child audiences before the advent of children's theatres in the late 19th and early 20th centuries. Fairy-tale plays suitable for children were certainly written and performed before then, such as Sarah A. Frost's *Aladdin, or, The Wonderful Lamp: A Fairy Tale for Little Folks* (1890s), but most of these works originated in the musical theatre tradition. 'Cinderella' and 'Sleeping Beauty' had appeared as children's opera in Vienna as early as 1853; later in the century, Adelheid Wette's *Hänsel und Gretel* (1893, with music by her brother Engelbert *Humperdinck) became an enduring classic still performed today. Like the Christmas fairy-tale play that assured the survival of theatres throughout the otherwise dry holiday seasons, the popularity of fairy-tale plays and their sure box-office success promoted stagings for social welfare benefits like the 1864 version of 'Cinderella' on behalf of the Sanitary Commission in New York or the Benefit of the Newark Orphan Asylum in 1876.

In the 20th century, the history of the fairy-tale play is inextricably linked with the history of children's theatre. Fairy-tale plays have been the backbone of many children's theatres, but their stage realizations have taken two directions: bourgeois theatres have typically presented traditional tales that reinforce the social and political status quo, while proletarian and progressive theatres have sought to upend the traditional tale and have rewritten them or produced original ones with radically revised messages. But whether bourgeois or progressive, children's theatres have used fairy tales to didactic purposes, for the performers and/or the audiences.

One of many such examples of children's theatre's mission as a pedagogical institution was the Federal Theater Project in the United States during the Great Depression. The founders' stated goals were to reach children not otherwise in theatres, to provide entertainment, and to help child audiences learn about problem-solving. They employed children in the rewriting and performance of fairy-tale plays as a way to encourage freedom of expression, to provide an emotional outlet, and to foster group cooperation. Of the plays the Project produced and staged around the country over a five-year period, *Aladdin*, *The Emperor's New Clothes*, *Hansel and Gretel*, **Jack and the Beanstalk*, and **Pinocchio* were the mainstays. The Federal Theater Project's objectives, goals, and productions are representative of much of children's theatre in the United States since that time.

Another part of the spectrum of didacticism in fairy-tale plays are the rewritings and adaptations to teach the audience. Perhaps the most interesting examples of this group were written and performed in the Soviet Union and later East Germany. In the 1920s in the Soviet Union, the traditional fairy tales were branded inappropriate for children's theatre because party officials considered them 'monarchist in orientation, mystic and religious in influence, and likely to encourage the child to rely on a supernatural power to solve all problems'. By the 1930s attitudes shifted and writers like Yevgeni Schwartz began writing adaptations like *Krasnaya Shapochka* (*Little Red Riding Hood*, 1937); *Snezhanaya Koroleva* (*The *Snow Queen*, 1939); and *Zolushka* (*Cinderella*, 1937) as true 'socialist fairy tales'; these works, and others like I. Karnaukova and L. Brausevick's adaptation of S. T. Aksakov's tale 'Alenikii tsvetochek' ('The Little Scarlet Flower', based on ***Beauty and the Beast') became part of the standard repertory of children's theatre. As the theatre tradition developed, there was a move towards intermingling of the real and the fantastic and reducing the use of the magical; S. **Prokofiev's *Pyot's polovinoy volshebnykh prevrashchenii* (*Five and a Half Magical Changes*) is a good example of this type: the one fantastic figure, the Kind Sorcerer, admonishes the child he aids to try to manage without magic, because every magical transformation is a kind of lie. By the 1950s Schwartz had turned from Western European classics to Russian folklore; in *Dvu klyona* (*The Two Maples*, 1954) Vassilissa, a proletarian worker, saves her sons from the Russian fairy-tale witch **Bába-Yagá. The main message of the play is defeating evil and not to run away from home. That message made *Dvu klyona* the most popular (or at least the most staged) play in children's theatre in East Germany.

In the West, fairy tales are embraced or eschewed for children's theatre depending on prevailing societal attitudes about children and their viewing needs, and the general role of theatre in society. Socio-political shifts in the 1980s and the connection to new psychoanalytical interpretations à la Bruno Bettelheim heralded a new 'poetic theatre' that distanced itself from the politically and socially engaged plays of the 1970s. It became possible to show the plot developments in fairy tales as psychic processes of universalized human, conflict-laden situations. Poetic theatre allowed a work of art to be independent of reality in favour of its own internal logic and it removed the work of art from social responsibility. Carlo Formigoni's 'Cinderella' adaptation and Paul Maar and Mauro Guindani's *Die Reise durch das Schweigen* (*The Trip through Silence*) on German stages were important pieces in this period. But by the 1990s fairy tales once again were enlisted into the service of social and political causes, as political correctness and cultural diversity became driving forces. The series by the Players' Press in California, for example, rehabilitates the bad guys and gals of traditional tales like *Rumpelstiltskin and the wolf of 'Peter and the Wolf', while Useni Perkins's *Black Fairy and Other Plays for African American Children* (1993) provides alternatives from under-represented traditions. Fairy-tale plays have once again become family theatre as many of the plays seem written more for the parents than for the children; fairy-tale plays allow a flight to childhood as an escape from the unpleasant political and social realities of adulthood.   SJ

> Morton, Miriam (ed.), *Through the Magic Curtain: Theater for Children, Adolescents and Youth in the U.S.S.R.* (1979).
> Nicholson, David B., *The Fairy Tale in Modern Drama* (1982).

Duane, Diane (1952–) American-born writer residing in Ireland, author of science fiction, fantasy, and media-related novels for children and adults. The 'Sorcerer's Apprentice' theme can be found throughout Duane's fantasy work. In the 'Tale of the Five' series—*The Door into Fire* (1979), *The Door into Shadow* (1984), and *The Door into Sunset* (1992)—five companions strive to control a powerful, elemental fire magic. *So You Want to Be a Wizard?* (1983), *A Wizard Abroad* (1993), and other books in the 'Wizardry' series are whimsical tales for young readers following the misadventures of wizards-in-training.   TW

Duclos, Charles Pinot (1704–72) French historiographer, moralist, and novelist. He was born into a wealthy family that lost its fortune with the collapse of Law's System (1720), and wrote treatises on Breton druids, French kings, and 18th-century morality. Despite a libertine best-seller (*Confessions du comte de* **, 1741), he was elected to the French Academy in 1746. He is also known for the parodic fairy tale *Acajou et Zirphile* (1744) and the bet surrounding its composition. The Comte de Tessin had commissioned engravings from Boucher for a fairy tale, but was recalled to Sweden. Boucher took them to Mlle Quinault's salon: a contest was held to write a fairy tale around his scenes of flying hands and genies in chamber pots. *Voisenon, *Caylus, and Duclos submitted entries: only Duclos's has survived. Its publication site of 'Minutie' ('Trifles') announces an aggressive preface that ridicules readers—a passage later omitted from the *Cabinet des fées* (*The Fairies' Study*, 1785) because of its rudeness. Unfortunately, this censorship destroys the parodic intent of this tale about two evil genies, a prince and princess (Acajou and Zirphile), and a good fairy. With ironic asides and clever puns, it burlesques the fairy-tale marvellous and motifs, pokes fun at the Duchesse du Maine and her fairy plays at Sceaux, and criticizes a shallow, libertine society. It inspired a response from Fréron and a comic-opera by Favart.   MLE

> Dagen, Jean (ed.), *Acajou et Zirphile* (1993).
> Meister, Paul, *Charles Duclos* (1956).
> Robert, Raymonde, *Contes parodiques et licencieux du 18e siècle* (1987).

Duffy, Carol Ann (1955–) Scottish poet and playwright who was appointed Britain's poet laureate in 2009. She has published a number of award-winning collections, such as *Standing Female Nude* (1985), *The Stolen Childhood and Other Dark Fairy Tales* (2003), and *The Lost Happy Endings* (2006). Duffy's *Grimm Tales* (1996) was successfully adapted by Tim Supple for the theater in 1997. Her other fairy-tale books include dark adaptations of *'Hansel and Gretel', 'The Golden Goose', and *'Rumpelstiltskin'.   KMJ and JZ

Dukas, Paul (1865–1935) French composer. In a small, carefully crafted *œuvre*

his major work, and only opera, is *Ariane et Barbe-Bleue* (1907), composed to accompany a short play of the same name published in 1901 by the Belgian symbolist Maurice *Maeterlinck. Intended from the start for musical elaboration, Maeterlinck's play joins Perrault's 'Barbe-bleue' (*'Bluebeard') with the myth of Ariadne. Despite being discovered and offered a vision of freedom by the eponymous heroine, Bluebeard's wives choose to continue living in the stifling opulence of their captor's castle. The story allows Dukas to conjure vivid impressions of gem-filled rooms and subterranean darkness.   SB

Dulac, Edmund (1882–1953) French-born, British-naturalized artist, illustrator, and stage designer. Dulac was one of the finest artists in a great age of illustration. Like his contemporary Arthur *Rackham, he specialized in fantasy, and their work has much in common—subdued yet softly glowing colour delicately outlined in black, an interest in pattern and texture, superb draughtsmanship, and a fascination with detail. Dulac's style, however, is more painterly; in his compositions, human figures are often subordinated to backgrounds executed in subtly textured watercolour washes. He has an affinity for oriental subjects, and his work shows the influence of Persian miniatures and Japanese prints as well as the Pre-Raphaelite tradition. Among his most notable illustrated books are *The *Arabian Nights* (1907), *Shakespeare's Comedy of the Tempest* (1908), **Sleeping Beauty and Other Fairy Tales from the Old French* (1910), **Stories from Hans Andersen* (1912), Laurence *Housman's retelling of *Princess Badoura: A Tale from the Arabian Nights* (1913), *Edmund Dulac's Fairy Book* (1915), and Alexander *Pushkin's *The Golden Cockerel* (1950). Dulac also designed costumes and scenery for dramatic productions, including several by his friend W. B. *Yeats. After the First World War, when the market for deluxe editions declined, he applied his versatile talents to interior design, caricatures, bookplates, playing cards, and postage stamps. SR

Larkin, David, *Dulac* (1975).

White, Colin, *Edmund Dulac* (1976).

Dumas, Philippe (1940–) French author and illustrator of children's literature. He composes witty and animated stories that often transpose quite literally classic fairy-tale elements. His suggestively titled collection *Contes à l'envers* (*Upside Down Tales*, 1977) includes 'La Belle au doigt bruyant' ('Boisterous Beauty'), a humorous reworking of *'Sleeping Beauty', in which the spell cast imposes blaring music and perpetual dancing instead of tranquil slumber. In 'Conte à rebours' ('Against the Grain Tale'), a story about conformity, walking backwards becomes the norm. The heroine of 'Le Petit Chaperon Bleu Marine' ('Little Navy Blue Riding Hood') is the grand-daughter of *Little Red Riding Hood. Envious of her ancestor's fame, she seeks the media spotlight by liberating a wolf from the Botanical Garden in Paris. The wary animal flees to Siberia where he avoids the fate of his great-great-uncle, who is none other than the wolf of *Perrault's tale. The story concludes with the moral that some men are more dangerous than wolves, and the accompanying illustration completes the allusion to Hitler. References to popular culture and contemporary institutions abound in these tales. Like other fairy-tale revisionists of the 20th century, Dumas creates unorthodox endings and challenges conventional fairy-tale wisdom and morals.   AZ

Malarte, Claire-Lise, 'The French Fairy-Tale Conspiracy', *The Lion and the Unicorn*, 12.2 (1988).

Dunsany, Edward John Moreton Drax Plunkett, Baron (1878–1957) Anglo-Irish writer of short stories, plays, and novels; he became 18th Baron of Dunsany (1899), and remained throughout his life one of the 20th century's most prolific writers of fantasy for adults. Influenced by the fairy tales of Oscar *Wilde and the romances of William *Morris, Dunsany began his literary career with the creation of his own mythical, quasi-mystical universe in *The Gods of Pegana* (1905) and *Time and the Gods* (1906). *The Sword of Welleran* (1908) contained some of his best fantasy tales including the title story and 'The Kith of the Elf-Folk', an account of a fairy-like creature who chooses to enter the world of late Victorian England, finds it hypocritical and ugly, and then renounces her soul to escape. The tale manifests two abiding characteristics of Dunsany, his dislike of organized religion and his loathing of the Industrial Revolution. In *A Dreamer's Tales* (1910), *The Book of Wonder* (1912) which contains 'The Hoard of the Gibbelins' known for its brilliant unhappy ending ('And, without saying a word . . . they neatly hanged him on the outer wall'), *51 Tales* (1915), *Tales of Wonder* (1916, called in America *The Last Book of Wonder*), and *Tales of Three Hemispheres* (1919), Dunsany expanded his mythopoeic vision. The impact of these early dreamland stories was heightened by the illustrations of Sime, whose pictures sometimes inspired Dunsany's tales. Later collections include *The Man who Ate the Phoenix* (1949), whose title story utilizes traditional Celtic motifs: encounters with a leprechaun, a Banshee, and the Fairy Queen; and another tale, 'Little *Snow White up to date', which modernizes the classic. More popular than the elaborately wrought, linguistically archaic fantasies are the Jorkens travel tales, which sometimes use folklore motifs for comic ends. Beginning with *The Travel Tales of Mr Joseph Jorkens* (1931), these records of a creative liar who entertains members of his club with his adventures—including, in 'Mrs Jorkens', his marriage to a mermaid—are among Dunsany's most amusing works.

Dunsany's second career, as a dramatist, associated him with Lady Gregory, W. B. *Yeats, and the revival of the Irish Theatre. Several of his non-realist plays, including *A Night at an Inn*, were popular, as were his short works utilizing fairy-tale themes. Moreover, he began writing novels in the 1920s; filled with quests, imaginary kingdoms, dream atmosphere, and the pseudo-medievalism of Morris's romances, these might be labelled fairy novels. Among them are a quest romance of fairyland, *The King of Elfland's Daughter* (1924) and the equally folkloric *Charwoman's Shadow* (1926), which reworks the traditional motif of the lost shadow. In *The Blessing of Pan* (1927),

Dunsany successfully fuses British folklore and pagan myth, while *The Story of Mona Sheehy* (1939) is an anti-fantasy, a novel of a young woman who wrongly believes she is of fairy birth.

As a fabulist who imaginatively transforms materials from *The *Arabian Nights*, classical mythology, Celtic, Germanic, and Hindu folklore as well as from medieval lays and quest romances, Dunsany is an important contributor to the fairy-tale tradition.   CGS

Anderson, Angelee Sailer, 'Lord Dunsany: The Potency of Words and the Wonder of Things', *Mythlore*, 15.1 (autumn 1988).

Joshi, S. T., *Lord Dunsany: Master of the Anglo-Irish Imagination* (1995).

Durand, Catherine (*née* **Bédacier**, *c*.1650–1712/15) French writer. The author of several novels and the creator of the dramatic proverb genre, she wrote three fairy tales: 'Histoire de la fée Lubantine' ('Story of the Fairy Lubantine'), which appeared in her novel *La Comtesse de Mortane* (*The Countess of Mortane*), as well as 'Le Prodige d'amour' ('The Miracle of Love') and 'L'Origine des fées' ('The Origin of Fairies'), both of which appeared in *Les Petits Soupers de l'année 1699* (*The Little Suppers of 1699*). In 'Le Prodige d'amour', Durand rewrites the basic plot of *Perrault's and *Bernard's *'Riquet à la houppe' by reversing gender roles. Her tales project a scepticism about love typical of French literature in this period.   LCS

Duvall, Shelley (1949–) American actress, director, and producer. Between 1982 and 1985 she produced *Faerie Tale Theatre*, a series of 26 fairy-tale adaptations, for the cable television network Showtime (*see* FILM AND FAIRY TALES). The series had been offered initially to Walt *Disney Productions, but Duvall was unwilling to relinquish artistic control, which Disney demanded. None the less, the series is not unified by Duvall's own style, interpretation, or artistic influence. Instead, each roughly 50-minute episode features famous actors and a well-known director, which results in a wide range of visual styles and approaches to the original fairy tales. The tales themselves also cover a broad territory, and diversity seems to be the guiding criterion for the selections. Drawing on the Brothers *Grimm, Hans Christian *Andersen, The *Arabian Nights, and other sources, the series includes adaptations of tales such as *'Hansel and Gretel', 'The Dancing Princesses', *'Sleeping Beauty', *'Snow White', *'Rapunzel', 'The Nightingale', 'The Emperor's New Clothes', 'The *Princess and the Pea', 'The *Snow Queen', '*Aladdin and his Wonderful Lamp', *'Jack and the Beanstalk', 'Goldilocks and the Three Bears', *'Beauty and the Beast', and other classic tales.

In only a few cases do the directors and actors take advantage of the live-action medium and exploit the limits imposed by the made-for-television format. A case in point is 'The Tale of the Frog Prince', which was written and directed by Eric Idle and features the actors Robin Williams and Terri Garr. Idle brings his television experience with Monty Python and his satirical vision to bear on the Grimms' tale. As a result he effectively blends the fairy tale with adult comedy and challenges the viewer's expectations. In addition, Idle's parody exposes traditional fairy-tale stereotypes, such as the equation of beauty with virtue, and ironically dissects the nature of power in society. The combination of Idle's irreverent humour and Williams's unpredictability creates an adaptation with surprises and new views of the traditional tale.

Despite the unevenness of the productions as significant fairy-tale adaptations, *Faerie Tale Theatre* has had considerable popular success, especially in syndication and the home video market. Duvall has produced other television fare aimed at an audience of children, including *Shelley Duvall's Tall Tales and Legends* (1985–8) and *Shelley Duvall's Bedtime Stories* (1992–3).   DH

Haase, Donald, 'Gold into Straw: Fairy Tale Movies for Children and the Culture Industry', *The Lion and the Unicorn*, 12.2 (December 1988).
Zipes, Jack, 'Once Upon a Time beyond Disney: Contemporary Fairy-Tale Films for Children', in *Happily Ever After: Fairy Tales, Children, and the Culture Industry* (1997).

Duve, Karen (1961–) German writer who is highly regarded for two books that deal with fairy tales, *Die entführte Prinzessin: Von Drachen, Liebe und anderen Ungeheuern* (*The Kidnapped Princess: About Dragons, Love and Other Monsters*, 2005) and *Grrrimm* (2012). *The Kidnapped Princess* is a light parody of conventional fantasy novels and fairy tales. A wealthy prince named Diego wants to irritate his parents by marrying Princess Lisvana, whose country is forlorn and impoverished. However, he discovers that the only way he can court and wed her is by kidnapping her. Meanwhile, his rival, the knight Bredur, hires a dragon to try to prevent him from marrying the princess. Their dual quests lead to hilarious adventures. In the end all the traditional fairy-tale roles and motifs are turned upside down through Duve's ironic style. *Grrrimm*, a collection of five unusual tales, is much different. Using various narrative voices that are blunt, colourful, and idiomatic, Duve retells five of the *Grimms' tales (*'Snow White', 'The *Frog King', *'Sleeping Beauty', 'Brother Lustig', and *'Little Red Cap') to explore hidden meanings that add greater social and philosophical depth to the stories. For instance, 'Zwergenidyll' ('Dwarf Idyll') is told in the first person by a dwarf who is in love with Snow White and tries to seduce her. In 'Die Froschbraut' ('The Frog's Wife') narrated by the princess, we learn that her tyrannical father is a criminal and maltreats his daughter. In the title story, 'Grrrimm', a tour-de-force retelling of 'Little Red Cap' combined with 'The Boy Who Set Out to Learn about Fear', she sets the tale in a contemporary village in the mountains of some apparent Slavic country, where conditions are very primitive. It is told from the alternating perspectives of Elsie ('Little Red Cap') and Stepan, Elsie's childhood friend, and we learn that Elsie is sent to her grandmother to obtain a cure for her father, who is dying from a poisonous wolf bite. However, her grandmother turns out to be a dangerous witch. Thanks to her friend Stepan, she is saved and then she saves him. Duve's narrative harks back to eighteenth- and nineteenth-century European versions of 'Little Red Riding Hood', and though the narrative is gruesome, she captures the heroic aspect of two young people born into a barbaric society. Duve clearly undermines expectations of readers of the classic versions of the Grimms' tales to cast light on the seamy side of 'real life'. JZ

Dvořák, Antonín (1841–1904) Czech composer. His music represents a meeting of the Viennese classical tradition with a style suffused with the landscape, speech patterns, and folk traditions of what was to become Czechoslovakia. Renowned for his symphonic and chamber works, Dvořák's fairy-tale inspired compositions include the operas *The Devil and Kate* (1898–9) and *Rusalka* (1900). The distinctively Czechoslovakian component of his music is also sharply evident in a set of four symphonic poems, referred to by the composer as 'orchestral ballads': *The Water Goblin*, *The Noon Witch*, *The Golden Spinning Wheel*, and *The Wild Dove* (all 1896). Each is based on a folk ballad from a collection entitled *A Bouquet of Folk Tales*, by the Czech poet and folklore specialist Karel Jaromír Erben. Dvořák's music broadly follows the outline of each story. As one critic wrote at the time, 'the orchestra recites Erben's poems'; indeed, certain of the instrumental lines are based on the rhythmic patterns of the verse.

The Water Goblin, composed as a rondo with seven scenes, tells of the marriage of a young girl and an evil goblin, identified by themes on the cellos and oboe respectively. Becoming homesick, the girl is granted permission to visit her mother, with the proviso that she leaves her child with its father. In the evening the goblin calls at the girl's mother's home. When the mother refuses to let her daughter go, a storm rises, and a thumping sound at the door proves to be the headless body of the child.

The Noon Witch begins quietly with a child playing while his mother prepares a meal. Angry with her son, the mother threatens him with mention of a witch who is thought to stalk during the hour before midday. The witch, a ghostly old woman, enters and demands the child, to the sound of muted strings, bass clarinet, and bassoon. After a struggle the mother collapses, as the midday bell rings. Returning home for his lunch, the father finds his wife, whom he revives; the child is dead.

The Golden Spinning Wheel is a complicated fairy tale to express in musical form. The only one of the four to have a happy ending, it involves a king and a young girl who has her hands and feet cut off and her eyes put out by her stepmother, so that the king will marry the stepmother's own daughter. The heroine is finally restored physically and reunited with the king, through the intervention of an old man, some magic water, and the eponymous spinning wheel.

Opening with a funeral march, *The Wild Dove* concerns the too hasty remarriage of a widow who, it transpires, poisoned her first husband. Tormented by the mournful cooing of a dove over the husband's grave—evoked by Dvořák using a combination of flutes, oboe, and harp—the woman drowns herself. SB

Clapham, John, *Antonin Dvořák: Musician and Craftsman* (1966).
Janáček, Leoš, 'A Discussion of Two Tone Poems Based on Texts by Karel Jaromír Erben: *The Wood Dove* and *The Golden Spinning Wheel*' (1897–8), trans. Tatiana Firkušný, in Michael Beckerman (ed.), *Dvořák and his World* (1993).

Egner, Thorbjørn (1912–90) Norwegian writer and illustrator of humorous fairy tales for children. His first and most famous book is a didactic story about evil trolls who live in a boy's teeth, *Karius og Baktus* (*Carius and Bactus*, 1949). A collection of funny animal fairy tales *Klatremus og de andre dyrene i Hakkebakkeskogen* (*Climbing-Mouse and Other Animals in the Hunchback Wood*, 1954) is inspired by Rudyard *Kipling. In *Folk og rvere i Kardemomme by* (*The Singing Town*, 1959) a British nonsense fairy-tale tradition can be traced. Egner has also translated the children's classics *Winnie the Pooh* and *Doctor Dolittle* into Norwegian.　　MN

Tveterås, Harald L. (ed.), *En bok om Thorbjørn Egner* (1972).

Eichendorff, Joseph Freiherr von (1788–1857) German poet and author who combined romantic nature mysticism with Christian faith. While studying at Heidelberg, he entered into friendship with Achim von *Arnim and Clemens *Brentano, whose German folk-song collection decisively influenced his subsequent literary production. In his early novel *Ahnung und Gegenwart* (*Presentiment and Actuality*, 1815), the mood and emotion of the characters often find expression in a lyric poetry that appropriates the form and metre of folk song, as is also the case in the story that has become a minor classic of world literature, 'Aus dem Leben eines Taugenichts' ('The Memoirs of a Good-for-Nothing', 1826). In Eichendorff's contribution to the genre of the artistic fairy tale (*Kunstmärchen*), 'Das Marmorbild' ('The Marble Statue', 1819), Florio no sooner falls in love with lovely young Bianca, and she with him, than he finds himself under the spell of a marble statue of Venus that has come alive in the person of a maturely alluring seductress. Florio is saved from succumbing to Venus' blandishments by his older friend Fortunato, and in the end young love triumphs.　　JMM

Blackall, Eric A., 'Images on a Golden Ground: Eichendorff', in *The Novels of the German Romantics* (1983).
Goebel, Robert O., *Eichendorff's Scholarly Reception: A Survey* (1993).
Hoffmeister, Gerhart, 'Eichendorff's *Ahnung und Gegenwart* as a Religious Development', in James N. Hardin (ed.), *Reflection and Action: Essays on the Bildungsroman* (1991).
McGlathery, James M., 'Magic and Desire in Eichendorff's "Das Marmorbild"', *German Life & Letters*, 42 (1989).
Schwarz, Egon, *Joseph von Eichendorff* (1972).

Elgar, Sir Edward (1857–1934) Major British composer; one of the last to represent music's long-lived romantic era. Active until early middle age as a local teacher and composer (he was self-taught), he won overnight success with his *Enigma Variations*, Op. 36 in 1899. There then followed over the next 20 years a prolific outpouring of large and small-scale works, including *Sea Pictures*, Op. 37 (1900); the oratorio *The Dream of Gerontius*, Op. 38 (1900); the First Symphony in A flat major, Op. 55 (1908); the Second Symphony in E flat major, Op. 63 (1911); the *Coronation Ode* of 1902 (containing the celebrated melody which later became 'Land of Hope and Glory'), the violin concerto of 1910, Op. 61; and the Violoncello Concerto, Op. 85 (1919).

Elgar's mystical approach to his life and art (hence the aforementioned *Enigma Variations*), found further expression in works based on other-worldly subjects. His two *Wand of Youth* orchestral suites (Op. 1a,

1907, and Op. 1b, 1908) originated from music he had written in his boyhood for a children's play set in a fairyland. In 1915 he wrote incidental music (Op. 78) for a children's play by Violet Pearn, *The Starlight Express*. Produced at the Kingsway Theatre, London, *The Starlight Express* was based on Algernon Blackwood's *The Prisoner in Fairyland*. TH

Ende, Michael (1929–95) Internationally known German author of fantasy literature and children's books. Ende was the son of the surrealist painter Edgar Ende and spent the years 1931–43 as a child in Munich's artist district, where he came under the influence of artists and writers associated with his father. Later, through the Waldorf School in Stuttgart, he became acquainted with the anthroposophic writings of Rudolf Steiner, who had developed esoteric interpretations of German fairy tales. He also studied acting in Munich, and his interest in theatre led him to the theoretical works of Bertolt Brecht. However, he ultimately abandoned Brecht's ideas because they advocated the destruction of illusion. Instead, Ende embraced fantasy as the creative force that would drive his work.

Although Ende published in a wide range of genres—including poetry, drama, short fiction, and picture books—he is best known for his fantasy novels, which incorporate fairy-tale structures and motifs. His first novel was published in two parts as *Jim Knopf und Lukas der Lokomotivführer* (*Jim Button and Luke the Engine Driver*, 1960) and *Jim Knopf und die Wilde 13* (*Jim Button and the Wild 13*, 1962). The two books chart the fairy-tale ascent of the black foundling Jim Knopf, whose fabulous journey leads him to discover his royal identity. In the fairy-tale novel *Momo* (translated into English as both *Momo* and *The Grey Gentlemen*, 1973), Ende describes a modern civilization that has been dehumanized by 'grey gentlemen' who have robbed people of their time. The novel's main character is a little girl named Momo, another orphan, who overturns the oppressive order of reason and technology, and restores imagination and human freedom to their rightful places.

In *Die unendliche Geschichte* (*The *Neverending Story*, 1979), Ende draws on the complex, self-reflexive fiction of the German romantics to create a book about the redemptive power of imagination and the act of reading itself. Using a frame story, Ende establishes two separate realities: the everyday world of his withdrawn juvenile hero, Bastian Balthasar Bux, and the fantasy world of the book Bastian is reading, *The Neverending Story*. The two worlds intersect when Bastian enters into the reality of the fantasy realm to prevent it from being lost in a void of nothingness, just as the actual reader gives life to Ende's book through an act of the imagination.

Following a German tradition that uses fairy tales to explore both social and aesthetic questions, Ende's fairy-tale works emphasize overall the importance of play and imagination in a society otherwise governed by rationality and utilitarian forces. However, despite his belief in the redemptive power of the imagination for the individual, Ende made clear in his play *Das Gauklermärchen* (*The Circus Clowns' Fairy Tale*, 1982), that he did not envision fantasy as an effective tool for pragmatic social change. DH

Haase, Donald, 'Michael Ende', in Wolfgang D. Elfe and James Hardin (eds.), *Contemporary German Fiction Writers*, 2nd ser. (1988).

Ensikat, Klaus (1937–) German illustrator who has won many national and international awards such as the Hans Christian *Andersen Medal in 1996. Ensikat does sharp black-and-white ink drawings and is known for his extraordinarily detailed work. Among his best illustrated fairy tales are Charles *Perrault's *Tom Thumb* (1977), Edward Lear's *The Story about the Four Small Children who Went around the World* (1992), Lewis *Carroll's *Alice in Wonderland* (1993), E. T. A. *Hoffmann's *Klein Zaches* (*Little Zaches*, 1994), and the *Grimms' *Bremen Town Musicians* (1994). Ensikat has also illustrated works by contemporary authors and has a predilection for creating characters in old-fashioned dress who often have trouble with strange machines like a mechanical cow or a broken-down car. The combination of quaint characters and modern technology lend his highly imaginative drawings a surrealistic quality filled with ironic innuendoes. KD

Erben, Karol Jaromír (1811–70) Czech historian, writer, and poet, who is best known for his book, *Kytice* (The Bouquet), a collection of Czech ballads, songs, and poems with folkloric and fairy-tale motifs. As member of the Bohemian Society of Sciences and the Academy of Sciences in Vienna, he collected more than 2,200 Slavic fairy tales. A selection was published in 1865, titled *Vybrané báje a pověsti národni, jiných větví slovenských* (Selected Folktales and Legends from other Slavic Branches), now regarded as a standard work of Czech fairy tale research. Inspired by this work Erben began to write fairy tales for children, which were published posthumously. *Česk pohádky* (*Czech Folktales*, 1905/1996), illustrated by Josef Lada, is often compared with the fairy tale collection *Kinder- und Hausmärchen* (1812–15) by the Brothers Grimm. JZ

Součková, Milada, *The Czech Romantics* (1958).

Ernst, Olga (1888–1972) Australian writer who, at the age of sixteen, wrote *Fairytales from the Land of the Wattle*. It was part of a new development in children's literature, which leaned towards the creation of an Australian Bush fantasy genre. Ernst sought to transpose traditional Old World faerie folk into the new Australian landscape and attempted to create a fairyland to which Australian children could relate. Ernst wrote two more books, *The Magic Shadow Show* (1913), a book of short fantasies with a mythological base, and *Songs from the Dandenongs* (1939), nursery rhymes set to music about the mountains of the Dandenong Ranges. It was published in 1939 under her married name of Waller. Ernst wrote sporadically over the course of her life, and though her literary output was small, she demonstrated great versatility. REF

Esterhazy, Daniska (1969–) Award-winning Canadian feminist independent film-maker (director, writer, editor, producer) based in Winnipeg, Manitoba. Inspired by her childhood interest in fairy tales, her short *The Snow Queen* (2005) tells the story of a young girl, growing up in Winnipeg's North End, who creates an alter ego based on Hans Christian *Andersen's character from 'The *Snow Queen' to escape her difficult life. Another short, *The Red Hood* (2009), offers a dark retelling of *'Little Red Riding Hood' set in the Canadian prairies during the Great Depression. Her feature *H&G* (2013) revisions *'Hansel and Gretel' in a present-day neorealist narrative about two resourceful children coping with unexpected threats. In keeping with her feminist perspective, Esterhazy regenders the witch character as male, alluding to fears about paedophiles and other contemporary bogeyman figures. In all these fairy-tale films, Esterhazy explores female characters' sometimes unexpected power. Her other films, including her first feature *Black Field* (2009), often incorporate fairy-tale allusions and themes. PG

Estes, Clarissa Pinkola (1943–) American psychoanalyst and writer whose book *Women who Run with the Wolves: Myths and Stories of the Wild Woman Archetype* (1992) was a best-seller in the United States and Europe. Estes uses Jungian psychology to analyse folklore and fairy tales and to explore the intuitive and creative drives that constitute the wild woman archetype. In *The Gift of Story: A Wise Tale about What Is Enough* (1993), she celebrates the counsel and therapeutic value of storytelling. JZ

Eulalie (Eulalie Banks, 1895–1999) British-American illustrator whose work for children spanned the entire 20th century. After moving to America from London, in 1919 she began to collaborate with Watty Piper and illustrated numerous fairy-tale books such as *Fairy Stories Children Love* (1922), *The Gateway to Storyland* (1925), *Famous Fairy Tales* (1932), and *Eight Fairy Tales* (1934), which she edited. She also provided the drawings for Homer Mitten's *The Enchanted Canyon Fairy Story* (1932). Eulalie blended all her ink drawings with bright and pleasant colours and depicted simple characters that gave her work a naïve quality. Aside from illustrating books, she also painted fairy-tale murals for libraries in California and Michigan and designed greeting cards. She is best known for the delightful pastel illustrations for *The Bumper Book: A Collection of Stories and Verses for Children* (1946), edited by Piper. JZ

Ewald, Carl (1856–1908) Danish journalist and novelist who grew up in Bredelykke ved Gram, a small Danish city under German rule in the 1850s and 1860s. His father, H. F. Ewald, was a well-known novelist and Danish nationalist. He moved his family to Elsinore, Denmark, in 1864 because he could not tolerate being governed by the Germans. A stern and didactic disciplinarian, he sent Carl to high school in nearby Fredricksborg and hoped his son would pursue a respectable career. However, in 1880, after Ewald tried his hand at forestry, he moved to Copenhagen and began earning his living as a journalist and freelance writer. Soon he made a name for himself with a series of novels that tended to expose the hypocrisy and corruption in Danish society. Strongly influenced by social Darwinism, Ewald depicted the brutal struggles for survival as a result of natural and social forces that shaped humankind's destiny. During the 1880s he effectively incorporated his social Darwinist principles into three important collections of fairy tales: *In det Fri* (*In the Open*, 1892), *Fem nye Eventyr* (*Five New Fairy Tales*, 1894), and *Die fire Fjendingsfyrsten* (*The Four Little Princes*, 1896). The public response was so favourable that he wrote another 20 volumes of fairy tales and also translated the fairy tales of the Brothers *Grimm in 1905. The major focus in Ewald's fairy tales is on enlightenment, survival of the fittest, and class struggle. In such tales as 'The Good Man', 'The Cuckoo', and 'The Wind', he depicts humans, animals, and elements that develop false notions of the world and experience disappointments because they cannot recognize and develop their true natures. In 'The Dragon Fly and the Lake Rose', Ewald critically alludes to *Andersen's 'The *Ugly Duckling' by showing how, despite their beautiful development, the dragonfly and rose must die because of the false illusions they cultivate about themselves and their environment.

By the turn of the 20th century Ewald became the most significant Danish fairy-tale writer in Europe next to Hans Christian Andersen. However, in contrast to Andersen's optimistic perspective, Ewald was much more sceptical and cynical. His tales do not exude a 'happy-ending' ideology, and it was precisely because of their grim realism that they had such a wide reception in Germany during the 1920s. His collected works were published there posthumously in five volumes: *Mutter Natur erzählt* (*Mother Nature Tells*, 1910), *Der Zweifüssler und andere Geschichten* (*Two Legs and Other Stories*, 1911), *Vier feine Freunde und andere Geschichten* (*Four Fine Friends and Other Stories*, 1913), *Meister Reineke und andere Geschichten* (*Master Renard and Other Stories*, 1919), and *Das Sternenkind und andere Geschichten* (*The Star Child and Other Stories*, 1925). Not only were his tales popular in Germany, but they also made their way to England and the United States. For instance, *Two Legs and Other Stories* was published in English in 1907, *The Old Willow-Tree and Other Stories* appeared in 1921. JZ

Ewing, Juliana Horatia (1841–85) English writer for children. The daughter of Margaret Gatty, in whose *Aunt Judy's Magazine* most of her work was first published, she wrote several stories about magic in everyday life, and a collection of shorter tales, *Old-Fashioned Fairy Tales* (1882), all of which had first appeared in *Aunt Judy*. Though from 1867 she was an army wife and obliged to lead a nomadic existence, she came from a large, closely knit vicarage family, and stories about family and country life, which she recalled with great nostalgia, form the greatest part of her *œuvre*. Her fantasy stresses family values. Thus in an early story,

Ewing, Juliana Horatia The giant believes the peasant's daughter will make a fine wife for him after tasting her soup in Juliana Horatia Ewing's 'The Ogre Courting', published in *Old-Fashioned Fairy Tales* (1882) and illustrated by A. W. Bayes.

'Melchior's Dream' (first published in the *Monthly Packet* in 1861, and one of the most powerful she ever wrote), the boy who wishes he were an only child finds in a terrible dream that he has become one. He fancies he is driving in a coach with Time, who puts down his brothers and sisters by the wayside until Melchior is left alone. 'Snap-Dragons' (1870) is more light-hearted but has much the same message. Here the Skradjt family who 'seldom seriously quarrelled, but never agreed about anything' are cured one Christmas when the brandy flames in the snap-dragon bowl turn into real dragons who force the children to snap and snarl with them. 'I doubt if the parents ever were cured. I don't know if they heard the story.' 'The Brownies' (1865), 'The Land of Lost Toys' (1869), 'Amelia and the Dwarfs' (1870), 'Benjy in Beastland' (1870), and 'Timothy's Shoes' (1870) all describe how children are cured of faults through the agency of magic. This was a frequently used convention of the time, though Mrs Ewing had a lighter and more humorous touch than most of her contemporaries. 'The Brownies', where two little boys decide to take on the role of the helpful house spirit, gave the name to the junior Girl Guide movement.

The preface to *Old-Fashioned Fairy Tales* defends the genre: 'They convey knowledge of the world, shrewd lessons of virtue and vice, of common sense and sense of humour ... They treat of the world at large, and life in perspective; of forces visible and invisible; of Life, Death, and Immortality.' Most are in the style of the German *Hausmärchen*, though a few have an Irish or Scots background. There is little fantasy but sound good sense.   GA

Avery, Gillian, *Mrs. Ewing* (1961).

Laski, Marghanita, *Mrs. Ewing, Mrs. Molesworth, and Mrs. Hodgson Burnett* (1951).

faerie (also known as **fairyland**) The realm inhabited by fairies. The delicate gossamer-winged creatures Europeans and North Americans associate with fairies are a Victorian invention. Those of European tradition are a more sinister or at best ambivalent lot. Human-like, they are smaller and, if visible, often misshapen or ugly. Possessing magical powers, they intervene in mortals' lives, with results ranging from destructive to helpful. Their practices on humans include taking lovers and/or spouses or stealing children (often substituting changelings), leading astray, stealing, invisibly performing tasks, transforming food, aiding or rewarding aid, paralysing, and playing pranks. Many fairy tales have no fairy characters, and stories about fairies are usually belief or personal experience narratives. Fairy belief was historically serious (and can remain so); in late nineteenth-century Ireland, Bridget Cleary's relatives burned her to death because they suspected she was a changeling. The faerie habitat is usually located in, or accessible via, specific locations, often prehistoric burial places, heights of land, caves, woods, or water. There time and its consequences—change, decay, illness, and ageing—are altered or absent. PG

Purkiss, Diane, *At the Bottom of the Garden: A Dark History of Fairies, Hobgoblins, and other Troublesome Things* (2003).
Narváez, Peter (ed.), *The Good People: New Fairylore Essays* (1997).

Faerie Tale Theatre *See* DUVALL, SHELLEY.

Fagnan, Marie-Antoinette (d. 1770?) Virtually all that is known about this French writer is that she probably wrote three fairy tales: *Kanor, conte traduit du turc* (*Kanor, Tale Translated from the Turkish*, 1750), *Minet bleu et Louvette* (*Blue Minet and Louvette*, 1753), and *Le Miroir des princesses orientales* (*Mirror of the Oriental Princesses*, 1755). The most notable of these, *Kanor*, features an unusual treatment of the monstrous spouse motif and a virulent critique of monarchy. Fagnan is one of the few French women writers of her time to use parody and eroticism, albeit ambiguously, in her tales. LCS

'Fairies, The' Charles *Perrault's tale 'Les Fées' ('The Fairies') appeared in his collection *Histoires ou contes du temps passé* (*Stories or Tales of Past Times*, 1697). An early version of this tale occurs in Ovid's *Metamorphoses*, where the goddess Latona transforms into frogs a group of mean-spirited peasants. Other antecedents include stories found in Giovan Francesco *Straparola's *Le *piacevoli notti* (*The Pleasant Nights*, 1550-3) and Giambattista *Basile's *Pentamerone* (1634-6). Perrault's tale portrays an unnamed younger sister who kindly does the bidding of a good fairy, disguised as a crone, and receives the gift of flowers and precious jewels issuing from her mouth. Her older sister, Fanchon, encounters the same fairy, this time magnificently apparelled, but rudely rebuffs her. The fairy ordains that toads and snakes pour from her mouth, and the exiled Fanchon dies alone in the forest. The tale's first moral extols the persuasive power of elegant discourse and addresses adult readers of French salon society, which cultivated a highly stylized form of polite conversation. The second moral emphasizes the rewards of courtesy and targets Perrault's young audience. Perrault's niece and fairy-tale author, Marie-Jeanne *Lhéritier, composed a longer, embellished variation, 'Les

Enchantements de l'éloquence', published in *Œuvres meslées* (*Assorted Works*, 1695). AZ

Fumaroli, Marc, 'Les Enchantements de l'éloquence: "Les Fées" de Charles Perrault ou de la littérature,' in Marc Fumaroli (ed.), *Le Statut de la littérature: mélanges offerts à Paul Bénichou* (1982).

Soriano, Marc, *Les Contes de Perrault: culture savante et traditions populaires* (1968).

fairy-tale blogs and websites Although most academic research on folk narratives on the Internet has focused on legends, cyberspace is also a major conduit for the circulation, exploration, and analysis of fairy tales. D. L. Ashliman's *Folktexts* site compiles and organizes fairy tales by ATU type (*see* AARNE-THOMPSON INDEX); Heidi Ann Heiner's *SurLaLune* presents and annotates multiple versions of well-known stories. Text-oriented blogs such as *Tales of Faerie, Doc-in-Boots, Breezes from Wonderland*, and *Once Upon a Blog* analyse fairy tales in a variety of media and engage with current scholarship in an accessible format; most online journal platforms allow for conversation and linkage across a variety of different spaces, and fairy-tale blogs take advantage of this ability to create interactive spaces for engagement and analysis. The blogging platform Tumblr enables a focus upon visual forms such as film, video, and visual art and is set up to allow easy circulation of entries. While a number of fairy-tale-oriented Tumblr blogs such as *Tabled Fables, Forest of Fairy Tales*, and *Fairy Tale Mood* curate the work of professional and amateur artists, the 'reblog' feature allows these works to circulate freely among all members of the site.

There is a thriving community of amateur writers, artists, and film-makers inspired by fairy tales who post their works on the Internet. Some of these creators revise, rework, and retell fairy tales directly. Others borrow elements from fairy tales to create stories and artwork responding to other media. Fan works engage not only with fairy-tale-centric media, such as the television series *Once Upon a Time*, but also use fairy-tale elements in creative work responding to media and literary texts such as *Sherlock*

and *The Hunger Games*. Sites such as *Archive of Our Own, Fanfiction.net*, and *Deviant Art* allow readers to search for stories and art involving fairy tales and fairy-tale elements. CT

Fallada, Hans (pseudonym of **Rudolf Ditzen**, 1893–1947) German writer who chose his pen name after two *Grimms' fairy-tale characters, 'Hans im Glück' ('Hans in Luck') and the talking horse Falada of 'Die Gänsemagd' ('The Goose-Girl'). He became famous for his novels of social criticism, but he also wrote the fairy-tale novel *Märchen vom Stadtschreiber, der aufs Land flog* (*Fairy Tale of the Municipal Clerk who Flew to the Countryside*, 1935). Hoping to sensitize children to moral concepts, Fallada additionally created stories for children, among them the collected fairy tales *Geschichten aus der Murkelei* (*Tales from the Murkelei*, 1938). CS

Schueler, Heinz J., *Hans Fallada: Humanist and Social Critic* (1970).

Fallen Fairies The dramatist W. S. Gilbert's last operatic collaboration. Based on Gilbert's own fairy play, *The Wicked World* (1871), *Fallen Fairies*, with music by Edward German, was premiered in 1909 at London's Savoy Theatre. Gilbert set his opera in Fairyland—above a cloud. In what becomes an ill-fated attempt to find love, fairies change places with mortals—a permissible exchange under fairy law as every fairy has a mortal lookalike. The work failed after less than a two-month run, partly, as was suggested at the time, through its unsuccessful mix of light comedy with near tragedy. TH

fantasy literature and fairy tales Fantasy is one of the most ambiguous notions in literary criticism, and it is often, especially in the context of children's literature, used to denote anything that is not straight realistic prose. It has been treated as a genre, a style, a narrative technique, and it is sometimes regarded as formulaic fiction. In handbooks, fairy tales and fantasy are frequently discussed together without precision, and no totally satisfactory and comprehensive definition of fantasy literature has been established so far. For many purposes, the difference is irrelevant; yet some theoretical considerations are necessary, since the two categories are distinct in some fundamental formal features as well as communicative and aesthetic functions. Three ways of distinguishing between fairy tales and fantasy seem fruitful: generic, structural (particularly spatio-temporal), and epistemological.

While fairy tales and fantasy are doubtlessly generically related—and it may even be argued that fantasy grows out of fairy tales—their origins and premises are radically different. Fairy tales have their roots in ancient society and thought, thus immediately succeeding myths. Fantasy literature is a modern phenomenon. Though we may view certain ancient authors in terms of fantasy (Homer, Ovid, Apuleius), and though features of fantasy can clearly be traced back to Jonathan Swift, fantasy literature basically owes its origins mostly to Romanticism, with its interest in folk tradition, its rejection of the previous, rational-age view of the world, and its idealisation of childhood.

Traditional fairy tales strive to preserve a story as close to its original version as possible, even though individual storytellers may convey a personal touch, and each version reflects its own time and society. Fantasy literature is a conscious artistic creation; authors choose the form which suits them best for their particular purposes, which may be instructive, religious, philosophical, social, satirical, parodical, or entertaining; yet fantasy has distinctly lost the initially sacral purpose of traditional fairy tales. Fantasy is also an eclectic genre, since it borrows traits from myths, romance, picaresque, science fiction and other genres, besides fairy tales, blending seemingly incompatible elements in one and the same narrative—for instance, pagan and Christian images, or magic wands and laser guns. The relation between fairy tales and fantasy is similar to that between epic and novel in Mikhail Bakhtin's theory: a fairy tale is a fully evolved and accomplished genre, fantasy a genre in evolution.

There is no consensus about 'the very first fantasy novel' ever published, and it is a matter of definition whether a text should be classified as fairy tale or fantasy. *The Nutcracker* (1816), by E. T. A. *Hoffmann, matches most criteria of fantasy and is therefore frequently acknowledged as a pioneering work. Fantasy becomes a strong tradition in Britain in the second half of the nineteenth century, with names such as Lewis *Carroll, Charles *Kingsley, and George *MacDonald, the last closest to fairy tales proper. At the turn of the twentieth century Edith *Nesbit, finding impulses from many predecessors, renewed and transformed the fantasy tradition, focusing on the clash between the magical and the ordinary, on the unexpected consequences of magic introduced into everyday life. Unlike fairy tales, fantasy is closely connected with the notion of modernity; for instance, the first time-shift fantasies by Nesbit are tangibly influenced by contemporary ideas in natural sciences, as well as by the science fiction genre, particularly H. G. Wells.

The Golden Age of the English-language fantasy arrived in the 1950s and 1960s, with names such as J. R. R. *Tolkien, C. S. *Lewis, Philippa *Pearce, Lucy M. Boston, Mary Norton, and Alan *Garner, whose work, while indebted to Nesbit, demonstrates a higher level of sophistication. Again, this tradition was affected by the tremendous changes undergone by the modern world. The development of science and technology, the theory of relativity and quantum physics, experiments with atomic energy and the first atomic bombs, achievements in space exploration, investigations of artificial intelligence, alternative theories in mathematics and geometry, new hypotheses about the origins of the universe—all this changed the very attitude towards natural laws. From a limited, positivist view of the world humankind has turned to a wider, more open view of life, willing to accept the possibility of the range of phenomena that fantasy deals with: alternative worlds, non-linear time, superhuman physical and mental abilities, and supernatural events which so far cannot be explained in terms of science, but which we are not prepared to ascribe to the traditional fairy-tale magic.

Most fantasy novels demonstrate similarities to fairy tales in form and content. They have inherited the fairy-tale system of characters, set up by Vladimir *Propp and his followers: hero, princess, helper, giver, antagonist. Unlike fairy-tale heroes, fantasy protagonists often lack heroic features, can be scared and even reluctant to perform the task, and can sometimes fail. The final goal of fantasy is seldom marriage and enthronement; in contemporary philosophical and ethical fantasy it is a matter of spiritual maturation. Fantasy also allows much freedom and experiments with gender transgression. Recent fantasy features protagonists endowed with supernatural powers, most prominently, but far from exclusively, Harry Potter. This is a significant deviation from the fairy tale, in which heroes are typically dependent on magical helpers to succeed.

Furthermore, fantasy has inherited superficial attributes of fairy tales: witches, genies, dragons, talking animals, flying horses and flying carpets, invisibility mantles, magic wands, swords and lanterns, and magic food and drink. However, fantasy transforms and modernises these elements: a genie may live in a beer can, flying carpets give way to flying rocking-chairs, and characters without fairy-tale origins are introduced such as animated toys. However, their function in the story is essentially the same.

Fantasy has also inherited the basic plot of fairy tales: the hero leaves home, meets helpers and opponents, goes through trials, and returns home having gained wealth and high social status. It has inherited some fundamental conflicts and patterns, such as quest or combat between good and evil. However, just as fairy tales are not a homogeneous genre category, featuring magic tales as well as animal and trickster tales, so is fantasy a generic heading for a range of narratives, some taking place in a magical realm, or immersive fantasy; some depicting travel between different worlds, or portal fantasy; some bringing magic into the everyday, or intrusive fantasy. There is, nevertheless, a principal difference in the way fairy tales and fantasy construct their spatio-temporal relations.

According to Mikhail Bakhtin, the particular construction of fictional space and time, the chronotope, is genre-specific; each genre has its own unique chronotope. With this structural approach, fairy tales and fantasy differ in their organisation of time and space. The characteristic feature of fantasy literature is the presence of magic, or any other form of the supernatural, in connection with a realistic, recognizable world. This presence may be manifest in the form of magical beings, objects, or events; it may be unfolded into a whole universe or reduced to just one magical element. This feature in itself is not different from fairy tales, but the anchoring in reality is.

Fairy tales take place in one magical world, detached from our own both in space and in time. The setting of a fairy tale is: 'Once upon a time' ('Es war einmal', 'Il était une fois', etc), 'in a certain kingdom', 'beyond thrice three realms', 'East of the moon, West of the sun'. The initial setting of fantasy literature is reality: a riverbank in Oxford (*Alice in Wonderland*, 1865), a farm in Kansas (*The Wonderful Wizard of Oz*, 1900), a country house in central England during Second World War (*The Lion, the Witch and the Wardrobe*, 1950) or a contemporary suburban area (the *Harry Potter* series, 1997–2007). From this realistic setting, the characters are transported into a magical realm, and most often, although not always, brought safely back. Alternatively, the magical realm itself intervenes in reality, in the form of magical beings (the Psammead, *Peter Pan, Mary Poppins, Merlin), magical transformations, or magical objects.

The time of fairy tales is the archaic, primordial, mythical time—*kairos*. For the recipient, this time is beyond reach. In fantasy literature, the characters are temporarily displaced from modern, linear time—*chronos*—into mythical archaic time and return to linearity at the end. The eternity of the fairy-tale time, expressed in the formula 'lived happily ever after', is alien to fantasy. Thus, the main characters in *The Lion, the Witch and the Wardrobe* live a long life in the archaic time space of Narnia, but are brought back and become children again.

The common denominator for the various representations of magic in fantasy literature is the concept of the secondary world, originating from J. R. R. Tolkien's essay 'On Fairy Stories' (1938). Thus, fantasy may be roughly defined as a narrative combining the primary and the secondary world(s), that is, our own real world and other, magical or fantastic imaginary worlds, single or multiple. Patterns of introducing magic into the everyday in fantasy literature vary from a complete magical universe with its own geography, history, and natural laws to a little magical pill that enables a character in an otherwise realistic story to become invisible or to understand the language of animals. Although fairy tales include similar features, they take place in one imaginary world, without any connection to the reader's reality.

A specific motif in fantasy literature, which may justify viewing the texts in which it occurs as a subcategory of fantasy, is time distortion. It appears presumably first in Nesbit's *The Story of the Amulet* (1906) and, more than any other fantasy motif, is influenced by the scientific thought of that time, especially the theory of relativity. The relationship between real and magic time in fantasy is the opposite of that in a fairy tale. A common folktale motif is the land (or island) of immortality where the hero spends what to him may seem a day, or three days, or a week. On return from the wondrous land or island, he discovers that many thousand years have elapsed. Here magical and mythical time become conflated and insignificant. In fantasy, characters may easily live a whole life in the imaginary world, while no time will pass in their own reality. The scope of time-related issues explored in fantasy is irrelevant in fairy tales: predestination and free will, the multitude of possible parallel times, time going at a different pace or even in different directions in separate worlds, the mechanisms of time displacement, and the various time paradoxes, such as meeting your own doubles or interfering with history. However, complicated time relations are present in all fantasy texts, independent of the dominant type or theme.

Scholars tend to make a distinction between secondary-world fantasy (The Narnia Chronicles, 1950-6, *The *Neverending Story*, 1979) and time-shift fantasy (*The House of Arden*, 1908, *A Traveller in Time*, 1939, *Tom's Midnight Garden*, 1958, *King of Shadows*, 1999). There is undoubtedly more obsession with time as such in time-shift fantasy: the very notion of time, its philosophical implications, its metaphysical character. But as to the construction of a magical universe and, as a direct consequence, the build-up of the narrative, there are more similarities than differences. The principal feature of time fantasy, time distortion, is also present in the secondary-world fantasy, while the principal pattern of the secondary-world fantasy, the passage between the worlds, is most tangible in time fantasy, where it is often connected with features such as doors, magic objects, and magic helpers, all of which are manifest in secondary-world fantasy and originate in fairy tales.

However, the most profound difference between fantasy and fairy tales is the position of the reader and the matter of belief. In traditional fairy tales, taking place in a detached time space, readers are not supposed to believe in the story. The addressee of a fairy tale is situated outside the text; the communication is based on a fictional contract between the sender and the addressee. Among others, Vladimir Propp maintains that the addressee of a fairy tale knows that the story is not true. This fact accounts for the recurrent final formulas, which, while assuring that the story is true, subvert its own conventionality. This is also the basic difference between myth and fairy tale: for the tellers and listeners of a myth, the events described are true; the myth is based on belief.

Fantasy, on the other hand, does not presuppose belief, while it does not directly subvert it either. Instead, it offers at least two possible interpretations of the events. They can be accepted mimetically, or objectively, as having actually taken place within the story, which means that recipients accept magic as part of the fictional world. Conversely, magic adventures can be accounted for metaphorically, or subjectively, as the protagonist's dreams, visions, hallucinations, or imagination, caused, for instance, by fever, or psychological or emotional disturbance; it can also be make-believe or pretence play. Such interpretations seek rational reasons for the irrational events. J. R. R. Tolkien was among the first to question the legitimacy of rational explanations. In his essay 'On Fairy Stories' he dismisses *Alice in Wonderland* because the heroine's adventures turn out to have been a dream. Tolkien's concept of fantasy literature (although he speaks of fairy stories rather than fantasy) is based on the suspension of disbelief; that is, unlike fairy tales, readers perceive fantasy, within its own premises, as 'true'. For Tolkien, genuine and skilful fantasy creates secondary belief (unlike the primary belief of myth or religion), putting the reader in a temporary state of enchantment. As soon as the suspension of disbelief is disturbed, the spell is broken, and, Tolkien adds, art has failed.

Fairy tales, on the other hand, often subvert their own credibility, either in initial or in final formulas: 'Once upon a time, when pigs drank wine...'. The protagonist (and the recipient) of a fairy tale does not experience wonder when confronted with magical events or beings: they are taken for granted. The characters of a fantasy novel, anchored in the real world, do not expect a rabbit to have a watch and wear a waistcoat; nor do they expect there to be magical realms behind the looking-glass or inside wardrobes. The essence of fantasy literature is a confrontation of the ordinary and the extraordinary, the familiar and the unfamiliar. In terms of readers' cognitive-affective engagement with fantasy, it is a powerful way to stimulate surprise, attention, imagination, memory, and other important mental activities.

Certain authors, notably C. S. Lewis, repeatedly emphasize the idea that secondary worlds are made up of characters, objects, and events which people on Earth have ceased to believe in. In *Peter Pan* belief seems to be a matter of life and death for fairies in the Neverland. Thus fantasy authors encourage readers to preserve belief and imagination as an essential part of spiritual growth.

The notion of secondary belief enables us to categorize a vast variety of fantasy literature, starting with Tolkien's own *Lord of the Rings* cycle (1954-6), developed by Lloyd *Alexander in his *Prydain Chronicles* (1964-8) and Ursula *Le Guin in *Earthsea* cycle (1968-2001), and achieving further popularity in the 1990s and beyond, with the works of Terry *Pratchett and Cornelia *Funke, which also contain playfulness, parody, and metafiction. These stories take place in a closed, self-contained secondary world without any connection with reality. However, unlike fairy tales, they are definitely based on secondary belief.

Tzvetan Todorov's theory of the fantastic offers another convenient approach, drawing a distinction between the marvellous, the fantastic, and the uncanny. The essence of the fantastic lies in the hesitation of the protagonist (and the reader) as confronted with the supernatural—which is anything that goes beyond natural laws. Fairy tales will, in this typology, fall into the category of the marvellous. Again, fairy-tale protagonists do not interrogate the existence of dragons or witches, because these are part of the fairy-tale build-up. For fantasy protagonists, the appearance of witches or unicorns in their own reality, or being transported into another world, presents a cognitive and moral dilemma, which readers share. Alternatively, the characters (or the reader) may decide that they are dreaming or hallucinating, but no definite answer is to be found in the text.

In more recent fantasy literature, the boundaries between the fictional reality and the secondary worlds become more elusive, and the passage often subtle, so that the hesitation is amplified. The *Chrestomanci* series (1977-2006), by Diana Wynne *Jones, and *His Dark Materials* trilogy (1995-2000), by Philip *Pullman, feature magical secondary worlds as familiar for the protagonists and our own real world as alien, a defamiliarization effect that tests readers' perception and imagination. These and many other novels portray multiple alternative worlds as equally real, so that the very concepts of reality, objectivity, and truth are questioned, in a postmodern manner. In contrast to the straightforwardness of fairy tales, fantasy celebrates plurality and ambiguity, where even concepts such as good and evil easily change places. Recently, the additional genre label of magical realism has been employed for texts that take place in the real world, but include strong elements of the uncanny, such as *Skellig* (1998), by David Almond, and *Miss Peregrine's Home for Peculiar Children* (2011), by Ransom Riggs. There is also a tangible tendency towards embedded secondary worlds, for instance in the *Inkheart* trilogy (2003-7), by Cornelia Funke. Not least, the dark magical forces, traditionally limited to secondary worlds, in recent fantasy leak into the primary world and thus threaten either the protagonist (*Coraline*, 2008, by Neil *Gaiman) or humankind (*Un Lun Dun*, 2007, by China Miéville).

Since the turn of the twenty-first century, fantasy has become a crossover phenomenon thanks to the works of acclaimed authors such as Pratchett, Gaiman, and Miéville, and particularly thanks to the international and transgenerational success of Pullman's *His Dark Materials* and Rowling's *Harry Potter*. While the latter was quickly picked up by the entertainment industry with blockbuster films, merchandise, and theme parks, Pullman's trilogy has been accepted into the high-culture canon. Yet, both works, together with the revived interest in Tolkien's *Lord of the Rings*, have made fantasy a literary and cultural phenomenon impossible to ignore or relegate to the sphere of pulp fiction. Paradoxically, as a side effect and, possibly, because of genre confusion, it has also stimulated a renewed interest in fairy tales.   MN

Bakhtin, Mikhail, *The Dialogic Imagination* (1981).
Jackson, Rosemary, *Fantasy: The Literature of Subversion* (1981).
Mendlesohn, Farah, *Rhetorics of Fantasy* (2008).
Nikolajeva, Maria, *The Magic Code: The Use of Magical Patterns in Fantasy for Children* (1988).
Swinfen, Ann, *In Defence of Fantasy: A Study of the Genre in English and American Literature since 1945* (1984).
Todorov, Tzvetan, *The Fantastic: A Structural Approach to a Literary Genre* (1973).
Tolkien, J. R. R., 'On Fairy Stories', in *Tree and Leaf* (1968).

Farjeon, Eleanor (1881-1965) English poet and author. Chiefly remembered for her stories for children, she began her literary career with a collection of fairy stories for adults, *Martin Pippin in the Apple-Orchard* (1921). (This was later reissued for children and was popular with adolescent girls.) Martin Pippin is a minstrel who helps a lovesick youth to regain his captive sweetheart. She is guarded by six milkmaids, one of whom he bribes each day with a tale. These gently romantic love stories all have a Sussex setting and were written during the First World War for a young soldier from Sussex. Her next novel, *The Soul of Kol Nikon* (1923) was very different. A bleak, even savage story, it is set in a Scandinavian village in some unspecified folkloristic age. Kol Nikon is convinced from early childhood that he is a changeling, born without a soul, and that his mother's true child has been stolen by the Hill People. Loathed by his mother, ostracized by the villagers, Kol's passionate purpose is to find or to steal a soul for himself and to turn his mother's hatred into love. Outraged villagers eventually stone him to death, and the ending suggests that the changeling stigma attached to him might have arisen from primitive superstition. Farjeon was never to write in this vein again, and her only other adult fantasy, *Ariadne and the Bull* (1945) is a facetious rendering of Greek legend in 1940s American idiom; it ends with the trial and acquittal of the Minotaur in American-style court proceedings.

There are several collections of tales for children. These are whimsical and imaginative, often with a lightly sketched deeper meaning. Thus the little fish in 'The Goldfish' (*One Foot in Fairyland*, 1938) who longs to 'marry the Moon, surpass the Sun, and possess the World' is put into a goldfish bowl by Neptune: 'He needed a world more suited to his size.' This collection also includes a poignant pastiche myth, 'Pannychis', prompted by a poem by Chénier. Pannychis and Cymon, 5 years old, play together happily. But Cymon, hearing stories about Europa, Persephone, and other stolen girls, dreads that Pannychis too will be snatched away. Oppressed by his fears for her, she runs away, calling: '"Look happy! Look happy!" And she was never seen again. They sought her in every glade, in every cave ... But which had taken her, sea, lake, or wood, they never knew.'

Martin Pippin in the Daisy-Field (1937), like its predecessor, consists of Sussex fairy tales; Rye, Wilmington, and Selsey Bill all feature in it. It contains one of her best-known stories, 'Elsie Piddock Skips in her Sleep'. As a child Elsie is so expert with a skipping rope that the fairies feel she is worthy of learning their own steps. At the age of 109 she uses this magic to defeat the landowner who wants to enclose Caburn Mount (an ancient camp on the South Downs) where village children had always skipped from time immemorial. GA

Colwell, Eileen H., *Eleanor Farjeon* (1961).
Greene, Ellin, 'Literary Uses of Traditional Themes: From "Cinderella" to "The Girl who Sat by the Ashes" and "The Glass Slipper"', *Children's Literature Association Quarterly*, 11.3 (fall 1986).
Sylvester, Louise, 'Women, Men and Words: Lexical Choices in Two Fairy Tales of the 1920s', *Essays and Studies*, 47 (1994).

Farmer, Philip José (1918–2009) American writer of science fiction and fantasy who often incorporates fairy-tale and trickster motifs into his works. In his famous *Riverworld* sequence (1965–93), comprised of novels and stories such as *To Your Scattered Bodies Go* (1965–6), *The Fabulous Riverboat* (1967–71), and *Quest to Riverworld* (1993), Farmer depicts a number of afterlife quests on another planet. One involves Richard *Burton, who, with the help of Lewis *Carroll's Alice, pursues the secret of afterlife existence. In one of his most poignant fairy-tale novels, *A Barnstormer in Oz* (1982), Farmer has Hank Stover, a 20-year-old pilot, happen upon Oz in 1923 while flying over Kansas. It turns out that Hank is the son of Dorothy, and he joins with Glinda of Oz to

protect Oz from being discovered by the American military and decides to settle in Oz forever. The utopian novel is a witty blend of social criticism and fantasy that reflects upon American political conditions during the 1970s and 1980s. JZ

Feist, Raymond E. (1945–) American writer of fantasy novels. While most of Feist's work consists of fantasy sagas set in invented worlds, *Faerie Tale* (1988), a horror novel, makes unusual use of British fairy lore, transplanting fairyland to the woods of modern America. The story follows a traditional 'changeling' plot: a child is abducted to the Erf King's court and a 'faerie changeling' left in his place. His twin brother must journey 'into the woods' and withstand many trials to win him back. Feist invigorates this standard tale by placing it in the present day, casting a dark glamour over the woods and its denizens. TW

feminism and fairy tales Feminists have an abiding interest in the socio-historical and cultural contexts in which literature arises and is received, how women have helped shape and contributed to traditions, and how women are represented in texts and scholarship. Feminist involvement with fairy tales falls roughly into two major categories: primary texts, and feminist theory as a critique of the genre and its production.

1. Primary texts

Feminist fairy tales, by definition, engage in a debate about literary conventions and societal norms. But they are also—and this is often ignored in the scholarship—a response to other tales by women, a *continuity* of narratives and concerns.

The first production of women's fairy tales for publication began in the French salons of the 1680s. Isolated from schooling and the body politic, the French *salonnières* created a vehicle to engage in the aristocratic discourse of the day, the 'Querelle des Anciens et des Modernes' ('Quarrel of the Ancients and the Moderns', 1687–96), a debate engendered by *Perrault's attack on classicism and defence of indigenous literary motifs and forms. Writing primarily for adults, Mme d'*Aulnoy, Mlle *Lhéritier, Mlle *Bernard, Mlle de *La Force, Mme de *Murat, and others, poked fun at classical literature by returning to the archaic and 'pre-logical' world of the Middle Ages, of nursemaids, and of children. These women were drawn to a genre which allowed them to explore alternative realities, create an ideal world that could exist only within the imagination, and engage in the intellectual discourse of the day from which they were officially excluded. These writers conceived of worlds inhabited by extraordinarily majestic and powerful *female* fairies, a mirror of their own omnipotence within the salon as contrasted with the conditions of their real lives. While set in make-believe realms, their stories were veiled critiques of contemporary society and dealt with issues such as choice of spouse, inheritance rights, and women's right to education. The French fairy-tale tradition waned with changing political and historical conditions in France, but the ideas begun in the female-penned fairy tales made their way to Germany and found fertile ground in the late Enlightenment and romantic periods.

While the salon-based fairy-tale tradition in France faded to re-emerge in the literature of edification, as professional governesses and tutors took over the genre as a teaching tool for girls, Benedikte *Naubert continued the tradition of storytelling for adults in the 1780s in Germany. Like her French predecessors, she sought inspiration not in classical sources, but in medieval Anglo-Saxon and Germanic traditions, and she was fascinated by powerful sorceress figures, 'a memory of that...which we once were, what heights our powers can reach without losing true femininity'. Themes in her works include women's rejection of marriage in favour of independence and communion with nature and magical powers; the creation of a female community outside traditional society; the mediating role of magical wisewomen; the positive rites of passage for females; and the rejection of patriarchal redemption. Naubert's work anticipates the themes and

narrative structures of women's fairy tales in the 19th and 20th century.

The history of fairy tales in 19th-century Germany is a case in point of how patriarchal practices have succeeded in diminishing the public perception of women's contribution to the genre; it also demonstrates the importance of revisionist scholarship in documenting the continuity of feminist concerns in literary history in order to reconsider the history of women and their contribution to the tradition. Writing contemporaneously with the *Grimms and perhaps in even greater numbers than their male contemporaries, women fairy-tale writers of 19th-century Germany dealt with issues anticipatory of those women writers and feminists would treat in the last three decades of the 20th century. These issues include: voice and voicelessness; the commodification of women; gender relations; the importance of female education; a questioning of the redemption motif of marriage as women's only salvation; and a series of other social malaises and gender inequities in patriarchy.

Their tales challenged both literary and social conventions, as in Bettina von *Arnim's 1808 untitled manuscript, in which a woman is robbed of a voice for human intercourse and learns instead the language of beasts. Other tales take issue with marriage conventions and patriarchal narratives, like Fanny Lewald's 'Ein modernes Märchen' ('A Modern Fairy Tale', 1841). Here Lewald stands the traditional story of the mermaid in search of a soul on its head when a slimy sea creature disguised as a cold fish of a man seeks redemption through a human mate, and the female protagonist thwarts his attempts to gain 'humanity'. Louise Dittmar's 'Affenmärchen' ('Tale of the Apes', 1845) tells of apes put on the market, an allegory for young women dressed up and trained for a competitive marriage market, levelling a scathing critique of female education, gender relations, and capitalist exploitation. A fascinating text by Marie Ebner-Eschenbach (one of the few 19th-century writers to make it into the standard canon) is in many ways the most modern: in *Die Prinzessin von Banalien* (*Princess Banalia*, 1872) a virtuous queen tries to break out of social expectations of her as queen, woman, and wife, and longs to join her beloved, a wild man, in his realm. Contemporary feminists would explore this as her return to her animal side (embracing her own sexuality), a notion Ebner-Eschenbach's time and own sensibilities could not yet actualize. Isolde *Kurz's satiric 'König Filz' ('King Tightwad', 1890) shows how women's skills could be used to triumph when the heroine kills her adversaries in a flourish of culinary cunning. By the end of the century, Ricarda Huch's 'Lügenmärchen' ('Pack of Lies', 1896) dissects the canon and an entire century of men's and women's fairy-tale writings. She criticizes the patriarchal attempt to usurp the female voice embodied in the siren's song and the fairy tale, an attempt which ultimately fails. The parry and jab of feminist revisions with received tradition had begun. In all these tales, as well as a myriad of others in Europe and North America, writers rewrote the patriarchal narrative to question reader expectations as well as literary and social conventions.

In the 20th century, women like Lou Andreas-Salomé, Hermynia *Zur Mühlen, Lisa *Tetzner, and Ina *Seidel continued to experiment with the form, but perhaps the most significant experimentation has been in response to the Women's Movement, beginning in the 1960s in the United States. Feminist tales are often wicked retellings, rewritings, and fundamental rejections of traditional gender roles and societal expectations; they lay bare the implausibility of gender roles in canonical texts by men and the stifling effects they have on women and their identity. Anne *Sexton's *Transformations* (1971) was an important first work because she recognized the impact of the socialization process on women and focused on the socio-cultural context of received tradition.

Certain canonical stories, especially those of female subjugation and voicelessness, have resonated internationally with late 20th-century feminist writers. *'Bluebeard'

provides the structuring narrative in poems by the Greek-American Olga *Broumas (*Beginning with O*, 1977); in stories from the Austrian Ingeborg Bachmann ('Der Fall Franza' ('The Case of Franza', 1978); the British Angela *Carter (*The Bloody Chamber*, 1979); the Canadian Margaret *Atwood (*Bluebeard's Egg*, 1983); the German Karin Struck (*Blaubarts Schatten* (*Bluebeard's Shadow*), 1991); the Austrian Elisabeth Reichart ('Die Kammer' ('The Chamber'), 1992); and the Irish Emma Donoghue (*Kissing the Witch*, 1997). *'Beauty and the Beast' has been another favourite: the American novelist Lynne Tillman, in 'The Trouble with Beauty' (1990) has her heroine retreat into autism after her father's sexual abuse and her consignment to his friend, the Beast, while works by Sylvia Plath (*The Bell Jar*, 1971), Alison Lurie (*The War between the Tates*, 1974), and Alix Kate Shulman (*Memoirs of an Ex-Prom Queen*, 1985) depict women who fall in love with beast-like men without the redemptive denouement.

The fairy tale has always been an important genre in the socialization of children, and it was in fact the work of a woman, Mme *Leprince de Beaumont and her *Magasin des Enfants* (*Magazine for Children*), that ushered the fairy tale into the nursery. Mainstream criticism has portrayed the anthologizing and writing for children in the 19th century as a predominantly male project initiated by the Grimms, but the study of women writers' publishing history reveals that they were at least as active as their male counterparts. For example, while many of the 19th-century German anthologies rework or present now-canonical tales from the French or German tradition, others by prolific writers like Amalie Schoppe and Agnes Franz include collected and original stories that question patriarchal values and virtues. Rather than recount the outward journey toward adventure and success, women's fairy tales often depict the internal voyage characterized by an interest in establishing firm familial bonds. The adventurous hero finds out that there is no place like home, and the heroine achieves education and a female community.

The 'patriarchal plot' has kept women's fairy tales for children from wide distribution, and modern feminists, perhaps unknowingly, are reinventing the weal of earlier women's works. In an attempt to change the cultural and social paradigms for future generations and to regain a sense of women's history, feminists since the late 1970s have organized their fairy-tale collections according to three categories: (1) anthologies of active heroines to counter the negative impact of passive female stereotypes promulgated by canonical texts on maturing adolescent girls; (2) 'alternative' or 'upside-down' stories with reversed plot lines and/or rearranged motifs; and (3) collections of feminist works or original tales based on well-known motifs. The first category includes titles like Rosemary Minard's *Womenfolk and Fairy Tales* (1975); Ethel Johnston Phelps's *The Maid of the North: Feminist Folk Tales from around the World* (1981); Alison Lurie's *Clever Gretchen and Other Forgotten Folk Tales* (1980); James Riordan's *The Woman in the Moon and Other Tales of Forgotten Heroines* (1985); Suzanne Barchers's *Wise Women: Folk and Fairy Tales from around the World* (1990); and Kathleen Ragan's *Fearless Girls, Wise Women, and Beloved Sisters: Heroines in Folktales from around the World* (1998). The second category includes original tales for younger audiences that stand conventional expectations on their heads: Jay *Williams's *The Practical Princess and Other Liberating Fairy Tales* (1969); Adela Turin, Francesca Cantarelli, and Nella Bosnia's *The Five Wives of Silverbeard* (1977); Jane Yolen's *Sleeping Ugly* (1981); Jeanne Desy's 'The Princess who Stood on her Own Two Feet' (1982); Babette *Cole's *Princess Smartypants* (1986); and Judy Corbalis's *The Wrestling Princess and Other Stories* (1986), among many, many others. Collections belonging to the third category include: Jack Zipes's *Don't Bet on the Prince: Contemporary Feminist Fairy Tales in North America and England* (1986); the Irish series 'Fairytales for Feminists', with titles like *Sweeping Beauties* (1990) and *Rapunzel's Revenge* (1995); Angela Carter's *Old Wives' Fairy Tale Book* (1990); Nina Auerbach's *Forbidden Journeys: Fairy Tales and Fantasies by Victorian Women Writers* (1992); Barbara *Walker's *Feminist Fairy Tales* (1996); Virginia *Hamilton's *Her Stories: African American Folktales, Fairy Tales, and True Tales* (1995); and Terry Windling's *The Armless Maiden and Other Tales for Childhood's Survivors* (1995).

2. Feminist theory

Feminist literary criticism has failed to keep pace with contemporary feminist fairy tales and, except for some revisionist scholarship, seems generally unaware of the tradition before the 1970s. Instead, feminist theory about fairy tales is fundamentally a critique of patriarchal literary and cultural practices in Western societies and concerns itself primarily with canonical tales, issues of gender, voice, and power in these tales, their impact on socialization and acculturation, as well as broader social issues like women's access to public discourse, the representation of women in literature and scholarship, and women's contribution to the fairy-tale tradition.

Historically, the feminist theoretical response to fairy tales is a product of the Women's Movement in the United States and Europe and grew out of attacks on patriarchy in the late 1960s by feminists like Simone de Beauvoir, Adrienne Rich, and Betty Friedan. This debate spawned a broad discussion about literary practices and their effects on the socializing process. In the popular press, texts like Madonna Kolbenschlag's *Kiss Sleeping Beauty Goodbye: Breaking the Spell of Feminine Myths and Models* (1979) and Colette Dowling's 1981 best-seller *The Cinderella Complex: Women's Hidden Fear of Independence* explored these issues, while within the academy, folklorists and literary critics developed critiques informed by the debate.

Some attacks addressed fairy-tale research at the structural level and found that research agendas, as well as major tools and apparatus for discussing folklore and fairy tales, have a clear gender bias against women. Feminist folklorists like Claire Farrer demonstrated how in the Western tradition patriarchal practices have kept men in the role of editors and compilers to the exclusion of women. She found that folklore collectors consulted men about stories and their experiences as raconteurs, but consulted females only for information on such subjects as 'charms, cures, and quaint beliefs'. Other feminists levelled attacks against the critical and research apparatus for working with fairy tales. Torborg Lundell, for example, argued that primary texts in folklore and fairy-tale research, like Antti *Aarne and Stith Thompson's *The Types of the Folktale* and Thompson's *Motif Index of Folk Literature*, have an inherent gender bias, ignoring strong heroines through selective labelling, misleading plot summaries, and placing the focus on male rather than female characters. Her concluding statement: there is work to be done, as evidenced by the following cross-references in the *Motif Index*: '*Man*, see also *Person*'. '*Woman*, see also *Wife*'.

Other work has been done on primary texts, most notably the *Kinder- und Hausmärchen* (*Children's and Household Tales*), to examine how editorial practices create traditions and how story selection perpetuates negative stereotypes of women. Some of the earliest research on 19th- and 20th-century anthologizing practices surrounding the Grimms' collection has been done by Kay Stone. She found that a dozen docile heroines are the 'overwhelming favourites', and that 'the passivity of the heroines is magnified by the fact that their stories jump from twenty percent in the original Grimm collection to as much as seventy-five percent in many children's books'. Growing out of research like that of Stone, writers and critics like Jane *Yolen not only anthologized collections with positive heroines, but also researched and wrote about positive models in less well-received stories ('America's Cinderella', 1972).

In the 1980s, critics like Ruth Bottigheimer and Maria Tatar launched another attack at the *Kinder- und Hausmärchen*, namely that not only is there an inherent sexism built into the collection, but this misogyny was the product of Wilhelm Grimm's *editorial*

intent. Working from the assumption that language and its use are social constructs, Bottigheimer backed up her study with a careful analysis of the verbs used in speech acts and found that female characters became increasingly mute in progressive editions, while evil female characters used their tongues with ever-increasing acerbity. The irrefutable conclusion: the *Kinder- und Hausmärchen* were *designed* to acculturate children and women into roles and models of behaviour patriarchy wanted to maintain. In addition to the critique of the Grimms' tales, there were also studies such as Jennifer Waelti-Walters's *Fairy Tales and the Female Imagination* (1982), which focused on seven French and French Canadian women writers whose novels illustrate the pervasive influence of fairy tales on women's lives.

Already as early as 1970, feminist discussion began to focus on the social and cultural effects fairy tales had on the children who listened to them, with respect to the child-rearing process in general, and the process of individuation in particular. Feminist critics like Maria Lieberman rejected the notion that fairy tales are 'universal stories', and argued instead that they acculturate girls to believe that passivity, placidity, and morbidity, along with physical beauty, will make them the 'best' kind of girl to be. Others like Karen Rowe maintained that fairy tales prescribe restrictive social roles for women and perpetuate 'alluring fantasies' of punishment and reward: passivity, beauty, and helplessness lead to marriage, conferring wealth and status, whereas self-aware, 'aggressive', and powerful women reap opprobrium and are either ostracized or killed. Whereas Bruno Bettelheim had suggested in his widely disputed and refuted work *The Uses of Enchantment* (1976), that fairy tales describe eternal truths about the disposition of the human psyche, and that the battles between evil older women and younger, helpless girls are therapeutic and gender-neutral for children, feminist and other literary critics maintained and still maintain that the 'eternal truths' in tales of the Western tradition are the story of women's subjugation and disenfranchisement under patriarchy.

The work from the reader-response school makes it possible to take stock of the progress made by the feminist cause and feminist rewritings of the tradition. Bronwyn Davies's *Frogs and Snails and Feminist Tales: Preschool Children and Gender* (1989) demonstrated how children's play, their conversation, and their responses to feminist stories can provide new insight into the social construction of gender. In addition, Ella Westland's 1993 study 'Cinderella in the Classroom: Children's Responses to Gender Roles in Fairy-Tales' included over 100 boys and girls aged 9–11 in five Cornish primary schools, whose perceptions of fairy tales were recorded through group discussions, pictures they drew, and stories they wrote. While the boys appeared to have little incentive to alter the standard fairy-tale structure (beyond enriching the mixture with added violence) because they had more to lose than to gain from the changes, the girls argued they would not want to be a princess because it was simply too boring and restrictive; their stories were closely moulded on published upside-down stories with independent, plain, and active heroines. The work of the past 30 years has indeed created a generation of 'resisting readers'.

That the long tradition of feminist fairy tales is as yet generally unknown to the larger public has to do with the methods of canon formation, publishing history, and the distribution of power and literature within patriarchy, as Marina *Warner has demonstrated in her significant study *From the Beast to the Blonde: On Fairytales and their Tellers* (1994). The question remains as to what the next step will be. The work by feminists such as Karen Rowe and Cristina Bacchilega suggests there have been significant advances brought about by the interactions between feminist theorizing and feminist practice. The anthologies of so-called alternative stories are, in fact, equally valid primary stories of realms of experience and longings for a better world the fairy tale can make real. It has been argued that fairy tales reflect lived realities of the writers and readers; perhaps future stories in keeping with the feminist project may one day reflect a new reality, a more prejudice-free world.   SJ

Bacchilega, Cristina, *Postmodern Fairy Tales: Gender and Narrative Strategies* (1997).

Bernheimer, Kate (ed.), *Mirror, Mirror on the Wall: Women Writers Explore their Favorite Fairy Tales* (1998).

Davies, Bronwyn, *Frogs and Snails and Feminist Tales: Preschool Children and Gender* (1989).

Haase, Donald (ed.), *Fairy Tales and Feminism: New Approaches* (2004).

Helms, Cynthia, 'Storytelling, Gender and Language in Folk/Fairy Tales: A Selected Annotated Bibliography', *Women and Language*, 10 (spring 1987).

Orenstein, Peggy, *Cinderella Ate My Daughter: Dispatches from the Front Lines of the New Girlie-Girl Culture* (2011).

Waelti-Walters, Jennifer, *Fairy Tales and the Female Imagination* (1982).

Warner, Marina, *From the Beast to the Blonde: On Fairytales and their Tellers* (1994).

Zipes, Jack (ed.), *Don't Bet on the Prince: Contemporary Feminist Fairy Tales in North America and England* (1986).

Fénelon, François de Salignac de la Mothe (1651–1715) Prominent French cleric and writer. Fénelon wrote several works for the Dauphin (Louis XIV's grandson and heir), to whom he was tutor. Among these early examples of children's literature (including his famous *Télémaque* (*Telemachus*, 1699) is his posthumously published *Recueil des fables composées pour l'éducation de feu Monseigneur le duc de Bourgogne* (*Collection of Fables Written for the Education of the late Monseigneur the Duke of Burgundy*, 1718), which contains moralizing fairy-tale stories that stress proper feminine and aristocratic conduct. Fénelon is the only French writer besides Mme *Leprince de Beaumont to have written fairy tales explicitly for children before the 19th century.   LCS

Ferra-Mikura, Vera (1923–97) Viennese author of stories, radio plays, and poems for children and adults. Ferra-Mikura's work is characterized by humour, playfulness, and imagination. Her fairy-tale-inspired, optimistic, and highly imaginative stories for children are written in gripping and easily accessible prose and soon became popular with young readers in Austria. Her artistic breakthrough as a writer for children came with the story *Zaubermeister Opequeh* (*Sorcerer Opequeh*, 1956), which was followed by many equally humorous and playfully absurd stories. EMM

Lexikon der österreichischen Kinder- und Jugendliteratur, i (1994).

Ferro, Martino (1974–) Italian writer who has written screenplays for the cinema and a popular comic series for television. In 2005 he won the Calvino Prize for his novel *Il primo che sorride* (*The First One Who Smiles*), and in 2011 he published a collection of humorous fairy tales, *C'era una svolta* (*Once upon a Turn*). These amusing modern stories recall the nineteenth-century folk tales collected by Italo Calvino. They are told by Tonino Buttalamare, a convict, who is to be executed in San Quentin prison in California, but his last wish is to tell stories, and if nobody wants him to continue telling them, he will be executed. His ironic fairy tales deal with the Mafia, homosexuality, nuclear war, and contemporary economic and social crises, and he succeeds in avoiding execution through storytelling. JZ

Ferron, Jacques (1921–85) Canadian doctor, novelist, short-storywriter, playwright, and essayist, whose fairy tales and stories have revitalized the Québécois folk tradition. Ferron led an active political life as doctor, often providing his services to working-class people in the province of Quebec and supporting the Quebec separatist movement. As a writer of tales, Ferron blends his real experiences as doctor and activist with the fabulous incidents and transforms traditional oral tales into short artful stories that question notions of normalcy and sanity. Many of his tales are philosophical and psychological fairy tales that are based in the daily life of common people. Ferron published two significant collections of his stories, *Contes du pays uncertain* (*Tales from the Uncertain Country*, 1962), which won the

Governor General's Award, and *Contes anglais et autres* (*English and Other Tales*, 1964). JZ

Bednarski, Betty, and McAlister, Vivian, 'Literature and Obstetrics: Reading Maternal Posture in Jacques Ferron's "Little William"', *Literature and Medicine* (fall 2002).

McAlister, Viviane, and McAlister, Christiane, 'In Search of the Anglophone Doctor in Jacque Ferron's Story "Le Petit William"', *Dalhousie Medical Journal* (fall 2006).

Fetscher, Iring (1922–2014) German political scientist and Professor at the University of Frankfurt am Main, best known for his numerous publications on the history and theory of marxism. In his 1972 collection of ironic fairy-tale adaptations and criticism, *Wer hat Dornröschen wachgeküsst? Das Märchenverwirrbuch* (*Who awakened Sleeping Beauty with a Kiss? The Book of Fairy Tale Confusion*), Fetscher explores alternative meanings and contexts for the *Grimms' tales. He employs what he terms *Verwirr-Methoden* (methods of confusion), borrowing playfully from serious scholarly approaches, such as philological, psychoanalytic, and historical materialist textual criticism, to produce a unique blend of imaginative storytelling and light-hearted criticism.

The collection contains reinterpretations of 13 of the best-loved Grimm tales, divided into three sections more or less corresponding to the methods of confusion: the rehabilitation of the wolf; the rise of the bourgeoisie, the anti-feudal revolution, and the problems of an antagonistic society; and the sexual problems of princesses. Traditional and adapted tales can be read nicely in relation to one another, for Fetscher begins with the Grimm version, then offers his tongue-in-cheek commentary, exposing a history of editorial censorship, class antagonism, and sexual anxiety. *Cinderella, for example, was a labour activist whose consciousness of 'irreconcilable class differences' causes her to reject the prince's offer of marriage; Lucky Hans was not stupid, but inadequately socialized in the ways of capitalist trade economy; the wolf of several fairy tales was a victim of character assassination;

and the kiss that awakened *Sleeping Beauty marked the end of her defloration phobia.

MBS

Fetscher, Iring, *Marx and Marxism* (1971).

Fielding, Sarah (1710–68) English novelist. *The Governess, or Little Female Academy* (1749), the first extended work of fiction for young readers, included two heavily moral fairy stories. 'The Story of the Cruel Giant Barbarico, the Good Giant Benefico, and the Pretty Little Dwarf Mignon' is the more original of the two, and was sometimes printed in chapbook form. 'The Princess Hebe' is in the high-flown romantic style of d'*Aulnoy. At a time when such stories were regarded by the enlightened as a relic of the dark ages, Fielding felt bound to apologize for their inclusion, and Mary Martha Sherwood in her recast 1820 version of the book excluded both stories.   GA

Figes, Eva (1932–2012) British writer who fled the Nazis in 1939 with her family as a seven-year-old girl, made London her home, and learned English to become a well-known writer of novels, literary criticism, and memoirs. During the 1960s she was associated with a group of experimental and feminist writers. Among her most prominent books are *Patriarchal Attitudes: Women in Society* (1970) and *Sex and Subterfuge: Women Writers to 1850* (1982). Her best-known fairy-tale work is *Tales of Experience: An Exploration* (2003), a stunning poetical memoir in the form of a dialogue between a grandmother and her granddaughter. Figes as narrator explores her past through the *Grimms' tales. Each short chapter in her memoir is a surrealistic interlude in which she dwells on haunting incidents in the tales and comes to terms with irresolution and death.   JZ

film and fairy tales The content, form, and reception of fairy tales in the modern Western world have been heavily influenced by the proliferation of adaptations for film. Many children now encounter folk literature predominantly as it is mediated by filmic versions, and film versions are produced in the shadow of the commercial and cultural dominance of the *Disney industry. Critical responses to fairy-tale films have in their turn been shaped by presuppositions about the nature and functions of fairy tale. Film is a relatively new medium for fairy tale, and to a great extent might be considered a different genre in its own right, with its own conventions and its own principles, although it may employ many narrative codes specific to literary fairy-tale schemata. Indeed, in *The Enchanted Screen*, Jack Zipes has gone so far as to suggest that classic European and Hollywood film traditions have been 'stamped' by the classic fairy tale narrative form. The expansion of a story to run for an hour or more may entail enhanced characterization, introduction of subplots or additional minor characters, and the development of strategies for maintaining audience engagement. At the same time, such expansions will need to address the overall coherence of the narrative and convey a sense that it has a pattern that moves to a meaningful outcome.

A criterion often adduced in discussing film adaptations is fidelity to source, but unlike film adaptations of literary classics, for example, fairy-tale films cannot always be referred back to a particular source or central tradition, but are part of a web of hypertextual links, as Cristina Bacchilega puts it in *Fairy Tales Transformed?*, or versions of an ever-evolving 'script'. Nevertheless, because fairy-tale film is dominated by versions of a small number of literary fairy tales and is often specifically allusive to preceding representations, there is much interest in the content of a film and in what is perceived to have been changed in the process of adaptation—what has been omitted, what added, how particular problems of representation have been addressed. Thus a comparison of Disney's The *Little Mermaid* with Hans Christian *Andersen's original tale, for example, discloses much about the ideological thrust of the Disney film, especially with respect to gender representations and assumptions about the global hegemony of Western (particularly North American) culture. Further, because a Disney transformation usually becomes the dominant known version of a tale and feeds back into literary retellings, a comparison offers insight into the nature of the hopes and aspirations that are being constructed for children in the modern era.

Commentary on fairy-tale film has grounded itself in two contrasting conceptions of fairy tale. On the one hand is the view that folk tales are stories with an essential form which convey universal and timeless truths capable of being reproduced, distorted, or lost in literary or filmic retellings. A fairy tale is thus invested with value as *story* for its own sake. That is, as a narrative which audiences may recognize as similar to other such narratives because it is patterned by archetypal situations and characterisations, a story transmits its latent value as a particular outworking of perennial human desires and destinies. It contains some instruction, some mechanism for helping us to understand and cope with the problems of everyday life. Audiences thus learn the roles which pattern their lives, that good always overcomes evil, and that proper behaviour is rewarded, usually by romantic marriage. The structural pattern itself signifies without needing to be interpreted, because the meaning lies in the repeatability and the deeply laid similarity amongst otherwise apparently diverse stories. A further assumption here is that fairy tale is not only germane to childhood but also forms an important part of a child's cultural heritage and inducts children into an understanding of their culture's grounding patterns of thought and behaviour. Such an assumption seems reflected in the propensity for fairy-tale films to incorporate visual quotations from the work of well-known illustrators of classic fairy tales. An extension of the notion of cultural heritage, well exemplified in the beautifully produced *We All Have Tales* series of the early 1990s, is the idea that fairy tales facilitate intercultural communication by bringing out the similarities between various world cultures and mediating elements of otherness. We all have tales, and both the impulse to story and the mutual comprehensibility of stories from different lands affirm the common humanity of the world's peoples. A potential flaw in such thinking is that otherness can be appropriated and transformed into sameness, and a charge frequently levelled at the Disney industry, in particular, is that it engages in a neocolonial co-opting of the folklore and stories of other peoples into the frame of North American society, politics, and capitalism. This process is identifiable in **Pinocchio, The Little Mermaid, *Aladdin, The Lion King, Pocahontas*, and *Mulan*.

A contrary view to this universalising perspective is the argument that folk tales only ever express conditions, attitudes, and values pertaining at specific sociocultural moments, and whenever collectors or rewriters turn folk tales into literary fairy tales, or invent new literary fairy tales, they express the social and moral assumptions of their own time and culture. At most, older meanings persist only in dialogue with those of the time of present production. Films are no exception, so that the significances attributable to fairy-tale films produced by the modern culture industry will be tied up with assumptions about social formations in contemporary society and will stand in some orientation towards areas of social change and social contestation, especially attitudes relating to ethnicity and race relations, economic (and political) stratifications within and across societies, and gender.

If we keep in mind that the sources for any fairy-tale film may be uncertain or multiple and are subject to influence from the multitude of retellings in general circulation at any one time, it is possible to identify four types of adaptation of fairy tale to film. First, there are renditions which strive to reproduce a particular version of a fairy tale with minimal addition or change. The second, and largest, group of adaptations consists of substantial reinterpretations of fairy tales. The third type treats its pre-text(s) as raw material for an original work and may combine various versions of a tale or several tales, or generate a new work in the genre. Examples are *The *Princess Bride* (1987), *Labyrinth* (1986), Disney's *The Lion King* (1994), adult films such as *Pretty Woman*

(1990), *Ladyhawke* (1985) or recent 'Sleeping Beauty' films directed by Catherine *Breillat (2011) and Julia Leigh (2011). Finally, fairy-tale film conventions evolved by the Disney corporation are used to frame other narratives, thus transposing them into a fairy-tale discourse—for example, *Alice in Wonderland* (1951), *Peter Pan* (1953), *Pocahontas* (1995), and *The Hunchback of Notre Dame* (1996). Discussion here will focus on the first two types.

The first type comprises a relatively small number of films, mostly brief, simple animations, which aspire to be literal or faithful renditions of a fairy tale which is considered to have 'classic' status, and which assume that there is something essential about the 'original' story which can be reproduced. Many films in this group are particularly ephemeral, and this type of adaptation also occurs in less thematically experimental films. 'Thumbelina', for example (in Shelley *Duvall's *Faerie Tale Theatre* series) is a humorous rewriting of Andersen's tale, rendered visually delightful by its extensive allusions to George *Cruikshank's nineteenth-century illustrations. The only substantial variations from Andersen's version—a gender switch of the field mouse from female to male, and the reuniting of Thumbelina with her foster-mother brought about by her prince bridegroom—firmly reinforce Thumbelina's status as an object of exchange and hence the tale's use of a male discourse to frame women's lives. This film also illustrates how the addition of humour masks and promotes passive acceptance of the ideological implications of discourse, as Thumbelina is finally coupled with someone of her own race and class.

The use in this 'Thumbelina' of classic illustrations reflects a common practice whereby simpler adaptations animate a picture-book version of a tale, and hence reproduce an intermediate version. By this means, a collection of three Andersen tales released by Weston Woods in the *Children's Circle* series (1991) achieved varying degrees of fidelity to the source text. For example, 'The Swineherd', based on illustrations by Bjorn Wiinblad, deftly reproduces Andersen's

narrative and dialogue, while using the visuals to convey narratorial attitude. The technique owes more to picture-book codes than to filmic codes, however. This comment also applies to the 1986 Bosustow Entertainment Production *Beauty and the Beast*, a curious presentation of two stories, Jay *Williams's *The Practical Princess* and a version of *Beauty and the Beast* taken from Marianna Mayer's 1978 picture book, now edited down to ten minutes. The presentation is framed by former child film star Hayley Mills as presenter and interpreter of the tales, which are both about 'common sense'. In *Beauty and the Beast* it is the common-sense position that people should not be judged by appearances. The framing didactic commentary effectively reinforces the deterministic patriarchy of the Mayer retelling: Beauty repeatedly dreams of a handsome prince destined to be her partner, while a fairy voice enjoins her to 'Look deep into others' beauty to find your happiness'. The outcome is thus always inevitable.

In the second type of adaptation a film reproduces the story, but in doing so either reinterprets or deconstructs the source materials. This group includes the best-known films, that is, those of Disney, Jim *Henson, Tom *Davenport, most of the *Faerie Tale Theatre* films, and many recent films. Disney corporation films loom very large here, despite the small number of fairy-tale feature films that have been produced by the company and a thirty-year hiatus between *Sleeping Beauty* (1959) and *The Little Mermaid* (1989). The films in the feature-length corpus are *Snow White* (1937), *Cinderella* (1950), *Sleeping Beauty* (1959), *The Little Mermaid* (1989), *Beauty and the Beast* (1991), *Aladdin* (1992), *Mulan* (1998), *The Princess and the Frog* (2009), *Tangled* (2010), and *Frozen* (2013).

A marked effect of Disney animated films has been to narrow and redefine what modern children (and adults) know as folk tale (or fairy tale), and what meanings they ascribe to folk tale. Disney films operate on the principle, as articulated by Christopher Vogler in *The Writer's Journey: Mythic Structure for Storytellers and Screenwriters* (1992), that all stories consist of a few common structural elements found universally in myths, fairy tales, dreams, and films. The nuances and significances given to these 'common structural elements', however, have the potential for great cultural influence, especially as the range of elements deployed has been reduced in the Disney films, which all employ a common set of features.

First, they draw on a schema in which a female protagonist is moved by desire for another, in some sense better, existence. That desire resembles a longing for agency, but the tales assert that it can only be attained within some version of a romance and marriage plot that denies the female characters individuality, self-determination and agency. The outcome—a happy ending in marriage—is reached only after the heroine is commodified, subjected to threat, rendered vulnerable, and finally rescued by her future husband. It is notable that one of the several ways *Aladdin* departs from its *Arabian Nights* source is to reshape the story and the role of the princess in it so that it conforms to this schema: Princess Jasmine is always the principal prize for which the males compete, and her marriage to Aladdin is part of the denouement, whereas it takes place at about the mid-point of the original tale, and her role in the defeat of the evil magician is substantially diminished (instead of being the instrument of his death, she herself has to be saved from death by Aladdin). Despite the illusion of nascent feminist impulses in the more recent heroines, they are always finally contained within a marriage plot moulded by a male discourse.

Second, the films add a comic element through the enhancement or addition of secondary characters—dwarfs, animals, fairy godmothers, animated kitchen utensils (*Beauty and the Beast*), or the genie (*Aladdin*). The comedy not only engages audience attention, and extends and varies an otherwise rather limited action, but also regulates audience response in relation to a third recurrent element in the films, a simple dichotomy between good and evil. Warm fuzzy humour generated by lovable animals

or teapots is associated with the good characters, while a more sardonic humour enters at the expense of evil characters. In other words, audiences laugh *with* the good characters but *at* the evil ones. The good-evil dichotomy has a powerful normative function as battle lines are drawn between good femininity and bad femininity, good masculinity and bad masculinity (the Beast and Gaston, respectively, in *Beauty and the Beast*), and American values and un-American values (in *The Little Mermaid* and *Aladdin*). Black-and-white contrasts, differentiating humour, and the unequivocal triumph of good over evil at the ending of a Disney film consistently replicate and effectively advocate a specific construction of what constitutes a good life.

The structural and thematic consistency of such a fairy-tale corpus spanning almost eighty years upholds the expression of what is generally an archaic world view. In so far as these fairy tales affirm what makes life meaningful, they do so by asserting a social structure which is patriarchal and capitalistic. Some limited space has been allowed for varieties of pseudo-feminism since *The Sleeping Beauty*, though this tends to be neutralized by conflating it with versions of teenage rebelliousness; and some small variations in conceptions of masculinity also began emerging with *Beauty and the Beast*. But ultimately these do not constitute recognition of any significant paradigm shift, and they are readily containable within a patriarchal discourse and traditional images of family life.

There have, however, been a number of attempts to challenge the dominance of the Disney film-fairy-tale formula through alternative films that offer a different vision of fairy tales and social conditions. Jack Zipes's comprehensive monograph, *The Enchanted Screen: The Unknown History of Fairy Tale Films* (2011), has made significant inroads in bringing some of these lesser-known films to critical attention. Georges *Méliès, for example, who Zipes suggests should be considered the founder and pioneer of fairy-tale film rather than Disney, drew on the theatrical tradition of the *Féerie* to make over 30 fairy-tale films long before Disney's *Snow White*. Méliès's comic films were characterized by a sense of the ridiculous which, as Zipes demonstrates, interrogated fairy-tale tradition and social reality, especially the abuse of power, resulting in 'utopian carnivalesques', themes which run counter to the Disney model. Brian Selznick's graphic novel *The Adventures of Hugo Cabret* (2007) retells a version of Méliès's life, interleaving it with the story of a young orphaned boy and a mystery plot. The recent film adaptation of that novel by Martin Scorsese, as *Hugo* (2011), emphasizes fairy-tale elements implicit in Selznick's novel, but also interweaves a history of the cinema (and of Parisian social life of the 1930s) by incorporating borrowed images from the period as well as films from the early silent-film period, most notably Méliès's 'masterwork' *Kingdom of the Fairies* (1903), the film which holds the key to the film's mystery plot. Scorsese's homage to Méliès is a splendid film in itself, but it also plays a role in displacing Disney's dominance in the cultural imagination.

Other attempts to produce fairy-tale films that evade the hegemony of the Disney formula include most notably the many productions of Jim Henson, Shelley Duvall's *Faerie Tale Theatre* series, and the boom in fairy tale films over the last decade or so. Filmic retellings which take a source from Grimm or Andersen and deliberately deviate from it may succeed in foregrounding stereotypical fairy-tale motifs and structures, and hence the roles and expectations imbricated within them, and subject them to interrogation or subversion, thus rendering visible the ideologies naturalized in the pre-text. *Faerie Tale Theatre* productions have been criticized for often privileging tour de force performances over narrative experimentation, but the juxtaposition of the distinctive acting styles of Liza Minnelli and Tom Conti in 'The *Princess and the Pea' effectively functions as a marker of difference as the characters renegotiate the metonymic social meaning of the term 'princess'. Overstatement is also a strategy in Henson's 'The Three Ravens' (from *The Storyteller*, 1988), a creative reworking of the Grimm tale 'The Six Swans' (scripted by Anthony Minghella). The plot structure is much tighter than in the Grimm story, as the stepmother/wicked witch's lust for power prompts her not only to transform her stepsons into ravens, but to murder her husband and move on to a new conquest. Both narrative and visual images emphasize the stereotypical contrast between the dark-haired witch and the long-haired, blonde princess. As further emphasis, as the ever-present and omniscient narrator (John Hurt) and his narratee (a talking dog) discuss the unfolding story, the dog frequently declares, 'I hate that witch!' A second convention foregrounded by the dog's interpolations is the equation of speech with individual power and autonomy in fairy tales: the heroine has an extended silence laid upon her as the only way to break the transformation spell that holds her brothers, but her inability to speak to defend herself against an accusation of witchcraft generates the danger of being burned at the stake. The outcome, a complete restoration of all she had lost, is offered as a reward for 'the girl who kept faith and had one face for everyone'. But the dog, as always in this splendid series, expresses his scepticism about the processes and outcomes of the tale. In such ways, narrative and filmic strategies alert the audience to the constructedness of story, and hence to the relationship between entertainment and pedagogy in fairy-tale films.

Another alternative to the Disney formula is the adaptation of non-Western fairy tales, though this risks accusations of cultural appropriation, a criticism made of Disney's *Mulan*. Michel *Ocelot's adaptations of West African folktales in *Kirikou and the Sorceress* (1998) and *Azur and Asmar: The Prince's Quest* (2009), while being censored by some American critics for being racist and for displaying nudity, are regarded by others as successfully challenging racial stereotypes and prejudices. Ocelot's more recent adaptations of international fairy tales compiled in *Tales of the Night* (2012) is also innovative stylistically through its use of silhouette animation.

There have been few radically experimental fairy-tale films, but three film-makers of note are Jan *Švankmajer, Nietzchka Keene (*The Juniper Tree*, 1990), and Pablo Berger (*Blancanieves*, 2012). An animator in the Czech surrealist tradition, Švankmajer combines live action and stop-motion animation to adapt Karel *Erben's 'The Wooden Baby' in *Otesanek* (2000), a story about a surrogate baby, Otik, who devours everything, including his parents. Švankmajer's filmic techniques are the antithesis of the conventions of 'classical' cinema. Furthermore, his interweaving of parallel narratives invites a political reading wherein Otik's hunger, violence, and cannibalism present the unrestrained consumerism of post-1989 Czechoslovakia.

Since the late nineties there has been a proliferation of films which seek to revise and modernize fairy tales. As Bacchilega has pointed out in *Fairy Tales Transformed?*, however, it does *not* (always) guarantee the articulation of new social possibilities for the genre. Disney's recent *Maleficent* (2014) and *Enchanted* (2007), for example, both seek to update, as well as self-parody in the case of the latter, earlier films; the extent to which either film interrogates the ideological paradigms of the Disney formula, however, is limited. In contrast, Breillat has brought her interest in gender politics and feminine sexuality to adaptations of Perrault's 'Bluebeard' and 'Sleeping Beauty' stories. In *Blaubart* (2009) she uses two parallel narratives, one set in the 1950s and the other in the 17th century, to construct a feminist critique of both periods. *La Belle endormie* (2010) is an expansion and continuation of the 'Sleeping Beauty' story which combines Perrault's story with elements drawn from Anderson's 'The Snow Queen' to depict the fantastic adventures that Princess Anastasia dreams as she sleeps. Anastasia falls asleep when she is 6 and wakes when she is 16, thus missing out on puberty. And so the narrative continues after she is awoken to explore not just the difficulty she has in negotiating the modern world, but also with her sudden transition into sexual maturity. Both films return an edging ambivalence and eroticism, alongside a feminist critique, to a fairy tale

world so thoroughly sanitized by the Disney tradition. Another recent modernized and provocative version of 'Sleeping Beauty' is Julia Leigh's version (2011) where the protagonist is paid to sleep alongside older men.

Other recent adaptations draw on and remix a range of film genres and traditions, in particular romance, comedy, fantasy-action, and horror. In the romance genre notable films are *Ever After* (1998), *Enchanted* (2007), *Snow White: The Fairest of them All* (2001), *Beastly* (2011), and *Mirror, Mirror* (2012). Each of these in various ways seeks to modernize the stories. Neil *Jordan's adaptation of Angela *Carter's re-version of 'Little Red Riding Hood', *The Company of Wolves* (1984), was one of the first fairy-tale horror films dealing with the violence and sexual undertones of the story. Such films have proliferated in the last ten years and are characterized by their moderate to excessive violence, epic battle scenes and fight-sequences, and a penchant for female warrior figures, for example Gretel in *Hansel and Gretel: Witch Hunters* (2013) and Snow White in *Snow White and the Huntsman* (2012). Many films also borrow freely from the epic fantasy-action style of Peter Jackson's *Lord of the Rings* films and Andrew Adamson's two *Chronicles of Narnia* films. Favoured tales are those which feature abused children, *'Hansel and Gretel', 'Snow White', 'Little Red Riding Hood', and 'The Story of Janghwa and Hongryeon' (a Korean folktale), though in many of these films the children now seek revenge in some way—Hansel and Gretel of *Witch Hunters* (a sequel to Grimm's story) are now bounty witch hunters; the children of Yim Pil-Sung's *Hansel and Gretel* (2007) lure adults to their house in the forest; Hailey of David Slade's *Hard Candy* (2005) compels Jeff (the wolf figure) to kill himself.

Such prolific film production and interest in fairy-tale stories and tropes in recent films are indicative of the great potential the fairy-tale film has for eliciting an intelligent audience engagement with story, processes, ideologies, and human values. In foregrounding their own generic multivalency films such as these for young viewers can stimulate critical literacy in young audiences, hence empowering them to look more sceptically at texts of other kinds and encouraging in them human qualities such as caring, trust, and reciprocity. Many of the recent fairy-tale films for teenagers and adults, however, offer quite pessimistic alternatives to the classic formula, leaving viewers with little hope. Instead, as Zipes has suggested of Yim Pil-Sung's *Hansel and Gretel* in *The Enchanted Screen*, 'these pessimistic films may be read as a critique of the brutal treatment of innocent children in . . . a world where barbarity often blends with civility or exists in high tension with civility' (2011).   RM/JAS

Aurouet, Carole (ed.), *Contes et légendes à l'écran* (2003).

Bacchilega, Cristina, *Fairy Tales Transformed? Twenty-First Century Adaptations and the Politics of Wonder* (2013).

Bazalgette, Cary, and Buckingham, David (eds.), *In Front of the Children: Screen Entertainment and Young Audiences* (1993).

Bell, Elizabeth, Haas, Lynda, and Sells, Laura (eds.), *From Mouse to Mermaid: the Politics of Film, Gender and Culture* (1995).

Greenhill, Pauline, and Matrix, Sidney Eve (eds.), *Fairy Tale Film and Cinematic Folklore: Fantastic Voyages, Monstrous Dreams, and Wonderful Visions* (2010).

Haase, Donald P., 'Gold into Straw: Fairy-Tale Movies for Children and the Culture Industry', *The Lion and the Unicorn*, 12.2 (1988).

Liptay, Fabienne, *WunderWelten. Märchen im Film* (2004).

Moen, Kristian, *Film and Fairy Tales: The Birth of Modern Fantasy* (2013).

Stone, Kaye F., 'Things Walt Disney Never Told Us', *Journal of American Folklore*, 88 (1975).

Warner, Marina, *Cinema and the Realms of Enchantment: Lectures, Seminars, and Essays.* (1993).

Zipes, Jack, *The Enchanted Screen: The Unknown History of Fairy-Tale Films* (2011).

Finian's Rainbow Successful stage musical which mixes fantasy with social commentary. Premièred in New York on Broadway in 1947, the show had a book by E. Y. Harburg (who also wrote the lyrics) and Fred Saidy, with music by Burton Lane. It achieved an initial run of 725 performances. A father and daughter leave Ireland for America's deep South, taking with them a crock of gold (stolen from the leprechaun Og) in the belief that, by burying it close to Fort Knox, it will grow abundantly. The show's social side deals with the defeat and rehabilitation of a negro-hating senator.   TH

Fiorentino, Giovanni (second half of 14th century) Italian novella writer. Many of the 20 novellas in his *Pecorone* (*The Big Sheep*) combine realistic and folkloric elements. In particular, in 4.1, 'La Donna di Belmonte' ('The Lady of Belmonte') a fairy-tale structure is transposed onto a historical setting; tales 4.2 and 10.1 present the familiar fairy-tale motif of a princess married against her will to an old man (a realistic version of the ogre found in similar tales by *Basile, for example); and tale 9.2 includes the motifs of a mysterious bridegroom, a princess closed in a tower, and a final double marriage. NC

Petrini, Mario, *La fiaba di magia nella letteratura italiana* (1983).

Fitzgerald, John Anster (1823–1906) Irish painter of highly original fantasy and fairy scenes who was known by his friends as 'Fairy Fitzgerald'. Little is known about his life and travels, but his grotesque goblin creations suggest that he must have been familiar with works by Brueghel and Bosch. It is also clear that his various 'dream' paintings refer to drug-induced hallucinations. 'The Artist's Dream' (1857), for instance, shows an artist asleep, dreaming of the fairy he is painting, while in the foreground nightmare figures caper round his chair, one of them offering him a potion in a glass. In 'Fairies in a Bird's Nest' (*c*.1860) the two fairy figures are dwarfed by the menacing Bosch-like aberrations that crowd the canvas.   GA

Flake, Otto (1880–1963) German writer and publisher. His extensive *œuvre* includes two volumes of naïvely-humorous fairy tales, reworking traditional folk-tale characters and beliefs. They appeared in several revised editions under changing titles: *Maria im Dachgarten und andere Märchen* (*Mary in* *her Roof-Garden and other Tales*, 1931); second edition *Kinderland* (*Children's Country*, 1948); third edition *Ende gut, alles gut* (*All's Well That Ends Well*, 1950), and *Der Strassburger Zuckerbeck und andere Märchen* (*The Baker of Strasbourg and Other Tales*, 1933); second edition *Der Mann im Mond und andere Märchen* (*The Man in the Moon and other Tales*, 1947); third edition *Der Basler Zuckerbeck* (*The Baker of Basle*, 1953).   KS

Fleischer Brothers Max Fleischer (1883–1972) and Dave Fleischer (1894–1979) were American pioneer animators and directors. Together they founded Inkwell Studios in 1921, later changed to Fleischer Studios. Max worked more as the producer, and Dave the director of animation. They invented such famous characters as Koko the Clown, Betty Boop, and Bimbo, and brought Popeye the Sailor and Superman to the screen. Early in the 1930s, they produced several hilarious and sexually loaded fairy-tale films featuring the fascinating Betty Boop in *Dizzy Red Riding Hood* (1931), *Jack and the Beanstalk* (1931), *Paradise of the Wooden Soldiers* (1933), *Snow White* (1933), and *Poor Cinderella* (1934). They also involved Popeye in several fairy-tale films such as *Popeye the Sailor Meets Ali Baba's Forty Thieves* (1937). The trait most characteristic of the Fleischer fairy-tale cartoons is irreverence. It is also this quality that characterizes the best of the carnivalesque fairy-tale cartoons up to the present. The Fleischers exploded the classical fairy tales, and out of the anachronistic dust created lively absurd narratives that stretched the imagination beyond belief. In doing so they diminished the authority of *Perrault's and the *Grimms' fixed narratives and relativized their meanings.   JZ

Fleischer, Richard, *Out of the Inkwell: Max Fleischer and the Animation Revolution* (2005).

Fleutiaux, Pierrette (1941–) French writer who began her career with the fantastic *Histoire de la chauve-souris* (*The Story of the Bat*, 1974) and later published a collection of fairy tales, *Métamorphoses de la reine* (*Metamorphoses of the Queen*, 1985), which

won the prestigious Prix Goncourt. In this latter volume, she rewrites several of *Perrault's stories, most notably by amplifying violence and eroticism, developing women's roles, and shifting narrative points of view. Above all, play with fairy-tale conventions allows Fleutiaux to reflect critically on expectations about feminine conduct.   LCS

Knapp, Bettina L., *Pierrette Fleutiaux* (1997).

Flinn, Alex (1955–) Author of numerous young-adult fairy-tale adaptations, including *Beastly* (2007), a retelling of *'Beauty and the Beast' set in New York City. The protagonist is Kyle Kingsbury, who is punished when he mistreats a modern-day witch. The novel was adapted and made into a film in 2011 and followed by a sequel, *Bewitching* (2012), the story of the witch who cast the spell. Flinn's other adaptations are: *A Kiss in Time* (2009), *Towering* (2013), and *Cloaked* (2011), which offer new versions of *'Sleeping Beauty', *'Rapunzel', and 'The Swan Princess'.   KMJ

Fokine, Michel (1880–1942) Russian dancer who became the 20th century's first important choreographer, spending the last two decades of his life in America, where he worked on Florenz Ziegfeld's 1922 *Follies*. Engaged as a choreographer earlier in the century by Diaghilev for his Ballets Russes, Fokine significantly developed newer styles of dancing, creating ballets to existing music, important among which was *Les Sylphides* (1908), with music by Chopin. *The Firebird* (1910) and *Petrushka* (1922), with music by *Stravinsky, are two works on fairy-tale themes for which Fokine is especially remembered.   TH

Folkard, Charles James (1878–1963) British children's illustrator and comic strip creator. A printer's son, he was enthralled by a conjuror at London's Egyptian Hall, learned magic, discovered a talent for designing programmes, and trained at Goldsmith's College and St John's Wood Schools of Art. He contributed to *Little Folks* and the *Tatler* before gaining notoriety for the fantastic naturalism of his illustrations for *The*

Folkard, Charles The mischievous puppet knocks the wig off poor Giuseppi, his creator and father, in Charles Folkard's illustration for Carlo Collodi's *Pinocchio* in the English version of 1911. Photo: Charles Folkard Collection/Mary Evans Picture Library.

Swiss Family Robinson (1910). This gift-book edition was followed by his definitive *Pinocchio* (1911): with 77 humorous drawings and 8 watercolour plates, it is still reprinted today. *The Children's *Shakespeare* (1911), *Grimm's Fairy Tales* (1911), *Aesop's Fables* (1912) and *The *Arabian Nights* (1913) followed, with the luminous 'Persian' plates of *Ottoman Wonder Tales* (1915) being especially noteworthy. In 1915 he created the first British comic strip. 'Teddy Tail' was an instant success, and appeared for the next 45 years in the London *Daily Mail* and in a series of adventure books, such as *Teddy Tail in Fairyland* (1916).

In addition to *Mother Goose rhymes and stories (1919, 1923), Folkard illustrated *British Fairy and Folk Tales* (1920), *Alice's Adventures in Wonderland* (1929), *The Princess and Curdie* and *The Princess and the Goblin* (1949), and *The Book of Nonsense by Many Authors* (1956), which featured Struwwelpeter and characters from Baron Münchhausen, Edward Lear, and Lewis *Carroll.

MLE

Dalby, Richard, *Golden Age of Children's Book Illustration* (1991).

Doyle, Brian, *Who's Who in Children's Literature* (1968).

Peppin, Brigid, and Micklethwait, Lucy, *Dictionary of British Book Illustrators* (1983).

folklore and fairy tales

1. The fairy tale as a subject of folklore study

Of the three main oral prose genres of folklore, fairy tale, myth, and legend, the fairy tale has received the most critical attention in folklore scholarship. Although early collectors of folk narrative did not draw fine distinctions, scholars have subsequently found it useful to define the fairy tale in relation to these other prose genres. Myths are narratives which are believed to be true about gods or supernatural beings who operate beyond the realm of human existence, and from whose experiences humans can draw moral lessons. Legends generally report on extraordinary events in the lives of ordinary humans, frequently in an encounter with the supernatural. Although there is

an inherent truth claim in the legend, there is often an element of scepticism or disbelief on the part of the narrator or audience. In contrast to legend and myth, fairy tales are narratives of magic and fantasy, which are understood to be fictional.

A distinction must also be made between 'folk tale' and 'fairy tale', for in spite of their frequent interchangeability, the terms have distinct etymologies and meanings. The words fairy tale can refer to both a category of oral folk tale and a genre of prose literature. As a term, it is often used by folk narrative scholars when referring specifically to 'magic tales', or tales listed under tale-type numbers 300–749 in the *Aarne–Thompson index. The term folk tale is reserved for any tale deriving from or existing in oral tradition and is generally preferred by folklorists and anthropologists. Literary scholars tend to use the word fairy tale to refer to a genre of prose literature, which may or may not be based on oral tradition.

Fairy tale is a translation of the French *conte de fée*, a form of oral narrative that became fashionable among the men and women of the French court in the late 17th century. The term first appeared in the title of Mme d'*Aulnoy's 1697 collection of tales and has been in the English language since the middle of the 18th century. The German word *Märchen* is a diminutive form of the Old High German *mär*, meaning report or story. In German academic and popular usage *Märchen* refers to the literary fairy tale as well as the traditional folk tale. Folk tale is a translation of *Volksmärchen* and first appeared in the English language in the 19th century. Although the word was not coined by him, 'Volksmärchen' first appeared in Johann Karl August *Musäus's *Volksmärchen der Deutschen* (*Folk Tales of the Germans*) published between 1782 and 1786.

The association of traditional narrative with *das Volk*, first articulated by Johann Gottfried Herder and later reinforced by the *Grimms, reflected a growing appreciation of the significance of folk culture for the development of the nation-state in the late 18th and early 19th centuries. For Herder, *Volkspoesie* (folk poetry) included all genres of literature and was synonymous with *Naturpoesie* (nature poetry), poetry that was natural and spontaneous. In contrast to *Kunstpoesie* (art poetry), literature produced by conscious creation, folk poetry represented the most sublime expression of the nation. Although Herder considered Homer and Shakespeare great folk poets, he believed folk poetry to be best preserved among the unlettered peasants, who had been least affected by the force of modern civilization. The Grimms fit the fairy tale into Herder's conceptual framework, distinguishing between *Volksmärchen* (folk tales) and *Kunstmärchen* (artistic or literary fairy tales) in their effort to establish the authenticity of their material, and set themselves apart from contemporary writers of fairy tales, who freely adapted folk tales for their own artistic creations. With the Grimms, the folk tale became exclusively associated with a narrative of anonymous origin existing in oral tradition.

2. Definition of a genre

Since the inception of folklore study, scholars have attempted to define the *Märchen* from different vantage points. The following definitions are not meant to be exhaustive, but to indicate the extent to which the problem of description and definition reflects different emphases in folk narrative research. The Grimms' holistic understanding of folk literature, evident in the inclusion of fables, legends, and anecdotes in their *Kinder- und Hausmärchen* (*Children's and Household Tales*), did not generate nuanced definitions on genre. Although the earliest statement on genre was Jacob Grimm's observation that 'the fairy tale is more poetic, the legend more historical', it was an idea that remained largely undeveloped. Following in the tradition of the Grimms, Johannes Bolte observed that since Herder and the Grimms, 'the *Märchen* has been understood as a tale created from poetic fantasy, particularly from the world of magic; it is a wonder story not concerned with the conditions of real life.' Kurt Ranke, founder of the *Enzyklopädie des Märchens*, adopted a similar view, defining the folk tale as 'a magic narrative that is independent of the conditions of the real world with its categories of time, place, and causality, and which has no claim to believability'. Stith Thompson, the American folklorist who published a six-volume index of motifs in folk literature and was convinced of the centrality of the motif as an element of folk tale analysis, defined the folk tale as 'a tale of some length involving a succession of motifs or episodes. It moves in an unreal world without definite locality or definite characters and is filled with the marvellous. In this never-never land humble heroes kill adversaries, succeed to kingdoms and marry princesses'. The Russian formalist Vladimir Propp viewed the fairy tale morphologically, that is, in terms of its component parts and their relationship to the overall structure of the tale. He suggested that 'any narrative can be a wonder tale that develops from an act of injury or state of lack, through certain mediating functions, to an eventual wedding or other concluding function'. The Swiss folklorist and professor of European literature Max Lüthi held that the *Märchen* was a 'universal adventure story with a clever and sublime style'. After nearly 200 years interest in the fairy tale has not been exhausted and scholarly definitions will continue to evolve as new perspectives and approaches are explored.

3. Methods of research and analysis

Scholarly interest in the fairy tale at the beginning of the 19th century was fuelled by Herder's appeal for the collection of folk literature and by the Grimms' belief that the custom of storytelling was on the decline. The study of the fairy tale began as part of a cultural and nationalist project to preserve and revive the German national spirit through its folk literature. From the beginning, fairy-tale research was text-centred: oral tradition was rendered as text, preserved in archives and published in collections for general as well as academic reading audiences. Only towards the middle of the 20th century did this paradigm, with the aid of modern recording technologies, yield to more context-sensitive and performance-centred aspects of storytelling.

The earliest type of fairy-tale scholarship was comparative in nature and grew out of the Grimms' understanding of oral tradition and interest in the problems of language and origin. Their study of comparative linguistics and mythology led them to believe that folk tales were the inheritance of a common Indo-European past containing 'fragments of belief dating back to the most ancient times'. Although their purpose in publishing the *Children's and Household Tales* was as a contribution to the history of German literature, they understood German folk narrative as part of an Indo-European cultural inheritance and were, therefore, also interested in the folk tales of other areas of Europe. Their appreciation of regional and cultural variation led to the publication in 1822 of a third volume of critical annotations, including notes on sources and variants of tales not included in the two volumes of *Household Tales*. The volume was significantly expanded in later editions and laid the foundation for subsequent comparative work.

Comparative folk-tale analysis continued into the early part of the 20th century through the efforts of Johannes Bolte and Georg Polívka, who elaborated upon the Grimms' critical notes in *Anmerkungen zu den* Kinder- und Hausmärchen *der Brüder Grimm* (*Annotations to the* Children's and Household Tales *of the Brothers Grimm*). Their five-volume work provided a more detailed list of variants and additional explanations to the texts and sources contained in the Grimms' third volume. It was with the historical-geographic method, a direction of folk-tale research developed by Finnish folklorists towards the end of the 19th century, that comparative analysis reached its apex. This method, which constituted the predominant research paradigm in the first half of the 20th century, was predicated on the assumption that every folk tale had a single origin (monogenesis), which could be determined by assembling all known oral and print versions and plotting the distribution of the tale over time and space. Versions of tales were broken down into their component parts called 'motifs' and then compared with one another. The goal

of this type of research was to arrive at the *Urform* (original or primeval form), which was believed to be the original tale. In addition to introducing key analytic concepts, an internationally recognized classification system, and rigorous methodological practice to the study of the folk tale, the other important contribution of this approach was the publication of *The Types of the Folktale* and *Motif Index of Folk Literature*, which remains the standard reference work for comparative scholarship.

Some of the most important research in the 20th century has come from European and American literary scholars, who introduced new methods of literary criticism to the study of the fairy tale. While remaining text-centred, these approaches have been innovative in the exploration of the fairy tale's form, style, and meaning. One type of comparative analysis, developed in the 1920s by Vladimir Propp, applied formalist criticism to Aleksandr *Afanasyev's collection of Russian fairy tales. Rather than examining the content of many versions of the same folk tale through the vehicle of the 'motif', a concept which he considered unscientific, Propp shifted the focus of analysis to the narrative structure of different folk tales. He determined that every folk tale consists of sequentially ordered 'functions', defined as the actions of a character as they relate to the development of the tale's plot, and numbering no more than 31 in a given tale.

The Swiss folklorist Max Lüthi employed the critical vocabulary of art historians in his examination of the folk tale as a particular art form. The style of the folk tale, according to Lüthi, is characterized by one-dimensionality (the unproblematic movement between real and enchanted worlds); depthlessness (absence of psychological feeling or motivation on the part of the fairy-tale characters); abstraction (lack of realistic detail and a tendency toward extremes, contrasts, and fixed formulas); and isolation and universal connection (abstract character types with no sustained relationships to other characters). A lively and productive re-examination of the Grimms' *Children's and Household*

Tales centred on the publication of John Ellis's *One Fairy Story Too Many* and continued through the 200-year anniversary observation of the births of Jacob and Wilhelm Grimm in 1984 and 1986. Important critical studies of this period include Jack Zipes's psycho-biographical examination of the life and work of the Grimms, and the feminist analyses of Maria Tatar and Ruth B. Bottigheimer, exploring the Grimms' editorial practices and gender-specific treatment of fairy-tale characters.

4. European fairy-tale scholarship

The purpose of this section is not to treat the collective efforts or research emphases of individual scholars or countries in detail, but to sketch in broad strokes the development of fairy-tale scholarship in Europe. Although the fairy tale has been the most extensively studied of folklore genres, it has not received equal critical attention and appreciation across Europe. Ironically, serious study of the genre faltered in areas where the earliest collections had appeared, and some of the most significant impulses for fairy-tale research have come from countries where interest in the genre was a relatively late development.

The formal study of the fairy tale began in Germany with Jacob and Wilhelm Grimm, whose statements on methodology and critical notes, including information on narrators and sources, made them the first systematic collectors and scholars in the field. The *Children's and Household Tales* exerted a powerful normative effect on oral tradition as well as on folk-tale collection and scholarship in other European countries. German scholars since the Grimms have continued to play a leading role, and until mid-century, German was the academic lingua franca for European folk-narrative research. The Finnish folklorist Antti Aarne published his tale-type index in German (*Verzeichnis der Märchentypen*) and the multi-volume *Enzyklopädie des Märchens*, based at the University of Göttingen, is published in German, although many of its contributors and users are not native German speakers. German scholars have also taken the lead in international institution-building. In 1957 Kurt Ranke, who laid the groundwork for the encyclopedia and served as its general editor until his death, founded the journal *Fabula*, dedicated to folk-narrative research. Ranke was also instrumental in organizing the International Society for Folk Narrative Research, which has met at regular intervals since the first conferences in 1959 in Kiel and Copenhagen.

In spite of the importance of *Basile and *Straparola for the development of the European fairy tale, there was relatively little interest in Italian folk literature until the end of the 19th century, when Benedetto Croce (1866–1952) translated Basile's *Pentamerone* from Neapolitan dialect into Italian. The Italian equivalent of the Grimms' *Children's and Household Tales*, *Fiabe italiane*, appeared only in the middle of the 20th century through the effort of the novelist Italo *Calvino (1923–88), who selected, translated, and annotated 200 texts from regional collections that had been published in the 19th century.

A similarly paradoxical situation developed in France, where, until approximately 1870, no fairy-tale collection with critical annotations had appeared, in spite of the fact that France was the first country to undertake a scholarly collection project on folk literature. Although the questionnaire of the Académie celtique, conducted between 1805 and 1814, was primarily concerned with local and historical legends, it also contained questions on the *conte de fée*. The questionnaire predated Jacob Grimm's *Circular wegen der Aufsammlung der Volkspoesie* (*Circular on the Collection of Folk Poetry*) by ten years and may have been the inspiration behind his own appeal for a similar undertaking in Germany. After this initial impulse, interest in the fairy tale dropped off and was not revived until the last quarter of the 19th century. The most significant work was carried out by Paul Sébillot (1846–1918), who edited the *Revue des traditions populaires*, and Emmanuel Cosquin (1841–1921), whose *Contes populaires de Lorraine* has come to be regarded as the French equivalent of the Grimms' classic.

According to Paul Delarue, the 'Golden Age of the French fairy tale' was between 1870 and 1914, and it was followed by a sharp decline in scholarly interest in the genre.

In Great Britain, Thomas Percy's *Reliques of Ancient English Poetry* (1765) had established the predominance of the ballad in the study of folk literature. Although there were early signs of interest in other forms of folk narrative, the impetus for the collection of fairy tales came towards the end of the century from outside the British Isles. None the less, as early as 1825, the Irish antiquarian Thomas Crofton *Croker published *Fairy Legends and Traditions of South Ireland*, a work translated into German by the Grimms. The extent to which Croker was influenced by the Grimms is unclear, but his detailed notes helped establish his collection as the first scholarly fairy-tale collection in Great Britain. Interest in the fairy tale was furthered by Andrew *Lang, the Scottish poet and philologist, who wrote introductions for the English translation of *Perrault's *Popular Tales* (1888) and the Grimms' *Children's and Household Tales* (1909). In addition, Lang published his own 12-volume fairy-tale collection, each named after a colour, beginning with *The Blue Fairy Book* in 1889 and ending with *The Lilac Fairy Book* in 1910. Although criticized for being unscientific, his fairy-tale books were enormously popular and did much to establish popular and academic interest in the fairy tale in Britain. Other late 19th-century scholars working on the fairy tale included several whom the American folklorist Richard Dorson identified as the 'Great Team' of British folklorists. Edwin Sydney Hartland published *English Fairy and Other Folk Tales* in 1890, a collection of English folk narrative based primarily on printed sources, and William Alexander Clouston's *Popular Tales and Fictions: Their Migration and Transformations* (1887) examined the history of the European folk tale.

Of the Scandinavian countries, the most enduring contributions to the development of folk-tale research have come from Finland. Although a Danish fairy-tale collection appeared just two years after the first Danish translation of the Grimms' *Children's and Household Tales*, the fairy tale received less scholarly attention in Denmark than the ballad and legend. In Sweden fairy tales and folk narrative have not fared well against the traditionally stronger interest in folklife. In Finland, interest in the fairy tale was initially overshadowed by the significance attributed to the national epic, the *Kalevala*. Towards the end of the 19th century the first systematic collection of fairy tales was undertaken by Kaarle Krohn, who also produced one of the first comprehensive statements on folklore methodology and, with Antti Aarne, began to develop a system for the classification of international tales. The development of the historical-geographic method, also known as the Finnish method, helped establish Finland as one of the most important European centres for folk-narrative research. Comparative folk-tale research, initiated by the intellectual interests of the Grimms and systematized through the critical annotations of Bolte and Polívka, was institutionalized by Finnish folklorists with the creation of the Aarne–Thompson *Tale-Type Index* and the founding of the Folklore Fellows, the first international association devoted to the study of folk narrative. Although the association itself was short-lived and has only recently been revived, its publication series, *Folklore Fellows' Communications*, has appeared more or less continuously since 1907 and has produced some important monographs and reference works.   MBS

Aarne, Antti, *The Types of the Folktale*, ed. and trans. Stith Thompson (2nd rev. edn., 1961).

Bolte, Johannes, and Polívka, Georg (eds.), *Anmerkungen zu den* Kinder- und Hausmärchen der Brüder Grimm (5 vols.; 1913–32).

Bottigheimer, Ruth B., *Bad Girls and Bold Boys: The Moral and Social Vision of the Grimms' Tales* (1987).

Ellis, John, *One Fairy Story Too Many* (1983).

Lüthi, Max, *The European Folktale: Form and Nature* (1982).

Propp, Vladimir, *The Morphology of the Folktale* (2nd edn., 1968).

Ranke, Kurt, *et al.* (eds.), *Enzyklopädie des Märchens* (1975–).

Tatar, Maria, *The Hard Facts of the Grimms' Fairy Tales* (1987).

Uther, Hans-Jörg (ed.), *The Types of International Folktales: A Classification and Bibliography* (3 vols., 3rd rev. edn., 2004).

Uther, Hans-Jörg, *Handbuch zu den 'Kinder- und Hausmärchen' der Brüder Grimm: Entstehung – Wirkung – Interpretation* (2008).

Thompson, Stith, *Motif Index of Folk Literature* (6 vols., 1932-6, 1955).

Thompson, Stith, *The Folktale* (1946).

Zipes, Jack, *The Brothers Grimm: From Enchanted Forests to the Modern World* (1988).

Zipes, Jack, *Grimm Legacies: The Magic Spell of the Grimms' Folk and Fairy Tales* (2014).

Fontana, Ugo (1921-1985) Prominent Italian illustrator who dedicated his life's work to children's books. From the 1940s until his death, Fontana worked for Italy's major publishers and produced illustrated fairy tales in large formats by such classic authors as Charles *Perrault, Jacob and Wilhelm *Grimm, Hans Christian *Andersen, Ludwig *Bechstein, Oscar *Wilde, and many other important writers of fairy tales. He was especially famous for two long-time book series, *Sonore Fiabe* (*Sonorous Fairy Tales*) and *I popoli e le loro fiabe* (*The People and their Fairy Tales*). His vast knowledge of the history of art was employed to produce sophisticated compositions and amazing interpretations. His dedication to what he considered the greatest challenge—illustrating for children— led him to illustrate more than 250 books. JZ

Grilli, Giorgia and Negrin, Fabian (eds.), *Ugo Fontana: Illustrating for Children* (2014).

'Foolish Wishes, The' ('**Les Souhaits ridicules'**, 1693) A verse fairy tale by Charles *Perrault about a couple who waste wishes from Jupiter. His only tale with mythological characters, it alludes to the Quarrel of the Ancients and the Moderns, and burlesques classical tradition by alternating between noble and vulgar registers.

Jean de La Fontaine had also treated this theme of a popular medieval fabliau. Perrault's silly wish that a sausage grow from the wife's nose recalls the obscene version in which genitalia sprout from the spouses' faces. The warning that his fairy tale is 'hardly delicate' reinforces this sexuality that

supposedly horrifies 'Mademoiselle' of his dedicatory preface. This is a good example of how Perrault adapted ribald folk tales for aristocratic readers.   MLE

Barchilon, Jacques and Flinders, Peter, *Charles Perrault* (1981).

Soriano, Marc, *Les Contes de Perrault* (1968).

Ford, Ford Madox (1873-1939) British author. Among his over 80 books are four for children, three of them written before his 21st birthday. Two of them are quite remarkable, combining classic fairy-tale themes and characters with sometimes poetic, sometimes comic invention. They also comment on—and in one case actually predict— the events of his own life.

Ford's first literary fairy tale, *The Brown Owl*, appeared in 1891, when he was barely 18. It is the story of an energetic young princess whose father has died, leaving her in the charge of an evil magician. She is protected by a brown owl who eventually turns out to be the spirit of her dead father. Two years before this story was written, Ford's father had also died. Ford and his brother went to live with their grandfather, the painter Ford Madox Brown, while their sister Juliet, then only 8, was sent to live with her uncle, William Rossetti, the most practical and conventional member of a very bohemian family. It seems possible that in this story Ford was sending a message to his sister Juliet, urging her to let their grandfather Brown, rather than their uncle, take the place of the lost father.

Ford's next literary fairy tale, *The Feather* (1892) is a complex and rambling story which mixes fairy-tale characters with Greek mythology. The protagonist, another independent and enterprising princess, goes on a supernatural voyage to the moon, where Diana lives in a temple made entirely of green cheese. The tale also seems to reflect Ford's courtship of Elsie Martindale, the 15-year-old girl whom he would marry two years later. The king in *The Feather*, like Elsie's rich, highly respectable father, opposes his daughter's suitor.

The Queen who Flew (1894), Ford's best book for children, is lively, imaginative, and highly untraditional. Its heroine, young Queen Elfrida, is subject to a sour, reactionary regent named Lord Blackjowl; later on another unpleasant black-bearded man called King Mark tries to kill her because she has refused to marry him. She escapes from both of these disagreeable father-figures with the help of a talking bat, and in the end marries a ploughman and goes off to live happily ever after in a country cottage. The story foreshadows real events: when Elsie was sent away to the country to put her out of her suitor's reach, she eluded her chaperone and returned to London, where she and Ford were quickly married; he was 20 and she 17. After the wedding, they went to live in the country.

Ford's last juvenile work, *Christina's Fairy Book* (1906), is a collection of stories and poems written for or about his and Elsie's two young daughters, Christina (born 1897) and Katherine (born 1900). Though it has moments of wit and charm, it is weaker and slighter than *The Brown Owl* or *The Feather*, and in many of the tales the fairies are tiny, silly, helpless creatures who wear cowslip caps, as in many then-popular, now forgotten books for children.   AL

Lurie, Alison, 'Ford Madox Ford's Fairy Tales', *Children's Literature*, 8 (1979).

MacShane, Frank (ed.), *Ford Madox Ford: The Critical Heritage* (1972).

Saunders, Max, *Ford Madox Ford: A Dual Life* (1996).

Weiss, Timothy, *Fairy Tale and Romance in Works of Ford Madox Ford* (1984).

Foreman, Michael (1938–) Born in Pakefield, Suffolk, Foreman graduated from the Royal College of Art, London, and lectured in various art schools and colleges between 1963 and 1972. His work as an illustrator has gained him such major awards as the Maschler (1982), the Kate *Greenaway (1983) and the Smarties prize (1993). He has illustrated fairy tales from the European classics—Charles *Perrault (1982), the *Grimms (1978), and Hans Christian *Andersen (1974); folk tales from around the world—Japan, New Zealand, India, Ireland, and Cornwall; and modern fairy tales by Oscar *Wilde, Terry *Jones, and himself (*All the King's Horses*, 1976). Foreman's distinctive fairy-tale illustrations assert their difference from more traditional styles. He works with watercolours and often restricts his palette to blues, browns, or pastels, for example; he makes minimal use of classical perspective, and often layers a scene as a series of planes moving towards a high horizon reminiscent of 19th-century Japanese woodcuts, while vertical lines are curved or wavy and lean away from the perpendicular; figures placed within the scene are abstracted towards caricature or the grotesque—by elongation of figure, by exaggeration of feature and gesture, or by excesses of beauty or ugliness. The style also enables depiction of delicate, lyrical beauty, however, counterpointing or offsetting ugliness or sentimentality in a story. His illustrations not only emphasize thematic implications but also enter into vigorous dialogue with those implications, accentuating their absurdities and monstrosities and exploring their comic potentialities. The often disconcerting effects of line, layout, and comic grotesquerie effectively discompose the spectator, prompting fresh and interrogative responses to the illustrated stories.   JAS

Forsyth, Kate (1966–) Australian author whose *œuvre* includes picture books, poetry (as Kate Humphrey), and novels. The bulk of her writing is fantasy, and she has written several fantasy series for both adults and children. Her best known work is probably *Bitter Greens* (2012), which mixes fairy-tale fantasy and historical fiction to retell the life story of Charlotte-Rose de Caumont de *La Force, author of *Le Contes des contes* (1698). The novel is scaffolded by La Force's 'Persinette' (*'Rapunzel' in the *Grimms' retelling). Forsyth's interest in storytellers is also demonstrated in *The Wild Girl* (2013), an imaginative account of the life of Dortchen Wild up until the time of her marriage to Wilhelm Grimm in 1825. Dortchen had been the source of many of the tales in *Kinder- und Hausmärchen*, and the novel includes scenes in which she tells Wilhelm simple versions of such tales as *'Hansel and

Gretel' and 'The Singing, Springing Lark', or in which they discuss the reception of the tales and processes of revision. For younger readers, Forsyth has collaborated with illustrator Fiona McDonald in *Two Selkie Stories from Scotland* (2014), in which she retells two familiar folktales, 'The Seal Wife' and 'The Seal Hunter'.   RM

Fouqué, Friedrich Freiherr de la Motte (1777–1843) Writer of fiction romanticizing and sentimentalizing the Germanic past. As a youth he was a lieutenant in the Prussian army and later served as an officer in a volunteer corps during the Wars of Liberation from French rule. Ideals of knighthood, chivalry, and noble virtue are a chief object of depiction in his novels, which were much esteemed and highly popular during the Napoleonic period, not least because of their patriotic sentiment. His novels, the most prominent of which were *Der Held des Nordens* (*The Hero of the North*, 1810) and *Der Zauberring* (*The Magical Ring*, 1813), were subsequently eclipsed by the Waverley novels of Walter Scott and their immense international popularity. In contrast to Scott's historical fiction, Fouqué's narratives incorporated a great deal of popular legend, folk superstition, and faith in miracles. A chief and most successful example of this practice of Fouqué's is his *Undine* (1811), a mermaid tale that became a minor world classic. Taking its idea from a treatise by Paracelsus (*c.*1494–1541) on elemental spirits (*Elementargeister*), the story is about a mermaid's receipt of a soul through marriage to a knight, her loss of him then to a haughty mortal woman, and her sorrow over his death in her embrace as, in the end, she wins him back at the moment he is about to join the new wife in the bridal chamber on their wedding night.   JMM

Lillyman, William J., 'Fouqué's Undine', *Studies in Romanticism*, 10 (1971).

Mornin, Edward, 'Some Patriotic Novels and Tales by La Motte Fouqué', *Seminar*, 11 (1975).

fractured fairy tales Traditional fairy tales, rearranged to create new plots with fundamentally different meanings or messages. Fractured fairy tales are closely related to fairy-tale parodies, but the two serve different purposes: parodies mock individual tales and the genre as a whole; fractured fairy tales, with a reforming intent, seek to impart updated social and moral messages.

Changes made to the English tales about *Jack and the giants offer a case in point. In its original chapbook versions, a plucky hero killed a series of (usually cannibalistic) giants, and afterwards enriched himself with their treasures. In the modern reformulation 'Jack and the Beanstalk', Jack's thievery proceeds piecemeal, first the giant's gold, then his golden egg-laying hen, and finally his magical golden harp. Like earlier man-eating giants, the Beanstalk giant also relishes human flesh:

> Fee, Fi, Fo, Fum,
> I smell the blood of an Englishman,
> Be he alive or be he dead,
> I'll grind his bones to make my bread.

The ancient Jack dispatched numerous giants, the Beanstalk Jack only one. Unlike the gorily detailed deaths of his 18th-century predecessors, Jack's 20th-century gigantic foe is neither swiftly decapitated, agonizingly disemboweled, nor stalwartly transfixed, but dies instead in an arranged accident: as the giant pursues Jack down the beanstalk, Jack chops through its trunk, the giant plunges to his death, and Jack and his mother live comfortably on the proceeds of his adventures.

In its fractured version one modern author (Alvin Granowski) reconfigured the Beanstalk's tale elements to present an altogether different message. His tale begins not in the poverty of Jack and his mother's hut, but with Mrs Giant and her husband, Herbert, a friendly old couple dressed in soft pastels, who tell the sad story of Jack's theft of their savings for retirement. Herbert's ritual quatrain now reads

> Fee, Fi, Fo, Fum,
> My wife's cooking is yum, yum, yum.
> Be it baked or be it fried,
> We finish each meal with her tasty pies.

On the final page, Mrs Giant speaks directly to the book's readers and explains that 'giants have feelings, too', and expresses the hope that they would never hurt a giant.

This example of a fractured fairy tale is one among many fairy tales—'The Little Red Hen', 'The Three Billy Goats Gruff', 'Goldilocks', and *'Hansel and Gretel'—that have been fractured and reconstituted to teach self-reliance, avoiding hasty conclusions, respect for others' privacy, and compassion for the old and poor. The process of producing a fractured fairy tale involves decoding a tale's words, motifs, and plot, and encoding them in a new pattern. Such reutilized fairy tales have entered elementary school writing curricula in some American states, such as New York.

In Germany after 1968, many fairy-tale parodies appeared which shared a common intent with fractured fairy tales. 'Hansel and Gretel' lent itself particularly well to character inversions (witch as pensioner, Hansel and Gretel as juvenile delinquents), and the mode was taken up vigorously in new collections, such as Paul Maar's *Der tätowierte Hund* (*The Tattooed Dog*, 1968).   RBB

Granowsky, Alvin (ed.), *Jack and the Beanstalk*, illus. Linda Graves/*Giants Have Feelings, Too*, illus. Henry Buerchkholtz (1996).

France, fairy tales in *See* p. 211.

France, Anatole (pseudonym of Jacques-Anatole-François Thibault, 1844–1924) French poet, novelist, critic, and Nobel laureate (1921). France had an abiding interest in fairy tales. An early story, 'L'Abeille' ('The Bee', 1882), features two young heroes who are eventually united by the King of the Dwarfs. Intended for children, the tale's mythological allusions and erudition appeal to adults as well. 'Dialogue sur les contes de fées' ('Conversation about Fairy Tales'), found in France's celebrated *Le Livre de mon ami* (*My Friend's Book*, 1885), is a passionate defence of the educational value and imaginative power of fairy tales. France's best-known tales are subversive reworkings of Charles *Perrault's *'Bluebeard' and *'Sleeping Beauty'. In 'Les Sept femmes de la Barbe-Bleue d'après des documents authentiques' ('The Seven Wives of Bluebeard according to Authentic Documents', 1909), Bluebeard is the unwitting victim of avaricious and adulterous wives. Here the revisionist narrator 'corrects' the 'errors' in Perrault's account, which he treats as fact rather than fiction. France's wilful confusion of these categories validates fiction by equating it with history and simultaneously undermines history's claims to accuracy and objectivity.   AZ

Bancquart, Marie-Claire, *Anatole France, un sceptique passionné* (1984).

Bresky, Dushan, *The Art of Anatole France* (1969).

Levy, Diane Wolfe, 'History as Art: Ironic Parody in Anatole France's *Les Sept Femmes de la Barbe-Bleue*', *Nineteenth-Century French Studies*, 4 (1976).

Tendron, Edith, *Anatole France inconnu* (1995).

Frank, Natalie (1980–) Talented American painter who has won many awards and has had numerous exhibits of her paintings, which often portray unusual figures and situations based on myths, fairy tales, and legends. In 2015 she held an important exhibition of 75 drawings of the *Grimms' fairy tales at the The Drawing Center in New York City that were also published as a book. In all her illustrations she touches on something raging in these tales that she extrapolates in vivid colours and configurations that transform the narratives into other stories. Instead of mirroring what we want to see, Frank's drawings of recomposed scenes from the Grimms' tales undress the banal charming images of yesteryear and redress the deep issues of the tales in sexually graphic and bizarre postures. Her images expose levels of the Grimms' tales that the Grimms would never have imagined. In short, Frank's drawings are ludic and extravagant, and are filled with distorted characters whose actions contest the canonical status of the Grimms' stories.   JZ

Franklin Brothers, the (Sidney, 1893–1972, and Chester, 1890–1949) Co-creators of silent pantomime films with virtually all-child casts. After a series of short 'kid pictures' they graduated to the Fox Film

France, fairy tales in (17th century to present) France has a long, rich, and diverse tradition of literary fairy tales.

Although the 'conte de fées' (fairy tale) first appeared so named at the end of the 17th century, what we would now call fairy-tale motifs are evident from the very beginnings of a written literature in French. Wonder tales and their elements are found throughout the fables and exempla used by the medieval Church. The 'marvellous' is also very much in evidence in medieval secular literature such as the *Lais* of *Marie de France, numerous *chansons de geste* (e.g. 'Huon de Bordeaux'), chivalric romances (e.g. those by Chrétien de Troyes), and plays, as well as in Renaissance prose fiction (e.g. Rabelais, du Fail, des Périers, *Cent nouvelles nouvelles*). Like the later literary fairy tales, almost all these precursors adapt motifs found in oral traditions. Yet, if the fairy tales that began to appear in France during the 1690s are part of a long-standing literary tradition, they were recognized at the time as being something new and different as well: these stories rework (what are presented as) indigenous, 'popular' narratives at a time when the dominant literary aesthetic prescribed ancient Greek and Roman models, and they unabashedly offer for adult consumption narratives readily associated with children.

1. BIRTH OF A GENRE: 1690–1715

Although Marie-Catherine d'*Aulnoy holds the distinction of publishing the first literary fairy tale in France ('L'Île de la félicité' ('The Island of Happiness'), published in her novel *L'Histoire d'Hypolite, comte de Duglas*, 1690), the flowering of the genre is actually a collective phenomenon. From at least the mid-17th century, members of Parisian salons and perhaps even the French court had played a society game in which they told stories (supposedly) resembling those of governesses and nurses. Once fairy tales along these lines began to be published, they appeared rapidly in what is best described as a 'vogue'. After a few more isolated stories (by d'Aulnoy, Catherine *Bernard, Marie-Jeanne *Lhéritier de Villandon, and Charles *Perrault), between 1697 and 1700 eight collections (by Louise d'*Auneuil, d'Aulnoy, Rose de *La Force, Jean de *Mailly, Henriette-Julie de *Murat, and Perrault) appeared with over 75 tales in all. Women writers dominated the vogue, with two-thirds of the tales published between 1690 and 1715 to their credit, which suggests that the genre offered them a means of expression and experimentation not available through other established literary forms. It was also women who coined the very expression 'conte de fées' (found in the title to d'Aulnoy's 1697–8 collection, *Les Contes des fées*, and Murat's 1698 *Nouveaux contes de fées*), which was translated to give the English 'tales of the fairies' (1699) and eventually 'fairy tale' (1724).

Perhaps most enduring legacy of the vogue was the mythic origin and the aesthetic its initiators created for the genre. Frontispieces and prefaces accompanying d'Aulnoy's, Lhéritier's, and Perrault's tales model the *conte* *de fées* on the storytelling by grandmothers, governesses, and nurses to young children. However real such storytelling may have been at the time and however undeniable the resemblance many *contes de fées* bear to folkloric narratives, the vogue's intertextual sources are diverse and decidedly literary. More than by oral traditions, the fairy tales of the first vogue were influenced directly or indirectly by Italian models, including the tales of *Straparola and *Basile but also the marvellous characters and episodes in works by Ariosto, Boiardo, and Tasso. The fairies, chivalry, and star-crossed lovers of these Italian sources provided the material with which to create a (hitherto non-existent) fairy-tale aesthetic that exerted considerable influence on subsequent fairy tales. As studied by Raymonde Robert, this aesthetic includes three components, which are found in most French fairy tales of the 17th and 18th centuries: (1) the tales state from the very outset that the hero and heroine will ultimately triumph over their adversaries; (2) they highlight the exemplary moral and social destiny of the heroic couple; and (3) they establish the self-sufficiency of the marvellous universe. For writers and readers of late 17th-century France, both the fairy tale's mythic origin and its aesthetic served a particular ideological function. The archetypal storytelling of lower-class women assimilated the popular oral tradition into élite literary practice so as to obscure the reality of hierarchical social relations. At the same time, the seemingly fantastical aesthetic of the *contes de fées* none the less served to celebrate the values of the self-contained social elite of late 17th-century France, values which are readily visible in characters and descriptions. Only in tales by Perrault and Eustache *Le Noble are the protagonists of this first vogue not royalty, and the other writers frequently incorporate the discovery of noble birth as a plot motif. Throughout these fairy tales, lengthy and tedious descriptions of luxurious settings recall (sometimes directly) the French court at Versailles. Given that French aristocrats and the court were experiencing severe economic difficulties at the time, both the protagonists and the settings of these fairy tales suggest that the genre was at least in part a form of compensation or escape from the pressures of the real.

Paradoxically, this aesthetic is much less evident in the most famous tales of the first vogue, those by Charles Perrault, than in those of his contemporaries. In fact, Perrault's are the most atypical of the first vogue. Unlike the other *contes de fées*, only half include a romantic plot, and almost all resemble folkloric tale types. Most distinctively, Perrault's *Histoires ou contes du temps passé* (*Stories or Tales from Past Times*, 1697), or *Contes de ma Mère l'Oye* (*Mother Goose Tales) as they are perhaps best known, feature an infantilizing narrative voice and a succinct neo-classical French style with limited description. Combined, these traits led 19th- and early 20th-century folklorists and literary critics to consecrate Perrault's enormously popular tales as the cultural monument they had already become through reprints and chapbooks. So doing, however, scholars exaggerated Perrault's 'faithfulness' to the oral tradition and oversimplified the tales' complex ideological and psychological meanings. The appearance of Marc Soriano's seminal *Les Contes de Perrault* (1968) addressed these issues straight-on and cleared the way for a critical reassessment of Perrault and his tales by historians, psychologists, semioticians, and feminists, among others. All of these approaches continue to shed light on the enduring popularity of Perrault's tales not only in France but throughout the world.

In spite of their instant success, the *Mother Goose Tales* did not inspire direct imitations among writers of fairy tales in 17th- and 18th-century France. Contrary to what is often asserted, the other writers were not following Perrault's but a different and parallel path. To be sure, like Perrault's, many of their tales can be traced (probably indirectly) to folkloric sources; yet, they are also far more indebted to motifs from novels and make more prominent use of magic characters and settings. While Perrault's collection was recognized from the beginning as being exceptional, if not inimitable, many tales by his contemporaries were no less popular well into the 19th century. Almost all of the fairy tales published between 1690 and 1715 were republished and anthologized later in the 18th century, but d'Aulnoy's tales came the closest to matching the popularity of the *Mother Goose Tales*. None the less, Perrault's and d'Aulnoy's fairy tales were popular for different reasons. Whereas the concision of Perrault's tales made them accessible to children and their irony simultaneously appealed to adults, d'Aulnoy's expansiveness, both in style and descriptions (e.g. variety of animals), resonated with adult readers steeped in the adventure novels popular at the time. And whereas Perrault recycles an age-old *gaulois* humour replete with misogynistic jibes, d'Aulnoy, like several other of the women writers of fairy tales, gives central billing to heroines and mothers, thereby probably appealing to women, the most avid readers of novels.

Notwithstanding the differences among their tales, all of these writers were conscious of developing a fashionable literary form for an élite public. Following the literary convention of their time, most of them presented their tales as 'pleasing' in order to be 'instructive', although their most immediate imperative was to create 'bagatelles' ('trifles') that entertained readers. Only a few critics took the trouble to dignify what they doubtless saw as a marginal and passing phenomenon, among them the austere abbé de Villiers, who in 1699 virulently denounced 'this heap of tales that has plagued us for a year or two'. What this dismissive critic failed—or refused—to see was that the vogue was by no means insignificant, and this for two reasons. First, it was intricately linked to the 'Quarrel of the Ancients and the Moderns' that was shaking French cultural life at this time. In separate manifestos, both Perrault and his niece Lhéritier argue that the literary fairy tale demonstrates the superiority of indigenous French culture over ancient Greek and Roman models. And, implicitly, all the fairy tales from this period illustrate the 'modernist' position. Secondly, the vogue cleared the way for new forms of fantasy fiction in 18th-century France, fantasy that is based only minimally on indigenous oral traditions and even less on Greek and Roman mythology and that is put to an ever-wider array of uses, from humorous escapism to social and political critique.

2. THE SECOND VOGUE: 1722–78

Although a steady stream of fairy tales appeared over a period of almost 100 years (1690–1778), it is useful to distinguish between the 17th- and 18th-century manifestations of the genre. After the explosion of 1697–1700, fairy tales were not published with anything resembling the same intensity until the 1740s. Overall, more tales appeared during the second vogue (approximately 144 between 1722 and 1778) than during the first (approximately 114). This increase in quantity was matched by an increase in diversity. In 18th-century France, the genre blossomed into a myriad of forms, including oriental, sentimental, philosophical, parodic, satirical, pornographic, and didactic tales. This diversity is an indication of the distinct social and intellectual groups that produced fairy tales in this period, as opposed to the collective effort that provided the impetus for the earlier vogue. Many of the 17th-century writers knew each other, met regularly in the same salons, and in some instances engaged in friendly competition with each other to compose stories based on the same plot (e.g. 'Les Fées' ('The *Fairies') by Perrault and 'Les Enchantements de l'éloquence' by Lhéritier). The same cannot necessarily be said of the 18th-century writers. Gatherings such as the salons of the duchesse du Maine at Sceaux, of Mme Le Marchand, and of Mlle Quinault, and the 'Société du bout du banc' were responsible for some of the fairy tales published during the second vogue (for example, Jean-Jacques *Rousseau probably composed 'La Reine Fantasque' for the salon of Mlle Quinault); but the majority of the writers of the second vogue conceived and published their tales independently. Moreover, a much smaller proportion of the 18th-century tales were written by women than during the first vogue, suggesting that the *conte de fées* had entered the male-dominated literary mainstream.

While respecting the aesthetic defined by their 17th-century predecessors, the 18th-century writers also produced fairy tales with far fewer discernible folkloric traces (one-tenth of the second vogue vs. one-half of the first vogue). It is a measure of both the genre's development and the changing literary climate that writers increasingly used it to give free rein to their imaginations rather than to adapt extant oral and written traditions. Numerous are the novel-like fairy tales that continue to rely on the sentimental romance scheme so frequently employed by the 17th-century women writers. However, in stories by Philippe de *Caylus, Marie-Antoin-ette *Fagnan, Louise *Levesque, Catherine de *Lintot, Mlle de *Lubert, Henri *Pajon, Gabrielle-Suzanne de *Villeneuve, and others, stock fairy-tale features are exaggerated and/or complicated; for instance, conflicts among good and evil fairies are sharply accentuated and the obstacles to the lovers' union become dizzyingly complex. Less apparent in these particular tales is the didactic imperative that their 17th-century counterparts seek to uphold, even if only superficially. Indeed, prefaces by Lintot and Lubert define the genre for the first time as pleasurable, but not necessarily instructive. This shift by no means implies that the 18th-century *conte de fées* was devoid of ideological, social, or philosophical import; rather, the ludic pleasure of fairy-tale writing, only timidly and discreetly suggested during the first vogue, was openly recognized and accepted during the second vogue.

In addition to these novel-like fairy tales, the 18th century produced other strains unlike those of the earlier period. Perhaps the single most significant of these is the *oriental tale. Between the first and second vogues appeared the immensely popular 12-volume translation/adaptation of The *Arabian Nights* (*Les Mille et une nuits*, 1704–17) by Antoine *Galland, which included the first (and most influential) version in a Western European language of such famous stories as *'Aladdin and the Magic Lamp', *'Ali Baba', and 'The Voyages of Sindbad'. If the fairy tales of the first vogue laid the groundwork for Galland's best-seller, this work in turn rekindled interest in the *conte de fées* and spawned stories that incorporate vaguely 'oriental' motifs, characters, and decors. More often than not, such oriental 'material' is superimposed upon Western European folklore, as in Thomas-Simon Gueulette's *Mille et un quarts d'heure* (*Thousand and One Quarter-Hours*, 1715) and the abbé de Bignon's *Aventures d'Abdallah* (*Adventures of Abdallah*, 1712–14). The reverse is apparent in Gueulette's *Soirées bretonnes* (*Breton Evenings*, 1712) in which authentic 'oriental' folklore is given French dress. Arguably, the vast numbers and immense popularity of 18th-century oriental wonder tales played a decisive role in the development of Western European 'orientalist' stereotypes that not only found their way into literary works of social critique (such as Montesquieu's *Lettres persanes* and *Voltaire's *Zadig*) but that also prepared the way, ideologically, for 19th-century European colonial expansion into North Africa and the Middle East.

No less numerous than the oriental tales were the 18th-century satirical and 'licentious' (or pornographic) tales. The *conte de fées* was hardly the only literary form to include satire and 'licentious' descriptions at this time. Yet, the genre's predictable structures and moralizing pretext lent themselves particularly well to these subversive uses. Capitalizing on its (purported) innocence, writers such as Louis de Cahusac, Jacques *Cazotte, Claude-Prosper de *Crébillon fils, Charles *Duclos, Charles de *La Morlière, Rousseau, Henri-Charles de Senneterre, and Claude-Henri de *Voisenon satirize religious and political personages and, occasionally, social and philosophical norms. In tales by Cahusac, Crébillon, Senneterre, and Voisenon especially, such satire is put in starker relief—or overshadowed—by (usually euphemistic) anatomical and sexual descriptions. Although often highly coded, the critique in these tales is conveyed through blatantly obvious humour. In addition, several *contes de fées* are explicit illustrations of Enlightenment thought (e.g. La Morlière, *Angola* (1746) and Rousseau, 'La Reine Fantasque' (1754)). On the whole, however, these tales are by no means the most radical form of social and political critique in pre-Revolutionary France, but instead portray the mores of the most privileged classes.

Central to the satirical and pornographic tales is parody of the fairy tale itself. Indeed, the humour in these strains of fairy-tale writing derives from ridiculing the characters, descriptions, and plots used so frequently during the first vogue. Parody was not a uniquely 18th-century phenomenon, however. In the midst of the first vogue, Anthony *Hamilton wrote three fairy-tale parodies (1703–4), although they were only published some 30 years later. In addition, two short fairy-tale comedies (one by Dancourt and another by Dufreny de la Rivière), staged in 1699, poke fun at fairies and their magic. Yet, it was only during the second vogue that the fairy-tale aesthetic was sufficiently well established to inspire numerous parodies. If the line between 'serious' and 'parodic' fairy tales is not always clear because some writers, notably Mlle de Lubert, delight in exaggerating the already hyperbolic features of the genre, several writers nevertheless state an unequivocal parodic intent through meta-commentaries on the stories made by storyteller and listeners (e.g. Crébillon's 'Ah quel conte!' and Rousseau's 'La Reine Fantasque'). That nearly one-third of all 18th-century fairy tales employ parody demonstrates the genre's significant contribution to the increasingly self-reflexive literature of this period.

Decidedly 'serious' and unparodic are the tales in Marie *Leprince de Beaumont's *Magasin des enfants* (*Young Misses Magazine*, 1757), which includes the most famous version of 'La Belle et la bête' (*'Beauty and the Beast'). These stories break with the established tradition of French fairy tales and blaze a new—and henceforth, dominant—path for the genre. Often considered to be the inaugural text of French children's literature, this primer written for English schoolgirls learning French is one of only two collections of tales written explicitly and exclusively for children during both the first and second vogues (the other is *Fénelon's *Fables*, published posthumously in 1718). For the most part, Leprince de Beaumont's collection adapts—that is, reduces and simplifies—previously published fairy tales (her version of 'Beauty and the Beast' is a rewriting of a longer and more complex tale by Villeneuve) and always presents a clear moral lesson for each of the stories. Alternating between fairy tales and Bible stories, this text features a series of conversations between a governess and young girls who draw practical moral lessons from the stories told. Such an explicitly pedagogical approach shifted emphasis away from the genre's aristocratic roots and promoted a complex of bourgeois Christian values that was to be at the core of 19th-century children's literature. In her own way, then, Leprince de Beaumont reinvigorated the injunction to 'please' and 'instruct' that was used by writers of the first vogue to justify the newly created genre but that was quickly and conveniently ignored as a conventional common-place. Coming at the very end of the second vogue (only two short tales, by Rétif de la Bretonne, were to appear after hers), Leprince de Beaumont's *Magasin des enfants* created a new model for fairy-tale writing in France. The pedagogical imperative it upholds even became a determining factor in the republication of fairy tales from the first and second vogues. At the end of the 18th century, when Charles-Joseph de *Mayer edited the massive 40-volume *Cabinet des fées* (1785–9), he was careful to defend the genre as being morally instructive and, simultaneously, to exclude almost all parodic and 'licentious' tales.

Notwithstanding these attempts to rejuvenate it, the *conte de fées* had been used overwhelmingly throughout the 17th and 18th centuries to advocate an aristocratic ethos incompatible with emerging democratic ideals. And so it is understandable that, by the time of the Revolution, writers had long since ceased publishing fairy tales.

3. THE 19TH CENTURY

Early 19th-century France did not share the enthusiasm for the literary fairy tale that swept romantic Germany. In France, unlike in Germany, folk and fairy tales were not used as a means of defining a national 'essence'. (Ironically, though, the 17th- and 18th-century *contes de fées* were an important source of inspiration for writers of the German romantic *Märchen*.) There was also resistance to including fairy tales in the growing corpus of children's literature. Several 18th- and early 19th-century writers for children, including Stéphanie-Félicité de Genlis, Arnaud Berquin, and J.-N. Bouilly were openly critical of the literary fairy tale. Some writers, such as Genlis and Berquin, were highly suspicious of fairy-tale magic and instead depicted natural wonders and Christian virtues. Institutional control of children's literature also thwarted the genre. Officially sanctioned children's literature for use in schools was controlled until 1871 largely by the Church, which was hostile to the idea of giving schoolchildren fiction, not to mention fairy tales. After the birth of the Third Republic (1871), control over schoolbooks was assumed by the State, whose ideological criteria were no less rigid than the Church's had been (although they were obviously of a different nature). The result was that little changed for the genre.

In spite of these obstacles, the fairy tale had a significant impact on readers from all walks of life, from the Parisian bourgeoisie to the provincial peasantry. With improvements in mechanical printing techniques came ever-cheaper and more widely distributed chapbook and broadsheet versions of fairy tales, especially—but not exclusively—of Perrault's *Mother Goose Tales*. Although they had appeared throughout the 18th century, these versions literally flooded 19th-century France (e.g. those published by the Oudot family of Troyes and the Imagerie d'Épinal), and it is difficult to overstate their importance. They transformed a small group of tales into 'classics' and engraved them into the collective French consciousness. They also had a knock-back effect on the very oral tradition from which the fairy tales had been adapted—mostly indirectly—in the first place. No less consequential was the conception of the genre they promoted: the *conte de fées*, like many of the texts in the *Bibliothèque bleue*, was reduced to the status of a didactic tool that promoted conservative social norms.

At the same time as republishing existing fairy tales, 19th-century France made its own contributions to the genre. Since they were excluded from both Church- and State-sanctioned school curricula, *contes de fées* were published for domestic consumption. Among the most notable of collections were those produced by Pierre-Jules Hetzel, perhaps the most prominent editor/publisher of secular, non-official children's literature during the first half of the century. Besides a collection of 40 tales from the *Cabinet des fées Livre des enfants* (*The Children's Book*), 1837, he published the *Le Nouveau Magasin des enfants* (*The New Children's Magazine*, 1844), which includes stories by Hans Christian *Andersen but also by many of the period's best-known French writers, including Honoré de Balzac, Alexandre Dumas père, Alfred de Musset, Charles *Nodier, and George *Sand. In addition to displaying their authors' deft use of a simple and direct style, the tales anthologized in this latter collection combine social realism with romantic fantasy. On the one hand, they repeatedly insist on the dignity of the economically disenfranchised; on the other, they depict a fantastical flight from modern life. Given the progressive bent (by the period's standards) of many of these tales, it is not surprising that they remained on the periphery of 19th-century French children's literature.

More prominent were collections by two women writers, George Sand and the comtesse de *Ségur. Although Sand's *Contes d'une grand-mère* (*Tales of a Grandmother*), 1876 and Ségur's *Nouveaux Contes de fées* (*New Fairy Tales*), 1857 share some superficial similarities (e.g. the minimal use of folkloric tale types and the nostalgic representation of country life), most aspects of their tales evince two very different conceptions of the genre. Sand's tales are by her own admission addressed to both children and adults and incorporate many of the philosophical and even scientific theories of her time. They are complex narratives that reveal a tension between social realism and nostalgic fantasy: Sand attempts to reconcile contemporary settings and characters with a muted fairy-tale magic and an idealized country existence. Very different are the seven tales in Ségur's collection. Written explicitly for children in a simple, direct style, Ségur's fairy tales utilize interdiction-transgression plots in order to convey a clear moral didacticism. In contrast with Sand and the other contributors to *Le Nouveau Magasin des enfants*, Ségur gives scant attention to social problems but instead presents ethical dilemmas, solutions of which are meant to uphold solid bourgeois values. The publication history of Ségur's volume further distinguishes it from Sand's. Whereas Sand was already a successful writer when she published her tales (first individually and then as a collection) and continued to incorporate fairy-tale motifs in subsequent works for both adults and children, Ségur used her *Nouveaux Contes de fées* to test the market before embarking on her phenomenally successful career as a writer of children's literature. However, never again did she return to the fairy tale.

Sand's and Ségur's examples notwithstanding, fairy tales constituted a relatively small portion of the overall output of children's literature by 19th-century French writers. Far more numerous were the fairy tales that were written for adults during the second half of the century by writers such as Paul *Arène, Théodore de *Banville, Anatole *France, Jules *Lemaître, Léo Lespès, Jean *Lorrain, and Catulle *Mendès. Between 1862 and 1922, approximately 500 tales were published in what might best be termed a third vogue. Issuing from the 'decadent' movement, this corpus of *contes de fées* departs sharply from the earlier vogues. Whereas the 17th- and 18th-century vogues respect the same basic aesthetic, the 19th-century 'decadent' tales meld literary naturalism with the marvellous. The result is fairy tales that undermine the self-sufficient, other-worldly universe so typical of the genre up to this point. The marvellous no longer comforts and reassures but rather disturbs and threatens as eroticism, ugliness, and sex wars take centre stage. In further contrast to their 17th- and especially 18th-century predecessors, the 19th-century writers do not create new plot scenarios as much as they rework Perrault's *Mother Goose Tales* by imagining sequels, developing minor characters or details, and juxtaposing fairy-tale and realistic settings. Their narrators also eschew the feigned naïveté of the earlier *contes de fées* in favour of a (supposedly) positivistic erudition, claiming to uncover intentions and details left unstated in the original. As the irony of this narrative stance indicates (obtaining as it does in wonder tales), this third vogue was in fact a reaction against the hegemony of science and realism in the late 19th century. Given a similar reaction in late 20th-century culture, it is perhaps not unexpected that many narrative features of the 'decadent' *contes de fées* reappear in contemporary fairy tales (particularly in English), even if the fin-de-siècle corpus seems to have had only a limited influence on subsequent writers.

4. THE 20TH CENTURY

As the 'decadent' movement waned, the literary fairy tale was reshaped by important institutional and scholarly developments. Beginning in the 1880s, fairy tales started to appear on recommended reading lists for pre-school and elementary school children. And to meet this need new collections were published, such as those by Maurice Bouchor (*Les Contes transcrits d'après la tradition française*, (*Tales Transcribed from the French Tradition*, 1911–13)), which aim to defend secular Republican ideals while simplifying the language and toning down the violence of his originals. More important still was the rise of folkloristics. During the period 1870–1914, folklorists hurried to transcribe oral narratives from regions all over France, aware that their country was far behind the similar projects of other European nations. If these transcriptions were intended primarily as enthnographic evidence affirming regional identity (in opposition to central State authority), many of them served as the basis for popularized series of folk tales. Among the most famous of these are Henri *Pourrat's *Le Trésor des contes* (*Treasury of Tales*, 1948–62), which in spite of Pourrat's claims are in fact artful retellings of folk tales, and the ongoing Gallimard collection *Récits et contes populaires* (*Popular Stories and Tales*), edited by Jean Cuisenier.

In scholarly circles, the painstaking fieldwork of fin-de-siècle folklorists culminated in the catalogue *Le Conte populaire français* (1957–85) by Paul Delarue and Marie-Louise Tenèze, which uses the *Aarne–Thompson index to classify French and Francophone oral narratives and is enormously useful to students of French folklore and literary fairy tales alike. Over the past 30 years, the fairy tale has become an increasingly dynamic field of study in France and has attracted scholars from a variety of disciplines and approaches, including literary criticism (Marc Soriano, Raymonde Robert), psychoanalysis (Jean Bellemin-Noël, François Flahault), semiotics (Claude Brémond, Louis Marin), and history (Catherine Velay-Vallantin).

For writers of the literary fairy tale, the 20th century has been no less productive than for folklorists and pedagogues. During the first half of the century, several major literary figures, notably Guillaume *Apollinaire and Jean *Cocteau, produced fairy-tale works designed, most decidedly, for adults. In different ways, both Apollinaire (poems in *Alcools* (1913) and *Calligrammes* (1918)) and Cocteau (film, *La Belle et la bête* (*Beauty and the Beast*, 1946)) were prominent exponents of the search for alternatives to conventional experience and reality and found in the fairy tale a convenient cultural reference for their projects. But it is for children that the vast majority of fairy tales have been written during the 20th century. Renowned series of children's books, such as the stories of Babar (created by Jean and François de Brunhoff) and Père Castor (created by Paul Faucher), both inaugurated in the 1930s, employ fairy-tale-like motifs and characters, even if they are not fairy tales in the strictest (i.e. folkloric) sense of the word. Moreover, the fairy tale has been the form of choice for scores of writers who devoted only part of their work to children's literature. Among the most significant of these are Marcel *Aymé, *Les Contes du chat perché* (*Tales of the Perched Cat*, 1937–9); Béatrix Beck, *Contes à l'enfant né coiffé* (*Tales for the Child Born with a Hairdo*, 1953); Léonce Bourliaguet, *Contes de la folle avoine* (*Wild Oat Tales*, 1946); Blaise Cendrars, *Petits contes nègres pour les enfants des blancs* (*African Tales for White Children*, 1928); Étienne *Delessert, *Comment la souris reçoit une pierre sur la tête et découvre le monde* (*How a Rock Falls on the Head of the Mouse and It Discovers the World*, 1961); Paul Éluard, *Grain d'aile* (*Little Wing*, 1951); Maurice *Maeterlinck, *L'Oiseau bleu* (*The *Blue Bird*, play, 1939); Antoine de *Saint-Exupéry, *Le Petit Prince* (*The Little Prince*, 1943); and Jules Supervielle, *La Belle au bois* (*Beauty in the Woods*, 1953).

Almost all of these fairy tales blend magic with realistic settings and psychology. More recent examples of the genre likewise use realism, but also make subversive use of the fairy-tale form. Notable are Philippe *Dumas and Boris Moissard (*Contes à l'envers* (*Upside Down Tales*, 1977)); Pierre *Gripari (*La Sorcière de la rue Mouffetard* (*The Witch of Mouffetard Street*, 1967), *Le Gentil petit diable* (*The Nice Little Devil*, 1984), and *Patrouille du conte* (*The Tale Patrol*, 1983)); Grégoire Solotareff (*Un jour, un loup* (*One Day a Wolf*, 1994)); and Michel *Tournier (*Sept contes* (*Seven Tales*, 1978–80)), who confront ecological, ethical, and social concerns through familiar day-to-day contexts, anti-conformist characters, and role-reversals. None of these writers hesitates to disturb rather than simply comfort young listeners/readers, sometimes through the depiction of vengeance and violence (e.g. Gripari); and all leave the 'moral' of their stories implicit rather than stating it explicitly. While such features underscore the double subversion at work in these tales (subversion of the 'classic' fairy-tale form in order to produce subversive personal and social effects), they constitute a constructive more than a destructive use of parody.

When contrasted with literatures in English especially, it is striking that late 20th-century French and Francophone literatures have produced so few literary fairy tales written primarily for adults. Be this as it may, those tales that have appeared attest to the rich diversity of contemporary writing in French. Beyond the use of fairy tales as important subtexts or cultural references (e.g. Daniel Pennac, *Au bonheur des ogres* (*The Ogres' Happiness*, 1985)) and *La Fée Carabine* (*The Fairy Gunsmoke*, 1987)), Jean-Pierre Andrevon (*La Fée et le géomètre* (*The Fairy and the Geometer*, 1978)), and Pierrette *Fleutiaux (*Métamorphoses de la reine* (*Metamorphoses of the Queen*, 1985)) have reworked fairy-tale plots so as to argue the necessity of ecological reform (Andrevon) and to depict erotic and even violent fantasies about feminine sexuality (Fleutiaux). By comparison, though, Francophone writers have of late contributed as much if not more to the genre than

French writers. Benefiting from their own considerable knowledge of folklore in their homelands, writers such as the French Canadian Germain Lemieux (*Les vieux m'ont conté* (*The Old People Told Me*, 1977)), the Senegalese Birago Diop (*Contes d'Amadou Koumba* (*Tales of Amadou Koumba*, 1947) and *Nouveaux contes d'Amadou Koumba* (*New Tales of Amadou Koumba*, 1958)), and the Martinican Patrick *Chamoiseau (*Au temps de l'antan: contes martiniquais* (*Creole Folktales*, 1988)) artfully blur the distinction between transcription and adaptation while highlighting the specificity of indigenous folklore from Francophone countries. Of course, in addition to literary fairy tales by French and Francophone writers, countless translations of folk tales from all regions of the world remain popular among adults and children alike. As France and Francophone countries ponder their roles in a global economy and a much-touted 'new world order', it is fitting that the fairy tale in French now encompasses such diverse—Francophone and non-Francophone—national and ethnic traditions.   LCS

Barchilon, Jacques, *Le Conte merveilleux français de 1690 à 1790* (1975).

Malarte-Feldman, Claire-Lise, 'La Nouvelle Tyrannie des fées, ou la réécriture des contes de fées classiques', *French Review*, 63.5 (April 1990).

Marin, Louis, *La Parole mangée* (1986?).

Palacio, Jean de, *Les Perversions du merveilleux: ma Mère l'Oye au tournant du siècle* (1993).

Perrot, Jean (ed.), *Tricentenaire Charles Perrault: les grands contes du XVIIe siècle et leur fortune littéraire* (1998).

Robert, Raymonde, *Le Conte de fées littéraire en France* (1982).

Seifert, Lewis C., *Fairy Tales, Sexuality, and Gender in France, 1690–1715* (1996).

Soriano, Marc, *Les Contes de Perrault* (1968).

Storer, Mary Elizabeth, *Un épisode littéraire de la fin du XVIIe siècle: la mode des contes de fées (1685–1700)* (1928).

Velay-Vallantin, Catherine, *L'Histoire des contes* (1994).

Zipes, Jack, *Beauties, Beasts, and Enchantments* (1989).

Corporation, where they jointly directed their first feature. It was a spectacular adaptation, faithful to literary sources rather than to stage versions, of *Jack and the Beanstalk (USA, 1917). In it all the actors were children, except the giant. Standing 8 ft 5 ins tall, and weighing 32 stone (450 lb.), the adult actor needed no camera trickery to make him look several times bigger than any of the 1,200 children (or so the publicity claimed) who played the inhabitants of the medieval kingdom at the top of the magic beanstalk. In its original cut the film gave free rein to the giant's habit of grinding bones to make his bread, and of putting babies on the chopping block, but before its UK release it was pruned from ten reels to eight because it was deemed too gory for children to see. With the same basic formula and the same lead actors—including 6-year-old Virginia Lee Corbin as the heroine, and 10-year-old Buddy Messinger as the heavy—the Franklins went on to make *Aladdin and his Wonderful Lamp (1917), full of sinuous oriental body movement and villainous moustache-stroking. Next came Babes in the Wood (1917, directed by Sidney alone) and *Ali Baba and the Forty Thieves (1918), which went on location and used forests, plains, and mountains as well as studio sets. After that, diminishing box-office returns prompted Fox to end the series.   TAS

Brownlow, Kevin, 'Sidney A. Franklin: The Modest Pioneer', *Focus on Film*, 10 (1972).

Frau Holle *See* MOTHER HOLLE.

Freeman, Mary E. Wilkins (1852–1930) American author, best known for her collections of short stories *A Humble Romance and Other Stories* (1887), *A New England Nun and Other Stories* (1891), *The Pot of Gold and Other Stories* (1892), and her novel *Pembroke* (1894). In Wilkin's lifetime, she published over a dozen collections of short stories, over fifty uncollected stories and essays, fourteen novels, eight children's books, three plays, and three volumes of poetry. Fairy-tale motifs remain prominent throughout her works in such stories as 'Princess

Rosetta and the Pop-corn Man', 'The Pumpkin Giant', and 'A Church Mouse'.   MF

Freleng, Fitz (1906–1995) American animator, cartoonist, director, and producer, who made major contributions to Looney Tunes and Merrie Melodies by creating such characters as Bugs Bunny, Porky Pig, Tweety Bird, Sylvester the cat, Yosemite Sam, and Speedy Gonzalez. Among his different fairy-tale cartoons, Freleng directed several fascinating *Red Riding Hood versions. In *The Trial of Mr. Wolf* (1941) the wolf, clearly a con man, is put on trial. Strangely, all the jurors are wolves, and the wolf is allowed to defend himself by telling a tale in which Little Red Hood is a demonic predator who lures him to her grandmother's house to be killed. As he finishes his obvious false testimony, he is run over by a trolley for lying. But it is not just the wolf who must pay for his 'crimes' in Freleng's cartoons. Red Riding Hood is so obnoxious in *Little Red Riding Rabbit* (1944) that Bugs Bunny and the wolf ignore her and leave her suspended in the air so that they can continue chasing each other without disturbance. In *Red Rodent Hood* (1952) Freleng put Sylvester the cat into the wolf's role. Freleng returned to ridiculing the wolf in *Red Riding Hoodwinked* (1955). This time he revised the tale with the celebrity cartoon characters Tweety and Sylvester. His other notable fairy-tale cartoons are: *Beauty and the Beast* (1934), *The Miller's Daughter* (1934), and *Jack-Wabbit and the Beanstalk* (1943), which all can be considered fractured fairy tales.   JZ

'Frog King, The' As the first fairy tale in the Brothers *Grimm, *Kinder- und Hausmärchen* (*Children's and Household Tales*), it has gained an incredible popularity as a didactic lesson for children as well as an erotic tale for adults. This tale of a king's daughter who promises a frog to let it eat and sleep with her if it retrieves a golden ball that she has dropped into a well becomes an exemplum for the fact that promises must be kept. In the German version the princess throws the frog against the wall, and this breaks the spell of a witch who had changed the prince into the frog. In most other versions the frog is kissed by the princess, and the prince appears. The relationship of this tale to the larger cycle of *'Beauty and the Beast' is much more prevalent here. But Wilhelm Grimm de-emphasized the sexual allusions in his various editions of the *Children's and Household Tales*, thus making the German variant above all an educational children's story.

The idea of a prince turned into a frog by a spell has been traced back to the Middle Ages, but the fairy tale itself was collected by Wilhelm Grimm, probably from Dortchen Wild. While its major purpose appears to be instructional, it has been pointed out that the princess also goes through a maturation process. She does not merely learn that promises must be kept, but she also comprehends that she must grow up and take matters into her own hands. It is the liberating and individualizing process that has been emphasized in the interpretation of this fairy tale by such psychologists as Bruno Bettelheim. When Anglo-American variants with the kiss scene are added to this view, then the tale also becomes an indirect expression of sexual development.

It is doubtless for the latter reason that 'The Frog King' has been reinterpreted to such a vast degree by literary authors in the form of serious poems and short stories or intriguing satires and parodies. Anne *Sexton's lengthy poem 'The Frog Prince' (1971) presents a sexual interpretation of the tale, but there are also poems by such authors as Sara Henderson *Hay, Robert Graves, Hyacinthe Hill, Phyllis Thompson, Elizabeth Brewster, Robert Pack, and Galway Kinnell. These poetic reactions to the traditional fairy tale abound with modern questions about love, marriage, identity, happiness, and interpersonal communication. In German poems by Marie Luise Kaschnitz and Franz *Fühmann, for example, questions of love and maturation are raised as well but with a lesser sexual implication owing to the fact that the 'kiss' variant has only become known in more recent years.

Nevertheless, the fairy tale has been usurped by the mass media and commercialism. In fact, the tale has been reduced to the internationally disseminated proverb 'You have to kiss a lot of toads (frogs), before you meet your handsome prince.' This slogan regarding the anxieties of modern relationships can be found on greetings cards, bathroom walls, T-shirts, bumper stickers, and posters. The scene of the frog being thrown against the wall or being kissed has also been used repeatedly in cartoons, comic strips, caricatures, and advertisements, where the topics range from economics to love or from politics to sex. Wishful thinking and realism are placed in striking confrontation by innovative manipulations of the traditional fairy tale. Most of these reinterpretations of the traditional 'Frog King' fairy tale are frustrated statements regarding the social and psychological problems of people whose dreams clash with reality. But by questioning the happy end of this extremely popular fairy tale, these people are barely hiding their hope for that redeeming kiss.   WM

Bettelheim, Bruno, *The Use of Enchantment: The Meaning and Importance of Fairy Tales* (1976).

Blair, Walter, 'The Funny Fondled Fairytale Frog', *Studies in American Humor*, 1 (1982).

Ellis, John M., *One Fairy Story Too Many: The Brothers Grimm and their Tales* (1983).

Mieder, Wolfgang, 'Modern Anglo-American Variants of The Frog Prince', *New York Folklore*, 6 (1980).

Mieder, Wolfgang, *Disenchantments: An Anthology of Modern Fairy Tale Poetry* (1985).

Röhrich, Lutz, *Wage es, den Frosch zu küssen! Das Grimmsche Märchen Nummer Eins in seinen Wandlungen* (1987).

Frølich, Lorenz (1820–1908) Danish artist, best known for his illustrations for Hans Christian *Andersen's fairy tales (1870–4). He also illustrated collections of Norse myths, folk tales, and folk songs, German folk ballads, fables by La Fontaine, as well as fairy tales by 19th-century Danish, French, and English writers. He also wrote some texts for his own illustrations. Frølich was active in Paris, and many of his fairy tales for children were initially published in French.   MN

Bergstrand, Ulla, *Bilderbokslandet Längesen* (1996).

Frost, Gregory (1951–) American science fiction and fantasy writer. His novel *Fitcher's Brides* (2002) sets the traditional story of an evil, supernatural serial killer in upper New York State in the 19th century. The sorcerer Fitcher becomes a preacher predicting apocalypse who marries three sisters in succession. As in the original tale, the youngest defeats him and revives her sisters. Frost has also written revisions of *'Rapunzel' and Hans Christian *Andersen's 'The Tinder Box'.   PG

Froud, Brian (1947–) English fantasy illustrator, artist, designer, and authority on faeries and faerie lore. His contributions to films such as *The Dark Crystal* (1982), *Labyrinth* (1986), and *The Storyteller* (1988) established innovative conceptual designs that in many ways revolutionized modern puppet and animatronic design. Froud is the author of and collaborator on a number of books focusing on mythical creatures, including *Good Faeries* (1998), *Trolls* (2012), and *Faeries* (1978), written in collaboration with illustrator Alan Lee. He also provided illustrations for *Lady Cottington's Fairy Letters* (2002), *Runes of Elfland* (2003), *Goblins!* (2004), and *Brian Froud's World of Faerie* (2007).   KMJ

Fuchs, Günter Bruno (1928–77) German writer, poet, and painter, noted for his surrealistic experiments. Fuchs helped found the avant-garde gallery Die Zinke in Berlin and produced works that parodied the bourgeois lifestyle. There are fairy-tale and fantastic elements in many of his works. Among his books that contain ironic fairy tales with extraordinary wordplay are *Einundzwanzig Märchen zu je drei Zeilen* (*Twenty-one Fairy Tales with Three Lines a Piece*, 1968) and *Bericht eines Bremer Stadtmusikanten* (*Report of a Bremen Town Musician*, 1968).   JZ

Fühmann, Franz (1922–84) East German poet, journalist, and author of children's and young adult books. After his return from Soviet prison camp following the Second World War, Fühmann settled in East Berlin, where he began his literary career by publishing poetry and writing for newspapers and magazines. In the early decades after the war, Fühmann strongly believed in the cause of communism. His retellings and recreations of Greek and Germanic myths as well as animal tales and folk tales, for which he became famous, reflect his ideological conviction. The specific qualities of Fühmann's reinterpretations rest on the originality of his approach and his stylistic elegance. Humour and playfulness mingle with horror and suspense. The mythical and everyday reality meet in his version of the Low German animal epic *Reineke Fuchs* (1964), in his retelling of the *Iliad* and *Odyssey*, *Das hölzerne Pferd* (*The Wooden Horse*, 1968), in his adaptations of *Shakespeare's fairy tales, (*Shakespeare-Märchen*, 1968), The Nibelungen epic (*Nibelungenlied*, 1971), and the tale of Prometheus (*Prometheus*, 1974). Also worthy of note are his idiosyncratic and very dark adaptations of *Grimms' fairy tales for radio, equipped with the warning label 'not for children'. In 1956, Fühmann received the Heinrich Mann Prize; in 1963 he was awarded the J.-R. Becher Prize; and in 1968, his Shakespeare fairy tales and *The Wooden Horse* were honoured for fostering socialist children's and youth literature.   EMM

Weise, Hans (ed.), *Franz Fühmann* (1972).

Funke, Cornelia (1958–) Bestselling author of fantasy novels for young readers, she is sometimes regarded as the German J. K. *Rowling. Her first success in Germany came with the publication of two children's series, *Die wilden Hühner* (*The Wild Chicks*, 7 volumes, 1993–2007) and *Gespensterjäger* (*Ghosthunters*, 4 volumes, 2006–7). But it was not until the appearance of the fantasy novels *Drachenreiter* (*Dragon Rider*, 1998) and *Herr der Diebe* (*Thief Lord*, 2002) that she became an international bestselling author. The prolific Funke soon became even more famous when she published her popular trilogy *Tintenherz* (*Inkheart*, 2003), which was awarded the 2004 BookSense Book of the Year in Children's Literature, *Tintenblut* (*Inkspell*, 2005), and *Tintentod* (*Inkdeath*, 2007). All three fantasy novels concern the teenager Meggie Folchart, who discovers that she and her father Mo (Mortimer), a professional bookbinder, have the extraordinary power of bringing characters from books into the real world when reading aloud. Meggie and Mo live in northern Italy, and the characters whom they bring to life with their 'silver tongues' involve them in all sorts of adventures and conflicts that they must eventually resolve through the art of reading. The first novel was made into a film in 2009, and parts of the trilogy have been adapted for the theatre. In anticipation of the bicentenary of the first edition of the *Kinder- und Hausmärchen* (1812/15) by the Brothers *Grimm, Funke published two novels *Reckless. Steineres Fleisch* (*Reckless*, 2010) and *Reckless. Lebendige Schatten* (*Fearless*, 2012). These works are a mishmash of fantasy and fairy tale and part of a trilogy 'Mirror World series' in which Funke depicts the Brothers Grimm as Jacob and Will Reckless in their early twenties. (The third novel has yet to be completed.) They enter a nineteenth-century fantasy world through a mirror, and in the first novel, *Reckless*, Jacob must rescue his brother, who is transformed into a Goyl, a member of a humanoid race with stone skin. In this fast-paced narrative Jacob encounters dwarfs, wicked and good fairies, and a female shape-shifting fox. Motifs from several Grimms' tales such as 'The *Frog King', *'Rapunzel', *'Sleeping Beauty', and *'Snow White' are thrown into the brew to enliven the plot. In the end Jacob can only save his brother by sacrificing his own life. He sends Will back to the 'real' world and has only a year to live unless he finds a cure for his curse. Of course, this ending leads to a new beginning in *Fearless*, in which Jacob falls in love with the shape-shifter fox, Celeste, while seeking to obtain an antidote to the deadly moth implanted in his heart. Again, motifs such as a miraculous apple, water of immortality, and magic blood are employed as possible cures for Jacob's curse. Whether he will ultimately find peace and happiness will be determined in the third novel. Funke's writing process includes a critical revision of the Grimms' tales, which Funke called somewhat reactionary in a 2010 interview.

However, it is difficult to assess whether Funke has transformed the Grimms' lives and their tales into a progressive fantasy because her 'grimm' novels are flawed, contrived, and, at times, ludicrous.   JZ

Furniss, Harry (1854–1925) Irish caricaturist and juvenile book illustrator who was educated at Dublin's Wesleyan College and studied art at the Royal Iberian Academy schools. At 19 he left Dublin to work as a cartoonist for numerous magazines such as the *Illustrated London News*, for which he covered the Chicago World's Fair. He was also a regular contributor to *Punch*, where he excelled at social realism, topical humour, and parliamentary caricatures: his popular cartoon about Gladstone and Irish Home Rule practically invented the Gladstone collar. He also gained notoriety for a Pear's Soap poster that became an advertising classic. In 1894 he left *Punch*—and his admission to the House of Commons—because of a salary dispute and founded *Lika Joko* and the *New Budget*. A popular lecturer, he later went to New York and worked as a writer, producer, and actor in Thomas Edison's films.

Furniss was hailed as one of the most gifted black-and-white artists, and his effortless, lightning execution and facility of rendering faces were ideally suited to caricature. Besides journals, he also illustrated Lewis *Carroll's *Sylvie and Bruno* books (1889, 1893), and the complete editions of Charles *Dickens (1910) and William Makepeace *Thackeray (1911); the latter includes *The Rose and the Ring*, a children's fairy tale about a fairy rose and enchanted ring.   MLE

Doyle, Brian, *Who's Who of Children's Literature* (1968).

Houfe, Simon, *The Dictionary of British Book Illustrators and Caricaturists 1800–1914* (1996).

Peppin, Brigid, and Micklethwait, Lucy, *Dictionary of British Book Illustrators* (1983).

Fuseli, Henry (1741–1825) Swiss-born British romantic artist; a man of letters as well as a painter. A history painter, Fuseli rendered themes he found embodied in literature, legend, and history, illustrating the works of Milton, Dante, Charles *Dickens,

William *Shakespeare, Sophocles, Virgil, Pope, and Homer in heroic style. In particular, his illustrations for Edmund *Spenser's *Faerie Queene* and Christoph Martin *Wieland's *Oberon* are notable. Classicism was integral to Fuseli's illustrative work. While his contemporaries described his art as bold, dreamlike, wild, grotesque, disturbing, they noted his genius.   SS

Auckland City Art Gallery, *A Collection of Drawings* (1967).
Knowles, John, *Life and Writing of Henry Fuseli* (1982/1831).
Weinglass, D. H., *Prints and Engraved Illustrations by and after Henry Fuseli* (1994).

Fyleman, Rose (Rose Amy Fyleman, 1877–1957) British children's poet, author, and playwright. Scores of Fyleman's deft, light-hearted fairy poems appeared in *Punch* in the 1920s, a period when belief in dainty, flower-dwelling fairies was fashionable even among adults. 'Fairies', which begins, notoriously, 'There are fairies at the bottom of our garden!' (*Fairies and Chimneys*, 1918) became a byword for this type of poetry and the whimsical mentality associated with it. Fairies also pervade Fyleman's children's stories in *The Rainbow Cat* (1923) and *Forty Good-Morning Tales* (1929), and her *Eight Little Plays for Children* (1925).   SR

Gaarder, Jostein (1952–) Norwegian writer, environmentalist, and author of children's books, who is primarily known for his unusual novel for young readers, *Sophie's World* (1991) about the history of philosophy. This book was such a success that it became the world's bestseller of 1995 and was translated into 54 different languages. Up until 1991, Gaarder had taught philosophy at a high school, and after the success of *Sophie's World* he became a full-time writer and has been active internationally in the environmentalist movement. Two of his more recent works can be regarded as fairy tales. Written as a novel for young adults, *Appelsinpiken* (*The Orange Girl*, 2004) concerns a young boy who receives a letter from his father eleven years after he had died from cancer, and the letter prompts the boy to see and live the world as a fairy tale. *De gule dvergene* (*Jonathan and the Little Yellow Dwarves from Outer Space*, 2006) is a children's book that begins with a bizarre situation: dwarves arrive from outer space searching for bananas and plan to send all the people of little Jonathan's town to their planet as a planet swap. Only Jonathan can save his townspeople if he rolls a seven with a dice. However, there is no seven on the dice. As in all his works, Gaarder seeks to stimulate his readers to contemplate difficult existential situations.   JZ

Gadda, Carlo Emilio (1893–1973) Italian writer and essayist, famous for his novels *Quel pasticciaccio brutto de via Merulana* (*That Awful Mess on Via Merulana*, 1957) and *La cognizione del dolore* (*Acquainted with Grief*, 1963). Earlier he had written *Il primo libro delle favole* (*The First Book of Fairy Tales*, 1952) and published collections of stories such as *Novelle del ducato in fiamme* (*Stories about the Duchy in Flames*, 1952) and *Accoppiamenti giudiziosi* (*Judicious Unions*, 1963). Gadda's renown for linguistic games and multilingualism is also present in his tales which are peopled with animals, real historical people, and objects such as flowers.

Gadda wrote over 186 fairy tales, some of which were published posthumously in *Favole inedite di Carlo Emilio Gadda* (*Unpublished Fairy Tales by Carlo Emilio Gadda*, 1983). Gadda's fairy tales are peculiar for, though he begins with imitations of Aesop and Phaedrus, and then borrows from Leonardo and other Italian authors, there remains nothing of the classical fairy tale. His fairy tales abound in aphorisms, epigrams, facetiae, anecdotes, and invectives against Mussolini. Some of his well-known tales include 'The English Horn', 'The Piglet', 'The Mouse', 'The Eagle', 'The Moon'.   GD

Gág, Wanda (1893–1946) American translator and illustrator of folk tales by the Brothers *Grimm, who was born in New Ulm, Minnesota, when German was spoken by the majority of inhabitants. While an adult living in New York City, Connecticut, and later in New Jersey, Gág translated the familiar fairy tales from the Grimms' collection in part to refresh her knowledge of the language. Aspects of her popular picture book *Millions of Cats* (1928) such as plot and refrains were reminiscent of the folklore style developed by the Grimms. Encouraged by her editor, Gág then translated the Grimms' tales with the intention of publishing them. She chose to rewrite 'freely', using her own words in English, rather than making a literal translation. Gág always completed the texts before embarking on the illustrations. Her

Gág, Wanda The Looker can see for miles, and the Listener can hear everything in the world in Wanda Gág's 'Six Servants' adapted from the *Grimms' 'How Six Made their Way Through the World' and published in *Tales from Grimm* (1946). Permission to reproduce granted by Norma Harm, Administrator, Wanda Gág Estate.

intention was to create an art product for adults as well as for children. Therefore, she developed 'dummies' or mock-ups for each book and designed the double-page spread of the book when opened. Only after completing studies in pencil did she draw the final pictures using an indian ink pen. Until she became ill, she always supervised the printer even for later editions.

Therefore her books have strong black-and-white illustrations; only the book jacket and frontispiece were printed in full colour.

She selected 16 stories for *Tales from Grimm* (1936) and illustrated each with one or usually several small ink illustrations. Among them were *'Hansel and Gretel', 'The Cat and Mouse Keep House', and 'The Fisherman and His Wife'. Out of consideration for the child reader, Gág avoided the more violent Grimm tales. The book is accessible in word choice to young readers, and the illustrations convey a sense of peasant life in the 19th century. *Gone is Gone* (1935) was Gág's reminiscence of a story she thought was German but could never verify, as the Norwegian source eluded her. This story about a capable woman who proposes that she and her complaining farmer husband exchange tasks for a day reveals how Gág saw herself as a woman. In the tale, the husband fails to cope with the feminine daily tasks of childcare, cooking, and house maintenance.

Urged by librarians and an editor to counteract the popular *Disney movie and book version of *Snow White and the Seven Dwarfs*, Gág created an exclusive single title published in 1938. She included the stepmother's three temptations, in contrast to Disney's one with the apple. Gág retained the folk image of the dwarfs; she depicted them as clean and orderly. Several years later she selected three more Brothers Grimm tales published during the midst of the Second World War as *Three Gay Tales* (1943).

Finally, her collection of *More Tales from Grimm* (1947) with 32 stories was published posthumously. As explained in the foreword, Gág had completed the text in her usual careful style, but several of the illustrations appear crude, as they were unfinished owing to her prolonged illness and death from lung cancer. Some art from her first Grimm publication was reused.   KNH

Hoyle, Karen Nelson, *Wanda Gág* (1994).

Gaiman, Neil (1960–) British experimental writer of graphic novels, comic books, screenplays, and fantasy. After working as a journalist and reviewer, Gaiman turned to writing comic books in 1987 and achieved almost instant notoriety with the publication of *Outrageous Tales of the Old Testament* that same year. He is most famous for his *Sandman* graphic novels (1991–6) in which he employs all kinds of fantasy and fairy-tale character motifs in highly original plots that recall traditional horror stories and romances. Owing to the innovative nature of the *Sandman* series and other graphic

novels, Gaiman has achieved cult fame in the United States and Great Britain.

Gaiman's writing tends to appeal to intellectuals because of his ironic humour and the intertextual nature of his stories that include references to folklore, myth, classical literature, and pop culture. He has also worked with musicians, film-makers, and illustrators on elaborate projects that deal with the fantastic in the arts, and he has collaborated with Terry *Pratchett in writing the comic novel *Good Omens, the Nice and Accurate Prophecies of Agnes Nutter* (1990). In 1996 Gaiman created the teleplay *Neverwhere* for the BBC, and in 1998 he rewrote and published it as a novel. Set in contemporary London, it deals with the problem of homelessness. The protagonist of this novel, Richard Mayhew, is an average businessman, who helps a young girl bleeding from a switchblade wound and takes her to his home, where he hopes she will recuperate. This good deed, however, propels him into a terrifying adventure, and he is transported into the nightmarish London underworld and compelled to deal with a culture that he never knew existed. In his next work, *Stardust* (1999), a fairy-tale novel based on a comic book that he created with the illustrator Charles Vess, Gaiman shifts the setting to Wall, a small English village during the Victorian period, where a young shopkeeper's assistant, Tristan Thorn, falls in love with a beautiful young woman named Victoria Forester, who will marry him only if he retrieves a fallen star. So lovestruck is Tristan that he embarks on a journey into the realm of faerie, where he must compete for the star with a dreadful and deceitful witch and decadent counts, who will kill anyone in their path. With magic and fortune on his side, Tristan defeats his opponents, but once he is successful in capturing the fallen star, a lovely but feisty young woman, and bringing her back to the quaint village of Wall, he learns that Victoria wants to marry someone else. At the same time he realizes that his future lies more in the realm of faerie with the pert star than in the charming but humdrum village. This novel was made into a film in 2007, and Gaiman also wrote the screenplay for the film *Mirrormask* (2005), directed by the artist David McKean, who has illustrated several of Gaiman's works. In this film, a young circus performer runs away from her parents and enters a fairy-tale world, where she realizes where her true place is—home in the circus. In two of Gaiman's fantasy children's books, *Coraline* (2002), also made into an animated film, and *Wolves in the* Walls (2003), the young protagonists need fantasy to unsettle them to come to terms with their realities. Gaiman's fantasy novels for adults also pick up on this theme. *American Gods* (2001) and *Anansi Boys* (2005) depict mythic figures and tricksters in contemporary American and British worlds in which storytelling becomes a mode to navigate chaotic circumstances. As in all his works, Gaiman takes a postmodern romantic stand in defence of other worlds of the imagination. Most of his fairy-tale stories and novels have a dark side to them, and in *The Ocean at the End of the Lane* (2013) Gaiman explores a frightening dilemma for a young boy revisited through the eyes of an adult. Here an older man in his forties returns to a small English town to find that his childhood home has been demolished. When he decides to go to a dilapidated farmhouse at the end of the lane, he recalls the events of his childhood that include murder and his strange encounter with eleven-year-old Lettie Hemstock and her sisters. Lettie takes the boy to a pond at the end of the lane that she calls an ocean, and she leads him to an alternative world. When he returns, he finds that evil in the form of a terrifying nanny has entered his home, and he must learn that sacrifice is the only way to get rid of this evil. Like many of Gaiman's other narratives, the journey to another world is a traumatic awakening that will mark the young hero for life.   JZ

Sanders, Joe, 'Of Storytellers and Stories in Gaiman and Vess's "A Midsummer Night's Dream"', *Extrapolation* (2004).

Galdone, Paul (1914–86) Hungarian-American author and illustrator of more than 30 folk tales among his 300 illustrated books. Galdone rewrote most of the folk tales he illustrated in terse repetitive language, selecting a wide rectangular shape especially suitable for adults to hold for children in a group. Productive in the field for 30 years, he interpreted English tales such as *Old Woman and her Pig* (1960), the *Grimms' The *Bremen Town Musicians* (1968), and *Perrault's *Puss-in-Boots* (1976) with whimsy and bold action. Galdone communicates the plot and mood clearly and delineates character differences in both word and picture.   KNH

Galland, Antoine (1646–1715) French orientalist, translator, philologist, numismatist, and epigraphist, whose version of the *Thousand and One Nights* (*Les Mille et une nuits*, 1704–17) was the first in a Western European language (*see* ARABIAN NIGHTS and ORIENTAL FAIRY TALES).

After studying at the Collège Royal and the Sorbonne, Galland, who was known for his gift with languages, spent 15 years in Constantinople as adviser to Louis XIV's ambassadors. In that capacity he had the opportunity to learn even more languages and to travel extensively throughout the Middle East. Upon his return to France, he devoted his energies to scholarly pursuits, writing extensively on Middle Eastern languages, cultures, and antiquities. Among his most important accomplishments were completing and publishing Herbelot de Molainville's encyclopaedic *Bibliothèque orientale* (*Oriental Library*, 1697) and translating the Koran. In 1701 he entered the prestigious Académie des Inscriptions, and in 1709 he was elected the first professor of Arabic at the Collège Royal.

Today Galland is known far less for his scholarly endeavours and much more for his version of the *Thousand and One Nights*, which he began in 1702 as a gift to a former pupil. He first translated the tales of Sindbad, but withdrew them from publication upon discovering they were part of a larger cycle. Working from a 14th-century Arabic manuscript, Galland set about to publish eight volumes of the *Thousand and One Nights* between 1704 and 1709. He completed another four volumes, published between 1712 and 1717, based on notes taken on stories told to him by Hanna, a Maronite from Aleppo.

Galland's translation has often been criticized for taking liberties with the original tales. This, however, oversimplifies the period's conceptions of literature and translation as well as the difficulties entailed in translating the disparate manuscripts that make up the Arabic *Alf Layla wa-Layla* (*One Thousand Nights and a Night*). At a time when the lines between literary creation and translation were not yet clearly drawn, it was hardly unusual for Galland to assert that 'putting into French' the *Thousand and One Nights* required 'circumspection' and 'delicacy'. Indeed, the enormous and immediate success of his translation was in great part due to the changes he made: toning down 'licentious' scenes; eliminating poetic interludes, repetitions, and enumerations; amplifying details of plot and decor to explain culture-specific material; and transposing stylistic registers (from the colloquial of the manuscript to French neoclassical literary style). It is a testimony to his success that even Galland's harshest critics praise the quality of his prose and acknowledge in him a 'born storyteller'. While cognizant of the need to adapt the tales, Galland was none the less careful to bring his wide erudition to the task. Many of his additions are explanatory descriptions. Furthermore, his text remains remarkably faithful to the original, even when the latter diverges from standard literary conventions of his day. Thus, for instance, lower-class characters, who have only rare counterparts in the literature of early 18th-century France, appear throughout the *Thousand and One Nights*. And yet faithfulness to the original manuscripts did not keep Galland from imposing a unity of tone and architecture they lacked as collections composed by multiple authors from the 9th to the 14th centuries. Not only does he rearrange the order of the tales found in the Arabic manuscripts, he also links and intercalates otherwise independent tales. Those in the last four volumes, including some of the best-known of the entire collection such as *'Aladdin', *'Ali

Baba', and 'Harun ar-Rashid', are not translations at all but adaptations of stories told to him orally and hence reflect most clearly his consummate literary skill.

Perhaps the most original aspect of Galland's work is his treatment of the theme of pleasure, which is apparent on many levels. Among the most obvious is the physical, if not erotic pleasure that Galland represents in spite of his tendency to tone down such descriptions. Unlike the predominant literary portrayal of the time, love is not as much a psychological passion as a physical attraction. No less obvious, however, is the pleasure of storytelling. Whereas writers of fairy tales (and in fact all literature) at this time present their works as both pleasurable *and* morally instructive (following the Horatian injunction *dulce et utile*), Galland unabashedly proclaims his tales to be 'pleasing and diverting', with no other pretence. Yet such a stance does not signify that the *Thousand and One Nights* are 'meaningless', as *Voltaire once quipped. The pleasure of storytelling in this collection serves many functions—to allay melancholy, to avert death, to satisfy curiosity, and to defend oneself, among others—and Galland's translation highlights this pleasure in the individual tales as well as the frame story with Scheherazade, Shahryar, and Dinarzade. Moreover, in the denouement that Galland gives to this story it is the pleasure of Scheherazade's storytelling—and not the children she had given birth to—that moves Shahryar to revoke his vow to kill her. In the end, then, it is pleasure that is the most important legacy of Galland's translation, and there is no doubt that it was among the most important influences in creating the Western stereotype of the 'Orient' (encompassing the Middle East, South East Asia, and China) as a place of exotic pleasures.

If Galland's tales met with such popular success upon their publication, it is also because they simultaneously resembled and differed from the fairy tales that had enamoured the French reading public since the 1690s. The convergence in Galland's translation of the familiar—many recognizable folkloric plots—and the unfamiliar—'oriental' local colour and seemingly gratuitous magic—paved the way for numerous collections of oriental tales by Jean-Paul *Bignon, Thomas-Simon *Gueulette, and Pétis de la Croix (among many others) and for the oriental motif exploited by prominent writers such as Montesquieu (in *Les Lettres persanes*) and Voltaire (in *Zadig*). Galland's *Thousand and One Nights* became a popular best-seller in many different languages. In the English-speaking world, the translation of the Galland version was better known than translations based on the original Arabic manuscripts until the mid-20th century. LCS

Abdel-Halim, Mohamed, *Antoine Galland: sa vie, son œuvre* (1964).
May, Georges, *Les Mille et une nuits d'Antoine Galland ou le chef-d'œuvre invisible* (1986).
Nurse, Paul McMichael, *Eastern Dreams: How the Arabian Nights Came to the World* (2010).

Garcia, Camille Rose (1970–) Provocative American artist and illustrator whose illustrations, paintings, and sculptures are influenced by cartoons and have a Gothic if not grotesque aura. Among her more notable illustrated books are *The Magic Bottle* (2006), *Alice's Adventures in Wonderland* (2010), and *Snow White* (2012). Her 'creepy' images tend to subvert classic tales and to bring out their outrageous aspects. Garcia's grim view of the world is particularly noticeable in her depictions of Alice and Snow White, young girls who are brutalized so much that their survival cannot be likened to a happy end. JZ

Landauer, Susan (ed.), *The Tragic Kingdom: The Art of Camille Rose Garcia* (2007).

García Márquez, Gabriel (1928–2014) Colombian novelist, short-story writer, and polemical journalist, who was awarded the Nobel Prize for literature in 1982. His literary works have influenced writers all over the world. In particular, his novel *Cien años de soledad* (*One Hundred Years of Solitude*, 1967) is a landmark in literary theory and history, since it gave rise to the term 'magic realism' and led many writers to imitate its style. As a major representative of 'magic realism', García Márquez always felt

suspicious of pure realism which, in his view, is unable to capture the essence of Latin America. Consequently, both his novels and short stories integrate the real and the fantastic, together with mythic, legendary, and magical elements. In fact, it is not uncommon for García Márquez's short stories to have their sources in *Märchen*, folklore, and myth. Formally austere and frequently located in rural settings, they are full of surprising elements that defy rational laws and make demands on the reader's imagination. His first volume of short stories, *Los funerales de la Mamá Grande* (*Big Mama's Funeral*, 1962) has been critically acclaimed as his best collection. It includes, among many others, two prodigious tales: 'La prodigiosa tarde de Baltazar' ('Balthazar's Prodigious Evening', 1962) and 'La viuda de Montiel' ('The Widow of Montiel', 1962). In the 1970s García Márquez published two other collections of short stories: *La increíble y triste historia de la cándida Eréndira y de su abuela desalmada* (*Innocent Eréndira and Other Stories*, 1972) and *Ojos de perro azul* (*A Blue Dog's Eyes*, 1972). Several critics have considered the title story of the former as a revision of 'The *Sleeping Beauty*', a tale that García Márquez goes back to in 'El avión de la bella durmiente' ('The Sleeping Beauty's Plane', 1982). This tale is included within his last volume of short stories, *Doce cuentos peregrinos* (*Twelve Wandering Tales*, 1992). Also incorporated into this collection is 'El rastro de tu sangre en la nieve' ('The Trace of Your Blood on the Snow', 1976), which is likewise related to the fairy-tale genre. CFR

Grullon, Carmen Amantina, 'Once There Was a Writer: The Narrative of Gabriel García Márquez and the Fairy Tale: A Comparative Study' (Diss., University of Connecticut, 1995).
Hancock, Joel, 'Gabriel García Márquez's *Eréndira* and the Brothers Grimm', *Studies in Twentieth Century Literature*, 3 (1978).
Jain, Jasbir, 'Innocent Eréndira: The Reversal of a Fairy Tale', in Alok Bhalla (ed.), *García Márquez and Latin America* (1987).
Linker, Susan Mott, 'Myth and Legend in Two Prodigious Tales of García Márquez', *Hispanic Journal*, 9 (1987).

Penuel, Arnold M., 'A Contemporary Fairy Tale: García Márquez's "El rastro de tu sangre en la nieve"', *Studies in Twentieth Century Literature*, 19 (1995).

Gardner, John (1933–82) American writer and scholar. He taught medieval literature and creative writing at a number of colleges and universities and eventually became the founder and director of the writing program at the State University of New York at Binghamton from 1978 until his death in 1982 in a motorcycle accident. His compelling and brilliant fiction—including *Grendel* (1971), *Nickel Mountain* (1973), *The King's Indian and Other Fireside Tales* (1981), and *Mikkelson's Ghost* (1982)—has earned him a respected place in the canon of contemporary American authors. In 1975, with the publication of *Dragon, Dragon and Other Timeless Tales*, he turned his attention to fairy tales for young readers. He followed that book with other witty and unusual fairy-tale works such as *Gudgekin the Thistle Girl and Other Tales* (1976) and *King of the Hummingbirds and Other Tales* (1977). Perhaps his major achievement in the genre is his fairy-tale novel *In the Suicide Mountains* (1977), in which three desperate protagonists intent on committing suicide meet by chance in the mountains, help each other, and learn to cherish their lives. JZ

Gardner, Sally (no dates available) British writer and illustrator for children and young adults who has written and illustrated a number of fairy-tale books for children such as *A Book of Princesses* (1998), *The Boy Who Could Fly* (2001), *The Glass Heart: A Tale of Three Princesses* (2002), *Magical Kids: The Invisible Boy and the Strongest Girl in the World* (2007), and *The Smallest Girl Ever* (2007). In her writings for young adults, she won several awards for *I, Coriander* (2005), a historical fairy-tale novel which deals with a young girl's difficult life in seventeenth-century England. Coriander is the daughter of a London merchant and a fairy-tale princess, and she narrates her adventures from early childhood through adolescence. After her mother dies and her father must flee political persecution, Coriander is left alone to deal with a nasty stepmother and a sinister Puritan minister. Fortunately, she discovers that she can move from the oppressive Cromwellian society to her mother's fairy-tale realm with the help of magic silver shoes. However, she encounters some of the same problems in the fairy realm as she does in Puritan England. Coriander is then faced with the task of finding a magic power that will enable her to overcome the oppressive regimes in both the fairy realm and London society. In another of her significant young-adult novels, *Tinder* (2013), she sets Hans Christian *Andersen's 'The Tinderbox'* in the time of the Thirty Years War (1618–48) and draws parallels with the wars in Iraq and Afghanistan by depicting how a common soldier is compelled to participate in devastating battles that are senseless. In her fantasy novel with political and fairy-tale motifs, *Maggot Moon* (2013), Gardner describes the plight of a fifteen-year-old boy living in a totalitarian society during the 1950s. Unlike *Tinder*, this novel offers a hopeful alternative to grim reality. JZ

Garner, Alan (1934–) Outstanding British novelist. Born in Cheshire, in a family of artisans, Garner was educated at Oxford, where he studied classics. In his first novel, *The Weirdstone of Brisingamen* (1960), he made use of a local legend from his birthplace, Alderley Edge, as well as motifs from Norse and Celtic folklore, including the Arthurian cycle. The child characters are quite ineffective, no more than lenses through which the colourful world of magic is described. What fascinated Garner in the legend was the idea of how it might influence contemporary life. This novel, like all his others, is about the 'here and now' rather than about magical countries or a remote past. The philosophical dilemma arising when Garner tries to retell a medieval legend in today's England can be summarized in his own words as: 'What if...?' This phrase is the key to Garner's work. What if the events of the legend are true? What would the consequences be, and what would happen if two ordinary children from today's England were to get involved in the strange world of the legend? And in his later novels: what would happen if magical objects were brought from another world into our own? How high is the price for meddling in the affairs of a magic realm? What would happen if modern young people were to get caught up in the tragic pattern of an ancient fairy tale?

Garner is one of the few writers who has managed to unite magical secondary worlds with a real landscape which can be found on a map. The magical world of Garner's books is projected onto the real world, and the boundary between the two is practically non-existent. In *The Weirdstone of Brisingamen* and its sequel, *The Moon of Gomrath* (1963), there is a clear sense of Garner's obsession with his native district and its numerous grave-mounds, standing stones, and churches oriented according to sunrise on the vernal equinox. These details are woven so subtly into the story that they often hamper the reader in following the plot. Like many beginning authors, Garner was too eager to put everything he knew into one and the same book. His first two novels, which were supposed to become a trilogy, have all the components of a successful adventure: mysteries, secret passages, pursuits, caves, false clues, as well as easily recognizable fairy-tale elements: magic amulets, good and evil wizards, dwarfs, and knights.

Elidor (1965), which has some elements from the legends of Childe Roland, begins in a church ruin on the outskirts of Manchester, where four siblings are enticed to enter a magical realm—the only magical realm in Garner's work that lies beyond the ordinary British landscape. The connections between the worlds are places of ruin and devastation where the boundary has been destroyed or weakened. Characteristically, the street where one of the passages emerges is called Boundary Lane. The children's treacherous guide, Malebron, a duplicitous magician, is prepared to sacrifice anything for the good of his country. After a very short stay in Elidor the children return to their own world carrying the four treasures of Elidor: a precious stone, a sword, a spear, and a cauldron, traditional magical objects of Celtic folklore. In the dull and uneventful reality of present-day Manchester, the treasures are transformed into a worthless cobble, splintered laths, a length of iron railing, and a broken cup. Nevertheless, even in this dilapidated form, they remain a bridge into mysterious Elidor, which, unlike the multicoloured world of *The Weirdstone of Brisingamen*, is rather vaguely depicted. Instead, the book is centred on the serious moral problems facing the main character. Because of Roland's fatal mistake, the front door of the house can serve as a passage from Elidor into the security of the real world. The threat of evil forces is felt as much stronger than if they had remained in the alternative world. In *Elidor*, the magical realm is like a shadow, a dreamworld, and the old church ruin the magical passage, the sound of the fiddle the Summons Call, and the four treasures the key to this realm. Garner is interested in reality and the way reality is affected by the intrusion of magic, in the form of Elidor's dark warriors and unicorn. This connection between worlds becomes the cornerstone of his later work.

It is easy to imagine Elidor existing not only in another spatial, but also in another temporal dimension. This is the link between Garner's first books, *Elidor*, and *Red Shift* (1973), a novel about the continuity of time and the simultaneous existence of all times. Although there is no direct reference to magic in *Red Shift*, there is a very strong sense of mythical thought, and the Stone Age axe portrayed in the story may be viewed as a magical amulet connecting the three historical layers of the plot.

The Owl Service (1967) is the only novel by Garner which does not have a direct connection to his native district and instead takes place in Wales. It is based on one of the stories from *The Mabinogion* while at the same time it examines the pain and anxiety of modern teenagers. This pain, described already in *Elidor*, reaches its peak in *Red Shift*; thus fairy-tale patterns are used by Garner exclusively as narrative devices for investigating his own time. For *The Owl Service* Garner was awarded the Carnegie Medal and Guardian Award.

The Stone Book Quartet (1976–8) has been praised as Garner's best work and regarded as his final conquest of realism. Superficially, these are indeed realistic stories about several generations of the Garner family, but it would be a mistake to view the *Quartet* as everyday realism. Everything that is typical of Garner as an artist, including his interest in the mystical and the inexplicable, and the legends, rites, and landscapes of his childhood, is present in these four stories and plays a most significant role. Here as well, the real and the magical landscapes are intertwined.

Besides original novels, Garner has also published a vast number of collections of retold fairy tales, always with his own characteristic tone and linguistic flavour, as can be seen in *The Guizer* (1976), *Alan Garner's Fairytales of Gold* (1980), *The Lad of the Gad* (1980), *Alan Garner's Book of British Fairy Tales* (1984), and *A Bag of Moonshine* (1986).

In his later novels, *Strandloper* (1996) and *Thursbitch* (2003), he continued writing tales about Cheshire, but they do not contain many of the fairy-tale and fantasy elements that had characterized his earlier work. They tend to combine patterns from Australian aboriginal and local Cheshire mythology. In 2012, he finally published a third book in the Weirdstone trilogy, *Boneland*, an adult sequel to the earlier volumes intended for young readers. In this work, which is filled with references to Cheshire and mythology, Garner focuses on Colin, who, now in his fifties, is a disturbed, brilliant scientist on a quest to locate his sister as well as to grasp his own place in the world. As in many of Garner's works, there are more unanswered questions than resolutions.   MN

'Alan Garner', spec. issue of *Labrys*, 7 (1981).
Gillies, Carolyn, 'Possession and Structure in the Novels of Alan Garner', *Children's Literature in Education*, 18 (1985).
Nikolajeva, Maria, 'The Insignificance of Time', *Children's Literature Association Quarterly*, 14 (1989).
Philip, Neil, *A Fine Anger: A Critical Introduction to the Work of Alan Garner* (1981).

Garner, James Finn (1960–) American writer whose adaptations of fairy tales and fables satirize the language and politics of political correctness. Garner's first collection, *Politically Correct Bedtime Stories*, appeared in 1994. It became an international best-seller, and he followed it up a year later with *Once Upon a More Enlightened Time* (1995). In his revisionist tales, millers and tailors are not poor, but 'economically disadvantaged'; witches are not wicked, but 'kindness impaired'; *Snow White's hosts are 'vertically-challenged'; and the wolf in *'Little Red Riding Hood' is 'unhampered by traditionalist notions of what was masculine or feminine'. Garner's hyperbole is most evident in his penchant for neologism: 'lookist', 'speciesist', and 'mer-persuns'.   MBS

Gaskell, Elizabeth (married name of **Elizabeth Cleghorn Stevenson**, 1810–65) English novelist, short-story writer, and biographer of Charlotte Brontë. She was a keen storyteller and lover of ghost stories. Charles *Dickens referred to her as his 'dear Scheherazade', and many of her short stories were published in his magazines *Household Words* and *All the Year Round*. Her fairy-tale-inspired short stories include 'Curious if True' (1860), in which an Englishman tracing his ancestry in France comes across a château full of strangely familiar guests, each of whom appears to be a realistic version of a fairy-tale character. Of her novels, *Wives and Daughters* (1864–6), left unfinished at her death, is most explicit in its use of fairy tales.   SB

Gautier, Théophile (1811–72) French poet, critic, and author of fantastic tales. He abandoned art studies to pursue poetry after Nerval introduced him to Hugo, for whom he led the legendary defence of *Hernani* (1830). A member of Le Petit Cénacle (literary salon of extreme romantics), he embraced the bohemian lifestyle represented in *Les Jeunes-France* (*The Young-France*, 1833) and caused a scandal with the 'art for art's sake' manifesto-preface to *Mademoiselle de Maupin* (1835). A lengthy journalistic career as a leading art critic followed, with success for his poetry: *Émaux et Camées* (1852; *Enamels and Cameos*, 1903) inspired the Parnassian poets and influenced Baudelaire, who dedicated to Gautier *Les Fleurs du mal* (*Flowers of Evil*, 1857).

Gautier also wrote novels (*Le Roman de la momie*, 1858/*The Romance of the Mummy*, 1863; *Le Capitaine Fracasse*, 1863/*Captain Fracasse*, 1880) and fantastic stories. They incorporate elements he defined in literary criticism on the fantastic (juxtaposition of realistic settings with mysterious phenomena, refusal to explain the impossible) and feature romantic quests for perfection and occult escapes from material worlds into altered states. His early stories show the influence of *Cazotte and *Hoffmann. 'La Morte amoureuse' ('The Vampire', 1836), for example, has a twisted *'Sleeping Beauty' motif: a young priest kisses the perfection of beauty—a ravishing corpse—and reanimates a vampire who falls in love with him. In this dark anti-fairy tale, beauty no longer signifies goodness, the ideal is neither attainable nor permanent, no one lives happily ever after. The priest must also lead both a real life and a dreamlife. Gautier elsewhere explores this double conflict of real vs. ideal in relation to madness ('Onuphrius, ou Les Vexations fantastiques d'un admirateur d'Hoffmann' ('Onuphrius', 1832) and to time and space. Past and present mingle whenever Regency art comes to life to seduce protagonists ('La Cafetière' ('The Coffeepot', 1831); 'Omphale', 1834) or when objects take men back to Ancient Egypt or Pompeii ('Le Pied de momie', 1840/'The Mummy's Foot', 1900; *Arria Marcella*, 1852/*Arria Marcella*, 1900).

Gautier also wrote lighter fairy tales. 'La Mille et deuxième nuit' ('The Thousand and Second Night', 1842) is a pastiche of the *oriental fairy tale written during the second phase of the oriental vogue in France (the first was occasioned by *Galland's translation of *Les Mille et une nuits* (*The Thousand and One Nights*) (*see* ARABIAN NIGHTS). Its frame story concerns Schéhérazade: she has run out of tales, begs one from the author, and learns about a man who has vowed to love a *péri* (a fairy in Middle Eastern mythology). Gautier later reworked this as a ballet (*La Péri*, 1843), written two years after

Giselle, ou Les Wilis (1841). This acclaimed ballet reworked Slavic legends told by *Heine: Gautier changed the *wilis* from fiancées' into dancers' spirits who lead men to their death. His other fantastic ballets dealt with alchemists, prophesying, and magic rings; unperformed scenarios treated undines, the Pied Piper, and the Pygmalion myth. MLE

Castex, Pierre-Georges, *Le Conte fantastique en France de Nodier à Maupassant* (1951).

Richardson, Joanna, *Théophile Gautier: His Life and Times* (1959).

Smith, Albert B., *Théophile Gautier and the Fantastic* (1977).

Todorov, Tzevtan, *The Fantastic: A Structural Approach to a Literary Genre*, trans. Richard Howard (1973).

Gavarni (pseudonym of **Guillaume Sulpice Chevalier**, 1804–66) Parisian illustrator and watercolourist. Trained as an architect, he was a popular and prolific illustrator whose engravings appeared in *La Mode* and *Le Charivari*. He was a close friend of Balzac, and his work was likewise praised for its encyclopaedic attention to detail in portraying all levels of society. In addition to *Robinson Crusoe* (1861) and *Gulliver's Travels* (1862), he illustrated E. T. A. *Hoffmann's fantastic tales (1843) and Mme *Leprince de Beaumont's fairy tales (1865). MLE

Landre, Jeanne, *Gavarni* (1970).

Stamm, Therese Dolan, *Gavarni and the Critics* (1981).

Gefaell, María Luisa (1918–78) Spanish author who wrote numerous books for children. Her prose has been constantly praised for its poetic nature, and her fairy tales in particular have been said to constitute a revolution within the genre of the *Märchen*. In 1951 Gefaell was given the Spanish National Literary Award for a collection of children's stories, *La princesita que tenía los dedos mágicos* (*The Little Princess who Had Magic Fingers*, 1951). In it there are a few fairy tales, such as the story from which the whole book takes its title and the one called 'Los cartuchos del abuelo' ('Grandpa's cartridges'). Gefaell's second most famous collection of fairy stories is *Las hadas de Villaviciosa de Odón* (*The Fairies of Villaviciosa de Odón*, 1953). It is made up of ten tales, each of which deals with a different kind of fairy: 'Las hadas del Mar' ('The Fairies of the Sea'), 'Las hadas de la Tierra' ('The Fairies of the Land'), and so forth.   CFR

Geras, Adèle (1944–) English writer for children and adults who has published over 75 books. Her significant contribution to the fairy-tale genre is the trilogy *Happy Ever After*, also known as the *Egerton Hall Trilogy*. It consists of *The Tower Room* (1990), *Watching the Roses (1992), and Pictures of the Night* (1992), retellings of **'Rapunzel', *'Snow White'* and **'Sleeping Beauty'*. These feminist novels portray the difficulties of adolescent girls in a boarding school. Geras has also written a picture book, *Sleeping Beauty* (2003).   JZ

Germany, fairy tales in *See* p. 239.

Gerstein, Mordecai (1935–) American illustrator and writer who began his career in animated films as a writer, director, and producer. During the 1980s he began writing and illustrating books for children. Among his fairy tales are *Prince Sparrow* (1984), *Tales of Pan* (1986), **Beauty and the Beast* (1989), and *The Giant* (1995). His imaginative use of ink and pastels gives his drawings a surrealist quality, and he has transformed some of his books such as *Beauty and the Beast* into award-winning animated films.   JZ

Gesta Romanorum (*Deeds of the Romans*) This collection of 181 Latin tales, each accompanied by a moral, composed in the late 13th century, is a preacher's guide. Although there were early English translations such as the one by Wynkyn de Worde in 1500, Charles Swan's version, published in Bohn's antiquarian library in 1824 (revised by Wynnard Hooper in 1876), is still useful.

Among the exempla are fairy tales of tasks or tests imposed on royal suitors: a princess announces that she will wed only the man who can outrun her in a race. Her challenger

diverts her with a ball inscribed 'Whosoever plays with me shall never satiate of play' (LX). Another princess tells a suitor how to remain safe in a garden guarded by a lion—smear his armour with gum to which the lion's paws will adhere (LXXIII). A princess will wed a man who solves a riddle: how many feet are in the length, breadth, and depth of the four elements (a supine servant composed of four elements measured).

Other stories have fairy-tale components. A wife tells her husband she will die if he leaves. He gives her a magic ring called 'Oblivion'. She forgets him (X). A child is born to barren parents after years of prayer (XV). A magic stag predicts that a man will kill his parents. He leaves home to avoid fate. Later he mistakes his visiting parents for his wife and a lover and kills them (XVIII). A compassionate executioner abandons a baby in woods, brings a hare's heart to his master, who had ordered the execution (XX). A bride's mother gives a groom a magic shirt that will 'neither be stained nor rent, nor worn' as long as he is chaste (LXIX). A fisherman's magic flute catches fish (LXXXV). While a husband is on a pilgrimage to Rome, his wife takes a lover, a necromancer, who makes an enchanted wax image of the husband to kill him *in absentia*. In Rome, an adviser gives the husband a magic mirror. When he sees the necromancer in the mirror prepared to shoot, he must immerse himself in water (CII). A king dies, leaving to the youngest son a magic ring with power to make the wearer beloved, a necklace to accomplish the heart's desire of any person, and a cloth that will transport anyone to any destination. He marries a woman who steals all three gifts. In his travels he acquires water that takes flesh off bones and fruit that causes leprosy. He finds a stream that restores the flesh of his feet, and a second tree that cures leprosy. Now a great healer, he is called to his wife's house to cure her. She must first confess her sins and restore all defrauded goods in exchange for a cure. He gives her the flesh-eating water and the fruit that causes leprosy.

Many different versions and translations of the *Gesta Romanorum* were disseminated

Germany, fairy tales in The roots of the German literary fairy tale can be traced to the ancient Egyptian and Graeco-Roman period of myths and oral storytelling as well as to the pagan Nordic and Slavic traditions of folklore. Though it is customary to credit Jacob and Wilhelm Grimm with fostering the study of folk and fairy tales in Germany and for providing the basis for the flowering of the fairy tale, this approach is somewhat misleading. The rise of the literary fairy tale in Germany can only be understood if we grasp the interaction between ancient European oral and literary traditions. The fairy tale in Germany is a hybrid genre closely associated with similar genres in other European countries. Therefore, it is necessary to grasp its cross-cultural history before discussing the unique development in Germany.

THE FAIRY TALE BEFORE THE BROTHERS GRIMM

Literary fairy tales are culturally marked: they are informed by the writers, their respective cultures, and the socio-historical context in which the narratives are created. Only by considering these factors can one point to the particular Italian, French, German, or English affiliations of a tale. Basically, fairy tales have a paradoxical disposition that accounts for their particularity: they contain 'universal' motifs and components that writers borrow consciously and unconsciously from other cultures in an endeavour to imbue their symbolical stories with very 'specific' commentaries on morals, mores, and manners. Fairy tales have always been truthful metaphorical reflections of the customs of their times, that is, of the private and public interrelations of people from different social classes seeking to determine the meaning of their lives. The truth value of a fairy tale is dependent on the degree to which a writer is capable of using a symbolical narrative strategy and stereotypical characterization to depict, expose, or celebrate the modes of behaviour that were used and justified to attain distinction and power in the civilizing process of a given society. Whether oral or literary, the tales have sought to uncover truths about existential conflicts and the intricacies of our civilizing processes.

For the past three hundred years or more scholars and critics have sought to define and classify the oral folk tale and the literary fairy tale, as though they could be clearly distinguished from each other, and as though we could trace their origins to some primeval source. This is an impossible task, because there are very few written records with the exception of paintings, drawings, etchings, inscriptions, and other cultural artefacts that reveal how tales were told and received thousands of years ago. In fact, even when written records came into existence, we have very little information about storytelling among the majority of people, except for bits and pieces that highly educated writers gathered and discussed in their works. It is really not until the late 18th century and the early 19th century that scholars began studying and paying close attention to folk tales and fairy tales, and it was also at this time that the Brothers Grimm, and many other intellectuals to follow, sought to establish national cultural identities by uncovering the 'authentic' tales of their so-called people, the folk, and their imagined nations.

From a contemporary perspective, the efforts of the Brothers Grimm— and the numerous efforts that they helped to inspire by Peter Christen *Asbjørnsen and Jørgen Moe, *Norwegian Folktales* (1841), George Stephens, *Swedish Folktales and Folk Stories* (1844-9), Ludwig *Bechstein, *German Fairy Tale Book* (1845), Johann Friedrich Wolf, *German Popular Tales and Legends* (1845), Ignaz Vinzenz and Joseph Zingerle, *Children and Household Tales from Tyrol* (1852), Aleksandr *Afanasyev, *Russian Fairy Tales* (1855- 63), Otto Sutermeister, *German and Household Tales* (Switzerland, 1869), Vittorio Imbriani, *Florentine Tales* (1871), Giuseppe Pitré, *Popular Sicilian Tales, Novellas, and Stories* (1875), Jerome Curtin, *Myths and Folk-Lore of Ireland* (1890), and Joseph Jacobs, *English Fairy Tales* (1890) to name but a few—led to a misconception about the nature of folk tales and fairy tales: there is no such thing as pure or authentic national folk tales or literary fairy tales, and neither genre, the oral folk tale and the literary fairy tale—if one can call them genres—is a 'pure breed'; in fact, they are both very much mixed breeds, and it is in the very way that they influenced each other historically through cross-cultural exchange that has produced fruitful and multiple versions of similar social and personal experiences.

Naturally, the oral folk tales that were told in many different ways thousands of years ago preceded the literary narratives, but we are not certain who told the tales, why, and how. We do know, however, that, well before the Judaeo-Christian era, scribes began writing down different kinds of tales that reflected an occupation with rituals, historical anecdotes, customs, startling events, miraculous transformations, and religious beliefs. The recording of these various tales was extremely important, because the writers preserved an oral tradition for future generations, and in the act of recording, they changed the tales to a greater or lesser degree, depending on what their purpose was in recording them. The literary fairy tale has deep roots in the oral tradition and was shaped in the early Christian era through the repeated transmission of tales that were written down and retold and mutually influenced one another. There is no evidence that a separate oral wonder-tale tradition or literary fairy-tale tradition existed in Europe before the Medieval period. But we do have evidence that people told all kinds of tales about gods, animals, catastrophes, wars, heroic deeds, rituals, customs, and simple daily incidents. What we call folk-tale or fairy-tale motifs are indeed ancient and appear in many pre-Christian epics, poems, myths, fables, histories, and religious narratives.

The formation of the narrative structure common to the oral wonder tale and the literary fairy tale does not begin to take shape in Europe until sometime during the early Medieval period. How this occurred, where it occurred, and exactly when it occurred—these are questions that are practically impossible to answer, because the tales developed as a process largely through talk, conversations, and performances that caught the imagination of many different people and were gradually written down first in Latin and then in different vernacular languages, when they became more acceptable in the late Middle Ages. This development has been examined in depth by Jan Ziolkowski in *Fairy Tales from Before Fairy Tales: The Medieval Latin Past of Wonderful Lies* (2006). Clearly, the literary fairy tale developed as an appropriation of a particular oral storytelling tradition of the wonder folk tale, often called the *Zaubermärchen* (magic tale) or the *conte merveilleux* (marvellous tale). As more and more wonder tales were written down from the 12th to the 15th centuries, they constituted the genre of the literary fairy tale, especially because they were conceived by a particular author, and writers began establishing distinct conventions, motifs, topoi, characters, and plots, based to a large extent on those developed in the oral tradition but altered to address a reading public formed largely by the aristocracy and the middle classes. Though the peasants, craftsmen, women, and slaves were excluded from the formation of this literary tradition, their material, tone, style, and beliefs were also incorporated into the new genre, and their experiences were recorded, albeit from the perspective of the literate scribe or writer. The secular wonder tales of the oral tradition that involved miraculous transformation formed the basis of the literary fairy tales. They were always considered somewhat suspect by the ruling and educated classes because the wonder tales indicated the need for change. The threatening aspect of wondrous change was something that the ruling classes always tried to channel through codified celebrations such as Carnival and religious holidays. Writers staked out political and property claims to wonder tales as they recorded and created them, and official cultural authorities sought to judge and control the new genre as it sought to legitimate itself.

The wonder tales provided the literary traditions with basic structures and artful facilitation for memory: their flexible structures have enabled people to store, remember, and reproduce the diverse plots over hundreds of years and to transform them to fit their experiences and desires because of the easily identifiable characters who are associated with particular social classes, professions, and assignments. The motifs, characters, topoi, and magical properties of the literary tradition can be traced back to tale collections from the Orient that predate Christianity. They are apparent in Indian, Egyptian, Greek, and Roman myths and in tales that constitute Oriental and Occidental religions. However, the wonder tales that became literary fairy tales were not collected or institutionalized in the short narrative forms that we recognize in the West until the late Middle Ages. It was at that time that male scribes began recording them in collections of tales, epics, romances, and poetry from the 10th century onwards.

The rise of the literary fairy tale as a short narrative form stemmed from the literary activity that flourished in Florence during the 14th century and led to the production of various collections of *novelle* in Italian and Latin under the influence of Boccaccio's *Decamerone*. The *novella*, also called *conto*, was a short tale which adhered to principles of unity of time and action and clear narrative plot. The focus was on surprising events of *everyday* life, and the tales (influenced by oral wonder tales, fairy tales, *fabliaux*, chivalric romances, epic poetry, and fables) were intended for the amusement and instruction of their readers. Before Boccaccio had turned his hand to writing his tales, the most famous collection had been the *Novellino* written by an anonymous Tuscan author in the 13th century. But it was Boccaccio who set a model for all future writers of this genre with his frame narrative and subtle and sophisticated style. It was Boccaccio who expanded the range of topics of the *novella* and created unforgettable characters, which led to numerous imitations by writers such as Ser Giovanni Fiorentino, Giovanni *Sercambi, Franco Sachetti, Piovano Arlotto, and Matteo Bandello, to name but a few.

It was undoubtedly due to Boccaccio's example and the great interest in the *novella* that Giovan Francesco *Straparola came to publish his collection, Le *piacevoli notti* (*The Pleasant Tales*, 1550/1553) in two volumes. Straparola is a fascinating figure, because he was the first European writer to include 14 fairy tales in his collection of 74 *novelle*. The allure of his work can be attributed to several factors: his use of erotic and obscene riddles, his mastery of polite Italian used by the narrators in the frame narrative, his introduction of plain earthy language into the stories, the critical view of the power struggles in Italian society and lack of moralistic preaching, and his interest in magic, unpredictable events, duplicity, and the supernatural.

Straparola's tales circulated throughout Europe and had a considerable influence on educated writers. The Neapolitan author Giambattista *Basile was apparently familiar with his book, and it is obvious that the French writers Mme d'*Aulnoy, Mme de *Murat, Eustache *Le Noble, and Jean de *Mailly knew his tales, and through them they spread to Germany and eventually influenced the Brothers Grimm, who wrote about Straparola and Basile. In short, Straparola initiated and influenced the genre of the literary fairy tale in Europe, and though it would be misleading to talk about a diachronic history of the literary fairy tale with a chain reaction that begins with Straparola, leads to Basile, then the French writers of the 1690s, and culminates in the work of the Brothers Grimm and the German Romantics, they do, indeed, form a historical frame in which the parameters of the early literary fairy tale were set, and within that frame there was an institutionalization of what we now call fairy-tale characters, topoi, motifs, metaphors, and plots. Their conventionalization enabled numerous writers (and story-tellers in the oral tradition) to experiment and produce highly original fairy tales at the same time. These writers were also tellers, for the split between oral and literary narrators was never as great as we imagine it to be, and their familiarity with the folklore of their respective societies played a role in their literary representations in the fairy tale.

In this regard, the French writers continued the remarkable experimentation with the marvellous that the Italians, namely Straparola and Basile, had begun many years before them, but they were able to ground them and institutionalize them as a genre more effectively than the Italians had done through the salon culture and the growth of the printing industry. Like Straparola and Basile, they exploited the marvellous in conscious narrative strategies to deal with real social issues of their time. The first French vogue of 1690–1700 was not a vogue in the sense of a fad, for shortly after the turn of the century it helped give rise to a second phase that consisted of Oriental tales and diverse experiments that consisted of farces, parodies, innovative narratives, and moral tales for the young. Perhaps the most momentous event was the publication of Antoine *Galland's Les *Mille et une nuits (1704–17) (The Thousand and One Nights, 1704–17) in 12 volumes.

By 1720 the literary fairy tale was firmly entrenched in France, and its dissemination was to increase throughout the 18th century in different forms. Perhaps the most significant way was through the chapbooks of the *Bibliothèque Bleue, which were series of popularized tales published in a cheap format in Troyes during the early part of the 17th century by Jean Oudot and his son Nicolas and Pierre Garnier. These collections (which were later translated and imitated in Germany as the *Blaue Bibliothek and spread to England in chapbook form) were at first dedicated to the Arthurian romances, lives of saints, and legends. They were carried by pedlars to towns and cities in the country and made works originally written for an upper-class audience available for all classes.

The French influence on the development of the literary fairy tale for young and old was prevalent throughout Europe and culminated in Charles-Joseph *Mayer's remarkable 40-volume collection, *Cabinet des fées (1785–9), which brought together a good deal of the most important fairy tales, including many of the Arabian tales by Galland, published during the past 100 years in France. His collection, which was reprinted several times, had a profound influence because it was regarded as the culmination of an important trend and gathered tales that were representative and exemplary for the institution of a genre.

THE FORMATION OF THE LITERARY FAIRY TALE IN GERMANY

Ironically, the most immediate impact of the Cabinet des fées was in Germany, where the literary fairy tale had not been flowering, and thanks to the French influence, it began to flourish in the last three decades of the 18th century. As Manfred Graetz has indicated in his significant study, *Das Märchen in der deutschen Aufklärung. Vom Feenmärchen zum Volksmärchen* (1988), the German educated class was largely fluent in French and could read most of the French works in the original. However, German translations of numerous French fairy tales helped German writers to form their versions in their own language to establish the 'German' literary genre in German-speaking principalities.

It should be noted that most of these early translated tales were very free and could be considered adaptations. The first translations began as early as 1710, and they were based on Galland's *Thousand and One Nights*. Some of the other more important translations were Friedrich Eberhard Rambachs' *Der Frau Maria le Prince de Beaumont Lehren der Tugend und Weisheit für die Jugend* (1758), based on Mme Leprince de Beaumont's *Le Magasin des enfants*; Justin Bertuch's *Ammen-Mährchen* (1790), based on Perrault's *Histoires ou contes du temps passé*; and *Feen-Märchen der Frau Gräfin von Aulnoy*, 4 volumes (1790–6), fairy tales by Mme d'Aulnoy. The most significant was the publication of the *Cabinet der Feen* (1761–6) in 9 volumes translated by Friedrich Immanuel Bierling. This collection provided the German reading public with key French fairy-tale texts and sparked imitations of different kinds. The work of Christoph Martin *Wieland was in part inspired by the French fairy tale, and he in turn was crucial as a cultural mediator. A famous German novelist and poet, closely associated with Weimar culture, Wieland published an important collection of tales titled *Dschinnistan* (1786–90), which included adaptations from the French *Cabinet des fées* as well as three original tales. Typical of all these narratives is the triumph of rationalism over mysticism. Among his other works that incorporated fairy-tale motifs are *Der Sieg der Natur über die Schwärmerei oder die Abenteuer des Don Sylvio von Rosalva*, (*The Victory of Nature over Fanaticism or the Adventures of Don Sylvio von Rosalva*, 1764), *Der goldene Spiegel* (*The Golden Mirror*, 1772), and *Oberon* (1780). Minor writers (Friedrich Maximilian Klinger, Christoph Wilhelm Guenther, Albert Ludwig Grimm, Friedrich Schulz) as well as major writers were influenced by the French tales, German translations, and Wieland's works. Though Johann Karl August *Musäus called his important collection of fairy tales *Volksmärchen der Deutschen* (*Folk Tales of the Germans*, 1782–6) and Benedikte *Naubert entitled her volume *Neue Volksmärchen der Deutschen* (*New Folk Tales of the Germans*, 1789–93), these works and others were pan-European and were also influenced by translations of Oriental tales into French and German. One of the first important collections for young readers, *Palmblätter* (*Palm Leaves*, 1786–90), four volumes edited by August Jakob Liebeskind with contributions by Johann Gottfried Herder and Friedrich Adolf Krummacher, had the subtitle 'erlesene morgendländische Erzählungen' ('selected oriental stories'), and one of the key romantic texts by Wilhelm Heinrich *Wackenroder had the title 'Ein wunderbares morgendländisches Märchen von einem nackten Heiligen' ('A Wondrous Oriental Tale of a Naked Saint', 1799).

In fact, by the time the German Romantics came on the literary scene in the last decade of the 18th century, the fairy tale had been more or less well established in Germany, and they could abandon the conventional structure and themes and begin to experiment in a vast number of ways. All the major romantic writers, Ludwig *Tieck, *Novalis, Clemens *Brentano, Joseph von *Eichendorff, Friedrich de la Motte *Fouqué, Adelbert *Chamisso, and E. T. A. *Hoffmann wrote fairy tales that reveal a great familiarity with the French and oriental literary tradition, as well as the oral tradition and folklore in Germany. In addition, the romantic writers were either inspired by or rebelled against Johann Wolfgang von *Goethe's 'Das Märchen' ('The Fairy Tale', 1795), a highly complex metaphorical depiction of the chaos wrought by the French Revolution and a call for a new enlightened society. Among the notable romantic writers who either responded to Goethe or went beyond him in proposing unusual ideal realms in their fairy tales were: Novalis, who wrote *Heinrich von Ofterdingen*, a fairy-tale novel of education; Tieck, who composed a series of fairy-tale plays such as *Der gestiefelte Kater* (*Puss in Boots*, 1797) and *Die Rotkäppchen* (*Little Red Riding Hood*, 1800) and published extraordinary fairy tales in *Phantasus* (1812–16); Brentano, whose *Fairy Tales of the Rhine* were written between 1809 and 1813 and were published posthumously in 1846–7; Eichendorff, who wrote several unusual tales such as 'Das Marmorbild' ('The Marble Statue', 1819). in which a young knight named Florio falls under the spell of Venus; de la Motte Fouqué, whose novella, *Undine* (1811) is one of the great classic fairy tales about a water nymph who seeks a soul to marry a young knight; Chamisso, who produced *Peter Schlemihls wundersame Geschichte* (*Peter Schlemihl's Amazing Story*, 1814) about a young man who sells his shadow to the devil; and Hoffmann, the greatest of the German writers of fairy tales, whose numerous fantastic fairy tales in *Nachtstücke* (*Nocturnal Pieces*, 1816–17) and in *Die Serapionsbrüder* (*The Serapion Brethren*, 1819–21) had a strong influence on European and American authors.

The Brothers Grimm were part of this Romantic movement, but they focused more on collecting and editing folk and fairy tales and produced the first of their great collections, *Kinder- und Hausmärchen* (*Children and Household Tales*) in 1812 and 1815. The first two volumes of *Children's and Household Tales* contained 156 tales and copious notes in the appendixes and were not at all intended for children. It was not until 1819, when the second edition appeared in one volume with 170 texts with the notes published separately, that the Grimms decided to cater to young readers as well as a growing middle-class reading audience of adults. After the publication of the second edition there were five more editions until 1857 as well as ten printings of a smaller edition of 50 tales, which were geared to the tastes of bourgeois families. The final edition of 1857 contained 210 tales, which had been carefully stylized by Wilhelm so that they reflected what he and Jacob considered a popular 'folk' tone and genuine customs and beliefs that the German people had cultivated. To a certain extent, their numerous editions and the republication of their tales throughout the 19th century not only made their tales the most popular in German history but also led to a kind of German cultural infatuation with the fairy tale.

Indeed, the 'love affair' of the German people with the Grimms' stories and with fairy tales in general reveals a great deal about the German national character, for the Brothers also imbued them with certain qualities that corresponded to the aspirations of the German middle class and peasantry. To a certain extent, the Grimms made a 'German' cultural institution out of the fairy-tale genre: they established the framework of the genre, one that has become a cultural field of production in which various writers convene to voice their personal needs and a social need for pleasure and power under just conditions. The most resilient genre in German literary history since the 18th century, the literary fairy tale has also been Germany's most democratic literary institution. The aesthetic nature of the symbolic discourse as consolidated by the Grimms enabled writers of all classes to use it, to voice their views without fear of reprisal, to seek to alter the dominant discourse, and to gain understanding from the discourse itself.

As a literary institution, the fairy tale assumed a secular educational role in the civilizing process of different German principalities that were forming a nation state. The overall social function of the literary fairy tale as institution at the beginning of the 19th century was to provide aesthetic formations of social redemption. Given the Napoleonic Wars, the censorship, the lack of unification of the German people, the ineffectual peasant revolts, and the gradual rise of bureaucracy, the literary fairy tale became a means for German writers and a bourgeois reading public to pose and explore more harmonious options for the creative individual experiencing the development of a free-market system, while also questioning such a system and the utilitarian purposes which the incipient bourgeois institutions began to serve. Unlike in France, where the literary fairy tale was first and foremost courtly and had declined by time of the French Revolution, and unlike in England, where the literary fairy tale was more or less banned by the bourgeois revolution of 1688 and did not revive until the Victorian period (partly because of German influence), the literary fairy tale in Germany became a major mode of expression for German bourgeois writers, a means of socio-religious compensation and legitimation.

More than Goethe and the German Romantics, whose complex, symbolical tales were not easily accessible for a large public—nor were they widely distributed—the Grimms were able to collect and compose tales that spoke to readers of all classes and age groups. Once the Grimms' fairy tales became established as the conventional model of the fairy tale in the 19th century, there was a kind of domestication of the fairy tale in the 19th century that represented a taming of the radical Romantic experimentation. This conservative trend can be seen in the works of Wilhelm Hauff, *Die Karawane* (The Caravan, 1825), Ludwig Bechstein, *Deutsches Märchenbuch* (*German Fairy Tale Book*, 1845) and the *Neues Deutsches Märchenbuch* (*New German Fairy Tale Book*, 1856), and Eduard Mörike, *Das Stuttgarter Hutzelmännlein* (*The Wrinkled Old Man from Stuttgart*, 1853), and many others. But there was still an abundant number of writers who sought to adapt the Grimms tales or experiment with the genre. For instance, numerous tales written by German women such as Karoline *Stahl, Clara Fechner, Sophie Albrecht, Dorothea Schlegel, Caroline Pichler, and Sophie Tieck-Bernhardi during the late 18th and 19th centuries reveal how widespread the interest in fairy tales was. Gisela von *Arnim formed a weekly Berlin salon in 1843, and the members wrote and read fairy tales as well as romances. Such literary salons and groups led to the publication of approximately 200 fairy-tale books by women in the 19th century.

The more the Grimms' tales and other popular fairy tales became part of German households, the more they also became pedagogical tools by the early 20th century. The use at home and at schools engendered numerous literary experiments so that almost all the significant German (including Swiss and Austrian) writers from the mid-19th century to the present have either written or endeavoured to write a fairy tale: Bettina von *Arnim, Gottfried *Keller, Fanny *Lewald, Theodor *Storm, Wilhelm *Raabe, Gisela von Arnim, Theodor *Fontane, Marie von Ebner-Eschenbach, Ricarda Huch, Hugo von *Hofmannsthal, Hermann *Hesse, Rainer Maria *Rilke, Franz *Kafka, Thomas Mann, Bertolt *Brecht, Ödön von *Horvàth, Carl Zuckmayer, Gerhart *Hauptmann, Alfred *Döblin, Georg Kaiser, Joachim *Ringelnatz, Kurt *Schwitters, Kurt Tucholsky, Walter Hasenclever, Hans *Fallada, Oskar Maria Graf, Erich *Kästner, Siegfried Lenz, Helmut Heissenbüttel, Ingeborg *Bachmann, Peter *Hacks, Günther *Kunert, Wolf Biermann, Christa Wolf, Stefan *Heym, Irmtraud Morgner, Peter *Härtling, Max *Frisch, Nicolas Born, Peter Handke, and Günter *Grass. They have all worked within the institution of the fairy tale and have viewed it as a viable means for reaching audiences and for expressing their opinions about the form itself and society.

After the First World War there was an unusual endeavour by progressive writers and artists during the Weimar Repulic (1919–22) to transform fairy tales along socialist and communist lines. Hermynia *Zur Mühlen started writing political fairy tales for children in 1921 with *Was Peterchens Freunde erzählen (What Little Peter's Friends Tell),* and she followed this with other collections, such as *Das Schloss der Wahrheit (The Castle of Truth,* 1924) and

Es war einmal, . . . und es wird sein (*Once Upon a Time . . . And It Will Come to Be*, 1930). In addition, Ernst Friedrich gathered some interesting political tales by Berta Lask, Carl *Ewald, and Robert Grötzsch in *Proletarischer Kindergarten (Proletarian Kindergarten,* 1921) while Bruno *Schönlank's *Grossstadt-Märchen (Big City Fairy Tales,* 1923), Walter Eschbach's *Märchen der Wirklichkeit (Fairy Tales of Reality,* 1923), Heinrich *Schulz's *Von Menschlein, Tierlein und Dinglein (Little People, Animals and Things,* 1925), Cläre Meyer-Lugau's *Das geheimnisvolle Land (The Mysterious Country,* 1925), and Lisa *Tetzner's *Hans Urian* (1931) demonstrated how fairy tales could be used to explain social contradictions to children in a highly illuminating way. However, the movement to radicalize fairy tales really never took root among children and adults in the Weimar Republic. The classic fairy tales of the Grimms, Andersen, and Bechstein reigned supreme and were imitated by a host of mediocre writers who fostered a canon of condescending, morally didactic tales which were used basically to sweeten the lives of children like sweets for consumption. Moreover, the classic fairy tale was now disseminated through radio and film, and this distribution made its impact even greater on children of all classes.

During the 1920s German writers moved in the direction of making the fairy tale more usable in the socialization process, and by 1933 such explicit use was expanded during the period of National Socialism, when the Nazis methodically exploited the fairy-tale genre in an ideological manner to uphold the racist and nationalist supremacy of the German people. Thus the schools, film industry, and publishers were induced to produce fairy tales that subscribed in text and image to *völkisch* ideology. And after 1945, the fairy tale continued to be employed directly by schools, literary organizations, theatres, psychologists, publishers—and, of course, by writers—to influence social attitudes. Albeit, this was not done in a fascist sense, although one cannot talk about a complete rupture with National Socialist thinking and methods in West Germany. The fairy tale retained something *völkisch* about it for many a German, and some Germans continued to identify with the Grimms' tales in a conservative nationalist manner after the Second World War. Generally speaking, however, fairy tales (primarily the Grimms' tales) were used widely in schools in a spiritual, religious, and aesthetic manner that downplayed the historical and social significance of the tales and stressed their 'marvellous' therapeutic and mystical qualities. Up until the late 1960s the social function of fairy tales in schools, endorsed by other outside organizations and societies, was to further the idealist notion of an inner realm of reality that is not connected to material conditions outside the self and can be shaped organically and morally by the fairy tale. Most striking here was the anthroposophical approach developed by followers of Rudolf Steiner in the Waldorf Schools, which had and still has a wide following outside those schools. Underlying the work of the Waldorf

Schools and similar pedagogical approaches was the belief that fairy tales reflect inner experiences related to natural conditions of primeval times, and that the symbols and images of fairy tales enable a child to imbibe and grasp the secret laws of nature. Such a spiritual approach to fairy tales, along with *völkisch* and psychological ones, was also common (at first) in one of the largest literary societies in West Germany, the Europäische Märchenge-sellschaft, which holds large annual meetings and sponsors a series of critical studies about fairy tales. This society, like many others, has become more realistic and historical in its approach to fairy tales since the late 1960s, when there was a major shift in the fairy tale as an institution; unlike in any other western country, the German fairy tale at that time underwent a politicization connected to the German infatuation with the fairy tale.

From 1948 to 1989 in East Germany, the Grimms' fairy tales were looked upon with suspicion at first because of their retrograde ideology associated with medieval absolutism. However, the socialist state and party gradually changed cultural policies on fairy tales, and the Grimms' tales and other German folk tales were approved by the mid-1950s because they contained positive elements of the class struggle and were part of a grand European tradition that corresponded to the internationalist aspect of communism. Moreover, the tales were considered helpful in developing the moral character of young people. In this regard, the East German film company, DEFA, played a major role in adapting the Grimms' tales by producing over 20 well-made and idealistic fairy-tale films.

In the meantime, by 1970, because of the West German student movement with its anti-authoritarian impulses, there was a crucial shift in the approach to fairy tales and their production—and this shift also occurred in East Germany. More progressive writers began formulating their socially symbolic discourse against the grain of the Grimms, while at the same time using the brothers' conventions. The conservative bourgeois value system in the Grimms' tales, which also incorporated feudal patriarchal notions, was viewed as anachronistic, banal, and escapist. Nevertheless, the fairy tale as an institution was not in and of itself considered escapist as long as one renovated, revised, and reutilized the Grimms' tales and others in the German cultural heritage. In addition to the critical approach taken by writers and publishing houses, young teachers in primary and secondary schools introduced socio-historical methods aimed at clarifying the relationship of the Grimms' tales and other fairy tales to social realities and to problems confronting contemporary Germans. With the development of a new sensibility, writers such as *Janosch, Friedrich Karl *Waechter, Kassa-jep, Karin Struck, Michael *Ende, Iring *Fetscher, Peter *Rühmkorf, Günter Grass, and numerous others designed their tales for a new German audience and with the hope that what they were criticizing and developing in the institution of the fairy tale would have some social impact.

The continuities of a dialogue within the institution of the fairy tale are astounding. If we consider just the productive side of fairy tales in both East and West Germany from the late 1960s until the present, we can grasp the significance the fairy tale as institution has retained for Germans. In the realm of children's literature numerous anthologies aimed at revising the Grimms' tales, while new types of provocative tales sought to upset the normative, traditional expectations of readers weaned on tales by the Grimms, Hauff, and Bechstein. Among the more interesting books here are Paul Maar's *Der tätowierte Hund* (*The Tattooed Dog*, 1968); Christine Nöstlinger's *Wir pfeifen auf den Gurkenkönig* (*We Don't Care a Bit about the Cucumber King*, 1972); Friedrich Karl Waechter's *Die Bauern im Brunnen* (*The Farmers in the Fountain*, 1979); Janosch's *Janosch erzählt Grimm's Märchen* (*Janisch Tells Grimm's* Tales, 1972, revised in 1991); Michael Ende's *Momo* (1973) and *Die unendliche Geschichte* (*The Neverending Story*, 1979); Hans Joachim Gelberg's anthology *Neues vom Rumpelstilzchen* (*Something New from Rumpelstiltskin*, 1976) with contributions from forty-three authors; Heinz Langer's *Grimmige Märchen* (*Grimm Fairy Tales*, 1984); Dieter Kühn's *Der fliegende König der Fische* (*The Flying King of the Fish*, 1996); Rotraut Susanne Berner's *Märchen-Stunde* (*Fairy-Tale Hour*, 1998); and Cornelia Funke's *Reckless: Steinernes Fleisch* (*Reckless: Stony Flesh*, 2010) and *Reckless: Lebendige Schatten* (*Fearless: Live Shadows*, 2012). The fairy tales written and collected for adults follow more or less the same pattern. Here the following works are significant: Iring Fetscher's *Wer hat Dornröschen wachgeküsst?* (*Who Kissed and Woke Up Sleeping Beauty?*, 1972), Jochen Jung's anthology *Bilderbogengeschichten* (*Broadside Tales,* 1974) with contributions by fifteen well-known authors, Peter Rühmkorf's *Der Hüter des Misthaufens: Aufgeklärte Märchen* (*The Guard of the Dung Heap: Enlightened Fairy Tales*, 1983), Rafik Schami's *Das Schaf im Wolfspelz* (*The Sheep in the Wolf's Fur,* 1989) and *Der Wunderkasten* (*The Casket of Wonders*, 1990), Roland Kübler's, *Der Märchenring* (*The Fairy-Tale Ring*, 1995), Felicitas *Hoppe's, *Picknick der Friseure: Geschichten* (*Picnic of the Barbers,* 1996) and *Iwein Löwenritter* (*Ivain, the Knight of the Lions*, 2011), and Karen *Duve's, *Die entführte Prinzessin* (*The Kidnapped Princess*, 2005) and *Grrrimm* (2012).

Finally, there has been a plethora of literary criticism dealing with folk and fairy tales which has matched the literary production itself. The major accomplishment of these critical works has been the elaboration of socio-historical methods with which one can analyse the contents and forms of the tales in light of their ideological meanings and functions in the specific German and the general Western socialization process. The focus is naturally more on Germany than on the West at large. Among the best books here are: Friedmar Apel's *Die Zaubergärten der Phantasie* (1978), Jens Tismar's *Das deutsche Kunstmärchen des 20. Jahrhunderts* (1981), revised in 1997 by Mathias Mayer, Walter Scherf's *Lexikon der Zaubermärchen* (1982) and *Das*

Märchen Lexikon (1995), Klaus Doderer's anthology *Über Märchen für Kinder von heute* (1983), with essays by various authors, Paul-Wolfgang Wührl's *Das deutsche Kunstmärchen* (1984), Volker Klotz's *Das europäische Kunstmärchen* (1985), Hermann Bausinger's *Märchen, Phantasie und Wirklichkeit* (1987), and Winfried Freund's *Deutsche Märchen* (1996).

It is not only German creative writers and scholars of folklore and literature who have responded to the fairy tale as institution, but also German philosophers. World-renowned, astute thinkers of the 20th century such as Walter Benjamin, Ernst Bloch, Theodor Adorno, Elias Canetti, Oskar Negt, and Alexander Kluge employed the fairy tale to register their insights about society and the potential of the tale itself to have a social impact. Thus, Benjamin wrote: 'Whenever good counsel was at a premium, the fairy tale had it, and where the need was the greatest, its aid was nearest. . . . The wisest thing—so the fairy tale taught mankind in olden times, and teaches children to this day— is to meet the forces of the mythical world with cunning and high spirits.'

This statement and others by Canetti and Bloch are not so much significant for their unique perspectives—although they are well worth studying— as they are for the manner in which they similarly focus on the social function of the fairy tale as prophetic and messianic. Indeed, these critics assume that the fairy tale is a special genre capable of revealing the true nature of social conditions. However, the power and communicative value which these critics attribute to the fairy tale is not typical of the way the majority of writers and thinkers outside Germany regard the genre. Undoubtedly the fairy tale as institution has its own special tradition in other countries, but it has not become such a 'sacred' convention and used as such a metaphorical medium to attain truth as it has been in Germany.   JZ

Apel, Friedmar, *Die Zaubergärten der Phantasie. Zur Theorie und Geschichte des Kunstmärchens* (1978).

Grätz, Manfred, *Das Märchen in der deutschen Aufklärung. Vom Feenmärchen zum Volksmärchen* (1988).

Haase, Donald, *The Reception of Grimms' Fairy Tales* (1993).

Jarvis, Shawn, and Blackwell, Jeannine (eds.), *The Queen's Mirror: Fairy Tales by German Women, 1780–1900* (2001).

Klotz, Volker, *Das europäische Kunstmärchen* (1985).

Tatar, Maria, *The Hard Facts of the Grimms' Fairy Tales* (1987).

Tatar, Maria, *The Annotated Brothers Grimm* (2012).

Tismar, Jens, *Kunstmärchen* (1977).

Wührl, Paul-Wolfgang, *Das deutsche Kunstmärchen* (1984).

Zipes, Jack, *The Brothers Grimm: From Enchanted Forests to the Modern World* (1988).

Zipes, Jack, *Fairy Tales and Fables from Weimar Days* (1989).

Zipes, Jack, *Grimm Legacies: The Magic Spell of the Grimms' Folk and Fairy Tales* (2014).

throughout Europe, and the tales were generally used to endorse religious morals and virtues and to expose vice. Yet, since they also stemmed in part from oriental culture and were filled with adventure, miracles, and romance, they were often secularized and changed in the oral tradition and were adapted by such great writers as Boccaccio, Chaucer, *Shakespeare, and *Schiller. HG

Marchalonis, Shirley, 'Medieval Symbols and the Gesta Romanorum', *Chaucer Review*, 8 (1974).

Roll, Walter, 'Zur Überlieferungsgeschichte der "Gesta Romanorum"', *Mittellateinisches Jahrbuch*, 21 (1986).

Gibbs, Cecilia May (1877–1969) Australian artist, cartoonist, author, and illustrator, who published under the name May Gibbs. She wrote and illustrated her first book, *Gumnut Babies* (1916), creating unique bush fairies; the iconic gumnut babies. Influenced by the art nouveau movement, her illustrations reflect the colours of the Australian bush and demonstrate her skill as an artist. In the best known of her books, *The Complete Adventures of Snugglepot and Cuddlepie* (1918), and in the books that followed, gumnuts, blossom babies, and Australian animals care for each other, share adventures, and meet villains, the Banksia Men. With a strong conservationist theme the popularity of these cherubic and original folk has seen Gibbs's books reproduced for successive generations of Australian children. Gibbs's bush fairyland has featured significantly in the imagination of magic for Australian children. In acknowledgement of her contribution to Australian children's literature Gibbs was awarded an MBE in 1955. REF

Gidwitz, Adam (1982–) American author of *A Tale Dark and Grimm* (2010), an original fairy-tale novel for young readers, which begins with the parents of Hansel and Gretel cutting off their heads. However, they manage to recover their heads and go into the forest of Grimm to seek better parents. In this comic fairy tale, they meet a dangerous stranger, a cannibal, the devil, a creepy moon, and a dragon. They even meet their parents again and manage to survive and return home in one piece. In his second fairy-tale novel, *In a Glass Grimmly* (2012), Gidwitz bases the story on 'Jack and Jill', while interweaving Grimms' tales such as 'The *Frog King' and tales by other authors such as Hans Christian *Andersen and Joseph *Jacobs. In both of these novels, Gidwitz touches on some very problematic aspects of child abuse in fairy tales. In the final novel of the trilogy, *The Grimm Conclusion* (2013), he relies heavily on the Grimms' tale 'Jorinda and Joringel', and sends the brother/sister pair on all kinds of perilous adventures that reveal how children must learn to fend for themselves and conceive their own world. JZ

Giraudoux, Jean (1882–1944) French novelist, playwright, and critic. Strongly influenced by German romantics, he wrote *Ondine* (1939), a play based on a tale by Friedrich de la Motte *Fouqué (*Undine*, 1811), which was itself a version of a 14th-century poem. Through the unsuccessful union of a nymph and a knight, Giraudoux suggests the difficulty of reconciling the natural and the human worlds. LCS

Glass, Philip (1937–) American composer whose *La Belle et la Bête: An Opera for Ensemble and Film* (première, 1994) is an innovative operatic adaptation of Jean *Cocteau's film *La Belle et la Bête* (*Beauty and the Beast*, 1946). Glass transforms Cocteau's film into a live production of music-theatre by eliminating the film's soundtrack, synchronizing his new operatic score with the film, and presenting live singers before their characters on screen. As an interpretation of the fairy-tale film, Glass's operatic score and media experiment stress the love story and the artist's inward journey towards creativity. DH

Glinka, Mikhail Ivanovich (1804–57) Russian composer. The history of Russian art music begins with Glinka's opera *A Life for the Tsar* (*Ivan Sussanin*), in 1836; in addition to its patriotic story, it was the first major composition to employ themes from

Russian folk music. His second opera, *Russlan and Ludmilla* (1842), also rich in folk themes, established the Russian national style. The story, from a poem by *Pushkin based on a Russian folk tale, relates how the Duke of Kiev's daughter Ludmilla is kidnapped by the evil flying dwarf Chernomor and rescued by the knight Russlan with his magic sword.   SR

Goble, Paul (1933–) English-born American illustrator and author who has retold many 19th-century Great Plains Indian myths and legends, primarily of the Sioux, Blackfoot, and Cheyenne cultures. Goble's works are well received by Native American readers. In fact, he has been adopted into the Yakima and Sioux tribes. *The Girl who Loved Wild Horses* (1979), a legend about a girl so impassioned by horses she is transformed into one, received the Caldecott Medal. It is a text epitomizing Goble's illustrative blend of Native American ledger book art and personal style, which stems from distinguished work as an artist and industrial designer in England. Among his other important books with fairy-tale motifs are: *Buffalo Woman* (1984), *Her Seven Brothers* (1988), and *Iktomi and the Boulder* (1988).   SS

Godoy Alcántara, José (1825–75) Spanish writer and scholar. His fame is due both to his work as a journalist and to several research works of his which received awards from the Spanish Academy of Language and the Spanish Academy of History. His tales appeared in periodicals such as *Semanario Pintoresco Español* (*Spanish Picturesque Weekly*). In 1849 Godoy published 'Un abad como hubo muchos y un cocinero como no hay ninguno. Cuento' ('An Abbot as There Have Been Many and a Cook as There Is No Other. Tale'. This story is a literary rendition of a popular European tale which had already been taken from the oral tradition and incorporated into the written one by the Spanish 16th-century writer Juan de Timoneda.   CFR

Goethe, Johann Wolfgang von (1749–1832) Germany's Olympian poet and dramatist, Goethe turned to literary fairy tales on several occasions in mid-life, integrating them into memoirs and novels. Chapbooks read in his childhood introduced him to popular tales like 'Fortunatus', *'Mélusine', 'Till Eulenspiegel', and 'The Wandering Jew', and storytelling at home made children's stories like 'The *Brave Little Tailor' familiar. In his twenties he made references in his correspondence to magical components recognizable from fairy tales such as 'The *Juniper Tree', 'One-Eye, Two-Eyes, and Three-Eyes', and 'The *Frog King'. Like all educated urban Germans of the 18th century, Goethe was also acquainted with French tales about fairies, both through his own reading and, by his own account, from stories his lively young mother had told him in his youth. In his first novel, *Die Leiden des jungen Werther* (*The Sorrows of Young Werther*, 1774), he developed this motif and had his protagonist Werther tell children stories.

As the 61-year-old author of *Dichtung und Wahrheit* (*Poetry and Truth*, part I, book 2), Goethe reported recounting to childhood playmates a 'fairy tale for boys', 'Der neue Paris' ('The New Paris'). A dream sequence, it embedded the narrative in a real and well-known location, the fortifications surrounding Frankfurt am Main. But the tale drew its elaborate magic, classic references, colourful cast of beautiful nymphs, and inventory of delicate crystal, exotic fruit, and courtly entertainments from the style and content of 18th-century French tales about fairies.

In part 2, book 10 of *Poetry and Truth*, Goethe recorded telling 'Die neue Melusine' ('The New Melusine') to a group of young friends near Strasbourg as a young man. Typical of the literary trajectory of many modern stories, it was a legend that had been published as a *Volksbuch* and developed by Mlle de *Lubert as 'Princess Camion' before it entered *Wilhelm Meisters Wanderjahre* (*Wilhelm Meister's Years of Travel*, 1821) as a novella (3.6). His final effort, 'Das Märchen' ('The Fairy Tale'), composed in 1795, became part of *Conversation of German Emigrants* (*Unterhaltungen deutscher Ausgewanderten*).

'The Fairy Tale' was Goethe's attempt to compose the consummate narrative of this genre and to address the chaos brought about by the French Revolution and Napoleonic Wars. The basic theme of the complex symbolical fairy tale concerns the golden age and the restoration of order and harmony on earth. In 'The Fairy Tale' two lands are separated by a river, and chaos reigns. A peasant man with a light is called upon to go to the temple on the other side of the river and to help cure the dying Lily. Various characters such as the ferryman, two will-o'-the-wisps, a beautiful green serpent, and a young man must make sacrifices and work together to bring about the establishment of a new enlightened realm. Goethe's 'Fairy Tale' has been interpreted as a religious, political, philosophical, and even economic allegory. *Novalis, the German romantic poet, wrote a fairy tale about Klingsohr to critique Goethe's work, and numerous German writers up to the present day have been influenced by it.

Like many others in 18th-century Germany, Goethe had been influenced by imports from France like The *Arabian Nights and tales about fairies. In high old age he enjoyed telling such stories to the princesses of the Weimar court and to his own grandchildren.

Respectful 19th-century contemporaries like J. G. Büsching and Wilhelm *Grimm kept Goethe informed about newly published German fairy-tale collections. Goethe's references to brief narratives and to fairy tales in theoretical terms are varied and various, admiring, analytical, and denigrating in turn. His remarks reflect the tension that fairy tales generate and express between competing realms: magic and morality, fantasy and reason. His utterances also embody his mixed experience with fairy tales, which included a notably failed effort to compose a sequel to the *Zauberflöte*.   RBB

Geulen, Hans, 'Goethes Kunstmärchen "Der neue Paris" und "Die neue Melusine": Ihre poetologischen Imaginationen und Spielformen', *Deutsche Vierteljahrsschrift für Literaturwissenschaft und Geistesgeschichte*, 59.1 (1985).

Hoermann, Roland, 'Goethe's Masked Masque in "Das Märchen": Theatrical Anticipations of Romanticism's Self-Reflexive Peril', in Clifford A. Bernd (ed.), *Romanticism and Beyond* (1996).

Mommsen, Katharina, '"Märchen der Utopien": Goethes Märchen und Schillers Ästhetische Briefe', in Jürgen Brummack (ed.), *Literaturwissenschaft und Geistesgeschichte* (1981).

Solbrig, Ingeborg H., 'Symbolik und ambivalente Funktion des Goldes in Goethes "Märchen"', *Jahrbuch des Wiener Goethe-Vereins*, 73 (1969).

Witte, Bernd, 'Das Opfer der Schlange: Zur Auseinandersetzung Goethes mit Schiller in den *Unterhaltungen deutscher Ausgewanderten* und in *Märchen*', in Wilfried Barner (ed.), *Unser Commercium: Goethe und Schillers Literaturpolitik* (1984).

Goldman, William (1931–) American screenwriter and novelist whose best-known fantasy works are the Morgenstern series: *The Princess Bride: S. Morgenstern's Classic Tale of True Love and High Adventure, The 'Good Parts' Version, Abridged by William Goldman* (1973) and *The Silent Gondoliers: A Fable by S. Morgenstern* (1983). Adapted for films in 1987, *The *Princess Bride* is a hilarious parody of the traditional fairy tale, soap operas, and popular romances. It involves the rescue of Princess Buttercup by a dashing pirate named Westley, her childhood sweetheart. Nobody is what she or he appears in this mock fairy tale, and Goldman leaves the reader up in the air as to whether Buttercup and Westley will live happily ever after.   JZ

Goldschmidt, Meïr Aron (1819–87) Goldschmidt grew up in a liberal Jewish community in Copenhagen. He may be best known for his novels, but some of his short stories rely heavily on folk beliefs. One such story is 'Bjergtagen' ('Bewitched', 1868), which stems from the belief that supernatural beings may 'take you into the mountain', to the world of 'the others'. This particular story uses folk belief in a most romantic way, for it demonstrates that a young woman who cannot be satisfied with her mundane life must strive to transcend it and find her soulmate in that other world.   NI

Goldstein, Dina (1969–) Canadian photographer who has produced two unusual conceptual series that present critiques of social and gender stereotypes. Her first and most provocative exhibition was staged in 2009 and was called *Fallen Princesses*. It includes disturbing and ironic photographs of classic fairy-tale female characters such as an obese *Little Red Riding Hood, a forlorn *Cinderella, a frustrated and flustered *Snow White, and a cancer-ridden *Rapunzel in contemporary settings. These glossy coloured photographs have received global attention as artworks that comment critically on the Disney world and raise many questions about the lives that women are expected to lead and the actual lives that they lead. Her photos are not optimistic. Rather, they are subtle, comic, and grotesque images that undo classic fairy-tale narratives and expose some of the negative results that are rarely discussed in public. In 2012 Goldstein produced another feminist series, *In the Dollhouse*, which shows the home and marriage of the iconic dolls Barbie and her partner Ken, to comment on gender stereotyping and changes in relations between the sexes.   JZ

Goldstein, Lisa (1953–) American writer who won the American Book Award for *The Red Magician* (1982), a novel with the homespun flavour of Jewish folk tales, set in a magical version of Eastern Europe prior to the Second World War. *Strange Devices of the Sun and Moon* (1993) is a delightfully quirky novel based on the 'changeling' motif, involving fairies and Christopher Marlowe in 16th-century London. Goldstein also works with folklore themes in two short stories: 'Breadcrumbs and Stones' (1993), a powerful look at *'Hansel and Gretel' as seen through the memories of a Holocaust survivor; and 'Brother Bear' (1995), inspired by 'Goldilocks' and the Native American legend 'The Girl who Married a Bear'.   TW

Golia (pseudonym of **Eugenio Colmo**, 1885–1967) Italian caricaturist, painter, and illustrator. Most of his ink drawings appeared in the leading satirical magazines of his times. He also provided pictures for journals for young readers, and his best fairy-tale illustrations can be found in *La princessa si spossa* (*The Princess Gets Married*, 1917) written by his good friend Guido *Gozzano. Golia experimented with different styles and was influenced by the Bauhaus school in the 1920s, but he always tended to stress the mock caricature in most of his works.   JZ

Gomez, Marie-Angélique Poission, dame Gabriel de (1684–1770) French writer. Married to an impoverished Spanish nobleman, she tried to live by her pen and published more than 50 volumes, including poetry, a play, and particularly novels. Her frame narrative *Les Journées amusantes* (*Amusing Days*, 1722–31) is unusual in that its storytellers are intent not so much on displaying their worldly graces as their bookish erudition through their tales and games. One of the tales in this collection, *Histoire de Jean de Calais* (*Story of Jean de Calais*, 1723) rewrites the folkloric tale type AT 506A.   LCS

Gonzenbach, Laura (1842–78) Storyteller and amateur collector of Sicilian folk tales. She was the daughter of a German Swiss merchant and grew up in Messina, Sicily. To help a German historian, Otto Hartwig, she gathered 92 Sicilian tales in dialect primarily from women peasants and translated them into high German. The tales were published as *Sicilianische Märchen* in 1875, and this German collection was ironically the first major collection of Sicilian folk tales. It is also apparent that the tales provided an unusual feminine perspective on women's hopes and fears and their struggle for recognition. The tales were translated into English by Jack Zipes in two volumes: *Beautiful Angiola: The Great Treasury of Sicilian Folk and Fairy Tales* (2004) and *The Robber with a Witch's Head: More Stories from the Great Treasury of Sicilian Folk and Fairy Tales* (2004).   JZ

Rubini, Luisa, *La raccolta di Laura Gonzenbach, la comunità di lingua tedesca a Messina nell'Ottocento* (1998).

Goodrich, Samuel (1793–1860) American publisher and author of over 100 juvenile books of instruction. The son of a Congregational minister, he encountered fairy tales late in his youth, and reacted with horror to 'these monstrosities', a view which he retained all his life, launching many attacks on them and on nursery rhymes. His pseudonym Peter Parley was taken up by several English authors of similar books of facts, and 'Peter Parleyism' became a term of abuse used by those who supported works of imagination. *Kingsley in *The Water-Babies* (1863) referred to him slightingly as 'Cousin Cramchild' of Boston.   GA

Gorey, Edward (1925–2000) Artist, illustrator, printmaker, and writer of macabre picture books, including many miniature books and alphabets. Gorey studied at the Chicago Art Institute and Harvard, and later worked for the publisher Doubleday Anchor Books as a designer and cover artist, and illustrated children's books, such as Florence P. Heide's *The Shrinking of Treehorn* (1971) and *Donald & the . . .* , with Peter F. Neumeyer. His real fame has come from humorously exaggerated Gothic tales, self-illustrated with his black-and-white ink drawings with heavy crosshatching. These books, including *The Unstrung Harp* (1953), *The Doubtful Guest* (1957), and *The Sopping Thursday* (1970), bear the look of Victorian illustrated texts but recount ominous events and strange disappearances. Although picture books, his works emphasize the adult nature of the content of fairy tales and satirize the conventions of didactic books, especially his many alphabet books. Of these, the most notorious is *The Gashlycrumb Tinies or After the Outing* (1963), which sardonically describes the deaths of 26 children, knocked off in alphabetical order; for example: 'O is for OLIVE run through with an awl | P is for PRUE trampled flat in a brawl.' Several anthologies have collected his work, including *Amphigorey* (1972), *Amphigorey, Too* (1975), and *Amphigorey Also* (1983). Also active in theatre design, Gorey won the 'Tony' award for his costume and set design of the 1977 Broadway production *Dracula*.   GRB

Ross, Clifford, and Wilkin, Karen, *The World of Edward Gorey* (1996).

Gourmont, Remy de (1858–1915) French writer and critic. He identified *Marie de France's *Lais* as a source for the French fairy tradition. His *Histoires magiques* (*Magic Stories*, 1894) includes several fantastic tales. The symbolist work 'Le Château singulier' ('The Singular Castle') reflects Gourmont's idealist philosophy as a princess tests her suitors, accepting only the one who can forgo sexuality; the others will be condemned to a life of physical drudgery. In 'L'Étable' ('The Stable', in *D'un pays lointain*, 1930) a serving girl also passes a test to become a prince's bride.   AR

Goverde, Thijs (1971–) Dutch writer and comedian who began writing children's books in 1998 after having studied philosophy at Nijmegen. Most of his works contain fairy-tale motifs and characters that he employs in highly innovative ways. His first book, *The Purple Royal Robe* (*De purperen konigsmantel*, 1998), concerns a colourful prince who struggles to brighten up a grey kingdom. In 2006 he published *The Revenge of the Master Thief* (*De wraak van de meesterdief*), the beginning of a trilogy, followed by *The Hunt for the Master Thief* (2007) and *The Hand of the Master Thief* (2008). Nominated for several awards, the trilogy is filled with tall tales that depict the fantastic adventures of Falco, who supposedly was born from an egg, raised by a child snatcher, and later becomes a master thief and the richest man in the world.   JZ

Govoni, Corrado (1884–1965) Important Italian poet, writer, and playwright. One of Italy's foremost futurist poets, Govoni wrote lyrical prose and novels influenced by d'Annunzio's style, namely, *Anche l'ombra è sole* (*Even the Shadow is the Sun*, 1920), *La terra contro il cielo* (*The Earth against the Sky*, 1921) and *La strada sull'acqua* (*The Street over the Water*, 1923). Govoni's tales, collected in *Le rovine del Paradiso* (*The Ruins of Paradise*, 1940) and *Confessione davanti allo specchio* (*Confessions in Front of the Mirror*,

1942), often blend the classical fairy tale and a Boccacciesque taste for the joke that victimizes the villain, as seen in 'La burla del nanino della Tofana' ('The Prank of the Little Dwarf from Tofana'), included in *I racconti della ghirlandàia* (*The Jay's Tales*, 1932).

MNP

Goytisolo, Juan (1931–) Spanish novelist whose works are written in a realistic but critical manner. Goytisolo is known for denouncing the bourgeoisie, the Catholic Church, capitalism, and other aspects of Spanish culture. He is likewise devoted to revising the national past and destroying its myths. From the 1960s onwards his narrative technique was enriched by all the innovations associated with the postmodern novel. Goytisolo has also published a few collections of short stories, but they are all written in a realistic manner. However, in *Reivindicación del Conde don Julián* (*Count Julian*, 1970), one of his most important novels, he makes incursions into folklore. In fact, at the beginning of the fourth and final section of this work there is a revision of *'Little Red Riding Hood'*, a tale which is repeatedly alluded to throughout the novel. This reworking is based on *Perrault's version, but there is one outstanding difference between the two stories, the fact that the main character in Goytisolo's story is a boy instead of a little girl.   CFR

Lee, Abigail E., 'La paradigmática historia de Caperucita y el lobo feroz: Juan Goytisolo's Use of "Little Red Riding Hood" in *Reivindicación del Conde don Julián*', *Bulletin of Hispanic Studies*, 65 (1988).
Ugarte, Michael, *Trilogy of Treason: An Intertextual Study of Juan Goytisolo* (1982).

Gozzano, Guido (1883–1916) Italian poet and writer, most known for his collections of poetry, *Via del Rifugio* (1907) and *I Colloqui* (*The Colloquies*, 1911). After Gozzano's death, four collections of his tales were published: *L'altare del passato* (*The Altar of the Past*, 1918), *L'ultima traccia* (*The Last Trace*, 1919), *I tre talismani* (*The Three Talismans*, 1914), and *La principessa si sposa* (*The Princess Gets Married*, 1916), which contains the classic tale 'Il re porcaro' ('The Pig King'), the story of the three beautiful princesses whose wicked stepmother seeks the aid of a sorceress to turn them into piglets. As they are about to be slaughtered, the three succeed in convincing the executioners to spare their lives and, after many trials and tribulations, they are restored to their rightful place with the aid of a magical lizard whom Chiaretta, one of the three princesses, had helped. The wicked Queen is turned to stone as a monument to her iniquity. Other fairy tales in this volume include: 'La cavallina del negromante' ('The Necromancer's Little Mare'), 'Il reuccio gamberino' ('The Little Shrimp King'), 'Nonso' ('Don't know'), and 'La leggenda dei sei compagni' ('The Legend of the Six Comrades'). Gozzano was greatly influenced by *Straparola, Charles *Perrault, Mme d'*Aulnoy, and the Brothers *Grimm.

GD

Carletto, M., 'Per uno studio del motivo fiabesco in C. Gozzano', *Italianistica*, 4 (1975).

Gozzi, Carlo (1720–1806) Venetian aristocrat, playwright, and memorialist, who reworked a number of old fairy tales for the theatre. Like his brother Gasparo, a distinguished journalist and writer of Aesopic fables, Carlo Gozzi was a leading figure in the literary circles of 18th-century Venice. Culturally conservative, he opposed Enlightenment innovation, especially when it radically changed the nature of the theatre. He held to the tradition of the *commedia dell'arte* with its improvisation, its stock situations and stock characters like Pantaloon, Punchinello, Harlequin, and Columbine; he was the sworn enemy of Carlo Goldoni, the greatest Venetian playwright, whose realistic scripted comedies swept away the old conventions. Gozzi espoused a sophisticated theatre of fantasy and set out to prove to Goldoni that this would attract the public away from the latter's social critiques. His sequence of successful *capricci scenici* or *fiabe drammatiche* began with *L'amore delle tre melarance* (*The Love of Three Oranges*, 1761), based on a story in *Basile's *Lo cunto de li cunti* (*The *Pentameron*, 1634–6). It was the first of ten fairy-tale plays written in the short period 1761–5, for which Gozzi drew upon existing collections of stories such as Basile's, as well as the oral folk tradition, oriental sources (especially *The *Arabian Nights*, published by Antoine *Galland in French as *Les Mille et une nuits* in the years 1704–17), and the *commedia dell'arte* itself which provided Gozzi with some of his characters. His *Turandot* was also performed in 1761, and among the later notable and seminal pieces were: *Il re cervo* (*The King Stag*), *Il mostro turchino* (*The Blue Monster*), *La donna serpente* (*The Serpent Woman*), and *L'augellin belverde* (*The Green Bird*). In these plays fairy-tale fantasy is wedded to comedy and satire. Later Gozzi modelled his work on Spanish theatrical precedents, nostalgically evoking a courtly mood. Finally, he left one of the great autobiographies of a period rich in such meditative and confessional writing: his *Memorie inutili* (*Useless Memoirs*, 1797–8) offer an insight into his views on the theatre.

Gozzi's work was highly influential abroad, if not in Italy, partly through the interest of northern romantics: Alfred de Musset and, earlier, Mme de Staël in France, and in Germany, *Goethe, Lessing and the Schlegels admired the plays, while *Schiller translated him, creating an adaptation of *Turandot* for Goethe to direct. From Gozzi's own times onwards, but especially in the early 20th century, numerous fairy-tale operas by composers of various nationalities were based upon his plays, most famously *Puccini's *Turandot* (1924); there are also an early *Wagner version of *La donna serpente* (*Die Feen*, started 1833, produced 1888), a Busoni *Turandot* (1917), *Prokofiev's *The Love of Three Oranges* (1919), and Henze's *König Hirsch* (*Il re cervo*, 1956).   ALL

Bentley, Eric (ed.), *The Genius of the Italian Theatre* (1964).

Gozzi, Carlo, *Fiabe teatrali: testo, introduzione e commento*, ed. Paolo Bosisio (1984).

Gozzi, Carlo, *Carlo Gozzi: Five Tales for the Theatre*, trans. Ted Emery, with introduction (1989).

Salina Borello, R., *Le fate a teatro: le Fiabe di Carlo Gozzi tra allegoria e parodia* (1996).

Grace, Patricia (1937–) Maori writer of novels and short stories for children and adults. She lives in New Zealand, where she has taught in different places while raising seven children. Her focus in writing has been on Maori culture, and she has published books of stories with folkloristic and fairy-tale motifs: *Waiariki* (1975), *The Dream Sleepers* (1980), and *Electric City and Other Stories* (1987). Her dual-language children's picture book, *Te Kuia me te Pungawerewere* (*The Kuia and the Spider*, 1981), which portrays a spinning contest between an old woman and a spider, was based on Maori folklore.   JZ

Grahame, Kenneth (1859–1932) English author of *The Wind in the Willows* (1908), who included a fairy story, 'The Reluctant Dragon', in *Dream Days* (1898), his second collection of stories about childhood. To the children in this book and its predecessor, *The Golden Age* (1895), fairy tales are reality, so that when the narrator in 'The Finding of the Princess' wanders into the garden of a great house, he assumes that the couple he finds there are a fairy princess and her prince. Similarly, he and his sister follow dragon footprints in the snow, and then are told a story about a peaceable and friendly dragon who is with much difficulty persuaded into a mock fight with St George to satisfy public expectation.   GA

Grass, Günter (1927–) German writer, poet, and artist. He was born and educated in Danzig until he was called up to the German army at the age of 16. He was captured by the Americans, and after his release in 1946, worked as a farm labourer and as a miner before he trained as a stonemason and sculptor, later studying art at Düsseldorf and Berlin. He then moved to Paris for some years, where he started his career as a writer. His first novel, *Die Blechtrommel* (*The Tin Drum*, 1959) is now recognized as the most important German post-war novel. In 1977 he published *Der Butt* (*The Flounder*), an epic novel that combines fairy-tale, mythological, and historical elements and that Grass actually wanted to designate as a fairy tale. It refers in its title and main motif to the *Grimm fairy tale 'Von dem Fischer un siine Fru' ('The Fisherman and his Wife'), the tale of a fisherman who spares the life of an enchanted flounder he has caught, but is sent back to the fish by his wife Ilsebill, who demands the granting of her wishes, until she is reduced to her former poverty after insisting on becoming God. In Grass's novel, the flounder has to face a tribunal of feminists who condemn the fairy tale as misogynistic, and accuse him of having caused the change from the matriarchy of mythological times to the patriarchal society that has prevailed since the neolithic period. In another fairy-tale novel, *Die Rättin* (*The Rat*, 1986), Grass experiments with the legend of *'The Pied Piper' and creates an apocalyptic narrative that involves characters from the Grimms' tales and the myth of the sunken city of Vineta. Fittingly, one of Grass's most recent works, *Die Wörter* (*The Words*, 2010), is a declaration of love to the Brothers Grimm. The book is a fictional biography of the Grimms, who appear more or less as fairy-tale heroes who preserved and enriched the German language.   CS

Brady, Philip, McFarland, Timothy, and White, John J. (eds.), *Günter Grass's Der Butt: Sexual Politics and the Male Myth of History* (1990).

Mews, Siegfried (ed.), *'The Fisherman and His Wife': Günter Grass's The Flounder in Critical Perspective* (1983).

Mouton, Janice, 'Gnomes, Fairy-Tale Heroes, and Oskar Matzerath', *Germanic Review*, 56.1 (winter 1981).

Pickar, Gertrud Bauer (ed.), *Adventures of a Flounder: Critical Essays on Günter Grass' Der Butt* (1982).

Preece, Julian, *The Life and Work of Günter Grass: Literature, History, Politics* (2004).

Rölleke, Heinz, *Der wahre Butt: Die wundersamen Wandlungen des Märchens vom Fischer und seiner Frau* (1978).

Gray, Nicholas Stuart (1922–81) British playwright, actor, and writer. His numerous fairy-tale plays include: *Beauty and the Beast* (1951), *The Tinder-Box* (1951), *The Princess and the Swineherd* (1952), *The Hunters and the Henwife* (1954), *The Marvellous Story of *Puss-in-Boots* (1955), *The Imperial Nightingale* (1957), *New Clothes for the Emperor* (1957), *The Other *Cinderella* (1958), *The Seventh Swan* (1962), *The Wrong Side of the Moon* (1968), and *New Lamps for Old* (1968). Gray rewrote *The Seventh Swan* as a fairy-tale novel of development, set in 16th-century Scotland, in which a young man learns to mature through his enchantment as a swan. Gray's other important fairy-tale novels are: *Down in the Cellar* (1961), *Grimbold's Other World* (1963), *The Stone Cage* (1963), *The Sorcerer's Apprentices* (1965), *The Apple Stone* (1965), and *The Further Adventures of Puss in Boots* (1971). Two of Gray's works feature cats that accompany young heroes who must perform great deeds. For example, in *Grimbold's Other World*, Grimbold the cat takes the young boy Muffler to a strange night world where he must rescue Gareth the sorcerer's son from a terrible spell, and in *The Stone Cage* the protagonist Tomlyn travels to the far side of the moon to cure a witch of her hatred of women. Gray's graceful narrative style is often juxtaposed to the serious themes of his fairy tales which often explore tense social struggles. His shorter fairy tales have been collected in *Mainly Moonlight: Ten Stories of Sorcery and the Supernatural* (1965), *The Edge of Evening* (1976), and *A Wind from Nowhere* (1978).   JZ

Green, Roger Lancelyn (1918–87) English writer and historian of children's literature, best known for his retellings of myths and legends for young readers. Like his hero, Andrew *Lang, his imagination had been kindled by Homeric legend, and he not only compiled several books of classical myths beginning in 1958 with *Old Greek Fairy Tales* and *The Tale of Troy*, but also wrote his own children's stories founded on these. He edited collections of fairy tales, of which the most wide-ranging is *Once, Long Ago: Folk and Fairy Stories of the World* (1962). His first publication was *Andrew Lang: A Critical Biography* (1946); in the same year he published *Tellers of Tales*, an account of children's writers which in later editions he expanded to include contemporaries. He also edited the diaries and later the letters of Lewis *Carroll. His fantasy stories for children, such as *The Wonderful Stranger* (1950) and *The Land of the Lord High Tiger* (1958) have strong echoes of favourite writers such as E. *Nesbit, Lewis Carroll, and Andrew Lang. *Fifty Years of Peter Pan* (1954) gives the history of the stage production.   GA

Greenaway, Kate (1846–1901) Influential English watercolourist and illustrator. She is most famous for her innovative use of colour wood engraving in her hugely successful illustrated children's rhymes *Under the Window* (1879) and *Marigold Garden* (1885), for which she also wrote the verse. These sensitive and intimate scenes of an idealized Victorian childhood in a rustic idyll were executed in a charming and innocent style which was widely copied. Among her illustrations of fairy tales are *Madam d'*Aulnoy's Fairy Tales* (*c.*1871), Kathleen Knox's *Fairy Gifts* (1874), and *Mother Goose or the Old Nursery Rhymes* (1881).   KS

greetings cards and fairy tales It has become quite fashionable to play with fairy-tale motifs on greetings cards. Especially birthday wishes as well as Valentine messages are couched in fairy-tale language together with the appropriate illustration. All greetings card companies take part in this mercantile exploitation of fairy tales, and a leading company like Hallmark Cards has an impressive repertoire to choose from. One of them proclaimed: 'Valentine, this card is just to tell you you're nothing but a wolf!—And I'm going through the woods to Grandmother's house this afternoon.' The humorous sexual message based on the fairy tale *'Little Red Riding Hood' surely was not missed. Another card based on *'Snow White' this time took the well-known verse of the mirror as a starting-point: 'Mirror, mirror on the wall who's the nicest, most wonderful, lovable person of them all?— That one! The one who's reading this card! Happy Valentine's Day!'

Two other 'Snow White' greetings cards added an ironic twist to the statement of the mirror: 'Mirror, mirror on the wall

Who's the fairest of them all?—It's still Snow White, but keep trying, kid!' and 'Mirror, mirror on the wall, who's the youngest of them all?—Oh, well, Happy Birthday, anyway!' Another card created a pun by employing a proverbial expression: 'This Birthday do as *Rapunzel—Let your hair down! (something exciting may come up)'. Once again there appears to be an indirect sexual message here.

The most popular fairy tale on greetings cards is 'The *Frog King', usually with the proverbial statement 'You have to kiss a lot of toads (frogs), before you meet your handsome prince.' But there are variations: 'It's Valentine's Day! Kiss the frog, and it will turn into a Handsome Prince!—The joke's on you, wart lips!', 'Some day our prince will come... but with our luck, we'll probably be down at the pond kissing toads', and 'I'll never forget the first time we kissed!—Weren't you supposed to turn into a handsome prince or something?' The intent of these cards is obvious: they use the format of the humorous understatement to deliver a nice message in an indirect fashion, always in the hope for a positive or even fairy-tale-like result. Since fairy tales are part of cultural literacy, the well-intended message will hopefully have its desired effect. No doubt producers of these cards have taken advantage of the commercial gold-mine of epistolary fairy-tale wishes.   WM

Mieder, Wolfgang, 'Survival Forms of "Little Red Riding Hood" in Modern Society', *International Folklore Review*, 2 (1982).
Mieder, Wolfgang, *Tradition and Innovation in Folk Literature* (1987).
Röhrich, Lutz, *Wage es, den Frosch zu küssen! Das Grimmsche Märchen Nummer Eins in seinen Wandlungen* (1987).

Grétry, André-Ernest-Modeste (1741–1813) Belgian, later French, composer whose comic operas enjoyed unequalled success in Paris and abroad. Among his 'marvellous' operas, Grétry set two fairy tales. His first, on Jean-François Marmontel's *'Beauty and the Beast', *Zémire et Azor* (1771), was the most successful fairy-tale opera of the century, and it was parodied, translated, and reworked numerous times. The characters derive from earlier fairy plays: Pierre-Claude Nivelle de La Chaussée's *Amour pour amour* (1742), and Jean-François Guichard's *L'Amant statue* (1759). Sandor, a Persian merchant, and his servant Ali are stranded on the island of Azor, a Persian prince and the king of Kamir, who has been transformed into a beast by a vengeful fairy. Azor spares their lives in exchange for Sandor's daughter Zémire, whose love redeems Azor at the end.

In 1776 Grétry began to set the encyclopedist Marmontel's opéra féerie, *Les Statues*, based on *The *Arabian Nights*, to music, but the project was abandoned after two acts were composed. His last fairy-tale opera, Michel-Jean Sedaine's *Raoul Barbe-bleue* (1789), based on Charles *Perrault's *'Bluebeard', was highly successful, although critics were disturbed by its violence, and perhaps by its implied social critique. The 'abominable tyrant' Raoul is of the ancient nobility, and the peasants celebrate his death at the end, caused by members of the newer nobility.

Grétry's operas utilize Italianate melody, symphonic instrumental writing, and dramatic musical setting of text. His *Mémoires* (2nd edn., 1797) and other writings are important primary sources.   DJB

A.-E.-M. Grétry, *Collection complète des œuvres* (1884–1936).

Charlton, David, *Grétry and the Growth of Opéra-Comique* (1986).

Grimault, Paul (1905–94) French animator and director who made several lyrical and ironical fairy-tale shorts and cartoons in the 1930s and 1940s. Among his best fairy-tale shorts are: *L'enchanteur est enchanté* (*The Magician Is Cast Under A Spell*, 1938); *L'épouvantail* (*The Scarecrow*, 1943); and *La flûte magique* (*The Magic Flute*, 1946). His greatest achievement, however, was *Le Roi et l'Oiseau* (*The King and the Bird*), an adaptation of Hans Christian *Andersen's 'The Shepherdess and the Chimney Sweep'. Although Andersen's story is not well-known in the US and Europe, it is still popular in France due to the brilliant

cinematic work of Grimault, who actually made two versions, *La Bergère et le Ramoneur* (1950; English version, *The Curious Adventures of Mr. Wonderbird*, 1952) and *Le Roi et l'Oiseau* (*The King and the Bird*, 1979), which does not have an English version. In both films he collaborated with the talented poet and screenplay writer, Jacques Prévert.

Andersen's tale can be interpreted as a story about the fear of freedom. The shepherdess and the chimney sweep rebel against a tyrant and run away, but they are so overwhelmed by the outside world that they return to the safe and comfortable parlor, where they submit to its social code. Only by accident do they become happy, if they really do at all. In contrast, Grimault's two films can be regarded as odes to freedom. In both renditions he celebrates the emancipation not only of the persecuted couple from a mean-spirited dictator but also the freedom of the oppressed populace living in darkness. First conceived in 1945, Grimault's two films hark back to the Second World War, the French occupation by the Nazis, and the atomic bomb. These events marked Grimault and Prévert to such an extent that they worked on the project for 24 years until they made the film as they desired and envisaged it. The reason why Grimault and Prévert re-titled the film 'The King and Mr. Bird' is because the film is no longer about the love between the shepherdess and the chimney sweep but about the struggle between the small oppressed people represented by the bird and his offspring and the cruel dictatorial king. Grimault himself said that the shepherdess and the chimneysweep are characters used as pretext: their very simple love sets off chain reactions. They are charming and nice, and everything that happens to them touches us. But it is the conflict between the king and the bird that gradually takes precedence. Clearly, Grimault and Prévert were influenced by the period of French and German fascism and were horrified by oppressive governments and the use of technology to intimidate people and cause mass destruction. Consequently, the tale in which Andersen re-confined his protagonists after they pursue freedom is transformed into a struggle for freedom and a transformation of technology to support the cause of freedom and instil a sense of hope in viewers. JZ

Lescarmontier, Jeanine, *Paul Grimault: Traits de mémoire* (1991).

Pagliano, Jean-Pierre, *Paul Grimault* (1986).

Pagliano, Jean-Pierre, *Paul Grimault* (1996).

Grimm, Albert Ludwig (1786–1872) A contemporary of Jacob and Wilhelm *Grimm, but unrelated, A. L. Grimm published numerous volumes of literary fairy tales that aimed at young readers' amusement and education. His 1809 *Kindermährchen* (*Children's Fairy Tales*) mixed fairy tales with fables and parables and was followed by *Lina's Mährchenbuch* (*Lina's Fairy Tale Book*, 2 vols.) in 1816. In 1820 he drew upon The *Arabian Nights* with *Mährchen der Tausend und Einen Nacht* (*Fairy Tales from the Thousand and One Nights*), after which he produced *Geschichten des Prinzen Kodadat und seiner 49 Brüder* (*Histories of Prince Kodadat and his Forty-Nine Brothers*, 1824); *Mährchen der alten Griechen* (*Tales of the Ancient Greeks*, 1824), classic myths told in fairy-tale style; a 7-volume *Mährchen-Bibliothek für Kinder* (*Fairy Tale Library for Children*, 1826); *Bunte Bilder* (*Colourful Pictures*, 1834); *Mährchen aus dem Morgenlande* (*Fairytales from the Orient*, 1843). After his retirement, Grimm published *Deutsche Sagen und Mährchen* (*German Legends and Tales*, 1867); and edited and republished the fairy tales of J. K. A. *Musäus (1868) and of Wilhelm *Hauff (1870) for young people.

Jacob and Wilhelm Grimm scorned A. L. Grimm's fairy tales, yet Jacob borrowed 'Die drei Königssöhne' ('The Three Princes'), editing and retitling it 'Die Bienenkönigin' ('The Queen Bee'); both incorporated *'Snow-White', but A. L. Grimm treated the Queen more gently. Like Jacob and Wilhelm, A. L. Grimm included numerous minor genres in his tale collections: magic tale, parable, fable, and literary fairy tale. RBB

Allgayer, Gustav, *Albert Ludwig Grimm: Sein Leben, sein öffentliches und literarisches Wirken* (1931).

Grimm, Albert Ludwig, *Kindermärchen*, ed. Ernst Schade (1992; orig. 1809).

Grimm, Brothers (Jacob Grimm, 1785–1863 and **Wilhelm Grimm**, 1786–1859) The Brothers Grimm produced a world-renowned tale collection, the *Kinder- und Hausmärchen* (*Children's and Household Tales*) and laid the foundations for the historical study of German literature and culture.

Their father, the son and grandson of Reformed (Calvinist) Protestant pastors, served the Count of Hanau as a magistrate, and from 1791 to 1796 Jacob and Wilhelm enjoyed an idyllic childhood in the spacious grounds and imposing house of their official residence. With their father's sudden death in January 1796 the family's fortunes sank dramatically, and in 1798 the two boys were put in the care of a Cassel aunt so that they could prepare for university entrance.

Intended for the law, Jacob and Wilhelm were both drawn instead to German medieval literature at the University of Marburg. In 1805 Jacob left Marburg before obtaining a degree to assist his mentor Friedrich Carl von Savigny with research in Paris. On his return to Cassel he was without regular employment, and it was in this period that Jacob and Wilhelm first began to search for traditional stories. The result was a handful of fairy tales preserved in letters sent to Savigny in the spring of 1808.

With Cassel ruled by Napoleon's brother Jérôme Bonaparte and newly designated (August 1807) the capital of the Kingdom of Westphalia, Jacob was hired first by the Commission for Army Provisioning, and subsequently as a generously paid private librarian to King Jérôme. With a light workload and able to support his brothers and sister (their mother had died shortly before), Jacob and Wilhelm together continued to collect tales, the beginning of Wilhelm's lifelong project of expanding and crafting the *Kinder- und Hausmärchen*.

Napoleon's eventual defeat and the Hessian Electoral Prince's 1813 return to power resulted in Jacob's being sent to Paris in 1813–14 to reclaim missing Hessian books and paintings carried off by retreating French troops, to the Congress of Vienna in 1814–15, and back to Paris in the autumn of 1815. Wilhelm worked as Cassel librarian from 1814 onward, and Jacob returned to his position in 1816, both continuing until 1829.

The brothers' librarianships facilitated their scholarship, and although overworked, underpaid, and repeatedly passed over for preferment, their remarkable output—*Altdänische Heldenlieder, Balladen und Märchen* (*Ancient Danish Hero Songs, Lays, and Tales*, 1811); *Children's and Household Tales* (1812, 1815); *Altdeutsche Wälder* (*Old German Forests*, 1813, 1815, 1816); and *Irische Elfenmärchen* (*Irish Folktales*, 1826), among many other publications—resulted in wide recognition, with honorary doctorates from Marburg (1819), Berlin (1828), and Breslau (1829). In 1825 Wilhelm married Dorothea Wild, a union that produced four children and a hospitable domestic sphere which Jacob shared to the end of his days.

As Jacob and Wilhelm undertook massive collaborative projects, such as their historical grammar of the German language and their study of German law and custom, their scholarly reputations grew beyond Germany. When the University of Göttingen offered Jacob a librarianship and professorship and Wilhelm a (slightly lesser form of) professorship, they accepted with alacrity, but within seven years they were summarily dismissed because of their refusal to abrogate an oath of fealty to the Constitution of the State of Hanover. Returning to Cassel, they lived with their younger brother, the artist Ludwig Emil *Grimm, and were in part sustained by a national subscription in support of the Göttingen Seven, as they and five other colleagues were called. Between 1837 and 1840 the brothers began work on their enduring achievement, the great dictionary of the German language.

In 1840 the Grimms' fortunes improved dramatically when the conservative king of Prussia Friedrich Wilhelm III died and was succeeded by his more liberal son, Friedrich Wilhelm IV. Through the good offices of their old friend Bettina von *Arnim, both

Jacob and Wilhelm were invited to Berlin as members of the Academy of Sciences, whose stipend enabled them to live and work in comfort. They were also allowed to teach at the Humboldt University.

From 1840 until their deaths (Wilhelm in 1859, Jacob in 1863), both brothers continued to work vigorously. After years of collecting and collating, Jacob began to publish his legal tradition project, which had been undertaken with the assistance of volunteers from all the German principalities. His history of the German language appeared in 1848, and in 1854 reissues of Jacob's legal tradition, mythology, and history of the German language appeared. Wilhelm continued to edit and publish medieval literature and to edit and to refine the *Children's and Household Tales*.

Jacob was also active beyond Prussia's borders. He presided over the first two conferences of Germanists (1846 and 1847) and was elected to the Frankfurt Parliament of 1848, whose principal purpose was to foster national unity. Ever independent, Jacob took a seat on neither the left nor the right but in the central gangway. In his later years, unshakeably convinced that language determined nationhood, he advocated Prussian annexation of Schleswig-Holstein.

Jacob coordinated pan-German research by mobilizing scores of volunteers who scoured local archives for evidence of ancient custom and folklore, mythology, religion, literature, linguistics, and law. Sitting at the pinnacle of massive amounts of detailed information from Germany's past, both Jacob and Wilhelm were persuaded that fairy tales, as they circulated in Germany in the 19th century, were remnants of ancient Germany's culture, and, decade after decade, they continued to use information from every area of their scholarly investigations to 'restore' 19th-century fairy tales to their 'original' state. Wilhelm incorporated Jacob's contributions and smoothed the language to transcend changes in usage, in the process creating a prose that came to define the fairy-tale genre. The result was a collection of constantly edited tales, which eventually numbered more than 210. Entitled the

Kinder- und Hausmärchen (*Children's and Household Tales*) the collection was published 17 times between 1812 and 1864, 7 times in its large form (with copious notes appended to the first edition, and in a separate volume in the second and seventh Large Editions), 10 times as a Small Edition with 50 tales initially illustrated by their brother Ludwig Emil, and intended specifically for children and families.　　　RBB

Bottigheimer, Ruth, *Grimms' Bad Girls and Bold Boys* (1987).

Martus, Steffen, *Die Brüder Grimm: Eine Biografie* (2009).

Rölleke, Heinz, *Die Märchen der Brüder Grimm: Eine Einführung* (2004).

Tatar, Maria, *The Hard Facts of the Grimms' Fairy Tales* (1987).

Tatar, Maria, *The Annotated Brothers Grimm* (2012).

Uther, Hans-Jörg, *Handbuch zu den 'Kinder- und Hausmärchen' der Brüder Grimm: Entstehung — Wirkung — Interpretation* (2008).

Zipes, Jack, The Brothers Grimm: From Enchanted Forests to the Modern World (1988).

Zipes, Jack, *Grimm Legacies: The Magic Spell of the Grimms' Folk and Fairy Tales* (2014).

Grimm, Ludwig Emil (1790–1863) The first illustrator (1825) for the fairy tales of Jacob and Wilhelm *Grimm. Before they were published in the Small Edition, Wilhelm Grimm suggested changes to his brother's seven initial studies (*'Red Riding Hood', 'The Goosegirl', *'Sleeping Beauty', 'Our Lady's Child', *'Cinderella', *'Snow White', *'Hansel and Gretel') to increase their Christian content (a Bible on grandmother's table in 'Red Riding Hood') and symbolic intent (less foliage and spiky dead limbs on the tree under which Our Lady's Child took shelter, a tearful Gretel). Later illustrators often quoted Grimm's designs.　　　RBB

Koszinowski, Ingrid, and Leuschner, Vera (eds.), *Ludwig Emil Grimm 1790–1863: Maler, Zeichner, Radierer* (1985).

Gripari, Pierre (1925–90) French author of modern fairy tales. Gripari observed that since his mother was a witch (a medium, actually), his interest in fairy tales was natural. His first collection of marvellous tales,

Contes de la rue Broca (*Tales from Broca Street*, 1967), was written in collaboration with children, while the *Contes de la rue Folie-Méricourt* (*Tales from Folie-Méricourt Street*, 1983) were adapted from Russian and Greek folk tales. But it is the parallel world of the *Patrouille du conte* (*Fairy Tale Patrol*, 1983) that pushed fairy-tale discourse to its subversive limits. To liberate classic tales and give them 'a second wind, a second truth', Gripari dismantled their dominant socio-psychological codes and updated them to reflect today's morality and civilizing process. Here, eight children are on a mission to right certain moral and ideological offences in the Kingdom of Folklore. But their politically correct agenda to eradicate sexism, bigotry, and feudalism backfires—with darkly humorous results. Each 'humanitarian' change (prohibiting wolves from eating little pigs, abolishing monarchies in the name of democracy) impacts successive tales, and the recodified world becomes yet more barbarous. Moving beyond parody, then, Gripari challenged not only the socialization models that are part of our collective unconscious, but our contemporary political agenda as well.　　　MLE

Malarte, Claire-Lise, 'The French Fairy Tale Conspiracy', *The Lion and the Unicorn*, 12 (1988).

Paucard, Alain, *Gripari: mode d'emploi* (1985).

Peyroutet, Jean-Luc, *Pierre Gripari et ses contes pour enfants* (1994).

Gripe, Maria (1923–2007) Swedish writer of books for young adults and children that contain fairy-tale and magical motifs. She is best known for her psychological realistic trilogy: *Josephine* (1961), *Hugo and Josephine* (1962), and *Hugo* (1966), for which she won the Hans Christian Andersen Prize in 1970. In addition, she has also written important fairy-tale novels such as *The Glassblower's Children* (1964), *In the Time of the Bells* (1965), and *The Land Beyond* (1967), which contain realistic details and settings in which her unique characters try to establish their place in supernatural worlds.　　　JZ

Gross, Milt (1895–1953) American illustrator and humorist who created popular cartoons for the *New York Evening Journal*, the *New York Tribune*, and the *New York World*. Among his best-known humorous works, in which he published phonetic Yiddish versions of classical fairy tales, are *Nize Baby* (1926) and *Famous Fimales from Heestory* (1928). Such delightful stories as 'Sturry from Rad Ridink Hoot' and 'Ferry Tale from Bloobidd, a Goot-for-Notting Nubbleman' are told to a baby to encourage him to eat his cereal and ridicule traditional fairy-tale plots.   JZ

Grötzsch, Robert (1882–1946) German writer who worked as a journalist for the social democratic newspaper *Die Sächsische Arbeiter-Zeitung* in Dresden. Aside from writing dramas and satires, he published political fairy-tale books for children: *Nauckes Luftreise* (*Naucke's Voyage in the Air*, 1908), *Verschrobenes Volk* (*Eccentric People*, 1912), *Muz der Riese* (*Muz the Giant*, 1913), and *Der Zauberer Burufu* (*The Magician Burufu*, 1922). These books were

popular with the general reading public and reprinted several times. Grötzsch employed comedy to depict the foibles of monstrous characters such as the evil magician Burufu or a great fish, and he expounded a deep faith in the potential of the common people to overcome despotism.   JZ

Gruelle, John Barton (1880–1938) Prolific American author and illustrator, best known for his *Raggedy Ann* and *Andy* stories. Inspired by his daughter Marcella's favourite doll, Raggedy Ann, Gruelle created them to offset the grief of her premature death at the age of 14. His writing and drawing emphasizes a gentle, optimistic view of life that reflects Gruelle's Midwestern, Victorian roots that lost touch with the dramatically changing America of the early 20th century.

Johnny Gruelle was born in Arcola, Illinois, but grew up in Indianapolis, Indiana, where gentle ideals, farm-life, nature, and family friends such as James Whitcomb Riley shaped his vision. He was a genuine

Grötzsch, Robert The little fish insists that he can save the town from the monster in this anonymous illustration to Robert Grötzsch's tale 'Felix the Fish', published in *Der Zauberer Burufu* (1922).

innocent who could be nothing but kind to anyone. Gruelle's father was a regional landscape painter of repute who encouraged his son, yet Johnny was largely self-taught. Initially, he worked for several midwestern publications as a cartoonist and caricaturist. His ability to capture the split-second gesture and fleeting nuance with a wry sense of humour epitomized his talent and versatility. Modest formal education deflected lofty ideas and ensured a down-to-earth approach.

In 1910 Gruelle won a contest that secured a position with the *New York Herald* creating a cartoon strip based on his elfin character Mr Twee Deedle. Gruelle's career blossomed, and he began creating illustrations for numerous commercial magazines. His daughter's death in 1918 triggered the Raggedy Ann (and Andy) books. Commercially potent, these works did little to secure respect. In the early 1930s, Gruelle moved his family to Florida for health reasons. Sadly, he took to drink and died at the age of 57.

One of Gruelle's earliest commissions was for illustrations to accompany Margaret Hunt's translation of *Grimm's Fairy Tales* (1914). Twelve full-colour illustrations and more than 50 pen-and-ink drawings demonstrate a sure draughtsmanship and debt to such models as Howard *Pyle, W. W. *Denslow, and John R. *Neill. Gruelle infused the work with American motifs and settings that provided familiarity to American readers. He embraced the humour and optimism of the tales, especially the happy endings. This sanguine approach, combined with the constant triumph of good over evil, provided the central focus of all his original writings. His output was shaped by two dominant features: the secretiveness of the 'real lives' of his inanimate characters and the complete eschewal of violence. Gruelle wrote and drew for a young audience, and he gave his stories a gentle, reassuring cast where examples were set through kind behaviour and courage. He tried to perpetuate these elements as part of the American dream, just when the dream was losing its validity and America its innocence. Gruelle had a profound affection for children and

identified with their world, creating humorous parables informed by an innate sense of whimsy. HNBC

Grimm, Jacob and Wilhelm, *The Complete Fairy Tales of the Brothers Grimm*, ed. and trans. Jack Zipes (1987).

Hall, Patricia, *Johnny Gruelle Creator of Raggedy Ann and Andy* (1993).

Williams, Martin, 'Some Remarks on Raggedy Ann and Johnny Gruelle', *Children's Literature*, 3 (1974).

Grundtvig, Svend (1824–83) Danish folklorist, professor at Copenhagen University, son of the famous writer N. F. S. Grundtvig, who was a champion of national culture and promoted the preservation of folklore. Svend Grundtvig started collecting fairy tales, legends, songs, traditions, and beliefs in the 1840s and published *Gamle danske Minder i Folkemunde* (*Old Danish Legends Alive on Folk Lips*, 1854–7). Grundtvig was the first in Denmark to systematize a folklore collection, meticulously noting the origins of texts within Denmark and abroad. His foremost achievement was the collection and publication of folk ballads which resulted in the first four volumes of *Danmarks gamle Folkeviser* (*The Old Folk Songs of Denmark*, 1853–83), completed by his disciple Axel *Olrik. It contains reprints of all previous transcripts of Danish folk songs and many new ones, as well as songs from Sweden, Norway, Iceland, and the Faroe Islands. The collection also includes indices and references to the ballads' correspondence to all European folk and fairy tales, which makes it a unique study of folklore. With the two collections of fairy tales, *Danske folkeeventyr* (*Danish Folktales*, 1876 and 1878), Grundtvig also made a significant contribution to the collecting of folklore in Scandinavia. The third posthumous volume of 1884 contains more literary retellings of fairy tales by Grundtvig. MN

Gueulette, Thomas-Simon (1683–1766) French magistrate and prolific writer of tales as well as plays. Gueulette's first collection of tales, the *Soirées Bretonnes* (*Breton Nights*, 1712), includes one story in which three men deduce without actually having seen it that a one-eyed camel with a limp carrying salt and honey had gone by. This tale, taken from Arab and Persian folklore, was later rewritten by *Voltaire in *Zadig* (1747). In the same year, Gueulette published the *Mille et un quarts d'heure, contes tartares* (*The Thousand and One Quarter-Hours, Tartarian Tales*), whose frame narrative imitates that of *The *Arabian Nights*: the doctor Abuleker goes to find a cure for the king's blindness; in the meantime, the doctor's son tells the king stories for a quarter of an hour every day and must satisfy the king until his father returns or be killed. Other collections by Gueulette include: *Les Aventures merveilleuses du mandarin Fum-Hoam, contes chinois* (*Chinese Tales; or, The Wonderful*

Adventures of the Mandarin Fum-Hoam, 1723), *Les Sultanes de Guzarate, ou Les Songes des hommes éveillés, Contes Mogols* (*The Sultanas of Guzarate, or The Dreams of Awake Men, Mogul Tales*, 1732), and *Les Mille et Une Heures, contes péruviens* (*Peruvian Tales related in One Thousand and One Hours*, 1733).   AD

Gueulette, J. E., *Thomas-Simon Gueulette* (1977).

Gulbransson, Olaf (1873–1958) Norwegian illustrator and painter who emigrated to Germany and drew delightful caricatures for the famous satirical journal *Simplicissimus* in Munich. In addition, he provided droll illustrations for an edition of Hans Christian *Andersen's fairy tales in 1927.   JZ

Di Napoli, Thomas, *The Children's Literature of Peter Hacks* (1987).

Hacks, Peter (1928–2003) East German playwright and author of fables, fairy tales, and verse for children. After receiving his doctorate in theatre studies in Munich in 1951, Hacks relocated to East Berlin in 1955, attracted by Brecht and his Berlin Ensemble. He served as dramaturg at the Deutsches Theater until 1963. Hacks is most renowned for his plays for adults (among them *Moritz Tassow*, 1961, *Amphitryon*, 1967, and *Omphale*, 1969). For his young audience he turned from ancient myths and legends to the minor genres of fable, parable, fantasy, and fairy tale, experimenting with the comical and the absurd. He pays tribute to children's playfulness and their power of imagination in his popular story about *Meta Morfoss* (1975), a girl who, as her name suggests, can change shape into just about anything, from angel to crocodile and from sock to locomotive. But even his most fantastic tales are laced with lessons readers should learn. In this as in other respects, Hacks remains indebted to his mentor Brecht. Most of Hacks's stories are firmly based in the Western fairy-tale tradition. In *Das Windloch* (*The Wind Hole*, 1956) and *Das Turmverlies* (*The Tower Prison*, 1962), the reader encounters a framework structure within which a multitude of tales unfold, reminiscent of the stories of James Krüss. *Der arme Ritter* (*The Poor Knight*, 1979) and *Der Wichtelprinz* (*The Dwarf Prince*, 1982) are more recent tales by Hacks. Only one of his tales, *Der Bär auf dem Försterball* (*The Bear at the Huntsmen's Ball*, 1966), has been translated into English. EMM

Hale, Shannon (1974–) American novelist and graphic novel co-author of *Rapunzel's Revenge* (2008) and *Calamity Jack* (2010), with Dean Hale. *Revenge* presents Rapunzel alongside Jack (*see* JACK TALES) in the Wild West with her hair doubling as both lasso and whip. Hale has written a number of fairy-tale novels, including *The Goose Girl* (2003), *Princess Academy* (2005), *Book of a Thousand Days* (2007), and the Ever After High book series, launched with Mattel. *The Storybook of Legends* (2013) and *The Unfairest of them all* (2014) are set at a boarding school attended by the children of famous fairy-tale characters. KMJ

Hamilton, Anthony (*c.*1646–1720) Exiled English writer of French parodic fairy tales. The son of expatriates from the court of Charles II of England, Hamilton was educated in France from an early age. He served in Louis XIV's army in France and then fought for James II in Ireland. Upon his return to France, he became well known in Parisian circles for his letters, light verse, and fairy tales. He is also the author of the fictionalized *Mémoires du comte de Grammont* (1713).

His three novel-length fairy tales, *Le Bélier* (*The Ram*), *Histoire de Fleur-d'Épine* (*Story of Mayflower*), and *Les Quatre Facardins* (*The Four Facardins*), were published posthumously in 1730, but written in all likelihood during 1703–4. Containing often obscure allusions to life at Louis XIV's court, Hamilton's tales are among the earliest examples of parodic French fairy tales. Indeed, their (usually) subtle wit is often compared to *Voltaire's, even if their use of satire is less explicit. Hamilton's use of parody takes numerous forms, all of which exaggerate established fairy-tale conventions. On a general level, farcical dialogue, frequent hyperbole, and play with onomastics are staple features of Hamilton's tales and set them apart from those of his contemporaries. Several other traits are particularly noteworthy for their influence on 18th-century French fairy tales. With the knight-errant motif, Hamilton creates plots of dizzying complexity, with numerous embedded stories, that render the protagonists more comical than exemplary. In *The Four Facardins*, for example, there are four different heroes, the first of whom is injured fighting a lion, must accomplish two tests to be healed, rescues a maiden in distress, battles a giant, and undertakes another series of tests for a nymph just in the first few pages! The nature of many of the adventures recounted is also comical and prefigures the 'licentious' tone of many later French fairy tales. In both *The Four Facardins* and *The Ram*, for instance, a princess is obliged to go naked until an intrepid knight defeats her adversary. The allegorization of historical events, persons, and places that was to become so popular later is especially evident in *The Ram*, which uses the fairy-tale form to relate anecdotes about a house in the gardens of Versailles that Louis XIV gave to the comtesse de Grammont, Hamilton's sister. But by far the most obvious parodic device is the frame narrative, which Hamilton uses to present *The Four Facardins* and *The Story of Mayflower* as continuations of *The Thousand and One Nights*, translated/rewritten and published by Antoine *Galland beginning in 1704. In his tales, Hamilton's Sultan and Dinarzade express impatience with the stories told by Scheherazade in Galland's work. And in so doing, Hamilton mocks *The Thousand and One Nights* and the French public's enthusiasm for it.

While obscure allusions and complex plots make Hamilton's tales difficult, their tone and stylistic features charted a new course for the literary fairy tale in France.

LCS

Clerval, Alain, *Du frondeur au libertin: Essai sur Antoine Hamilton* (1978).

Hamilton, Virginia (1936–2002) African-American author of fiction, folklore

collections, and biographies for children. Her most important novels, including *The Planet of Junior Brown* (1971), *M. C. Higgins, the Great* (1974), *Sweet Whispers, Brother Rush* (1982), and *The Magical Adventures of Pretty Pearl* (1983), increasingly incorporate aspects of folklore tradition: the first portrays an urban homeless culture; the second, an Appalachian mountain community; the third, a ghostly visitation; and the fourth, an epic journey by an African goddess and her brother John de Conquer during southern Reconstruction. Hamilton's fiction is distinguished by innovative language, rhythmically blending African-American idiom with her own imaginative style. From the mid-1980s she has concentrated on folklore anthologies such as *The People Could Fly: American Black Folk Tales* (1985), *In the Beginning: Creation Stories from around the World* (1988), *The Dark Way: Stories from the Spirit World* (1990), *Her Stories: African American Folktales, Fairy Tales, and True Tales* (1995), *When Birds Could Talk and Bats Could Sing: The Adventures of Bruh Sparrow, Sis Wren, and their Friends* (1996), and *A Ring of Tricksters: Animal Tales from America, the West Indies, and Africa* (1997). Her original short stories, collected in the *All Jahdu Storybook* (1991), are a cycle of literary myths guest-starring Bruh Rabbit, Hairy Man, *Red Riding Hood, and other folk-tale figures. Hamilton has been recognized in the United States and internationally with major awards, including the Hans Christian *Andersen Award, the National Book Award, the Newbery Medal, the Coretta Scott King Award, and the Laura Ingalls Wilder Award.

BH

Mikkelsen, Nina, *Virginia Hamilton* (1994).

Handel, George Frederick (1685–1759)

German baroque composer, naturalized as a British subject in 1726. Handel's Italian operas, which dominated the London musical scene from 1711 to 1741, were notable for complex plots and depth of characterization. *Rinaldo* (1711), the sensation of Handel's first London season, and *Alcina* (1735) are based on parallel episodes from Tasso's *Gerusalemme Liberata* and Ariosto's

Orlando Furioso, in which the knight Rinaldo becomes a willing captive of the sorceress Armida (or Alcina) in her enchanted palace. *Orlando* (1733) and *Ariodante* (1735) are also drawn from Ariosto.   SR

Hannover, Heinrich (1925–) German lawyer and writer. He studied law at Göttingen and since 1954 he has been a lawyer in Bremen, having made his name as a defence counsel in prominent political trials. From 1962, Hannover published political and judicially critical papers and books, but he became especially successful as a children's author. His stories, originally tales he had invented for and together with his own six children, are published in several collections such as *Das Pferd Huppdiwupp und andere lustige Geschichten* (*The Horse Huppdiwupp and Other Funny Tales*, 1968), *Der vergessliche Cowboy* (*The Forgetful Cowboy*, 1980), and *Hasentanz* (*The Dance of the Hare*, 1995). In his tales Hannover combines fantastic and fairy-tale elements with elements of everyday life to produce original stories which aim to stimulate the imagination and creativity of children so that they continue the tales and create their own stories. The stories are intended to revive the oral tradition of fairy-tale telling and, in his prefaces and annotations, Hannover therefore recommends to parents not simply to read the stories out loud to their children, but to retell them in their own words. In the book *Riesen haben kurze Beine* (*Giants Have Short Legs*, 1976) and the tale 'Die Rosen des Herrn Funkelstein' ('Mr Funkelstein's Roses', in *Frau Butterfelds Hotel*, 1994), Hannover employs characteristic fairy-tale structures and components, combined with a partly real political and socio-critical background, to create unusual tales about reigns of terror and their outwitting by courageous people.   CS

Hans Christian Andersen (film: USA, 1952) This film announces itself not as a biopic, but as a fairy tale about the Danish spinner of fairy tales. Within a framing narrative about a trip to Copenhagen are embedded songs and a ballet that bring to the screen a few of Andersen's 156 tales. As played by Danny Kaye, Hans is whimsical, charming, innocent, and fonder of making up fanciful stories than of getting on with his work as a cobbler. Persuaded to leave the town of Odense because his storytelling is keeping the children away from school, he goes to Copenhagen and meets a little match girl, a chimney sweep, and other characters he will one day write about.

When he gets a job making shoes for the Danish State Ballet's prima ballerina, Doro, he immediately falls in love with her. Seeing her quarrelling with her husband, who is also the impresario, Hans mistakenly assumes that they hate each other and writes 'The *Little Mermaid' as an expression both of his love and of his belief that she is married to the wrong man. The story reaches Doro who, unaware of its meaning for Hans, accepts it simply as the basis for a new ballet. Next season the production opens to great acclaim, but Hans at last realizes that he has deluded himself. Doro will never love him. Dejected and wiser, he returns to Odense only to find that, as a published author, he is now welcomed even by the schoolmaster.

Among the Frank Loesser songs that wrap up Andersen tales as memorable, hummable nuggets are 'The King's New Clothes' (changed for metrical reasons from 'The Emperor's New Clothes'); *'Thumbelina', which Hans makes up and performs, using his thumbs as visual aids, for a lonely little girl he sees outside the jail where he is languishing; and 'The *Ugly Duckling', sung to a shaven-headed boy who is being mocked and shunned by his schoolmates.

The songs, however, are secondary to the 15-minute Little Mermaid cine-ballet, which is the emotional centrepiece of the film. Danced by the newcomer Zizi Jeanmaire and the film's choreographer, Roland Petit, to music by Liszt, it has 28 supporting dancers and six vast sets. Its text is not authentic Andersen: already tweaked by the screenplay so that Hans can think of it as being simply about a woman who seeks love in the wrong place, it is further modified to accommodate the limitations of ballet. The mermaids' tails have to be imagined, for if they really had them they would not be able to dance. Likewise, the heroine cannot leave her voice behind with the witches, for as a dancer she has none; she is therefore able to get from the witches a magic veil which makes her human, without having to give anything in payment. And at the end, having not been recognized by the prince as his saviour, she is free to run back into the waves and resume mermaid form without fear of dissolving into foam.

Andersen did in fact come from Odense, but otherwise the film, as it admits, offers no reliable information about him or his stories. It does, however, give an accurate depiction of the screen Danny Kaye at the height of his career.   TAS

'Hansel and Gretel' German folk tale, with analogues all over the world. The tale combines several important motifs: the wicked stepmother, the abandoned children, the trail of crumbs or peas that are eaten, the edible house, and the tricking of the witch/ogre. Parts of it closely resemble *Perrault's 'Petit Poucet' (with an analogue in the Italian tale 'Chick') and d'*Aulnoy's 'Finette Cendron', as well as the candy houses in the medieval Land of Cockaigne.

The tale was first published by the Brothers *Grimm in the first edition of their *Kinder- und Hausmärchen* (1812); their source was their neighbour Dortchen Wild, later Wilhelm Grimm's wife. It bears striking resemblances to other tales in their collection: 'Brother and Sister', 'God's Food', and 'Children of Famine', and to the recently published tale 'Dear Mili'. They persistently lengthened and altered the tale from the early terse manuscript version (1810), adding names for the children and Christian motifs in 1812, transforming the mother to a stepmother in 1819, and further rationalizing the abandonment of the children in 1843 and 1857. Their final version (1857) goes like this: A woodcutter is persuaded by his wife to abandon his children, Hansel and Gretel, in the forest because the family faces near-starvation in a time of famine. The first time

the children find their way back to the family cottage by following the trail of pebbles Hansel has strewn on their path. The second time, however, they are unable to return because birds eat the crumbs Hansel has scattered. They walk deeper and deeper into the forest, subsisting on berries, until a bird leads them to a house made of bread, with 'cake for a roof and pure sugar for windows'. Hansel gorges himself on a large piece of the roof, while Gretel eats a piece of the window pane in spite of the voice from inside the house crying:

> Who's that nibbling at my house?
> Nibble, nibble, I hear a mouse.
> Who's that nibbling at my house?

They answer that it's just the wind, but then are appalled to see the witch emerge from the house. She invites them in, feeds them pancakes and milk, and puts them to bed in clean white sheets. They think they are 'in heaven', but the witch's cannibalistic intentions are clear. The next morning she puts Hansel in a cage to fatten him up; Gretel must cook him nourishing meals, while eating only crabshells herself. The near-sighted witch regularly tests one of Hansel's fingers to see if he's getting fatter, but he cleverly gives her a chicken bone to feel. After a month she decides to eat him anyway and commands Gretel to build the fire in the oven. Gretel tearfully follows her orders, but when the witch tells her to climb in to see if the oven is hot enough, she pretends not to understand and asks the witch to demonstrate. The witch climbs in, Gretel slams the door shut, and then releases Hansel from his cage as the witch, howling, is burned to death. They fill their pockets with gold and jewels from the witch's house, are carried over a wide river by a friendly duck, and finally reach the family cottage again. Their stepmother has died, and they live with their father (and the jewels they've brought) 'in utmost joy'.

Some scholars have focused on the biographical origins for the Grimms' investment in the tale and the changes they made, stressing their own closeness as siblings, their reverence for their mother, their 'abandonment' by their long-dead father,

'Hansel and Gretel' 'Nibble, nibble, I hear a mouse, who's that nibbling at my house?' asks the witch in Hermann Vogel's illustration to 'Hansel and Gretel' in *Kinder- und Hausmärchen gesammelt durch die Brüder Grimm* (1894).

and the importance of domestic harmony and security in their lives. Others have stressed the historical background of the tale: the repeated famines in the early 19th century in Germany, the tradition of the abandonment of children, the ubiquity of stepmothers because so many mothers died young, the brooding presence of real forests that were always threatening, uncivilized places. (This urge to see the tale as a historical source has been brilliantly parodied by Hans Traxler in *Die Wahrheit über Hänsel und Gretel* (*The Truth about Hansel and Gretel*); he provides mock-documentation for the location of the family hut near the Frankfurt–Würzburg autobahn, of the witch's cottage and oven in the forest nearby, and of fossilized biscuits from its roof.)

Other scholars have focused on the psychological states and childish impulses the story represents. Bruno Bettelheim insists that the story, his favourite tale, is really about dependence, oral greed, and destructive desires that children must learn to overcome. They arrive home 'purged of their oral fixations'. Other interpreters have stressed the satisfying psychological effects of the children vanquishing the witch or of the wicked stepmother's death. Jack Zipes argues that the Grimms' final version of the tale celebrates the Oedipus complex and the symbolic order of the father, systematically denigrates the adult female characters (who may in fact be the same person), and rationalizes the abuse of the children.

Engelbert *Humperdinck's opera (1893) is based on the Grimms' version, though his librettist omits the deliberate abandonment of the children and transforms the wicked stepmother back into a mother; Maurice *Sendak designed a new production of the opera in 1997. The *Disney industry has not yet attacked 'Hansel and Gretel', but there is a film version in Tom *Davenport's series of Grimm movies (1975). Several recent writers have played variations on the tale, among them Robert *Coover in 'The Gingerbread House' in *Pricks and Descants* (1970), Anne *Sexton in a poem in *Transformations* (1971), Garrison Keillor in 'My Grandmother, My Self' in *Happy to Be Here*

(1982), Emma *Donoghue in 'A Tale of the Cottage' in her *Kissing the Witch* (1997), and Louise Murphy, *The True Story of Hansel and Gretel: A Novel of War and Survival* (2003).   EWH

Böhm-Korff, Regina, *Deutung und Bedeutung von 'Hänsel und Gretel': Eine Fallstudie* (1991).

Khader, Jamil, 'Humanizing the Nazi? The Semiotics of Vampirism, Trauma, and Post-Holocaust Ethics in Louise Murphy's *The True Story of Hansel and Gretel: A Novel of War and Survival*', *Children's Literature*, 39 (2011).

Mieder, Wolfgang, *Hänsel und Gretel: Das Märchen in Kunst, Musik, Literatur, Medien und Karikaturen* (2007).

Tatar, Maria, 'Table Matters; Cannibalism and Oral Greed', in *Off with their Heads!* (1992).

Weber, Eugen, 'Fairies and Hard Facts: The Reality of Folktales', *Journal of the History of Ideas*, 42 (1981).

Zipes, Jack, 'The Rationalization of Abandonment and Abuse in Fairy Tales', in *Happily Ever After* (1997).

Harris, Joel Chandler (1848–1908) American author of the Uncle Remus stories. Brought up in rural Georgia, in 1862 he became printer's devil on the *Countryman*, a plantation newspaper. 'It was on this and on neighboring plantations that I became familiar with the curious myths and animal stories that form the basis . . . of Uncle Remus.' He created the character of Uncle Remus, an elderly ex-slave, in 1876 in a sketch for the *Atlanta Constitution*, but the first appearance in that paper of Uncle Remus the storyteller was on 20 July 1879, the idea having been suggested to him by an article, 'Folklore of the Southern Negroes', in *Lippincott's Magazine* of December 1877. The stories about how the cunning and anarchic Brer Rabbit defeats his enemies (and sometimes his friends) were immediately popular; *Uncle Remus, his songs and his sayings* was published in 1880, *Nights with Uncle Remus* in 1883. Later Uncle Remus stories were directed primarily at children. They are trickster tales, a type common to all folklore, embellished by Harris with elaborate dialogue and set in a framework of idealized plantation life. Though adapted to the Afro-American experience, it has been shown that over half of the 220 stories retold by Harris originated in Africa.   GA

Baer, Florence, *Sources and Analogues of the Uncle Remus Tales* (1980).

Bickley, R. Bruce (ed.), *Critical Essays on Joel Chandler Harris* (1981).

Hemenway, Robert (ed.), *Uncle Remus: His Songs and his Sayings* (1982).

Keenan, Hugh, 'Joel Chandler Harris' Tales of Uncle Remus: For Mixed Audiences', in *Touchstones: Reflections on the Best in Children's Literature* (1987).

Keenan, Hugh, 'Rediscovering Uncle Remus Tales', *Teaching and Learning Literature*, 5.4 (March–April 1996).

Montenyohl, Eric L., 'Joel Chandler Harris and American Folklore', *Atlanta Historical Journal*, 30.3–4 (fall–winter 1986–7).

Hartzell, Päivi (1949–) Finnish screenwriter and film director, a crucial participant in 1980s children's fantasy feature film-making in Finland, in which symbolic, allegorical readings of themes of war and power unfold in worlds of fantasy and dark reality. Her artistically ambitious, innovative *Lumikuningatar/The Snow Queen* (1986), a secular reinterpretation of Hans Christian *Andersen's Christian moral tale, features fantastical sets and a strong orchestral soundtrack, combined with excellent performances by youthful and adult actors. *Kuningas jolla ei ollut sydäntä/The King Without a Heart* (1982), which Hartzell co-directed with Liisa Helminen, offers both a light-hearted narrative of 'once upon a time' and a parable about the dangers of capitalism in government.   PG

Hartzenbusch, Juan Eugenio (1806–80) Spanish romantic playwright, especially famous for one play, *Los amantes de Teruel* (*The Lovers of Teruel*, 1837). In 1845 Hartzenbusch began to write tales and legends which were published in the collection *Las mil y una noches españolas* (*The Spanish Thousand and One Nights*). From 1848 onwards he published several tales in a periodical called *Semanario Pintoresco Español* (*Spanish Picturesque Weekly*). *Cuentos y Fábulas* (*Tales and Fables*, 1861) is yet another collection of Hartzenbusch's short narratives

that show the author's preference for historic and legendary tales, as well as for stories of popular origin, such as 'Palos de Moguer' ('Palos de Moguer', 1861) and 'La novia de oro' ('The Golden Bride', 1861).   CFR

Hauff, Wilhelm (1802–27) Early 19th-century German writer, one of the most popular German writers of literary fairy tales. Although his literary and editorial activities spanned little more than three years, he was extraordinarily productive. Hauff's stories rank just behind the *Grimm brothers' *Children's and Household Tales* (*Kinder- und Hausmärchen*) in German language editions. His three fairy-tale almanacs, containing 14 novella-length tales, are as well known to German-speaking audiences as *Huckleberry Finn* or *Alice in Wonderland* are to Anglophones.

In 1820, at the age of 18, Hauff undertook theological studies at Tübingen seminary. He received his Ph.D. in 1824 but was not disposed to become a parish pastor. For the next two years he worked as a tutor for the young sons of the Württemberg Minister of War, Baron von Hügel, and did freelance writing. He began modestly, in 1824, by editing a volume of *War and Folksongs* (*Kriegs- und Volkslieder*). Over the next three years, in addition to the three collections of fairy tales, the young writer produced numerous works demonstrating a remarkable range and variety: journal entries, letters, parodies, poems, sketches, half a dozen novellas, a two-part Rabelaisian satirical novel, and a historical romance.

By 1826 he had earned enough money freelancing to undertake an extended educational tour through France, Flanders, and Germany. He made contacts with literary and intellectual circles in Paris, Hamburg, Bremen, Leipzig, and Berlin. Upon his return in 1827, after a four-year courtship, Hauff married his cousin Luise. Hired by the publisher J. F. (Baron von) Cotta as editor of the well-established *Morning Newspaper for the Educated Classes* (*Morgenblatt für gebildete Stände*), Hauff undertook the difficult task of reforming and raising the intellectual level of the newspaper. But the autocratic

Hauff, Wilhelm With the help of his magic shoes Little Muck wins the race against the sultan's best runner in Wilhelm Hauff's 'Little Muck'. An anonymous illustration from the English translation of *Arabian Days' Entertainments* (1858).

publisher interfered with his editor, bypassing Hauff in important editorial decisions. Conflicts over editorial policy ensued, resulting in a stalemate. Hauff's older brother, Hermann, approached Cotta, offering to edit the paper in his brother's stead, and stating in a letter that he would prove more decorous and pliable than Wilhelm. Cotta granted the editorship, a position Hermann held for 37 years.

In September 1827 Wilhelm Hauff fell ill. He was bedridden by October, and he died in November of the same year, eight days after the birth of his daughter, Wilhelmine.

Hauff is best known for his literary fairy tales. He initially told the tales as entertainment for his two younger sisters and later, as a tutor for the von Hügel family, he continued storytelling for his two young charges. Their mother, the Baroness von Hügel, was impressed by his talent and encouraged Hauff to write his stories down. In late 1825 he published the first cycle, entitled *The Caravan* (*Die Karawane*). Two additional collections followed: *The Sheik of Alexandria and his Slaves* (*Der Scheik von Alessandria und seine Sklaven*) published in 1827, and *The Inn in the Spessart* (*Das Wirtshaus im*

Spessart), published posthumously in 1828. Structured somewhat like Chaucer's *The Canterbury Tales*, each cycle features not only multiple narrators, but also a frame tale in which the individual novellas are embedded.

Hauff's tales were greeted enthusiastically by his contemporaries and have continued to enjoy unabated popularity for close to two centuries. But, while puzzling over his popularity, academic critics have for the most part rejected them as the flawed reflection of Hauff's petty bourgeois and philistine spirit. However, recent studies have argued for a re-evaluation of Hauff's tales as the work of a sophisticated cross-writer who intentionally speaks to a dual audience of children and adults. In this view, Hauff's tales draw on traditional folk- and fairy-tale motifs, and they evoke a magical world which allows for a childlike play of fantasy. But the writer also provides numerous clues signalling the possibility of a more complex and sophisticated 'adult' reading of Hauff's multi-layered texts. The child is invited to engage the imagination; the adult is invited to recognize Hauff's concealed subversive and often critical intent.

In a brief preface to the first cycle of tales, a narrative entitled 'Fairy Tale as Almanac' ('Märchen als Almanach'), Hauff signals his critical and subversive intent to bypass contemporary censorship laws: Fairy Tale has been barred entrance into the city by guards (censors) with sharp pens, who malign or even kill those who disagree with accepted opinions. To circumvent the censors, Fairy Tale dons a disguise, the fabulous cloak of 'Almanac'. (Hauff referred to his three cycles as Almanacs.) Her true identity concealed, Fairy Tale lulls the guards to sleep with the images she evokes, and passes undetected. A sympathetic adult guides her to his house, where she can tell her tales to his children and the neighbourhood children, and thus carry out her subversive activities undisturbed.

As this allegorical preface suggests, the tales in the three collections interweave fantasy and finely wrought ironies in a marvellous and complex interplay. The frame tale frequently provides a critical foil for the tales.

The multiple narrators in each cycle are played off against each other with consummate skill, while the individual narratives hover suggestively in that magical and ambiguous space between childhood innocence and adult experience.

Dwarf Long Nose (*Der Zwerg Nase*), one of Hauff's best-known tales, appears to be a conventional tale in which a wicked witch takes revenge on a little boy. The Herb Fairy transforms little Jacob into an ugly dwarf because he has publicly derided her grotesque appearance. After a series of adventures, Jacob is restored to his human form and lives a contented life. The tale does not seem to swerve from the expected happy ending and restoration of order. However, on a different level, Jacob's knee-jerk response to the stranger is representative of the prejudices of an entire community. The Herb Fairy, like the tale itself, is not quite what she seems. She is not a wicked witch, but a wise, if stringent, mentor who demonstrates to Jacob and the empathetic reader what it is like to walk in the shoes of the grotesque outsider. Jacob discovers the pain of ostracism as he is cast out by his parents, and rejected by the townspeople who fail to recognize him in his new incarnation. As Dwarf Long Nose, the formerly handsome Jacob discovers the injuriousness of the prejudices he had previously shared with his fellow townsfolk. Despite the restoration of order at the conclusion of the narrative, the child reader is left with the vivid impression of Jacob's suffering, while the adult is invited to recognize the mechanisms of prejudice, and to detect the irony of a 'happy ending' which does not resolve, but merely sets aside, the problems raised in the narrative.

In each of the collections, vivid tales evoke a fantasy world for children even as Hauff examines questions of social identity, criticizes provincial narrowness, and raises probing questions about communal prejudice. Unfortunately, there are very few translations of Hauff's tales into English. Thus, for most Anglophones, Hauff's 14 tales remain unexplored territory waiting to be discovered.   DMT

Hinz, Ottmar, *Wilhelm Hauff: Mit Selbstzeugnissen und Bilddokumenten* (1989). Schwarz, Egon, 'Wilhelm Hauff: "Der Zwerg Nase", "Das Kalte Herz" und andere Erzählungen (1826–27)', in Paul Michael Lützeler (ed.), *Romane und Erzählungen zwischen Romantik und Realismus* (1983). Thum, Maureen, 'Misreading the Cross-Writer: The Case of Wilhelm Hauff's "Dwarf Long Nose"', *Children's Literature*, 25 (1997).

Haugen, Tormod (1945–2008) Norwegian writer, Andersen Medal winner (1990), author of several remarkable fairy-tale novels for young readers. In *Slottet det hvite* (*The White Castle*, 1980) he tells what happened after the prince and princess started 'living happily ever after'. *Dagen som forsvant* (*The Day that Disappeared*, 1983) is a modern version of *Peter Pan. Farlig ferd* (*A Dangerous Ride*, 1988) and *Tsarens juveler* (*The Tsar's Jewels*, 1992) contain many elements of traditional quest fairy tales. All Haugen's books show a deep interest in myth and fairy tale in combination with social and existential problems of today's young people.   MN

Losløkk, Ola and Øygarden, Bjarne (eds.), *Tormod Haugen—en artikkelsamling* (1995). Metcalf, Eva Maria, 'The Invisible Child in the Works of Tormod Haugen', *Barnboken*, 1 (1992).

Hauptmann, Gerhart (1862–1946) German dramatist and Nobel Prize winner. Though Hauptmann was regarded as the leading representative of German naturalism, he was deeply influenced by the traditions, myths, and legends of his Silesian home. Having become famous for his naturalist dramas, he increasingly integrated mystical and fairy-tale elements in his work. This development led to the dramatic fairy tale *Die versunkene Glocke* (*The Sunken Bell*, 1896), telling of the enchantment and rescue of the bell-founder Heinrich in a region populated by wood- and water-sprites; and the glassworks fairy-tale drama *Und Pippa tanzt!* (*And Pippa Dances*, 1906). Towards the end of his life he wrote 'Das Märchen' ('The Fairy Tale') as a conscious attempt to vary *Goethe's 'Das Märchen' for the purpose of criticizing fascism. Yet his tale about Theophrast, a wandering pilgrim, remains too obtuse to be considered effective.   CS

Clouser, Robin A., 'The Pilgrim of Consciousness: Hauptmann's Syncretistic Fairy Tale', in Peter Sprengel and Phillip Mellen (eds.), *Hauptmann-Forschung: Neue Beiträge/ Hauptmann Research: New Directions* (1986). Nicholson, David, 'Hauptmann's Hannele: Naturalistic Fairy Tale and Dream Play', *Modern Drama*, 24.3 (September 1981).

Haviland, Virginia (1911–88) American critic and compiler of many collections of fairy tales for children. Each of her collections consists of tales taken from compilations of well-known writers and folklorists which are retold with a child reader in mind: the language of the tales is simplified, and the narration is in large print with many illustrations. Her first collection, *Favorite Fairy Tales Told in England* (1959), which includes *'Jack and the Beanstalk' and *'Tom Thumb', are retellings of tales taken from Joseph *Jacobs's *English Fairy Tales* (1890). In 1959 Haviland published *Favorite Fairy Tales Told in Germany*, in which she adapts the *Grimms' version of *'Rumpelstiltskin' and *'Hansel and Gretel' and *Favorite Fairy Tales Told in France* (1959), which includes retellings of Charles *Perrault's *'Puss-in-Boots' and *'Sleeping Beauty in the Wood'. Other *Favorite Fairy Tales* collections include: *Told in Ireland* (1961) with tales from Seumas *MacManus's collections; *Told in Russia* (1961) with tales from R. Nisbet *Bain's collections; *Told in Spain*, with an adaptation of Cecilia *Bohl de Faber's 'The Carlanco'; *Told in Italy* (1965), with an adaptation of the 'Cenerentola' (*'Cinderella') by Giambattista *Basile and tales from Andrew *Lang's collections; and *Told in Czechoslovakia*, with illustrations by Trina S. *Hyman. In 1979 Haviland published *North American Legends*, which includes American tall tales, tales of European and African immigrants, and folklore of American Indians and Eskimos.   AD

Hawthorne, Nathaniel (1804–64) American man of letters and author of two retellings of Greek legends for children, *A Wonder-Book for Girls and Boys* (1852), and *Tanglewood Tales for Girls and Boys* (1853). The first set of stories is told against a background of the Berkshire Hills of Massachusetts where Hawthorne was living at the time. Both books reflect an idealized American domesticity rather than the savagery of the original legends. Hawthorne removed the gods (except Mercury, disguised as 'Quicksilver'), eliminated all evil and sexuality, and introduced child characters wherever he could, so that Proserpina and Pandora become children, and Midas is given a little daughter, Marygold, with whom he shares a lavish New England breakfast. The student narrator in *The Wonder-Book* defends this treatment of the stories, saying that a modern Yankee had the same right as the ancient poets to remodel the myths. Charles *Kingsley was so affronted by Hawthorne's renderings that he produced his own, *The Heroes* (1856).

Among Hawthorne's short stories are allegorical tales of the supernatural and a few examples of fantasy. 'Feathertop' (*Mosses from an Old Manse*, 1846) describes how a witch brings a scarecrow into life and makes him so personable that he impresses everyone he meets; 'The Snow-Image' (*The Snow-Image and Other Twice-Told Tales*, 1851) is an allegory. Two children create another child out of snow. She comes to life and plays with them, but their matter-of-fact father refuses to believe she is made of snow, and, trying to warm her, destroys her.   GA

Alsen, Eberhard, 'Hawthorne: a Puritan Tieck; a Comparative Analysis of the Tales of Hawthorne and the Märchen of Tieck' (Diss., Indiana University, 1967).

Bailey, Herbert S., Jr., 'On "Rappaccini's Son": A Note on a Twice Told Tale', *Nathaniel Hawthorne Review*, 17.1 (spring 1991).

Brown, Gaye, 'Hawthorne's "Rappaccini's Daughter": The Distaff Christ', *Nathaniel Hawthorne Review*, 22.2 (fall 1996).

Hundley, Clarence Carroll, Jr., 'Fairy Tale Elements in the Short Fiction of Nathaniel Hawthorne' (Diss., University of North Carolina-Greensboro, 1994).

Laffrado, L., *Hawthorne's Literature for Children* (1992).

Rucker, Mary E., 'The Art of Witchcraft in Hawthorne's "Feathertop: A Moralized Legend"', *Studies in Short Fiction*, 24.1 (winter 1987).

Hay, Sara Henderson (1906–87) American poet. Known for her collection of fairytale sonnets *Story Hour* (1963; 2nd edn., 1982), Hay uses them to comment acerbically on the questionable moral stance of famous fairy tales. In the title poem, the speaker suppresses a child's question about *'Jack and the Beanstalk': 'Was no one sorry for the murdered Giant?' Hay often shifts the point of view from hero to villain, offering ironic commentary on our desire for fairy-tale closure. Frequently anthologized are 'Interview,' a monologue by *Cinderella's stepmother, and 'Juvenile Court,' positing *Hansel and Gretel as juvenile delinquents.   NJW

Haymon, Ava Leavell (no dates available) American author of four collections of poetry, including *Why the House Is Made of Gingerbread* (2010), in which images, characters, and concepts from *'Hansel and Gretel' organize poems from an adult Gretel's perspective. Haymon explores the violence of contemporary American women's experiences via the dark fairy-tale themes of hunger, child abuse, betrayal, cannibalism, and murder.   PG

Hearn, Lafcadio (1850–1904) American author and journalist, born in the Ionian islands of Irish/Maltese parents. In 1869, Hearn moved to the United States, where he wrote on subjects he called 'exotic, strange, and monstrous'. Emigrating to Japan in 1890, he renamed himself *Koizumi Yakumo*, married into a samurai family, became a citizen, wrote, and held a chair in English literature at Tokyo University. The author of many sketches, essays, and several novels, Hearn is noted for sensitive interpretations of Japanese traditions, especially about spirits and ghosts. Most frequently read today are probably *Kwaidan* (*Ghost Tales*), and *Japan: an Interpretation* (1904).   JSN

Hayley, Barbara 'Lafcadio Hearn, W. B. Yeats and Japan', in Robert Welch and Suheil Badi

Bushrui (eds.), *Literature and the Art of Creation* (1988).

McNeil, William K., 'Lafcadio Hearn: American Folklorist', *Journal of American Folklore*, 91 (1978).

Hegenbarth, Josef (1884–1962) German illustrator, known for his highly innovative drawings and interpretations of fairy tales and fables. Hegenbarth's illustrations were influenced by Impressionism and make use of unusual movement and striking colours to form new constellations that comment on the text in highly original ways. He did drawings for the works of many great authors such as *Goethe, *Tolstoy, Cervantes, *Shakespeare, and Swift, and among his best illustrated fairy-tale books are J. K. A. *Musäus, *Volksmärchen der Deutschen* (*Folk Tales of the Germans*, 1947–9), Jacob and Wilhelm *Grimm, *Die goldene Gans* (*The Golden Goose*, 1951), Giambattista *Basile, *The Pentameron* (1954), Wilhelm *Hauff, *Die Karawane* (*The Caravan*, 1966), and Jacob and Wilhelm Grimm, *Märchen* (*Fairy Tales*, 1969).   JZ

Heidelbach, Nikolaus (1955–) German illustrator who has won many awards owing to his ability to mix realistic and fantastic motifs in unusual combinations. He has illustrated the works of both classic and contemporary authors. For example, he contributed unique drawings for Christine *Nöstlinger's version of *Pinocchio* (1988) and for the *Märchen der Brüder Grimm* (*The Fairy Tales of the Brothers *Grimm*, 1995). He endows his figures with a striking and sober everyday physiognomy and a symbolical ambience. He gave the wooden puppet Pinocchio lifelike eyes, and the dwarf who guards *Snow White's casket in the night is surrounded by empty wine bottles. Heidelbach's pictures tell entire stories, reveal the inner depths of characters, and depict contrasting incidents that have horrifying and shocking features to them. Among his other notable illustrated books are: *Die dreizehnte Fee* (*The Thirteenth Fairy*, 2002), *Andersens Märchen* (*Andersen's Fairy Tales*, 2004), and

Märchen aus aller Welt (*Fairy Tales from Everywhere in the World*, 2010).   KD

Heine, Heinrich (1797–1856) German poet and author, many of whose poems have been set to music by Franz Schubert, Felix *Mendelssohn, Robert *Schumann, and Johannes Brahms, among others. He received a doctorate of law from Göttingen, at which time he converted from Judaism to Christianity to improve his prospects for a post in government or at a university. Unsuccessful in these efforts, he lived from his pen, with subsidies from a wealthy uncle and other sources. Literary fame came rather early, with the publication of his first volume of *Reisebilder* (*Travel Sketches*), *Die Harzeise* (*Journey through the Harz Mountains*, 1826), and with the volume of collected poems *Buch der Lieder* (*Book of Songs*, 1827). In 1831 he went to Paris to report on events in the wake of the July Revolution and remained there permanently. His interest in myth, legend, and folk tale is evident in much of his work, most prominently in two fanciful renditions that became sources for operas by Richard Wagner: the story of the Flying Dutchman, in 'Aus den Memoiren des Herren Schnabelewopski' ('From the Memoirs of Herr Schnabelewopski', 1834, in *Der Salon I*) and the legend of Tannhäuser, in 'Elementargeister' ('Elemental Spirits', 1837, in *Der Salon III*). The folk song, especially in the literary form pioneered by his contemporary Wilhelm Müller (1794–1827), exerted a considerable influence on Heine's lyric poetry.   JMM

Reeves, Nigel, *Heinrich Heine: Poetry and Politics* (1974).

Sammons, Jeffrey L., *Heinrich Heine: The Elusive Poet* (1969).

Sammons, Jeffrey L., *Heinrich Heine: A Modern Biography* (1979).

Heine, Helme (1941–) German author and illustrator of picture books. This popular author/illustrator is known for his playful, charming, cartoon-like illustrations, which enchant child readers. Among his picture books are new, zany, and funny interpretations of myths, morality tales, fables, and

parables, such as *Das schönste Ei der Welt* (*The Most Wonderful Egg in the World*, 1983), in which three hens quarrel about who is the most beautiful, while the king decides to honour the hen that produces the best egg instead. Heine's favourite themes, which he revisits in many of his picture books, are friendship and tolerance.
EMM

Heine, Thomas Theodor (1867–1948) German caricaturist, writer, and editor, known for his satirical illustrations in the periodical *Simplicissimus*. Forced into exile by the Nazis, Heine composed sardonic tales that criticized the social and political ills of his day. His first collection, *Die Märchen* (*Fairy Tales*, 1935), was followed by a revised and expanded edition, first published in Danish as *Sällsamt händer* (1946) and later in German as *Seltsames geschieht* (*Strange Things Happen*, 1950). Illustrated with his own drawings, Heine's pessimistic tales caricature the abuses of government, science, business, and the military, as well as the weakness of human nature.   DH

Haase, Donald P., 'Thomas Theodor Heine's Exile Märchen', in Uwe Faulhaber, Jerry Glen, Edward P. Harris, and Hans-Georg Richert (eds.), *Exile and Enlightenment: Studies in German and Comparative Literature* (1987).

Hiles, Timothy W., *Thomas Theodor Heine: Fin-de-Siècle Munich and the Origins of Simplicissimus* (1996).

Hélias, Pierre Jakez (1914–1995) A Breton stage actor, journalist, author, poet, and writer for radio, who worked in French and Breton languages. Hélias became a prominent literary figure in the late 20th century, and is best known for his novel *Le Cheval d'orgueil* (*The Horse of Pride*, 1978), which was adapted for the cinema by Claude Chabrol in 1980. He also collected Breton oral folktales for publication, including *Contes bretons du pays bigouden* (*Breton Tales of Bigouden*, 1967), *Contes bretons de la Chantepleure* (*Breton Tales of Chantepleure*, 1971), and *Contes du vrai et du semblant* (*Tales of Truth and Appearance*, 1984). Hélias also published collections of Celtic fairy tales titled *Mojennou Breiz: Ar Mor* (Folktales of Brittany: The Sea, 1957).   MF

Henson, Jim (1936–90) American creator of a puppetry style involving remote animatronic control and whole human bodies as well as the more traditional hands and rods. Buoyed by the international success of *Sesame Street*, *The Muppet Show*, and their spin-off features, Henson and his team devised a range of creatures and narratives which pushed back the boundaries of the possible. In the two decades before Henson's death, his company produced two original fantasies and some characters in **Alice in Wonderland* for the cinema, and various Muppet variations on Grimm and nine invocations of the fireside storytelling tradition for television.

After Kermit the Frog became a favourite with American children following the 1969 start of the *Sesame Street* TV series, it was natural that one of the tales customized for him and other Muppet characters to perform would be 'The Frog Prince' (1971). However, Kermit does not play the hero; instead, he is the narrator, giving a frog's-eye-view of Grimm. Sitting by a pond, he recalls Robin, a frog he once met, who claimed to be really an enchanted prince and proved it by showing how he was unable to swim. A princess who could restore Robin lived nearby, but she, too, was bewitched and could only speak backwards. Kermit continues his recollections and recalls how he saved Robin from being eaten by an ogre and how all the other frogs rallied around to thwart an evil witch who was the cause of Robin's problems. Kermit reveals that once the princess kissed Robin, who became human and succeeded to the throne, the two were married. As the film ends, the royal couple arrive with their baby, Prince Kermit. The story thus becomes, in Henson's hands, a fairy tale about friendship and trust enlivened by comedy and songs.

During the rest of the 1970s Henson's energies went mainly into *Sesame Street* and *The Muppet Show*, but with the cinema feature *The Dark Crystal* (UK, 1982) he broke away from them completely, seeking to create a comprehensive other world, free of both Muppets and humans. In its conception there was inspiration from the bleak terrain and carrion-eating birds of Dartmoor, from the fantasy illustrations of the artist Brian Froud, and from skills, such as stilt-walking, that particular performers happened to have. Out of this mixture came such creatures as the Skeksis, decadent reptilian predators; the Garthim, crab-like enforcers of the Skeksis law; two Gelflings, survivors of an elf-like race; and the Landstriders, spidery long-legged carriers. Around them Henson wove a complex story of a world under threat, ultimately saved by the triumph of Good over Evil.

Labyrinth (UK, 1986), Henson's second cinematic fantasy, differs from its precursor by having human characters at its centre: Henson had decided that puppet creatures are good at being funny or nasty, but do not work as protagonists, because an audience cannot satisfactorily identify with them. Chief among the humans are Sarah, a teenager who wishes herself rid of her grizzling baby brother; and David Bowie playing Jareth, the goblin king who grants Sarah's wish. The plot gives her 13 hours in which to find her brother in Jareth's labyrinth. She makes friends (an unreliable gnome, a gentle lumbering giant), who more or less help her. At the climactic moment, Sarah realizes that Jareth exists only because her mind has created him; when she states firmly that he has no power over her, he disappears. As well as this Wonderland/Oz scenario, the film contains some traditional fairy-tale elements—an uncaring stepmother, a piece of poisoned fruit, a ballroom where Sarah dances precious hours away.

In 1988, as producer of an animated TV series about the Muppets as babies, Henson offered a critique of Disney in an episode called 'Snow White and the Seven Muppets'; then, in the same year, he showed how he thought innovative fairy-tale cinema could be done with *The Storyteller* (UK). Encouraged by a daughter who had recently studied folklore, Henson aimed to cut through 19th-century bowdlerizations and try to recapture not only the essential meaning, but also the

original mode of delivery, of some seminal tales. The focus was to be on a storyteller, with a dog as audience, seated by the fire in a large hall. Parts of each story would be dramatized, but the storyteller's spoken words would begin it, end it, and hold it all together.

Commissioned to write scripts for this blend of telling and showing, Anthony Minghella sifted stories from across Europe, comparing each version with others, homing in on the essence. In this he was helped by Stith Thompson's standard reference work, which groups together folk and fairy tales, with the same basic theme and structure, from all over the world. In particular, Minghella noted differing transition points within a grouping; for example, in a princess's search for her alienated husband ('Hans My Hedgehog'), the number of pairs of shoes she wears out varies from version to version, as do what they were made of, and how long it was before she finds him.

Minghella selected nine basic narratives which dealt with strong themes such as he and Henson wanted—promises kept, promises broken, lust for power, parental rejection of children, the fear of incest, oneness with nature—and set about developing them into vehicles for television storytelling. Except for 'The Soldier and Death', which is derived from an Arthur *Ransome translation of a Russian tale, they are each credited on screen as coming from 'an early German folk tale'. However, Minghella's method was more ambitious than that phrase implies: he mixed and matched freely, added and subtracted with no heed for academic niggles, and allowed the storyteller and the dog to comment on the characters and their actions. The result is a fresh re-creation of the tales, rather than a straightforward adaptation of Grimm or any other pre-existing texts.

Each programme is introduced by the storyteller's voice invoking a time when stories were used to keep the past alive, explain the present, and foretell the future. The language he uses to tell the tale—which never begins with the phrase 'Once Upon a Time'—is full of devices designed to make it, for teller and listener, memorable and thrilling. Among them are alliteration (a journey takes in 'cliff and cavern, crevasse and chasm, cave and canyon'); imagery (a princess who falls for her gardener 'felt little fish swim up and down her back'); repetition (about a boy who is tempted to tell someone's secret, the storyteller says, 'but he can't, so he mustn't, so he won't'); and new-minted words (a woman who at long last got the baby boy she had pined for 'snoodled him to bits'). There is back-and-forth interplay between the storyteller and the listening dog, who follows false trails ('I thought the babies had been killed'), insists that the teller has got a story wrong, or points out that a character has broken her vow of silence before the expiry of the time-limit ('Yes, clever-clogs, the princess spoke three minutes too soon'). Teller and dog alike are visually linked to the dramatized segments in a continuing variety of ways: arte-facts pass between storyteller and character, a king sheds a tear which falls on the dog's head.

One example of the nine tales presented in this style is 'Sapsorrow', which combines aspects of the Cinderella story with a different one, variously called 'Rushie Coat' and 'All Kinds of Fur', about a girl who escapes human society by turning herself into an animal. As Henson and Minghella present it, a widower king has three daughters, of whom two are bad, one good. Fearing to be lonely when his daughters leave him, the king proclaims he will wed the woman whose finger fits the late queen's ring. Nobody's does except that of the good daughter, Sapsorrow, who only tries it on by accident. Both of them shrink from such a union, but the law insists. Stalling, Sapsor-row insists on three dresses being made—one the colour of the moon, one that of the stars, one that of the sun—but when the wedding day dawns, she is gone. Three years later, now covered in filthy fur and known as Straggletag, she is in another country, scrubbing pots in a king's kitchen. Upstairs, at a grand ball, the prince will dance with no one until a beautiful woman in a moon-coloured dress turns up; at the next ball she is in silver, then gold. A golden slipper is the only clue to her identity. The bad sisters turn up to try it on, and from them Straggletag learns that her father has died. She slips her foot into the shoe and secures the prince's promise that he will marry her as Straggletag, before revealing that she is also the princess he loves.

Since Henson's untimely death, the Crea-ture Shop that he founded has remained pre-eminent in the world of animatronics. The 1990s, however, have seen these skills being put to work primarily in the service of other people's films; as a result bears, mice, a gorilla, and an Oscar-winning pig—all as zoologically accurate as possible—have ousted hedgehog princes and heartless giants. TAS

Bacon, Matt, *No Strings Attached: The Inside Story of Jim Henson's Creature Shop* (1997).
Minghella, Anthony, *Jim Henson's 'The Storyteller'* (1988).
Ransome, Arthur, *The War of the Birds and the Beasts* (1984).
Thompson, Stith, *Motif Index of Folk Literature* (6 vols., 1932–6; 1955).
Zipes, Jack, *Happily Ever After: Fairy Tales, Children, and the Culture Industry* (1997).

Hessel, Franz (1880–1941) German writer and translator. He dabbled with fairy tales, and in his unusual collection of stories, *Teig-waren leicht gefärbt* (*Noodles Slightly Coloured*, 1926), he included 'Der siebte Zwerg' ('The Seventh Dwarf'), a retelling of *'Snow White and the Seven Dwarfs', in which the youngest dwarf claims to have saved Snow White and to have been neglect-ed by history. JZ

Hetmann, Frederik (pseudonym of **Hans-Christian Kirsch**, 1934–2006) German editor, scriptwriter, translator, and author of books for young people and adults. Kirsch retells myths and folk tales adapted from the Native American, African American, and Irish-Celtic cultural traditions in such works as *Die Reise in die Anderswelt. Feen-geschichten und Feenglaube in Irland* (*The Journey to the Other World: Fairy Stories and Fairy Belief in Ireland*, 1981), *Die Büffel kommen wieder und die Erde wird neu. Märchen, Mythen, Lieder und Legenden der* *nordamerikanischen Indianer* (*The Buffaloes Return and the Earth Becomes New: Fairy Tales, Myths, Songs and Legends of the North American Indians*, 1995), and *Der Junge, der die Sonne fing. Märchen der nordamerikanischen Indianer* (*The Boy Who Caught the Sun: Tales of the North American Indians*, 2003). His retellings are well researched and have an authentic feel. In 1965 Hetmann was awarded the German State Prize for children's and youth literature for *Amerika Saga* (1964), a rich and varied collection of American myths, anecdotes, ghost and trickster stories, and personal narratives. He has also written theoretical articles about fairy tales and fantasy literature.   EMM

Hetmann, Frederik, *Traumgesicht und Zauberspur. Märchenforschung, Märchenkunde, Märchendiskussion* (1982).
Hetmann, Frederik, *Die Freuden der Fantasy. Von Tolkien bis Ende* (1984).

Heym, Stefan (pseudonym of **Helmut Flieg**, 1913–2001) Controversial (East) German writer who moved from American exile to East Berlin in 1952 and became a member of the German Parliament after unification. Often using a historical framework, his satirical stories, novels, and drama criticized social and political conditions in East Germany. He also published three volumes of ironic fairy tales for children: *Casimir und Cymbelinchen* (*Casimir and Little Cymbeline*, 1966), *Cymbelinchen oder der Ernst des Lebens, Vier Märchen für kluge Kinder* (*Little Cymbeline, or Real Life: Four Fairy Tales for Bright Children*, 1975), *Erich Hückniesel und das fortgesetzte Rotkäppchen* (*Erich Hückniesel and Little Red-Riding-Hood Continued*, 1977).   KS

Hindemith, Paul (1865–1963) German composer, theorist, teacher, and viola player. His dauntingly copious output, encompassing a huge variety of forms and instrumental combinations, includes the three-act opera *Cardillac* (1926; revised, 1952), with libretto by Ferdinand Lion adapted from E. T. A. *Hoffmann's novella *Das Fräulein von Scuderi* (1819). The story,

set in 17th-century Paris and telling of a fatally gifted goldsmith whose murderous obsession with his own creations proves his undoing, is told via a series of neo-baroque musical numbers, characteristic of Hindemith's essentially anti-romantic compositional ethos at this time.   SB

Hines, Jim (1974–) American fantasy writer, author of the Goblin Quest fantasy series, which includes *Goblin Quest* (2006), *Goblin Hero* (2007), *Goblin War* (2008), and *Goblin Tales* (2011). Hines is known for his female-empowering novels from his Princess Series, which features *The Stepsister Scheme* (2009), *The Mermaid's Madness* (2009), *Red Hood's Revenge* (2010), and *The Snow Queen's Shadow* (2010) (*see* 'SNOW QUEEN, THE'). The first of the collection presents a fairy-tale trio that includes *Cinderella, martial-arts expert *Sleeping Beauty, and powerful mage, *Snow White. Hines has also written numerous short stories and was awarded the Hugo Award for Best Fan Writer in 2012.   KMJ

Histoires ou contes du temps passé avec des moralités (*Stories or Tales of Past Times, with Morals*, 1697) The best-known French fairy-tale collection today. It includes 'La Belle au bois dormant' (*Sleeping Beauty'), 'Le Petit Chaperon rouge' (*Little Red Riding Hood'), 'La Barbe-bleue' (*Bluebeard'), 'Cendrillon ou La Petite Pantoufle de verre' (*Cinderella'), 'Le Petit Poucet' (*Little Tom Thumb'), 'Riquet à la houppe' (*Riquet with the Tuft'), 'Le Maître chat ou Le Chat botté' (*Puss-in-Boots'), and 'Les Fées' ('The *Fairies'). Later editions were called *Contes de ma Mère l'Oye* (*Mother Goose Tales*) and included the previously published verse fairy tales 'Grisélidis', 'Les Souhaits ridicules' ('The *Foolish Wishes') and 'Peau d'âne' (*Donkey-Skin'). Published under the name of P[ierre Perrault] Darmancour, the 1697 stories are also attributed to his father, Charles *Perrault.

Which Perrault wrote the *Tales*? The uneven levels of style between the prose stories and verse morals suggest the 19-year-old prodigy and not the French Academy polemicist. And yet, this stylistic inconsistency plus worldly social commentary on the court, fashion, and marriage may indicate a father–son collaboration. Then again, the *Tales* were not mentioned in Pierre's obituary, and Charles was the acknowledged author of the verse fables and rumoured author of the collection. For these reasons, critics now champion his literary paternity. The dedicatory preface by 'P. Darmancour' to Mademoiselle (Elisabeth-Charlotte d'Orléans) was therefore a trick to present the son to society and to curry favour with her uncle, Louis XIV. Similarly, his change in publisher (to Claude Barbin) was a way to sidestep authorship and avoid reinvolvement in the Quarrel of the Ancients and Moderns (which debated the merits of classical over contemporary literature). Despite these ruses, the 'Ancient' partisan Boileau still derided these 'trifles' as the work of the 'Modern' Perrault.

Like La Fontaine's *Fables*, these moralizing *Tales* were unabashedly modern, and reflected the preoccupations of a widower rearing four sons. They were to 'civilize' a new public (children) of a new social class (the emerging bourgeoisie) in what he deemed the accepted political, social, and moral codes of 17th-century France. In short, the progressive Perrault was continuing the kind of cultural absolutism that he had enforced during 20 years as secretary to finance minister Jean-Baptiste Colbert.

Situated between the earliest literary fairy tales by *Straparola and *Basile and those of the Brothers *Grimm and *Andersen, the *Tales* are at the historical and literary crossroads of lower-class vs. upper-class culture. They were written when the rigid classical hierarchies were beginning to dissolve, and thus they incarnated the social and artistic hybridization characteristic of the period. The voguish appropriation of peasant tales by aristocratic women in literary salons is a case in point. Just as Mme d'*Aulnoy and other women were transforming oral folk tales into written fairy tales, so did Perrault refine his sources by respecting *bienséance* (propriety). He eliminated gore, obscenity, and paganism that would have frightened children or offended sensibilities: for example, a werewolf no longer seduced Little Red Riding Hood into drinking grandma's blood, stripping and joining him in bed. He also polished language, upgraded social status, and added touches of realism. He named fairies and introduced contemporary themes, such as famine or the scores of widowed mothers with dowry-dependent daughters. He anchored allegorical portraits in history as well, and patterned ogres on aristocrats like Gilles de Rais (Bluebeard). Finally, by including references to Versailles, he provided social commentary ranging from the necessity of appearances and the shallowness of courtiers to women's fashions and gourmet sauces. In short, at every juncture Perrault added 'civilizing' social references to please and educate the salon public and emerging bourgeoisie.

What could youngsters learn from this nascent genre of children's literature? The tales presented the same information as period manner books and pamphlets, offering models of social comportment that were broadly divided along gender lines. Questionably moral boys' stories like 'Little Tom Thumb' and 'Puss-in-Boots' had active heroes who used their wits to trick opponents: small size and low birth were no obstacles to achieving social success if one knew how to present oneself. Likewise, passive heroines like Sleeping Beauty and Cinderella taught girls the virtues of patience, grace, and charity, while Little Red Riding Hood and Bluebeard's bride showed the importance of filial and spousal obedience. Perrault also stressed these qualities in his writings in defence of women. Indeed, the humble Grisélidis and incest-fleeing Donkey-Skin were feminist role models for their time, although they are not considered so today.

Why are Perrault's handful of tales still popular, whereas the hundreds by female authors dominated the 18th century? In general, children's literature has become a consumer market. Youngsters can more easily understand his shorter, linear, timeless narratives—as opposed to the longer, minutely detailed sub-plots that preoccupied women two centuries ago. French children also enjoy his tongue twisters, like 'tire la chevill-ette, la bobinette cherra' ('pull the cord and the latch will fall', from 'Little Red Riding Hood'). Moreover, from a psychoanalytic viewpoint, his tales of conflict resolution—from famine, war, and social oppression to sibling rivalry, adolescent sexuality, and Oedipus complexes—offer a cathartic experience, while women's stories did not always end happily. Finally, the increasing availability during the 19th century of cheaper paper and inks made illustrated tales more available, and the tri-colour Épinal cartoons favoured tales like 'Little Tom Thumb'. Nor can the influence of Gustave *Doré's 1864 edition of Perrault be stressed enough. His 36 engravings of pop-eyed ogres and baroque decor defined Perrault for generations, so well did they complement his moral and 'bourgeoisified'—yet timeless—stories. Today, there are hundreds of editions of Perrault's *Tales* in scores of languages, while the fairy tales by 17th-century Frenchwomen comprise a relatively limited and erudite market.   MLE

Barchilon, Jacques, and Flinders, Peter, *Charles Perrault* (1981).

Lewis, Philip, *Seeing through the Mother Goose Tales: Visual Turns in the Writings of Charles Perrault* (1996).

Malarte-Feldman, Claire-Lise, 'Perrault's *Contes*: An Irregular Pearl of Classical Literature', in *Out of the Woods: The Origins of the Literary Fairy Tale in Italy and France* (1996).

Seifert, Lewis, *Fairy Tales, Gender, and Sexuality in France, 1690–1715* (1996).

Soriano, Marc, *Les Contes de Perrault: Culture savante et traditions populaires* (1968).

Zipes, Jack, *Fairy Tales and the Art of Subversion* (1983).

Hoban, Russell (**Russell Conwell Hoban**) (1925–2011) Award-winning American writer, widely acclaimed for his modern fantasy classic, *The Mouse and his Child* (1967). He was born in Lansdale, Pennsylvania, of Russian Jewish descent. His early talent for drawing foreshadowed a career in art and illustration. After studying at the Philadelphia Museum School of Industrial Art, and army war service, he worked as a television art director, freelance illustrator, and advertising copywriter. Discovering a preference for writing, he became a full-time writer in 1967.

Generically diverse and prolific, Hoban's writing is particularly notable for its intelligence and wit, and his works are multi-layered, highly allusive, and have strong allegorical threads. His recurrent themes of identity, finding a place in the world, and being true to oneself mirror the central concerns of fairy tales, with the emphasis that characters' intellectual processes and assistance from others generate independence. Into his stories Hoban imaginatively weaves the common fairy-tale motifs of loss and violent retribution, recovery, innate fears, and quests or journeys where chance meetings hold the key to self-knowledge. In *The Mouse and his Child* two tin clockwork mice, broken and rejected, begin life anew when revived by a tramp. On their quest to regain their lost home and to become self-winding, they meet good and evil, and survive against all odds. Helped by animals they meet, they finally outsmart and overcome their adversary, the predatory villain Manny Rat, whose last violent act of destruction rebounds on himself. Still, the toys accept 'Uncle Manny' into their household, a situation echoed in the sorcerer's closing words in *La Corona and the Tin Frog* (1979). 'They'll want me too,' he said. 'Everyone can't be nice.'

Although Hoban uses the main structures of traditional fairy and folk tales, most of his work has a postmodern edge in that it self-consciously explores how words and language shape our response to the world. Narrative strategies foreground a distinction between the fantasy world of fairy-tale events and endings, and the real world of less fixed outcomes. However, *The Sea-Thing Child* (1972) works within more traditional structures to express its theme metaphysically. In *The Marzipan Pig* (1986) a parodic twist to the mouse's independence challenges the wisdom of conventional tales. The verbal and visual cues of *La Corona and the Tin Frog* evoke the style of traditional fairy tale, while a closer reading of how its codes are used situates the text more radically. In the first three stories words and images present the means whereby characters succeed in their quests. Through the last story, 'The Clock', all the stories cohere, justly so, as temporality in a text holds all the story parts together. The clock, silent witness to the action in all the stories, exerts his influence to arrest time. When this happens, all the characters from the book leave through a window, composed visually by the text. Thus, in each story in *La Corona* the fictional framework metafictively carries the tale's insights into the real world and exposes the text's constructedness.   CM

Hoernle, Edwin (1883–1952) German writer and politician who helped politicize the fairy tale during the Weimar Republic. In 1918 he became one of the founders of the Communist Party and a prominent leader in the revolutionary educational movement. In 1920 he published *Die Occuli-Fabeln*, an anthology of radical fables and fairy tales, written during the war, which stress the necessity for revolutionary action. In particular, his short, terse tales contain a critique of the Social Democratic Party for compromising the goals of socialists and communists alike and undermining the power of the working classes. During the 1920s he wrote numerous articles about progressive education, eventually published in his book *Grundfragen der proletarischen Erziehung* (*Basic Questions about Proletarian Education*, 1929), which contained a key theoretical piece about radical fairy tales and the need to 'proletarianize' the traditional fairy tale.   JZ

Hoffman, Alice (1952–) Considered one of the foremost writers in America, Hoffman has written over 30 novels for adults and teenagers and has also written three children's books. Her works range from historical fiction and fantasy to magic realism, and four of her narratives, *Practical Magic, Acquarmarine, Independence Day*, and *The River King* have been made into films. *Practical Magic* (1995), written for adults, is a novel that concerns two fabulous young women who grow up in a small town in Massachusetts. Accused of witchery, they flee their home to escape charges of black

magic and to form new identities. However, they discover that they can never deny their marvellous powers. In her young-adult novels, Hoffman's protagonists are often beset by problems connected to their other worldly natural gifts and desires to determine their own destinies. In *Aquarmarine* (2001) a mermaid flees her underwater realm to find love with a human and transforms herself through this love; in *Indigo* (2002) two brothers with web hands who have vague memories of their lives as mermen, join with a young girl to uncover their hidden identities; in *Green Angel* (2003) a young girl loses her family in a major disaster recalling 9/11, and she withdraws into a devastated garden where a mute boy and a white dog enable her, through love and magic, to overcome the trauma that she suffered; in *Green Witch* (2010) Hoffman recalls the former character Green, who overcomes loss and tragedy by gathering stories from some mysterious women branded as witches. Almost all Hoffman's young-adult books are works of magic realism, as are many of her novels and stories for adults. In *The Ice Queen* (2005) a cool young woman expresses a wish to be struck by lightning, and her wish is granted, which turns her into a more compassionate and passionate person who falls in love with a mysterious man who had also been struck by lightning. *The Red Garden* (2010) is full of fabulous tales about people who grow up in an American town founded three hundred years ago by a courageous Englishwoman. *The Museum of Extraordinary Things* (2014) is set in 1911. Eighteen-year-old Coralie, a gifted swimmer, plays a mermaid in her father's Coney Island sideshow called the Museum of Extraordinary Things. Like some other characters in Hoffman's novels, she has webbed fingers. Among the performers in the sideshow are the wolfman, the butterfly girl, the goat boy, the bee woman, the Siamese twins, and a one hundred-year-old turtle. At one point Coralie accompanies her father, Professor Sardie, who is part magician and part mad scientist, to search for freaks in New York city, and she meets Eddie Cohen, a photographer, who has run away from his father's orthodox Jewish community on the lower East Side. They fall in love, and as their romance develops, Eddie photographs the disastrous Triangle Shirtwaist Factory fire, which took the lives of 146 garment workers, and he becomes involved in a murder mystery. Throughout the novel the marvellous becomes real, and Hoffmann combines social issues involving the rights of children and women workers with drugs, alcoholism, and mysterious parents to form a surrealist fairy-tale plot. Almost all of Hoffmann's novels and stories are haunting fairy tales that deny conventional happy endings even when persecuted characters survive sadistic manipulation and torment through love.   JZ

Hoffmann, E. T. A. (1776–1822) Writing name of arguably the world master of the genre of fantastic tales, Ernst Theodor Wilhelm Hoffmann (he adopted the initial 'A.' in his pen name out of reverence for the composer Wolfgang Amadeus *Mozart). He was born in Königsberg, East Prussia (since 1945 Kaliningrad, Russia) into a family of lawyers and completed a course of study in law at the university in his native city. Following family tradition he entered upon a career in the Prussian judiciary, passing successfully through the several stages of apprenticeship, first in Königsberg, then in Glogau (now Glogów, Poland), in Berlin, and finally in Posen (now Poznan, Poland). There in 1802 he was promoted to full rank as councillor (*Rat*), but then was given an unwelcome posting to Plock, as punishment for having participated in a prank ridiculing governing officials in Posen. He was happy to be posted two years later to Warsaw, then in Prussian hands as a result of the third partition of Poland in 1795. There he participated enthusiastically in the active cultural life of the city, through which he became acquainted with the works of German romantic authors and had the opportunity to further his cherished musical ambitions as composer and conductor. A chance to fulfil that dream presented itself with Napoleon's occupation of Poland in the autumn of 1806, which necessitated the dismissal of most

Prussian officials there, including Hoffmann. After a period of discouragement and poverty, he moved in 1808 to Bamberg, where he was able to support himself and his wife through work as composer, music teacher, and music critic, the latter activity leading him to embark on the literary career that made him famous. That acclaim dated from the publication of his *Fantasiestücke* (*Fantasy-Pieces*, in 4 vols., 1814–15), which included republication of his much debated hailing of Beethoven as the most romantic of composers (in the 'Kreisleriana') and his equally much discussed romantic interpretation of Mozart's opera *Don Giovanni* (in the fantasy-piece entitled 'Don Juan'). His achievement of literary fame coincided with his reinstatement in the Prussian judiciary, following the defeat of Napoleon; with an appointment at the *Kammergericht* in Berlin (1816); and also with the successful première (also 1816) of his pioneering romantic opera *Undine to a text by *Fouqué (based on the latter's mermaid story of that title). In the half-dozen years that remained before his life was cut short by death from a relatively sudden onset of paralytic illness, Hoffmann enjoyed both continued popularity and acclaim as an author and distinction as a high judiciary official.

As Hoffmann repeatedly explained to his readers, his aim as an author was to offer an experience of poetic transport by depicting the entry of a magical spirit realm into the confines of earthly existence in such a way as to make that realm seem as vivid as familiar reality. The transport created by such mingling of fantasy and reality involved an element of horror, vertigo, or sense that one was perhaps surrendering to insanity. His immediate literary precursor in this regard was his romantic contemporary Ludwig *Tieck, but Hoffmann's interest in the relation between fantasy and insanity was much deepened by his acquaintance in Bamberg with psychiatric physicians there and the relevant medical literature. Important, too, in this regard was his own experience of fantasy and fear of insanity regarding his romantic infatuation with the niece of one of these physicians, his adolescent voice pupil—a devotion that found various depictions in the *Fantasiestücke* and later in the autobiographical novel *Lebensansichten des Katers Murr* (*Views on Life of the Tomcat Murr*, 2 vols., 1819, 1821). The theme of the threat of insanity in connection with erotic passion is dominant as well in his other novel, *Die Elixiere des Teufels* (*The Devil's Elixirs*, 2 vols., 1815, 1816) and in his two volumes of tales entitled *Nachtstücke* (*Nocturnal Pieces*, 1816, 1817). He collected and published his numerous tales written—often in a lighter vein—for almanacs and other periodicals in the four volumes entitled *Die Serapionsbrüder* (*The Serapion Brethren*, 1819–21), for which he provided a narrative frame of the sort familiar since Boccaccio's *Decameron*.

The most popularly famous of the seven of his stories that Hoffmann considered to be fairy tales is 'Nussknacker und Mausekönig' ('Nutcracker and the Mouse-King', 1816), on which the *Tchaikovsky ballet is based. Hoffmann, however, considered the very first of these *Märchen*, *Der goldne Topf* (*The Golden Pot*, 1814), to be his masterpiece. It is indeed in that tale that Hoffmann most brilliantly succeeds at his programmatic intermingling of fantasy and reality, using lore about elemental spirits familiar to him from Fouqué's *Undine* and other literary sources, as he did again in the later fairy tale 'Die Königsbraut' ('The King's Bride', 1821). In the Nutcracker story, the magical realm is that familiar from literary folk fairy tales like those of *Perrault and the *Grimms, while in Hoffmann's other four *Märchen*—'Das fremde Kind' ('The Strange Child', 1817), *Klein Zaches* (*Little Zachary*, 1819), *Prinzessin Brambilla* (*Princess Brambilla*, 1820), and *Meister Floh* (*Master Flea*, 1822)—the element of fantasy is taken from pious legend, French literary fairy tales, the *commedia dell'arte*, and lore about ghosts, respectively. In addition, the fantastic in Hoffmann's *Märchen* is usually connected with elements from nature mysticism as found in the writings of his German romantic contemporaries, especially the philosopher Schelling, the poet *Novalis, and others influenced by them.   JMM

Daemmrich, Horst S., *The Shattered Self: E. T. A. Hoffmann's Tragic Vision* (1973).

Hewett-Thayer, Harvey W., *Hoffmann: Author of the Tales* (1948).

Klessmann, Eckart, *E. T. A. Hoffmann oder die Tiefe zwischen Stern und Erde* (1988).

McGlathery, James M., *E. T. A. Hoffmann* (1997).

Safranski, Rüdiger, *E. T. A. Hoffmann: Das Leben eines skeptischen Phantasten* (1984).

Steinecke, Helmut, *Die Kunst der Fantasie: E. T. A. Hoffmanns Leben und Werke* (2004).

Hoffmann, Heinrich (1809–94) German physician, satirist, and author of picture books and fairy tales. Hoffmann never thought of himself as a writer and considered his political and cultural satires and his children's books as amusing pastimes that were secondary to his profession as a medical doctor. Yet the first of several picture books he wrote, *Der Struwwelpeter* (*Slovenly Peter*, 1845), not only allowed him to pay off his debts, but brought him instant fame. He did not achieve renown as a physician as he did with *Struwwelpeter*, but even in his chosen profession he was something of a pioneer, initiating reforms in psychiatric treatment at the Frankfurt insane asylum over which he presided from 1851 until his retirement in 1888. It could even be argued that *Struwwelpeter* was inspired by his medical practice.

Hoffmann had often used funny drawings and stories as a way of distracting sick and terrified children and had perfected this manner of amusing children through the years. Thus he was not a complete novice when he decided to write and illustrate a picture book of his own for his 4-year-old son. His collection of diverse, mostly cautionary tales became the predecessor of the modern cartoon and the modern picture book. Its short, exciting, and amusing rhymed tales unfold over several pages and are supplemented by naïve, cartoon-like illustrations.

Published as *Lustige Geschichten und drollige Bilder* (*Funny Stories and Amusing Pictures*) under the pseudonym Reimerich Kinderlieb, Hoffmann's collection of tales took the children's book market by storm. It was renamed *Struwwelpeter* in 1847, but the picture book by that name that became an international classic did not take final shape until 1858, when it was furnished with new illustrations inspired by those that appeared in the Russian translation. *Struwwelpeter* was widely read and became part of childhood lore well into the 20th century, fostering many imitations and parodies. In the 1970s *Struwwelpeter* was sharply criticized for its authoritarian message and for the drastic nature of punishment in its cautionary tales (*see* WAECHTER, FRIEDRICH KARL, *Anti-Struwwelpeter*). Yet the book, which has become part of German folklore, seems to have survived this onslaught as well, perhaps because, like any good tale, it allows for contradictory interpretations.

The fairy tales Hoffmann wrote later in life, including *König Nussknacker und der arme Reinhold* (*King Nutcracker and Poor Reinhold*, 1851) and *Prinz Grünewald und Perlenfein mit ihrem lieben Eselein* (*Prince Grünewald and Perlenfein with their Dear Little Donkey*, 1871) were much more conventional in content and style; and although amusing and beloved by their author, none of them were as creative or became as popular as *Struwwelpeter*.   EMM

Hoffmann, Heinrich, *Lebenserinnerungen* (1985).

Müller, Helmut, 'Struwwelpeter und Struwwelpetriaden', in Klaus Doderer (ed.), *Das Bilderbuch* (1973).

'*Struwwelpeter* and Classical Children's Literature', spec. issue of *The Lion and the Unicorn*, 20.2 (1996).

Zipes, Jack, 'The Perverse Delight of *Shockheaded Peter*', in *Sticks and Stones: The Troublesome Success of Children's Literature from Slovenly Peter to Harry Potter* (2002).

Hofman, Wim (1941–) Dutch author, poet, and illustrator, who has written and illustrated a number of ironic fairy-tale narratives for young readers. Among his notable books are *Koning Wikkepokluk der merkwaardige zoekt een rijk* (King Wikkepokluk the Odd, Who Is Searching for his Kingdom, 1974), *Klein Duimpje* (*Little Tom Thumb*, 1992), and *Zwart als inkt is her verhaal van Sneeuwwitje en de zeven dwegeren* (*Black as Ink is the Story of Snow White and the Seven Dwarfs*, 1998). Written in verse and self-illustrated, these stories all involve protagonists who take journeys of self-discovery. In his most important fairy tale, *Black as Ink*, which Hofman transformed into a long verse epic, *Snow White must flee her real mother, not her stepmother, writes notes and letters during a seven-year stay with the dwarfs, and eventually avoids her mother's murderous attempts only to discover that she will probably repeat her mother's history when she looks into the magic mirror.   JZ

Hofmannsthal, Hugo von (1874–1929) Austrian writer and dramatist. With his drama *Jedermann* (*Everyman*, 1911) and the essay 'Der Brief des Philipp Lord Chandos an Francis Bacon' ('Letter of Philip Lord Chandos to Francis Bacon', 1925), he became one of the leading writers of the 'Jung-Wiener Gruppe'. His esteem for the *Thousand and One Nights* (*see* ARABIAN NIGHTS) is evident in his early fairy tale 'Das Märchen der 672. Nacht' ('Fairy Tale of the 672nd Night', 1895). In this narrative a rich young man gets lost in a labyrinthine town and meets his death in a nightmarish atmosphere. Whereas this fairy tale is determined by the *fin-de-siècle* mood, Hofmannsthal turned to the romantic tradition in his posthumously published fairy-tale fragments 'Das Märchen von der verschleierten Frau' ('Fairy Tale of the Veiled Woman') and 'Die Prinzessin auf dem verzauberten Berg' ('The Princess on the Enchanted Mountain'). In addition, Hofmannsthal rewrote his libretto for Richard *Strauss's fairy-tale opera *Die Frau ohne Schatten* (*The Woman without a Shadow*, 1919) as a prose version, which is often regarded as his best fairy tale. Influenced by *Novalis and Johann Wolfgang von *Goethe, this allegorical work reveals a social utopian dimension and thus deviates from the early works' pessimistic tenor.   BKM

Csúri, Károly, 'Hugo von Hofmannsthals späte Erzählung "Die Frau ohne Schatten". Struktur und Strukturvergleich', *Studia Poetica*, 2 (1980).

Kümmerling-Meibauer, Bettina, *Die Kunstmärchen von Hofmannsthal, Musil und Döblin* (1991).

Hogg, James (1770-1835) Known as the 'Ettrick Shepherd' and viewed as a 'peasant poet', Hogg was a collector of authentic Scottish folklore. Famous for his novel *Confessions of a Justified Sinner* (1824), he incorporated local fairylore into such works as *The Brownie of Bodsbeck and Other Tales* (1817). His most famous poem, *The Queen's Wake* (1813), contains a literary ballad called 'The Witch of Fife' and the verse tale 'Kilmeny' about the fairies' abduction of a perfect maiden. 'Kilmeny' was extremely popular throughout the 19th century. CGS

Holt, Tom (1961-) British mythopoetic novelist, born in London, best known for his parodic fantasy novel *Who's Afraid of Beowulf?* (1988). Holt has also produced *Snow White and the Seven Samurai* (2004), a comedic science fiction fairy-tale novel, featuring three children hacking an evil queen's computer system to uncover the supposed truths about fairy tales; it includes retellings of *'Little Red Riding Hood', 'The Three Little Pigs', and more. MF

Hoppe, Felicitas (1960-) German author who won the prestigious Georg Büchner prize in 2012, the most important literary prize for German-language books. Known for her interest in extraordinary events that happen abruptly, Hoppe has written two works connected with the fairy-tale genre. The first is *Picknick der Friseure* (*Picnic of the Barbers*, 1996), a collection of unusual miniature sketches, which includes short Kafkaesque fairy tales, often involving absurd situations and the flight of children from their parents and from a hostile world. In *Iwein Löwenritter*, (*Yvain, the Knight of the Lion*, 2008) Hoppe retold the medieval Arthurian romance *Yvain, the Knight of the Lion* (*c*.1200) by Hartmann von Aue for young readers. In the traditional Arthurian romance, the emphasis is placed on Yvain's quest to gain honour and maintain his role as the best knight of King Arthur's court. However, in Hoppe's modern rendition the emphasis shifts and focuses on the friendship formed between Yvain and the dazzling lion he meets as he does battle with dragons and a giant. JZ

Hopper, Nora (1871-1906) Irish poet and participant in the 'Celtic Twilight'. Praised by William Butler Yeats for her early poems and tales, she incorporated Irish fairylore into her works. *Ballads in Prose* (1894) and *Under Quicken Boughs* (1896) contain a number of elegiac farewells to members of various fairy tribes. Significant works include the poems 'The Wind among the Reeds', 'The Fiddler', and 'The Lament of the Last Leprechan' as well as the prose tale 'Daluan'. CGS

Horvàth, Ödon von (1901-38) Austrian writer. With his *Sportmärchen* (sport fairy tales) 'Der Faustkampf, das Harfenkonzert und die Meinung des lieben Gottes' ('The Boxing Match, the Harp Concert, and God's Opinion', 1924) and 'Legende vom Fussballplatz' ('Legend of the Football Pitch', 1926), he created unusual fairy tales for adults in which he causes the reader to be sceptical about the relevance of fairy tales in modern times. BKM

Baur, Uwe, 'Sport und Literatur in den zwanziger Jahren. Horvàths "Sportmärchen" und die Münchner Nonsense-Dichtung', in Kurt Bartsch, Uwe Baur, and Dietmar Goltschnigg (eds.), *Horvàth-Diskussion* (1976).

Hosemann, Theodor (1807-75) German painter and illustrator acknowledged as one of the great graphic artists of the 19th century. Hosemann also established a distinguished reputation as an illustrator of children's books and produced numerous drawings for fairy-tale collections by J. K. A. *Musäus (*Volksmärchen der Deutschen*, 1839), by Hans Christian *Andersen (*Märchen*, 1844-9), and by Wilhelm *Hauff (*Märchen*, 1877). Known for his realistic style, Hosemann was also a caricaturist and contributed pictures to a series of German broadsheets with fairy tales towards the end of the 19th century. JZ

Housman, Laurence (1865-1959) English dramatist, illustrator, and author of literary fairy tales for adults. Housman was the more sociable and outspoken younger brother of the poet A. E. Housman. He attended the Lambeth School of Art in London and was initially more interested in illustration than writing; at 30 he became the art critic for the *Manchester Guardian*. As an art critic, Housman championed book illustration and design as a serious art form and praised the work of earlier illustrators, such as Arthur *Hughes and Arthur Boyd Houghton. Housman's illustrated edition of Christina *Rossetti's *Goblin Market* (1893), with its stunningly sensual series of black-and-white drawings, continued the tradition of Pre-Raphaelite book design. The elegant book design and strikingly grotesque images, which Housman credited as coming from his 'freakish imagination', surpass the initial illustrations done by Dante Gabriel *Rossetti for the original edition of 1862 and are considered the classic visual interpretation of the poem. Housman's illustrations of *Goblin Market* were widely praised in the press and resulted in an invitation from Aubrey Beardsley to contribute artwork to the *Yellow Book*, although Christina Rossetti was less impressed and remarked, 'I don't think my Goblins were quite so ugly.' Housman's illustrations to Jane Barlow's *The End of Elfintown* (1894) show the strong visual influence of Beardsley. Housman also illustrated Edith *Nesbit's *A Pomander of Verse* (1895) and provided her with the concept which she later developed into her fantasy novel *The Phoenix and the Carpet* (1904). Housman—along with Nesbit, George Bernard Shaw, and H. G. *Wells—was a founding member of the Fabian Society. He was critical of the social condition of England, and his fairy tales and plays frequently question the sexual double standard for men and women as well as the hypocrisy of the upper classes. Housman thought of himself as a romantic socialist and broke from the political conservatism of his family. He was an early active supporter of women's rights. After the First World War he promoted pacifism. He actively campaigned for more toleration for homosexuals and remained friends with Oscar *Wilde after the latter's sensational trial. Housman was also a member of the artistic circle of authors and writers clustered around the publisher John Lane and the short-lived but influential

journal, *Yellow Book*, which included Wilde, Beardsley, and Kenneth *Grahame. The *fin de siècle* celebration of eroticism, decadence, and excess are apparent in both Housman's plays and his literary fairy tales. A successful and productive dramatist, Housman has the distinction of being England's most censored playwright, since his dramas dealt directly with sexuality and provided unflattering portrayals of royalty and religious figures. Housman's best-known drama *Victoria Regina* remained censored until 1935.

Housman published four collections of literary fairy tales: *A Farm in Fairyland* (1894), *The House of Joy* (1895), *The Field of Clover* (1898), and *The Blue Moon* (1904). He illustrated his first two collections, but eventually stopped producing book illustration since the strain of his intricate drawings affected his poor eyesight. The latter two volumes were illustrated by his sister Clemence Housman, who had attended art school with her brother and was an accomplished wood engraver; her illustrations echo the sensuality found in such fairy tales as 'The Bound Princess', 'The Passionate Puppets', 'The Rat-Catcher's Daughter', and 'White Birch'. Clemence Housman also published *The Were-Wolf* (1896), a children's fantasy novel.

Characteristic of the late 19th-century literary fairy tale, Housman's tales are intended for adults rather than children, and are written in a lyrical but somewhat haunting and bitter-sweet tone. They reflect the highly wrought style and literary excesses of Walter Pater's aesthetic of 'art for art's sake'. Their decadence, or attempts to titillate if not shock middle-class readers, are reminiscent of the literary fairy tales found in Wilde's *The Happy Prince and Other Tales* (1888) and *A House of Pomegranates* (1891). Housman's exotic selection of *Stories from the Arabian Nights* (1907) was exquisitely illustrated by Edmund *Dulac and became one of the most sought-after gift books of the period.   JS

Egan, Rodney, *Laurence Housman* (1983).
Kooistra, Lorraine Janzen, 'The Representation of Violence/The Violence of Representation: Housman's Illustrations to Rossetti's *Goblin Market*', *English Studies in Canada*, 19.3 (1993).

THE BLUE MOON
BY LAURENCE HOUSMAN
LONDON: JOHN MURRAY 1904

ENGRAVED BY
CLEMENCE HOUSMAN

Housman, Laurence Clemence Housman, Laurence's sister, provided this *Jugendstil* illustration of a magic door for her brother's book, *The Blue Moon* (1904).

Houssaye, Arsène (1815–96) French writer, editor, and theatre director. A *fantaisiste* (fantasist) like many other 'Generation of 1830' romantics, Houssaye exploited contemporary tastes for the imaginative. His popular songs, prose, poetry, and drama include fantastic and fairy themes as in *La Pantoufle de Cendrillon* (*Cinderella's Slipper*, 1851), and his *Arabian Nights*-inspired *Les Mille et une nuits parisiennes* (*The Thousand and One Parisian Nights*, 1876). Although considered a second-rate talent, he gained considerable power as director of reviews like *L'Artiste* and administrator of the Comédie Française (1849–56), forcing a generation of dramatists and poets, including Baudelaire, to court Houssaye while they covertly ridiculed him.   AR

Hughes, Arthur (1823–1915) British illustrator and artist, associated with Lewis *Carroll, George *MacDonald, and the Pre-Raphaelite Brotherhood. Heeding the call of Dante Gabriel *Rossetti to create art which could be reproduced for the mass media, Hughes was one of the artists who produced pictures for wood engravings for the growing serial publications of Victorian England. He illustrated *Tom Brown's Schooldays* (1869 edition) and Christina *Rossetti's *Sing-Song* (1872) and *Speaking Likenesses* (1874). His most realized work was with MacDonald, including his fairy stories, such as 'The Light Princess' and *The Princess and the Goblin* (1871), which first appeared in the magazine *Good Words for the Young* with illustrations by Hughes. Following the conventions of Victorian wood engraving, Hughes's pictures were printed in sharp black and white, using a thin outline with texture provided with heavy crosshatching, often with light streaming in from a window or fireplace. His drawings were often engraved by the illustrious Dalziel Brothers firm. Wood engraving, which Hughes used skilfully throughout his career, allowed a sharper line than the more cumbersome woodblock and was most popular before common inexpensive use of colour and photographic reproduction. Hughes's dark and brooding pictures for fairy tales treat the stories seriously, often emphasizing their frightening nature. Because many of his illustrations first appeared in magazines with two columns, they often appear in half-page width. Hughes's paintings were less famous since his output was small, but Lewis Carroll is known to have owned one. His printed work has influenced the 20th-century American artist Maurice *Sendak.   JS

Hughes, Richard Arthur Warren (1900–76) British poet, novelist, and critic, of Welsh descent. He began his literary career as a poet and playwright, but received critical acclaim as a novelist with *A High Wind in Jamaica* (1929). Hughes was preoccupied by the question of children's literature which, he believed, was written much too often with an adult audience in mind. He wrote several collections of stories for children: *The Spider's Palace* (1931), *Don't Blame Me* (1940), and *The Wonder-Dog* (1977).

Hughes considered Morocco 'almost a second home', and in the 1930s wrote several stories inspired by his sojourns there. They were first published in various magazines. It was only after his death, however, that they were published together as *In the Lap of Atlas: Stories of Morocco* (1979). The collection includes 'The Fool and the Fifteen Thieves', whose trickster-simpleton Ish-ha resembles the popular Arab folk hero Djuha, and 'The Story of Judah Ben Hassan', a magical tale based on the folklore of djinns.   AD

Hughes, Ted (**Edward James Hughes**, 1930–98) English poet and poet laureate from 1984. Renowned for its evocation of the natural world, Hughes's poetry is deeply influenced by mythology, and volumes such as *Crow* (1970) seem to distil the stark unsentimentality of folk tale and fable. His explicit dealings with the fairy tale include the children's play, *Beauty and the Beast* (broadcast 1965; first produced 1971), and the short story 'The Head' (1978). His writing for children also includes *Tales of the Early World* (1988) and a number of animal fables.   SB

Hughes, Arthur The evil witch seeks revenge in George *MacDonald's 'Day Boy and Night Girl' published in *The Light Princess and Other Stories* (1862) and illustrated by Arthur Hughes.

Humperdinck, Engelbert (1854–1921) German composer who wrote mainly operas and music for plays. He was strongly influenced by Richard *Wagner, for whom he worked during the première of *Parsifal* in Bayreuth. Humperdinck's greatest accomplishment was the creation of the most significant German romantic fairy-tale opera, *Hänsel und Gretel* (*Hansel and Gretel*, 1893). He wrote three other fairy-tale operas, *Die sieben Geisslein* (*The Seven Little Kids*, 1895), *Königskinder* (*The Royal Children*, 1897), and *Dornröschen* (*Sleeping Beauty*, 1902), but they could not match the enormous international success of *Hansel and Gretel*, which was first performed in Weimar on 23 December 1893 and directed by Richard Strauss.

The libretto for the opera was originally written by Humperdinck's sister Adelheid Wette for a family gathering, and it was later transformed into a three-act opera. In Wette's version of the Grimms' tale, the children of a broom-maker neglect their chores and, as punishment, they are sent into the woods by their mother to gather berries. When the father learns about this, he is horrified because he has heard about a witch in the woods who eats children. So the parents go in search of Hansel and Gretel. In the meantime, the children have become lost and, since they are exhausted, they lie down to sleep while a guardian angel keeps watch over them. The next day the children come upon the gingerbread house of the witch and begin to nibble on the gingerbread and sweets. The witch catches them and locks Hansel in a cage to fatten him up for a meal. When Gretel is asked by the witch to heat the oven, the girl pretends to be clumsy. The witch goes over to the oven to show Gretel what to do, and then the girl pushes the witch into the oven. The magic oven explodes into many pieces, and Gretel utters a magic spell and frees all the children who had been changed into gingerbread. The broom-maker and his wife arrive, and they celebrate the reunion with their children in a festive happy ending.

Humperdinck used many of Wagner's compositional techniques and elements of folk music to write this opera. Moreover, he included numerous children's songs and repeated these melodies as leitmotivs throughout the opera. Among his other operas, *The Royal Children* is the only one that continues to be performed. The first versions with the libretto by Ernst Rosmer was a melodrama and was performed in Munich in 1897. The second version was expanded into an opera and had its première in the New York Metropolitan Opera House. The plot is an original one that combines various fairy-tale figures: goose girl, prince, witch, knight, fool, broom-maker. The goose girl flees a witch and encounters a wandering prince who falls in love with her. Both of them are driven from the city and die because they eat poisoned bread given to them by the witch.   THH

Hurston, Zora Neale (1891–1960) Preeminent American author and anthropologist. Although she died in obscurity and was buried in an unmarked grave, her groundbreaking work continues to influence writers and ethnographers. On a scholarship to Columbia University, she studied and worked with Ruth Benedict, Franz Boas, Melville Herskovits, and Gladys Reichard. They convinced her to collect traditions from African-American communities, but Hurston also incorporated her own recollections, which pervade her fictions as well as her scholarly studies. Her autobiography *Dust Tracks on a Road* (1942), a play *Mule Bone, A Comedy of Negro Life* (with Langston Hughes, 1931), the novels *Jonah's Gourd Vine* (1934), *Their Eyes Were Watching God* (1937), *Moses, Man of the Mountain* (1939), and *Seraph on the Sewanee* (1948), and ethnographic collections *Mules and Men* (1935) (on African-American folktales and hoodoo), *Tell My Horse: Voodoo and Life in Haiti and Jamaica* (1938), and the posthumous *Every Tongue Got to Confess* (folktales from the Gulf States, 2001) offer invaluable sources for understanding African-American and Caribbean cultures. They demonstrate trickster characters and other clever, coded uses of language by slaves and marginalized Black folks to challenge and resist White oppression and oppressors. PG

Cotera, María Eugenia, *Native Speakers: Ella Deloria, Zora Neale Hurston, Jovita González, and the Poetics of Culture* (2008).

Husain, Shahrukh (1950–) British–Pakistani psychotherapist, folklorist, storyteller, author, and playwright, who adapted *A Thousand and One Nights* (*The Story of Shehrazad*) for the theatre in 2001. Husain has published multiple collections of fairy tales about transgressive women, including *Handsome Heroines: Women as Men in Folklore* (1996), *Women Who Wear the Breeches: Delicious and Dangerous Tales* (1995), and *Daughters of the Moon* (1994). With co-author Bee Wiley, Husain published *Stories from Ancient Civilisations*, an eight-volume series of Egyptian, Indian, African, Ancient Roman, Chinese, Greek, and Aztec myths, legends, folktales, and fairy tales. MF

Hyman, Trina Schart (1939–2004) American illustrator of children's books. A timorous little girl whose favourite story was *'Little Red Riding Hood', Hyman grew up to become one of the most distinguished late 20th-century illustrators to specialize in picture-book versions of traditional and literary fairy tales. These include Howard *Pyle's *King Stork* (1973), *Snow White (1974), **The Sleeping Beauty* (1977), *Little Red Riding Hood* (1983), the Caldecott Award-winning *Saint George and the Dragon* (1984, retold by Margaret Hodges from *Spenser's *Faerie Queene*), *Swan Lake* (1989), *Hershel and the Hanukkah Goblins* (1989) by Eric Kimmel, *The Fortune-Tellers* (1992) by Lloyd *Alexander, *Iron John (1994), and *Bearskin* by Howard Pyle (1997). Hyman's dark, sensuous, romantic style, reminiscent of early 20th-century illustration, is informed by a highly individual and feminist consciousness. Her illustrations for *The Water of Life* (1986), for example, endow the Princess with a vivid personality, two pet lions, and a black cat (Hyman's own cat, Marty) and a more powerful role than she plays in the Grimms' text. One of her castle guards happens to be dark-skinned—the other, a woman. Even Hyman's retelling of *The Sleeping Beauty* liberates Briar Rose from the cliché of passivity by making her 'mischievous and clever' as well as 'gracious, merry, beautiful, and kind'. SR

Hyman, Trina Schart, 'Caldecott Medal Acceptance', *Horn Book*, 61 (1985).

Hyman, Trina Schart, 'Illustrating The Water of Life', *Children's Literature Association Conference Proceedings*, 13 (1986).

Hyman, Trina Schart, *Self-Portrait: Trina Schart Hyman* (1989).

Illés, Béla (1895–1974) Hungarian writer who, after participating in the First World War, became a pacifist and joined the Communist Party in Hungary. After the failure of the soviet republic in Hungary in 1920, he emigrated to Vienna and later settled in the Soviet Union, where he became a leading member of the International Organization of Revolutionary Writers. Many of his novels and stories were published in German for the German-speaking ethnic groups in the Soviet Union, and in 1925 his collection *Rote Märchen* (*Red Fairy Tales*) appeared in Leipzig. Illés made use of traditional oral tales and fables and expressionist techniques to draw parallels with political conditions in Europe. His major purpose was to illustrate in symbolic form the lessons that the oppressed classes had to learn if they were to triumph in the class struggle. JZ

Imbriani, Vittorio (1840–86) Italian folklorist, writer, and literary historian. He dedicated much of his life to the study of Italian oral traditions such as folk poetry, folk songs, fairy tales, and folklore. He coined the term 'demopsicologia', which was subsequently applied to the new field of the history of folk traditions. His earliest works were collections of folk songs in various Italian dialects, compiled in *Canti popolari delle province meridionali* (*Folk Songs of the Southern Provinces*, 2 vols., 1871–2). Imbriani maintained, similarly to the *Grimms and other romantic scholars, that these songs had their roots in ancient epic poetry; that they thus documented, in mediated form, the cultural 'infancy' of Italy; and that their study was a crucial part of the formation of a modern national culture. His most significant fairy-tale collections are the *Novellaja fiorentina* (*Florentine Tales*, 1871) and the *Novellaja milanese* (*Milanese Tales*, 1872), in which he revealed himself to be scrupulously faithful to his oral sources;

Imbriani himself termed his method one of 'stenographic transcription'. He also wrote a number of original fairy tales, such as *Mastr'Impicca* (*Master Hangman*, 1874), in which he incorporated allusions to contemporary society into a fantastic frame. Imbriani was one of the first to publish a serious critical study of Giambattista *Basile's *Pentamerone* (1875); he also edited an edition of Pompeo *Sarnelli's *Posilicheata* (1885). NC

Cirese, Alberto Maria, 'Paragrafi su Vittorio Imbriani demopsicologo', *Problemi: Periodico Quadrimestrale di Cultura*, 80 (1987).
Cocchiara, Giuseppe, *Popolo e letteratura in Italia* (1959).

Ingelow, Jean (1820–97) English poet and novelist, and writer of children's stories. The initial inspiration for her one full-length fairy story, *Mopsa the Fairy* (1869), which F. J. Harvey Darton in *Children's Books in England* described as 'pure artless fantasy', perhaps came from *Alice's Adventures in Wonderland*, which had appeared four years earlier. A little boy, out for a walk with his nurse, climbs up a hollow tree and finds a nestful of fairies. He pockets them and flies off to Fairyland on the back of an albatross. Then follows a dreamlike maze of events, during which his favourite fairy, Mopsa, grows until she is older than he. After a long journey they reach the castle where she is to be queen, and he sorrowfully realizes that he must leave her and return home. Though some of the dialogue and characters in the early pages are Carrollian and the plot is as inconsequential, it is a gentler, more romantic story than either of the *Alices*.

In contrast, Ingelow's other writing for children—mostly domestic tales and allegories—has a strong moral element. *The Little Wonder-Horn* (1872) contains a fairy story, 'The Ouphe of the Woods', in which the cottagers who are offered fairy gold in return for hospitality ask for a spinning wheel and a hive of bees instead. 'Nineteen seventy-two' is an apt guess at what London might be like a hundred years on.   GA

Attebery, Brian, 'Women Coming of Age in Fantasy', *Extrapolation*, 28.1 (spring 1987).
Peters, Maureen, *Jean Ingelow: Victorian Poetess* (1972).

Ingemann, Bernhard Severin (1789–1862) Ingemann achieved popularity as a Danish Walter Scott, but in several stories he revealed a profound knowledge of the German *Märchen*, and it is obvious that E. T. A. *Hoffmann was a notable inspiration to him. In some tales Ingemann lets harmony rule, but in others he uses the form of the tale to study a person who is at odds with himself. In 'Sphinxen' ('The Sphinx', 1816), a young man is caught between the ordinary world of everyday life and a fantastic world, and he cannot reconcile those two until he finally accepts life as a mystery.   NI

Innocenti, Roberto (1940–) Italian illustrator known for his exquisite, detailed paintings that border on surrealism. In particular, his illustrations for *Cinderella* (1983), *The *Adventures of Pinocchio* (1988) and *Nutcracker* (1996) are all highly innovative and range from setting Cinderella in an English village during the roaring twenties and Pinocchio in 19th-century Florence with palpable reality. His most important experimental book is undoubtedly *Rose Blanche* (1986) written with Christophe Gallaz. The story concerns a young German girl named Rose Blanche, the name of a German Resistance movement, who is confronted by the horrors of the Holocaust and dies while trying to help concentration camp victims. Though not a fairy tale in any traditional sense, this tale has a symbolical and magical quality that recalls 'Briar Rose' only to challenge the notion of the sleeping princess by introducing an ordinary German girl whose goodness is illuminated at the end of the tale. In 2012 he provided unusual illustrations for Aaron Frisch's *The Girl in Red*, which recounts the strange adventures of a modern-day Little Red Riding Hood in a city portrayed as a wilderness.   JZ

Brezzo, Steven L., *Roberto Innocenti: The Spirit of Illustration* (1996).

Into the Woods A 1987 Broadway musical by James Lapine (libretto) and Stephen Sondheim (music and lyrics) that utilized familiar and original fairy tales. In a storybook setting, various characters set off into the woods with particular tasks. *Jack goes to sell the family cow, *Little Red Riding Hood travels to see her grandmother, *Cinderella steals away to visit the grave of her mother and, in an original sub-plot, a baker and his wife search for specific items demanded by a witch that has rendered the couple childless. The same witch holds her daughter *Rapunzel a prisoner in a tower. Once in the forest, Jack obtains the magic beans that allow him to climb the beanstalk to kill the giant. Cinderella goes to the festival and meets her Prince while Little Red outwits the wolf and he is killed, and Rapunzel is rescued by her Prince. The first act ends with everyone singing 'Happily Ever After', but in the second act the characters must face up to the responsibilities brought on by their earlier actions. The giant's wife seeks revenge, killing Red's grandmother, and terrorizing the countryside. The baker's wife has a brief affair with Cinderella's shallow Prince, and the disenchanted Rapunzel runs off and is trampled by the giant. The survivors eventually kill the female giant and the musical ends on a bitter-sweet note with parents learning about the power of their words on their offspring and children finding that 'No One Is Alone' in this world.   TSH

Iolanthe, or The Peer and the Peri
(1882) English operetta with libretto by William S. Gilbert and music by Arthur Sullivan. The story is based loosely on one of Gilbert's *Bab Ballads* (1869), 'The Fairy Curate'. By the late 19th century, the fairy bride motif beloved of the romantics had become a cliché and, for Gilbert, an object of parody. Iolanthe, a fairy (in Persian, 'peri'), has been banished by the Fairy Queen for marrying a mortal—a crime which 'strikes at the root of the entire fairy system'. Her son Strephon is 'a fairy down to the waist—but his legs are mortal'. In the end, Iolanthe is reunited with her husband, now Lord Chancellor, while the entire House of Peers marry fairy brides as well and are magically transformed into a 'House of Peris'. The operetta hints slyly at a family relationship between Wagner's Ring and the 'fairy system'; the chorus of fairies are likened musically to the Rhine maidens, while the statuesque Fairy Queen wears a winged helmet and corslet like Brunhilda's.   SR

Irish fairy-tale films These films are as often made and set in America as in Ireland. In the post-war period Irish gold, magic, blarney, and little people were popular both in Hollywood and on Broadway: 1947 gave rise not only to a match-making leprechaun, but also to a successful stage musical in which a granted wish delivers a lesson about racial prejudice. *The Luck of the Irish* begins with an American on holiday in Ireland. Encountering a leprechaun, he wins gratitude by not stealing his gold. Back in New York, he falls for an Irish woman but is uncertain how to approach her, till guidance comes from a manservant who turns out to be the leprechaun. The path to romance is cleared, the three return to Ireland, and the leprechaun's help is acknowledged by the nightly gift of a bottle of whiskey. One of his kin, Og, is likewise far from home in the musical *Finian's Rainbow* (which crossed from stage to screen

in 1967). Og has followed Finian to the multiracial community of Rainbow Valley, in the vicinity of Fort Knox, because Finian has stolen Ireland's gold. Finian intends to plant it, convinced that near Fort Knox it will quickly multiply. Og (whose name means 'young') has been watching over Ireland for 459 years, and wants the gold back, because without it wishes cannot be granted, a blight has fallen on the old country, and the leprechauns are turning mortal (he himself is already human size). In the end Finian's scheme comes to nothing, and Og has to choose between using the last of three wishes to make himself immortal again, or using it to save Finian's daughter from being burned as a witch for turning a white man black. A similar idea of leprechauns can be seen in *Disney's *Darby O'Gill and the Little People* (1959), except that in this they are shown as being only 21 inches tall, and have a flame-thrower, as well as magic, in their arsenal. After being kicked into a deep hole by a pookah (ghost horse), Darby is allowed three wishes when he sets free the king of the leprechauns. As soon as he wishes for wealth his daughter becomes gravely ill, and he rescues her by wishing to die in her place. At the climax the king saves them both, and Darby discovers within himself a changed sense of priorities.

In the 1990s two films invoking Irish myth were shot on location in Eire itself, and centred on animals rather than leprechauns. *Into the West* (Eire, 1992) begins in contemporary Dublin, when the traveller grandfather of two motherless boys living in a high-rise flat brings a white horse which has followed him from the sea. The horse and its name, Tir na nOg ('country of eternal youth'), invoke the legend of Oisin, who was taken through the sea, on a horse, to the land of the ever-young. Hunted by the police, the two boys ride westwards until they can go no further. On the coast the horse takes one of the boys out to sea where, beneath the waves, he is temporarily reunited with his late mother. Tir na nOg disappears for a while, then emerges from flames and gallops away. In the following year a similar perception—of the sea as preserver of life rather than destroyer—imbued *The Secret of Roan Inish* (USA, 1993). Set in 1940s Donegal, it tells, through the eyes of 10-year-old Fiona, of her family's kinship with seals. One of her ancestors was saved from a shipwreck by a seal; another took a selkie (half-human, half-seal) as his bride, and had many children with her until she tired of being human and resumed seal form. Fiona even finds her brother Jamie, presumed dead since he was swept out to sea in a wooden cradle as a baby. He has been looked after by seals, who now gently drive him back to his human family. The film presents the selkie myth not as empty whimsy, but as the product of a collective guilt engendered by centuries of tension between a recognition of the seals' beauty, and the economic necessity of clubbing them to death. TAS

'Iron Hans' (German, 'Eisenhans') First incorporated into the *Kinder- und Hausmärchen* (*Children's and Household Tales*)

by the Brothers *Grimm in 1850. It is also known as 'The Wild Man', 'Goldener', 'The Golden Boy' and can be found in the oral and literary traditions of different European countries.

In the Grimms' version there is a king whose forest is inhabited by some mysterious creature, and he kills all who enter it. After many years a stranger finally arrives and disenchants the forest by capturing a wild man, who had been dwelling in a deep pool. The man was brown as rusty iron, and his hair hung over his face down to his knees. The king has the wild man imprisoned in an iron cage in the castle courtyard, gives the key to the queen, and forbids anyone to open it under the penalty of death. However, one day the king's 8-year-old son loses his golden ball, and it bounces into the cage. Consequently, the wild man tells him that the only way he can regain his ball is by stealing the key from under his mother's pillow and emptying the cage. When the boy frees the wild man, he is so terrified of his father's wrath

'Iron Hans' The wild man haunts the king's pond in the Grimms' 'Iron Hans' illustrated by Otto *Ubbelohde and published in *Kinder- und Hausmärchen gesammelt durch die Brüder Grimm* (1927).

that he asks the wild man to take him along on his escape.

The wild man carries the boy to a golden spring in the forest and tells him that he must not allow anything to fall into it or else the water will become polluted. However, the boy's finger, which had become stuck while he was freeing the wild man, begins to hurt, and he dips it into the spring. The finger turns to gold, as does his hair after the wild man gives him two more chances. Therefore the boy must leave the forest. But the wild man reveals his name to the boy and tells him that whenever he needs something he is to return to the forest and cry out, 'Iron Hans'.

The prince covers his golden hair with a little cap and eventually obtains a job as a gardener's helper at another king's castle. One day, while working in the garden, he takes off his cap, and the king's daughter notices his golden hair from her window. She invites him to her room and rewards him for bringing flowers to her. Soon after this, with the help of Iron Hans, who gives him a magnificent steed and knights, the boy helps the king win a war. Disguised in armour, he leads a troop of knights into battle and then disappears quickly, returning the stallion and knights to Iron Hans to resume working as the simple gardener's helper.

In order to discover the strange knight's identity, the king holds a tournament. The princess throws out a golden apple three days in a row, and the disguised prince, helped by Iron Hans, who gives him red, white, and black armour and horses, rides off with the prize each time. However, on the third day the king's men give pursuit and manage to wound him and catch a glimpse of his golden hair before he escapes. The next day, the princess asks her father to summon the gardener's helper, and she reveals his golden hair. Consequently, he produces the golden apples to show that he was indeed the true hero of the tournament. As a reward, the young man asks to marry the princess, and on the wedding day

his mother and father attend and are filled with joy. During the celebration, Iron Hans suddenly appears, embraces the bridegroom, and reveals that he had been made wild by a magic spell, and since the prince had brought about his release from that spell, he wanted to reward him with all the treasures that he possessed.

Up until 1843, the Grimms had published a different version of this tale in the *Kinder- und Hausmärchen* called 'The Wild Man'. In 1850 they eliminated it in favour of 'Iron Hans', a tale which Wilhelm Grimm virtually wrote by himself using a dialect version collected from the Hassenpflug family of Kassel and a tale entitled 'Der eiserne Hans' ('Iron Hans') from Friedmund von Arnim's *100 neue Mährchen im Gebirge gesammelt* (*One Hundred New Fairy Tales Collected in the Mountains*, 1844). Wilhelm synthesized literary and oral versions that folklorists have traced to two basic tale types, 314 (*The Youth Transformed into a Horse*, also known as *Goldener* in German, or *The Golden-Haired Youth at a King's Court*) and 502 (*the Wild Man*) according to the *Types of the Folk-Tale* by Antti *Aarne and Stith Thompson. Given the evidence that we have from the Brothers Grimm, Wilhelm's 'Iron Hans' is mainly based on tales that stem from type 314, *The Golden-Haired Youth*. As usual, there is a debate among folklorists about the origins of this type. Some place the tale's creation in India, while others argue that it originated during the latter part of the Roman Empire. However, almost all folklorists agree that, as far as Wilhelm Grimm's version is concerned, the major plotline and motifs of the tale were formed during the Middle Ages in Europe. Furthermore, they were strongly influenced by a literary tradition, in particular a 12th-century romance entitled *Robert der Teufel* (*Robert the Devil*), which gave rise to many different literary and oral versions in medieval Europe.

There have been numerous stories associated with 'The Wild Man' which have nothing to do with the Grimms' 'Iron Hans', in which the focus is mainly on the young boy. In the Western imagination, the wild man is often associated with the noble savage, the dangerous gigantic monster, the mysterious uncivilized barbarian, or the loner who refuses to be civilized. In more recent times 'Iron Hans' has been associated with men's groups. In Germany Otto Höfler began using the tale during the 1950s in connection with men's initiation rituals. In 1990 the American poet Robert *Bly published his book *Iron John* based on a mythopoeic interpretation of 'Iron Hans' to outline how American men could recapture their manliness in New Age fashion, and the book became an international best-seller.   JZ

Dammann, Günter, 'Goldener', in Kurt Ranke et al. (eds.), *Enzyklopädie des Märchens* (1987).

Scherf, Walter, 'Der Eisenhans', *Lexikon der Zaubermärchen*, i (1982).

Zipes, Jack, 'Spreading Myths about Iron John', in *Fairy Tale as Myth/Myth as Fairy Tale* (1994).

'Iron John' *See* 'IRON HANS'.

Irving, Washington (1783–1859) American author of essays, travel books, biographies, and true and legendary histories. His first notable success, *A History of New York* (1809), supposedly written by the fictitious Diedrich Knickerbocker, created a legendary history for his native city while satirizing both its early Dutch inhabitants and contemporary American politicians. Irving's strong interest in folklore also influenced *The Alhambra* (1832), which incorporates several Moorish legends, gracefully retold, into an account of his stay in Granada. He is most famous for two stories included in *The Sketch Book of Geoffrey Crayon, Gent.* (1819–20): 'The Legend of Sleepy Hollow' and 'Rip Van Winkle'. While the 'Legend' pokes fun at Ichabod Crane's superstitious credulity, 'Rip Van Winkle' is a genuine fairy tale—the first with a distinctively American flavour. Irving successfully transposed the European motif of the enchanted sleeper to his own Hudson River Valley, substituting for the traditional fairy revellers the explorer Hendrick Hudson and his crew. Both stories have inspired numerous painters, illustrators (including Arthur *Rackham and N. C. Wyeth), cartoonists, and dramatists. A stage version of *Rip Van Winkle* (1860) starring Joseph Jefferson was one of the longest-running hits in the history of the American theatre, while the plots of 'Rip' and 'The Legend' were ingeniously interwoven in Robert Planquette's opera *Rip Van Winkle* (1882).   SR

Attebery, Brian, *The Fantasy Tradition in American Literature* (1980).

Rubin-Dorsky, Jeffrey, *Adrift in the Old World: The Psychological Pilgrimage of Washington Irving* (1988).

Tuttleton, James W. (ed.), *Washington Irving: The Critical Reaction* (1993).

Irwin, Robert (1946–) English scholar and writer whose academic works such as *The Arabic Beast Fable* (1992) and *The *Arabian Nights: A Companion* (1994) have made major contributions towards understanding and interpreting literature of the Middle East. In addition, he has written a remarkable fairy-tale novel, *The Arabian Nightmare* (1983, rev. 1987), in which the hero Balian explores Cairo in the 15th century, becomes entangled in the labyrinth of the city, and falls into a nightmare that is never-ending. Irwin combines his erudition on the Middle East with conventions of Western fantasy to explore the boundaries between dream and story.   JZ

Italy, fairy tales in *See* p. 303.

Italy, fairy tales in Italy can pride itself on having the earliest and one of the richest collections of literary fairy tales in Giambattista *Basile's *Lo cunto de li cunti*. The seminal experimentations with the fairy tale as an independent literary genre in the Renaissance and baroque periods on the part of Basile and *Straparola did not, however, provide the impetus for the blossoming of a subsequent fairy-tale 'vogue', as was the case in France of the 17th and 18th centuries. Even Basile's *Lo cunto*, though recognized by scholars for centuries as an artistic and folkloric masterpiece, never achieved the status of beloved national treasure that the collections of Charles *Perrault, the Brothers *Grimm, or Aleksandr *Afanasyev did. Although Italy has abounded in important fairy-tale collections as well as fairy-tale authors, a national collection of Italian fairy tales akin to those published in other European countries in the 19th century appeared only in 1956. Up to this day Italian folklorists, literary scholars, and writers continue to grapple with the question of how to assimilate the vast storehouse of dialect narratives of oral tradition, still in part unfamiliar to the modern reading public, into literate culture.

1. UP TO 1400

The oldest example of an 'Italian' literary fairy tale is the story of 'Cupid and Psyche', embedded in *Apuleius' 2nd-century Latin novel *The Golden Ass*. During the millennium that followed, oral tales continued to circulate in the same fashion that they had for hundreds, if not thousands, of years, but due to various factors, among which figured the lack of a secular literate culture, there were few further experiments with the literary fairy tale. The advent of vernacular culture, especially from the 13th century on when the novella became a predominant genre, marked the point at which the mediation between popular and literary traditions began to manifest itself in the presence of fairy-tale elements in short narrative, even if the first integral fairy tales appeared only three centuries later.

The anonymous late 13th-century *Novellino* (*The Hundred Old Tales*), for example, draws on materials from diverse cultural traditions and thematic areas. Although many of the tales have the structure of medieval exempla, the collection also includes animal fables and fantastic motifs. In other contemporary manuscripts we find more explicit fairy-tale elements, but in general the exemplum flavour of many of these earliest novellas did not allow for the full expression of the secular supernatural and marvellous that permeates the fairy tale.

We find the most significant early use of fairy-tale motifs, and perhaps the first explicit reference to fairy tales, in Giovanni Boccaccio's works. Boccaccio had a pivotal role as mediator between the feudal-chivalric and the emerging bourgeois cultures; thematically, his tales frequently feature ordinary protagonists who triumph over hardship, thus expressing a fairy-tale-like optimism. In chapter 10 of book 14 of his treatise on ancient mythology *Genealogia deorum gentilium* (*The Genealogies of the Gentile Gods*, 1350–75), he affirms that we may find wisdom not only in the works of great 'official' poets like Virgil, Dante, and Petrarch, but also in popular narratives: 'there has never been a little old woman . . . as she invents or recites tales of ogres, fairies, or witches around the hearth on winter nights . . . who has not been aware that under the veil of her narrative lies some serious meaning, with which she can frighten children, or amuse maidens, or at least demonstrate the power of fortune.' Among his works of fiction, the prose novel *Filocolo* (1336?) adapts the French tale of Florio and Biancofiore's troubled but ultimately happy-ended love story, and includes such fairy-tale functions as an initial lack, antagonists and helpers, a difficult quest and series of tasks, the magic gift, and a final reward and marriage. But it is above all in his most famous work, the *Decameron* (1349–50), that the fairy tale is used most cogently as a compositional device. No surprise when we consider the variety of materials, many of which share characteristics with the fairy tale, that Boccaccio drew from: classical literature, medieval lais and fabliaux, *chansons de geste*, and other popular narratives. As is well known, the entire book has a consolatory function, for its tales are told by a group of young people in order to escape the physical and psychological ravages of the plague. Although they are presented as examples of the power of fortune, individual enterprise, and love, the tales often borrow the structure of the fairy tale, especially in day 2, dedicated to the wiles of fortune, and day 5, which features love stories with happy endings. Among such tales are 2.3, the story of three brothers who miraculously ascend from rags to riches; 'Andreuccio of Perugia' (2.5), with its tripartite series of adventures; 'Bernabò of Genoa' (2.9), the tale of a woman wrongfully accused of adultery by her husband; 'Giletta of Nerbona' (3.9), which bears resemblance to Basile's 'La Sapia'; 'Nastagio degli Onesti' (5.8); 'Torello of Stra and the Saladino' (10.9); and 'Griselda and the Marquis of Saluzzo' (10.10), which combines motifs common to 'Cinderella' and 'Beauty and the Beast' and was later rewritten in verse form by Perrault.

Several other early novella collections offer further examples of the entrance of fairy-tale motifs into the literary arena. Four of the 20 novellas in Ser Giovanni Fiorentino's *Pecorone* (*The Big Sheep*, second half of the 14th century) bear strong resemblance to fairy tales, even if in realistic garb (4.1, 4.2, 9.2, and 10.1); just as fairy-tale motifs are evident in the tales 'De bono facto', 'De vera amicitia et caritate', and 'De bona ventura' of Giovanni *Sercambi's *Novelle* (*Novellas*, 1390–1402). Fairy-tale compositional techniques informed two other genres which were increasingly transported from the oral to the literary sphere towards the end of this period. A number of the *cantari*, epic or romantic ballads which in their early form were recited in town squares by minstrels, have an integral fairy-tale structure, such as the anonymous *Il bel Gherardino* (*The Fair Gherardino*), *Ponzela Gaia* (*The Gay Maiden*), and *Liombruno*, each of which is composed of two 'movements' including the typical elements of initial lack, helpers, departures, battles, donors and magic gifts, and elimination of lack. The *sacre rappresentazioni*, or religious dramas, were also performed in squares or churches, and had as their subject biblical stories, Christian legends, and saints' lives. Unjust persecution was a favourite topic of several of the most renowned of these dramas, such as *Santa Guglielma*, which with its persecution of an innocent wife is similar to tale 10.1 of the *Pecorone*; *Santa Uliva*, in which a daughter's victimhood involves having her hands cut off, and which includes motifs later found in tales by Basile ('The She-Bear' and 'Penta of the Chopped-Off Hands'), Perrault, and the Grimms; and *Stella*, whose evil stepmother is, of course, present in innumerable fairy tales.

2. 1400–1600

The *cantari* were the single most important influence on the Italian chivalric epic, which emerged in this period, and accordingly, the fairy-tale motifs present in the former were often transposed to the latter. In Luigi Pulci's comic epic *Morgante* (1483) we find dragons and ogrish wild men; in particular, the story of Florinetta in canto 19 shares characteristics with Basile's 'The Flea' and 'Cannetella'. Matteo Maria Boiardo's *Orlando innamorato* (*Orlando in Love*, 1495), is similarly populated by miraculous animals, ogres, and fairies, and Ludovico Ariosto's entire *Orlando furioso* (*The Frenzy of Orlando*, 1516–32), with its interminable search for the elusive female object of desire, is structured like an extended fairy tale.

Although a general interest in popular culture and folk traditions permeated the Renaissance, at least until the second half of the 16th century novellas generally favoured realistic subjects, often taking up the favourite Boccaccian theme of the *beffa*, or practical joke. From the second half of the 15th century on there was also an increasing interest in fables of the Aesopian type, which culminated in a work like Giacomo Morlini's Latin *Novellae* (*Novellas*, 1520). It is, however, Giovan Francesco Straparola who for the first time and in undisguised fashion included entire fairy tales in a novella collection. His enormously popular *Le *piacevoli notti* (*The Pleasant Nights*, 1550–3), adopts a frame similar to that of the *Decameron*, in which, after the ex-bishop of Lodi Ottaviano Maria Sforza leaves Milan for political reasons, he assembles an aristocratic company at his palace near Venice to tell tales over the course of 13 nights. The tales are an eclectic mix of various genres; of the 74 tales, 14 are fairy tales, whose materials were probably gleaned from *oriental fairy tales, animal fables, and oral tradition; these are: 'Cassandrino' (1.2), 'Pre' Scarpacifico' (1.3), 'Tebaldo' (1.4), 'Galeotto' (2.1), 'Pietro pazzo' ('Crazy Pietro', 3.1), 'Biancabella' (3.3), 'Fortunio' (3.4), 'Ricardo' (4.1), 'Ancilotto' (4.3), 'Guerrino' (4.5), 'Tre fratelli' ('The Three

Brothers', 7.5), 'Maestro Lattanzio' (8.5), 'Cesarino de' Berni' (10.3), and 'Soriana' (11.1). Although Straparola's versions of the tales are nowhere near as innovative as Basile's experiment with the genre a century later, there is no doubt that he had a great influence not only on Basile, who reworked several of his tales, but also on Perrault and the Brothers Grimm; all of the fairy tales from the *Nights*, in fact, find later counterparts in the above collections and others.

3. 1600–1800

The spread of print culture, the anthropological interest that the continuing geographical discoveries inspired, and the attraction to the marvellous that permeated late Renaissance and baroque culture were among the most significant factors that resulted in a re-evaluation of native folkloric traditions and the attempt to transport them into the realm of literature. And Giambattista Basile's *Lo cunto de li cunti overo lo trattenemiento de peccerille* (*The Tale of Tales, or Entertainment for Little Ones*, 1634–6), the first integral collection of fairy tales in Europe, is the work that truly marks the passage from the oral folk tale to the artful and sophisticated 'authored' fairy tale. Written in Neapolitan dialect and also known as the **Pentamerone*, this work is composed of 49 fairy tales contained by a 50th frame story, also a fairy tale. In the frame tale, a slave girl deceitfully cheats Princess Zoza out of her predestined prince Tadeo, and the princess reacts by using a magic doll to instil in the slave the craving to hear tales. The prince summons the ten best storytellers of his kingdom, a motley group of old women, and they each tell one tale apiece for five days, at the end of which Zoza tells her own tale, reveals the slave's deceit, and wins back Tadeo. In many ways the structure of the *Pentamerone* mirrors, in parodic fashion, that of earlier novella collections, in particular Boccaccio's *Decameron*, suggesting that Basile was well aware of the radically new course he was taking: there are five days of telling that contain ten tales each; the tales are told by ten grotesque lower-class women; the storytelling activity of each day is preceded by a banquet, games, and other entertainment; and verse eclogues that satirize the social ills of Basile's time follow each day's tales.

Despite its subtitle, the *Pentamerone* is not a work of children's literature, which did not yet exist as a genre, but was probably intended to be read aloud in the 'courtly conversations' that were an elite pastime of this period. Moreover, Basile did not merely transcribe oral materials, but transformed them into original tales distinguished by an irresistible presence of the comic; vertiginous rhetorical play, especially in the form of extravagant metaphor that draws on diverse stylistic registers; abundant references to the everyday life and popular culture of the time; final morals that often poorly fit their tales; characters who, likewise, often betray our sense of what they should be, as fairy-tale characters; and a subtext of playful critique of courtly culture and the canonical literary tradition. The *Pentamerone* contains the earliest literary versions of many celebrated fairy-tale types—*'Cinderella', *'Sleeping Beauty', *'Rapunzel', and others—although they are far more colourful, racy, imbued with sheer exuberance, and open-ended than their canonical counterparts. Indeed, Basile does not offer easy answers to the problem of how an archaic, oral narrative genre can, or should, be re-proposed in literary form; in the *Pentamerone* 'high' and 'low' cultures intersect to create a 'carnivalesque' text in which linguistic and cultural hierarchies, as well as the conventional fairy-tale hierarchies, are rearranged or made to show their weak spots. Besides being one of the most suggestive expressions of the search for new artistic forms and the attraction to the marvellous theorized by baroque poetics, Basile's work exerted a notable influence on later fairy-tale writers such as Perrault and the women writers of his generation, and the Grimms.

In the century following its publication the *Pentamerone* inspired much admiration but few further experiments with the genre. Basile's friend Giulio Cesare Cortese included several fairy-tale episodes in his *Viaggio di Parnaso* (*Voyage to Parnassus*, 1620), one of which closely resembles the first story of the *Pentamerone*, which was probably already in progress at this time. Salvatore Rosa made reference to many of the themes present in the *Pentamerone* in his *Satire* (*Satires*), written in the mid-17th century, and in Lorenzo Lippi's mock-epic *Malmantile riacquistato* (*Malmantile Recaptured*, 1676) we also find an episode borrowed from Basile. The only other fairy-tale collection of the 17th century is Pompeo *Sarnelli's *Posilicheata* (*An Outing to Posillipo*, 1684), composed of five tales told in Neapolitan dialect by peasant women at the end of the country banquet that the frame story narrates.

The enormous production and popularity of fairy tales in 17th- and 18th-century France saw no parallel phenomenon in Italy, and it was over 100 years after Basile, when the fairy-tale 'vogue' was in full fervour in France, that another Italian author wrote a major work based on fairy tales. From 1760 to 1770 the Venetian Carlo *Gozzi published his ten *Fiabe teatrali* (*Fairy Tales for the Theatre*): *L'amore delle tre melarance* (*The Love of Three Oranges*), based on Basile's tale 5.9; *Il corvo* (*The Crow*), based on Basile's tale 4.9; *Il re cervo* (*The King Stag*); *Turandot*; *Il mostro turchino* (*The Blue Monster*); *La donna serpente* (*The Snake Woman*); *L'augellin belverde* (*The Green Bird*); *I pitocchi fortunati* (*The Fortunate Beggars*); *La Zobeide*; and *Zeim re dei geni* (*Zeim, King of the Genies*). Besides Basile, Gozzi's sources included French tales, oriental tales and romances such as the recently translated *The Thousand and One Nights* (*see* ARABIAN NIGHTS), and popular oral tradition. The particularity of his plays lies in their juxtaposition of fairy tales with the conventions, improvisational techniques, and masks of the *commedia dell'arte*, a mix that, somewhat paradoxically, often results in a rather cerebral interpretation of the marvellous. Gozzi, a political conservative and literary traditionalist, wrote his satirical and pointedly ideological plays in polemical response to his arch-rival Carlo Goldoni's dramas of bourgeois realism, and considered his fairy tales negligible 'children's' stories chosen precisely for their distance from the everyday world depicted in Goldoni's plays and for their ability to stimulate curiosity and surprise. Gozzi's *Fairy Tales* proved to be greatly suggestive from a theatrical point of view, as is evidenced by their inspiration of operas by Richard *Wagner, Ferruccio Busoni, Giacomo *Puccini, and Sergei *Prokofiev.

4. 1800–1900

The early 19th-century romantic interest in archaic popular traditions, which supposedly most genuinely represented the 'spirit of a nation', expressed itself in Italy above all in the study of folk songs and oral poetry, and in investigations of popular customs, beliefs, superstitions, and other practices. Fairy tales were generally not included in this sort of research, and foreign endeavours in this field, such as the Grimms', aroused interest principally for their aesthetic value. Only later in the century, during the period of Italian unification (1860–70), did tales and legends become the focus of positivistic and comparativistic studies and ethnographic collections. Among the first fairy-tale collections to appear were Vittorio *Imbriani's *Novellaja fiorentina* (*Florentine Tales*, 1871) and *Novellaja milanese* (*Milanese Tales*, 1872); these were followed by what is arguably the most important Italian collection of the century, the four-volume *Fiabe novelle e racconti popolari siciliani* (*Fairy Tales, Novellas, and Popular Tales of Sicily*, 1875) by Giuseppe *Pitrè. From the last decades of the 19th century to the beginning of the 20th century a wealth of other collections appeared that, along with the above, became precious documents for later anthologists of Italian fairy tales such as Italo *Calvino. These include: Carolina Coronedi-Berti's *Novelle popolari bolognesi* (*Bolognese Popular Tales*, 1874), Domenico Comparetti's *Novelline popolari italiane* (*Italian Popular Tales*, 1875), Isaia Visentini's *Fiabe mantovane* (*Mantuan Fairy Tales*, 1879), Gherardo Nerucci's *Sessanta novelle popolari montalesi* (*Sixty Popular Tales from Montale*, 1880), Pietro Pellizzari's *Fiabe e canzoni popolari del contado di Maglie in terra d'Otranto* (*Fairy Tales and Popular Songs from the Countryside of Maglie in Terra d'Otranto*, 1881), Antonio De Nino's *Fiabe* (*Fairy Tales*, 1883), Pitrè's *Novelle popolari toscane* (*Tuscan Popular Tales*, 1888), Domenico Giuseppe Bernoni's *Fiabe popolari veneziane* (*Venetian Popular Fairy Tales*, 1893), Giggi Zanazzo's *Novelle, favole e leggende romanesche* (*Roman Tales, Fables, and Legends*, 1907), and Letterio di Francia's *Fiabe e novelle calabresi* (*Calabrian Fairy Tales and Stories*, 1929–31).

There were also a number of writers at this time who benefited from the huge amount of 'prime materials' newly at their disposal to produce highly suggestive creative elaborations of fairy tales, for the first time written for a young audience. The most famous of these is Carlo *Collodi's novel *Le avventure di *Pinocchio: Storia di un burattino* (*The Adventures of Pinocchio: Story of a Puppet*, 1883). In short, *Pinocchio* tells of how its homonymous protagonist, a wooden puppet, is induced both by the harsh socio-economic conditions in which he lives and by his own cheerfully transgressive nature to undergo a series of perilous adventures that eventually lead to his transformation into a real boy. *Pinocchio*, though it shares with the fairy tale its structure of a journey of initiation fraught with obstacles that ultimately leads to rebirth on the higher plane of adulthood, as well as the common motifs of a fairy godmother, talking animals, magical helpers and donors, and other marvellous beings, also has much in common with the more realistic genres of the picaresque novel, the moralizing family drama so prevalent in children's literature of this period, and even the *Bildungsroman*, or novel of formation. Pinocchio's adventures are essentially traumatic, for the social world that Collodi depicts is coloured by privation, violence, and indifference, and even in the more intimate, familial sphere, self-interest and cruelty often reign. *Pinocchio* has, in fact, been considered an 'anti-Cinderella' tale for its ostensible message that the only way to achieve social validation is through hard work, self-reliance, and obedience to one's superiors; and that even when it comes, it is far from the enchanted happy ending of fairy tales. Indeed, *Pinocchio* nearly became a cautionary tale along the lines of *'Little Red Riding Hood' since, when it was first being published serially in a children's journal, Collodi ended his tale at the end of chapter 15, when Pinocchio is hanged and left for dead, victim of his own unruly ingenuousness. Ultimately, though, Pinocchio's lasting attraction has much less to do with the puppet's metamorphosis into a responsible member of society than with the affirmation of the unleashed vitality and essential humanity of childhood of which he gives constant and poignant proof up until the very last chapter. Although the best-known re-adaptation of *Pinocchio* is Disney's film, there have been many imaginative contemporary rewritings of Collodi's classic tale in Italy, among which figure Carmelo Bene's 1962 dramatized version and Luigi Malerba's *Pinocchio con gli stivali* (*Pinocchio in Boots*).

The birth of Pinocchio coincided with the publication of the Sicilian Luigi *Capuana's first collection of original fairy tales, *C'era una volta* (*Once Upon a Time*, 1882), which was then followed by many others, including *Il regno delle fate* (*The Kingdom of Fairies*, 1883), *La reginotta* (*The Princess*, 1883), *Il Raccontafiabe* (*The Fairy Tale-Teller*, 1894), *Chi vuol fiabe, chi vuole?* (*Who Wants Fairy Tales, Who Wants Them?*, 1908), and *Le ultime fiabe* (*The Last Fairy Tales*, 1919); as well as by the theatrical fairy tales *Rospus* (*Toad*, 1887) and *Spera di sole: Commedia per burattini* (*Sunbeam: A Comedy for Marionettes*, 1898). Capuana used his familiarity with Sicilian folklore to create tales that evoked the oral tales of tradition, although it is his innovative elaboration of these materials through the use of humour, whimsical fantasy, and realistic detail that gives his work its true flavour. This flavour best emerges in the 19 tales of *Once Upon a Time* where, alongside princes and princesses, fierce antagonists, enchanted objects, and marvellous metamorphoses, we find loving depictions of domestic tableaux and Sicilian landscapes, surprisingly earthy fairies and wizards, and lower-class protagonists consumed by their primary needs whose final triumph is guaranteed, however, by their simple virtues of perseverance, goodness of heart, and humility.

The children's author Emma *Perodi's experimentations with the genre closed the century. Among her numerous fairy-tale collections should be remembered *Le novelle della nonna* (*Grandmother's Tales*, 1892), whose frame tale narrates the life of the Marcuccis, a peasant family that lives in the Tuscan countryside. The narratives, many of which are fairy tales, are told around the family hearth by the Marcucci matriarch Regina from one Christmas Eve to the following November, punctuating the 'real' stories of the Marcucci family; indeed, Regina often chooses her tales on the basis of the consolation or instruction that they may offer to members of the family. Perodi's tales are distinguished by a vividly expressive style, the juxtaposition of reassuringly domestic scenarios and uncanny fantastic topographies, the attraction to the dark and the cruel, and the presence of bizarre and macabre figures. Although within the frame Regina may stress the didactic function of her tales, Perodi ultimately resists any socializing project in favour of the celebration of the pleasures of narration and of the delectable indeterminacy of the fantastic worlds that her tales depict.

5. 1900–PRESENT

By the start of the First World War, the flurry of collection and compilation of tales had died down somewhat, although it again resumed after the Second World War. The 'rediscovery' of the popular narratives of the various Italian regions in the 20th century has been distinguished, on the one hand, by a more painstakingly philological approach to the source materials and, on the other, by the relatively recent attempt to determine 'ecotypes' of tales based on the principal cultural areas of Italy. Furthermore, figures such as Benedetto Croce and Antonio Gramsci have had an enormous influence in redirecting folkloric and fairy-tale scholarship of this century. Croce, above all in his seminal studies of Basile's *Pentamerone* published in the first decades of the century, maintained that the investigation of folk tales as historical and aesthetic entities should supersede questions of origin or comparativistic analysis of motifs, and thus opened the door to a full-fledged literary analysis of fairy tales. Gramsci, in his essay 'Osservazioni sul folclore' ('Observations on Folklore', 1950), put forth the idea that popular folklore expresses a 'concept of the world' that is radically different from the 'official' world view, and that by studying these perspectives we may better understand the contradictions of a society based on class divisions, an idea that would then be taken up by ideological criticism.

Notwithstanding the abundant tale collections and theoretical reflection on the material contained therein, a definitive 'master collection' of Italian tales was not published until 1956, when Italo Calvino, one of the most eminent literary figures of the 20th century, filled the gap with his *Fiabe italiane* (*Italian Folktales*). The 200 tales were chosen with the criteria of offering every major tale type, of which *Folktales* includes about 50, often in multiple versions; and of representing the 20 regions of Italy. Fairy tales predominate, but there are also religious and local legends, novellas, animal fables, and anecdotes. Calvino selected his materials primarily from 19th-century tale collections, and by 'touching up', imposing 'stylistic unity', and translating from Italian dialects created his own versions of the tales. This procedure was likened to the Grimms' by the author himself, but Calvino is entirely self-conscious about his 'half-way scientific' method, discussing at length his techniques of recasting the tales and integrating variants so as to produce the 'most unusual, beautiful, and original texts'.

Calvino motivates his endeavour by maintaining that folk tales are the thematic prototype of all stories, just as he finds an essential structural paradigm for all literature in the multiple narrative potentialities that folk tales offer, with their 'infinite variety and infinite repetition'. The Italian corpus that Calvino discovers is, in his eyes, comparable in richness and variety to the great Northern European collections; at the same time, it possesses a distinctly personal and 'unparalleled grace, wit, and unity of design'. He also identifies a series of more specific characteristics of the Italian tales, though critics have pointed out that they may be in part Calvino's own invention: a sense of beauty and an attraction to sensuality, an eschewal of cruelty in favour of harmony and the 'healing solution', 'a continuous quiver of love' that runs through many tales, a 'tendency to dwell on the wondrous', and a dynamic tension between the fantastic and the realistic. Regarding the vital importance of his material, Calvino maintains that 'folktales are real', since they encompass all of human experience in the form of a 'catalogue of the potential destinies of men and women'. From folk tales we learn, ultimately, that 'we can liberate ourselves only if we liberate other people'; that we must salvage 'fidelity to a goal and purity of heart, values fundamental to salvation and triumph'; 'beauty, a sign of grace that can be masked by the humble, ugly guise of a frog'; and 'the infinite possibilities of mutation'.

In the introduction to his *Folktales* Calvino exhorts his readers to consult the original sources he used, and scholars to publish the tales they contain. Since the 1970s, especially, this challenge has been met on multiple fronts:

there have been re-editions of the classic 19th-century collections, new compilations of tales and indices of tale types, the emergence of children's writers with a predilection for fairy tales, and suggestive 'retellings' of traditional tales by well-known contemporary authors.

The most ambitious of the attempts to catalogue Italy's wealth of popular tales was a series of 16 volumes published by Mondadori from 1982 to 1990 dedicated to the fairy tales of the various Italian regions, in which an author and scholar teamed up to translate and edit the material. This sort of endeavour has led to an ever more precise consideration of both the influences that merge to form the common types of Italian tales and of their distinguishing regional characteristics. In this same period there have also been noteworthy experiments with rewriting the classic fairy-tale canon for children, which in the case of the pedagogue and children's writer Gianni *Rodari also encompassed a theoretical discussion of how fairy tales could assume a creative and liberating function in the hands of both children and educators (*Grammatica della fantasia* (*A Grammar of Fantasy*, 1973)). Rodari's own most suggestive encounters with the fairy tale include *Favole al telefono* (*Tales on the Telephone*, 1962), *Tante storie per giocare* (*Lots of Stories for Play*, 1971), and *C'era due volte il barone Lamberto* (*Twice Upon a Time There Lived Baron Lamberto*, 1978). Rodari's teachings served as an ideal model for numerous authors who have, over the past decades, continued to transform the increasing interest in fairy tales into the invention of original works often distinguished by the treatment of contemporary social and political issues within the traditional narrative structure of the fairy tale. Among these authors should be remembered Beatrice Solinas Donghi, whose playful approach to tradition is most evident in *Le fiabe incatenate* (*The Linked Fairy Tales*, 1967) and *La gran fiaba intrecciata* (*The Great Interlaced Fairy Tale*, 1972); Bianca Pitzorno, whose revisitation of fairy-tale commonplaces often focuses on the development of positive female protagonists, as in *L'incredibile storia di Lavinia* (*The Incredible Story of Lavinia*, 1985) and *Streghetta mia* (*My Little Witch*, 1988); Roberto Piumini, whose extensive fairy-tale corpus includes both traditional material and innovative tales which engage with social transformations and political myths of our time (for example, *Il giovane che entrava nel palazzo* (*The Youth Who Entered the Palace*) and *Fiabe da Perserèn* (*Fairy Tales from Perseren*), both written in the early 1980s); and Luigi Malerba, whose *Pinocchio con gli stivali* (*Pinocchio in Boots*, 1977) is a pastiche in which the itineraries of a modern Pinocchio lead to encounters with classic fairy-tale characters such as Little Red Riding Hood and Cinderella. And, finally, there have also been a number of initiatives in which authors and poets whose principal activity is not children's literature have tried their hands at fairy tales, as in the 1975 anthology *Favole su favole* (*Fairy Tales upon Fairy Tales*).

The cataloguing of popular tales in the second half of the 19th century was in some sense a response to national unification and the inevitable weakening of local traditions that its linguistic and educational standardization would bring. So today the cultural homogenization that our late-industrial, globalized society thrives on makes the need to retrieve the narrative remnants of local traditions seem even more urgent. This urgency stems not from a romantic nostalgia for preserving the past, but from the hope that the cultures which produced these legacies may regain their fading vitality and continue to tell their life-affirming tales and that, therefore, we may all continue to experience and to recreate the power of fairy tales to delight, instruct, and promote human communication.   NC

Aristodemo, Dina, and de Meijer, Pieter, 'Le fiabe popolari fra cultura regionale e cultura nazionale', *Belfagor*, 34 (1979).

Bacchilega, Cristina, 'Calvino's Journey: Modern Transformations of Folktale, Story, and Myth', *Journal of Folklore Research*, 26 (1989).

Beckwith, Marc, 'Italo Calvino and the Nature of Italian Folktales', *Italica*, 64 (1987).

Beniscelli, Alberto, *La finzione del fiabesco: Studi sul teatro di Carlo Gozzi* (1986).

Boero, Pino, and De Luca, Carmine, *La letteratura per l'infanzia* (1995).

Bronzini, Giovanni Battista, 'Italien', *Enzyklopädie des Märchens*, vii (1992).

Bronzini, Giovanni Battista, *La letteratura popolare italiana dell'Otto–Novecento: Profilo storico-geografico* (1994).

Calabrese, Stefano, *Fiaba* (1997).

Canepa, Nancy L., *From Court to Forest: Giambattista Basile's 'Lo cunto de li cunti' and the Birth of the Literary Fairy Tale* (1999).

Cirese, Alberto Maria, 'Folklore in Italy: A Historical and Systematic Profile and Bibliography', *Journal of the Folklore Institute*, 11 (June/August 1974).

Cocchiara, Giuseppe, *Popolo e letteratura in Italia* (1959).

Emery, Ted, 'The Reactionary Imagination: Ideology and the Form of the Fairy Tale in Gozzi's *Il re cervo*', in Nancy L. Canepa (ed.), *Out of the Woods: The Origins of the Literary Fairy Tale in Italy and France* (1997).

Faeti, Antonio (ed. and intro.), *Fiabe fantastiche: Le novelle della nonna* by Emma Perodi (1993).

Massini, Giulia, *La poetica di Rodari: Utopia del folklore e nonsense* (2011).

Mazzacurati, Giancarlo, 'La narrativa di G. F. Straparola e l'ideologia del fiabesco', in *Forma e ideologia* (1974).

Perella, Nicolas, 'An Essay on Pinocchio', *Italica*, 63 (spring 1986).

Petrini, Mario, *La fiaba di magia nella letteratura italiana* (1983).

Petrini, Mario, *Il gran Basile* (1989).

Pisanty, Valentina, *Leggere la fiaba* (1993).

Robuschi, Giuseppina, *Luigi Capuana, scrittore per l'infanzia* (1969).

Rodari, Gianni, *The Grammar of Fantasy*, trans. Jack Zipes (1996).

Jack and the Beanstalk (film version) A 1952 adaptation of the folk tale directed by Jean Yarbrough and starring the comedy team of Bud Abbott and Lou Costello. Beyond the requisite Hollywood love story, the movie explores imagination and acting through the unrestrained childlike behaviour of Costello, who plays Jack, an adult 'problem child'. In the story of 'Jack and the Beanstalk', which a child reads to him, Jack acts the part of the giant killer and imagines the power and social acceptance that he cannot achieve in reality. In the end, play and fantasy give way to the real world of adult authority.   DH

Jack tales A constellation of traditional events and motifs, newly formed in early 18th-century England, in which a quick-witted boy, son of a (wealthy Cornish) farmer, meets and vanquishes numerous giants, acquiring their wealth and marrying a noble wife.

Notably absent from 17th-century folk amusement such as puppetry and chapbooks, the first Jack tale documented was *Jack and the Gyants* [*sic*] in 1708. An immediate success, Jack and his giants were frequently alluded to in familiar terms by 18th-century writers like Henry Fielding, John Newbery, Dr Johnson and Boswell, and William Cowper.

Jack's 18th-century cycle of adventures breaks down into three groups of tales. In the first, Jack defeats his foes physically. Using familiar tools of hunters (horn), farmers (spade or shovel), and Cornish miners (pick), Jack overpowers the 18-foot tall Cornish giant Cormilan and wins his treasure. Subsequently Cormilan's gigantic brother Blunderboar, seeking revenge, captures Jack and invites a brother giant to a feast at which he proposes to serve Jack's heart with pepper and vinegar. Instead, Jack contrives to throttle both giants and to cut off their heads, much as did David after his battle with Goliath.

In the second group of tales, Jack sets off to fight Welsh giants. In his first encounter he doubly outwits his gigantic host, first saving his own life and then tricking the giant into killing himself: 'Soon after the Giant arose, and went to his Breakfast with a Bowl of Hasty-Pudding, containing four Gallons, giving *Jack* the like Quantity, who being loth to let the Giant know he could not eat with him, got a large Leathern Bag putting it artificially under his loose Coat, into which he secretly conveyed the Pudding, telling the Giant he would shew him a Trick; then taking a large Knife ript open the Bag, which the Giant supposed to be his Belly, and out came the Hasty-Pudding, which the Giant seeing cried out, *Cotsplut, hur can do that Trick hurself*: then taking a sharp Knife he ript open his own Belly from the Bottom to the Top, and out dropt his Tripes and Trolly-bubs, so that hur fell down dead. Thus *Jack* outwitted the *Welsh* Giant, and proceeded forward on his Journey.'

In the second part of this tale cycle, Jack encounters a son of King Arthur, whose generosity so impresses him that he 'desired to be his servant'. Together they proceed to a castle inhabited by a gigantic uncle of Jack's, and in a comic episode Jack acquires his uncle's magic sword of sharpness, shoes of swiftness, cloak of invisibility, and cap of knowledge. With these, Jack defeats Lucifer himself to free a captive princess from an evil spirit, after which the Prince marries her and Jack is made a Knight of the Round Table.

In the third group of tales 'honest Jack', now in King Arthur's service, continues to fight Welsh giants 'yet living in remote parts

Jack tales Little Jack has no mercy for the giant in Richard *Doyle's fabulous illustration in *The Marvellous History of Jack the Giant Killer* (1842).

of [his] kingdom...to the unspeakeable damage of your majesty's liege subjects'. The first unnamed giant falls to Jack's unstoppable attack: 'at length, giving him with both hands a swinging stroke, cut off both his legs, just below the knee, so that the trunk of his body made not only the ground to shake, but likewise the trees to tremble with the force of his fall...Then had *Jack* time to talk with him, setting his foot on his neck, saying, thou savage and barbarous wretch, I am come to execute upon you the just reward of your villainy. And with that, running him through and through, the monster sent forth a hideous groan; and so yielded up his life into the hands of the valiant conqueror *Jack* the Giant-Killer.' Wearing his coat of invisibility Jack cuts off the nose of the next giant he encounters, then 'runs his sword up to the hilt in the Giant's fundament, where he left it sticking for a while, and stood himself laughing (with his hands a kimbow) to see the Giant caper and dance the canaries, with the sword in his arse, crying out, he should die, he should die with the

griping of the guts.' As ritual seemingly requires, Jack cuts off both Giants' heads, sends them to King Arthur, releases the captives they had been fattening for slaughter, feeds them, and distributes the giants' gold and silver. Jack's third giant in this group of tales is the two-headed Welsh Thunderdel, who utters the now-familiar verse

Fee, fau, fum,
I smell the blood of an *English* man,
Be he alive, or be he dead,
I'll grind his bones to make my bread.

before Jack lures him to his destruction using his magic cloak, cap, and shoes. His heads, too, are sent to King Arthur.

Jack's last giant, the 'huge and monstrous' Galigantus, is the one whose telling is most evidently influenced by the elaborate magical devices of French fairy tales, for instance, an old conjuror whose 'magick art' transforms knights and ladies into 'sundry shapes and forms'. Amongst them was 'a duke's daughter, whom they fetched from her father's garden, by magick art, and brought ...through the air in a mourning chariot, drawn as it were by two fiery dragons, and having secured her within the walls of the castle, she was immediately transformed into the shape of a white hind, where she miserably mourned her misfortune; and tho' many worthy knights have endeavoured to break the inchantment, and work her deliverance, yet none of them could accomplish this great work, by reason of two dreadful Griffins, who are fixed by magick art; at the entrance of the castle-gate, which destroyed them . . . as soon as they had fixed their eyes upon them: but you, my son, being furnished with an invisible coat, may pass by them undiscovered; where on the brazen gates of the castle, you shall find it engraved in large characters, by what means the inchantment may be broken.' Jack soon cuts off this giant's head and (once again) sends it to King Arthur, who 'prevailed with the aforesaid Duke to bestow his Daughter in Marriage on honest *Jack*, protesting that there was no Man living so Worthy of her as he' and 'he and his Lady lived the Residue of their Days in great Joy and Happiness'.

When Jack tales were rewritten for refined sensibilities later in the 18th and 19th centuries, the crudity of their gory killings disappeared, King Arthur faded away, Jack became an earthly Everyboy, and the Giant a geographically unlocalizable married oaf, reachable only by the magic of a bean that grew endlessly heavenward. Thus revised, Jack tales incorporated modern fairy-tale elements of social rise through magical enrichment.

In the southern Appalachians, 'Jack' became the generic hero of innumerable tales of cunning of disparate origin. Some, such as 'Lazy Jack and his Calf Skin', 'Old Catskins', and 'Old Gally Mander', are grounded in *Grimm tales; 'Jack the Giant Killer', on the other hand, descends directly from English chapbooks, changes its English Hasty Pudding into American mush, but ends identically to its English forebears. In North Carolina Jack tales have been collected from the Ward, Hicks, and Harmon families over several decades. RBB

Carter, Isabel Gordon, 'Mountain White Folklore: Tales from the Southern Blue Ridge', *Journal of American Folklore*, 38 (1925).

Chase, Richard, *The Jack Tales* (1943).
Opie, Peter and Iona, *The Classic Fairy Tales* (1974).
McCarthy, William Bernard (ed.), *Jack in Two Worlds* (1994).

Jacobs, Joseph (1854–1916) Jewish historian and folklorist who made several notable collections of fairy tales. Born in Australia, educated and long resident in England, he was from 1900 an American citizen. His earliest writings were on Jewish anthropological studies; this led to a general interest in folklore. From 1889 to 1900 he edited the British journal *Folk-Lore* and drew on many contributions there for his collections of stories. In 1888 he published an edition of the fables of Bidpai, and in 1890 he began a series of retellings of folk tales for children, which rank in importance with those of Andrew *Lang. *English Fairy Tales* (1890) had a sequel *More English Fairy Tales* (1893); *Celtic Fairy Tales* (1891) was followed by *More Celtic Fairy Tales* (1894). These were all illustrated by John D. Batten. There was also a volume of *Indian Fairy Tales* (1892) and *Europa's Fairy Book* (1916), a collection of 'common folk-tales of Europe', some of which he softened more than his wont. His six-volume edition of *The Thousand and One Nights* appeared in 1896 (*see* ARABIAN NIGHTS).

In his preface to the first *English Fairy Tales* he said that he wanted to write 'as a good nurse will speak' when she recounted tales. He had rewritten those where there was dialect (many stories came from Lowland Scots sources); elsewhere he had 'cobbled together' different variants, reduced 'the flatulent phraseology of chapbooks', simplified literary English, arriving at an easy colloquial style that suggested their folk origins. He did not attempt to prettify, though in some cases he admitted to modifying particularly strong material. More orthodox folklorists disapproved, and in the preface to *More English Fairy Tales* (1894) he defended himself against the criticism that he had unduly tampered with sources. This second book, which mostly went over 'hitherto untrodden ground', included *Märchen*,

TATTERCOATS

Jacobs, Joseph The prince declares to his father, the king, that he wants to marry Tattercoats in John Batten's illustration published in *More English Fairy Tales* (1894).

romantic legends, drolls, cumulative stories, beast tales, and nonsense.

The Celtic tales are more elaborate and detailed, and are mostly drawn from Scotland and Ireland, Wales contributing only a handful and Cornwall one. In prefaces to them he spoke of the long oral tradition in the Celtic culture which led to a richness only equalled by the Russian folk tale. Unlike Lang, he left in all his books a record of his sources, with comments on variants and parallels. These were not always specific enough: an edition of 1968 remarks that 'Jacobs' enthusiasm as a collector of stories sometimes exceeded the care he took in assembling his Notes and Sources.' They were printed as an appendix to each volume, and in his first book were divided from the main text by a drawing of a town crier announcing that 'Little Boys and Girls must not read any further'. The fairy tales were all published by the firm of David Nutt, whose head in Jacobs's day was Alfred Nutt (1856–1910), a distinguished folklorist and Celtic scholar whose help with the Celtic tales Jacobs warmly acknowledged. GA

Fine, Gary Alan, 'Joseph Jacobs: A Sociological Folklorist', *Folklore*, 98.2 (1987).

Shaner, Mary E., 'Joseph Jacobs', in Jane Bingham (ed.), *Writers for Children* (1987).

Stewig, John Warren, 'Joseph Jacobs' *English Fairy Tales*: A Legacy for Today', in Perry Nodelman (ed.), *Touchstones: Reflections on the Best in Children's Literature: Fairy Tales, Fables, Myths, Legends, and Poetry* (1987).

Janáček, Leoš (1854–1928) Czech composer, much influenced by the language of his native Moravia, and of its folk songs, which he collected. Renowned for his highly distinctive operas, including *The Cunning Little Vixen* (1924), adapted by the composer from a novel by the Czech writer Rudolf Tesnohlídek (first published in serial form in a daily newspaper, as accompaniment to line drawings by the artist Stanislav Lolek). The fantastical story of the life and exploits of a vixen cub involves a host of vividly observed human and animal characters, including parts written specifically for children's voices and several ballet scenes. SB

Janosch (pseudonym of **Horst Eckert**, 1931–) Extremely prolific and internationally renowned German author illustrator of books for young children. Janosch has written and/or illustrated close to 200 books. His works have appeared in 47 languages and an estimated 5 million copies have been sold world-wide. Most of these are playful and grotesquely funny tales for young children, but Janosch has written several novels for adults as well. In his autobiographical novel *Janosch: Von dem Glück, als Herr Janosch überlebt zu haben* (*About the Luck to Have Survived as Mr Janosch*, 1994), Janosch talks about his life and his dream of becoming a painter. Born into a working-class family, he was apprenticed as a blacksmith and later worked for several years in a textile factory. His attempt to study at the Art Academy in Munich in 1953 failed, but he remained in Munich, designing wallpaper and writing and illustrating stories for the *Süddeutsche Zeitung*, *Die Zeit*, and the satirical journal *Pardon*.

Janosch has stated that he merely stumbled into writing children's books. He still sees himself as illustrator first and author second, yet he is extraordinarily talented as both. Social satire and parody have always been his preferred means of expression, but much warmth and gentle fun can also be found in his tales for the young. The menagerie of whimsical, endearing, sly, and clever anthropomorphized animal characters who come to life in his faux-naïve drawings are lifted right out of fable and folk-tale tradition. Many of his stories are in fact playful, demythifying, and anarchist recreations of German folk tales and fairy tales. *Janosch erzählt Grimms Märchen* (*Not Quite as Grimm*, 1972) belonged to the most controversial and successful children's books in Germany in 1972. The fairy tales in Janosch's collection are imaginative, creative, original, and turn morals upside down and inside out, and they invite readers familiar with the classic tales to productive comparisons.

One of Janosch's best-known books is perhaps *Oh, wie schön ist Panama* (*The Trip to Panama*, 1978) which won the Deutscher Jugendliteraturpreis (German Prize for

Children's and Youth Literature) in 1979. It is an account of an unsuccessful quest undertaken by the two friends, Little Bear and Little Tiger, that ultimately proves to be fully satisfying and rewarding for both. Friendship is also the theme of *Die Fiedelgrille und der Maulwurf* (*The Cricket and the Mole*, 1982), a 'de-moralized' fable in which the cricket carelessly fiddles the summer away only to be taken in for a jolly winter by her good friend the Mole. This tale and its illustrations have the perfect blend of naïve sweetness and humorous grotesque that characterizes all of Janosch's production.   EMM

    Children's Literature Review, 26 (1992).
    Something about the Author, 72 (1993).

Janssen, Susanne (1965–) German illustrator who studied art in Düsseldorf and began her career as a professional artist in the 1990s. After illustrating three fairy tales by Italo *Calvino and two by the Dutch writer and painter *Armando, she turned to the Brothers Grimm and produced two startling picture books of *'Little Red Riding Hood' ('Rotkäppchen', 2000) and 'Hansel and Gretel' (2008). These books are notable for their unconventional, bold, and surrealistic images, as is her stunning illustration of *Peter Pan* (2005). In 2008 she was awarded the German Children's Literature Prize for 'Hansel and Gretel'.   JZ

Jansson, Tove (1914–2001) Finno-Swedish writer and Andersen Medal winner, internationally famous for her novels about the Moomins. Raised in a family of artists within the tiny Swedish-speaking minority in Finland, she constructs her fairy-tale universe in order to emphasize the national identity of this group. Situated in post-war Finland, the Moomin novels also clearly reflect their time, combining traumatic memories of the past with optimistic hopes for the future. The significance of family bonds is accentuated in the Moomin novels, where separation is apprehended as a tragedy and reunion as a cause for celebration. This apparently expresses the idea of national identity in a minority culture being preserved primarily through the family. Generosity and hospitality

are two other characteristic features. There is also a casual attitude towards material things that may be a reflection of the repetitive loss of property during the war, as well as the author's general bohemian view of life.

Unlike most so-called high fantasy worlds, with which Moominvalley has often been compared, it is loosely anchored in the Finnish archipelago and has many concrete geographical and climatic features of real Finland. In the picturebook *Den farliga resan* (1978; *The Dangerous Journey*, 1978), attached to the novels, an ordinary child is granted entry into Moominvalley, which implies that the Otherworld is open to those having a key to it. It is thus a more realistic realm than, for instance, Tolkien's. The Moomin characters, although imaginary, more closely resemble ordinary people, with their faults and virtues, than fairy-tale trolls, elves, or dwarfs.

Moominvalley is the utopian world of childhood, paradise before the Fall. Home signifies security. The harmonious community of the Moomin figures is completely happy; they have no enemies, and they do not have to think about their daily bread. As in traditional Arcadian children's novels, it is always summer in Moominvalley, and time stands still. The world of the Moomins is static, its time is cyclical, with recurrent events and habits. Eternal summer is interrupted by winter hibernation, which is not depicted as anything more remarkable than going to sleep at night. The Moomins do not grow up or age, and there is no death, at least not in the early novels. This may be also seen as part of the national identity, as an attempt to preserve the Finno-Swedish idyll without taking into account the changes in the surrounding world, for instance, the diminishing Swedish-speaking population in Finland.

However, time, changes, and the notion of death in Nordic mythology and imagery, closely connected with winter, appear in *Trollvinter* (1957; *Moominland Midwinter*, 1962). In the late Moomin novels, *Pappan och havet* (1965; *Moominpappa at Sea*, 1967) and *Sent i november* (1970; *Moominvalley in November*, 1971), there is suddenly a clear progression of linear time. They take place in the autumn, the time of decay and farewell, which, however, is necessary for the coming winter (death) and spring (resurrection). In the last Moomin novel, the Moomin family itself is absent and is only seen in a glimpse at the end, maybe returning home, but more likely taking the last view of their childhood paradise before leaving it definitively behind. This can be interpreted as the awakening from enchantment on the Island of Immortality, the well-known fairy-tale motif, and the return to reality. The circular fairy-tale time is transformed into modern linear time, which has a beginning and an end. *Moominvalley in November* was the last Moomin novel. Since then, the author has wholly devoted herself to writing adult fiction. However, many of her adult novels and short stories also have a certain fairy-tale structure.

With a few exceptions, like the Hobgoblin's hat in *Trollkarlens hatt* (1949; *Finn Family Moomintroll*, 1965), there is no magic in Moominvalley, and the magic, although tricky and unpredictable, is basically good and creative, initiating an endless string of enjoyable adventures. When Moominvalley is threatened, the threat does not come from dark, evil forces, but from natural catastrophes: a comet in *Kometjakten* (1946; *Comet in Moominland*, 1968), a volcano eruption and subsequent flood in *Farlig midsommar* (1954; *Moominsummer Madness*, 1961) or—typically Nordic—an extremely cold winter in *Moominland Midwinter*.

There are several clear-cut fairy-tale patterns in the Moomin novels, such as the quest, the dragon-slayer, the wish-fulfilling magical object, the hero–princess relation between Moomintroll and Snork Maiden, and many typical helping and guiding figures. However, most of these patterns are presented in a parodical or ironical manner. The Moomin novels lack the heroic pathos of Tolkien's Hobbits, being much more domestic and down-to-earth. They depict the maturation of the central character, not through heroic deeds and struggles between good and evil, but through slow psychological development. While in *Comet in Moominland* the protagonist takes the very first

cautious steps towards liberation from his parents, the sequels show him at various stages of breaking away from home. In the early novels, the Moomintroll's trials are depicted rather as innocent games and adventures, and the security of home and family is reinforced. In the later texts, serious moral dilemmas are put before him, and his sexual awakening plays a central role. Thus the thematic structure of the Moomin novels repeats the basic structure of fairy tales, illuminating the necessity to leave childhood and proceed into adulthood, in a fairy-tale-like rite of passage.

Finn Family Moomintroll is the most idyllic novel, the one in which the idyll is slightly disturbed but soon brought to order. *Moominsummer Madness* takes the character a bit further away from home, keeping the parents and friends close at hand. *Comet in Moominland* is the most explicit quest novel. Also *Moominland Midwinter*, which introduces the protagonist to death, nevertheless brings him back to idyll. *Moominpappa at Sea* breaks up into linearity, where idyll is forever left behind, and *Moominvalley in November* depicts the total disintegration of childhood paradise. The suitability of the later novels for a young audience has often been questioned.

Jansson, who illustrated her own books, also illustrated *Alice in Wonderland, fairy tales by Zacharias *Topelius, and a vast number of fairy stories by Finno-Swedish authors.   MN

Huse, Nancy Lyman, 'Equal to Life: Tove Jansson's Moomintrolls', in Priscilla A. Ord (ed.), *Proceedings of the Eighth Annual Conference of the Children's Literature Association* (1982).
Huse, Nancy Lyman, 'Tove Jansson and her Readers: No One Excluded', *Children's Literature*, 19 (1991).
Jones, W. Glyn, *Tove Jansson* (1984).
Westin, Boel, *Familjen i dalen. Tove Janssons muminvärld* (1988).

Japan, fairy tales in *See* p. 321.

Jarrell, Randall (1914–65) American poet, novelist, critic, and writer for children. Reviewing Jarrell's *Selected Poems* (1955), Karl

Japan, fairy tales in The Japanese fairy tale, if conceived as a written text conveying a narrative of wondrous transformation, should probably date to 'The Tale of the Bamboo Cutter', believed to have been completed by the mid-10th century (it is mentioned in the early 11th-century *Tale of Genji*). In the tale, a humble bamboojack discovers a tiny girl from the moon in a segment of bamboo; she brings a wealth of gold nuggets, and then grows into a beautiful princess wooed by five princes and the Mikado himself. Following this early example were two important medieval collections. One is the thirty-volume mid-12th century collection *Tales of Times Now Past* (*Konjaku monogatari-shū*), which includes short vignettes such as 'Rashōmon', which Akutagawa Ryūnosuke rewrote with modern psychological realism in 1915 (before Kurosawa reworked it again in his most famous film). The second medieval anthology is the *Otogizōshi* (*Companion Tales*) collection of tales from the 15th and 16th centuries, the most famous being 'Issun-bōshi', about a one-inch-tall boy who defeats a monster and marries a princess.

Shibukawa Seiemon coined the term 'otogizōshi' when he collected these hand-scroll narratives into a 23-volume set published sometime in the years 1716–36 (the Kyōhō period). This is significant both as an early modern effort to preserve and market a printed version of an oral tradition, but also as the *locus classicus* for the term 'otogi-banashi' (companion story), now one of the two standard terms (along with 'dōwa' or 'children's story') that most closely approximates 'fairy tale' in Japanese. The two terms seem to have been largely interchangeable through the 18th and 19th centuries, but diverged with the children's literature movement led by the 1918 launch of a magazine called *The Red Bird*. This magazine offered a mix of translations of Western fairy tales alongside newly commissioned dōwa by important authors such as Akutagawa, Izumi Kyōka, and Tanizaki Jun'ichirō. This rise of serious interest in fairy tales occurred in tandem with efforts to collect and preserve regional folk legends, such as Yanagita Kunio's 1910 *Legends of Tōno*.

After the Second World War the elite of the Japanese literary establishment continued to embrace fairy tales, and many authors playfully engaged with the form. In the years 1958–9 Kawabata Yasunari, who won the Nobel Prize for literature in 1968, and Nogami Akira translated all of Andrew *Lang's fairy books. Shibusawa Tatsuhiko and Terayama Shūji both wrote several pieces on *'Bluebeard' in the 1960s, the same time that Awa Naoko began publishing her fairy tales for children. Mizuki Shigeru and Takahashi Rumiko wrote manga in the fairy-tale mode, Ōba Minako and Kurahashi Yumiko wrote dark, erotic updates to fairy tales in a manner similar to Angela *Carter, and contemporary authors like Ogawa Yōko and Tawada Yōko continue to utilize the recombinant logic of fairy-lore in their fiction.   SCR

Keigo, Seki (ed.), *Nihon mukashi-banashi taisei*, 12 volumes (1978–80).

Saburō, Kuwabara, and Shunjii, Chiba (eds.), *Nihon jidō bungaku meisakushū*, 2 vols (1994).

Sebastian-Jones, Marc (ed.), *Marvels & Tales: The Fairy Tale in Japan*, 27:2 (2013).

Takejirō, Hasegawa (ed.), *Japanese Fairy Tale Series*, 25 volumes (1885–1903).

Tyler, Royall, *Japanese Tales* (1987).

Shapiro remarked that the book's subtitle should be '*Hansel and Gretel in America'. Jarrell's fairy-tale poetry blends advocacy for children with an intense interest in psychoanalysis. The title of his 1951 collection *The Seven-League Crutches* evokes the difficulty of 'learning from tales' ('The Märchen', 1948) in a post-war world where wishing no longer does much good. Jarrell's poems update tales such as Andersen's 'The *Little Mermaid', 'La Belle au Bois Dormant' (*'Sleeping Beauty'), and *'Cinderella', and the *Grimms' tale 'The *Juniper Tree' plays a crucial role in his only novel, *Pictures from an Institution* (1954). In the early 1960s Jarrell began translating the Grimms' tales collected in *The Golden Bird and Other Fairy Tales* (1962) and those of Ludwig *Bechstein in *The Rabbit Catcher* (1962). Before his untimely death, he went on to write his own children's fairy tales, *The Gingerbread Rabbit* (1964) illustrated by Garth Williams, *The Bat-Poet* (1964), *Fly By Night* (1976), and *The Animal Family* (1965), all illustrated by Maurice *Sendak. The last is a haunting and disturbing variation on motifs from Hans Christian *Andersen and the Grimms in which a hunter and a mermaid invent a family.   RF

Ferguson, Suzanne, *The Poetry of Randall Jarrell* (1971).

Flynn, Richard, *Randall Jarrell and the Lost World of Childhood* (1990).

Griswold, Jerome, *The Children's Books of Randall Jarrell* (1988).

Pritchard, William, *Randall Jarrell: A Literary Life* (1990).

Jones, Adrienne and **Allen, Peter** Editors of *Grimm & Grimmer: Dark Tales for Dark Times* (2009), a collection of short stories with fairy-tale characters and themes. The stories featured in the collection introduce a bourbon-guzzling *Pinocchio, a heroin-addicted *Snow White, among other modernized renditions of *Rapunzel and *Hansel and Gretel, alongside newfangled dystopian stories. Jones has also authored fiction works involving ghosts, shape-shifters, and demons, while Allen serves as the editor of the Amityville House of Pancakes anthologies.   KMJ

Jones, Diana Wynne (1934–2011) British author of more than 30 highly original fairy-tale novels, an indisputable innovator of the genre. Even when using typical motifs like the struggle between good and evil, journeys into alternative worlds, or time shifts, she uses quite subtle means, which turn the conventional and well-known into something unexpected. Her novels are intellectually demanding, since they operate with paradoxes, different dimensions, and complicated temporal and spatial structures, but this also makes them stimulating reading. One of her favourite devices is to give the protagonist magical powers, thus breaking the traditional fairy-tale pattern in which the protagonist is an ordinary person assisted by a magical helper. In several novels the narrative perspective lies with a witch or wizard. Jones portrays otherness, including Other Worlds, from the inside, while our own reality becomes, for the protagonist, the other world. This device, known as 'estrangement', is extremely unusual in fairy-tale novels for children. Playing with alternative worlds enables Jones to discuss existential questions such as: What is reality? Is there more than one definite truth? The recurrent idea in her novels is the existence of an infinite number of parallel worlds, which may recall our own but are different in essential ways, depending on the development in each particular world. This idea is in accordance with contemporary scientific views of the universe. In Diana Wynne Jones's model of the universe, the difference between worlds implies that in some of them magic is a common trait. In a group of loosely connected novels, *Charmed Life* (1977), *The Magicians of Caprona* (1980), *Witch Week* (1982), *The Lives of Christopher Chant* (1988), and *Conrad's Fate* (2005), our own reality is featured in the background as a parallel world, bleak and dull, since it lacks magic. The world of her novels is a combination of medieval and modern, where magic is a natural part of the everyday, and magical power is a skill to be developed in a child, just like languages or maths.

In *The Power of Three* (1976) the characters are supernatural creatures who work magic by incantations, can see into the future, and sense danger. There are other creatures in this world, Giants, who eventually appear to be humans, and their so-called magic, which the protagonist admires, takes the form of radios, cars, and dishwashers. There is also a more traditional magic object involved in the story, connected with a curse. Thus Jones always combines elements of the heroic fairy tale with irony and humour. The device of making the protagonist alien is especially invigorated in *Archer's Goon* (1984), where a young boy, the central character of the plot, appears in the end to be one of the seven evil wizards striving to take over the world. The story is told from Howard's point of view, and he is facing a hard dilemma: he has been trying to reveal the villain, and discovers to his dismay and horror that he himself is this villain, against his knowledge and will.

In *Howl's Moving Castle* (1986) we meet a young girl who is enchanted and turned into an old woman. This common motif, however, acquires a different tone since we are given a detailed description of Sophie's rheumatism and age fatigue, which traditional fairy tales usually omit. Sophie is the eldest of three sisters and therefore knows that according to fairy-tale rules she is bound to fail. The story is built upon Sophie's and the reader's anticipation, which naturally is disrupted. The novel is set in the magical land of Ingaria, and the enchanted Sophie lives in a strange moving castle belonging to Howl, a powerful magician. The castle door opens into four different dimensions, one of which is our own reality, where Howl comes from. In Howl's childhood home in Wales, his nephew is playing a computer game involving a magical castle with four doors (Diana Wynne Jones was among the first to use the image of computers in fairy-tale novels). She thus questions our common notions of the here and now and the far away, of time and space. There are all sorts of magic in the novel, both good and evil, and many magical creatures, both traditional and original. *Castle in the Air* (1991), an independent sequel, is more of a magical adventure story, inspired by *The *Arabian Nights*, with its vaguely oriental setting and tokens such as flying carpets and genies in bottles. The young protagonist sets out on a quest after his kidnapped princess and is assisted by several helpers, all of whom appear to be enchanted humans.

In many of Diana Wynne Jones's novels, the struggle between good and evil takes on cosmic dimensions, and humans are merely pawns in the hands of higher powers. This disturbing idea, most explicit in *The Homeward Bounders* (1981), *Fire and Hemlock* (1984), and *Hexwood* (1993), is often counterbalanced by reflections about Earth being the most beautiful place in the universe. In *Dogsbody* (1975), the protagonist and narrator, the star Sirius, is exiled on Earth in the form of a dog. There is thus a double perspective in the story, both the point of view of a powerful deity and that of a helpless, speechless animal. The protagonist's dilemma is the usual one in Jones's books; the magician's loyalty to ordinary people, the burden, and responsibility of unlimited power are themes in *Deep Secret* (1997) and its sequel *The Merlin Conspiracy* (2003). In her novels, to be a magician and use magic is a painful and laborious process with ethical implications. There are never any clear-cut boundaries between good and evil, and the readers, like the characters, are encouraged to take sides. The protagonist of *The Lives of Christopher Chant* has nine lives and loses them one after another during his adventures in alternative worlds. This recalls the structure of computer games which allows players to continue to play the game after having 'died'. It is, however, more fruitful to view this motif as a child's training, in his imagination, to live his own life, to discover his identity. Christopher learns eventually that besides their lives people also have a soul, which holds all lives together.

In all of Diana Wynne Jones's novels we see unconventional solutions, sharp observations, and a deep penetration of human nature. There are never magical adventures for their own sake, and the traditional struggle between good and evil is merely a background for an inner struggle within the character. Among Jones's strengths, her portraits of young girls are drawn in a true feminist spirit.   MN

Kondratiev, Alexei, 'Tales Newly Told: A Column on Current Modern Fantasy', *Mythlore*, 19.2 (spring 1993).

Mendlesohn, Farah, *Diana Wynne Jones: Children's Literature and the Fantastic Tradition* (2005).

Nikolajeva, Maria, 'Fairy Tale and Fantasy: From Archaic to Postmodern', *Marvels & Tales* (2003).

Rosenberg, Teya, Hixon, Martha, Scapple, Sharon, and Whites, Donna (eds.), *Diana Wynne Jones: An Exciting and Exacting Wisdom* (2002).

Waterstone, Ruth, 'Which Way to Encode and Decode Fiction', *Children's Literature Association Quarterly*, 16 (1991).

Jones, Terry (1942–) Welsh humorist and children's author. Educated at Oxford, he was a founding member of the comedy troupe Monty Python; he wrote and acted for their television series, records, and films (which he also directed). He later collaborated with Pythoner Michael Palin for a BBC series and sequels *Ripping Yarns* (1977, 1979), whose tall tales were later published and issued on videocassette. He began his second career as a children's writer with *Fairy Tales* (1981). Accompanied by Michael *Foreman's delightful watercolours, their refreshing humour and inventiveness contrasts with the sombreness and violence of the traditional European fairy tale. These loopy tales reinvent the genre, and while some are as dark as the *Grimms', they all offer positive models for children. These stories have been adapted for television, issued on videocassette (as *East of the Moon*, 1987), and republished separately. His *Fantastic Stories* (1993) are in the same vein. Jones has also updated the legend genre with the whimsically didactic *Saga of Erik the Viking* (1983; filmed as *Erik the Viking*, 1989). The irreverent *Nicobobinus* (1985) followed, taking a youngster to the Land of Dragons via a literary parody of 19th-century adventure books, swashbucklers, and nonsense tales. Similarly, the 18th century's

fictive historicity of elaborate prefaces and supposed memoirs is hilariously lampooned in *Lady Cottington's Pressed Faery Book* (1994, diary of a woman who presses fairies instead of flowers) and *Strange Stains and Mysterious Smells: Quentin Cottington's Journal of Faery Research* (1996, in which her brother preserves their odours). Both are co-written and wittily illustrated by Brian Froud (*Faeries*), with whom Jones previously worked while writing the screenplay for Jim *Henson's film *Labyrinth*.   MLE

Johnson, Kim 'Howard', *The First 200 Years of Monty Python* (1989).

Lesniak, James (ed.), *Contemporary Authors*, New Revision Series, 35 (1992).

Olendorf, Donna (ed.), *Something About the Author*, 67 (1992).

Perry, George, *Life of Python* (1983).

Jonson, Ben (1572–1637) English dramatist known for his biting social satire. Jonson's masques often contained elements of the marvellous taken from classical mythology. In *Lord Haddington's Masque, or The Hue and Cry after Cupid* (1608), Venus descends from her star to look for her son Cupid, who has united the couple for whom Jonson wrote the masque. *Oberon, the Faery Prince* (1611) was written for Prince Henry upon his investiture as Prince of Wales and concerns Prince Oberon, who emerges from his palace the night of a full moon with his fairies and elves only to disappear at daybreak.   AD

Jordan, Neil (1950–) Irish-born filmmaker and novelist whose film *The Company of Wolves* (1984) adapts Angela *Carter's literary reworking of *Little Red Riding Hood tales. Using dreams and stories told within dreams, Jordan's film explores the subconscious of an adolescent female in order to question popular wisdom about sexuality, especially as transmitted by fairy tales. While affirming the 'beastly' side of women, who are shown to be equally capable of being transformed into wolves, the film simultaneously challenges viewers to reflect critically not only on the power of sexuality but also on the limits of the visual experience. In a recent film, *Ondine* (2009), based on the European mythic and folklore figures of *Undine and the mermaid, Jordan transforms the story into a contemporary mystery about international drug dealing. A fisherman rescues a woman trapped in some nets only to discover later that she is a Romanian drug mule who is fleeing criminals after having stolen their drugs.   DH

Joyce, Graham (1954–) British writer of stories and novels who has won many awards for his speculative fiction and fantasy narratives. Among his works related to fairy tales are *House of Lost Dreams* (1993), *The Tooth Fairy* (1996), *The Limits of Enchantment* (2005), *The Silent Land* (2011), *Some Kind of Fairy Tale* (2012), and *The Year of the Ladybird* (2013). Joyce's mysterious narratives often conflate the borders between reality and fantasy to question general expectations and assumptions about normality. In one of his early coming-of-age novels, *The Tooth Fairy*, a young boy from the working classes named Sam suddenly encounters an enigmatic tooth fairy with sharp teeth, dressed in fatigues, flashy leggings, and boots. Only Sam can see the mischievous fairy, who changes sexes and haunts him as he grows older and learns to deal with tragic incidents that have marked his life. In *Some Kind of Fairy Tale*, there is a similar situation, but this time the action takes place in a small town on the edge of a forest in the English Midlands. Two young men in their forties, Peter and Richie, must come to terms with the return of Tara Martin, who had been missing for twenty years and then suddenly reappears looking exactly as she did when she had disappeared. Peter, her brother, and Richie, her former boyfriend, who had been suspected of killing her, must listen to Tara's mysterious stories of how she had been kidnapped by fairies. Her incredible storytelling changes the young men, as they begin to doubt the verities in their own lives. In all of Graham's fantasy writing, the intrusion of mysterious

fairy-tale figures alters normal perceptions of reality and normality.   JZ

Juan, Ana (1961–) Spanish illustrator, sculptor, painter, and writer, who has created over 20 unusual covers for the *New Yorker Magazine*. Juan studied fine arts in Valencia and later moved to Madrid, where she made a name for herself by publishing illustrations in newspapers and magazines. By the 1990s she had had major exhibitions of her paintings and illustrations in Geneva, New York, and Madrid. Known for its ironic and surreal style, Juan's work is often enigmatic, and her illustrations question the stories that they are intended to depict, or enhance the plots with magic realism. She has rewritten and illustrated three classic fairy tales, *Snowhite* (2001), *La bella durmiente* (*Sleeping Beauty*, 2007), and *Caperucita roja* (*Little Red Riding Hood*, 2011) predominantly in stark black-and-white ink and tends to subvert the happy endings. For instance, in *Snowhite*, which takes place sometime during the beginning of the twentieth century, the young princess is drugged by her stepmother and raped by a wealthy and sadistic Mr. Prince. Lost and listless, *Snow White yearns for a daughter, while her stepmother accidentally drowns herself. Aside from creating such provocative fairy tales, Juan has contributed fascinating illustrations to the five fantasy novels in Catherynne *Valente's *Fairyland* series.   JZ

Juan Bobo stories Puerto Rican folk tales documented extensively by anthropologist J. Alden Mason (1885–1967) in Puerto Rico. Often a fool, though occasionally a trickster, Juan Bobo is a 'jibaro', an archetypical Puerto Rican peasant. In the Juan Bobo stories, the protagonist perpetually fails at the most remedial tasks, which results in humorous misadventures. Although 'Bobo' implies an unintelligent figure, the character's innocent naivety is occasionally revealed as good-natured and clever. Many of the tales are remarkably similar to stories found around the world. Be the protagonist a 'Foolish John', Jack, Jean, or Juan, the fables frequently offer moral conclusions reflecting their origins. Contemporary adaptations of the tales include *Los Cuentos de Juan Bobo* (Tales of Juan Bobo, 1981) by Puerto Rican author Rosario Ferré and Marisa Montes' children's picture book, *Juan Bobo Goes to Work* (2000).   KMJ

Jung, Carl Gustav (1875–1961) Swiss psychiatrist and psychotherapist who posited that myths and fairy tales represent the human unconscious and their motifs express archetypes—cross-cultural images, thoughts, and ideas. Stored as cognitive universals in the human collective unconscious, archetypes also appear symbolically in dreams and fantasies. Analysing expressive culture determines its archetypal basis and reflection of personal and sociocultural growth. Jung is criticised for reductivism, presuming the biological universality of European folkloric motifs, and believing that traditions reveal individual, cultural, and social development towards an ideal state of self-awareness, the well-adjusted unconscious, and creativity. His ideas influenced Robert *Bly's and Marie-Louise von Franz's fairy-tale reflections.   PG

'Juniper Tree, The' The first literary version of the entire tale was written in a Low German dialect (*Plattdeutsch*) by the painter Philip Otto Runge, and published in Achim von *Arnim's *Journal for Hermits* (*Zeitung für Einsiedler*) in 1809. The *Grimms then included it in their first collection of tales in 1812. Some critics argue that Runge's economical yet poetic versions of this tale and of 'The Fisher and his Wife' profoundly influenced the Grimms' treatment of their tales.

Runge's version goes like this: A mother, who has long wished for a child, at last becomes pregnant, but dies (after eating juniper berries) as her son is born and is buried under the juniper tree. Her son is mistreated and finally decapitated by his stepmother, who then serves his mangled body to his father in a stew. His half-sister, however,

convinced that she is responsible for his death, remains faithful to his memory, buries his bones under the juniper tree, and watches as a bird rises through mist and fire from the grave. The bird then sings a song recounting a compressed version of his story:

> My mother, she killed me.
> My father, he ate me.
> My sister Marlene
> Gathered up my bones,
> Put them in a silken scarf,
> Buried them under the juniper tree.
> Keewit, keewit, what a fine bird am I.

The bird repeats the song to a goldsmith, to a shoemaker, and to some millers, and receives a gold chain, a pair of red shoes, and a millstone in return. He then flies back to the juniper tree and, singing his song again, drops the gold chain around his father's neck, the red shoes in his sister's lap, and the millstone on his stepmother's head. Her eyes and hair shoot fire, but after she is crushed the brother appears in the flames and smoke. The father, sister, and brother joyfully return to the house to eat together.

The tale was certainly well known in German-speaking cultures long before Runge and the Grimms wrote it down. Beginning with the earliest versions of *Faust* (1774), *Goethe has his Gretchen sing a version of the bird's song in prison, strangely appropriating the voice of her murdered child as her own.

Many versions of this tale are told in cultures around the world. In Russia the juniper tree becomes a birch, in England a rose-tree; in England the murdered child is usually a girl. But the motifs of family violence and cannibalism, of death, retribution, and resurrection are always present.

Maurice *Sendak, Randall *Jarrell, and Lore Segal chose 'The Juniper Tree' as the title tale for their two-volume collection of the Grimms' tales (1973). Margaret *Atwood uses motifs from the tale in her poem 'The Little Sister' and in some of the legendary folk material in her 1972 novel *Surfacing*. In her film, *The Juniper Tree* (1990), the American director Nietzchka Keene used a desolate region of Iceland for the setting of the story and transformed it into an unusual dark tale about witchcraft.   EWH

Belgrader, Michael, *Das Märchen von dem Machandelbaum* (1980).
Greenhill, Pauline, and Brydon, Anne, 'Mourning Mothers and Seeing Siblings: Feminism and Place in *The Juniper Tree*', in Pauline Greenhill and Sidney Eve Matrix (eds.), *Fairy Tale Films: Visions of Ambiguity* (2010).
Tatar, Maria, 'Telling Differences: Parents vs. Children in "The Juniper Tree"', in *Off With Their Heads!* (1992).
Wilson, Sharon Rose, *Margaret Atwood's Fairy-Tale Sexual Politics* (1993).

Kaffeterkreis (Coffee Circle) Initially an exclusively female literary salon established by Gisela, Armgart, and Maximilia von *Arnim in Berlin in 1843. The circle produced numerous fairy tales and fantasy plays. The members were daughters of Berlin's intellectual and political aristocracy and bourgeoisie. Their anonymously submitted art works and literary and musical compositions appeared in final form in the *Kaffeterzeitung* (*Coffee Circle News*). The group also often wrote and performed fairy-tale plays to the likes of the Prussian monarch, the Prussian Minister of Justice, Eduard *Mörike, Hans Christian *Andersen, and the Prussian crown prince. Plays featured strong female characters like *Frau Holle, Loreley, *Undine, and *Mélusine.

The *Kaffeterzeitung* was lost sometime between the world wars; today only a few drafts of writings survive in archives. One piece by Gisela von Arnim, 'Die Rosenwolke' ('The Rose Cloud', c.1845), may be representative of works by the group. Her literary rendition of a girl's rite of passage, in which the girl, whose aunt serves as her guiding spirit, confronts her mother, suggests a deconstruction of the *Grimms' model of female maturation. Von Arnim's protagonist seeks intellectual rather than material riches. The *Kaffeterkreis* broke the ban of silence imposed on Grimm girls as the virtuous path to adulthood. The last meeting took place in 1848. SJ

Jarvis, Shawn C., 'Trivial Pursuit? Women Deconstructing the Grimmian Model in the *Kaffeterkreis*', in Donald Haase (ed.), *The Reception of Grimms' Fairy Tales: Essays on Responses, Reactions, and Revisions* (1993).
Jarvis, Shawn C. (trans.), 'The Rose Cloud', *Marvels and Tales*, 11 (1997).

Kafka, Franz (1883–1924) Influential 20th-century German-language writer from Prague. Kafka's life and works epitomize the alienated individual in the modern world. To portray that world in his fiction, Kafka adapted the dreamlike conditions of the fairy tale with an ironic twist. Whereas fairy-tale characters are at home in the magical landscapes they inhabit, Kafka's blend of the irrational and the realistic disorientates his confused characters and alienates them from the very society they are trying to join. By inverting the classical fairy tale and playing with its motifs, Kafka created what has been called the anti-fairy tale, which questions the certainties and optimism of the classical genre.

For example, the protagonist of his novel *Das Schloss* (*The Castle*, 1926) does not progress like the conventional fairy-tale hero from the peasant village to the castle, but remains dislocated between these fairy-tale extremes without achieving a happy end. In 'Die Verwandlung' ('The Metamorphosis', 1915), Kafka adapted the fairy-tale motif of transformation by depicting a travelling salesman who has been transformed into a giant insect-like creature. In contrast to the traditional enchanted prince, however, Kafka's middle-class anti-hero experiences no conventional disenchantment. Instead, his one-way transformation from human to 'beast' ironically frees him from life in modern society and liberates his family to achieve happiness without him. Kafka experimented with a variety of related short forms in his writings, including parable and animal fable, and these too explore the ambiguities of life in the early 20th century. DH

Kalevala (1835) Finnish national epic constituted of popular songs, folk tales, myth, and fairy-tale motifs. The first literary version of some 12,000 verses was compiled and edited in unrhymed alliterative trochaic metre by the Finnish philologist and district health officer Elias Lönrott (1802–44), who wove the individual songs that he recorded in Karelia, a large region on both sides of the Russo-Finnish border, into a continuous narrative. The second edition of the *Kalevala*, published in 1849, was composed of 22,900 verses and based on additional research by Lönrott. Kalevala, the abode of Kaleva, an obscure gigantic ancestor like the Greek Titans, is the mythic name of Finland, and the narrative concerns the mythical founding of the country featuring the singer/shaman Väinämöinen, a culture hero, who has numerous marvellous adventures and saves Finland from pestilence and its enemies. The focus throughout the epic is on the heroic feats of Väinämöinen and other legendary characters such as his brother Imarinen, the great smith and craftsman, and, Lemminkainen, the wanton ladies' man. Lönrott changed many episodes based on fairy-tale motifs such as the beautiful maiden Aino, who was seduced by the old man Väinämöinen in a forest. However, she refuses to marry such an old man, commits suicide in the sea, and becomes a wondrous salmon that tantalizes Väinämöinen, who catches and then loses her, causing him to seek another bride and to engage in conflict with his brother. In Lönrott's adaptation and transformation of the oral songs he mixed Christian elements with apparent Scandinavian and Germanic pagan beliefs and mythology to justify the arrival of Christianity in Finland. Though many of his changes were inconsistent and jarring, it is this strange mixture of superstition, paganism, Christianity, and literature that makes the *Kalevala* such a fascinating national epic. JZ

Kane, Alice (1908–2003) Canadian librarian, storyteller, and writer, who published a collection of wonder tales, *The Dreamer Awakes* (1995). These tales were well-known Irish and European tales and were adapted by Kane, a prominent storyteller, who has told them at many events in North America. JZ

Kawabata, Yasunari (1899–1972) Japanese writer, winner of the Nobel Prize in Literature (1968). His poetic, sombre, usually realist work deals with conflicts between tradition and modernity. The novella *The House of the Sleeping Beauties* (1961) alludes to the *Sleeping Beauty tale, describing a secret establishment in which old men pay to share the beds of beautiful, naked, sleeping—indeed, unconscious—virgin women. It partly inspired Australian film-maker Julia Leigh's *Sleeping Beauty* (2011). His short stories frequently invoke the problematic kinship relations explored in fairy tales. Kawabata also supervised and edited a 1958–9 translation of Andrew *Lang's twelve-volume *Fairy Books*. PG

Keary, Annie (1825–79) English writer of children's books. Though she endowed her works with strong didactic messages, Keary was a fine stylist and offset her moralism with fanciful inventions in her stories. Her major fairy-tale work is *Little Wanderlin and Other Fairy Tales* (1865), which combines her interest in natural history and religion and reveals how the imagination can be used for moral improvement. JZ

Keats, Ezra Jack (1916–83) Celebrated American writer/illustrator of children's books. Largely a self-taught painter with experience as a muralist (WPA), comic-book illustrator, and camouflage designer, Keats is hailed not only for his artistic originality and innovation, principally his use of collage, but also for featuring children of colour as central characters. His most acclaimed text, *The Snowy Day*, 1963 Caldecott Medallist, which tells the story of a young child's experience with snow, is the first full-colour picture book to feature a black child; the book has met with some controversy, for Keats was Caucasian. Of note in Keats's career is *John Henry* (1965), the tale of a larger-than-life African American railroad worker, 'who died with his hammer in his hands'. The illustrations have been regarded as some of

Keats's finest, particularly for their vibrancy, size, and consequent force. In evidence as well is his collage insignia, particularly here, the marbling of cut or torn paper. Among his best illustrated fairy-tale books are *Wonder Tales of Dogs and Cats* (1955), *The Little Drummer Boy* (1968), and *The King's Fountain* (1971), written by Lloyd *Alexander.   SS

Alderson, Brian, *Ezra Jack Keats: Artist and Picture-Book Maker* (1994).

Engel, Dean, and Freedman, Florence B., *Ezra Jack Keats: A Biography with Illustrations* (1995).

Nikola-Lisa, W., 'Scribbles, Scrawls and Scratches: Graphic Play as Subtext in the Picture Books of Ezra Jack Keats', *Children's Literature in Education*, 22 (1991).

Keene, Nietzchka (1952–2004) An American film-maker and Communication Arts Professor at the University of Wisconsin. Her feature film *The Juniper Tree*, based on the Brothers *Grimm version of 'The *Juniper Tree', was shot in Iceland, with Icelandic actors speaking English. Keene's moody, dreamlike version, set in medieval Iceland, deals sympathetically with stepmother Katla's perhaps accidental homicide of her stepson Jónas, in an attempt to keep her husband Jóhan's love. Singer Björk, in her first cinematic role, plays Margit, Katla's sister, who sees visions of their mother, executed as a witch. Keene wrote a full-length *'Sleeping Beauty' film script, and at the time of her death, she was working on a project entitled 'Belle', based on late 19th/early 20th-century American female serial killer, Belle Gunness.   PG

Greenhill, Pauline, and Brydon, Anne, 'Mourning Mothers and Seeing Siblings: Feminism and Place in *The Juniper Tree*,' in Pauline Greenhill and Sidney Eve Matrix (eds.), *Fairy Tale Films: Visions of Ambiguity* (2011).

Keightley, Thomas (1789–1872) Irish author of *The Fairy Mythology* (1828). He had earlier contributed much material to Thomas *Croker's *Fairy Legends of the South of Ireland* (1825). While Croker gathered tales, Keightley compared them; his book is among the most significant studies of comparative folklore written in the first half of the 19th century. Often re-published, it was enjoyed for its lively retellings of fairy tales ranging from the Persian to the Danish and valued for its faithful acknowledgment of sources. In *Tales and Popular Fictions* (1834), Keightley showed his indebtedness to the *Grimms' theory that the source of lore was primitive Gotho-Germanic religion.   CGS

Dorson, Richard M., *The British Folklorists* (1968).

Kennedy, Patrick (1801–73) Irish folklorist, Dublin bookseller, and collector and preserver of the varied tales of County Wexford. Author of the important *Legendary Fictions of the Irish Celts* (1866), Kennedy is thought of as one of the fathers of the Irish folklore revival and is thus associated with the Celtic literary renaissance. Much of his early work was originally written for the *Dublin University Magazine*, though he used the pseudonym of Harry Whitney to publish *Legends of Mount Leinster* in 1855. Fearing that the tales he had heard as a child were in the process of being lost, he produced not only *Legendary Fictions* but *The Banks of the Boro* (1867), *The Fireside Stories of Ireland* (1870), and *The Bardic Stories of Ireland* (1871). His *Fireside Stories* are reminiscent of the *Grimms' *Kinder- und Hausmärchen* (*Children's and Household Tales*) in implications of origin; they suggest the domestic circumstances in which folk tales were told. Kennedy did not attempt to capture the flavour of the original Irish stories or the tone of their tellers, nor does he cite specific sources or informants. He did, however, offer to the public a wide range of traditional narratives including *Märchen*, ghost stories, local legends, and Ossianic heroic adventures. Especially interested in the witches and fairies of Ireland, he effectively retells many tales of changelings and fairy abductions. He was praised by Douglas Hyde for not further adulterating Gaelic stories, already impaired by their English idiom, and by William Butler *Yeats for preserving Irish lore as a writer rather than as a scientist.   CGS

Kennedy, Richard (1932–) Prolific American children's writer, with a keen ear for the folkloristic rhythms of the language, and an ironic sense of humour. Many of Kennedy's literary folk tales thematically invoke the misadventures in the quest for 'true love', and the redemptive powers of that love when it is found. In the 1990s Kennedy wrote a successful Oregon production of a musical based on Hans Christian *Andersen's 'The *Snow Queen'. Sixteen of Kennedy's bitter-sweet tales and novellas are collected in *Richard Kennedy: Collected Stories* (1987). His mythopoeic and apocalyptic *Amy's Eyes* (1985), a novel marketed for children, was awarded the German Rattenfänger (Rat Catcher, i.e. Pied Piper) award as best foreign book translated in 1988.　　PFN

Neumeyer, Peter F., 'Introducing Richard Kennedy', *Children's Literature in Education* (1984).

Kent, Jack (1920–85) American author-illustrator of humorous fables, folk tales, rhymes, and other picture books. After freelancing as a commercial artist and cartoonist, known for the comic strip 'King Aroo', he began to write and illustrate children's books in 1968. He uses a similar technique in his books, with heavy outline and flat colour. Kent's *Fables of Aesop* (1972) and *More Fables of Aesop* (1974) are uniquely his in selection and interpretation, appropriate for younger readers. Kent retold *The Fat Cat* (1971) from a Danish tale. The hilarious consecutive scenes describe the cat becoming increasingly obese as he eats what comes into sight. Kent's cartoon-like art makes the classic folk-tale texts, frequently reduced in length and depth, accessible to the young. While Kent retold some stories, he illustrated the work of other authors, too. *The *Bremen Town Musicians* (1974) and *Seven at One Blow* (1976), based on *Grimms' tales, follow a simple plotline and introduce familiar characters in a witty manner. He also did a splendid book illustration of Hans Christian *Andersen's *The Emperor's New Clothes* (1977), simplifying it for younger children. Attentive to the concerns of parents, Kent included only non-violent rhymes for the young in *Merry Mother Goose* (1977) and was careful not to introduce conflict into his works.　　KNH

Kerner, Justinus (1786–1862) German poet, writer, and doctor, who was one of the foremost members of the Swabian romantics. Though primarily known for his sentimental lyrics and folk ballads, Kerner also wrote fairy tales and stories that reflected his interest in magnetism, mysticism, and clairvoyance. His most notable fairy tale is 'Goldener' ('The Golden Boy'), which is a variant of the *Grimms' *'Iron Hans', and depicts how the golden boy, who becomes lost in the forest, eventually fulfils the prophecy of a mysterious lady and becomes king of a realm that was his destiny.　　JZ

Kerr, Peg (1959–) An American fantasy fiction author of *Emerald House Rising* (1997) and *The Wild Swans* (1999), a retelling of Hans Christian Andersen's literary fairy tale 'The Wild Swans' (ATU 451), which offers two parallel narratives of a 17th-century New England heroine suffering to save her cursed brothers and a 20th-century New Yorker diagnosed with AIDS. Her short stories have been published in magazines such as *Tales of the Unanticipated, Amazing Stories, Pulphouse*, and *Weird Tales*.　　KMJ

Bear, Bethany Joy, 'Struggling Sisters and Failing Spells: Regendering Fairy Tale Heroism in Peg Kerr's The Wild Swans', in *Fairy Tales Reimagined* (2009).

Kilworth, Garry (1941–) English writer of fantasy, science fiction, horror, and mystery. Kilworth's major work in fairy tales is generally addressed to young readers. In his collection *Dark Hills, Hollow Clocks* (1990) Kilworth often uses dialect and traditional folklore to relate stories about changelings, dragons, goblins, and wizards. He is most adept at crossing the boundaries of different genres such as the fairy tale, mystery, and science fiction, as can be seen in his collections for adults, *Songbirds of Pain* (1984), *In the Hollow of the Deep-Sea Wave* (1984), *Moby Jack and Other Tall Tales* (2005), and *The Fabulous Beast* (2013). One of his most innovative novels for young readers is *The Phantom Piper*, a revision of 'The Pied Piper', in which the adults of a Scottish village answer the call of a mysterious piper and leave their children behind to run their own lives and eventually to confront two evil travellers. JZ

Kinder- und Hausmärchen (*Children's and Household Tales*, 1812–15) Compiled by Jacob and Wilhelm *Grimm and edited by Wilhelm Grimm, this is one of the most influential tale collections in the Western world. Translated into scores of languages, *Children's and Household Tales* has enriched children's literature world-wide.

Many of the tales of volume I of the first edition (1812) came from young acquaintances in the Grimms' bourgeois circle in Cassel and nearby towns. Volume II (1815) had a radically different character, its stories stamped by the plots and diction of Dorothea Viehmann, a tailor's widow from the neighbouring village of Zwehrn.

Children's and Household Tales appeared in seven Large (1812–15, 1819, 1837, 1840, 1843, 1850, 1857) and ten 50-story Small Editions (1825, 1833, 1836, 1839, 1841, 1844, 1847, 1850, 1853, 1858). Often adding new tales from published sources, occasionally substituting more authentic versions, and constantly smoothing their literary style, Wilhelm set an international standard for fairy tales, the *Gattung Grimm* (Grimm genre).

Within Germany *Children's and Household Tales* was also published as popular poster-sized *Bilderbogen* (broadsides). Single-text editions, such as *'Hänsel und Gretel'* appeared early, as did illegal pirated editions of the Small Edition. In addition, other tale collectors frequently incorporated the Grimms' tales into their own works. From the early 19th century, *Children's and Household Tales* attracted the interest of the world's principal illustrators of children's literature.

The publishing history of *Children's and Household Tales* falls into two clearly demarcated segments. During nearly the whole of the 19th century (1806–93) the *Tales* continued under the legal control of Jacob and Wilhelm and, after their deaths, of Wilhelm's son Hermann. The family marketed the *Tales* conservatively, in complete editions, whether Large or Small, and apparently without offering cheaply printed editions for mass consumption. When copyright lapsed in 1893, 30 years after Jacob's death, an explosive increase in the number and kinds of editions followed. This wave of printings, in addition to the tales' historical inclusion in school readers in the preceding decades, brought *Children's and Household Tales* into the 20th century on a crest that remained high till a generation ago.

The history of publishing and reading in Germany reveals that a flood of fairy-tale books (*Märchenbücher*) had inundated Germany's women readers from the late 1700s onward. In the 19th and 20th century, however, widespread belief in unbroken chains of oral transmission, reaching from the present to antiquity, made critics ascribe the tales' simple and simplified plots to the 'childhood of man' and view them as the folk equivalent of ancient Greek myth. Nationalists of the 19th century exploited this approach to posit a continuous link between the fragmented 19th-century German nation and its medieval past. Much of the influence exerted by *Children's and Household Tales* in the 20th century stemmed from a related conviction among psychologists and educators that the tales metaphorically represented universal stages of children's psychological maturation. RBB

Bastian, Ulrike, *Die 'Kinder- und Hausmärchen' der Brüder Grimm in der literaturpädagogischen Diskussion des 19. und 20. Jahrhunderts* (1981).
Hennig, Dieter, and Lauer, Bernhard (eds.), *Die Brüder Grimm. Dokumente ihres Lebens und Wirkens* (1985).
McGlathery, James, *Grimms' Fairy Tales: A History of Criticism on a Popular Classic* (1993).
Rölleke, Heinz, *Die Märchen der Brüder Grimm: Eine Einführung* (2004).
Sennewald, Jens, *Das Buch, das Wir Sind: Zur Poetik der 'Kinder- und Hausmärchen', gesammelt durch die Brüder Grimm* (2004).
Zipes, Jack (ed.), *The Original Folk and Fairy Tales of the Brothers Grimm: The Complete First Edition* (2014).
Zipes, Jack, *Grimm Legacies: The Magic Power of the Grimms' Folk and Fairy Tales* (2015).

Kinder- und Hausmärchen The charming prince parts the briars on his quest to wake the enchanted princess in E. H. Wehnert's illustration of *‘Sleeping Beauty’ in *Household Stories Collected by the Brothers Grimm* (*c.*1900), the English edition of *Kinder- und Hausmärchen*. The Bodleian Library, University of Oxford (Opie C 897).

Uther, Hans-Jörg, *Handbuch zu den 'Kinder- und Hausmärchen' der Brüder Grimm: Entstehung—Wirkung—Interpretation* (2008).
Zipes, Jack (ed.), *The Original Folk and Fairy Tales of the Brothers Grimm: The First Edition* (2014).
Zipes, Jack, *Grimm Legacies: The Magic Spell of the Grimms' Folk and Fairy Tale* (2014).

Kingsley, Charles (1819–75) English novelist, Anglican clergyman, and author of *The Water-Babies* (1863), one of the most celebrated Victorian fantasies for children. Subtitled 'a fairy tale for a land-baby', it is a curious but vivacious jumble of moral instruction, scientific fact, pronouncements on the nature of scientific thought and Darwin's theory of evolution, references to forgotten mid-Victorian controversies, and choleric outbursts of prejudice on topics ranging from 'frowzy monks' to the absurd new fashion of dining at eight. Brian Alderson has pointed out how much the book owes to Rabelais, greatly admired by Kingsley, not just with the famous word lists, but also with the deliberate digressions and the satiric fantasy. A striking example of the latter is the fable of the Doasyoulikes which puts evolution into reverse.

It has always been a perplexing story. The dedication to his youngest son Grenville is followed by the couplet 'Come read me my riddle, each good little man: | If you cannot read it, no grown-up folk can.' Kingsley gives the same weight to his vehement arguments that water-babies are a fact as he does to his descriptions of natural phenomena, like the hatching of a dragonfly. While his enthusiasm for the wonders of nature is one of the most attractive features of the book, the most coherent section and the best-remembered now is the first, where Tom, a little chimney sweep, goes with his master to sweep the chimneys of Harthover Place. He loses his way in the maze of flues, and comes down into the bedroom of a little girl named Ellie. Here for the first time he sees himself in a looking-glass—'a little black ape', and is horrified at the contrast between himself and the white purity of Ellie. Pursued over the moors, he finally scrambles down a cliff face and seems to drown in the stream below. But the reader knows that he has become a water-baby. At this point the narrative becomes chaotic. It might seem that Tom's trials and travels are a spiritual pilgrimage, and that the two fairies Mrs Bedonebyasyoudid and Mrs Doasyouwouldbedoneby (representing Law and Love?) are preparing him for heaven, but it could also be taken as an allegory of evolution, or a plea for reverence for nature (a favourite topic with Kingsley), while at least two critics have suggested that it is a masturbation fable. Nor does Kingsley help by telling his readers to remember 'that this is all a fairy tale, and all fun and pretence; and, therefore, you are not to believe a word of it, even if it is true'.

Kingsley's retellings of Greek myths, *The Heroes* (1856), subtitled 'Greek fairy tales for my children', is far more straightforward. It was written as a corrective to Nathaniel *Hawthorne's *Tanglewood Tales* (1853), which he found 'distressingly vulgar', and which undoubtedly falsified the originals. 'No one', wrote Roger Lancelyn *Green in *Tellers of Tales* (1946), 'has caught the magic and the music and the wonder of the old Greek legends as Kingsley did.'   GA

Alderson, Brian (ed.), *The Water-Babies* (1995).
Chitty, Susan, *The Beast and the Monk* (1974).
Cunningham, Valentine, 'Soiled Fairy: The Water-Babies in its Time', *Essays in Criticism*, 35.2 (1985).
Leavis, Q. D., 'The Water-Babies', *Children's Literature in Education*, 23 (winter 1976).
Manlove, C. N., 'Charles Kingsley and the Water-Babies', in *Modern Fantasy: Five Studies* (1975).

Kingston, Maxine Hong (1940–) Chinese-American author who was given the Lifetime Achievement Award from the Asian American Literary Awards Committee in 2006. She wrote the fairy-tale novel *The Woman Warrior: Memoirs of a Girlhood Among Ghosts* (1975), a retelling of the traditional Chinese fairy tale 'Hua-Mulan'. Similarly, her novel *Tripmaster Monkey* (1989) was an American modernization of the mythical Chinese character Sun Wukong (the Monkey King) based on the Chinese epic *Journey to the West*.   MF

Kipling, Rudyard (1865–1936) English author who used Puck to introduce the characters from the past in *Puck of Pook's Hill* (1906) and *Rewards and Fairies* (1910). Two children, Dan and Una, are acting scenes from *A Midsummer Night's Dream* in a fairy ring on Midsummer's Eve, when they find they have conjured up 'a small, brown, broad-shouldered, pointy-eared person'. He is the last of the Old Things who once were pagan gods and then became the People of the Hills; he is contemptuous of the word 'fairy'—'little buzz-flies with butterfly wings and gauze petticoats'. In the succeeding stories he produces for the children people who have lived in their part of Sussex, and in 'Dymchurch Flit' tells them how the Reformation frightened the last fairies ('Pharisees') out of England. GA

Kirsch, Sarah (1935–2013) German writer and lyric poet. Born in the former German Democratic Republic, Kirsch studied biology at Halle and literature at the Johannes R. Becher Institute for Literature in Leipzig. In 1977 she emigrated to West Germany, where she continued to work as a freelance writer. Kirsch also wrote the texts for a number of illustrated children's books, among them two retellings of Grimm fairy tales: *Hänsel und Gretel* (1972) and *Hans mein Igel* (*Hans my Hedgehog*, 1980). Fairy-tale motifs also frequently feature in her prose and poetry, as in *Allerlei-Rauh* (1988), which includes a modern version of 'Manypelts'. CS

Kismet Visually spectacular show with a score based on the music of the Russian composer Alexander Borodin (1833–87). The writers George Forrest and Robert Wright created their own lyrics, having founded their musical on Edward Knoblock's *Kismet* of 1911. *Kismet* the musical opened at the Ziegfeld Theatre, New York in 1953, achieving a first run of over 500 performances. Its *Arabian Nights setting follows the adventures of Hajj, a public poet who, in the space of an adventurous 24 hours, ascends from his lowly and disreputable position to a place of high influence with the Caliph in Baghdad. TH

Knatchbull-Hugessen, Edward, first Baron Brabourne (1829–93) English politician, man of letters, and author of 15 books of fairy tales for children, in which, the *Dictionary of National Biography* declared, 'he failed to distinguish himself'. His first book, *Tales for my Children*, appeared in 1869, his last, *Friends and Foes from Fairy-Land*, in 1885. His stories are slow-paced and verbose, often macabre and sometimes sadistic; in *Crackers for Christmas* (1870) he refers to criticism evoked by 'Pussy-Cat Mew' in the previous volume, with its description of an ogre preparing human meat. 'The Pig-faced Queen' (*Queer Folk*, 1874) is a savage attack on feminism. GA

Knipfel, Jim (1965–) American novelist and journalist, famous for his three memoirs, *Slackjaw* (1999), *Quitting the Nairobi Trio* (2000), and *Ruining It for Everybody* (2004), which recount his numerous attempts to commit suicide and some of his other exploits. Knipfel has also written offbeat, comic fairy tales in *These Children Who Come at You with Knives, and Other Fairy Tales* (2010). JZ

Korczak, Janusz (pseudonym of **Henryk Goldszmidt**, 1878–1942) Polish writer and educator, author of the utopian fairy-tale novel *Król Macuis I* (1923; *King Matt the First*, 1986). He was the director of an orphanage in the Warsaw ghetto and voluntarily followed the children into the gas chambers of the concentration camp at Treblinka.

The novel is set in a fictional European kingdom. Little Matt is 6 years old when his father the king dies and Matt becomes king. In an adventurous plot, reminiscent of *The Prince and the Pauper*, Matt runs away and learns about the real needs of his people. He tries to be a just and generous ruler and to provide for the children of his country. However, his reforms fail, mostly owing to his inexperience and idealism, and the betrayal of adults. After a long series of adventures and trials, Matt is defeated in a war, captured by the neighbouring king, and exiled to a desert island.

Knatchbull-Hugessen, Edward, first Baron Brabourne Little Charlie is entranced by a magical world in 'Charlie and the Elves' in Edward Knatchbull-Hugessen's *Moonshine* (1871), illustrated by William Brunton.

Korczak's fairy tale is based on his firm belief in children's rights as well as his profound knowledge of their psychological needs. However, the pessimistic ending of the novel leaves no illusions as to the possibility of the fulfilment of his ideals. There are no magical or supernatural elements in the novel, but most episodes are built up as a typical fairy-tale quest, and the heroic character of the young king is emphasized. This is an inverted *Little Tom-Thumb plot in which the child character, his wits and sincere wishes notwithstanding, is unable to defeat the ogres.   MN

Joseph, Sandra, *A Voice for the Child: The Inspirational Words of Janusz Korczak* (1999).
Lifton, Betty Jean *The King of Children: The Life and Death of Janusz Korczak* (1988).
Lypp, Maria, 'Kindheit als Thema des Kinderbuchs. Die Metapher des kindlichen König bei Janusz Korczak', *Wirkendes Wort*, 3 (1986).

Koser-Michaels, Ruth (1896–1968) and **Koser, Martin** (1903–71) German illustrators who produced charming illustrations for fairy-tale editions of Jacob and Wilhelm *Grimm (1937), Hans Christian *Andersen (1938), Aldelbert von *Chamisso (1938), Wilhelm *Hauff (1939), Ludwig *Bechstein (1940), and Hans Friedrich Blunck (1942). Through detailed ink drawings and bright aquarelles they produced lovable folk characters and cosy scenes that have a quaint quality, and their illustrated books have remained popular up to the present.   JZ

Koslow, Ron (1947–) American television writer and producer. Koslow was responsible for *Beauty and the Beast, (1987–90), a dramatic fantasy series inspired by Jean *Cocteau's 1945 film version of the fairy tale. 'Beauty' is Catherine (played by Linda Hamilton), a young lawyer who works for New York City's District Attorney. Attacked and left for dead one night in Central Park, she is found by 'the Beast'—Vincent, a man with a lion's face (Ron Perlman)—who carries her to his home in the hidden tunnels beneath the city and nurses her back to health. The two form a telepathic bond that deepens into a profound but hopeless love; although neither can live in the other's world, Vincent always knows when Catherine is in danger and comes to rescue her. The series was given little chance of success, but achieved a surprising degree of 'cult' popularity, particularly among women viewers, who fell in love with Vincent, fangs and all.   SR

Kotzwinkle, William E. (1938–) American writer of fantasy who often incorporates fairy-tale motifs in such works as *Fata Morgana* (1977) and *Herr Nightingale and the Satin Woman* (1978). Kotzwinkle also wrote the novels on which the films *E.T.—The Extra Terrestrial* (1982) and *Superman III* (1983) were based. His fairy tales for children have been collected in *The Oldest Man and Other Timeless Stories* (1971) and introduce conventional characters into mysterious situations. Thus in 'Hearts of Wood' a troll uses magic to make a carousel come alive, and in 'The Dream of Chuang' a butterfly catcher dreams he becomes a butterfly but also comes to think he may be a butterfly who dreams he is a man. Nothing is ever certain in Kotzwinkle's tales, as he demonstrates in 'The Fairy King', who leaves his throne empty for anyone to become king.
                JZ

Kredel, Fritz (1900–73) Popular woodcutter and illustrator, born in Michelstadt-im-Odenwald, Germany. He attended the Real Gymnasium, entered the military, was apprenticed to a pharmacist, and cared for horses in Pomerania before his family finally permitted him to enter art school. He studied under the master illustrator Rudolf Koch at the Kunstgewerbeschule in Offenbach-am-Main. Koch encouraged him to become a woodcutter, and the left-handed Kredel taught himself to cut 'on the plank' by using discards from the neighbouring Klingspor Typefoundry. Their first collaboration was a compendium of liturgical and craft symbols called *Das Zeichenbuch* (*A Book of Signs*, 1923), for which Kredel cut Koch's illustrations. By the time they had finished the incomparable *Das Blumenbuch* (*The*

Book of Flowers, 1930), Kredel was an acknowledged master at cutting smooth, delicate lines. A huge wall map of Germany, printed from joined woodblocks, lithographed and then hand-coloured, was another collaboration—but the Hitler regime had the 1933 prints recalled for undisclosed reasons. At that time, violence was erupting between the Nazis and the Communists at the studios of the Offenbacher Werkstatt. After the death of Koch, who had long acted as a buffer between the opposing groups, politics forced Kredel to flee to Austria, and then to the United States. He arrived in 1938 to find that American book illustration had already been influenced by his *Fairy Tales by the Brothers Grimm* (1931). These hand-coloured woodcuts have a lively airiness that he would later capture in pen drawings with watercolour wash for works such as *Baron Münchausen's Adventures* (1950). Quite different are his linear woodcuts for the *Decameron* (1940) and *Aucassin and Nicolette* (1957), whose medieval flavour reflect the Florentine chapbooks that he deemed the height of the decorated book.

Kredel became a US citizen, taught at Cooper Union Art School (1940–2), and illustrated a number of popular works characterized by an economical, caricature-like line and flowing spontaneity. In addition to his own books about soldiers, puppets, and folk tales about his native Odenwald, he illustrated the classic *Slovenly Peter* (*Der Struwwelpeter*, 1936), more tales by the Grimms (1937), *Andersen's Fairy Tales* (1942), *The Complete Andersen* (1949), *Pinocchio* (1946), *Tales of Aesop* (1947), and *Fables of a Jewish Aesop* (1966). Kredel also illustrated a Christmas tale by First Lady Eleanor Roosevelt, and for President Kennedy designed the woodcut of the presidential eagle for the print of his inaugural address.

His many honours include the Golden Medal for Book Illustration (Paris, 1938), the Silver Jubilee Citation of the Limited Editions Club (New York, 1954), and the Goethe-Plakatte and Johann-Heinrich Werk-Ehrung (Germany, 1960).   MLE

Chappell, Warren, 'Fritz Kredel', *Gazette of the Grolier Club* (1973).

Foster, Joanna, *Illustrators of Children's Books: 1957–1966* (1968).

Kent, Norman, 'Fritz Kredel, Master Xylographer', *American Artist* (May 1946).

Koch, Rudolf, *Der Holzschneider Fritz Kredel* (1932).

Standard, Paul, 'Fritz Kredel: Artist, Woodcutter, Illustrator', *Motif*, 4 (1960).

Kreidolf, Ernst (1863–1956) Swiss illustrator who developed the craft of making picture books into an art. Kreidolf produced over 25 illustrated books for children during his lifetime and generally wrote the text, conceived the total design, and prepared the script, type, and binding. He was strongly influenced by the work of William *Morris and Walter *Crane as well as the *Jugendstil* movement. His very first book, *Blumen-Märchen* (*Flower Fairy Tales*, 1898), was representative of all the work that he was to produce throughout his career. The characteristic features included idyllic settings, anthropomorphized plants and animals, and intricate decoration. Other important works include: *Der Gartentraum* (*The Garden Dream*, 1911), *Alpenblumenmärchen* (*Alp Flower Fairy Tales*, 1922), *Ein Wintermärchen* (*A Winter Fairy Tale*, 1924), and *Bei Gnomen und Elfen* (*With Gnomes and Elves*, 1928).   JZ

Kress, Nancy (1948–) American writer of science fiction and fantasy who uses many fairy-tale motifs in her works. Her three fantasy novels, *The Prince of Morning Bells* (1981), *The Golden Grove* (1984), and *The White Pipes* (1985), deal with gender issues, magical transformation and the power of story to change people's lives, often in disturbing ways.   JZ

Krúdy, Gyla (1878–1933) Hungarian journalist and novelist whose numerous works have been rediscovered and have received greater attention and praise in the 21st century than during his lifetime. In the early part of the 20th century he produced a series of stories, *The Travels of Sinbad* (1912), *The*

Resurrection of Sinbad (1916), and *The Youth and Grief of Sinbad* (1917), which were collected in one book *The Adventures of Sinbad* (1998) and translated into English by the Hungarian-born British poet George Szirtes. Throughout the magical tales Sinbad is portrayed as a melancholic godlike figure who drifts through Budapest and often transforms himself in inconclusive anecdotes that reveal the decaying foundations of the Old World traditions. Sometimes he dies and is miraculously resurrected, but he is never saved. Ironically, Krúdy fills his modernist fairy tales with a sense of loss.   JZ

Krüss, James (1926–97) German author of children's and picture books, illustrator, poet, dramatist, scriptwriter, translator, and collector of children's poems and folk songs. First and foremost, Krüss is a storyteller, whose fantastic and whimsical tales are deeply rooted in folk-tale and oral storytelling tradition. Many of his books are actually collections of tales held together by a frame story. Such is the case with *Mein Urgrossvater und ich* (*My Great Grandfather and I*, 1959), for which he received the Deutscher Jugendliteraturpreis (German Prize for Children's and Youth Literature), with its sequel *Mein Urgrossvater, die Helden und ich* (*My Great Grandfather, the Heroes, and I*, 1967), and with *Der Leuchtturm auf den Hummerklippen* (*The Lighthouse on the Lobster Cliffs*, 1956).

Storytelling and language itself not only keep the protagonists in these books entertained, but provide them with new insights and at times the means to survive. Stories flatten the differences and shrink the distances between children and adults. By way of stories Krüss can and does address his young readers as equals. With *Timm Thaler oder das verkaufte Lachen* (*Timm Thaler or the Sold Laughter*, 1962), a modern version of the pact with the devil, Krüss prepared the ground for social criticism in children's literature. With Timm, who sells his laughter to the devil, Krüss criticizes the growing materialism and consumerism of Germany's economic miracle years. Krüss received the

Hans Christian Andersen Medal for his body of work in 1968.   EMM

Doderer, Klaus, *Zwischen Trümmern und Wohlstand. Literatur der Jugend 1945–1960* (1988).
Doderer, Klaus, *James Krüss: Insulaner und Weltbürger* (2009).

Kubin Alfred (1877–1959) Austrian author and illustrator. His disturbing art with its Bosch-like grotesques is said to reflect the search for meaning amid contemporary social, technological, and political upheavals. He was fascinated by dreams and the subconscious in both his verbal and his visual art, detailed in *Die andere Seite* (*The Other Side*, 1909). He illustrated a work about Münchausen's adventures and numerous fantastic tales by Honoré de Balzac, Edgar Allan Poe, and E. T. A. *Hoffmann.   MLE

Kallir, Jane, *Alfred Kubin: Visions from the Other Side* (c.1983).
Raabe, Paul, *Alfred Kubin* (1977).
Rhein, Phillip H., *The Verbal and Visual Art of Alfred Kubin* (1989).

Kuitenbrouwer, Kathryn (1965–) Award-winning Canadian author of novels including *All The Broken Things* (2014) and *Perfecting* (2009), the short story collection *Way Up* (2003), and short fiction in *Granta Magazine*, *The Walrus*, and *Storyville*. While much of her work evokes a fairy-tale ethos and feel, *The Nettle Spinner* (2005) in particular draws on the French/Flemish narrative of the same title collected by Charles Deulin in the 19th century and published by Andrew *Lang in *The Red Fairy Book* (1890). Kuitenbrouwer juxtaposes the fairy tale with a present-day story about rape and pregnancy; in both narratives, the protagonists weave a tapestry using nettle fibre.   PG

Kumin, Maxine (1925–2014) American poet, novelist, and essayist. Kumin advised her close friend Anne *Sexton on *Transformations* and also occasionally experimented herself with fairy-tale motifs. Poems like 'Changing the Children' and 'Seeing the Bones' in her 1978 volume *Retrieval System*

dwell on *Grimm-like spells and metamorphoses. 'The Archaeology of a Marriage', also in that volume, is the sardonic story of a 50-ish suburban *Sleeping Beauty who suddenly wakes to contemplate her 'Planned Acres Cottage', her husband, and her long marriage: 'Why...should any | twentieth-century woman | have to lie down at the prick of | a spindle etcetera etcetera'.   EWH

Kunert, Günter (1929–) German writer who was recognized at one time as one of the leading poets of East Germany. Kunert also developed a unique talent as a prose writer who uses concrete and striking images in succinct, terse narratives. Among his best works are *Tageswerke* (*Day's Works*, 1961), *Die Beerdigung findet nicht statt* (*The Funeral Does Not Take Place*, 1968), *Tagträume* (*Daydreams*, 1972), *Die geheime Bibliothek* (*The Secret Library*, 1973), *Der andere Planet* (*The Other Planet*, 1974), and *Lesearten* (*Ways of Reading*, 1987). Though he lived in East Germany until 1977, Kunert's works have always been received well in both parts of Germany and continue to have success in reunified Germany. He has often experimented with fairy tales in his work and endowed them with subtle social and political meanings. For instance in his version 'Dornröschen' (*'Sleeping Beauty') he alludes to the hedge as the Berlin Wall that conceals not a utopian socialist society in the figure of the sleeping princess but a snoring trollop.   JZ

Kunze, Reiner (1933–) German writer and lyric poet. He was born in the former German Democratic Republic, where he lived and worked as a freelance writer until his emigration to West Germany in 1977. His prose and poetry have been translated into 30 languages. He also wrote several children's books, among them the fairy-tale collection *Der Löwe Leopold* (*The Lion Leopold*, 1970), including a sequel to *'Snow White', in which he provides a different ending for the wicked stepmother, and the fairy-tale volume *Eine stadtbekannte Geschichte* (*A Story Known All Over Town*, 1982).   CS

Kurahashi, Yumiko (1935–2005) Japanese author of *Cruel Fairy-tales for Adults*, a 1984 collection of dark, sexual manipulations of Western and Japanese tales. Her version of 'Snow White', for example, finds the hero unable to cook, clean, or mend for the dwarfs (as a princess, she never acquired those skills), but she is able to contribute sexually, and ends up embroiled with all seven of them. The evil queen smashes her mirror, Snow White turns ugly after applying to herself a potion meant for an enemy, and yet the ending is happy with Snow White bringing up her brood of dwarf children.   SCR

Cardi, Luciana, 'Kurahashi's Retelling of 'Snow White'', *Marvels & Tales*, 27:2 (2013).
Kurahashi, Yumiko, *Otona no tame no zankoku dōwa* (1984).

Kurz, Isolde (1853–1944) German writer and translator. She explored religious and philosophical ideas in her three volumes of fairy tales, *Phantasieen [sic] und Märchen* (*Fantasies and Fairy Tales*, 1890), *Zwei Märchen* (*Two Fairy Tales*, 1914), *Die goldenen Träume* (*Golden Dreams*, 1929). The story 'Der geborgte Heiligenschein' ('The Borrowed Halo') gently satirizes Christianity, while 'Vom Leuchtkäfer' ('The Glow-Worm') is a bitter-sweet tale of love and reincarnation: a shooting star is turned into a glow-worm who falls in love with a firefly but dies only to be reborn as a human child. Recognizing the baby's grief, the narrator finds the firefly and gives it to the child.   KS

Kushner, Ellen (1955–) American writer of fantasy novels for children and adults. Kushner's first novel, *Swordspoint*, makes deft use of the language of fairy tales to relate a melodrama of manners, concerning a swordsman and his male paramour in the imaginary city of Riverside. With her second novel, *Thomas the Rhymer* (1990), Kushner turns directly to folklore themes in an impressive retelling of this Scottish Border ballad and fairy tale. The novel closely follows the plot of the traditional tale: a talented young harper is seduced by the Queen of Faery and willingly agrees to seven years of service in her court. Several things make Kushner's rendition of this familiar tale distinctive. One is her prose, as exquisitely musical as a harper's song. Secondly, she draws upon a wealth of traditional ballads to tell her story, ingeniously incorporating elements of 'Jack Orion', 'The Famous Flower of Serving Men', 'Tam Lin', 'The Unquiet Grave', and many others into the novel. Thirdly, she invests the story with a delicious sensuality in the lush descriptions of the faery court, and the complex, enigmatic relationship between Thomas and his Queen. Finally, Kushner is too fine a writer not to know that the best fantasy novels are ones we can read on two levels at once. Her novel entertains and enchants as we follow the harper 'into the woods'—but Kushner is also exploring a theme relevant to all creative artists: the story of a man who follows his muse to the point of danger—and beyond. TW

Kyber, Manfred (1880–1933) German writer, theatre critic, and editor. He was deeply influenced by Rudolf Steiner, and anthroposophic ideas are evident in all his work but especially in his extremely popular fairy tales, which he saw as the reality of another world. His fairy-tale works include: *Drei Waldmärchen* (*Three Sylvan Fairy Tales*, 1903), *Der Königsgaukler, ein indisches Märchen* (*The King's Magician, an Indian Tale*, 1921), *Märchen* (1921), *Der Mausball und andere Tiermärchen* (*The Mice's Ball and Other Animal Tales*, 1927), *Puppenspiel, Neue Märchen* (*Puppet Theatre: New Fairy Tales*, 1928), *Das wandernde Seelchen, Der Tod und das kleine Mädchen*, and *Zwei Märchenspiele* (*The Little Wandering Soul, Death and the Little Girl*, and *Two Fairy Tale Plays*, 1920). KS

Lackey, Mercedes (1950–) American author of fantasy fiction, lyricist, and poet, best known for her science fiction fairy tales and novels. She has published individual stories in collections such as *Witches: Wicked, Wild & Wonderful* (2012). Lackey has also published a fairy-tale fiction series, The Five Hundred Kingdoms Series, which includes *The *Snow Queen* (2008), a retelling of Hans Christian Andersen's tale of the same name; *The Sleeping Beauty* (2010), a science fiction version of *'Sleeping Beauty'; and *Beauty and the Werewolf* (2011), a hybrid retelling of *'Beauty and the Beast' and *'Little Red Riding Hood'. Lackey's Fairy Tale series also includes two titles: *The Firebird* (1996), a retelling of the Russian fairy tale of the same name, and *Black Swan* (1999), a retelling of the ballet *Swan Lake*, adapted from the Russian fairy-tale type 'The Swan-Maiden'. MF

Lacombe, Benjamin (1982–) French illustrator renowned for his fairy-tale artwork included in collections such as *Le Petit Chaperon Rouge* (*Little Red Riding Hood*, 2004) and *Blanche-Neige* (*Snow White*, 2010). Lacombe produced the critically acclaimed pop-up book *Il Était Une Fois* (*Once Upon a Time*, 2010) which includes eight classic fairy tales rendered in three-dimensional illustrations/paintings and has been published in over a dozen languages. He also illustrated and co-authored *L'Herbier des Fées* (*The Fairy Herbarium*, 2011) and *Généalogie d'une Sorcière* (*Geneology of a Sorceress*, 2008), among others with Sebastian Perez. Lacombe's artwork—particularly his fairy-tale-themed work—is also available on stationery, accessories, and prints. KMJ

Lada, Josef (1887–1957) Czech writer and illustrator, best known for his illustrations for *Soldier Schwejk* (1924) by Jaroslav Hasek. His *In-and-outside Tales* (1939) and follow-up *Naughty Tales* (1946) are collections of fractured fairy tales parodying famous Czech folk tales. *About the Cunning Uncle Fox* (1937) is a parody of Reynard the Fox, set in the contemporary Czech countryside. *Purrkin the Talking Cat* (1934–6) is an original fairy-tale story featuring an intelligent pet. Lada illustrated all his books himself. His illustrations are inspired by the style of caricature, as he was a gifted cartoonist. He also illustrated many collections of traditional folk tales. In 1947 he was awarded the title of 'National Artist'. MN

La Force, Charlotte-Rose Caumont de (1654–1724) French writer born to a high-ranking noble family known for defending the Protestant cause during the Wars of Religion. She converted to Catholicism in 1686, which allowed her to nurture numerous connections important for her subsequent career as a writer: she was lady-in-waiting to the Dauphine, was intimately acquainted with Mademoiselle (Elisabeth Charlotte, duchesse d'Orléans), dedicated several of her novels to the princesses of Conti, and even received a pension from Louis XIV. Like several other late 17th-century French women writers (notably Mme d'*Aulnoy and Mme de *Murat), her name was associated with several public scandals: she was known to have had love affairs; her marriage, which had been contracted without parental consent, was annulled by her father-in-law; and she was exiled for a time to a convent for composing impious *Noëls*. This period of exile was particularly productive, for during it she wrote several historical novels and a

La Force, Charlotte-Rose Caumont de The two lovers in Mlle de la Force's 'The Good Woman' (1697) find safety in the woods. An illustration by Eduard Courbould published in *Fairy Tales by Perrault, De Villeneuve, de Caylus, De Lubert, De Beaumont and Others* (1860).

volume of fairy tales, *Les Contes des contes* (*The Tales of the Tales*, 1697).

La Force's fairy tales are witty commentaries on conventions of novels and *contes de fées* of late 17th-century France. Although none of them are parodic, several of them deftly poke fun at metaphorical and mythological portrayals of love. In 'La Puissance d'Amour' ('The Power of Love'), for instance, literal flames become the pleasurable flames of love for both hero and heroine. Such playfulness allows La Force to defy the period's almost exclusively psychological representations of love with physical and, sometimes, erotic descriptions. Thus, in 'Vert et bleu' ('Green and Blue'), perhaps the most daring of her collection, the narrator describes with delectation the heroine bathing nude all the while exchanging impassioned glances with her voyeuristic admirer.

La Force's eight fairy tales span a wide range of narrative sub-genres, including the mythological ('Plus Belle que fée' ('More a Beauty than a Fairy'), 'The Power of Love', 'Tourbillon' ('Whirlwind'), 'Vert et bleu' ('Green and Blue')); the pastoral ('La Bonne Femme' ('The Good Woman'), 'Le Pays des délices' ('The Country of Delights')); the chivalric ('L'Enchanteur' ('The Sorcerer')); and the folkloric ('Persinette'). Among her contemporary writers, perhaps only d'Aulnoy wrote a greater variety of fairy tales. Particularly noteworthy are 'The Sorcerer', a retelling of an episode in the medieval *Perceval* romance in which La Force pastiches old French (an innovation at the time), and 'Persinette', an early literary version of the *Grimms' more famous *'Rapunzel'. In La Force's 'Persinette' the heroine's secret marriage is revealed not by her naïveté (as in 'Rapunzel') but by her pregnant state, and at the end of their punishment it is the fairy's powers and not the princess's tears that restore their happiness. Overall, La Force's fairy tales stand out among those of her fellow fairy-tale writers for their diversity, wit, and sensuality, as well as their (relative) brevity.   LCS

Vellenga, Carolyn, 'Rapunzel's Desire: A Reading of Mlle de la Force', *Merveilles et Contes*, 6.1 (May 1992).

Welch, Marcelle Maistre, 'L'Éros féminin dans les contes de fées de Mlle de la Force', *Actes de Las Vegas* (1991).

Lagerkvist, Pär (1891–1974) Swedish Nobel Prize winner who started as an expressionist playwright, but went on to become one of the most famous Swedish novelists of the 20th century. *Dvärgen* (*The Dwarf*, 1944) and *Barabbas* (1950) are parables of the modern human being's moral and religious dilemmas.

In *Onda sagor* (1924, included in *The Marriage Feast*), Lagerkvist uses the form of the parable and tends to give the folk tale a nasty intertextual twist. One text is tellingly called 'Prinsessan och hela riket' ('The Princess and All the Kingdom'), and makes the point that life continues in all its complexity and ambiguity after the formulaically happy, but shallow, ending of the magic tale.

In other texts, Lagerkvist tends to revise legends by giving them surprise endings, such as in 'Den onda änglen' ('The Evil Angel'), in which an angel of darkness, who hatefully announces that human beings will perish, is simply met with the laconic response that they are perfectly aware of their mortality. In 'Kärleken och döden' ('Love and Death'), a young couple walk down the street when suddenly Cupid appears—a brutish, hairy fellow who shoots an arrow into the young man's chest. As the man's blood runs in the gutter, until none is left, his sweetheart walks on unaware of what has happened to him. Lagerkvist's texts play with metaphysics and religion, but without a belief in anything beyond the present reality. His texts are funny, bleak, and artistically well-wrought.

NI

Lipman-Wulf, Barbara Susanne, 'Die Zwergfiguren in Pär Lagerkvists *Dvärgen* und Gunter Grass' *Die Blechtrommel*' (Diss., State University of New York–Stony Brook, 1979).
Schwab, Gweneth B., 'Herod and Barabbas: Lagerkvist and the Long Search', *Scandinavica*, 20.1 (May 1981).
Scobbie, Irene, 'The Origins and Development of Lagerkvist's Barabbas', *Scandinavian Studies*, 55.1 (1983).

Lagerlöf, Selma (1858–1940) Swedish novelist and Nobel Prize winner (1909), the first woman admitted into the Swedish Academy of Letters. She was born and lived most of her life in the Swedish province of Värmland, famous for its storytelling traditions. In all her novels and short stories Lagerlöf makes use of folktales and legends, weaving them into everyday surroundings. Her most internationally well-known book, *Nils Holgerssons underbara resa genom Sverige* (1906-7; *The Wonderful Adventures of Nils*, 1907, *The Further Adventures of Nils*, 1911), originally a geography schoolbook, has several layers of fairy-tale matter. The frame of the book is a traditional fairy-tale plot in which a lazy boy is punished by being transformed into a midget and must improve in order to become human again. His journey with the wild geese borrows many traits from the animal tale, notably Reynard the Fox, and from Rudyard *Kipling's *The Jungle Book*. Like a folk-tale hero, Nils is able to understand animal language when he is enchanted, and he acquires both friends and enemies in the animal realm. He is significantly nicknamed *Little Tom Thumb, and in many of his adventures performs the function of the so-called culture hero. He also has a typical fairy-tale guide and mentor, the old wise goose Akka. Places which Nils visits are described in terms of etiological folk tales, explaining the origin of geographical features of the landscape, and of uncanny local legends. Finally, some well-known plots are involved, such as 'Pied Piper of Hamelin' and the sinking of Atlantis, here both connected with concrete settings in Sweden.

Lagerlöf has served as a model and a source of inspiration for Michel *Tournier.

MN

Edström, Vivi, *Selma Lagerlöf* (1984).
Rahn, Suzanne, 'The Boy and the Wild Geese', in *Rediscoveries in Children's Literature* (1995).
Sale, Roger, *Fairy Tales and After: From Snow White to E. B. White* (1978).

Lamb, Charles (1775-1834) British critic, essayist, and poet, also known for hosting literary circles frequented by Coleridge and Wordsworth, Leigh Hunt, William Hazlitt, and Robert Southey. Over the course of his lifetime, Lamb cared for his sister Mary who, in a moment of insanity, killed their mother in 1796. Together they composed *Tales from Shakespeare* (1807), prose versions of *Shakespeare's plays intended as an introduction to the dramatist's works, with an audience of young girls in mind. He also collaborated with his sister on *Mrs Leicester's School* (1809), another work aimed at young girls in which several 'young ladies' relate their personal histories.

In 1811 Lamb published two fairy tales in verse, *Prince Dorus: Or, Flattery Put out of Countenance*, and *Beauty and the Beast: A Rough Outside with a Gentle Heart*. *Prince Dorus*, a tale inspired by 'The Emperor's New Clothes', tells the story of Prince Dorus who, cursed with a long nose, is made to believe that it is in fact quite beautiful by his mother and the entire court. It is not until he overcomes the flattery of others and realizes the true nature of his nose that the spell is broken, and he is granted a beautiful nose. Lamb's *Beauty and the Beast* closely follows Mme *Leprince de Beaumont's version, but Lamb gives it an exotic twist: Beast turns out to be a Persian prince and takes Beauty back to Persia at the end of the tale. AD

La Morlière, Charles-Jacques-Louis-Auguste Rochette de (1701-85) French writer. In addition to several novels and plays, he is attributed with authorship of *Angola, histoire indienne, ouvrage sans vraisemblance* (*Angola, an Indian Story and an Implausible Work*, 1746). This work's fairy-tale plot is used to satirize with considerable viciousness society life, the nobility, and the bourgeoisie of 18th-century Paris. Its critique of the period's barriers to social mobility are distinctly pre-Revolutionary in tone.

LCS

Lanagan, Margo (1960-) Australian writer of speculative fiction who, after an early career writing children's genre fiction under pseudonyms, published two well-received realist young-adult novels, *The Best Thing* (1995) and *Touching Earth Lightly* (1996). Then she shifted focus to dark fantasy short stories with *White Time* (2000), followed by *Black Juice* (2004) and *Red Spikes* (2006). The genre of these stories is fantasy, with elements of fairy tale and fable blended in, as in 'Daughter of the Clay' (*Red Spikes*), a reflection on parental love and the expectations which hold us in thrall, told through the story of a changeling and her return to fairyland. The mixing of genres and traditions underlies Lanagan's capacity to make the weird seem strangely familiar. Such mixing constitutes one of the strengths of *Tender Morsels* (2008): this novel is not a fairy-tale fantasy, but its narrative isomorphically reflects the classic fairy tales 'All Kinds of Fur' and *'Sleeping Beauty'. The protagonist, a teenage victim of incest and repeated rape, is mysteriously spirited away into another, safer world, along with the two daughters she has borne, where they remain until one of her daughters finds a route back into the original world. In addition, encounters with bears which have humanoid characteristics evoke folklore about bears and shamanic practices, as reflected, for example, in the shape-changer Beorn in *Tolkien's *The Hobbit*. Interactions which cross the borderline between human and animal are also at the core of Lanagan's highly imaginative crossover novel *Sea Hearts* (2012; also published as *The Brides of Rollrock Island*), an adaptation of the Scottish seal wife legend, which has a curious fascination for Australian writers. Lanagan has won numerous awards for her writing and is a four-time winner of the prestigious World Fantasy Award.   RM/JAS

Landolfi, Tommaso (1908–80) Italian writer, poet, playwright, and critic. From his first work, *Dialogo dei massimi sistemi* (*Dialogue On Great Systems*, 1937), Landolfi showed his inclination for paradoxical humour and grotesque surrealism. His ten volumes of tales and novellas reveal his remarkable talent, whether it is bent to achieve stylistic preciousness, or to blend together fantastic, sardonic, and surreal elements to create a sense of anguish and of looming nightmares, as Landolfi does in *Nel mar delle blatte* (*The Sea of Cockroaches*, 1939), *La spada* (*The Sword*, 1942), and *Racconto*

d'autunno (*An Autumn Story*, 1947). In this last tale the author recalls the atmospheres of the gothic narrative of such writers as E. T. A. *Hoffmann, Edgar Allan Poe, and Barbey d'Aurevilly. Moralistic and metaphysical concerns permeate instead the science-fiction tale *Cancroregina* (*Cancerqueen and Other Stories*, 1950), while a certain didactical tendency prevails in his allegoric fables for young readers such as *La ragnatela d'oro* (*The Cobweb of Gold*, 1950) and *Il principe felice* (*The Happy Prince*, 1950). The most distinctive aspect of Landolfi's tales—the shocking effect—is captured by Italo *Calvino, who writes: 'the first rule of the game established between reader and writer is that sooner or later a surprise will come; and that surprise will never be pleasant or soothing, but will have the effect of a fingernail scraping glass, or of a hair-raising, irritating caress, or an association of ideas that one would wish to expel from his mind as quickly as possible.' Two representative collections are *Gogol's Wife and Other Stories* (1963) and *Words in Commotion and Other Stories* (1986).   MNP

Lang, Andrew (1844–1912) Scottish folklorist, scholar, poet, and man of letters. Ironically for someone of his vast output, he is now remembered mainly for his fairy tales, and for his Fairy Book series. Born in Selkirk in the Scottish Borders, he was steeped in the ballads and legends of those parts. He was sent to school in Edinburgh where Greek, which 'for years seemed a mere vacuous terror', became a passion once he discovered Homer. He studied classics at St Andrews University, and one of his earliest books was a translation of the *Odyssey* (with S. H. Butcher), published in 1879. Later he was to collaborate with Henry Rider Haggard in *The World's Desire* (1890), a romance chronicling the wanderings of Odysseus in search of Helen, and the evil magic of Meriamun, queen of Egypt, who tries to foil him.

He had been a comparative mythologist since his youth with a strong interest in anthropology, and his earliest statement of his anthropological theory was in an essay, 'Mythology and Fairy Tales', in the

Prince Comical spies the sleeping King

Lang, Andrew Prince Comical spies the sleeping king in Andrew Lang's *The Princess Nobody* (1884), illustrated by Richard *Doyle.

Fortnightly Review (May 1873), described by Reinach as 'the first full statement of the anthropological method applied to the comparative study of myths'. He was to return to it again and again in *Custom and Myth* (1884), *Myth, Ritual and Religion* (1887), and lengthy polemical essays in Margaret Hunt's edition of the *Grimms' tales (1884), in *The Marriage of Cupid and Psyche* (1887), *Perrault's Popular Tales* (1888), and *The Secret Commonwealth of Elves, Fauns, and Fairies* (1893) by Robert Kirk, a Perthshire Presbyterian minister who, according to local legend, was spirited away by the fairies after he trod on a fairy hill.

His Fairy Book series began in 1889 with *The Blue Fairy Book*. He had overcome his early distaste for literary tales, and though the series was mostly to contain only traditional folk tales, this first volume oddly included an abridged version of Gulliver's voyage to Lilliput. There were 37 tales, from Mme d'*Aulnoy, Charles *Perrault, the Grimms, as well as Norse, Scottish, and English stories. Though

Lang himself had chosen the stories, nearly all the translation and rewriting had been done by others. This was to be the case throughout the series, Mrs Lang latterly undertaking most of the work. *The Blue Fairy Book* also contained 'The Terrible Head', a retelling by Lang himself of the story of Perseus and the Gorgon. He did much the same with 'The Story of Sigurd' in the next volume, but did not include this sort of mythological material again in the series. *The Red Fairy Book* followed in 1890, and the *Green* in 1892, finishing with *Lilac* in 1910, by which time the tales had moved from exclusively European sources to take in African, American, American Indian, Berber, Brazilian, Indian, Japanese, Persian, Sudanese, and Turkish examples. Though he had included invented stories by authors such as d'Aulnoy, Hans Christian *Andersen, and Zacharias *Topelius, by far the greater part of the Fairy Books was derived from traditional folklore. The immense popularity of the series did much to revive interest in fairy tales.

Lang himself wrote several fairy stories. His first, *The Princess Nobody* (1884) was commissioned to provide a text for illustrations by Richard *Doyle, originally published in 1870 with poems by William Allingham. The most striking is *The Gold of Fairnilee* (1888), inspired by Border ballads and legends. The fairies here are the shadowy, feared spirits who seek to steal humans, and Fairnilee is an actual ruined house on the Tweed known by Lang as a boy. Ranald Ker, whose father has died at the battle of Flodden Field, grows up 'in a country where everything was magical and haunted; where fairy knights rode on the leas after dark, and challenged men to battle'. His great wish is to meet the Fairy Queen and to be taken into her world, and one Midsummer's Eve he disappears, carried off to Elfland. Here he is held captive, and though it charms him at first, he comes to see it as hollow and desolate. (In its account of Elfland the story resembles Dinah Mulock's *Alice Learmont*, which it is possible Lang had read.) At the end of seven years Jean, his childhood companion, succeeds in rescuing him. *Prince Prigio* (1889), *Prince Ricardo of Pantouflia* (1893), and *Tales of a Fairy Court* (1906) are light-hearted *jeux d'esprit* in the Thackeray manner, sometimes, especially in the last of these, verging on the burlesque. Prince Prigio, cursed by a fairy at his christening by being made 'too clever', antagonizes all around him. Having spurned the gifts brought by the more benevolent fairies—seven league boots, a wishing cap, a magic carpet—in a dire emergency he learns their value, and eventually wishes himself to *seem* no cleverer than other people. In contrast, Prigio's son Ricardo relies too much on magic and has to be taught self-reliance. *Tales of a Fairy Court* are further chronicles of Prigio and Pantouflia.   GA

Burne, Glenn S., 'The Blue Fairy Book', in Perry Nodelman (ed.), *Touchstones* (1987).
Green, Roger Lancelyn, *Andrew Lang* (1946).
Montenyohl, Eric, 'Andrew Lang's Contributions to English Folk Narrative', *Western Folklore*, 47 (1988).
Zipes, Jack, 'Introduction' in Andrew Lang (ed.), *The Green Fairy Book* (2009).

Lasswitz, Kurd (1848–1910) German writer, philosopher, and scientist. Although Lasswitz is considered one of the pioneers of science fiction in Germany, he also wrote experimental fairy tales. In *Seifenblasen: Moderne Märchen* (*Soap Bubbles: Modern Fairy Tales*, 1890) and *Nie und Nimmer: Neue Märchen* (*Nevermore: New Fairy Tales*, 1902) he tried to integrate ethical, political, and scientific thinking that broke with traditional fairy-tale patterns. For example, in 'Tröpfchen' ('Little Drop', 1890) the 'romantic hero' of this tale is a drop of water that reflects critically about his bizarre encounters as he journeys through the world and observes injustices, exploitation, and suicide as well as courage and love.   JZ

Last Unicorn, The (film: USA, 1982) Animated fable about beauty, duty, and ecology. Peter Beagle himself adapted his 1968 'hip *Tolkien' novel in which a female unicorn hears that all others of her kind, though immortal, have vanished from the face of the earth. Helped by Schmendrick, who aspires to be a magician but initially can manage only tricks, she sets out to find them. At the climax, having been turned human by Schmendrick as an escape device, she has to make a stark moral choice: either to rejoin her species and save them from watery incarceration, or to remain mortal and marry the prince she loves.   TAS

Lazare, Bernard (1865–1903) French writer and journalist. He is best known for his decisive role, along with Zola, in the appeal of the Dreyfus case and for his pioneering studies of anti-Semitism. Written for adults, the stories in his collection, *Le Miroir des légendes* (*The Mirror of Legends*, 1892), reinterpret biblical and classical myths, and several incorporate fairy-tale motifs. In 'Les descendents d'Iskendar' ('The Descendants of Iskender') and 'Les Fleurs' ('The Flowers'), the accumulation of enchanted beings and objects complements Lazare's evocative and richly descriptive narrative style.   AZ

Lee, Tanith (1947–2015) Prolific English writer of novels, short story collections, radio plays, and television scripts. Born and educated in London, she had completed the manuscripts of several books by the time she was 25. Initially she was known principally as a children's writer, having published *The Dragon Hoard* (1971), *Princess Hynchatti and Some Other Surprises* (1972), and a picture book, *Animal Castle* (1972), although her first published work, *The Betrothed* (1968), was a collection of short stories for adults. At 25 she began study at an art college, but writing remained her primary focus and she soon became a full-time writer. Her continued interest in art, especially painting, seems reflected in the powerful visual imagination which characterizes most of her writing. Her career in the 1970s was evenly divided between books for young readers, with nine appearing between 1971 and 1979, and adult fantasies. After *Shon the Taken* (1982), Lee had appeared to abandon children's writing, but has made an impressive return with *Black Unicorn* (1991) and *Gold Unicorn* (1994). Altogether, Lee has written more than 70 novels and 250 short stories.

Lee's output is diverse, but the genres which dominate her work are fairy tale, fantasy, and science fiction, often intermingled in very creative ways. Her contribution to fairy tale is of three main kinds: playful original stories for young readers, which adduce familiar conventions for comic or parodic purposes; retellings for an adult audience of classic tales, placing the tales in a new context, or giving them a startling new twist or point of view; or more allusive uses of known tales within other genres, especially fantasy. Her propensity for playing with the fairy tale is quickly evident in her first foray into the genre, *The Dragon Hoard*. This humorous novel for younger children exploits the comic potential in many fairy-tale motifs by a mixture of pastiche and absurdity. Prince Jasleth is sent out to seek his fortune in the hope of alleviating a spell cast on himself and his twin sister by a wicked witch who was not invited to their 17th birthday party (and who of course still bore a grudge over being left out of the christening), but discovers that all the fairy-tale quests he expects have been performed

years ago, and the quest he finally joins (itself a parody of the story of the Argonauts) becomes a series of comic adventures. The novel has more than its quota of talking animals, helpers, and opponents, and is littered with allusions to fairy tales, classical mythology, and the Bible. Storytelling is pushed to an ironic self-reflective absurdity when the 50 questers, captured by an evil sorcerer, escape by boring him with an utterly pointless fairy tale concocted by passing the story to a new teller every few sentences, with each speaker uttering 'the first things that came into his head', pursuing various fairy-tale schemata in random ways.

Princess Hynchatti and Some Other Surprises continues in a similar vein of absurdity, but now as 12 original fairy tales, alternately about Princesses and Princes. These tales deal with quests solved by ingenuity or cunning, comic or foolish quests undertaken by inept heroes and heroines, helpful talking animals, malicious spells and accidental metamorphoses, and female and male **'Cinderella'* figures who win happiness not by magic but by intelligence. Throughout these tales, the heroes' victories always affirm particular qualities necessary for their happiness—consideration for others, altruism, humility, thoughtfulness. These values are intrinsic to Lee's human insight, even within her most macabre adult Gothic fantasies.

The adult fairy tales, a good selection of which were gathered together in *Red as Blood, or Tales from the Sisters Grimmer* (1983), are parables about the human psyche. The significances of the nine stories in this volume are readily evident in those tales which are reworkings of classics, that is, in 'Paid Piper' ('The Pied Piper'), 'Red as Blood' (**Snow White*), 'Thorns' (**Sleeping Beauty*), 'When the Clock Strikes' ('Cinderella'), 'The Golden Rope' (**Rapunzel*), 'The Princess and her Future' ('The **Frog King*'), and 'Beauty' (**Beauty and the Beast*). Here the comedy of Lee's children's tales is replaced by grim irony, the blithe archaic settings by medievalist wastelands, Gothic ruins, and deserts of the mind, and the simple conflicts between good and evil are teased out into a kind of psychomachia. Lee's adult writings deal in almost overwhelming emotions, and human desires are figured by supernatural horrors and illuminations. Thus in the opening tale, 'Paid Piper', the Piper from Robert Browning's poem subsumes the lost gods of fertility and ecstasy, Pan and Dionysus, and the sterility visited on the village that rejects him symbolizes the aridity of mundane, material lives lived without joy and love for others. The tales evince a pervasive desire for transcendence, but in attributing to human beings an endemic propensity for evil acknowledge a danger that this may be won at the cost of humanity. Elsewhere, in 'Bloodmantle' (in *Forests of the Night*, 1989), a tale loosely connected with *'Little Red Riding Hood'*, the main character recognizes that the ghostly werewolf she has met is stranded with 'no self to become' and that the human quest is 'not to find the bestial in humankind, but...to be free of it'. Sometimes in Lee's adult fairy tales characters meet the bestial, in paranormal or supernatural forms, and are devoured by it. Thus 'The Princess and her Future'—in which the creature from the well fulfils the 'young and handsome Prince' cliché but eats his bride on their wedding day—challenges banal psychoanalytic readings of 'The Frog King' which assert that the frog, representing a fear of sexuality, will be transformed into an ideal life partner. Conversely, in the science-fiction retelling of 'Beauty' the heroine's relationship with the 'monster', who figures a fusion of mind and body transcending mundane existence, lifts her above the superficiality and ennui of aimless being. In *White as Snow* (2000), Lee combines the classic Grimms' *'Snow White'* with the Persephone myth to create a dark medieval novel about savage love and brutality.

Common to all of Lee's fairy tales, whether for children or adults, and whether they explore the positive or negative aspects of human desire, is a faith in what she has elsewhere called 'the rays of human love and human ability, that are the best of all of us' (author's foreword to *Eva Fairdeath*, 1994).   JAS

Haut, Mavis, *The Hidden Library of Tanith Lee: Themes and Subtexts from Dionysos to the Immortal Gene* (2001).
Lefanu, Sarah, 'Robots and Romance: The Science Fiction and Fantasy of Tanith Lee', in Susannah Radstone (ed.), *Sweet Dreams: Sexuality, Gender and Science Fiction* (1988).

Le Guin, Ursula (1929–) American author. She is probably most famous for her brilliant fantasy novels for children: *A Wizard of Earthsea* (1968), *The Tombs of Atuan* (1971), and *The Farthest Shore* (1972). In 1990, 18 years later, a fourth and final volume of the story, *Tehanu*, appeared.

The Earthsea books draw on many of the conventions of the fairy story and the quest tale. They take place in an imaginary island archipelago where magic exists and is practised by both official wizards and village witches. In the first three volumes, the boy Ged, who travels to distant lands and overcomes both internal and external obstacles to become a famous wizard, is a central character.

The final volume of the series, *Tehanu*, as Le Guin has said, marks a shift in her vision of the world away from the male tradition of heroic fantasy. Here, as in many European fairy tales, it is women who have supernatural ability; and their magic is of a very different sort. The emphasis is on knowledge, kindness, and patience, rather than strength and violence, as a way of defeating evil.

Among other features of the Earthsea books that recall fairy tales are the magic power of names and naming (as in *'Rumpelstiltskin'*), and the animal helpers: dragons whose ancient wisdom aids the protagonists. Le Guin has also written some remarkable variations on classic fairy tales, such as 'The Poacher' (1996), in which a peasant boy chops his way through the thorny hedge surrounding *Sleeping Beauty's* castle, but decides not to wake her.

Le Guin has also explored themes from Native American and trickster tales in her works. In her utopian novel *Always Coming Home* (1985) she makes great use of oral traditions, and in the short stories of *Buffalo Gals and Other Animal Presences* (1987)

there are motifs taken from trickster and animal tales.   AL

Attebery, Brian, 'Gender, Fantasy, and the Authority of Tradition', *Journal of the Fantastic in the Arts*, 7.1(25) (1996).

Cadden, Mike, *Ursula K. Le Guin Beyond Genre: Fiction for Children and Adults* (2004).

Hatfield, Len, 'From Master to Brother: Shifting the Balance of Authority in Ursula K. Le Guin's *Farthest Shore and Tehanu*', *Children's Literature*, 21 (1993).

McLean, Susan, 'The Power of Women in Ursula K. Le Guin's *Tehanu*', *Extrapolation*, 38.2 (summer 1997).

Reid, Suzanne Elizabeth, *Presenting Ursula K. Le Guin* (1997).

Rochelle, Warren, *Communities of the Heart: The Rhetoric of Myth in the Fiction of Ursula K. Le Guin* (2001).

Leibovitz, Annie (1949–) An American photographer, known for her celebrity portraiture and photojournalism with *Rolling Stone* magazine in the 1970s. The Walt Disney Company hired Leibovitz in 2007 to produce celebrity portraits of characters from Disney fairy-tale films for their ongoing 'Year of a Million Dreams' campaign. Basically the fairy-tale characters are turned into fashion models for Disney and *Vogue Magazine*. A limited selection of these portraits include actor Scarlett Johansson as Cinderella (2007); Jennifer Lopez and Marc Anthony as Jasmine and Aladdin (2008); Queen Latifah as Ursula (2011); Russell Brand as Captain Hook (2012); and Jennifer Hudson as princess Tiana from Disney's *The Princess and the Frog* (2009).   MF

Leland, Charles Godfrey (1824–1903) American journalist, folklorist, and artist. According to family legend, soon after Leland was born, his nurse took him to the attic and performed a ritual that included a Bible, a key, a knife, lighted candles, money, and salt to ensure a long life as a scholar and a wizard. Indeed, Leland had a long and illustrious life as folklorist and artist. He was one of the first folklorists in the 19th century to write extensively about witches in *Etruscan Roman Remains in Popular Tradition* (1892) and *Aradia, or the Gospel of the Witches*

(1899). During his long stay in Europe in the 1870s and 1880s, he published important collections of folklore such as *The English Gipsies* (1873), *Johnnykin and the Goblins* (1879), *The Gypsies* (1882), and *Gypsy Sorcery and Fortune Telling* (1891). In 1892, he published his own unique book, *The Hundred Riddles of the Fairy Bellaria*, which he designed and illustrated. It concerns a fairy who outwits a prince who cannot answer all her riddles. When Leland returned to the US he played an important role in the Arts and Crafts Movement and founded the Public Industrial Art School, which later became the Philadelphia University of the Arts.   JZ

Lem, Stanislaw (1921–2006) Polish writer and philosopher, physician by education, author of several popular science-fiction novels and short stories. He lived in West Berlin in 1980–3 and in Austria in 1983–8. His early novels, such as *The Astronauts* (1951) and *The Magellan Cloud* (1953–5), are utopian fairy tales, depicting interplanetary communist paradise. Lem's best-known works, *Eden* (1959) and *Solaris* (1961), also adapted for film by Andrei Tarkovsky, are more like contemporary existential novels, reflecting on the essence of human civilization, possible contacts with other worlds, and the problems and dilemmas of mutual understanding. These 'serious' novels are deeply psychological and display the writer's extreme erudition and keen insight into human nature.

By contrast, quite a number of his novels and stories, for instance, *Robot Fairy Tales* (1964) or *Cyberiade* (1965), are full of humour and the grotesque. Closest to traditional fairy tales are *Star Diaries of Ijon Tichy, Space Vagabond* (1957), a parody on themes, characters, and stylistic clichés of contemporary science fiction, which draws inspiration from *Munchausen* and *Gulliver's Travels*. Among Lem's humorous works are also several collections of reviews and prefaces to non-existent books, such as *Provocation* (1984).

Lem received a vast number of national and international literary awards, including a medal from the International Association of Astronauts (1995).   MN

Berthel, Werner (ed.), *Stanislaw Lem. Der dialektische Weise aus Krakow* (1976).

Nikolchina, Miglena, 'Love and Automata: From Hoffmann to Lem and from Freud to Kristeva', in Joe Sanders (ed.), *Functions of the Fantastic: Selected Essays from the Thirteenth International Conference on the Fantastic in the Arts* (1995).

Ziegfeld, Richard E., *Stanislaw Lem* (1985).

Lemaître, Jules (1853–1914) French writer and influential theatre critic. His collection of stories *Contes blancs* (*White Tales*, 1900) includes several fairy tales, such as 'Les Amoureux de la princesse Mimi' ('Princess Mimi's Suitors'), in which *Little Tom Thumb and the cyclops Polyphemus compete for the hand of *Cinderella's daughter, the eponymous Mimi. The young narrator of 'Les Idées de Liette' ('Lietta's Ideas') protests at the unjust endings of some classic fairy tales. In her imaginative revisions of *'Little Red Riding Hood' and *'Bluebeard', the Virgin Mary and Jesus intervene on behalf of the persecuted heroines.   AZ

Lemon, Mark (1809–70) English writer and the first editor of *Punch*. Among a handful of books for children he wrote two fairy stories, described by F. J. Harvey Darton in *Children's Books in England* (1932) as 'jocularly moral'. In *The Enchanted Doll* (1849), illustrated by Richard *Doyle, a grasping old doll-maker is reformed by fairy means and by the altruistic kindness of the neighbour he despises. Lemon was a close friend of Charles *Dickens, and characters and setting have echoes of *A Christmas Carol* (1843). The strange story of *Tinykin's Transformations* (1869) describes how the fairy queen, Titania, aids a boy to take on various animal shapes and thereby gather experience and wisdom to rule over a Saxon kingdom.   GA

Le Noble, Eustache (1643–1711) French writer. After a tumultuous early life that included banishment, prison, and love affairs, Le Noble began a prolific writing career. He inserted two fairy tales, 'L'Apprenti magicien' ('The Apprentice Magician') and

'L'Oiseau de vérité' ('The Truth Bird'), into a collection of intercalated stories, *Le Gage touché* (*The Wager Paid*, 1700). Like his contemporaries Mlle *Lhéritier and Charles *Perrault, Le Noble avows and idealizes the popular origins of his two fairy tales, both of which are narrated by young girls who in turn had been told these stories by their governesses. The plot of 'The Apprentice Magician' resembles somewhat 'The Sorcerer's Apprentice' in that an apprentice, Alexis, experiments with the magic of his master, La Rancune. Here the resemblance stops, for it is metempsychosis that Alexis tries. Changing into a myriad of forms to escape La Rancune's wrath, he finally succeeds in killing his master, which frees him to marry a captive princess. 'The Truth Bird' shares the same plot as Mme d'*Aulnoy's 'La Princesse Belle-Étoile et le prince Chéri'. A central feature of this story is the search for identity by three royal children who were banished from court at birth by an evil queen mother. Both d'Aulnoy's and Le Noble's retellings use this plot to introduce the theme of incest. But whereas d'Aulnoy makes the hero and heroine fear, for a time, their mutual inclination (they are raised as brother and sister but are actually cousins), Le Noble explores the more troubling scenario of a father pursuing his daughter until he discovers who she is. Compared with d'Aulnoy's tale, Le Noble's is considerably more concise in terms of length and style, which has led some scholars to suggest that he may have had access to popular versions of this tale. What is certain is that both of Le Noble's tales come close to Perrault's attempts to combine the concision of oral storytelling with classical French literary style.   LCS

Lenski, Lois (1893–1974) American illustrator and artist, best known for her realistic regional books and her books for very small children. Early in her career, which stretched over 50 years, Lenski illustrated five books of fairy tales, three edited by Veronica Hutchinson and two by Kathleen Adams and Frances Atchinson. The style for which she became famous depends on place, except for these books. She also used colour in interesting ways; her work is detailed and suggestive, as well as economical. Her faces are often similar, even interchangeable.

Lenski was born in Ohio, the fourth child of a Lutheran minister who was given to eclectic interests, which ranged from raising cacti to photography. She attended and graduated from Ohio State, receiving a B.Sc. in Education. Lenski was expected to become a teacher, but found herself increasingly drawn to art. Prompted by the head of the Art Department at Ohio State, she went to New York to study at the Art Students League. There she met her lifelong friend Mabel Pugh and her future husband, Arthur Covey. Encouraged by Pugh, Lenski studied for two years in London at the Westminster School of Art, where she was given her first book commission, *The Green Faced Toad* by Vera Birch, followed by Kenneth *Grahame's *The Golden Age*. She travelled and sketched in Italy, returning to the USA to marry Arthur Covey in 1921.

The Golden Age contains four coloured tipped-in plates on brown paper with tissue covers. They feature children, the girls in dresses and the boys in sailor suits. The colours are solid; a blue dress is completely blue. Coloured outlines are used on curtains and clothing. Complementing the coloured plates are black-and-white ink drawings as chapter heads and endings. Some, such as the decorations for 'Alarms and Excursions', feature dragons, knights, castles, and princesses. These were precursors to the three Hutchinson books, the first, *Chimney Corner Stories*, appearing in the United States in 1925. All three books are a mixture of folk and fairy stories representing rhymes, pourquoi tales, cumulative tales, silly tales, and reward-for-virtue tales. The first contains *'Cinderella', in which the fairy godmother appears as a kindly witch. Each story begins with a chapter picture and a decorated first letter. *Candle-Light Stories* and *Fireside Stories* were both published in 1927, each with six colour plates. The two books are composites of various kinds of folk tales, including North American Indian, Black tales, and tall tales like 'Paul Bunyan', and anticipate

Lenski's regional books. Although there is a European peasant quality, such as wooden shoes, tights on the men, patterned aprons, and odd hats, the interiors resemble those of New England, where Lenski was living at the time.

In 1927, Dodd, Mead published *A Book of Princess Stories* and in 1928, *A Book of Enchantment*. In these books Lenski commented that she could indulge her passion for the medieval and make use of the tapestries and medieval costumes which she had seen in England and Italy. Most of Lenski's work was preceded by sketches; she recorded visits in sketchbooks, and whenever possible she worked from models. Thus her characters, whether animal or human, appear realistic even if dressed in quaint clothing and put into fairy-tale backgrounds.   LS

Lenski, Lois, *Journey into Childhood* (1972).

Leprince de Beaumont, Jeanne-Marie

(1711–80) Popular French writer of didactic literature. Educated in a convent school in Rouen, she later became a teacher in the schools which, at that time, were being developed for children of all social classes. In 1741 she married M. de Beaumont, a dissolute libertine, and the marriage was annulled after two years. In 1745 she departed for England, where she earned her living as a governess. During her long residence in London, she made a name for herself by publishing short stories in magazines and producing collections of anecdotes, stories, fairy tales, commentaries, and essays directed at specific social and age groups, all with a strong pedantic bent. For instance, she published a series of pedagogical works with the following titles: *Le Magasin des enfants* (1757), *Le Magasin des adolescents* (1760), *Le Magasin des pauvres* (1768), *Le Mentor moderne* (1770), *Manuel de la jeunesse* (1773), and *Magasin des dévotes* (1779). In 1762 she returned to France, where she continued her voluminous production, and retired to a country estate in Haute-Savoie in 1768. Among her major works of this period were *Mémoires de la Baronne de Batteville* (1776), *Contes moraux* (1774), and *Œuvres mêlées* (1775). By the time of her death, she had written over 70 books.

Leprince de Beaumont, Jeanne-Marie Beauty modestly refuses the beast's marriage proposal in Eleanor Vere *Boyle's adaptation of Mme Leprince de Beaumont's 'Beauty and the Beast', which she also illustrated in *Beauty and the Beast: An Old Tale New-Told* (1875). The Bodleian Library, University of Oxford ((OC) 250 e.67).

Mme Leprince de Beaumont's major fairy tales were all published in *Le Magasin des Enfants* (translated as *The Young Misses' Magazine*), which was designed to frame stories, history lessons, and moral anecdotes told by a governess to young girls. Among the fairy tales were: 'La Belle et la Bête' (*'Beauty and the Beast'), 'Le Prince Chéri' ('Prince Darling'), 'Le Prince Désir' ('Prince Desire'), 'Le Prince Charmant' ('Prince Charming'), 'La Veueve et les deux filles' ('The Widow and her Two Daughters'), 'Aurore et Aimée', 'Le Pêcheur et le Voyageur' ('The Fisherman and the Traveller'), 'Joliotte', and 'Bellotte et Laidronette'. Her version of 'Beauty and the Beast', which was based on Mme Gabrielle-Suzanne de *Villeneuve's longer narrative of 1740, is perhaps the most famous in the world. Here Belle, the youngest daughter of a bankrupt merchant, is willing to sacrifice herself to a savage beast to save her father. Her conduct at the beast's palace is so exemplary that she not only provides the means to restore her father's good name, but she also saves the beast from certain death. Mme Leprince de Beaumont's emphasis in all her fairy tales was on the proper upbringing of young girls like Beauty, and she continually stressed industriousness, self-sacrifice, modesty, and diligence in all her tales as the qualities young ladies and men must possess to attain happiness. Aside from 'Beauty and the Beast', several other fairy tales have remained somewhat popular in France and reflect Mme Leprince de Beaumont's major theme: the transformation of bestial behaviour into goodliness. For instance, 'Prince Darling' concerns a conceited and tyrannical prince who is turned into various animals until he resolves to be good and gentle. 'Prince Desire' depicts a prince who does not want to accept the fact that he has a huge nose but learns that he must accept his faults if he wants to marry the Princess Mignonne. Mme Leprince de Beaumont was one of the first French writers to write fairy tales explicitly for children, and thus she kept her language and plot simple to convey her major moral messages. Though her style was limited by the lesson she wanted to teach, she was careful not to destroy the magic in her tales that triumphs despite her preaching. JZ

Clancy, Patricia, 'A French Writer and Educator in England: Mme Le Prince de Beaumont', *Studies on Voltaire*, 201 (1982).

Hearne, Betsy, *Beauty and the Beast: Visions and Revisions of an Old Tale* (1989).

Kempton, Adrian, 'Education and the Child in Eighteenth-Century French Fiction', *Studies on Voltaire*, 124 (1974).

Pauly, Rebecca M., 'Beauty and the Beast: From Fable to Film', *Literature/Film Quarterly*, 17.2 (1989).

Stewart, Joan Hinde, 'Allegories of Difference: An Eighteenth-Century Polemic', *Romantic Review*, 75 (May 1984).

Wilkins, Kay S., 'Children's Literature in Eighteenth-Century France', *Studies on Voltaire*, 176 (1979).

Zipes, Jack, 'The Origins of the Fairy Tale', in *Fairy Tale as Myth/Myth as Fairy Tale* (1994).

Lermontov, Mikhail (1814–41) Major Russian romantic poet and writer. In his romantic poems and ballads, such as 'The Demon' (1830–41), 'Tamara' (1841), and 'The Combat' (1841), he used motifs from folklore, mainly Transcaucasian, which he knew well from his travels. Also, his only fairy tale in prose, *Ashik-Kerib* (1837, pub. 1846) is based on an oriental folk story, with its specific poetic style and exotic setting. MN

Lerner, Alan Jay (1918–86) American lyricist and librettist for such Broadway musicals as *My Fair Lady* (1956) and *Camelot* (1960). In these musicals Lerner followed the practice of other Broadway librettists in adapting an existing literary work into a musical, but in his first major show, *Brigadoon* (1947), Lerner claimed to have created his own original story about a Scottish village that only comes to life for one day every hundred years. He acknowledged that he was influenced by James Barrie's books about his native Scotland, but it was a remark by his musical collaborator, Frederick (Fritz) Loewe, that inspired the story of *Brigadoon*. 'Faith moves mountains', Loewe had said, and Lerner created a tale of two Americans on a hunting trip in Scotland who come upon the magical village. They fall in love with two of the village girls, but at first they are not able to give up their own world to join the village in its 100-year sleep. After they return to New York, however, the men realize their mistake and seek out the site of Brigadoon again. There the power of their love brings the village back to life. The prominent drama critic George Jean Nathan accused Lerner of taking his plot from a German story, 'Germelschausen', by Friedrich Wilhelm Gerstacker, but Lerner always maintained *Brigadoon* was his original creation. Whatever the source, *Brigadoon* is characteristic of Lerner's idyllic and romantic approach to the American musical and produced such enduring songs as 'Almost Like Being in Love'.   PF

> Lees, Gene, *Inventing Champagne: The Worlds of Lerner and Loewe* (1990).
>
> Lerner, Alan Jay, *The Street Where I Live* (1980).

Levesque, Louise Cavelier (1703–45) French writer. Her *Le Prince des Aigues marines* (*The Prince of the Sea Waters*) and *Le Prince invisible* (*The Invisible Prince*), published in 1722, feature the more complicated plot scenarios that were to dominate 18th-century French fairy tales. In *The Invisible Prince* Levesque incorporates vague allusions to cabalistic magic in an otherwise conventional plot. And in *The Prince of the Sea Waters* she uses the killing glance motif both as an obstacle to the union of two lovers and as a means of 'civilizing' an island of 'primitive' peoples.   LCS

Lewis, C. S. (Clive Staples Lewis, 1898–1963) British author, scholar, and popular theologian. Lewis and his older brother Warren, sons of a Belfast solicitor, enjoyed a protected middle-class childhood whose happiness and security were destroyed by the death of their mother from cancer in 1908, followed by a grim succession of boarding schools. After the First World War, Lewis returned to Oxford, where he achieved a triple First Class degree at University College. In 1925 he became a Fellow of Magdalen College. His scholarly reputation in medieval and Renaissance English

literature was established when his book *The Allegory of Love* won the Hawthornden Prize in 1936. In 1954 he was offered a professorship at Cambridge University, where he taught until his retirement. Meanwhile, he was becoming increasingly well known as a popular theologian. A militant atheist in his teens, as he relates in his spiritual autobiography *Surprised by Joy* (1955), Lewis finally surrendered to Christianity in 1931. After recasting his spiritual journey as a fantastic allegory in *The Pilgrim's Regress* (1933), he began experimenting, more successfully, with other modes. *The Problem of Pain* (1940) and *Mere Christianity* (1952) were straightforward expository works. *The Screwtape Letters* (1942), on the other hand, inspired by his study of *Paradise Lost*, entertains the reader with a series of letters from a senior devil, instructing his junior in effective techniques of damnation. *Out of the Silent Planet* (1938) was the first of a science-fiction trilogy in which spiritual concepts were expressed in terms of an original mythology. A struggle between cosmic good and evil that begins on Mars continues on Venus in *Perelandra* (1943) and concludes on Earth in *That Hideous Strength* (1945), subtitled *A Modern Fairy-Tale for Grown-Ups*. Lewis's planets are vividly imagined; not surprisingly, he went on to create an entirely imaginary world in his fantasy series for children, The Chronicles of Narnia.

Narnia, as Doctor Cornelius tells Prince Caspian, was not made for human beings. 'It is the country of Aslan, the country of the Waking Trees and Visible Naiads, of Fauns and Satyrs, of Dwarfs and Giants, of the gods and the Centaurs, of Talking Beasts' (*Prince Caspian*). Lewis filled Narnia with all the mythical creatures that appealed to him, whatever their origin—gods and centaurs from Greek mythology, giants and dwarfs from Germanic folklore, talking animals from Beatrix *Potter and Kenneth *Grahame. Contributing to the eclectic effect is the variety of literary sources, from Homer, Malory, and Milton to Hans Christian *Andersen, J. R. R. *Tolkien, E. *Nesbit, and *The *Arabian Nights*. George *MacDonald, in particular, taught Lewis how to infuse the literary fairy tale with Christian meaning. Aslan the Lion, the Son of the Emperor-beyond-the-Sea, represents the animal form that divine incarnation might assume in a world like Narnia. In the first of the series, *The Lion, the Witch, and the Wardrobe* (1950), four children from our world enter a Narnia frozen in perpetual winter by the White Witch (clearly inspired by Andersen's *Snow Queen). Aslan dies voluntarily at the Witch's hands, trading his life for one of the children's, but he is miraculously resurrected and leads his forces to victory against her. Despite the unmistakable analogy to Christ's crucifixion and resurrection, Lewis did not begin the story consciously intending to teach Christianity. 'Suddenly', he says, 'Aslan came bounding into it...But once He was there He pulled the whole story together, and soon He pulled the six other Narnian stories in after Him' (*Of Other Worlds*). Lewis realized that he might circumvent children's negative associations with religious subjects by 'stripping them of their stained-glass and Sunday school associations' and recasting them in an imaginary world. Although the Narnian stories are not allegories—and have been misused by being treated as such—they are permeated with Christian concepts. *Prince Caspian* (1951), for example, raises the question of faith in a secular age. The four children return to Narnia only to learn that several hundred years have passed; human beings have taken over, the trees are 'asleep', and the surviving mythical creatures, driven into hiding, are unsure whether Aslan even exists. The triumphant return of Aslan, however, and the restoration of Narnia to its former self can represent the victory of imagination over materialism as readily as that of faith over disbelief. *The Voyage of the 'Dawn Treader'* (1952) and *The Silver Chair* (1956) follow the classic fairy-tale pattern of the quest-journey. The former is both the most 'Arthurian' of the series, with its echoes of the Grail quest, and the most Homeric, in its voyaging among strange islands. In *The Magician's Nephew* (1955), Lewis depicted the creation of his imaginary world, and in *The Last Battle* (1956), a Carnegie Award-winner, its final apocalypse. As a whole, *The Narnia Chronicles*—beautifully illustrated by Pauline Baynes—are considered one of the finest achievements of 20th-century children's fantasy.

Lewis's last novel for adults, *Till We Have Faces: A Myth Retold* (1956), is an interesting reworking of 'Cupid and Psyche', set in a small kingdom on the fringes of ancient Greek civilization, and narrated by Psyche's ugly sister Orual, whose deep but possessive love for Psyche makes her hostile to the Divine Love towards which her sister, an *anima naturaliter Christiana*, is instinctively drawn.

Lewis's essays on children's literature and fairy tales, though few, have had considerable influence. In 'On Three Ways of Writing for Children' he argued that children's literature should be judged as literature—a radical view in 1952—and defended the fairy tale from charges of being escapist and too frightening for children. 'Sometimes Fairy Stories May Say Best What's to Be Said' described Lewis's attraction to the genre and its special power. Both essays appear in *Of Other Worlds* (1966).   SR

Manlove, Colin, *The Chronicles of Narnia: The Patterning of a Fantastic World* (1993).

Schakel, Peter J., *Reading with the Heart: The Way into Narnia* (1979).

Wilson, A. N., *C. S. Lewis: A Biography* (1990).

Lhéritier de Villandon, Marie-Jeanne

(?1664–1734) French writer. Daughter of a Royal Historiographer and the niece of Charles *Perrault, Lhéritier received an exceptional education for a woman of her day. Although little is known of her early life, she became a prominent participant in literary circles of the 1690s and 1700s, contributed frequently to the *Mercure Galant*, won prizes sponsored by the Académie française, was given honorary membership in literary academies, and is said to have inherited Madeleine de Scudéry's salon upon that writer's death. Throughout her lifetime, she published several collections of her works— poetry, letters, novellas, and fairy tales. She also edited the memoirs of her protectress, the duchesse de Nemours (1709), and translated Ovid's *Heroides* into French (1723).

Lhéritier was a key player in the group of writers who inaugurated the late 17th-century 'vogue' of fairy tales. The tales in her *Œuvres meslées* (*Assorted Works*, 1695)— 'L'Adroite Princesse' ('The Discreet Princess'), 'Les Enchantements de l'éloquence' ('The Enchantments of Eloquence'), and 'Marmoisan'—were published even before Perrault's **Histoires ou contes du temps passé* (1697). In this same collection, Lhéritier offers glimpses into the environment that fostered the writing of *contes de fées*. Among other things, she gives indications that the 'vogue' was a collective phenomenon. Besides encouraging other women to write fairy tales in letters and poems, Lhéritier cites phrases from Perrault's 'Les Fées' ('The *Fairies') in 'The Enchantments of Eloquence', which is based on the same folk tale and was written at about the same time as her uncle's, probably as a friendly competition with him. Lhéritier also includes a manifesto-type 'Lettre à Mme D.G.' in which she links fairy tales to novels, traces their common origins to troubadours' poetry, and calls for moral and literary renewal through the élite rewriting of indigenous French stories. In this text and others, Lhéritier uses the example of the fairy tale to defend the 'modernist' position in the Quarrel of the Ancients and the Moderns that marked late 17th-century French cultural life. None the less, she held ambivalent views about the value of (what we would now call) oral folklore. Although she, like Perrault, idealized the image of the nurse or grandmother telling tales to children, she unapologetically rewrote (i.e. expanded) stories whose origins she recognized as popular. This is especially true of her last two tales, 'Ricdin-Ricdon', the first literary version of the story made famous by the *Grimms as *'Rumpelstiltskin', and 'La Robe de sincérité' ('The Truth Dress'), both of which were published in *La Tour ténébreuse* (*The Dark Tower*, 1705).

Of all the late 17th-century French women writers, Lhéritier was arguably the most overtly feminist. Besides celebrating the accomplishments of prominent women writers and responding to the satirist Boileau's misogynistic attacks, she repeatedly defended women's education in her fiction. This latter defence can be found in 'The Enchantments of Eloquence', in which she explicitly defends women's reading and outlines a classically inspired 'feminine' rhetoric. Lhéritier also repeatedly employed the figure of the female cross-dresser to denounce inequalities between the sexes (e.g. 'Marmoisan'). Yet she also attempted to reconcile such feminist arguments with traditional 'feminine' virtues such as submission and obedience (e.g. 'The Discreet Princess'). More than perhaps any of her contemporaries, then, Lhéritier used the fairy tale not simply to convey conventional moral lessons but also to address real social concerns.

LCS

Fumaroli, Marc, 'Les *Contes* de Perrault, ou l'éducation de la douceur', in *La Diplomatie de l'esprit: de Montaigne à La Fontaine* (1994).
Seifert, Lewis, 'The Rhetoric of Invraisemblance: Lhéritier's "Les Enchantements de l'éloquence"', *Cahiers du Dix-septième*, 3.1 (1989).
Velay-Vallantin, Catherine, *La Fille en garçon* (1992).

Liestøl, Knut (1881–1952) Norwegian folklorist, professor at Oslo University 1917–51, minister of church and education 1933–5, director of the Norwegian Collection of Folklore 1914–51. His most important contributions to folklore studies include *Norske trollvisor och norrøne sogor* (*Norwegian Fairy Songs and Old Scandinavian Sagas*, 1915) and *Norske aettesogor* (*Norwegian Clan Sagas*, 1922). In his studies, Liestøl combined philological and folkloristic approaches with high artistic quality. He was especially interested in the evolution and regularities of folklore texts. He wrote a biography of P. C. *Asbjørnsen in 1947 and of Moltke *Moe in 1949.   MN

Linati, Carlo (1878–1949) Italian writer and literary critic, known for his novel *Duccio da Bontà* (1912). He wrote autobiographical tales, allegoric and psychological tales, and fairy tales. In *Storie di bestie e di fantasmi* (*Animal and Ghost Stories*, 1925), he draws from the fantastic and the animal world to create such original tales as 'Favola Marina' (*A Sea Fairy Tale'), a fast-paced story of the marine kingdom in which a clever little fish fools a voracious shark.   MNP

Lindgren, Astrid (1907–2002) The most prominent contemporary children's author in Sweden, Andersen Medal-winner, and translated into more than 70 languages. The appearance and success of her first books immediately after the Second World War was prepared by the vast interest in pedagogy and child psychology in Sweden during the 1930s, as well as a general awareness about children's rights. Lindgren stands wholly on the child's side, rejecting the early didactic and authoritarian ways of addressing young readers. In terms of literary tradition, her fairy tales came in the wake of the many translations into Swedish of world fairy-tale classics. At the same time, the war experience presented earlier idyll and adventure in a new light, bringing her writing closer to everyday reality and giving it a more optimistic tone.

Although Lindgren has written in almost every possible genre and style, her foremost achievements are in the field of the modern fairy tale. Her internationally best-known work is *Pippi Långstrump* (*Pippi Longstocking*, 1945), featuring the strongest girl in the world, independent and defiant, empowering the child in an unheard-of manner.

In *Lillebror och Karlsson på taket* (*Karlsson-on-the-roof*, 1955) Lindgren also brings the fairy tale into daily life, presenting an unexpected solution to lonely children in the image of the selfish fat man with a propeller on his back. Adult critics often get irritated by Karlsson and wonder why the boy puts up with him. But Lindgren's deep confidence in her readers makes her sure that they will see through Karlsson and learn from his misbehaviour.

The same merging of the everyday and the extraordinary is true of Lindgren's collection of short fairy tales, *Nils Karlsson Pyssling* (1949, sometimes translated as *Simon Small*), in which supernatural figures appear in contemporary Stockholm, often providing help and consolation for lonely children. Another collection of fairy tales, *Sunnanäng* (*South Wind Meadow*, 1959), is more traditional, based on local legends and heroic tales, although firmly anchored in the 19th-century Swedish landscape. They stand closer to Lindgren's two major contributions to the fairy-tale novel genre, *Mio, min Mio* (*Mio, My Son*, 1954) and *Bröderna Lejonhjärta* (*The Brothers Lionheart*, 1973). In both novels, Lindgren uses first-person narrative, an unusual perspective in fairy tales, which provides stronger identification with the reader and signals the radical transformation of conventional patterns.

At first sight, *Mio, My Son* is a typical contemporary fairy tale: an ordinary boy is transported to a distant country beyond space and time, where he is sent away on a quest in order to meet an evil enemy. But his ties to the real world are never lost. The boy constructs his imaginary world after the model of his own reality, at the same time furnishing it with the brilliance of a fairy tale. Nevertheless, many inhabitants of Farawayland definitely come from fairy tales: the genie in the bottle, the magical helpers and donors, and the antagonist, the cruel Sir Kato.

Unlike the traditional fairy-tale hero, Mio is at times scared and ready to give up. The most important battle takes place within himself. Lindgren rejects the basic pattern of the fairy tale with a safe homecoming. She never brings Mio back to his own world, but lets him stay in Farawayland because nobody and nothing waits for him in his own world. Mio's quest is caused by his profound unhappiness in the real world. But the magical journey is not an escape into daydreams; it is a psychodrama which makes the protagonist strong enough to cope with his inner problems. The ending is open: as readers we are allowed to decide whether the boy is still sitting on a park bench and has invented the whole story, or whether he is happy and safe with his loving father the King in Farawayland. The ending evokes Hans Christian *Andersen's fairy tale 'The Little Match Girl'.

Almost 20 years later Astrid Lindgren ventured on a similar theme in *The Brothers*

Lionheart, in which the force of the psycho-drama is stressed by the shadow of death. The features of the heroic fairy tale are even stronger in this novel; however, it also breaks from the conventional linear pattern of safe homecoming and instead sends the two heroes further on a path of trials. Fairy-tale monsters, like the female dragon Katla, represent evil; but, typically for Lindgren, her protagonist is a pacifist. The impact of the story is all the stronger since the two characters have less of the valiant fairy-tale hero about them. The final sacrifice of the brothers has no parallels in traditional fairy tales, and has been criticized by some scholars as escapist and defeatist.

Likewise, the seemingly 'realistic' novels by Lindgren show a clear fairy-tale structure. For instance, the protagonist of *Emil i Lönneberga* (*Emil in the Soup Tureen,* 1963) and its sequels bears close resemblance to the traditional fairy-tale trickster, also evolving from a fool or a *Little Tom Thumb into a hero. In the *Kalle Blomkvist* (*Bill Bergson*) series, which takes the form of a detective story, traces of the dragon-slayer motif can be found. Most important, all of Lindgren's characters share common traits with the traditional folk-tale hero: they are generally the youngest son or daughter; they are of the oppressed, the powerless, the underprivileged; and they gain material and spiritual wealth during a period of trials. This feature of Lindgren's writing, seldom acknowledged by scholars, has gained her a special appreciation in the former totalitarian states of Eastern Europe, where the rebellious pathos of her children's books and the subversive questioning of all forms of authority was recognized.

Lindgren's last full-length novel, *Ronja Rövardotter* (*Ronia, the Robber's Daughter,* 1981) is a fairy tale of female maturation, featuring a number of imaginary creatures, only slightly resembling traditional folklore: harpies, goblins, dwarfs, rumphobs, and murktrolls. Unlike so many female characters in modern fairy tales, who are forced by the authors into conventional male roles as dragon-slayers or space-ship pilots—a simple gender permutation, tokenism—Ronia's

dilemma is to reconcile her independence with the female identity, which among other things will not permit her to become a robber chieftain. The novel sums up all the specific traits of Lindgren's writing, such as her superb mastery of the fairy-tale plot, her poignant and poetic language, powerful characterization, and a deep understanding of human relationships.   MN

Bamberger, Richard, 'Astrid Lindgren and a New Kind of Books for Children', *Bookbird* (1967).
Edström, Vivi, *Astrid Lindgren—vildtoring och lägereld* (1992).
Edström, Vivi, *Astrid Lindgren och sagans makt* (1997).
Metcalf, Eva-Maria, *Astrid Lindgren* (1995).

Link, Kelly (1969–) American writer and editor who co-founded Small Beer Press. After graduating from Columbia University in 1991, Link studied creative writing at the University of North Carolina in Greensboro and began her career as a freelance writer and editor. She has published two important collections of contemporary fairy tales, *Stranger Things Happen* (2000) and *Magic For Beginners* (2005) for adults and one for young readers, *Pretty Monsters: Stories* (2008). Stamped by magic realism and post-modernism, Link's tales generally reveal a feminist perspective and great originality. Her title tale, 'Pretty Monsters', won the Locust award for best novella in 2009. It depicts the problematic situation of adolescent girls who believe in werewolf romances and cannot distinguish between misleading fiction and dangerous reality. For Link, fairy tales and fantasy expose the dark side of societies that limit the autonomy of young women.   JZ

Lintot, Catherine Caillot, dame de (*c.*1728–?) French writer about whom virtually nothing is known. She is the author of *Trois nouveaux contes de fées, avec une préface qui n'est pas moins sérieuse* (*Three New Fairy Tales, with a Preface that is No Less Serious,* 1735), which contains 'Timandre et Bleuette', 'Le Prince Sincer', and 'Tendrebrun et Constance'. The sentimental plots, allusions to cabbalistic magic, and abundance of fairies in these tales are fairly typical of 17th- and 18th-century 'serious' French fairy tales. In 'Prince Sincer' and 'Tendrebrun and Constance', she develops the monstrous spouse motif, like several women writers of fairy tales in this period, including Mme *Leprince de Beaumont, Marguerite de *Lubert, and Mme de *Villeneuve. The preface to her collection, purportedly written by l'abbé Prévost, defends the genre by shifting emphasis toward the pleasures of fantasy and away from its (conventionally invoked) didactic value.   LCS

'Little Mermaid, The' The figure of a mermaid who strives to gain an immortal soul was made famous by Hans Christian *Andersen in his 'Den lille Havfrue' ('The Little Mermaid', 1837). The tale is based on the Christian-inspired folk belief that supernatural beings are not endowed with a soul but will vanish into nothingness when they die. Although sea creatures in folklore tend to be depicted as demonic and seductive, this mermaid reflects romanticism's longing for transcendence. She sacrifices an alluring voice to become human so that she can make a prince fall in love with her, for only then can she gain an immortal soul. She fails in her quest, but when given the chance of returning to her former element—by killing the prince—she refuses. Feeling a love for the prince that he cannot feel for her and acting accordingly, she passes a test and is rewarded by the divine being with the promise of an immortal soul. The story glorifies suffering and self-denial, and its ending may seem sentimental, but the tale has proved to be tremendously popular. When adapted to other media—such as in the *Disney production of 1989, which turned the plot into a close approximation of a magic tale—its philosophical overtones tend to be lost.   NI

Johansen, Jørgen Dines, 'The Merciless Tragedy of Desire', *Scandinavian Studies*, 68 (1996).

Zipes, Jack, *Fairy Tales and the Art of Subversion* (1983).

Zipes, Jack, *Hans Christian Andersen: The Misunderstood Storyteller* (2005).

'Little Nemo' Comic strip character created by Winsor *McCay whose adventures appeared weekly in the Sunday Supplements of the *New York Herald* (1909-11), the *Herald Tribune* (1924-7), and were reissued by McCay's son in 1947. Influenced by Jonathan Swift's *Gulliver's Travels*, Lewis *Carroll's *Alice in Wonderland*, and Freud's ideas about dreams and their relationship to the unconscious, *Little Nemo in Slumberland* is a ground-breaking departure from the coarse slapstick humour of contemporary strips. Structured around the unexpected logic of dream association, each episode tells an adventure experienced in his sleep by 5-year-old 'Little Nemo', who anticipates these with excitement each night.   KS

Little Prince, The (film: USA, 1974) An adaptation of the book by French aviator/writer Antoine de *Saint-Exupéry, who died in 1944 on a flying mission over the Mediterranean. In the story a pilot crash-lands in the desert and meets a small boy who has come to earth from the small, distant asteroid he rules. Seeking fidelity to the book, the director Stanley Donen filmed on location in the Sahara rather than create a desert in a studio. Even Saint-Exupéry's drawings are used, both as part of the credits and in a short animation sequence. Only the songs, by Lerner and Loewe, have no counterpart in the original.   TAS

'Little Red Riding Hood' The first literary version of this tale, 'Le Petit Chaperon Rouge', was published by Charles *Perrault in his collection, *Histoires ou contes du temps passé* (*Stories or Tales of Past Times*, 1697). Though it is not certain, Perrault probably knew an oral tale that emanated from sewing societies in the south of France and north of Italy. This folk tale depicts an unnamed peasant girl who meets a werewolf on her way to visit her grandmother. The wolf asks her whether she is taking the path of pins or needles. She indicates that she is on her way to becoming a seamstress by taking the path of the needles. The werewolf quickly departs and arrives at the grandmother's house, where he devours the old lady and places some of her flesh in a bowl and some of her blood in a bottle. After the

'Little Red Riding Hood' The curious wolf seeks to know where Little Red Riding Hood is going in Gustave *Doré's famous illustration to Charles *Perrault's tale, published in *Les Contes de Perrault* (1867).

peasant girl arrives, the werewolf invites her to eat some meat and drink some wine before getting into bed with him. Once in bed, she asks several questions until the werewolf is about to eat her. At this point she insists that she must go outside to relieve herself. The werewolf ties a rope around her leg and sends her through a window. In the garden, the girl unties the rope and wraps it around a fruit tree. Then she escapes and leaves the werewolf holding the rope. In some versions of this folk tale, the werewolf manages to eat the girl. But for the most part the girl proves that she can fend for herself.

Perrault changes all this in 'Little Red Riding Hood' by making the girl appear spoiled and naïve. She wears a red cap indicating her 'sinful' nature, and she makes a wager with the wolf to see who will arrive at grandmother's house first. After dawdling in the woods, she arrives at her grandmother's house, where she finds the wolf disguised as the grandmother in bed. She gets into bed with him and, after posing several questions about the wolf's strange appearance, she is devoured just as her grandmother was. Then there is a verse moral to conclude the tale that indicates girls who invite strange men into their parlours deserve what they get. After the translation of Perrault's tale into many different European languages in the 18th century, the literary and oral variants mixed, and what had formerly been an oral tale of initiation became a type of warning fairy tale. When the Brothers *Grimm published their first version, 'Rotkäppchen' ('Little Red Cap') in *Kinder- und Hausmärchen (*Children's and Household Tales*) in 1812, they introduced new elements such as the *Jäger* or gamekeeper, who saves Little Red Cap and her grandmother. In turn, they cut open the belly of the wolf and place stones into it. When he awakes, he dies. There is also an anticlimactic tale that the Grimms attached to this version in which another wolf comes to attack Little Red Cap and her grandmother. This time they are prepared and trick him into jumping down the chimney into a pot of boiling water.

Since the Grimms' version of 'Little Red Riding Hood' appeared, their tale and Perrault's version have been reprinted in the thousands in many different versions, and they have also been mixed together along with oral variants. Most of the new versions up to the present have been directed at children, and they have been somewhat sanitized so that the wolf rarely succeeds in touching or gobbling the grandmother and the naïve girl. On the other hand, there have been hundreds of notable literary revisions by such gifted authors as Ludwig *Tieck, Alphonse *Daudet, Joachim *Ringelnatz, Milt *Gross, James *Thurber, Anne *Sexton, Tomi *Ungerer, Angela *Carter, and Tanith *Lee in which the nature of sexuality and gender stereotypes have been questioned and debated in most innovative ways. For instance, there are tales in which a rambunctious grandmother eats up everyone; the wolf is a vegetarian and the girl a lesbian; the girl shoots the wolf with a revolver; and the girl seduces the wolf. Needless to say, these literary alternatives and many films, such as the adaptation of Angela Carter's *In the Company of Wolves* (1985) directed by Neil *Jordan and *Freeway* (1996) written and directed by Matthew Bright, reflect changes in social mores and customs; as one of the most popular fairy tales in the world, 'Little Red Riding Hood' will most likely undergo interesting changes in the future, and the girl and her story will certainly never be eliminated by the wolf.   JZ

Beckett, Sandra, *Red Riding Hood for All Ages: A Fairy-Tale Icon in Cross Cultural Contexts* (2008).

Dundes, Alan (ed.), *Little Red Riding Hood: A Casebook* (1989).

Jones, Steven Swann, 'On Analyzing Fairy Tales: "Little Red Riding Hood" Revisited', *Western Folklore*, 46 (1987).

Mieder, Wolfgang, 'Survival Forms of "Little Red Riding Hood" in Modern Society', *International Folklore Review*, 2 (1982).

Orenstein, Catherine, *Little Red Riding Hood Uncloaked: Sex, Morality, and the Evolution of a Fairy Tale* (2002).

Zipes, Jack (ed.), *The Trials and Tribulations of Little Red Riding Hood* (1983; 2nd rev. edn., 1993).

'Little Tom Thumb' ('Le Petit Poucet') This tale by Charles *Perrault, published in the *Histoires ou contes du temps passé* (*Stories or Tales of Past Times*, 1697), is an amalgam of folk-tale motifs. An early literary version by *Basile ('Nennillo et Nennilla' from the *Pentamerone*, 1634) concerns two children abandoned in the woods. Perrault enlarges the family and shrinks his hero. Tom, the youngest of seven sons, overhears his impoverished parents planning to lose their children in the forest because they cannot feed them. The self-reliant boy first leads his brothers home thanks to a trail of stones, but the second time, his trail of crumbs is eaten by birds. Spying a light in the distance, he leads his siblings to the castle of an ogre, and begins a David-and-Goliath confrontation of wits. He tricks the ogre into murdering his seven daughters and steals his treasure and seven-league boots. With these, he secures a post as a courier doing reconnaissance for armies and lovers, and buys positions at court for family members. The concluding moral of this rags-to-riches tale reassures even the smallest boy that looks can be deceiving: quick wits can help the underdog triumph, advance in society, and bring honour to one's family. It also stresses that large families don't have to be a burden.

Perrault's insistence on hardship anchors this tale in the socio-economic climate of 17th-century France. The plague had reappeared, droughts had caused disastrous harvests, famine was widespread, and an extra mouth to feed could literally mean the difference between life and death. Children were sometimes abandoned; widows with children needed to remarry, and became stepmothers. Reversal of fortune affected the upper classes as well: such is the background of a version by Mme d'*Aulnoy, who includes a *Cinderella variant. 'Finette-Cendron' (1697) features a king and queen in economic straits who abandon their three daughters: the youngest saves her sisters, tricks the ogre into an oven, and decapitates his wife. The *Grimms' version of *'Hansel and Gretel' also repeats elements of these tale types, while Michel *Tournier's 20th-century parody, 'La Fugue du petit Poucet' ('Tom Thumb Runs Away', 1978) subverts Perrault's tale with politically correct commentary on materialism and ecology.

Next to *'Little Red Riding Hood', 'Little Tom Thumb' has enjoyed the greatest popularity beyond the salon public thanks to the widespread distribution of 19th-century chapbooks and *images d'Épinal*, and Gustave *Doré's illustrations. Most of the more than 80 regional French versions, however, have little in common with Perrault's tale save the name of his hero. This is also the case with the Grimms' 'Tom Thumb' and 'Tom Thumb's Travels' or *Tragedy of Tragedies, or, The Life and Death of Tom Thumb*. Indeed, from P. T. Barnum's diminutive entertainer to celebrated locomotives to foodstore chains, the name 'Tom Thumb' remains popular.   MLE

Darnton, Robert, 'Peasants Tell Tales: The Meaning of Mother Goose', in *The Great Cat Massacre* (1984).

Delarue, Paul, and Tenèze, Marie-Louise (eds.), *Le Conte populaire français* (1997; orig. 4 vols., 1957–85).

Soriano, Marc, *Les Contes de Perrault* (1968).

Lo, Malinda (no dates available) Chinese-born American writer of young-adult novels and stories. Lo often adapts classic fairy tales from a feminist and lesbian perspective. In *Ash* (2009), a teenager named Ash reads fairy tales as a means of escaping and surviving the abuse of her stepmother. When a fairy prince named Sidhean suddenly arrives, he promises salvation but must depart and leave her alone for some time. Then Ash meets Kaisa, the king's royal huntress, and gradually falls in love with her. As a result, upon Sidhean's return, he and Kaisa struggle to win Ash's heart. In the end Ash declares her love for Kaisa. Lo has also written a prequel to *Ash* called *Huntress* (2011) in which two seventeen-year-old girls, Kaede and Taisin, are called upon to save the human world from disaster. They must take a journey to the city of the fairy queen and learn that, though they are very different from one another, their destinies are connected, and they are able to deal with the forces that threaten the stability of the human world. As in her other science fiction works, Lo characteristically depicts the uncommon strengths of young women.   JZ

Lobe, Mira (1913–95) Popular and highly esteemed Austrian children's book author. Born into a Jewish family in Silesia, Lobe spent her childhood in Germany and emigrated to Palestine in 1936. There she began writing for children, which she resumed in 1950 after her move to Vienna. Her story *Die Omama im Apfelbaum* (*Granny in the Apple Tree*, 1965) is considered a milestone in the development of the humorous, fantastic children's tale in Austria. Lobe's work displays strong social commitment and a deep psychological understanding of childhood and its difficulties.   EMM

Lobel, Anita (1934–) Polish-born American illustrator, best known for her interpretation of folk tales as both writer and artist. She began illustrating children's books in 1965 after a seven-year career as a freelance textile designer. Lobel carried the design and textures into her illustrations. For example, in her early *Troll Music* (1966), borders of flowers and leaves surround the text and illustrations as though the viewer were looking through a window at the action. Some 30 years later, in *Toads and Diamonds* (1995) retold by Charlotte Huck, the concept of looking at stop-action drama is still present, although the surrounding flowers have been replaced by a full-page illustration and a box-line around the pages with text. In her earlier work, Lobel worked with pen and ink and watercolours that did not always stay within the lines. In her most recent work, she uses watercolour and gouache paints which give the illustrations a chalky texture.

In both periods, she is extremely detailed in her presentation of flowers and vegetables—and attentive to her child viewer. For example, in her award-winning collaboration with her husband Arnold *Lobel, *A Treeful of Pigs*, twelve pigs appear in each of her pictures.

Lobel conveys an old-world charm in her illustrations. Even the beautiful maidens in *Princess Furball* (1989) are not particularly beautiful; the noses are too big, the eyes too expressive. It is easy to believe that beauty is internal, resides in the personality. Strongly influenced by the theatre, Lobel transformed her illustrations into frozen scenes. The action is stopped, but the viewer knows that action preceded the picture and will continue after the page is turned. 'I wanted to be in the theatre at one time. When I am illustrating a manuscript, I do it as if it might be a stage play.' It is an unusual quality in children's picture books. A further development in one of her latest works, *Toads and Diamonds*, is to incorporate the younger daughter Renée's thoughts into four different scenes all pulled together by clouds of smoke, rounded trees, and a figure-eight picture fence on a black background.

Incarcerated in a concentration camp in Germany, she and her brother were reunited with their parents in Sweden and then came to the United States in 1952. She was awarded a degree in fine arts from Pratt Institute in 1955 where she met her husband, Arnold Lobel. Her work continues to add new elements while retaining the recognizable quality that characterizes most of her work.   LS

Hopkins, Lee Bennett, *Books are by People* (1969).

Lobel, Arnold (1933–87) Award-winning American writer and illustrator of works for children. Among his honours are the Caldecott and Newbery Medals and Honor Book selections; National Book Award; New York Times Best Illustrated Book of the year; American Institute of Graphic Arts Children's Book Showcase. In her review of *Hansel and Gretel* (1971), the folklorist Anne Pellowswki stated that Lobel was one of only a few who came 'close to the spirit of

intimacy and homeliness in the *Grimm stories', home being a predominant image in Lobel's work. Although Lobel illustrated tales told by others, several of his texts are modern tales that reflect a wide repertory of styles. His storytelling is pastoral and Victorian. In fact, Lobel has said that while Beatrix Potter was his artistic mother, Edward Lear was his artistic father; the latter is particularly evident in 'The Man Who Took the Indoors Out' (1974), a fantastical nonsense rhyming poem about Bellwood Bouse, who loved all things in his house and so one day he invited all of it to spend the day outdoors. Of his more than 100 texts, Lobel is best noted for his beginning reader books, the Frog and Toad quartet, folk-style tales of two best friends: Frog the more reasonable and worldly; Toad the more impulsive and innocent. The marriage of setting and theme, of the pastoral and friendship (and whimsy), distinguish these tales of daily life dramatized.   SS

Shannon, George, *Arnold Lobel* (1989).

Loorits, Oskar (1900–61) Estonian folklorist who published two important collections of folklore: *Livonian Fairy Tales and Fables* (1926) and *Estonian Folk Poetry and Mythology* (1932).

His German edition, *Estnische Volkserzählungen* (1959), provided non-Estonian readers with a comprehensive anthology of diverse Estonian folk tales. He also published a significant source book in German, *Grundzüge des estnischen Volksglaubens* (*The Basic Features of Estonian Folk Beliefs*, 3 vols., 1949–57), which contains vital information about Estonian fairy tales, legends, religious mores, and customs.   JZ

López Salamero, Nunila (1966–) Spanish storyteller and short-story writer. Her works are transmitted orally in her public performances, although she has also had some of them recorded on a CD entitled *Cuentos para antes de despertar* (*Stories to Wake Up To*), which appeared in book format in 2012 and can be freely listened to and read on the Internet. However, it was her feminist rewriting of the Cinderella story that made her especially popular in Spain and other Spanish-speaking countries. Written by her and illustrated by Myriam Cameros Sierra, *La Cenicienta que no quería comer perdices* (*The Cinderella Who Did Not Want to Live Happily Ever After*) became first an Internet viral phenomenon and in 2009 a bestseller that since then has inspired thousands of readers to demythologize the notion of romantic love. CFR

Lorrain, Jean (1855–1906) French writer and critic, born Paul Duval. Notorious for his flamboyance, Lorrain often reveals the dark side of *fin-de-siècle* Paris in his works. The collection *Princesses d'ivoire et d'ivresse* (*Princesses of Ivory and Intoxication*, 1902) reflects his decadent taste for ephebes and *femmes fatales*, but also includes versions of traditional fairy tales like *Snow White, 'La Princesse Neigefleur' ('Princess Snowflower'), and *Sleeping Beauty, 'La Princesse sous verre' ('The Princess Under Glass'). *'Mélusine enchantée' ('Melusina Enchanted', 1892) and 'La Mandragore' ('The Mandrake', 1899) reveal the Norman author's interest in the fairy tradition of his region. AR

Lortzing, Albert (1801–51) German composer of *Undine a romantische Zauberoper* (romantic magic opera). Lortzing wrote and composed (one of the first German composers before Richard *Wagner to do so) comic operas whose music and humour owed much to German folk traditions. A partisan of German music, Lortzing imported appropriate elements such as plots and devices from French comic opera and the *buffo* from the Italian, though he publicly inveighed against the pervasive influence of Italian opera. Lortzing's opera *Regina* celebrated the revolutions erupting around Europe in 1848, but the political liberalism it expressed cost him a crucial position in Vienna, and he subsequently died in poverty, notwithstanding the popularity of his operas. *Undine* was something of an aberration for Lortzing, whose works are more generally comic. Freely adapted from the literary fairy tale of the same name by Friedrich de la Motte *Fouqué (who had died in

1843), the opera was premièred in Magdeburg in 1845. *Undine* combines the robust German humour for which Lortzing is famous with an uncharacteristically romantic theme. Lortzing altered Fouqué's plot to introduce comic parts for new minor characters (the squire Veit and cellarer Hans) and a happier ending, in which, rather than dying, the lovers Undine and Hugo are taken to live under the sea by her watchful father Kühleborn. NJW

Schlöder, Jürgen, *Undine auf dem Musiktheater. Zur Entwicklungsgeschichte der deutschen Spieloper* (1979).
Subotnik, R. R., 'Lortzing and the German Romantics: a Dialectical Assessment', *Musical Quarterly*, 62 (1976).

Lover, Samuel (1797–1868) Irish novelist, dramatist, song-writer, and painter. Primarily known for his miniature paintings, Lover was also a gifted musician and writer, who took a strong interest in Irish folklore. For instance, he collected tales and anecdotes from the Irish peasantry in *Legends and Stories of Ireland* (1831), and his two novels, *Rory O'More* (1837) and *Handy Andy* (1831), incorporate a great deal of Irish folklore. In 1844, after his eyesight began to fail, he began touring England and America performing Irish ballads, songs, and tales that were very successful and contributed to the rise of Irish national consciousness. JZ

Bernard, W. B., *The Life of Samuel Lover* (1874).
Symington, A. J., *Samuel Lover* (1880).

Lubert, Marguerite de (*c.*1710–79) One of the most important women writers of 18th-century French fairy tales. She is said to have been acquainted with Fontenelle and *Voltaire and to have spurned marriage so as to pursue a writing career. Beyond this, little is known of her life.

Lubert wrote six novel-length fairy tales: *La Princesse Camion* (1743), *La Princesse Couleur-de-Rose et le prince Céladon* (*Princess Rose Colour and Prince Celadon*, 1743), *Le Prince Glacé et la princesse Étincelante* (*Prince Frozen and Princess Sparkling*, 1743), *La Princesse Lionnette et le prince Coquerico* (*Princess Lionnette and Prince*

Cockadoodledoo, 1743), *La Princesse Sensible et le prince Typhon* (*Princess Sensitive and Prince Typhoon*, 1743), and *Sec et Noir, ou la Princesse des fleurs et le prince des autruches* (*Dry and Black, or the Flower Princess and the Ostrich Prince*, 1737). In addition, Lubert inserted shorter tales in frame narratives, such as 'Le Petit chien blanc' ('The Little White Dog') in *La Veillée galante* (*The Galant Gathering*, 1747); 'Étoilette' ('Starlet') and 'Peau d'ours' ('Bearskin') in her edition of Mme de *Murat's *Les Lutins du château de Kernosy* (*The Ghosts of the Castle of Kernosy*, 1753).

Lubert develops and pushes to its limits the fairy-tale discourse of her time. Like d'*Aulnoy, d'*Auneuil, and Murat before her, Lubert writes tales that are sentimental love stories that highlight magical opponents and helpers. Yet, she adds more twists and turns to her plots and, especially, amplifies several stock features consecrated by her precursors. Magical objects and characters proliferate at every turn, which accentuates the implausibility of her stories. Lubert also delights in lengthy descriptions of luxurious but also horrifying settings. On the level of narrative structure, her stories place particular emphasis on the opposition between 'good' and 'evil'—so common to fairy tales—by multiplying the rivalries among characters. 'Prince Frozen and Princess Sparkling', for instance, features rivalries between the hero and another man, the heroine and another woman, two fairies, as well as a sorcerer and a sylph. Particularly noteworthy is the frequency with which Lubert depicts conflicts among fairies, who are decidedly more ambivalent than their counterparts in late 17th-century fairy tales. These and other characteristics exaggerate the implausibility of the obstacles to love and, thus, underscore their phantasmagorical quality. Sometimes these obstacles include monstrosity if not sadism, as in 'Princess Camion'. In whatever form, they always give the *appearance* that the lovers are incompatible, an appearance Lubert is careful to sustain until the last possible moment. Thus, in 'Dry and Black', the heroine, destined to love a man who does not love her, is eventually united with the hero, whose indifference was only caused by a fairy's spell.

In the preface to 'Dry and Black', Lubert is the first writer to defend the fairy tale in terms of pleasure alone. It is not surprising, then, that didacticism is not much in evidence in her tales. Nor is it surprising that they contain highly original and often comical situations and characters that none the less conform to the fundamental structure of the wonder tale. In the end, Lubert's corpus is perhaps best described as playful. Her light-hearted approach to the genre and its conventions borders—but never crosses the line of—parody. For enthusiasts and detractors alike, hers were the epitome of nonparodic, non-satirical literary fairy tales in 18th-century France. LCS

Duggan, Maryse-Madeleine-Elisabeth, 'Les Contes de Mlle de Lubert: les textualités du ludique' (Diss., University of British Columbia, 1996).

Lynch, P. J. (Patrick James Lynch, 1962–) Irish illustrator. He was born in Belfast and received his art education there and in England. While not all of his work has focused on fairy-tale material, he has shown a particular affinity with this genre. Among the most striking of his illustrations have been those for William Butler *Yeats's *Fairy Tales of Ireland* (1990; a compendium of *Fairy and Folk Tales of the Irish Peasantry* and *Irish Fairy Tales*), Oscar *Wilde's *Stories for Children* (1990), Hans Christian *Andersen's **The Steadfast Tin Soldier* (1991) and **The Snow Queen* (1993), the traditional *East o' the Sun and West o' the Moon* (1991), and *The Candlewick Book of Fairy Tales* (1995). RD

Lynch, Patricia (1894–1972) Irish children's writer. She was born in Cork and spent her early years moving between Ireland, England, Scotland, and Belgium, before eventually returning to settle in her native land in the 1920s. As her autobiographical *A Story-Teller's Childhood* (1947) makes clear, she grew up in Cork in an environment where the oral and literary tradition of native story was remarkably strong.

In particular, she pays tribute to a Mrs Hennessy, described as 'a shanachie, one of the real old story-tellers', who was a very strong influence on the young child, transmitting to her a wonderful treasure of Irish stories and imbuing her with what was to be a lifelong fascination with them. In virtually all of the 50 or so children's novels which Lynch wrote, this indebtedness to childhood memories of story is obvious, affecting even those of her books which set out to be realistic in tone and setting. Her fictional world is a place where reality and fantasy are very closely linked, and the picture of Ireland which emerges is of a place where the possibilities of magical experience are to be found around every corner. Many of her full-length fantasy stories are, in effect, extended fairy tales, testifying to Lynch's fondness for employing the structures and motifs of the genre. Her most successful books in this category include *The Grey Goose of Kilnevin* (1939) and *Jinny the Changeling* (1959), both characterized by a Yeatsian sense of longing to recapture a lost childhood. In a lengthy sequence of novels, especially popular in Ireland over a number of generations, she featured the adventures of the fairy folk who live in the Fort of Sheen, especially those involving Brogeen, the leprechaun cobbler. Among the best known of these titles are *Brogeen Follows the Magic Tune* (1952), *Brogeen and the Green Shoes* (1953), and *Brogeen and the Lost Castle* (1956). Several of the characters from these stories appear also in various Lynch novels dealing with the resourceful and omniscient Long Ears, the donkey making his debut in 1934 in *The Turf-Cutter's Donkey*. These and the Brogeen books are typified by a level of activity which borders on the frenetic and by a fondness for the kind of transformational magic which ensures a rapidly changing plotline. In addition to these full-length novels, Lynch produced a collection of 19 short stories entitled *The Seventh Pig and Other Irish Fairy Tales* (1950), subsequently reissued (with one extra story, 'The Fourth Man') as *The Black Goat of Slievemore and Other Irish Fairy Tales* (1959). The stories in these volumes (dedicated, incidentally, to her old mentor, Mrs Hennessy) rank among Lynch's greatest achievements, combining her usual exuberance with a discipline in the telling and a sense of other-world atmosphere which is frequently haunting. The emphasis in such stories as 'The Shadow Pedlar', 'The Cave of the Seals', and 'The Golden Comb' is on the misty veil which separates our waking existence from our dreams and on the sadness which marks our understanding of the differences between them. RD

Watson, Nancy, 'A Revealing and Exciting Experience: Three of Patricia Lynch's Children's Novels', *The Lion and the Unicorn*, 21.3 (September 1997).

Maar, Paul (1937–) German author, translator, and illustrator of children's books for all ages, who also scripts plays for radio, theatre, film, and television. Maar has created the libretto for an opera and musicals and designed sets for the theatre. He had great success with his first book, *Der tätowierte Hund* (*The Tattooed Dog*, 1968), a tale about bad *Hansel and Gretel and the good witch. But by far his most popular fictional creation is the 'Sams', an uppity fantastic creature with blue spots who represents Mr Taschenbier's suppressed ego in *Eine Woche voller Samstage* (*A Week Full of Saturdays*, 1973), *Am Samstag kam das Sams zurück* (*Sams Returned on Saturday*, 1980), and *Neue Punkte für das Sams* (*New Spots for Sams*, 1992). In 1996 Maar was awarded the Deutscher Jugendliteraturpreis (German Prize for Children's and Youth Literature) for the entire body of his work.   EMM

Tabbert, Reinbert, 'Kindergeschichten von Paul Maar—nicht nur für Kinder', *Kinderbuchanalysen I* (1989).

McCarthy, Paul (1945–) American multimedia contemporary artist, known for his irreverent and witty critiques of American popular culture, especially Disney fairy-tale film icons. His 2013 multimedia exhibition 'White Snow' ('WS') presents a sexually explicit re-evaluation of *'Snow White' that provides social commentary on consumer excess. McCarthy includes himself in some photographs as 'Walt Paul', a fictional persona that, as McCarthy claims, combines Walt Disney, Hugh Hefner, and Adolf Hitler.   MF

McCay, Winsor (1867–1934) American pioneer of comic books and animation. He began his career as editorial cartoonist for the *Cincinnati Commercial Tribune* in 1898 and drew national attention with his experimental cartoon strip 'The Tales of the Jungle Imps by Felix Fiddle' in 1903. As a result, the *New York Herald Tribune* offered him a job, and his first major work was a cartoon strip for adults, *Dreams of the Rarebit Fiend* (1904), composed of nightmare episodes with characters in excruciating situations. Soon afterward McCay became famous for his creation of *Little Nemo in Slumberland* (1905–11), which was continued in William Randolph Hearst's *New York American* as *In the Land of Wonderful Dreams* (1911–14), and then concluded in the *Herald Tribune* under the original title (1924–7). Influenced by Art Nouveau, McCay drew meticulously intricate scenes describing the fantastic voyages and adventures of his protagonist Little Nemo. The plots ranged from dream fantasies to futuristic sketches based on science fiction and appealed to children and adults. All McCay's stories about Little Nemo have a fairy-tale quality to them, but he transcended the traditional stories and brilliantly adapted the fairy-tale motifs to modern developments. A prolific artist and inventor, McCay did almost all the drawings for a series of animated films (*Little Nemo*, 1911, *How a Mosquito Operates*, 1912, *Gertie the Dinosaur*, 1914, and *The Sinking of the Lusitania*, 1918), which are unusual for their graphic details, extraordinary plots, and burlesque humour. Unfortunately, McCay, who set high standards of quality for animation, abandoned this medium after 1918 and worked primarily as a comic strip artist and illustrator until the end of his life.   JZ

Canemaker, John, *Winsor McCay: His Life and Art* (1987).

McDermott, Gerald (1941–2012) American film-maker and writer and illustrator of children's books and mythology. An early prodigy in Detroit where he studied art at the Detroit Institute of Arts, acted in plays, and made films while in high school, McDermott went on to study on the Pratt Institute of Art in New York City, where he produced his first animated film, *The Stonecutter*, based on a Japanese folk tale. After graduation from Pratt in 1964, he produced three more animated films, *Sunflight* (1966), *Anansi the Spider* (1969), and *The Magic Tree* (1970), all based on folk or fairy tales. By 1972, he had begun his successful career as an illustrator and/or writer. He had a special affinity for trickster tales, and among the books he adapted and illustrated were *Papagayo, the Mischief Maker* (a Brazilian folktale, 1980), *Raven, A Trickster Tale from the Pacific Northwest* (1993), *Jabuti, the Tortoise, a Trickster Tale from the Amazon* (2001), and *Monkey, a Trickster Tale from India* (2011). As an illustrator he collaborated with Marianne Mayer on *The Adventures of Pinocchio* (1981), *Aladdin and the Enchanted Lamp* (1985), and *The Spirit of Blue Light* (1985). In addition to all these accomplishments, McDermott wrote two works consisting of mythological creation stories and books that dealt with his Irish heritage such as *Daniel O'Rourke* (1986) and *Tim O'Toole and the Wee Folk* (1990). Among the finest American award-winning author/illustrators, McDermott was known for his visual storytelling and witty illustrations. JZ

MacDonald, George (1824–1905) Scottish author of many notable fantasies. He was born in Huntly, Aberdeenshire, where his family attended the Missionary Kirk, whose Calvinistic teaching MacDonald was later to discard, though traces of this can be found in the retribution theme in a few of his children's stories, notably *The Wise Woman* (1875).

His mother died when he was 8, and, significantly, his fantasy works were to be peopled with beautiful women who appear to symbolize a semi-divine motherhood. Educated at King's College, Aberdeen, where he was already regarded as a visionary, he was, through family money troubles,

obliged to spend one of his undergraduate years 'in a nobleman's mansion' cataloguing the library. This has never been identified, but it is probable that it was Thurso Castle, owned by Sir George Sinclair, whose father had been a German scholar, educated at Göttingen, and that it was here that MacDonald first encountered the works of such writers as *Novalis, *Hoffmann, *Tieck, and de la Motte *Fouqué who were to have such an influence on his writing. After less than two years at Highbury Theological College, where he left without receiving a degree, he was ordained as a Congregational minister, and took over the charge of a chapel at Arundel, Sussex. But his unorthodoxy displeased the congregation and he resigned in 1853.

Thereafter he depended on writing and lecturing for a living, which for many years was very meagre. *Phantastes*, subtitled 'a faerie romance', his earliest prose work, was published in 1858. It is a quest story, ostensibly for a beautiful marble lady, but behind this it is a search for spiritual perfection, and a repudiation of Calvinism which seems to be represented by the idol that Anodos topples in the last pages. Anodos makes his way into fairyland through the agency of a fairy woman, the prototype of the grandmother figures of his fantasies. (His Greek name is usually translated as 'pathless', a rare usage, and is much more likely to be intended as 'a spiritual ascent', one of its other meanings.) In a series of dreamlike adventures he acquires a malignant black shadow that blights and diminishes everything it falls upon, and when he finally awakes in the ordinary world, it is only to find that this has gone. 'Thus I, who set out to find my Ideal, came back rejoicing that I had lost my Shadow.' It was the first MacDonald work that C. S. *Lewis encountered, and was to have a profound influence on him.

Lilith (1895), MacDonald's only other fantasy for adults, was his last major work, and like *Phantastes* is an exploration of the unconscious. It took him five years to write and went through eight drafts. Full of sexual imagery, it was much disliked by his wife, who at this stage of his life was increasingly

MacDonald, George The prince is astonished to see the floating princess in George MacDonald's 'The Light Princess', published in *The Light Princess and Other Stories* (1862), illustrated by Arthur *Hughes.

disturbed by his state of mind. Lilith (a name uncomfortably like that of Lilia, his much-loved dead daughter) is the demon figure of Jewish mythology, used by MacDonald to represent death as well as sexual desire. It is another spiritual journey where Vane, the central character, moves through a night-mare landscape from which he can only es-cape when the evil in Lilith has been exorcized. As he at last seems to be entering Paradise, he wakes. The book finishes with a quotation from Novalis: 'Our life is no dream, but it should and will perhaps be-come one.'

The theme of a search for spirituality re-curs in most of MacDonald's fairy stories for children, which like *Phantastes* are full of hidden symbolic meaning, but cannot prop-erly be called allegories. His first children's novel, *At the Back of the North Wind* (serial-ized in *Good Words* 1868–9, published 1871) has as its central character a Christ-like child (a feature also of MacDonald's *Sir Gibbie*, 1879) regarded by those around him as sim-ple. The North Wind visits him at night and sweeps him off to her own country, which MacDonald himself likens to Dante's Purga-tory. She is a mother-figure, but also a per-sonification of death. (Arthur *Hughes did striking illustrations for this book and the two that follow.) Finally she carries him off for ever. 'They thought he was dead. I knew he had gone to the back of the north wind.'

Only Diamond sees the North Wind, and in *The Princess and the Goblin* (serialized in *Good Words* 1870–1, published 1872) the Princess Irene alone can see the glorious being who calls herself Irene's great-great-grandmother. Her nurse is angry and con-temptuous, and Curdie the miner's son, still earthbound, can only see a bare garret with a tub, a heap of musty straw and a withered apple. In the sequel *The Princess and Curdie* (serialized 1877, published 1883) Curdie, growing out of sceptical adolescence, sees the grandmother at last, and though at first she seems a bent old woman, as he watches she becomes beautiful and straight and strong. The unusual presence of mines and miners in these two books, and indeed Mac-Donald's frequent use of mountains as a

setting, owe much to German romantic writ-ing such as Novalis's *Heinrich von Ofterdin-gen* and E. T. A. Hoffmann's 'The Mines of Falun'.

'The Golden Key', a short story first pub-lished in *Dealings with the Fairies* (1867), is the most concise and accessible of all Mac-Donald's fantasies. Here two children, Mossy and Tangle, set out to find the lock which their golden key will open, and which they hope will bring them into a land where the beautiful shadows they have seen on the journey at last become reality. They grow old as they go, become separated, but at the last stage Mossy finds Tangle waiting for him, and they climb together up the stairs out of the earth: 'They knew they were going up to the country whence the shadows fall.'   GA

Carpenter, Humphrey, 'George MacDonald and the Tender Grandmother', in *Secret Gardens* (1985).

Goldthwaite, John, 'The Name of the Muse', in *The Natural History of Make-Believe* (1996).

Raeper, William, *George MacDonald* (1987).

Raeper, William (ed.), *The Gold Thread: Essays on George MacDonald* (1990).

McKillip, Patricia A. (1948–) American writer of fantasy novels for children and adults. While none of McKillip's many fine books are direct retellings of fairy tales, this author's prose is so thoroughly steeped in the language of folk and fairy tales that all of her work has the flavour of stories passed down through the generations. McKillip es-tablished her reputation with the award-winning novel *The Forgotten Beasts of Eld* (1974), a mysterious tale of a young enchant-ress who wields a powerful magic yet lies emotionally frozen, awaiting the kiss that will wake her human heart. *The Riddlemas-ter Trilogy* (1976–9) uses riddles and snip-pets of invented folklore as it follows a poetic young prince on a quest—and his stubbornly down-to-earth sister, engaged in a quest of her own. The award-winning *Something Rich and Strange* (1994), based on fairy art by Brian Froud, spins mermaid tales, British fairy lore, and oceanography into a romantic contemporary story set on the coast of the Pacific Northwest. *The Book* *of Atrix Wolfe* (1995) makes beautiful use of the 'lost child' theme in an original adult fairy tale set in a woodland of wolves and magicians. 'The Lion and the Lark' (1995) reworks motifs from 'East of the Sun, West of the Moon'. *Winter Rose* (1996) is not only the author's finest work to date, but the one most closely aligned to a single fairy-tale theme. This novel, set in an English wood, makes skilful use of traditional 'Tam Lin' material—written in the gorgeously sensual prose which has earned McKillip recognition as a modern master of the fantasy form. TW

McKinley, Robin (Jennifer Carolyn McKinley, 1952–) American fantasy writer for young adults. McKinley's work falls into two overlapping categories: the fictionalization of fairy tales and the creation of fantasy kingdoms. Prominent among the former are her novels based on *'Beauty and the Beast', Beauty* (1978) and *Rose Daughter* (1997), both realizing Beauty—in different depths of detail—as the strong, independent central figure of a fantastical romance, with the 1997 version harbouring a surprise conclusion. *Deerskin* (1993), patterned on *Perrault's *'Donkey-Skin', explores faerie's darker side in portraying the heroine's escape from her father's incestuous rage. McKinley's fast-paced fantasy *The Blue Sword* (1982) and its sequel *The Hero and the Crown* (1984), which won the Newbery Honor and Newbery Medal respectively, develop the kingdom of Damar as the setting for exploits by two bold young women, Hari (or 'Harry', as she prefers to be called) the warrior and Aerin the dragon slayer. McKinley's signature creation is a blend of the magical and the mundane in the shape of dramatic, resourceful, adventurous heroines who begin with a mark against them and end triumphantly, with a true love as well. It is an appealing formula that she fosters smoothly and imaginatively, often with a prominent animal helper in the form of a beloved dog or horse, along with various symbolic objects. In *Spindle's End* (2000), an adaptation of *'Sleeping Beauty', the princess is raised without knowing her parents and the curse. It is only when she discovers her true identity that her troubles begin. However, an animal helper comes to her rescue. One of McKinley's collections of short stories, *The Door in the Hedge* (1981), incorporates several fairy-tale retellings, while *A Knot in the Grain and Other Stories* (1994) features stories from Damar. She has also written a number of fantasy novels, *Sunshine* (2003), *Dragonhaven* (2007), *Chalice* (2008), and *Shadows* (2013), which are rich in fairy-tale motifs. BH

Cadden, Michael, 'The Illusion of Control: Narrative Authority in Robin McKinley's *Beauty and The Blue Sword'*, *Mythlore*, 76 (spring 1994).

Cadden, Michael, 'Home Is a Matter of Blood, Time, and Genre: Essentialism in Burnett and McKinley', *Ariel*, 28.1 (1997).

Hains, Maryellen, 'Beauty and the Beast: 20th Century Romance?', *Merveilles et Contes*, 3.1 (May 1989).

Rutledge, Amelia, 'Robin McKlinley's *Deerskin*: Challenging Narcissisms', *Marvels & Tales* (2001).

Woolsey, Daniel P., 'The Realm of Fairy Story: J. R. R. Tolkien and Robin McKinley's *Beauty'*, *Children's Literature in Education*, 22.2 (June 1991).

MacManus, Seumas (*c*.1868–1960) Irish dramatist, poet, and prolific writer of popular stories, who played an important role in the rise of Irish national literature. Son of a poor farmer, MacManus became a schoolteacher in County Donegal and began contributing articles and stories to many Irish newspapers in the 1890s. Some of his best retellings of Irish fairy tales are in *In Chimney Corners: Merry Tales of Irish Folk-lore* (1899). During the 20th century MacManus travelled back and forth between Ireland and the United States and became one of the most popular interpreters of Irish folklore for Americans through his collections of tales. Among his best works are *The Bewitched Fiddle and Other Irish Tales* (1900), *Donegal Fairy Stories* (1900), *Tales that Were Told* (1920), *The Donegal Wonder Book* (1926), *Tales from Ireland* (1949), and *The Bold Heroes of Hungry Hill, and Other Irish Folk Tales* (1951). Though MacManus often exaggerated the Irish aspects of the tales with a mannered style, he also expanded upon the Irish fairy-tale tradition in innovative ways. JZ

McNeal, Tom (1950–) American writer who has written a number of books and stories for young adults. His unique fairytale novel, *far far away* (2013), delves into the 'secret' life of Jacob *Grimm and portrays him as more sensitive and fallible than most biographies about this famous 'bachelor', which generally depict him as a supremely confident and unperturbed scholar. In McNeal's tour-de-force work, however, he transforms Jacob Grimm into a very sympathetic ghost who undertakes the task of protecting a young nerdy teenager named Jeremy Johnson living in a small town called Never Better, a microcosmic representation of American small-town life that bears the marks of petty minds and generous hearts at the same time. Throughout the novel, McNeal introduces relevant Grimm tales to guide Jacob and Jeremy, and even Jacob learns to listen to tales that he never really appreciated. Reintroducing Jacob Grimm to the tales that he collected and that still maintain their deep value and power in contemporary times forms the unusual quality of his exceptional novel.   JZ

Maeterlinck, Maurice (1862–1949) Belgian poet, playwright, and essayist. Consistent with his ties to the symbolist movement, Maeterlinck displays a distinct attraction for fantasy, dreams, and the imaginary throughout his *œuvre*. Going against the prevailing *fin-de-siècle* theatrical aesthetic of realism and naturalism, many of his plays draw on pseudo-chivalric romance and folklore (e.g. *Les Sept Princesses* (*The Seven Princesses*, 1891), *Pelléas et Mélisande* (1893), *Ariane et Barbe-Bleue* (1901). Maeterlinck's most famous fairy-tale work is *L'Oiseau bleu* (*The *Blue Bird*, 1909), a play for children. The plot, which bears no resemblance to the tale by d'*Aulnoy with the same title, concerns two children, Tyltyl and Mytyl, who are sent by the fairy Bérylune to find the Blue Bird that will cure her sick daughter. In many magical adventures, the children are set against forces of darkness, and at one point the Blue Bird plots to keep Tyltyl and Mytyl from learning the 'great secret of all things and happiness' which it holds. The children eventually return home, without the Blue Bird, only to watch in amazement as their pet dove turns blue. Bérylune takes the Blue Bird home for her daughter, but it escapes, prompting Tyltyl at the end of the play to ask the audience to find it so that they can be happy. With the quest for the Blue Bird, Maeterlinck confirms the adage that 'the grass is not greener on the other side of the fence' and invites adults to discover spirituality through a childlike state of mind. Popular in the United States, *The Blue Bird* was twice made into a film (in 1940 and 1976). Maeterlinck wrote a much less successful sequel to this play, *Les Fiançailles* (*The Engagement*, 1922), in which Tyltyl is an adolescent in search of love.   LCS

Maguire, Gregory (1954–) American writer for adults and children who has published several important fairy-tale novels, adaptations of classical fairy tales. Among them are radical re-interpretations of *The *Wonderful Wizard of Oz*: Wicked: The Life and Times of the Wicked Witch of the West* (1995), *Son of a Witch* (2005), *A Lion Among Men* (2008), and *Out of Oz* (2011); a historical tragic rendition of *'Cinderella', called *Confessions of an Ugly Stepsister* (1999); and a more optimistic 16th-century adaptation of *'Snow White', with the title *Mirror, Mirror* (2003). Two of his books for children include delightful fairy tales: *Leaping Beauty: And Other Animal Fairy Tales* (2004) and *What-the-Dickens: The Story of a Rogue Tooth Fairy* (2007). His novel *Wicked* was turned into a very successful Broadway musical in 2003. In all his works, Maguire shows a distinct disposition to defend outsiders and underdogs, including sentient animals. Unlike L. Frank *Baum's utopian vision, Maguire's perspective in writing his series of Oz adaptations called *The Wicked Years* is somewhat critical, if not realist and dystopian.   JZ

Mahfouz, Naguib (1911–2006) Nobel Prize-winning and prolific Egyptian novelist. *Arabian Nights and Days*, the 1995 English translation of his 1982 novel *Layali Alf Layla* (literally 'The Nights of the Thousand Nights'), adapts *The *Arabian Nights* from within the Islamic tradition, rather than from an orientalizing (John *Barth) or a hybridizing (Salman *Rushdie) perspective. It explores what happens after the happy ending, what Shahryar must do to purify himself, and how ordinary people succumb to and struggle against the power abuses and corruption of absolutism. The Café of the Emirs, rather than the Sultan's palace, is the storytelling heart of the novel. Mahfouz retells specific tales (e.g. 'Marouf the Cobbler', 'The Pseudo-Caliph', the Jewish Doctor's tale in the Hunchback's cycle) and traces Sufi-based spiritual transformations, as both 'believing' and mischievous genies test the minds and souls of humans.

The author of more than 30 novels, ranging from historical to socialist and existentialist, and of several volumes of short stories, Mahfouz was also an active journalist. His well-known *Cairo Trilogy* was serialized for the Cairo daily. A defender of Rushdie in 1989, Mahfouz continued to promote the coexistence of religion and democracy within Islam. Condemned as a blasphemer by one religious group for his controversial novel translated as *Children of Gebelawi* (1981), he survived an attempt on his life in 1994.   CB

Al-Mousa, Nedal, 'The Nature and Uses of the Fantastic in the Fictional World of Naguib Mahfouz', *Journal of Arabic Literature*, 23.1 (1992).

Mahy, Margaret (1936–2012) New Zealand author of juvenile fiction. A children's librarian, Mahy counts the Order of New Zealand among her awards for folklore and fantasy for all reading levels. Her humorous and didactic picture books were illustrated by award-winning artists (Quentin *Blake, Steven Kellogg), and she twice won the Carnegie Medal for young adult novels about family relationships (*The Haunting*, 1982; *The Changeover: A Supernatural Romance*, 1984). A fairy tale of sorts, *The Changeover*'s metatextual references to *Alice in Wonderland*, *The Wizard of Oz* and *'Sleeping Beauty' underscore the heroine's inner journey (from mortal to witch, from child to adult) as she awakens the magical powers within.   MLE

Lawrence-Pietroni, Anna, 'The Trickster, the Changeover, and the Fluidity of Adolescent Literature', *Children's Literature Association Quarterly* (1995).

Norton, Lucy, 'Seeing is Believing: Magical Realism and Visual Narrative in Margaret Mahy's *The Changeover*', *Bookbird* (1998).

Wilkie-Stibbs, Christine. '"Body Language": Speaking the Feminine in Young Adult Fiction'. *Children's Literature Association Quarterly* (2000).

Mailly, Jean, chevalier de (?–1724) French writer. A military officer and godson of Louis XIV, Mailly published widely, including a collection of 11 fairy tales, *Les Illustres Fées, contes galans* (*The Illustrious Fairies, Galant Tales*, 1698). (It is uncertain whether or not he contributed to a later collection, *Nouveau recueil de contes de fées* (*New Collection of Fairy Tales*, 1730).) In *The Illustrious Fairies* Mailly displays a wide knowledge of the literary (and perhaps folkloric) sources of the 17th-century French 'vogue' of fairy tales. For example, at least three of the tales in this volume ('Fortunio', 'Blanche Belle' ('White Beauty'), and 'Le Prince Guerini') are versions of stories found in *Straparola's *Pleasant Nights*; the plots of 'White Beauty' and 'Guerini' are also retold by his contemporaries d'*Aulnoy and *Murat; and four of Mailly's tales have discernible folkloric traces (the aforementioned, plus 'Le Bienfaisant ou Quiribirini' ('The Benefactor or Quiribirini'). In addition, his stories feature a wide range of the motifs commonly found in fairy tales of the period, including chivalric adventures, cabbalistic magic, enchanted islands, metamorphosis, and metempsychosis. Mailly makes frequent and deft use of the last two. In both 'Le Prince Roger' and 'Le Roi magicien' ('The Magician King'), for example, a main character changes form to pursue love interests. And in 'The Benefactor or Quiribirini' the power of souls to travel from body to body is central to the plot. Metamorphosis of a more figurative kind occurs in 'Le Prince Guerini' when the hero, an uncouth but gentle 'savage', blossoms into a predictably incomparable hero-prince. Without being parodic, many of Mailly's tales treat fairy-tale scenarios with humour. Indeed, his tales often make use of 'galanterie', a refined but light-hearted deference for women that is none the less androcentric; hence, the tongue-in-cheek criticism of husbands who do not tolerate their wives' extramarital affairs in 'White Beauty'. For their variety and humour, Mailly's fairy tales evince a conception of the genre shared by d'Aulnoy, *La Force, and *Perrault.   LCS

Hannon, Patricia, 'Feminine Voice and the Motivated Text: Mme d'Aulnoy and the Chevalier de Mailly', *Merveilles et Contes*, 2.1 (1988).

Maitland, Sara (1950–) British writer of novels and stories who experiments with fairy tales and magic realism. In 2003 she published a collection of short stories, *On Becoming a Fairy Godmother*, which deals with menopausal woman. In *Far North & Other Dark Tales* (2008) she re-creates dark mythological tales taken from around the world. One of her tales, 'True North', was made into a film in 2007. In *Gossip from the Forest: The Tangled Roots of Our Forests and Fairytales* (2012), a highly original and poetical rendition of twelve Grimms' fairy tales, she weaves stunning essays about the relationship of the tales to British forests. Her observations of places, plants, trees, and animals are subtly embedded in her stories, which lend a new vitality to the Grimms' 19th-century tales. Moreover, Maitland does not shy away from a political critique of deforestation and other 'inhumane' ways in which we regard and treat our natural environment. There is also a strong feminist current in her essays and tales.   JZ

Malamud, Bernard (1914–86) American writer known for his novels and tales based on Jewish social and cultural experience. Malamud made his reputation with the novel *The Assistant* (1957), which uses the legend of St Francis of Assisi to address questions of anti-Semitism and Jewish identity in New York during the 1930s. In two superb collections of stories, *The Magic Barrel* (1958) and *Idiots First* (1963), he draws upon eastern European folklore, Franz *Kafka, and New York Jewish humour to create unique kinds of stories and modern fairy tales. Thus, in 'The Jewbird', a talking bird named Schwartz flies into the kitchen of the Cohen family to escape anti-Semeets (anti-Semites) but ironically meets his end in the hands of the Jewish salesman Cohen.   JZ

Malerba, Luigi (1927–2008) Contemporary Italian writer and screenwriter. His first book, *La scoperta dell'alfabeto* (*The Discovery of the Alphabet*, 1963), which anticipates the fantastic type of narrative that he later develops, is a collection of tales in which the old Ambanelli decides to learn how to read and write when he discovers that he can move around the letters of the alphabet. The novel *Il serpente* (*The Serpent*, 1966) deals with a stamp collector who realizes that, by using his imagination, he can become a king, an explorer, an emperor—anything he wishes.

Malerba's 'Millemosche' ('A Thousand Flies'), a series of stories for children written in cooperation with Tonino Guerra in 1969, was published under the title *Storie dell'anno Mille* (*Stories of the Year One Thousand*, 7 vols., 1973). This work together with *Mozziconi* (1975) represents the author's attempt to try to reach young people and propose to them an alternative type of reading. 'Millemosche' is also an attempt to reread history from the lower ranks of society. The three protagonists, Millemosche, Pannocchia ('Cob') and Carestia ('Famine') are unable to defeat their hunger, and through their eyes we relive the Middle Ages from the point of view of the oppressed. Mozziconi ('Butts') is an uprooted person, a *clochard* who decides to dismantle his house and throw everything out of the window, and then the window itself. This way he can create his fairy tale and enter it. Something similar takes place in *Pinocchio con gli stivali* (*Pinocchio with the Boots*, 1977), in which *Pinocchio leaves his own fairy tale and enters that of *Little Red Riding Hood, *Cinderella, and then is brought back by guards to the same point from which he departed, between chapters 35 and 36. Malherba's stories deal with the question of freedom and of creating one's own fairy tale in the modern world.

The author's predilection for this type of narrative is evident in his other collections of stories such as: *Le rose imperiali* (*The Imperial Roses*, 1975), *Storiette* (*Little Stories*, 1977), and *Nuove storie dell'anno Mille* (*New Stories of the Year 1000*, 1981). *Storiette e storiette tascabili* (*Little Stories and Pocket Stories*, 1994) contain perhaps the author's best modern tales, from 'La favola di Orestone', in which the father writes a fairy tale for his son, to 'La maiala' ('The Sow'), the story of a professor of letters, history, and geography who goes to teach every day to take revenge on her husband.   GD

Cannon, JoAnn, *Postmodern Italian Fiction: The Crisis of Reason in Calvino, Eco, Sciascia, Malerba* (1989).
Colonna, Marco (ed.), *Luigi Malerba* (1994).
Sora, S., *Modalitäten des Komischen: Eine Studie zu Luigi Malerba* (1989).

Mameli, Paolo (1956–) Italian illustrator, graphic artist, and writer, who has focused on comic adaptations of classic fairy tales in two books, *Storie così: Ciniche e spietate realtà tra principesse, lupi e giganti* (*Stories Like This: Cynical and Cruel Reality Tales among Princesses, Wolves, and Giants*, 2005) and ... *E Biancaneve Avvelenò la Strega: 32 Meta-fiabe Disincantate tra Cinismo, Dabbenna-gine E...Sfiga* (*And Snow White Poisoned the Witch: 32 Disenchanted Meta-Fairy Tales amidst Cynicism, Simple Mindedness and...Misfortune*, 2012). Mameli illustrates and rewrites tales and fables from the works of Aesop, Charles *Perrault, the Brothers *Grimm, Hans Christian *Andersen, and Andrew *Lang with an ironic emphasis on the realistic and humorous aspects of the characters and incidents.   JZ

Mardrus, Joseph Charles (1848–1949) Caucasian doctor and scholar born in Cairo, responsible for an important French translation of *Les Mille et Une Nuits* (*Thousand and One Nights*, 1899–1904) based primarily on the 1835 Egyptian edition of *The *Arabian Nights* by Boulak. Mardrus studied classics and Arabic literature in Beirut, and went on to receive a doctorate in medicine at the Sorbonne in 1895. While working as a doctor on shipping lines, which took him from the Middle East to South-East Asia, he began to translate and publish *Les Mille et Une Nuits*, the revenues from which allowed him to settle permanently in Paris by 1899. Within Parisian literary circles, Mardrus frequented Stéphane Mallarmé, Paul Valéry, Maurice *Maeterlinck, André Gide, and Marcel *Schwob, and dedicated to each of them a volume of his 16-volume work. Mardrus's translation became the object of critical debate, which opposed the partisans of Antoine *Galland, who claimed the superiority of the latter's classical style, to those who favoured Mardrus's more sensual, unexpurgated version. Unlike Galland, Mardrus did not Frenchify the Arabian tales but retained much of their cultural specificity.   AD

Marie de France 12th-century French poet. The first known European woman writer to compose vernacular narrative poetry, Marie was best known for her Aesop-based *Fables* and her twelve widely translated *Lais* (*c.*1160–1215). Short verse romances, the *Lais* are sophisticated retellings of traditional Breton oral lais. In several, the supernatural plays a key role: 'Lanval', a fairy bride story whose hero is one of Arthur's knights; 'Bisclavret', the story of a virtuous werewolf; and 'Yonec', an animal-groom tale whose captive heroine is visited by a lover in the form of a hawk.   SR

Marinuzzi, Gino (1882–1945) Italian conductor and composer, widely praised for his conducting of *Wagner and Richard *Strauss, but also important as an interpreter of works by his countrymen, directing the première of *Puccini's *La rondine* in 1917. He studied at the Palermo Conservatory and made his conducting debut in Catania. Among the several posts he held was artistic director of Chicago Opera Association (1919–21), and chief conductor La Scala, Milan, from 1934. Active as a composer, he wrote the ballet *Le avventure di *Pinocchio*, which was later reworked by his son, Gino Marinuzzi (1920–), in 1956 and entitled *Pinocchio, storia di un burattino*.   TH

Marshak, Samuil (1887–1964) Russian children's writer and translator, one of the pioneers of Soviet children's literature. Besides being one of the foremost translators of *Shakespeare's sonnets into Russian, he translated English nursery rhymes and ballads, R. L. *Stevenson, *Kipling, Edward Lear, and A. A. *Milne. He wrote a number of original versified fairy tales, often featuring animals, for instance *The Tale of the Stupid Mouse* (1923), *The Tale of the Clever Mouse* (1956), or *Why the Cat was Called a Cat* (1939). Many of them are based on traditional Russian folk tales, as well as Ukrainian, Lithuanian, and *oriental folk and fairy tales. He has also retold in rhyme some fairy tales by Hans Christian *Andersen.

Most of his fairy tales are clearly didactic. For instance, in one of them animated books run away from a lazy and slovenly boy. Marshak has written several plays based on Slavic folk tales, the most famous being *The Twelve Months* (1943), a Slovak fairy tale, reminiscent of *'Mother Holle'; and an original play *Pussy-cat's House* (1945). Marshak's status in Russian children's literature is comparable to that of Milne in Britain or Dr *Seuss in the United States; his fairy tales are among the very first literary texts young readers encounter. As an editor of a literary magazine for children, and later the chairman of the Soviet Children's Writers' Guild, Marshak made an outstanding contribution to the promotion of Soviet fairy tales and the introduction of international fairy tales in the Soviet Union.   MN

Bode, Andreas, 'Humor in the Lyrical Stories for Children of Samuel Marshak and Korney Chukovsky', *The Lion and the Unicorn*, 13.2 (December 1989).

Marshall, James (James Edward Marshall, 1942–92) American author-illustrator of numerous books for young children. In addition to his popular 'Stupids' series (1974 onwards)—'simpleton' tales transposed to contemporary America—Marshall has reinterpreted several individual *Mother Goose rhymes and folk tales as humorous picture books. His colourful, cartoonlike illustrations expand and comment on the stories, à la *Caldecott—the cat tucked up with Granny in *Red Riding Hood* (1987), for example, or the crocodile hopefully pursuing the heroine on the last page, or the books piled by the three beds in *Goldilocks and the Three Bears* (1988).   SR

Martín Gaite, Carmen (1925–2000) Spanish writer highly regarded for her novels and short stories. She has also experimented with other literary genres, and her work in the field of children's literature is exemplified by fairy tales such as 'El castillo de las tres murallas' ('The Castle of the Three Walls', 1981) and 'El pastel del diablo' ('The Fiend's Cake', 1992). In addition, she is the author of *La reina de las nieves* (*The Snow Queen*, 1994), a novel based on Hans Christian *Andersen's *'The Snow Queen'. Of all her fairy stories, the most successful has been *Caperucita Roja en Manhattan* (*Little Red Riding Hood in Manhattan*, 1990), a short novel in which she rewrites the story of *'Little Red Riding Hood' with feminist overtones.   CFR

Masson, Sophie (1959–) Australian author, born in Indonesia of French parents, Masson is the author of over fifty novels, primarily for young adults and children, written mostly in various subgenres of speculative fiction, including fairy-tale fantasy. Her adaptations of fairy tales draw on various traditions and incorporate historical contexts transferred to an alternate world. Her narratives not only blend fairy tale and history, but also explore analogies with literary classics, as in *Cold Iron* (1998; also published as *Malkin*), which locates a blend of *Tattercoats* and *Shakespeare's *A Midsummer Night's Dream* in a parallel Elizabethan England. Classic fairy tales are often reworked as frames or pre-texts in highly inventive ways: *The Crystal Heart* (2014) blends *'Rapunzel', the Irish legend *Deirdre of the Sorrows*, and George *MacDonald's *The Princess and the Goblin*. Other classic tales adapted by Masson are *'Sleeping Beauty' in *Clementine* (1999), *'Puss-in-Boots in *Carabas* (1996; also published as *Serafin*), *'Cinderella' in *Moonlight and Ashes* (2012), and *'Beauty and the Beast' in *Scarlet in the Snow* (2013). The blending in *The Hollow Lands* (2004) of Breton folk-tale motifs and topoi with the medieval English proto-fairy tale, *The Marriage of Gawain and Dame Ragnell*, along with Scottish folklore and French history, shows Masson at her most creative. JAS

Mateos, Aurora (no dates available) Spanish 20th-century writer. For years she was the editor of *Bazar*, a magazine for adolescent girls that began to be published after the Spanish Civil War (1936–9) and became a transmitter of the feminine ideal as it was defined by the official ideologists of Franco's military regime. In *Bazar*, Mateos published children's plays, saints' lives, and numerous fairy tales of her own. Two recurring characters in Mateos's works became very well known: Doña Sabionda, a good-hearted and plump fairy, and Guillermina, a candid and naughty girl whose life was full of adventures. A great number of Mateos's plays can be considered as fairy tales in dramatic form. Some examples of these are: *La hija de Blanca Nieves* (*Snow White's Daughter*, 1947), *El reino de la felicidad* (*The Kingdom of Happiness*, 1948), and *La princesa Remilgadina* (*Princess Remilgadina*, 1949). CFR

Matthiessen, Wilhelm (1891–1965) German writer and librarian. Although his popularity has waned, Matthiessen was once among the best-selling authors for children, with a vast production of quaint fairy tales that includes: *Das alte Haus* (*The Old House*, 1923), *Deutsche Hausmärchen* (*German Household Fairy Tales*, 1927), *Turm der alten Mutter* (*Tower of the Old Mother*, 1930), *Die grüne Schule* (*The Green School*, 1931), and *Die alte Gasse* (*The Old Alley*, 1931), *Das geheimnisvolle Königreich* (*The Mysterious Kingdom*, 1933), and *Die glücklichen Inseln* (*The Happy Islands*, 1949). Most of these collections of tales are set in frame narratives and take place in a mysterious realm called 'Mythikon'. Matthiessen was fond of repeatedly introducing the same anthropomorphized characters, among them little firemen, cellar men, mother pine tree, and the great magician ventilator into his tales. These had a clear symbolical relationship to Aryan mythology and mysticism. JZ

Matute, Ana María (1925–2014) One of the most talented 20th-century novelists in Spain. She received numerous literary awards, including the Cervantes Award in 1959. Besides writing novels for adults, Matute is well known for her children's stories in which she made frequent use of traditional fairy-tale motifs and stylistic features. Among Matute's fairy tales are: 'El aprendiz' ('The Apprentice', 1961), 'Caballito loco' ('Crazy Little Horse', 1961), 'Carnavalito' ('Little Carnival', 1961), and 'El saltamontes verde' ('The Green Grasshopper', 1969). More recently, Matute participated in the fairy-tale revisionist trend popular in Western literature since the 1970s. Her contribution to this phenomenon is a rewriting of Charles *Perrault's 'The *Sleeping Beauty' entitled *La verdadera historia de la Bella Durmiente* (*Sleeping Beauty's True Story*, 1995). In this short novel Matute tries to stick as closely as possible to her source, but she introduces certain changes. To start with, she pays little attention to the first part of the story that concludes when Beauty is wakened by the prince. She is mainly interested in narrating the second and least known part, that in which we are told about the prince's mother's murderous drives towards her grandchildren and daughter-in-law. Matute's major contribution consists in giving extra information on the biographies of the prince's parents. CFR

Ellenberger, Madeleine Michell, 'Reality and Fantasy in Three Tales for Children by Ana María Matute' (Diss., University of Virginia, 1973).

Ulyatt, Philomena, 'Allegory, Myth and Fable in the Work of Ana María Matute' (Diss., University of Newcastle upon Tyne, 1977).

Mayer, Charles-Joseph, chevalier de (1751–1825) French writer and editor of the 40-volume *Cabinet des fées* (1785–9). This massive collection brought together fairy tales written and published over a period of 100 years in France. Although Mayer rejected almost all 'licentious' tales, he nonetheless included *oriental fairy tales. In addition to his work as editor, Mayer also wrote for this collection useful biographical essays on 17th- and 18th-century writers of fairy tales and an essay ('Discours préliminaire') that is one of the first attempts at a critical synthesis of the literary fairy tale in France. Mayer speculates on the social and literary origins of the genre, defines its function as primarily didactic, and extols it as an expression of French refinement. Both this essay and the *Cabinet* as a whole are marked by a sense of nostalgia for (what is perceived to be) the decline of the French literary fairy tale at the end of the 18th century. However, this collection made it possible for a broad European public to become acquainted with the tradition of 17th- and 18th-century French fairy tales and was a particularly important source of inspiration for romantic fairy tales in Germany.   LCS

Mayer, Mercer (1943–) American author and illustrator of children's books. His father was in the navy, and Mayer spent his childhood in the South, and his adolescence in Hawaii. *Rackham, *Tenniel, Beardsley and *Ford were his favourite illustrators, and he studied at the Hawaii Academy of Arts and the Art Students' League in New York. He worked with an advertising agency before devoting himself full-time to his art.

Mayer has received numerous awards for his more than 100 books that humorously represent a child's world from a child's perspective. He developed the wordless children's picture book with *A Boy, a Dog, and a Frog* (1967), which led to a five-book series. Feeling more comfortable with words, he added text to plots with the classic *There's a Nightmare in my Closet* (1968; UK, *There's a Nightmare in my Cupboard*, 1969), eventually producing only the text for unconventional silliness, such as the *Appelard and Liverwurst* books illustrated by Steven Kellogg.

Mayer is best known for two self-illustrated series that address children's frustrations and fears. The *Little Monster* and *Little Critter* books with their menagerie of minority protagonists reject both racial and sex stereotyping, and feature topics ranging from jealousy of new siblings to the responsibility of keeping pets, to fear of the dentist. Important socialization tools, these mass-marketed titles target a variety of reading levels and media. In addition to books, there are audio cassettes, film adaptations, and interactive CD-ROMs (such as *Little Monster at School*, 1994; *The Smelly Mystery*, 1997).

In 1991 Mayer published three fairy-tale adaptations in the *Little Critter* series: *Little Red Riding Hood, *Hansel and Gretel*, and *Jack and the Beanstalk*. These highly detailed board books for toddlers all feature his 'Critter-Monster' style of deft, scratchy pen strokes and bold colours. Very different are his earlier books for older children, which feature a richly muted 'Victorian' palette and design: these include *The Sleeping Beauty* (1981) and *East of the Sun and West of the Moon* (1980), a Norwegian folk tale. He has also illustrated other authors' retellings of *Favorite Tales from Grimm* (1978) and *Beauty and the Beast* (1978). Retold by Marianna Mayer (his first wife), the latter shows the influence of *Villeneuve's version with its dreams of the prince and fairy warnings. Here, text and illustration beautifully complement each other as tension, foreboding, loneliness, and metamorphosis are dramatically reflected by foreshortened figures, Gothic surroundings, sombre colours, or Egyptian motifs of death and rebirth.   MLE

Hearne, Betsy, *Beauty and the Beast: Visions and Revisions of an Old Tale* (1989).

Lesniak, James, and Trosky, Susan M. (eds.), *Contemporary Authors*, New Revision Series, 38 (1993).

Montreville, Doris de, and Crawford, Elizabeth D., *Fourth Book of Junior Authors and Illustrators* (1978).

Meckel, Christoph (1935–) German writer and artist. Born in Berlin, Meckel studied graphics and painting in Freiburg and Munich. Aside from producing outstanding art work, Meckel has written experimental poetry, stories, and novels with strong surrealist and fairy-tale elements. Among his best works are *Tarnkappe* (*The Invisible Cap*, 1956), *Tullipan* (1965), *Kranich* (*Crane*, 1973), *Der wahre Muftoni* (*The True Muftoni*, 1982), and *Ein roter Faden* (*A Red Thread*, 1983). He has a predilection for the absurd situation, and his stories have a bizarre Kafkaesque quality to them. In 'Die Krähe' ('The Crow', 1962), for example, the narrator attempts to save a talking crow from persecution, but fails because of the prejudices of small-minded people.   JZ

Méliès, Georges (1861–1938) Influential French film producer and director of numerous films, many of which were adaptations of classical fairy tales. He was the accidental inventor of trick photography and thus what we today call special effects. Méliès's most famous fantasy film—or *féerie*—is undoubtedly the 30-scene science-fiction adventure *Le Voyage dans la lune* (*A Trip to the Moon*, 1902) in which a rocket launched from earth lands in the moon's eye. However, Méliès, a stage magician and illusionist by training

who became one of the first directors to use film techniques such as dissolve, time-lapse photography, and artificial lighting, also adapted *The Grasshopper and the Ant* (from Aesop's *Fables*) in 1897, made a 20-scene version of *Cendrillon* (**Cinderella*) in 1899, and completed versions of *Barbe-Bleue* (**Bluebeard*) and *Le Petit Chaperon Rouge* (**Little Red Riding Hood*) in 1901. In 1903, Méliès made *Kingdom of the Fairies*, 15 minutes long and 1,080 feet in length. He remade *Cinderella* in 1912.

Owner of the appropriately named Star Film company, Méliès, at his zenith between 1896 and 1902, influenced European and American directors. Edwin Porter, popularly known for his *Life of a Fireman* (1902) also made **Jack and the Beanstalk* in 1902. Porter's version of *Jack* is modelled on Méliès's version of *Bluebeard*. Ferdinand Zecca further developed the trick photography techniques 'invented' by Méliès in the fairy-tale adaptations *Ali Baba et les 40 Voleurs* (**Ali Baba and the Forty Thieves*) (1902) and *Aladin* (**Aladdin*) (1906). Charlie

Méliès, Georges The water fairy observes the shipwreck in Georges Méliès's film *The Kingdom of the Fairies* (1903).

Chaplin and D. W. Griffith ('I owe him everything') also testified to the influence of Méliès. The French film director René Clair's 1947 tribute to Méliès was called *Le Silence est d'or* (*Silence is Golden*). Initially, Méliès's films were so successful that they were pirated, until his brother, Gaston Méliès, began registering them with the Library of Congress.

Film historians argue that whilst the Lumières invented realist narratives, or *actualities*, in films like *Sortie des ouvriers de l'usine Lumière* (*Workers Leaving the Lumière Factory*) and *L'Arrivée d'un train en gare de la Ciotat* (*Train Arriving at the Station*), Méliès invented fantasy narratives. David Shipman writes: 'The Lumières photographed nature; Méliès photographed a reconstructed life.' Méliès was declared bankrupt in 1923—a fallen star. In true fairy-tale style, though, he later married Jeanne d'Alcy, a former actress and protégée. For his considerable contributions to film, including the fairy-tale film, Méliès was awarded a Legion of Honour medal in 1931.   IWA

Ezra, Elizabeth, *Georges Méliès: The Birth of the Auteur* (2000).

Hammond, Paul, *Marvellous Méliès* (1974).

Jenn, Pierre, *Georges Méliès cinéaste* (1984).

McKlaren, Norman, 'Homage to Georges Méliès,' in David Shepard (ed.), *Georges Méliès: First Wizard of Cinema (1896–1913)* (2008).

Malthête, Jacques, and Mannoni, Laurent, *L'Œuvre de Georges Méliès* (2008).

Robinson, David, *Georges Méliès: Father of Film Fantasy* (1993).

Shephard, David (ed.), *Georges Méliès: First Wizard of Cinema (1896–1913)* (2008).

'Mélusine' French legend that has inspired numerous literary works. The essential elements of the plot are laid out in two medieval versions of *Le Roman de Mélusine* (*The Romance of Mélusine*), one in prose by Jean d'Arras (1392–3), and one in verse by Coudrette (*c*.1402). Mélusine, the daughter of a fairy, marries Raymondin on the condition that he never look at her on Saturdays. She bears him ten sons, who pursue chivalric adventures all over Europe and constitute the Lusignan dynasty. Eventually Raymondin breaks his promise and sees Mélusine transformed into a serpent, who then disappears.

The story holds that she keeps a watchful eye over her descendants from her château at Lusignan. While these medieval versions are more genealogical myths than wonder tales, later rewritings place greater emphasis on the marvellous. After a German version by Thüring von Ringoltingen (*Die Geschichte von der schönen Melusine* (*The Story of the Beautiful Melusine*, 1456), Paul-François *Nodot was the next writer to rework the legend in his pseudo-historical novels *Histoire de Mélusine* (*Story of Mélusine*, 1698) and *Histoire de Geofroy* (*Story of Geoffroy*, 1700). Later versions tend to take greater liberties with the story, often setting the interdiction-transgression and metamorphosis motifs in less magical and more contemporary contexts (e.g. *Arnim, *Goethe, La Roche). The composers *Mendelssohn and Hoffmann each wrote pieces inspired by Ringoltingen's version of the legend. More recently, A. S. *Byatt used the Melusine story as a subtext in *Possession* (1990), and both historians and literary critics have turned their attention to the meanings and uses of the legend in medieval and early modern culture.   LCS

Harf-Lancner, Laurence, *Les Fées au Moyen Âge: Morgane et Mélusine. La naissance des fées* (1984).

Lundt, Bea, *Mélusine und Merlin im Mittelalter: Entwürfe und Modelle weiblicher Existenz im Beziehungsdiskurs der Geschlechter* (1991).

Maddox, Donald, and Sturm-Maddox, Sara (eds.), *Melusine of Lusignan: Founding Fiction in Late Medieval France* (1996).

Mendelssohn, Felix (1809–47) German romantic composer. As children, the four young Mendelssohns staged their own outdoor performances of *Shakespeare's plays. *A Midsummer Night's Dream* was their favourite, and at 17 Felix Mendelssohn wrote an *Overture* for it which ensured his fame. In 1843 he was requested by King Frederick William IV of Prussia to provide complete incidental music for a production of the play, and used themes from his overture to create interludes, entr'actes, dances, a nocturne, and a wedding march. *Incidental Music to 'A Midsummer Night's Dream'* remains one of the finest musical realizations of a literary fairy tale. Mendelssohn's *Märchen von der Schönen Melusina* (*Fair Melusina Overture*, 1834) was inspired by the French legend of the mermaid who married a nobleman. Its opening theme, suggestive of flowing water, was borrowed by *Wagner for the Prelude to *Das Rheingold*.   SR

Mendès, Catulle (1841–1909) French writer. Unable to establish a lasting reputation for himself, Mendès none the less played a role in the Parnassian and symbolist movements. As literary editor of *La Revue fantaisiste* (1861) and *Le Parnasse contemporain* (1866–76), he provided opportunities for writers now considered important. Cultivating contemporary tastes for *la fantaisie* (fantasy), Mendès published works with fairy themes for himself and others like *Banville and *Daudet. His 'Les Mots perdus' ('Lost Words', 1886) recounts a wicked fairy's vengeance upon a nation by removing the words 'I love you' from its memory. Only when she falls in love with a young poet does she release the land from the curse. His marvellous and fantastic stories generally reflect this *fin-de-siècle* taste for the 'cruel'. In 'Le Miroir' ('The Mirror', 1886), an ugly queen who has forbidden all mirrors in her realm condemns a beautiful princess to death. The girl refuses to believe in her beauty until she sees it reflected in the hangman's sword. The double-bind moral of 'Les Deux Marguerites' ('The Two Daisies', 1886) further illustrates his pessimistic decadent aesthetic. A fairy gives two young men each a magic flower which will provide them with various sensations. One man rapidly uses up his share of pleasure, while the other hoards the daisy; this delay results in the flower dying and thus losing its power. Of the two choices, using up all of one's happiness in youth or never experiencing it at all, neither appears satisfactory.   AR

mermaid fairy-tale films A sub-genre derived directly or indirectly from Hans Christian *Andersen's 'The *Little Mermaid'. None of the films is interested in the metaphysical ideas of that story; instead, they concentrate on exploring the comic and tragic potential of beautiful voices, tails versus legs, cross-species relationships, and slippery sex.

In Andersen, the mermaid has her tongue cut off as the price to be paid for entering the human world, but in the comedy *Miranda* (UK, 1948) that idea is turned on its head. Throughout, the mermaid's tongue is her chief strength. Initially, she uses it to persuade a handsome doctor she has rescued to take her to London. There she gives voice to any desires she has, telling men how strong they are, and what nice ears they have; and she takes what she wants when she sees it, devouring bowl after bowl of cockles. Such conduct charms, excites, and seduces three men, who vie with each other for the pleasure of carrying her around in their arms—an operation rendered necessary by the fact that, in order to keep her tail permanently draped, she is posing as an invalid unable to walk. When her secret gets out, she returns to the sea, fearing to be made an aquarium exhibit. In any case, she has got what she really came for: whereas Andersen's mermaid wants an immortal soul, all Miranda wants from her contact with humans is impregnation.

Another mermaid comedy begins a bit like Andersen: the heroine of *Splash* (USA, 1984) loses her voice—albeit temporarily—and acquires the ability to walk. Andersen's ending, however, is reversed. Twice Madison saves Allen from drowning, once when he is 8 and again 20 years later: her presence magically gives him the power to breathe underwater. When she comes to New York to find him, her tail dries out and is transformed into a pair of legs. At first unable to communicate with Allen, she learns English from watching television. Allen falls in love with her, not realizing she is a mermaid. The idyll ends when Madison's legs get wet and her tail returns; she suffers the fate that Miranda feared—being exhibited and experimented on—before Allen comes to the rescue and plunges into the deep with her so that they can be together forever. Instead of dying in an attempt to become human, she has caused a human to renounce humanity and become aquatic.

A range of other films (including *Hans Christian Andersen*) have based themselves more closely on 'The Little Mermaid', but none has stuck with that text to the end. *Disney's *The Little Mermaid* (USA, 1989), because its medium is animation rather than live action, is able to follow Andersen in presenting the underwater world and its characters in considerable detail, illuminated by songs, before Ariel goes to see the witch Ursula. The deal they strike is the standard one—Ariel gives up her beautiful voice in exchange for legs—but a time limit is added to it: Ariel has only three days in which to win Prince Eric's love. If she fails, she will not die (as in Andersen); instead she will become Ursula's possession. By using Ariel's voice, Ursula thwarts her attempts to charm the prince. When the time limit expires, Ariel's distraught father relinquishes his kingdom in order to save her from perpetual enslavement. At the climax, Prince Eric's ship kills Ursula. Ariel becomes human again, and the prince marries her. Only a final shot of Ariel's father, realizing sadly that he has lost his daughter not just to a husband but to a species that lives in a different element, suggests that this happy ending is not happy for everyone.

Andersen himself appears as a character in *Rousalochka* (USSR/Bulgaria, 1976), telling the story to a little girl in a stagecoach. He presents a new side to the fabled beauty of mermaids' voices—it is their siren singing, rather than a storm, that causes the prince's ship to be dashed against rocks in the first place—before dwelling on the particular mermaid who saves the prince. Andersen then inserts himself, as a troubadour, into the story he is telling, and persuades a witch to make the mermaid human. In exchange, the mermaid has to give up her voice before trying to win the prince's love. During the attempt, she is exposed as a mermaid, and condemned to be burned at the stake. The prince rescues her, but is killed in a duel, till the witch intercedes at the mermaid's behest and revives him. For this she must pay with her life, unless someone is willing to die in her place. The troubadour does. As a result she will live forever, but not with the prince;

she returns to the sea alone, to be seen in future only by believers. In stressing that love requires sacrifice, and in not endorsing miscegenation, this adaptation comes closest in spirit to Andersen's original story.

In a more contemporary adaptation, loosely based on Andersen's tale, *Mermaid* (2008) by the gifted Russian director, Anna Mlikyan, the story begins in post-1989 Russia on a seacoast. As the credits run, we see a very large, fat woman meander through bathers on a beach to an isolated rocky spot, where she strips and walks naked into the sea. Once in the sea, she swims happily, almost like a porpoise. Meanwhile, a sailor comes by and sits down by her clothes. He is tired and dozes. After a few minutes he slowly opens his eyes and is stunned when this huge woman emerges from the sea, stark naked like an enormous mermaid. He is obviously entranced. What happens next is not shown on the screen, but it is apparent that they will sleep together and produce a daughter, Alisa (Alice). The sailor will depart and will never be seen again except in Alisa's dreams. Melikyan's film turns into a realistic fairy-tale allegory that uses Andersen's 'Little Mermaid' to comment on the hopeless situation of working-class youth, in particular, girls, who find themselves ignored in the 'New Russia'. However, this is not a simplistic allegory but a complex rethinking of different fairy tales and how they might shed light on the drastic condition of Russian youth looking for possibilities to activate themselves and to grab a bit of happiness. This is an enlightening fairy-tale film, not Andersen's didactic Christian sermon about how a mermaid must sacrifice herself to win the Lord's approval.   TAS

Meyer, Stephenie (1973–) American author of the *Twilight* saga, a bestselling young-adult series which depicts the romance between teenaged human Bella Swan and vampire Edward Cullen. The first novel, *Twilight*, published in 2005, was a huge success and was quickly followed by *New Moon* (2006), *Eclipse* (2007), and *Breaking Dawn* (2008). Altogether, the *Twilight* series is regarded as having sparked the popularity of the 'dark romance' genre, which drew on elements of romance, fantasy, myth, and fairy tale, in many of the episodes. The series has been heavily criticized for what many view as a negative representation of female sexuality and its portrayal of the controlling and domineering Edward as an ideal partner. These problematic elements, however, have not prevented the books' adaptation into an equally popular film franchise.   ST

Meyrink, Gustav (1868–1932) Austrian writer. Meyer, who later changed his name to Meyrink, went to Prague at the age of 16 to attend the business school and stayed there for a number of years. He was deeply influenced by the atmosphere of the city, and it was here that he started his career as a writer of fantastic literature. He began with grotesque satires, which he later combined with occultism and mysticism, culminating in his most famous novel *Der Golem* (1915). He also wrote several fables like 'Der Fluch der Kröte' ('The Curse of the Toad', 1903).   CS

Michelstaedter, Carlo (1887–1910) Italian poet and philosopher of Jewish ancestry who committed suicide soon after writing his dissertation, later published as *La persuasione e la rettorica in Platone e Aristotele* (*Persuasion and Rhetoric in Plato and Aristotle*, 1913). His complete works, published in 1958, include poems and some tales, one of which, entitled 'La bora' ('The North Wind'), personifies this famous wind as the benevolent sister of Slavic warriors. 'La bora' was used by Michelstaedter as an exemplum in his philosophical works, and he customarily used his tales to embody his pessimistic thought.   GD

Midsummer Night's Dream, A (film versions) It has been filmed more than 30 times, with a wide range of approaches, often derived from a stage production. The best-known screen adaptation was only the second *Shakespeare play to be filmed with sound; other interpretations include speechless, erotic, and postmodern.

In 1934 the Austrian stage producer Max Reinhardt (1873–1943) put on in the Hollywood Bowl a popular and acclaimed *Midsummer Night's Dream*, which included dancing fairies choreographed to the music Mendelssohn had written for the play in the previous century. When Warner Bros. invited Reinhardt to co-direct a film of it (USA, 1935), they did not want a straightforward record of the stage production. Nor did Reinhardt. He aimed instead to continue to show respect for Shakespeare's text but use some of Warners' established movie stars— such as James Cagney (Bottom), Dick Powell (Lysander), Joe E. Brown (Flute), and 14-year-old Mickey Rooney (Puck)—rather than his stage actors. Equally, Reinhardt wanted to exploit cinema's unlimited space, and the camera's technical possibilities, to create a world of magic and enchantment. A large troupe of gossamer fairies—nearly 1,000 extras were used, according to the publicity—is shown skipping up to the stars on a spiral pathway of clouds, then floating down on a moonbeam; Bottom's head is transformed into that of a donkey before the viewer's eyes, by means of overlapping dissolves; and some of the forest scenes are shot through a lens partially coated in oil, to enhance perception of the story as a hazy dream. This cinematography won an Academy Award.

About 20 years later the celebrated Czech animator Jiří *Trnka started work on a nonverbal CinemaScope puppet version (Czechoslovakia, 1958). Shakespeare's dialogue was cut out completely, except for the occasional few words of plot explanation. In place of dialogue Trnka relied on visual richness and inventiveness to convey character. Puck, for example, shows his impish humour in the way he transforms himself into little animals from time to time; and Oberon's moods are implied by a succession of costume changes. A twist not found in Shakespeare is that in the final scene, when the artisans are performing their play before Theseus and the court, Puck uses magic to transform their acting from silly to sublime for a few brief moments.

In the 1980s came a radical reworking (UK/Spain, 1984) which used more of Shakespeare's text than Trnka had done, but not by much. Directed by Celestino Coronado, and based on a well-travelled stage production, it posits the dream as being that of Puck in a lascivious and voyeuristic mood. The only bits of text used are those which Puck as satyr likes, and they are enhanced for him by the addition of sex, mime, and transvestism. No longer are the fleeing lovers, Demetrius and Helena, separated during their night in the forest—they lie together. Next morning, when he wakes with eyes befuddled by Puck's magic, the first person Demetrius sees and fancies is not Helena, but his rival Lysander. However Hermia, when she opens her eyes, does fall for Helena. They all make love, then change partners. In other parts of the wood Bottom, instead of acquiring an ass's head, turns into a horned Beast who excites and satisfies Titania (played by a man); and Oberon carries off the changeling boy—cause of his problems with Titania—for private pleasures.

A Royal Shakespeare Company production transferred to film (UK, 1996) similarly interprets it as one particular person's dream. In this case it is a sleeping boy, in ancient Athens, who becomes a silent onlooker. The production thus reaches out to touch and join earlier other-land excursions such as The *Wizard of Oz and *Alice in Wonderland. There are also, in the visuals, invocations of Beatrix *Potter, Arthur *Rackham, E.T., and Mary Poppins. This child's-eye perception is extended by a presentation of the enchanted Athenian wood as a virtual world generated by computer. The dreaming boy is also, like Puck in the 1984 version, interested in the sexual potential of the comings and goings in the wood, but not so deeply.

Perhaps because of its fairy-tale elements, A Midsummer Night's Dream seems to be the most versatile and adaptable of all Shakespeare's plays.   TAS

Millar, Harold Robert (1869–1942) British illustrator of the Black and White School who trained at the Birmingham School of Art. Known for his work for books by E. *Nesbit and Rudyard *Kipling, he also provided fairy-tale illustrations for the Strand Magazine and Little Folks from 1890 until the 1920s. Beginning in 1893 with Aunt Louisa's Book of Fairy Tales and concluding with Our Old Fairy Stories by Mrs Herbert Strang (1939), Millar illustrated over 15 books of fairy stories, along with many reissues of these books. Especially popular were The Golden Fairy Book (1894), The Silver Fairy Book (1895), The Diamond Fairy Book (1897), and The Ruby Fairy Book (1900). Millar was noted for his faultless line, his perspectives, and his attention to detail. His early background as a civil engineer served him well in depicting fairy buildings such as castles.   LS

Millhauser, Steven (1943–) American writer. His extraordinary novels Edwin Mullhouse (1972), From the Realm of Morpheus (1986), and Martin Dressler: The Tale of an American Dreamer (1996) explore and transcend the boundaries between realism and fantasy. Clearly influenced by the work of Jorge Luis *Borges, Millhauser has subtly revised classic fairy tales and challenged our interpretations of these tales in various collections of short stories: In the Penny Arcade (1986), The Barnum Museum (1990), Little Kingdoms (1993), The Knife Thrower (1998), and Dangerous Laughter: Thirteen Stories (2008). For instance, 'The Eighth Voyage of Sinbad' and 'Alice Falling' in The Barnum Museum are droll and highly sophisticated investigations of classic fairy tales that uncover new meanings in the exploits of Sindbad and *Alice. In 'The Princess, the Dwarf, and the Dungeon' (Little Kingdoms) Millhauser transforms a fairy tale into a Gothic tale of jealousy and horror. 'The New Automaton' in The Knife Thrower recalls E. T. A. *Hoffmann's tales and highlights a major theme in all of Millhauser's unusual 'postmodern' fairy tales: the exhaustion and abuse of the imagination. One of Millhauser's best stories, 'Eisenheim the Illusionist', was based on the mythical career of a unique Viennese magician who mystified audiences at the end of the 19th century, and it was made into the film The Illusionist in 2006. Paradoxically, Millhauser's compelling tales of magic realism seek to save humanity from nihilistic tendencies in imaginations run amok.   JZ

Fowler, Douglas, 'Steven Millhauser, Miniaturist', *Critique*, 37 (winter 1996).
Kinzie, Mary, 'Succeeding Borges, Escaping Kafka: On the Fiction of Steven Millhauser', *Salmagundi*, 92 (fall 1991).
Salzman, Arthur M., 'In the Millhauser Archives', *Critique*, 37 (winter 1996).

Milne, A. A. (Alan Alexander Milne, 1882–1956) British humorist, playwright, and children's writer. Best known for his children's poetry and for his toy stories, *Winnie-the-Pooh* (1926) and *The House at Pooh Corner* (1928), Milne was also intrigued by the form and conventions of the fairy tale and wrote a number of literary fairy tales for adults and for children. Indeed, according to his own account in *It's Too Late Now* (1939), as the youngest of three sons, he grew up half-expecting the charmed future fairy tales predicted for him. At Henley House, the small school run by his father in London, he showed outstanding promise in mathematics and won a scholarship to Westminster School at the remarkably early age of 11. Deprived of his father's imaginative teaching, however, he soon lost interest in schoolwork. His hobby of writing light verse in collaboration with his brother Ken became an avocation, and at Cambridge University his chief ambition was to edit *Granta*, then known as the *Cambridge Punch*. Having scraped through with a Third Class degree in mathematics, Milne spent several precarious years in London as a freelance writer before being invited, at 24, to be *Punch*'s assistant editor. Although his Liberal politics prevented his being asked to join the Punch Table (where editorial policy was determined) until 1910, his witty and light-hearted sketches found an enthusiastic audience and were repeatedly collected and republished. Milne married Daphne de Sélincourt in 1913, but this happy period ended with the First World War. Although Milne survived the trenches, the degrading years of military service left him a committed pacifist. After the war, he turned to playwriting—in the early 1920s, he was Britain's most popular dramatist—and, at the suggestion of Rose *Fyleman, to writing light verse for children. The phenomenal success of *When We Were Very Young* (1924), *Now We Are Six* (1927), and the *Pooh* books left Milne unwillingly but permanently typecast as a children's writer, though he continued to publish plays, novels, stories, and essays into the early 1950s.

Like *Thackeray's *The Rose and the Ring* and *Dickens's *The Magic Fishbone*, the handful of fairy tales for adults Milne published in *Punch* before the First World War and included in *Those Were the Days* (1929) satirized the conventions of the genre. In 'The King's Sons', a fairy tests the three sons by transforming herself into a dove pursued by a hawk. The youngest son, kind-hearted Prince Goldilocks, is prompt with his bow; unfortunately, he is a poor shot, and hits the dove. 'A Modern Cinderella' transposes the story to present-day London. A blasé debutante, Milne's *Cinderella, is tired of balls; she kicks off her shoes at a dance—and loses one—simply because her feet are hurting. In 'A Matter-of-Fact Fairy Tale', Prince Charming sets out to kill the Giant Blunderbus and rescue Princess Beauty's brother Udo, transformed by the giant into a tortoise seven years before. Here, as in the other tales, Milne associates the fairy-tale tradition with a sentimental and unrealistic view of life and human nature. Udo is unromantically preoccupied by his ignorance of what tortoises are supposed to eat. Prince Charming is disillusioned when the dying giant reveals that Udo is not Beauty's brother, while the lovers, reunited at last, discover that they are no longer attracted to each other.

Milne's *A Gallery of Children* (1925) includes his few and disappointing fairy tales for children, some of which were originally published in the annual *Joy Street*. Lacking the ironic bite of his fairy tales for adults, such stories as 'Prince Rabbit' and 'The Princess and the Apple Tree' seem insipid imitations of traditional folk tales. Clearly, Milne needed the fresh inspiration of his son's toy animals before he could realize his gifts as a children's writer.

His most successful experiment with the fairy tale was written for the pleasure of himself and his 'collaborator' Daphne, during the wartime months when, as a signals officer, he was expecting at any moment to be shipped out to France. *Once on a Time*, which appeared, virtually unnoticed, in 1917, takes place in the imaginary kingdom of Euralia. When King Merriwig sets off to war with the neighbouring kingdom of Barodia, the wicked but delightful Countess Belvane attempts to seize power from Merriwig's shy young daughter, Hyacinth. The Princess sends to Prince Udo of Araby for help, but Belvane uses a wishing ring to transform him into a ridiculous composite animal—part-rabbit, part-lion, and part-sheep. Like his predecessor in 'A Matter-of-Fact Fairy Tale', Udo becomes egotistically obsessed by the problem of what to eat, and easily succumbs to Belvane's manipulations. But Hyacinth discovers an ally—and a lover—in Udo's more intelligent companion, Coronel, and the two succeed in putting the Countess in her place. Merriwig returns triumphantly from a bloodless war and marries Belvane, Hyacinth marries Coronel, and Udo returns to Araby in his proper shape but alone.

In *Once on a Time*, which can be enjoyed by both adults and children, the fairy tale is no longer the target of Milne's satire but the medium through which he observes human foibles and pretensions (including such foibles as absurd and unnecessary wars). The imaginary kingdom 'once on a time' frees his characters from the constraints of time, place, and social milieu, while a light touch of magic reveals more clearly what they are. Having discovered this new capability of the fairy tale, Milne made similar use of it in several plays for adults. *Portrait of a Gentleman in Slippers* (1926), *The Ivory Door* (1927), and *The Ugly Duckling* (1941), while unsuccessful as stage plays, are closet dramas of high quality.   SR

Milne, A. A., *It's Too Late Now: The Autobiography of a Writer* (1939).

Swann, Thomas Burnett, *A. A. Milne* (1971).

Thwaite, Ann, *A. A. Milne: The Man Behind Winnie-the-Pooh* (1990).

Mitchison, Naomi (1897–1999) British politician and prolific writer who published short stories, novels, poetry, plays, essays, biographies, memoirs, and political articles. Among her works are fantasy novels and collections of fairy tales that are stamped by her feminist and socialist perspective. There is always social commentary in her fantasy. For example, in *The Bull Calves* (1947), which takes place in Scotland during 1747, a good woman becomes a witch in opposition to the conformity of her times. In *The Big House* (1950), a fairy-tale novel for children, Su from a rich family and the fisherman's boy Winkie overcome class differences and take a magical journey through space and time, and Su learns to make up for the sins of her proud forebears. *To the Chapel Perilous* (1955) is a retelling of the Grail legend that develops into a satire of the contemporary press. *Not by Bread Alone* (1983) is a science-fiction novel and critique about the multinational corporation PAX, which seeks to produce free food for the entire world and yet causes many people to die. Although most of her fairy-tale plays such as *Nix-Nought Nothing* (1928) and *Kate Crackernuts* (1931) and her fairy tales such as *Graeme and the Dragon* (1954), *The Fairy who Couldn't Tell a Lie* (1963), and *The Two Magicians* (1978), were intended for young readers, Mitchison also published two superb collections of political tales for adults, *The Fourth Pig* (1936) and *Five Men and a Swan* (1957). In her version of *'Hansel and Gretel'*, the witch's Rolls Royce stops in Corporation Street, Birmingham, and lures children of the unemployed workmen to the dangerous house of Capital, and in *'The Snow Maiden'* the talented young Mary Snow, who had won scholarships at the university, abandons her plans, sacrifices her career to marry plain George Higginson, and melts away. All of the tales in this volume are intended to provoke the reader to think about the social conditions of the Depression years and combine unique social commentary with traditional fairy-tale motifs.   JZ

Calder, Jenni, *The Nine Lives of Naomi Mitchison* (1997).

Miyazaki, Hayao (1941–) Japanese animator and film director whose fantasy and fairy-tale films are considered among the most original and profound artworks of the last 40 years. Early in his career Miyazaki was chief animator and scene designer for *Hols: Prince of the Sun* (1968), a pioneer animated film directed by Isao Takahata, with whom he continued to collaborate for the next three decades. In Kimio Yabuki's **Puss-in-Boots* (1969), Miyazaki again provided the designs, storyboards, and story ideas for key scenes in the film. In 1971, Miyazaki made the designs for *Ali Baba and the 40 Thieves*. By 1984, he was able to produce the first animated feature film written and directed by himself. It was an unusual adventure film, *Kaze no Tani no Naushika* (*Nausicaä of the Valley of the Wind*), based on his Manga book series, which he had written, and dealt with key themes that run throughout his works: pacifism, environmentalism, feminism, and morality. In 1985 Miyazaki co-founded the animation production company Studio Ghibli with Takahata, and embarked on a career marked by great ingenuity and sophistication. Of his first three films, *Laputa: Castle in the Sky* (1986) concerns two orphans who seek a magic castle that floats in the sky; *Tonari no Totoro* (*My Neighbor Totoro*, 1988) recounts the exploits of two girls and their relationship with forest spirits; and *Kiki's Delivery Service* (1989) portrays a provincial girl who leaves her home, travels to a large city, and learns to become a witch. After a temporary retirement, Miyazaki directed *Mononoke-Hime* (*Princess Mononoke*) in 1997, similar in its themes to *Nausicaä of the Valley of the Wind*. Here animal spirits of the forest must struggle with the humans who exploit the forest for industry. It was followed by an even greater animated feature film: *Sen to Chihiro no Kamikakushi* (*Spirited Away*, 2001), which concerns a young girl who is depressed because her parents have compelled her to move to a new city. Along the way they stop at an abandoned amusement park that turns into a bathhouse for utterly weird spirits. In the meantime her parents are turned into pigs by the sorceress who owns the bathhouse. The young girl must work in the bathhouse to free her parents and is assisted by a young water spirit who enables her to realize how complex the world is and how much she loves her parents. This film was an international success and received many awards, including Best Picture at the 2001 Japanese Academy Awards, Golden Bear (First Prize) at the 2002 Berlin Film Festival, and the 2002 Academy Award for Best Animated Feature. In 2004 Miyazaki directed *Howl's Moving Castle*, an adaptation of Diana Wynne *Jones's fantasy novel. His most recent film is *Ponyo* (*Gake no Ue no Ponyo*, literally 'Ponyo on the Cliff', 2008), based on Hans Christian *Andersen's '*The *Little Mermaid'. Here a little female goldfish named Ponyo is saved by Sosuke, a five-year-old boy, who befriends her. As their friendship develops, Ponyo, whose real name is Brunhilde, seeks to become human against her father the sea-king's wishes. He does not trust humans because they have caused great damage to nature. However, after testing Sosuke and Ponyo, he relents and allows his daughter to live with Sosuke and his mother.   JZ

Cavallaro, Dani, *The Anime Art of Hayao Miyazaki* (2006).

McCarthy, Helen, *Hayao Miyazaki: Master of Japanese Animation* (1999).

Miyazaki, Hayao, *Starting Point: 1979-1996* (2009).

Odell, Colin, and Le Blanc, Michelle, *Studio Ghibli: The Films of Hayao Miyazaki and Isao Takahata* (2009).

Mizuki, Shigeru (1922–) Japanese manga artist of yōkai monster tales, including the long-popular *Gegege no Kitarō* series that ran throughout the 1960s. Mizuki began cartooning after military service in Papua New Guinea, an experience he credits with sparking his interest in folk legends and the supernatural. His magnum opus *Gegege no Kitarō* served largely as a vehicle to unearth and preserve Japan's rich collection of yōkai tales, and has now itself become a base text for an industry of remakes in several media.   SCR

Foster, Michael Dylan, *Pandemonium and Parade: Japanese Monsters and the Culture of Yōkai* (2009).

Papp, Zilia, *Animé and its Roots in Early Japanese Monster Art* (2010).

Shamoon, Deborah, 'The *Yōkai* in the Database' *Marvels & Tales*, 27:2 (2013).

Mizuno, Junko (1973–) Japanese-born artist and manga creator. Her art incorporates *kawaii* (sweet, cute, adorable) comic characters into chaotic horror, fantasy, grotesque worlds of sex and violence. Three manga begin with fairy tales and their characters and themes. *Cinderalla* (Japanese 2000; English 2002) (unlike her *Cinderella counterpart), doesn't want to be a princess: she wants to be a zombie; she loses an eyeball, not a glass slipper, and one of her tasks is feeding her ravenous zombie stepmother. Voracious eaters and preternatural appetites also abound in *Hansel & Gretel* (Japanese 2000, English 2003) and *Princess Mermaid* ('The *Little Mermaid', Japanese 2002, English 2003).   PG

Moe, Jørgen See ASBJØRNSEN, PETER CHRISTIAN AND MOE, JØRGEN.

Moe, Moltke (1859–1913) Norwegian linguist and folklorist, son of Jørgen Moe (*see* ASBJØRNSEN PETER CHRISTIAN AND MOE, JØRGEN), and professor at Christiania (Oslo) University. He was assigned by P. C. Asbjørnsen to revise the language for a new edition of Asbjørnsen and Moe's collection *Norske Folkeeventyr* (*Norwegian Folktales*). Moe's greatest achievement was a three-volume collection, *Norske Folkeviser* (*Norwegian Folk Songs*), published posthumously in 1920–4 by Knut *Liestøl. Moe coined the notion of 'epic laws' in folklore studies. MN

Liestøl, Knut, *Moltke Moe* (1949).

Molesworth, Mary Louisa (1839–1921) English writer, popular in late Victorian and Edwardian nurseries. Her first published work for children, *Tell me a Story* (1875) included 'The Reel Fairies', based on her own childhood imaginative games with the reels in her mother's workbox, and 'Con and

the Little People', about a boy who is stolen by the fairies, one of her few to use folk-tale elements, and the only one where she shows fairyland as sinister rather than benevolent. But her large output of 87 children's books is mostly made up of small domestic chronicles and teacup dramas in which she closely identifies with her child characters. Edward Salmon said (*Juvenile Literature as it is*, 1888) that her greatest charm was her realism: 'On this ground her stories of everyday child life are preferable to her fairy stories.'

Though she had enjoyed the *Grimms, Hans Christian *Andersen, and E. T. A. *Hoffmann's *Nutcracker and Mouse King* as a child, she wrote that 'save for an occasional flight to fairyland, children's books should be *real*' (*Atlanta*, May 1893). She also understood young children's desire for security and a solid background, and her fantasy stories reflect this. There is nothing frightening or strange—in the article above she wrote of the care with which the scrupulous writer for children 'banished from the playground . . . all things unsightly, or terrifying, or in any sense hurtful'. Thus her child characters who visit such places as butterfly-land, an eagles' eyrie, or a squirrel family find everyone courteous, friendly, and hardworking; tempting meals are served at regular intervals but no one is ever greedy, and even the eagles turn out to be fruitarian. She liked children to be polite, well-behaved, and above all contented, and most of her fairies, such as the Cuckoo in *The Cuckoo Clock* (1877), behave like governesses and insist on good manners. This was her first full-length fairy story and her most popular. It begins with a favourite formula: 'Once upon a time in an old town, in an old street, there stood a very old house.' Here motherless Griselda goes to live with her greataunts, and is irked by the orderly life and the discipline imposed on her (a favourite Molesworth theme). The fairy cuckoo in the clock made by her great-great-grandfather takes her on magic adventures through which she becomes happier and more contented, and she is also provided by the end with a child companion to ease her loneliness, and a surrogate mother.

Molesworth, Mary Louisa Aureole has a magical relationship to animals in Mary Louisa Molesworth's
Christmas-Tree Land (1884), illustrated by Walter *Crane. The Bodleian Library, University of Oxford (Opie AA 1936).

The Tapestry Room (1879) was almost equally popular. It is set in an old house in Normandy where Jeanne and Hugh find themselves in the tapestry that hangs in Hugh's bedroom. Their guide in their adventures there is Dudu, the autocratic old raven who belongs to the house. In one of their dreamlike adventures they meet a lady at a spinning-wheel who tells them the traditional tale of 'The Black Bull of Norrowa'. In *Christmas-Tree Land* (1884), set in an ancient castle in Thuringia where Rollo and Maia are sent to stay with their elderly cousin, there is another inset fairy tale, 'The Story of a King's Daughter', this time by Molesworth herself. It is told to them by

their fairy mentor who calls herself their godmother, and who bears some resemblance to George *MacDonald's wise women. The influence of MacDonald is also evident in *Four Winds Farm* (1887), more subtle than most of her fantasies. Here the four winds appoint themselves Gratian's preceptors and gently nudge him out of his dreamy ways. *The Children of the Castle* (1890) is less successful in its imitation of MacDonald; spiritual mysteries were not her line. For the great-great-grandmother of *The Princess and the Goblin* she substitutes the Forget-me-not Lady (also in a turret room), who succeeds in making wilful Ruby and odious Bertrand feel remorse. In

The Ruby Ring (1904) a magic ring helps spoilt Sybil to become more contented, and in 'The Groaning Clock' (*Fairies—of Sorts*, 1908) an old clock is inhabited by a brownie who groans and growls if children are ill-tempered or careless.

Some of her most attractive fairy stories are the short ones. In three tales in *An Enchanted Garden* (1892)—'The Story of the Three Wishes', 'The Summer Princess', and 'The Magic Rose', and in '"Ask the Robin"', 'A Magic Table' and 'The Weather Maiden' in *Fairies Afield* (1911), all with a timeless folk-tale background, she sheds the governess manner, and writes warmly of good people rewarded.   GA

Green, Roger Lancelyn, *Mrs. Molesworth* (1961).
Keenan, Hugh T., 'M. L. S. Molesworth', in Jane M. Bingham (ed.), *Writers for Children* (1988).
Laski, Marghanita, *Mrs. Ewing, Mrs. Molesworth, and Mrs. Hodgson Burnett* (1950).

Moncrif, François-Auguste Paradis de

(1687–1770) French writer of Scottish descent who served as secretary to several notable personages, including Marie Leszcynska, and eventually became secretary-general of the French postal system. Besides plays, and moral and scientific treatises, he wrote *Les Aventures de Zéloide et d'Amanzarifdine* (*The Adventures of Zeloide and Amanzarifdine*, 1715). In this tale, which includes numerous embedded stories, Moncrif combines an oriental setting and the marvellous to portray a sentimental love plot with detailed psychological descriptions.   LCS

Assaf, Francis (ed.), *Les Aventures de Zéloide et d'Amanzarifdine* (1994).

Montresor, Beni

(1926–2001) Celebrated Italian writer of radio plays (including adaptations of fairy tales), book illustrator, and stage designer. Montresor was knighted by the Italian government for distinguished contribution to the arts. Born in Bussolengo, Italy, he moved to the United States in 1960, where he developed his great talent for picture-book illustration. His studies of art at the Accademia di Belle Arti in Venice and of set and costume design at the Centro Sperimentale di Cinematografia in Rome and his work staging European films and theatre—operas, ballets, and musicals—prepared him for children's book illustration. Because Montresor filled a book's blank pages with the colour, movement, and lighting as he did the stage, the reading of his books is akin to experiencing all the splendour of a theatrical event. Among his most notable achievements are the illustrations for *The Princesses* (1962), **Cinderella* (1967), *Nightingale* (1985), *Witches of Venice* (1989), and **Little Red Riding Hood* (1991).   SS

Moomin characters (or Moomintrolls)

Portrayed in the fairy-tale novels by Tove *Jansson, beginning with *Kometjakten* (1946; *A Comet in Moominland*, 1968), the Moomins are a variety of imaginary creatures, half-animals, half-dwarfs or trolls, inhabiting the self-contained world of the Moomin valley. They are clearly human beings in disguise and often have prototypes in real life. The core of the family consists of Moominmamma, Moominpappa, and their son Moomintroll, who can be viewed as the central character of the novels. Otherwise, the Moomin figures function as a collective character, representing different human traits. Thus Sniff is cowardly, selfish, and greedy. Snufkin is an artist who despises material possessions and values his independence most of all. Snork is bossy and pedantic, and his sister Snork Maiden kind, vain, and a little silly, a parody on a female stereotype. Hemulen is a bore and a numskull, Muskrat a caricature of a cynical philosopher, and Fillyjunk a neurotic spinster. Little My is a strong and independent female. The Groke is the only evil, or rather ambivalent, character in the Moomin gallery, who can be viewed as the dark side of Moominmamma and interpreted in terms of Jungian Shadow. Moominmamma changes most throughout the Moomin suite, abandoning her nurturing role and finding her identity as an artist.

The Moomins have no magic powers themselves; however, in *Trollkarlens hatt* (1949; *Finn Family Moomintroll*, 1965) they come into the possession of magical objects and meet a wizard who can grant wishes.   MN

Jones, W. Glyn, *Tove Jansson* (1984).

Lowe, Virginia, 'Snufkin, Sniff and Little My: The "Reality" of Fictional Characters for the Young Child', *Papers*, 2 (1991).

Westin, Boel, *Familjen i dalen. Tove Janssons muminvärld* (1988).

Moravia, Alberto (pseudonym of **Alberto Pincherle**, 1907–90) Italian novelist, playwright, and essayist. He achieved immediate success with his first novel *Gli indifferenti* (*The Time of Indifference*, 1929). The popularity of his novels—many of which were made into films—has somewhat obscured the merits of his remarkable production of short stories and tales. Some of the very best, written between 1935 and 1945, now appear in *Racconti surrealistici e satirici* (*Surrealistic and Satirical Tales*, 1982). Here the abstract, the metaphysical, the absurd, the grotesque, and the fantastic are used to pose important questions for the reader to ponder. Whether he draws sketches of Roman life, as he does in *Racconti romani* (*Roman Tales*, 1954), *Nuovi racconti romani* (*More Roman Tales*, 1959), or writes tales of sex and eroticism as he does in *Il paradiso* (*Paradise and Other Stories*, 1971), and *Racconti erotici* (*Erotic Tales*, 1983), Moravia probes aspects of reality and reveals them as a multitude of kaleidoscopic images that are as varied and mutable as human experience.   MNP

Morgan le Fay A sorceress most familiar through Sir Thomas Malory's 15th-century *Le morte d'Arthur*. Here, she is Arthur's malignant sister, aunt, or mother (as Morgawse) of Mordred, and mother of Agravain, the knight who reveals Lancelot and Guinevere's adultery. Her offspring are instrumental in destroying Camelot.

Starting with Geoffrey of Monmouth's 12th-century *Vita Merlini*, Morgan, whose name may be a Welsh form of the Irish Morrigan, appears in various guises in works ranging from 12th-century romances to 20th-century novels. Although Morgan may be human or supernatural, ugly or beautiful, her talents are relatively consistent. She often learns magic from Merlin, is a shapeshifter and an enchantress who, as Morgan

the Wise, compounds magic healing balms. She transports the dying to her other-world island, Avalon, to heal them, so that, like Arthur, they may sleep to return to earth when they are needed.

Vindictive toward Guinevere and Arthur, Morgan sometimes administers chastity tests, using a drinking horn or a mantle. In *Sir Gawain and the Green Knight, Morgan tests Arthur's court, later appearing as a hag at Sir Bercilak's castle. Whenever a mysterious being threatens Arthurian society, cognoscenti should suspect Morgan. She is called Morgana in *Orlando Inamorata* and *Orlando Furioso*, where she is also the Lady of the Lake.   JSN

Fries, Maureen, 'From the Lady to the Tramp: The Decline of Morgan le Fay in Medieval Romance', *Arthuriana* (1994).

Harf-Lancner, Laurence, *Les Fées au Moyen Âge, Morgane et Melusine, La Naissance des fées* (1984).

Morgin, Kristen L. (1968–) American visual artist working primarily in sculpture and the recipient of the Joan Mitchell Award in 2005. Morgin's exhibit 'Snow White in Evening Wear and Other Works' (2012) featured pieces crafted from old-fashioned toys and other children's ephemera. The broken bodies of children's toys refashioned with ad hoc prosthetics created a carnivalesque pastiche of Disneyesque characters such as Mickey Mouse, Popeye, and Jiminy Cricket salvaged from the scrapyard.   KMJ

Morgner, Irmtraud (Irmtraud Elfriede Schreck, 1933–90) East German feminist writer who investigated in her highly innovative writing the condition of women in the German Democratic Republic. Weaving together elements of myth, fairy tale, legend, superstition, and even biblical motifs, her montage novel *Leben und Abenteuer der Trobadora Beatriz nach Zeugnissen ihrer Spielfrau Laura. Roman in dreizehn Büchern und sieben Intermezzos* (*Life and Adventures of Troubadour Beatriz as Chronicled by her Minstrel Laura: A Novel in Thirteen Volumes and Seven Intermezzi*, 1974) has as its main theme the impossibility of female subjecthood under patriarchy. Using the motif of the sleeping princess from 'Dornröschen' ('Briar Rose' or *'The Sleeping Beauty'), the eponymous Beatriz, a historical 12th-century French countess, decides to withdraw from her unbearable life by sleeping for 800 years in the hope of awaking in a world not determined by men. In Morgner's parodic treatment of the fairy-tale motif, her sleep is abruptly cut short by two years—not to be rescued by a prince—but when her castle is blown up by engineers to make way for a modern development. Beatriz's disenchantment is fully effected when she is raped, and the fairy-tale figure is forced into the 20th century to engage with its problems and disappointments as a woman in a world still run by and for men—even in the 'ideal' conditions of the GDR. In another mock fairy tale, *Der Schöne und das Tier: Eine Liebesgeschichte* (*Beauty and the Beast: A Love Story*, 1991), Morgner subverts traditional gender expectations with a male beauty.   KS

Biddy, Martin, 'Socialist Patriarchy and the Limits of Reform: A Reading of Irmtraud Morgner's Life and Adventures of Troubadora Beatriz as Chronicled by her Minstrel Laura', *Studies in Twentieth Century Literature*, 5.1 (1980).

Cardinal, Agnes, '"Be realistic: Demand the impossible": On Irmtraud Morgner's Salman trilogy', in Martin Kane (ed.), *Socialism and the Literary Imagination: Essays on East German writers* (1991).

Lewis, Alison, *Subverting Patriarchy: Feminism and Fantasy in the Works of Irmtraud Morgner* (1995).

Mörike, Eduard (1804–75) Swabian novelist and poet. Mörike published three prose narratives explicitly called 'fairy tales'. 'Der Bauer und sein Sohn' ('The Farmer and his Son', 1856) chronicles the supernatural punishment and redemption of an animal-abusing farmer. In 'Die Hand der Jezerte' ('Jezerte's Hand', 1853), the king's jealous consort is supernaturally deformed and killed for defiling her late rival's grave. Both picaresque and fairy-tale-like, the novel *Das Stuttgarter Hutzelmännlein* (*The Wrinkled Old Man from Stuttgart*, 1853) employs the entire fairy-tale arsenal (water sprites,

helpful dwarfs, magic shoes, spell of invisibility) in the story of a shoemaker seeking the right wife.   WC

Morin, Henry (1873–1961) French illustrator. Born in Strasbourg, he studied at the École des Beaux-arts in Paris, worked for magazines (*Mon Journal, Le Petit Français Illustré, La Semaine de Suzette*), and specialized in illustrating children's books (1906–25) before turning to religious art. In addition to La Fontaine's *Fables*, he illustrated the fairy tales of Mme d'*Aulnoy, Mme *Leprince de Beaumont, and Charles *Perrault ('La Barbe-bleue' (*'Blue Beard') as well as French editions of the Brothers *Grimm and Lewis *Carroll's *Alice books.
MLE

Morris, William (1834–96) British author, designer, and socialist. Although Morris did not write original fairy tales, he used fairy-tale and folk materials throughout his literary career, beginning with the pseudo-medieval tales he wrote for the *Oxford and Cambridge Magazine* (1856) and the Arthurian and supernatural poems for the *Defence of Guenevere* volume (1858). The 24 tales that comprise *The Earthly Paradise* (1858–70) use plots, motifs, and characters from *The *Arabian Nights, *Gesta Romanorum*, the *Grimms' *Kinder- und Hausmärchen/ Children's and Household Tales*, and Scandinavian saga and folklore. His late romances or 'fairy novels', especially *The Wood beyond the World* (1894) and *The Well at the World's End* (1896) influenced the work of William Butler *Yeats, Lord *Dunsany, C. S. *Lewis, J. R. R. *Tolkien, and others.   CGS

Mother Goose Legendary female figure often associated with fairy tales. Some scholars believe her origins may lie in the stories and representations of Queen Blanche (d. 783), the mother of Charlemagne, called 'La Reine Pédauque' for her large, flat, goose-like foot. Others have connected her with the Queen of Sheba (also sometimes represented with a webbed foot or a mermaid's tail), or with the classical sibyls, or with St Anne, the good, wise grandmother of the child Jesus. All of these figures are ambiguously associated with story-telling, spinning, and female, sometimes bawdy mystery.

Whatever her origins, Mother Goose was certainly linked with fairy tales in France. They were often referred to as 'contes de ma Mère l'Oie' (in a letter Mme de Sévigné wrote her daughter in 1674, for example); Charles *Perrault used the phrase as the subtitle of his 1697 collection *Histoires ou contes du temps passé (*Stories and Tales of Times Past*). On the frontispiece three children, under a placard bearing the subtitle, listen to a nurse with a distaff—a representation of the motherly, lower-class storytellers Mother Goose, Mother Bunch, Gammer Grethel, Fru Gosen, and all the other 'old wives' and gossips.

In England and America, however, Mother Goose became the icon of nursery rhymes during the 18th century, probably following John Newbery's publication of *Mother Goose's Melody, or Sonnets for the Cradle* (*c.*1765). (The old story that she was a Mrs Elizabeth Goose of Boston has been discredited; no copy of the collection of rhymes bearing her name supposedly published in 1719 has ever been found.) Mother Goose continues to be illustrated, usually as a large goose with an apron or bonnet and spectacles, in endless collections of verses for children and is also still a popular drag role in British pantomime.   EWH

Opie, Iona and Peter (eds.), *The Oxford Dictionary of Nursery Rhymes* (1951).
Warner, Marina, *From the Beast to the Blonde* (1994).

Mother Holle (German: *Frau Holle*) Also known as Mother Holda/Hulda. The definitive version came from the hands of the Brothers *Grimm, who first heard the tale about her from the 18-year-old Dortchen Wild in 1811.

In their final version of 1857, published in *Kinder- und Hausmärchen* (*Children's and Household Tales*), the Grimms took material from other versions to compose a synthetic tale about a young maiden, who is lovely and industrious but is unfortunately the stepdaughter of a nasty woman, whose own daughter is ugly and lazy. The good girl, unnamed in the tale, sits by a well all day long and spins until her fingers bleed. One day she drops the spindle down the well, and her stepmother compels her to find it. So, out of fear, she jumps down into the well and discovers herself in an underworld. As she wanders in this strange country, she encounters an oven that asks her to take out some hot buns, otherwise they will burst. She accommodates the oven. Next she meets a tree full of ripe apples that asks her to knock the apples off of it because they are ready to be eaten. She does this, too. Finally, she comes to a cottage where she meets a fearful-looking old woman with big teeth. This woman, Mother Holle, asks her in a friendly way to help her keep house, and the maiden complies and works very hard. Whenever she makes up Mother Holle's bed and shakes her quilt, the feathers fly, and in the upper world, it snows.

Despite the fact that she is treated well by Mother Holle, the maiden is homesick and would like to return home. The old woman then takes her to a gate and rewards her with a shower of gold that sticks to her, and she is also given the lost spindle. Once the girl returns home, her stepmother gives her a warm welcome because of the gold. After she explains what happened to her, the stepmother decides to send her own daughter down the well. However, once the ugly, lazy maiden arrives in the underworld, she refuses to help the oven and the tree. Moreover, when she is offered a job by Mother Holle to help her clean her house, she slacks off, and Mother Holle dismisses her. As 'reward' for her behaviour, Mother Holle has a big kettle of pitch poured over her. When she returns home, the pitch does not come off her and remains on her for the rest of her life.

There are important literary precursors to 'Mother Holle'. Giambattista *Basile published 'Three Fairies' in the *Pentamerone* (1634–6) and Charles *Perrault *'The Fairies' in *Histoires et contes du temps passé* (1697). In their more baroque versions the lovely stepdaughter is rewarded with gold and jewels for helping a poor helpless woman/

fairy, and these gems fall out of her mouth when she speaks, while the ugly daughter spits out toads and snakes. The stepdaughter marries a prince, and the ugly daughter experiences a horrible death. There are hundreds if not thousands of oral versions that involve the friendly and the unfriendly maidens, and the rewards they reap are based on their behaviour. In both the oral and the literary traditions, the myth about Mother Holle has little significance. In *Deutsche Mythologie* (*German Mythology*) Jacob Grimm wrote that Mother Holle was a mythical creature who could do good or evil depending on whether one maintained an orderly household. She can be found in lakes and fountains, and stories about her circulated in Hesse and Thuringia. This mythical aspect is virtually forgotten in the literary tales and adaptations that followed the Grimms' tale. Ludwig *Bechstein published a version, 'Die Goldmaria und die Pechmaria' (1853), which virtually neglects the mythical aspect and stresses the contrast between the good and bad sisters. This theme is also at the basis of Ferdinand Hummel's opera of 1870, and in the 20th century there have been numerous adaptations for the stage, screen, and television, and books for children that combine the Perrault version of 'The Fairies' with the Grimms' 'Mother Holle' to illustrate the rewards that kindness to old ladies can bring.   JZ

Hagen, Rolf, 'Der Einfluss der Perraultschen Contes auf das volkstümliche Erzählgut' (Diss., Göttingen, 1955).

Jones, Steven Swann, 'Structural and Thematic Applications of the Comparative Method: A Case Study of "The Kind and the Unkind Girls"', *Journal of Folklore Research*, 23 (1986).

Roberts, W. E., *The Tale of the Kind and Unkind Girls* (1958).

Rumpf, Marianne, 'Frau Holle' in Kurt Ranke *et al.* (eds.), *Enzyklopädie des Märchens*, v (1987).

Wienker-Piepho, Sabine, 'Frau Holle zum Beispiel', *Jahrbuch der Brüder Grimm Gesellschaft*, 2 (1992).

Mozart, Wolfgang Amadeus (1756–91) Austrian musician and composer. Born in Salzburg, though seldom remaining long in one place, he travelled extensively throughout Europe, where he performed or conducted many of his compositions. In his short life of only 35 years, Mozart wrote over 600 works in every kind of musical form available to him, including 22 operas. The last of these, and his final completed composition, is the famous 'magic opera', *Die Zauberflöte* (*The Magic Flute*, 1791), principally based upon a fairy tale by A. J. Liebeskind (originally, *Lulu, oder die Zauberflöte*) in *Wieland's collection of oriental tales called *Dschinnistan* (1786). Other sources for the magical and ritual elements may have included Philipp Hafner's play *Megära* (1763) and the novel *Sethos* (1731) by Jean Terrasson. Emanuel Schikaneder (1751–1812), long-time friend of the Mozart family and a well-known actor who had toured south Germany and Austria (playing especially such Shakespearian roles as Hamlet, King Lear, and Macbeth), settled finally in Vienna in 1789 where he managed the Theater auf der Wieden, and fostered there the fashionable *Singspiel* ('song-play', often comic, in which musical numbers are separated by dialogue). Schikaneder, as actor-manager and librettist (possibly assisted by the obscure C. L. Giesecke), eager to promote his theatre, suggested to Mozart that the two of them should collaborate in an opera for Schikaneder's theatre. Having recently composed the three Italian comic operas to libretti by Lorenzo da Ponte (1749–1838)—*Le nozze di Figaro, Don Giovanni*, and *Così fan tutte*—Mozart was eager to write a German opera again. Also, he had just completed, supposedly in only 18 days, a commission to write an *opera seria* (a 'serious opera'). This was *La Clemenza di Tito*, composed for the coronation of the emperor Leopold II as king of Bohemia, in Prague on 6 September 1791. But Mozart was thinking now most of all about *Die Zauberflöte*. He had written *Singspiele* before this one, but nothing so ample—fairy tale, magic, quasi-religious devotion, low comedy all generously combined. Mozart's previous best of this kind was *Die Entführung aus dem Serail* (*The Abduction from the Harem*, 1782) with its exotic Turkish setting (reminiscent of another foreign location in *Idomeneo*, 1781, placed in ancient Crete). But *Die Zauberflöte* is the apotheosis of the *Singspiel* and of the exotic fairy tale, a remarkable grafting together of forms that was to prove an important influence on later German opera, such as Richard *Strauss's *Die Frau ohne Schatten* (*The Woman without a Shadow*, 1919).

Mozart was attracted to Schikaneder's libretto partly because he could develop a number of contrasting dramatic roles. Moreover, like Schikaneder, Mozart was an earnest Freemason, having been initiated into the Craft in 1784. He evidently believed that his new opera should exalt Masonic ideas and principles in a way meaningful for both initiated and uninitiated, and he transforms much of the original fairy tale into musical writing of considerable solemnity, ritual, magic, and symbolism. The overture to the opera opens in E flat major, with its three flats in the key signature, three being an important number to 18th-century Freemasons. But there are many other features of *Die Zauberflöte* generally descriptive or interpretive of Freemasonry, most notably the lofty idealism and super-denominational religious spirit that permeates the whole opera. Yet Mozart combines such seriousness with farcical clowning, presenting the opera on two levels, the spirituality of Tamino–Pamina and the earthy Papageno–Papagena relationship.

The opera begins with the entrance of Tamino, who is pursued by a huge serpent but lacks the arrows with which to defend himself. He calls for help, falls unconscious, and at this moment three Ladies dressed in black and carrying spears enter and kill the serpent. When Tamino recovers consciousness, he meets the bird-catcher Papageno, who boasts that he has killed the serpent himself. The Ladies return, lock up the lying Papageno's mouth with a padlock, and show Tamino a portrait of Pamina, daughter of the Queen of the Night, who is alleged to have been abducted by Sarastro. Tamino falls at once in love with Pamina and determines to find and release her. Now the Ladies remove the padlock from Papageno's mouth, give him a chime of magic bells, and

to Tamino a magic flute, bidding them to carry on their journey to find Pamina, which will be guided safely by three boys or Genii. In subsequent scenes, we discover that Sarastro ('Zoroaster') is no monster, but rather the chief priest of the Temple of Wisdom, and the Queen of the Night is in fact the wicked character. Tamino is put through three tests by which he is made worthy of Pamina, while Papageno parodies this grand journey of initiation on a very different level, being united at last with his bird-wife Papagena. At the same time, the unholy Queen of the Night is vanquished, while the reign of knowledge and the just law of nature endures. Tamino and Pamina thus represent ideal beings who seek to realize an ideal union, while Papageno and Papagena are children of nature who yet long for and achieve a simple union of a lesser kind; for all sorts and conditions of people may live in Sarastro's world of harmony and true wisdom. Mozart's opera was first performed on 30 September 1791; the composer died nine weeks later, in Vienna, on 5 December.   PGS

Angermüller, Rudolph, *Mozart's Operas* (1988).

Dent, Edward J., *Mozart's Operas: A Critical Study* (2nd edn., 1947).

Einstein, Alfred, *Mozart: His Character; His Work* (1945).

Mann, William, *The Operas of Mozart* (1977).

Mrs Pepperpot Title character in the fairy-tale collection by the Norwegian writer Alf *Prøysen, published in 1956–66 and translated into all major languages. Mrs Pepperpot ('Teskjekjerringa' in Norwegian, literally 'Teaspoon Lady'), an old farmer's wife, turns into a lilliputian the size of a pepperpot at whim, and in this shape experiences all sorts of funny adventures, acting as a magical helper and assisting both people and animals. In a true fairy-tale spirit, she is able to understand the language of animals when she turns small and loses this ability upon regaining her normal size.   MN

Mueller, Lisel (1924–) American poet and translator, born in Hamburg, Germany. Winner of the 1997 Pulitzer Prize for her

Staying Alive: New and Selected Poems, Mueller has often returned to her German roots, particularly to the tales of the Brothers *Grimm, which she also studied as a graduate student in the folklore department at Indiana University. Poems that reflect her interest in the tales include her long sequence 'Voices from the Forest', 'Reading the Brothers Grimm to Jenny', 'The Story', and 'Immortality' (based on *'Sleeping Beauty'). EWH

Mulder, Elizabeth (1904–87) Spanish novelist and translator. She wrote a couple of books for children: *Los cuentos del viejo reloj* (*The Old Clock's Tales*, 1941) and *Las noches del gato verde* (*The Green Cat's Nights*, 1963). The former is a collection of beautifully written tales, many of which can be considered fairy stories. The teller of the tales is an old clock set on entertaining two children on a rainy afternoon. Most of the tales have a traditional happy ending as in 'Los tres gigantes tristes' ('The Three Unhappy Giants'), 'La princesa que no podía llorar' ('The Princess who Didn't Know How to Cry'), and 'Cuento de una reina que estaba triste' ('Tale of an Unhappy Queen'). Nevertheless, other fairy stories in the collection, such as 'El niño que encantó al sol' ('The Child who Cast a Spell on the Sun'), end on a sad note in much the same vein as Hans Christian *Andersen's tales. CFR

Munro, Alice (1931–) Canadian author who is considered one of the foremost writers of short stories in the English-speaking world and was awarded the Nobel Prize for literature in 2013. Although Munro has not written as many clearly recognizable fairy tales as her compatriot Margaret *Atwood, her tales are nevertheless filled with motifs from folklore, myth, and fairy tales. Such stories as 'The Lady of Shalott', 'My Mother's Dream', 'Save the Reaper', and 'The Children Stay' resonate with fairy-tale echoes. Writing in a succinct, lucid prose, Munro is a local colour writer who focuses on girls' coming of age, sexual relations, and the loneliness of middle-aged women. Among her best collections of stories are:

Who Do You think You Are? (1978), *The Progress of* Love (1986), The *Love of a Good Woman* (1998), and *Too Much Happiness* (2009). JZ

Carscallen, James, *The Other Country: Patterns in the Writing of Alice Munro* (1993).

Cox, Alisa, *Alice Munro* (2004).

Hallvard, Dahlie, *Alice Munro and Her Works* (1984).

Hebel, Ajay, *The Tumble of Reason: Alice Munro's Discourse of Absence* (1994).

Hooper, Brad, *The Fiction of Alice Munro: An Appreciation* (2008).

Munsch, Robert (1945–) Canadian writer for children. His non-sexist fairy tale *The Paperbag Princess* (1980), about a princess who carries paper bags and rejects a status-conscious prince, had a major impact among writers and educators in the 1980s. Since his success with *The Paperbag Princess*, Munsch has become one of the most popular authors and storytellers for children in North America. He writes about various controversial topics with a wry sense of humour and a propensity for the fantastic. For example, *Good Families Don't* (1990) concerns a child who discovers a great big purple, green, and yellow fart in her home. While her parents refuse to acknowledge the fart's existence, claiming that good families like theirs do not have farts in their house, the fart monster takes over the house and overcomes the police. Only the quick-thinking girl manages to find a way to drive the fart from the house. JZ

Murat, Henriette Julie de Castelnau, comtesse de (1670-1716) French writer from an old noble family of Brittany, whose works can be situated within the late 17th-century fairy-tale vogue. At the age of 16 Murat was sent to court in Paris to marry the comte de Murat and soon became known as a woman of little virtue. Later in life, Murat contested the narrow confines and contradictory expectations her society placed on women, which resulted in the kind of reputation she had to endure, in the pseudo-autobiographical *Mémoires de Madame la comtesse de M**** (1697). In 1694

Murat published her first work, *Histoire de la courtisane Rhodope*, which was considered a libel against the court and resulted in her exile from the capital in that same year to the provincial city of Loches, a sentence which was not revoked until the death of Louis XIV in 1715.

Her husband having since died, Murat went to Loches on her own and pursued her career as a writer. In 1698 she published *Contes de fées* (*Fairy Tales*) comprised of 'Le Parfait Amour' ('Perfect Love'), 'Anguillette', and 'Jeune et Belle' ('Young and Beautiful'). That same year *Les Nouveaux Contes des fées* appeared, containing 'Le Palais de la Vengeance' ('The Palace of Revenge'), 'Le Prince des feuilles' ('The Prince of Leaves'), 'Le Bonheur des moineaux' ('The Happiness of Sparrows'), and 'L'Heureuse peine' ('The Happy Sorrow'). Her final collection of tales, *Histoires sublimes et allégoriques* (*Sublime and Allegorical Stories*, 1699) included 'Le Roy Porc' ('The Pig King'), 'L'isle de la Magnificence' ('The Island of Magnificence'), 'Le Sauvage' ('The Savage'), and 'Le Turbot'. Murat also wrote a novel, *Les Lutins du château de Kernosi* (*The Elves of Kernosi Castle*, 1710).

Murat often combined traditional French fairy lore with Graeco-Roman mythology. For instance, the fairy Danamo of 'Le Parfait Amour' is a descendant of Calypso, and the princess of 'Anguillette' becomes a second Hebe, the Greek goddess of youth. Murat also borrowed from *Straparola, as the very title 'Le Roi Porc' would suggest, and for her tale 'Le Sauvage', the plot of which follows closely Straparola's story about Constantine, the daughter of the king of Egypt who disguises herself as a man—a source which was also the likely inspiration for Mme d'*Aulnoy's 'Belle-Belle, ou le Chevalier Fortuné' ('Belle-Belle, or the Chevalier Fortuné').

In many of her tales Murat grappled with the question of love, which she treated from different perspectives. In 'Anguillette', for instance, the princess Plousine is kind to a fairy who, in the tradition of *Mélusine, is transformed into an eel for a few days each month. Plousine is rewarded with both beauty and wit, but learns that fairies are powerless in matters of love. She is caught between her passionate love for Atimir and her more tempered love for the Prince of the Peaceful Island; passion overrides temperance, and the tale ends tragically. In 'Le Palais de la Vengeance', Murat explores another tragic end to passionate love: boredom. When the dwarf Pagan falls in love with the princess Imis, he places obstacles between her and her lover Philax until he realizes that condemning the two lovers to live together perpetually in a crystal palace is the surest way to put out the flames of their passion.

In her tales Murat emphasized the connection between the fairies and the fates, for fairies constantly foresee and even try to control the destinies of the tales' protagonists. However, there is one domain in which fairies have no control, which is the lesson of 'Le Prince des feuilles': the domain of love.   AD

Cromer, Sylvie, '"Le Sauvage"—Histoire sublime et allégorique de Madame de Murat', *Merveilles et Contes*, 1.1 (May 1987).

Welch, Marcelle Maistre, 'Manipulation du discours féerique dans les Contes de Fées de Mme de Murat', *Cahiers du Dix-septième*, 5.1 (spring 1991).

Murphy, Louise (1943–) American writer. Her most significant and acclaimed work is *The True Story of Hansel and Gretel: A Novel of War and Survival* (2003). This adaptation sets *'Hansel and Gretel' in Poland during the Second World War, following connections between Jewish, Romani, and Polish peasant characters and their experiences of the Holocaust. The two main characters are given the pseudonyms Hansel and Gretel to obscure their Jewish names, and their narrative sometimes mirrors, and sometimes contrasts with, the traditional fairy tale. Writing against stereotype, Murphy makes the Witch character the children's saviour and the story's moral compass. The Stepmother also acts heroically in defence of her husband and stepchildren. The villain, not surprisingly given the context, is a male Nazi SS officer.   PG

Musäus, Johann Karl August (1735–87) One of the leading cultural figures at the

Weimar court, Musäus published *Volks-märchen der Deutschen* (*Folktales of the Germans*) in five volumes between 1782 and 1786. The 14 tales include magical elements and embrace disparate genres. Despite their title, the tales are literary rather than 'folk' and many derive from non-German sources. Musäus's playfully sophisticated literary style met the approval of his contemporary Christoph Martin *Wieland, who noted that 'all fairy tales did not have to be told in the childlike style of my *Mother Goose'. Like the *Grimms, Musäus excluded the fairy world and populated his tales with now-traditional characters such as transformed animals, sorcerers, giants, animal bridegrooms, and wicked stepmothers.

Musäus personified his characters as cleverly as did Ludwig *Bechstein, in a stylistically expansive text. One canny hero who understands fairy-tale magic recognizes that talking animals must be creatures under an enchantment, and quickly marries all three of his daughters to beasts, who enrich him and eventually return to human shape. In one form or another, all of Musäus's tales explore love and the married state.

Claiming to be the first to rework German *Volksmärchen*, that is, fairy tales told by the people, Musäus stressed that the tales were all thoroughly native, transmitted orally through numberless generations. However, 9 of Musäus's 14 tales derive demonstrably from prior literary sources:

1. *Basile, 'Li tre ri anemale' → d'*Aulnoy, 'La Belle aux cheveux d'or' → Musäus, 'Bücher der Chronika der drei Schwestern'
4. Johannes Prätorius, *Volksbuch* → Musäus, 'Rübezahl'
5. *Perrault, 'Peau d'âne' (*Donkey-Skin') + 'La belle au bois dormant' (*Sleeping Beauty') + Mme de *Villeneuve, 'Les Nayades' → Musäus, 'Nymphe des Brunnens'
6. Piccolomini, *Historia Bohemica* + Johannes Dubravius, *Historia regni bohemiae* → Musäus 'Libussa'
7. *Thousand and One Nights* + motifs from Swan Maidens → Musäus, 'Der geraubte Schleier'
8. 'Die Matrone von Ephesus' → Musäus, 'Liebestreue'
10. various French versions of *'Riquet à la Houppe' (Perrault, *Bernard, Lheritier) → Musäus, 'Ulrich mit dem Bühel'
12. Bodmer, Graf von Gleichen → [*Volks-bücher?*] → Musäus, 'Melechsala'
14. Erasmus Francisci, 'Höllischer Proteus' → Bürger, 'Lenore' → Musäus, 'Die Entführung'

The most enlightening source about Musäus's fairy-tale production comes from his own pen. To a correspondent he wrote that fairy tales were back in fashion and that he was therefore preparing a collection 'that will bear the title, *Fairy Tales of the Folk: a Reader for Big and Little Children* (*Volksmärchen, ein Lesebuch für grosse und kleine Kinder*). For it I'm gathering the most hackneyed old wives' tales that I'm inflating and making ten times more magical than they originally were. My dear wife has high hopes that it will be a very lucrative product.' Manfred Grätz, historian of the emergence of fairy tales in Germany, notes that Musäus used the word 'Volksmärchen' in the older sense of fanciful tales (*Lügengeschichte*) and that Musäus's purpose paralleled Perrault's, in that he wished to praise ancient virtues while depicting the medieval period as less simple than his romantic contemporaries wished to believe.

Musäus's collection, reprinted in 1787–8, 1795–8, and 1804–5, enjoyed a long popularity, which many contemporaries attributed to his humorous style. In 1845 it was translated into English as *The Enchanted Knights*.
                                                                      RBB

Grätz, Manfred, *Das Märchen in der deutschen Aufklärung: Vom Feenmärchen zum Volksmärchen* (1988).
Klotz, Volker, *Das europäische Kunstmärchen* (1985).
McGlathery, James M., 'Magic and Desire from Perrault to Musaus: Some Examples', *Eighteenth-Century Life*, 7.1 (October 1981).
Miller, Norbert (ed.), *Johann Karl August Musäus. Volksmärchen der Deutschen* (1976).
Tismar, Jens, *Kunstmärchen* (1977).

Musil, Robert (1880–1942) Distinguished Austrian writer. Aside from the fairy-tale novellas in his trilogy *Drei Frauen* (*Three Women*, 1924) which show his interest in the romantic tradition, Musil also incorporated fairy-tale motifs into his collection of stories *Nachlass zu Lebzeiten* (*Posthumous Papers while Alive*, 1936). In his major work *Der Mann ohne Eigenschaften* (*The Man without Qualities*, 1930–43), Musil developed a mode of cognition in which the fairy tale functions as a preliminary stage to his *Utopie des anderen Zustands* (Utopia of the Other Condition).   BKM

> Kümmerling-Meibauer, Bettina, *Die Kunstmärchen von Hofmannsthal, Musil und Döblin* (1991).

myth/mythology and fairy tales In the late 20th century, the proliferation of reading materials for young people and significant paradigm shifts within Western societies have led to a re-evaluation of the status of myth and folk tale. Once considered a standard element within a child's reading, these interrelated genres have undergone rather different fates. In the West, myth usually denoted Greek, Roman, and Norse mythologies, recognizable by story elements or motifs. These mythologies have been relegated to a minor position in the body of children's literature and have been replaced by 'myth' in the very different sense of grand cultural narratives. Folk tale has also shrunk in scope, but with the difference that a relatively small number of 'literary' folk tales—that is, *fairy* tales derived for the most part from the collections of Charles *Perrault, the Brothers *Grimm, and Hans Christian *Andersen—still remain very widely known and frequently reproduced in modern Western society. Instead of the range of tales available in, for example, the 12 volumes of Andrew *Lang's *Fairy Book* series (published between 1889 and 1910), late 20th-century children are likely to know few fairy tales other than a reduced corpus of 10 or 15. These tales are often only those popularized by *Disney films, although more local conditions, such as the continuance of the Christmas pantomime tradition in England, also play a part in determining which fairy tales survive. The modern corpus includes

*'Snow White', *'Cinderella', *'Sleeping Beauty', *'Beauty and the Beast', *'Little Red Riding Hood', *'The Frog King', *'Hansel and Gretel', *'Aladdin', *'The Ugly Duckling', and *'The Little Mermaid'; also well known but slightly less familiar are tales such as *'Rapunzel', 'The Dancing Princesses', *'Puss-in-Boots', *'The Princess and the Pea', and *'Rumpelstiltskin'.

These literary stories have become mythic, not in the old sense of the term, but in the sense that they have naturalized particular and formulaic ways of thinking about individuals and social relationships. In other words, they have become the bearers of grand cultural narratives. The tales listed above constitute a mythic matrix constructed around three assumptions: gender and sexuality, and hence male and female behaviour, are ordered according to a patriarchal hierarchy; good will always conquer evil; and the meritorious individual will rise in the world, winning prestige, riches, and power. Howsoever a retold tale varies in its focus and emphasis, its processes and outcome will normally be a configuration of these assumptions. Disney films have tended to naturalize this matrix by reaffirming conservative social structures, and especially through a 'disequilibrium between good and evil', such that the forces of evil dominate events until the denouement, when the final victory of the forces of good restores the proper or 'natural' order (that is, normative social values) and distributes rewards to the deserving. Where the instrument of victory is male, his power lies in courage and resourcefulness; where female, her strength is in her beauty, sensibility, and compassion. In *Aladdin*, for example, once evil has overreached and brought about its own destruction, the film swiftly comes to a close by instantiating all three elements of the mythic matrix. Such a close represents social ideology as if it were simply the way things are.

The concentration of fairy tale into a relatively small number of frequently reproduced examples is not merely a historical accident. Because such tales have a long history within the civilizing process whereby a society determines its own structures of behaviour and relationships, the tales most likely to have endured are those which most aptly reflect the social and political assumptions of the social groups which control a community's economic, political, educational, and media institutions. Other tales have been effectively excluded, and the late 20th-century fairy-tale canon seems to be virtually closed. Newly created tales, even those which conform closely with the structures and forms of the classic tales, do not enter the canon, and are soon forgotten. Of course, problems of copyright inhibit reproduction and reworking of such stories, but their lack of underpinning by tradition is probably a greater barrier. On the other hand, the classic canon also resists the reintroduction of 'forgotten' traditional works which are not subject to copyright restrictions.

A pertinent example is afforded by Jim *Henson's television series *The Storyteller*, which included some very inventive recreations and combinations of less familiar stories such as 'All Fur', 'The Six Swans', 'The True Bride', and 'The Soldier and Death'. Although it reached a wide audience through television and a subsequent video release, there has been no indication that the series changed the contemporary classic canon, either through incorporation of some of these new versions or recuperation of the stories lying behind them. A plausible reason for this lack of effect is that the Henson retellings deviated in both form and theme from the tales characteristic of the canon. The intrusive presence of the storyteller and his talking dog might have served to evoke the oral and folk origins of fairy tales, but instead the comic and frame-breaking aspects of their dialogue drew attention to the constructedness of the genre and its tendency to become inadvertently comic or melodramatic. For example, the pervasive comic wordplay in *The True Bride*—a tale woven mainly out of a combination of motifs from the Grimms' 'The True Bride' and the Scandinavian 'East of the Sun, West of the Moon'—is a clear indicator of the tale's self-reflective character. More important,

however, is the tales' departure from the familiar mythic significances of the canon, as in *Sapsorrow*, for example, which is a degradation-and-disguise story woven from elements of three related tales: Perrault's *'Donkey-Skin', the Grimms' 'All Fur', and (for the ending) the Scandinavian 'Kari Woodengown' (from Lang, *The Red Fairy Book*). The tale type is a complex depiction of male domination and female submission, in that its central figure is a princess whose widowed father attempts to marry her, and to avoid this she flees in the guise of a base and ugly creature and hides by taking up a menial occupation. Her period of degradation before marriage to the local prince and reinstatement to her proper rank seems to represent a period in which she expiates the guilt of the female sexuality which has made her an object of attention and hence a victim in the first place.

Sapsorrow arrives at its happy outcome by developing a potentiality in the structure of 'Kari Woodengown', whereby Kari has dealings with the prince three times in her wooden gown and three times in magnificent clothing, but *Sapsorrow* transforms this pattern by depicting its heroine as a resourceful young woman who not only arouses the prince's desire when she appears in her beautiful, ballroom form, but also brings about a growth of his humanity by repeatedly challenging structures of social and gender hierarchy in her conversations with him when she is in her 'Straggletag' disguise. Hence the tale is no longer about a forlorn princess whose destiny is to gain a high-ranking husband as recompense for her patient suffering, but about forging an equal and companionate relationship, for the prince now must implicitly prove himself worthy of Sapsorrow/Straggletag. Unlike the princes of both 'Donkey-Skin' and 'Kari Woodengown', this prince neither knows nor suspects that Straggletag is his dream princess, and willingly agrees to marry her before her identity is revealed. This outcome (redemption through romance) does not represent a radical reworking of the basis of relationships between male and female in fairy tales, but in that it is reached through a combination of female agency and a modification of masculinity, it deviates significantly from the mythic matrix.

Fairy tales pose a particular challenge for storytellers, illustrators, and critics who wish to use literature to disseminate contemporary forms of humane values. They often pivot on or incorporate world views antithetical to those preferred by many members of modern societies, an aspect they share with mythological narratives. For a long time myth was generally (though not universally) considered to be an older form than folk tale, and ever since the Grimm brothers proposed that *Märchen*, or folk tales, were vestiges of ancient myths, the thought has persisted that these tales often preserve in their story structures elements of an older, intuitively figurative vision of being and existence, and have an innate cultural value for that reason. Hence it can be claimed that well-known tales such as 'Sleeping Beauty' or 'Rapunzel', in which the main character undergoes a long period of dormancy which is perhaps a figurative death, reflect a fertility myth pivoting on images of death and rebirth. What has disappeared from the folk tales, in this view, is some anterior religious significance. In this context, an essential premiss for the identification of myth is that it deals with the irruption of the sacred, and especially supernatural beings, into the world. The effect of such irruptions is to bring something into the world, to be a beginning. The Greek death-and-rebirth myth about the abduction of Persephone by Hades, for example, signifies the origin of seasonal climatic change, as the world 'dies' with Persephone's winter descent to the Underworld, and revives with her return in spring. Once the process has been set in motion, it goes on being repeated as an aspect of human experience of the world, as in many other fertility myths.

Further, because the process has its origins in the actions of supernatural beings, it is exemplary for all significant human activities, from birth, through the social life of people, to death, and imbues such incidents with the qualities and value of a religious experience. As such, it guarantees that human experience of the world is not random and meaningless, but repeatable and significant. Such a structuring of thought has crucial implications in the modern era, either because we return to the ancient myths seeking a sense of purpose and order we find lacking from our own everyday narratives, or because traditional tales are reframed in conformity with new cultural codings so that they express myths of another kind. The strands which go to make up what was referred to above as a mythic matrix are more properly referred to as metanarratives. That is, narrative forms—fictions, histories, personal narratives, and, of course, myths and fairy tales—are shaped so that they conform in terms of theme and outcome with values and norms which are assumed to be central or common within a society at a particular historical moment. A metanarrative thus supplies presuppositions about what are proper social and material objects of desire and what behaviours will produce an appropriate outcome. Its function as such is quite similar to ancient myth in its capacity to offer exemplary models for life.

The fairy tales which modern scholars most often discuss in relation to an antecedent myth are those which involve an animal as bridegroom, best known by versions of 'Beauty and the Beast'. These tales can be related back to the myth of Cupid and Psyche retold by *Apuleius in the 2nd century, and so there exists a textual tradition which includes both myth and fairy tale and which has common structures and motifs. Where the genres most clearly diverge, however, is in theme. Apuleius' retelling portrays the marriage of Psyche to a mysterious husband who visits her only in the dark, and who is possibly a monster. As in many subsequent versions of the story, when she attempts to see him one night she loses him and can only win him back by undergoing a quest involving many tests and tribulations. In fairy tale versions the quest normally ends with a disenchantment motif as the heroine regains her partner by ending the spell which has enchanted him. As myth, 'Cupid and Psyche' was probably a narrative about a process of initiation, or rite of passage, whereby faith was tested and confirmed as the initiate grew in spiritual stature. In the version which comes down to us, the names of the characters were a cue for Apuleius to recast the story as a 'philosophical allegory of the progress of the rational soul towards intellectual love' (Robert Graves) or 'the journey of the soul towards the concealed godhead' (Marina *Warner), though as a forerunner of the Beauty and Beast tale it has been interpreted rather as a quintessential account of gender role modelling.

For adults who retell traditional stories, both myth and fairy tale are attributed with value as *story* itself. That is, as a narrative which audiences may recognize as similar to other such narratives because it is patterned by archetypal situations and characterizations, a story transmits its latent value as a particular working out of perennial human desires and destinies. The pattern seems meaningful in itself without need of explanation, because signification inheres in the repeated structures and motifs. This combination of structure and assumptions about reception facilitates the transformation of story from one kind of mythic significance to the other. Amongst other functions, the story of a myth or a fairy tale can be conventionally thought of as pointing towards five key areas of signification, all of which can be discerned in both 'Cupid and Psyche' and later animal bridegroom narratives. Story alerts audiences to the distinctions between surfaces and depths and hence between material and transcendent meanings; it fosters responses to the numinous or mysterious; it suggests ways of making sense of being and existence; it helps define the place of the individual in the world; and it offers social and moral guidance. In practical terms, the distance between transcendent meanings and social behaviour can be very great indeed, but their co-presence within a bundle of significations indicates that the business of such story is to produce versions of subjective wholeness. Thus the social behaviours inscribed within story are naturalized, on the grounds that 'this is how things are' and that 'this organization is confirmed by

its link with the timeless and transcendent'. The apparent seamlessness of the complex masks the fact that myth and fairy tale are structured ideologically by such things as individualism, imperialism, masculinism, and misogyny. New metanarratives which are developed either by retelling or reinterpreting the stories are apt to emerge within and reproduce those ideological structures. Hence, as with the older myths, they present their thematic implications as an inherent property of human experience of the world.

In the modern era, there have been four main ways in which tellers and interpreters of fairy tales have attempted to preserve the genre while reforming the metanarratives which have shaped it since the 17th century. The first is by the invention of new tales which employ traditional structures and motifs—for example, the formulaic beginnings and endings, the general recourse to character stereotypes, the recurrent patterns of action—but seek outcomes no longer shaped by patriarchal or bourgeois ideology. Second, because the conventionalized forms of fairy tales tend to reinforce existing metanarratives and so make it difficult to reshape the stories without recourse to drastic processes of revision, many attempts are made to transform the tales through parody, or in the form of the 'fractured' fairy tale. The usual objects of parody are the most widely known tales. Parodies have nevertheless had only limited success in questioning contemporary social formations, both because the parodied story is inevitably reinscribed as a normative pre-text, and because they continue to conform with conventional outcomes dependent on happy endings and the evocation of an orderly society.

The third method is to group carefully refashioned tales in anthologies so that their conjunction instantiates metanarratives of other kinds, or to embed them within a frame which constructs a point of view from which the gathered tales are to be interpreted. An example of the former type is Robert Leeson's *Smart Girls* (1993), a bundle of tales in which meritorious females deftly overturn patriarchal hierarchy; an example of the latter is Susan Price's *Head and Tales*

(1993), in which the frame narrative focuses on issues of social class and draws attention to the volume's pervasive themes of social justice, personal freedom, and human responsibility. Such strategies successfully instantiate alternative metanarratives, but usually at the cost of wide audience appeal because the tales included are generally drawn from outside the classic literary canon.

Finally, the fourth approach to altering the metanarrative of fairy tales begins as acts of interpretation and thence impacts on processes of retelling. This approach is grounded in modern myths derived from psychoanalysis. Just as the Oedipal myth of psychosexual development was fashioned from an appropriation of an ancient Greek myth, so fairy tales are subject to retrospective interpretation as narratives addressing the psychological problems of childhood: narcissistic disappointments; Oedipal dilemmas; sibling rivalries; learning to relinquish childhood dependencies; gaining a feeling of selfhood and self-worth, and a sense of moral obligation. From this perspective, the animal bridegroom tales become, psychoanalytically, 'illustrations of a process where guilt and fear because of the sexual desires are followed by sublimation of those wishes into something pure and fine' (Heuscher), or an account of how the aspects of 'sex, love and life' are wedded into a unity (Bettelheim).

Such conclusions have often met with a sceptical response, especially from feminist critics who question the presumption that fairy tales express universal values, and argue instead that they reflect distinct culturally and historically determined developmental paradigms for boys and girls, and these paradigms are products of gendered social practices. Hence the tales are apt to simplify what is in practice a complicated process of socialization. What still remains unresolvable is whether the meaning of the tales lies in their story structures—where, for example, boys are usually active and resourceful, and girls are passive and dependent—or their metanarratives, that is, from textual representations or cultural assumptions.

All attempts to redirect the metanarratives of fairy tales are based on the assumption that the tales are one of culture's primary mechanisms for inculcating roles and behaviours, symbolically portraying basic human problems and social prescriptions. The different ways of rewriting and rereading them accept that they function to help children find meaning in life, but the history and contemporary contestation of myths and metanarratives associated with fairy tales is a salutary reminder that meaning, subjectivity, and sociality are historically produced and subject to whatever assumptions about gender, class, and so on prevail at moments of production and reproduction.   JAS

Anderson, Graham, *Fairytale in the Ancient World* (2000).

Anderson, Graham, *Greek and Roman Folklore: A Handbook* (2006).

Bettelheim, Bruno, *The Uses of Enchantment: The Meaning and Importance of Fairy Tales* (1976).

Eliade, Mircea, *Myth and Reality* (1963).

Heuscher, Julius E., *A Psychiatric Study of Myths and Fairy Tales* (1963; 2nd edn., 1974).

Rose, Ellen Cronan, 'Through the Looking Glass: When Women Tell Fairy Tales', in Elizabeth Abel, Marianne Hirsch, and Elizabeth Langland (eds.), *The Voyage In: Fictions of Female Development* (1983).

Thompson, Stith, *The Folktale* (1946).

Warner, Marina, *From the Beast to the Blonde* (1994).

Zipes, Jack, *Fairy Tales and the Art of Subversion: The Classical Genre for Children and the Process of Civilization* (1983).

Zipes, Jack, *Fairy Tale as Myth/Myth as Fairy Tale* (1994).

Napoli, Donna Jo (1948–) Professor of linguistics and leading American writer of fairy tales for young readers. Her first work, *The Hero of Barletta* (1989), based on an Italian folk tale, concerns a clever giant who saves his village from a hostile army. Since the publication of this humorous story, Napoli has focused on the retelling of classical fairy tales with great originality and extraordinary depth. *The Prince of the Pond: Otherwise Known as De Fawg Pin* (1992), is a revision of 'The *Frog Prince' told from the viewpoint of Jade, a female frog, who recalls how she helped a bewildered prince, who was transformed into a frog by a wicked hag, to survive in the wilderness and regain his human form. Napoli followed this fairy-tale adaptation with two sequels: *Jimmy, the Pickpocket of the Palace* (1995), involves a frog who was sired by the prince when he was a frog. He is turned into a human when he tries to save the pond from the hag and discovers that he does not like human life in the palace; *Gracie, the Pixie of the Puddle* (2004) deals with a tiny female frog who saves Jimmy, the pickpocket, from all sorts of dangers and also makes him realize his love for her. In *The Magic Circle* (1993), a powerful retelling of *'Hansel and Gretel', Napoli investigates the prehistory of the witch with great sympathy, and she reveals that the witch was at one time a good healer but became transformed into an ogress by evil spirits. The dark side of fairy tales is also examined in *Zel* (1996), a revision of *'Rapunzel', in which Napoli explores the psychology of the three main characters—the girl locked in the tower, the prince who wants to save her, and the witch/mother, who wants to keep her—by allowing each one to tell the story and shift perspectives. Napoli also uses shifting perspectives in *Spinners* (1999), an adaptation of *'Rumpelstiltskin', except that the tale ends on a tragic note because of the selfishness of all three main figures in the story. In *Crazy Jack*

(1999), an original interpretation of *'Jack and the Beanstalk', she adds a romantic element to a profound tale about a young man's intense desire to prove himself and overcome the giant who represents more than just voraciousness. *Beast* (2000), a retelling of *'Beauty and the Beast', which draws on Persian folklore for its setting, involves the son of a shah, cursed for his arrogance. *Bound* (2004), based on *Cinderella variants, takes place in Ming China and critically depicts the negative effects of foot binding. Napoli's latest experiment with fairy-tale classics is *The Wager* (2010), a fascinating re-creation of a Sicilian folk tale and the Grimms' 'Bearskin'. The setting is medieval Italy, and a young nobleman named Don Giovanni loses his fortune after a tsunami. To recover his wealth he makes a bet with the devil and learns how to rid himself of arrogance and become humane and civilized in his struggle with demonic forces. Napoli's fairy tales are subtle and complex and can be considered crossover works that appeal to young readers and adults.   JZ

Naubert, Benedikte (b. Hebenstreit; m. Holderieder, widowed; m. Naubert, 1756–1819) A popular and prolific German novelist, Naubert was born in Leipzig and after marriage lived in Naumburg. She used fairy-tale motifs extensively in her fictional works; she stands with *Musäus and *Wieland in the tradition of the German Enlightenment fairy tale. Her work characteristically combines the genres of historical novel (particularly medieval), Gothic novel, legend, and fairy tale. She is noted for her care with historical sources, using such works as Tacitus' *Germania*, Percy's *Reliques*, and archival material from the university library of Leipzig, provided by male friends with access. Following the success of Musäus's collection of German tales (1782–6), Naubert wrote the four-volume *Neue Volksmährchen der Deutschen* (*New German Tales*, 1789–93), which feature creative versions of the following tales or figures: St Julian; Queen Guinevere and tales of Arthur's court in tandem with the *Mother Holle tale; the legends of the British and German supernatural spirits Mother Ludlam and Rübezahl; the lady in white; St Ottilie; the Oldenburg Horn; the Pied Piper of Hamelin; the daughter of the Elf King; St George, and the Nibelung treasure. A second, smaller collection of fairy tales, *Heitere Träume in kleinen Erzählungen* (*Delightful Dreams in Short Tales*, 1806), shows the influences of the French women writers around Charles *Perrault in the tales 'Fanchon vielleuse', 'Persin-Persinet', and 'Blanca Bella'. Her 'magic novel' *Velleda* (1795) treats legendary women of Anglo-Saxon and Germanic tales. Boadicea, Queen of ancient Britain, strives to rescue her seven daughters, coming into conflict with the Germanic enchantress, Velleda, who is protecting them. This novel also contains two other stories of ancient legend and magic in ancient Egypt, a favourite locale for Naubert's tales. Her other collections also combine detailed narrative, legend, and magic or mystery: *Wanderungen der Phantasie in die Gebiete der Wahrheit* (*Fantastic Excursions into the Realm of the Truth*, 1806) and the 'mythological tale', 'Die Minyaden' (1806). Many of her historical novels combine elements of magic and legend with fact and fiction: *Amalgunde, Königin von Italien oder das Märchen von der Wunderquelle* (*Amalgunde, Queen of Italy or the Tale of the Magic Fountain*, 1787), *Gebhard Truchses von Waldburg Churfürst von Cöln oder die astrologischen Fürsten* (*Gebhard, Steward of Waldburg, Elector of Cologne, or the Astrological Princes*, 1791) and *Ottilie, oder das Schloss Zähringen* (*Ottilia, or The Castle Zähringen*, 1791). Some of her other works have

more affinity with magical romantic fiction: *Almé oder Egyptische Mährchen* (*Almé or Egyptian Tales*, 5 vols., 1793–7). Although well known for the more than 50 novels she published, Naubert carefully maintained her anonymity until 1819; widely esteemed as 'the author of Walter von Montbarry and Thekla von Thurn', her most popular works, she was read by such writers as Sir Walter Scott, Achim von *Arnim, and the *Grimms. Wilhelm Grimm discovered her identity through a friend of her publisher and travelled to Naumburg to interview her about her works in December 1809. After republications and translations into French and English during the period from the 1780s to the 1820s, her work was largely forgotten until the 1980s.   JB

Blackwell, Jeannine, 'Die verlorene Lehre der Benedikte Naubert: die Verbindung zwischen Fantasie und Geschichtsschreibung', in Helga Gallas and Magdalene Heuser (eds.), *Untersuchungen zum Roman von Frauen um 1800* (1990).

Dorsch, Nikolaus, *Sich rettend aus der kalten Würklichkeit: die Briefe Benedikte Nauberts: Edition, Kik, Kommentar* (1986).

Grätz, Manfred, *Das Märchen in der deutschen Aufklärung: Vom Feenmärchen zum Volksmärchen* (1988).

Jarvis, Shawn C., 'The Vanished Woman of Great Influence: Benedikte Naubert's Legacy and German Women's Fairy Tales', in Katherine R. Goodman and Edith Waldstein (eds.), *In The Shadow of Olympus: German Women Writers from 1790–1810* (1991).

Runge, Anita, *Literarische Praxis von Frauen um 1800: Briefroman, Autobiographie, Märchen* (1997).

Schreinert, Kurt, *Benedikte Naubert: ein Beitrag zur Entstehungsgeschichte des historischen Romans in Deutschland* (1941; repr. 1969).

Sweet, Denis, 'Introduction to Benedikte Naubert, "The Cloak"', in Jeannine Blackwell and Susanne Zantop (eds.), *Bitter Healing: German Women Writers 1700–1830. An Anthology* (1990).

Neill, John R. (John Rea Neill, 1877–1943) Definitive illustrator of *Oz* books. Trained at the Pennsylvania Academy of Fine Arts, Neill was 25 when he got his big break—little suspecting that he would spend the next

41 years as 'Imperial Illustrator of Oz'. He was hired to succeed W. W. *Denslow as L. Frank *Baum's illustrator after a bitter copyright dispute over *The *Wonderful Wizard of Oz* (1900). Insolvent, Baum hoped that a sequel would solve his financial woes. It did (temporarily). *The Marvelous Land of Oz* (1904), a profusely illustrated text with 16 colour plates, 24 full-page line drawings, and over 100 smaller pictures, was an immediate success, and Neill continued his collaboration. He had a beautifully detailed style similar to Arthur *Rackham's and an economy of line, evidenced in his trademark designs of Oz (an encircled Z) and his name ('Jno'). In addition to the hundreds of characters he brought to life in book illustrations, he also designed promotional materials ranging from posters to celluloid buttons. After *The Emerald City of Oz* (1910), which Baum wrote as his last Oz story, Neill illustrated his *Sea Fairies* (1911) and *Sky Island* (1912). But disappointing sales forced the author and artist to return to Oz for annual sequels. Marketing became aggressive when the publishers Reilly & Britton suggested that Neill produce a book of cardstock dolls (*The Oz Toy Book, Cut-outs for the Kiddies*) to promote *The Scarecrow of Oz* (1915). Unfortunately, they neglected to secure Baum's permission. The 'Royal Historian of Oz' was furious that he might be embroiled in another copyright dispute, but accepted an apology none the less. The relationship became strained, however, and he tried to replace Neill because he did not feel the illustrations were whimsical enough for young readers. But Neill collaborated on the rest of Baum's novels plus all 19 titles by Ruth Plumly *Thompson, the Second Royal Historian of Oz.

After drawing Oz for 38 years, Neill had his chance to describe it when he became the Third Royal Historian. *The Wonder City of Oz* (1940), *The Scalawagons of Oz* (1941), and *Lucky Bucky in Oz* (1942) differed radically from previous books. His somewhat unbridled imagination modernized Oz with elections, automobiles, and animate, warring houses. Allusions to the Second World War were further underscored by a dustjacket letter from Bucky of Oz: he tells boys and girls that 'The Nazis and Japs are harder to beat than the Gnomes' and urges them to buy Victory Bonds and Stamps. Slumping wartime sales and a paper shortage prompted the publishers to postpone a fourth Neill title, *The Runaway in Oz*. Published in 1995 by Books of Wonder, it is the 36th Oz book that Neill either illustrated or wrote.   MLE

Greene, David L., and Martin, Dick, *The Oz Scrapbook* (1977).
Snow, Jack, *Who's Who in Oz* (1954).

Němcová, Božena (1820–62) Czech writer who some consider to be the mother of Czech prose. She married at a very early age and had a difficult relationship with her authoritarian husband. Both were involved in the Czech national revival and suffered from persecution because of their political beliefs. After 1845, Němcová and her husband had to move frequently, and they lived in small towns in different parts of Bohemia. Sometimes Němcová travelled by herself and gathered folklore material in Bohemia and Slovakia. Her research enabled her to write many books, including collections of Czech and Slovak folktales and fairy tales. Němcová's first published works were the patriotic poem *To the Czech Women* (1843) and the book *Folk Fairy Tales and Legends* (parts 1–7, 1845–7). In the 1850s, she published realistic short stories and novellas about common people. Among her best works are 'Baruška', 'Wild Bára', *In and Near the Castle*, and her most popular work, the novella *The Grandmother* (1855), which portrays a remarkable woman in an ideal Czech community. In addition she collected Slovak fairy tales and published them in Czech translation in 1857–8. In the course of time after her death, she became a legendary heroine, and there are three museums dedicated to her in northeastern Bohemia. JZ

Morava, Jirí, *Sehnsucht in meiner Seele: Božena Němcová, Dichterin: Ein Frauenschicksal in Alt-Österreich* (1995).
Součková, Milada, *The Czech Romantics* (1958).

Nerval, Gérard de (pseudonym of **Gérard Labrunie**, 1808–55) A French writer best known for his poetry and fantastic tales. Reared in the country, he felt that the 'old French ballads' of the provinces should be preserved, yet feared being labelled too 'historic' or 'scientific'. None the less, his work between 1842 and 1854 included 26 folk songs and many legends: some were collected as *Chansons et légendes du Valois* (1842). The occult and delirium, which ultimately led to his suicide, also influenced his writing.

The German romantics inspired Nerval's early work. His translation of *Faust* at 19 was praised by *Goethe, and he later penned *Hoffmann-inspired fantastic stories set in the Valois, such as 'La Main enchantée' ('The Enchanted Hand') and 'Sylvie' (in *Les Filles du feu* (*Daughters of the Fire*, 1854)). After collaborating with Dumas père and obsessing about an actress, Nerval led a bohemian existence throughout Germany and the Orient. He suffered his first breakdown in 1841, and recorded the resulting confusion between dream and reality, illusion and delusion in *Aurélia* (1855), his masterpiece. Religious syncretism of mythology, the Cabbala, and Swedenborgian theosophy, plus a metaphysical 'descent' into the psyche, gave Nerval's work an Orphic quality whose Illuminism prefigured symbolism. *Les Illuminés* (1852) and *Les Chimères* (1855) typify his esoteric poetry.   MLE

Bénichou, Paul, *Nerval et la chanson folklorique* (1970).

Knapp, Bettina, *Gérard de Nerval: The Mystic's Dilemma* (1980).

Richer, Jean, *Nerval: expérience vécue & création ésotérique* (1987).

Strauss, Walter A., *Descent and Return: The Orphic Theme in Modern Literature* (1971).

Nesbit, Edith (1858–1924) English writer whose children's books include many fantasies with a contemporary setting. Obliged to support herself and the family in the early years of her marriage to Hubert Bland in 1880, she did much hack work before she began writing stories for children. Initially these were about the Bastable family, genteelly poor like the Blands, and their efforts to restore the family fortunes. But in 1899 she contributed a series of modern fairy tales

to the *Strand* under the title 'Seven Dragons'—the beginning of a long association with that magazine, in which all her fantasies were to be serialized. The dragon stories, light-hearted and inventive, collected under the title of *The Book of Dragons* in 1900, may have been suggested by Kenneth *Grahame's anti-heroic 'The Reluctant Dragon'. There is a fabulous creature, a manticore, in the opening story 'The Book of Beasts', who is very like Grahame's dragon in his extreme reluctance to fight. The drawings were by H. R. *Millar, always to be her favourite illustrator. *Nine Unlikely Tales* followed in 1901. It contains the remarkable 'The Town in the Library in the Town in the Library', where two children build a town out of books and picture blocks and toy bricks. They walk up the steps of books into it and find their own house there, and on the library floor the same town as they had built and realize that this could repeat itself into infinity. She was to develop the theme in the full-length *The Magic City* (1910). Significantly, the cities are built from books, and people both friendly and hostile emerge from them. Books play an enormous part in her child characters' lives; Stephen Prickett writes of 'a network of literary cross-references to other writers', and in her last fantasy, *Wet Manic* (1913), there is a Battle of the Books between her favourites and those she despised.

Nesbit's first full-length fantasy, *Five Children and It*, was published in 1902. Its comedy and magic are reminiscent of F. *Anstey, and indeed the children speak of *The Brass Bottle*. 'It' is a Psammead, a sand fairy, a furry creature with eyes on antennae. It was to be the prototype of two other Nesbit fairies who orchestrate events—the Mouldiwarp and the Phoenix. All are touchy, vain, and caustic, but are presented with humour, unlike Mrs *Molesworth's fairy cuckoo (*The Cuckoo Clock*) from which they may have been derived. The Psammead condescends to allow the children one wish a day. In the style of the Three Wishes folk story, their rash choices—to have wings, to be as beautiful as the day—inevitably lead to disaster, and their final wishes have to be used to undo the havoc. Nesbit returned to the theme in *The Phoenix and the Carpet* (1904), where the children find an egg in an old carpet—in fact a magic travelling carpet, with a phoenix inside the egg. The narcissistic Phoenix, one of her best comic creations, much resembles the ludicrously vain Dodo in G. E. Farrow's *The Little Panjandrums Dodo* (1899), who bursts into a London office in the same way as the Phoenix was to do at the Phoenix Fire Office. (Like *The Enchanted Castle*, this now forgotten fantasy also featured prehistoric creatures from the Crystal Palace dinosaur park which opened in 1854.)

The Psammead reappears in *The Story of the Amulet* (1906), when the children, in London now, find it in a pet-shop near the British Museum. It leads them to a charm—half an Egyptian amulet which, if they can only find the other half, will be able to give them their hearts' desire. To search for it, the children use their half of the amulet and the Word of Power inscribed on it to step back into the remote past. The story owes its origins and historical details to Wallis Budge, Keeper of Egyptian and Assyrian Antiquities at the British Museum. Himself the author of *Egyptian Magic* (1901), he suggested that she should use a form of amulet which supposedly gave its dead wearer access to the different regions of the underworld. Such an amulet carries a word of power, and he invented one for her, Ur Hekau Setcheh, which might be translated as 'Great of magic is the Setcheh-snake' (a mythological serpent named in some early spells for the dead).

Time travel was then an innovation in children's books, and Nesbit may have been inspired by H. G. *Wells's *The Time Machine* (1895). She was to use it in *The House of Arden* (1908) and its companion *Harding's Luck* (1909). In the first, two children move back into the past by dressing up in clothes they find in an old chest. In the second book, the central character, a poor lame boy from a London slum who discovers that he is in fact the heir of the Arden estates, elects to go back forever to the great Jacobean household which he has visited with the help of the Mouldiwarp.

Her most elaborately constructed fantasy is *The Enchanted Castle* (1907). It starts, like many of her books, with children in search of magic. They find a castle, and in it a magic ring. This brings misadventures which at first are comic, but gradually become more serious, even terrifying, as when the children make dummy figures and idly wish they were alive. The ring also allows the wearers to enter a world where the statues in the castle garden come to life, and in the last pages the children and two sympathetic adults have a vision of eternity.

The Wonderful Garden (1911) also shows children pursuing magic, but here, though they cast spells which apparently work, this is brought about by luck and outside intervention.   GA

Briggs, Julia, *A Woman of Passion* (1987).
Knoepflmacher, U. C., 'Of Babylands and Babylons: E. Nesbit and the Reclamation of the Fairy Tales', *Tulsa Studies in Women's Literature* (1987).
Lurie, Alison, 'E. Nesbit', in Jane Bingham (ed.), *Writers for Children* (1988).
Prickett, Stephen, *Victorian Fantasy* (1979).
Robson, W. W., 'E. Nesbit and *The Book of Dragons*', in Gillian Avery and Julia Briggs (eds.), *Children and their Books* (1989).
Sircar, Sanjay, 'The Generic Decorum of the Burlesque Kunstmärchen: E. Nesbit's "The Magic Heart"', *Folklore* (1999).

Nestroy, Johann (1801–62) Austrian actor and dramatist who wrote approximately 83 plays and was highly regarded for his acerbic wit. Nestroy employed dramatic forms ranging from fairy-tale play and farce to political satire. He was a master of the Viennese dialect and folk tradition and mixed high and low culture to startling effect. Among his most notable fairy-tale plays are *Die Verbannung aus dem Zauberreiche oder Dreissig Jahre aus dem Leben eines Lumpen* (*The Banishment from the Magic Kingdom or Thirty Years in the Life of a Tramp*, 1828), *Der konfuse Zauberer oder Treue und Flatterhaftigkeit* (*The Confused Wizard or Fidelity and Fickleness*, 1832), *Die Zauberreise in die Ritterzeit oder die Übermüthigen* (*The Magic Journey into the Days of Knights or the Exuberant Ones*, 1832), *Genius, Schuster und*

Markör oder die Pyramiden der Verzauber-ung (*Genius, Shoemaker and Waiter or The Pyramids of Enchantment*, 1832), *Der Feen-ball oder Tischler, Schneider und Schlosser* (*The Fairy Ball or Carpenter, Tailor and Locksmith*, 1832), *Der Zauberer Sulphurelek-tromagnetikophosphoratus und die Fee Walburgiblocksbergiseptemtriolanis oder des ungeratenen Herrn Sohnes Leben, Taten und Meinungen wie auch dessen Bestrafung in der Sklaverei und was sich alldort Ferneres mit ihm begab* (*The Wizard Sulphurelektromag-netikophosphoratus and the Fairy Walburgi-blocksbergiseptemtriolanis or the Life, Deeds and Opinions of the Spoiled Master Son as Well as his Punishment in Slavery and All the Rest that Happened with him There*, 1834), *Das Verlobungsfest im Feenreiche oder die Gleichheit der Jahre* (*The Engagement Feast in Fairyland or the Equality of Years*, 1834), *Die Familien Zwirn, Knieriem und Leim oder Der Welt-Untergangs-Tag* (*The Zwirn, Knier-iem and Leim Families or The Day the World Ended*, 1834), and *Der Koberl oder Staberl im Feendienst* (*The Goblin or Staberl in the Ser-vice of the Fairies*, 1838). Undoubtedly his most famous fairy-tale play is *Der böse Geist Lumpazivagabundus oder Das Liederliche Kleeblatt* (*The Evil Spirit Lumpazivagabun-dus or the Roguish Trio*, 1833), which begins with the fairy goddesses Fortuna and Amorosa making a bet to see whether man can be improved by riches. According to the wager, if two out of three vagabonds improve themselves, Fortuna wins, but if only one changes, Amorosa wins, and For-tuna must give her daughter Brillantine to the magician's son Hilarus, who maintains that only love can reform the evil ways of man, as does Amorosa, who wins the bet and sets out to reform the two vagabonds who have led dissolute lives. Many of the folk characters reappear in Nestroy's plays, and many of his other farces have strong elem-ents of the fairy tale in them. But magic was always employed by Nestroy to make fun of humankind's foibles and to expose the ab-surd nature of reality. JZ

Corriher, Kurt, 'The Conflict between Dignity and Hope in the Works of Johann Nestroy', *South Atlantic Review*, 46 (1981).

Decker, Craig, 'Toward a Critical Volksstück: Nestroy and the Politics of Language', *Monatshefte*, 79 (1987).

Diehl, Siegfried, *Zauberei und Satire im Frühwerk Nestroys* (1969).

Hein, Jürgen, *Das Wiener Volksstück: Raimund und Nestroy* (1978).

Hein, Jürgen, *Johann Nestroy* (1990).

Neverending Story, The (*Die unen-dliche Geschichte*) A multi-million-selling fairy tale about the death of fairy tales. Much to the author Michael *Ende's disgust, it has spawned three films (West Germany, 1984; Germany, 1989; and Germany, 1994). First published in West Germany in 1979, Ende's 428-page novel became a cult book; it contains echoes of earlier writers—comprehensive mythology like *Tolkien's, a talkative Carrollian giant tortoise, reader-involvement such as that which *Barrie in-vokes—but also enough originality for the novel to sell over a million copies in German alone, and go on to be translated into 27 other languages.

It tells two parallel stories which gradually interlock. Bastian Balthasar Bux, an anxious overweight German boy whose mother has recently died, takes refuge from bullies by hiding in a bookshop. There he finds 'The Neverending Story' and borrows it. Reading in an attic when he should be in class, he gets drawn into the world of Fantasia, which is in imminent danger of being destroyed by the Nothing. People are losing their hopes and forgetting their dreams. Only the Child-like Empress can save Fantasia, but she is too ill, so Atreyu the boy-warrior sets out to find the one person who can cure her. When Atreyu, journeying across the plains, needs refreshment, Bastian in the attic opens his lunch-box. On his quest Atreyu is variously helped or opposed by a rockbiter, a racing snail, a vicious black beast called Gmork, the Southern Oracle, and Falkor the flying luck-dragon. Despite his bravery, however, Atreyu loses heart and fails in his mission; extinction looms for Fantasia until at last Bastian realizes that he is the saviour the Empress needs, and heals her by giving her his mother's name.

For film-makers, the book's international popularity made it irresistible, but its length made it impossible. Wolfgang Petersen, director and co-screenwriter of the first adaptation, cut out the digressions, simplified the plotline and characters, turned Bastian into a fit and bright American boy, shot in English, and made no attempt to encompass more than just the first half of the book. The apocalyptic conflict with the Nothing is downgraded to secondary dramatic status: the climax is instead provided by Bastian coming back from Fantasia on Falkor and using him to get his private revenge on the bullies.

Feeling betrayed, Ende angrily rejected this treatment of his book, but had sold the rights and could not stop it. He therefore took his name off the film completely and wished a plague on its producers. It was none the less a commercial success and prompted two sequels, neither of which finishes the job of filming Ende's book. The first—*The Next Chapter*—largely replicates the original, taking Bastian back to Fantasia where he and Atreyu, aided by Falkor and some new characters, battle to save the realm from the Emptiness created by the evil sorceress Xayide, who works by persuading people to give up their memories in exchange for miracles. In *Escape from Fantasia* it is Nastiness that is the threat, causing everyone to become selfish and avaricious. However, it can be fought only in the outside world. When Bastian returns home to begin the task, he inadvertently takes with him two gnomes, a baby rockbiter, a talking tree, and Falkor. These creatures end up scattered across the North American continent, and must find Bastian in order to get back.

These two sequels must have seemed to Ende empty and nasty. Certainly they did nothing to mollify his sense of betrayal. A book which had been intended to illustrate the importance of nourishing the individual imagination, and the danger of it being stultified by mass-production and literalmindedness, had in his eyes become on screen part of the problem rather than the solution.   TAS

Nielsen, Kay Rasmus (1886–1957) Danish illustrator and designer. He studied in Paris at the Académie Julienne under Jean-Paul Laurence and later with Kristian Krog and Lucian Simon, became fascinated by the work of Aubrey Beardsley and, like others in the golden age of children's book illustration, was deeply influenced by Japanese art. He lived and worked in London, Copenhagen, and from 1939 to 1957 in southern California.

Nielsen was drawn early on to fairy tales and illustrated many volumes for Hodder & Stoughton: *In Powder and Crinoline* (1913), *East of the Sun, West of the Moon* (1914), Hans *Andersen's Fairy Tales (drawings completed in 1912, but first published in 1924), *Hansel and Gretel* (1925), and *Red Magic* (Jonathan Cape, 1930), a collection of fairy tales from around the world.

Nielsen's designs unite strong linearity with delicate colouring. For example, the heroine of 'Prince Lindworm' in *East of the Sun* kneels in a perfect arc of physiologically impossible grace before a tree whose weeping branches echo her curves. In the same volume in 'The Lassie and her Godmother' the heroine, shoulders hunched, turns to watch the splendidly coloured sun flying away through the forbidden chamber door she has just opened.

Characterized by a sense of two-dimensional flatness, Nielsen's objects and people are highly stylized: foxglove blossoms hang in measured asymmetry; princes and princesses stand on improbably long legs; and their garments billow in gravity-defying parabolas. The power of his illustrations lies in his uncanny ability to retrieve a story's emotional effect on its reader and to recreate it visually in two dimensions.   RBB

Larkin, David (ed.) and Keith Nicholson (intro.), *Kay Nielsen* (1975).
Poltarnees, Welleran, *Kay Nielsen: An Appreciation* (1976).

Nimue A nymph or fay in Malory's *Morte d'Arthur*, also referred to as Nymanne, Ninien, Niniane, or Vivienne, etc., depending on the work in which she appears. These works range, in both date and language,

Nielsen, Kay An image by Kay Nielsen from *East of the Sun and West of the Moon* (1914), showing his characteristic strength of composition and design. The 15 Nordic tales in the collection, written by Gudrun Thorne-Thomsen, have become forever associated with Nielsen. Photo: Epic/Mary Evans Picture Library.

from the 12th-century romances of Chrétien de Troyes through the later romances of Hartman van Aue and Ulrich von Zatzikhoven, to Renaissance Italian and English Victorian poetry. In the 13th-century *Prose Lancelot*, she is the Lady of the Lake who rears Lancelot and gives him a white steed.

Nimue has several salient traits. In the *Huth Merlin*, she gallops a palfrey into Arthur's court to demand the head of the murderer of her brother. Described there as 'the most beautiful woman that ever rode into Arthur's court', she is granted her wish, picks up the severed head, and rides off.

Nimue has supernatural powers and is romantically linked with Merlin, of whose attentions she eventually tires. In the *Vulgate Lancelot*, she encloses Merlin in a wall of air. Malory portrays her as an enchantress who restrains Merlin's ardour by imprisoning him under a stone. Like Viviane in *Tennyson's Idylls of the King*, she pursues Merlin for the spell that enables her to enclose him in an oak tree. As in the case of Morgan, whom many scholars believe to be her model, Nimue is often supposed to have learned magic from Merlin.   JSN

Lacy, Norris J. (ed.), *The New Arthurian Encyclopedia* (1993).
Paton, Lucy Allen, *Studies in the Fairy Mythology of Arthurian Romance* (1903, 1960).

Nix, Garth (1963–) Australian author who specializes in fantasy novels for children and young adults. A prolific writer, he has received much acclaim for his Old Kingdom Series, also known as The Old Kingdom Chronicles, The Abhorsen Trilogy and The Abhorsen Chronicles. He has also published a six-part Seventh Tower series and seven-part The Keys to the Kingdom series. Nix's collection of previous-published short stories, *Across the Wall: A Tale of the Abhorsen and Other Stories* (2006) includes 'Hansel's Eyes', a retelling that features an organ-harvesting witch, and 'Three Roses', a fable about a grieving gardener and a greedy king.   KMJ

Nodier, Charles (1780–1844) French lexicographer and author of fantastic tales. A child prodigy who had published two Jacobin speeches by the age of 10, he experienced the Terror at first hand: his magistrate father regularly guillotined the condemned. These executions led Nodier to reject the Revolution (he eventually became an ultraroyalist) and explore death in fantastic stories. His non-fiction interests ranged from compiling dictionaries to writing on entomology, botany, history, geography, and linguistics. Librarian of the Arsenal, he was the first head of the French romantic movement, hosted its first *cénacle* (salon) from 1824 to 1827, and advanced the careers of Vigny, Musset, and Hugo. He was elected to the French Academy in 1833.

Nodier's early fiction imitated *Crébillon and *Goethe; *Cazotte inspired his collaboration on 'Le Vampire' (1820), a supernatural melodrama. He became increasingly fascinated by occult folklore, the Cabbala, Freemasonry, Illuminism, and metempsychosis—as shown by *Smarra, ou Les Démons de la nuit, songes romantiques* (1821; *Smarra or The Demons of the Night*, 1893) and *Trilby ou le Lutin d'Argail* (1822; *Trilby, The Fairy of Argyle*, 1895). These tales go beyond Cazotte's in blurring the demarcation between reality and illusion, and were among the first French works to address dreams and the unconscious (thus prefiguring Freud and Jung). They also influenced the symbolists and surrealists in free-associative explorations of inner truths.

In 1830, after the July Monarchy and during the vogue of *Hoffmann, a politically disenchanted Nodier published an essay on the fantastic. In addition to addressing German romanticism, he chronicled the marvellous in literature, and likened Ulysses and Othello to *Perrault's Petit Poucet and Barbe-Bleue (*Little Tom Thumb and *Bluebeard). He also praised fairy tales and the fantastic as salutary genres necessary in political times of transition, when society must escape grim reality and take refuge in the imagination. Nodier elsewhere proclaimed that he would write nothing but fairy tales. His first was *La Fée aux miettes* (1832; *The Crumb Fairy*), now considered his masterpiece. It is about an insane asylum inmate and an aging hag: he saves her with a magical mandrake and metamorphoses her back into a beautiful fairy. Its interpretations range from alchemical to psychoanalytical, centre on integrating the fragmented self, address the theme of madness and insight, and juxtapose dreams and reality, time and space—ideas that would fascinate *Nerval. Nodier also wrote a simpler fairy tale for children, *Trésor des fèves et fleur des pois* (1837; *The Luck of the Bean-Rows*, 1846), about an elderly, childless couple, a tiny boy, and an even tinier princess. It underscores love and constancy, and has, says Nodier, 'the usual lucky ending of all good fairy tales'.   MLE

Castex, Pierre Georges, *Le Conte fantastique en France de Nodier à Maupassant* (1951).

Crichfield, Grant, 'Charles Nodier', *Dictionary of Literary Biography*, 119 (1992).

Hamenachem, Miriam S., *Charles Nodier: Essai sur l'imagination mythique* (1972).

Juin, Hubert, *Charles Nodier* (1970).

Vodoz, Jules, *'La Fée aux miettes': Essai sur le rôle du subconscient dans l'œuvre de Charles Nodier* (1925).

Nodot, Paul-François (*fl.* 1695–1700) French writer. His novels *Histoire de Mélusine* (*Story of Mélusine*, 1698) and *Histoire de Geofroy* (*Story of Geofroy*, 1700) embroider on the legend of the fairy *Mélusine and continue a tradition of literary rewritings that began as early as the 14th century with

Jean d'Arras's *Le Roman de Mélusine* (*The Romance of Mélusine*, 1392–3). Unlike the medieval Mélusine, who combines Christian belief with magic, Nodot's fairy and son Geofroy possess—and are dominated by—powers of occult magic. Above all, Nodot tailors the legend to the period's taste for sentimental historical fiction.   LCS

Nooteboom, Cees (1933–) Dutch novelist, journalist, and poet, who is also a well-known travel writer and essayist. A prolific and experimental author, Nooteboom has won many literary awards and has been nominated for the Nobel Prize. Among his many novels, he has written a surrealist adaptation of Hans Christian *Andersen's 'The Snow Queen' with the title *In the Dutch Mountains* (*In Nederland*, 1984). In this strange version narrated by a Spanish government official, who has ambitions to become a writer, two circus performers, the beautiful blonde Lucia and handsome dark-haired Kai, lead a happy life as illusionists until the Snow Queen kidnaps and enslaves Kai. But this is not an ordinary 'snow queen', but a witch-like mobster, and as Lucia sets out to free Kai from the snow queen's enchantment, Nootebom explores the metaphysical and aesthetic quandaries that plague modern life. Though the novel ends happily, the narrator is somewhat pessimistic about his fairy tale when he comments, 'In myths everything is solved in some way or other; in novels nothing is ever solved; and in fairy tales the solution is postponed, but if it ever takes place it will be outside the scope of the fairy tale. That is the lie.'   JZ

Norstein, Yuri (1941–) Russian animator who has produced two major animated fairy-tale shorts, *Hedgehog in the Fog* (1975) and *Tale of Tales* (1979). Some critics have praised *Tale of Tales*, which has been awarded many international prizes, as the best animated film in modern times. It is an autobiographical and metaphorical journey about the impact of the Second World War in Russia, and it involves a nationally known

'lullaby' wolf who tenderly protects an infant and carries him into a better future.   JZ

Kitson, Clare, *Yuri Norstein and Tale of Tales* (2005).

North American and Canadian fairy tales *See* p. 417.

Norton, Mary (1903–92) English writer of fantasy books for children and creator of the Borrowers, minuscule beings who live by 'borrowing' items that humans leave around. Her first book, *The Magic Bed-Knob*, was published in New York in 1943 while she and her four children were living in America. Subtitled 'How to Become a Witch in Ten Easy Lessons', it shows the genteel Miss Price struggling to master the black arts, and a bed-knob which through her spells will take a bed and its occupants on magic travels. The comic misadventures that follow were clearly inspired by E. *Nesbit, as was the sequel, *Bonfires and Broomsticks*, published in London in 1947. Here the bed is used to travel back to the past, where Miss Price eventually elects to stay. A combined version of the two, *Bed-Knob and Broomstick*, appeared in 1957.

The Borrowers (1952) and the five subsequent books about them, can be read at different levels. Children are fascinated by a perspective of the world observed at six inches from the ground, and by the wealth of practical details; for adults it is a poignant parable of the struggle for survival of the stateless, displaced, and homeless. The three Borrowers, the parents Pod and Homily, and their daughter Arrietty (even their names are borrowed and have become transmuted in the process) are among the handful of their kind who have survived. They are not fairies, but miniature people; symbionts, dependent on humankind for all the essentials of existence. They search for stability and permanence and they echo the follies and delusions of the upper world. The last chapter of *The Borrowers* sees them driven out of the big old house where they have lived under the floorboards, and fleeing across the fields. *The Borrowers Afield* (1955) describes their Robinson Crusoe existence in the open air, enjoyed by Arrietty alone—she

North American and Canadian fairy tales (1900 to present)

Even though it is often dismissed as infantile and non-serious literature, the fairy tale pervades 20th-century American culture in a variety of forms and media, operates in multiple contexts from education to therapy as well as entertainment, and performs contradictory but significant ideological functions. The following overview of fairy tales in 20th-century North America and Canada seeks to provide an understanding of social dynamics affecting the national production and reception of fairy tales, the institutionalization of fairy tales both through the dominant role of fairy-tale films and in the schools as children's literature, the rethinking of gender in fairy tales, the radical but marginal role of literary fairy tales for adults, and the relatively recent revival of storytelling. While the general parameters of this overview apply to all of North America, Canadian specifics will also be addressed.

'When I first saw The *Wizard of Oz', writes Salman *Rushdie, 'it made a writer out of me.' It may be inevitable that a presentation of the 20th-century fairy tale in North America should begin with L. Frank *Baum's 1900 The Wonderful Wizard of Oz novel, but Rushdie's tribute to its 1939 MGM screen adaptation—which he saw in Bombay in the 1950s—also underscores the radically foreign even though central character of fairy tales in modern and contemporary North America as well as the wide dissemination of American fairy-tale films.

In the 19th century American publishers marketed translations or adaptations of European fairy tales for children with some caution, following a puritan and utilitarian suspicion of make-believe. Such versions often emphasized the moralizing aspect of these tales and developed a contemporary setting for them. It is only in the 20th century that—through the effective combination of the genre's adaptation to American concerns and its otherworldly vision—the fairy tale becomes an institution of American culture, playing significant and contradictory functions within it.

Commonly dubbed the first great American fairy tale, Oz exhibits the fairy tale's typical journey and initiation patterns in both its printed and its cinematic versions. Dorothy leaves her grey and threatening Kansas farm world to explore the colourful and wonderful world of Oz, where she discovers her own strengths, empowers others, and defeats the forces of evil. Transformed by this new understanding of herself and her possibilities, she clicks her ruby shoes three times and returns home. Baum also incorporated familiar details of American Midwestern agrarian life and focused on a resourceful and curious female protagonist whose common sense and frankness bear a distinctly American imprint. Clearly, Oz Americanized the fairy tale, but the continuing appeal of this narrative rests on its forceful commentary on America itself. Scholars disagree as to the interpretation of this meta-national commentary. For Paul Nathanson in Over the Rainbow: The Wizard of Oz as a Secular Myth of America (1991), it is Dorothy who requires changing so as to appreciate the wonders of Kansas; thus, when reading Baum's novel and especially when watching the film on TV as it has been regularly offered starting in the 1950s, Americans participate in a collective initiation ritual confirming the value of 'home', their own nation. For others, including Selma Lanes (1971), Brian Attebery (1980), and Jack Zipes (1994), Baum's novel and its various sequels expose the failure of the American dream—Kansas is no land of milk and honey and, by the fifth volume of the Oz series written by Baum, Dorothy moves to Oz permanently— at a time when it was visible at the turn of the century, and the film in turn asserts the validity of hope and the possibility of social change in the continued pursuit of that dream precisely when the depression of the 1930s and the ideological rigidity of the 1950s seemed overpowering. Along the assertive lines suggested by the latter reading, gay male American audiences in the 1980s appropriated the 1939 film, particularly its representation of the Lion.

The fairy tale as genre has elsewhere served nation-building projects because of its ethnically marked distribution and its culture-specific values. In America, the genre's association with the nation as it develops in the 20th century is different: either America itself is glorified as the fairy-tale realm where wishes come true, or the utopian project of the fairy tale works to remark on the failed American dream and at the same time rekindle hope for change. Thus, on the one hand, the glitter and happy ending of fairy tales promote an acritical consent to the ideological, economic, and social status quo; on the other hand, the transformative dynamics both within the tales and through their multiple tellings enable alternative visions.

Film has been the most powerful medium for the mythifying workings of the American fairy tale. As we have already seen with *The Wizard of Oz*, and as other film-makers have proven, the fairy-tale film can make different uses of its magic. Nevertheless, it is abundantly clear that, as Donald Haase states, the 'normative influence of *Disney's animated fairy tales has been so enormous, that the Disney spirit ... [has] become the standard against which fairy tale films are created *and* received.' State-of-the-art animation, fireworks displays of ever-improving technology, aggressive marketing and distribution, and the double-voicing strategy that allows for spellbinding children while entertaining adults with off-colour or political jokes are the not so magic ingredients that have ensured the success of Disney movies all over the world. Disney's celebrated and money-making animated films, from *Snow White and the Seven Dwarfs* (1937) to *Beauty and the Beast* (1991), are an institution and one that has not only dominated the fairy-tale film, but also influenced fairy tales on television, on video, in print through the Disney Books series, on audiotape, etc. These films have consistently promoted a certain 'Disneyfied' image of the fairy tale, specific social values, and definite gender roles.

Drawing from diverse sources such as Charles *Perrault's and Hans Christian *Andersen's literary tales, Carlo *Collodi's 19th-century fairy-tale novel *Pinocchio*, and The *Arabian Nights* (and consistently avoiding the *Grimms' texts), Disney's films have clearly privileged the fairy-tale genre. If metaphor, as the magically immediate verbal expression of an image, is the core of classic European fairy tales, in the Disney 'classics' the image dominates the word and the song subordinates narrative. Furthermore, even though films are the product of teamwork, each Disney fairy-tale film contributes to and confirms its own image, naturalizing its particular brand of fairy tale: minimal character development, humour and cuteness to fill in the storyline, an unequivocal happy ending, no ties to the historicity or cultural specificity of the chosen tales. Overall, the strategies and effects of Disney's industry have been to enforce sameness on fairy-tale diversity and to put storytelling at the service of spectacle or passive entertainment.

Disney films have also explicitly intervened in the socialization at first of American children, but increasingly—given the globalization of the market in the second half of the 20th century—all children. One can say that these films' values are morally good (truthfulness, courage, love, and loyalty) and as such these successful films are a significant communal reference point for 20th-century generations. One can also say that Disney films have celebrated American individualism and enterprise as universally normative behaviour, have stereotyped other cultures (even in Disney's apparently multicultural projects such as *Aladdin* 1992 and *Mulan* 1998 which are as basically ahistorical as the 1940 *Pinocchio* was), and have blatantly promoted consumerism through the association of fairy-tale films with brand products for children and, of course, the Disneyland or Disneyworld theme parks.

It is perhaps on matters of gender, however, that Disney fairy-tale films have attracted the strongest criticism and at the same time exerted the greatest influence. Between the late 1930s and the early 1950s, Disney canonized a few fairy tales which glamorized anachronistic gender roles. The passive heroines of *Snow White and the Seven Dwarfs*, *Cinderella*, and The *Sleeping Beauty* simply wished for love and found in the prince a solution to all their problems; in turn the prince was one-dimensional (either a status symbol or a man of action) and attracted to the heroine's beauty. Fairy-tale heroines and heroes were reduced to this simplistic formula. In response to feminist criticism in the 1970s and a growing gender awareness in the 1980s, Disney presented more assertive and active heroines (Ariel in The *Little Mermaid*, Beauty in *Beauty and the Beast*, and Jasmine in *Aladdin*), but the romance plot has continued to submerge that of personal development and to assert a visible uniformity of desirability.

Rather than imitate the Disney look (as in the Cannon Group movies from the late 1980s and the 1998 *Quest for Camelot*) or reproduce the 'my prince will come' mentality in fairy-tale films for adults (as in Gary Marshall's romanticized *Pretty Woman*), a few American films have employed diverse strategies to break the Disney monopoly on fairy tales. Unlike Disney, first of all, these film-makers have drawn on the Grimms' texts or on modern fairy-tale novels, and have also incorporated storytelling to encourage a more interactive response on the part of the audience. Second, their use of humour is often pointed at outdated social arrangements or questionable values within the tales instead of acting as a simple diversion. Third, rather than creating a fantasy world which implicitly advertises American values and products, these films Americanize the fairy tale explicitly either by featuring well-known actors, or by adapting North American folk versions, or by setting the action in a recognizably specific time of American history. In practice, these strategies have not been uniformly successful, but beginning with the iconoclastic and often repeated *Fractured Fairy Tales* series that was part of the 1960s *Rocky and his Friends* and *The Bullwinkle Show* on American television, there is an identifiable counter-tradition that includes Jim *Henson's various Muppet fairy-tale films and *The Storyteller* (1987), Shelley *Duvall's live-action *Faerie Tale Theatre* episodes aired in the 1980s, the strikingly historicising work of Tom *Davenport (from *Hansel and Gretel* in 1975 to *The Step Child* in 1997), and a few other films like *The *Never-ending Story* (1984), *The *Princess Bride* (1987), and the 1997 *Snow White* featuring Sigourney Weaver and Sam Neill.

While it did not explicitly replicate Disney patterns, the popular 1980s CBS television series *Beauty and the Beast* belongs only marginally to the counter-tradition outlined above. Set in a violent New York City, the series portrays the strong tie between Vincent—a vaguely leonine Beast who lives in the uncorrupted under world of 'Father' Jacob's community of outcasts—and Catherine, a rich lawyer who after being kidnapped and raped becomes committed to fighting for social justice. Catherine is brave, and Vincent has depth, but the series participates in the romance replotting of fairy tales and reproduces the violent solutions of most crime shows.

In the more traditional media of storytelling and print, schools and libraries constitute another significant context for the institutionalization of fairy tales in 20th-century North America. From the beginning of the century, children were reading fairy tales at school; and in the 1990s it is still through fairy tales that American children, both as listeners/readers and tellers/writers, are often first encouraged to achieve an understanding of narrative within the educational system. Overall, in terms of the 19th-century debate over the value of fairy tales for children, one can say that fairy tales in North America have done well for a variety of reasons. The European fairy tale has been Americanized through books like the *Oz* series,

Eva Katharine Gibson's *Zauberlinda the Wise Witch* (1901), Carl *Sandburg's *Rootabaga Stories* (1922), James *Thurber's tales in the 1940s and 1950s, as well as the popular novels for girls with a fairy-tale plot such as *Rebecca of Sunnybrook Farm* (1903), *Daddy Long-Legs* (1912), and, later, literary adaptations of the fairy tale's magic for younger children such as the extremely popular Dr *Seuss's *The Cat in the Hat* (1957) and Maurice *Sendak's *Where the Wild Things Are* (1984). Other factors working to promote fairy tales with North American children in the 20th century include a consistent emphasis on storytelling as part of the training of children's librarians; the increasingly aggressive marketing of quality picture books illustrated by American artists; the bowdlerization and simplification of tales; and, in more recent years, thanks to the proliferation of 'new' fairy tales in response to multicultural critiques of the curriculum, the recognition that folk and fairy tales are powerful points of entry into other cultures and not exclusively into the lofty realm of the imagination.

In approaching the fairy tale as children's literature more broadly, several trends are especially notable. First, some adults select fairy tales for their children because they are classics, in a nostalgic reaction against the perceived shallowness of the present; for many others, fairy-tale books are the extension of Disney and its glamorous world. In either case, the fairy tale is still a measure of 'cultural literacy' and is most in demand because of its socializing functions. It is also important to note in this context that, perhaps paradoxically, it is through the simplified Disney fairy-tale books, as well as the popular *Sesame Street* TV series, that many American children in the latter part of the century learned to read before attending school. Secondly, modern American illustrators—such as Nancy Ekholm *Burkert, Tomie *De Paola, Michael Hague, Trina S. *Hyman, Gerald McDermott, and Maurice Sendak—have played a crucial role in both the marketing and aesthetic success of fairy tales. Thirdly, the representation of gender in fairy tales has been the foremost challenge to this genre in the 20th century, and it has profoundly affected the production and consumption of fairy tales for both children and adults.

In her 1949 ground-breaking study *The Second Sex*, Simone de Beauvoir had already identified passive and docile fairy-tale heroines as pernicious role models for women. In North America the discussion of acculturation in fairy tales began in the 1970s as part of the growing feminist movement, and was initially (with, for instance, Andrea Dworkin's influential study *Woman Hating*) a blanket rejection of fairy tales as narratives that promote rigid, hierarchical, and limiting gender roles (the helpless princess and the heroic prince). The debate has developed since then along the lines of the larger feminist frameworks and as enhanced by various complementary feminist projects: consciously expanding the repertoire of fairy tales for children to include stories with clever and resourceful heroines; editing traditional fairy tales so as to de-emphasize beauty and marriage; writing new fairy tales which question conventional gender roles and other social conventions; and providing scholarly critiques of gender politics and representation in fairy tales.

Fairy-tale anthologies—which together with expensively illustrated single fairy-tale books are most prevalent in the contemporary market for children—played a particularly significant role in the context of the first two overlapping feminist projects outlined above. Rosemary Minard's *Womenfolk and Fairy Tales* (1975), Ethel Johnston Phelps's *Tatterhood and Other Tales* (1978), Alison Lurie's *Clever Gretchen and Other Tales* (1980), and Jack Zipes's *Don't Bet on the Prince: Contemporary Feminist Fairy Tales in North America and England* (1986) are just a few of the collections that exemplified the wits of fairy-tale heroines not as well known as Cinderella or Sleeping Beauty. As editor, Phelps went further to launder the traditional tales of undesirable or anachronistic character features. A similar spirit of feminist revisionism animated writers for children in North America, especially from the 1970s on, to promote the values of gender equality and women's assertiveness in contrast to the dominant pattern of women's oppression as seen in the Perrault or Disney fairy-tale classics. In particular, several writers chose to rework well-known fairy tales; role reversal, humour, and a new ending are some of the most common strategies in adaptations such as Jane *Yolen's *Sleeping Ugly* (1981) or Harriet Herman's *The Forest Princess* (1974). Others (e.g. Jay *Williams with 'Petronella' in 1979, Jeanne Desy with 'The Princess who Stood on Her Own Two Feet' in 1982, and Wendy *Walker with her psychological probing of fairy-tale characters in the 1988 collection *The Sea-Rabbit, or The Artist of Life*) sought to transform the genre by writing new stories which imitate general fairy-tale patterns and themes, but promote innovative gender and other social arrangements. Jane Yolen's contribution in particular stands out. Though her lyricism at times seems to counter the project of unmasking women's oppression, Yolen has widely experimented with adapting the fairy tale to feminist uses (see her 1983 collected *Tales of Wonder*), published an impressive fairy-tale novel *Briar Rose* in 1993 for young adults, and written a study of fairy tales, *Touch Magic* (1986).

As the presence of women's studies, feminist theory, and children's literature became stronger in academia in the 1980s, American feminist research on fairy tales also continued in interdisciplinary ways to question the genre's magic spell, but in historically framed projects such as Ruth B. Bottigheimer's and Maria Tatar's various studies of the Grimms' tales, Sandra M. Gilbert and Susan Gubar's influential analysis of 19th-century British literature as re-enacting the innocent child/manipulating woman conflict in 'Snow White', and Jack Zipes's extensive *œuvre* on the changing ideological functions of the genre both in Europe and the United States.

These critics have recontextualized the analysis of gender within the tales by asking other important questions: who is telling or publishing the story? when? and for whom? The folklorist Kay Stone in particular has contributed to a specific understanding of gender and fairy tales in a North American context. She observed early on that North American folk-tale heroines were not as passive as their European counterparts but, owing to the Disney influence, these heroines have remained largely unknown within modern American popular or mass culture. Through extensive interviewing, she also noted how North American women often reinterpreted seemingly victimizing plots to emphasize and identify with the female protagonist's heroics.

Because, on the one hand, the fairy tale continues to provide a convenient repertoire of stock characters and plots as well as a short cut to presumably shared cultural knowledge if not values, and because, on the other hand, the revision of fairy tales in both the individual's mind and historically framed ideologies is an ongoing and unpredictable practice, the influence of fairy tales on 20th-century North American literature for adults is considerable and remarkably diversified, extending to the use of fairy tale as structuring frame for novels such as William Faulkner's *Absalom, Absalom!* (1936), and to writers occasionally experimenting with the genre, as E. E. *Cummings did with poems for his young daughter. But this influence has also developed in clearly recognizable directions. As Brian Attebery has argued, the strong 20th-century fantasy tradition in America has stretched fairy-tale magic into the creation of a whole world which can stand in different relations to the contemporary social world. For instance, out of an intense disappointment in the American dream, James Branch Cabell's *Jurgen* (1919) offered an alternative world of bookish origins to the exploration of a witty, excessively ironic, and hollow hero. James Thurber, who highly praised L. Frank Baum's *Oz* and strongly politicized the fairy tale, composed a playfully self-reflective world in his *The White Deer* in which words themselves weave a spell and rather complex heroes reach only tentatively happy endings. And after the Second World War and the publication of J. R. R. *Tolkien's *The Lord of the Rings*, we see the explosion of disturbing and radical fantasies by writers such as Philip K. *Dick and Ursula *Le Guin. Another recent development of the fairy-tale fantasy not 'for children only' combines elements of fantasy and gender politics to address young adults, especially adolescent girls, as their select audience. The novel *Beauty* (1978) by Robin *McKinley, the imaginative Ohio-born fantasist, and the 1993 *Snow White, Blood Red* anthology edited by Ellen Datlow and Terri Windling have been particularly popular within this genre. Fantasy, like fairy tales, then, is rarely a simple escape in this tradition; rather it holds an unflattering mirror up to our own world and at the same time envisions possibilities for change.

Extending the fairy tale in a different direction, postmodern literary texts from the late 1960s to the beginning of the 21st century hold a mirror up to the foundational narratives of Western literature and culture, those fictions that, like the fairy tale, have framed and naturalized the social arrangements of the contemporary Western world. Beginning with John *Barth's 'Once upon a time' Möbius-strip frame for the experimental *Lost in the Funhouse*, these highly self-reflexive fictions have sought to question and unmake the rules of narrative itself while paradoxically exploiting, in an anti-modernist move, the wonders of folk narrative and pre-modern traditions. While Barth remained tied to *The Arabian Nights*, which he has appropriated throughout his career in sophisticated but self-indulgent novelistic tours de force, Donald Barthelme in *Snow White* (1967) and 'The Glass Mountain' (1970) experimented with parodying the Western tale of magic. Some of Robert *Coover's most successful fictions also use the fairy tale as their point of departure. Humorous, disruptive of expectations, intensely political, and persistently confronting the entanglements of sexuality and power in fairy tales, Coover's work from *Pricksongs & Descants* (1969) to 'The Dead Queen' (1973), *Pinocchio in Venice* (1991), *Briar Rose* (1996), and *Stepmother* (2004) unmakes and remakes the fairy tale within the framework of a rigorous critique of American mainstream politics and consumeristic mentality.

From a feminist perspective, Anne *Sexton's collection of poems, *Transformations* (1971), stands out as a violent and modern revision of the Grimms' tales; Olga *Broumas's haunting woman-centred poems in *Beginning with O* (1977) foreshadow the experimental vitality of *Kissing the Witch*, the 1997 lesbian collection by the Irish writer Emma *Donoghue; Ursule Molinaro's 'The Contest Winner' (1990) exposes the 'void' of Snow White's 'helpless purity'; and Karen Elizabeth Gordon plays with the fabric of tales by Hans Christian Andersen and the Brothers Grimm in her witty *The *Red Shoes and Other Tattered Tales* (1996). But, overall, in the United States there is no 20th-century sorceress or white witch of the literary acclaim or popularity of, for instance, the British Angela *Carter or the Canadian Margaret *Atwood, while in the 21st century there appears to be a resurgence of feminist fairy-tale experimentation, as can be seen in the works of Kelly Link and Catherynne Vallente.

Turning back to the larger picture, it is important to underline that both postmodern and feminist literary experiments with the fairy tale play only a marginal role in the production and reception of fairy tales for adults in late 20th-century North America, where humorously benevolent parodies and conservative updates of classic fairy tales are far more popular in the entertainment industry, whether it be literature (e.g. *The Frog Prince Continued* and the 1994 *Politically Correct Bedtime Stories*) or the performance arts (e.g. the 1987 Broadway musical *Into the Woods*). Furthermore, as the

British author Angela Carter noted, it is as joke—especially the dirty joke—
that the fairy tale ironically flourishes as we move into the 21st century; and
it is in association, not only with Disney, but with television soap operas and
royalty tabloid stories that the fairy-tale stereotype continues to gain
credence.

A different non-literary medium that has also become central to adult
consciousness of fairy tales during the last 30 years of the century is storytelling in non-traditional contexts. Rooted in the training of librarians and
teachers from the early 20th century on and exploding in the 1970s with the
popularity of storytelling festivals and the rise of professional organizations,
the revival of storytelling has attracted a large number of adults seeking
cultural roots, forgotten values, community interaction, therapy, stage experience, and entertainment. Folk and fairy tales from all over the world
constitute a large part of these storytellers' repertoires. Kay Stone's *Burning
Brightly: New Light on Old Tales Told Today* (1998) describes four storytelling approaches—the traditional, the dramatic, the educational, and the
therapeutic—as streams that have contributed to the energy of organized
contemporary storytelling communities in North America, including the two
largest ones: the National Association of Storytelling, which held its first
festival in 1973 in Tennessee; and the Storytellers' School of Toronto, first
established in 1979. According to Stone's statistics, by 1995 over 800 individuals and approximately 300 groups were listed in the National Storytelling Association.

Within this context, the therapeutic uses of professional storytelling have
been particularly controversial. Bruno Bettelheim's influential Freudian
analysis *The Uses of Enchantment: The Meaning and Importance of Fairy
Tales* (1976), and two Jungian best-sellers, providing gendered readings of
fairy tales to heal contemporary American men and women—Robert *Bly's
Iron John: A Book about Men (1990), and Clarissa Pinkola *Estés's *Women
who Run with the Wolves: Myths and Stories of the Wild Woman Archetype*
(1993)—have exemplified the popular appeal and scholarly dangers of such
approaches. But Susan Gordon has also powerfully described her use of
Grimms' tales with groups of abused adolescents, and the practice of
storytelling in therapeutic situations is certainly more complex than anything that books modelled on self-help and ahistorical mythification might
indicate.

Other complicated matters evolving from the professional dimension of
this storytelling revival include the role of the storyteller as stage performer
rather than as member of a community, as well as questions of cultural
appropriation, and increasingly of copyright. Internet discussion groups and
fairy-tale web pages simply multiply the possibilities of exchange and exploitation of sources. Nevertheless, more traditional storytellers have also
been featured at organized festivals, and—because many professional tellers

work from printed sources—the revival process has put into wider circulation regional and ethnic collections of North American narratives, such as Vance *Randolph's Ozark tales, the many Jack tales, Native American tales, and recent immigrants' adapted traditions.

Stone argues that in Canada this organized storytelling revival has been less commercialized and more community-oriented than in the United States. Perhaps the shape of this recent development can be related to the diversified fairy-tale tradition for children that developed in Canada: from Howard Kennedy's 1904 *The New World Fairy Book*, which wove materials from various indigenous and immigrant traditions together, to Cyrus Macmillan's important *Canadian Wonder Tales*, a 1918 collection of tales recorded just before the First World War and edited to conform to a European fairy-tale style; from French-Canadian tales as collected most notably by Marius Barbeau in *The Golden Phoenix and Other French-Canadian Fairy Tales* (1958), to Celtic fairy beliefs. This is not to say that *The Wonderful Wizard of Oz*, for instance, was not influential—Baum's successful formula has been adapted to a northern Canadian setting—or that the orphan-heroine novel for girls modelled on 'Cinderella' and *Jane Eyre* was not also produced in Canada, as proven by the well-known 1908 *Anne of Green Gables* by L. M. Montgomery. But, perhaps because of the different kinds of magic alive in Canadian traditions and the patchwork Canadian approach to immigrant cultures as distinctive from the American melting pot, Disney has not had as domineering an effect on the perception of what a fairy tale is or does.

However, the 'Rapunzel syndrome', as Margaret Atwood called it, has imprisoned many Canadian heroines in a tower from which no hero can liberate them. In this sense, the fairy tale has mythified the image of Canada itself as the great and threatening unknown. In more experimental fairy tales, whether for children or adults, feminism and metanarrative are as strongly at work in Canada as in the United States, while fantasy is not as strong a tradition. The following stand out: *The Paper Bag Princess* by Robert *Munsch, a tongue-in-cheek 1980 fairy tale for children; the hauntingly meta-fictional *Truly Grim Tales* by Priscilla Galloway (1995); and Margaret Atwood's many acclaimed revisions of the Grimms' tales, in which disturbing fairy-tale themes become tools for demanding change in gender and social dynamics. The Hungarian-born Canadian illustrator Laszlo Gal is also notable.

At the beginning of the 21st century in North America, the fairy tale has found a new operative context in the Internet—where parodies and jokes are often exchanged and multiple versions of a tale are made instantly available on web pages. The question of whether the normative and commodified uses of the fairy tale or its 'antimythic' and transformative powers will prevail can only be addressed within a broadly political and social framework of analysis; given the increasing power of technology and of a global culture industry, however, the multifarious permutations of the fairy tale in the 20th century offer some hope that the fairy tale's wonderful diversity will survive and thrive. CB

Attebery, Brian, *The Fantasy Tradition in American Literature: From Irving to Le Guin* (1980).

Atwood, Margaret, *Survival: A Thematic Guide to Canadian Literature* (1972).

Avery, Gillian, *Behold the Child: American Children and their Books 1621–1922* (1994).

Davenport, Tom, and Carden, Gary, *From the Brothers Grimm: A Contemporary Retelling of American Folktales and Classic Stories* (1992).

Davies, Bronwyn, *Frogs and Snails and Feminist Tales: Preschool Children and Gender* (1989).

Grant, Agnes, 'A Canadian Fairy Tale: What Is It?', *Canadian Children's Literature/ La Littérature Canadienne pour la Jeunesse*, 22 (1981).

Haase, Donald P., 'Gold into Straw: Fairy Tale Movies for Children and the Culture Industry', *The Lion and the Unicorn*, 12.2 (1988).

Jones, Steven Swann, *The Fairy Tale: The Magic Mirror of Imagination* (1995).

McCarthy, William, *Jack in Two Worlds* (1994).

McCarthy, William (ed.), *Cinderella in America: A Book of Folk and Fairy Tales*. (2007).

Mieder, Wolfgang, *Disenchantments: An Anthology of Modern Fairy Tale Poetry* (1985).

Mieder, Wolfgang, *Tradition and Innovation in Folk Literature* (1987).

Rushdie, Salman, *The Wizard of Oz* (1992).

Schickel, Richard, *The Disney Version* (1968; rev. edn., 1985).

Stone, Kay, 'Feminist Approaches to the Interpretation of Fairy Tales', in Ruth B. Bottigheimer (ed.), *Fairy Tales and Society* (1986).

Stone, Kay, *Burning Brightly: New Light on Old Tales Told Today* (1998).

Zipes, Jack (ed.), *Don't Bet on the Prince: Contemporary Feminist Fairy Tales in North America* (1986).

Zipes, Jack (ed.), 'The Fairy Tale', spec. issue of *The Lion and the Unicorn*, 12.2 (1988).

Zipes, Jack (ed.), *Spells of Enchantment: The Wondrous Fairy Tales of Western Culture* (1991).

Zipes, Jack, *Fairy Tale as Myth/Myth as Fairy Tale* (1994).

Zipes, Jack, *Happily Ever After: Fairy Tales, Children, and the Culture Industry* (1997).

Zipes, Jack, *Why Fairy Tales Stick: The Evolution and Relevance of a Genre* (2008).

has always longed to escape from houses. In *The Borrowers Afloat* (1959) they are forced out of the gamekeeper's cottage where they have sheltered during the winter, and voyage downstream in an old kettle. *The Borrowers Aloft* (1961) sees them captured by rapacious humans who want to exhibit them. Imprisoned in an attic, they use all their borrower ingenuity to construct a balloon in which they can float out of the window. Offered a comfortable house in a model village by a sympathetic human with whom Arrietty—to her parents' horror—has fraternized, Pod insists that they must move on—humans can never be trusted. '"Where are we going to?" asked Homily, in a tone of blank bewilderment. How many times, she wondered now, had she heard herself ask this question?' *The Borrowers Avenged* (1982) takes up the story for the last time; they are leaving this house with all its comforts in search of a new resting-place away from human eyes. They find one, behind a grate in an old rectory, but we know, as do the Borrowers, that inevitably they will have to move on. GA

Nöstlinger, Christine (1936–) Prolific, popular, and versatile postwar Austrian children's book author. She has published more than 100 books in all categories, from picture books to young adult novels, and has written countless weekly newspaper glosses and articles, film scripts, popular children's radio programmes, and poems in both High German and the Viennese dialect. Many of these books have broken new ground, won prestigious awards, and become classics of modern children's literature. All of her stories, both the fantastic and the realistic ones, contain sharp social commentary and critique. What has made her books appealing to both critics and millions of devoted readers are her boundless imagination, her deep insight into the human psyche, her willingness to defend and fight for the rights of the powerless and outsiders, her free-flowing, off-beat, spirited, and sometimes masterful prose, and, above all, her wit and humour which ranges from slapstick to sophisticated irony, laced, at times, with a shade of sarcasm.

Nöstlinger was born in 1936 in a working-class district of Vienna, which became the setting for many of her stories. She studied art and design before she took up writing. Already her first book, *Die feuerrote Friederike* (*Fiery Frederica*, 1970), won her recognition. Friederike is teased and taunted by the other children on account of her raspberry-red hair which, however, has magic qualities that allow her to defend herself and finally to fly off to a better world.

Despite this heroine's escape from a troubled world, Nöstlinger's books are anything but escapist. Her brand of fantasy is emancipatory, distorting reality in order to draw attention to things that are in need of change. Gender roles, the economic structure, parent–child relations, and the status and treatment of the child in society are burning issues in post-1968 Europe that she addresses in *Die Kinder aus dem Kinderkeller* (*The Disappearing Cellar*, 1971), *Wir pfeifen auf den Gurkenkönig* (*The Cucumber King*, 1972), *Konrad oder das Kind aus der Konservenbüchse* (UK, *Conrad: The Factory-Made Boy*; USA, *Konrad*, 1975), and *Rosa Riedl, Schutzgespenst* (*Rosa Riedl, Guardian Ghost*, 1979). They all feature shy, lonely, or too well-adapted and well-behaved children who, with the help of a magic agent or understanding friends, turn into assertive, socially engaged, and self-assured young people. In *The Disappearing Cellar*, the optimism and idealism that runs through Nöstlinger's early work is embodied in the down-to-earth fairy godmother Pia Maria Tiralla. She helps the children step out into the world and take charge as opposed to Ferri Fontana, the representative of the conventional, escapist kind of fantasy literature, who lulls children into sweet dreams in his cellar.

The Cucumber King, a novel of greater complexity, was awarded the Deutscher Jugendbuchpreis (German Prize for Children's and Youth Literature) in 1973. It takes a stab at the patriarchal and authoritarian structure of the Hogelmann household that is mirrored in the dictatorial rule of the Cucumber King over his Kumi-Ori people in the Hogelmann's cellar. The nasty behaviour of the Cucumber King and the example of the Kumi Oris, who have thrown out their oppressor, inspire the Hogelmann children to do the same and open the road to an uneasy, fledgling family democracy.

In *Konrad* the fantastic acquires an element of science fiction. The instant-boy Konrad is sent out as canned goods by a mail-order company specializing in the production of well-behaved children. He is delivered to the wrong address, and what follows is a hilarious account of mishaps and misunderstandings in an upside-down world in which the child acts like an adult and the parent like a child. Although the book's criticism is aimed at a bourgeois, authoritarian education in the grip and service of a technocratic consumer society, Nöstlinger's ultimate message is more balanced. The truth lies somewhere in the middle, as the book's ending suggests.

Despite Nöstlinger's strong political convictions, her books are never didactic. Her superior narrative talent, and especially her subversive humour, undo the intentionality that fuelled her stories during the early and most creative part of her career. She is a master of the short narrative, and her poems are intense, witty, and full of imagination and wordplay. Nöstlinger has a special affinity for the grotesque that permeates her writing and dominates her novel *Hugo, das Kind in den besten Jahren* (*Hugo, the Child in the Prime of Life*, 1983), fantastic tales spun around absurdist drawings by the Austrian artist Jörg Wollmann.

Two major phases can be discerned in Nöstlinger's writing. Her militant social revolutionary stance during the 1970s and early 1980s slowly gave way in the mid-1980s to a stage of deep despair and pessimism about the effect fiction can have on readers and a state of resignation in the 1990s. Yet Nöstlinger continues writing. In *Der Hund kommt* (*The Dog Arrives*, 1987) she portrays her own situation in the fate of an anthropomorphized old dog who travels the country to help the young and powerless, but has only limited success. The story ends in a way that is reminiscent of *Janosch's bear and tiger tales, when the dog retreats into privacy together with his friend, the bear. A more fairy-tale-like atmosphere reigns in *Der gefrorene Prinz* (*The Frozen Prince*, 1990), in which conventional magical motifs are interspersed with grotesque ideas.

Perhaps one of Nöstlinger's most beautiful modern fairy tales about love's uneasy give and take is the picture book *Einer* (*Someone*, 1980), which is illustrated by Janosch. It starts out in the traditional fairy-tale manner: 'Once upon a time …', but does not use magic and has an unconventional plot. Like all of Nöstlinger's modern fantasy and fairy tales, this tale rests firmly in today's reality and takes issue with today's problems. Nöstlinger has received many prizes and recognitions, the most prominent of which was the 1984 Hans Christian Andersen Award.   EMM

Altschaffel, Stefan, *Zur Darstellung der Erziehungsproblematik unter besonderer Berücksichtigung des Generationenkonflikts in ausgesuchten Texten Christine Nöstlingers* (2008).
Dilewsky, Klaus Jürgen, *Christine Nöstlinger als Kinder- und Jugendbuchautorin. Genres, Stoffe, Sozialcharaktere, Intentionen* (1993).
Kaminski, Winfred, 'Fremde Kinder—Zwei moderne Klassiker', in *Einführung in die Kinder- und Jugendliteratur* (1994).

Novalis (pseudonym of **Friedrich von Hardenberg**, 1772–1801) An important German romantic writer who pioneered a revolutionary new aesthetic for the literary fairy tale. Born on the family estate in Oberwiederstedt, Novalis was the eldest son in a family dominated by a strict father, who belonged to the pietistic *Herrnhuter* sect. Despite being drawn to philosophy and literature, Novalis studied law in deference to his father's expectation that he pursue an administrative career. After receiving his law degree from the University of Wittenberg in 1794, Novalis was apprenticed by his father to the district director of Thuringia so that he could pursue his administrative training. In the course of an official visit to a landowner's estate, Novalis met the 12-year-old Sophie von Kühn, with whom he fell in love. The two were secretly engaged, but she died in 1797. Sophie's death, coupled with the loss of his brother Erasmus less than one month later, devastated Novalis, who entered a period of mourning and deep introspection. He emerged from this life-changing experience prepared not only to embrace the fullness of life, but also to overcome life's reverses through the creative power of the imagination.

Novalis immersed himself in the dynamic philosophical, scientific, and aesthetic currents of his time. He resumed his study of philosophy, especially the work of Immanuel Kant and Johann Gottlieb Fichte; he pursued his scientific interests and prepared for a new career as a mining engineer by undertaking technical studies at the Freiberg Mining Academy; and he experimented with new forms of literary expression and interacted with writers such as Friedrich and August Wilhelm Schlegel, Ludwig *Tieck, and Friedrich Schleiermacher, who were the vanguard of early romanticism in Germany.

Novalis, whose pen name means 'preparer of new land', experimented with a broad spectrum of genres, including aphorisms, essays, poetry, novels, and fairy tales. With the exception of some poetry and two collections of aphorisms, most of Novalis's writings were first published after he died at the age of 28. His contributions to the development of the fairy tale come from posthumously published notebook entries and from drafts of two fragmentary novels.

In his notebooks, Novalis began to articulate a theory of the fairy tale, which he considered the quintessential genre of romantic literature. In contrast to many writers of the 18th century, Novalis did not view the fairy tale as a children's genre with a morally didactic purpose. Nor did he value the fairy tale because it preserved the oral tradition of the folk. Instead, he conceived of a literary fairy tale that was written according to a radically new aesthetic for a highly literate audience. Novalis believed the fairy tale should not be characterized by simplicity and predictable order, but by chaos and 'natural anarchy', which would require new, more challenging modes of imaginative perception on the part of his readers. So the romantic fairy tale envisioned by Novalis was a progressive, not a regressive, genre. It was not meant to recapture the ancient spirit of the folk and merely restore the lost harmony of the simple past. Rather, it was to be the prophetic expression of the creative individual, whose imagination could synthesize the chaos and contradictions of the present and project a utopian future on a more complex, higher level. By engaging the imagination of its sophisticated readers, this romantic fairy tale would liberate them from the constraints of one-dimensional rationality and allow them to envision a new world. So, in an era of revolutions, the utopian fairy tale that Novalis theorized was not only an epistemological and aesthetic innovation, but a social and political gesture as well.

The fairy tales that Novalis wrote are embedded in his two uncompleted novels. His philosophical novel *Die Lehrlinge zu Sais* (*The Disciples of Sais*, 1802) contains the story of 'Hyazinth und Rosenblütchen' ('Hyacinth and Rosebloom'). This deceptively simple tale embodies Novalis's fairy-tale theory of history as a triadic progression: a youth separated from his family and his beloved wanders in search of his lost past and re-achieves his original state on a much higher level. This plot is repeated in *Heinrich von Ofterdingen* (1802), a novel of education based on Heinrich's fairy-tale journey towards ever higher levels of poetry and imagination. The novel includes three tales, each of which mirrors the larger narrative and elaborates the profound connections between Heinrich's own story and the fairy tale of history itself. The first tale, which is told to Heinrich by a group of merchants, alludes to the ancient Greek myth of Arion and depicts the triumph of art over narrow-minded materialism. The next, also told by the merchants, is more elaborately constructed and adapts the myth of Atlantis to suggest the rebirth of a society ruled by the spirit of poetry. The last tale, known as 'Klingsohrs Märchen' ('Klingsohr's Fairy Tale') after the master poet who tells the story, is a narrative of extreme complexity. It draws eclectically on world mythologies, science, and philosophy in order to break traditional aesthetic boundaries and create a utopian vision through an act of imagination. In the end, all of Novalis's fairy tales proclaim the legitimacy of the imagination and its power to transcend restrictive realities and to create a new state ruled by love and imagination.

Novalis's multifaceted and very complex work has been often oversimplified and misunderstood. None the less, his innovative theories and sophisticated literary fairy tales prepared the way for writers such as E. T. A. *Hoffmann, Joseph von *Eichendorff, Hermann Hesse, Maurice *Maeterlinck, George *MacDonald, Ursula *Le Guin, and many others, who discovered in his work strategies for producing new forms of fantasy and fairy tale for the times in which they lived.   DH

Birrell, Gordon, *The Boundless Present: Space and Time in the Literary Fairy Tales of Novalis and Tieck* (1979).

Calhoon, Kenneth S., *Fatherland: Novalis, Freud, and the Discipline of Romance* (1992).

Mahoney, Dennis F., *The Critical Fortunes of a Romantic Novel: Novalis's 'Heinrich von Ofterdingen'* (1994).

Neubauer, John, *Novalis* (1980).

O'Brien, William Arctander, *Novalis: Signs of Revolution* (1995).

Novaro, Angelo Silvio (1868–1938) Italian writer and poet whose first literary effort was a volume of sea tales entitled *Sul mare* (*At Sea*, 1889). The collection of tales entitled *La bottega dello stregone* (*The Sorcerer's Shop*, 1911) contains the story of a man (a sorcerer, according to the local women) whose shop is cursed since everyone who rents it fails to succeed in business. A young shoemaker, however, who is in love with a beautiful maid with golden tresses, has great success and is rewarded with marrying the maid and keeping the shop.

Novaro's most successful work is, however, the prose poem *Il Fabbro armonioso* (*The Harmonious Blacksmith*, 1919) which deals with his son's death at war. Novaro wrote the collection of poems *Il cestello* (*The Little Basket*, 1910) for children, as well as the stories *Garibaldi ricordato ai ragazzi* (*Garibaldi Recorded for Children*) and *La festa degli alberi spiegata ai ragazzi* (*The Feast of Trees Explained to Children*, 1912).   GD

nursery comics These have included many fairy tales. *The Chicks' Own*, the first nursery comic, was initially published in 1920 and continued until 1957. Gifford's records are incomplete for this comic but show that 'The Three Bears' (1936), 'Fairy Fay and Eddie Elf' (1939) and *'Hansel and Gretel' (1957) occurred in picture stories, as did 'Babes in the Wood' (1957), *'Peter Pan' (1959), and 'Wizard Weezle' (1966) when the comic was incorporated with *Playhour*.

A number of other nursery comics have published fairy stories, the most prolific being *Bimbo* which between 1962 and 1972 included 'Tom Thumb', *'Snow White', 'Mandy the Mermaid', *'Aladdin', *'Jack and the Beanstalk' and *'Puss-in-Boots'. These stories have tended to be harmless, pleasant, well illustrated versions which have avoided material which might prove frightening.

Today's nursery comics are much more focused on early learning. One comic is unique because it has based its approach wholly on folk and fairy tales, including both text and picture stories alongside the puzzles and problems. *I Love to Read—Fairy Tales* has been published monthly since 1995. Recent issues have included 'Dick Whittington', 'The *Ugly Duckling', 'The Frog Prince', 'Puss in Boots', 'Hansel and Gretel' and 'The Dragon and his Grandmother'. This comic changed its title to *Storyland* in 1998, although the emphasis on fairy tales has remained.   GF

Nyblom, Helena (1843–1926) Pioneer of the Swedish literary fairy tale and author of more than 80 fairy tales written between 1896 and 1920. Her most famous fairy tales include versions of *'Beauty and the Beast' and a variant of Hans Christian *Andersen's 'The *Little Mermaid'. Many of her tales, in which she mixes Swedish folklore, ancient myths, and romantic motifs, contain clear feminist messages, typical of her time; they also reflect the general didacticism of turn-of-the-century Swedish literature for children.　　　　　　　　　　　　　MN

Nordlinder, Eva, *Sekelskiftets svenska konstsaga och sagodiktaren Helena Nyblom* (1991).

Nyström, Jenny (1854–1946) Pioneer of Swedish fairy-tale illustrations. She illustrated one of the very first Swedish literary fairy tales, *Lille Viggs äfventyr på julafton* (*Little Viggs' Adventure on Christmas Eve*,

1875) by Viktor Rydberg. Her most famous book, *Barnkammarens bok* (*The Nursery Book*, 1882), is a collection of folk songs and nursery rhymes. She also created the figure of the Swedish Christmas 'tomten' (corresponding to Santa Claus) in numerous magazine covers, posters, and cards.　　　MN

Forsberg Warringer, Gunnel, *Jenny Nyström: konstnärinna* (1992).

Gynning, Margareta, *Jenny Nyström: målaren och illustratören* (1996).

Oates, Joyce Carol (1938–) Prolific American writer whose work includes plays, novels, stories, poetry, and literary criticism. Her first collection of short stories, *By the North Gate*, appeared in 1963, and since then she has published many other collections such as *The Land of Abyssalia* (1980) and *Raven's Wing* (1986), in which she has woven fairy-tale motifs into her narratives. Other works such as *Bellefleur* (1980) and *A Bloodsmoor Romance* (1982) reflect her interest in supernatural and Gothic fiction. Her collections, *Night-Side: Eighteen Tales* (1977), *Haunted: Tales of the Grotesque* (1994), and *Demon and Other Tales* (1996), include dark fantasy and weird fiction. In 1988 she published two fairy tales, 'Blue-Bearded Lover' and 'Secret Observations on the Goat Girl' in *The Assignation*, and 'The Crossing' (1995) and 'In the Insomniac Night' (1997) appeared in the *Ontario Review*. All her fairy tales have a dreamlike quality to them and develop psychological and surprising twists to traditional narrative plots. Thus *'Bluebeard' is revisited from the perspective of a woman who wins his trust and will bear him children. JZ

Ōba, Minako (1930–2007) Japanese author of several reworked versions of traditional Japanese folktales. In her 1976 appropriation of the 'yamauba' myth of an old mountain widow who preys on vulnerable men, Ōba layers in a backstory explaining how years of mistreatment by men and internalization of misogyny created the monster. In her 1986 rewrite of 'The Tale of the Bamboo Cutter', Ōba largely leaves the narrative intact, but emphasizes the moon-princess's rebuff of her five suitor-princes and the Mikado himself as a rejection of marriage as a compulsory social system. SCR

Ōba, Minako, 'The Smile of the Mountain Witch', *Japanese Women Writers* (1991).
Wilson, Michiko, 'Refashioning a *Yamauba* Tale', *Marvels & Tales*, 27:2 (2013).

O'Casey, Sean (1880–1964) Irish dramatist and younger rival of William Butler *Yeats. O'Casey's career took off with the Abbey Theatre's production of *The Shadow of a Gunman* (1923), a realistic play about pre-independence Ireland. With the *Silver Tassie* (1929), O'Casey began experimenting with expressionism and allegory, but it was not until later in his career that he experimented with fantasy, resulting in *Cock-a-Doodle Dandy* (1949), in which an enchanted cock, whom the village priest believes to be the incarnation of the devil, represents 'the joyful, active spirit of life'. *Figuro in the Night* (1961) is a fantasy written in much the same vein. AD

Ocelot, Michel (1943–) French animator, director, and writer, who has created several fascinating films that are influenced by West African folklore. Ocelot spent his childhood in Guinea, West Africa, and after returning to France he studied at the École nationale supérieure des arts décoratifs in Paris and later the California Institute of the Arts in Los Angeles. When he returned to Paris, he began making short animated films and then established a name for himself with two feature films, *Kirikou and the Sorceress* (1998) and *Kirikou and the Wild Beasts* (2005), that rely on two-dimensional hand drawings that recall the unusual paintings of Henri Rousseau. The protagonist of these two films is a tiny naked West African child who is born with wisdom beyond his years and also has the capacity to speak. He literally bursts from his mother's womb and scoots about the village to declare that he is there, ready to help the needy villagers. In the first film Kirikou quickly learns that his tiny village is threatened by the sorceress Karaba, who uses an army of robots and automatons to take gold and kill any of the men who dare to oppose her. Kirikou decides to save the village, and everyone mocks him, but when he succeeds and outwits Karaba with his adroit speed and cunning, they begin celebrating him with songs that extol his deeds. This also occurs in the second Kirikou film, in which the boy defeats wild beasts. One of Ocelot's more recent films, *Azur and Asmar* (2006), continued to provide substantial cultural difference in animation and to present bodies in unusual images and situations that challenge stereotypes and social prejudices. Set in the Middle Ages, the film takes place first in Andalusia, where a young boy named Azur is being nursed and educated by a North African woman Jénane because the infant's mother has died. Jénane has her own son, Asmar, the same age. The two boys play together and become close 'brothers', despite class and ethnic differences. Ocelot depicts the relationship between the blue-eyed blond-haired Azur and the dark-skinned, brown-eyed Asmar as natural and free of prejudice. The boys are both enraptured by a tale that Jénane tells them about the fairy of the jinnis, who is encased in glass and needs to be saved by a valiant knight. As Azmur grows older, however, his father, a nobleman, abruptly and violently banishes Jénane and Asmar from Andalusia because he wants his son to receive a royal education appropriate for a young nobleman and believes that the dark son of a servant has had a bad influence on Azmur. Later, when Azmur has matured, he rebels against his racist father and sets out on a quest to free the fairy of the jinnis, who resides across the sea in Jénane's home country, where there is a happy reunion and the fairy is rescued. Ocelot has also produced a series of short-fairy-tale films for television called *Dragons and Princesses* (2010) and a feature film *Contes de la Nuit* (*Tales of the Night*, 2010), which brings together three fairy tales. In 2012, Ocelot produced a prequel to his Kirikou films titled *Kirikou et les Hommes et les Femmes* (*Kirikou and the Men and Women*), which recalls several early adventures of Kirikou and how he cleverly helps the people of his village. JZ

Gudin, Christine, 'La genèse des contes de Michel Ocelot', in Carole Aurouet (ed.), *Contes et légendes à l'écran* (2005).

Neupert, Richard, 'Kirikou and the Animated Figure/Body', *Studies in French Cinema* (2009).

Oehlenschläger, Adam (1779–1850) Poet and playwright who tends to be considered the Danish Wordsworth. His writings reveal his fascination with folklore, and in 1816 he translated *Märchen* by *Musäus, *Fouqué, *Hoffmann, and *Chamisso into Danish, thus stimulating such writers as *Ingemann and *Andersen. His plays *Aladdin* (1806) and *Aly og Gulhyndy* (*Aly and Gulhyndy*, 1813) are romantic adaptations from The *Arabian Nights, in which, true to the tradition of the multi-phased magic tale, Oehlenschläger takes his protagonists through a process of *Bildung*. NI

Offenbach, Jacques (1819–80) German-French composer, one of the most important representatives of the *opéra bouffe* and the French operetta. Born in Cologne, the son of a Jewish cantor, Offenbach went with his father to Paris in 1833 and was admitted to study at the Paris Conservatoire at 14 because of his extraordinary talent. Once he had completed his studies, he worked as a cellist and conductor. In 1853 he produced his first operetta, and during the following years he was the head of two theatres and also lived in the United States for a long time. His greatest successes, however, were in Paris, where he was regarded as a pioneer of musical comedy of the kind created by Johann Strauss in Austria and Gilbert and Sullivan in England. What made Offenbach's operettas so distinctive was his social critique. He combined satire and irony with an unusual compassion and understanding for his characters.

Among his approximately 90 operettas, Offenbach wrote a parody of the *Bluebeard tale, *Barbe-bleue* (1866). This fascinating and mysterious fairy-tale character, created by Charles *Perrault, has been adapted in operas many different times: *Raoul Barbe-bleue* (*King Bluebeard*, 1789) by André-Ernest-Modeste *Grétry, *Ariadne et Barbe-bleue* (1907) by Paul *Dukas, *A Kékszakállú herceg vára* (*Duke Bluebeard's Castle*, 1918) by Béla *Bartók, *Ritter Blaubart* (*Knight Bluebeard*, 1920) by Emil Nikolaus von Reznicek. In Perrault's tale, Bluebeard wants to kill his disobedient wife because she has opened the forbidden door behind which the other murdered wives of Bluebeard are concealed. Offenbach collaborated closely with his librettists Henri Meilhac and Ludovic Halévy in his adaptation, and he set the action in the south of France during the crusades, but he made references through caricatures to the conditions in France during the reign of Napoleon III and he depicted the affable relations between the aristocracy and the common people while also revealing the servility of the nobles. The knight Bluebeard has six wives killed by his Alchemist Popolani so that he can marry the daughter of the king. However, Popolani had instead given the wives sleeping tablets and eventually brings them alive and well to the king. Bluebeard's marriage is then nullified, and as 'punishment' he must live the rest of his life with his sixth cranky and angry wife.

Offenbach did not write only operettas. He also composed important operas. One fairy-tale opera, *Die Rheinnixen* (*The Nixies of the Rhine*, 1864), commissioned by the Viennese Court Opera, was not particularly successful. However, during his last years Offenbach was working on his *opus summum*, the great fantastical opera, which he never completed, *Les Contes d'Hoffmann* (*The Tales of Hoffmann*, 1880). The composer died during the rehearsals on 5 October 1880. The opera was completed by Ernest Guiraud and produced in Paris in February 1881. The librettists, Jules Barbier and Michel Carré, took episodes from various tales by the German writer E. T. A. *Hoffmann, whom Offenbach greatly admired, and they fused them together in a frame story. The central figure of the opera is the writer Hoffmann, who tells drinking companions about three adventures with women whom he had loved. Olympia, a mechanical doll, whom Hoffmann views through magical glasses and mistakes for a live woman, is destroyed because of a mysterious duel between her inventors. The fragile and beautiful singer Antonia dies from consumption. The courtesan Giuletta, who has a liaison with a sorcerer, mocks and deceives Hoffmann, who is left forlorn and alone at the end of the opera. Offenbach combined reality, magic, and the grotesque in his final work, which is one of the greatest fairy-tale operas ever composed.

THH

Faris, Alexander, *Jacques Offenbach* (1980).
Gammond, Peter, *Offenbach* (1980).
Harding, James, *Jacques Offenbach: A Biography* (1980).
Yon, Jean-Claude, *Jacques Offenbach* (2000).

Ogawa, Yōko (1962–) Japanese author of contemporary stories and novels on the Gothic everyday, mathematics, and fairy tales. Her *Revenge*, a 1998 release in Japan, weaves together eleven narratives that initially appear unrelated into a complex and perhaps temporally impossible text. The Japanese title is considerably more suggestive: *Reticent Corpse, Lewd Requiem* (Kamoku na shigai, midara na tomurai). She rewrites and embellishes 'The *Little Mermaid', *'Little Red Riding Hood', *Alice's Adventures in Wonderland*, and 'Wild Swans' in a 2006 collection (*Otogibanashi no wasuremono*), adding, for example, self-sacrificing mermen devoted to serving the mermaid.　　SCR

Fraser, Lucy, 'Transformations of "The Little Mermaid"', *Marvels & Tales*, 27:2 (2013).
Ogawa, Yōko, *Otogibanashi no wasuremono* (2006).

Okri, Ben (1959–) Nigerian novelist, poet, and essayist, best known for his otherworldly and imaginative fiction. His works focus on African folklore and African experience, especially political strife in Nigeria. His best-known work, *The Famished Road* (1991), won the Booker Prize in 1991 and is the first in a three-part trilogy that includes *Songs of Enchantment* (1993) and *Infinite Riches* (1998).

The trilogy centres on the life of a spirit child in Yoruba mythology. Okri's emphasis on allegory and magic plays a major role throughout his career and most notably in *Astonishing the Gods* (1995), *Starbrook* (2007), and *Tales of Freedom* (2009). KMJ

Ole Lukkøje Title character of one of the most popular fairy tales by Hans Christian Andersen (1841; translated into English as 'Willie Winkie', 'The Sandman', 'The Dustman', 'Old Luke'). The name means literally 'Ole, close your eyes', 'Ole' being a boy's name. The origin of the figure goes back to the German folklore character Sandmännchen, a little man or dwarf who makes children go to sleep. Ole Lukkøje carries two umbrellas, one with beautiful pictures, giving children interesting dreams, and a plain black one. He may be viewed as one of Andersen's many self-portraits as a storyteller. Ole Lukkøje has a brother whose name is Death. MN

Olrik, Axel (1864–1917) Professor of folklore at the University of Copenhagen, Denmark; his international claim to fame rests mainly on the article 'Episke love i folkedigtningen' ('Epic Laws of Folk Narrative', included in Allen Dundes, *The Study of Folklore*). Olrik, whose observations foreshadowed many of Vladimir Propp's, was thereby one of the initiators of the structural study of folk narratives, and his analysis of narrative laws clarifies the differences between oral tales and literary imitations. NI

Dundes, Allen, *The Study of Folklore* (1965).
Olrik, Axel, 'Episke love i folkedigtningen', *Danske Studier* (1908).
Thompson, Stith, *The Folktale* (1946).

Ontiveros, José Rodolfo Loaiza (1982–) Self-taught visual artist of Mexican origin famous for his subversion of Disney Studios' fairy-tale film canon. His paintings replicate stills from Disney films altered to feature characters engaging in atypical activities, ranging from same-sex affection to using illicit drugs. Adult-oriented in theme, the works often rely on intertextual references drawn from Hollywood cinema and celebrity culture. The portrait 'Love the Way You Lie' from Ontiveros' 'DisHollywood' exhibition (2013) is a portrait of *Princess and the Frog*'s Tiana, dishevelled and bruised, reminiscent of popstar Rhianna's domestic violence scandal. Other exhibitions include 'Disenchanted' (2011) and 'Disasterland' (2012). KMJ

opera and fairy tales Opera is a sung dramatic work designed for theatrical performance. While opera's broad appeal is expressed mainly through music and drama, its complete theatrical experience frequently relies on costume, scenery, and movement: in France, a ballet sequence was long considered a crucial part in any opera's construction. After a 400-year history, opera now has a long list of constituents, of which the foregoing are among the most significant. For at least half that time, fairy tales have provided a rich source of inspiration for composers when selecting subjects for their works.

Part of opera's continuing fascination lies in its ever-changing complexity, reflecting contemporary tastes in music and drama, styles of singing, and scale of production. Opera has seldom been free from controversy. While one view maintains that it is an invaluable part of civilized society, another holds that it is an irrelevance—a diversion which has no connection with everyday life. What is undeniable, however, is that it has the ability to uplift audiences, inspiring in them an almost religious devotion.

1. History

Opera has played a pivotal role in theatrical entertainment not just for centuries, but for several millennia, dating back to the ancient Greeks. The prototype of its present-day form began to appear in late Renaissance Italy—the first surviving acknowledged operatic work being Jacopi Peri's *Euridice* in 1600. Peri belonged to a select group of musicians and learned nobles whose aim was the reinstatement of clearly declaimed sung text, rather as it had been in ancient Greece. Consolidating Peri's work, Claudio Monteverdi (1567-1643), a far more historically important composer, produced *La Favola d'Orfeo* (*The Fable of Orpheus*) in 1607.

Opera's rapid growth during the 17th century, first in Italy and shortly after throughout the rest of Europe, owed much to the encouragement of the aristocracy, whose taste for grand festive occasions gave it an important platform. Italian influence led to early enthusiasm for the new art form in France and Germany, although, initially at least, attempts by centres such as Paris and Dresden to found an indigenous school were invariably rooted in the Italian style. At first the spread of opera was greatly assisted by travelling troupes, usually from Italy. This was later mirrored in America, where early opera was largely a matter of what was provided by visiting European companies. Mid-17th-century French opera and ballet (for a considerable time in France the two were virtually indivisible), is invariably remembered today through the Italian-born composer Jean-Baptiste Lully (1632–87), a musician of great influence at the court of Louis XIV.

In the early 18th century, London enjoyed the double benefit of German-born George Frederic *Handel, who composed and conducted operas in the Italian manner, and the Royal Academy of Music—a business enterprise which promoted them. Later in the same century both Christoph Willibald von Gluck (1714–87) and Wolfgang Amadeus *Mozart made Vienna their centre of operations, although some of their important works received premières in other leading European cities. Gluck sought to 'reform' Italian opera with a more natural form of expression: it had lapsed into a somewhat stilted form. Mozart, the incomparably superior composer, tapped deeper emotional currents through detailed character development. Dresden flourished in the early 19th century owing to Carl Maria von *Weber, who as Royal Saxon *Kapellmeister* was not only active as a composer but undertook wide-ranging reforms to opera-house practices.

From the mid-17th until the early 20th century, Paris was a significant centre for opera, reaching its zenith in the 19th century, having attracted the Italian composer Gioacchino *Rossini and the German

Giacomo Meyerbeer (1791–1864) to settle there. But Paris was rich, too, in native-born talent: Hector Berlioz (1803–68); Charles Gounod (1818–93); Georges Bizet (1838–75); and Jules Massenet (1842–1912). That said, one of the most popular 'Parisian' composers of all time was German-born Jacques *Offenbach. This period was remarkable also for the number of theatres presenting opera in Paris. Some sources claim a figure as high as 30.

As opera grew more international, countries such as Germany, Russia, and Czechoslovakia became more musically nationalistic in character, as did Hungary and Poland. Czechoslovakia, an important part of the Austro-Hungarian Empire, had a long tradition of importing musical talent and experience from Germany and Austria. Now native composers such as Bedrich Smetana (1824–84) and Antonin *Dvořák emerged, followed later by the highly individual Leoš *Janáček. In Russia the national movement was led by Mikhail *Glinka, succeeded by Alexander Borodin (1833–87), Modest Mussorgsky (1839–81), Piotr *Tchaikovsky, and Nikolai *Rimsky-Korsakov. Many of these Slav composers produced a conspicuous number of fairy-tale operas in an astonishingly short space of operatic history.

Meanwhile, as the 19th century unfolded, the arrival of Giuseppe Verdi (1813–1901) and Richard *Wagner focused musical attention as never before on Italy and Germany. For a time Verdi was almost certainly the world's most popular composer, a belief which has changed little in 100 years. His wonderful melodic gifts, unerring sense of theatre, and expert knowledge of the voice make his works instantly accessible. Wagner based many of his operas on Nordic mythology and German legends, and as such has more relevance to this article on fairy tales.

The pattern of a contemporaneous Italian and German each individually breaking new ground was repeated again with Giacomo *Puccini and Richard *Strauss. Puccini, a significant figure in the 'Verismo' movement, gave opera a much-needed 'naturalist' impetus, as did Ruggero Leoncavallo (1857–1919), and Pietro Mascagni (1863–

1945). Like these composers, Strauss too dealt frequently in highly charged emotion which was liable to take a violent turn. Indeed, some of his early operas such as *Salomé* and *Elektra* frequently touched on extremes of brutality.

The closest he came to a fairy-tale opera was *Der Rosenkavalier* (*The Rose Cavalier*, premièred 1911), a believable fantasy set in 18th-century Vienna with text by Hugo von *Hofmannsthal. Sophie is doomed to a pre-arranged marriage with the ageing, licentious Baron Ochs and is rescued by her lover Count Octavian. Strauss was also a noted conductor and in 1893 conducted the première of Engelbert *Humperdinck's *Hansel and Gretel*, arguably the most famous of all fairy-tale operas.

The 20th century has been characterized by the appearance of many more sharply defined styles of composition, including the vogue for small-scale works, such as *The Soldier's Tale* by Igor *Stravinsky. Premièred in 1918, it is without doubt a curiosity—an opera with speech and drama and no singing. Stravinsky's fellow Russians, however, still thought on the grand scale. Sergei *Prokofiev's lyrical yet rhythmically invigorating manner complemented Dmitri Shostakovich's (1906-75) rousing and often satirical style. Both at various times fell foul of Soviet censure.

Germany has been well represented by Hans Werner Henze (1926-2012). His *The Bassarids* (premièred 1966) is very much on the grand scale and continues the long tradition of basing a work on Greek legend. In contrast to former times, France has not been so fortunate. François Poulenc (1899-1963), a brilliant and popular composer, wrote a quantity of songs and was strongly identified with Les Six, a group of French composers. His operatic output was small, but powerful: *Les Mamelles de Tiresias* (*The Mammaries of Tiresias*, 1944) and *Dialogues des Carmélites* (*Dialogues of the Carmelites*, 1957), for example. The most significant contributions by the so-called Second Viennese School led by the composer of *Moses und Aron*, Arnold Schoenberg (1874-1951) came, ironically, from one of Schoenberg's pupils, Alban Berg (1885-1935), who wrote *Wozzeck* (premièred 1925) and *Lulu* (premièred 1937).

When the mid- to late 20th century is assessed, it will be seen that lasting impacts were made by Gian Carlo Menotti (1911-) and Benjamin Britten (1913-76), and to a lesser extent Michael Tippett (1905-98). Writing for both small and large scale, Britten revitalized British opera, giving it a new self-assuredness. Menotti's greatest successes have tended to be with small-scale works, in which stories are often highly focused. They are heavily endowed with powerful drama, made more naturalistic by choosing a contemporary setting.

2. Opera stories

From opera's earliest times its stories or plots have been as varied as storytelling itself. Greek and Roman myths and legends were early favourites, and have continued to be so through to the present day. Other operas deal in power and corruption, such as Beethoven's *Fidelio* (1805), or Puccini's *Tosca* (1900). Love stories, usually with unhappy endings, abound. Among the most prominent are Verdi's *La Traviata* (1853) and Puccini's *La Bohème* (1895). Gaetano Donizetti (1797-1848) often took historical figures as his subjects (almost invariably female), portraying, among others, Anna Bolena, Lucrezia Borgia, and Mary Stuart

3. Early 'fantastic' subjects

Henry *Purcell's *The Fairy Queen* (1692), an adaptation of *Shakespeare's *A Midsummer Night's Dream*, is an early example of an existing 'fantastic' story set to music. Yet another is his *King Arthur* (1691). Some sources claim a tally of around 30 operas on the Arthurian legends. Purcell's best-known opera is *Dido and Aeneas* (1689), whose story places great reliance on witches and sorcery.

The 17th century was also a time for the so-called 'Slumber Scene'. Popular in Italian opera, it was a dramatic device requiring a character to fall asleep. In this state, characters would receive welcome news or otherwise from an apparition, or impart the same to eavesdroppers by talking in their sleep.

The vogue for such theatricality continued for some considerable time, eventually producing a whole opera on the subject, *La Sonnambula* (*The Sleepwalker*, 1831) by Vincenzo Bellini (1801–35).

4. Fairy tales

Fairy tales, with their strong dramatic opposites of good/evil, love/hate make appealing operatic material. *Cinderella* (French *Cendrillon*, Italian *Cenerentola*, German *Aschenbrödel*), was one of the first fairy tales as such to receive staged musical treatment— Rossini's *Cenerentola* of 1817 being the best known. It remains popular to the present day. Other versions from the mid-18th to late 19th century are by Laruette (1759); Isouard (1810); Steibelt (1810); Garcia (1826); C. T. Wagner (1861); Cheri (1866); Conradi (1868); Langer (1874); Rokosny (1885); Massenet (1899, a rival in popularity to Rossini's). At the beginning of the 20th century, six appeared in quick succession: Wolf-Ferrari (1900); Albini (*c*.1900); Forsyth; Blech (1905); Asafyev (1906); and Butykay (1912).

During the last year of his life, 1791, Mozart produced his remarkable *Die Zauberflöte* (*The Magic Flute*). It is a story steeped in allegory and Masonic symbolism. Some directors produce the work emphasizing its fairy-tale side; certainly in the right hands it does take on this form with its magic flute which can charm animals and magic bells that subdue enemies.

Mozart's death coincided with the emergence of 'romanticism'—a development in literature and the arts which found a deep response among a rising generation of composers: Beethoven, Berlioz, Schubert, *Mendelssohn, *Schumann, and Chopin. Among its achievements in literature, romanticism helped re-examine old fairy tales and ghost stories, thus stimulating composers into creating the 'romantic opera'.

In 1821 Weber composed *Der Freischütz* based on a story from a collection, *Gespensterbuch* (*Ghost Book*, 1810), by Johann Apel and Friedrich Laun. It tells of a shooting contest, an evil spirit, magic bullets, and redemption through confession. Not so well remembered as Weber, but nevertheless important in the history of German romantic opera, was Heinrich Marschner (1795–1861), whose best-known opera, *Hans Heiling* (1833), is based on a folk tale. It relates how a mortal girl is wooed, unsuccessfully, by a supernatural being. Marschner's contemporary Albert *Lortzing composed one of several operas on the subject of *Undine* (1845)—a water spirit (female), famous in Central European folk myth, who seeks to marry a mortal. Earlier in the century E. T. A. *Hoffmann, who like Lortzing was active in several other areas as well as composing, also took Undine as an operatic subject (1816).

It could be argued that one major accomplishment of Weber, Marschner, Lortzing, and Hoffmann was to prepare the way for Richard Wagner, who in 1833–4 produced his first complete opera, *Die Feen* (*The Fairies*). Based on *Gozzi's comedy *La donna serpente* (1762), Wagner's opera deals with the familiar theme of the tribulations which can arise when a mortal and a fairy fall in love. While Wagner did not turn out to be a setter of fairy tales as such (he invariably wrote his own librettos), magic often plays a significant part in many of his plots, which were synthesized from Nordic and Teutonic myths and sagas.

For instance, the supernatural runs right through the whole of *Der Ring des Nibelungen*, a cycle of four operas. Thus Alberich (a dwarf), changes his appearance by means of a magic helmet in *Das Rheingold*. Siegmund in *Die Walküre* is the only one who can draw a sword left embedded in a tree. In the third opera, Siegfried slays a dragon, but burns his finger in the creature's blood. He nurses the wound, discovering thereby that he can understand a warning given him by a woodbird. The final opera, *Götterdämmerung*, sees a return of the magic helmet which plays a vital part in Hagen's plot to kill Siegfried. Wagner's awesome originality in the use of the orchestra, innovative harmonic language, and dramatic presentation marked a turning-point in opera worldwide. One unfortunate side effect was that contemporary German composers found themselves overlooked.

Nevertheless, Engelbert Humperdinck did manage to make an impact with one opera in particular, even though his music bears superficial similarity to that of Wagner, for whom, early in life, he worked as a copyist. Based on the *Grimm brothers' story in *Kinder- und Hausmärchen*, *Hänsel und Gretel* was highly successful when first produced, and has stayed in the repertoire, being greatly popular in Germany, Britain, and America. Humperdinck's *Königskinder* (*The Royal Children*, 1910), also explored the realms of fairy tale, being concerned with a goose girl who loves a king's son. Their love is thwarted by a witch.

The strong operatic mix of the romantic with the supernatural in 19th-century Germany was not matched in France, although Jacques Offenbach's *The Tales of Hoffmann* (premièred posthumously in 1881), is an outstanding exception. Offenbach based his opera on stories by E. T. A. Hoffmann, the work's eponymous 'hero', whose quest for love is doomed. He is either ensnared by magic or frustrated by it.

Almost all the composers associated with the blossoming of Russia's national school wrote operas. Some were most prolific in this area. No doubt because of that country's literature, fairy tales were often a prominent feature of their work. Mikhail Glinka's *Russlan and Ludmilla* (1842), is based on *Pushkin's poem of 1820. A fairy-tale opera on a grand scale, it is cast in five acts. Ludmilla's abduction by a dwarf sets Russlan off on a series of fabulous adventures in which he encounters fairies (good and bad) and acquires a magic sword. He finally discovers Ludmilla and awakens her from her trance with the aid of a magic ring.

Among Rimsky-Korsakov's 14 operas (some sources claim 15), are several which take fairy tales or folk stories as their theme. In *May Night* (1880) water nymphs (Rusalki) help Levko overcome his father's objections in marrying Hanna. Other operas that kept Rimsky occupied with fairy tales and magic are *The *Snow Maiden* (1882), *Sadko* (1898), *The Tale of Tsar Saltan* (1900), and *The Legend of the Invisible City of Kitezh* (1907). His last opera, *The Golden Cockerel* (premièred

posthumously in 1909), tells of a miraculous golden cockerel that crows at the sign of impending danger. Tchaikovsky's best-known operas, on the other hand, are based on characters who behave like real people in believable surroundings, although *Iolanta* (1892) does have a blind princess who recovers her sight through finding love.

Russian composers did not lose their taste for fairy tales in the 20th century. Prokofiev's *The Love for Three Oranges* (1921) is based on Gozzi's play of 1761. A series of adventures befall a melancholic prince after attempts are made to induce him to laugh.

In Czechoslovakia, too, nationalism had set itself on an unstoppable course, commencing with Smetana. It was Dvořák, however, who in writing his masterpiece *Rusalka* (1900) also gave the world a great fairy-tale opera, perhaps the finest of all works on the subject of love between a water sprite and a mortal. Janáček took Czech opera into the 20th century, producing in the last decade of his life a highly individual series of works. *The Cunning Little Vixen* (1924), has animals and humans invading each other's social domain.

Native opera, which had long been dormant in Britain (with the exception of the phenomenal Gilbert and Sullivan partnership in the late 19th century) suddenly began a revival with the astonishingly successful *The Immortal Hour* (1914) by Rutland Boughton. Intended as the centrepiece of an 'English Ring', it was a tragic love tale set in fairyland. Benjamin Britten produced no fairy tales as such, but did provide another operatic version of *A Midsummer Night's Dream*. He also set a ghost story, *The Turn of the Screw* (1954), based on Henry James's story of 1898.

In America, the Italian-born Gian Carlo Menotti wrote an opera with fairy-tale ingredients, *Amahl and the Night Visitors* (1951). It was the first opera written especially for television and relates the story of a crippled boy who is cured on joining the three kings on their way to Bethlehem.

Hans Werner Henze (1926–2012) is one of the 20th century's most prolific German composers. His *König Hirsch* (*The Stag*

King, 1956), narrates the adventures of a king who as a child was abandoned in the forest and brought up by animals as a result of which he has the gift of moving in and out of human and animal form.

During the second half of the 20th century composers, directors, and producers creating operas to focus on social issues have emerged. While such operas do not tend to employ the traditional fairy tale as such, they follow the custom of moralizing through colourful fiction.   TH

Ardoin, John, *The Stages of Menotti* (1985).

Carpenter, Humphrey, *Benjamin Britten: A Biography* (1992).

Gammond, Peter, *Offenbach: His Life and Times* (1981).

Harewood, George Henry Hubert Lascelles, Earl of (ed. and rev.), *Kobbe's Complete Opera Book* (10th edn., 1987).

Headington, Christopher, Westbrook, Christopher, and Barfoot, Terry, *Opera: A History* (1987).

Holden, Amanda, Kenyon, Nicholas, and Walsh, Stephen (eds.), *The Viking Opera Guide* (1993).

Kloiber, Rudolf, and Konold, Wulf, *Handbuch der Oper* (1993).

Landon, H. C. Robbins, *1791: Mozart's Last Year* (1988).

Warrack, John, and West, Ewan, *The Concise Oxford Dictionary of Opera* (1992).

operetta and fairy tales Operetta is a form of opera in which the style is essentially light-hearted with tuneful music. The translation from Italian is 'little opera', indicating that in the 18th century short entertainments were frequently performed in the middle of a serious work. Apart from 'operetta' various other names describing the form, which could be extremely varied depending on country of origin, became attached, including 'intermezzo', 'opera buffa' (Italy), 'opéra bouffe', 'opéra comique' (France), and 'Singspiel' (Germany).

In time, operetta separated itself from its parent, turning into a stage genre in its own right and often taking as long as an opera to perform. One main difference to emerge was the lighter form's reliance on spoken dialogue. Thus while 'singing actors' are to be found only intermittently in opera, their absence in operetta is unimaginable. The 'musical' grew out of operetta, gradually, finding its place in the 20th century. Its most recognizable ingredients are tuneful scores, upbeat stories, spoken dialogue, and lavish productions—a scenario which has often enhanced the fairy tale.

The evolution, however, had more intermediate stages than is often realized. For a time there was a vogue for descriptive titles. Designations such as 'a musical play', 'a fantastic musical play', or 'a play with music' were encountered (at least in Britain), during the years encompassing the 1890s and the early 20th century. This is not to say that a line may be drawn between the end of one species and the beginning of another. Indeed, there have been times when they have co-existed quite happily, influencing each other at crucial periods in their development.

1. Operetta in the 19th century in France, Britain, Austria, and Germany

The second half of the 19th century, moving into the early 20th, marked operetta's heyday. Its antecedents were to be found in the light stage works popular during the 18th century by Italian composers such as Giovanni Pergolesi (1710–36) and Domenico Cimarosa (1749–1801). Wolfgang Amadeus *Mozart, and Antonio Salieri (1750–1825) were far more substantial composers, but wrote *opera buffa* too: Mozart's *Le nozze di Figaro* (*The Marriage of Figaro*) which premièred in 1786, is generally described as 'opera buffa'.

Comedy was still the mainstay of such entertainments, and was continued into the 19th century by Gioacchino *Rossini, by which time a vogue for other subjects was emerging. A point worth remembering is that Rossini made his name with *opera buffa*, but later turned his attention to more serious subjects. His *La Cenerentola* of 1817 is a rather darker version of the *Cinderella story than is represented by the familiar pantomime variant. Rossini's popularity in Paris probably helped create a taste for a lighter form of opera. His energetic, melodious style influenced many contemporaries, so that by the time composer, actor, and singer Florimund Ronger (1825–92) appeared, the time was ripe for a more individual kind of operetta—France being generally considered as the country which gave it birth.

Ronger took the pseudonym Hervé, composing over 100 operettas, among which was *Les Chevaliers de la Table Ronde* (*The Knights of the Round Table*, 1866). Although Hervé was an important figure in the emergence of operetta, it was Jacques *Offenbach, older by six years, who consolidated its position, partly by tapping into the contemporary taste for satire. His lasting popularity, however, has more to do with his brilliance as a composer.

Premièred in 1858, *Orphée aux Enfers* (*Orpheus in the Underworld*), Offenbach's most enduring work, was a caricature of the Orpheus story. The demand for Offenbach's satirical operettas was especially strong during France's Second Empire. With the Franco-Prussian War (1870–1), and the fall of Napoleon III, the public lost its appetite for such entertainments, as Offenbach soon found out. The composer's foray into the realms of fairy tale came with *Le Roi Carotte* (*King Carotte*, 1872), containing a scene in which a witch turns vegetables into humans. The drama by Victorien Sardou was based on a tale by E. T. A. *Hoffmann, whose tales Offenbach incorporated later in his great posthumous opera *The Tales of Hoffmann* (1881).

After Offenbach, late 19th-century French operetta continued to go from strength to strength, resulting in an upsurge of composing talent, although few could match Offenbach's genius and wit. Born in Paris, Robert Planquette (1848–1903), wrote *Les Cloches de Corneville* (*The Chimes of Normandy*, 1877). It became his most popular work, with a story concerning the marquis de Corneville, a political exile from his estate in Normandy. A local legend proclaims that a set of ghostly bells will ring out on the owner's return.

A later work from Planquette, *Rip* (1882) was based on Washington *Irving's *Rip Van Winkle*. As realized by Planquette and the librettists H. Meilhac, Philippe Gille, and H.

B. Farnie, Rip, a mortal, finds himself in the company of ghostly mariners. Enticed by a water nymph to drink wine which has a spell upon it, he falls asleep for 20 years. After waking, he returns home an aged man and succeeds in righting some old wrongs.

Reminiscent of a popular theme in fairy tales, *La Poupée* (*The Doll*, 1896), by Edmond Audran, takes up the theme of a toymaker who manufactures a lifelike doll—an exact replica of his own daughter.

The craze for operetta, especially works by Offenbach, spread quickly throughout Europe, resulting not only in many imitators but, crucially, stimulating what can best be described as national schools of light opera, not least the legendary Gilbert and Sullivan partnership in Victorian Britain. Ironically, it was poor box-office receipts for Offenbach's *Perichole* at London's Royalty Theatre which led the impresario Richard D'Oyly Carte to invite W. S. Gilbert (1836–1911) and Arthur Sullivan (1842–1900) to collaborate on the one-act *Trial by Jury* (1875).

This operetta was no fairy tale, but plots with magic lozenges, etc., were never far from Gilbert's dramas. Hence the partnership's next collaboration, *The Sorcerer* (1877), included Mr John Wellington Wells, of J. W. Wells & Co., Family Sorcerers. *Iolanthe* (1882), was billed as 'An Entirely New and Original Fairy Opera in Two Acts' and reworked the oft-repeated theme in myth and drama of a fairy who marries a mortal. Five years later, in 1887, the partnership produced *Ruddigore*, containing a scene in which portraits of dead ancestors come to life.

The Beauty Stone (premièred in 1898), a collaboration between Sullivan and Arthur W. Pinero (1855–1934), lived up to its description of a 'romantic musical drama', being the story of a stone which has the power to transform ugliness into beauty. Sullivan's last work for the stage, *The Rose of Persia* (a collaboration with Basil Hood), took various themes from *The *Arabian Nights*. Premièred in 1899, it contained a scene in which several persons under sentence of death endeavour to think of a story with which to entertain the Sultan, thus hoping to spin out their lives. In their ensemble 'It has reached me', they consider various fairy-tale options such as 'Old Mother Hubbard', 'Little Miss Muffet', and 'The Cat and the Fiddle'.

The triumphs of French and British operetta found a parallel in Vienna, where Johann Strauss the second (1825–99) first came to prominence as a composer of waltzes. His first operetta, *Indigo und die vierzig Räuber* (*Indigo and the Forty Thieves*), was premièred in 1871, to be followed three years later by his most famous and enduring work for the stage, *Die Fledermaus* (*The Bat*). Strauss's fame ensured a spectacular first night for *Indigo* which, in containing the character *'Ali Baba', owed much to *The Arabian Nights*. *Indigo* was revised a number of times. One version appeared in 1906 after Strauss's death, entitled *Tausend und eine Nacht* (*Thousand and One Nights*).

As the old 19th century prepared to bow out, Paul Linke's *Frau Luna* (*Castles in the Air*, premièred in 1899 in Berlin), took its characters on a trip to the moon—in a balloon. *Frau Luna* effectively marked the beginning of what has been called the Berlin School of Operetta.

2. Musical comedy and comic opera

Although operetta was the begetter of the musical, there was an intermediate stage to be gone through. The era c.1890–1939 saw operetta expanding in many directions at once. Generally, such developments may be identified with the single title, musical comedy. That said, operetta did not die out completely during this time, certainly not the Viennese variety thanks to Franz Lehar (1870–1948), who revived it with his phenomenally successful *The Merry Widow* (1905).

Lehar operettas are peopled with real characters, who find themselves in generally believable circumstances. His style and melodic gifts set a benchmark for a great number of composers such as Oscar Straus (1870–1954), Leo Fall (1873–1925), Robert Stolz (1880–1975), and Emmerich Kalman (1882–1953), who all produced a considerable number of works, forming the core of the genre known as 'Viennese Operetta'.

In Britain, during the 20th century's first decade, Edward German (1862–1934) kept the flag of British Operetta flying with works such as *Merrie England* (1902). Set in the 16th century, it was written by Basil Hood and styled a 'comic opera', as were all German's collaborations with this dramatist. The following year (1903), German and Hood produced *A Princess of Kensington*. Owing something to *Shakespeare's *A Midsummer Night's Dream*, it describes the exploits of fairies who occupy Kensington Gardens, London, for a day—Midsummer Day. As might be imagined, they take to interfering in the love lives of mortals. A happy end follows a series of trials and tribulations. Thanks to a collaboration with W. S. Gilbert, German wrote another fairy operetta—*Fallen Fairies* (premièred in 1909). As in *Iolanthe*, a quarter-century earlier, Gilbert's drama dealt with the theme of love between fairies and mortals. Intriguingly, Gilbert advanced the theory (in the drama), that every mortal has a fairy doppelgänger.

The rise of musical comedy in Britain is often linked to *The Shop Girl* of 1894. Lionel Monkton (1861–1924), who co-wrote some of its music, also contributed to the highly popular *The Arcadians* of 1909, in which beings from an imaginary world (Arcadia) invade London with the intention of improving its ways. Monkton's contemporaries included Leslie Stuart (1864–1928), composer of *The Silver Slipper* of 1901, a version of the Cinderella story. *Chu Chin Chow* (1916), billed as 'A musical tale of the East told by Oscar Asche and set to music by Frederic Norton', turned out to be a mixture of pantomime, operetta, and musical comedy, with a story beholden to 'Ali Baba and the Forty Thieves'.

Parallel to what was happening in Britain, around the turn of the century America was developing its own operetta/musical comedy style. Reginald De Koven (1859–1920), whose *The Begum* has been hailed as an 'American First', wrote *Robin Hood* in 1891. Based on the legendary adventures of the Sherwood Forest outlaws, *Robin Hood* had book and lyrics by Harry B. Smith. De Koven and Smith continued to collaborate, producing in 1894 another folk-hero operetta, *Rob Roy*. Of interest later was De Koven's sequel to *Robin Hood*: *Maid Marian* was premièred in 1902.

By now, the composer Victor Herbert (1859–1924), had overtaken De Koven in popularity. Herbert was an Irish-born, German-trained musician who settled in America. A cellist and conductor of symphony orchestras, Herbert gradually turned his attention to operetta in the 1890s, enjoying some success with a number of works. His first significant triumph came with *Babes in Toyland* (1903; book and lyrics by Glen MacDonough). Its music and story—generally a procession of fairy-tale and nursery-rhyme characters, made a spectacular impact on audiences of all ages. Intriguingly, *Babes in Toyland* was an attempt to capitalize on the success in that same year of *The *Wizard of Oz* (music by A. Baldwin *Sloane, and Paul Tiejens, book and lyrics by L. Frank *Baum, adapted from Baum's novel). Among Herbert's highly prolific output is a variation on the Cinderella story, *The *Lady of the Slipper*, produced in 1912.

3. The 20th century: the emergence of the musical

The 1920s in Britain and America were typified by a brand of stage work signalling the beginnings of the modern musical. Romantic operetta in America was still able to hold its own, as was proved by composers from the old world such as the Czech-born Rudolf Friml (1879–1972), and the Hungarian-born Sigmund Romberg (1887–1951). Friml's *The Vagabond King* of 1925 was based on the play and novel *If I Were King* and followed the story of François Villon—an outlaw who cheats the gallows and succeeds in becoming King of France for a day.

But now something else was added to the crucible of old-style operetta and the new musical comedies by American composers such as Jerome Kern (1885–1945; two songs by Kern were included in one of many musical adaptations of *Peter Pan*), Cole Porter (1891–1964), George Gershwin (1898–1937), and Richard Rodgers (1902–79). Emerging

almost simultaneously in Britain and America, the new development was termed variously as either a show or a revue, and its vitality and extravagance reflected the new world's growing self-confidence in its own culture, and the old world's desire to share in it. Irving Berlin (1888–1989), perhaps America's most prolific writer of songs, was closely associated with many such Broadway ventures over several decades.

One American impresario, Florenz Ziegfeld (1867–1932), refined the medium by devising 'The Ziegfeld Follies', commencing a series of such productions in 1907. Almost invariably, they were a concoction of celebrated performers, popular music, glamorous women, and lavish staging. In 1930 Ziegfeld also produced *Simple Simon* with music by Richard Rodgers and lyrics by Lorenz Hart (1895–1943). The book, by the American comedian Ed Wynn and the British dramatist Guy Bolton, deals with a newspaper vendor who finds escapism in a sort of fairyland.

Three years before, in 1927, Rodgers and Hart, who were already an established team, wrote *A Connecticut Yankee*, based on Mark *Twain's original tale entitled *A Connecticut Yankee in King Arthur's Court*. Audiences warmed to the story of a modern American who dreams he is back in Camelot.

Running parallel with Ziegfeld in America, Britain's C. B. Cochran (1872–1951) became his country's foremost producer of musicals, revues, and operettas. For a time he was associated with the multi-talented Noël Coward (1899–1973). He also produced a number of shows by the composer and librettist Vivian Ellis, with the exception of Ellis's gender-reversal musical *Mr Cinders* (1929).

The 'Jazz Age' of the 1920s had, by now, reached its peak and straightforward treatments of fairy tales were becoming a thing of the past. Indeed the syncopated rhythms of jazz itself had already made deep inroads into American musical comedy.

In the years prior to the Second World War, Britain became accustomed to a steady diet of musicals by Noël Coward and composer/actor Ivor Novello (1893–1951), who forged his own kind of eye-catching operetta with the accent on romance. In storyline these works had much in common with their contemporary German, French, and Viennese counterparts. Tales of young lovers divided by rank and station were popular, as were exotic locations far removed from the country in which the work originated.

4. Post-1945 developments

If in the decades following the end of hostilities in 1945 the American musical seemed to dominate audiences world-wide, there were good reasons for this. America's vitality was in stark contrast to a Europe tired by war: the energy and escapism which the American musical radiated suited the contemporary mood exactly. Almost immediately, as if to aid the desire for escapism, a number of musicals appeared which concerned themselves with the supernatural.

In 1945 Richard Rodgers and Oscar Hammerstein (1895–1960) collaborated on the second of their many hit shows, *Carousel*. Here the hero, Billy Bigelow, having killed himself to avoid capture for theft, is allowed to leave Purgatory for a day. He returns to Earth, seeking to help his daughter, as a result of which he finds Redemption and is finally allowed into Heaven. Two years later, in 1947, two musicals steeped in fantasy were premièred in New York. *Finian's Rainbow* had a book by E. Y. Harburg and Fred Saidy, lyrics by Harburg, and music by Burton Lane. A crock of gold is taken from Ireland to a mythical part of America's deep South and has the power to grant three wishes.

By contrast, *Brigadoon*, by the lyricist Alan J. Lerner (1918–86), and the composer Frederick Loewe (1904–88), was set in Scotland, taking the theme of a mythical village which materializes just for a day once every 100 years. *Kismet* (1953), noted for its opulent production, was a return by the lyricists George Forrest and Robert Wright to *The Arabian Nights*. They adapted music by the Russian composer Alexander Borodin (1833–87).

The Faustian story was given a new twist by Jerry Ross and Richard Adler with *Damn Yankees* in 1955. A senator sells his soul to the devil in exchange for his favourite baseball team being allowed to win. Lerner and Loewe continued their run of successes with *Camelot* (1960), which was based on a fresh approach to the Arthurian legend as contained in T. H. White's story *The Once and Future King*.

In the previous year the composer Mary Rodgers (daughter of Richard Rodgers), collaborated with the lyricist Marshall Barer to produce *Once Upon a Mattress*, an enlarged musical version of the humorous fairy tale 'The *Princess and the Pea'. A highly significant musical appeared in 1987, namely Stephen Sondheim's *Into the Woods*, in which a series of fairy-tale characters are involved; they confront the evil force of a giant with tragic results but help a baker and his wife have a child. Another important musical was created by Tim Rice, who became part of the team which produced *Beauty and the Beast* in 1994.

Although the foregoing would suggest that the musical's immediate past has been dominated by America, shows by Britain's Andrew Lloyd Webber, including fantasy subjects such as *Phantom of the Opera*, and *Starlight Express*, have been just as popular and in many cases more commercially successful world-wide. With a few exceptions, such successes have not been matched by home markets in other European countries, which frequently prefer to import American and British shows.

In conclusion, a point worth bearing in mind is that in the second half of the 20th century it is chiefly America, through the medium of the musical, which has helped extend the European fairy-tale tradition.   TH

Bailey, Leslie, *The Gilbert and Sullivan Book* (4th edn., 1956).

Block, Geoffrey, *Enchanted Evenings: The Broadway Musical from* Showboat *to* Sondheim (1997).

Gammond, Peter, *Offenbach: His Life and Times* (1981).

Larkin, Colin (ed.), *The Guinness Who's Who of Stage Musicals* (1994).

Lubbock, Mark, *The Complete Book of Light Opera* (1962).

Rees, Brian, *A Musical Peacemaker: The Life and Work of Edward German* (1986).

Traubner, Mark, *Operetta: A Theatrical History* (1984).

oral tradition and fairy tales Oral tradition refers to the sum of folklore that is verbally communicated as well as to the process of transmission, by which a given item of folklore is learned, recreated, and disseminated. In societies without writing, oral tradition accounts for much of the cultural transmission from one generation to the next. In societies with writing, it has been heavily influenced but seldom entirely replaced by print culture as a mode of communication. Anonymous in origin and transmitted through face-to-face communication, fairy tales deriving from oral tradition exist in multiple, standardized versions and exhibit patterns of stability and variation over time and space.

Since the *Grimms, scholars have distinguished between oral and literary traditions of the fairy tale, with the terms reflecting differences in the origin and style of a tale. In identifying their tales as *Volksmärchen* (folk tales) in contrast to the *Kunstmärchen* (literary fairy tale), Jacob and Wilhelm Grimm not only elaborated upon Johann Gottfried von Herder's differentiation between *Volkspoesie* (folk poetry) and *Kunstpoesie* (art poetry), but claimed an authenticity for their material that set the *Kinder- und Hausmärchen* (*Children's and Household Tales*) apart from the collections of their contemporaries. Literary fairy tales were defined as the conscious creations of a single author of middle- or upper-class background, as opposed to fairy tales from oral tradition, which were considered to be the natural and spontaneous expression of illiterate or semi-literate peasants. The assumptions underlying the oppositions of folk versus élite and natural versus artful continue to be modified as research sheds new light on the complex, often reciprocal, relationship between oral and literary traditions.

There has been much debate over whether the Grimms' tales were recorded from oral tradition, though they claimed that most of them were collected from 'oral traditions in Hesse and in the Main and Kinzig regions of the duchy of Hanau'. Contrary to popular perception, the Grimms did not travel the German countryside collecting tales directly from the mouths of peasants. Some of their best sources were people from the lower and middle class familiar with printed fairy-tale editions, who were invited to the Grimms' home to recite their stories. They also received versions of fairy tales mailed to them by friends and colleagues, in response to Jacob's appeal for assistance in his 'Circular on the Collection of Folk Poetry'.

Although they were the first systematic scholars of folk literature who conscientiously documented the sources of their material, particularly printed sources, the annotations to their tales often consisted of no more than the word 'mündlich' (oral), along with the region where it was recorded and the identity of the storyteller. Because they destroyed their original notes, most of what is known about their research methods is limited to their own programmatic statements in the prefaces to the editions of the *Kinder- und Hausmärchen* or has been deduced by analysing the unwritten editorial practices that shaped the development of their collection through subsequent editions. The Grimms reconstructed the tales on the basis of their recorded notes and in comparison with other variants, which they included in the bibliographic information in the third volume. They were careful to preserve, sometimes even provide, what they perceived to be the authentic oral style of the folk tale and omitted from later editions tales which, in their opinion, did not pass the test of traditionality.

Ironically, although their research was fuelled by the desire to preserve the oral tradition of folk tales and the custom of storytelling that they feared was on the decline, Jacob and Wilhelm Grimm were in many ways instrumental in blurring the distinctions between the oral and literary traditions. Over the course of the seven editions published during their lifetime, they refashioned and revised the tales, creating a uniquely stylized folk tale that has been subsequently termed *Buchmärchen* (book folk tale) because it is not entirely oral or literary. The popularity and pedagogical value of their collection, the rise of literacy rates in Europe, and the growing affordability of books combined both to stabilize the oral tradition and to create an eager readership in the German middle class for fairy tales from the oral tradition.

Until the middle of the 20th century, the study of the oral tradition and fairy tales was essentially text-centred. This tended to minimize the role of narrators to that of tradition-bearers, who were judged according to their adherence to tradition, rather than for their expressive artistry or innovation. The stability of tradition was privileged over variation, with stability viewed as an ideal and variation as the degeneration from that hypothetical ideal. Theories advanced to explain the remarkable stability of oral tradition include Axel *Olrik's epic laws of folk literature and Walter Anderson's law of self-correction.

An appreciation for expressive creativity within the parameters of oral tradition was initiated through the ground-breaking insights of Milman Parry and A. B. Lord into the composition of Classical and Serbo-Croatian epics. Parry and Lord outlined a theory 'oral-formulaic' composition, based on their observation that formulas, groups of words regularly employed under the same metrical conditions to express the same idea, constitute the building blocks of oral composition. These formulas make up the generic knowledge of an individual epic singer and reflect the traditional character of the orally composed epic. With each performance the singer creates a new song; each performance is both creation and re-creation.

Although their research was confined to the epic, the ideas of Parry and Lord prompted folk-tale scholars to investigate the dynamic processes of composition in performance. Beginning in the 1960s, sociolinguistic and ethnographic perspectives introduced a shift from text-centred to contextual analyses of storytelling and oral tradition. The focus of performance-centred folkloristic research was no longer limited to the item of folklore *per se*, but embraced the storytelling event, the expressive and aesthetic function of storytelling, and the role of narrative in the social and cultural life of a community.   MBS

Cocchiara, Giuseppe, *The History of Folklore in Europe* (1981).
Dégh, Linda, 'What did the Grimm Brothers Give to and Take from the Folk?', in James M. McGlathery (ed.), *The Brothers Grimm and Folktale* (1988).
Gatto, Giuseppe, *La Fiaba di tradizione orale* (2006).
Kamenetsky, Christa, *The Brothers Grimm and their Critics* (1992).
Zipes, Jack, *The Irresistible Fairy Tale: The Cultural and Social History of a Genre* (2012).

oriental fairy tales Things oriental since time immemorial have constituted a source of inspiration for Western imagination and creativity. Geographically, the East is not only the direction of sunrise ('ex oriente lux'), and thus the immediate source of life, but also—as has aptly been expressed by George Eliot (1856)—the place where beautiful flowers, strange animals, precious fabrics, and valuable spices originated, besides the great religions—and the world's internationally renowned collections of tales ('ex oriente fabula').

Historically, the notion of how to define the Orient has been shifting in accordance with the changing centres of power. In antiquity, the encounter between the Greeks and the Persians in the 5th century BC is one of the starting-points of the ensuing relationship between the East and the West, which until the very present has remained essentially political. While Herodotus still preserves fragmentary testimonies that the early Greeks regarded the Northern barbarians as similarly exotic as, for example, the Egyptians, the Hellenistic era inaugurated by Alexander the Great's conquests to some extent integrated the Orient, shifting its eastern boundaries to the far side of the River Indus. In Roman times, when the whole Mediterranean belonged to a single dominion, the Orient constituted a minor factor on the outskirts of a strong and highly self-conscious empire. When, in the Middle Ages, the European centres of power had shifted to the north, not only had Greek antiquity largely been obscured, but also the reality of the Orient had been relegated to the realm of fantasy, largely nourished by fictitious narratives based on the oral tradition of merchants, pilgrims, and travellers. The crusades brought parts of the Islamic Orient back into European consciousness, but the fall of the crusader states and the ensuing political development once more prevented the free flow of information between the East and the West that alone could have contributed to creating an unbiased mutual apprehension of both sides. The conquest of Constantinople by the Turks (1453) documented the imminent 'oriental' threat to the whole of Europe, whereas, on the other hand, the political consolidation at the end of the 17th century engendered an unprecedented enthusiasm for everything oriental, be it food, clothing, music, architecture, or tales. The introduction of *The *Arabian Nights* to Europe at the beginning of the 18th century until the present constitutes the single most important event in the inspiration of Western creativity through oriental models and elements. Though Napoleon's expedition to Egypt (1798–9) is usually interpreted as having inaugurated a more scientific line in creative orientalism, still at the turn of the 20th century exact and reliable first-hand information about the Orient appears to be available to fewer specialists than would be needed to liberate the Orient from being exploited as a mine of fictitious and often heavily biased depictions.

Psychologically, the Other has contributed as much to the definition of the Self as the relevant individual's or culture's own apprehension of itself. In this respect, the Orient as the West's neighbouring Other has always served as a matrix for Western creative projections, whether they be purely invented and innocent in an uncompromising and friendly way, or whether they be ignorant, malicious, and aggressive. None of these projections was seriously intended to make available or distribute knowledge about the Other. Rather, as Edward Said has argued in his highly influential study *Orientalism* (1978), in attempting to document the Orient (the Other, the opposite), the Occident came to document itself. At the same time, paradoxically, the West has yet fully to acknowledge the fact that its culture relies on a threefold legacy, constituted by Greek, Latin, and Arab elements, of which the latter is largely ignored. Since exact knowledge in certain ways is counter-productive to imagination, the lack of knowledge appears as a prerequisite to imaginative reception. Imagination, on the other hand, relies on specific preconceived conditions, which in their turn are outlined by the accessibility of information as well as the cultural background of the informant, writer, or artist. This implies certain misconceptions and prejudices, since all parties implied are highly susceptible to the influence of their societies. Their presentation of the Orient as well as the resulting literary production proved that obviously, in the Western mind, imagination and reality possessed little overlap, or rather that imagination overruled reality.

These are, in terms of cultural history, the general outlines one has to consider when researching the reception of oriental narratives in Western literature.

Oriental fiction in the European literatures prior to 1700 had contributed to a more or less vague and general imaginative acquaintance with the Orient. As for English literature, as far back as the 11th century, fictitious descriptions of the marvels of India are found in Anglo-Saxon translations of legends concerning Alexander the Great; moreover, the romance of Alexander itself, so popular all over Europe (and the Islamic Orient), to a large extent is indebted to oriental sources. The Middle Ages witnessed scholarly (Latin) translations of some of the great oriental collections of tales, such as *Sendebar* (*Syntipas*), *Kalila and Dimna* or *The Fables of Bidpai* (the Persian/Arabic adaptation of the Indian *Panchatantra*). The *Disciplina Clericalis* of Petrus Alphonsi, a Spanish Jew converted to Christianity, while drawing on oriental material, constitutes the first European collection of short novellas, inaugurating a new genre in European literature. The narrative of *Barlaam and Josaphat*, one of the most popular legends in medieval Europe, derived largely from an Indo-Persian version of the legend of Buddha's youth. Medieval romances, apologues, legends, and tales of adventure drew heavily on oriental motifs. Famous English examples besides Arthurian romance include John Mandeville's *Travels* or Chaucer's 'Squire's Tale'. Romances of chivalry, travel (such as the *Navigatio Sancti Brendani*), and adventure all over Europe, even up to the Icelandic saga incorporate oriental motifs. Collections of jocular tales such as the *Facetiae* by Poggio Bracciolini (compiled around 1450) constitute a precursor to European literature of the chapbook and *vademecum* genre and document the fact that even minor genres such as jokes and anecdotes formed part of the large narrative stock exchange taking place between Europe and the Orient. Beginning with the 16th century, the great period of translation, popular versions of the important narrative collections were produced in the regional languages and continued to transmit oriental motifs to the Western readership.

A case in point here is the collection *Peregrinaggio di tre giovani figliuoli del re di Seren* (*Voyage of the Three Young Sons of the King of Ceylon*), published 1557 in Venice and written by a certain Christoforo Armeno. This author, whose identity has only recently been confirmed, compiled an adaptation of the Persian *Hasht Behesht* (*Eight Paradises*) by Amir Khosrau of Delhi (1253–1325), itself inspired by the famous *Haft Peikar* (*Seven Portraits*), by Nezami (d. 1209). The *Peregrinaggio*'s frame story is about three princes who prove their extreme sensitivity and cleverness to the Persian emperor Bahram Gur; within this frame, a number of tales are told, the best known of which probably became the 'tall tale' about the lucky hunter who shoots the foot and the ear of a deer with one arrow. The *Peregrinaggio* was extremely popular in late 17th- and 18th-century Europe. Following several Italian editions (1577, 1584, etc.), it was translated into German (1583, 1599) and French (1610). A French reworking was published by the chevalier de *Mailly (1719), again inspiring German (1723), English (1722), and Dutch (1766) translations. It was Horace Walpole (1717-97) who after reading what he labelled a 'silly fairy tale' coined the term 'serendipity', defined as 'the faculty of making happy and unexpected discoveries by accident'. In the 17th century one of the most influential authors with respect to the adaptation of oriental narrative was the French poet Jean de La Fontaine (1621-95). His *Fables*, published in 1668-93 in twelve books, notably in their latter half draw on the oriental collection of fables *Kalila and Dimna*. La Fontaine in the course of the 18th century was translated and adapted into most major European languages.

All previous instances of the adaptation of oriental narrative in the West are outshone by the overwhelming success staged by the reception of *The Arabian Nights* in Europe. Though single tales from the *Nights*, as well as its frame tale, had already been known in Europe at least from the 14th century onwards (Giovanni *Sercambi (1347-1424), *Novelle*; Ludovico Ariosto (1474-1533), *Orlando furioso*), a comprehensive edition was published by the French orientalist scholar Antoine *Galland only at the beginning of the 18th century. Two arguments help to understand the extraordinary success Galland's publication met with. The French interest in the Orient had been growing throughout the 17th century in connection with the colonial and commercial expansion of France in the reign of Louis XIV; moreover, *The Arabian Nights* were 'discovered' in an atmosphere thoroughly impregnated by the narrative conventions and fashion of the *conte de fées* and their craving for the extravagant. The magic elements in the *Nights* combined with the explicit and unpretentious representation of sexuality created a powerful inspiration for the European imagination. Contrary to the widespread depreciation of contemporary oriental people (who were predominantly characterized as proficient liars and thieves, at best as culturally degenerate), the *Nights* represented things oriental in an attractive garb which was all the more appealing to the European taste since in Galland's adaptation the tales were Europeanized (and, in fact, Frenchified).

No serious author of French, English, or German literature of the 18th and 19th centuries could avoid the challenge of the *Nights*, and most of them in some way have shown that they read (and loved) the *Nights*. In France, the *Nights* first of all prompted the publication of other similar collections, such as the *Mille et un jours* (*Thousand and one days*, 1710–12) by François Pétis de la Croix, and Thomas-Simon *Gueulette's numerous compilations (*Les mille et un quarts d'heure*, 1712; *Aventures merveilleuses du mandarin Fum-Hoam*, 1723; *Sultanes de Guzarate*, 1732; *Mille et une heures, contes peruviens*, 1733). The oriental mode these works inaugurated also inspired Montesquieu's *Lettres persanes* (1721), and *Voltaire claimed to have read the *Nights* 14 times—though he did not necessarily share the sympathetic attitude towards the contemporary oriental craze.

W. F. Kirby in his survey of 'Imitations and miscellaneous works having more or less connection with the Nights' (1885) classified the aftermath of the *Nights* according to seven categories, which are not always clearly defined: (1) Satires on the Nights themselves, e.g. Anthony *Hamilton; (2) Satires in an oriental garb, e.g. William Beckford (1760–1844), *History of the Caliph Vathek* (French original 1787, unauthorized English translation 1786); (3) Moral tales in an oriental garb, e.g. Frances Sheridan, *Nourjahad* (1767); (4) Fantastic tales with nothing oriental about them but the name, e.g. Robert Louis *Stevenson, *New Arabian Nights* (1882); (5) Imitations pure and simple, e.g. George Meredith (1828–1909), *Shaving of Shagpat: An Arabian Entertainment* (1855); (6) Imitations more or less founded on genuine oriental sources, e.g. the *Tales* of the comte de *Caylus; (7) Genuine oriental tales, e.g. *Mille et un jours* by Pétis de la Croix.

The literary merit of the European production inspired by oriental fairy tales has been evaluated highly divergently over the centuries. While W. A. Clouston (1843–96) regarded Frances Sheridan's *Nourjehad* as 'one of the very best of the imitations of Eastern fiction', Robert Irwin (1994) concedes only with a certain reluctance 'strangeness and originality' to this moral tale, a genre he evaluates as boring, extremely exasperating, and 'leadenly moral'. Irwin, in his chapter on 'Children of the *Nights*', presents a number of European authors who alluded to, borrowed from, or were influenced in one way or another by the *Nights*. The list of names he discusses in addition to those already named includes Joseph Addison (1672–1719), Samuel Johnson (*Rasselas: Prince of Abyssinia* (1759), John Hawkesworth (1715–73), Jean Potocki (1761–1815), Jacques *Cazotte (*Les Mille et une fadaises*, 1742), Robert Southey (*Thalaba the Destroyer*, 1800), Thomas Moore (*Lalla Rookh*, 1817), Samuel Taylor Coleridge (1772–1834), Washington *Irving, Edgar Allan Poe ('The Thousand-and-Second Tale of Scheherazade'), James Joyce (1882–1941), Marcel Proust (1871–1922), Jorge Luis *Borges (1899–1986), and Salman *Rushdie (*Haroun and the Sea of Stories*, 1990). Many more writers were influenced by the *Nights*, such as the French Flaubert, Stendhal, Dumas, and Gobineau; the English Walter Scott, *Thackeray, *Dickens, Conan Doyle, and Angela *Carter; the Russian *Pushkin and *Tolstoy; the German *Goethe, *Wieland, Mirger, E. T. A. *Hoffmann, Rückert, *Hauff, Grillparzer, and *Chamisso. Indeed, according to Irwin, it might be easier to discuss those writers who were *not* influenced by the *Nights*.

The term 'orientalism', in the coinage it has acquired in recent decades, primarily denotes the Near East or Middle East. Taken in a wider sense, a similar attitude of cultural and intellectual hegemony applies to other areas of the Orient, and terms such as 'Egyptomaniac', 'Chinoiserie', or 'Japonaiserie' have been coined to denote comparable uncritical and self-revealing attitudes of exploiting the oriental Other. One specific aspect that separates oriental fairy tales in Western literature (or fairy tales *à l'orientale*) from the literature of other regions is that the tales in general are evaluated as the Islamic Orient's major contribution to world literature. In the Western evaluation, they are foreign enough to be appealing, yet they appear familiar enough not to remain entirely exotic. It might, however, be useful to keep in mind that the Orient as depicted in its tales portrays a narrative world with a similar degree of fantasy and imagination as do its Western adaptations. Especially in the 19th century, many Europeans believed the world of *The Arabian Nights* to present a faithful reproduction of oriental reality, so they confused the real East with the East of the stories. The decidedly negative response of the Arab-American community to the depiction of oriental reality in *Disney's *Aladdin* proved, if such a proof be needed after the affair (1989) initiated by Salman *Rushdie's *Satanic Verses*, that towards the end of the 20th century a different kind of sensitivity might be required in dealing with the narrative adaptation of oriental fairy tales.   UM

Caracciolo, Peter L. (ed.), *The Arabian Nights in English Literature* (1988).

Conant, Martha P., *The Oriental Tale in England in the Eighteenth Century* (1908).

Irwin, Robert, *The Arabian Nights: A Companion* (1994).

Kabbani, Rana, *Europe's Myth of Orient: Devise and Rule* (1986).

Marzolph, Ulrich (ed.), *The Arabian Nights Reader* (2006).

Meester, Marie E. de, *Oriental Influences in the English Literature of the Nineteenth Century* (1915).

Sardar, Z., and Davies, M. W., *Distorted Imagination: Lessons from the Rushdie Affair* (1990).

Ossorio y Bernard, Manuel (1839–1904) Writer and distinguished journalist who collaborated with several magazines and newspapers, both for adults and for children. He devoted much attention to improving children's education, and for this reason wrote several children's books full of short stories, tales, epigrams, and short poems, all of which had a clear moralistic intention.

Three collections are: *Lecturas de la infancia* (*Childhood Readings*, 1880), *Cuentos novelescos* (*Fantastic Tales*, 1884), and *Cuentos ejemplares* (*Exemplary Tales*, 1896). The fairy tale of 'The Fisherman and his Wife' was revised twice by Ossorio y Bernard, first in 'Un cuento de viejas' ('An Old Crone's Tale', 1862) and secondly in 'La mujer del pescador. Balada' ('The Fisherman's Wife. Ballad', 1859).   CFR

Othoniel, Jean-Michel (1964–) French visual artist who specialises in sculpted art installations. Othoniel's retrospective exhibit at the Brooklyn Museum of Art, 'My Way' (2010), surveyed the artist's twenty-five-year career with installations like 'The Precious Stonewall' (2010), a tower of glass bricks and 'The Secret Happy End' (2008), a vintage carriage adorned with metal, murano and mirror glass. The exhibit is said to have evoked a fantastic universe through themes of mythology and metamorphosis. Another noteworthy project, 'Le Petit Théâtre de Peau d'Ane' (The Little Theatre of Donkey Skin, 2004), features thirty-five intricate glass models inspired by Pierre Loti's puppet collection.   KMJ

Outhwaite, Ida Rentoul (*fl.*1920–35) Australian writer and illustrator who collaborated with her husband Grenbry in several picture books about fairies. These differ from English fairy books of the period only by the occasional introduction of kookaburras, koalas, and gum trees. In *The Enchanted Forest* (1921) Anne joins in fairy revels and sees 'a ducky little baby-boy', which later turns out to be her own new little brother. In *The Little Fairy Sister* (1923) Bridget visits her dead sister Nancy in 'the lovely country of the Fairies'. *The Little Green Road to Fairyland* (1922) has a rather more lively story by Outhwaite's sister, Annie Rentoul.   GA

Oyeyemi, Helen (1984–) Nigerian-born British writer whose work offers a postcolonial feminist melding of myth, fantasy, and reality. Her novels *The Icarus Girl* (2005), *The Opposite House* (2007), and *White is for Witching* (2009) integrate Yoruba and

English literatures and mythologies in Gothic explorations of cultural hybridity. *Mr. Fox* (2001) uses the traditional *'Bluebeard' tale type, 'The Robber Bridegroom', making the eponymous homicidal character a writer who kills his novels' heroines. The plot links Fox, his wife Daphne, and muse Mary Foxe, whose individual and collective variations on the fairy tale subvert conventions. *Boy, Snow, Bird* (2014) recasts *'Snow White' in the context of American racism.   PG

Pacovská, Květa (1928–) Czech artist and illustrator who is known for her extraordinary paperwork, collages, and surrealist experiments. She follows very much in the tradition of Paul Klee, Vassily Kandinsky, Joan Miró, and the Bauhaus, has published over 70 books, and her work has been exhibited throughout the world. Among her extraordinary fairy-tale picture books are *The Little Match Girl* (1994), *Little Red Riding Hood* (2007), and *Cinderella* (2010). The graphics, drawings, figures, and colours are juxtaposed to the text in such a surprising fashion that the illustrations lend and create a new meaning to the stories. JZ

Paget, Francis (1806–82) English clergyman and author of *The Hope of the Katzekopfs* (1844), the first published fantasy for children. Written under the name 'William Churne of Staffordshire', it contains the poem 'Farewell, rewards and fairies' by Bishop Richard Corbet (1582–1635). It is a lively burlesque which concludes on a moral note, telling the story of the spoilt Prince Eigenwillig (Self-willed), who is wrenched away from his doting parents by the fairy Abracadabra. She rolls him into a rubber ball and bounces him to Fairyland where he has to submit to the grave old man, Discipline, before he can return home. GA

Paine, Albert Bigelow (1861–1937) Editor and author of a biography of Mark *Twain, Paine also wrote a number of children's books, including *The Arkansaw Bear* (1898), an original fantasy about a homeless boy who meets a fiddle-playing bear. They wander through Arkansas, fiddling and dancing for their keep, the bear's music having Orpheus-like powers over listeners. Paine's 'Hollow Tree' series consists of short stories about animals, reminiscent of Joel Chandler *Harris's Uncle Remus tales. GA

Pajon, Henri (?–1776), French lawyer who enjoyed an early career as a successful author of fabliaux. He wrote several fairy tales, including 'Eritzine & Parelin' (1744), 'L'Enchanteur, ou la bague de puissance' ('The Sorcerer or the Magical Ring', 1745), and 'Histoire des trois fils d'Hali Bassa' (The Story of Hali Bassa's Three Sons', 1745), which were first published pseudonymously in the monthly *Mercure de France*. Incorporating the oriental setting and characters of *A Thousand and One Nights* (*see* ARABIAN NIGHTS), his tales are distinguished by their elaborate plots, embedded narratives, and proliferation of magical objects and beings.
AZ

Pal, George (1908–80) Oscar-winner in 1943 for the development of new film animation techniques which, along with Cinerama, he later employed partly in service of the *Grimms. Born in Hungary, Pal made his first film—an advertisement showing cigarettes marching in and out of their packages—in 1934. During the next five years, working in Holland, he developed a series of short films which he called Puppetoons. They were cartoon-style stories told by means of three-dimensional animation, in which Pal achieved fluency of movement by having a different puppet made for each frame of film. For each eight-minute Puppetoon, around 6,000 wooden figures had to be individually carved and painted. This system was expensive, but the results it achieved were popular; Pal moved to the

USA in 1939, where his Oscar helped him carry on making Puppetoons for another ten years.

All this time he wanted to go beyond the eight-minute format and make a full-length Puppetoon feature, but the enormous cost deterred potential backers. In the 1950s in England, he was finally able to direct an adaptation of the Grimms' 'Thumbling' (*'Little Tom Thumb'), under the title *Tom Thumb* (UK, 1958). It was, however, mainly live-action, with Russ Tamblyn in the title role. Only a small Puppetoon element remained.

The attraction of the story to Pal lay in the size difference between Tom and the other characters, not in the original narrative, virtually all of which he jettisoned. Tom's adventures inside a cow's stomach, and later inside a wolf, were omitted as being distasteful and unfilmable. His method of riding a horse—sitting inside its ear and giving instructions from there—is one of the few details retained. There are also two robbers who, as in the original, use Tom to help them steal from the town's coffers. The rest of the screen time is taken up by a romance between a mortal (Woody the piper) and an immortal (the Forest Queen); by Tom singing and dancing; by Tom's efforts to prove that his parents are not thieves; and by a sequence involving Puppetoon characters—Con-Fu-Shon (an oriental sage), Thumbella (a female counterpart to Tom), and a Yawning Man.

Four years later Pal returned to the Grimms as co-director of a romantic musical which was about Wilhelm and Jacob themselves as well as what they collected. Called *The Wonderful World of the Brothers Grimm* (USA, 1962), it had been chosen as a good subject for exploiting the potential of a new three-directional cinematography and projection system called Cinerama, which produced an image up to 10 metres (30 feet) high and 30 metres (90 feet) wide on a curved screen. Within the film are embedded dramatizations, directed by Pal, of three of the stories the brothers record: 'The Dancing Princess' (reduced to one from the twelve of the original), 'The Cobbler and the Elves', and 'The Singing Bone'.

The first in particular was shaped to maximize its Cineramic possibilities. For one sequence the three-in-one Cinerama camera was strapped underneath four coach-pulling horses, in order to capture for viewers the sensation of being surrounded by flying hooves; for another it was mounted inside a giant drum careering down a hillside, to convey the experience of falling and rolling. In the second story Pal went back to his Puppetoon technique to bring the elves to life; in the last one, to animate the mighty dragon, he resorted to a rival, cheaper, system which was based on having just one creature-model, with movable parts. Developed in 1933 for *King Kong*, it had been revived with spectacular success in the 1950s, under the name Dynamation, for *The Seventh Voyage of Sinbad*.

Pal carried on working in films for more than another decade, but did not revisit either the Grimms or the Puppetoons.   TAS

Palacio Valdés, Armando (1853–1937) Spanish novelist who belonged to the school of literary realism. His works are characterized by his profound longing for a simple world, his relish for the idyllic, and his unconditional defence of traditional virtues. As well as writing novels, Palacio Valdés composed a good number of short stories, 20 of which were published in a collection called *Aguas fuertes* (*Etchings*, 1884). None of his stories can be said to be literary renditions of the folk-tale tradition, the exception being 'El crimen de la calle de la Perseguida' ('The Crime of La Perseguida Street', 1884), which is based on a Spanish popular tale.   CFR

Panchatantra (Sanskrit: *Five Books*) Famous Indian collection of fables and other morally instructive tales. The *Panchatantra* belongs to the literary genre of mirror for princes, intending to teach wisdom to future rulers. Its five books treat the following topics: (1) disunion of friends, (2) gaining of friends, (3) war and peace, (4) loss of possession, (5) consequence of rash action. The author of the *Panchatantra* is unknown. The book's original text, now lost, was probably compiled between the 1st and 6th centuries;

the oldest extant version, which is regarded as quite close to the original, is the *Tantrakhayika* (Tales containing a system of wisdom), attributed to a certain Vishnusharman. The *Panchatantra* was circulated in the West by a series of adaptations and translations in various languages: the Persian physician Burzoy (6th century) prepared a (now lost) middle-Persian adapted version, which also incorporated tales derived from the Indian national epic *Mahabharata* (The great [tale about the war of the] Bharata family); this text in turn served as the basis for the Arabic adaptation by Ibn al-Muqaffa (first half of the 8th century), named after two jackal protagonists *Kalila and Dimna*. The most influential text for Western tradition was the Latin version of *Kalila and Dimna*, the *Directorium vitae humanae* (*Manual of instructions for human life*; compiled 1263–78) by the converted Jew John of Capua.

Neither the *Panchatantra* nor its later versions contain fairy tales in the narrow sense, nor even tales of magic. On the other hand, some of its tales have circulated widely, since they offer moral instruction in an attractive narrative garb. Among the best-known tales are 'Llewelyn and his Dog' (in which a faithful dog is killed by rash action; 5.2) and 'The Man who builds air castles' (5.13).   UM

Benfey, Theodor, *Pantschatantra* (2 vols., 1859).
De Blois, François, *Burzoy's Voyage to India and the Origin of the Book of Kalilah wa Dimna* (1990).
Edgerton, Franklin, *The Panchatantra Reconstructed* (2 vols., 1881).
Hertel, Johannes, *Tantrakhyayika* (2 vols., 1909).

Pancrazi, Pietro (1893–1952) Italian literary critic, journalist, and writer. Primarily known for his penetrating critical essays, Pancrazi left two collections of tales, *L'Esopo moderno* (*The Modern Aesop*, 1930) and *Donne e buoi dei paesi tuoi* (*Women and Oxen of your Home Countries*, 1934). Many of Pancrazi's tales, especially the 'Aesopian' ones, are short and amusing, but do not disguise the author's social commentary and ironic intent, as seen in 'Le età dell'uomo' ('The Age of Man'), 'Politica del

pipistrello' ('The Politics of the Overcoat'), and 'Critici' ('Critics').   MNP

Panzini, Alfredo (1863–1939) Italian writer and literary critic. Panzini's conservative idea of society, as it transpires from *La Lanterna di Diogene* (*The Lantern of Diogenes*, 1907) and *Il padrone sono me* (*I Am the Boss*, 1922), stands in contrast with his masterful rendering of women characters in his best works, namely *Santippe* (1913) and *Il bacio di Lesbia* (*The Kiss of Lesbia*, 1937). Panzini's interest in the fantastic is evident in *Le fiabe della Virtù* (*The Fairy Tales of Virtue*, 1911) and *I tre re con Gelsomino buffone del re* (*The Three Kings with Gelsomino, the King's Clown*, 1927). His tales, often based on classical models, speak of kings and villains, and of the wisdom of rewarding ingenuity. 'Il tesoro rubato' ('The Stolen Treasure'), from *Novelline divertenti per bambini intelligenti* (*Amusing Stories for Intelligent Children*, 1937) is a good example.   MNP

Pardo Bazán, Emilia (1851–1921) Spanish novelist and short-story writer and major proponent of naturalism in her country. She wrote several hundred short stories that have been unanimously praised by the critics and considered, in most cases, perfect models of the genre. Her *œuvre* includes stories ranging from the humorous to the historical, from the romantic to the religious. She also wrote fantasy tales, some of which may be said to have been influenced by the fairy-tale genre, such as 'El príncipe amado' ('The Beloved Prince', 1884), 'El llanto' ('The Weeping', 1905), and 'El balcón de la princesa' ('The Princess's Balcony', 1907). 'Agravante' ('The Aggravating Circumstance', 1892) is an example of a literary narration inspired by a traditional story, that of 'La matrona de Efeso' ('The Matron of Ephesus').   CFR

Parrish, Maxfield (1870–1966) Encouraged by his father, an etcher, and by Howard *Pyle, Parrish began his long and phenomenally successful career in 1895 with a cover for *Harper's Magazine* and a mural of *Old King Cole* for the Mask and Wig Club in

Philadelphia. From the outset, he specialized in fantasy—in idyllic landscapes and cloud castles peopled with whimsical or idealized figures, controlled by a strong sense of design and rendered in a luminous, photo-realistic style entirely his own. Often, his pictures are suffused with colour—gold, crimson, or the intense 'Parrish blue'. The first book Parrish illustrated was L. Frank *Baum's first as well, *Mother Goose in Prose* (1897), followed by *The Golden Age* (1899) and *Dream Days* (1902) by Kenneth *Grahame. These illustrations were executed in black and white, using a stippled pen-and-ink technique; improvements in colour printing enabled Parrish to illustrate later books with glowing full-colour plates. Among his most notable were Eugene Field's *Poems of Childhood* (1904), *The *Arabian Nights* (1909), *Tanglewood Tales* (1910), and *The Knave of Hearts* (1925). For *Hearst Magazine*, Parrish created a series of covers based on fairy tales, including 'The *Frog Prince', *'Snow White', and *'Sleeping Beauty', now much sought after by collectors. Eventually, Parrish grew tired, as he said, of 'girls on rocks' and devoted the remainder of his life to landscapes.   SR

Gilbert, Alma, *Maxfield Parrish: The Masterworks* (1992).
Ludwig, Coy, *Maxfield Parrish* (1973).

Pasolini, Pier Paolo (1922–75) Italian poet, writer, and film director. In 1974 he directed *Il fiore delle mille e una notte* (*The Flower of The Thousand and One Nights*), part of the 'trilogy of life' which also included the *Decameron* (1971) and *I racconti di Canterbury* (1972). Pasolini does away with *The *Arabian Nights* frame tale, and adapts a number of its tales into a complexly embedded narrative structure. The film is a celebration of sexual delights, and in its polemic mythicizing of a homoerotic, non-Western, peasant society is one of the most suggestive rewritings of the *Nights*.   NC

Rumble, Patrick, 'Stylistic Contamination in the *Trilogia della vita*: The Case of *Il fiore delle mille e una notte*', in Patrick Rumble and Bart Testa (eds.), *Pier Paolo Pasolini: Contemporary Perspectives* (1994).

Paton, Joseph Noël (1821–1901) Scottish illustrator and painter whose works have strong religious features. He achieved fame as an illustrator with his drawings for Charles *Kingsley's *Water-Babies* (1863). His other successful illustrated fairy-tale books are *Compositions from *Shakespeare's Tempest* (1845) and *The Princess of Silverland and Other Tales* (1874). He frequently mixed motifs from Celtic myths and Arthurian romance in his paintings. His most famous work, *The Reconciliation of Oberon and Titania*, hangs in the National Gallery of Scotland.   JZ

Paulding, James Kirke (1778–1860) American satirist and writer of realistic stories. He published his only fantasy, *A Christmas Gift from Fairyland*, anonymously in 1839, seemingly the first fairy stories in a New World landscape. It contains four tales inside a frame story about a Kentucky trapper who finds in his trap 'the queerest little vermint women I ever did see'. The stories the fairies leave reflect Paulding's views about the value of imagination, and the God-given freedom of the New World. 'The Nameless Old Woman', set in New Amsterdam, introduces such American elements as witches and St Nicholas.   GA

Peacock, Thomas Love (1785–1866) British novelist, poet, and satirist, who composed two romances inspired by British and Welsh folklore in which he adeptly combined romanticism with biting political satire. *Maid Marian* (1822), as the title suggests, is based on the folklore of Robin Hood, Peacock's main source being Joseph Ritson's *Robin Hood: A Collection of All the Ancient Poems, Songs, and Ballads Now Extant Relative to that Celebrated Outlaw* (1795). In 1822 *Maid Marian* was made into a comic opera, with libretto by J. R. *Planché. For *The Misfortunes of Elfin* (1829), Peacock drew heavily from Welsh folklore, the sources of which his Welsh wife, Jane Gryffydh, helped him translate. Here Peacock intertwined traditional Welsh folk ballads with ironic parodies of contemporary political discourse, resulting in one of his most acclaimed works.   AD

Peake, Mervyn Laurence (1911–68) Author of three Gothic fantasy novels, *Titus Groan* (1946), *Gormenghast* (1950), and *Titus Alone* (1959), which describe the life of Titus, 77th earl of Groan in his decaying ancestral home of Gormenghast castle and his struggle to escape from it and find a new identity. Peake in his lifetime was better known as an illustrator. He excelled at the grotesque and macabre, and his drawings for Lewis *Carroll's *The Hunting of the Snark* (1941) and the two *Alice* books (1946 and 1954) are among his finest work, as are those for the *Grimm Brothers' *Household Tales* (1946).   GA

Pedley, Ethel (1859–1898) An English-born musician and writer who emigrated with her parents to Australia as a young girl. Although primarily a violinist and music teacher, Pedley wrote an Australian children's book *Dot and the Kangaroo* (1899), Australia's first animal fantasy. With a strong conservation theme, Pedley's story of a small girl, Dot, who becomes lost in the Australian bush and is rescued by a kangaroo is more than an imaginative tale of talking animals. As an early environmentalist Pedley presents an eloquent appeal for humans to stop their destructive ways and live in harmony with nature. Her work was published posthumously.   REF

Peele, George (*c.*1558–96) English dramatist, regarded as one of the 'university wits' who made a major contribution to the development of English drama during the Elizabethan period. Aside from writing several of the lord mayor's pageants in London, Peele wrote five plays representative of different genres: *The Arraignment of Paris* (*c.*1584), a court pageant; *Edward I* (1592–3?), a chronicle play; *The Battle of Alcazar* (*c.*1589), a patriotic drama; *The Love of King David and Fair Bethsabe* (*c.*1589), a biblical piece written in verse; *The Old Wives' Tale* (1591–4?), a burlesque and parody of chivalric romance, which could be considered a fairy-tale play. Three wandering knights, Antic, Frolic, and Fantastic, become lost in a forest and are rescued by Old Clunch, who takes them to his cottage. After Madge, his wife, serves them supper, she regales them with a marvellous fairy tale, and, as she begins speaking, the characters of the tale arrive and act it out. The story concerns the evil magician Sacrapant, who has imprisoned the lovely maiden Delia in a castle. Other characters include her sister who has been driven insane, and her husband transformed into an old man by day and a bear that guards a crossroads by night. Not until the virtuous knight Eumenides, who is assisted by the ghost of *Jack the Giant Killer, arrives on the scene can Sacrapant be defeated.   JZ

Pentamerone Secondary title of Giambattista *Basile's *Lo cunto de li cunti overo lo trattenemiento de peccerille* (*The Tale of Tales, or Entertainment for Little Ones*, 1634–6). The name *Pentamerone* appeared on the dedication page of the first edition, published posthumously. It was subsequently included on the title-page in Pompeo *Sarnelli's 1674 edition of *Lo cunto*; whether Basile had anything to do with this alternative title is uncertain.

The *Pentamerone* is composed of 49 fairy tales contained by a 50th frame story, also a fairy tale, and is the first such framed collection of literary fairy tales to appear in European literature. The tales are told in Neapolitan dialect by ten grotesque old women over five days; the end of the frame tale closes the collection. Days 2–5 are preceded by a banquet and entertainment, and days 1–4 conclude with eclogues in dialogue form that satirize contemporary social ills.

The frame tells of Princess Zoza, who has never laughed. Once she does laugh, a mysterious old woman tells her that she must rescue a certain prince Tadeo from a sleeping spell and then marry him. As she is completing the task necessary to wake him, she falls asleep and a black slave, Lucia, finishes the job. Tadeo awakes and marries Lucia. Zoza then moves into a palace facing Tadeo's and tempts Lucia, now pregnant, with three magic objects previously given to her by fairies. Lucia demands to have them; the last object instils in her the need to hear tales. Tadeo summons the best storytellers of his kingdom, and the first day begins.

The *Pentamerone* contains many famous fairy-tale types, such as *'Sleeping Beauty', *'Puss-in-Boots', and *'Cinderella', and held great interest for later fairy-tale writers (in particular, the *Grimms) and scholars. It constituted a culmination of the interest in popular culture and folk traditions that permeated the Renaissance, and was one of the most significant expressions of the baroque poetics of the marvellous and its thirst for discovering new inspirations for and forms of artistic expression. Structurally, Basile's tales are close to the oral tradition from which they draw. But through the use of Neapolitan as a literary language, the extravagant metaphor, and the abundant representations of the rituals of daily life, Basile's versions of these tales become a laboratory of rhetorical experimentation as well as an encyclopaedia of Neapolitan popular culture. In his work Basile also engages in a playfully polemical dialogue with contemporary society—especially courtly culture—and the canonical literary tradition, above all the Italian novella tradition, whose most illustrious exponent was Boccaccio.   NC

Basile, Giambattista, *The Tale of Tales, or Entertainment for Little Ones*, trans. and ed. Nancy Canepa, illustr. Carmelo Lettere (2007).

Canepa, Nancy L., *From Court to Forest: Giambattista Basile's 'Lo cunto de li cunti' and the Birth of the Literary Fairy Tale* (1999).

Croce, Benedetto, Intro. to Giambattista Basile, *Il pentamerone* (1982).

Guaragnella, Pasquale, *Le maschere di Democrito e Eraclito: Scritture e malinconie tra Cinque e Seicento* (1990).

Petrini, Mario, *Il gran Basile* (1989).

Rak, Michele, Intro. to Giambattista Basile, *Lo cunto de li cunti* (1986).

Pereda, José María de (1833–1906) Spanish realistic novelist who had an idyllic vision of the rural world which he opposed to the corrupt urban world. Pereda's style is characterized by linguistic archaisms, and

his descriptions of the northern Spanish landscape have received much praise. As a writer of short stories, Pereda published several collections, such as *Escenas montañesas* (*Mountainous Scenes*, 1864) and *Tipos y paisajes* (*Types and Landscapes*, 1871), in which he included two stories worth mentioning: 'Para ser buen arriero...' ('If You Want To Be a Good Muleteer...', 1871), based on the popular Spanish tale 'El zapatero pobre' ('The Poor Cobbler'), and 'Al amor de los tizones' ('By the Fireside', 1871). The latter is a story about a gathering of country people who enjoy listening to Uncle Tanasio's famous fairy stories.   CFR

Pérez Galdós, Benito (1843–1920) Most important Spanish novelist in the 19th century. His contribution to the short-story genre has been traditionally overlooked, and not until recently have his tales been published together and regarded as a valuable corpus. Out of his 20 stories, twelve are of a fantastic nature. The latter, recently published in a collection entitled *Cuentos Fantásticos* (*Fantastic Tales*, 1996), suggest that Pérez Galdós was influenced at least in part by E. T. A. *Hoffmann and Edgar Allan Poe. In particular, his tale 'La princesa y el granuja' ('The Princess and the Urchin', 1977) bears some resemblance to Hoffmann's 'The Sandman' (1817) to the extent that the central male characters in both stories fall in love with a wax doll.   CFR

Perodi, Emma (1850–1918) Italian writer and journalist. She devoted most of her life to children's literature, serving as editor of the most important children's periodical of her time, *Giornale per i bambini* (*Children's Journal*), editing scholastic books for use in elementary schools, and, above all, producing numerous collections of fairy tales. Among these collections are: *Al tempo dei tempi...Fiabe e leggende del Mare, delle Città e dei Monti di Sicilia* (*In Days of Old... Fairy Tales and Legends from the Sea, Cities, and Mountains of Sicily*), *Fate e Fiori* (*Fairies and Flowers*), *Il Paradiso dei folletti* (*The Paradise of Elves*), *La Bacchetta Fatata* (*The Enchanted Wand*), *Le Fate Belle* (*The*

Beautiful Fairies), *Le Fate d'Oro* (*The Golden Fairies*), *Nell'antro dell'orco* (*In the Ogre's Cave*), and *Le novelle della nonna* (*Grandmother's Tales*). Although Perodi was active in the years when major folkloric collections were being assembled in Italy, her tales were not the product of scientifically conducted field research, but offered a creative re-elaboration of the oral tradition.

Le novelle della nonna (1892), her most important work, comprises 45 tales, many of which are fairy tales. The realistic frame tale narrates the life of the Marcuccis, a peasant family that lives in the Tuscan countryside. The first tale is told around the family hearth on Christmas Eve by the Marcucci matriarch and designated storyteller Regina, and the tales continue into the following November. The *Novelle* are generally told on Sundays or holidays, and are punctuated by the 'real' stories of the Marcucci family, which include marriages, new jobs, and food shortages; indeed, Regina often chooses her tales on the basis of the consolation or instruction that they may offer to members of the family. The conclusion to the frame takes place a year later, on Christmas Day, when the birth of a baby brings new hope to the Marcucci family, although we also learn that six months later Regina dies.

Perodi's tales are distinguished by a vividly expressive style, by the juxtaposition of credible and incredible scenarios and domestic and fantastic topographies, by the attraction to the dark and the cruel, and by the presence of bizarre and macabre figures, as we see, for example, in the tales 'Il morto risuscitato' ('Risen from the Dead'), 'Il teschio di Amalziabene' ('Amalziabene's Skull'), 'La fidanzata dello scheletro' ('The Skeleton's Fiancée'), 'Mona Bice e i tre figli storpi' ('Lady Bice and her Three Crippled Sons'), 'Il ragazzo con due teste' ('The Boy with Two Heads'), 'L'impiccato vivo' (''Hung Alive'), and 'Il lupo mannaro' ('The Werewolf'). Although within the frame Regina may stress the didactic function of her tales, Perodi's tales are too contradictory and uncanny to be considered as exempla in the 'literature of acculturation' for children that was being created in this period in Italy and in Europe.

Ultimately, the *Novelle* celebrate the pleasures of narration and the delectable indeterminacy of the fantastic worlds that they depict in order to resist any socializing project, and it is perhaps for this reason that they still hold appeal for us today.   NC

Faeti, Antonio, Intro. to Emma Perodi, *Fiabe fantastiche: Le novelle della nonna* (1993).

Perrault, Charles (1628–1703) French writer, poet, and academician. He was born in Paris into one of the more celebrated bourgeois families of that time. His father was a lawyer and member of Parliament, and his four brothers—he was the youngest—all went on to become renowned in such fields as architecture and law. In 1637 Perrault began studying at the Collège de Beauvais (near the Sorbonne), and at the age of 15 he stopped attending school and largely taught himself all he needed to know so he could later take his law examinations. After working three years as a lawyer, he left the profession to become a secretary to his brother Pierre, who was the tax receiver of Paris. By this time Perrault had already written some minor poems, and he began taking more and more of an interest in literature. In 1659 he published two important poems, 'Portrait d'Iris' and 'Portrait de la voix d'Iris', and by 1660 his public career as a poet received a big boost when he produced several poems in honour of Louis XIV. In 1663 Perrault was appointed secretary to Jean-Baptiste Colbert, controller general of finances, perhaps the most influential minister in Louis XIV's government. For the next 20 years, until Colbert's death, Perrault was able to accomplish a great deal in the arts and sciences owing to Colbert's power and influence. In 1671 he was elected to the Académie Française and was also placed in charge of the royal buildings. He continued writing poetry and took an active interest in cultural affairs of the court. In 1672 he married Marie Guichon, with whom he had three sons. She died in childbirth in 1678, and he never remarried, supervising the education of his children by himself.

When Colbert died in 1683, Perrault was dismissed from government service, but he

Perrault, Charles The cunning cat approaches the ogre in Gustave *Doré's illustration of Charles Perrault's 'Puss in Boots' in *Les Contes de Perrault* (1867).

had a substantial pension and was able to support his family until his death. Released from governmental duties, Perrault could concentrate more on literary affairs, and in 1687 he inaugurated the famous 'Quarrel of the Ancients and the Moderns' ('Querelle des Anciens et des Modernes') by reading a poem entitled 'Le Siècle de Louis le Grand'. Perrault took the side of modernism and believed that France and Christianity could progress only if they incorporated pagan beliefs and folklore and developed a culture of enlightenment. On the other hand, Nicolas Boileau, the literary critic, and Jean Racine, the dramatist, took the opposite viewpoint and argued that France had to imitate the great empires of Greece and Rome and maintain stringent classical rules in respect to the arts. This literary quarrel, that had great cultural ramifications, lasted until 1697, at which time Louis XIV decided to end it in favour of Boileau and Racine.

However, this decision did not stop Perrault from trying to incorporate his ideas into his poetry and prose.

Perrault had always frequented the literary salons of his niece Mlle *Lhéritier, Mme d'*Aulnoy, and other women, and he had been annoyed by Boileau's satires written against women. Thus, he endeavoured to write three verse tales 'Grisélidis' (1691), 'Les Souhaits Ridicules' (*'The Foolish Wishes', 1693) and 'Peau d'âne' (*'Donkey-Skin', 1694) along with a long poem, 'Apologie des femmes' (1694) in defence of women. Whether these works can be considered pro-women today is another question. However, Perrault was definitely more enlightened in regard to this question than either Boileau or Racine, and his poems make use of a highly mannered style and folk motifs to stress the necessity of assuming an enlightened moral attitude toward women and exercising just authority.

In 1696 Perrault embarked on a more ambitious project of transforming several popular folk tales with all their superstitious beliefs and magic into moralistic tales that would appeal to children and adults and demonstrate a modern approach to literature. He had a prose version of *'Sleeping Beauty' ('La Belle au bois dormant') printed in the journal *Mercure Galant* in 1696, and in 1697 he published an entire collection of tales entitled *Histoires ou contes du temps passé*, which consisted of new literary versions of 'Sleeping Beauty', *'Little Red Riding Hood' ('Le Petit Chaperon Rouge'), 'Barbe Bleue' (*'Bluebeard'), 'Cendrillon' (*'Cinderella'), 'Le Petit Poucet' (*'Little Tom Thumb'), 'Riquet à la Houppe' (*'Riquet with the Tuft'), 'Le Chat botté' (*'Puss-in-Boots'), and 'Les Fées' ('The *Fairies'). All of these fairy tales, which are now considered 'classical', were based on oral and literary motifs that had become popular in France, but Perrault transformed the stories to address social and political issues as well as the manners and mores of the upper classes. Moreover, he added ironic verse morals to provoke his readers to reflect on the ambivalent meaning of the tales. Although *Histoires ou contes du temps passé* was published under the name of Pierre Perrault Darmancour, Perrault's son, and although some critics have asserted that the book was indeed written or at least co-authored by his son, recent evidence has shown clearly that this could not have been the case, especially since his son had not published anything up to that point. Perrault was simply using his son's name to mask his own identity so that he would not be blamed for re-igniting the 'Quarrel of the Ancients and the Moderns'. Numerous critics have regarded Perrault's tales as written directly for children, but they overlook the fact that there was no children's literature *per se* at that time and that most writers of fairy tales were composing and reciting their tales for their peers in the literary salons. Certainly, if Perrault intended them to make a final point in the 'Quarrel of the Ancients and the Moderns', then he obviously had an adult audience in mind that would understand his humour

and the subtle manner in which he transformed folklore superstition to convey his position about the 'modern' development of French civility.

There is no doubt but that, among the writers of fairy tales during the 1690s, Perrault was the greatest stylist, which accounts for the fact that his tales have withstood the test of time. Furthermore, Perrault claimed that literature must become modern, and his transformation of folk motifs and literary themes into refined and provocative fairy tales still speak to the modern age, ironically in a way that may compel us to ponder whether the age of reason has led to the progress and happiness promised so charmingly in Perrault's tales.   JZ

Barchilon, Jacques, and Flinders, Peter, *Charles Perrault* (1981).

Burne, Glenn S., 'Charles Perrault 1628–1703', in Jane M. Bingham (ed.), *Writers for Children: Critical Studies of Major Authors since the Seventeenth Century* (1988).

Lewis, Philip, *Seeing through the Mother Goose Tales: Visual Turns in the Writings of Charles Perrault* (1996).

McGlathery, James M., 'Magic and Desire from Perrault to Musäus: Some Examples', *Eighteenth-Century Life*, 7 (1981).

Marin, Louis, 'La cuisine des fées: or the Culinary Sign in the Tales of Perrault', *Genre*, 16 (1983).

Seifert, Lewis C., 'Disguising the Storyteller's "Voice": Perrault's Recuperation of the Fairy Tale', *Cincinnati Romance Review*, 8 (1989).

Soriano, Marc, *Les Contes de Perrault. Culture savante et traditions populaires* (1968).

Peterfreund, Diana (1979–) American writer of young-adult literature, some of whose work incorporates magic, including novels (*Rampant* 2009 and *Ascendant* 2010) and short stories about killer unicorns. These and her post-apocalyptic science fiction fantasy, *For Darkness Shows the Stars* (2012, based on Jane Austen's *Persuasion*) and *Across a Star-Swept Sea* (2013, based on Baroness Orczy's *The Scarlet Pimpernel*) integrate girl-power themes. For the latter books, Peterfreund's website provides free prequel short-story paratexts. She offers writing workshops on how to use folklore, mythology, legends, and fairy tales. Among her influences she cites C. S. *Lewis and Lucy Maud Montgomery. PG

Peter Pan Eternal youth created by Sir James Matthew *Barrie. He was first mentioned in an adult novel (*The Little White Bird*, 1902): Peter used to be a bird, flew away from his parents when they were discussing his future, and settled in Kensington Gardens. Barrie expanded this idea in the play, *Peter Pan, or The Boy who Wouldn't Grow Up* (1904), which was inspired by Victorian fairy dramas, Drury Lane pantomimes, and five young boys. Here, Peter and the fairy Tinkerbell help the Darling children fly to Neverland where they have adventures with Lost Boys, Indians, and Pirates. The play was immediately successful. But while Barrie had Arthur *Rackham illustrate earlier short stories for *Peter Pan in Kensington Gardens* (1906), others were already adapting his play. Barrie's *Peter and Wendy* did not appear until 1911; the finalized play, in 1928. In short, 'Peter Pan' was a classic fairy tale even before Barrie published it for children!

Some critics feel that Peter owes his life to the death of Barrie's brother. Because his mother became obsessive over her dead child (who never aged) and ignored the one who matured, Barrie immortalized an ageless youth who longs for a mother figure. Interestingly, early versions (written when Freud was defining adolescent sexuality) have the female characters rejecting this maternal role. They favour a sexual relationship, one to which the boy cannot or will not commit emotionally. Avoidance of responsibility (the 'Peter Pan syndrome'), is also symbolized by confrontations of youth and maturity whenever Peter battles Hook. When each unconsciously mimics the other, Hook represents Peter's adult self. At other times, because the same actor usually plays Hook and the Father (Mr Darling), an Oedipal confrontation arises. Finally, perhaps Hook wants Peter to remain a boy, too—for paedophilic reasons. This reading prompts conservatives to ban the book from schools, and is supported by claims that Barrie was abnormally attracted to the Llewelyn Davies boys. (The brothers, whom Barrie eventually adopted, always denied improper behaviour.)

Peter Pan was a Christmas tradition in London's West End from 1904 to 1990, with only nine seasons on hiatus. After Hamlet, Peter is the most sought-after role and is usually played by a woman: female casting is in the tradition of pantomime, and a child star necessitates proportionately smaller Lost Boys, perhaps too young to act. Nina Boucicault, Maude Adams, and Betty Bronson created the role in London, on Broadway, and on film. Other notable Peters include Eva Le Gallienne, Elsa Lanchester (with husband Charles Laughton as Hook), Dame Maggie Smith, and Cathy Rigby.

Barrie's play has undergone many changes over the years. Leonard Bernstein added music (1950), Walt *Disney animated it (1953), and Jerome Robbins created a flying ballet (1954). This Mary Martin–Cyril Ritchard musical made history when it was televised live and in colour in 1955, and remains the definitive version for post-war American Baby Boomers. In 1982 Miles Anderson broke the 'Peterless Pan' tradition with the Royal Shakespeare Company, which restored the 1928 stage direction, added a narrator resembling Barrie, and incorporated his epilogue in which Wendy grows up. Steven *Spielberg expanded this idea in *Hook* (1990), a film about Wall Street pirate Peter (a father married to Wendy's granddaughter) who fights Hook for their children. Finally, an aged Peter and his wife Alice are allegorized in *Death Comes for Peter Pan* (1996), a study of America's Neverland/Wonderland of Medicare. No longer merely the hero of a fairy play, then, Peter Pan has become a transcendent myth for all generations of (former) children. MLE

Birkin, Andrew, *J. M. Barrie & The Lost Boys: The Love Story that Gave Birth to Peter Pan* (1979).

Brady, Joan, *Death Comes for Peter Pan* (1996).

Hanson, Bruce K., *The Peter Pan Chronicles* (1993).

Kelley-Lainé, Kathleen, *Peter Pan: The Story of Lost Childhood* (1997).

Rose, Jacqueline, *The Case of Peter Pan, or The Impossibility of Children's Fiction* (1984).

Stirling, Kirsten, *Peter Pan's Shadows in the Literary Imagination* (2012).

Peter Pan (film) The celebrated British play of 1904 has rarely been tackled by the cinema. For the major silent version (USA, 1924), the author J. M. *Barrie himself approved the casting of boyish 18-year-old newcomer Betty Bronson as Peter. The Chinese-American actress Anna May Wong, playing the redskin princess Tiger Lily, was only 17 but had appeared on screen before, notably in Fairbanks's *The *Thief of Bagdad*. Complementing these youngsters were veterans such as the eye-rolling Ernest Torrence as Hook, and George Ali who, inside a dog costume, repeated a performance as Nana the nurse that he had given many times on stage. Most other elements of the film, including the use of wires to accomplish the flying scenes, also followed the stage production closely. The only significant difference is that whereas on stage Tinker Bell the fairy is represented simply by a darting spot of light, in the film she is fleshed out by Virginia Brown Faire, who was miniaturized by photographic multiple-exposure techniques. In the UK the film's director was praised for not having Americanized the play, but in fact some scenes were shot with alternative versions: for British audiences the flag the Lost Boys raised was the Union Jack, while in the USA it was the Stars and Stripes.   TAS

Peter Pan (musical) J. M. *Barrie's enduring children's story has inspired a number of musical adaptations, mostly American; the first appeared in 1905 in New York. A production in 1924 contained two songs by Jerome Kern. Another version in 1950 was again notable for musical contributions from an important composer, Leonard Bernstein; it ran for 321 performances. A more lasting version appeared in 1954 opening at the Winter Garden, New York, with music by Moose Charlap and Carolyn Leigh. Jule Styne, among others, later contributed additional numbers. A German translation appeared at the Theater des Westens, Berlin, in 1984. Meanwhile, American interest in the story continued with another production in 1979, which overtook previous versions by achieving a run of 551 performances. London's West End saw a similar version in the mid-1980s. Yet another *Peter Pan* opened in New York in 1990 for a short six-week season, forming part of the show's nationwide tour.   TH

Petrushevskaya, Lyudmila (1938–) Russian writer, novelist, singer, and playwright, who is considered one of the foremost writers in contemporary Russia. A translation of some of her best fairy tales, written between 1970 and 2000 and published in the famous Moscow magazine *Novy Mir*, appeared in English for the first time in 2009 under the title *There Once Lived a Woman Who Tried To Kill Her Neighbor's Baby*. It was followed by *There Once Lived a Girl Who Seduced Her Sister's Husband, and He Hanged Himself* (2009). Many of her stories are grotesque tales about weird everyday events. For instance, 'Marilena's Secret' concerns a magician who turns two skinny ballerinas into one fat circus performer, and in 'The Fountain House' a father uses a blood transfusion to bring his dead daughter back to life. 'The New Robinson Crusoes' plays with Daniel Defoe's classic novel and depicts a family desperately trying to escape something. All Petrushevskaya's tales are about survival and include implicit and explicit critiques of living conditions under Soviet rule. Petrushevskaya also co-wrote the screenplay of Yuri Norstein's brilliant film, *Tale of Tales* (1979).   JZ

piacevoli notti, Le (1550–3) Translated by W. G. Waters in 1894 as *The Facetious Nights of Giovanni Francesco Straparola*. Other possible titles are *The Entertaining Nights* or *The Pleasant Nights*. Little is known about the author Giovan Francesco *Straparola. However, his collection of tales was very popular in the 16th century and went through 20 editions and influenced numerous European writers of fairy tales. Not all the *novelle* are fairy tales in this collection. Similar to Boccaccio's *Decameron*, the *Notti* has a framework: thirteen ladies and several

piacevoli notti, Le The ladies and gentlemen gather together to tell stories in the English edition of Giovan Francesco Straparola's *Le piacevoli notti*. Illustrated by E. R. Hughes.

gentlemen flee to the island of Murano near Venice during the last 13 days of Carnival to avoid political persecution. To amuse themselves, they dance and tell 75 stories. Each one ends with a riddle with multiple meanings. Of the 75 tales there are 14 fairy tales: 'Cassadrino' ('The Master Thief'), 'Pre Scarpafico' ('The Little Farmer'), 'Tebaldo' ('All Fur'), 'Galeotto' ('Hans My Hedgehog'), 'Pietro' ('The Simpleton Hans'), 'Biancabella' ('The Snake and the Maiden'), 'Fortunio' ('The Nixie in the Pond'), 'Ricardo' ('Six who Made their Way into the World'), 'Aciolotto' ('The Three Little Birds'), 'Guerrino' (*'Iron Hans'), 'I tre fratelli' ('The Four Skillful Brothers'), 'Maestro Lattantio' ('The Thief and his Master'), 'Cesarino' ('The Two Brothers'), and 'Soriana' (*'Puss-in-Boots'). These tales were either European or oriental in origin, and their translations in the 16th, 17th, and 18th centuries influenced French and German writers. Straparola's 'Soriana' is the first literary version of 'Puss-in-Boots'. Straparola was not a great stylist, but his succinct, witty narratives have effective dramatic structures and contain biting social commentary. Indeed, some of the narratives about priests offended the Church during the Counter-Reformation in the 17th century, and the *Notti* was placed on the Index in 1624.   JZ

Boscardi, Giorgio, 'Le Novelle di G. F. Straparola', *Rassegna Lucchese*, 3 (1952).

Pozzi, Victoria Smith, 'Straparola's Le piacevoli notti: Narrative Technique and Ideology' (Diss., University of California-Los Angeles, 1981).

Rua, Giuseppe, 'Intorno alle Piacevoli Notti dello Straparola', *Giornale Storico della Letteratura Italiana*, 15 (1890).

Straparola, Giovan Francesco, *The Pleasant Nights*, ed. Donald Beecher, 2 vols (2012).

Waters, W. G. (trans.), *The Facetious Nights of Giovanni Francesco Straparola* (2 vols., 1894).

Pinborough, Sarah (1972–) British writer of horror, mystery, and fantasy works for young adults. She also writes under the pen name Sarah Silverwood. Pinborough has written mystery episodes for TV and has won a number of awards for her young-adult novels. In 2013, she began writing a fairy-tale trilogy for adults, *Poison* (2013), *Charm* (2014), and *Beauty* (2014), with great success. *Poison* is a rewriting of *'Snow White'* in which Lilith, the queen, is portrayed with more empathy, while Snow White, only slightly younger than her stepmother and free-spirited, shows that she knows how to fend for herself without the help of dwarfs. *Charm* is an adaptation of *'Cinderella', and the portrayal of the characters is completely reversed. Cinderella is somewhat ignorant and determined to get what she wants, while her stepsisters only want what is good for her, as do her stepmother and father, who care for one another. Finally, *Beauty* is a reimagining of *'Sleeping Beauty'* in which the prince discovers that the princess he wants to save has inherited luring witch-traits from her mother and has thrown decadent soirées in the castle before the prince arrives to try to save her. In all three novels, Pinborough displays unusual originality that will surprise many a reader's conventional expectations of fairy tales.   JZ

Pinkney, Brian (1961–) American illustrator of children's books who is committed to exploring African-American culture in his works. He has collaborated with Robert *San Souci in producing the important anthology *Cut from the Same Cloth: American Women of Myth, Legend, and Tall Tale* (1993) and has also illustrated San Souci's *Sukey and the Mermaid* (1992). Pinkney uses scratchboard techniques to sculpt stark black-and-white images, and he also endows his lines and figures with an unusual rhythm. Pinkney has also provided drawings for Lynn Joseph's *A Wave in her Pocket: Stories from Trinidad* (1991) and Patricia McKissack's *The Dark Thirty: Southern Tales of the Supernatural* (1992).   JZ

Pinkney, Jerry (1939–) American illustrator who has dedicated himself to producing highly original multicultural books. Pinkney's major works have led to a rediscovery and celebration of the African-American heritage. Among his fairy-tale books are: *The Adventures of Spider: West African Folk*

Tales (1964) by Joyce Cooper, Folktales and Fairytales of Africa (1967) edited by Lila Green, The Beautiful Blue Jay and Other Tales of India (1967) edited by John Spellman, *The King's Ditch: A Hawaiian Tale* (1971) by Francine Jacobs, *Prince Littlefoot* (1974) by Berniece Freschet, *Tonweya and the Eagles and Other Lakota Indian Tales* (1979) by Rosebud Yellow Robe, and *The Talking Eggs* (1989) by Robert San Souci. He has also collaborated with Julius Lester in reinterpreting the Uncle Remus tradition in America with *The Tales of Uncle Remus* (1988), *More Tales of Uncle Remus* (1988), and *Further Tales of Uncle Remus* (1990). Pinkney's illustrations are characterized by bold action, extraordinary colours, and compelling interpretations of the texts.   JZ

Pinocchio, The Adventures of (*Le avventure di Pinocchio*) Carlo *Collodi first published his vivacious masterpiece as a serial story in a children's weekly paper, *Il Giornale per i bambini*, between 1881 and 1883. In February 1883 it was issued as a volume with black-and-white illustrations by Enrico Mazzanti, who had collaborated with Collodi in earlier work. The serial was originally entitled *La storia di un burattino* (*The Story of a Puppet*) and ended tragically with chapter 15; the definitive title was adopted on the relaunching of the serial, the whole eventually reaching 36 short chapters. *Pinocchio* is a fairy story not only because the 'Fairy with indigo hair' is prominent as a kind of fairy godmother to the puppet who longs to become a real boy; in addition, many of the other characters and some narrative devices link it to the age-old web of oral and literary storytelling concerning the marvellous, and not just to those strands identified with the complex art of the fairy tale. Among the fairy-tale features of Collodi's fantasy of picaresque adventure are the many talking animals and birds which mix with human beings, the monstrous creatures and ogre-like humans, the transformations and illogical happenings, the showing of bravery in the face of repeated dangers, and the coming of good from evil. Specifically, the rewarding of virtue is part of a rags-to-comfort-if-not-riches theme which evolves from within the social ambit of the very poor. Six years before writing *Pinocchio*, Collodi had translated Charles *Perrault's French fairy tales into Italian, but his wide reading made his children's story into a palimpsest of cultural allusions. If the Fairy encourages and protects and sometimes surprises with magic, as the fairy godmother does in *'Cinderella' (to which there are several references), then Collodi's Fox and Cat belong to the Aesopic tradition of fables with morals, as filtered through the verse versions of Perrault's contemporary and compatriot, La Fontaine. Though Ovid is not absent from *Pinocchio*, the specific metamorphosis of the puppet into a donkey more closely mirrors the circumstances and moral purpose of *Apuleius' *The Golden Ass*. Collodi's inspiration, while not religious, was deeply moral; good and evil are ever-present, sometimes accompanied by Dantesque imagery. His sense of fun was regarded as emulating the 'English humour' of Lewis *Carroll and the Nonsense school. The whole story is imbued with the theatrical, whether it be dramatic use of light and dark or overt reference to the *Commedia dell'arte*. With its apparently direct and natural manner, *Pinocchio* is a highly sophisticated tale rendered sparkling by the wordplay and renowned irony. As in Carroll, the allusions are not all literary; Collodi was prompted by his commitment to political and social reform. The episodes of the doctors called to diagnose Pinocchio's condition and of the judge pronouncing on the theft of his coins are akin to the fairy tale and the fable (and *Alice in Wonderland*) in the use of talking animals and in the danger threatening the protagonist, but at a deeper level these episodes pungently criticize professional malpractice and the shortcomings of society. Paradoxically, *Pinocchio* has the timelessness and universality of the fairy tale and yet was pertinent to matters of moment in Collodi's place and time.

Collodi died before producing any strict sequel to *Pinocchio*, but the book's best-seller status in Italy ensured that new editions were constantly available, with illustrations by numbers of different artists; between 1883 and 1983 in Italy alone there were 135 different illustrated editions, well over one per year. From early days, there were many emulators and imitators, a distinguished disciple being Collodi's nephew. Sons, brothers, friends galore of the puppet were spawned, as was even a fiancée. Pinocchio was subjected to an inexhaustible sequence of adventures in many named lands, as an explorer, hunter, policeman, mountaineer, magistrate, journalist, diver, spaceman, dancer, soldier, castaway, and in 1927–8 as a Fascist. He was a wooden Everyman.

The original *Pinocchio* quickly began to be translated around the world in innumerable editions and adaptations. At any one time there are many English versions available, the majority abridgements. Some are even modifications of the first English translation of 1892 by Mary A. Murray, as the 1996 North American version by Ed Young is. More than 100 years on, *Pinocchio* also appears in many non-literary guises: toys, trinkets, publicity, and numerous films. Interesting and faithful film versions are still being made, but the one that dominates world-wide perceptions of *Pinocchio*, even after 50 years, is Walt *Disney's 1940 animated interpretation. While countless children have loved it for itself, it bears little resemblance to Collodi's *Pinocchio*; the story is fundamentally altered, the mood softened and Hollywoodized, and the puppet deprived of his personality. Disney is sentimental where Collodi is uncompromising, challenging, and exhilarating. Whether or not prompted by cinematic or illustrators' images, readers and critics of different times and places have understood *Pinocchio* in a myriad different ways, according to the political, religious, or cultural imperatives informing their perception. Interpretations have been variously Christian, marxist, anti-communist, Freudian, and the product of many other 'isms'. This capacity to mean many things to many people, to provide metaphors for the frightening and the incomprehensible, but always with a bearing upon the real world, makes *Pinocchio*

an authentic scion of the fairy-tale tradition.   ALL

Citati, Pietro, 'Una fiaba esoterica' and 'La fata dai capelli turchini', in *Il velo nero* (1979).
Collodi, Carlo, *The Adventures of Pinocchio*, trans. and ed. Ann Lawson Lucas (1996).
Goldthwaite, John, *The Natural History of Make-Believe* (1996).
Perella, Nicolas J., 'An Essay on *Pinocchio*', in Carlo Collodi, *Le avventure di Pinocchio—The Adventures of Pinocchio* (1986).
Pizzi, Katia (ed.), *Pinocchio, Puppets and Modernity: The Mechanical Body* (2011).
Wunderlich, Richard, and Morrissey, Thomas, 'Carlo Collodi's *The Adventures of Pinocchio*: A Classic Book of Choices', in Perry Nodelman (ed.), *Touchstones: Reflections on the Best in Children's Literature* (1985).
Wunderlich, Richard, and Morrissey, Thomas, *Pinocchio Goes Postmodern: Perils of a Puppet in the United States* (2002).

Pippi Longstocking Title character of three novels by Astrid *Lindgren, *Pippi Långstrump* (*Pippi Longstocking*, 1945) and sequels, the strongest girl in the world, independent and free in confrontation with the world of adults. Pippi lives on her own in a little town with her horse and her monkey; she does not go to school and defies the dictatorship of norms and conventions, of dull reality, of authority, of structure and order. Although many critics have viewed the character as an expression of escape, her spirit is chiefly anti-authoritarian, which signals her strong links with brave and clever fairy-tale heroines, such as Molly Whuppie, or the princesses of contemporary feminist fairy tales.

Pippi has no magic powers and no magic objects to assist her, and she uses her wits rather than her physical strength to win over impertinent adults. Unlike the typical underdog heroine or hero of the fairy tale, Pippi is secure, self-assured, strong, and rich from the beginning. Thus her role is not of a hero, but rather that of a magical helper or donor in a fairy tale, bringing colour and joy into ordinary children's lives. She is also the source of unlimited wealth, fulfilling the wildest dreams of any child.

Like *Peter Pan, Pippi does not want to grow up, but mainly because she refuses to be socialized. When she offers her friends magical pills which will prevent them from growing up, she acts like a witch enticing them with enchanted food into an eternal childhood akin to death. Thus Pippi is a highly ambivalent figure.   MN

Edström, Vivi, 'Pippi Longstocking: Chaos and Postmodernism', *Swedish Book Review*, suppl. (1990).

Hoffeld, Laura, 'Pippi Longstocking: The Comedy of the Natural Girl', *The Lion and the Unicorn*, 1 (1977).

Lundqvist, Ulla, *Århundradets barn. Fenomenet Pippi Långstrump och dess förutsättningar* (1977).

Metcalf, Eva-Maria, *Astrid Lindgren* (1995).

Moebius, William, 'L'Enfant Terrible Comes of Age', *Notebooks on Cultural Analysis*, 2 (1985).

Reeder, Kik, 'Pippi Longstocking—a Feminist or Anti-feminist Work?' *Racism and Sexism in Children's Literature* (1979).

Pitrè, Giuseppe (1841–1916) Italian folklorist and ethnographer. He was the foremost figure in 19th-century Italian folklore studies, and had a central role in establishing the study of popular traditions as an independent discipline in Italy. He opposed a strictly aesthetic approach to folklore, maintaining that folk traditions offered precious historical information on national heritages that often revealed different realities from 'official' history. His homeland of Sicily offered him an especially rich corpus of materials, which he studied and collected throughout his life. Pitrè's major works include the 25-volume *Biblioteca delle tradizioni popolari siciliane* (*Library of Popular Sicilian Traditions*, 1870–1913); *Fiabe novelle e racconti popolari siciliani* (*Fairy Tales, Novellas, and Popular Tales of Sicily*, 1875); the journal *Archivio per lo studio delle tradizioni popolari* (*Archive for the Study of Popular Traditions*, 1882–1909), which he founded and edited; the 16-volume *Curiosità popolari tradizionali* (*Curiosities of Popular Traditions*, 1885–99); and *Bibliografia delle tradizioni popolari d'Italia* (*Bibliography of Italian Popular Traditions*, 1894). Pitrè's principal source for the *Fiabe* was the oral storyteller Agatuzza Messia, whose tales he transcribed with precision, opposing his method to that of more 'creative' scholars like the *Grimms. The *Fiabe* became a precious document for later anthologists of Italian fairy tales such as Italo *Calvino.   NC

Cocchiara, Giuseppe, *Pitrè, la Sicilia e il folklore* (1951).

Cocchiara, Giuseppe, *The History of Folklore in Europe* (1981).

Pitrè, Giuseppe, *The Collected Sicilian Folk and Fairy Tales of Giuseppe Pitrè*, ed. and trans. Jack Zipes and Joseph Russo (2008).

Zipes, Jack, 'The Indomitable Giuseppe Pitrè', *Folklore* (2009).

Pitzorno, Bianca (1942–) Prominent Italian author of children's literature. Pitzorno's feminism and her interest in both history and contemporary issues have often produced works with realistic settings and strong female characters, such as *Ascolta il mio cuore* (*Listen to My Heart*, 1991), which depicts daily life in post-Second World War Italy as seen through the eyes of a little girl. But Pitzorno is also attracted to the marvellous. For instance, in *L'incredibile storia di Lavinia* (*The Incredible Story of Lavinia*, 1985), Pitzorno adapted Hans Christian *Andersen's 'The Little Match Girl' by transforming it into a delightful tale about an orphan named Lavinia living and begging in contemporary Milan. Instead of dying because of the neglect of people who pass her by, as in Andersen's story, she is helped by a gracious fairy who gives her a ring that transforms everything into excrement. This strange, powerful ring leads Lavinia into many comical situations. Most importantly, the ring enables Lavinia to become a celebrity who uses her fame to fight against injustices. In the sequel to this book, *Una Scuola per Lavinia* (*A School for Lavinia*, 2005), Pitzorno depicted Lavinia living in the Grand Hotel and attending an exclusive school for daughters of millionaires. However, she still sells matches as a beggar and refuses to use her magic ring to promote herself. When her friend Teo disappears, however, Lavinia resorts to using the ring to find him. And this search brings about many exciting and amusing adventures. Other important books by Pitzorno include *Clorofilla dal Cielo blu* (*Clorophyll from the Blue Sky*, 1974) an 'ecological fantasy' which was adapted for the cinema, and *Streghetta Mia* (*My Little Witch*, 1997). Pitzorno was the head of production for children's programming for RAI television in the 1970s and later worked on the children's show *L'Albero azzurro* (The Blue Tree). NC

Garavini, Melissa, 'Bianca Pitzorno: Imagination and Feminism', *Bookbird* 50.4 (2012).
Salvadori, Maria Luisa, 'Apologizing to the Ancient Fable: Gianni Rodari and His Influence on Italian Children's Literature', *The Lion and the Unicorn* 26.2 (2002).

Piumini, Roberto (1947–) Italian author of children's and adult fiction and poetry. Piumini has reworked well-known fairy-tale types to explore genre (ballads, theatre, music) and address contemporary concerns. His original tales include *Le fiabe infinite* (*Infinite Fairy Tales*, 2011), *Poco prima della notte* (*Just Before Night*, 2011), the series *L'albero delle fiabe* (*The Tree of Fairy Tales*, 2009-11), *Tre fiabe d'amore* (*Three Fairy Tales of Love*, 2005), and *Fiabe per occhi e bocca* (*Fairy Tales for the Eyes and the Mouth*, 1995). A former teacher, Piumini has collaborated on projects aimed at the experimental use of narrative and language in the classroom. He has also written for RAI television's *L'Albero Azzurro* (*The Blue Tree*), Italy's longest-running children's programme. NC

Planché, James Robinson (1796–1880) English dramatist and translator of French fairy tales. Planché was a highly productive and popular dramatist of the London stage who created nearly 180 productions from 1818 to 1856, and is best known for his theatrical extravaganzas which were frequently based on French fairy tales. Planché acknowledged his sources for the extravaganzas as the *folie féerie* (fairy comedy) which he borrowed from the Paris stage, English pantomime, and burlesque. Planché suggested the essential elements of a successful fairy extravaganza were: 'A plot, the interest of which is sustained to the last moment, and is not in the least complicated, a series of startling and exciting events, the action which required no verbal explanation, and numerous opportunities for scenic display and sumptuous decoration—What more could be desired?' Planché produced his first extravaganza in 1825 using mythological subjects, but turned to French fairy tales for his plots beginning with **Riquet with the Tuft* (1836). Other fairy extravaganzas quickly followed including comic adaptations of **Puss-in-Boots* (1837), **Bluebeard* (1839), **Sleeping Beauty in the Wood* (1840), **Beauty and the Beast* (1841), and *The White Cat* (1842). Planché eventually wrote 44 extravaganzas that combined song, dance, spectacle, and topical allusions.

While pantomime was considered a working-class genre, the extravaganza was thought to be middle-class in its appeal, despite the fact that both forms of entertainment relied on transformation scenes, fantastic plots and lavish costumes, and numerous changes of scenery. Both became British theatrical institutions during the Christmas and Easter seasons, and Planché's extravaganzas in particular were influential in the creation of Gilbert and Sullivan's comic operettas. The fairy extravaganza is a pantomime with the harlequinade removed, new lyrics written for popular songs, extensive use of puns, and an elaborate concluding transformation scene involving spectacular changes in scenery and costumes. While the extravaganza was considered respectable family entertainment, some of the adult appeal was due to the sometimes revealing costumes of the actresses. Planché took care to produce historically accurate costumes and eventually published *History of British Costumes* (1834) and *An Encyclopaedia of Costume or Dictionary of Dress* (1876–9).

Planché's theatrical adaptations of fairy tales were published shortly before his death in the five-volume *The Extravaganza of J. R. Planché, Esq.* (1879). In addition to his extravaganzas, Planché translated two collections of French fairy tales, *The Fairy*

Planché, James Robinson The charming prince is about to kiss Sleeping Beauty in James Robinson Planché's unusual adaptation of *Perrault's tale in *An Old Fairy Tale Told Anew* (1865), illustrated by Richard *Doyle.

*Tales of the Countess D'*Aulnoy* (1855) and the companion volume *Four and Twenty Fairy Tales* (1858), which was reprinted as *Fairy Tales by Perrault, De Villeneuve, De Caylus, De Lubert, De Beaumont* [*Leprince de Beaumont], *and Others*. He also wrote a version of 'Sleeping Beauty' in verse which accompanied Richard *Doyle's illustrations in *An Old Fairy Tale Told Anew* (1865).   JS

Booth, R. Michael, *Prefaces to English Nineteenth-Century Theatre* (1980).

Buczkowski, Paul, 'J. R. Planché, Frederick Robson, and the Fairy Extravaganza', *Marvels & Tales* (2001).

Planché, James Robinson, *The Recollections and Reflections of J. R. Planché* (1872).

Roy, Donald (ed.), *Plays by James Robinson Planché* (1986).

Pocci, Franz von (1807–76) German dramatist, poet, painter, and composer, who wrote numerous fairy-tale plays for the puppet theatre. Aside from drawing illustrations for collections of fairy tales by *Perrault, the *Grimms, and *Andersen, Pocci wrote over 40 plays for the Munich Marionettentheater. Some were based on traditional classical plots, and some were his own inventions. Among his best fairy-tale plays are *Blaubart* (*Bluebeard*, 1845), *Schattenspiel* (*Shadow Play*, 1847), *Hänsel und Gretel* (1861), *Zaubergeige* (*The Magic Violin*, 1868), *Eulenschloss* (*The Castle of Owls*, 1869), *Kasperl wird reich* (*Punch Becomes Rich*, 1872). At his best, Pocci combined comic features of the Punch and Judy shows with fantastic elements of the traditional fairy tales to create social farces aimed at enlightening and amusing children.   JZ

Dreyer, A., *Franz Pocci, der Dichter, Künstler und Kinderfreund* (1907).

Lucas, A., *Franz Pocci und das Kinderbuch* (1929).

poetry and fairy tales It is no secret that literary authors frequently reach back to classical and traditional stories and motifs to create their own poetic works. The tragic stories of Tristan and Isolde or Romeo and Juliet have been retold many times, and this is certainly true for the short fairy tales which most authors know extremely well from personal childhood experiences. The *Grimms' *Kinder- und Hausmärchen* (*Children's and Household Tales*) are in fact so ubiquitous that it would be surprising if there were no entire literary works in the form of novels, dramas, short stories, and poems based on them. And where this is not the case, it will not be difficult to find at least short verbal allusions to traditional fairy tales, especially in lyric poetry with its interest in metaphorical and indirect communication.

There existed a tradition of fairy-tale poetry already in the 19th century, with authors primarily being interested in retelling the tale quite literally in poems of numerous stanzas. Ludwig Uhland, August Heinrich Hoffman von Fallersleben, Heinrich *Heine, Eduard *Mörike, and Wolfgang Müller von Königswinter are German poets who were intrigued and influenced early by the Grimms' fairy tales. From the Anglo-American world Alfred *Tennyson, Samuel Rogers, Bret Harte, Frances Sargent Osgood, Ethel Louise Cox, John Greenleaf Whittier, James N. Barker, Tom Hood, and Guy Wetmore Carryl come to mind for such lengthy poetic retellings. For the most part their poems are nothing more than stylistic variations of the traditional fairy tales, and they add little to a deeper or differentiated understanding of the psychological underpinnings of the tales' messages.

This changed considerably at the turn of the century when authors were no longer satisfied in mechanically retelling the entire fairy tales in verse. Modern authors recognized early that although fairy tales depict a supernatural world with miraculous, magical, and numinous aspects, they also present in a symbolic fashion common problems and concerns of humanity. Fairy tales deal with all aspects of social life and human behaviour: not only such rites of passage as birth, courtship, betrothal, marriage, old age, and death, but also episodes that are typical in most people's lives. The emotional range includes in part love, hate, distrust, joy, persecution, happiness, murder, rivalry, and friendship, and often the same tale deals with such phenomena in contrasting pairs—good versus evil, success versus failure, benevolence versus malevolence, poverty versus wealth, fortune versus misfortune, victory versus defeat, compassion versus harshness, modesty versus indecency; in short, black versus white. That is indeed rich material for lyric poets, especially as they critically confront the basic idea of fairy tales that all conflicts can be resolved at the end. The fairy tales end with happiness, joy, contentment, and harmony in a world as it should be, where all good wishes are fulfilled. In the more modern fairy-tale poems this world is regrettably more often than not anything but splendid and perfect. The basic message of most 20th-century poems based on or at least alluding to fairy tales is one that this is a world of problems and frustrations, where nothing works out and succeeds as in those beautiful stories of ages past. And yet, by composing their poems around fairy-tale motifs, these authors if only very indirectly seem to long for that miraculous transformation to bliss and happiness.

Realistic reinterpretations of entire fairy tales or certain motifs have become the rule in modern fairy-tale poetry, a subgenre of lyric poetry that has received little attention from the scholarly world. Even though some literary historians have commented on the fairy-tale poems by such acclaimed poets as Franz *Fühmann, Günter *Grass, Randall *Jarrell, and Anne *Sexton, the fact that many modern poets have written fascinating poems either based on fairy tales or at least alluding to them has been overlooked. At the beginning of the 20th century James Whitcomb *Riley composed a number of generally traditional fairy-tale poems, and his 'Maymie's Story of Red Riding Hood' was even written in dialect. But contrast such a poem with the recent retelling of several popular fairy tales for children and adults by Roald *Dahl. In his lengthy poems the fairy tales are restated in the jargon of the modern world, so that one finds in them such words as 'discos', 'pistols', and 'panty hose'. Dahl has brought fairy tales up to date, somewhat as James Thurber did in his short prose texts based on fairy tales and fables.

A few poems do exist that contain somewhat positive reactions to the perfect world of fairy-tale endings. As an example, Joy Davidman's *'Rapunzel' poem, 'The Princess in the Ivory Tower', comes to mind; though even in this poem it is not clear whether the prince will reach his beloved or not: 'Let down your hair, let down your golden hair, | that I may be free . . .'. And the poem 'Reading the Brothers Grimm to Jenny' by Lisel *Mueller, clearly written by a mother for a child, also does not remain unproblematic, juxtaposing as it does the wonderful world of fairy tales and the dangerous world of reality: 'Knowing that you must climb, | one day, the ancient tower | where disenchantment binds | the curls of innocence, | that you must live with power | and honor circumstance, | that choice is what comes true— | O, Jenny, pure in heart, | why do I lie to you?'

Only a few poems retain the peace and harmony reached in the conclusions of the original tales. And with the exception of some humorous poems that are in fact ridiculous nonsense verses, the modern German and Anglo-American fairy-tale poems are critical reactions to fairy tales that are no longer believed or accepted. Transformed into parodistic, satirical, or cynical anti-fairy tales, these poems often contain serious social criticisms. By reading these modern renderings the readers are supposed to re-evaluate societal problems. The unexpressed hope is perhaps that such alienating anti-fairy tales might eventually be transformed again to real fairy tales in a better world. Many fairy-tale poems are therefore deeply felt moral statements, varying from subjective statements to more general claims. And yet, there are also poems of natural beauty, both in language and spirit, as can be seen from Aileen Fisher's 'Cinderella Grass' poem: 'Overnight the new green grass | turned to Cinderella glass. | Frozen rain decked twigs and weeds | with strings of Cinderella beads. | Glassy slippers, trim and neat, | covered all the clover's feet . . . | just as if there'd been a ball | with a magic wand and all.'

Modern fairy-tale poems concern themselves with every imaginable human problem.

There are poems about love and hate, war and politics, marriage and divorce, responsibility and criminality, and also emancipation as well as sexual politics. Such productive fairy-tale poets as Sara Henderson *Hay, Anne Sexton, and Olga *Broumas deal specifically with women's concerns and do not shrink from making explicit sexual comments. Their poems are never vulgar or promiscuous but rather sincere personal expressions. Hay's book *Story Hour* (1982) contains primarily poems alluding to such Grimm tales as 'The *Frog King', *'Snow White', *'Rumpelstiltskin', and *'Hansel and Gretel', where the titles of 'The Marriage', 'One of the Seven Has Somewhat to Say', 'The Name', and 'Juvenile Court' only allude to the underlying tale. But other poems are called explicitly 'The Goosegirl' or 'Rapunzel'. Each poem is composed of two rhymed stanzas of unequal length, with the second one presenting a realistic twist to what appears to be like a fairy tale in the first stanza. Here is the second stanza of Hay's 'Rapunzel' poem: 'I knew that other girls, in Aprils past, | Had leaned, like me, from some old tower's room | And watched him clamber up, hand over fist . . . | I knew that I was not the first to twist | Her heartstrings to a rope for him to climb. | I might have known I would not be the last.'

Anne Sexton treats numerous fairy tales in much longer poems of free verse, and she does not shy away from calling them directly 'The Frog Prince', 'Rapunzel', *'Little Red Riding Hood', 'Snow White and the Seven Dwarfs', etc., in her celebrated book *Transformations* (1971). These are indeed transfigured tales in which questions of sexuality, sexual politics, and emancipation all add up to a feministic statement against gender stereotypes. While her poems might be shocking and aggressive at times, Sexton is without doubt a genius at lyrical reinterpretations of Grimm tales. The titles of several poems in Olga Broumas's book *Beginning with O* (1977) are the same as Sexton's. Clearly inspired by the latter, Broumas looks at fairy tales from a lesbian point of view in her long poems of free verse. While her poems might be disagreeable to some, she presents deeply felt emotions and illustrates the psychosexual meaning of fairy tales to women.

But sex is only one major theme of fairy-tale poems. Many of them also deal with such problems as vanity, deception, lovelessness, materialism, and power. The adult world is simply not a perfect fairy tale. The philosophical fairy-tale poems by Randall Jarrell especially capture the frustrations that modern people experience in a world void of happy endings. But again, many of the pessimistic statements conceal a quiet hope for a better world. As Jarrell puts it at the end of his poem 'The Märchen (Grimm's Tales)': 'It was not power that you lacked, but wishes. | Had you not learned—have we not learned, from tales | Neither of beasts nor kingdoms nor their Lord, | But of our own hearts, the realm of death—Neither to rule nor die? to change, to change!' Changes are necessary in an increasingly complex world, and the transformations depicted in these poems might just be guideposts for humanity to find positive solutions to its difficult problems.

While Randall Jarrell wrote searching fairy-tale poems in America, Franz Fühmann approached the Grimm tales in a similarly philosophical way in Germany. Together with Anne Sexton, these two authors belong to a group of truly outstanding poets whose works contain numerous fairy-tale poems. There are other poets who must be mentioned, though. From the German-speaking countries the following poets are included with more than one poem in Wolfgang Mieder's anthology *Mädchen, pfeif auf den Prinzen! Märchengedichte von Günter Grass bis Sarah Kirsch* (*Girls, Don't Care about the Prince! Fairy-Tale Poems from Günter Grass to Sarah Kirsch*, 1983): Franz Josef Degenhardt, Günter Bruno *Fuchs, Albrecht Goes, Ulla Hahn, Rolf Kreuzer, Karl Krolow, Helmut Preissler, Josef Wittmann, etc. But well-known authors like Bertolt Brecht, Paul Celan, Hans Magnus Enzensberger, Günter Grass, Erich Kästner, Marie Luise Kaschnitz, Sarah *Kirsch, Elisabeth Langgässer, Eva Strittmatter, Martin Walser, Rudolf Otto Wiemerh, to name a few, are represented as well. In fact, most modern lyric poets have at least one fairy-tale poem or at least a poem or two alluding to a Grimm tale in passing in their published poems.

The same is true for the Anglo-American world, as can be seen from W. Mieder's anthology *Disenchantments: An Anthology of Modern Fairy Tale Poetry* (1985). Among the many poets not yet mentioned but represented in this book are such distinguished authors as Elizabeth Brewster, Hayden Carruth, William Dickey, Robert Gillespie, Louise Glück, Robert Graves, William Hathaway, Robert Hillyer, Paul R. Jones, Galway Kinnell, Walter *de la Mare, Eli Mandel, Robin Morgan, Howard Nemerov, Wilfred Owen, Robert Pack, Sylvia Plath, David Ray, Dorothy Lee Richardson, Stevie Smith, Phyllis Thompson, Louis Untermeyer, Evelyn M. Watson, and Elinor Wylie. Many more names could be added to this list, indicating once and for all that the subgenre of fairy-tale poetry is something to be reckoned with by scholars and poetry enthusiasts. Moreover, it has become abundantly clear in a later anthology, *The Poets' Grimm: 20th Century Poems from Grimm Fairy Tales* (2003), edited by Jean-Marie Beaumont and Claudia Carlson, that fairy-tale poetry has become much more than just a subgenre.

Hundreds of German and English fairy-tale poems reveal that they can be grouped according to the specific tale being discussed or mentioned. But there are also those poems which deal in general with the sense of fairy tales in the modern world. The following four lines from Alfred Corn's poem 'Dreambooks' give a flavour of this approach: 'Grim fairy tale. 'Once upons' are always | Puns, double understandings for | The double life, to be read and dreamed | Until the secret order appears.' A second more general group could be termed fairy-tale potpourris in that their authors create *tour-de-force* combinations of various fairy-tale allusions. Gail White's poem 'Happy Endings' might serve as an appropriate example: 'Red Riding Hood and her grandmother | made the wolf | into a big fur coat | and Gretel | shoved Hansel into the oven |

and ate him with the witch | and the Beauty enjoyed | her long sleep | quite as much | as the awakening kiss | and the Prince might take | Cinderella to the palace | but she would insist | on scrubbing floors | and scouring pots | and getting her good clothes | covered with ashes | after all | it was what | she was used to.' There are more serious poems of this type, but clearly their authors delight in the montage of various fairy-tale motifs.

Of the many poems dealing with one specific fairy tale it can be stated that the tales 'Briar Rose' (usually called *'Sleeping Beauty'), *'Cinderella', 'The Frog King', 'Snow White', and 'Little Red Riding Hood' have inspired the greatest number of poets. For the most part, these poems carry those exact titles, thus indicating from the outset that the poem will occupy itself with a traditional tale. But often the surprise comes immediately after the title, as for example in Charles Johnson's short poem 'Sleeping Beauty', where only the title is a direct allusion to the tale itself: 'A Beautiful Black man | Sleeping in a corner | His mind wandering into the deepest of | Darkness | His suffering eyes closed | His mouth open wide as if he | Wants to eat up the White world | And spit it out into the hand | of the White man and then | wake up.' The harmless title had clearly conjured up the image of the sleeping princess, only to be utterly destroyed by this social wake-up call. Another short poem entitled 'Ella of the Cinders' by Mary Blake French also debunks the passive world of the fairy-tale character Cinderella: 'I am not physically perfect: | I have no spherical symmetry. | I need no Prince Charming to awaken me. | I am fully conscious of your happily-ever-after! | My feet grow large to break your glass slippers; | I shall use the shivered glass for my own collage.' These few lines represent numerous poems that address the emancipatory goals of independence for modern women.

The poems based on 'The Frog King' centre primarily on transformations with an obvious emphasis on sexual matters. A few lines out of Anne Sexton's poem 'The Frog Prince' show to what grotesque imagery some of the reinterpretations might lead: 'Frog has no nerves. | Frog is as old as a cockroach. | Frog is my father's genitals. | Frog is a malformed doorknob. | Frog is a soft bag of green. | The moon will not have him. | The sun wants to shut off | like a light bulb. | At the sight of him | the stone washes itself in a tub. | The crow thinks he's an apple | and drops a worm in. | At the feel of frog | the touch-me-nots explode | like electric slugs. | Slime will have him. | Slime has made him a house.' But Sexton can also be much more realistic and less repulsive, as for example in the last few lines of her long poem about Snow White. Her evil stepmother is just dancing herself to death in the red-hot iron shoes, and 'Meanwhile Snow White held court, rolling her china-blue doll eyes open and shut | and sometimes referring to her mirror | as women do.' The question about and wish for beauty appear to be indestructible.

Other fairy tales that have found their way into modern poetry with somewhat less frequency are 'Hansel and Gretel', 'Rapunzel', 'Rumpelstiltskin', and 'Snow White and Rose Red'. Those are also the fairy tales best known in the English-speaking world. While in German poetry a few additional tales appear, the ones mentioned here are dealt with the most. In both languages there are also a few poems about Hans Christian *Andersen's two best-known tales of 'The Emperor's New Clothes' and 'The *Princess and the Pea' by such authors as Rolf Haufs, Maurice Lindsay, Christoph *Meckel, Paul Muldoon, Gerda Penfold, Jane Shore, Carolyn Zonailo, etc. A poem by Joy Kogowa with the first line being identical with its title, may serve as an example: 'I think I am that fabled princess | Who could not sleep | Upon layers of soft mattresses | Because of that one hard pea beneath | And I am wondering, my love, | If we will discover | That you are that prince | Who sought me. | For if you are not | Then I am a silly saint | And you are a bed of nails.' What all of the authors of fairy-tale poetry seem to have taken to heart is an aphorism by Elias Canetti from the year 1943: 'A closer study of fairy tales would teach us what we can still expect from the world.' Collectively

their poems acknowledge that modern life is not a fairy-tale existence and point out disenchantments everywhere. But by doing so they offer the hope that people will learn from their experiences and from the fairy tales which have couched them in such poetic language. The interplay of traditional fairy tales and innovative fairy-tale poems certainly results in a meaningful process of effective communication.   WM

Beaumont, Jean Marie, and Carlson, Claudia, *The Poets' Grimm: 20th Century Poems from Grimm Fairy Tales* (2003).

Bechtolsheim, Barbara von, 'Die Brüder Grimm neu schreiben: Zeitgenössische Märchengedichte amerikanischer Frauen' (Diss., Stanford University, 1987).

Horn, Katalin, 'Heilserwartung im Märchen und ihre Spiegelung in einer Auswahl moderner Lyrik', *Neophilologus*, 73 (1989).

Hösle, Johannes, 'Volkslied, Märchen und moderne Lyrik', *Akzente*, 7 (1960).

McClatchy, J. D. (ed.), *Anne Sexton: The Artist and her Critics* (1978).

Mieder, Wolfgang (ed.), *Grimms Märchen—modern: Prosa, Gedichte, Karikaturen* (1979).

Mieder, Wolfgang (ed.), *Mädchen, pfeif auf den Prinzen! Märchengedichte von Günter Grass bis Sarah Kirsch* (1983).

Mieder, Wolfgang (ed.), *Disenchantments: An Anthology of Modern Fairy Tale Poetry* (1985).

Mieder, Wolfgang, *Tradition and Innovation in Folk Literature* (1987).

Ostriker, Alicia, 'The Thieves of Language: Women Poets and Revisionist Mythmaking', *Signs* (1982–3).

Pogány, Willy (1882–1955) Hungarian-born artist; distinguished painter, illustrator, muralist, architect, stage designer, film art director, sculptor; naturalized US citizen, 1921. Pogány illustrated more than 100 books and was noted for his stylistic variety. While living in London, he produced—designed and executed—what have been regarded as masterpieces: Coleridge's, *Rime of the Ancient Mariner* (1910) and the Wagnerian trilogy: *Tannhäuser* (1911), *Parsifal* (1912), and *Lohengrin* (1913). An anecdote about Pogány notes that when he was preparing for his departure from London and immigration to America, he illustrated 'Story of Hiawatha' (*c*.1914), an exceptional panoramically designed text. He also did singular illustrations of traditional fairy tales such as *'Little Red Riding Hood' and *'Cinderella', and provided the artwork for W. Jenkyn Thomas's *The Welsh Fairy Book* (1907) and Nandor Pogány's *Magyar Fairy Tales from Old Hungarian Legends* (1930). SS

Pogodin, Radi (1925–93) Outstanding Russian children's writer, author of philosophical and existential fairy tales. Unlike most Soviet fairy tales, Pogodin's are totally free from ideology and didacticism. He makes use of the traditional Russian fairy-tale patterns and characters, blending them with contemporary settings and allowing ordinary children to experience adventures in fairy-tale countries. He also employs elements from animal tales, both using traditional figures, such as a mouse, and inventing his own imaginary creatures. The central idea in his tales is the tension between the innocence and creative power of childhood and the burden and corruption of adulthood. MN

Nikolajeva, Maria, 'On the Edge of Childhood', *Bookbird*, 35 (1997).

Polívka, Jiří (1858–1933) Czech folklorist and professor of Slavic studies at Karl University in Prague. He wrote several major studies of Slavic folk tales such as *Slavic Fairy Tales* (1932), in which he paid great attention to the narrative form of the folk tale. Together with his German colleague Johannes Bolte, he edited the highly significant, five-volume annotated study of the *Grimms' fairy tales, *Anmerkungen zu den 'Kinder- und Hausmärchen'* (1913–32). MN

Pontiggia, Giuseppe (1934–2003) Italian writer and critic who, from the start of his literary career, showed an interest in fairy tales, publishing 'La morte in banca' ('The Death in the Bank') in 1959 (republished in 1979 with six other short stories). 'Cichita la scimmia parlante' ('Cichita the Talking Monkey') is a modern fairy tale originally published in 1979, in which Cichita comes to the financial rescue of the circus she belongs to by becoming a talking sensation.

Bandits kidnap her for ransom, but Cichita manages to escape and have the bandits arrested.

Pontiggia edited and prefaced Carlo *Collodi's *I racconti delle fate* (*Fairy Tales*), with illustrations by Gustave Doré. His novels *Il giocatore invisibile* (*The Invisible Player*, 1978), and *La grande sera* (*The Great Evening*, 1989) won the Campiello and Strega prizes, respectively. The author's fondness for the fantastic was still apparent in his latest work, *L'Isola volante* (*The Flying Island*, 1996). GD

popular song and fairy tales Popular song is a short vocal item whose melodic line is performable by singers of all standards—from amateur to professional. Thus, an important element in what makes a song popular is the ease with which it can be sung. Closely allied to this is the nature of the words—a successful fusing of text and music frequently produces the most memorable songs. Yet another ingredient is the character of the song's accompaniment. As the European art song developed, German romantic composers especially cultivated a particularly fluent style in establishing and maintaining the mood of a song through the piano accompaniment.

1. History

Singing is the most natural form of all human music-making, with its origins in prehistoric times. Most early surviving music dates from around the 13th century, being a variety of church music, and secular songs, notated either by clergy, or aristocratic laity educated by clergy. The 13th century also saw the rise of the troubadours—singers and poets, who frequently performed their own material at important court functions, or for the delight of a favoured lady. Originating in France, the art of the troubadour spread quickly throughout Europe, helped immeasurably, no doubt, by the great mobility of knights and their armies *en route* to the crusades.

By the late Middle Ages, part-singing (a group of singers with one or more of its number assigned to a series of individual parts, which when performed together create a satisfying whole), had developed to the point where it was a fashionable social pastime. This is not to overlook the evolving importance of religious choral music, which for many Christian denominations was central to their acts of worship. Meanwhile, stage plays in late Renaissance Britain often helped individual secular songs achieve popularity through the widespread habit of inserting them into the drama. William *Shakespeare made extensive use of music in his plays, including a great quantity of song.

2. Appearance of songs with supernatural-related texts

As the Age of Reason dawned (18th century), the Italian solo art song was already well established. Later, during the 19th century, the form found its greatest expression in Germany and to some extent in Russia also. This was a time when poems dealing in supernatural elements began to interest composers. Schubert's *Erlkönig* (*The Erl King*) of 1817 is a setting of *Goethe's celebrated ballad, concerning a young boy who is lured to his untimely end by an evil goblin. The same composer's *Der Alpenjäger* (*The Alpine Hunter*), another Goethe setting, invokes the spirit of the mountains.

3. Nursery and cradle songs

A point worth bearing in mind is that many leading composers of the 18th, 19th, and 20th centuries wrote cradle songs—*Mozart, Schubert, *Schumann, Brahms (his *Wiegenlied*, Op. 49 No. 4, being especially famous), and Richard *Strauss. The Russian composer Modest Mussorgsky (1839–81) set a cycle of five nursery songs. (He also composed a setting of Goethe's *The Flea*.)

4. Folk song and community songs

The folk song tradition is widespread throughout Europe and Russia, being most often at its strongest in rural and industrial communities. For centuries it relied for its continuation on transmission from parent to child. Many leading composers in the 20th century have turned to arranging such material. Manuel de Falla's collection *Seven Spanish Folk Songs* contains a cradle song, 'Nana', as does Béla *Bartók's Hungarian collection, *Village Scenes*.

The arrival of printed collections, as distinct from the arrangements mentioned above, indicated that countries were becoming more aware of their cultural heritage, including indigenous folk or fairy tales. With the absorption of traditional airs into the public consciousness, together with a heavy reliance on contemporary popular commercial song, community singing arose in the early 20th century, attaining an especial vogue in the United States, Britain, and Australia. During the First World War, in both America and Britain, the practice was a popular pastime within the armed services.

The movement went on to gain impetus with the publication of special song books. In Britain it reached a peak of popularity, helping to draw vast crowds to public events such as in 1926 when 10,000 people attended London's Royal Albert Hall to inaugurate the Daily Express Community Singing Movement. The repertoire was, by and large, an amorphous collection of traditional airs, interspersed with hymns and carols, sea shanties, and Negro spirituals, including songs which had fairy-tale-style narratives, such as 'Old King Cole', 'Who Killed Cock Robin?', or the nursery rhyme 'Hot Cross Buns'.

5. The 20th century

Through the continuing demand for pantomime in the 20th century, many popular songs have found themselves allied to fairy tales, while not in themselves dealing with the subject. Thus a pantomime about *'Cinderella' or, say, *'Jack and the Beanstalk', might not contain a vocal item which relates to the story as such. A good example of this is the 1937 Walt *Disney film *Snow White and the Seven Dwarfs*, although it could be argued that the song, 'Some Day my Prince Will Come', is part of the narrative.

Elsewhere, fairy-tale references were to be found, including a show with a fairy-tale title, *Cinderella on Broadway* (1920), and a song, 'Cinderella stay in my arms', written by Michael Carr and Jimmy Kennedy in 1938. Before that, in 1933, Kennedy, in collaboration with Harry Castling, wrote what became probably the most popular of all songs in the fairy-tale tradition: 'The Teddy Bears' Picnic'. The song has long been established as a 'classic', being a favourite among young and old alike.

A modern fairy tale created especially for popular song was 'Rudolf the Red-Nosed Reindeer'. Based on a story by Robert L. May written in 1939, Rudolf the Red-Nosed Reindeer was fashioned into a song by Johnny Marks in 1949. An enduring favourite, especially at Christmas time, it first gained popularity with a recording made by the renowned American actor and singer Gene Autry. A similar tale of an animal disadvantaged by its physical appearance, yet who eventually wins acceptance, emerged with a song made famous by the British actor and dancer Tommy Steele in 1959. 'The Little White Bull', which he sang in the film, *Tommy the Toreador*, became one of his greatest hits. Hans Christian *Anderson's 'The *Ugly Duckling' found its way into song thanks to the 1952 film based on the life of the Danish writer of fairy tales. With music by Frank Loesser, the film *Hans Christian Andersen* starred the celebrated American comedian and singer, Danny Kaye.

The rise and eventual domination by 'pop' and 'beat' music in the last few decades has not tended to include the traditional fairy tale. Nevertheless, it continues to have a firm place in commercial ventures, as can be seen with the number of musical shows and films (such as *Beauty and the Beast* from Walt Disney Studios), based on such stories.   TH

Fischer-Dieskau, Dietrich, *Book of Lieder* (1976).
Gammond, Peter, *The Oxford Companion to Popular Music* (1991).
Goss, John (ed.), *Daily Express Community Song Book* (1927).
Larkin, Colin (ed.), *The Guinness Who's Who of Stage Musicals* (1994).
Sadie, Stanley, (ed.), *The New Grove Dictionary of Music and Musicians*, xvii (1980).

pornography and fairy tales While fairy tales were historically intended for audiences of all ages, the present-day assumption that fairy tales are the domain of childhood has led writers, artists, and film-makers to explore the potentials for 'adult' readings and creating of fairy tales, particularly with regard to sexuality and desire. A good deal of scholarship has examined eroticism in literary retellings of fairy tales, but little attention has been paid to the genre of hard-core pornographic films, many of which have borrowed the plots and imagery of traditional narratives; fairy tales, with their linear plots and flat characters, lend themselves easily to the pornographic film structure.

Fairy-tale pornography is a subtype of the broader category of the porn parody. While many porn parodies limit their reference to the target text to the title (i.e. *Beauty and the 14-Inch Beast*), other films engage more closely with the object of parody—especially the Disney version, if it exists. These porn parodies address the sexuality that Hollywood films often erase. Like other adult-oriented genres such as horror, fairy-tale pornography derives much of its power from invoking the frisson of 'innocent' stories of childhood and then subverting that perceived innocence through the display of explicit sexuality.   CT

Portuguese fairy tales *See* p. 479.

postcards and fairy tales Picture postcards were first introduced in Europe and North America during the 1890s. Given the popularity of fairy tales and the craze for picture postcards at the turn of the century, there were numerous fairy-tale postcards printed by international firms such as Birn Bros., Davidson Bros., Max Ettlinger & Co., C. W. Faulkner, S. Hildesheimer & Co., W. Mack, Misch & Stock, Raphael Tuck, Uvachrom, Valentine, and others. Cards were mainly sold in envelopes or in sets of six or twelve. Some fairy-tale postcards were signed, but most remained anonymous. Since payment for postcard illustration was very low and provided only supplementary income, women were more likely to accept the job. This was certainly the case in England, where the early illustrators were Hilda Miller

Portuguese fairy tales No one has yet written a history, definitive or otherwise, of Portuguese fairy tales ('histórias da Carochinha'), and studies of children's literature are a relatively recent development. Yet there is a wealth of material—incontrovertible evidence of a deep-rooted, vigorous tradition which parallels and frequently interacts with other popular genres such as the proverbial saying or the ballad—that demands commentary and analysis.

The earliest collection of stories in Portuguese dates back to the late 14th or early 15th century: the *Horto do Esposo* (*The Orchard of the Husband*), an exemplum collection in which we find some tales of devils, magicians, and spells. Portugal also has its own compilation of Aesopian fables in a 15th-century manuscript known as the *Fabulário Português* (*Portuguese Fable Book*). Many of these tales seem to have taken root in the collective consciousness—possibly as a direct consequence of the pulpit—and reappear later in collections of popular tales.

The current situation can be summed up as follows. Two distinct tendencies coexist and occasionally compete, at least in terms of readership. On the one hand, we find numerous translations into Portuguese from French, German, and English of the 'canonical' literary fairy tales. Ana de Castro Osório (1872–1935), described by some literary historians as the founder of Portuguese children's literature, collected traditional folklore and was also responsible for numerous translations of foreign authors including the Brothers *Grimm and Hans Christian *Andersen. In fact, translations of the Grimms and Andersen, who himself visited and wrote about Portugal, are still being produced in abundance, either as single tales or in compilations. The fairy tales of Charles *Perrault are also found in countless editions, one of the most recent being the lavishly illustrated *Três contos de Perrault* (1997), translated by Luiza Neto Jorge and Manuel Joao Gomes. Of the three tales selected for translation, 'A Pele de Burro' (*'Donkey-Skin') has been rendered in verse, while 'O Barba Azul' (*'Bluebeard') and 'O Polegarzinho' (*'Little Tom Thumb') are in prose.

The tales of the comtesse de *Ségur, at one time extremely fashionable, were re-edited up to the mid-1980s, but are now less widely read, having been displaced by mystery and adventure stories. Lewis *Carroll has also attracted some attention: *Alice's Adventures in Wonderland* was first translated in 1936 under the title *Alice no pais das fadas* (*Alice in the Country of Fairies*), an abridged edition intended for young children. Successive translations of varying quality and length have followed, and the Portuguese fortunes of Alice have recently been the subject of critical essays by Glória Bastos and José António Gomes.

On the other hand, there exists a substantial corpus of traditional folk tales in Portuguese. Little is really known about Portuguese fairy tales outside Portugal—some might even argue within the country as well—because of the language barrier and as a result of 'a continuing failure to archive, catalogue and publicize the available material' (Cardigos, 1996). Where tales have been collected, published, and analysed, this has been very much the labour of love of a handful of intellectual pioneers writing at the end of the 19th century or in the early years of the 20th. Several major collections exist, but these were published in academic journals or scholarly editions never intended for the lay reader and are now out of print. But four scholars in particular deserve mention. The works of Ana de Castro Osório continue to be published, even as recently as 1997, making traditional Portuguese stories available to new generations of readers. The same holds true of Adolfo Coelho (1847–1919), author of *Contos populares portugueses* (*Popular Portuguese Tales*, 1879); Zófimo Consiglieri Pedroso (1851–1910), compiler of *Contos populares portugueses* (*Popular Portuguese Tales*, 1910); and Teófilo Braga (1842–1924), author of *Contos tradicionais do povo portugués* (*Traditional Tales of the Portuguese People*, first published in two volumes in 1883).

Adolfo Coelho and Consiglieri Pedroso are also notable, and their works have been widely disseminated. Thirty of Pedroso's 500 or so unpublished *Portuguese Folk-Tales* appeared in English before they were published in Portugal, while Coelho's tales appeared in London six years later under the title *Tales of Old Lusitania from the Folklore of Portugal*. Many of the Portuguese stories are variants of internationally known fairy tales. The narratives collected by Pedroso derived from the Aesopian tradition, the Renard Cycle, and La Fontaine, among other sources. They include a Portuguese variant of *'Beauty and the Beast', 'A menina e o bicho' ('The Maiden and the Beast'), in which first the beast, then the maiden dies. Pedroso's 'Os dois pequenos e a bruxa' ('The Two Children and the Witch'), also published as 'Os meninos perdidos' in Coelho's collection, is obviously a version of *'Hansel and Gretel'. Pedroso's 'A rainha orgulhosa' ('The Vain Queen') and 'A estalajadeira' ('The Innkeeper') display a marked resemblance to *'Snow White'. Pedroso's tale 'As tias' ('The Aunts'), known as 'As fiandeiras' in Braga, has several points of contact with *'Rumpelstilt-skin'. 'Branca Flor' ('White Flower'), which exists in at least 13 Portuguese versions, has been identified as 'The Girl as Helper in the Hero's Flight' (AT 313, Cardigos, 1996). The same author's 'A princesa que nao queria casar com o pai' ('The Princess Who Did Not Want to Marry her Father') is a Portuguese example of 'Donkey-Skin', who becomes 'Pele-de-cavalo' ('Horse-Skin') in Coelho. *'Cinderella' is known as 'The Hearth Cat' or 'A gata borralheira' in Pedroso, and Pedroso has his own version of *'Little Red Riding Hood', 'A menina do chapelinho vermelho'. 'Cara de boi' ('Ox Face') has strong echoes of the Grimms' *'Rapunzel'.

Nevertheless, not all of the fairy tales match the types classified by Antti *Aarne and Stith Thompson in *The Types of the Folktale*. Some may well be exclusive to Portugal, while others are certainly unusual in their degree of deviation from the established version. Portuguese scholars are now beginning to investigate these questions; the last decade has seen a handful of theses on Portuguese fairy tales or related topics, and the journal *Estudos de Literatura Oral*, published by the University of the Algarve, seems set to stimulate fresh interest in Portuguese folklore.   PAOB

Bastos, Glória, *A escrita para crianças em Portugal no Século XIX* (1997).

Cardigos, Isabel, 'Stories about Time in Four Fairytales from Portuguese Speaking Countries', *Portuguese Studies*, 11 (1995).

Cardigos, Isabel, *In and Out of Enchantment: Blood Symbolism and Gender in Portuguese Fairytales* (1996).

Gomes, José António, *Literatura para crianças—alguns percursos* (1991).

Gomes, José António, *Towards a History of Portuguese Children's and Youth Literature* (1998).

Lopes, Ana Cristina Macário, 'Literatura culta e literatura tradicional de transmissao oral: a bipartiçao da esfra literária', *Cadernos de Literatura*, 15 (1983).

(1876–1939), Millicent Sowerby (1878–1967), Susan Pearse (1878–1959), Margaret *Tarrant (1881–1959), Lilian Govey (1886–1974), and Joyce Mercer (1896–1965). Both Tarrant and Sowerby, gifted artists, illustrated editions of the *Grimms' fairy tales. Another important illustrator, Charles *Folkard (1878–1963), had his illustrations for *Grimms' Fairy Tales* (1911) made into picture postcards. In Germany Otto Kubel had his oil paintings of the Grimms' tales transformed into picture postcards.

Throughout the 20th century artists in all countries worked in different modes to produce fairy tales for postcards. Many French photographers, especially at the beginning of the 20th century, used posed live characters and animals in photographs to illustrate *Perrault's tales. Scenes from the Épinal fairy-tale broadsides were published as postcards. There are art deco cards, black-and-white ink drawings, woodcuts, silhouettes, and comic-strip cards as well as advertisements for products and department stores printed as chromolithographs. In the latter half of the 20th century reproductions have been made of famous illustrated books, and theme parks and films have printed fairy-tale postcards to complement their products. Cards from the beginning of the 20th century have become valuable collectors' items and are remarkable for their originality and exquisite artistic qualities. Among the best artists are: Mabel Lucie *Attwell (UK), G. L. Barnes (UK), Fritz Baumgarten (Germany), Margret Boris (The Netherlands), Frances Brundage (USA), Oskar Herrfurth (Germany), Paul Hey (Germany), Ernst Kutzer (Austria), Jenny *Nyström (Sweden), Heinz Pingerra (Austria), Bernhard Tohn (Germany), Louis Wain (UK), and Lisbeth *Zwerger (Austria).   JZ

Cope, Dawn and Peter, *Red Riding Hood's Favorite Fairy Tales* (1981).
Mashburn, J. L., *Fantasy Postcards* (1996).
Willoughby, Martin, *A History of Postcards* (1992).

Potócki, Jan (1761–1815) Polish folklorist/ethnologist, linguist, adventurer, and author. His works include *Histoire primitive des peuples de la Russie* (*Early History of the Russian*

Peoples, 1802) and reports on his philological/historical research in Turkey, Egypt, Morocco, the Caucasus, and Mongolia, prefiguring modern anthropological stances by approaching cultures via their own ideas and values. Potócki's novel *The Manuscript Found in Saragossa* (*Manuscrit trouvé à Saragosse*) reflects his cross-cultural interests. It was originally written in French and published in fragments in the early 19th century, and its frame tale surrounds Gothic horror, picaresque, comic, erotic, and moral stories. Described as modern, postmodern, non-realistic, Gothic, and romance, *Saragossa* reflects Potócki's use of *The *Arabian Nights* for structure, theme, characters, and narrative. It inspired the film *The Saragossa Manuscript* (*Rękopis znaleziony w Saragossie*, 1965), a French television miniseries, Romanian- and English-language plays, and an episode of an Italian television series.   PG

Potter, Beatrix (1866–1943) Author of the 'Peter Rabbit' books. Her first book, *The Tailor of Gloucester*, printed privately in 1902 and published by Warne in 1903, is in effect a fairy story: an old tailor has his incomplete work finished on Christmas Eve, not by the traditional brownies, but by grateful mice. *The Fairy Caravan*, her penultimate book, was published in America in 1929, in England in 1952. A long and rambling tale about an animals' travelling circus, it has two inset fairy tales, 'Fairy Horseshoes' and 'The Fairy in the Oak'.   GA

Pourrat, Henri (1887–1959) Collector-author of French folk and fairy tales. Born in the town of Ambert, Pourrat spent 50 years amassing regional tales of his native Auvergne. As with *Perrault and the *Grimms, he wanted to record and preserve folk heritage. But unlike Perrault, who transcribed but a dozen tales for aristocrats of literary salons, Pourrat in his *Trésor des contes* (*Treasury of Tales*) passed on 1,009 rustic stories for everyday readers—an audience somewhat closer to the bourgeois public of the Grimms.

Ironically, it is to ill health that we owe his astounding collection, for tuberculosis at the age of 18 prevented him from pursuing a career as an agricultural engineer. Thereafter, he passed his sedentary mornings resting and writing, with more physical afternoons devoted to walking the countryside and interviewing storytellers. From them he collected some 30,000 regionalisms, which he recorded in a succession of notebooks and later used to enrich his numerous essays, folk-tale collections, and historical romances.

Pourrat achieved fame with his first novel, *Gaspard des montagnes* (*Gaspard from the Mountains*, 1922–32), which won the Prix Figaro (1922) and the French Academy's Grand Prix for Best Novel (1931). Each of its four volumes spans seven nights in which 'Old Marie' tells numerous tales of courageous country folk who outwit Evil. The frame story for this 'folk Scheherazade' is set after the French Revolution, and is based on several versions of the folk tales 'Les Yeux rouges' ('Red Eyes') and 'La Main coupée' ('The Severed Hand'). Alone one night during her parents' absence, Anne-Marie Grange discovers that an intruder has entered her Auvergne farmhouse. She outwits the thief by cutting off his hand, and he swears vengeance. Seasons later, she is unwittingly married to this violent bandit chief, who eventually steals away their child born of her rape. Throughout a thousand pages of harrowing and melodramatic adventures, Anne-Marie's cousin Gaspard is her constant support. Chaste, star-crossed lovers of sorts, this couple's strength, spirituality, and folk wisdom incarnate the ennobling simplicity of rustic life.

After *Gaspard*, Pourrat continued to write extensively about the Auvergne. Recognized as a major French author during the Second World War, he was awarded the Prix Goncourt in 1944 for *Le Vent de mars* (*March Wind*), an essay concerning wartime Auvergne. But it is *The Treasury of Tales* (1948–62) that sealed his reputation as a folklorist. Published at a time when postwar France was battling rising fascism, its 13 volumes incarnate what Pourrat termed 'the original mythology of the French people'. The tales are divided into categories about fairies, the devil, bandits, village life, the mad and the wise, beasts, and love and marriage. As complete as this thousand-tale collection may seem, however, the *Treasury* never attained prominence among the 'academic' folklorists. Indeed, it occasioned a rather violent debate. First, ethnologists who had published regional folk tales had commented on the rarity of those in the Auvergne: they were sceptical that 'new *Mother Goose tales' continued to be told. Pourrat, in his comprehensive picture of regional folklore, did indeed include not only stories, but fables, proverbs, jokes, and songs from oral sources (some 106 storytellers and 86 singers) as well as printed matter (regional chapbooks, almanacs, texts from Rabelais to La Fontaine). Like Perrault and the Grimms, Pourrat thus found himself at the crossroads of the existing traditions of the oral folk tale and literary fairy tale. But in trying to transform these genres through ingenious methods of translating their orality, he committed two major 'sins'. Unlike the academics who scrupulously recorded and published their sources along with the tales, Pourrat resolutely kept such documentation for his personal records. He hoped this 'anonymity' would impart a timelessness to the tales, instead of reducing them to dry accounts told by a certain person of a certain age at a certain time. Secondly, the ethnologists felt he violated the sacred rules of 'never omit anything, never add anything' when transcribing sources. This is precisely what Pourrat could not bring himself to do. Rather than strictly recording tales told by, say, ageing lacemakers, Pourrat was faithful to their spirit by inventing an oral, 'rustic style' uniquely his own. He recreated the atmosphere of storytelling itself in confidential asides to the reader and reproduction of sounds, smells, and tactile sensations: the clicking of needles or the ringing of the angelus, the aroma of freshly mown hay, the humidity of a late-summer evening. He would also combine several versions of a folk tale, flesh out psychological portraits, and pepper his stylized narratives with colloquialisms and minute details of local colour. Because of these modifications to original source material, critics regarded him more as an author than folklorist, and felt that his attention to detail worked against his goal of rendering the tales timeless. They also criticized his censuring of data: the devout Pourrat downplayed the bawdy or anticlerical elements of fabliaux-inspired tales, and eliminated verses of songs when translating from Occitan (a dialect of Provençal) into standard French.

Today, Pourrat's ethno-literary ode to the Auvergne is undergoing a long-overdue reappraisal. A journal dedicated to Pourrat studies, as well as new French editions of the *Treasury* and an English translation, are now available to the public. His celebration of 19th-century peasant life, with its 20th-century post-war agenda of revitalizing the French national spirit, is now universally acclaimed as a milestone in French folklore studies.　　　　　MLE

Bricout, Bernadette, *Le Savoir et la saveur: Henri Pourrat et Le Trésor des contes* (1992).

Cahiers Henri Pourrat (1981–present).

Gardes, Roger, *Un écrivain au travail: Henri Pourrat* (1980).

Plessy, Bernard, *Au pays de Gaspard des montagnes* (1981).

Zipes, Jack, 'Henri Pourrat and the Tradition of Perrault and the Brothers Grimm', in *The Brothers Grimm: From Enchanted Forests to the Modern World* (1988).

Powell, Michael (1905–90) and **Pressburger, Emeric** (1902–88) Film-makers whose company twice turned its attention to producing cinematic works inspired by literary tales. For *The *Red Shoes* (UK, 1948) the idea of creating an original ballet that was pure film and could never be reproduced on stage was the reason for the whole project. The result was *The Ballet of the Red Shoes*. Derived from *Andersen's story of the girl whose new shoes dance her to death, it compresses numerous changes of scene and time into 13 minutes, and uses special-effects techniques to show her dancing in two places at once, or coming down from a leap so slowly that she floats. The story filling the other two hours parallels this central ballet: a young student becomes

a great ballerina but is driven to suicide when forced to choose between love of her husband and love of her art.

Three years later Powell and Pressburger followed up this cine-ballet with a cine-opera, *The Tales of Hoffmann* (UK, 1951), but this time used existing texts. Adapted from *Offenbach's operatic version of a play based on the life and stories of E. T. A. *Hoffmann, it starts with a prologue in which Hoffmann, having just had old wounds reopened, offers to tell the students in a tavern three tales of the follies he has committed in the name of love. In the first, as a very young man, he is tricked into an infatuation with Olympia, only to find out eventually that she is merely a mechanical doll. In the second, now older, he is enslaved by a beautiful courtesan, Giulietta, who gains possession of his soul by capturing his reflection, then goes off with another man. Finally, having reached maturity, he falls in love with Antonia, a singer dying of consumption, who promises him she will not sap her strength by performing again; however, she is misled by a quack doctor, breaks her promise, and dies in Hoffmann's arms. The epilogue shows how Hoffmann, seeing his audience spellbound, realizes that his true destiny is to be a poet, not a lover.　　　　　TAS

Pratchett, Terry (1948–2015) English writer of comic fantasy novels. He worked as a journalist and then as a press officer between 1965 and 1987, when he became a full-time writer. Most of his novels are intended primarily for adults, but like much popular fantasy they also have a strong appeal to adolescent readers. Stories, themes, and motifs are drawn from very diverse areas of history, literature, popular culture, and traditional story, whether the novels are set in the Discworld he has invented as the setting for most of his adult novels, or whether the fantastic irrupts into the everyday modern world, as in his trilogy for young readers, *Truckers* (1989), *Diggers* (1990), and *Wings* (1991). Amongst his many inventive and engaging rereadings of literature, culture, and society, Pratchett has presented readers with playful and at times parodic versions of

Homer and Dante (*Eric*, 1989), of Shake-speare (*Wyrd Sisters*, 1988, and *Lords and Ladies*, 1992), of *The Phantom of the Opera* (*Maskerade*, 1995), and the origins of pop music in the 1950s (*Soul Music*, 1994). Specifically fantastic elements are drawn extensively from myths, legends, and fairy tales, and borrowings or allusions appear throughout the novels. Part of the game is to draw attention to the processes of borrowing and refashioning, as when a character in *Guards! Guards!* (1989) explains an item of knowledge as 'Well known folk myth'.

Folk-tale motifs pervade the novels, but their function is usually comic or ironic. *Guards! Guards!*, for example, pivots on a legend about the finding of a descendant of a vanished royal line, and this heir to the throne is easily identified by readers because he is an orphan possessing a special sword and a birthmark. He himself never realizes the truth, however, remaining in his humble station and so exemplifying a point Pratchett made overtly in his note to the 1992 revision of *Carpet People* (originally 1971): 'the *real* concerns of fantasy ought to be about not having battles, and doing *without* kings.' The Truckers trilogy has elements of the folk-tale quest narrative, but is largely a parody of Tolkienesque 'high fantasy', with touches of science fiction. The first volume, *Truckers*, introduces a world on the periphery of human society inhabited by nomes, small beings whose various social formations reflect and parody the familiar human 'real' world (the spelling foregrounds their difference from the 'gnomes' of fairy tale). Through his depiction of the nomes Pratchett critiques familiar social systems and behaviours, especially customs associated with religion, class, and gender. He does this by means of parodic citation of familiar texts and discourses and by playing with signs and meanings. The nomes have a society, culture, and religion which is a bricolage of discourses misappropriated from department store signs and advertising, mixed with parodic forms of biblical and religious discourse, philosophical and pseudo-scientific discourse, and clichéd everyday utterances. The parody draws attention to the constructedness of the represented world and, through that, to the ways in which representations of the world outside the text are similarly constructed and ascribed with meanings.

The novels which make most particular and extensive use of folk and fairy tale are *Witches Abroad* (1991) and *Hogfather* (1996). *Hogfather* can in part be read as a manifesto about the value and functions of fairy tales within culture. The Hogfather of the title is a Santa Claus figure in danger of disappearing because of the pervasive failure of belief under the hegemony of rationalism. Against this threat, the novel's protagonists assert a kind of ontology of the fantastic whereby belief brings concepts into being. Death, for example, whose character has evolved through the Discworld series into the embodiment of a deeply humanistic view of existence and the imagination, asserts that 'Humans need fantasy to be human. To be the place where the falling angel meets the rising ape.' The point is to be able to imagine a different world, other possibilities. Thus elsewhere in the novel, Death interrogates and dismisses *Andersen's 'The Little Match Girl' because its recourse to religious consolation constitutes an evasion of social justice and responsibility. In a more light-hearted way, the novel mocks the rationalizing binary opposites of structural anthropology: if there is a Tooth Fairy who collects there can also be a Verruca Gnome who delivers, and all it takes to bring the latter into being is a linguistic formulation of the idea of it.

Earlier, in *Witches Abroad*, Pratchett had examined the more negative possibilities of fairy tales, their capacity to be implicit purveyors of ideology within powerful teleological structures. In this novel, Lilith, an evil-minded magic-worker, has set herself up as a fairy godmother and compels people to live their lives as if they were fairy-tale characters. The frame tale is a version of *'Cinderella', with various other tales incorporated, from classics such as *'Little Red Riding Hood' to modern tales like *The *Wizard of Oz*. Three 'good' witches set out to oppose Lilith, striving to bring about endings other than the traditional ones, and hence striving to avert the ideological implications of the tales. Fairy-tale schemata have their own momentum, however, so on their way to a successful outcome the three witches must resist becoming absorbed into Lilith's version of the narrative, whereby she is the 'good' one and they are assigned the adversarial function and are hence destined for defeat.

Beyond the comic turns and surface humour, Pratchett's refashioning of familiar fairy tales addresses large themes: the responsibility of authors in shaping stories, the role of readers in challenging the grand cultural narratives which inhere in fairy tales, and finally the central importance of creativity and imagination to the humanity of human beings.　　　　　JAS

> Broderick, Kirsten, 'Past and Present: The Uses of History in Children's Fiction', *Papers: Explorations into Children's Literature*, 6.3 (1996).
> Butler, Andrew, James, Edward, and Mendlesohn, Farah, *Terry Pratchett: Guilty of Literature* (2000).
> Stephens, John, 'Gender, Genre and Children's Literature', *Signal*, 79 (1996).
> Stephens, John, 'Not Unadjacent to a Play about a Scottish King: Terry Pratchett Retells *Macbeth*', *Papers: Explorations into Children's Literature*, 7.2 (1997).
> Stephens, John, and McCallum, Robyn, *Retelling Stories, Framing Culture: Traditional Story and Metanarratives in Children's Literature* (1998).

Pratt, Tim (1976–) Prolific, award-winning American science fiction and fantasy writer and poet, and senior editor at *Locus* magazine. His debut short-story collection was *Little Gods* (2003) and his first novel, *The Strange Adventures of Rangergirl* (2005). His series of urban fantasies featuring indomitable sorcerer Marla Mason began with *Blood Engines* (2007) and is ongoing, with seven more books, including the online prequel novella *Bone Shop* (2009). His prose often features magical characters and themes, but his titles sometimes reference the genre as in 'Unfair Tale' (a version of **Sleeping Beauty*') and 'Fairy Tale of Oakland'.　　PG

Préchac, Jean de (1676–?) French writer. Author of numerous novels, Préchac published *Contes moins contes que les autres* (*Tales Less Tale-like than the Others*, 1698) at the height of the 'vogue' of fairy tales in late 17th-century France. Reflecting Préchac's excellent court connections, his 'Sans Parangon' ('Without Equal') and 'La Reine des fées' ('Queen of the fairies') are panegyrics of Louis XIV's court. 'Without Equal' contains an allegory about many of the high points of Louis's reign, including the construction of Versailles, which is erected by fairy magic; and 'La Reine des fées' describes the banishment of bad fairies and the praise of good fairies, who are none other than prominent aristocratic women of Préchac's day. These tales are extreme examples of ways the fairy-tale form could be used to promote official propaganda. Préchac is the first French writer of fairy tales to make such explicit and sustained allusions to historical reality, a technique frequently employed during the 18th century (albeit more often in the satirical mode).　　LCS

Prelusky, Jack (1940–) American writer of children's poetry who was named the inaugural winner of the Children's Poet Laureate by the Poetry Foundation in 2006. He has published over 50 poetry collections, and several of his picture books such as *The Dragons Are Singing Tonight* (1993), illustrated by Peter Sis, *Monday's Troll* (1996), illustrated by Peter Sis, *The Beauty of the Beast from the Animal Kingdom* (1997), illustrated by Meilo So, and *Awful Ogre's Awful Day* (2001), illustrated by Paul *Zelinsky, *The Wizard* (2007), illustrated by Brandon Dorman, and *Awful Ogre Running Wild* (2008), illustrated by Paul Zelinsky, are based on fairy tales or have fairy-tale motifs. Prelusky's style is marked by inventive word play, so that in *The Dragons Are Singing Tonight*, which has a series of poems about dragons of every size and colour, he writes: 'If you don't believe in dragons, | It is curiously true | That the dragons you disparage | Choose to not to believe in you.' In *Awful Ogre's Awful Day*, he transforms the ogre from a fearful giant into a humane creature by describing an ordinary day in the life of an ordinary ogre in short verses. Most of his poems connected to fairy-tale characters depend on the clever subversion of stereotypes and of the general expectations of young readers. JZ

Preus, Margi (no dates available) An American writer of stories, plays, opera libretti, and novels for young adults. Many of her works, such as *The Peace Bell* (2008) and *Heart of a Samurai* (2010), have historical settings. This is also the case with her remarkable fairy-tale novel, *West of the Moon* (2014), influenced by the great Nordic folklore tradition of *Asbjørnsen and Moe. Preus focuses on a feisty young girl named Astri, bent on escaping to America from deplorable conditions in the rural regions of 19th-century Norway. She recounts Astri's adventures in the first person with humour and gusto and depicts how this remarkable girl overcomes numerous obstacles to save her sister and make her way to America, the land of her dreams. Not only does Preus endow Astri with great imagination and wit, but she also shows how Astri creatively uses Norwegian folk and fairy tales to give herself hope. JZ

Preussler, Otfried (1923–2013) German author of children's books. During his years as a schoolteacher and headmaster in Bavaria, Preussler wrote a series of popular children's books using traditional fairy-tale characters and motifs, including *Der kleine Wassermann* (*The Little Water Sprite*, 1956), *Die kleine Hexe* (*The Little Witch*, 1957), *Der Räuber Hotzenplotz* (*The Robber Hotzenplotz*, 1962), and *Das kleine Gespenst* (*The Little Ghost*, 1966). Demythified traditional folk-tale and fairy-tale villains are the main protagonists of these stories. The child-sized, spunky, and zany witches, robbers, and ghosts, who are stripped of the dark, evil, and threatening side of their character, are entertaining rather than threatening. Ample use of suspense, slapstick, and situation comedy further endeared these books to children so that they remained best-sellers for several decades.

To a somewhat older audience Preussler is perhaps best known for *Krabat* (*The Satanic Mill*, 1971), a fantastic tale of suspense and romance about a miller's apprentice who succeeds in breaking the evil spell surrounding the mill through friendship and love. Preussler received the Deutscher Jugendbuchpreis (German Prize for Children's and Youth Literature) twice; once in 1963 for *The Robber Hotzenplotz* and again in 1972 for *Krabat*, which was adapted for the cinema as a Czech animated feature film with the title *The Sorcerer's Apprentice* (1978) and as a German live-action film with the title *Krabat* (2008). EMM

Baumgärtner, Clemens Alfred, and Pleticha, Heinrich, *ABC und Abenteuer. Texte und Dokumente zur Geschichte des deutschen Kinder- und Jugendbuches* (2 vols., 1985).
Doderer, Klaus, *Zwischen Trümmern und Wohlstand. Literatur der Jugend 1945–1960* (1988).
Scharioth, Barbara, 'Auch im dritten Jahrtausend: Geister sind "in"', *Börsenblatt für den Deutschen Buchhandel*, 33 (1977).

'Princess and the Pea, The' ('Prindsessen paa Ærten') One of Hans Christian *Andersen's shortest yet best-known stories, which appeared in his first collection of tales for children, *Eventyr, fortalte for Børn* (*Tales, Told for Children*, 1835). In a Swedish folk-tale analogue, 'Princessa' som lå' på sju ärter' ('The Princess who Lay on Seven Peas'), an orphan girl pretends to be a princess on the advice of her pet cat. Subjected to a series of tests, the last consisting of seven peas under her mattress, the girl claims to have slept poorly, as befits a true princess.

In contrast to the folk-tale heroine, who relies on deception, Andersen's is genuinely sensitive. One stormy night, a bedraggled girl seeks refuge at the castle. Although the girl claims to be a princess, the sceptical queen tests her claim by placing a single pea under 20 mattresses and 20 featherbeds. Upon arising, the girl laments her sleeplessness, bemoaning the presence of 'something so hard that I am black and blue all over'. With everyone thus persuaded that she is 'a real princess', she and the prince are married and the pea enshrined in a museum. Though suffused with bourgeois domesticity (the king opens the gate, the queen makes the bed), the tale is told from the aristocratic perspective of the young prince seeking a royal bride. It thus reflects Andersen's preoccupation with issues of class as well as, by his own direct admission elsewhere, his feelings of personal fragility.

The tale gained wide popularity with *Once Upon a Mattress*, a 1960 musical burlesque starring Carol Burnett as the irrepressible Princess Winnifred, which has had numerous professional and amateur revivals. Other dramatic versions abound, for radio, television, and the stage, most addressed to children. There are also several recent ballet versions.   JGH

Princess Bride, The (Rob Reiner, 1987) Film based on a book of the same title by William *Goldman (1973). Framed by a grandfather reading to his sick grandson, the high-adventure plot includes many fairy-tale characters and motifs, including swashbuckling musketeers, a captive princess, an enchanted forest, a giant, and magic. A cult classic in some circles, this film wavers between parodic and serious treatment of fairy-tale conventions and highlights the pleasure storytelling can afford to children.   LCS

Prineas, Sarah (no dates available) Contemporary American writer who has published an important trilogy of fairy-tale novels for young readers: *The Magic Thief* (2008), *The Magic Thief: Lost* (2009), and *The Magic Thief: Found* (2010). The novels concern a young pickpocket by the name of Conn, who steals a wizard's *locus magicalus*, a stone used to create magic. After he is caught, Conn becomes the wizard's apprentice and must learn to use his magical skills to oppose a predator magician called Arihonvar bent on destroying the city of Wellmet. After Conn has been exiled from Wellmet, he is arrested and sentenced to death when he returns to the city with a baby dragon. But it is this dragon that

enables Conn to block the evil magic of Arihonvar. Prineas's lively style and unique imagination lend new depth to the folklore tradition about the master and his apprentice.   JZ

Prokofiev, Sergei Sergeievitch (1891–1953) Russian composer. Prokofiev studied under *Rimsky-Korsakov and Liadov, both noted for their use of Russian folklore materials. He spent the First World War in London, then moved to the United States, but in 1934 was induced by the Soviet government to return permanently to Russia. His *Peter and the Wolf* (1936), a 'symphonic fairy tale' for which he wrote the accompanying text, is designed to teach children the components of an orchestra. Peter (represented by a string quartet) and his friend the Bird (flute) cleverly capture the Wolf (French horns). Beneath its cheery musical surface, the tale weaves a dark pattern of predator–prey relationships; the Cat (clarinet) stalks the Bird, hunters (tympani) stalk the Wolf, and the Wolf devours the Duck (oboe), still mournfully quacking inside him as the piece ends. Prokofiev's ballet *Cinderella (1945) also undermines the conventional expectations of the fairy tale. While Cinderella is portrayed as an innocent child of nature, the Prince's court is as corrupt and materialistic as her stepmother's house; she and her Prince will only find their happy ending in a world yet to come. *The Stone Flower* (1954), based on a Russian tale, is the story of a craftsman who yearns to create a perfect stone vase and follows the Mistress of the Copper Mountain into her underground realm to learn her secrets, whence he is rescued by his peasant sweetheart. SR

Prokofiev, Sergei, *Autobiography* (1960).

Propp, Vladimir (1895–1970) Russian folklore scholar who published numerous folk and fairy-tale studies. His *Morphology of the Folktale* (1928) derived a syntagmatic (sequential) narrative structure common to Russian traditional oral wonder tales—numbers 50–150 of Aleksandr *Afanasyev's *Russian Fairy Tales* (1855–63). Propp argued that these folktales contained a finite series of 31 repeating motifs, which he called functions, comprising actions such as interdiction or flight. For example, two functions are: at the beginning a member of a family absents himself from home; at the end, the hero is married and ascends the throne. These functions are undertaken by six categories of characters/dramatis personae—villains, mediators, heroes, gift-givers, helpers, and objects of a quest—in a relatively fixed sequence. Translated into English in 1958, *Morphology* quickly became influential in American folklore studies and beyond. The application of Propp's structure to all traditional fairy tales remains controversial, and Propp himself would no doubt be scandalized to learn that it has also been applied to English poetry, Hollywood films, the works of James Joyce, Scottish and Spanish traditional ballads, literary fairy tales and fantasy, novels, television series, and games.   PG

Propp, Vladimir Yakovlevich, *The Russian Folktale*, ed. and trans. by Sibelan Forrester (2012).

proverbial language and fairy tales
The use of folk speech in folk tales should come as no surprise. Tales of any type collected from folk tradition exhibit the use of formulaic language in the form of proverbs, proverbial expressions, proverbial comparisons, proverbial exaggerations, and twin formulas as part of everyday speech and colloquial communication. Obviously didactic stories abound in the use of traditional proverbs to express traditional wisdom handed down from generation to generation. But proverbs also play a role in humorous tall tales, jokes, riddles, legends, and fairy tales.

In general, fairy tales employ proverbs and proverbial expressions rather sparingly. The unreal and imaginary world of fairy tales is perhaps not especially suited to the mundane and didactic proverb. And yet, fairy tales have their lessons to present, and a careful search through the *Grimms' *Kinder- und Hausmärchen* (*Children's and Household Tales*) reveals a considerable number of proverbial statements used as part of the direct discourse or in the narrative prose. While proverbs add wisdom and didacticism to the individual tales, proverbial expressions, comparisons, and exaggerations seem to reflect the folk speech of the common people from whom the Brothers Grimm claimed to have collected their stories. It has been noted, however, that the tales of the Brothers Grimm contain a higher frequency of proverbial language than those folk tales collected and recorded by others in Germany and other countries. This fact has led scholars to a number of studies regarding the surprisingly large number of proverbial texts in the Grimm versions, and it has been established that both brothers added proverbial materials to their sources with Wilhelm being the more fervent proverbialist of the two.

A study of the role of proverbs in the complete works of the Brothers Grimm has shown that they were very interested in proverbial language. They used them in their letters, they cited them as references in their scholarly works, they quoted dozens of them in their voluminous dictionary of the German language, and they commented upon them whenever the occasion arose in lectures and essays. In fact, it was Wilhelm Grimm who gained a special expertise in medieval proverbs, commenting in detail on them in his edition of *Vridankes Bescheidenheit* (*Vridankes' Modesty*, 1834), a medieval collection of gnomic verses by the poet Freidank. Wilhelm even put together his very own collection of medieval proverbs which has now been published. Jacob Grimm had his special interest in proverbs as well, excelling primarily in the codification of Germanic law in proverbs. He cited and commented on many of them in his invaluable legal treatise *Deutsche Rechtsaltertümer* (*German Legal Proverbs*, 1828). The Brothers also had most of the standard proverb collections in their private library, and it is known that they made ample use of these treasures of folk wisdom.

There is no doubt that Wilhelm Grimm in particular was cognizant of the proverbial character of some of the fairy tales that he and his brother had assembled. In his own detailed notes to his fairy-tale collection he explains that the tale 'The Sun Will Bring It to Light' obviously also exemplifies the German proverb 'Nothing is so finely spun that it won't come to light' and even traces it back to medieval documents. This tale clearly exemplifies a proverb, and Wilhelm did not 'tinker' with its proverbial language. This, however, is not the case in the many instances where he added ever more proverbial language to the tales. It has in fact been shown very convincingly that he enriched the tales in the progression of their seven editions from 1812/1815 to 1857. He had a definite proverbial style in mind for the *Children's and Household Tales*, and by making his own additions he altered some of the traditional tales to become fairy tales in language and form as he saw fit.

A short passage from three different editions of the fairy tale 'The Magical Table-cloth, the Gold-Ass, and the Cudgel' may serve as an example of Wilhelm Grimm's work as a proverbial stylist. In this case Wilhelm did not add the proverb (unless he did so when he recorded the text originally), but he continued to work on the proper integration of the proverb until he found the fairy-tale style he wanted.

> 1812: The innkeeper was curious, told himself that all good things would come in threes, and wanted to fetch this third treasure that same night.
> 1819: The innkeeper pricked up his ears and thought, what can this be? All good things come in threes, and by rights I should have this one as well.
> 1857: The innkeeper pricked up his ears: 'What in the world can that be?' he thought to himself. 'The sack surely is filled with nothing but jewels. I should have this one, too, for all good things come in threes.'

As can be seen, Wilhelm intentionally changed the proverb from its syntactically awkward wording 'all good things would come in threes' to the usual statement 'all good things come in threes'. In the seventh edition he even introduces the proverb with the conjunction 'for', which as a short introductory formula emphasizes this bit of

proverbial wisdom. Furthermore, he adds the proverbial expression 'to prick up one's ears' and the colloquial interjection 'what in the world' that help to clarify the short statement of the first edition through popular folk speech. Even though he may have found the actual proverb already in his source, he changed its subjunctive form to the normal text and surrounded it with additional proverbial material. These are conscious stylistic variations in accordance with the fairy-tale style that Wilhelm Grimm felt to be appropriate.

Wilhelm started primarily with the second edition of 1819 to add proverbial materials, and he made considerable further additions even for the seventh edition of 1857. Thus the well-known proverb 'we learn by experience' was incorporated into the fairy tale 'The Golden Goose' in 1819; the proverb 'he who has begun a thing must go on with it' was added to *'Hansel and Gretel' in 1843; and the proverb 'well begun is half done' found its way into 'The Clever Little Tailor' only in 1857. It should be noted that Wilhelm Grimm did not add these proverbs in a manipulative or deceptive fashion. In the introduction to the sixth edition of the *Children's and Household Tales* of 1850, he states quite openly: 'In the sixth edition, too, new tales have been added and individual improvements made. I have been ever eager to incorporate folk proverbs and unique proverbial expressions, which I am always listening for.' There is thus no conscious deception as far as the proverbial additions to the fairy tales are concerned. Since proverbs and proverbial expressions belong intrinsically to the fairy-tale style, Wilhelm Grimm felt justified in making suitable additions and clearly enriched the *Children's and Household Tales* with this proverbial language.   WM

Bluhm, Lothar, 'Sprichwörter und Redensarten bei den Brüdern Grimm', in Annette Sabban and Jan Wirrer (eds.), *Sprichwörter und Redensarten im interkulturellen Vergleich* (1991).

Mieder, Wolfgang, *'Findet, so werdet ihr suchen!' Die Brüder Grimm und das Sprichwort* (1986).

Mieder, Wolfgang, 'Wilhelm Grimm's Proverbial Additions in the Fairy Tales', in

James McGlathery (ed.), *The Brothers Grimm and Folktale* (1988).

Röhrich, Lutz, 'Sprichwörtliche Redensarten aus Volkserzählungen', in Wolfgang Mieder (ed.), *Ergebnisse der Sprichwörterforschung* (1978).

Röhrich, Lutz and Mieder, Wolfgang, *Sprichwort* (1977).

Rölleke, Heinz, and Bluhm, Lothar (eds.), *Das Sprichwort in den Kinder- und Hausmärchen der Brüder Grimm* (1988; 2nd edn., 1997).

Wilcke, Karin, and Bluhm, Lothar, 'Wilhelm Grimms Sammlung mittelhochdeutscher Sprichwörter', in Ludwig Denecke (ed.), *Brüder Grimm Gedenken*, suppl. vol. xix. *Kasseler Vorträge in Erinnerung an den 200. Geburtstag der Brüder Grimm, Jacob und Wilhelm Grimm* (1987).

Prøysen, Alf (1914–70) Norwegian writer, internationally renowned for his many collections of humorous fairy tales about Little Old *Mrs Pepperpot, published in 1956–66. He also wrote a number of fairy tales involving traditional folklore characters like trolls and dwarfs, as well as animal tales, especially about mice. Continuing the tradition of Hans Christian *Andersen, Prøysen uses everyday language and tone and combines everyday settings with folktale elements, for instance when he lets his comic figure Mrs Pepperpot meet the most famous Norwegian folktale character Valemon the White Bear (from the Norwegian version of *'Beauty and the Beast'). MN

Prussian, Claire (1930–) American painter and digital media collage artist who based a digital print series on fairy tales and nursery rhymes. When exhibited, the prints hang upon ornate wallpaper matching the milieu of the digital print; the uncanny repetition truncates the distance between the fairy-tale site and its viewer. The pieces also compel the viewer to reflect on the glib happiness of the fairy tale. For example, in 'Three Blind Mice' (1998), a woman carries a blood-stained sword, blankly gazing at three defenceless mice; the work encourages reflexivity in considering the human-centeredness of the tale's moral trajectory. KMJ

psychology and fairy tales The psychological significance of fairy tales has been one of the most pervasive topics in the history of fairy-tale studies. There are many different theories concerning the fairy tale's psychological meaning and value, but most start with the premiss that the stories are symbolic expressions of the human mind and emotional experience. According to this view, fairy-tale plots and motifs are not representations of socio-historical reality, but symbols of inner experience that provide insight into human behaviour. Consequently, the psychological approach to fairy tales involves symbolic interpretation, both for psychoanalysts, who use fairy tales diagnostically to illustrate psychological theories, and for folklorists and literary critics, who use psychological theories to illuminate fairy tales.

Although the psychological approach to fairy tales is usually associated with Freudian psychoanalysis and other 20th-century theories, it actually had its beginnings in the previous century, when nationalistic awareness motivated collectors and scholars to study folk tales as expressions of the folk soul or psyche. Focusing on the relationship of folk tales to myth, scholars looked to these stories for evidence of the values, customs, and beliefs that expressed a specific people's cultural identity. Over the course of the 19th century and into the 20th, mythic and anthropological approaches to the fairy tale relied on the notion that the study of folk tales could reveal the 'psychology' of ethnic cultures, especially that of so-called primitive people. This form of ethnopsychology is exemplified in Wilhelm Wundt's *Völkerpsychologie* (*Folk Psychology*, 1900–9), which maintained that the fairy tale is the oldest of all narrative forms and reveals fundamental aspects of the primitive mind.

In contrast to ethnopsychology, Sigmund Freud's psychoanalytic theory attempted to discern the more universal psychology of human behaviour and culture. Freud found fairy tales especially useful for illustrating his theories of the mind because they seemed so much like dreams. According to Freud, both fairy tales and dreams used symbols to express the conflicts, anxieties, and forbidden desires that had been repressed into the unconscious. In writings such as *Die Traumdeutung* (*The Interpretation of Dreams*, 1900), 'Das Motiv der Kästchenwahl' ('The Theme of the Three Caskets', 1913), and 'Märchenstoffe in Träumen' ('The Occurrence in Dreams of Material from Fairy Tales', 1913), Freud demonstrated that fairy tales used a symbolic language that could be interpreted psychoanalytically to reveal the latent or hidden content of the mind. For example, in his famous analysis of the Wolf Man—described in the essay 'Aus der Geschichte einer infantilen Neurose' ('From the History of an Infantile Neurosis', 1918)—Freud noted that his patient's dreams used the same symbolism as the Grimms' stories of 'The Wolf and the Seven Young Kids' and *'Little Red Riding Hood' to express sexual anxiety resulting from traumatic childhood experiences.

Freud's earliest followers produced numerous psychoanalytic studies of fairy tales, in which they elaborated on different aspects of his theories. Franz Riklin's *Wunscherfüllung und Symbolik im Märchen* (*Wishfulfilment and Symbolism in Fairy Tales*, 1908) pursued Freud's idea that fairy tales are a form of wish fulfilment that use dream symbolism to express repressed sexual desires. Riklin's work was supported by Herbert Silberer, who similarly argued that fairy tales demonstrate the pathology of sexual repression. In essays on 'Phantasie und Mythos' ('Fantasy and Myth', 1910) and 'Märchensymbolik' ('Fairy-Tale Symbolism', 1912), Silberer analysed 'The *Frog King' and a female patient's sexual dream of animal transformation to show that the fairy-tale pattern of enchantment and disenchantment mirrors the psychological phenomenon of repression followed by the healing release that comes from psychoanalysis. In a 1928 paper on 'Psycho-Analysis and Folklore', Ernest Jones also offered a psychoanalytic reading of 'The Frog King'. In typical Freudian fashion, Jones's interpretation stressed the female's aversion to sexual intimacy, symbolized by the princess's reluctance to allow the phallic frog into her bed.

Otto Rank expanded the discussion about the psychological origin of fairy tales in his influential study *Der Mythus von der Geburt des Helden* (*The Myth of the Birth of the Hero*, 1909) and in his *Psychoanalytische Beiträge zur Mythenforschung* (*Psychoanalytic Contributions to Myth Research*, 1919). Rank proposed that fairy tales are adult projections of childhood fantasies, and he specifically examined mythological and fairy-tale heroes in the light of Freud's theories about the Oedipus complex and Family Romance. Freud's idea that fairy tales use the symbolic language of dreams received an intriguing twist in the prolific research of Géza Róheim. In works like *The Gates of the Dream* (1952) and 'Fairy Tale and Dream' (1953), Róheim did not simply agree that fairy tales resembled dreams; he asserted that fairy tales were dreams that had been retold by the dreamer. Applying the psychoanalytic principles of dream interpretation to variants of tales from Europe and around the world, Róheim produced intriguing readings of stories such as *'Hansel and Gretel', *'Mother Holle', and 'Little Red Riding Hood'.

Carl Gustav Jung, who had also been a disciple of Freud, developed a new branch of analytic psychology that has had an enormous impact on fairy-tale scholarship and the popular reception of fairy tales. While Freudian psychoanalytic theory generally viewed pathological behaviours and symbolic expressions as manifestations of the individual's unconscious, Jung looked beyond pathology and beyond the individual mind for the source and meaning of symbols. Jung posited the existence of an impersonal and ahistorical collective unconscious that was a reservoir of images and forms universally shared by all humans. According to Jung, the symbolic language of myths, dreams, and fairy tales was composed of these timeless symbolic forms, which he called archetypes. From the Jungian perspective, archetypes were universal symbols showing the way to transformation and development.

Jung described the archetypal basis of fairy tales in works like 'Zur Phänomenologie des Geistes im Märchen' ('The Phenomenology of the Spirit in Fairy Tales', 1948),

'Zur Psychologie des Kind-Archetypus' ('The Psychology of the Child Archetype', 1941), and 'Zur Psychologie der Schelmenfigur' ('On the Psychology of the Trickster-Figure', 1954). His ideas have not only influenced the literary fairy tales of writers such as Hermann Hesse, they have also generated a great number of fairy-tale interpretations. One of the best-known studies is Hedwig von Beit's three-volume work on the *Symbolik des Märchens* (*The Symbolism of the Fairy Tale*, 1952–7), which examines the archetypal basis of fairy-tale motifs and the quest for self-realization and redemption. The psychological quest for self-realization is also taken up by Julius Heuscher in *The Psychiatric Study of Fairy Tales* (1963) and by Joseph Campbell in *The Hero with a Thousand Faces* (1949). The difference between the Freudian and Jungian approaches to symbols is especially well illustrated in Campbell's interpretation of 'The Frog King'. Campbell reads 'The Frog King' not specifically as a story of sexual anxiety and maturation, as the Freudian Jones had done, but as an illustration of the broader archetypal theme of the call to adventure—the individual's awakening to unconscious forces and a new stage of life.

The archetypal studies by Marie-Louise von Franz have been widely recognized as classic works of Jungian fairy-tale analysis. Von Franz, too, has dealt with individual development and redemption in *Individuation in Fairytales* (1977) and *The Psychological Meaning of Redemption Motifs in Fairytales* (1980). She illuminates the classic shadow archetype in *Shadow and Evil in Fairy Tales* (1974) and explores the basis of the female archetype in *Problems of the Feminine in Fairy Tales*.

The Jungian treatment of male and female archetypes has been criticized by feminists, who point out that Jung's archetypes are actually socio-cultural constructions, not timeless psychological truths. Nonetheless, some feminist scholars and psychoanalysts have followed the lead of von Franz and used Jungian analysis to elucidate women's issues in fairy tales. This is the case in Sibylle Birkhäuser-Oeri's study of *Die Mutter im*

Märchen (*The Mother*, 1976) and Torborg Lundell's examination of *Fairy Tale Mothers* (1989). In *Leaving my Father's House* (1992), Marion Woodman, a feminist psychoanalyst, presents a Jungian interpretation of Grimms' 'All Fur' and includes commentaries by her patients to show women how to take control of their lives in a male-dominated society.

Because Jungian psychology stresses universal myths of higher consciousness and redemption, it has quasi-religious or spiritual overtones, which has given it a wide popular appeal. Eugen Drewermann has combined the perspectives of theology and analytical psychology in a popular series of fairy-tale interpretations called *Grimms Märchen tiefen psychologisch gedeutet* (*Grimms' Fairy Tales Interpreted According to Depth Psychology*, 1981–). Drewermann's volumes have been criticized for relying too much on archetypal associations and too little on literary or folkloric expertise. Another example of Jungian psychology being mixed with religious beliefs is Arland Ussher and Carl von Metzradt's book *Enter These Enchanted Woods* (1954), which interprets selected Grimms' tales from a Jungian-flavoured Christian perspective. Fairy tales have also been interpreted by adherents of anthroposophy, a spiritual movement that grew out of the work of Rudolf Steiner under the influence of psychoanalytic theories. The readings that Steiner included in *The Interpretation of Fairy Tales* (1929) sought to reveal spiritual truths and became a model for his followers, who considered fairy tales a kind of scripture that could inspire spiritual development. The unusual nature of anthroposophic fairy-tale interpretation is evident in Paul Paede's book of anthroposophic medicine *Krankheit, Heilung und Entwicklung im Spiegel der Märchen* (*Disease, Healing and Development in the Mirror of Fairy Tales*, 1986). Paede's interpretation of **'Cinderella'* contends that the story's symbolism deepens our appreciation of feet and their role in maintaining spiritual and physiological harmony in the human organism.

The psycho-spiritual claims of Jungian analysis and anthroposophy are echoed in the many self-help books of fairy-tale interpretation published for the popular book trade, especially since the advent of New Age philosophy in the 1980s. For example, in the eclectic German series *Weisheit im Märchen* (*Wisdom in the Fairy Tale*, 1983– 8), each volume is written by a different author who interprets a single tale to show readers how to achieve better relationships, self-confidence, self-acceptance, and other improvements in their lives. The Jungian psychotherapist Verena Kast claims to show the way to personal autonomy and better interpersonal relationships in her popular books of fairy-tale interpretation, including one entitled *Wege aus Angst und Symbiose* (*Through Emotions to Maturity*, 1982). From a Christian perspective the American authors Ronda Chervin and Mary Neill published *The Woman's Tale* (1980), a self-help book of pop psychology that promotes the idea that reading fairy tales can help women develop their personal identities. From another perspective, Robert *Bly's *Iron John* (1990) offers Grimms' tale as a story that helps men heal their psychic wounds and realize their true masculine personality.

Although the psychotherapeutic value of reading fairy tales is speculative, some analysts have presented case histories as evidence of the fairy tale's efficacy in treating patients. The Jungian analyst Hans Dieckmann, for example, advocated in many different publications the diagnostic and therapeutic importance of the *Lieblingsmärchen*—the favourite fairy tale—based on his clinical experience with patients. According to Dieckmann, the neuroses of adults are exposed in their favourite childhood stories. Consistent with his Jungian orientation, Dieckmann maintained that therapy is facilitated when the patient consciously recognizes the identity that exists between the personal psyche and the cosmos. On the other hand, the psychoanalyst Sándor Lorand used a case history in 1935 to point out that fairy tales experienced in childhood can also have adverse effects that cause psychological trauma. He cites in particular a patient whose fear of castration was traced to the tale of 'Little Red Riding Hood'.

Typically, however, psychologists view the fairy tale as having a significant and positive role in the psychological development of children. These developmental psychologists consider the fairy tale not simply as a useful therapeutic tool in clinical practice, but as children's literature that should be part of every child's experience. The basic premiss is that children learn how to overcome psychological conflicts and grow into new phases of development through a symbolic comprehension of the maturation process as expressed in fairy tale. Among the earliest studies of this kind was Charlotte Bühler's *Das Märchen und die Phantasie des Kindes* (*The Fairy Tale and the Child's Imagination*, 1918), which identified psychological connections between the fairy tale and the mind of the child. Bühler pointed out that both the formal and the symbolic aspects of the fairy tale corresponded to the child's imaginative mode of perception, and that because of this correspondence the genre assumed a special function in the mental life of the developing child. In *Der Weg zum Märchen* (*The Pathway to Understanding the Fairy Tale*, 1939), Bruno Jöckel stressed the fairy tale's symbolic depiction of the conflicts and sexual maturation that occur during puberty. Josephine Bilz's study of *Menschliche Reifung im Sinnbild* (*Symbols of Human Maturation*, 1943) emphasized the maturation process more generally and showed how *'Rumpelstiltskin' symbolically enacts the female's development from youth to motherhood. Walter Scherf has made the case in numerous essays and in his book *Die Herausforderung des Dämons* (*Challenging the Demon*, 1987) that magic tales are dramas of family conflict in which children can identify their own problems. According to Scherf, these magic stories engage the dramatic imagination of children and allow them to overcome their conflicts, separate from the parents, and integrate themselves into society.

The discussion about the fairy tale's place in child development has been dominated by Bruno Bettelheim's book *The Uses of Enchantment* (1976). No study of fairy tales has been as popular or as controversial as

Bettelheim's. His Freudian readings are based on the idea that fairy tales are existential dramas in which children subconsciously confront their own problems and desires on the path to adulthood. Oedipal conflicts and sibling rivalry play especially important parts in Bettelheim's analyses. Bettelheim's critics object that his psychoanalytic readings are not only reductionist but also blatantly moralistic. Opponents note, too, that Bettelheim proposes a model of socialization that is repressive and sexist. They also point to his ignorance of the fairy tale's historical development and his failure to take into account the many variants of the stories that he discusses—factors that would complicate his premiss that the fairy tale communicates timeless truths. While Bettelheim's influential work has been the focus of much criticism, these objections are typical of those lodged against the psychoanalytic view of fairy tales.

As an alternative to Bettelheim's psychoanalytic view, F. André Favat's study of *Child and Tale* (1977) used Jean Piaget's ideas about the stages of development to consider the affinity between fairy tales and child psychology. What draws the child to the fairy tale, according to Favat, is not the opportunity to confront conflicts symbolically as part of the socialization process. Instead, the fairy tale relaxes the tensions brought on by socialization and change, and provides a fictional realm where children can re-experience the pleasure of a magical, egocentric world ordered according to their desires. Experimental psychologists have also worked in various ways with the fairy tale to test the theoretical claims and assertions made about the psychological importance of fairy tales for children. For example, Patricia Guérin Thomas's 1983 dissertation on 'Children's Responses to Fairy Tales' used Piaget's theory of cognitive development and Erik Erikson's theory of psycho-social development to analyse the responses of children to the Grimms' stories 'Brother and Sister' and 'The Queen Bee'. Although Thomas found that children do respond to the stories based on the inner conflicts and moral understanding they have at a given stage of development, she could find no evidence to support the psychoanalytic claim that fairy tales aid children in resolving psychological conflicts.

Some recent psychological studies of fairy tales have attempted to avoid the reductionism typical of psychoanalytic fairy-tale interpretations, while others have applied new models as alternatives to Freud and Jung. The folklorist Alan Dundes has argued throughout his research that psychoanalytic theory in the study of a folk tale can be very valuable when adequately informed by a rigorous comparative analysis of the tale's variants. In her book *The Hard Facts of the Grimms' Fairy Tales* (1987), the literary scholar Maria Tatar illuminated psychological themes by using Freud's idea of the Family Romance within the interpretive constraints demanded by formal aspects, socio-historical factors, and the editorial history of the Grimms' collection. In *Fairy Tales and the Art of Subversion* (1983), Jack Zipes used Freud's theory of the uncanny in tandem with ideas from Favat, Piaget, and the philosopher Ernst Bloch to develop a theory of the fairy tale's liberating potential; and in his book on *The Brothers Grimm* (1988), he advocated a new psychoanalytic approach to violence in fairy tales that would build on the work of the Swiss psychoanalyst Alice Miller. In *Du sollst nicht merken* (*Thou Shalt Not Be Aware*, 1981), Miller challenged the Freudian notion that violence inflicted by fairy-tale parents is an inverted projection of the child's own negative feelings towards the parent. Instead, using 'The Virgin Mary's Child' and 'Rumpelstiltskin' as examples, Miller theorized that some fairy tales are adults' censored projections of abuse that they actually experienced as children, a fantasy possibly more in tune with socio-historical and familial reality than adults can admit.

Postmodern literary fairy tales for adults have also stimulated new ways of thinking about fairy tales and psychology. Peter Straub's revision of 'The *Juniper Tree' (1990), for example, links fairy-tale violence with child abuse in a way that confirms Miller's theory. Other writers like Margaret

*Atwood, Angela *Carter, and Robert *Coover have understood the socio-historical dynamics of the fairy tale and produced fairy-tale adaptations that complicate, undercut, and frustrate conventional psychoanalytic readings—especially as they relate to the psychology of identity, socialization, gender, and sexuality. Such revisions challenge readers to rethink classical psychoanalytic premises and search for new models to understand the psychological implications of the fairy tale in social, historical, and cultural contexts.   DH

Dundes, Alan, 'The Psychoanalytic Study of Folklore', *Annals of Scholarship*, 3 (1985).

Dundes, Alan, 'The Psychoanalytic Study of the Grimms' Tales', in *Folklore Matters* (1992).

Grolnick, Simon A., 'Fairy Tales and Psychotherapy', in Ruth B. Bottigheimer (ed.), *Fairy Tales and Society: Illusion, Allusion, and Paradigm* (1986).

Laiblin, Wilhelm (ed.), *Märchenforschung und Tiefenpsychologie* (1969).

Lüthi, Max, 'Psychologie und Pädagogik', in *Märchen*, rev. Heinz Rölleke (8th edn., 1990).

Puccini, Giacomo (1858–1924) Italian composer. His opera in three acts, *Turandot* (libretto by Adami and Simoni), remained uncompleted at his death and was performed, with the last scene completed by another composer, in 1926. *Turandot* is based on Carlo *Gozzi's play of the same name (1762), which in turn was in part adapted from The *Arabian Nights. The plot revolves around Princess Turandot's promise to marry whoever can answer three riddles that she poses.   NC

Ashbrook, William, *Puccini's Turandot: The End of the Great Tradition* (1991).

Pullman, Philip (1946–) British writer whose famous fantasy trilogy, *His Dark Materials*, contains numerous folkloristic and fairy-tale motifs. The three books, *Northern Lights* (also known as *The Golden Compass*) (1995), *The Subtle Knife* (1997), and *The Amber Spyglass* (2000), depict the trials and tribulations of two young protagonists, Lyra and Will, in other worlds, seeking to grasp how and why evil has come about and how humanity and humanism can be preserved. *The Golden Compass* was made into a film in 2007. Pullman has also written sequels to *His Dark Materials* and shorter fairy-tale books such as *The Wonderful Story of Aladdin and the Enchanted Lamp* (1993), *The Firework-Maker's Daughter* (1995), *Mossycoat* (1998), *Puss in Boots: The Adventures of That Most Enterprising Feline* (2000), and *The Scarecrow and his Servant* (2004) along with the amusing fairy-tale novel, *I was a Rat! or The Scarlet Slippers* (1999), a parody of 'Cinderella' that is set in modern-day England and recounts the strange adventures of Cinderella's pageboy, who was never turned back into a rat by the fairy godmother. It was adapted for a television series by the BBC in 2001. In the bicentenary year celebrating the first edition of the Grimms' *Kinder- und Hausmärchen* (*Children's and Household Tales*, 1812–15), Pullman published 50 of their tales, which he eloquently rewrote in *Grimm Tales: For Young and Old* (2013).   JZ

Tucker, Nicholas, *Darkness Visible: Inside the World of Philip Pullman* (2003).

Purcell, Henry (1659–95) English court composer, especially of vocal works, but also well known for anthems and liturgical works. Purcell was a chorister of the Chapel Royal, London, in 1669, eventually becoming organist at Westminster Abbey in 1680. Late in his career, he composed music for the theatre, in particular settings for masques and so-called 'semi-operas'. Most important amongst these are *Diocletian* (1690; properly known as 'The Prophetess; or, The History of Diocletian'), with its representation of various mythical figures, Flora, Bacchus, Pomona, and the Sun God; *King Arthur* (1691), with a text by John Dryden, featuring both good and evil spirits; and the *Fairy Queen* (1692), an anonymous adaptation of *Shakespeare's *A Midsummer Night's Dream*. Not a single line of the play actually occurs in the *Fairy Queen*, but Purcell highlights Titania, queen of fairyland, by providing music appropriate for her and the fairy train, and an elaborate dance setting for the Followers of the Night. Purcell's final achievements include *The Indian Queen*

(1695), with its famous conjuring scene in Act III, Scene ii, in which Zempoalla consults the magician Ismeron, who summons the God of Dreams to reveal her fate. *Bonduca* is probably Purcell's last major work (also of 1695), which tells of the struggles of the British heroine Boadicea, with an impressive temple scene of praying Druids.   PGS

Holman, Peter, *Henry Purcell* (1994).
Pinnock, A., 'Play into Opera: Purcell's The Indian Queen', *Early Music*, 18 (1990).
Savage, R., 'The Shakespeare–Purcell Fairy Queen', *Early Music*, 1 (1973).

Pushkin, Alexander (1799–1837) Russian national poet and a major writer of fairy tales. In his versified fairy tales he used some common plots, as in *The Tale of the Dead Princess and the Seven Heroes* (1833), a version of *'Snow White', or in *The Tale of the Fisherman and the Fish* (1833), a well-known tale of the Brothers *Grimm. However, unlike the Grimms, Pushkin lets the woman benefit from the wish-granting, while the man remains poor and oppressed, thus emphasizing social injustice. *The Tale of Tsar Saltan* (1831) is based on a popular Slavic chapbook, but it also has many recognizable elements from European fairy tales. In *The Tale of the Golden Cockerel* (1834), Pushkin retold the story of the Arab astrologer from the *Alhambra* by Washington *Irving, making it into a biting political satire of Tsarist Russia. *The Tale of the Priest and Balda, his Hired Hand* (1830, pub. 1840), the plot of which is also found in the Brothers Grimm, is another example of his satirical use of the fairy tale; the tale was banned owing to its disrespectful portrayal of the clergy and published posthumously with many alterations: for instance, the priest was changed into a merchant.

Foreign sources notwithstanding, Pushkin's fairy tales have very tangible details of Russian settings and historical and social context. They also have brilliant characterizations, unusual for traditional fairy tales. The language, often imitating folk songs or ballads, is distinctly colloquial and abounds in poetical figures. Many punchlines from the fairy tales have entered the treasury of Russian proverbs. Although the fairy tales were not primarily addressed to children, they have been widely used in schoolbook texts, thus becoming a notable part of the national heritage. The significance of Pushkin for the Russian fairy-tale tradition cannot be overestimated.   MN

Debreczeny, Paul, *The Other Pushkin: A Study of Alexander Pushkin's Prose Fiction* (1983).
Edmunds, Catherine J., 'Pushkin and Gogol as Sources for the Librettos of the Fantastic Fairy Tale Operas of Rimskij-Korsakov' (Diss., Harvard University, 1985).
Eimermacher, Karl, 'Aspekte des literarischen Märchens in Russland', in Klaus-Dieter Seemann (ed.), *Beiträge zur russischen Volksdichtung* (1987).

'Puss-in-Boots' Archetypal folk tale in which an inherited cat rescues an impoverished youngest son and civilizes him to curry royal favour, gain power, and win a princess. Nuances in early literary versions reflect societal variations on this trickster cat/fox motif.

*Straparola's tale of social mobility appears in Night 11 of *Le *piacevoli notti* (*The Pleasant Nights*, 1550). Constantino Fortunato is a peasant whose cat (actually a fairy in disguise), rescues him from cruel siblings. To help him gain a royal audience, she repeatedly traps prey as presents in her master's name. To make him presentable to Society, she licks away his stress-induced acne and tricks the king into lending him fine garments. The entire court is duped by his appearance. Constantino marries the princess, receives her dowry, and lives in a castle which the cat coerces everyone to say is his. Because the former peasant eventually inherits the throne (which is passed down through his children), this tale legitimizes patriarchy through duplicitous power politics. Its rags-to-riches treatment would have interested élite Renaissance readers in the Venetian republic and Italian city-states.

Some 80 years later, the Neapolitan *Basile stressed ingratitude in Day 2 of the *Pentamerone* (1634). Emphasizing local colour and reality over fantasy, he presents a real cat—albeit a talking one, in good

'Puss-in-Boots' The clever cat cries for help to save his master in Charles *Perrault's 'Puss-in-Boots',
illustrated by Gustave *Doré and published in *Les Contes de Perrault* (1867).

folklore tradition. This animal-heroine's manners and flattering speech are much finer than her master's, whose drivel she stifles while arranging his marriage of convenience. On the advice of this ever-loyal, hard-working servant, he gains yet more riches after the dowry, and promises to reward her. She tests his sincerity, finds him ungrateful, and flees her non-existent job security. Critiquing all classes of feudal society, she observes that reversals of fortune can ruin character. She may have socialized, but not civilized, her master.

The French Academician Charles *Perrault modified these storylines in 'Le Chat botté ou le Maître chat' for *Histoires ou contes du temps passé* (*Stories or Tales of Past Times*, 1697). He upgraded the son's social rank, conferred status-symbol boots on his (male) cat, omitted post-marriage scenes and 'sincerity test', had the cat threaten peasants with death, and reinvested the tale with magic. The castle of his 'Marquis de Carabas' is inhabited by an ogre, whom the conniving cat has changed into a mouse before eating him. Cunning, confiscation of lands, murder—all are featured in this portrait of society under Louis XIV (which, unlike Basile's, rewards the loyal servant/secretary). Two morals conclude the text. The first ironically values ingenuity and hard work (neither of which is displayed by the son) over inherited wealth as a means to attain power; the second somewhat misogynistically suggests that mere appearances and civility can seduce women and society. MLE

Seifert, Lewis, *Fairy Tales, Sexuality, and Gender in France, 1690-1715* (1996).
Soriano, Marc, *Les Contes de Perrault* (1968).
Zipes, Jack, 'Of Cats and Men', in *Happily Ever After: Fairy Tales, Children, and the Culture Industry* (1997).

Pyle, Howard (1853–1911) Well-known American illustrator and author. Pyle lived in Delaware's Brandywine Valley near Wilmington for most of his life except for a brief apprenticeship in New York City and the ill-fated European journey that ended with his death. Pyle's first successful book was *The Merry Adventures of Robin Hood* (1883), a beautifully designed, illustrated and retold edition of the classic tales. Published simultaneously in Britain and America, the book's design won widespread critical accolades— even from William *Morris, dean of the beautiful book. Pyle's Arthuriad, published 1903–10, demonstrates his continuing fascination with English tales of chivalry. The stylized medievalesque diction in which Pyle chose to relate these tales has been variously admired and criticized, but it does lend a tone of high seriousness to his rendition. In both the Robin Hood and Arthurian cycles, Pyle altered the stories in order to enhance his heroes' virtues, particularly emphasizing chastity and leadership in keeping with contemporary bourgeois norms. The potential irony that medieval English stories should be offered to American youth is partially explained by Pyle's support of 'The Knights of King Arthur', an early precursor to the Boy Scout movement, and his friendship with President Theodore Roosevelt. Valuing the republican, civilizing (or colonizing) themes of the old tales, Pyle emphasized social order and the rule of law. In addition to revising English legends, Pyle published three collections of folk tales: *Pepper & Salt* (1886), *The Wonder Clock* (1888), and *Twilight Land* (1895). Rendered in the avuncular style of the Brothers *Grimm and Joseph Jacobs, the collections are more accessible than the legendary exploits of Robin Hood and King Arthur. They emphasize the democratizing aspects of the folk tradition, but also justify the unequal distribution of wealth by appeals to fate and a social-Darwinist view of individual value. Pyle's illustrations evolve from rather static Morris-influenced woodcut designs in the first collection to impressionistic pen-and-ink drawings in the last. In *Twilight Land* and *A Modern Aladdin* (1892), Pyle moves away from English and Germanic influences and draws on 18th-century French orientalism for his inspiration, particularly *The *Arabian Nights*. In all these collections, Pyle recombines old folk motifs into new stories supporting the American Dream. Finally, Pyle wrote literary fairy tales, most notably *The Garden behind the Moon* (1895), a Swedenborg-influenced fantasy in part inspired by the untimely death of his oldest son. An extended parable about death and imagination indebted to the fantasies of George *MacDonald, *The Garden behind the Moon* is unusual in that it begins with a primary, everyday world, moves to a magical faerie plane, and then demonstrates the mutual interpenetration of the two worlds by unexpectedly resolving the plot in the primary world. Pyle exerted further influence through teaching, notably of Maxfield *Parrish and N. C. Wyeth.   NJW

Agosta, Lucien L., *Howard Pyle* (1987).
Howard Pyle Commemorative Issue, *Children's Literature Association Quarterly*, 8 (summer 1983).
Pitz, Henry C., *Howard Pyle: Writer, Illustrator, Founder of the Brandywine School* (1965).

Quiller-Couch, Sir Arthur Thomas
(1863–1944) English critic, writer, and compiler of Cornish descent who published under the pseudonym 'Q'. Among his many anthologies, Quiller-Couch put together three collections of fairy tales. In 1895 he published *Fairy Tales Far and Near Re-told*, with illustrations by H. R. *Millar. For his *The Sleeping Beauty and Other Fairy Tales from the Old French Retold* (1910), illustrated by Edmund *Dulac, Quiller-Couch translated and retold tales by Charles *Perrault (*'Bluebeard', *'Cinderella', and *'Sleeping Beauty') and Mme de *Villeneuve (*'Beauty and the Beast') taken from the French *Cabinet des fées* (1785–9). His third collection, *In Powder and Crinoline: Old Fairy Tales Retold* (1913), illustrated by Kay *Nielsen, includes a version of 'The Twelve Dancing Princesses'.　　　AD

Rackham, Arthur (1867–1939) British illustrator whose gift for gracefully portraying fairy world inhabitants within familiar settings, captured the affection of his contemporaries, and continues to elicit the admiration of critics.

Rackham's first fairy-tale illustrations, in the *Fairy Tales of the *Brothers Grimm* (1900), included 95 drawings whose immediate popularity led him to revise some of its illustrations for colour reproduction. In 1902 he illustrated *The Little White Bird*. His subsequent illustrations for *Rip van Winkle* (1905) established him as 'the leading decorative illustrator of the Edwardian period', in the words of his biographer Derek Hudson. A torrent of illustrations followed: *Peter Pan in Kensington Gardens* (1906), *Alice in Wonderland* (1907), *A Midsummer Night's Dream* (1908) visually based on the Suffolk landscape where he vacationed, de la Motte *Fouqué's *Undine* (1909), *Aesop's Fables* (1912), *Mother Goose* (1913), *Arthur Rackham's Book of Pictures* (1913), which included many goblins, elves, and fairies, *The Allie's Fairy Book* (1916), *Little Brother and Little Sister* (1917), 40 additional Grimm tales in *Cinderella* (1919), *The *Sleeping Beauty* (1920), which displayed his gift for silhouette, *Irish Fairy Tales* (1920) by James Stephens, and finally *The Arthur Rackham Fairy Book* (1933).

In 1910 Rackham expressed the idea that an illustrator's partnership with an author reached its highest level when illustrations communicated the 'sense of delight or emotion aroused by the accompanying passage of literature' (Hudson, 88). His work was regularly exhibited in Europe and won international recognition in Milan (1906) and Barcelona (1912).

As a child Rackham had drawn indefatigably. On a journey to Australia at 17 to strengthen his delicate health, he sketched uninterruptedly and determined to make drawing his lifework. Trained at the Lambeth School of Art, he began his career in the 1890s with journalistic illustrations of social and political life for two London weeklies, the *Pall Mall Budget* and the *Westminster Budget*. He also illustrated travel books and brochures, memoirs, gardening and nature books, which required a high degree of realism, as well as mystery novels and literary books (by Anthony Hope, Washington *Irving, Maggie Browne, Fanny Burney, Ingoldsby, Charles and Mary *Lamb, and *Shakespeare) which gave scope to his penchant for the fantastic. Exhibiting his technical versatility, his illustrations for Hans Christian *Andersen's tales mixed dramatic silhouette, expressively detailed black-and-white pen-and-ink drawings, and watercolour.

Rackham achieved financial independence early and enjoyed a steady income from commissions from the publisher Heinemann. In 1903 he married Edyth Starkie, herself an accomplished painter who won a gold medal in Barcelona in 1911, a year before her husband did, and who encouraged his bent for the fantastic. His goblins embody emotions that range from sombre malevolence to malicious glee; his human characters can be tenderly beautiful or touchingly earnest, like Gerda and Kay in 'The *Snow Queen'.   RBB

Gettings, Fred, *Arthur Rackham* (1975).
Hamilton, James, *Arthur Rackham: A Life with Illustration* (1990).
Hudson, Derek, *Arthur Rackham: His Life and Work* (1974).

Rackham, Arthur Since he thinks no one will guess his name, the mysterious little creature dances happily in the Grimms' *'Rumpelstiltskin', illustrated by Arthur Rackham in *Fairy Tales of the Brothers Grimm* (1910). The Bodleian Library, University of Oxford (Castello 32).

Raimund, Ferdinand (pseudonym of Jakob **Raimann**, 1790–1836) Austrian dramatist, actor, and director who, along with Johann *Nestroy, cultivated the fairy-tale farce and transformed it into high art. Raimund was strongly influenced by the baroque theatre and the *commedia dell'arte* and combined elements of social satire with romance to write unique dramas about Austrian society and the folk tradition. His first two plays, *Der Barometermacher auf der Zauberinsel* (*The Barometer Maker on the Enchanted Island*, 1823) and *Der Diamant des Geisterkönigs* (*The Diamond of the King of Spirits*, 1824) were rough experiments in the fairy-tale genre. Beginning with *Das Mädchen aus der Feenwelt oder der Bauer als Millionär* (*The Maiden from Fairyland or The Farmer as Millionaire*, 1827), Raimund showed his remarkable ability to endow the fairy-tale play with deeper meaning and great humour. In this farce the powerful fairy Lacrimosa is stripped of her magic powers because she falls in love with a human and gives birth to a daughter. She can only regain her powers if her daughter marries a poor young man before she reaches her 18th birthday. In another fascinating play, *Der Alpenkönig und der Menschenfeind* (*The King of the Alps and the Enemy of Man*, 1828), Raimund depicts a rich, misanthropic landowner named Rappelkopf, who refuses to allow his daughter to marry an artist. In order to punish Rappelkopf and reform him, Astralagus, King of the Alps, transforms Rappelkopf into his own brother-in-law, and the king assumes Rappelkopf's identity to show the misanthrope how cruel he was. In the end, Rappelkopf reforms and becomes kind and gentle, and allows his daughter to marry the artist. Raimund's last great play, *Der Verschwender* (*The Spendthrift*, 1834), concerns a nobleman named Julius von Flottwell, endowed with great wealth by the fairy Cheristane. However, Flotwell likes to spend his money without regard for the consequences despite Cheristane's warnings. Soon he loses his fortune, and his friends and servants turn on him. Gradually he learns his lesson, and Cheristane helps him regain his wealth and position in society. Raimund wrote three other fairy-tale plays, *Moisasurs Zauberfluch* (*The Magic Curse of Moisasur*, 1827), *Die gefesselte Phantasie* (*The Fettered Imagination*, 1828), and *Die unheilige Krone oder: König ohne Reich, Held ohne Mut, Schönheit ohne Jugend* (*The Unholy Crown or: King without Kingdom, Hero without Courage, Beauty without Youth*, 1829), which were unsuccessful attempts to introduce tragic elements into the fairy-tale tradition.   JZ

Crockett, Roger, 'Raimund's *Der Verschwender*: The Illusion of Freedom', *German Quarterly*, 58 (1985).

Harding, Laurence V., *The Dramatic Art of Ferdinand Raimund and Johann Nestroy: A Critical Study* (1974).

Hein, Jürgen, *Ferdinand Raimund* (1970).

Holbeche, Yvonne, 'Raimund and Romanticism: Ferdinand Raimund's "Der Alpenkönig und der Menschenfeind" and E. T. A. Hoffmann's "Prinzessin Brambilla"', *New German Studies*, 18 (1994).

Jones, Calvin N., *Negation and Utopia: The German Volksstück from Raimund to Kroetz* (1993).

Ralston, William Ralston Shedden (1828–89) English translator and specialist in Russian folklore, librarian and scholar with the British Museum, and founding member of the Folk-Lore Society. Modelled on Jacob *Grimm's *Deutsche Mythologie* (1835), Ralston's first compilation, *The Songs of the Russian People, as Illustrative of Slavic Mythology and Russian Social Life* (1872), is an attempt to reconstruct from peasant tradition the mythological underpinnings of Slavic folklore. *Russian Folk-Tales* (1873), consisting of tales mainly from Aleksandr *Afanasyev's collections, again reflects Ralston's interest in the relation between mythology and folk and fairy tales. Ralston also wrote introductions to *Indian Fairy Tales* (1880 edn.), *Portuguese Folk-Tales* (1882), and *Tibetan Tales* (1882) in which he proves to be a rigorous comparatist and typologist, demonstrating his vast knowledge in both Eastern and Western folk traditions.   AD

Randolph, Vance (1892–1980) American folklorist and expert on Ozark folklore and culture. Randolph was an accomplished storyteller and self-trained scholar, who worked outside of the academic setting most of his life. His fieldwork among the Ozark mountain people began in 1919 and spanned more than four decades, yielding publications on numerous folklore topics: *Ozark Folksongs* (1946–50), *Ozark Superstitions* (1947), *We Always Lie to Strangers: Tall Tales from the Ozarks* (1951), *Down in the Holler: A Gallery of Ozark Folk Speech* (1953), *Hot Springs and Hell, and Other Folk Jests and Anecdotes from the Ozarks* (1965) and *Pissing in the Snow, and Other Ozark Folktales* (1976). The latter, a collection of bawdy tales omitted from earlier publications at the insistence of his editors, marked an important departure from the practice of censoring folklore's erotic or obscene content. Ironically, Randolph's insistence on preserving the colourful idiom of folk speech did not translate into a rigorous fieldwork methodology. As a folk-tale collector, Randolph eschewed the widely accepted practice of providing verbatim transcripts of recorded storytelling events, choosing instead to rely upon his handwritten notes of a folk-tale performance. Censored material from two unpublished manuscripts, *'Unprintable' Songs from the Ozarks* and *'Vulgar Rhymes from the Ozarks'*, was published posthumously in *'Roll Me in Your Arms'* and *'Blow the Candle Out'*. MBS

Cochran, Robert, *Vance Randolph: An Ozark Life* (1985).

Legman, G., 'Unprintable Folklore? The Vance Randolph Collection,' *Journal of American Folklore*, 103 (1990).

Ransome, Arthur (1884–1967) English journalist and author of children's adventure stories. His first substantial book was *Old Peter's Russian Tales* (1916). In his autobiography he describes how he had seen the richness of the material in W. R. S. *Ralston's Russian Folk Tales* (1873), and had gone to Russia in 1913 to collect folklore material, subsequently becoming Russian correspondent for the *Daily News*. The tales—written mostly from memory, Ransome says in his introduction—are supposedly told by a grandfather to two children, and skilfully incorporate explanations of the Russian background for the benefit of young English readers. GA

'Rapunzel' The best-known version of 'Rapunzel' was published in the *Grimms'* *Kinder- und Hausmärchen* (*Children's and Household Tales*, 1812) from which the title originates. In the Grimms' version, a king climbs into the garden of a witch to steal some of her Rapunzel salad leaves which his pregnant wife craves. Upon being caught by the witch, he promises her their child, whom the witch keeps in a doorless tower. One day, a prince observes the witch climbing up the girl's long golden hair and, doing likewise, he enjoys a secret relationship with Rapunzel until she becomes pregnant and the tightness of her clothes uncovers her deceit to the witch. In later editions, the Grimms revised this motif so that a naïve Rapunzel gives herself away when she unfavourably compares the witch's weight to that of the prince. The witch banishes Rapunzel to a desert and lures up the prince by letting down the girl's hair which she had cut off and tied to a window hook. To save himself, he throws himself out of the tower and, blinded by thorns, he wanders the world for many years until he finds Rapunzel with her twin children. When her tears fall on his eyes, he regains his sight.

The Grimms' source was a translation of a French literary version by Charlotte-Rose de *La Force entitled 'Persinette' ('Parsley', *Les Contes des contes*, 1697), and the tale's plot is also contained in Marie-Catherine d'*Aulnoy's 'La chatte blanche' ('The White Cat', *Contes nouveaux ou les fées à la mode*, 1698). The sentimental ending following the victimization of the lovers is a literary motif not found in oral precursors of the tale, in which the lovers successfully escape the witch because of the girl's magical powers. In *Basile's 'Petrosinella' (*Pentamerone*, 1634–6), the girl throws three oak-galls behind her which turn into a dog, a lion, and finally a wolf, who tears up the witch; and in a Catalan version, white and red roses, thrown in the path of the pursuing giant, turn into a stream and fire.

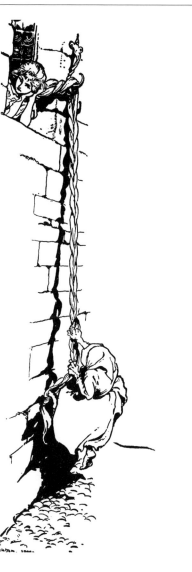

'Rapunzel' Rapunzel pulls up the witch into the tower with her long hair in the illustration by Arthur Rackham in *Fairy Tales of the Brothers Grimm* (1910).

Versions of the tale are found throughout Europe, Russia, and the Americas in which the girl is blinded or turned into a frog. In a recent literary revision, Emma *Donoghue uses the motif of the blind girl in 'The Tale of the Hair' (*Kissing the Witch*, 1997), but her version focuses on the old woman's care for the self-centred girl, fulfilling all her wishes from building the tower to even

impersonating the desired prince. In Anne *Sexton's lesbian reading of 'Rapunzel' (*Transformations*, 1972), the older woman is left by her young lover, who gives in to social pressure for a conventional heterosexual relationship. Edith *Nesbit's 'Melisande: or, Long and Short Division' (1908), in contrast, is an ironic interpretation where the princess's over-abundant hair-growth is pragmatically treated as the kingdom's most valuable export, but romantic interest requires a prince who can stop her hair growing. He achieves the desired happy end after the initial misfortune of the girl growing to immense height—which, however, allows her to defend her father's kingdom against invasion.   KS

Auerbach, Nina, and Knoepflmacher, U. C., *Forbidden Journeys: Fairy Tales and Fantasies by Victorian Women Writers* (1992).
Bolte, Johannes, and Polívka, Georg, *Anmerkungen zu den* Kinder- und Hausmärchen *der Brüder Grimm* (5 vols., 1913–32).
Lüthi, Max, 'Die Herkunft des Grimmschen Rapunzelmärchens', *Fabula*, 3:1–2 (1959).
Warner, Marina, *From the Beast to the Blonde: On Fairy Tales and their Tellers* (1994).

Rapunzel Let Down Your Hair (film: UK, 1978) A feminist discourse on the images of female enslavement created by cinema and television. Using the *Grimms' tale as a jumping-off point, it starts with a plain acting-out of the original text, as read by a mother to a child. A woodsman's daughter, *Rapunzel, has for years been imprisoned by a witch in a room at the top of a high tower in which there are no stairs. A passing prince, attracted by her singing, gets up by climbing her long hair. When the witch finds out, she strikes the prince blind and exiles him, but her triumph is cut short when Rapunzel bears twins. Exiled herself, Rapunzel takes her babies, seeks the prince, finds him, and cures his blindness with her tears.

The film then goes on to present four different perceptions of what the tale could be about in relation to the 1970s. The first, from the child's point of view, shows Rapunzel as the princess-heroine of a *Disney animated feature. In the second, shot in *film* *noir* style, the prince sees himself as a detective, and Rapunzel as a good girl needing to be rescued from a lesbian protector who has turned her into a junkie living at the top of a tower block. Prefacing the third viewpoint is a dissertation on the evolution of witches, arguing that the idea of witchcraft derives from patriarchal societies in which women endowed with exceptional skills or insights were stigmatized and persecuted. Following this the witch casts herself as a gynaecologist in a television melodrama; in this script, Rapunzel is her wayward teenage daughter. Finally, the fifth section offers Rapunzel's own reading of the situation: she begins as a singer forced to earn her living by working in a supermarket as a check-out girl. Falling in with a group of like-minded female performers, she finds fulfilment doing gigs which attract women of all persuasions. As the film ends she is singing a song called 'Let Down Your Hair', which she has written to express the joy she feels in her discovery of female solidarity. The naturalist style in which the last scenario is shot emphasizes that, for the women's cooperative that made the film, this interpretation is reality.   TAS

Ravel, Maurice (1875–1937) French composer. Along with several other influential artists working in Paris in the early years of the 20th century, Ravel in his early works exhibits an attraction to the exotic. Of a projected opera inspired by The *Arabian Nights*, only the overture, *Shéhérazade* (1898), was written. The lush orchestral song cycle *Shéhérazade* (1903), in which no reference is made to the eponymous heroine, sets three orientally inspired poems from a collection of the same name by Tristan Klingsor. Ravel's interest in fairy tales was part of a general fascination he had with the remembered world of childhood. *Ma Mère l'Oye* (*Mother Goose*, 1908–10), originally written as a set of five piano duets for children, was inspired by characters from Charles *Perrault, Mme d'*Aulnoy, and Mme *Leprince de Beaumont. Orchestrated in 1911, the suite was also expanded to act as a ballet score, based around the

story of *Sleeping Beauty (1912). The carefully crafted evocation of a child's viewpoint is further developed in the opera, or 'fantasie lyrique', *L'Enfant et les sortilèges* (*The Child and the Spells*, 1925). The libretto, by Colette, involves a naughty young boy who, having been reprimanded by his mother, finds the objects in his room coming to life, singing of their maltreatment at the hands of the young terror. In the second scene, after demonstrating his better nature by dressing a wounded squirrel, the child is tearfully reunited with his 'Maman'. Ravel's ingenious score includes a foxtrot for the Chinese cup and the famous cats' duet.   SB

Nichols, Roger, *Ravel* (1977).

Redgrove, Peter (1932–2003) British poet and novelist. Though known mainly for his poetry, Redgrove wrote several erotic and occult fantasies: *The God of Glass* (1979), *The Sleep of the Great Hypnotist* (1979), *The Beekeepers* (1980), and *The Facilitators, or Mister Hole-in-the Day* (1982). In 1989 he published *The One who Set Out to Study Fear*, a collection of revised classical fairy tales which have a metaphysical and Jungian flavour to them. Set in contemporary England, the tales address the need for changing sexual and social relations while raising the issue of psychological transformation. In a 'Job at Holle Park', a contemporary version of *'Mother Holle', the maltreated younger daughter breaks with her mother and sister to become the manager of an amusement park, thereby overcoming the monsters of her past. In 'The Rose of Leo Mann', based on *'Beauty and the Beast', a young woman rescues her beastly husband Leo from drugs and alcohol. Most of Redgrove's tales depict voyages and quests in which the protagonists become at one with themselves and exhibit great spiritual determination.   JZ

'Red Shoes, The' ('De Røde Sko', 1845) Known to modern audiences largely through the haunting 1948 film of the same name, directed by Michael *Powell and Emeric Pressburger, Hans Christian *Andersen's 'The Red Shoes' tells the story of a girl whose vanity and obsession with her red shoes lead to grotesque punishment and then death.

'Little Karen' is given a pair of makeshift red cloth shoes, which she wears to her mother's funeral. She is pitied and adopted by a wealthy woman who has the red shoes burnt. Taking advantage of her guardian's poor eyesight to buy another pair for her confirmation, Karen goes through the ceremony thinking only of the shoes. Forbidden to wear them to church, she disobeys. At the church door the following Sunday, a red-bearded soldier taps the soles of her shoes, both as she enters and as she leaves, saying: 'My! what lovely dancing shoes! Stay on tight when you dance!' While kneeling at the altar, Karen thinks only of the red shoes, forgetting to sing the hymns and to pray. But as she leaves the church, Karen begins to dance. Once started, she cannot stop until the shoes are forcibly removed and hidden in a cupboard.

Rather than tend her sick guardian, Karen accepts an invitation to a ball, again donning the red shoes. But once she starts dancing, the shoes take on a power of their own, clinging to her feet despite her efforts to tear them off and dancing her into the forest and churchyard. In the church, an angel appears, his face 'stern and solemn'. 'Dance you shall,' he proclaims, 'dance in your red shoes until you are cold and pale, until your skin shrivels up like a skeleton's!' Dancing ceaselessly, Karen feels abandoned by humans and cursed by God. Desperate, she implores the executioner to cut off her feet, and, as he does so, the shoes and feet dance off alone, across the fields and into the forest. Now with wooden feet and crutches, she is afraid to enter the church, which is barred by the red shoes still dancing before her eyes. Modest and pious, she becomes the parson's servant. As she prays, the angel reappears, transforming her simple room into the glorious church she had so feared to enter. 'Full of sunshine and peace and joy', her heart at last breaks, her soul flying 'to heaven, where there was no one to ask about the red shoes'.

Andersen ascribed this harsh and puritanical story to his own childhood guilt over

caring more about a pair of new boots than the confirmation to which he wore them. However, the red shoes seem to symbolize not merely vanity but also normal sensuality, which the narrative seeks unremittingly to expose and punish.

While employing Andersen's symbolic language, the film offers a more complex story, with the red shoes representing the lure of the artistic life. The heroine of the ballet dances herself to death, beguiled into wearing the shoes by the sorcerer-like 'shoemaker'. The ballerina-heroine of the frame narrative must choose between art (represented by a forceful and hypnotic director) and love (her temperamental composer husband). Irrevocably torn between art and life, wearing the red shoes of her signature ballet, she dances wildly to a parapet and leaps in front of a passing train. A 1993 Broadway musical, choreographed by Lar Lubovich, was based on the film. A new ballet, choreographed by Flemming Flindt for the Royal Danish Ballet, premièred in January 1998.   JGH

Régnier, Henri de (1864–1936) French writer. Once a leader of the symbolist movement, Régnier produced volumes of prose and poetry drawing upon a classical pantheon of nymphs, satyrs, and demigods. In *Contes à soi-même* (*Tales to oneself*, 1894), his 'Le Sixième Mariage de Barbe-Bleue' ('*Bluebeard's Sixth Marriage*') grafts a happy ending onto a dark legend. Régnier's novel *Le Passé vivant* (*The Living Past*, 1909) has been considered a fairy story, while collections like *La Canne de jaspe* (*The Jasper Cane*, 1897), and *Histoires incertaines* (*Uncertain Tales*, 1919) juxtapose naturalist detail with supernatural events.   AR

Rego, Paula (1935–) Portuguese-born painter who trained at the Slade School of Art in Britain and settled permanently in London in 1976, where she has also taught at the Slade. She represented Britain and Portugal in the São Paolo Bienal, and, in 1990, was appointed the first associate artist for the National Gallery in London. After a grant from the Gulbenkian Foundation in 1976 to research fairy tales, she illustrated

Portuguese fairy tales in *Contos Populares* (1974–5) and the more successful 1989 etchings of English *Nursery Rhymes*. Her inspired illustration of **Peter Pan* (1992) and the **Pinocchio* paintings (1995–6) are typical in their exploration of the murky underside and emotional conflicts of these familiar stories. To paint, Rego must have a story, found in fairy tales, **Disney*'s films, opera, magazines, nightmares, and from sights in the street. Rego's work is figurative, often using caricatured, anthropomorphic animals to express psychological states where the story functions as shared cultural knowledge, providing an entry to the exploration of conflicting emotions. Often of a personal nature, they confront childhood terror and the violence of family relationships; the 1995 **Snow White* series, where the narrative across the four paintings shifts the sites of power between Snow White and her stepmother, shows the contradictory intersections of love and hate, nurturing and torture, rather than resolving them in a conventional happy ending. In contrast to the Snow White series, Rego's **Little Red Riding Hood* series of 2003 represents a very optimistic view of a mother and grandmother protecting a girl from male predators. In a series of six coloured pastels, she comically illustrates how a mother dressed in red arrives to cut open the belly of a middle-aged man with a pitchfork. Indeed, she is elegantly dressed, and in the final image, the mother sits in an office chair elegantly dressed with a wolf fur wrapped around her neck. Numerous women artists have been drawn to *'Little Red Riding Hood'* because of the gender conflict and because the Perrault and Grimm versions tend to make little girls responsible for their own rape and or demise. Rego recreates a version in which women are capable of saving themselves.

All her remakes of classical fairy tales question how women and children are raised and treated and project borderline images of loving care and brutality, joy in life, and sadistic punishment. The complex sensual ambiguity of human behaviour is at the heart of other fairy-tale re-creations such as *The Little Mermaid* (2003), a pastel on paper that depicts a grown woman in a bathing suit as refuse on a beach, or the three **Pinocchio* pastels on paper, which blur the affection of the Blue Fairy and Gepetto for a lifelike boy, and *Prince Pig's Courtship* (2006), a coloured lithograph based on Giovan Francesco **Straparola*'s 'The Pig Prince', that marks the oppression of a disheartened woman. Rego bores into the troubled psyches of the characters of her tales, and she is not afraid to spill blood and guts in her re-creations.   KS

Coldwell, Paul, *Paula Rego Printmaker* (2005).
McEwen, John, *Paula Rego* (2nd edn., 1997).
McEwen, John, *Paula Rego behind the Scenes* (2008).
Rego, Paula, *Paula Rego* (1988).
Rego, Paula, *Tales from the National Gallery* (1991).

Reid Banks, Lynne (1929–) British novelist and writer of fantasy for young adults who is mainly known for her Omri series: *The Indian in the Cupboard* (1980), *The Return of the Indian* (1986), *The Secret of the Indian* (1989), and *The Mystery of the Cupboard* (1993). These works centre on a cupboard with a magic key, and whenever the young boy Omri puts his plastic Indian named Little Bear or other things inside, they either come to life or are reduced in size. The key also brings about time-travel adventures into the past, and Omri himself becomes involved in them. The series was transformed into the **Disney* film *The Indian in the Cupboard* (1995). Lynne Reid Banks has also written fairy-tale novels such as *The Farthest-Away Mountain* (1976), which involves a girl and a frog, who travel together to break the frog's spell; *The Fairy Rebel* (1985), which concerns a fairy who defies her queen by helping a woman have a baby girl; and **Melusine: A Mystery* (1988), which depicts a young boy's sexual awakening in a French château and his encounters with a teenage girl who has mysterious powers of transformation.   JZ

Reinick, Robert (1805–52) Much loved German poet and writer for children. Originally a painter, Reinick started writing—primarily for children—in the 1840s when bad health forced him to give up painting, but his early training remains evident in his closely observed and lovingly portrayed descriptions of nature. His output is not large but is very varied; his first collection of rhymes, poems, and stories appeared in 1845, *ABC-Buch für grosse und kleine Kinder* (*ABC-Book for Children Big and Small*), and he contributed to three volumes of the *Deutscher Jugendkalender* (*Calendar for German Youth*, 1849–52). He was close to the romantic poets whose interest in nature and folklore he shared, and his work is characterized by its simplicity, purity, naïve joyfulness, and a lyrical style. Although he is not considered the equal of his contemporaries, his work was as often set to music as that of Heinrich *Heine. Reinick's fairy tales tend to be didactic, but the moral is balanced by humour, and his interest in the romantic literary fairy tale, especially E. T. A. *Hoffmann's work. Hoffmann's 'Nussknacker und Mausekönig' ('The Nutcracker') provided the model for Reinick's first fairy tale, 'Die Wurzelprinzessin' ('The Root Princess', 1847). While he tells one oral tale, 'Die Hausgenossen' ('The Housemates'), and 'Prinz Goldfisch und das Fischermädchen' ('Prince Goldfish and the Fishergirl') follows the *Grimms' 'Aschenbrödel' (*'Cinderella'), most of his work is literary. His lastingly popular anthology *Märchen-, Lieder- und Geschichtenbuch, Gesammelte Dichtungen für die Jugend* (*A Book of Fairy Tales, Songs, and Stories*, 1873) contains most of his work, and all of his fairy tales.   KS

Sturm, K. F., *Robert Reinick der Kinderdichter* (1907).

Reiniger, Lotte (1899–1981) Pioneer exponent of silhouette films and director of the world's first animated feature, a fantasy culled from *The *Arabian Nights*. Born in Berlin, she had developed her free-hand scissor technique, and made her first short film, by the age of 20. Her method of animation was simple: having designed and cut out her protagonists from paper, she joined together the different parts of each body by means of wire hinges. The figures were then arranged directly beneath the camera on a horizontal glass table lit from below. After exposing one frame of film, she would slightly modify the position of the figures, and then expose the next.

Her feeling for character and how to communicate it in a silhouette extended right down to the fingertips: an evil character would be given wicked hands as well as an evil face and posture. This art can be seen gradually reaching its peak in her 65-minute feature *Die Abenteuer des Prinzen Achmed* (*The Adventures of Prince Achmed*), made over three years between 1923 and 1926. It is based on 'The Tale of the Ebony Horse' which Reiniger blends with *'Aladdin' and some original material as well.

The story starts when an ugly and powerful sorcerer appears on the caliph's birthday with a magic flying horse he has created. The caliph wants to possess it at once, but the sorcerer will part with it only in exchange for the hand of the caliph's beautiful daughter Dinarsade. This proposal incenses Achmed, her brother, and he persuades the caliph to reject it, thereby causing the sorcerer to retaliate by casting a spell which lures him to mount the horse and set off on a flight which, the sorcerer intends, will be fatal. However, Achmed averts disaster, lands on the enchanted island of Wak Wak, and falls in love with its ruler, the princess Pari Banu.

For the rest of her life, most of which was spent working in England because of Nazi persecution in her homeland, Reiniger carried on producing silhouette films, all of them shorts rather than features, many of them made for television. Among the fairy tales that she adapted to suit her medium were several from the *Grimms (e.g. *'Snow White and Rose Red', 'The Golden Goose', 'The Three Wishes'), and some from *Andersen (e.g. 'The Little Chimney Sweep', 'The Flying Suitcase'). One such 10-minute film, 'The Gallant Little Tailor', won her recognition at the 1955 Venice Biennale where, in the short television film category, she was awarded a Silver Dolphin.   TAS

Ricard, Jules (1848–1903) French novelist and playwright. His collection of short stories, *Acheteuses de rêves* (*Buyers of Dreams*,

Reiniger, Lotte Aladdin confronts the monster in Lotte Reiniger's 1926 silhouette film, *The Adventures of Prince Achmed*, inspired by several stories in *The Arabian Nights*. Photo: BFI Stills.

1894), contains 'Contes de la fée Morgane' ('Tales of the Fairy Morgane'). Here the Celtic fairy Morgane recounts five stories that examine the nature of love, including a retelling of *'Cinderella'. A curious mix of reality and fantasy, the narrative framework for the stories consists of conversations between the earthy, ironic fairy, who grouses about silly human wishes, and the first-person narrator, a writer whom she accuses of plagiarizing her stories. AZ

Rice, Anne (1941–) American author of horror and erotica. She was born Howard Allen O'Brien and grew up in the 'Irish Channel' section of New Orleans, just blocks away from the genteel quarter of her horror novels. A modern-day myth maker, she synthesized a variety of folk legends for her *Vampire Chronicles* (1976–95), which includes *Interview with a Vampire, The Vampire Lestat, The Queen of the Damned, The Tale of the Body Thief,* and *Memnoch the Devil.* Her originality lies in their sympathetic treatment: vampires are philosophizing victims who must spend eternity debating good and evil. These supernaturally erotic heroes find special favour with gays, who identify with their banishment from mainstream society. Her *Lives of the Mayfair Witches* series (1990–4) also has a cult following, and includes *The Witching Hour, Lasher,* and *Taltos.*

She penned erotica under the pseudonym Anne Rampling, and as A. N. Roquelaure fashioned the ultimate subversion of a beloved fairy tale. Awakened not by a kiss but by sexual initiation, her *Sleeping Beauty becomes a sado-masochistic sex slave in the pornographic *Sleeping Beauty Novels* (1982–5; *The Claiming of Sleeping Beauty, Beauty's Punishment, Beauty's Release*). Her self-proclaimed 'Disneyland of S & M' is meant to be a psychological portrait of dominance and submission, sexuality and spirituality. MLE

Ramsland, Katherine, *Prism of the Night: A Biography of Anne Rice* (1991).

Ramsland, Katherine, *The Roquelaure Reader: A Companion to Anne Rice's Erotica* (1996).

Roberts, Bette B., *Anne Rice* (1994).

Smith, Jennifer, *Anne Rice: A Critical Companion* (1996).

Richter, Ludwig (Adrian Ludwig Richter, 1803–84). A phenomenally popular 19th-century German illustrator of *Bechstein's fairy tales, Richter's illustrations were sought for other fairy tale collections and were later borrowed for the *Grimms' *Tales.* From the age of 12 Richter learned draftsmanship in his father's copperplate engraving workshop. At 17 his precocious artistic accomplishment won him a position recording the French journeys of a Russian prince. Sent subsequently by a Dresden patron to Italy for three years (1823–6), he joined the German community of artists in Rome, which included the influential Julius Schnorr von Carolsfeld. Called the 'St Luke Brotherhood' (*Lukasbrüder*), their work was generally Nazarene in style.

On his return to Germany, Richter instructed aspiring porcelain painters, concentrating on Saxon scenes. In meeting a demand for 'German' art, Bechstein's landscapes made his reputation. Appointment to the professorship of landscape painting at the Dresden Academy of Art (1836) was followed by commissions from the Leipzig publishers Wigand for engravings which culminated in a 21-volume reprint series of 15th- and 16th-century German chapbooks.

Richter's illustrations for August *Musäus's *Volksmärchen der Deutschen* (*Folktales of the Germans,* 1842) established his fame, and calls for further fairy-tale illustrations followed. About his work on Musäus's *Tales,* Richter wrote that, while he worked on one scene, he imagined three more and regretted having to lay his pencil down at evening. His fertile imagination resulted in 2,600 woodcuts in nearly 150 books during his professional career. By his own account, the influence of Albrecht Dürer, which is everywhere apparent in his most fully realized cityscapes, loomed large in his artistic development.

Richter's best-known illustrations were undoubtedly those for the fairy tales of Ludwig Bechstein. Reused in poster editions of Bechstein's fairy tales and pirated for editions of Grimms' tales, they contributed lastingly to German visual culture. RBB

Hand, Joachim Neidhardt, *Ludwig Richter* (1969).

Stubbe, W. (ed.), *Das Ludwig Richter Album: Sämtliche Holzschnitte* (1971).

Rickert, M. (**Mary Rickert**, 1959–) American writer of postmodern fantasy fiction. Her short-story collections, *Map of Dreams* (2006) and *Holiday* (2010), and novel *The Memory Garden* (2014) offer dark Gothic narratives populated by ghosts, human/animal transformation, and other mythic and fairy-tale protagonists and processes. Commenting that 'the modern fairy tale is arguably the extreme romance of our time, generally founded on impossible beauty, perfect affection and happy endings' (*Numéro Cinq Magazine* 3, 2012), Rickert argues in this essay on the Gothic that fairy-tale imagery can be found in unexpected locations.　　　　　　　　　　PG

Riley, James Whitcomb (1849–1916) American poet. During his lifetime, Riley enjoyed enormous popularity. Known as 'The Hoosier Poet' or 'the people's poet', he drew material from Midwestern literature, fairy tales, and speech patterns. His verses, written in folk dialect, expressed the myth of rural America, with phrases such as 'When the frost is on the punkin' and 'the old swimin'-hole'. Riley's 'Raggedy Man' inspired Johnny *Gruelle's Raggedy Ann and Andy books. His most enduring creation, 'Little Orphan Annie'—'the Gobble-uns'll git you | Ef you | Don't | Watch | Out'—became part of childhood folklore and the name of a classic comic strip (the source of the Broadway musical *Annie*).　　　　AS

> Morrow, Barbara Olenyik, *From Ben-Hur to Sister Carrie: Remembering the Lives and Works of Five Indiana Authors* (1995).
> Revell, Peter, *James Whitcomb Riley* (1970).

Rimsky-Korsakov, Nikolai Andreievich (1844–1908) Russian composer. As a young man with virtually no musical training, Rimsky-Korsakov sought advice from Mili Balakirev, who welcomed him into the small group of Russian nationalist composers he had founded—the 'Mighty Handful', which also included Borodin and Mussorgsky. Family tradition pointed him toward the navy, however; not until returning from a three-year cruise as an officer could he rejoin his musical friends and complete his first symphony (1865). In 1871 he was invited to become a professor of composition at the St Petersburg conservatory—somewhat to his dismay, as he still knew almost nothing of structure or theory. Prudently retaining his commission, he accepted, studying all night to keep ahead of his classes; eventually, he became an outstanding teacher, among his pupils being Igor Stravinsky.

Rimsky-Korsakov's music is known for vitality and brilliant orchestration. Many of his melodies came directly from the folk songs he collected, and of his 15 operas, 14 were inspired by Russian folklore. His first opera, *Sadko* (1867; revised 1897), was based on the folk tale of 'Sadko the Sailor'. *The *Snow Maiden* (1882), *The Tsar Saltan* (1900), and *The Invisible City of Kitezh* (1906) also have folk-tale origins. *Tsar Saltan*, from *Pushkin's poetic version of the tale, contains Rimsky-Korsakov's best-known musical moment, 'The Flight of the Bumblebee'. In the story, Tsar Saltan, falsely informed that his wife has borne a monster, has them put in a barrel and thrown into the sea. The son grows up on a desert island, acquires magical powers, and transforms the island into a place of wonders. This is possibly the only opera in which a squirrel sings a Russian folk song while cracking golden nuts and extracting emeralds from them. Rimsky-Korsakov's last opera, *The Golden Cockerel* (*Le Coq d'Or*, 1908), originated in the folk tale of the foolish Tsar Dadon, transformed by Pushkin into a biting satire on autocracy. Rimsky-Korsakov created the musical equivalent of satire by parodying military marches and other popular tunes, while Ivan *Bilibin parodied cheap popular prints in his set designs and costumes.

Reading *The *Arabian Nights* inspired Rimsky-Korsakov's most famous orchestral work, *Scheherazade* (1888). This symphonic poem consists of four movements tied together by passages for solo violin, representing the voice of Scheherazade as she tells her stories to the misogynistic sultan, whose loud and threatening theme is heard at the beginning of the piece. The first movement is titled 'The Sea and Sind-bad's Ship'; the second, 'The Story of the Calender Prince'; the third, 'The Young Prince and the Young Princess'; and the fourth, 'The Festival of Bagdad; The Sea; The Ship Goes to Pieces on a Rock Sur-mounted by a Bronze Warrior'. The piece ends serenely as Scheherazade concludes, having finally won the love of her lord. In 1910 *Scheherazade* became the musical setting for one of Diaghilev's most famous ballets, with a new plot superimposed on the music. SR

> Abraham, Gerald, *Rimsky-Korsakov* (1945).
> Rimsky-Korsakov, Nikolai, *My Musical Life* (1947).

Ringelnatz, Joachim (pen name of **Hans Bötticher**, 1883–1934) German writer and cabaret performer whose connection to the Dada movement was reflected in the satirical children's tales and nonsense rhymes he created. His Kuttel Daddeldu character, found in Ringelnatz's poems and short stories, is a cynical seaman and storyteller whose colourful stories often blend dialect and foreign phrases with political criticism and nonsense, while sub-verting narrative conventions and audience expectations. MBS

> Pape, Walter (ed.), *Joachim Ringelnatz: Das Gesamtwerk in sieben Bänden* (1983).
> Ringelnatz, Joachim, *Kuttel Daddeldu erzählt seinen Kindern das Märchen vom Rotkäppchen* (1923).
> Zipes, Jack (ed.), *Fairy Tales and Fables from Weimar Days* (1989).

'Riquet with the Tuft' ('Riquet à la houppe') A variant of the 'Cupid and Psyche' and *'Beauty and the Beast' motif, 'Riquet with the Tuft' has three French versions writ-ten for a literary salon contest. An ugly-yet-brilliant gnome king, prince, or devil loves a beautiful-yet-stupid princess on whom he bestows intelligence in exchange for mar-riage. *Perrault's princess renders Riquet handsome: Love blinds her to his faults. *Bernard's heroine takes a lover, whom Riquet transforms into his double: she iron-izes that all lovers eventually become

husbands. In *Lhéritier's 'Ricdin-Ricdon' (precursor of *'Rumpelstiltskin'), the woman must guess the devil's name. MLE

Ritchie, Anne Thackeray (1837–1919) Daughter of British Victorian novelist Wil-liam Makepeace *Thackeray, aunt to Virginia Woolf, and a significant author and editor in her own right. Best known for her biograph-ical introductions to her father's works, she also wrote several 'domestic novels', numer-ous essays on her contemporaries, and two collections of modern fairy tales. *Five Old Friends and a Young Prince* of 1868 (published in America as *Fairy Tales for Grown Folks*) and *Bluebeard's Keys* (1874) are *Märchen* in Victorian dress for adult audiences. Ritchie's versions of classic tales including *'Beauty and the Beast', 'The *Sleeping Beauty in the Wood', *'Cinderella', and *'Little Red Riding Hood' have been criticized as heavily moralized and pedes-trian, lacking the magic of their originals. But they are always realistic in setting, rev-elatory of Victorian middle- and upper-class manners and mores, and clever in their psychology. They are sometimes feminist in orientation. Ritchie's female protagonists, young women journeying to maturity (often aided by wise old spinsters) awake to the problems of society's foolish and superficial judgements or battle against marriages of convenience. Her villains: misers, fanatics, *nouveau riche* industrialists, and hard-heart-ed materialists of both sexes are the ogres, monsters, and witches of traditional fairy lore transformed. Ritchie also provided a valuable introduction to *The Fairy Tales of Madame d'*Aulnoy* in 1895. CGS

> Auerbach, Nina, and Knoepflmacher, U. C. (eds.), *Forbidden Journeys* (1992).
> Zipes, Jack (ed.), *Victorian Fairy Tales* (1987).

'Robber Bridegroom, The' Told to the Brothers *Grimm by Marie Hassenpflug, 'Der Räuberbräutigam' is closely related to another tale from *Kinder- und Haus-märchen* (*Children's and Household Tales*), 'Fitchers Vogel' ('Fitcher's Bird'), as well as to *Perrault's 'Barbe bleue' (*'Bluebeard'). In addition, the 1812 volume of the first edition of the Grimms' tales included 'Das Mords-chloss' ('The Castle of Murder', omitted in subsequent editions), which reads as an amalgam of 'The Robber Bridegroom' and 'Fitcher's Bird'.

In the version of 'The Robber Bridegroom' which appears in *Children's and Household Tales*, a rich but slightly unnerving suitor becomes engaged to a miller's daughter at her father's behest. Invited to the forest home of her husband-to-be, the girl warily marks her tracks with peas and lentils. On arriving at the forbidding, seemingly deserted house she is warned by a caged bird that she should turn back, as the house belongs to murderers. In the cellar she comes across an old woman who confirms the bird's warning: the house is a cannibals' den, and the young girl is to be their victim. Hidden behind a barrel, she then watches as the murderous crew, including her future husband, return home with their latest catch. As they chop her up, a finger flies into the young heroine's lap. However, having had their drinks spiked by the old woman, the murderers are soon asleep, and the girl is able to escape.

At the wedding feast a round of storytelling is proposed. Asked by her bridegroom to contribute, the young girl proceeds to recount a dream, which turns out to be the tale of her trip to the murderers' den. Reaching the point in the story at which the chopped finger landed in her lap, she miraculously produces the real thing. The robber and his gang are duly arrested.

A particularly gruesome tale, 'The Robber Bridegroom' is also relatively lacking in fairy-tale magic (as is 'Bluebeard'), which is the reason why, in terms of tale type, it has been categorized as a novella. Variants have been recorded throughout Europe, notably the witty and poetic English tale, 'Mr Fox', in which the eponymous villain is merely a murderer rather than a cannibal, acting alone, and which includes the notable refrains 'Be bold, be bold, but not too bold', and 'It is not so, nor it was not so'.

The Grimms' tale has served as the source for a novel by Eudora Welty (*The Robber Bridegroom*, 1942). More recently, the elements it shares with 'Bluebeard'—including dismembered female victims and a cunning female heroine—have been explored in fiction by Angela *Carter and Margaret *Atwood, the latter of whom has given 'The Robber Bridegroom' a late 20th-century twist in the form of her novel *The Robber Bride* (1993). SB

Robinson, Charles (1870–1937) British illustrator, son of Thomas Robinson who was an artist and engraver; along with his two brothers William Heath *Robinson and Thomas Heath *Robinson, he worked in the Arts and Crafts tradition. In 1899 he and his brothers illustrated *Fairy Tales from Hans Christian *Andersen* for Dent. Before that he had already illustrated *Stevenson's *A Child's Garden of Verses* and Aesop's *Fables*. In the same year, he also drew illustrations for Charles *Perrault's *Tales of Past Times*, and in 1900–2 Dent published a three-volume set, The True Annals of Fairy-Land, edited by William Canton with Charles Robinson's illustrations.

In 1908 he illustrated Evelyn Martinengo Cesaresco's *The Fairies' Fountain, and Other Stories* and another two-volume *True Annals of Fairyland in the Reign of King Cole* for Dent in 1909. Two particular fairy-tale books appeared in 1910 and 1913: the first, Jacob and Wilhelm *Grimms' *Grimms' Fairy Tales*, and the second, Oscar *Wilde's *The Happy Prince, and Other Tales*.

Largely self-taught, he was apprenticed as a lithographic artist and was dedicated to the ideal of the book beautiful, an ideal which encompassed the text, layout, illustrations, and cover. He worked primarily in black and white and watercolour, and was one of the first to integrate the text with illustration. According to Tessa Chester and Irene Whalley, his work was characteristic of the Art Nouveau period with its 'interweaving, curving line, the solid black areas relieved by white, and the careful use of stylised pattern'.

His works were exhibited at the Royal Academy and he was a lifelong member of the London Sketch Club. Altogether, he illustrated over 100 books, one of the last of which was *Granny's Book of Fairy Stories* (1930).   LS

Whalley, Joyce, and Chester, Tessa Rose, *A History of Children's Book Illustration* (1988).

Robinson, Thomas Heath (1869–1950) British illustrator, second of the Robinson brothers to achieve prominence in illustration. With his two brothers, Charles and William Heath, Robinson illustrated *Fairy Tales from Hans Christian *Andersen* (1899). The brothers were dubbed the three musketeers.

Educated at Cook's Art School and the Westminster Art School, T. H. Robinson went on to illustrate *Fairy Tales from The *Arabian Nights* in 1899. His talent resided more with realistic art than with the fantasy ability of his two brothers, so his work was better applied to such books as *The Scarlet Letter* by Nathaniel *Hawthorne, and works by Laurence Sterne, Mrs *Gaskell, and William Makepeace *Thackeray. He contributed to boys' adventure stories in numerous magazines as well as to books with religious subjects, such as George R. Lees, *The Life of Christ* (1920).   LS

Robinson, William Heath (1872–1944) British illustrator, youngest of the three talented Robinson brothers. He collaborated with his two brothers on *Fairy Tales from Hans Christian Andersen* (1899). A volume of *Andersen's tales appeared in 1913, *Hans Andersen's Fairy Tales*, with 16 tipped-in colour illustrations by W. H. Robinson. Trained at the Islington School of Art (1887), he initially planned on being a landscape artist, but then followed in his brothers' footsteps. He developed a talent for humorous drawings, often contributing designs of dotty contraptions to periodicals. Although he began under the influence of Beardsley and Art Nouveau, he experimented with various styles and the use of light, sometimes backlighting the subjects. He also used the circular frame for his illustrations. He was one of the most versatile of British illustrators.   LS

Rodari, Gianni (1920–80) The most distinguished and original of writers for children in Italy in the 20th century; Rodari has been widely translated abroad and is greatly respected among scholars and *cognoscenti*. While his subject-matter is unequivocally identifiable with the 20th century, his connection with the fairy tale resides in the markedly fantastic inclination of his work and in his (often parodic) re-use of traditional forms and devices. Brought up in the era of fascism in Italy, Rodari began reading philosophers, including Marx, while still at school and was always drawn to novel and radical ideas. Musically gifted, his career was begun as a teacher, but towards the end of the Second World War he joined the Communist Party and participated in the Italian Resistance movement. Like so many Italian intellectuals, he saw utopian marxism as the country's political salvation, a guarantee against future authoritarian oppression. After the war he committed himself full-time to the communist cause, launching a new Party journal, *L'ordine nuovo*, in 1945. So began his lifelong work as a journalist. In 1947 he began to write for the leading communist daily newspaper, *L'Unità*, in Milan, one assignment being the composition of some pieces for children. In 1950 the Party sent him to Rome to co-edit *Il pioniere* (*The Pioneer*), a weekly paper for the young, whose future he was dedicated to improving. The 1950s were an intensely creative time for Rodari, during which he published hundreds of poems and stories for children, as a journalist moving away from communist control but still working for the press of the Left. His first book, *Il libro delle filastrocche* (*The Book of Rhymes*, 1950), contained comic verses in the manner of Edward Lear and Lewis *Carroll, and the second, *Il romanzo di Cipollino* (1951), was a fantastic narrative about a tyrant prince, but for him 'Nonsense' and fantasy were methods of addressing the political and social evils of the time. Throughout the decade the Church saw him as a threat to youthful minds and urged the banning of his books in schools. The eminent publisher Einaudi of Turin first handled Rodari's work in 1960, a turning-point, and during the 1960s Rodari worked in close contact with both children and teachers through the Educational Cooperation Movement. In the same period he helped to advance educational reforms. Some of his most noted and popular works now began to appear; *Favole al telefono* (*Telephone Tales*, 1962; a selection, 1965), the brief stories of a commercial traveller nightly phoning his family, illustrates both Rodari's concern with contemporary reality and the surreal quality of his humour. *Il libro degli errori* (*The Book of Errors*, 1964), *La torta in cielo* (1966; *A Pie in the Sky*, 1966; 1971), and *Novelle fatte a macchina* (*Tales Told by a Machine*, 1973; a selection, 1976) followed amongst many others. In 1973 he published an important personal statement and wittily probing exploration in *Grammatica della fantasia: Introduzione all'arte di inventare storie* (*The Grammar of Fantasy: An Introduction to the Art of Inventing Stories*), in which he illustrates the power and riches of the imagination and elucidates his own ideas and methodology; he shows language to be as important as imagination, and sometimes synonymous with it. The work was to become a touchstone handbook for teachers and parents. In it Rodari repeatedly discusses the pleasures and uses of familiar fairy tales, ancient and modern, from *'Little Red Riding Hood' to *Pinocchio. He refers to Italo *Calvino, whose life and work exhibited some significant parallels with his own. From the 1950s, this eminent close contemporary had been evolving new approaches to fantasy and fairy-tale narratives in his major works for adults, as well as minor pieces for children, thus establishing a liberating alternative to the prevailing literary mood of neorealism. Calvino had been responsible, too, for the first compendious national collection of folk tales, rewritten from their regional dialects into Italian (*Fiabe italiane*, 1956), a revelatory work for Rodari as for the cultural establishment. Some of Rodari's later titles clearly demonstrate his kinships within the fairy-tale family tree: *Marionette in libertà* (*Marionettes at Liberty*, 1974), *La filastrocca di Pinocchio* (*Pinocchio's Rhyme*, 1974), *C'era due volte il barone Lamberto* (*Twice Upon a Time There was Baron Lamberto*, 1978), and *La gondola fantasma* (*The Phantom Gondola*, 1978). The imaginative inheritance which Rodari elaborated and enriched did not, for him, provide a diverting escape route but instead an empowering and liberating approach to civilized modern life. Rodari's purpose was not to disguise and sweeten through fantasy, but to use imagination to teach children the truth about reality.   ALL

Argilli, Marcello, del Cornò, Lucio, and de Luca, Carmine (eds.), *Le provocazioni della fantasia. Gianni Rodari scrittore e educatore* (1993).

Bini, G. (ed.), *Leggere Rodari* (1981).

Boero, Pino, *Una storia, tante storie: guida all'opera di Gianni Rodari* (1992).

Massini, Giulia, *La poetica di Rodari: Utopia del folklore e nonsense* (2010).

Petrini, Enzo, Argilli, Marcello, and Bonardi, Carlo (eds.), *Gianni Rodari* (1981).

Rodari, Gianni, *The Grammar of Fantasy*, trans. with intro. Jack Zipes (1996).

Roi et l'oiseau, Le (*The King and the Bird*) While in keeping with the tradition of the fairy tale, this animated film reflects the changing values of its time. Adapted from *Andersen's 'The Shepherdess and the Chimney Sweep', and first released in France (1953) under the title *La Bergère et le ramoneur*, *Le Roi et l'oiseau* is a remake of the first full-length film by Paul Grimault with a screenplay by Jacques Prévert (1950). Grimault's 33 mm., 87-minutes-long film, in colour, was produced in France (1979) and was awarded the Louis Delluc prize in 1980.

The Grimault–Prévert production diverges from its Danish model in respect to gender roles and ideology. Andersen stressed the paradigm of the unassertive female, and the acceptance of one's destiny. Overwhelmed by the sight of the world, the shepherdess returns to an anti-climactic self-inflicted captivity. In contrast, in the French animated film, the shepherdess and the chimney sweep equally aspire to their freedom. Grimault's film, a witty satire against tyranny, celebrates the formidable power of peace. Particularly stirring is the closing image of the redeemed bulldozer destroying the bird's cage, which eloquently synthesizes Prévert's message of freedom.

Roi et l'oiseau, Le The chimney sweep and the shepherdess escape from the tyrannical king in Paul Grimault's animated film *Le Roi et l'oiseau* (1953). Jacques Prévert's screenplay transformed the Hans Christian *Andersen tale 'The Chimney Sweep and the Shepherdess' into a political commentary about contemporary fascism. Photo: © Les Films Paul Grimault/Les Films Gibe/The Kobal Collection.

Grimault (1905–94) was the originator of French animated films. He founded 'Les Gemeaux' (1936), the first French corporation of animated films and the most prominent one in Europe. Grimault left 'Les Gemeaux' (1951) to found his own film association: 'Les Films Grimault'. Prévert (1900–77) was a multifaceted artist: a poet, a film-maker, and a song writer. Throughout his art, he tirelessly denounced the oppressive power of the rich—a prevalent theme of 'The King and the Bird'—with a judicious blend of provocative humour and endearing simplicity.   AMM

Lescarmontier, Jeannine, *Paul Grimault: Traits de mémoire* (1991).

Pagliano, Jean, *Paul Grimault* (1996).

Romano, Lalla (1906–2001) Italian poet, painter, translator, and critic. She is best known for her autobiographical narrative *Le parole tra noi leggere* (*The Words between Us Weightless*, 1969, Strega Prize), which resembles in its conclusion the morals of fairy tales. Romano's flirting with fairy tales is most evident in *Le Metamorfosi* (1951, rev. 1983), a collection of short prose narratives based on dreams. Some of them are truly fairy tales, since the author believes that dream-transformations are of the same material one finds in myths and fairy tales. Other works with a fairy-tale atmosphere include *L'ospite* (*The Guest*, 1973) and *Ho sognato l'ospedale* (*I Dreamed the Hospital*, 1995).   GD

Rosen, Michael (1946–) British poet, writer of children's books, and broadcaster. Known for his humorous verse, Rosen is regarded as one of the most significant poets for children in England. He was the fifth British Children's Laureate from June 2007 to June 2009. Rosen has also written several witty fairy-tale books in verse and prose for children. Among his better works are: *Hairy Tales and Nursery Crimes* (1985), *The Wicked Tricks of Till Owlyglass* (1989), *The Man With No Shadow* (1994), and *Arabian Frights and Other Stories* (1999). JZ

Rossetti, Christina (1830–94) English poet. She is best known today for her brilliant long poem *Goblin Market* (1862), an extended tale about two sisters who meet a band of sinister half-human, half-animal creatures who tempt them to buy exotic fruit. Laura eats the fruit, and then craves more and more—but the next day she cannot find the goblins, and she begins to waste away from longing. Lizzie, who can still see and hear the goblin men, buys their fruit but refuses to eat it; instead, she hurries home to Laura, who licks the juice from Lizzie's face and is cured. The poem draws upon legends about humans who are lost in fairyland after eating enchanted food; but it is also clearly an allegory of sexual sin and redemption that has been interpreted in many ways. AL

DeVitis, A. A., 'Goblin Market: Fairy Tale and Reality', *Journal of Popular Culture*, 1 (1968).

Kooistra, Lorraine Janzen, 'Goblin Market as a Cross-Audienced Poem: Children's Fairy Tale, Adult Erotic Fantasy', *Children's Literature*, 25 (1997).

Marsh, Jan, 'Christina Rossetti's Vocation: The Importance of *Goblin Market*', *Victorian Poetry*, 32.3–4 (autumn–winter 1994).

Smulders, Sharon, *Christina Rossetti revisited* (1996).

Watson, Jeanie, '"Men Sell Not Such in Any Town": Christina Rossetti's Goblin Fruit of Fairy Tale', *Children's Literature*, 12 (1984).

Rossetti, Dante Gabriel (1828–82) English painter and poet. A founding member of the Pre-Raphaelite Brotherhood (1848), Rossetti developed a highly personal subject-matter and symbolism inspired by medieval poetry (particularly Dante). Although his later work was almost entirely devoted to sensuous allegorical images of women, earlier paintings included many subjects from medieval literature, including the Arthurian cycle. Closest in feeling to a fairy tale is 'The Wedding of St George and Princess Sabra' (1857); Rossetti gives the legend a magical happy ending in a gold-and-crimson chamber, with the dragon's head nearby in a wooden box. SR

Rossini, Gioacchino (1792–1868) Italian composer. Among his many operas is the two-act *La Cenerentola* (*Cinderella*, 1817), whose libretto by Jacopo Ferretti was adapted from Charles *Perrault's fairy tale. In Rossini and Ferretti's version of this tale, Angelina (Cinderella) is maltreated by her father Don Magnifico and her stepsisters Clorinda and Tisbe. Prince Ramiro, disguised as his servant Dandini, falls in love with Angelina. The Prince's tutor Alidoro has the role of magic helper as he assists Angelina in her attempt to go to the Prince's ball. Angelina finally proves that she is the object of the Prince's desire by means of a silver bracelet, a variation on the glass slipper found in Perrault's tale. NC

Osborne, Richard, *Rossini* (1986).

Rousseau, Jean-Jacques (1712–78) pre-eminent Swiss Enlightenment philosopher and writer. His witty salon fairy tale 'La Reine Fantasque' ('Queen Fantastic', 1754) reflects many of his educational, social, and political theories. The tale is told by a druid to the arab Jalamir and recounts the capriciousness with which a queen enlists a fairy's help to become pregnant and endow her offspring, a boy and a girl. Making effective use of narrative suspense and parenthetical dialogue, Rousseau's story critiques monarchy, but also pokes fun at women. LCS

Rowling, J. K. (Joanne Rowling, 1965–) British children's book author whose seven Harry Potter novels, published from 1997 to 2007, have broken all children's book publishing records.

In addition, all the novels have been adapted for the cinema from 2001 to 2010 with great success. Neither the novels nor the films are fairy tales, but their magic is closely (spell)bound with fairy-tale elements. Above all, the power of the fairy-tale 'family romance' plays a major role in the phenomenal success of the series: the outcast child living with horrible grown-ups, the Dursleys, who cannot possibly be his real parents. With the help of his fairy godmother (Hagrid), Harry discovers his true, ideal parentage, which places him in the privileged world of the Hogwarts School of Wizardry with special status. This structure of split parentage, so central to the first volume of the series, *Harry Potter and the Philosopher's Stone* (1997; US title, *Harry Potter and the Sorcerer's Stone*), continues from volume to volume as the orphaned Harry starts out from and returns to the unpleasant Dursley family, his only living relatives, with whom he lives, at the end of each novel. The series traces the psychological growth that ultimately breaks the idealization of his parents and Professor Dumbledore, who heads the Wizardry School which Harry attends each of the seven years that he learns about magic and himself. Eventually, Harry comes to accept his parents and Dumbledore as imperfect people in ways that allow him to accept himself and others as fallible human beings. Harry Potter's successful family romance, prominently recalling *'Cinderella', stands in powerful contrast to the failure of the evil wizard Voldemort's story; he is the inverted image of Harry himself. Voldemort, too, is outcast and orphaned. But he never comes to accept and embrace the father who repudiated him, murdering him instead—the give-away signs of failed family romance are unresolved rivalry, aggression, and the need to dominate. These uncontrollable psychological urges govern Voldemort's entire being and his relation to others. He has no friends but only servants who vie with each other for his attention, which they also fear. His only intimacy is possession, reducing others utterly to his objects. In contrast, Harry creates and is part of a society of commitment, transforming the classic fairy-tale heroism into a society of friends. Fairy tales contain not only social and psychological types of character but also historical references, reflecting famines, class conflicts, and family structures. The *Harry Potter* novels are similarly shaped and metaphorically reflect world wars, the terror of contemporary life, the corruption of the press, ministry, and school. But the novels also imagine a different society. Gender roles, so rigid in classic fairy tales, which 'incarcerate' girls into gendered spaces and domestic work—in both *Harry Potter* and classic fairy tales housework is punishment and enslavement—are altered to include a diversity of gendered paths that can be seen in the development of his good friend Hermione Granger as joint heroine with Harry and Ron Weasley, a schoolmate and dependable companion. Together the three young people resist Voldemort, but also his desire for celebrity and domination, in mutual commitment to a common, better world embodied in Dumbledore's Army. The fairy-tale ending of marriage and kinship with its fantasy of power and elevation here becomes a heroism not of personal glory but of friendship, shared goals, moral values, and mutual love.   SW

Anatol, Giselle Liza, *Reading Harry Potter: Critical Essays* (2003).
Gupta, Suman, *Re-Reading Harry Potter (2003).*
Nel, Philip, *J. K. Rowling's Harry Potter Novels: A Reader's Guide* (2001).
Wolosky, Shira, *The Riddles of Harry Potter: Secret Passages and Interpretive Quests* (2010).
Zipes, Jack, *Sticks and Stones: The Troublesome Success of Children's Literature from Slovenly Peter to Harry Potter* (2001).

Rubino, Antonio (1880–1964) Italian writer who became an important illustrator in 1908 when he could not find anyone to draw pictures for his poems. One of the founders of *Corriere dei Piccoli*, a magazine for children, Rubino became famous for his cartoon characters Pierino, Burattino, Quadratino, Barbabucco, and many others. Strongly influenced by *Jugendstil*, Rubino developed a highly unusual comic style that employed pastels, ink, and caricatures to illustrate numerous fairy tales and his own original works filled with ironic depictions of eccentric figures.   JZ

Rühmkorf, Peter (1929–2008) German poet, essayist, and editor. Known for his socialist commitment and ironical wit, Rühmkorf published two books of fairy tales for adults that reflect his satirical critique of German society. In *Auf Wiedersehen in Kenilworth* (*Until We Meet Again in Kenilworth*, 1980) Rühmkorf transforms the steward of a castle named Jam McDamm into a cat and his cat Minnie into a beautiful maiden, sends them off to Rome, and reveals how difficult it is to have happy endings in happy homes. In *Der Hüter des Misthaufens* (*The Caretaker of the Dung Heap*, 1983), he published 13 'enlightened fairy tales' that make use of traditional *Grimms' fairy tales to parody capitalist greed and to mock the provincialism of Germans. Rühmkorf suggests through the magical transformations in his fairy tales that it is only through cunning and the imagination that social change can come about.   JZ

'Rumpelstiltskin' When a poor miller boasts that his daughter can spin straw into gold, the king places her into a chamber full of straw to prove this claim under threat of death. An ugly little man appears and performs this impossible task for her in exchange for her ring and, on the second night, her necklace. On the third night, the king puts her into the largest chamber yet and promises to marry her if she succeeds. With nothing left to trade, she is forced to promise the dwarf her first child. When he comes to claim it, he is moved by her tears to let her keep the baby if she can find out his name in three days' time. Failing to answer correctly on the first two nights, the young queen is told by her messenger at the last moment how he had overheard a strange little man calling himself 'Rumpelstiltskin' as he was dancing round a fire in the woods. When the queen confronts 'Rumpelstiltskin' with the correct name, he tears himself apart in his fury.

The best-known version of this tale, 'Rumpelstilzchen', was published by the Brothers *Grimm in their collection *Kinder- und Hausmärchen* (*Children's and Household Tales*, 1812), but there are many other variants, mainly European, such as the English 'Tom-Tit-Tot', the Italian 'Zorobubù', or the Swedish 'Titteli Ture'; the name-guessing motif also links it to *Puccini's opera *Turandot*. The Grimms' story is an amalgamation of three sources, one of which is similar to the influential 'Ricdin-Ricdon' (*Bigarrures ingénieuses*, 1696) by Marie-Jeanne *Lhéritier, in which it is the king or prince who discloses the name. The Grimms' printed version differs from oral variants in which the girl's predicament lies in her inability to spin anything but gold. She acts on her own behalf when she willingly accepts the little man's help to perform her work and, as spinning was a marriage test in rural communities, gain a husband. Emma *Donoghue in her revision, 'The Tale of the Spinster' (*Kissing the Witch*, 1997), takes up the theme of spinning as productive work and translates her version into an entirely female context; however, it is also a critique of materialistic self-interest and entrepreneurial exploitation. A widow's daughter continues her mother's successful spinning business after her death, but needs to take on a slow-witted girl, Little Sister, to carry out the fine spinning. When the widow's daughter becomes pregnant in the course of soliciting more work, Little Sister agrees to pretend to be the mother to protect the business. But she finally leaves when the baby is punished for damaging the wool, taking the child with her, since the widow's daughter had shown so little interest in either of them that she had not even asked their names. Anne Sexton interprets her 'Rumpelstiltskin' (*Transformations*, 1972) as a figure of interiorized infantile rage and despair, while William Hathaway's 'Rumpelstiltskin' (*Disenchantments*, 1985) is an angry meditation on contemporary pressures on men to be good at sports and physically beautiful to win the girl.   KS

Bolte, Johannes, and Polívka, George, *Anmerkungen zu den* Kinder- und Hausmärchen der Brüder Grimm (5 vols., 1913–32).
Mieder, Wolfgang (ed.), *Disenchantments: An Anthology of Modern Fairy Tale Poetry* (1985).
Röhrich, Lutz, 'Rumpelstiltskin. Vom Methodenpluralismus in der Erzählforschung', in *Sage und Märchen, Erzählforschung heute* (1976).
Zipes, Jack, 'Spinning with Fate: Rumpelstiltskin and the Decline of Female Productivity', *Western Folklore* (January 1993).

'Rumpelstiltskin' The little man asks the queen to guess his name in the *Grimms' 'Rumpelstiltskin'
illustrated by Ernst Liebermann in *Rumpelstilzchen* (1911).

Rushdie, Salman (1947–) Indian-born
novelist. Born in Bombay to a Muslim family,
Rushdie was sent to school in England in
1961. After reading history at Cambridge,
he spent some time as an advertising copywriter. His first novel, the allegorical *Grimus*
(1975), already demonstrates two distinctive
elements: the use of a fantastical narrative
idiom—notably less restrained in *Grimus*
than elsewhere—and the exploration, in
both form and content, of the meeting of
the cultures of East and West (he has since
published a collection of stories entitled
East, West, 1994).

However, it is in *Midnight's Children*
(1981) that Rushdie's mode of storytelling
appears fully formed. A dense, discursive
epic of post-Independence India, it fuses
baroque realism and a Shandean narratorial
voice with a spirit of storytelling deeply informed by oral and folk traditions. It draws
heavily on The *Arabian Nights*, both as a

model for fantastical, expansive tale-spinning against a background of personal and
national disorder, and, in the form of the
one-thousand-and-one children born in the
first hour of independence, as an expression
of manifold possibility, of new, untold, and
retold stories: '1001, the number of night, of
magic, of alternative realities'.

Rushdie's third novel, *Shame* (1983), another fictionalized history, experiments further with a form of written orality, conjuring
a host of fairy-tale characters and motifs
from both European and Arabic/Indian traditions, and using the ingredients and techniques of traditional storytelling, notably the
juxtaposition of comedy and violence, to tell
a story of 'Peccavistan', the narrator's 'looking-glass Pakistan'.

Rushdie's use of folk- and fairy-tale material is always integral to the work as a
whole: the use of non-Western traditions
and modes of storytelling in novels dealing

with the legacies of colonial rule, and the use of genuinely popular culture to tell the unofficial stories lying beneath orthodox histories. Nowhere is this more apparent than in *Haroun and the Sea of Stories* (1990), the children's novel Rushdie wrote in the wake of the *fatwa* issued against him for what was seen as blasphemy against Islam in *The Satanic Verses* (1988). *Haroun* takes its basic conceit from Somadeva's enormous Sanskrit story cycle, *Kathasaritsagara* (*The Ocean of the Sea of Story, c.*1070), the title of which is literalized in the form of the ocean visited by the eponymous young hero, in his quest for the solution to his storyteller father's mysterious narrative sterility. An Arabian night in its own right, it is an argument against the silence that follows when storytelling ends, and a reminder of the continued relevance of the wellsprings of narrative tradition.

In 2010, Rushdie produced a sequel to *Haroun* called *Luka and the Fire of Life*. In this fairy-tale novel, the storyteller Rashid and another one of his sons, Luka, walk home from Luka's school in the fictional land of Alifbay, and as they pass the Great Rings of Fire circus they are distressed by the pitiful state of the animals. Luka curses the circus. Soon his curse works, and the animals are liberated. Two of them, Dog and Bear, become Luka's loyal pets and protect him. However, one month later Rashid falls asleep and doesn't wake up. Luka is informed via vultures from Aag, owner of the circus, that he cursed Rashid. In the ensuing action Luka must enter the World of Magic with Dog and Bear to rescue Rashid just as his brother Haroun did in the previous novel. Written as a crossover work for young and adult readers, this novel is more a pastiche of fairy-tale motifs with a traditional plot than a substantial exploration of storytelling, as was the case in *Haroun*.   SB

Batty, Nancy E., 'The Art of Suspense: Rushdie's 1001 (Mid-) Nights', *Ariel*, 18 (1987).
Brennan, Timothy, *Salman Rushdie and the Third World: Myths of the Nation* (1989).
Cundy, Catherine, 'Through Childhood's Window: *Haroun and the Sea of Stories'*, in D. M. Fletcher (ed.), *Perspectives on the Fiction of Salman Rushdie* (1994).
Deszcz, Justyna, *Rushdie in Wonderland: Fairytaleness in Salman Rushdie's Fiction* (2004).
Rushdie, Salman, *Imaginary Homelands: Essays and Criticism 1981–1991* (1991).

Rushforth, P. S. (Peter Scott Rushforth, 1945–2005) English writer whose first novel *Kindergarten* (1979) was awarded the Hawthornden Prize in 1980. Using the *Grimms' tales 'Fitcher's Bird' and *'Hansel and Gretel', Rushforth weaves together two incidents of violence: a small girl taken hostage in Berlin has her image broadcast on television, and it compels three boys in Suffolk, England, to recall their mother lying dead on the concourse of Rome airport, victim of an attack by the same terrorist organization that is threatening the girl in Berlin. Rushforth's novel of realism and fairy tales also recalls the Holocaust to address the problem of senseless cruelty.   JZ

Ruskin, John (1819–1900) English author and artist whose *The King of the Golden River* might be regarded as the first English fairy story for children. Though it was not published until 1851, seven years after Francis *Paget's *The Hope of the Katzekopfs*, it was in fact written in 1841 for 12-year-old Effie Gray, whom he later married. It is a story of the three brothers of tradition, two bad, the youngest good, and their reception of a supernatural visitor, the South West Wind. Ruskin described it himself as 'a fairly good imitation of *Grimm and *Dickens, mixed with some true Alpine feeling of my own', but the South West Wind is a powerful and original character, described by Stephen Prickett as the 'first magical personage to show that combination of kindliness and eccentric irascibility that was to appear so strongly in a whole tradition of subsequent literature'. Richard Doyle, who illustrated the original edition, made a striking drawing of him.

Edgar *Taylor's translation of the Grimms' stories with illustrations by George *Cruikshank was published in 1823; in *Praeterita* Ruskin recorded how he had copied these when he was 10 or 11. The book was

Ruskin, John The idyllic countryside of Stiria is portrayed before the onset of tempestuous times in John Ruskin's *The King of the Golden River* (1841), illustrated by Richard *Doyle. The Bodleian Library, University of Oxford (AA 2294).

reissued in 1868 with an introduction by Ruskin in which he spoke of the value of the traditional tales, with their power 'to fortify children against the glacial cold of selfish science'—a sentiment which lies at the heart of his own story. GA

Burns, Marjorie J., 'The Anonymous Fairy Tale: Ruskin's King of the Golden River', *Mythlore*, 14.3 (spring 1988).

Coyle, William, 'Ruskin's *King of the Golden River*: A Victorian Fairy Tale', in Robert A. Collins and Howard D. Pearce (eds.), *The Scope of the Fantastic: Culture, Biography, Themes, Children's Literature* (1985).

Dearden, James S., '*The King of the Golden River*: A Bio-Bibliographical Study', in Robert E. Rhodes and Del Ivan Janik (eds.), *Studies in Ruskin: Essays in Honor of Van Akin Burd* (1982).

Filstrup, Jane Merrill, 'Thirst for Enchanted Views in Ruskin's *The King of the Golden River*', *Children's Literature*, 8 (1979).

Prickett, Stephen, *Victorian Fantasy* (1979).

Ruy-Vidal, François (1931–) French author of children's literature. He creates unusual fairy tales, such as 'Le Voyage extravagant de Hugo Brise-Fer' ('The Secret Journey of Hugo the Brat', 1968), in which enchanted creatures help mend the selfish ways of an unlikable brat. 'Le Petit Poucet' (**Little Tom Thumb*', 1974), an elaborate retelling of Perrault's tale, foregrounds the socio-historical and political causes of the woodcutter's poverty and misery. The inclusion of such details is designed to disrupt the seductive power of fairy tales and thereby subvert their authoritarian and conformist messages. AZ

S., Svend Otto (real name **Svend Otto Sörensen**, 1916–96) Danish illustrator of fairy tales, notably those by Hans Christian *Andersen. His first picture books based on Andersen's fairy tales were 'The Fir Tree' (1968), 'The Tinder Box' (1972), and 'The *Ugly Duckling' (1975). He also illustrated a collection, *Børnenes H. C. Andersen* (*Children's Andersen*, 1972).

Svend Otto S. has published a number of picture books based on famous fairy tales, such as *'Little Red Riding Hood' (1970), *'Puss-in-Boots' (1972), *'Sleeping Beauty' (1973), 'The *Bremen Town Musicians' (1974) *'Snow White' (1975), *'Little Tom Thumb' (1976), and many others. Most of his books have also been published in English and are highly praised internationally. His illustrations are characterized by a richness of detail, elaborate technique, and warm humour. They also show a clear tendency to counterbalance the *Disney style. Unlike many illustrators of classical fairy tales, Svend Otto S. addresses primarily an audience of children, avoiding adult connotations or allusions. He has also written and illustrated original fairy tales, exploring characters from Norse mythology, like trolls. He won the Andersen Medal for illustration in 1978.   MN

Saint-Exupéry, Antoine Jean-Baptiste Marie Roger de (1900–44) French aviator and author of autobiographical novels and metaphysical fantasy. 'St-Ex' was an impoverished aristocrat who had a mystical communion with aviation, the source of his creativity. His sparse, spiritual works all record the transcendence of perspective he experienced while flying over North Africa or being stranded in the desert—events that crystallized for him man's responsibility towards others.

He worked as a mail pilot, negotiated airline routes on two continents, ran rescue missions in the desert, and reported on the Spanish Civil War. While convalescing from various crashes, he wrote aviation novels such as *Courrier sud* (*Southern Mail*, 1929) and the prize-winning *Vol de nuit* (*Night Flight*, 1931). *Terre des hommes* (*Wind, Sand and Stars*, 1939), winner of the French Academy's prize for Best Novel and the (American) National Book Award, was based on his mystical near-death epiphany in the Sahara; a reconnaissance sortie that earned him the Croix de Guerre inspired *Pilote de Guerre* (*Flight to Arras*, 1942), which Vichy banned as a 'Gaullist manifesto'. Exiled for two years, he lived in New York before returning to North Africa to train pilots. He perished during his 10th reconnaissance flight and was posthumously awarded a second Croix de Guerre.

Saint-Exupéry is best remembered as the author-illustrator of *Le Petit Prince* (*The Little Prince*, 1943), the number one best-selling children's book. Dedicated to a friend who was at the time a Second World War hostage, it is a fairy tale addressed to children and to the children that grown-ups had once been. A boy-prince has fled a vain rose on asteroid B-612. In his interplanetary travels, he encounters other allegorical characters, meets a marooned pilot in the Sahara, and asks him to draw a sheep. Because the only acceptable sketch is of a closed box with the (invisible) animal inside, the adult learns from the child that that which is truly meaningful can only be perceived by the spirit—a theme that resonates throughout Saint-Exupéry's work. Likewise, the boy learns about social responsibility and returns home to tame his rose.

This slim volume has elicited scores of divergent analyses. Because the Little Prince sacrifices himself and his (transfigured) body is not found, theologians note analogies to Christ, the Prince of Peace. Philosophers cite parallels to Plato's 'Allegory of the Cave', Aristotle's *Ethics*, and Heidegger's phenomenology. Social critics refer to the imaginary voyages of 'Candide', *Gulliver's Travels*, and *Alice in Wonderland, while psychoanalysts posit models of solitude, memory, and maturation. Finally, those arguing against over-interpretation urge us to accept this lyrical fable with childlike wonder, lest its magic be destroyed.   MLE

Capestany, Edward J., *The Dialectic of The Little Prince* (1982).

Higgins, James E., *The Little Prince, A Reverie of Substance* (1996).

Monin, Yves, *L'Ésotérisme du Petit Prince* (1975).

Robinson, Joy D. Marie, *Antoine de Saint-Exupéry* (1984).

Schiff, Stacy, *Saint-Exupéry: A Biography* (1994).

Sand, George (pseudonym of **Amandine-Aurore-Lucile Dudevant,** *née* **Dupin,** 1804–76) French romantic novelist and writer. In her pastoral novels like *La Mare au diable* (*The Devil's Pool*, 1846), Sand included scenes of storytelling and references to folklore. Sand was raised on tales by Charles *Perrault and Mme d'*Aulnoy, whose impact on her *œuvre* resides primarily in her idealized representations of the countryside and nature, but her specific brand of the marvellous clearly was influenced by E. T. A. *Hoffmann's fantastic tales. It was not until Sand was herself a grandmother that she put together a collection of tales for her granddaughters Aurore and Gabrielle, entitled *Contes d'une grand-mère* (*Tales of a Grandmother*, 1873).

Her tales have an overriding pedagogical function, in which children who have been abandoned in some way by their parents learn to overcome their weaknesses, often with the help of surrogate parents and a belief in the supernatural. In 'Le Château de Pictordu' ('Pictordu Castle'), for instance, the feeble Diane, rejected by her stepmother and whose father is unimaginative, is brought back to life by the intervention of the veiled lady of the castle, who becomes her artistic inspiration. Characters often embody nature and anti-nature, as in the case of Marguerite and her false cousin Mélidor in 'La Reine Coax' ('Queen Coax'). In this tale, the fantastic is limited to the talking frog Queen Coax, who is in fact a projection of Marguerite's penchant for the unnatural which she must overcome. Other tales in the collection include 'Le Nuage rose' ('The Pink Cloud'), 'Les Ailes de courage' ('Wings of Courage'), 'Le Géant Yéous' ('Yeous the Giant'), 'Le Chêne parlant' ('The Talking Oak Tree'), and 'La Fée Poussière' ('The Fairy Dust').   AD

Lane, Brigitte, 'Les Contes d'une grand-mère I: 'Les Ailes de courage', *George Sand Studies*, 11.1–2 (spring 1992).

Persona, Mariangela, 'L'Imaginaire pédagogique dans les *Contes d'une grand'mère* de George Sand', *Quaderni di Lingue e Letterature*, 11 (1986).

Sandburg, Carl (1878–1967) American poet, biographer, and folklorist. His humorous tales for children, *Rootabaga Stories* (1922) and *Rootabaga Pigeons* (1923), were originally told to his two young daughters. Sandburg's best stories are as full of poetic invention and comic nonsense as Edward Lear, but they take place in an American Midwest where trains, skyscrapers, and a farm buried in popcorn mix with classic fairy-tale motifs and magic objects like the Gold Buckskin Whincher, which causes Blixie Bimber to fall in love with the first man she meets with an x in his name.   AL

Lynn, Joanne L., 'Hyacinths and Biscuits in the Village of Liver and Onions: Sandburg's *Rootabaga Stories*', *Children's Literature*, 8 (1979).

Niven, Penelope, *Carl Sandburg: A Biography* (1991).

Thistle, Mary S., 'Carl Sandburg's *Rootabaga Stories*: American Fairy Tales' (Diss., Florida Atlantic University, 1991).

Sanderson, Ruth (1951–) One of the most creative and prolific American illustrators who has published over 80 different kinds of fantasy and fairy-tale books for children of all ages. In addition to illustrating works by Jane *Yolen and other notable American authors, Sanderson has written her own fairy tales or has freely adapted folk tales. She attended the Paier School of Art in Connecticut and was influenced by famous traditional American painters such as Howard Pyle, N. C. Wyeth, and Normal Rockwell. After graduation in 1974, she did some work for textbook companies, advertisers, and Golden Books. In 1986, she began to make a name for herself by illustrating Yolen's *The *Sleeping Beauty*, and in 1990 she had a major breakthrough as an independent illustrator with the publication of the Brothers *Grimm's *Twelve Dancing Princesses*, which displayed her talents as an exquisite realist painter. From this point onwards, she produced a wide array of fairy-tale books including *Beauty and the Beast* (1993), *Papa Gatto* (1995), *The Golden Mare, The Firebird, and the Magic Ring* (2001), *Cinderella* (2002), *Rose Red and Snow White* (2013), and *The Snow Princess* (2014). In her early fairy tale *The Enchanted Wood* (1991), in which three brothers embark on a quest to discover 'the heart of the world', Sanderson's illustrations were regarded as sumptuous and meticulous, qualities that can be found in almost all of her works up to the present. Working with live models portrayed in oil paintings, she transports them into medieval settings to give them 'new' lives in tales that are recreated for contemporary readers.   JZ

San Souci, Robert (1946–) American writer of books for children and young adults who is widely regarded as one of the finest adapters of folk tales and legends in the US. In particular, San Souci has carefully woven a multicultural repertoire of books that also includes a feminist agenda. He has adapted tales from Eskimo, Native American, African American, European, and oriental lore. Among his best-known fairy-tale books are: *The Legend of Scarface: A Blackfeet Indian Tale* (1978), *The Enchanted Tapestry: Adapted from a Chinese Folktale* (1987), *The Six

Swans (1988), *The Talking Eggs* (1989), *The White Cat* (1990), *Sukey and the Mermaid* (1992), *Sootface* (1994), *Cinderella Skeleton* (2000), *As Luck Would Have It* (2008), and *The Firebird* (2011). He has collaborated with such fine illustrators as Daniel San Souci, Jerry *Pinkney, and Brian *Pinkney to produce his fairy-tale books, and he has also written his own texts such as *Nicholas Pipe* (1997) about a marvellous merman, who falls in love with the daughter of an ordinary fisherman. In keeping with his innovative approach to fairy tales, San Souci has compiled an important anthology of tales about remarkable American women entitled *Cut from the Same Cloth: American Women of Myth, Legend, and Tall Tale* (1993).   JZ

Sanvitale, Francesca (1928–2011) Italian playwright, essayist, and translator, who showed a particular interest in fairy tales. Her tales, however, are sad for, as she said, they cannot be otherwise, as they concern ghosts and death. Her first novel, *Cuore borghese* (*Bourgeois Heart*, 1972), was an immediate success which steadily increased with titles such as *Madre e figlia* (*Mother and Daughter*, 1980), *L'uomo del parco* (*The Man in the Park*, 1984), *Verso Paola* (*Towards Paola*, 1991), and *Il figlio dell'Impero* (*The Son of the Empire*, 1993).

Her collections of tales include *La realtà e un dono* (*Reality Is a Gift*, 1987), *Tre favole dell'ansia e dell'ombra* (*Three Fairy Tales of Anxiety and Shadow*, 1994), and *Separazioni* (*Separations*, 1997). 'Fanciulla e il gran vecchio', 'Bambina', and 'Rosalinda' are imbued with a sense of anguish characterizing the plight of women, typical of Sanvitale's tales.   GD

Sargood, Corinna (1941–) London-born artist. She illustrated two collections of woman-centred fairy tales edited by Angela *Carter, *The Virago Book of Fairy Tales* (reprinted as *Old Wives' Fairy Tale Book*, 1990) and *The Second Virago Book of Fairy Tales* (reprinted as *Strange Things Sometimes Still Happen*, 1992). Informed by folk art traditions, especially from Mexico and Italy,

Sargood's lino cuts conflated the natural and human worlds to bizarre effect. She also did the paintings for *The Magic Toyshop*, the 1987 fairy-tale film based on Angela Carter's screenplay and directed by David Wheatley.

CB

Bacchilega, Cristina, 'In the Eye of the Fairy Tale: Corinna Sargood and David Wheatley Talk about Working with Angela Carter', *Marvels & Tales*, 12.1 (1998).

Sarnelli, Pompeo (1649–1724) Italian writer and bishop. His edition of Giambattista *Basile's Lo cunto de li cunti* (1674) used for the first time the title **Pentamerone*, by which Basile's work would subsequently be best known. His later work, the *Posilicheata* (*An Outing to Posillipo*, 1684), is composed of five fairy tales, probably of oral origin, that are told in Neapolitan dialect by peasant women at the end of a banquet in the country. The tales are: 'La pietà ricompensata' ('Mercy Recompensed'), 'La serva fedele' ('The Faithful Servant'), 'L'ingannatrice ingannata' ('The Deceiver Deceived'), 'La gallinella' ('The Young Hen'), and 'La testa e la coda' ('The Head and the Tail'). NC

Sarnelli, Pompeo, *Posilicheata*, ed. Enrico Malato (1986).

Scandinavian countries, fairy tales in
See p. 529.

Scarry, Richard (1919–94) American author and illustrator of children's picture books. Scarry's career was launched in 1948 when he signed with the Artists and Writers Guild, responsible for the Little Golden Books series published by Simon and Schuster. Scarry illustrated several Little Golden Books for which his wife Patricia wrote the text, including *The Country Mouse and the City Mouse, the Dog and His Bone, the Fox and the Crow: Three Aesop Fables* (1961). Scarry's claim to fame is his use of animal characters like Lowly Worm, Wild Bill Hiccup the racoon, and his stock of pigs, rabbits, dogs, cats, and bears. It comes as no surprise that he illustrated tales like 'The Little Red Hen' and 'The *Ugly Duckling' (*Nursery Tales*, 1958); *'Little Red Riding Hood', 'The

Three Little Pigs', 'Goldilocks and the Three Bears', and 'The Musicians of *Bremen' (*Richard Scarry's Animal Nursery Tales*, 1975). In his 'Tinker and Tanker' series for young children, which follows the adventures of a rabbit and a hippopotamus, Scarry drew from the genres of fantasy (*Tinker and Tanker and their Space Ship*, 1961), adventure (*Tinker and Tanker and the Pirates*, 1961), and medieval romance (*Tinker and Tanker Knights of the Round Table*, 1963). Medieval romance was also the inspiration for *Richard Scarry's Peasant Pig and the Terrible Dragon: with Lowly Worm the Jolly Jester* (1980). Scarry also wrote *The Animals' *Mother Goose* (1964), containing a selection of popular nursery rhymes, and *Teeny Tiny Tales* (1965), a collection of animal stories.

AD

Schami, Rafik (1946–) Syrian-born German satirist and storyteller. Schami, born Suheil Fadél, emigrated from Syria to Germany in 1971. There he shared the fate of German guest workers before taking a doctorate in chemistry at Heidelberg. In 1982 he left his job at a German chemical company to devote himself full-time to storytelling and writing. Around that time, Schami cofounded two literary organizations for guest workers, *Südwind* and *PoLiKunst*, which allowed him to publish some of his stories. His genre of choice is the modern fairy tale or fantastic tale whose style he has perfected since he began writing in German in 1978. The stories he tells are indebted to the oral storytelling tradition he grew up with and keeps alive during extensive lecture tours in Germany. His tales are only committed to print after they have withstood the test of many public performances.

Schami tells stories about everyday people and everyday courage. Some stories could be called trickster tales, in which a powerless person outwits the high and mighty, while others end in failure and disappointment. Lodged between modern-day reality and fantasy land, between Orient and Occident, between adult and children's literature, his story collections, such as *Der erste Ritt durchs Nadelöhr* (*The First Ride Through

Scandinavian countries, fairy tales in Scholars in the Scandinavian region began relatively early to collect, classify, and comment on folk tales. As in Germany, this movement was inspired by romanticism with its interest in and idealization of folk literature. Although each of the Scandinavian countries had its own political and cultural peculiarities, they were all very much influenced by Germany. Therefore, the publication of the Grimms' collection, *Kinder- und Hausmärchen*, was the chief stimulus toward collecting folk tales among the Scandinavian people. Denmark, the southernmost and closest country to Germany and Western Europe, as always took the lead. In 1816 the major Danish romantic poet and playwright Adam *Oehlenschläger (1779–1850) published a collection, which contained six fairy tales by the Brothers Grimm as well as several fairy tales by *Musäus and *Tieck. Among early endeavours, mostly aimed at preserving the national treasury of folklore, the four volumes of *Danske Folkesagn* (*Danish Folk Legends*, 1819–23) by Just Mattias Thiele (1794–1874) should be mentioned. This collection was important as a source for Hans Christian *Andersen. In addition, Svend *Grundtvig made his major contribution to the classification and study of Scandinavian folklore with his collections of Danish legends and folk tales (1853–83).

In Norway, which was part of Denmark until 1814 and afterwards united with Sweden up to 1905, the collection and study of folklore was intimately connected to the emergence of a national identity. The first collections of Norwegian folk tales marked a significant step towards the establishment of a national written language, which did not emerge until the mid-19th century. Norwegian folklorists were most active during the 1840s, by which time the Grimm tradition was firmly rooted in Scandinavia. The world-famous collection by P. C. *Asbjørnsen and Jørgen Moe, *Norske Folkeeventyr* (*Norwegian Folktales*), appeared between 1841 and 1844; and Asbjørnsen's collection *Norske huldreeventyr og folkesagn* (*Norwegian Fairy Tales and Folk Legends*) in 1845–8. Both collections reflect the striving to accentuate specific Norwegian cultural features rather than present variants available also in other European countries. This is especially apparent in the settings. While many Danish folk tales are of trickster-type, Norwegian fairy tales abound in magic: magical adventures and magical creatures, mainly trolls. The major protagonist of Norwegian narratives is Askeladden ('Ashlad'), the 'low' hero who wins fortune at the end.

Swedish scholars were slow in showing interest in folklore collecting. During the Enlightenment, fairy tales were used for political and educational purposes—for instance Olof Dalin (1708–63) produced *Sagan om hästen* (*The Tale of a Horse*) in 1740, and some anonymous collections with translated fairy tales by the Grimms and the German romantic writers appeared in the early 1820s. However, it was not until the 1840s that Gunnar Olof Hyltén-Cavallius (1818–89) and his Scottish colleague George *Stephens published

Svenska folksagor och äfventyr (*Swedish Folk Tales and Folk Stories*, 1844–9). This collection had a purely scholarly purpose, and never achieved the same popularity with readers as the Grimms' or Asbjørnsen's collections. Unlike their Danish and Norwegian counterparts, Swedish collectors retold folk tales in an accurate literary language. Many Swedish folk tales are animal tales, especially the cycle about the cunning fox; a vast number are aetiological tales, accounting for the peculiarities of landscape. The first collection for children was published by Fridtjuv Berg (1851–1916) in 1899.

A significant contribution to the initial collection of folk tales was made by the Swedish-speaking scholars in Finland; the publication in 1835–6 of the Finnish national epic *Kalevala* was an important source of inspiration, as well as the collection of Finnish folk tales published in 1852–66 by Eero Salmelainen (1830–67). Between 1809 and 1917, Finland was a part of the Russian Empire as a separate grand duchy, but culturally part of Scandinavia. The first Finnish folk-tale collection addressed to children was published in 1901–23 by Anni Swan (1875–1958).

The father of the literary fairy tale in Scandinavia was Hans Christian Andersen. With his four collections published between 1835 and 1872, Andersen indeed created a completely new literary genre which inspired many generations of writers not only in Scandinavia, but throughout the world, since his fairy tales were translated into many languages already during his lifetime.

Although most of Andersen's fairy tales are based on well-known sources and exploit familiar plots, they show a totally new approach to the folklore material. First, he gave the fairy tale a personal touch, using everyday, colloquial language, individual narrative voice, and obvious irony. Secondly, with very few exceptions, his fairy tales have realistic settings, concrete geographical locations, and details incompatible with the fairy-tale atmosphere. Further, Andersen invented several new types of fairy tale which have no origins in folklore, but which have been widely used by his successors: for instance, stories about animated toys ('The *Steadfast Tin Soldier') and objects ('The Darning Needle'). His animal tales are original as well, devoid of the conventional moral of a fable, but instead presenting satirical sketches of human ways and opinions. 'The *Ugly Duckling' may be seen as an autobiography, describing the thorny path of a washerwoman's son to world fame.

Although Andersen primarily addressed his fairy tales to children, they are free from didacticism and very often lack happy endings, notably in 'The *Little Mermaid' or 'The Shadow'. It is remarkable that he is universally considered a children's writer. Indeed, only a small portion of his most famous fairy tales is included in contemporary volumes for children. His late fairy tales, which he himself preferred to call 'Stories', are definitely too complicated for children, in subject-matter as well as in style. Also, many others have a clear dual audience, where children will enjoy the plot, while adults may note irony and satire, for instance, 'The Emperor's New Clothes'.

The impact of Andersen on the world fairy-tale tradition cannot be overestimated, although it is hardly his pessimistic world view to which his followers have paid most attention. For the Scandinavian fairy-tale tradition Andersen's heritage has been decisive, and can also be seen in the work of the other popular Danish fairy-tale writer, Carl *Ewald.

Zacharias *Topelius is considerably less known internationally than Andersen; however, he should be regarded as the creator of Swedish-language literary fairy tales. Topelius belonged to the Swedish-speaking minority in Finland and thus contributed to the genre in both countries. Topelius's *Läsning för barn* (*Reading Matter for Children*, 8 vols., 1865–96) contained a variety of magical, moral, and animal tales, showing a clear influence by Andersen. Another significant Swedish writer of the 19th century was Victor Rydberg (1828–95), whose fairy tale *Lille Viggs äfventyr på julafton* (*Little Vigg's Adventure on Christmas Eve*, 1875) introduced the figure of the brownie ('tomten').

The turn of the century in Sweden saw the heyday of fairy tales, reflecting the strong neo-romantic movement beginning in the 1890s. Helena *Nyblom was the most prominent of a large number of fairy-tale writers; among others, Anna Maria Roos (1862–1938), Anna Wahlenberg (1858–1933), Alfred Smedberg (1850–1925), Hugo Gyllander (1868–1955), Cyrus Granér (1870–1937) should be mentioned. At that time, the abundance of children's and Christmas magazines provided new channels for the publication of fairy tales; one of them, called *Bland Tomtar och Troll* (*Among Brownies and Trolls*) specialized in fairy tales and is still being published every year. Several outstanding illustrators, like John Bauer (1882–1918) and Jenny *Nyström, contributed to these publications; however, the quality of the texts was often very poor.

At the same time, picture books for children became a prominent genre, many based on fairy-tale plots. The most famous, still read and enjoyed today, were written and illustrated by Elsa Beskow (1874–1953): *Tomtebobarnen* (*Elf Children of the Woods*, 1910), *Puttes äfventyr i blåbärskogen* (*Peter's Adventures in the Blueberry Patch*, 1901), *Resan till landet Längesen* (*Travels to the Land of Long Ago*, 1923), and many others. Magical adventure was the subject of *Kattresan* (*Journey with a Cat*, 1909) by Ivar Arosenius (1878–1909).

The major early 20th-century contribution to the Scandinavian fairy-tale tradition was made by Selma *Lagerlöf, an outstanding Swedish novelist, the winner of the Nobel Prize in 1909, and, together with Andersen, the most internationally well-known Scandinavian writer. Her *Nils Holgerssons underbara resa genom Sverige* (1906–7; *The Wonderful Adventures of Nils*, 1907, *The Further Adventures of Nils*, 1911), originally a schoolbook in geography, has several layers of fairy-tale matter. The frame of the book is a traditional fairy-tale plot in which a lazy boy is punished by being transformed into a midget and forced to improve in order to become human again. His journey with wild geese borrows many traits from the animal tale. Places which Nils visits are described in terms of aetiological folk tales, explaining the origin of the landscape, and the history of uncanny local legends. Finally, some well-known plots are involved, such as 'The Pied Piper of Hamelin' and the sinking of Atlantis. Unlike Andersen's tales, Selma Lagerlöf's novel made little impact in Sweden itself, chiefly because it has been regarded as a schoolbook; it has, however, inspired many fairy-tale writers abroad.

After the explosive development of Swedish fairy tales around the turn of the century, the period between the wars is characterized by the decline of the genre. The only author worth mentioning is probably Gösta Knutsson (1908–73) with his series of animal fables, starting with *Pelle Svanslös* (*Peter No-Tail*, 1939). They depict anthropomorphic cats and occasionally dogs in realistic Swedish settings, mainly the university town of Uppsala; the characters are supposed to reflect the academic world of Uppsala.

The year 1945, often called 'Year Zero' in the history of modern Swedish children's literature, marks the appearance of two major fairy-tale authors, Astrid *Lindgren and Tove *Jansson.

Astrid Lindgren is the most prominent and famous contemporary children's author in Sweden. Her highly original modern fairy tales can roughly be divided into two groups. One brings the marvellous into the everyday, for instance in her internationally best-known book *Pippi Långstrump* (*Kinder- und Hausmärchen*, 1945), featuring the strongest girl in the world; or in *Lillebror och Karlsson på taket* (*Karlsson-on-the-roof*, 1955), presenting an unexpected solution to lonely children in the image of the selfish fat man with a propeller on his back. The same merging of the everyday and the extraordinary is manifest in her short fairy tales, in which supernatural figures appear in contemporary Stockholm, often providing help and consolation for lonely children.

The other group takes the protagonist from the everyday into a magical realm, thus adhering to the traditional heroic fairy tale. However, there are several ways in which Lindgren's two major contributions to the fairy-tale novel genre, *Mio, min Mio* (*Mio, My Son*, 1954) and *Bröderna Lejonhjärta* (*The Brothers Lionheart*, 1973), present a radical transformation of conventional patterns. In both novels, Astrid Lindgren uses first-person narrative, an unusual perspective in fairy tales. Further, she makes her characters scared and even reluctant to perform their heroic deeds, thus allowing a considerable psychological development. She also rejects the traditional happy ending and safe homecoming, instead leaving the readers in hesitation as to whether the described events have actually taken place or are merely products of daydreams and fancies.

If these two novels are based on the typical male quest, *Ronja Rövardotter* (*Ronia, the Robber's Daughter*, 1981) is a fairy tale of female maturation, featuring a number of imaginary creatures. Also, the seemingly 'realistic' novels show a clear fairy-tale structure, *Emil i Lönneberga* (*Emil in the Soup Tureen*, 1963) drawing from the trickster tale, *Mästerdetektiven Kalle Blomkvist* (*Bill Bergson Master Detective*, 1964) from the dragon-slayer. Most important, all of Lindgren's characters have common traits with the traditional folk-tale hero, the youngest son or daughter, the oppressed, the powerless, the underprivileged gaining material and spiritual wealth during a period of trials.

Fairy-tale novels by Tove Jansson are of a different kind. Like Topelius, Jansson represents the Swedish-speaking minority in Finland, and her novels about *Moomintrolls, although sometimes compared to *Tolkien's works, are a reflection of this minority's marginal and isolated position in relation to Sweden as well as Finland. Appearing in post-war Finland, the Moomin novels also clearly reflect their time, combining traumatic memories of the past with optimistic hopes for the future. The significance of family bonds is accentuated in the Moomin novels, which apparently expresses the idea of national identity in a minority culture being preserved primarily through the family.

The Moomin cycle comprises seven novels, a collection of short fairy tales, and three picture books. Unlike most so-called high fantasy worlds, Moominvalley is loosely anchored in the Finnish archipelago and has many concrete geographical and climatic features of real Finland. The Moomin characters, although imaginary, resemble ordinary people, with their faults and virtues, more than fairy-tale trolls, elves, or dwarfs. With a few exceptions, there is no magic in Moominvalley, and the little magic there is, although tricky and unpredictable, is basically good and creative, initiating an endless string of enjoyable adventures. When Moominvalley is threatened, the threat does not come from dark evil forces, but from natural catastrophes: a comet, a flood, or an extremely cold winter.

Tove Jansson's Finno-Swedish compatriot, Irmelin Sandman Lilius (1936–), writes a very different kind of fairy tale, clearly inspired by international tradition, but at the same time highly original. *Enhörningen* (*The Unicorn*, 1962) starts a sequence of fairy-tale novels portraying a young girl and her adventures in an imaginary realm. In her series about the town of Tulavall, beginning with *Gullkrona Gränd* (*Gold Crown Lane*, 1969), Sandman Lilius builds up a mythical universe, firmly rooted in reality and using traits of Scandinavian folk legends.

Another Finno-Swedish writer worth mentioning is Christina Andersson (1936–) who published several collections of *fractured fairy tales during the 1970s. Unfortunately, they went almost unnoticed.

Among the Finnish-language writers, Marja-Leena Mikkola (1939–) is the author of remarkably original fairy-tale novels such as *Anni Manninen* (*Anni Manninen*, 1977), based on Finnish folklore. Stories about the failed magician Mr Huu by Hannu Mäkelä (1943–) are humorous and parodical. Because of the language barrier, there is seldom any interaction between Finnish and other Nordic literatures.

Still another outstanding Swedish author of fairy-tale novels is Maria Gripe (1923–), the 1974 Andersen Medal winner. Her *Glasblåsarns barn* (*The Glassblower's Children*, 1964) is a powerful and poetic story, using elements of Norse mythology. *I klockornas tid* (*In the Time of the Bells*, 1965) combines medieval setting with extensive symbolic imagery. *Landet Utanför* (*The Land Beyond*, 1967) is an experimental fairy tale: the same story is told twice, the second version being more sophisticated and presenting a sort of comment on the first.

The 1960s in Sweden were the years of social commitment in literature, and all imaginative writing was pronounced harmful and undesirable by many critics. Several parodical fairy tales, labelled as 'socialist', were published during this time. During the 1970s and 1980s, occasional fairy-tale novels appeared, which exploited conventional motifs like journeys into magical realms or magical objects; they were rather colourless and mediocre compared to their apparent British models. Later some heroic tales, imitating Tolkien, appeared, for instance by Eva Uddling (1944) and Bertil Mårtensson (*fl.* 1945).

Unlike their Swedish colleagues, Norwegian writers seem to prefer humorous and entertaining fairy tales, among which stories about little Old *Mrs Pepperpot by Alf *Prøysen are best-known internationally. Another renowned master of the genre is Torbjørn *Egner with his animal tales and absurd adventures. More like British models is *Trapp med 9 trinn* (*Staircase with 9 Steps*, 1952), a time-shift fairy tale by Odd Bang-Hansen (1908–84). However, the most original author is Zinken Hopp (1905–87) with her *Trollkrittet* (*The Magic Chalk*, 1948), a remarkable nonsensical story about a boy who gets hold of a magical piece of chalk, and whatever he draws becomes real. In the sequel, *Jon og Sofus* (*Jon and Sofus*, 1959), the same boy and his drawn and animated friend find a wish-granting wand. Both books have a strong satirical tone. One of Zinken Hopp's followers in this respect was Tor Åge Bringsvaerd (1939–), with a series of socially critical fairy tales.

Tormod *Haugen belongs to a totally different tradition, closer to Astrid Lindgren and clearly influenced by the contemporary British fairy tale. *Slottet det hvite* (*The White Castle*, 1980) tells what happened after the prince and princess started 'living happily ever after' and had children of their own. *Dagen som forsvant* (*The Day that Disappeared*, 1983) brings *Peter Pan into today's Norwegian capital. Children's rights and adults' responsibility is Haugen's primary concern, much like Astrid Lindgren's. He works extensively with symbols and metaphors, transforming traditional fairy-tale patterns into moral and ethical issues. Several novels contain elements of quest fairy tales, while still others successfully combine magical and science-fiction motifs. Haugen stands out considerably in light of the predominantly realistic contemporary literature in Norway.

The most recent addition to the Norwegian fairy-tale genre is Jostein Gaarder (1952–), the author of the international best-seller *Sophie's World*. His fairy-tale novels, for instance, *Kabalmysteriet* (*The Solitaire Mystery*, 1990), bear resemblance to the German romantic tale, but they may also have been influenced by Michael *Ende.

Remarkably, in Denmark, the home country of Andersen, the modern fairy-tale tradition is virtually non-existent. It may partly be explained by Andersen filling the need, since his fairy tales are widely published and illustrated by many contemporary Danish artists. In the second half of the 20th century, especially during the 1960s and later, Denmark has been significantly more politically radical than Sweden and Norway. As a result, the realistic tradition is much stronger in Denmark than a fairy-tale or fantastic one. Indeed, a great deal of criticism has been aimed against Astrid Lindgren by Danish critics. The only well-known modern Danish fairy tale is the cautionary dream-story *Palle alene i verden* (*Palle Alone in the World*, 1942) by Jens Sigsgaard (1910–91). With some reservations, a series by Cecil Bodker (1927–), beginning with *Silas og den sorte hoppe* (*Silas and the Black Mare*, 1967), can be considered in terms of the fairy tale.

In summary, it should be pointed out that, with a few exceptions, Scandinavian countries cannot boast of a significant and persistent fairy-tale tradition, and there is definitely no continuity comparable to the modern British fairy-tale tradition. One of the reasons may be that the need for fairy-tale and fantastic literature is satisfied by translations of English-language texts, with which native writers cannot compete. When, in the early 1980s, after a period of social commitment, a new wave of translated fantasy and fairy tales entered Sweden, Swedish writers reacted primarily by switching from contemporary to historical settings; thus the historical novel partly plays the role of the fairy tale in Scandinavia. Strange as it may seem, the rich history, mythology and epic writing of the Scandinavian people have not inspired writers to create anything similar to Middle Earth or explore the device of time travelling. Moreover, the notion of the fairy tale is mainly associated with the works of *Perrault and the Grimms than with any native texts.   MN

the Eye of a Needle, 1985) and *Eine Hand voller Sterne* (*A Hand Full of Stars*, 1990), reflect Schami's childhood years in Damascus in their setting and flavour, and his adopted homeland and culture in literary style. His tales are pared down to the bare essentials and told matter-of-factly with humour, irony, and a hint of cynicism. He often combines the oral Arabic storytelling tradition with the German fairy-tale narrative style, and in such collections as *Erzähler der Nacht* (1989), translated as *Damascus Nights* in 1993, he frames his tales in much the same manner as the **Arabian Nights*. He has also written often about problems of xenophobia and integration of outsiders in Germany, alluded to in his fairy tales, and he has written a novel about the dictatorships in Syria with the title *Die dunkle Seite der Liebe* (*The Dark Side of Love*, 2004).								EMM

Amin, Magda, 'Stories, Stories, Stories: Rafik Schami's *Erzähler der Nacht*', *Alif: Journal of Comparative Poetics* (2000).
Deeken, Annette, 'Der listige Hakawati', *Deutschunterricht* (1995).
Schami, Rafik, 'The Magic Lamp', trans. and intro. Alfred Cobbs, *Marvels & Tales* (2002).

Scheherazade Female character within the frame story and narrator of all tales but the frame of *The *Arabian Nights* (also known as the *Thousand and One Nights*). The sultan Shahryar, disillusioned by the sexual infidelity of women, has decided to marry a new wife every night only to kill her the next morning. Three years later, all marriageable women have either been killed or deserted the town, and none are left except the vizier's own daughters Scheherazade and Dinarzade. Scheherazade, the elder one, is well educated and has read a thousand books of histories and tales. Against her father's advice she insists on challenging the king. After the consummation of their marriage, Scheherazade has her sister ask her to tell a tale in order to pass the time. Scheherazade narrates a fascinating tale, but breaks off without reaching the end. Out of curiosity the king decides not to kill her and listens to the continuation next night. This strategy of suspense goes on for a thousand nights, until Scheherazade in the thousand and first night discloses her ruse and presents to the king the three children to whom she meanwhile has given birth. The king pardons her, renounces his former habit, and all rejoice.

In Western literary criticism, *The Arabian Nights* was regarded for a long time as equivalent of 'Scheherazade's tales', a label that veils the quality of Scheherazade herself constituting the protagonist of a narrative. On the other hand, the narrator Scheherazade has been subjected to various interpretations largely from a feminist perspective. Though Shahryar appears the supreme ruler commanding life and death, he readily falls victim to a (daring, yet simple) female ruse. By arousing the ruler's curiosity, Scheherazade inadvertently educates him. Generally speaking, Scheherazade is the perfect threefold woman: mother, whore, and friend. The male she confronts is brutal and insensitive and has to be tricked into allowing his own positive qualities to unfold. The fact that the male authors of the *Nights* have a female narrator educate a male wrongdoer contains more than an obvious simple moral and has continued to inspire literary reworkings of Scheherazade's background, motivation, and fate, notably in the modern Arabic novel.					UM

Gerhardt, Mia I., *The Art of Story-Telling* (1963).
Lahy-Hollebecque, Marie, *Scheherazade, ou l'éducation d'un roi* (1927, 1987).
Malti-Douglas, Fedwa, 'Shahrazad feminist', in Richard G. Hovannisian and George Sabagh (eds.), *'The Thousand and One Nights' in Arabic Literature and Society* (1997).

Schenck, Johann Baptist (1753–1836) Austrian composer and teacher who is remembered partly for his association with Wolfgang Amadeus **Mozart* and chiefly for his opera Der Dorfbarbier (*The Village Barber*). *Der Dorfbarbier* was premièred in Vienna in late 1796, enjoying popular success well into the 19th century. It belongs firmly to the *Singspiel* genre, to which Schenk's not inconsiderable number of stage works belong. The story's brush with fairy lore encompasses a village barber's unsuccessful attempt to marry his young ward, Suschen, and his claim that he has a wondrous bacon-cure which will alleviate ills.   TH

Schiller, Friedrich von (1759–1805) Classical German poet, dramatist, and historian, who wrote one major fairy-tale play, *Turandot, Prinzessin von China* (*Turandot, Princess of China*, 1802), based on Carlo Gozzi's play *Turandot* (1762). Schiller's tragicomedy concerns the gifted but cruel Princess Turandot of China who will marry only the man who can solve three riddles. A daring prince named Calaf, who is travelling incognito, solves the riddles, but the enraged princess demands a retaliatory trial. Calaf must demonstrate his integrity one more time, and after a near tragedy the princess agrees to marry him.   JZ

> Snook, Lynn, 'Auf den Spuren der Rätselprinzessin Turandot', in Jürgen Janning, Heino Gehrts, and Herbert Ossowski (eds.), *Vom Menschenbild im Märchen* (1980).
> Witte, W., 'Turandot', *Publications of the English Goethe Society*, 39 (1969).

Schönlank, Bruno (1891–1965) German journalist and writer known especially for his chorus works. Schönlank's commitment to social justice for the working class found expression in his two fairy-tale collections, *Grossstadt-Märchen* (*Big City Fairy Tales*, 1923) and *Der Kraftbonbon und andere Grossstadtmärchen* (*The Power Candy and Other Big City Fairy Tales*, 1928). In the modern urban setting of these Berlin-based tales, Schönlank's characters surmount problems through their shared sense of community. His *Schweizer Märchen* (*Swiss Fairy Tales*, 1938), written in exile from Nazi Germany, incorporate aspects of the Swiss culture and landscape, but remain focused on this ideal vision of community.   DH

schools of folk-narrative research The different theories and schools of thought that have attempted to explain the historical development of folk narrative date back to the early collections and analyses of folk literature in the late 18th century and extend up to present-day considerations about the nature of storytelling in modern, technological societies. In the history of folk narrative scholarship, the main prose genres have been folk tale, legend, and myth. The folk tale continues to be the most extensively studied of the prose genres. Although many theoretical perspectives have evolved directly from the study of the folk tale, they have often been applicable to other genres as well. An overview of research on folk narrative can be grouped according to four general directions of inquiry, which do not always constitute separate schools, concerning the question of origin, form, meaning, and style.

1. Precursors

The formal study of folk narrative began with Jacob and Wilhelm *Grimm, who were the first systematic collectors and scholars. Others predated them, but it was the Grimms who provided the earliest theoretical and methodological statements on folk narrative, from Jacob's initial observations on genre to Wilhelm's description of their sources and research methods. For the Grimms, their research on folk narrative was part of a conceptually holistic project of *Germanistik* (German studies) encompassing the areas of philology, law, mythology, and literature. Although their fairy tales were appropriated by the German middle class, who saw in them an instrument for the socialization of children, their primary purpose in publishing the *Kinder- und Hausmärchen* (*Children's and Household Tales*) was first and foremost as a contribution to the history of German folk poetry.

Collections of literary fairy tales, such as Giambattista *Basile's *Pentamerone* and Charles *Perrault's *Contes de ma Mère l'Oye* had already enjoyed considerable popularity by the time the first collections of folk literature, focusing initially on poetry, ballads, and folk songs, were published. Thomas Percy's *Reliques of Ancient English Poetry*, a three-volume collection of traditional English and Scottish ballads, appeared in 1765, the same year as James Macpherson's *Poems of Ossian*, which would later be denounced as the fraudulent fabrication of the editor. The collections of Percy and Macpherson had a profound impact on the German philosopher and writer Johann Gottfried von Herder, who in turn inspired the Grimms.

Herder was convinced that *Volkspoesie* (folk poetry), which included prose and lyric genres, was the only true poetry, because its natural vitality and simplicity were uncorrupted by the destructive forces of modern civilization. For Herder, folk poetry constituted the genuine expression of national character. He believed that German literature had lost touch with its native traditions, and that only through studying folk poetry, which still survived among the German peasants, could Germany recover its true national and cultural identity. He articulated his goal of reviving the nation's past in *Fragmente über die neuere deutsche Literatur* (*Fragments on Recent German Literature*) and published his own collection of international folk songs, *Lieder* (*Songs*), later retitled *Stimmen der Völker in Liedern* (*The Voice of People in Songs*) in 1778–9.

2. Origin

In the mid-19th century the prevailing intellectual climate was concerned with the question of origins. Rapidly developing technology brought about increased travel to and greater knowledge of other places in the world, and with it investigations into the origins of the human race as well as that of language and culture. Related to the question of origins for folk-narrative scholars were the issues of distribution and dissemination, as these processes constituted the traceable links between past and present forms of folk narrative.

Both the Grimms and Friedrich Max Müller, a Sanskrit scholar who translated the *Rig-Veda*, were proponents of the Indo-European theory of mythic origins, which held that European folk tales were the fragmented remains of the myths of Indo-European peoples. The aim of research was to reconstruct the Indo-European parent language, and by extension Indo-European folk tales and their original meanings. On the basis of comparative linguistics and comparative mythology, they attempted to reconstruct the myths and the mythic-religious beliefs that gave rise to these narratives.

Statements expressing the belief that folk tales were part of the cultural inheritance from a common Indo-European past can be found in Jacob Grimm's 1834 *Deutsche Mythologie* (*Teutonic Mythology*) and in the preface to the 1856 edition of the Grimms' *Kinder- und Hausmärchen*. In the latter, Wilhelm Grimm observed that folk tales contain 'fragments of belief dating back to the most ancient times'. Demonstrating his penchant for naturalistic metaphors, he compared the mythic in folk tales to 'small pieces of a shattered jewel which are lying strewn on the ground all overgrown with grass and flowers, and can only be discovered by the most far-seeing eye'.

Müller and George Cox were also proponents of 'solar mythology', the idea that folk tales derive from myths about natural phenomena. They posited that early humans were fascinated by the dramas of nature, specifically the movement of the sun, and that early language described natural processes in concrete and personified terms. Myth evolved as language became increasingly abstract and rational, in the attempt to explain obsolete concepts and linguistic forms no longer comprehensible to modern man.

Another school of thought on the origins of the folk tale was proposed by Theodor Benfy, a German orientalist whose reading of the *Kinder- und Hausmärchen led him to believe that India was the probable source of the European folk tale. Rather than rely on the philological speculation practised by Müller, Benfy examined Indic texts as well as the relationship between oral and literary traditions. He concluded that the dissemination of tales from India to Europe occurred through three avenues: first through oral tradition before the 10th century, later through the vehicle of Persian and Arabic translations of Indian literary texts, and finally through contact between Muslim and European populations. Present-day scholars consider India as one of several important sources for the European folk narrative tradition and subscribe to the theory of polygenesis (many origins) when accounting for the similarity of narrative traditions throughout the world.

The search for origins acquired greater rigour in the hands of Finnish folk-tale scholars, who developed what is known as the historical-geographic method of folk-tale analysis. Eschewing preconceptions about the origin and meaning of folk tales that characterized much of 19th-century thought, this approach consisted of assembling all known variants of a single folk tale from archival and literary sources as well as oral tradition, isolating the tale by its component parts, and plotting the distribution of the tale over time and space. The central premiss of this method was that each tale had a single origin (monogenesis). Multiple variants of a particular tale were attributed to diffusion, with the best tales travelling the furthest in wave-like circles from their point of origin.

The goal of the researcher working within the Finnish school was to reconstruct the history of a particular tale and determine its hypothetical *Urform* (original form). The central units of historical-geographic analysis consisted of the 'motif', defined as the smallest narrative element capable of persisting in tradition, and 'type', a traditional tale comprising many motifs and having an independent existence. In addition to developing key analytic concepts in folklore scholarship, this direction of folk narrative research produced important research tools and reference works for comparative analysis, most notably Antti Aarne's *Types of the Folktale*, expanded and translated by Stith Thompson and therefore known as the *Aarne–Thompson index, and Stith Thompson's six-volume *Motif-Index of Folk Literature*. Although their usefulness is greatest when analysing European and European-derived traditions, they offer the most widely recognized classification system for the identification of international folk narratives. In 2004, the German folklorist, Hans-Jörg Uther revised the Aarne-Thompson Index and published it in three volumes as *The Types of International Folktales: A Classification and Bibliography*. He expanded the international coverage of tales beyond Europe and North America, changed titles and descriptions, and added new bibliographical information. In addition to the different compilations of indices, several other important handbooks and methodologies developed out of the Finnish school, among them Kaarle Krohn's *Die folkloristische Arbeitsmethode* (*Folklore Methodology*) and Stith Thompson's *The Folktale*.

3. Form

Folk-narrative scholars have also asked themselves why certain ideas and experiences take a particular form. Andre Jolles approached the problem of form as a category of poetic expression in *Einfache Formen* (*Simple Forms*). Narrative, he suggested, originates in and takes its form from the expression of fundamental human experiences, which exist in the mind of the individual as a *Geistesbeschäftigung* (mental occupation) until they are expressed linguistically in a particular narrative form. Social change brings about different experiences, and this has prompted scholars to re-examine the analytic categories and typologies developed in earlier times from the study of traditional narrative. The German folklorist Hermann Bausinger demonstrated in 'Strukturen des alltäglichen Erzählens' ('Structures of Everyday Narration') and *Folk Culture in the Technical World* that contemporary storytelling, while often non-traditional in form and content, none the less is created out of many of the narrative impulses outlined by Jolles.

Considerations of form have contributed to the analysis of narrative structure. Structuralist approaches to folk narrative had their heyday from the 1950s to the 1970s and were applied primarily to the study of the folk tale and myth. Folk-narrative scholars generally distinguish between two types of structuralism, one developed by the Russian formalist and literary scholar Vladimir Propp, the other by the French anthropologist Claude Lévi-Strauss.

Propp's *The Morphology of the Folktale* applied Russian formalist criticism to the relatively small corpus of tales in Aleksandr *Afanasyev's collection of Russian fairy tales. Rejecting Aarne's classification system based on categories of the motif and type, which he considered inconsistent and unscientific,

Propp devised a method of identifying the structure of narrative elements in relation to one another and to the tale as a whole. His basic unit of analysis was the 'function', defined as the actions of a character from the point of view of its significance for the development of the course of action. Propp determined that functions occur in a fixed sequential order, often in pairs constituting an action and its consequence, and that there is a maximum of 31 possible functions, although not all 31 will necessarily occur in a given tale. He demonstrated that folk tales with very different content have a similar structure, consisting of a series of 'moves' from conflict to the resolution of that conflict. Although Propp's *Morphology of the Folktale* appeared in 1928, its importance for international folk-tale scholarship was only fully realized with the first English translation in 1968. The American folklorist Alan Dundes applied Propp's system to North American Indian folk tales as well as in investigations into the structure of proverbs.

For Lévi-Strauss, who analysed myths within the study of comparative religion, myths reflected the logical structure of the human mind. In 'The Structural Study of Myth', he compared the structure of the Oedipus myth with Zuni origin myths, concluding that the logic of mythological thought and the structure of narrative were based on the mediation of binary opposites, such as nature and culture or man and woman. Unlike Propp, for whom structure remained a question of syntax, Lévi-Strauss sought to relate structure to cultural context and symbolic meaning.

4. Meaning

Most studies of folk narrative have ultimately been driven by the search for meaning, although only a few theories about the meaning of folk narrative led to fully developed schools of thought. Herder and the Grimms, convinced that folk narrative was the purest expression of national character, attributed great cultural importance to the collection and interpretation of folk narrative for all nations, in particular for Germany. Their belief that folk narrative reflected cultural values did not translate into a detailed analysis of specific tales, but rather contributed to the general applied nature of their work. Meaning was as much a question of political and cultural application in their contemporary context as it was a problem of historical development.

Theories of meaning in the 19th century were also linked to questions of origins and often conceived within paradigms of progress: the Grimms believed that the meaning of tales was linked to the Indo-European past; solar mythologists held that myths and folk tales developed out of early man's explanations of natural phenomena; and British anthropologists, adopting the evolutionary theories of the day that all societies pass through the same stages of culture at different historical moments, concluded that folk tales were survivals of primitive myths. All held that while the forms of narrative persisted, their original meanings had been lost.

In the 20th century psychoanalytic interpretations, following in the tradition of Sigmund Freud and Carl Jung, have claimed to uncover the meanings of folk narrative in the unconscious desires of individuals, often in the correlation between dreams, fairy tales, and myths. This direction of analysis began with Freud's 1913 essay 'The Occurrence in Dreams of Material from Fairy Tales', analysing a patient's dreams containing motifs from *'Little Red Riding Hood' and 'The Wolf and the Seven Kids'. It was supported by Karl Abraham's assertion that 'the dream is the myth of the individual' and extended in Géza Róheim's conclusion that dreams provide the raw substance for myths and tales. Where solar mythologists saw nature symbolism in myths and folk tales, Freudian psychoanalytic readings see symbolism of a sexual nature. Carl Jung, however, rejected the narrow emphasis on sexual symbolism in favour of what he called the 'collective unconscious'. One of his more important essays for folk narrative research analyses the psychology of the trickster figure in the mythology of North American Indians.

In *The Uses of Enchantment* the Freudian-trained child psychologist Bruno Bettelheim concluded that fairy tales speak to the unconscious of a child, thereby aiding the child in overcoming inner struggles, such as sibling rivalry and Oedipal conflicts, through the presentation of simple situations, polarities that are easy to comprehend, and solutions to conflicts in the form of happy endings. In the United States, the most prolific proponent of psychoanalytic interpretations of folk narrative has been the folklorist Alan Dundes.

5. Style

Stylistic considerations have been textual and contextual in nature, with text-centred approaches predominating from the beginning of folk narrative research up through the first half of the 20th century. The earliest conceptions of folk narrative, defined alternately by Herder as *Naturpoesie* (natural poetry) and *Volkspoesie* (folk poetry), derived from his philosophy of aesthetics and contributed to the romantic idea that folk literature, with its strong rhythms and vibrant imagery, was closer to nature because the peasants, who retained the folk-narrative traditions, remained tied to the land and were less affected by the force of civilization. Similar statements can also be found with the Grimms, whose understanding of the style of folk narrative was both romantic and rigorous. The romantic underpinnings of their ideas derived from the period of romanticism in which they lived, while their rigour was the result of their comprehensive knowledge of and extensive study into German language, literature, and culture. Influenced as they were by Herder, they held that the style of *Volkspoesie*, in contrast to the deliberate and conscious creation of *Kunstpoesie* (art poetry), was organic, resembling the 'half-unconscious growth of plants watered by the source of life itself'. Prefaces to editions of the *Kinder- und Hausmärchen*, for example, praised the simplicity, innocence, and purity of the oral traditions they sought to preserve. For them the inherent style of folk literature derived from its social and cultural context and resided in the text. Their work on German grammar, the history of the German language, and

particularly on their *Deutsches Wörterbuch* (*German Dictionary*) provided them with an impressive knowledge of the evolution of German language and the place of folk literature within that framework. Jacob's *Deutsche Grammatik* (*German Grammar*) included a comparison of German regional dialects and Wilhelm's appreciation for folk speech and idiom was reflected in later editions of the *Kinder- und Hausmärchen*. Jacob also addressed the question of generic styles, when he observed that the fairy tale is more poetic, the legend more historical.

In the 20th century, important contributions to the study of folk narrative style have come from literary scholars as well as ethnographers. In *The European Folktale*, the Swiss folklorist and professor of literature Max Lüthi identified the central stylistic features of the folk tale as: one-dimensionality (the unproblematic coexistence of real and enchanted worlds); depthlessness (an absence of psychological depth and motivation); abstraction (the lack of realistic detail and a proclivity towards extremes, contrasts, and fixed formulas); and isolation and universal connection (the lack of sustained relationship between characters).

As style was thought to be inherent in the narrative itself, the text-centred approaches of the Grimms and later scholars viewed story-telling from the vantage point of an abstract ideal, favouring stability and adherence to tradition over individual artistry and innovation. Storytellers were seen as 'bearers of tradition', whose role it was faithfully to reproduce stories they had learned. Although the Grimms appreciated Frau Dorothea Viehmann, one of their main sources, for her ability to narrate 'carefully and confidently and in an unusually lively manner', their praise was based more on her accuracy while adapting to their recording needs than her actual performance style. Later theories explaining the stability of oral tradition, such as Walter Anderson's 'law of self-correction', regarded stylistic variation as an error corrected by a communal aesthetic.

In the 20th century ethnographers introduced a shift in focus from text-centred studies of folk narrative to the social context and creative process of storytelling. Ethnographies from the Russian and Hungarian schools of folklore examining the personality of storytellers and the social function of storytelling in a community, such as Mark Aadowskij's *Eine Siberische Märchenerzählerin* (*A Siberian Teller of Fairy Tales*) and Linda Dégh's *Folktales and Society: Storytelling in a Hungarian Peasant Community*, contributed towards a richer understanding of the meaning of storytelling for narrator and audience. In the United States, context-sensitive ethnographers from various disciplines began to conceive of performance as an aesthetically marked event, in which narrators assume responsibility for artistic communication. Viewing performance as an emergent event in which aesthetic aspects of communication predominate, researchers in this tradition are as much interested in the process of storytelling as the text produced through performance. Precursors to this 'performance-centred' approach include the work of Prague School linguists emphasizing actual performance over rule-based competence, and the 'oral-formulaic' theory of Milman Parry and A. B. Lord delineating the complex technique of oral composition by which lengthy epics are created and recreated in performance through the use of 'formulas', groups of words regularly employed under the same metrical conditions to express a given idea.   MBS

Aarne, Antti, *The Types of the Folktale* (1910; enl., with Stith Thompson, 1928; 2nd rev. edn., 1961).

Bauman, Richard, *Verbal Art as Performance* (1978).

Bauman, Richard, and Scherzer, Joel, *Explorations in the Ethnography of Speaking* (1974).

Bettelheim, Bruno, *The Uses of Enchantment* (1976).

Jolles, Andre, *Einfache Formen* (1930).

Lord, A. B., *The Singer of Tales* (1960).

Lüthi, Max, *The European Folktale: Form and Nature* (1982).

Propp, Vladimir, *The Morphology of the Folktale* (1968; orig. 1928).

Thompson, Stith, *The Folktale* (1946).

Thompson, Stith, *Motif-Index of Folk Literature* (1955–8).

Uther, Hans-Jörg, *The Types of International Folktales: A Classification and Bibliography*, 3 vols. (2004).

Schröder, Binette (1939–) German illustrator and photographer who has gained an international reputation, especially in Japan. In 1997 she won the German Literature Prize for her collected works. Her fantastic fairy-tale world is strikingly stylized and filled with graceful dolls and artificial landscapes. She frequently depicts charming futuristic scenes on a well-ordered but lifeless theatrical stage. Her first illustrated fairy-tale book, *Lupinchen* (1977), was translated into 17 languages and established her international fame. She has also illustrated Hans Christian *Andersen's fairy tales (1974), *Kinder- und Hausmärchen* (1986), The *Frog King* (1987/9), and The *Juniper Tree* (1997), which she endowed with mythic proportions.   KD

Schulz, Heinrich (1872–1932) German educator and writer who became head of the cultural ministry in 1920 when the Social Democrats came to power in the Weimar Republic. At the same time he began writing books for children. Among his books are *Der kleine Jan* (*Small Jan*, 1920), *Aus meinen vier Pfählen* (*Out of my Four Posts*, 1921), and *Von Menschen, Tierlein und Dinglein: Märchen aus dem Alltag* (*About People, Little Animals, and Little Things: Fairy Tales from Every Day Life*, 1924). This last book, a collection of fairy tales, was most important because the tales were conceived to clarify social relations and to offer possibilities for the solution of political conflicts. In such tales as 'The Castle with Three Windows' and 'The Quiet Engine' Schulz focused on the necessity to encourage solidarity among workers and introduced proletarian elements into traditional folk tales and fables.   JZ

Schumann, Robert (1810–56) Regarded as one of the great German romantic composers, known for his piano music, chamber music, songs, and symphonies. Although Schumann wrote some operas, the only one he finished, *Genoveva* (1850), was never as successful as his other works that often had strong fairy-tale elements.

Influenced by E. T. A. *Hoffmann, Schumann wrote two important fairy-tale piano compositions during the 1830s: *Phantasiestücke* (*Fantasy Pieces*), a collection of poetic mood pieces based on Hoffmann's tales, and *Kreisleriana*, fantasy pieces that recall the mad musician Kreisler, who appears in several of Hoffmann's stories.

In his choral work *Das Paradies und die Peri* (*Paradise and the Peris*, c.1850), Op. 50, Schumann set to music one of the poems from Thomas Moore's *Lalla Rookh* (1817). The Peris are descendants of fallen angels, related to fairies and elves, and have been banished from heaven. One of these fallen angels endeavours to complete three tasks so that she will be allowed to return to heaven, and she succeeds. Another choral composition by Schumann, *Der Rose Pilgerfahrt* (*The Pilgrimage of the Rose*, 1851, Op. 112), places the listener in the sphere of magic. The queen of the fairies grants the wish of a rose to become a human being. Once the rose becomes a beautiful maiden, she travels through the world on a kind of pilgrimage and experiences rejection and pain but also love and happiness. In the end, she dies while giving birth to a child and then is received in heaven by angels.

Schumann also composed music for Lord Byron's verse drama *Manfred* (1849, Op. 115). Here the magician Manfred conjures up earth and sky spirits that make him restless. After numerous adventures in the Alps and a battle with the spirits, Manfred finally regains his peace of mind and dies.   THH

Schwartz, Yevgeni (1896–1958) Russian playwright, author of several plays based on Hans Christian *Andersen's fairy tales. *The Naked King* (1934, pub. 1960) follows the basic plot of Andersen's 'The Emperor's New Clothes', incorporating some elements from 'The Swineherd' and 'The *Princess and the Pea'*, as well as a good deal of social satire. *The *Snow Queen* (1939) and *The Shadow* (1940) are closer to the originals, while they have a clear satirical focus, the latter portraying a country ruled by a dictator. However, unlike the original, Schwartz's version of *The Shadow* has a happy ending. Many of Schwartz's plays were banned when Communist censorship detected possible satires of the regime in their motifs of power and falseness.

Schwartz's *Little Red Riding Hood* (1937) may be one of the earliest contemporary versions of this fairy tale where the little girl is brighter than the wolf; she also receives help from a number of animals to whom she has been kind. *Cinderella* (1947), originally a film script, abounds in funny, everyday details and introduces a number of colourful secondary characters, especially the absent-minded and charming king. In this play, figures from other famous fairy tales appear, such as *Little Tom Thumb*.

Schwartz also wrote several original plays loosely based on fairy-tale motifs, such as the lyrical comedy *The Ordinary Miracle* (1956), an inversion of *'Beauty and the Beast'. *The Dragon* (1943) makes use of the dragon-slayer motif to show how slavery corrupts people and how easily the oppressed become oppressors. During the war, it was easy for official Soviet criticism to declare that the play was a satire on Germany; however, the true target was obvious. The most subtle satire is probably to be found in Schwartz's original fairy-tale play, *The Two Maple-Trees* (1953). In the play a conceited witch, the traditional *Bába Yagá of Russian folklore, transforms two brothers into trees, effectively hiding them from their mother, although they are within her reach. Like all of Schwartz's plays, it appeared to be addressed to children; however, adult audiences recognized at once the millions of innocent people hidden forever in Stalin's prisons and labour camps amidst everyday life. The witch was a brilliant satirical portrait of the Communist Party: admiring herself, boasting, promising too much, and never keeping her promises.

Schwartz also wrote some prose fairy tales, most notably an original sequel to *'Puss-in-Boots' (1937), in which he places the main character in a contemporary Soviet setting and has him defeat an evil frog-witch, who has enchanted a little boy, turning him into a villain. At the end of the tale, Puss attends the May Day parade on Red Square. 'Two Brothers' (1943) is based on the common motif of enchantment and rescue, introducing a parody of the Father Frost figure, the cruel and cynical wizard Great-Grandfather Frost. 'A Tale of Lost Time' (1948) portrays a lazy schoolboy who is enchanted by wicked wizards and turned into an old man. All three fairy tales have a clear didactic tone.   **MN**

Corten, Irinia H., 'Evgenii Shvarts as an Adapter of Hans Christian Andersen and Charles Perrault', *Russian Review*, 37 (1978).

Schwind, Moritz von (1804–71) Austrian painter, illustrator, and writer, who was famous for his prodigious fairy-tale paintings and drawings and his fairy-tale contributions to the *Münchner Bilderbogen* (*Munich Broadsheets*), one of the most popular series of broadsheets in the 19th century. After studying art and philosophy in Vienna, Schwind moved to Munich in 1828 and began to make a career for himself as painter and illustrator. He is best known for three cycles of fairy tales that he wrote and illustrated: *Aschenputtel* (*Cinderella, 1854), an oil painting, *Von den sieben Raben und der treuen Schwester* (*The Seven Ravens and their Faithful Sister*, 1857–8), 15 aquarelles, and *Von der schönen Melusine* (*The Beautiful* *Melusine, 1869), 11 aquarelles. Schwind's work has a classical, monumental quality to it. The lines of his drawings are strong and graceful, and his figures are realistically drawn. His classical style can especially be seen in the eight woodcuts that he did for the *Münchner Bilderbogen* between 1848 and 1855. Among his best fairy-tale broadsheets are 'Puss-in-Boots' and 'The *Juniper Tree'. Schwind's interpretations of the fairy tales were not particularly original. Rather, his illustrations endowed the tales with formidable traditional features.   **KS**

Bredt, E. W. (ed.), *Moritz von Schwind: Fröhliche Romantik* (1917).

Schwitters, Kurt (1887–1948) German Dadaist painter, performance artist, and writer. He developed innovative forms of printing and became one of the leading experimental artists in Berlin after the First World War. He created unusual fairy tales for children and adults, such as 'Der Hahnenpeter' ('Peter the Rooster', 1924), 'Die Märchen vom Paradies' ('The Fairy Tales of Paradise', 1924), and 'Die drei Wünsche' ('The Three Fairy Tales'). He called his special type of stories Merz fairy tales, publishing them in newspapers and journals and performing them in small theatres. In 1920 he declared that Merz desires freedom from all fetters in order to shape things artistically. Freedom is not unrestraint, but rather the result of strict artistic discipline. Merz also means tolerance towards any kind of limitation for artistic reasons. Every artist must be permitted to compose a picture, even if it is just made out of blotting paper, provided that he knows how to create. All of Schwitters' fairy tales and artworks were provocative and displeased the Nazis when they came to power in 1933. Schwitters escaped the Nazis in 1938 and eventually landed in England, where he spent the rest of his life and wrote some Merz fairy tales in English.   **JZ**

McBride, Patrizia, 'The Game of Meaning: Collage, Montage, and Parody in Kurt Schwitter's Merz', *Modernism/Modernity* (April 2007).

Meyer-Büser, Susanne, and Orchard, Karin (eds.), *In the Beginning Was Merz: From Kurt Schwitters to the Present Day* (2000).

Steinitz, Kate Trauman, *Kurt Schwitters: A Portrait from Life* (1968).

Webster, Gwendolen, *Kurz Merz Schwitters: A Biographical Study* (1997).

Zipes, Jack, 'Kurt Schwitters, Politics, and the Merz Fairy Tale', in Kurt Schwitters, *Lucky Hans and Other Merz Fairy Tales* (2009).

Schwob, Marcel (1867–1905) French essayist, critic, and novelist, who was strongly influenced by Edgar Allan Poe and wrote haunting tales that incorporated fairy-tale motifs. Schwob wrote his unusual tales for various Parisian newspapers and journals and collected them in three important books, *Cœur double* (*Double Heart*, 1891), *Le Roi au masque d'or* (*The King with the Golden Mask*, 1893), and *Les Vies imaginaires* (*Imaginary Lives*, 1896). Schwob's tales were brief reveries with ironic twists, such as the king who wears

Schwind, Moritz von The complete triumphant story of *'Puss-in-Boots' is portrayed by Moritz von Schwind in this Munich broadside of 1848.

a golden mask unaware that he has leprosy. By discarding the mask, he purifies himself; and with his own blood he heals the leprosy, but thereby causes his death. In most of Schwob's tales there is a paradoxical connection between horror and truth.   JZ

Champion, Pierre, *Marcel Schwob et son temps* (1927).

Trembley, George, *Marcel Schwob, faussaire de la nature* (1969).

science fiction and fairy tales Science fiction (SF) and the fairy tale both deal with situations that are contrary to fact, a quality Samuel R. Delany calls 'subjunctivity'. Although the term '*science* fiction' might seem automatically to exclude any meaningful contact with the fairy tale, both are subsets of the mode called fantastic. Rosemary Jackson defines mode as a set of general rules not limited to a particular literary type (genre) or time period, and the critics Brian Aldiss and Damien Broderick have found it more useful to speak of SF as a mode than as a genre or story type, since one can then focus on what SF does instead of on what elements—space travel or aliens—it includes. At the same time, SF is marketed as a genre separate from fantasy in recognition of the distinctive formulaic elements of each type.

SF is the most recent addition to the fantastic mode. It began in the 19th century as narrative response to scientific enquiry and the increasing application in society of the results of experimentation. SF came into its own in the works of H. G. *Wells and Jules Verne, and addresses the anxieties not only of the destabilizing effects of industrialization but also those of evolutionary theory. Even if the dominant cultural attitude was hopeful belief in the progressive amelioration of the human condition, serious consideration of the implications of Darwin's theories, for example, that the devolution depicted in *The Time Machine* (1895) was a possibility, served only to heighten the tension between hope and fear. If Jules Verne produced exuberant fantastic voyages, the writings of Wells, even if he called them 'scientific romances', presented a darker vision. The apparent changes of fortune in

fairy tales bring the world back to a (possibly better) sameness, whereas SF moves its worlds into an uncertainty and difference. Darko Suvin speaks of SF as a literature dependent on an 'imaginative framework alternative to the author's empirical environment' based on a creative departure he calls a 'novum' that both generates and grants an inner logic to the plot; its value rests not in sheer novelty but in its genuine alternatives to what we know and to the social structures we now inhabit.

The boundaries between SF and fantasy are the subject of numerous debates because SF does not always achieve the level of purity from the purely fantastic desired by its most rigorous proponents. For example, the practice most often associated with SF narratives is *extrapolation* from our current state of science. Problems in disentangling SF from fairy tale arise, however, when a futuristic device is employed as a substitute for a magic wand, as it tends to be in the variety of SF known as 'space opera'. The resulting narrative becomes a fairy tale with futuristic hardware.

One basic constraint separates the SF mode from the fairy tale: both fairy tales and SF are rule-based, but the rules of SF either replicate or are modelled upon the empirical physical principles of our everyday world. One will not find witches, mages, elves, or dragons in those pseudo-medieval aspects they present in traditional fairy tales; nor will one find the supernatural or magical agencies that dominate the fairy-tale mode of writing. George *MacDonald describes the fantastic environment as an 'inverted world, with laws of other kinds'. MacDonald's own fantasies occasionally touched upon elements of science, as in the arrangement of mirrors used in *Lilith*, which was praised for its ingenuity by H. G. Wells, but the 'laws' of the narrative world are not the central focus. MacDonald called his fantasies 'fairy stories', and even the scientific romantic tales of *Hawthorne such as 'Rappacini's Daughter' or 'The Birthmark' have the individual soul, so to speak, at their narrative centre. In 'Do-It-Yourself Cosmology', Ursula K. *Le Guin describes fantasy as 'introverted', lending itself to private fantasizing, and SF as a modern, extraverted variety of fantasy more suited to address issues of technology in society.

The fairy tale has two primary functions in SF: it offers a structural formula, following to a greater or lesser degree the motif patterns of quest and initiation (departure–test–return) described by Vladimir Propp, and it provides the reader with appealing compensatory fantasies. In his essay 'Fairy Tales and Science Fiction', Eric Rabkin discusses the psychoanalytical and developmental concepts shared by fairy tales and science fiction: wish fulfilment, the illusion of centrality, and omnipotence of thought. In fairy tales, the 'happy ending' is the most common element of wish-fulfilment, but the triumph of the downtrodden, the possession of extraordinary or preternatural talents or a talisman, or the victory against incredible odds—Rabkin cites 'The *Brave Little Tailor*'—make up the plots that culminate in such endings.

In terms of setting, the world of the fairy tale tends to be positively oriented towards the protagonist, providing helpers as needed, a detail noted both by Northrop Frye and somewhat differently by Stanislaw *Lem; the world of an SF tale tends to be neutrally oriented, it is a *place* and nothing more, even if populated by beings inimical to the protagonist. The SF tale does not demand the 'happy ending' as an absolute criterion, and the most empirically-oriented tales do not provide it. At best, the more utopian SF will be open-ended, with future positive results contingent on continued struggle for social change.

In traditional fairy tales the utopian content is attenuated to an improvement in the social condition of the protagonist (most often an unmarried female) within the existing social structure, a situation quite different from the more obvious utopianism of traditional folk tales which advocates the destabilizing of social hierarchies. Fairy-tale individualism persists in a great deal of SF, although the hero takes on the enemies of an oppressed or beleaguered world as often as not, and the SF monster-slayer encounters ever more exotic opponents and uses the most up-to-date weaponry. Such tales, the 'galactic empire' stories, show SF at its most conservative; victory means the restoration of the existing social order by destroying the invading or disruptive element.

SF contains a strong and essential admixture of the fantastic; time travel and propulsion beyond the speed of light, both patently impossible, are SF commonplaces. Brian Aldiss designates Mary Shelley's *Frankenstein* as arguably the first work of SF, but one must deal with the novel's notable lack of rigour in the 'science' surrounding the fabrication of Victor Frankenstein's creature. At the same time, Shelley's manipulation of Gothic fiction's dread of the Other effectively uses the fantastic to highlight the anxieties provoked by technological advances. Aldiss's definition of SF insists on its Gothic content: 'Science fiction is the search for a definition of mankind and his status in the universe which will stand in our advanced but confused state of knowledge (science), and is characteristically cast in the Gothic or post-Gothic mode.' This definition serves to underscore SF's continuity with an older narrative tradition while taking account of the demands of empiricism. Fairy tales do not offer explanations of their magic; it is simply part of the narrative world of the stories. SF arises in an interrogative context, so to speak, and its departures from accepted 'reality' are more evident, since its narrative universe shares its basic principles with our own.

The issues of probability, possibility, and plausibility focus on the reader's expectations of and responses to SF. We read a fantasy/fairy story with a different set of protocols from those active when we read SF; the 'enabling devices' of SF are different from those of the fairy tale; the distinguishing features—multi-sun solar systems or silicon-based physiology—are not at all trivial; rather, they signal to the reader SF's narrative universe and its attendant rules. For instance, in a much-quoted example, Samuel R. Delany notes that the phrase 'her world exploded' means one thing in a mainstream novel and something entirely different in SF. SF has made strategic use of fairy-tale conventions since they are older, more widely available, and more a part of the experience of the general reader; hence, fairy-tale elements have served to make arcane content more accessible to its readers. Mainstream fiction abandoned fantasy in the name of 'realism', but for a long time the isolation of American SF within a community of 'fans' kept a large proportion of its narratives closer to the conventions of fairy tales than might be evident to casual readers put off by too-evident hardware; these are the narratives known as 'space operas'.

The 'space opera' was canonized in the pulp magazines begun in the 1920s by Hugo Gernsback's *Amazing Stories*, and brought to its fullest development in John W. Campbell's magazines of the 1930s, most notably *Astounding Science-Fiction*. Gernsback's novel *Ralph 124 C41+* (1925) set the pattern for many to follow: the super-scientist with a device for every situation and the wits and courage to conquer foes of any size and anatomical configuration, who defends a heroine predictably attractive to the opposite sex—Martian or human.

The space opera, aptly named since it is an elaborately costumed spectacle—Aldiss calls it 'power fantasy'—features the radically polarized conflict of good vs. evil of the fairy tale; imperilled worlds and maidens are rescued by clean-cut heroes. In the earlier stories, for every device that was a rigorous extrapolation from known principles—the then hypothetical radar was described with uncanny accuracy in Gernsback's *Ralph*— many were carried over from medieval romance. For example, in E. E. Smith's 1930s 'Lensman' series, his warriors wear 'space armour' and wield 'space axes' as well as their blasters. A more up-to-date version of medievalism, heroics, and SF hardware is Frank Herbert's *Dune* (1965), the first and most successful in a series that combined creative extrapolation—the desert world of Arrakis—with a solid story of initiation.

The use of fairy-tale motifs ensured SF's success among those readers who craved adventure along with the detailed technical discussions that sometimes halted the progress of the plot, but that very success led to the stagnation of American SF. There were a few twists to the standard imitation heroic epic such as the doctor-as-hero stories of Murray Leinster, written in the late 1950s and early 1960s, which featured the human and animal team of Calhoun and the monkey-like Murgatroyd, companion and biosynthesizer in one, or, in the 1940s, stories such as Fritz Leiber's stories of Fafrhd and the Grey Mouser, for which he coined the term 'sword-and-sorcery'. On the whole, however, for every novel by Alfred Bester such as *The Stars My Destination* (1956) with its space-warping mode of personal travel, *More than Human* (1953) by Theodore Sturgeon, which presented the next stage of human evolution as a composite psyche, Homo Gestalt, or the evolution-as-apocalypse of *Childhood's End* (1953) by Arthur C. Clarke, there were scores of writers content simply to provide the fans with more of the formulaic fiction they craved.

The presence of fairy-tale elements in SF suggests that it might be especially attractive to younger readers. The 'power fantasies' of space opera tend to be described, pejoratively, as 'adolescent', and the SF reader is caricatured as an alienated young male. The straightforward action-oriented narratives of SF, as well as its avoidance, especially from the 1930s to the 1960s, of any adult sexuality made SF accessible and appealing to young and older readers alike, with the result that both groups read the same stories. To this day, book club notices tend to place warnings about explicit language, violence, or sexual content after their promotional statements in recognition of this dual audience.

There has been, nevertheless, a relatively small amount of SF directed to pre-adolescent readers. These stories use space travel and off-world settings for stories of quests and initiation, with a generous portion of world-saving heroics. In the 1950s, Isaac Asimov (writing as 'Paul French') published the 'Lucky Starr' series; Robert Heinlein's *Bildungsromane* such as *Citizen of the Galaxy* (1957) or *Red Planet* (1949) anticipated the revolution-centred *The Moon is a Harsh Mistress* (1966). In the young adult fiction of these two authors, the quality of the prose is strikingly high, in general less hackneyed than classic pulp SF repackaged as novels. On the other hand, novels by Alan E. Nourse, notably *Rocket to Limbo* (1957), or Lester del Rey's *Marooned on Mars* and *Rocket Jockey* (both 1952) replicated the tried and true space opera formulas.

For much younger readers, Eleanor Cameron's 'Mushroom Planet' books (the first was written in 1954 for her 9-year-old son) followed the 'boy explorer' pattern. Although SF is traditionally male-oriented fiction, it was read by girls, who admittedly found very few females except those waiting to be rescued. Still, they had Heinlein's *Podkayne of Mars: Her Life and Times* (1963) with its female protagonist, and *Have Spacesuit— Will Travel* (1958), in which the girl is a prodigy, surpassing the boy in intellect if not in strength. In the 1970s, James H. Schmitz used the popular pattern established by the 'Nancy Drew' stories in his short stories and novels featuring Telzey Amberdon; earlier, in 1965, he published 'Balanced Ecology', combining a serious topic with a satisfying story of effectively heroic children.

Today, the fairy-tale adventure has, to a great extent, been taken over by role-playing and computer games. The work of Sylvia Louise Engdahl, such as *Enchantress from the Stars* (1970), the *Tripod Trilogy* (1980) of John Christopher, or the 'Torin' series of Cherry Wilder, which began with *The Luck of Brin's Five* (1977), continue the tradition of heroic SF adventures for children. Young adult SF in print tends to focus more on utopias and dystopias than on wish-fulfilment, which is now mostly the province of fantasy fiction, flourishing for this market more than ever before. There are elements of dystopia in Engdahl's later work and in Christopher's trilogy; Lois Lowry's *The Giver* (1993) is a more recent example of this tendency.

Part of the attraction of the young audience to SF and fantasy can be attributed to the popular films from the 1970s to the present; it is here that the links between SF and the fairy tale have been deliberately affirmed and exploited. George Lucas's four 'Star Wars' films, *Star Wars* (1977), *The Empire Strikes Back* (1980), *The Return of the Jedi* (1983), and *The Phantom Menace* (1999), replay a

version of Freud's 'Family Romance' (the child as hidden royalty) in a quasi-Arthurian *Bildungsroman*. The wish-fulfilment of finding the absent father and gaining a magical friend is the central motivation of Steven *Spielberg's *E.T.: The Extra-Terrestrial* (1982), and Spielberg's *Close Encounters of the Third Kind* (1977) offers similar compensatory fantasy for the adult audience.

If wish fulfilment is enlarged to the concepts of adult desires, fears, or hopes, and the self-knowledge that is the ideal goal of the fairy-tale quest is enlarged to agency in social transformation, then fairy-tale content remains a viable structuring element in contemporary SF. The monster-slayer, or the (generally) Male *Cinderella, of whom George Lucas's Luke Skywalker is but the latest exemplar, do not exhaust the relationship of fairy tale to SF.

Three such stories are Samuel R. Delany's *Babel-17* (1966), Vonda N. McIntyre's *Superluminal* (1984), and Marge Piercy's *He, She, and It* (1991). In the 1960s, SF's 'New Wave' brought deliberately self-reflexive literary techniques to the forefront in SF writing. In addition to the older structures, fairy tales among them, these writers experimented with aligning techniques from contemporary fiction with the narrative content of SF. In *Babel-17* Delany addresses the effects of linguistics on our perceptions of reality as his heroine, the poet Rydra Wong, her accomplice, the Butcher, who seems more humanoid than human, and her crew—12 teenagers, a married 'triple', and three 'discorporates' (i.e. dead persons)—seek the source of a mechanical language linked with successful enemy sabotage; theoretical complexity and freewheeling traditional narrative structures function here in unison. Vonda N. McIntyre invokes many of the conventions of adult romance, yet the love stories among humans so radically altered for survival in the oceans or in deep space that they can no longer sustain meaningful relationships with the unaltered, undermine reader expectations as often as they fulfil them; thus she recuperates what would otherwise be banality. Piercy reflects on the nature of story itself, interweaving the political and ecological struggles of an imperilled colony of Jewish descent against world-controlling corporations, with the 'bubbe meise', or 'granny tales' of the Golem of the Prague ghetto—not simple fairy tales, to be sure, but told by an elderly programmer as part of the socialization of the android warrior she has helped to create—a re-enactment of the ancient cultural work of the fairy tale.

Although the most transparent appropriations of the fairy tale appear in American SF, the utopian potential of fairy-tale structure was also exploited in the former Soviet Union, primarily in the 1960s and early 1970s by the brothers Boris and Arkady Strugatsky, notably *The Snail on the Slope* (1966–8) and *Roadside Picnic* (1972), to express the hope that technology would help to reduce the gap between socialist utopian dreams and human reality. The Polish writer Stanislaw Lem, one of the most stringent critics of SF's dissipation of its critical potential in the 'empty games' of space opera, used fairy-tale structures to parody the foibles of his robot inventors in the short stories collected as *The Cyberiad* (1967).

All of these stories attest to the durability of the fairy tale while not replicating SF's earlier trite use of the old motifs. The 'story' of SF has never been separate from that of the fairy tale; these contemporary works speak of some of the best that that long association has to offer.   AAR

Aldiss, Brian, and Wingrove, Owen, *Trillion-Year Spree* (1986).
Broderick, Damien, *Reading by Starlight* (1995).
Csicsery-Ronay, Jr., Istvan, 'Towards the Last Fairy Tale: On the Fairy-Tale Paradigm in the Strugatskys' Science Fiction, 1963–72', *Science-Fiction Studies*, 13.1 (1986).
Delany, Samuel R., 'About 5,750 Words', *The Jewel-Hinged Jaw: Notes of [sic] the Language of Science Fiction* (1977).
Jackson, Rosemary, *Fantasy: The Literature of Subversion* (1981).
Le Guin, Ursula K., 'Do-It-Yourself Cosmology', in *The Language of the Night* (1979).
Rabkin, Eric, 'Fairy Tales and Science Fiction', in George E. Slusser *et al.* (eds.), *Bridges to Science Fiction* (1980).
Scholes, Robert, 'Boiling Roses: Thoughts on Science Fantasy', in George Slusser and Eric Rabkin (eds.), *Intersections: Fantasy and Science Fiction* (1987).
Suvin, Darko, *Metamorphoses of Science Fiction: On the Poetics and History of a Literary Genre* (1979).

Scieszka, Jon (1954–) American picturebook author who satirizes folk and fairy tales with a humorous postmodern twist. *The True Story of the Three Little Pigs by A. Wolf* (1989) parodies the traditional villain as an unreliable narrator, while *The *Frog Prince, Continued* (1991) challenges the premiss of living 'happily ever after' with the *Grimms' witches lurking about. *The Stinky Cheese Man and Other Fairly Stupid Tales* (1992), including the *Ugly Duckling* that grew into an ugly duck, was selected by the American Library Association as a Caldecott Honor Book for its sophisticated, surrealistic paintings by the illustrator Lane Smith.   BH

Apseloff, Marilyn Fain, 'The Big, Bad Wolf: New Approaches to an Old Folk Tale', *Children's Literature Association Quarterly*, 15.3 (fall 1990).
Stevenson, Deborah, '"If You Read This Last Sentence, It Won't Tell You Anything": Postmodernism, Self-Referentiality, and The Stinky Cheese Man', *Children's Literature Association Quarterly*, 19.1 (spring 1994).

Scott, Sir Walter (1771–1832) Novelist, poet, and essayist of the romantic period, concerned with Scottish Border legends and traditions throughout his lifetime. His *Minstrelsy of the Scottish Border* (1802–3) was a collection of folk and literary ballads in three volumes and contained his important early essay 'The Fairies of Popular Superstition'. While the elfin people play a role in his poetry, notably in 'The Lay of the Last Minstrel', they and their lore are featured even more prominently in his novels. *The Monastery* (1820) discusses the nature of elemental spirits and presents a fairy-sylph in the form of the White Lady of Avenel. A fairy changeling appears in *Peveril of the Peak* (1822), and a *Rumpelstiltskin-like supernatural dwarf in *The Pirate* (1822). Discussions of fairy lore permeate other novels.

Scott's most important contribution, however, is to folklore analysis and theory. In his *Letters on Demonology and Witchcraft*

(1820), he examines the possible origins of the fairies, the connections between fairies and witches, the evidence for fairy abductions, and the ways of avoiding elfin malice. He suggests a rational and historical basis for supernatural beliefs, thus popularizing the euhemerist position. He plays a significant role in legitimizing the 19th-century study of fairies.   CGS

Dorson, Richard M., *The British Folklorists* (1968).
Parsons, Coleman O., *Witchcraft and Demonology in Scott's Fiction* (1964).
Silver, Carole G., *Strange and Secret Peoples* (1998).

Scudder, Horace (1838–1902) American editor and author. He was a passionate supporter of imaginative literature, at a time when American opinion was uncertain about its value. He wrote three volumes of fairy stories, much influenced by writers such as Hans Christian *Andersen, George *MacDonald, and Charles *Dickens, and in his Bodley Family series of books (which began in 1875) incorporated many traditional tales. In 1867 he became editor of the new *Riverside Magazine for Young People* and later persuaded Hans Christian Andersen to contribute. *Childhood in Literature and Art* (1894) contains a long essay about fairy tales and Hans Andersen.   GA

Ségur Sophie, comtesse de (1799–1874) French writer of children's books. The daughter of Count Rostopchine who served as minister during the reign of Tsar Paul I and as governor of the City of Moscow in 1812, she spent her childhood in Moscow and on the vast family estate in Voronono. In 1817 her father fell into disgrace, and the family went into exile to France. Two years later she married Count Eugène de Ségur, who soon preferred the glamour of Paris, while Sophie spent most of her time at Les Nouettes, the country estate in Normandy that would be the setting for most of the stories she wrote. Neglected by her husband, Ségur devoted herself entirely to the education of the couple's eight children. The countess was 58 years old when she launched her literary career. First, she wrote two fairy tales, 'Histoire de Blondine'

and 'Le bon petit Henri', which were originally published in *La Semaine des Enfants*, a weekly magazine for children published by Louis Hachette, who eventually bought the copyrights to a manuscript that included three other tales: 'Histoire de la Princesse Rosette', 'La Petite Souris grise' ('The Little Grey Mouse') and 'Ourson'. The five fairy tales appeared under the title *Nouveaux Contes de fées* (*New Fairy Tales*, 1857) with 20 illustrations by Gustave *Doré. All the heroes in these tales, which combine an exuberant taste for the marvellous with a rigorous moral intention, are children who must overcome great difficulties and their human weaknesses to earn the happiness they will surely find at the end of their adventures. After the publication of *Nouveaux Contes de fées*, Ségur left behind the realm of fairy tales in favour of a different literary genre: the realistic novel for children, in which she gives an accurate rendition of French society during the Second Empire. The 20 novels she produced between 1857 and 1869 secured her a founding place in the tradition of French children's literature. The trilogy consisting of *Les Malheurs de Sophie* (*The Misfortunes of Sophie*), *Les Petites Filles modèles* (*Model Little Girls*) and *Les Vacances* (*Vacation*, 1859) is one of Ségur's most popular works, which still today find an enthusiastic audience among young readers. Legend once portrayed Ségur as a sweet grandmother writing stories for her grandchildren. Recent scholarship has shown, however, that she was a true novelist whose career was closely associated with the Hachette publishing house and the creation of the famous Bibliothèque Rose, a collection of books aimed at the largest possible children's audience.   CLMF

Doray, Marie-France, 'Cleanliness and Class in the Countess de Ségur's Novels', *Children's Literature*, 17 (1989).
Doray, Marie-France, *La Comtesse de Ségur: une étrange paroissienne* (1990).
Kreyder, Laura, *L'Enfance des saints et des autres. Essai sur la comtesse de Ségur* (1987).
Lastinger, Valérie, 'Of Dolls and Girls in Nineteenth-Century France', *Children's Literature*, 21 (1993).

Malarte-Feldman, Claire-Lise, 'La Comtesse de Ségur: A Witness of Her Time', *Children's Literature Association Quarterly*, 20 (fall 1995).

Seidel, Heinrich (1842–1906) Much loved German writer of children's stories and songs. He is best known for his novels on the Biedermeier idyll of the eponymous *Leberecht Hühnchen* (1882–90). Influenced by Robert *Reinick and Hans Christian *Andersen, he wrote his first fairy tale 'Schmetterlingskönigin Wieglinde' ('Wieglinde, Queen of the Butterflies') in 1864. Although didactic-moral tales, the exquisite stories in his two-volume collection *Wintermärchen* (*Winter Tales*, 1885) are also entertaining and have been published in various collections since 1945: *Zitrinchen und andere Märchen* (*Citronella and Other Fairy Tales*, 1958, 1969) and *Das Zauberklavier* (*The Magic Piano*, 1959).   KS

Seidel, Ina (1885–1974) German writer who wrote numerous poems, novels, essays, and memoirs. Her major contribution to the fairy-tale tradition in Germany was *Das wunderbare Geissleinbuch* (*The Wonderful Book about the Little Kids*, 1925), which has the subtitle 'New Stories for Children who Are Well-Acquainted with the Old Ones'. Seidel portrays a child who visits the seven kids and their mother, and he encounters other characters from the *Grimms' tales in adventures that do not involve magic, bewitchment, and punishment. In this way Seidel sought to modernize the Grimms' tales and make them more cheerful and soothing for young children. During the difficult post-war years in Germany, parents and educators were attracted to the non-violent nature of the book, which was reissued in 1949, and remained very popular until the early 1960s.   JZ

Sélis, Nicolas (1737–1802) French teacher and royal censor. He annotated La Fontaine's fables and wrote one fairy tale, 'Le Prince désiré' ('The Coveted Heir', n.d.), presented to Marie-Antoinette on the birth of the dauphin. A beloved king and queen rejoice when a long-awaited heir is born. A good fairy and benevolent genies, former monarchs who have been granted supernatural power, endow the newborn with all the virtues of an ideal prince. A panegyric to the French and Austrian royal families, this brief tale reiterates royalist ideology on the eve of the French Revolution.   AZ

Sendak, Jack (1923–95) American writer and illustrator who began writing children's stories in the 1950s. His first two books, *The Happy Rain* (1956) and *Circus Girl* (1958), were illustrated by his brother Maurice. Among his other works are *The Second Witch* (1965), *Martze* (1968), and *The Magic Tears* (1971), selected by the *New York Times* as one of the best illustrated children's books of the year. His collection, *The King of Hermits and Other Stories* (1966), contains several tales with a bizarre and charming Central European atmosphere.   JZ

Sendak, Maurice (1928–2012) American illustrator, writer, and set designer. Sendak was easily the most important designer of children's books in the English-speaking world; winner of the Hans Christian Andersen prize in 1970, he continued to evolve as a writer and illustrator.

Early in his career Sendak illustrated many books written by contemporaries (Ruth Krauss and Elsie Minarik among them). Later, however, he turned to older books, often fairy tales: *Seven Tales* by Hans Christian *Andersen (1959), tales by Wilhelm *Hauff and Clemens *Brentano (1960–2), *The Golden Key* and *The Light Princess* by George *MacDonald (1967, 1969). He also illustrated a collection of stories based on Jewish folk material by Isaac Bashevis *Singer (*Zlateh the Goat*, 1966). He seemed most drawn to the strange mixture of realism and fantasy, piety and violence, in the *Grimms' tales: he produced *The *Juniper Tree*, 27 tales in two volumes, with translations by Lore Segal and Randall *Jarrell (1973); *King Grisly-Beard* (1974); and *Dear Mili*, a tale found in an 1816 letter by Wilhelm Grimm (1988). The influence of romantic artists like William Blake, Samuel Palmer, Philipp Otto Runge, and Caspar David Friedrich—as well as of 19th-century book illustrators like Walter *Crane and George

*Cruikshank and of American popular culture—became steadily more evident in his work, as did his love for *Mozart.

In his own picture books, Sendak drew deeply on fairy-tale motifs and impulses. His elegiac fantasy *Higglety Pigglety Pop!* (1967) traces the journey of a terrier, Jennie, to a wider world of artistic experience, including a climactic performance in the *Mother Goose World Theater. The three books in his major 'trilogy'—*Where the Wild Things Are* (1963), *In the Night Kitchen* (1970), and *Outside Over There* (1981)—differ markedly in style and texture, but all feature a child's movement from anger or fear into a fantastic inner world where the child's own actions resolve the conflicts.

In the late 1970s Sendak began designing sets and costumes for operas in collaboration with the director Frank Corsaro: first Mozart's *Magic Flute* in 1979, then *Janáček's *Cunning Little Vixen* (1981), *Prokofiev's *Love of Three Oranges* (1982), Mozart's *Idomeneo* (1990), and *Humperdinck's *Hansel and Gretel* (1997). All of them show his delight in the theatrical and the fantastic—speaking animals, battles of polarized forces, symbolic objects and figures. Some of these operas later became picture books, as his designs for the ballet *The Nutcracker* in 1984. He also collaborated in turning his own books into television shows (*Really Rosie, Starring the Nutshell Kids* in 1975) and into operas (*Where the Wild Things Are* in 1979 and *Higglety Pigglety Pop!* in 1985, both with music by Oliver Knussen).   EWH

Cech, John, *Angels and Wild Things: The Archetypal Poetics of Maurice Sendak* (1995).
Lanes, Selma G., *The Art of Maurice Sendak* (1980).
Tatar, Maria, 'Wilhelm Grimm/Maurice Sendak: *Dear Mili* and the Art of Dying Happily Ever After', in *Off with their Heads!* (1992).

Sercambi, Giovanni (1348–1424) Italian novella writer and historian. Many of his *Novelle* (*Novellas*, 1390–1402) borrow from popular genres such as fabliaux, anecdotes, oral poetry, and fairy tales. Fairy-tale motifs are most evident in 'De bono facto' ('On a Happy Event'), the story of a simpleton who ends up marrying the daughter of the king of France; 'De vera amicitia et caritate' ('On True Friendship and Charity'), which adopts the fairy-tale motif of 'the two brothers'; and 'De bona ventura' ('On Good Luck'), in which fairies and tripartite trials are incorporated into a fabliau.   NC

Petrini, Mario, *La fiaba di magia nella letteratura italiana* (1983).

Seton, Ernest Thompson (1860–1946) Canadian naturalist, artist, and author of numerous realistic animal stories. Inspired by his own close observations, *Wild Animals I Have Known* (1898), *Biography of a Grizzly* (1900), *Lives of the Hunted* (1901), and *Animal Heroes* (1905) are among the most famous of their kind and helped to create the beginnings of an environmental consciousness in North America. *Woodmyth and Fable* (1905), a collection of short tales based on animal lore, stands apart from the main current of his work as Seton's one experiment with the fairy tale.   SR

Seuss, Dr (pseudonym of **Theodor Seuss Giesel**, 1904–91) Popular American author and illustrator of children's books. In his stories Seuss plays on the imaginative powers of children, which adults often dismiss or repress, and uses the stylistic techniques of accumulation and *mise-en-abyme* to create his fantasies. In his verse tale *And To Think That I Saw It on Mulberry Street* (1937), Marco prepares for his father a tall tale about what he saw coming home from school that day. A horse-drawn cart becomes in Marco's imagination a circus wagon with a brass band, and fantastic details progressively accumulate in his mind; but when his father indifferently asks him what he has seen that day, Marco replies, 'Nothing . . . But a plain horse and wagon on Mulberry Street'. Marco later returns in *McElligot's Pool* (1947) to tell a tall fish tale.

In his first prose tale *The Five Hundred Hats of Bartholomew Cubbins* (1938), fantasy is not stifled by indifference but is the pretext for questioning the arbitrariness of power. Bartholomew has a magical hat which is quite plain and shaped like that of Robin Hood. When Bartholomew takes off his hat to pay his respects to the king, another hat appears in its place, which he subsequently removes, and another then appears, until by the end of the story he has accumulated 500 hats. Seuss again employs the technique of accumulation to present his tale, which pits a simple but imaginative man against an easily threatened king. Bartholomew also makes an appearance in *Bartholomew and the Oobleck* (1949), an ecology story in which Bartholomew saves the kingdom from the threatening 'oobleck' (a sticky ooze) invented by the king's magicians.

In *Horton Hears a Who!* (1954), an allegory for the situation of Japan after Hiroshima, Seuss points to the potential dangers of people's lack of imagination. Horton the elephant, who previously appeared in *Horton Hatches the Egg* (1940), hears a noise coming from a speck of dust, which he discovers to his surprise to be the voice of the mayor of Who-ville asking for Horton's protection. The other animals in the jungle, who fail to understand why Horton is protecting the speck of dust, ridicule and torture him until Horton gets the Whos to make themselves heard to the other animals. The story ends with a *mise-en-abyme*, the mayor of Who-ville himself discovering an entire world on a speck of dust.

Seuss wrote *The Cat in the Hat* (1957), perhaps his most famous book, as a reading primer, using a total of 237 words. The two children in the story encounter the Cat, who appears to entertain them, juggling various household objects, conjuring up the rambunctious Things, and generally creating chaos in their home while their mother is gone. Like Marco, the children of *The Cat in the Hat* hesitate to explain to their 'realistic' mother their fantastic adventures with the Cat when she asks them, 'Did you have any fun? Tell me. What did you do?'

The Cat in the Hat Comes Back (1958) came out in the same year as *How the Grinch Stole Christmas!*, which recalls *Dickens's A Christmas Carol. Other fantasy stories by Seuss include *The Lorax* (1971), a parable about pollution; and *The Butter Battle Book* (1984), an allegory about the arms race.   AD

Lurie, Alison, 'The Cabinet of Dr. Seuss', *Popular Culture: An Introductory Text* (1992).

MacDonald, Ruth K., *Dr. Seuss* (1988).

Sexton, Anne (1928–74) Major American poet whose book *Transformations* (1971) was one of the most significant 'subversive' adaptations of the Grimms' tales from a woman's perspective. Sexton was born Anne Grey Harvey into an upper-middle-class family in Newton, Massachusetts; after attending a Boston finishing school, she eloped with Alfred Muller Sexton and worked for a time as a model. In the early 1950s, during which time she gave birth to her two daughters, she had a series of mental breakdowns, and she was advised by her psychiatrist, Dr Martin Orne, to write poetry. Consequently, Sexton began taking courses in John Holme's poetry workshop at the Boston Center for Adult Education, and her talent was immediately recognized. She received a scholarship in 1958 to the Antioch Writers' Conference, and later that year she was accepted into Robert Lowell's graduate writing seminar at Boston University, where she met and became friends with Sylvia Plath, Maxine Kumin, and George Starbuck. In 1960 she published her first important collection of poetry, *To Bedlam and Part Way Back*, and she also began teaching poetry at Harvard and Radcliffe. Throughout the 1960s Sexton won numerous prizes and published several collections of poetry, but she also suffered from severe depressions, attempted suicide, and was hospitalized on occasion. She won the Pulitzer Prize for *Live or Die* in 1967, and she taught at Boston University, worked at the American Place Theatre, and conducted poetry workshops in her home. However, she continued to feel disturbed and tried to commit suicide again in 1970, the year before she published *Transformations*, which was performed in an operatic adaptation in Minneapolis in 1973. This was also the year in which she divorced her husband and was hospitalized at the McLean's Hospital. The following year she took her life in the garage of her home by carbon monoxide poisoning.

All Sexton's poems are intensely personal and reflect the pain and suffering she endured during her life. *Transformations* is unique in that she gains distance on her personal problems by transposing them on to fairy-tale figures and situations. The book consists of 17 poems taken from the *Grimms' Children's and Household Tales*, and among them are such classics as *'Snow White and the Seven Dwarfs', 'The *Frog Prince', *'Rumpelstiltskin', *'Rapunzel', 'Red Riding Hood', *'Cinderella', and *'Hansel and Gretel' as well as such lesser-known ones as 'The White Snake' and 'The Little Peasant'. In each of the poems, written in free verse, Sexton has a prologue in which she addresses social and psychological issues such as sexual abuse, abandonment, incest, commodification, alienation, and sexual identity. Then she retells the Grimms' tale in a modern idiom with striking and frequently comic metaphors and with references to her own experiences. Instead of a moral at the end, there is a coda that raises disturbing questions about the issues with which she has dealt. Thus 'Cinderella' does not end on a happy note. Instead Sexton writes:

> Cinderella and the prince,
> lived, they say, happily ever after,
> like two dolls in a museum case
> never bothered by diapers or dust,
> never arguing over the timing of an egg,
> never telling the same story twice,
> never getting a middle-aged spread,
> their darling smiles pasted on for eternity.
> Regular Bobbsey Twins.
> That story.

Indeed, Sexton retold 'that story' or fairy stories because she wanted to unveil the ugly truths they contained to question the deadliness of bourgeois life, the power relations between the sexes, and the oppression of women. Her outlook on women's liberation was not optimistic, but her fairy-tale poems can be considered 'feminist' in the manner in which they seek to deal with the 'true situation' of women during the 1950s and 1960s and undermine the false promises of the classical fairy tales.   JZ

Hall, Caroline King Barnard, *Anne Sexton* (1989).
McGowan, Philip, *Anne Sexton & Middle Generation Poetry: The Geography of Grief* (2004).
Middlebrook, Diane Wood, *Anne Sexton: A Biography* (1992).
Salvio, Paula, *Anne Sexton: Teacher of Weird Abundance* (2007).
Sexton, Linda Gray, *Searching for Mercy Street: My Journey Back to my Mother, Anne Sexton* (1996).

Shakespeare, William (1564–1616) English playwright, poet, director, and actor, who uses forms of the word 'fairy' in at least ten of his plays, as well as in *Venus and Adonis*. Shakespeare mentions elves in five plays; nymphs in eight plays, *Venus and Adonis*, *The Passionate Pilgrim*, and the Sonnets; sprites or supernatural spirits in 20 plays, *Venus and Adonis*, *Troilus and Cressida*, and *The Rape of Lucrece*; goblins and hobgoblins in five plays. These references, as well as marked presence of fairies in the works of Spenser, Drayton, and Lyly, among many other contemporaries, indicate that fairy folk and legends were familiar to Shakespeare's audience.

In *The Anatomy of Puck*, thus far the longest recent study of Shakespeare's general use of fairy material, K. M. *Briggs maintains that the Elizabethan era was a golden age of fairy lore. She ascribes this to an increasing number of yeoman writers who had learned fairy lore from their ancestors and felt freer to articulate it in an age less intimidated by fears of heresy. Briggs hints at, but does not elaborate upon, the tenor of humanism and humanists who, like Marlowe's Dr Faustus, were intrigued by opportunities to tinker with the supernatural. The alchemical and necromantic interests of such scholars are but further evidence of a growing fascination with the human power to affect, even to command, the universe. In such an atmosphere, fairies, sprites, and elves were more innocent familiars than devils, while nymphs and nature spirits evoked ancient Greek and Roman beliefs harmonious with the taste for the classical past.

With rare exceptions, however, the origins of Shakespeare's fairy lore remain uncertain. Celtic legend is the most frequently invoked, though often questionable, source. Perhaps the Shakespearian fairy with the clearest genealogy is Oberon of *A Midsummer Night's Dream*, whose avatar is Auberon, the fairy king of *Huon de Bordeaux*, a 15th-century romance.

Generally, Shakespeare's fairies serve as light embellishments with a strong appeal for audiences. Pageantry, so entrancing to Elizabethan ceremony and theatre, was enhanced by the addition of glittering creatures with magic powers. As Shakespeare's *A Midsummer Night's Dream* illustrates so well, portrayals of fairies were highly effective in creating the atmosphere desirable in masques.

Shakespeare's fairies appeared in several sizes and guises: in a stature equal to that of very young children, as full-sized or even outsized mortals, as miniature creatures, as hobgoblins, as good and as evil spirits. In general, however, fairies in the literature of this period were meant to be charming figures of fun, and the frequent appearance of full-length portraits of wicked fairies was, with rare exceptions (*see* MORGAN LE FAY), a later phenomenon.

Most of Shakespeare's references to fairies are brief. There are three notable exceptions: *A Midsummer Night's Dream*, *The Tempest*, and *The Merry Wives of Windsor*. Outstandingly fey among Shakespeare's plays is, of course, *A Midsummer Night's Dream*, two of whose chief characters are Oberon and Titania, king and queen of the fairies. The same play features Puck, also known as Robin Goodfellow. His appeal to generations of theatregoers may be attributed to his mischief-making charm as a hobgoblin or his philosophical unmasking of 'What fools these mortals be'. In this play, the actions of fairies both divide and unify three worlds—the dreamworld, the world of the fairies, and the world of ordinary mortal affairs. The intervention of the fairies in the lives of mortals is part of the dreamworld that unites the lovers with their desired partners and solves all the problems in the play, partly by potions and spells, but ultimately by means of the fairy *ex machina*.

The Tempest is densely populated with strange creatures, some of whom are fairy-like, but some of whom, like Caliban, seem to challenge or even defy classification. Prospero, the typical humanist scholar, spends too much time on his books. Becoming a wizard king, he conjures Ariel, the airy spirit whom many call an elemental. 'As swift as thought', Ariel can make his master's wishes come true, creating illusions, charming mortals and monsters alike, and controlling the weather. The air surrounding the island is 'full of spirits', as Caliban, the resident monster and colonial, complains. The play's masque includes goddesses like Iris and features a pageant of supernaturals.

The tiniest of all Shakespeare's fairies is Mab, recognized in Shakespeare's England as queen of the fairies. In *Romeo and Juliet* she drives a nutshell coach drawn by ants and small enough to light on suitors' noses. She is touted here for her ability to make men dream of love and courtship.

Perhaps the strongest Shakespearian proof that fairies were conventional enough in the lore and literature of the era to be mocked and parodied appears in *The Merry Wives of Windsor*. Here the fairies, though the size of children and ruled by an adult-sized queen, are not real fairies. Briggs has pointed out how faithfully these false fairies reflect popular beliefs. They carry torches of glow worms and rattles for fairy bells. Like good legendary fairies of their era, they dance around in a circle and control the order of things. But the ultimate Shakespearian evidence of the fairy fashion may be that Macbeth's witches know the traditional terpsichorean kinship of fairies and witches. Both witches and fairies dance, as the witches sing, like 'elves and fairies in a ring'.   JSN

Blount, Dale M., 'Modifications in Occult Folklore as a Comic Device in Shakespeare's *A Midsummer Night's Dream*', *Fifteenth-Century Studies*, 9 (1984).

Briggs, Katherine M., *The Anatomy of Puck* (1959).

Levy, Michael-Marc, 'The Transformations of Oberon: The Use of Fairies in Seventeenth Century Literature' (Diss., University of Minnesota, 1982).

Milward, Peter, 'Fairies in Shakespeare's Later Plays', *English Language and Literature*, 22 (1985).

Tave, Stuart M., *Lovers, Clowns and Fairies: An Essay on Comedies* (1993).

Sharp, Evelyn (1869–1955) English writer and suffragette who joined the famous *Yellow Book* staff in 1895 and began publishing stories, articles, novels, and books for children. As a pacifist and feminist, she became deeply committed to doing relief work in Germany after the First World War, and her concern in the welfare of children led her to writing *The London Child* (1927) and *The Child Grows Up* (1929), two studies of working-class life, and *The African Child* (1931), which deals with social conditions in Africa. Her fairy-tale books for children, *Wymps and Other Fairy Tales* (1897), *All the Way to Fairyland* (1898), *The Other Side of the Sun* (1900), *Round the World to Wympland*

(1902), were written early in her career and were not as explicitly political as her other writings. Yet there is a sense in many of her tales that rebellion against the accepted notions of behaviour and propriety will lead to greater self-awareness on the part of the young protagonists. Certainly in one of her best tales, 'The Spell of the Magician's Daughter', Firefly, the young heroine, realizes her full potential as a unique woman by exercising her imaginative powers and overcoming tyranny.   JZ

Shepard, Ernest Howard (1879–1976) British illustrator and author, best remembered for the black-and-white ink drawings

Sharp, Evelyn An unusually mild dragon who loves to read features in Evelyn Sharp's 'The Last of the Dragons', collected in *Round the World to Wympland*, illustrated by Alice *Woodward.

accompanying A. A. *Milne's Christopher Robin and Winnie-the-Pooh stories. A consummate professional whose output was constant and consistent, Shepard illustrated nearly 100 books while contributing regularly to *Punch* and other periodicals.

The son of an architect and a mother whose father was a distinguished watercolourist, Shepard's ability was innate. His mother's untimely death disrupted the family, and Shepard was enrolled at the prestigious St Paul's School in London (under the auspices of an uncle who taught there). His talent for drawing surfaced here, and he enjoyed free range to explore his visual imagination. Despite significant success at the Royal Academy Schools, Shepard lacked confidence to pursue a career as an oil painter and followed the more pragmatic course of illustration. This calling was marked with the acceptance of a drawing by *Punch* in 1907. He also began illustrating books at this time, including *David Copperfield* and *Aesop's Fables*, but the First World War interrupted his career, and he joined the artillery. Shepard continued to submit drawings to *Punch*, and after the armistice he was invited to a regular position on its staff. Here he was connected with A. A. Milne to illustrate verses for *When We Were Very Young*, submitted to the magazine in 1923. Despite initial misgivings, Milne capitulated, and the complete book appeared in 1924. This forged the alliance that resulted in *Winnie-the-Pooh* (1926); *Now We Are Six* (1927); and *The House at Pooh Corner* (1928). Although based on photographs and visits to Milne's farm, Shepard was acutely aware of a child's 'power to transform reality into something magical'. The success of these books engendered creative frustrations for both men. Shepard did very solid work in subsequent years, but the Pooh books overshadowed all subsequent efforts.

Most memorable was *Wind in the Willows* (1931), which Shepard considered his favourite drawings. He visited the aged Kenneth *Grahame and sketched the riverbank and meadows where the characters lived and cavorted. He brought them alive in a manner that Grahame especially liked.

Having lost his wife suddenly in 1927, Shepard threw himself into his work, and in the 1930s he illustrated 14 books as well as executing his regular work for *Punch* and various other projects.

In the late 1940s, commissions began to decline and he was let go by *Punch* in 1953. This invigorated him, however, and he illustrated nine books in 1954 and 1955 alone (*Modern Fairy Tales*, 1955; *Pancake*, 1957; *Briar Rose*, 1958). Shepard interpreted some traditional fairy tales including those by Hans Christian *Andersen in 1962, but his last project was to create coloured editions of *Winnie-the-Pooh* and *The House at Pooh Corner*. Shepard's gentle observation of life was combined with a penchant for accuracy. His sensitive draftsmanship contained a delicacy which generated a whimsical sense of magic.   HNBC

Knox, Rawle (ed.), *The Works of E. H. Shepard* (1980).

Meyer, Susan E., *A Treasury of the Great Children's Book Illustrators* (1983).

Shepard, E. H., *Drawn from Memory* (1957).

Sherman, Cindy (1954–) American photographer and filmmaker who has challenged the manner in which women are portrayed in society through unusual, often disturbing photographs. In two of her major series of photos, *Fairy Tales* (1985) and *Disasters* (1986-9), Sherman used prostheses and mannequins in her studio to reveal some of the more gruesome aspects of fairy tales. Her focus was not on specific fairy tales but on abductions and murders, and characters such as witches and ogres. Her intention was to make the real horrors of the world easier to absorb through artifice. She also used grotesque images in her photographic book, *Fitcher's Bird* (1992), an adaptation of a *Grimm fairy tale, which had first appeared in *Vanity Fair*.   JZ

Bronfen, Elisabeth, *et al. Cindy Sherman: Photographic Works 1975-1995* (2002).

Burton, Johanna (ed.), *Cindy Sherman* (2006).

Cruz, Amanda Cruz, *et al., Cindy Sherman: Retrospective* (2000).

Sills, Leslie, *et al., In Real Life: Six Women Photographers* (2000).

Sherman, Delia (1951–) American writer of historical fantasy novels. In *Through a Brazen Mirror* (1989), Sherman uses a traditional English ballad ('The Famous Flower of Serving Men') as the basis for an elegant exploration of gender issues. In *The Porcelain Dove* (1993), she works motifs from classic French fairy tales into a study of socio-sexual mores during the French Revolution. She also uses fairy-tale themes extensively in short fiction and poetry, including 'The Printer's Daughter' (1995), based on the Russian story 'The Snow Child'; 'Snow White to the Prince' (1995), a poignant look at mother–daughter relationships; and 'The Fairy Cony-Catcher' (1998), a bawdy account of the Elizabethan fairy court.   TW

Shrek (films) Four computer animated films, based on William *Steig's picture book *Shrek!*, have been produced by DreamWorks Studio: *Shrek* (2001), *Shrek 2* (2004), *Shrek the Third* (2007), and *Shrek Forever After* (2010). A short 3D film, *Shrek 4-D*, was released in 2003. The Christmas television special *Shrek the Halls*, premiered in 2007, and was followed by a Halloween television special, *Scared Shrekless*, in 2010. A spin-off film *Puss in Boots* was released in 2011. Only the first film comes close to following the plot of Steig's book about a frightening, ugly ogre, who finds happiness when he encounters a female ogre who is just as ugly as he is. The directors and the producers transformed the story into that of a likeable looking ogre who is overwhelmed by well-known fairy-tale characters in a swamp when they are banished from the nasty Lord Farquaad's realm. Annoyed by them and especially by his sidekick, Donkey, Shrek goes to Lord Farquaad, who promises him to get rid of the fairy-tale characters, if he kills a dragon and rescues Princess Fiona so that she can become Farquaad's bride. Shrek agrees, but he does not kill the dragon because it falls in love with Donkey, and it turns out that Fiona has a curse: she is a beautiful princess during the day and an ugly ogress at night. Shrek falls in love with her and reluctantly brings her to Farquaad's castle. However, the dragon eats the evil

king, and Fiona kisses Shrek and is turned completely into an ogress. The couple then marry in the swamp in the presence of all the fairy-tale characters. The films that follow *Shrek* are all stories that threaten the love and happiness of Shrek and Fiona. While the computer animation and characters retain a certain originality, the plots of the three sequels become stale, and the charm of the *Shrek* series fades.   JZ

Shua, Ana Maria (1951–) Argentine journalist and writer of novels, short stories, and books for children. Among her interesting work in the field of fairy tales are four collections of micro fiction *Casa de geishas* (*Geisha House*, 1992), *Botánica del caos* (*Botany of Chaos*, 2000), *Temporada de fantasmas* (*Ghost Season*, 2004), *Cazadores de letras* (*Dream Catchers*, 2009), and *Fenómenos de circo* (*Phenomena of the Circus*, 2011). Selections from these books have been gathered in an English translation, *Quick Fix: Sudden Fiction* (2008) and *Microfictions* (2009). The stories are rarely more than a paragraph long and are a mixture of fairy tales, dreams, and absurd anecdotes.   JZ

Shulman, Polly (1963–) American author of the young-adult novel *The Grimm Legacy* (2010), which follows a girl's adventures working at the 'New-York Circulating Material Repository', a lending library of historical artefacts that include magical objects collected by the Grimms. In 2013 Shulman published a sequel, *The Wells Bequest*, an adventure about the Repository's collection of objects from the science fiction of H. G. Wells, Jules Verne, and others. Shulman also writes for and edits a variety of publications.   KMJ

Shwartz, Susan (1949–) American writer of science fiction and fantasy novels. Shwartz specializes in sagas set in thoroughly detailed 'alternative-worlds' in which the history of the Orient has been changed by the addition of magic. *Silk Roads and Shadows* (1988), set in lands resembling Byzantium and China, weaves 'Tulku' legends into the story of a woman involved in the silk trade. *The Grail of Hearts* (1992), inspired by Arthurian legends, tells the story of Kundry (from *Wagner's *Parsifal*) and the Fisher King. Shwartz is also the editor of *Arabesques* (2 vols.; 1988, 1989), collections of original stories based on the tales of *The *Arabian Nights*.   TW

Sibelius, Jean (1865–1957) Highly individual Finnish composer whose importance was recognized by a government decision to grant him a pension for life when he was 32. His eight symphonies (written between 1899 and 1924) offered new thinking on the symphonic form, while his early interest in the Finnish national epic, *Kalevala*, led to compositions, such as the symphonic poems *En Saga*, *Finlandia*, and *Tapiola*, which either deal with Finnish nationalism, or (as in the case of *Tapiola*), draw on images of supernatural figures from the forest. Direct influence from the *Kalevala* emerged with the *Kullervo Symphony* of 1892 and the *Lemminkäinen Suite* of 1896, whose third movement, 'The Swan of Tuonela', describes Lemminkäinen's quest for the Swan on the river of death (Tuonela).   TH

Sierra, Judy (1945–) American children's book author, folklorist, poet, and editor of *Cinderella* (1992), an international collection of *Cinderella fairy tales representing a broad range of cultures and geographical areas, with illustrations by Joanna Caroselli. She also wrote *The Gift of the Crocodile: A Cinderella Story* (2000), an Indonesian retelling of 'Cinderella', with illustrations by Reynold Ruffins. Sierra's *Can You Guess My Name?: Traditional Tales Around the World* (2002), an international folk-tale collection, including tales resembling 'The Three Pigs' and *'Rumpelstiltskin', won the American Folklore Society's Aesop Prize for best folklore book for children.   KMJ

Silko, Leslie Marmon (1948–) Native American writer. In 1981, she published *Storyteller*, a collection of poems and short stories, strongly influenced by Native American folklore. In addition, she has also produced a significant work of non-fiction,

Yellow Woman and a Beauty of the Spirit: Essays on Native American Life Today (1997).   JZ

Sinclair, Catherine (1800–64) Scottish writer whose children's book, *Holiday House* (1839), includes 'Uncle David's Nonsensical Story about Giants and Fairies'. Though her preface to *Holiday House* looks back wistfully to the days when children were like 'wild horses on the prairies' instead of being stuffed with knowledge, Uncle David's story is a moral one, about how indolent and gluttonous Master No-Book rejects education and is seized by Giant Snap-'em-up. The gruesome details of how the giant prepares him for dinner may have influenced Edward *Knatchbull-Huguessen in his stories about ogres and their eating habits.   GA

Singer, Isaac Bashevis (1904–91) Writer of Yiddish stories, novels, memoirs, and children's books. Most of his work has been translated into English, with his own careful direction and participation, and much of it reflects motifs of Jewish folklore. Singer was born in Poland but emigrated to the United States before the Second World War. His fiction is populated with demons, dybbuks, imps, witches, ghosts, angels, magicians, and other traditional figures (including the Golem) summoned in part from the mystical vision of his father, a Hassidic rabbi, but drawn with the sharp-edged realism that characterized his mother. Fuelled by his parents' active storytelling and his own experience of shtetl culture, Singer believed that all good literature has roots in ethnic lore. *Zlateh the Goat and Other Stories* (1966), *The Fearsome Inn* (1967), and *When Shlemiel Went to Warsaw and Other Stories* (1968) won critical acclaim as Newbery Honor Books, while *The Fools of Chelm* (1973) remains an all-time favourite with children. A deceptively simple style, rhythmic pace, and orally tuned narrative patterns contribute to the folkloric tone of his work. (Singer's distinguished illustrators include Maurice *Sendak, Uri Shulevitz, Margot *Zemach, and Nonny Hogrogian.) In his adult books, too,

Singer juggled fantastical dreams and desperate plights, with the ultimate miracle often depending on the wisdom of innocents, as in 'Gimpel the Fool' (1954). Singer won a US National Book Award for *A Day of Pleasure: Stories of a Boy Growing up in Warsaw* (1969) and received the Nobel Prize for Literature in 1978. BH

Allison, Alida, *Isaac Bashevis Singer: Children's Stories and Childhood Memoirs* (1996).

Collar, Mary L., 'In His Father's House: Singer, Folklore and the Meaning of Time', *Studies in American Jewish Literature*, 1 (1981).

Lenz, Millicent, 'Archetypal Images of Otherworlds in Singer's "Menaseh's Dream" and Tolkien's "Leaf by Niggle"', *Children's Literature Association Quarterly*, 19.1 (spring 1994).

Schwarz, Martin, 'Two Practitioners of the Grotesque: Sherwood Anderson and Isaac Bashevis Singer', in Olena H. Saciuk (ed.), *The Shape of the Fantastic* (1990).

Sir Gawain and the Green Knight Late 14th-century alliterative Arthurian romance. Its anonymous English author—whose work survives in a single manuscript (Cotton Nero A10)—fused two source motifs from Celtic legend to create a dazzling literary fairy tale. Sir Gawain, challenged to a Beheading Game by the supernatural Green Knight, travels into the northern wilderness to keep his pledge, finding hospitality at the castle of Sir Bertilak and temptation from Bertilak's wife. The magical elements and threefold repetitions of a folktale are combined with vivid description, psychological insight, sly humour, and the moral complexity characteristic of classic fantasy. SR

Sir Orfeo 14th-century anonymous English verse romance which audaciously transforms the Greek myth of Orpheus into a charming fairy tale. Queen Heurodis (Eurydice) is stolen from her husband Orfeo by the King of Fairyland (the god Hades) and taken to his underground realm. Like Orpheus, Orfeo is a superlative harper, whose music wins back his wife. Unlike the myth, however, the romance ends happily; the two return triumphantly to the kingdom which

their loyal steward has kept safe for them. The poem contains much authentic fairy lore, including the strong traditional association of fairies with the dead. SR

Slater, Lauren (1963–) American clinical psychologist, freelance writer, and award-winning author. Among works which include the memoirs *Love Works Like This: Moving from One Kind of Life to Another* (2002) and *Prozac Diary* (2011), Slater wrote *Blue Beyond Blue: Extraordinary Tales for Ordinary Dilemmas* (2005), a collection of creative fairy tales. The book demonstrates Slater's commitment to narrative psychotherapy, in which fairy-tale allegories and themes are applied to clinical psychology through writing as therapeutic practice. KMJ

Slavic and Baltic countries, fairy tales in *See* p. 562.

'Sleeping Beauty' ('Briar Rose') This tale appears in the Catalan *Frayre de Joy e Sor de Placer* (14th century), as 'Troylus and Zellandine' in the French *Perceforest* (16th century), as 'Sole, Luna e Talia' in *The *Pentamerone* (1634–6) by Giambattista *Basile, as 'La Belle au bois dormant' in **Histoires ou contes du temps passé* (*Stories or Tales of Times Past*, 1697) by Charles *Perrault, and as 'Dornröschen' in **Kinder- und Hausmärchen* (*Children's and Household Tales*, 1812–15) by Jacob and Wilhelm Grimm.

The story begins with a royal couple's wish for a child. When the baby is born, the parents plan a celebration but invite only 12 of the 13 wise women (godmothers, fairies) in the realm. Perrault makes the uninvited fairy a disgruntled old woman, long absent from the court, and creates a good fairy who hides so that she can counteract any harmful gift. Eleven fairies had given the baby such gifts as beauty, virtue, wealth, and wisdom when the 13th interrupts with a prophecy: the girl will die at the age of 15 when she pricks her finger with a spindle.

The 12th fairy modifies the prophecy to a sleep of 100 years. The king tries to evade fate by banning all spindles in the realm. The story deals with the futility of trying to escape

Slavic and Baltic countries, fairy tales in A systematic collection of folk tales did not start in Eastern Europe until the middle of the 19th century, which reflects the late development of national literatures in this region as compared to most Western countries. Among the first collections in the Russian Empire were *Russian Fairy Tales* (1860) by Ivan Khudyakov (1842–76), and the famous eight-volume collection of *Russian Fairy Tales* (1855–63) by Aleksandr *Afanasyev, the first serious Russian scholar of Slavic folklore. Unlike the *Grimms' collection, these publications never reached a wide audience; however, many of the subsequent retellings were based on Afanasyev's versions.

On the other hand, already at the beginning of the 19th century, the first literary fairy tales appeared in Russia, clearly influenced by German romantic writers. *The Black Hen, or The Underground People* (1829) by Antony Pogorelsky (pseudonym of Aleksei Perovsky, 1777–1836), bears a close resemblance in plot and style to *The Nutcracker*; Pogorelsky was a good friend of E. T. A. *Hoffmann. Like its model, this didactic story starts in the everyday and takes its young protagonist into a magical realm. A similar plot and overt didacticism is to be found in *The Town in the Music-Box* (1834) by Vladimir Odoyevsky (1803–63). Unlike most fairy tales from the same period, often written by less talented female authors, these two are still popular today.

In his versified fairy tales, Alexander *Pushkin, Russian national poet, used well-known European plots in *The Tale of the Dead Princess and the Seven Heroes* (1833), *The Tale of the Fisherman and the Fish* (1833), and *The Tale of the Priest and Balda, his Hired Hand* (1830, pub. 1840) as well as popular chapbooks in *The Tale of Tsar Saltan* (1831) and romantic literary sources in *The Tale of the Golden Cockerel* (1834). Pushkin's fairy tales contained a biting political satire of Tsarist Russia, and some of them were banned by the censorship. They have tangible Russian settings in a historical and social context, and they were the first to introduce colloquial language into the literary fairy tale.

Many 19th-century Russian writers wrote fairy tales for children and adults. One of the most popular was *The Scarlet Flower* (1859) by Sergei Aksakov (1791–1859), a version of *'Beauty and the Beast'. The contribution of Lev *Tolstoy is especially significant. An ardent educationalist, Tolstoy published several school primers, which contained retellings of folk and fairy tales from all over the world. These collections, addressed to peasant children, are very simple in structure and style and also use typical Russian settings. Another classic was *Frog the Traveller* (1887) by Vsevolod Garshin (1855–88), the forerunner of animal tales.

Fairy tales flourished during the so-called Silver Age of Russian literature from the turn of the century to 1917, when many symbolist poets wrote fairy tales addressed to an adult audience. Parallel to this highly artistic trend, a vast number of sentimental and didactic tales were written for children.

During the communist regime in the Soviet Union, fairy tales occupied an ambivalent position. On the one hand, they were treated with suspicion, as a 'bourgeois' form, and pronounced dangerous, escapist, and undesirable reading matter. Kornei *Chukovsky and Samuil *Marshak, both translators of foreign classics, educationalists, and authors of verse fairy tales, worked hard for the preservation of the Russian fairy-tale tradition and the creation of new, modern fairy tales. Chukovsky's pedagogical pamphlet *From Two to Five* (1928) contains a chapter on the importance of fairy tales for the imagination and psychological development of young children.

On the other hand, fairy tales for children were the only genre where authors, including major adult authors, were relatively free from the pre-scriptions of 'socialist realism', the approved method in literature and art. The tradition of camouflaged criticism of the authorities, going back to Afanasyev, Pushkin, and Tolstoy, was prominent in the 20th-century Russian fairy tale and yielded some excellent results.

As early as 1928, Yuri Olesha (1899–1960) published a fairy-tale novel entitled *The Three Fat Men*, an allegorical story of struggle against oppression. Especially during the 1930s, the worst years of communist terror, fairy tales became a legitimate genre for many writers. Most of them depict the abstract struggle between good and evil. Veniamin Kaverin (1902–87) was rather transparent in his *The Tale of Mitya and Masha, of the Merry Chimney-Sweep and Master Golden Hands* (1939), where a girl is kidnapped by evil forces and carried away to a distant country where everything is brown. The connotation of the colour brown was obvious in the late 1930s. The kidnapper is Kashchey the Immortal, the traditional evil figure of Russian folk tales. However, both the evil country and the villain could be easily related to contemporary Soviet conditions. Other fairy tales by Kaverin are more firmly anchored in reality, where good and evil magical forces intrude. The tales focus on ethical issues and often portray artists— poets, painters, musicians—as possessing magical powers, which in the Soviet context was quite a subversive idea. In this regard, Kaverin was by far the most original fairy-tale writer of his generation.

Most of his contemporaries exploited the motif of the infinite fulfilled wishes, as in *The Rainbow Flower* (1940) by Valentin Katayev (1897–1986). The tendency to use the everyday contemporary setting rather than send the protagonist to a magical world, dominant in the Western fairy tale, is typical of Soviet writers, presumably as a compromise to the demands of 'realism'. Thus, in *The New Adventures of *Puss-in-Boots* (1937), Yevgeni *Schwartz places the famous character in a communist youth summer camp and lets him defeat an evil frog-witch, representing the capitalist past. Another familiar fairy-tale figure appears in *Old Man Khottabson* (1938) by Lazar Lagin (1903–79), a free adaptation of a minor British classic, *The Brass Bottle* by F. *Anstey. A genie is released from his bottle-prison by a Russian boy and sets out to fulfil his rescuer's wishes. Naturally his ways and morals come into conflict with the young communist, and his obliging magic causes many funny, but awkward situations. At the end the old man is 'reformed' and becomes an exemplary Soviet citizen.

Using foreign sources and adapting them to the declared needs of the Soviet audience was a common practice among Russian writers, possibly due to the cultural isolation of the Soviet Union, where most contemporary Western fairy tales were totally unknown at least until the 1960s. Thus, the most popular Russian fairy-tale novel, *The Wizard of the Emerald City* (1939) by Aleksandr *Volkov, is a slightly adapted version of *The *Wonderful Wizard of Oz*. Such adaptations focus mostly on social improvements and group achievements rather than individual development manifest in their models. In the Russian version of *Pinocchio*, entitled *The Golden Key, or The Adventures of Burattino* (1935) by Aleksei *Tolstoy, the object of the quest is a key to a secret door concealing a puppet theatre, which Burattino and his puppet friends happily take into possession. No psychological change is allowed or even suggested. The puppet remains a puppet, and individual fulfilment is replaced by collective happiness, achieved through socially beneficial labour.

Thus, the fairy-tale form became in the Soviet Union the main channel for subversive literature. Quite a number of books followed the traditional folk-tale pattern: the hero comes to a country oppressed by a tyrant or devastated by a dragon and delivers it from evil. In the plays by Yevgeni Schwartz, loosely based on Hans Christian *Andersen's fairy tales and other famous plots, political undertones are promptly amplified. Many of Schwartz's plays were banned when the Soviet censorship detected a possible satire on the regime: *The Emperor's New Clothes* (1934, pub. 1960) and *The Shadow* (1940) both deal with power and falseness; *The Dragon* (1943) makes use of the dragon-slayer motif to show how liberators can become tyrants. An implicit critique of the ruling 'revolutionary élite in the Soviet Union', the play was produced during the Second World War and accepted by official Soviet criticism as a satire on Germany; however, the true target was obvious.

It is sometimes debatable as to whether the writers consciously included political satire in their narratives. It is clearly the case, however, whenever the falsehood of the tyrant is emphasized. One such example is *The Land of Crooked Mirrors* (1951) by Vitali Gubarev (1912–81), which could exploit the motif of a Looking-Glass country because Carroll's classic was at that time practically unknown in the Soviet Union. Behind the looking glass, the main character Olga finds not only her own reflection (which magnifies all her worst traits) but a country where crooked mirrors serve the purpose of unscrupulous rulers, distorting reality and making beautiful things ugly and vice versa—a more tangible form of Orwell's Newspeak. Naturally, Olga triumphs over evil and witnesses a revolution. As with Schwartz's plays, the depicted country allegedly embodied hateful capitalism, and Olga—wearing a Soviet school uniform with a red tie—supposedly represented the victorious ideas of communism.

The practice of reading between lines and assuming that words always meant something other than their dictionary definition became a habit with the Soviet adult audience, resuscitating the old phenomenon called in Russian 'Aesopian language', and partially reminiscent of the notion of palimpsest in contemporary feminist criticism. Unfortunately, like any artistic device which is abused, the satirical arrowhead became more and more blunt as time went by. Likewise, the obtrusive didacticism of Russian fairy-tale writers eventually resulted in a vast number of fairy-tale novels exploiting the same motif of a wish-granting magical object used for the purpose of teaching the protagonist a moral lesson, as in the works by Yuri Tomin (1929–), Sofia Prokofieva (1928–), or Valeri Medvedev (1925–). In all of these texts, the struggle between 'right' and 'wrong' values, always explicitly or implicitly connected with Soviet versus Western ideology, is the central theme. Individualism is condemned and collectivism praised as a virtue.

Another popular strategy for a successful fairy tale was educational. In these works, the protagonist was sent to a country inhabited by numbers, colours, or musical instruments so that the readers acquired some useful knowledge alongside the hero. The subversive effect of such fairy tales was considerably less, if any.

At best, fairy tales could be entertaining, creating a childhood utopia comparable with the utopian promises of the communist doctrine, as in the trilogy by Nikolai Nosov (1908–76), portraying an idyllic society of miniature people, *Dunno and his Friends* (1954). A much later, but likewise popular author, Eduard Uspensky (1937–), showed possible influences from Western humorous and nonsensical fairy tales, notably Astrid *Lindgren, especially in *Uncle Theodor, the Dog and the Cat* (1974).

More often, the limited access to fairy tales from the West stimulated Soviet writers to fill in the gaps with their own products, occasionally resulting in quite original works. However, the isolation inevitably led to stagnation. In the 1980s Russian fairy tales, lacking inspiration and insight from Western authors, were still primarily didactic and politicized. This pertains even to the best writers such as Irina Tokmakova (1929–). Two prominent exceptions are Radi *Pogodin and Vladislav Krapivin (1938–), authors of philosophical, existential fairy tales, completely free from any foreign influences, as well as from ideology or didacticism. The popular novels of Kir Bulychov (1934–) combine elements of fairy tale and science fiction.

In other Eastern European countries, the collection and publication of fairy tales were closely connected with movements of independence, the emergence of national identity, and the establishment of a written literary language.

The first collectors of folktales in Poland were Zorian Chodakowski (1784–1825), Kazimierz Wojticki (1807–79), and Antoni Glinski (1817–66). Glinski's collection *The Polish Storyteller* (1853) also contained Belorussian and Lithuanian folklore. One of the first authors of literary fairy tales was Maria Konopnicka (1842–1910), the author of *The Tale about the Gnomes and Marysia the Orphan* (1895), the pioneering work of Polish national children's literature. Based on folklore, this fairy tale used colloquial language, many everyday details, and warm humour.

In the period between the wars, the most outstanding work was the children's utopian novel *King Matt the First* (1923) by Janusz *Korczak. In communist Poland, as in other Eastern European countries, fairy tales were often a means of avoiding censorship, while presenting the faults of society. Such are the novels by Jan Brzechwa (1900–66), with their eccentric wizards Mr Lens and Mr Blot, also featuring characters from traditional tales, like *'Little Red Riding Hood' and *'Sleeping Beauty'. *Little Carole* (1959) by Maria Krüger (1911–) is based on the motif of a capricious wish-granting object.

Of all Slavic peoples, Czech folklore was greatly influenced by the German tradition. The characteristic feature of Czech folk tales is a cunning peasant or servant. They were first collected and retold by the poet and folklorist Karel Erben (1811–70). The most famous Czech collector and author of fairy tales was Bozena Nemcová (1820–62), whose retellings were characterized by the striving to overcome the romantic view of folklore and create a more realistic and everyday touch. She also amplified the female heroines of traditional fairy tales. Both Erben and Nemcová published Slovak fairy tales, often similar to Czech ones, but sometimes with a national flavour. Alois Jirásek (1851–1930) published *Old Czech Legends* (1894). Contemporary fairy tales, often with satirical and political overtones, were written between the wars by Jiri Volker (1900–24), Marie Majerová (1882–1967), Karel *Čapek, Vítezslav Nezval (1900–58), Vladislav Vancura (1891–1942), and Josef *Lada (1887–1957). Among post-war works, *Three Bananas* (1964) by Zdenek Slaby (1930–) should be mentioned. It seems that Slovak authors were less interested in fairy tales than their Czech colleagues.

Yugoslavian (Serbian, Croatian, Slovenian, Bosnian, Macedonian) fairy tales were collected by Vuk Karadzic (1787–1864). They show a strong influence of ancient Greek and oriental sources. For instance, the oriental trickster hero Hodja Nasreddin is also popular in Yugoslavian folk tales. The specific mixture of Christian and Islamic tradition makes them different from other Slavic folklore. Literary fairy tales did not appear until after the Second World War. *The Gnome from the Lost Country* (1956) by Ahmet Hromadzic (1923–) is based on a Bosnian legend.

Bulgaria was an agrarian country until the end of the 19th century, and its fairy tales reflect motifs from peasant life. Half a millennium of Turkish occupation made the liberation pathos of Bulgarian fairy tales prominent. The two best-known characters of Bulgarian tales are Krali Marko (featured also in Yugoslavian fairy tales), an authentic historical figure, who became mythologized as a heroic image, and Cunning Peter, a typical trickster. There is also a cycle of humoristic tales about the lazy and greedy inhabitants of the town of Gabrovo, similar to the German Schildbürger. Among animal tales, cats play a significant role. Systematic collection and publication of folk tales in Bulgaria began in the late 19th century. The Bulgarian writers Elin Pelin (1877–1949) and Angel Karalijcev (1902–72) both retold traditional fairy tales and wrote many original ones.

In the three Baltic countries, the development of fairy tales has been closely connected with political history. Estonia and Latvia existed as independent states only for a short period between the two world wars, while Lithuania has a long history as a powerful European realm, first as an independent state, later in union with Poland.

The Estonian national epic *Kalevipoeg* (1862, similar to the Finnish *Kalevala*) marks the origin of national literature. The first collection of fairy tales for children, *Old Tales of the Estonian People*, was published in 1866 in Finland. It was followed by *Estonian Fairy Tales* in 1884. Around the turn of the century many writers retold or imitated folk tales. During independence, realistic prose dominated the fairy tale. During the Soviet occupation, on the contrary, fairy tales became a powerful vehicle of subversive literature, often based on allegory and animal fable. The 1960s and 1970s saw the heyday of the literary fairy tale. The most important work was the four-volume *Three Jolly Fellows* (1972–82) by Eno Raud (1928–96), depicting three imaginary beings, trolls or dwarfs, called Muff, Half-Shoe, and Mossbeard, and their funny adventures in an otherwise realistic world.

In Latvia folklore, especially the specific Latvian folk song, *dainas*, was collected by Krisjanis Barons (1835–1923). An early literary tale was *Little Devils* (1895) by Rudolfs Blaumanis (1863–1908). Karlis Skalbe (1879–1945) was also a renowned author of fairy tales based on Latvian and international folklore. During the period of independence, several allegorical fairy tales appeared (otherwise literature from this period was mostly realistic, focusing on class struggle). During the Soviet occupation, folk and fairy tales were considered the most 'safe' genres, and the most popular ones. In most instances, writers composed fairy tales intended for children, as in the case of Imants Ziedonis (1933–). These fairy tales naturally have many dimensions, addressing both an adult and a young audience. Some fairy tales were written by Latvian writers in exile; these were for the most part quite conventional, showing clear influence from Western writers such as *Tolkien or Michael *Ende.

Lithuania was closely connected to Poland for a long time, and shared much of its folklore. Strange as it may seem, this connection delayed the emergence of national literature. The first literary tale, based on Lithuanian folklore, appeared in 1905, written by Vincas Píetaris (1850–1902). During independence the foremost author of fairy tales was Pranas Masiotas (1863–1940). Under Soviet occupation many writers, such as Kazys Boruta (1905–65), sought inspiration in folklore and published stories and novels based on folklore motifs. Contemporary fairy tales, depicting magical realms or portraying humanized animals and animated toys, often with didactic tones, were written by Vincas Giedra (1929–), Vitautas Petkevicius (1930–), and Kazys Saja (1932–). The major author of fairy-tale plays was Violeta Palcinskaite (1943–). An important landmark was the allegorical fairy tale *Clay Matthew, the King of Men* (1978) by Petkevicius, which described Lithuania's history in disguise. Short, philosophical fairy tales were published by Vytaute Zilinskaite (1930–), who also wrote an allegorical fairy-tale novel set in the country of broken toys, *Travels to Tandadrika* (1984).

After the fall of communism in the 1990s, the former Soviet republics and satellites have tried to re-establish and emphasize their national identity and language. Fairy tales have proved to be an important part of their national heritage, while the fairy-tale form appears to be the best artistic device to treat the traumatic past and the complicated present. They often have an optimistic tone, reflecting the countries' hope for a better future. On the other hand, a huge wave of translated Western fairy tales and fantasy has inspired national authors to write original works especially noticeable in the new trend of 'sword and sorcery' fantasy in Poland. Also in Russia, new attempts are being made to create indigenous fantasy, inspired by Tolkien, but based on traditional Russian epics. MN

'Sleeping Beauty' The entire court is still asleep as the prince approaches the lovely sleeping princess in Charles *Perrault's 'Sleeping Beauty'. This anonymous illustration was published in *Les Contes des fees offerts à Bébé* (*c.*1900).

one's fate, a theme familiar in Eastern literature. Despite precautions, the princess violates the interdiction by pricking a finger on a spindle belonging to an old woman in a hidden room in the castle. All the residents of the castle, both human and animal, share her sleep. Perrault's good fairy returns to ensure that the princess will return to an unchanged world, unlike the monk who followed a bird for 300 years, and returned to a strange world ('Monk Felix').

The storytellers play with the idea of halted time, describing the comic attitudes of the servants whose daily chores had been interrupted at the onset of the sleep. Although time has stopped within the castle, a briar thicket had grown around it hiding it from sight. During the 100 years, bold knights had made attempts to brave the thicket but had died in the attempt. Finally a prince was able to pass through it to the palace and to find the sleeping princess. In the early versions her discoverer rapes her, and she awakens when her baby is born. But the awakening is more chaste in the Perrault version. Just the prince's proximity arouses the sleeping princess while the Grimms have their prince bestow a kiss upon her lips, and the entire castle bustles with resumed activities that are related with comic joy. This story of an interruption in time has the strange advantage of the sleeper's being able to take her whole world with her into the lapse. More common is the situation of a sleeper who awakens to find a world empty of familiar faces. Here there is an important difference between the Perrault and the Grimms' versions, for Perrault (like Basile) extends the story by having the princess give birth to a girl ('Dawn') and a boy ('Day'). The prince is afraid to bring his bride home to his parents because his mother is an ogress. When his father dies, and he becomes king, he finally does bring his wife and children to his court. Soon, however, he must go off to do battle with his neighbour, and his mother seeks to have the cook make meals out of the prince's children and his wife. The cook uses a subterfuge to save them, and in the end it is the queen mother who dies in a vat filled with vipers, toads, and snakes.

This ending has generally been eliminated in the fairy-tale tradition of the 19th and 20th centuries, especially when the tale has been rewritten or retold for children. Generally speaking, most traditional literary versions have sanitized the tale and place great emphasis on the unfortunate plight of the helpless princess and the valour of the rescuing prince. The most sentimental version is, of course, the *Disney film of 1959, but almost all of the classic picture books for children are no different. The great break in the tradition of the comatose princess and the daring prince comes in the 1970s when contemporary writers began to explore the political implications and sexual innuendoes of the tale. Thus, Olga *Broumas and Emma *Donoghue turn the tale into a story about lesbianism. Anne *Sexton explores sexual abuse, and Jane *Yolen transforms it into a novel about the Holocaust. In his novella *Briar Rose* (1996) Robert *Coover repeats and varies the narrative *ad nauseam* to question the veracity of the traditional tale. Given the social changes with regard to gender roles in Western societies, it is inconceivable for the fairy-tale princess of the classical 'Sleeping-Beauty' tradition to serve as a model for female readers in contemporary fairy tales. More appropriate, it would seem, would be a tale in which the princess has nothing but sleepless nights.					HG

Franci, Giovanna, and Zago, Ester, *La bella addormentata. Genesi e metamorfosi di una fiaba* (1984).

Romain, Alfred, 'Zur Gestalt des Grimmschen Dornröschenmärchens', *Zeitschrift für Volkskunde*, 42 (1933).

Vries, Jan de, 'Dornröschen', *Fabula*, 2 (1959).

Zago, Ester, 'Some Medieval Versions of "Sleeping Beauty": Variations on a Theme', *Studi Francesi*, 69 (1979).

Zipes, Jack, 'Fairy Tale as Myth/Myth as Fairy Tale' in *The Brothers Grimm: From Enchanted Forests to the Modern World* (1988).

Sloane, A. Baldwin (Alfred Baldwin Sloane, 1872–1925) American theatre composer. The most prolific Broadway composer at the turn of the century, Sloane scored some two dozen New York musicals between 1896 and 1912. Born in Baltimore, where his songs were first heard in such semi-professional theatres as his own Paint and Powder Club, he arrived in New York in 1894 and soon had his melodies interpolated into others' scores, such as the successful *Excelsior, Jr.* (1895). His first full score in New York was for the children's extravaganza **Jack and the Beanstalk* (1896), which featured such familiar characters as King Cole, Miss Muffett, Old Mother Hubbard, Sindbad the Sailor, and **Puss-in-Boots. Sloane's most famous Broadway musical was The **Wizard of Oz* (1903), in which he collaborated with the author L. Frank **Baum. Because they were played by popular stars, Dave Montgomery and Fred Stone, the characters of the Scarecrow and the Tin Man dominated the show. Other Sloane musicals that contained fairy-tale or fantasy elements include *The Hall of Fame* (1902), *The Gingerbread Man* (1905), and *Tillie's Nightmare* (1910), which featured his most famous song, 'Heaven Will Protect the Working Girl'. Sloane was not a distinguished composer and few of his songs became popular, but he was a competent craftsman with a sound theatrical sense.   TSH

Smith, Harry B. (1860–1936) American playwright and lyricist. The most prolific of all American theatre librettist/lyricists, Smith wrote 123 Broadway musicals and operettas between 1887 and 1932, often with such distinguished composers as Victor Herbert and Jerome Kern. Among his works that dramatized fairy tales and used fantasy extensively were a version of **Cinderella called The Crystal Slipper* (1888), *Robin Hood* (1891), *Jupiter* (1892), *The Wizard of the Nile* (1895), *The Caliph* (1896), *Sinbad, or The Maid of Balsora* (1898), *Maid Marian* (1902), *The White Cat* (1905), and *The Enchantress* (1911).   TSH

Smith, Jessie Willcox (1863–1935) American illustrator instantly recognized for her sweet yet realistic portrayals of children; also popular in Britain. She was noted for her portraiture, her 180 covers for *Good Housekeeping Magazine*, her advertisements, and

particularly for her illustrations to George **MacDonald's *The Princess and the Goblin* and *At the Back of the North Wind*, and Charles **Kingsley's *Water-Babies*. Educated as a kindergarten teacher, she discovered her drawing talent accidentally. Trained first in the School of Design for Women in Philadelphia in 1884, and then at the Pennsylvania Academy of Fine Arts under Thomas Eakins, she fortuitously studied with Howard **Pyle in his first class at Drexel Institute of Arts in Philadelphia. He encouraged her to think of illustration as an art, to emphasize the reality of background and surroundings, and importantly, to regard the commercial end of illustration.

In 1909 a Smith painting entitled *Goldilocks and the Three Bears* appeared in *Thirty Favorite Paintings*. The standing bears are stuffed, with bows around their necks; Goldilocks is seated in front of them. This work first appeared in *Collier's Magazine* in 1907. Subsequently, full-colour pictures for **'Beauty and the Beast', 'A Modern **Cinderella', **'Little Red Riding Hood', **'Sleeping Beauty', **'Jack and the Beanstalk', and **'Hansel and Gretel' appeared in *Collier's Weekly* between 1907 and 1914. *Woman's Home Companion* also featured Smith's illustrations for 'The Goose Girl', 'Hansel and Gretel', 'Cinderella', 'Goldilocks', 'Jack and the Beanstalk', and **'Snow White and the Seven Dwarfs' from 1910 to 1915. The full-page colour illustrations were painted in oil over the charcoal drawings.

Through publication in family magazines, readers became familiar with Smith's style of illustration for fairy tales. These illustrations are still available today in books such as *A Child's Book of Stories* (1986), published by Children's Classics but first issued in 1911 by Duffield and Company with ten full-page illustrations. That same year saw the *Now-a-Day's Fairy Book* by Anna Alice Chapin, issued with six full-page tipped-in illustrations by Smith, including the 'Three Bears', 'Beauty and the Beast', 'Little Red Riding Hood', and 'A Modern Cinderella'. In this book, three children interact with various fairy-tale characters. These two collections were published in Britain by Chatto and Windus (1913) and Harrap (1917).   LS

Nudelman, Edward D., *Jessie Willcox Smith: A Bibliography* (1989).

Schnessel, S. Michael, *Jessie Willcox Smith* (n.d.).

Smith, Kiki (1954–) American artist who has experimented widely in the creation of fairy-tale sculptures, paintings, and lithographs generally from a feminist perspective. Smith tells all sorts of stories through her art, and they keep changing as the modalities of her art change. Smith focuses on bodies and blood, fluidity and flexibility, surprising formations through rearrangement of object relations, and the provocation of new associations within spectators who are challenged and might be stimulated to form their own stories. In her installation *Telling Tales* (2001) and the exhibit *Prints, Books, & Things* (2003) she demonstrates multiple approaches to *'Little Red Riding Hood'. In her stunning four-feet-tall sculpture *Daughter* (1999) made out of nepal paper, bubble wrap, methyl cellulose, hair, fabric, and glass, we are presented with a young girl wearing a red wool cape and hood that contrasts with her white dress. She appears to be a mutant, the daughter of Little Red Riding Hood and the wolf. In the glass paintings of *Gang of Girls and Pack of Wolves* (1999), the bronze sculpture *Wolf* (2000), and the lithographs *Companions* (2001), the wolves are noble, sturdy, and larger than life, but they are more friendly and protective than threatening. Smith often suggests that, if women are born of wolves, they may inherit their intrepid character. They are certainly not fearful, and neither is Smith in the enigmatic photos of herself as a witch dressed in black in *Sleeping Witch* (2000); nor are the nude women in the *Spinster Series I and II* (2002) the typical miller's daughter. Though they appear to be tied to their spinning wheels, they have a quiet confidence about them. Smith's transformation of the female protagonists of fairy tales into confident and self-possessed women is brought about by a transformation of their bodies, dress, function, format, and their relationship to their environments. In her *Blue Print* series (1999), consisting of 15 etchings and aquatints, she portrayed a disturbed Dorothy from The *Wizard of Oz*, which reflects not only the dilemmas of the young girl swept off to a strange land but also the struggles of Judy Garland, for Dorothy is Judy and Judy, Dorothy, American fairy-tale icons of the twentieth century. In two other etchings based on Lewis *Carroll's *Alice's Adventures Under Ground*, created in 2000 and 2002, Alice appears in two contexts: in the first engraving she appears in a pool of her own tears, anxiously fleeing some danger that obviously has frightened a strange group of fowls and animals; in the second she sits on a hill and watches a flock of geese fly away from her. It is not clear why, but this Alice seems self-composed. In each instance, in the etchings of Dorothy and Alice, Smith wants us to wonder what is bothering the girls and to rethink the stories that we have been told about these young women. JZ

Haenlein, Carl (ed.), *Kiki Smith: All Creatures Great and Small* (1998).

Posner, Helaine, and Smith, Kiki, *Kiki Smith: Telling Tales* (2001).

Weitman, Wendy, *Kiki Smith: Prints, Books & Things* (2003).

Snow, John Frederick 'Jack' (1907–56) American author of *Oz* books. At L. Frank *Baum's death, 12-year-old Jack wrote to the publishers Reilly & Lee and offered to continue the *Wizard of Oz* series. Nineteen years later, he got his wish. As the Fourth Royal Historian of Oz, he imitated Baum's writing style and purified Oz of non-Baum characters in *Magical Mimics in Oz* (1947) and *The Shaggy Man of Oz* (1949). By this date, however, post-war America was losing interest in Oz, and Snow's novels were not popular. He later compiled *Who's Who in Oz* (1954), an illustrated encyclopaedia based on his extensive collection of Baumiana and Oziana. MLE

Greene, David L., and Martin, Dick, *The Oz Scrapbook* (1977).

Snow, Jack, *Who's Who in Oz* (1954).

'Snow Queen, The' ('Sneedronningen') 'The Snow Queen' was published in Hans Christian *Andersen's second collection of tales: *Nye Evyntyr, Anden Samling* (*New Tales, Second Collection*, 1845). Composed of seven individual stories and thus one of Andersen's longest tales, it is an imaginative blend of the natural and supernatural and of Christian and folk elements.

In the devil's mirror, what is good and beautiful diminishes while what is evil and ugly intensifies. When the mirror accidentally smashes into 'hundreds of millions, billions and even more pieces', two of the glass splinters pierce the eye and heart of a little boy named Kay. Hitherto content to play simply and affectionately with little Gerda next door, Kay now disdains everything he previously valued, his heart a lump of ice. Science displaces imagination, and he prefers the neighbourhood boys to his former playmate. One day, a sleigh appears in the square, its driver barely visible. Recklessly hitching his small sled to the larger one, Kay is drawn through ice and snow to the realm of the Snow Queen. Terrified, he tries to escape but when 'he tried to say the "Our Father", all he could remember was the multiplication table'. Enchanted by the Snow Queen's beauty, his protests stilled by her chilling kiss, he forgets his past and devotes himself to arithmetic and science.

The rest of the story follows Gerda's quest for her beloved playmate. Fully at home in the natural world, her faith in Kay's survival never waning, she is assisted on her journey north by several fantastic companions, including talking flowers, an assertive princess, two bourgeois crows in domestic service, and a wild robber girl. At the Snow Queen's palace, she finds Kay, almost black with cold, beside a frozen lake (named the 'Mirror of Reason'), where he tries in vain to arrange pieces of ice into the one word—'Eternity'— that can free him from the Snow Queen's domination. Gerda embraces him, and her hot tears penetrate his heart, 'melting the lump of ice and burning away the splinter of glass'. When she sings a favourite hymn, Kay bursts into tears, washing the splinter from his eye. Now 'both adults, yet children still— children at heart', they retrace Gerda's journey, arriving at last at their old home where 'it was summer, warm, glorious summer'.

Juxtaposing doctrinaire piety with colloquialism, sentimentality with irony, 'The Snow Queen' addresses both child and adult audiences. On one level about 'the victory of the heart over cold intellect' (Andersen, in a letter), it is also a perceptive psychological allegory of male adolescence, depicting an evolution from alienation to sensibility through the power of love. In modern times, the story has inspired a science-fiction novel by Joan Vinge (1980), several dramatic and ballet versions, an orchestral suite, an interactive video game, and a song by Elton John (1976).   JGH

Andersen, Celia Catlett, 'Andersen's Heroes and Heroines: Relinquishing the Reward', in Francelia Butler and Richard Rotert (eds.), *Triumphs of the Spirit in Children's Literature* (1986).

Bredsdorff, Elias, *Hans Christian Andersen: The Story of his Life and Work 1805-75* (1975).

Conroy, Patricia L., and Rossel, Sven H. (trans. and intro.), *Tales and Stories by Hans Christian Andersen* (1980).

Lederer, Wolfgang, *The Kiss of the Snow Queen: Hans Christian Andersen and Man's Redemption by Woman* (1986).

Rubow, Paul V., 'Et Vinterevyntyr' ('A Winter's Tale') in *Reminiscencer* (1940).

'Snow White and the Seven Dwarfs'

This tale deals with an 'innocent persecuted heroine'. Early written versions appeared in Giambattista *Basile's The *Pentamerone* (1634-6), J. K. *Musäus's *Volksmärchen der Deutschen* (1782), and Wilhelm and Jacob *Grimm's *Kinder- und Hausmärchen* (*Children's and Household Tales*, 1812-15). It has circulated widely in Africa, Asia Minor, Scandinavia, Ireland, Russia, Greece, Serbo-Croatia, the Caribbean, and North, South, and Central America. The tale consists of stable elements: origin, jealousy, expulsion, adoption, renewed jealousy, death, exhibition of corpse, resuscitation, and a multiplicity of incidental variant details.

Snow White's origin is marked by a magical sequence of events. Her mother, longing for a child, pricks her finger while sewing; three droplets of blood fall on the snow (or she eats a rose leaf, a pomegranate seed, a tangerine). She wishes for a child as red as blood, as white as snow, and as black as ebony. The wish fulfilled, she dies in childbirth. Snow White's father remarries, and this generates jealousy between stepmother and stepdaughter, creating a surrogate mother towards whom Snow White can direct hostility, while revering her birth mother's image. Her stepmother, aware that beauty declines with years, is jealous of the girl's youth and beauty. In the Grimms' version she has a magic mirror she consults to verify who is the fairest in the land. When the girl passes from infancy to girlhood (seven years) the mirror acknowledges Snow White as the fairest. Elsewhere the stepmother consults an omniscient trout in a well, the sun, or the moon; she overhears passers-by remarking on the stepdaughter's beauty; a visiting nobleman prefers her daughter; guests declare the girl more beautiful than she.

Anxious to restore her primacy, the queen orders the heroine's execution, a terminal expulsion from the family. A huntsman is to kill her and bring back her lungs and liver. Instead, as the traditional compassionate executioner, he stabs a boar (stag, dog) and substitutes the animal's lungs and liver (heart, intestines). He brings a blood-soaked dress (undershirt, hands, eyes, tongue, intestines, hair, bottle of blood stoppered with her little finger) to prove he has completed the task. The queen, determined to consume her rival's essence, has the parts cooked and served. A unique motif has the father lead her into the forest and abandon her as in *'Hansel and Gretel'. The adoption phase begins when she finds a home with seven dwarfs (thieves, woodsmen, ogres, Jinns, bears, bandits, giants, monkeys, cannibals, brothers, wild men, old women).

In almost all the versions Snow White sweeps the house, washes the dishes, and prepares a meal for the occupants. These domestic tasks represent the young woman's first assumption of responsibility. Renewed jealousy occurs when the mirror or the queen's other informants continue to name Snow White as the fairest. The stepmother's rage and her determination to find Snow White confirm the idea that the daughter cannot escape, but must learn how to cope with danger. The queen makes various attempts to kill her rival. She disguises herself as a pedlar (sends a beggar woman in her stead) to sell lethal items: poisoned staylaces, a poisoned comb, a poisoned apple (flowers, corsets, shoes, raisins, grapes, needles, rings, belts, neckbands, shirts, wine, gold coins, headbands, hats, cakes, shoes, white bread, brooches) that Snow White eats and apparently dies. Musäus has the stepmother, the Countess of Brabant, order a physician to kill the girl with poisoned pomegranate soap, and then with a poisoned letter. Her death (death-like sleep) occurs despite the precautions of her companions, who warn her against strangers. In the Grimms' version the dwarfs rescue her twice, once from the staylaces and then from the comb. In an English text, the robbers also save her twice. They take away the pedlar's basket and burn the flowers that she offers to her victim. Then the pedlar throws poisoned apples in a glade, and Snow White picks one up and eats it. An ingenious pedlar puts a poisoned dart in the keyhole, and entices Snow White to insert her finger so that it might be kissed. In a Mexican version, the storytellers recognize the temporary nature of her death. She dons poisoned slippers one at a time. With the first she starts to shake, and with the second she is stunned and looks dead.

The Grimms have the dwarfs mourn her apparent death in the exhibition episode and display her corpse in a glass coffin on a mountain top in a sort of wildlife shrine to which animals come to weep. In another tale it is cast into the sea. In Basile's version she is placed in seven nested crystal chests. Elsewhere her bejewelled casket is carried on a horse that will stop only if someone gives it a magic command (in a golden coffin in an oxcart, suspended between elk's antlers). Her casket is variously left on a windowsill or on a doorstep. Her body is placed in a four-poster bed surrounded by candles or on a stretcher suspended between two trees. A Mexican storyteller confuses her with the Virgin Mary and places her on an altar in church. The chance arrival of a prince (a hunter, a nobleman) brings about her resuscitation. In the Grimms' tale he convinces the dwarfs to give him the coffin. When his men carry it, they stumble. The jolt causes the piece of poisoned apple to be released from the sleeping princess's throat. In other versions someone removes the lethal instrument, and she revives. The resolution is marriage with the prince, and punishment of the stepmother (immolation, immuration, decapitation).

Like all the great classical fairy tales, 'Snow White' has undergone numerous literary transformations in the 19th and 20th centuries. Two of the more important adaptations were films: Walt *Disney's *Snow White and the Seven Dwarfs* (1937) and Howard Hawks's *Ball of Fire* (1941), starring Gary Cooper and Barbara Stanwyck (*see* BURLESQUE FAIRY-TALE FILMS). In an important literary study, Sandra Gilbert and Susan Gubar used the fairy tale as a theoretical paradigm about how 19th-century literature depicted older women being pitted against younger women within the framework of a male mirror and were driven mad. During the 1970s and 1980s numerous writers such as Anne *Sexton, Olga *Broumas, Tanith *Lee, and Robert *Coover have focused on the sexual connotation of this tale in different ways. Central to all the reworkings of the classical tale is the theme of jealousy.   HG

Baeten, Elizabeth M., *The Magic Mirror: Myth's Abiding Power* (1996).
Girardot, N. J., 'Initiation and Meaning in the Tale of Snow White and the Seven Dwarfs', *Journal of American Folklore*, 90 (1977).
Gilbert, Sandra M., and Gubar, Susan, *The Madwoman in the Attic: The Woman Writer and the Nineteenth-Century Literary Imagination* (1979).
Holliss, Richard, and Sibley, Brian, *Walt Disney's Snow White and the Seven Dwarfs and the Making of the Classic Film* (1987).
Jones, Steven Swann, *The New Comparative Method: Structural and Symbolic Analysis of the Allomotifs of 'Snow White'* (1990).
Stone, Kay, 'Three Transformations of Snow White', in James M. McGlathery (ed.), *The Brothers Grimm and Folktale* (1988).

socialization and fairy tales Though fairy tales often seem to be products of

pure fantasy, they always have designs on their audiences and readers, defining proper behaviour and enforcing codes of conduct. As Maria Tatar says, 'Any attempt to pass on stories becomes a disciplinary tactic aimed at control.' Following Norbert Elias's work on the civilizing process, many recent scholars have focused on the ways fairy tales shape social expectations and individual actions in different periods. As fairy tales became primarily a genre for children, their socializing function became more and more explicit.

Certainly oral tales have always been told in part to instruct, to ensure that the hearers, particularly children, would act in approved ways. But literary fairy tales, at least since the 1690s in France, have more insistently reinforced (and sometimes questioned) existing social arrangements. The earliest written tales in France in fact always ended with a verse 'moralitez', though these morals often seem deliberately flat or out of tune with the tale itself. *Perrault's tales (1697) in general both prescribe and reinscribe sharply differentiated roles for men and women; for example, he takes *Bluebeard's power and violent history as an acceptable given, while stressing his wife's dangerous curiosity. In contrast, the tales written by women like d'*Aulnoy and *Lhéritier at the same time often feature adventurous cross-dressing heroines, powerful fairies, and unconventional marriage arrangements by the standards of the times. They implicitly question dominant patriarchal and heterosexual norms. Though both Perrault and his female contemporaries were products of the literary salons, they saw the social potential of the fairy tale very differently.

During the 18th century, the fairy tale became even more explicitly a disciplinary genre. Sarah *Fielding's *The Governess* (1749) and Jeanne-Marie *Leprince de Beaumont's anthology for children *Le Magasin des enfants* (1757; translated as the *Young Misses' Magazine* in 1761) both included many tales framed by edifying dialogues between a governess and her charges. Though unadulterated fairy tales lived on in the popular imagination, chapbooks, and new editions (particularly in the 40-volume *Cabinet des fées*, 1785–9; *see* MAYER, CHARLES-JOSEPH), they often became occasions for clumsy didactic interventions.

Jacob and Wilhelm *Grimm, writing in the first half of the 19th century, continued this didactic, socializing tradition, though somewhat more subtly. In the preface to the second volume of their *Kinder- und Hausmärchen* (1815), they refer to their collection as an 'Erziehungsbuch' (conduct book, or manual of manners). In the successive versions of tales from 1810 to 1857, as critics like Heinz Rölleke, Maria Tatar, and Jack Zipes have shown, they carefully reshaped or 'sanitized' the tales to be more effective instruments for the education of middle-class children. They often omitted or softened sexually explicit material. Though they excised many of the most violent episodes, they retained much punitive violence, making sure that powerful older women would dance in red hot shoes, or that Cinderella's wicked sisters would have their eyes pecked out. Women's transgressive acquisition of knowledge and power is often severely punished. The Grimms also stressed good behaviour, differing for boys and girls: *Little Red Riding Hood must not stray from the orderly path prescribed by her mother, while young heroes like the *Brave Little Tailor are encouraged to be resourceful, independent, and cunning. Though the Grimms often show a lower-class boy rising to a higher social station, their tales, Perrault's, and Hans Christian *Andersen's in fact reinforce the existing structures of power and of gender relations, affecting generations of children throughout Europe and North America. The *Disney films based on their tales have continued to reinforce these ideological patterns.

In his 1976 book *The Uses of Enchantment*, Bruno Bettelheim claims that the Grimms' tales help children accept their necessary place in the social and family order. His readings of the tales focus on the dark antisocial impulses that children must learn to resist, from oral greed in *'Hansel and Gretel' to jealousy of the mother (strangely enough) in *'Snow White'.

Feminist literary critics have exposed Bettelheim's late-Victorian and rigidly Freudian assumptions—often simultaneously condemning the patterns in fairy tales that doom women to passivity, narcissism, and inactivity (sleeping for 100 years, lying in a glass coffin). They prescribe new patterns that will socialize women in different ways—calling for reclaimed, new, or rewritten tales for children that stress women's independence and resourcefulness. Marxist critics have also promoted tales that have a 'liberatory' function and contribute to the formation of new social attitudes and social structures or a 'utopian' future.

Most writers on fairy tales assume, whatever their ideological position, that tales will have effects on their child audiences; reader response always includes reader acculturation. The current controversies focus on the cultural projects and norms, often seen as conservative or reactionary, that traditional tales promote and their value in the late 20th century.   EWH

Bottigheimer, Ruth, *Grimms' Good Girls & Bad Boys* (1987).

Rowe, Karen, 'Feminism and Fairy Tales', *Women's Studies*, 6 (1979).

Stone, Kay F., 'The Misuses of Enchantment: Controversies on the Significance of Fairy Tales', in Rosan Jordan and Susan J. Kalcik (eds.), *Women's Folklore, Women's Culture* (1985).

Tatar, Maria, *Off With Their Heads!* (1992).

Zipes, Jack, *Fairy Tales and the Art of Subversion* (1983).

Solinas Donghi, Beatrice (1923–) Italian author of children's and adult fiction. Solinas Donghi has cultivated creative and scholarly interests in folk and fairy tales, evident in *Fiabe a Genova* (*Folktales in Genoa*, 1972) and *Fiabe liguri* (*Ligurian Folktales*, 1982) as well as in her original works *Le fiabe incatenate* (*The Linked Fairy Tales*, 1967), *La gran fiaba intrecciata* (*The Great Interlaced Fairy Tale*, 1972), and *Sette fiabe dentro una storia* (*Seven Fairy Tales inside One Story*, 1993), which offer a modern take on the permeability of fairy-tale narratives. Her monograph *La fiaba come racconto* (*The Fairy Tale as Story*, 1976) investigates the pre-history of European fairy tales and presents comparative readings of several tale types. It was highly regarded by Italo *Calvino as integral to the understanding of Italian folklore. In 2003, Solinas Donghi received the Andersen Prize in recognition of her extensive and original collection of Italian literature for children.   NC

Solomon, Fred (Frederick Charles Solomon, 1853–1924) British-born playwright-composer-director. Born in London to a musical family, Solomon had an extensive career as a performer first in London and, after emigrating to America in 1886, on Broadway. Soon he was conducting musicals and later writing them, often adapting British pantomimes for the Broadway stage. Among his works with fantasy or fairy tale subjects were *Captain Kidd* (Liverpool, 1883), *The Fairy Circle* (London, 1885), *King Kalico* (New York, 1892), *The *Sleeping Beauty and the Beast* (New York, 1901), *Mr *Bluebeard* (New York, 1903), *Mother Goose* (New York, 1903), and *Humpty Dumpty* (New York, 1904).   TSH

Sørensen, Villy (1929–2002) Danish writer. Extremely well-versed in philosophy, he delighted in reworking texts of the past, be they about Greek or Old Norse mythology or the gospels, by giving them a modernist turn. In such collections as *Sære historier* (*Strange Stories*, 1953) or *Formynderfortællinger* (*Tutelary Tales*, 1964), he may invoke a *Märchen*, and then turn it topsy-turvy. The brief 'Fjenden' ('The Enemy', 1955) demonstrates that Sørensen's knowledge of the conventions of the folk tale was so facile that he could wickedly play with them.   NI

Spain, fairy tales in *See* p. 578.

Spenser, Edmund (1552–99) English poet. Spenser's magnificent marriage poem, *Epithalamion* (1594), with its Greek nymphs, Christian angels, and English hobgoblins, foreshadows the multiple mythologies of his unfinished allegorical epic *The Faerie Queene* (1590–6), where Greek goddesses and satyrs share the forest with giants, dragons, and enchanted castles.

Inspired by the epics of Ariosto and Tasso, Spenser planned a multi-levelled 12-book structure, its 12 heroes corresponding to the 12 virtues of the perfect Christian gentleman. Linking their interwoven adventures is Arthur, the King to be, and his quest for Gloriana, the Fairy Queen, who represents both true Glory and Queen Elizabeth I.   SR

Spielberg, Steven (1946–) American director of two films of fantasy which both evoke J. M. *Barrie's play and novel *Peter Pan*. The first was *E.T.: The Extra-Terrestrial* (USA, 1982), which has joined *The *Wizard of Oz*, *King Kong*, and a few other films in achieving a fixed place in Western cultural consciousness. One interpretation is that Spielberg and the scriptwriter Melissa Mathison conceived the character of E.T. as a combination of both Peter Pan and his fairy companion Tinkerbell. Before E.T. is domesticated and identified, the children in the film speculate that he might be an elf, or a goblin, or—most Peter-like—a leprechaun. There is, after all, a forest just outside their house. Like Peter, E.T. comes from afar, enters his new friend's bedroom, and flies away with him across the face of the moon. Later, the film explicitly acknowledges *Peter Pan* as one of its reference points when the mother reads to Gertie the chapter in which Tinkerbell, having drunk poison to save Peter's life, is herself saved from death by children all over the world clapping in affirmation of their belief in fairies. Soon after, when both E.T. and Elliott are near death, E.T. saves Elliott by breaking the empathic bond which links them; as a result Elliott revives while E.T. is pronounced clinically dead. Alone with the body, in a scene which caused cinema audiences around the world to weep, Elliott tells E.T. that he loves him. Almost immediately, E.T.'s inner light begins to glow. Within the narrative, this resuscitation is ascribed to his having received a telepathic energy injection from his mothership; but to audiences it is quite plain that their tears, and Elliott's love, are the real cause of E.T.'s resurrection.

Nine years later, with *Hook* (USA, 1991), Spielberg returned to Barrie. He had long

Spain, fairy tales in Since there were no notable compilers of fairy tales in Spain like the Brothers *Grimm, these fanciful narratives must be sought either in isolated texts or in literary allusions to familiar tales. Although the universally recognized stories of 'Cenicienta' (*'Cinderella'), 'Blanca Nieve' (*'Snow White'), 'La bella durmiente' (*'Sleeping Beauty') 'Caperucita Roja' (*'Little Red Riding Hood'), and 'Los niños abandonados' (*'Hansel and Gretel') have been circulating in Spain and in Latin America for some time now, it is not clear when they became part of the native canon of wonder tales.

1. THE 11TH CENTURY TO THE 17TH CENTURY

Nevertheless, Spain produced its share of wonder tales, some of which reflect the 800-year Arab presence in the Iberian peninsula. An important collection of tales of Arabic origin is *Disciplina Clericalis*, translated into Latin by Moisés Sefardí (born in Huesca in 1056, converted, christened Petrus Alphonsi in 1106). In 'The Rustic and the Bird' a man captures a bird. To gain her freedom she gives him some words of advice: 'Do not believe everything that is said' (a precious stone in her body), 'what is yours you will always possess' (she is in the sky; he cannot possess her), 'do not sorrow over lost possessions' (he must not lament loss of the stone). This tale was disseminated widely with variants and was interpolated in a chivalric text, in a translation of the life of Buddha, and in a compilation of sermonic exempla. Also from *Disciplina* is the tale of 'Dream Bread' (whose literary trajectory led it to the Golden Age dramatist Lope de Vega's *San Isidro labrador de Madrid*, 1599), in which a clever rustic tricks his urban travelling companions by pretending to have had a miraculous dream.

Fadrique, Alfonso X's brother, was the patron in 1253 for a translation of another Arabic text, *Seven Sages* (modern Spanish title *Sendebar*). *Sendebar* includes three tales set in a perilous forest: 'The Hunter and the She-Devil', 'The Three Wishes', and 'Spring that Changes Prince into a Woman'. The common element is a prince or nobleman who leaves home to go hunting and comes to grief in a forest.

In another Arabic text, *Kalila and Dimna* (translated as *Calila e Dimna* by order of Alfonso X, 1221–84), a sage leaves home on a quest. He journeys to India seeking a resuscitative herb. The topic reappears in a 13th-century poem, *Razón de amor*, in which the scent of magical flowers in an enchanted meadow will revive the dead. *Calila* contains two transformation tales. In 'The Rat Maiden' a monk raises a tiny rat and prays that she be transformed into a young woman. Old enough to wed, she wants the most powerful mate of all. He offers her the sun, but it is covered by clouds; the clouds are controlled by winds; a mountain blocks the winds, but the mountain is gnawed by rodents. Therefore, she must marry a rat. He prays that she will return to her previous shape. In 'The Frog-King's Mount', a serpent's arrogance is punished by a transformation into serving as a frog-king's mount, condemned to eat only those frogs given him by the king.

A chivalric novel, *Cavallero Zifar* (1300, translated as *The Book of the Knight* in 1983) strings together a number of fairy tales. The good knight's adventures begin when he is unable to serve any royal master for long because he had been cursed. Any horse or other beast that served him as a mount dies after ten days ('Equine Curse'). He seeks a new post repeatedly since he represents a considerable expense for his royal masters. One day a son is carried off by a lioness, nurtured by her until he is adopted by kind strangers ('Child Nurtured by Lioness'). His wife, captured by pirates, defeats her captors, throws their corpses overboard, and sails magically to a safe port. In another episode Zifar's squire becomes a knight, and is lured into the underwater realm of the 'Lady of the Lake', whom he marries. His fairy wife orders him not to speak to anyone in her realm. He disobeys the interdiction. In this land parturition follows conception by seven days. Fruit trees bear fruit every day, and beasts have young every seven days. Having violated her interdiction against speech, he and his adult son are ejected violently from his underworld kingdom soon after his arrival. In a parallel episode, Zifar's son, Roboán, is at the court of the emperor of Tigrida, a monarch who never laughs. Roboán is punished for asking why the emperor does not laugh. He is set adrift in an oarless, rudderless boat to a magic kingdom, the Fortunate Isles. There he is chosen by the empress, Nobility, to be the emperor with the understanding that if he completes a year successfully on the throne, he will never lose the empire. Three days before his year ends, an enchantress seduces him with a magical mastiff, an enchanted hawk, and finally a horse that can outrun the wind. Mounted on the magical horse faster than the wind, he touches its flanks lightly with his spurs, and the horse carries him away from his empire back to Tigrida. There he learns that he and the doleful emperor were two in a long succession of unlucky men who had lost the empire of the Fortunate Isles in the same demonic way.

In the chivalric novel *Amadís de Gaula* (1508) lovers are tested for constancy and nobility in another enchanted kingdom (Ínsola Firme). Before the noble Apolidon and his bride Grimanesa leave their enchanted realm, they must select successors who match them in nobility, skill in arms, and in governance as well as in physical beauty and loving constancy. As a test they build an enchanted arch leading to four chambers. Unworthy pairs passing under the arch are ejected by a horrific mechanical trumpeter and terrible flames and smoke. The same trumpeter plays wonderfully sweet music for the deserving couple, Amadís and Oriana. An evil enchanter, Arcalaus, disguised as a mysterious stranger, devises a test to tempt Amadís and Oriana to come out of hiding. Two magnificent gifts are offered: a magic sword that can be taken from its sheath only by a lover whose devotion to his beloved is greater than any other's in the world, and a headdress adorned with flowers that will bloom only when worn by a woman whose devotion to her beloved equals his. To counter the efforts of Arcalaus, a good enchantress, Urganda the Unknown, guides and protects Amadís throughout his life. Every time he needs her help she appears. Similarly, the evil enchanter, Arcalaus, appears when the storyteller needs a limit to his hero's almost unlimited powers; for example, he tricks Amadís into entering an enchanted chamber whose power causes him to faint and appear to die. Arcalaus comes to court to trick King Lisuarte into permitting him to wed Oriana. He lends the king two magical objects: a crown that guarantees its wearer perpetual honour and power, and an enchanted cloak for the queen that ensures that there can never be discord between the wearer and her mate. They may retain the gifts until Arcalaus comes to claim them. If for any reason Lisuarte cannot return them, he must promise to grant him whatever he wants. The evil enchanter sends an emissary to the queen for the crown and cloak, and then comes in person to claim the missing items. Unable to return them, Lisuarte must surrender his only daughter Oriana to the evil magician.

A traditional paradisaical land of abundance, *La Tierra de Jauja*, where the streets are paved with eggs and sweets, rivers run with wine and honey, roast partridges fly by with tortillas in their beaks saying 'Eat Me' is described by Luis Barahona de Soto (1548–95) in *Diálogo de la montería* (also in Lope de Rueda's *La Tierra de Jauja*, 1547). Mateo de Alemán alludes to this territory in the picaresque novel *Guzmán de Alfarache*, as does Fray Juan de Pineda in *Diálogos familiares de la agricultura cristiana* (1589).

Heroes kill two grotesque, horrific monsters, another feature of fairy tales. One in *Amadís* is the hideous fruit of an incestuous union between the giant Bandaguido and his daughter Bandaguida, and the other is a fearsome dragon said to have consumed a whole town, in the crusade narrative *Gran Conquista de Ultramar*. In a ballad, a dragon abducts a princess ('El culebro raptor'), and in another a seven-headed serpent gnaws at a penitent sinner ('Penitencia del rey don Rodrigo'). The fantasy of a grotesque mountain woman, who preys on travellers, appears in many tales. Her horrible nature is best described, in a ballad, as a lamia with the head and breast of a woman and the body of a serpent ('La Gallarda, matadora').

Time is manipulated magically in many ballads and tales. In a ballad, a captive's magic sleep makes him think only minutes have passed. In reality seven years have gone by ('El conde Arnaldos'). In prose this motif occurred in the tale of 'Don Illán and the Dean of Santiago' in *El Conde Lucanor* (1335) by Don Juan Manuel (1282–1347). In a 15th-century compilation of sermonic exempla a friar follows a bird to paradise and returns 100 years later (*Libro de los enxenplos por a.b.c.* by Clemente Sánchez de Vercial, 1370–1426, translated as *The Book of Tales by A.B.C.* in 1992). In the most famous Golden Age drama, *La vida es sueño* (1631–2), Pedro Calderón de la

Barca (1600–81) has his hero Segismundo fall into a magic time-distorting sleep.

Storytellers interpolated fairy tales in larger narratives. The *Libro de Apolonio* (1235–40) begins with a princess who is the prize offered to the solver of a hermetic riddle. In *Gran conquista de Ultramar* (1295–1312), 'The Swan Knight' is inserted into a crusade story. Princess Isomberta's family arranges a marriage for her, and she escapes in a rudderless boat without sails. She lands on a deserted island where Count Eustacio finds her in a hollow tree. He is uneasy about this strange apparition and consults his mother Ginesa about marriage to her. His mother disapproves, but they wed anyway. While Eustacio is away Isomberta has seven babies. Multiple births were thought to be results of adulterous behaviour, but an angel comes to save her and the babies putting a gold collar on each child. Ginesa orders a servant to kill the children, but he takes them to a wilderness and abandons them. A deer nurses them until a hermit adopts them and raises them. Ginesa spies six of the boys, takes them to her palace, and orders her servants to kill them, but first to remove their collars. Their collars removed, the boys turn into swans and fly away. She takes the gold (silver) to a metalworker who melts it and makes a goblet. He keeps the metal from the five collars since one suffices for the goblet. When their father learns the truth, the five remaining collars are restored. The seventh lad, still wearing his collar and accompanied by his swan brother, spends his life defending those who need him, including his calumniated mother. When he marries, he imposes an interdiction on his bride. She may never ask him for his name, nor his origin. If she does, he must leave forever, carried away by his swan brother.

Sometimes fairy tales leave only traces of themselves in the form of allusions. Allusive passages in literary works are signs that the tale had spread widely enough in the community to be familiar to the average reader. For instance, the anonymous author of a 16th-century picaresque novel *Lazarillo de Tormes* alluded to an Arabic tale 'The House Where No One Eats Nor Drinks' in a chapter where his hero serves an impoverished squire. Cervantes refers to the 'Frogs who asked Jupiter for a King' and the 'Princess Rescued by a Half-Man, Half-Bear' in *Don Quixote*. Later Fernán Caballero (pseudonym of Cecilia *Böhl de Faber) and Alonso de Morales related the same story as 'Las princesas encantadas'.

Many stories like 'The *Tale of a Youth who Set Out to Learn What Fear Was' were part of Spain's cultural heritage (*Quinquagenas*, Gonzalo Fernández de Oviedo, 1478–1557). Lope de Vega (1562–1635) alluded to it in two dramas (*Los porceles de Murcia*, *c.*1604–8), *Quien ama no haga fiero*, *c.*1620–2), and later Juan de Ariza wrote a story 'Perico sin Miedo' (1848).

While the interest for the modern reader of the antonomastic lover, Don Juan, is his indefatigable pursuit of women, in *El burlador de Sevilla*, the public for Tirso de Molina (pseudonym of Friar Gabriel Téllez, 1571–1648) was more concerned with his lack of repentance as evidenced in his invitation to dinner to the dead Comendador's statue, a situation paralleled in the tale of 'The Skull Invited to Dinner'. Antonio de Zamora (1664–1728) wrote a version *No hay plazo que no se cumpla, ni deuda que no se pague, y convidado de piedra* (*No Agreement Goes Unfulfilled, nor Any Debt Unpaid*). A dead person grants good fortune to his benefactor and returns to demand the reward promised him in Lope de Vega's *Don Juan de Castro* (*c.*1604–8), a theme also used by Calderón in *El mejor amigo el muerto* (1636).

Similarly, proverbs that enjoyed popular currency are evidence that the tales to which they refer existed in the oral tradition. For example, a fanciful story tells of an encounter between a giant who reproached Pedro de Urdimales when he tried to carry off a mountain full of firewood, telling him to be satisfied with one tree. A 17th-century proverb collection lists the tale's echo, 'Pedro de Urdimales, o todo el monte, o nonada' ('Either the Whole Mountain or Nothing').

Another source of information about fairy tales is the oral-traditional ballad. These brief narratives were first written down in the 16th century, but it was not until 1832 that Agustín Durán published his *Romancero general* and Ferdinand Wolf and Conrad Hoffman collected them in *Primavera y flor de romances* (1856). Among these popular narratives, we find the tale of a hunter who comes upon an enchanted princess in a tree. Like the princess in *'Sleeping Beauty' ('Briar Rose') she had been cursed at birth by one of seven fairies who had come to bring her gifts. She was compelled to spend seven years in an enchanted tree. Like the count in the 'Swan Knight' story, the frightened hunter must first consult his mother (aunt) before he can agree ('La infantina'). In variant versions, he makes sexual demands on her. She reveals she is the Virgin Mary ('El caballero burlado a lo divino'). In another ballad he comes upon a magical dove and promises that her offspring and his will be brothers and sisters ('El mal cazador'). In still another, a deer is really an enchanted princess who asks him to marry her ('La niña encantada').

A serpent appears to a woman at a fountain. He is a king enchanted for six years ('La inocente acusada'). In a Portuguese ballad, a man falls in love with a Moorish woman in a castle. He captures the castle, but she disappears magically ('A moura encantada'). Echoing the experience of the 'Bold Knight' and Prince Roboán, a fairy takes her lover to her bed in a far-off land and keeps him enchanted. He has a son with her ('Los amores de Floriseo y de la reina de Bohemia'). Extraordinary people are said to be other-worldly. A man whose beauty rivals the stars causes the goddess of beauty to fall in love with him ('Romance del infante Troco').

Strange, magical happenings are often associated with the sea. A sailor's song calms the sea and the winds, causes fish to leap out of water, and birds to perch on a ship's mast ('El conde Arnaldos'). The protagonist of several ballads travels in a magic boat. Just as in the chivalric novel *El caballero Zifar*, in which the knight's wife single-handedly steers a boat whose sails fill miraculously and whose rudder takes her to a safe harbour, a galley without sails and oars is invincible in battle ('La toma de Galera'). In a Portuguese ballad, an exiled woman returns home in a boat without sails ('A filha desterrada'). Hero seeks Leander in a boat using her sleeves as sails, and her arms as oars ('Hero y Leandro'). Reminiscent of *Rapunzel, imprisoned in a tower, Leander lets down her long hair so that her lover can climb ('Hero y Leandro'), and still another woman uses her long tresses as a lifeline for a drowning man ('Repulsa y compasión').

Other unusual objects have migrated from fairy tales to ballad narratives. A gigantic sapphire adorns a castle tower and illuminates the area, promising marvellous events. Night becomes day ('Romance de Rosaflorida'). A magic sword promises that the hero need only brandish it to cut a swath through the enemy ranks ('El conde Niño'). Just as fairy-tale objects had migrated to ballads, they also made their way into prose narratives. Cervantes alluded to magic wands in two of his *Exemplary Novels*: *El casamiento engaños* (*The Deceitful Marriage*) and *Los baños de Argel* (*The Bagnios of Algiers*).

Magic animals figure in many ballads. A marauding deer leads seven lions and a lioness to kill knights and their horses ('Romance de Lanzarote'). A speaking horse will aid the hero if given winesop and not fodder ('Gaiferos libera a Melisendra', 'Pérdida de don Beltrán', 'Passo de Roncesval', 'Conde Olinos'). Birds carry messages from captives to their potential rescuers ('El Conde Claros en hábito de fraile', 'La esposa de D. García'). Another bird warns men not to trust women ('La tórtola del peral'). A dove sustains a shepherdess for seven years with a magic flower ('A pastora devota de María', 'La devota del rosario'). Problem pregnancies in ballads are attributed to inhaling the magic fragrance of some flowers or treading upon magic grass ('Romance de don Tristan', 'La mala hierba').

2. THE 18TH CENTURY

As far as fairy tales are concerned in Spanish literature, the 18th century constitutes a tremendous gap; the almost total absence of fantasy short narrative in that period comes to an end in the next century. However, before exploring the main tendencies and writers of the *Märchen* in the 19th century, it is worth recounting the reasons why the Spanish Age of Reason showed such a negative attitude towards a genre that was otherwise profusely used in neighbouring countries, above all in France.

In 18th-century Spanish literature, both the short novel and the short story failed to develop any degree of quality, and therefore they offer little interest to contemporary readers and scholars. Writers of the 18th century tended to devote their talents to other genres. While scarcely any attention was paid to short narrative genres, the Spanish literary heritage was enriched by many a writer's devotion to such genres as diaries, travel literature, speeches, journalistic essays, and utopias, as the critic Esther Lacadena Calero has pointed out.

According to Juan Antonio Ríos Carratala, one of the reasons why imaginative narrative genres were neglected in 18th-century Spain is that an omnipresent censorship controlled all kinds of publications and was especially vigilant with respect to periodicals and translations, mainly from French into Spanish. Such censorship, of both a civil and a religious nature, made it very difficult for editors to publish unauthorized works; however, there were some exceptions to this. Mariano José Nipho, for example, was an editor who went against the grain, supporting several publications which regularly published short narratives and some moralistic tales addressed to a female reading public.

Ríos Carratala also affirms that short narratives were despised by most important literary figures of the period as non-respectable genres, on the basis that they lacked the support of a classical literary tradition. Moreover, the same critic points out that literary theorists and writers of the time showed great mistrust of pure fiction; for them, literature had to play a moral and instructive role that short narratives of a fictitious nature could never perform, since they were considered to be simply destined to entertain their readers.

Despite the forces working against the development of short narrative in 18th-century Spain, some examples of it can still be traced. Thus, Professor Antonio Fernández Insuela of the University of Oviedo (Spain) studied the small corpus of short narrative publications in the 18th century, particularly in *Tertulia de la aldea* (*A Village Literary Gathering*). This journal was structured in several sections, one of which included brief texts under the heading of 'tales', 'jokes', 'sayings', 'funny stories', etc., which had a historical or pseudo-historical origin and also sometimes a traditional or folk one. Ríos Carratala (1993) mentions yet another 18th-century periodical which gave some attention to the short-story genre: *El Correo de Madrid* (*The Madrid Post*). In this periodical, apart from some moralistic stories, jokes, and anecdotes, it was likewise possible to read brief tales with a folk source.

3. THE 19TH CENTURY

With the advent of the 19th century, the situation of short narratives radically changed. In fact, it was during this century that the short story became an autonomous literary genre. Excellent examples of short narrative were produced at the time, and most of the great literary figures of the century tried their hand at writing short stories. It is Ríos Carratala (1993) again who best summarizes the reasons why this change took place. First of all, he mentions the end of censorship during the 1830s. Secondly, he points out the enormous development of the press, since it benefited all literary genres, particularly the short story. In fact, the 19th-century short story was almost always initially published in literary sections of periodicals. Throughout the 19th century the short story gained a degree of acceptance that it had lacked in the past; moreover, it received some critical attention, this being especially true in the case of the literary tale based on folk material.

One aspect concerning the short stories produced in 19th-century Spanish literature is that they can be categorized according to many different types, as Baquero Goyanes has demonstrated in his seminal study *El cuento español en el siglo XIX* (*The Spanish Short Story in the 19th Century*, 1949). Some of the categories that he has distinguished are: literary versions of folk tales, fantastic tales, children's tales (in which the main character is a child), legendary tales, rural tales, historical and patriotic tales, religious tales, and humoristic and satiric tales. It is worth pointing out for our purposes that literary versions of folk tales were not often cultivated by Spanish 19th-century writers. In fact, Baquero Goyanes is quite convinced that this category might just be comprised of Cecilia Böhl de Faber's works as well as those of a couple of her followers, Antonio de Trueba (1819–89) and Luis Coloma (1851–1914).

Nevertheless, it would seem that the list of 19th-century Spanish writers who appropriated folk material for their literary purposes could be further expanded so as to include the names of those who, in the history of Spanish literature, tend to figure prominently in categories distinct from that of the literary folk tradition. This would be the case of Emilia *Pardo Bazán and Vicente *Blasco Ibáñez, generally regarded among the ranks of the naturalist school; Pedro Antonio de *Alarcón, who is otherwise grouped with romantic novelists; and writers like José María de *Pereda, Armando *Palacio Valdés, and Benito *Pérez Galdós, who were part of the realist tradition; all of these writers cultivated to some degree the genre of the literary fairy tale. Furthermore 19th-century scholars and journalists such as Manuel *Ossorio y Bernard and José *Godoy Alcántara can be added to the list, as can Juan Eugenio *Hartzenbusch, the famous romantic playwright. Mainly known for his poetry, Gustavo Adolfo *Bécquer nevertheless should be accorded a place within the history of the Spanish literary tale on account of his *Leyendas* (*Legends*, 1871), for which he drew motifs from Spanish legends as well as from the European folk tradition. A special case is that of Leopoldo *Alas 'Clarín'; he was not a writer of literary fairy tales himself, but was none the less a major defender of the genre, and was also responsible for some of the best short stories of the 19th century.

There were no notable compilers of fairy tales like the Grimm brothers in Spain; yet, it should be pointed out that the romantic impulse to collect folk tales systematically did produce some outstanding results, if not as noteworthy as those gathered in Germany. Cecilia Böhl de Faber, generally referred to by her male pseudonym 'Fernán Caballero', is the most important figure to have transformed this impulse into an actual compilation of folk stories entitled *Cuentos y poesías populares andaluzas* (*Popular Andalusian Tales and Poems*, 1859). Her project was not as ambitious as that of the Grimms', since she did not aim at gathering folk tales from the whole of Spain, but only from one of its regions, Andalusia. However, like the Grimms, she transcribed the stories she collected from different folk sources and subsequently adapted them to her own literary taste.

4. THE 20TH CENTURY

In the 20th century it becomes much more difficult to make a comprehensive analysis of literature written in Spanish owing to the influence of other cultures and literatures. In fact, after gaining their independence, all South American countries began to develop their own sense of identity, out of which new forms of literature grew.

At the turn of the century, two writers figure prominently in Spain: Pío *Baroja and the Nobel Prize-winner Jacinto *Benavente. As was the trend in the 19th century, neither of them was associated explicitly with the fairy-tale genre, but both had some connection to it. Baroja, one of the greatest contemporary Spanish novelists, wrote some short narratives of a fantastic nature akin to those by Edgar Allan Poe, while Benavente's plays for children were almost always inspired by one classical fairy tale or another.

From the 1940s to the 1960s, however, a good number of writers began to devote themselves more specifically to the fairy-tale genre. It should be noted that many of them were women writers who had in mind an adolescent audience, or who were simply writing for children. Thus appeared collections of fairy stories by writers like María Luisa *Gefaell, Concha *Castroviejo, María Luisa *Villardefrancos, and Elizabeth *Mulder. During these decades of Franco's dictatorship, the fairy tale was often used to convey a traditional ideology that was being promoted by the followers of the regime. The girls' magazine *Bazar*, for instance, was intended to inculcate in its readers an ideal of femininity characterized by docility, passivity, and piety. It promoted a kind of woman who had no other interests beyond household and marital duties, whose body was to conform to canonical beauty, and who duly fulfilled the precepts of Catholicism. Aurora *Mateos, for years the editor of *Bazar*, made sure that one or several fairy tales imbued with such an ideology filled some of the pages of each issue.

For the most part, the approach to folk and fairy-tale materials underwent a dramatic change from the 1970s onwards in Spain, although examples can still be found, such as that of Ana María *Matute, of writers who venerate the established fairy-tale canon and do not wish to subvert it. With the beginnings of democracy, the censorship imposed by the Franco regime was brought to an end, with the result that many themes, until then considered taboo, could be freely dealt with in literature. Fairy-tale material was used in works that tried to deconstruct traditional discourses concerning the national past, Catholic morals and manners, and a good number of sexual taboos, as in Juan *Goytisolo's work. Feminist ideology was also soon easily identifiable in much of post-Franco literature, and feminist writers were often inspired by the genre of the fairy tale, as is the case of a good number of Sara *Suárez Solís's short stories, and also of Carmen *Martín Gaite's novels and fairy tales; some famous publishing houses even produced whole collections in which the best-known traditional fairy tales were rewritten with a feminist bias, of which the series 'The Three Twins', published by Planeta, is an excellent example.

Feminist revision of fairy tales is a phenomenon that has likewise affected the production of several Latin American writers from the 1970s onwards. The Puerto Rican Rosario Ferré and Luisa *Valenzuela, and Marco Denevi, both Argentinian, figure among those writers who have used fairy-tale material in their short stories in order to socialize their reading public according to values other than the patriarchal ones, or at least, to make their readers conscious of the patriarchal ideology inscribed in many traditional narratives.

In Chile, during Salvador Allende's presidency (1970–3), a publishing house called Quimantú working under the auspices of the *Unidad Popular* (Allende's political party) published *Cabrochico* (*Small Child*), a children's magazine in which several classical fairy tales appeared; they were all refashioned according to the socialist ideology that the leaders of the country wanted to disseminate.

Leaving aside the socializing aim which fairy stories have often been intended to fulfil in contemporary South American literature, what is undeniable about the genre is that it has ignited such movements as magical realism in Spanish. Moreover, in the case of the short story, a number of South American writers are reputed to have produced the best examples of the literary fairy tale in the Spanish language. The three names most often cited are: Gabriel García *Márquez, Julio *Cortázar, and above all Jorge Luis *Borges. In their works, folk and fairy-tale material are intertwined with features borrowed from the genres of the fantastic and magic realism, the fundamental South American contribution to contemporary world literature. Borges, one of the best short-story writers in the Spanish language, adds yet another element to his literary production—the inspired touch of *The *Arabian Nights*, the masterpiece which influences almost all of his works.   HG/CFR

Baquero Goyanes, Mariano, *El cuento español en el siglo XIX* (1949).
Baquero Goyanes, Mariano, *El cuento español. Del Romanticismo al Realismo* (1992).
Boggs, Ralph Steele, *Index of Spanish Folktales* (1930).
Bravo-Villasante, Carmen, *Historia de la literatura infantil española* (1972).
Bravo-Villasante, Carmen, *Antología de la literatura infantil española* (1979).

Cerda, Hugo, *Ideología y cuentos de hadas* (1985).

Chevalier, Maxime, *Cuentos folklóricos españoles del Siglo de Oro* (1983).

Chevalier, Maxime, *Cuentos maravillosos*, Biblioteca Románica Hispánica (1995).

Espinosa, Aurelio, *The Folklore of Spain in the American Southwest: Traditional Spanish Folk Literature in Northern New Mexico and Southern Colorado* (1985).

Fernández Insuela, Antonio, 'Notas sobre la narrativa breve en las publicaciones periódicas del siglo XVIII: Estudio de la *Tertulia de la aldea*', *Estudios de historia social*, 52-3 (1990).

Garcia Collado, Marian, 'El cuento folklórico y sus adaptaciones: Entre la tradición oral y la fijación escrita. Tres apropiaciones del cuento "Juan el oso" (cuento tipo AT 301b)', *Revista de Dialectología y Tradiciones Populares*, 47 (1992).

Goldberg, Harriet, *Motif-Index of Medieval Spanish Narrative* (1998).

Lacadena Calero, Esther, *La prosa en el siglo XVIII* (1985).

Ríos Carratala, Juan Antonio, 'La narrativa breve en España (siglos XVIII y XIX)', in J. L. Alonso Hernández, M. Gosman, and R. Rinaldi (eds.), *La Nouvelle Romane (Italia–France–España)* (1993).

wanted to film the play more or less straight, but seems to have decided that modern audiences could not take its whimsy or its political incorrectness, so approached the play obliquely, using a script based on two suppositions. The first of these was that Peter eventually left Neverland so that he could have children of his own, got married to Wendy's niece, became a cellphone-addicted lawyer in America, and erased all memory of his former life. The second was that Hook did not perish inside the crocodile at the end of the original story, but survived, and reopens the old battle by abducting Peter's children. Thanks to Tinkerbell's continuing devotion to him, Peter manages to pursue them to Neverland, win over the Lost Boys and get back into fighting shape—except that he cannot fly—within the allotted three days. Having once again saved his life, though less dramatically than before, Tinkerbell lets Peter go, accepting with sorrow that he will never be hers. He finally becomes airborne, and able to defeat Hook, as a result of having a happy thought about his children. Reunited with his family, he throws his cellphone away to symbolize that he intends never again to lose contact with the child within. The Boy who Would Not Grow Up has become The Man who at Last Learned to Grow Up.   TAS

Springer, Nancy (1948–) American writer of fantasy novels for children and adults. Although standard folklore and fantasy tropes (wizards, fairies, magical beasts) can be found throughout this author's early fiction, it is Springer's powerful mature work on which her reputation rests. In *The Hex Witch of Seldom* (1988), she makes highly original use of Pennsylvania Dutch folklore. In *Fair Peril* (1996), Springer creates a droll modern fairy tale for adult readers. The novel concerns a middle-aged woman, her daughter, an annoying talking frog, and the magical realm of Fair Peril which lies between two stores at the mall.   TW

Stahl, Karoline (*née* **Dumpf**, 1776–1837) Livonian writer of fairy tales and didactic literature for children. Much in the tradition

of the French tales she partially emulated, Stahl's fables and reworkings of fairy-tale and saga motifs included moral instruction for upper-class children, enjoining them to avoid the seven deadly sins of childhood: envy, tattling, vanity, prattling, unhealthy snacking, dangerous play, and haughtiness. A few of the tales from her *Fabeln, Märchen und Erzählungen* (*Fables, Fairy Tales and Stories*, 1818) found their way in altered form into the second edition of the **Kinder- und Hausmärchen* (*Children's and Household Tales*).   SJ

stamps and fairy tales Many national postal services have recognized what pleasure it would bring to children and adults if they were to produce series of stamps depicting certain fairy-tale motifs. In addition to the pragmatic aspect of selling stamps needed to post mail, the postal services also appreciated the commercial advantage of these stamps since many customers purchased them as collectors' items. Fairy-tale stamps are thus part and parcel of the mercantile exploitation of the traditional tales, no matter how delightful the images on the stamps might be.

The German postal services issued a series of fairy-tale stamps, starting with a single stamp illustrating the Brothers *Grimm, between 1959 (Wilhelm Grimm died 100 years earlier) and 1967. Choosing always four major motifs of each individual tale, these sets depicted such well-known fairy tales as 'The Star Coins', *'Little Red Riding Hood', *'Hansel and Gretel', *'Snow White', 'The Wolf and the Seven Young Kids', *'Sleeping Beauty', *'Cinderella', *'The Frog King', and *'Mother Holle'. But there was a positive price to be paid for these stamps. In addition to their value of 10, 20, and up to 50 pfennigs, purchasers had to pay between 5 and 25 pfennigs extra for the purpose of helping needy children: a clever idea by the national postal service, and one that benefited children throughout the country. In 1985 (Jacob Grimm's 200th birthday) the Swiss postal service followed a similar approach using such tales as 'Cinderella', 'Hansel and Gretel', 'Snow White', and 'Little Red Riding Hood'.

Also in 1985 the East German postal service issued a set of six Brothers Grimm commemorative stamps. Once again there was one stamp depicting Jacob and Wilhelm, while the other five stamps each illustrated one scene out of *'The Brave Little Tailor', 'The Seven Ravens', 'Lucky Hans', *'Puss-in-Boots', and 'The Sweet Porridge'. The Hungarian postal service also remembered the Grimms with similar stamps during that year, and stamps have also been issued in Bulgaria, Czechoslovakia, Denmark, Finland, Luxembourg, Poland, and Romania. At least such stamps were affordable and brought joy and memories to many. One wonders how many people will ever see the 1,000 German marks bill that depicts the Brothers Grimm and which was put into circulation in 1990 shortly after reunification. WM

Partington, Paul, *Fairy Tales and Folk Tales on Stamps* (1970).

Starewicz, Ladislaw (1882–1965) Russian stop-motion animator, best known for his short film titled *Mest' kinematograficheskogo operatora* (*The Cameraman's Revenge*, 1912), and *Lucanus Cervus* (1910), the first puppet-animated film. Starewicz is credited as one of the inventors of stop-motion animation and is also known for his dark sense of humour. In his adaptation of Aesop's 'The Ant and the Grasshopper', for example, the film concludes with the grasshopper's unceremonious on-screen death. Starewicz also garnered renown for his reanimation of taxidermied animals, insects, and amphibians, as in *Les Grenouilles qui demandent un roi* (*The Frogs Who Demand a King, or Frogland*, 1922) and his hand-tinted, *La Voix du rossignol* (*The Voice of the Nightingale*, 1923), which was awarded the Hugo Riesenfield medal in 1925. Similar techniques were used in Starewicz's adaptation of other Aesop's Fables, including *The Dragonfly and the Ant* (1912) and *Le Roman de Renard* (*Tale of the Fox*, 1941). KMJ

'Steadfast Tin Soldier, The' ('Den Standhaftige Tinsoldat') Published in the third collection of *Eventyr, fortalte for Børn* (*Tales, Told for Children*, 1838), 'The Steadfast

Tin Soldier' remains among the most popular of Hans Christian *Andersen's tales. It is the first of several stories to animate inanimate objects; others include 'Grantræet' ('The Fir Tree') and 'Stoppenaalen' ('The Darning Needle').

One of 25 tin soldiers in a box, the protagonist lacks one leg 'as he was the last to be made and there wasn't enough tin to go round'. Despite this handicap (or perhaps because of it), his devotion to military decorum is uncompromising, and he never slackens in his erect and stoical demeanour. Falling in love with a paper ballerina—both for her beauty and because he thinks that she, too, has only one leg—he spends his days gazing longingly at her but never betraying his feelings. Whether by accident or through the ill will of a jealous goblin, the soldier falls from the window. When the owners look for him, he refrains from calling out, thinking such action unbecoming his uniform. Several misadventures follow: two urchins place him in a paper boat; he is swept into a culvert and, Jonah-like, swallowed by a fish. Through all, he remains silent, staunchly shouldering his weapon and always standing erect. Miraculously returned to the toy room (the fish is caught, then purchased by the cook), he is overjoyed to find the dancer still in the doorway of her castle and almost weeps 'tears of tin' at what he sees as her fidelity, though he restrains himself. One of the children suddenly seizes him and throws him into the fire. Still erect, the soldier begins to melt, but whether the heat consuming him 'came from the actual fire or from love, he had no idea'. Almost simultaneously blown into the fire by a gust of wind, the paper dancer is similarly consumed. Though the two are united at last, all that remains are a lump of tin in the shape of a heart and the dancer's spangle 'burnt black as coal'.

The story is unusual among Andersen's early tales both in its emphasis on sensual desire and in its ambiguities. Blind fate, not intention, determines all events. Moreover, the narrative questions the very decorum it praises. The tin soldier's passive acceptance of whatever happens to him, while exemplifying pietistic ideals of self-denial, also contributes to his doom. Were he to speak and act, the soldier might gain both life and love. Restrained, however, by inhibition and convention, he finds only tragedy and death. The tale is often read autobiographically, with the soldier viewed as symbolizing Andersen's feelings of inadequacy with women, his passive acceptance of bourgeois class attitudes, or his sense of alienation, as an artist and outsider, from full participation in everyday life. A ballet version, set to music by Georges Bizet, was choreographed by George Balanchine in 1975. The tale has inspired several short children's films, as well as a feature-length science-fiction fantasy film, *The Tin Soldier* (1975), and several orchestral compositions.   JGH

Bredsdorff, Elias, *Hans Christian Andersen: The Story of His Life and Work 1805-75* (1975).

Rossel, Sven Hakon (ed.), *Hans Christian Andersen: Danish Writer and Citizen of the World* (1996).

Rubov, Paul V., 'Idea and Form in Hans Christian Andersen's Fairy Tales', in *A Book on the Danish Writer Hans Christian Andersen: His Life and Work* (1955).

Zipes, Jack, 'Hans Christian Andersen and the Discourse of the Dominated', in *Fairy Tales and the Art of Subversion* (1983).

Steiber, Ellen (1955–) American writer of fantasy novellas with fairy-tale themes. Japanese folklore permeates *Shadow of the Fox* (1994) and 'The Fox Wife' (1995), illuminating the boundaries between husbands and wives, passion and madness. 'Silver and Gold' (1994), based on *Little Red Riding Hood*, examines the allure of the wolves in our lives. 'In the Night Country' (1995) turns 'Brother and Sister' into a powerful novella about troubled teenagers. 'The Cats of San Martino' (1998) sets an Italian fairy tale in modern Tuscany. 'The Season of the Rains' (1998) works 'Lilith' legends into the story of a scientist whose heart is as dry as the desert he studies.   TW

Steig, William (1907–2003) An American artist whose cartoons in the *New Yorker* led to success as a children's book illustrator and author. Steig's stories are often talking-beast tales in which the good-hearted young protagonist displays the attributes of a fairy-tale hero(ine) in undertaking a journey and overcoming adversity with the aid of magic. He won the Caldecott Medal for *Sylvester and the Magic Pebble* (1969), the story of a donkey turned to stone because of a misguided wish, and a Caldecott Honor for *The Amazing Bone* (1976), about a pig rescued from the clutches of a fox by a bone that speaks in several languages, including at least one effective witch spell. His Newbery Honor Book *Dr DeSoto* (1982) is a trickster tale about a mouse dentist who outsmarts another foxy adversary, this one with a toothache as well as a taste for raw rodent 'with just a pinch of salt, and a dry white wine'. Although Steig has also proved adept at longer fantasies, including the Newbery Honor Book *Abel's Island* (1976), his most prolific genre was the picture book, in which spontaneous pen-and-wash illustrations project his clear plots and witty narrative with equally clear colours and witty line-work. Steig's send-ups of traditional lore are clearly reflected in *Shrek!* (1990), which includes a witch, a dragon, and a princess who is just as ugly as the dragon himself, with whom she lives 'horribly ever after'; and *The Toy Brother* (1996), a cross between *Little Tom Thumb* and the sorcerer's apprentice theme. *Shrek!* was adapted for the screen in 2001, and its great commercial and artistic success led to three sequels. Steig also illustrated his wife Jeanne Steig's fractured fairy tales, *A Handful of Beans*, in 1998.   BH

Bottner, Barbara, 'William Steig: The Two Legacies', *The Lion and the Unicorn* (1978).

Moss, Anita, 'The Spear and the Piccolo: Heroic and Pastoral Dimensions of William Steig's *Dominic* and *Abel's Island*', *Children's Literature* (1982).

Topliss, Iain, *The Comic Worlds of Peter Arno, William Steig, Charles Addams and Saul Steinberg* (2005).

Wilner, Arlene, '"Unlocked by Love": William Steig's Tales of Transformation and Magic', *Children's Literature* (1990).

Stein, Gertrude (1874–1946) American poet and writer. In the 'Transatlantic Interview' (1946), Gertrude Stein insisted that all her poetry was 'children's poetry'. Clearly, she often experimented with children's genres, such as the alphabet book. Her most famous work for children, *The World is Round* (1939), experiments with fairy-tale discourse by juxtaposing the linear narrative of a fairy tale within the tale (chapters 29–34) to the 'rounder' narrative of the book as a whole. Stein's satire of narrative and gender stereotypes in children's literature is wittily reinforced by Clement Hurd's pink-and-blue colour scheme. RF

DeKoven, Marianne (ed.), 'Gertrude Stein Special Issue', *MFS: Modern Fiction Studies*, 42.3 (fall 1996).

Rust, Martha Dana, 'Stop the World, I Want to Get Off! Identity and Circularity in Gertrude Stein's *The World Is Round*', *Style*, 30.1 (spring 1996).

Watts, Linda S., 'Twice upon a Time: Back Talk, Spinsters, and Re-Verse-als in Gertrude Stein's *The World Is Round* (1939)', *Women and Language*, 16.1 (spring 1993).

Stephens, George (1813–95) Scottish linguist and folktale collector, resident of Sweden 1834–51, professor at the University of Copenhagen beginning in 1855. Stephens edited and published collections of Swedish folk tales and songs. Together with Gunnar Olof Hyltén-Cavallius, he founded the Swedish Society for Ancient Writings in 1843, and published *Svenska folksagor och äfventyr* (*Swedish Folktales and Folk Stories*, 1844–9). This collection, having a purely scholarly purpose, never achieved the same popularity with readers as those compiled by the *Grimms or *Asbjørnsen and Moe. MN

Stevenson, Robert Louis (1850–94) Scottish writer of adventure stories and travel essays, especially known for *Treasure Island* (1883) and *The Strange Case of Dr Jekyll and Mr Hyde* (1886), both of which have become Western cultural icons. Over the course of his lifetime, Stevenson published three collections of tales. His first collection, *New Arabian Nights* (1882) includes 'The Suicide Club' and 'The Rajah's Diamond', in which Prince Florizel of Bohemia and Colonel Geraldine parody *The *Arabian Nights*' Harun ar-Rashid and his grand-

vizier. The title story of *The Merry Men and Other Tales and Fables* (1887) draws from Scottish lore, and his third collection, *Island Nights' Entertainments* (1893), contains a Faustian tale set in Hawaii, 'The Bottle Imp', in which Keawe buys a magic bottled imp and is granted all he desires, but must sell it before he dies or 'burn in hell forever'. AD

Stewart, Sean (1965–) Canadian writer of thoughtful, well-crafted fantasy novels in the tradition of Ursula *Le Guin. *Nobody's Son* (1993) is a compelling 'post-fairy-tale' story, following its commoner-hero *after* the quest is done and the princess won. *Clouds End* (1996) takes place in a vivid invented world and includes the folk tales of that land—original to the text but clearly modelled on traditional European folk tales. The 'changeling' and 'lost child' motifs can be found threaded throughout Stewart's work, in *Resurrection Man* (1995) and *The Night Watch* (1997) as well as the two novels listed above. TW

Stockton, Frank (1834–1902) American author, particularly noted for his humorous stories for adults and his fairy tales for children. Although, at his father's insistence, Stockton was trained as a wood-engraver, he soon began writing short stories in his spare time; by his mid 30s, he was supporting himself as a freelance writer and journalist. His first book of fairy tales, *Ting-a-ling* (later *Ting-a-ling Tales*), was published in 1870; rather crude and violent in comparison to his later work, the adventures of the diminutive fairy Ting-a-ling also suggest the humour and imagination that were to become his special strengths. In 1873 he was invited to become the assistant editor to Mary Mapes Dodge of the new children's magazine *St. Nicholas*. He held this position for five years, until ill health forced him to take an easier job with *Scribner's Monthly*, and continued to write for *St. Nicholas* well into the 1890s—so prolifically, in such a variety of genres, that he was obliged to adopt two additional pseudonyms. During the 1880s and 1890s Stockton was also one of America's most popular authors for adults,

Stockton, Frank The majestic griffin carries away the canon in Frank Stockton's 'The Griffin and the Minor Canon', collected in *The Queen's Museum* (1887), illustrated by Frederick Richardson. Photo: Mary Evans Picture Library.

best known for such humorous novels as *Rudder Grange* (1879) and *The Casting Away of Mrs. Lecks and Mrs. Aleshine* (1886) and for wild and ingenious short stories, sometimes bordering on science fiction. His single most famous short story was the classic teaser 'The Lady or the Tiger?'

In addition to *Ting-a-ling*, Stockton produced four volumes of literary fairy tales, most of which were originally published in the *St. Nicholas*: *The Floating Prince and Other Fairy Tales* (1881), *The Bee-Man of Orn and Other Fanciful Tales* (1887), *The Queen's Museum* (1887), and *The Clocks of Rondaine and Other Stories* (1892). His role was pivotal in the development of the American fairy tale. Before 1880 little fantasy had been written in America, even for children;

Stockton became the first American author to develop a species of fairy tale with a distinctively American character. Although he drew liberally from the stock plots and characters of European and Near Eastern folk tales, he had, he says, ideas of his own about the 'fanciful creatures' of tradition, which he consciously incorporated into his stories: 'I did not dispense with monsters and enchanters, or talking beasts and birds, but I obliged these creatures to infuse into their extraordinary actions a certain leaven of common sense.' The incongruity of common sense in a monster became not only a source of wry humour, but also a reflection of American scepticism towards the irrational. Stockton's fairyland is essentially democratic, too, despite its kings and queens;

there is little of the jockeying over status or social class characteristic of Lewis *Carroll's imaginary worlds. And while the 'fanciful creatures' may play a traditional animal-helper role in assisting the protagonist on a quest, they are in no way subject to him; often, they are pursuing quests of their own. In this, as in other respects, Stockton's fairy tales may well have influenced those of L. Frank *Baum.

Most of Stockton's tales are based on familiar folk-tale patterns. Some, the simplest, are about children who encounter a 'fanciful creature' and earn some reward from it, like the heroines of 'Toads and Diamonds' or 'Snow White and Rose Red'. A larger and more interesting group of stories is based on such tales of quests and journeys as 'The Water of Life' and 'The Seven Ravens'. In these, the protagonists are royal; their quests often take them to distant lands, where they may encounter a wide variety of creatures—from the dryads of Greek myth, to the giants, fairies, and hobgoblins of European folklore, to the sphinxes and genies of the East. The third group is farthest from folktale origins and contains some of Stockton's most original and philosophical tales. Their protagonists are of lowly social status, their problems are universal—old age in 'Old Pipes and the Dryad', destiny in 'The Bee-Man of Orn', the failure of goodness to redeem human nature in 'The Griffin and the Minor Canon'—and their outcomes are not conventional happy endings.

There is an underlying melancholy in many of Stockton's best fairy tales, and the quest-journey, his favourite plot device, is generally given an ironic twist. Quests tend to go awry, and many end inconclusively or in failure. The Bee-Man's long search for his 'original form' results in his discovery that his original form was that of a bee-man. The king, who begins his travels under the direction of a sphinx in 'The Banished King', intending to learn how to rule more wisely, never returns to his kingdom, leaving it in the competent hands of his queen. The prince of 'Prince Hassak's March' becomes hopelessly lost in his attempt to march from one kingdom to another in 'a

mathematically straight line'. The three conceited princes in 'The Sisters Three and the Kilmaree' are unable to reach the three beautiful sisters on their island until they have learned humility and built a fairy 'kilmaree', a boat shaped like a ram's horn that cannot possibly sail straight. Those characters who do succeed in Stockton's metaphor for life do not march arrogantly toward their goal; like Prince Nassime, 'The Floating Prince', they must be willing to 'float'—to be flexible and take what comes to them in their journey, and to learn from all the strange creatures they meet along the way.

SR

Golemba, Henry L., *Frank Stockton* (1981).
Griffin, Martin I. J., *Frank Stockton: A Critical Biography* (1939).
Rahn, Suzanne, 'Life at the Squirrel Inn: Frank Stockton's Fairy Tales', in *Rediscoveries in Children's Literature* (1995).
Zipes, Jack, 'Afterword', in *The Fairy Tales of Frank Stockton* (1990).

Storm, Theodor (1817–88) German novelist and lyric poet who studied law at Kiel and Berlin. During this time he fell in love with the 11-year-old Bertha von Buchan, who later rejected his proposal. For her, he composed numerous poems and his first fairy tale, 'Hans Bär' (1837), written in the *Grimm tradition. Storm gained renown for novellas of poetic realism, but he also kept on writing fairy tales, resulting from a lifelong interest in mythology and folklore. His most popular fairy tale, *Der kleine Häwelmann* (*The Little Häwelmann*, 1849), written for his 1-year-old son, is the story of a child's nocturnal journey in its cradle. 'Hinzelmeier' (1857), a tale about the choice between the philosopher's stone and the rose maiden, deviates from the traditional fairy-tale pattern in not providing a happy ending. In 1866 Storm published the book *Drei Märchen* (*Three Fairy Tales*, 1873), consisting of three tales previously published individually in magazines: 'Bulemanns Haus' ('Bulemann's House'), 'Die Regentrude' ('The Rain Maiden'), and 'Der Spiegel des Cyprianus' ('Cyprianus' Mirror'). 'Bulemanns Haus' is the uncanny tale about the literal decline of a stingy misanthropist. In 'Die Regentrude', Storm combines an old folk tale with the love story of two young peasants who are sent to wake up the rain maiden in order to avert the drought caused by her deep sleep. 'Der Spiegel des Cyprianus' is based on a theme that recurs in Storm's later works: unbridled passion as destructive power.   CS

Artiss, David S., 'Theodor Storm's Four Märchen: Early Examples of his Prose Technique', *Seminar: A Journal of Germanic Studies*, 14 (1978).

Freund, Winfried, 'Rückkehr zum Mythos: Mythisches und symbolisches Erzählen in Theodor Storms Märchen "Die Regentrude"', *Schriften der Theodor-Storm-Gesellschaft*, 35 (1986).

Hansen, Hans-Sievert, 'Narzissmus in Storms Märchen: Eine psychoanalytische Interpretation', *Schriften der Theodor-Storm-Gesellschaft*, 26 (1977).

Storr, Catherine (1913–2001) Born in London, Storr earned degrees in English and medicine, practised as a psychiatrist and psychologist from 1948 until 1962, and then devoted herself full-time to writing. Her treatment of fairy tales occurs mainly in her four books about Polly and the Wolf, beginning with *Clever Polly and the Stupid Wolf* (1955) and concluding with *Last Stories of Polly and the Wolf* (1990). In these stories the wolf attempts to capture Polly by replaying the events and conventions of fairy tales or other familiar narratives (a hijack, for example), and the theme which most commonly emerges from this pattern is that individuals achieve agency by comprehending society's cultural and linguistic codes and handling them flexibly and adaptively. Polly always wins by reordering the narrative sequence, by pushing it to a logical outcome detrimental to the wolf, or because fairy-tale conventions do not apply in the 'real' world. In 'Thinking in Threes' (*Last Stories*), she advises the wolf to read fewer fairy tales and 'face real life instead'. Here the series' pervasive scepticism about fairy tales as blueprints for life experience emerges most overtly, though the idea also surfaced in a separate collection, *It Shouldn't Happen to a*

Frog (1984), in which the main character attempts to replay four well-known fairy tales with the advantage of already knowing the tale, and discovers that to have the blueprint is not enough, as changing social circumstances produce either different outcomes or a different route to the expected outcome.   JAS

Stephens, John, *Language and Ideology in Children's Fiction* (1992).

Storr, Catherine, 'Folk and Fairy Tales', *Children's Literature in Education*, 17 (1986).

storytelling and fairy tales Fairy stories occupy an important place in storytelling. Anne Pellowski's 1977 survey revealed the existence of the activity in every part of the inhabited world. In the past, storytelling required an apprenticeship in some places, and in others it was passed down by families of storytellers from one generation to the next. Storytelling encompasses oral history, religion, mythology, legends, fables, folk tales, and fairy stories. Distinctions between the last three are blurred. Elizabeth Cook acknowledged that critics have spent much time trying to identify the differences between them. She claimed that, in fact, all three were about human behaviour in a world of magic. If this definition is accepted, then it becomes obvious that Anne Pellowski found that fairy tales were being told in countries as diverse as Russia, Ireland, China, Australia, India, and Morocco, as well as many others.

Storytelling can be defined in a number of ways. It might be regarded as telling a tale to an audience without depending on the written word, or it might be seen as taking the printed words from a book and giving them life by reading them orally to one or more listeners.

In pre-literate societies, fairy tales would be told and passed down from one generation to the next. As a consequence, the content of the stories would gradually change. Once books became more common and people more literate, fairy stories were collected in printed form. Thereafter, storytelling began to incorporate story reading, and it is likely that most fairy stories are now told in this way. That is not to say that this newer approach meets with universal approval. Some folklorists claim that a fairy story loses its power and authority once it is recorded in print, and there are still storytellers who believe that a story should be the property of its creator. Although these are minority opinions and reading aloud must now be acknowledged to be the mode, there are still powerful arguments for fairy stories being told rather than read.

One of the most convincing cases for telling rather than reading fairy stories comes from Bruno Bettelheim in his classic book on fairy tales, *The Uses of Enchantment: The Meaning and Importance of Fairy Tales* (1976). Bettelheim claimed that fairy tales should be told rather than read because their meanings are interpersonal. This applies particularly to older fairy tales as opposed to newly created ones. The ancient fairy tales have been shaped and reshaped through millions of tellings, whereas newer versions, being committed to print, are more static. Telling, claimed Bettelheim, is preferable to reading because it allows for greater flexibility.

It is clear that Bettelheim is mainly concerned with family storytelling in this respect, preferably on a one-to-one basis. This allows both teller and listener to empathize with the story and make subtle changes to it. That is not to say that the story should be used in a didactic way; the child will be able to derive meanings which are individually related. There is no need for the teller to explain the story. Although Bettelheim advocates telling rather than reading fairy stories mainly in a family setting, Eileen Colwell—herself a distinguished storyteller—also recommends this approach with larger audiences. She regards the use of a book as a barrier to the intimate relationship with the audience which the storyteller should have.

Audiences who listen to the telling of fairy stories vary from culture to culture, as do the venues for the activity. Anne Pellowski (1977) found that in some societies storytelling occurred in the workplace, at festivals, and in the street and market-place. Examples of the last named can still be found in Morocco, notably in the city of Marrakesh. Audiences in these places will at times be mainly adult, at other times mixed. In Western society the telling of fairy tales is much more likely to take place in the home or school and, to a much lesser extent, in parks, around camp fires, and in libraries. The main reason for this is probably that once fairy stories were recorded in writing they lost some of their vigour, became less frightening and more genteel, and were consequently regarded as being mainly for a juvenile audience.

Fairy stories are often thought to be mainly for young children, but in 1971 Elizabeth Cook claimed that pupils aged between 8 and 14 also enjoyed them. She mentions many of the stories from the collections by the Brothers *Grimm, *Andersen, and *Perrault in this respect, but also the more recent works of Oscar Wilde, George *MacDonald, C. S. *Lewis, and J. R. R. *Tolkien. Certainly Tolkien's books *The Hobbit* (1937) and *The Lord of the Rings* (1954–5) have been very popular in recent years. The length of both Tolkien's and Lewis's books results in most of the associated storytelling being confined mainly to reading from the books.

Many children demonstrate the ability to retell fairy stories from an early age. Arthur Applebee's study in 1973 revealed that even at the age of 2 a considerable number could make use of a formal beginning and the past tense consistently. It is, in all probability, the established pattern of fairy stories which helps children to retell them with some competence. Standardized beginnings and endings, the rapid identification of principal characters, a crisis or challenge followed by a rapid chain of events followed by a successful resolution all assist in this process, as does the frequent repetition of words and phrases.

Applebee also found that at the ages of both 6 and 9 fairy tales were the most frequently chosen stories for retelling. Among the most popular with 6-year-olds were *'Cinderella' and 'Goldilocks'. At nine the most popular choices were 'The Three Little Pigs', Bedknobs and Broomsticks', 'The Lion, the Witch, and the Wardrobe', *'Sleeping Beauty', *'The Princess and the Pea', and

*'Snow White'. A significant difference between the 6- and 9-year-olds was that the former were far less likely to be able to distinguish between fantasy and reality. They were far more likely to think that Cinderella was real or to be certain that they had personally encountered a real giant.

Some of Applebee's findings have been confirmed by Goeff Fenwick. He found young children to be enthusiastic about the retelling of fairy tales, although before the age of 5 they encountered some trouble with providing a satisfactory ending. They found fairy tales much more easy to retell than other kinds of stories, and improved with practice. Although their retellings were in the main accurate, they added their own individual touches in much the same way as adult storytellers do. For example, there might be four rather than three little pigs, the wise pig might trick the wolf by going to pick apples at '40 o'clock' in the morning, one of the pigs might be rescued from the same cauldron in which the wolf is being boiled, Cinderella's coach can be motorized, and Goldilocks might steal the little bear's teddy bear. Many children retell their stories dramatically, adopting the appropriate mode. Their growing competence often seems to influence their ability to record the same material in writing.

Jack Zipes in *Creative Storytelling* suggests that children might recognize the dynamic nature of fairy stories by being asked to provide their own endings. In addition, characters and plots from different fairy stories might be mixed up to illustrate the same point. For example, *Little Red Riding Hood and Snow White might be included in the same story. Alternatively, different versions of the same story might be considered. By these means, children are likely to understand the personal nature of fairy stories and how they can change from one telling to the next. Teresa Grainger also underlines the creative element in children's storytelling. By retelling fairy tales, they are not only demonstrating their powers of recall and comprehension, they are developing the power of their own language. Grainger recommends the use of fairy tales from

different parts of the world and suggests that children should share the telling of a fairy story or dramatize it. Nor should the audience be confined to the classroom. Children might tell fairy tales to pupils younger or older than themselves or to selected groups of adults.

The media's contribution to storytelling in Great Britain has been considerable. From 1922 until 1966 *Children's Hour*, aired each day in the early evening on British radio, told many types of stories, including fairy tales. The best-known was probably the long-running series 'Toy Town'. *Children's Hour* was particularly important during the Second World War when books and other forms of entertainment were in short supply. Another well-known radio programme, also broadcast by the BBC, was *Listen with Mother*, which was on the air weekday afternoons. Fairy tales were also a part of its corpus of stories. The programme lasted from 1950 until 1982.

For large audiences to be captured by unseen readers is an indication of the power of story. A medium even more unlikely than radio for communicating stories is television, unless those stories are dramatized. Yet from 1964 until the early 1980s, a British programme specializing in storytelling, *Jackanory*, had a weekday slot in the late afternoon. Often the readers were accomplished actors, such as the late Kenneth Williams. On one occasion Prince Charles read his own folk tale, 'The Old Man of Lochnagar'. *Jackanory* lasted for 15 minutes, an ideal time for a storytelling programme.

Storytelling associations exist in many countries. Their aims are to preserve, promote, and develop this ancient art. There has been a resurgence of interest in storytelling on both sides of the Atlantic since the early 1980s. Many groups have been formed in North America, one of the best-known being the Canadian-based Storytelling School of Toronto. The interest has been so great that National Festivals of Storytelling have been held from time to time in the United States.

In Great Britain there are a number of influential societies. One of them, the Company of Storytellers, comprises some 200 professionals who make some part of their living by giving public performances of their art. Other associations include Common Lore, the Crick-Crack Club, the National Association for Storytelling, and the Society for Storytelling. All of these groups make use of well-known fairy and folk tales, and extend the range of their expertise to material from many ethnic groups. Storytellers who have helped to extend the range of storytelling in Great Britain include Ben Haggerty, Beula Candappa, Grace Hallworth, and Duncan Williamson. The revival of storytelling might be due to some extent to a reaction against the passive nature of much modern entertainment. Although all of the associations mentioned regard work with children as being important, their involvement with teenagers and adults has demonstrated that fairy tales are by no means exclusively for the very young.

The public library service has been influential in the development of storytelling in both the United States and Great Britain. The activity can be traced as far back as 1896 in the Free Library in Brooklyn, New York, but it was probably a visit by Marie Shedlock in 1900 which gave it the impetus which resulted in it becoming established in public libraries across the nation.

Marie Shedlock (1854–1935) spent most of her life in England, becoming a professional storyteller in 1885. A versatile practitioner, she specialized in telling the stories of Hans Christian Andersen such as 'The Swineherd', 'The *Steadfast Tin Soldier', and 'The Princess and the Pea'. Her warm, natural style was a departure from the stilted dramatics of the day. She demonstrated this cleverly by telling Andersen's story 'The Nightingale', in which the song of the live bird is contrasted with that of its clockwork rival. She claimed that, to tell a story effectively, you had to convey the impression that you were part of it. Marie Shedlock made further visits to the United States, including an extended one between 1915 and 1920. Her book *The Art of the Story-Teller*, first published in 1913, is regarded as a classic of its kind.

Others noted for their work in promoting storytelling include Ann Carroll Moore and Ann Cogswell Tyler. Mainly through their efforts, storytelling became a popular feature in the public libraries of New York. In 1909, for example, stories were told to over 28,000 children in the city's libraries. Ruth Sawyer (1886–1970) also collaborated on this work. Her source was mainly Celtic and her version of 'The Voyage of the Wee Red Cap' was a much-loved feature at Christmas in the libraries of New York. Her book *The Way of the Storyteller* (1942) is regarded, like Shedlock's, as a classic.

In Great Britain, Eileen Colwell and Grace Hallworth made outstanding contributions to the development of storytelling in libraries. Eileen Colwell became a librarian in 1920, and in 1926 assumed responsibility for children's libraries in Hendon, North London, making them well known for their pioneering work. She became a friend of John Masefield, the then Poet Laureate, who helped to establish an annual festival of the spoken word at Oxford. Eileen Colwell's style of storytelling is quiet and undemonstrative, with no use of visual aids. She published several collections of stories for telling, including *A Storyteller's Choice* (1961) and *A Second Storyteller's Choice* (1963). Her range of stories includes modern tales such as Ursula Moray Williams's 'The Clever Little Christmas Tree', and the *Celtic Tales* of Joseph *Jacobs. Colwell eventually became a lecturer at the Loughborough School of Librarianship. Grace Hallworth came from Trinidad in 1957 to work in a library in Hertfordshire, where she developed storytelling, specializing in West Indian folk tales. Her book *Stories to Read and to Tell*, written in collaboration with J. Marriage, was published in 1970. Another librarian notable for her work was Janet Hill, who encouraged outdoor storytelling in the London parks in the 1970s.

Storytelling in schools in Great Britain takes place mainly in the early years. Many of the stories which teachers tell are traditional fairy tales. Beyond the first two years of schooling, the incidence of both fairy tales and storytelling decreases markedly. Thereafter, if fairy tales are employed in the classroom, they are likely to be read rather than told. Fairy tales in general are thought to be for young children.

Fairy tales play an important part in the teaching of reading. Their structure, especially the frequent repetition of words and phrases and the use of rhyme, make them ideal subjects for books within reading schemes. These books are read aloud when children are learning to read. A fairly recent innovation in the teaching of reading has been the use of Big Books. These are outsize with attractive pictures and a small amount of very large print. Many of them consist of simple fairy tales with a great deal of repetition, often with only one new word on each successive page. Several children can read a Big Book at once. They can learn the content so quickly that they can tell the stories with ease.

Teachers have not developed storytelling to the same extent as librarians, probably because they face a wider, less voluntary audience. Influenced by a statutory National Curriculum which includes both storytelling and fairy tales, there are indications that teachers are now developing considerable expertise. They have been assisted in this respect by the National Oracy Project, which was established in 1987 and which placed considerable emphasis on storytelling, including work with older pupils. Children as old as 16 were encouraged to tell local folk tales.

Both audiotape and videotape also play a part in storytelling in schools. Videotapes usually present dramatized versions of stories, whereas audiotapes use narration, often by accomplished actors, and can be used by either groups or single listeners.   GF

Applebee, Arthur, *The Child's Concept of Story: Ages Two to Seventeen* (1973).
Bettelheim, Bruno, *The Uses of Enchantment: The Meaning and Importance of Fairy Tales* (1976).
Colwell, Eileen, *A Storyteller's Choice* (1961).
Colwell, Eileen, *A Second Storyteller's Choice* (1963).
Colwell, Eileen, *Storytelling* (1980).
Cook, Elizabeth, *The Ordinary and the Fabulous: An Introduction to Myths, Legends and Fairy Tales for Teachers and Storytellers* (1969).
Fenwick, Geoff, *Teaching Children's Literature in the Primary School* (1990).
Grainger, Teresa, *Traditional Storytelling in the Primary Classroom* (1997).
Hallworth, Grace, and Marriage, J., *Stories to Read and to Share* (1970).
Howe, Alan, and Johnson, John, *Common Bonds. Storytelling in the Classroom: The National Oracy Project* (1992).
Pellowski, Anne, *The World of Storytelling* (1977).
Sawyer, Ruth, *The Way of the Storyteller* (1942).
Shedlock, Marie, *The Art of the Story-Teller* (1913).
Zipes, Jack, *Creative Storytelling: Building Community, Changing Lives* (1995).

Straparola, Giovan Francesco (*c.*1480–1558) Italian writer and poet, generally considered the 'father' or progenitor of the literary fairy tale in Europe. He was born in Caravaggio, Italy, but left few documents, so that little is known about his life. Even the name 'Straparola' itself may be a penname, for it indicates someone who is loquacious. Whoever he was, Straparola was the first truly gifted author to write numerous fairy tales in the vernacular and cultivate a form and function for this kind of narrative to make it an acceptable genre among the educated classes in Italy and soon after in France, Germany, and England. Aside from a small volume of poems published in Venice in 1508, his major work is Le **piacevoli notti* (1550–3), translated variously as *The Pleasant Nights*, *The Entertaining Nights*, *The Facetious Nights*, or *The Delectable Nights*. The collection has a framework similar to Boccaccio's *Decameron*. In this case, the tales are told in 13 consecutive nights by a group of ladies and gentlemen gathered at the Venetian palace of Ottaviano Maria Sforza, former bishop of Lodi, who has fled Milan with his widowed daughter Lucretia to avoid persecution and capture by his political enemies. The framework and tales influenced other Italian and European writers, among them Giambattista *Basile, Charles *Perrault, and the Brothers *Grimm. Of the 73 stories, there are 14 fairy tales, which can be traced to the Grimms' *Children's and Household Tales* and many other collections: 'Cassadrino' ('The Master Thief'), 'Pre Scarpafico' ('The Little Farmer'), 'Tebaldo' ('All Fur'),

Straparola, Giovan Francesco The princess talks to her serpent sister in a garden in Giovan Francesco Straparola's tale 'The Snake and the Maiden' (1550), illustrated by E. R. Hughes in the English edition *The Facetious Nights of Gian Franco Straparola* (1888). © The British Library Board (BL Gen Ref Coll K.T.C.22.c.7., Vol 1, p. 128).

'Galeotto' ('Hans my Hedgehog'), 'Pietro' ('The Simpleton Hans'), 'Biancabella' ('The Snake and the Maiden'), 'Fortunio' ('The Nixie in the Pond'), 'Ricardo' ('Six who Made their Way into the World'), 'Aciolotto' ('The Three Little Birds'), 'Guerrino' (*'Iron Hans'), 'I tre fratelli' ('The Four Skilful Brothers'), 'Maestro Lattantio' ('The Thief and his Master'), 'Cesarino' ('The Two Brothers'), and 'Soriana' (*'Puss-in-Boots').   JZ

Bottigheimer, Ruth B., 'Straparola's *Piacevoli notti*: Rags-to-Riches Fairy Tales as Urban Creations', *Merveilles et Contes*, 7 (December 1994).

Gillet, Anne Motte, 'Giovan Francesco Straparola: Les Facétieuses Nuits. Notice', in Anne Motte Gillet (ed.), *Conteurs de la Renaissance* (1993).

Mazzacurati, Giancarlo, 'La narrativa di G. F. Straparola e l'ideologia del fiabesco', in *Forma & Ideologia* (1974).

Piejus, Marie-Françoise, *Individu et societé. Le Parvenu dans la nouvelle italienne du XVI siècle* (1991).

Squarotto, Giorgio Bàberi, 'Problemi di tecnica narrativa cinquecentesca: lo Straparola', *Sigma* (March 1965).

Straparola, Giovan Francesco, *The Pleasant Nights*, ed. Donald Beecher, 2 vols. (2012).

Stratton, Helen (*fl.* 1892–1925) British illustrator who worked primarily with children's stories and fairy tales. Although she lived in Kensington, London her work was strongly influenced by the Art Nouveau school of Glasgow, particularly with regard to children's clothing and backgrounds. Her animals and birds were quite realistic. She worked both in black and white and in colour, and illustrated at least five editions of Hans Christian *Andersen's fairy tales for Blackie between 1896 and 1908, an edition of *Grimms' Fairy Tales* (1903), and finally *Stories from Andersen, Grimm and the Arabian Nights* (1929). Also notable were her watercolour illustrations for George *MacDonald's *The Princess and the Goblin* (n.d.) and *The Princess and Curdie* (1912) for Blackie.   LS

Strauss, Gwen (1963–) Haitian-born American writer and poet. In *Trails of Stone* (1989), a unique collection of poetry inspired by classical fairy tales and illustrated by Anthony Browne, Strauss gives each poem its own 'voice': 'Their Father' is told from the point of view of *Hansel and Gretel's father; 'The Waiting Wolf' from that of *Little Red Riding Hood's wolf; and 'Her Shadow' from that of the miller's daughter in *'Rumpelstiltskin'. Strauss does not simply retell the tales from the perspective of a particular character; rather, she makes of the tales psychological allegories for the inner life, exploring such issues as 'fear of love, shame, grief, jealousy, loneliness, joy'.   AD

Strauss, Richard (1864-1949) Bavarian composer, the most important successor of Wagner, who wrote 15 operas, numerous *Lieder*, and much instrumental music. His early symphonic poem *Till Eulenspiegels lustige Streiche* (*Till Eulenspiegel's Merry Pranks*, 1895) recalls the exploits of the 14th-century north German peasant clown and vagabond hero, immortalized in many chapbooks, the first appearing about 1500. Strauss's collaboration with the Viennese poet Hugo von *Hofmannsthal resulted in several works based on classical or mythological themes, including *Elektra* (1909), *Ariadne auf Naxos* (1912, revised 1916), and especially *Die Frau ohne Schatten* (*The Woman without a Shadow*, 1919). In this ambitious opera, which pays general homage to *Mozart's *Die Zauberflöte* (*The Magic Flute*, 1791), Hofmannsthal provided Strauss

with a fairy tale vaguely inspired by Wilhelm *Hauff's *Das Kalte Herz* (*The Stone Heart*, 1887), expanded by various ideas from *Goethe's *Hafiz* poems, from Bachofen's *Myths of the Occident and the Orient*, *The *Arabian Nights*, and other sources, but above all from his fertile imagination.

Hofmannsthal's verse libretto for Strauss's opera, which he also expanded into a prose narrative (*Erzählung*), is a story of enchantment set vaguely in a region called the South Eastern Islands where a certain emperor reigns. He will lose his wife, the daughter of the mysterious Keikobad of the spirit world, unless she conceives a child within 12 months—that is, casts a shadow—and at the same time he will turn to stone. The opera describes how the empress finds her shadow, or becomes fully human. Meanwhile, in the mundane and materialistic world live Barak the dyer and his wife. She has a shadow but wants to renounce it. The point is that neither the empress nor Barak's wife understands her potential for life, which is not merely the desire or the ability to bear children, but rather to have compassion and sympathy for humankind—this is to have a shadow. Strauss composes music of astonishing brilliance that well illustrates these different spheres of action. The empress in her first scene, for example, has music of shimmering coldness and translucence, emphasizing her connection with the spirit world; but Barak's music is more thickly and deeply orchestrated. Both couples—the emperor and empress, and Barak and his wife—must undergo tests of confession and repentance to become worthy of possessing a shadow. At the triumphal end of the opera, with trials completed, the two couples are shown to be worthy of love by possessing virtuous desire and purity of motive. The Dyer's wife now may properly embrace her shadow, while the empress gains her very own shadow. Strauss's glorious music interprets and elevates Hofmannsthal's marvellous tale at every stage in what may be the greatest achievement of his career and one of the most successful of all operatic fairy tales.

PGS

Del Mar, Norman, *Richard Strauss: A Critical Commentary on his Life and Works* (3 vols., 1962–72).

Mann, William, *Richard Strauss: A Critical Study of the Operas* (1964).

Pantle, Sherrill Hahn, '*Die Frau ohne Schatten*' *by Hugo von Hofmannsthal and Richard Strauss: An Analysis of Text, Music, and their Relation* (1978).

Stanwood, Paul G., 'Fantasy and Fairy Tale in Twentieth-Century Opera', *Mosaic*, 10.2 (1977).

Stravinsky, Igor Fyodorovich (1882–1971) Russian-born composer. He left Russia in 1913, living in Switzerland and France until finally moving to the United States in 1939. Stravinsky had already begun working on what was to become the opera *Le Rossignol* (*The Nightingale*, 1914), based on the Hans Christian *Andersen fairy tale, when Sergei Diaghilev, founder of the hugely influential Ballets Russes, requested a score for a ballet based on the Russian legend of 'The Firebird'. With scenario by Michel *Fokine, choreographer for the Ballets Russes, *L'Oiseau de feu* (*The Firebird*, 1910) tells of the defeat of the ogre Kashchei by the young Prince Ivan, with help from the Firebird. Written for large orchestra, Stravinsky's colourful score simultaneously looks back to the music of his teacher *Rimsky-Korsakov, and forward to the violent rhythmic innovations of *Le Sacre du printemps* (*The Rite of Spring*, 1913). *The Firebird* proved to be the first in a series of fairy-tale-based ballet scores written by Stravinsky for Diaghilev's company. Before *The Rite* came *Petrushka* (1911), with scenario by Stravinsky and Alexandre Benois, set during a vividly realized Shrovetide Fair in St Petersburg in the 1830s, and featuring the traditional figure of the fairground puppet (danced in the original production by Vaslav Nijinsky).

Following two idiosyncratic stage works based on Russian tales from the collections of A. N. *Afanasyev—*Renard* (composed 1915–16; first performed 1922), an animal fable involving Reynard the Fox, and *Histoire du soldat* (*The Soldier's Tale*, 1918)—Stravinsky composed music for the one-act ballet *Pulcinella* (1920). With costumes and sets designed by Pablo Picasso, *Pulcinella* tells a simple story involving the hero of the Neapolitan *commedia dell'arte*. The score is one of the first examples of Stravinsky's neoclassicism, based as it is on music from the Italian baroque; he later referred to it as 'my discovery of the past'. Such creative interaction with the music of previous centuries also formed the basis of *Le Baiser de la fée* (*The Fairy's Kiss*, 1928), which draws on some of the less familiar music of *Tchaikovsky, to accompany a condensed version of Hans Christian Andersen's 'The Ice Maiden'. Dedicating it to the memory of Tchaikovsky, Stravinsky conceived of the story as an allegory of his predecessor's work.   SB

Stravinsky, Igor, *An Autobiography* (1936).

Stravinsky, Igor, *Selected Correspondence*, ed. Robert Craft, iii (1984).

Taruskin, Richard, *Stravinsky and the Russian Traditions: A Biography of the Works through 'Mavra'* (2 vols., 1996).

White, Eric Walter, *Stravinsky: The Composer and his Works* (1966).

Strindberg, August (1849–1912) Swedish playwright. His early drama *Lycko-Pers Resa* (*Lucky Per's Journey*, 1881) suggested that Strindberg was familiar with narrative folklore; and various folk beliefs make their way into such late symbolic plays as *Spöksonaten* (*The Ghost Sonata*, 1907). Admiration for Hans Christian *Andersen reveals itself in *Sagor* (*Tales*, 1903), in which Strindberg imitates the Dane's whimsical and experimental use of the folk tale and *Märchen*.   NI

Mays, Milton A., 'Strindberg's *Ghost Sonata*: Parodied Fairy Tale on Original Sin', *Modern Drama*, 10 (1967).

Syndergaard, Larry, 'The *Skogsra* of Folklore and Strindberg's *The Crown Bride*', *Comparative Drama*, 6 (1972).

Stuckenberg, Viggo (1863–1905) Danish novelist who dealt mainly with intricate marital relationships. In his *Vejbred* (*The Plantain*, 1899), he demonstrates, however, a critical turn of mind that uses the tale form to censure bourgeois society. In 'Klods Hans' ('Clod Hans', 1855)—a continuation of Hans Christian *Andersen's tale—Stuckenberg reveals that the farmboy who, by his forth-right manner had won the hand of the prin-cess, has now become bored with life at court. This anti-tale concludes with the pro-tagonist eloping with a lusty country girl and, thereby, regaining his freedom. Stuckenberg offers a savage intertextual criticism of Andersen.   NI

Suárez Solís, Sara (1925–2000) Spanish writer who is best known as a novelist. Influ-enced by fairy tales, she has publicly advo-cated that *Märchen* should be revised from a feminist point of view and has published some unusual fairy tales herself. All three of them revise the story of *'Cinderella': 'Cen-icienta 39' ('Cinderella '39', 1989), 'Las Cen-icientas ya no son lo que eran' ('Cinderellas Are No Longer What They Used To Be', 1990), and 'Bibicenicienta' ('Bibicinderella', 1991). 'Cenicienta 39' brings the story of Cinderella to Spain and sets it during the years of the Spanish Civil War (1936–9). It is an ironic tale in which the happiness of those who won the war is contrasted with the calamities that befell the losers. Pili, the Cinderella in this story, is a young girl who has been mutilated by a cannon ball and will therefore never be rescued by a charming prince. More clearly feminist are Suárez Solís's two other revisions of 'Cinderella'. The author's intention in both texts is to unveil the patriarchal stereotypes that per-meate classical versions of the story, and to supply humorous commentaries, often spoken by a fairy godmother, about the re-fusal of contemporary young women—con-temporary Cinderellas—to follow the traditional patterns that contributed to their mothers' subjection.   CFR

Sutermeister, Otto (1832–1901) Swiss folklorist and professor who collected and revised numerous folk tales, legends, fables, and proverbs. His major works are *Frisch und Fromm: Erzählungen, Märchen, Fabeln, Schwänke für die Jugend* (*Fresh and Pious: Stories, Fairy Tales, Fables, and Anecdotes for the Young*, 1863), *Kinder- und Hausmärchen* (*Children's and Household Tales*, 1869), and *Kornblumen: Fabeln und Märchen*

(*Cornflowers: Fables and Fairy Tales*, 1870). Strongly influenced by the Brothers *Grimm, Sutermeister emphasized the didactic aspect of Swiss folklore and rewrote many of the tales to suit young readers.   JZ

Svankmajer, Jan (1934–) Czech film-maker, director, and artist, known for his inventive use of stop animation and surreal-istic adaptation of fairy tales. There are also strong socio-political critiques in all his films. In 1988 he produced a stunning *Alice* (*Něco z Alenky*), which brought out the dark side of Lewis *Carroll's *Alice in Wonder-land*. As is his custom, he mixes stop anima-tion with live action so that all the inanimate objects assume a threatening life of their own. Svankmajer's scintillating fairy-tale film, *Little Otik* (2000), is perhaps the most perfect film to initiate viewers into the bi-zarre happenings of the 21st century. Not only is it a dark comedy about how the Czechs stumbled into a global capitalism that may swallow them alive, but the film digs deep into Czech folklore and transforms a delightful fairy tale into a harrowing filmic critique of voracious consumerism that can be best grasped and fully enjoyed as parody. Svankmajer's film is based on the great Czech folklorist, Karel *Erben's folk tale 'The Wooden Baby', published in 1865. 'The Wooden Baby' concerns poor peasants, a nameless man and wife, who live on the edge of a village and yearn to have a baby despite their poverty. One day the husband digs up a tree stump shaped like a baby. He trims it until it looks just like a real baby. Then he brings it home and presents it to his wife, who sings a lullaby that apparently gives life to the wooden stump. The woman is overcome with joy, but the baby wants food and vast amounts of it. In fact, the baby turns out to be insatiable and soon eats his 'mother' and 'father'. And the more he devours, the more voracious he becomes. Soon he eats the dairymaid, a wheelbarrow, a peasant with his cart of hay, a swineherd with his pigs, and a shepherd with his sheep. Gigantic, the baby moves into a field of cab-bages where he begins digging up the plants. An old woman warns him to stop destroying her cabbages, and when he tries to eat her as well, she strikes him with her hoe and slits open his stomach. Out pop all the people, animals, and articles that the now dead baby had swallowed, and the peasant couple never again wish for a child. Svankmajer modernizes the story to take place in Prague during the 1990s, and *Little Otik* becomes a film about consumption and consumerism on many different levels. It is about a tree stump turned into a baby that devours his parents; it is an inverse if not perverse interpretation of the Cronos myth; it subverts Carlo *Collodi's *Pinocchio* by depicting how it is impossible for a piece of wood, that is, a piece of nature, to be tamed and civilized; and it is about unrestrained consumerism in the post-1989 Czech Republic in which consumption is related to cannibalism and barbarianism.   JZ

Furniss, Maureen, 'Adapting Alice: Two Contexts', *Art and Design* (1997).

Hames, Peter (ed.), *The Cinema of Jan Svankmajer: Dark Alchemy* (2nd edn., 2008).

Reid, Tina-Louise, 'Něco z Alenky (Alice)', in Peter Hames (ed.), *The Cinema of Central Europe* (2004).

Uhde, Jan, 'The Film World of Jan Svankmajer', *Cross Currents* (1989).

Svevo, Italo (pseudonym of **Ettore Schmitz**, 1861–1928) Italian writer of novels, short stories, plays, and essays, born in Trieste. He introduced the psychological novel in Italy with his first novel *Una vita* (*A Life*, 1892), followed by *Senilità* (*As a Man Grows Older*, 1898). Both novels were greatly admired by James Joyce, whom Svevo met in 1905, and whose influence was visible in the stream of consciousness of *La coscienza di Zeno* (*Zeno's Conscience*, 1923). Svevo had read and translated Freud's *Interpretation of Dreams*, which had a direct impact on his novels of introspection and interior monologues, and which fuelled his fascination and cultivation of fairy tales and short stories. During his lifetime Svevo published only seven stories and left many unpublished. His fairy tales have been collected in *Racconti, Saggi, pagine sparse* (*Stories, Essays, Sparse Pages*, 1968). His earliest story, 'Una lotta' ('A Contest', 1888), is a parody of chivalric romances peopled with names such as Arturo, Ariodante, and Rosina, a character keep out of *Don Quixote*. This was followed by 'L'assassinio di via Belpoggio' ('Murder on Belpoggio Street', 1890), a psychological thriller, and 'La tribù' ('The Tribe', 1897), a political allegory about the life of a nomadic tribe and its leader Hussein.

Svevo had a predilection for fairy tales and wrote *La madre* (1910, rev. 1927), a tale about chicks who are very upset because they were hatched in an incubator and do not have a mother. One of them is named Curra (*Roller* or *Runner*), for he was the first to run for food. This fairy tale symbolically depicted Svevo's relationship with 'mother' Italy who had ignored him for a very long time before his literary recognition. 'Una burla riuscita' ('A Successful Hoax', 1926) is the story of a 70-year-old author whose novel *Giovinezza* has had no recognition, thus forcing him secretly to write tales about sparrows. Another very short tale is 'Un eroe salvò una fata' ('A Hero Saved a Fairy'). In general, fairy-tale motifs can be found in most of his works and were always endowed with unique meanings.   GD

Swan, Anni (1875–1958) Finnish journalist and author of young adult and children's books. She is regarded as one of the foremost writers of fairy tales in Finland. In 1901 she published her first book, *Satuja* (*Fairy Tales*) and followed it with additional volumes in 1906, 1917, 1920, and 1923. She also translated the tales of the Brothers *Grimm into Finnish as well as *Alice's Adventures in Wonderland*.   JZ

Tabart, Benjamin (*c.*1767/8–1833) London bookseller and proprietor of the Juvenile Library who published many notable children's books including fairy tales, at a time when moral tales and books of instruction prevailed. In 1804 he began issuing a sixpenny series of fairy and popular stories, including tales by *Perrault, d'*Aulnoy, and from *The *Arabian Nights*, and also versions of chapbook tales such as Valentine and Orson, Fortunatus and Robin Hood. His 1807 publication, *The History of *Jack and the Beanstalk* was perhaps the first time this story had appeared in print. *Popular Tales* (1804), published in four volumes, included many of these. **GA**

Taglioni, Filippo (1778–1871) Italian choreographer whose *La Sylphide* (*The Sylph*, 1832) is considered the first romantic ballet. The story of a Scottish farmer whose possessive love for a sylph causes her death, *La Sylphide* became the prototype for innumerable ballets based on the motif of the fairy bride. Taglioni created the role of the sylph for his daughter Marie, whose ethereal grace and elevation made her unusually convincing in supernatural roles. He also featured her in his fairy ballet *La Fille du Danube* (*The Daughter of the Danube*, 1836) and in *L'Ombre* (*The Shadow*, 1839), whose heroine becomes a ghost. **SR**

Taglioni, Paul (1808–84) Dancer and choreographer, born in Vienna, the son of Filippo Taglioni. The younger Taglioni created over three dozen romantic ballets, several of which were variations on the fairy-bride motif first utilized in dance by his father. His *Coralia, or The Inconstant Knight* (1847), based on de la Motte *Fouqué's *Undine*, was far more faithful to the original than the earlier ballet *Ondine* (1843). Other fairy ballets included *Thea, ou la fée aux fleurs* (*Thea, or the Flower Fairy*, 1847) and

Fiorita et la reine des elfrides (*Fiorita and the Queen of the Elves*, 1848). **SR**

Takahashi, Rumiko (1957–) Japanese manga artist of several decade-long series including *Urusei yatsura*, *Ranma ½*, and *Inuyasha*. *Inuyasha* is of particular interest, as its subtitle was *Warring States Fairy Tale* (Sengoku otogizōshi), and the narrative involves a modern girl transported to the 15th and 16th centuries, adventuring with a half-dog-demon, half-human guide. Other companions in the series include a familiar shape-shifting fox found throughout Asian folklore and the more domestic 'tanuki' raccoon-dog. *Inuyasha*'s magical red robe is a reference to the 'Tale of the Bamboo Cutter', Japan's earliest fairy tale. **SCR**

Shamoon, Deborah, 'The *Yōkai* in the Database', *Marvels & Tales*, 27:2 (2013).

Tale of a Youth who Set Out to Learn What Fear Was, The (*Von einem, der auszog, das Gruseln zu lernen*) A prize-winning puppet film based on the *Grimms, and used for teaching Nazi values. In its written form the story is about a young man who has a tender heart but is such a simpleton that he cannot even understand what people mean when they talk about something 'giving them the shivers'. Reproached for his stupidity by his father, he protests that he is very willing to learn, and would like to start by finding out how to get the shivers. A sexton guarantees to frighten him inside a church tower at midnight, but that has no effect. Nor does sleeping under a gibbet from which seven bodies are hanging. The youth even passes three nights in a haunted castle, thereby winning the king's daughter in marriage, without anything giving him the shivers. Finally his new wife solves the problem by emptying a bucket of small fish over his naked body. Told like this, it embodies folk-wisdom—'He who does not know fear is a fool'—and at the same time it is a comic tale about the superiority of female tactics over male.

However, Paul Diehl's 1935 adaptation of this story gives it a different inflection. His was one of a range of silent short films made for the Reichstelle für den Unterrichtsfilm (State Office for Educational Films) and widely shown in German schools. The scene of the night in the castle, though it follows Grimm closely in parts, shows clearly this altered ideological orientation. The youth, now given the name Hans, is swift and violent in his dispatch of a variety of grotesque creatures. He skewers one on a fork and holds it over a flame. He fastens a cat in a vice, cuts its head off, and tosses it into the moat. Unlike the written text, in which the youth feels sorry for a dead body and tries to warm it up, Diehl presents him as pitiless. Since the film has no sound-track, teachers could talk over it and impose an interpretation: children were taught that the action in the film symbolized the necessity for German fearlessness in stamping out enemies of the state (Jews, gays, Gypsies, non-Aryans). In 1937 the film was given a gold medal by the government department for which it was made. Nine years later, however, a Unesco commission, charged with the task of de-Nazifying the teachers and materials that were to be employed in post-war German schools, came to a different verdict: 'Though there is nothing that is specifically subversive in this film, there is much that is typically Nazi in outlook, with its approbation of killing and force, coupled with callousness.' The film was therefore suppressed, and is today little known, despite the technical proficiency of its animation.   TAS

Lang, Andrew, *Blue Fairy Book*, ed. Brian Alderson (1975).

Warner, Marina, *Cinema and the Realms of Enchantment* (1993).

Tarrant, Margaret (1888–1959) British illustrator noted for her innovative work for the Medici Society in the 1920s. Her colour illustrations accompanied Marion Webb's poems about unusual fairies such as insects and wild fruits. Altogether 13 little books, about 10 by 13 cm (4 by 5 inches), were produced from 1917 to 1929. They featured glued-in watercolour illustrations with decorative and varied borders surrounding the illustration. Tarrant dressed her fairies in varied garb. For instance, the caterpillar in *The Insect Fairies* sported a sunshade, veil, bag, purse, and sailor's hat, and carried a seaside spade and pail.

Born in Battersea, London, Tarrant studied at the Clapham School of Art and later at Heatherley's School of Art. In 1935 she took another course at the Guildford School of Art. She began her career by designing cards and calendars, gaining her first commission in 1908 for Charles *Kingsley's *The Water-Babies*. In 1910 she illustrated both *Fairy Stories from Hans Christian *Andersen* and *Charles *Perrault's* Contes. She exhibited at the Royal Academy and the Walker Royal Society of Artists. In 1936 she went to Palestine to collect material for her work.

Tarrant produced three editions of Hans Christian Andersen stories, the first in 1917 and the last in 1949 for Ward Lock as part of the Sunshine Series. Altogether in this latter book there are 24 colour plates, some in circle form. In 'The Swineherd', she depicts the princess wearing stilts when asking the price of the pipkin, which saves the princess's feet from becoming embedded in the mud.

As an author and editor, Tarrant produced six books beginning with *Autumn Gleanings from the Poets* in 1910 and concluding with *The Margaret Tarrant Story Book*, first published in 1947. In the latter, all the stories are either traditional or by women. Her black-and-white illustrations are all shaded around the edges, making them softer and filled-in, while the colour illustrations are watercolours with washes softening the images and making the background slightly blurry, as though the reader were looking into a magical mirror.

Tarrant was considered an accessible and popular illustrator. Her illustrations were naturalistic, sometimes humorous, and warm. Besides illustrating tales by Webb, Andersen, Perrault, as well as her own retellings, she also illustrated fairy-tale books by Harry Golding (*Fairy Tales* (1930) among others) and Mary Gann's *Dreamland Fairies* (1936), which contained 35 original short stories such as 'House Goblins' and 'Garden of Dreams'. The frontispiece of the latter shows a child in a bathrobe and slippers sliding hand-in-hand with a fairy down a moonbeam. Like other original work she illustrated, this book was sentimental and often too sweet, but her illustrations never demonstrated that aspect of the text. Instead they conveyed warmth and humour.

In 1978 Ward Lock printed *Fairy Tales by Margaret Tarrant* which contained six fairy tales accompanied by 18 colour plates. These illustrations showcased Tarrant's innovative talent. For example, the first of her two illustrations for 'The Three Bears' depicts mama and papa bear facing baby bear holding his empty porridge bowl, while steam spirals up from theirs. Over this picture is a frieze-type border showing the three bears approaching a table set with three appropriately sized porridge bowls. The second illustration is a circle outlined in golden bear brown representing little bear hanging on the end of his bed while Goldilocks sleeps in it. Circular shaped pictures appear in 'The *Sleeping Beauty*', 'Tom Thumb', and 'Babes in the Wood'. Borders with additional characters complement the illustrations. The most unusual is keyhole-shaped in which Beauty bends over the collapsed Beast.   LS

Tawada, Yōko (1960–) Contemporary Japanese author who has resided in Germany since 1982 and writes in both Japanese and German. Her 1993 *The Bridegroom was a Dog*, a playful spin on a Japanese folk tale called 'The Crane Wife', won Tawada the Akutagawa Prize for new writers and established her reputation for playful reappropriation of the fairy tale as theme and literary form. She reworks Till Eulenspiegel into a stage play performed in German and Japanese (*Till*) and a Japanese short story ('Fukuchi otoko') in which the scatological trickster encounters a group of Japanese tourists.   SCR

Mitsutani, Margaret, 'Tawada Yōko's "The Man with Two Mouths"', *Marvels & Tales*, 27:2 (2013).

Taylor, Edgar (1793–1839) First English translator of the *Grimms' fairy tales. Taylor's two-volume collection *German Popular Stories* (1823–6), illustrated by George *Cruikshank, was composed, as he explained in a letter to the Grimms, with 'the amusement of some young friends principally in view'. Taylor translated a third volume of the Grimms' tales, *Gammer Grethel, or German Fairy Tales and Popular Stories* (1839), illustrated by Cruikshank and Ludwig Emil *Grimm. The popularity of *German Popular Stories* helped to make fairy tales an acceptable form of children's literature in England. However, Taylor's tales were not literal or faithful translations. Rather, they were adaptations, for Taylor took great liberties and changed most of the tales. Consequently, his so-called translations that are still in circulation today are not really representative of the Grimms' style and intentions.   JS

Blamires, David, 'The Early Reception of the Grimms' *Kinder- und Hausmärchen* in England', *Bulletin of the John Rylands University Library of Manchester* (1989).

Michaelis-Jena, Ruth, 'Edgar and John Edward Taylor, die ersten englischen Übersetzer der *Kinder- und Hausmärchen*', in *Brüder Grimm Gedenken*, ed. Ludwig Denecke (1975).

Schacker, Jennifer, *National Dreams: The Remaking of Fairy Tales in Nineteenth Century England* (2003).

Sutton, Martin, *The Sin-Complex: A Critical Study of English Versions of the Grimms' Kinder- und Hausmärchen in the Nineteenth Century* (1996).

Taylor, Edgar. *German Popular Stories*, ed. Jack Zipes (2012).

Tchaikovsky, Piotr Ilyich (1840–93) Russian composer. Although Tchaikovsky's works include six symphonies, two piano concertos, a violin concerto, and several operas, none are more highly regarded than his fairy-tale ballets; his music for *Swan Lake* (*Le Lac des cygnes*, 1877), *The *Sleeping Beauty* (*La Belle au bois dormant*, 1890), and *The Nutcracker* (*Casse noisette*, 1892) is considered incomparable of its kind. His father, a government official in the Department of Mines, allowed him piano lessons as a child, but planned a career in the civil service for him. Tchaikovsky spent seven years at the School of Jurisprudence and obtained a clerkship at the Ministry of Justice in 1859. Before long, however, he was attending classes at St Petersburg's new music conservatory, and in 1863 he resigned his unrewarding position to study music full-time. Although he became friends with Balakirev's 'Mighty Handful', particularly with *Rimsky-Korsakov, he never shared their commitment to Russian folk sources, but remained primarily oriented towards the European musical mainstream. In 1866 he became a professor of harmony at the new music conservatory in Moscow; within a few years he was a well-known, though not always successful, composer. Tchaikovsky suffered all his life from mental instability and depression, exacerbated by the need to conceal his homosexuality. In 1877 he made a desperate attempt at marriage, which ended a few weeks later when he waded into an icy river, vainly hoping to catch pneumonia, and then fled to St Petersburg in a state of mental collapse; he never saw his wife again. A far more congenial and productive relationship was his long epistolary friendship with the wealthy widow Nadezhda von Meck. Although they never met—save for a few accidental glimpses—she supported him both artistically and financially for years. When she abruptly broke off their correspondence, he was devastated. Three years later, he was dead of cholera, after drinking a glass of unboiled water—possibly, a suicide.

No one knows who had the initial idea or wrote the scenario for *Swan Lake*, but it may have been Tchaikovsky himself. Although the story is nominally set in Germany, swan maidens recur in many Russian folk tales, and Tchaikovsky had apparently devised a children's ballet on this theme for his nieces six years earlier, from which he drew the swan theme introduced by the oboe in the finale of Act I. The situation of the hero, Prince Siegfried, is even reminiscent of the composer's—only months before his disastrous marriage. The Prince, too, is reluctant to marry, though he resigns himself to his mother's command that he choose a bride at her next ball. His love for Odette, the enchanted swan, is in the romantic fairy-bride tradition, in which such a relationship represents no earthly sexual passion but the yearning for an ideal that exists only in the imagination. When he succumbs to Odile at the ball, it is only because she resembles Odette, and this unfaithfulness to his ideal brings about his destruction as well as hers. Odette loses her magical protection and they are drowned together in the lake.

The first production was not a success. The choreography was poor, and Tchaikovsky's bold attempt to realize the dramatic possibilities of the story through his music was puzzling both to the dancers and to the audience, who expected ballet to be primarily a decorative spectacle with an incidental plot. *Swan Lake* was not produced again until 1895, when it was completely re-choreographed by Marius Petipa and Lev Ivanov and its scenario revised—including the substitution of a happy ending for Tchaikovsky's tragic and powerful conclusion.

The collaboration of Tchaikovsky with Petipa in *The Sleeping Beauty*, however, was a true partnership, to a degree unheard of at that time. Petipa gave Tchaikovsky a complete programme to work from, specifying the character, tempo, and exact duration of each dance, and Tchaikovsky invented brilliantly within this framework. For dancers, Petipa's masterpiece requires, above all other ballets, the greatest command of classical technique. It is also the ballet which most strongly emphasizes its relationship with the fairy tale. Petipa uses only the first half of *Perrault's 'Sleeping Beauty'—omitting the long episode of the Prince's ogrish mother. He greatly elaborates what remains, in effect constructing a literary fairy tale of his own based on Perrault's—

assigning new names to the characters, creating additional characters and episodes, and enhancing the magical aspect of the story. (For example, Prince Florimund first sees Princess Aurora in a vision, dancing amid a band of fairies, then voyages to her castle in the Lilac Fairy's magic boat.) Petipa's homage to the fairy tale reaches a climax in the final scene (sometimes performed independently as *Aurora's Wedding*), in which characters from several other tales join the wedding celebration: the White Cat dances with *Puss-in-Boots, the *Bluebird with the Enchanted Princess, even *Little Red Riding Hood with her Wolf.

Tchaikovsky was less satisfied with the Petipa–Ivanov collaboration which produced *The Nutcracker*. The scenario, based on a simplified version by Alexandre Dumas père of E. T. A. *Hoffmann's fairy tale *The Nutcracker and the Mouse King* (*Nussknacker und Mausekönig*), seemed incoherent and pointless. Act II, for example, consisted of a series of unrelated dances performed for the entertainment of the heroine and her Prince. Tchaikovsky felt enthusiasm only for his new instrument, the celeste, which he had ordered from its Parisian inventor to play the tinkling music of the Sugar Plum Fairy. Since its unimpressive première, however, *The Nutcracker* has become the most widely performed of all ballets and, for innumerable children, an unforgettable introduction to ballet's magic world. Each ballet company has tackled the problematic scenario in its own way—two famous solutions being George Balanchine's and the Kent Stowell–Maurice *Sendak production, which attempts to reinstate Hoffmann's version of the story. What remains constant and timeless is Tchaikovsky's music.   SR

Anderson, Jack, *The Nutcracker Ballet* (1979).
Brown, David, *Tchaikovsky* (1982).
Sendak, Maurice, Introduction to E. T. A. Hoffmann, *Nutcracker* (1984).
Wiley, Roland John, *Tchaikovsky's Ballets* (1985).

Tegner, Hans Kristian (1853–1932) Danish artist and illustrator, professor, member of the Danish Academy of Arts, mainly known for his illustrations of Hans Christian *Andersen's fairy tales. His first watercolours of Andersen's 'The Tinderbox' were shown at an art exhibition in 1882. A selection of Andersen's fairy tales with Tegner's exquisite illustrations was produced in a so-called international publication (in various languages) up to 1901.   MN

television and fairy tales Television has significantly influenced the production and reception of the fairy tale during the latter half of the 20th century. Like other technologies—from the printing press and graphic illustration to film and radio—television provided a new medium for the adaptation, presentation, and consumption of the genre. Just as the technology of print publication produced the classic fairy tale and promoted the oral tale from folklore to the literary canon, so television's wide distribution of fairy tales has made the genre an enduring part of late 20th-century popular culture. A 1976 German survey confirms that contemporary knowledge of fairy tales comes mainly from television.

Before television, the reception of the classic fairy tale depended to a large degree on literacy. The televised fairy tale, however, does not essentially require that its viewers be able to read. Involving principally sight and sound, television is a visual and oral-aural medium. It has the potential to address a wider and more diverse audience than the printed tale, especially since television sets have become accessible to a broad range of socio-economic groups. Relying on performances that are visually and aurally experienced, the televised fairy tale bears some affinity to the medium of storytelling. Consequently, when broadcast to an audience, the televised fairy tale might seem to be a social event reminiscent of the oral tradition. Some broadcasts intentionally invoke this affinity by framing stories with a narrator's voice or images of a storytelling event. For instance, episodes of the American series *Amazing Stories* (NBC, 1985–7) opened with images of prehistoric people gathered around a fire and listening to a storyteller, a tableau which was gradually revealed to be a scene on a television screen, around which a modern family of viewers was assembled.

The literary affinities of the televised fairy tale, however, are equally evident. Not only does the televised fairy tale frequently draw on stories from the print tradition, it is also a scripted presentation that has none of the spontaneity or variability associated with traditional notions of oral storytelling. Similarly, viewers are clearly not engaged in a face-to-face, two-way social relationship with the narrator, performers, or creators. In this sense, although the reception of the televised fairy tale may simulate a communal event, it is in many ways a private act. Fairy-tale broadcasts sometimes recall the authority of the print tradition by beginning with the image of a book, which opens up as an authoritative voice-over intones a traditional introductory formula such as 'once upon a time'.

Like the literary fairy tale, the televised fairy tale is essentially a middle-class phenomenon. Television emerged as a viable technology after the Second World War, and in the United States the number of households with television sets grew dramatically in 1948, when nation-wide network broadcasts became possible. From the beginning, television's target audience was the middle-class family, those consumers with the means to purchase the products advertised on the broadcasts. With the post-war baby-boom, conducive socio-economic developments, and the rapidly developing role of children as consumers, the appeal of fairy tales as children's and family fare grew. At the same time, the cultural values and commercial interests it embodied were broadcast to all segments of society.

While the fairy tale is certainly a commodity in both the oral and print traditions, the commercial nature of network television has made the televised fairy tale not only a valuable commodity but also a vehicle for other commercial interests. In fact, the television advertisement itself is a form that makes frequent and significant use of the fairy tale. Fairy tales are well suited to television commercials because they are popular and easily recognized. Their familiar motifs can be truncated and adapted for brief commercials while still remaining meaningful. In Germany even the animated *Mainzelmännchen*, whose antics provide transitions among commercials during advertising segments, are reminiscent of fairy-tale characters. Moreover, basic fairy-tale elements like magic, transformation, and happy endings lend themselves perfectly to the advertiser's pitch that the featured product will miraculously change the viewer's life for the better. Products act as magic helpers who assist the heroes and heroines of the mini-fairy tale overcome whatever dilemma they face.

Much like commercials, television situation comedies have also imitated the basic plotline of the fairy tale—especially in those traditionally based on family situations. Required by generic necessity to complete its story within a limited period of time, the typical situation comedy replicates the economy of the fairy tale by using recognizable character types who experience and resolve a dilemma against a background of explicit contrasts and values. As in the fairy tale, the protagonist's happiness is achieved less through personal action than through the requirements of the genre itself. The structuralist formula 'lack-lack liquidated', which has been used to characterize the fairy tale, applies as well not only to the 'plot' of the television commercial, but also in general to the situation comedy.

The fairy tale and television situation comedy, however, sometimes differ in their utopian thrust. Whereas the classic fairy tale frequently depicts a triumph over an unjust familial or social order, the plot of the situation comedy usually restores the conventional order of family and society after it has been disrupted. So commercial television adapts the basic structure of the classic fairy tale in both advertising and the situation comedy to promote a specific notion of personal, familial, and social happiness.

The popular American programme *Bewitched* (ABC, 1964–72) actually took the intersection of family situation comedy, advertising, and fairy tale as its basic theme. The sitcom's premiss involved the marriage of an advertising executive to a witch, who promises to give up her magical powers in order to live as a mortal. While the wife's magic frequently profits her husband in his business dealings, her power also regularly disrupts the order of the family and their suburban neighbourhood. Adapting the fairy-tale witch and the supernatural maiden who is supposed to deny her true identity in order to become mortal, *Bewitched* mirrored American attitudes towards business, family, and gender during a time of shifting social values in the late 1960s and early 1970s.

As this example suggests, the fairy tale and its motifs have played a significant role in television programming. The fairy tale appears in many different formats for both children and adult audiences—from animated cartoons and dramatic series to feature films and other special broadcasts. Despite the tendency to produce adaptations that are familiar, predictable, and consistent with viewers' expectations, television has also produced remarkable adaptations that experiment with the fairy tale in innovative ways.

Relying on the fairy tale's popularity, television specials have long featured the fairy tale as mass entertainment. Since the 1950s, American networks have produced numerous musicals based on popular tales and starring well-known actors. These musical specials have included *Pinocchio with Mickey Rooney and Fran Allison (NBC, 1957); *The Pied Piper* with Van Johnson and Claude Rains (NBC, 1957); *Hansel and Gretel with Red Buttons and Rudy Vallee (NBC, 1958); *Once Upon a Mattress with Carol Burnett (CBS, 1964 and 1972); *The Dangerous Christmas of Red Riding Hood* with Liza Minnelli, Vic Damone, and the musical group the Animals (ABC, 1965); and *Alice in Wonderland* with Sammy Davis Jr., Telly Savalas, Sid Caesar, Shelley Winters, and Carol Channing (CBS, 1985). The story of *'Cinderella' has been a particular favourite on American television. Richard Rodgers and Oscar Hammerstein's musical adaptation of *Cinderella was broadcast by CBS in 1957 with Julie Andrews in the starring role and again in 1965, this time featuring Lesley

Ann Warren. In 1997 Walt *Disney Corporation and Whitney Houston produced a live action version of Rodgers and Hammerstein's *Cinderella* with pop singers Brandy and Houston cast in the title role and as the fairy godmother, respectively. Other historically important fairy-tale specials include the musical version of *Peter Pan with Mary Martin, which was originally broadcast by NBC in 1960 and rerun in 1989, and the frequent televised showings of the 1939 film adaptation of L. Frank *Baum's *The *Wizard of Oz*, starring Judy Garland. Popular telecasts such as these have played an enormous role in defining the post-war generations' experience of the fairy tale.

Echoing a European tradition that presents fairy-tale theatre during the winter holiday season, many American fairy-tale specials are broadcast between Thanksgiving and Christmas, which also makes them a significant vehicle for holiday advertising. Telecasts of fairy-tale musicals, ballets, and operas are especially common during the winter holidays on both commercial and public television. For example, *The Enchanted Nutcracker*, adapted from *Tchaikovsky's ballet and featuring musical stars Carol Lawrence and Robert Goulet, aired on ABC in December 1961 as a special production of Westinghouse Presents; and the New York City Ballet production of *The Nutcracker* was shown on CBS in December 1965. The Public Broadcasting Service (PBS) regularly broadcasts fairy-tale ballets during the Christmas season, such as its December 1972 presentation of Rudolf Nureyev and the National Ballet of Canada in *Sleeping Beauty*. Along with Tchaikovsky's fairy-tale ballets, especially *The Nutcracker*, and ice ballet adaptations of Hans Christian *Andersen's *'Snow Queen', performances of Engelbert *Humperdinck's opera *Hänsel und Gretel* are trotted out on the television screen as part of this holiday tradition. How far television networks will go to adapt fairy tales to the successful holiday format is evident in *The Trial of Red Riding Hood* (1993), a special December broadcast by the Canadian Broadcasting Corporation that adapted the classic story about *Little Red Riding

Hood and set it in the Klondike in order to create a holiday musical on ice.

Despite the conservative tendency of commercial interests to stick with proven formulas, televised fairy tales have occasionally produced technological or generic innovations, especially in the medium of animation. In 1967, for example, Hanna-Barbera produced a special presentation of *Jack and the Beanstalk* (NBC), which was the first American television special to mix animation with live action. Animation has also produced some of the most interesting generic and thematic revisions of the fairy tale on American television. In some cases, these innovations actually have their roots in films from the years before television. Just as segments of Disney's animated feature films found their way to television and more recently to home video, so have the cartoons of important animators such as Walter Lantz and the Warner Brothers studio been serialized for television and re-packaged for the home video market. These 1940s fairy-tale cartoons were televised on series such as *The Bugs Bunny Show* (ABC, 1960-7) and *The Woody Woodpecker Show* (ABC, 1957-8). With titles like 'Little Red Riding Rabbit' (1944) from Warner Brothers Merrie Melodies, these zany cartoons resist the Disney model and offer no romantic love stories or conventional morals. Instead they demystify the classic tales by mixing allusions to social trends with self-conscious irony and generic humour. These irreverent cartoons were the forerunners of Jay Ward's *Fractured Fairy Tales*, one of television's most significant contributions to the modern revision of the fairy tale. A regular feature on the popular children's programmes *Rocky and his Friends* (ABC, 1959-61) and *The Bullwinkle Show* (NBC, 1961-4), 'Fractured Fairy Tales' consisted of 91 episodes that revel in wordplay, poke fun at traditional storytelling conventions, and destroy fairy-tale illusions with irony and references to contemporary reality.

Anthology series featuring classic fairy tales are staples of commercial, public, and cable television, but they have rarely produced innovative forms of storytelling. Fairy-tale anthologies have included syndicated series like *The Amazing Tales of Hans Christian Andersen* (1954) and *Story Theatre* (1971), *Once Upon a Classic* (PBS, 1976-9), Shelley *Duvall's *Faerie Tale Theatre* (Showtime, 1982-5), and *Happily Ever After: Fairy Tales for Every Child* (HBO, 1995). None of these generated adaptations is as remarkable as those of Jim *Henson in his series *The Storyteller* (NBC, 1987). In re-envisioning nine fairy tales for television, Henson, working with puppets and actors, shed new light on traditional tales by experimenting creatively with visual and musical aspects; and he engaged viewers to a new degree by questioning the authority of the storyteller. Henson also creatively interpreted fairy tales and fairy-tale motifs in other television programmes, including *Sesame Street* (NET/PBS, 1969-), *The Frog Prince* (CBS, 1971), *The Muppet Show* (syndicated, 1976-81), and *Muppet Babies* (CBS, 1984-92).

The challenges to traditional representations of the fairy tale that are characteristic of Henson's work reflect the reassessment of the genre that began in the 1970s in European and Anglo-American society. Many cultural critics, writers, and film-makers questioned the traditional authority and values of classic tales, and looked for ways to encourage readers and viewers to regain control over the genre. For example, an innovative special on German television in 1987 encouraged public participation in re-visualizing the Grimms' fairy tales for television. In the wake of the bicentennial celebration of the births of the Brothers Grimm in 1984 and 1986, the German television network ZDF (Zweites Deutsches Fernsehen) collaborated with Japanese state television and the Goethe Institute, a German cultural organization, on a contest that invited young film-makers up to the age of 30 to submit their own video adaptations of the Grimms' classic tales. Selected videos were shown in Germany in December 1987 on a special broadcast entitled *Von Fröschen, Freaks und Video-Hexen* (*Frogs, Freaks, and Video Witches*), where they were discussed by the psychoanalyst Bruno Bettelheim.

The critical and creative reassessment of the fairy tale resulted in renewed possibilities for the genre in the 1980s. In addition to anthology series like *Amazing Stories* and Henson's *The Storyteller*, several dramatic and adventure series based on fantasy and fairy-tale motifs emerged on America's commercial networks, including *Wizards and Warriors* (CBS, 1983), *The Wizard* (CBS, 1986–7), *Werewolf* (Fox, 1987–8), and *Beauty and the Beast* (CBS, 1987–90). The most successful of these was **Beauty and the Beast*, which depicted the relationship between Catherine, a socially conscious New York attorney, and Vincent, a half-man-half-lion from a society of outcasts living in tunnels below the city. Although the series used the fairy tale to explore problems of American society and urban life, the romantic relationship dominated the series. Other dramatic series such as *L.A. Law* (NBC, 1986–94) and *thirtysomething* (ABC, 1987–91) based some episodes explicitly on fairy-tale motifs from stories such as 'Little Red Riding Hood', *Alice in Wonderland*, and 'The **Little Mermaid*'. These fairy-tale allusions were used in different ways to exploit sexual themes, to explore gender stereotypes, and to frame the baby boomers' adult rites of passage ironically in terms of childhood stories. In addition, a 1980s situation comedy entitled *The Charmings* (ABC, 1987–8) transplanted Snow White and Prince Charming to a suburban American neighbourhood, where they lived with other fairy-tale characters such as Snow White's evil stepmother, a dwarf, and the magic mirror. Unlike the much earlier situation comedies *Bewitched* and *I Dream of Jeannie* (NBC, 1965–70), which had also moved magical fairy-tale characters into suburbia, *The Charmings* did not enchant the viewing public. Unable to evolve beyond its basic premiss, it developed no significant reinterpretation of the fairy-tale genre for its postmodern era.

Since the 1980s the growth of new national networks, cable television, and home videos has also provided new opportunities for fairy-tale production and reception. Cable television has not only enabled the showing of theatrical films, it has also facilitated the production of made-for-cable series, such as

Duvall's *Faerie Tale Theatre*, and made-for-cable films, such as **Snow White: A Tale of Terror* (1996). Even important commercial television series such as *Fractured Fairy Tales* are being reprised on cable for new audiences. In addition, films and made-for-cable fairy tales can now be purchased and owned by viewers. No longer limited entirely by television programmers, consumers use their television sets to view videos of fairy-tale films that were once available to them only rarely or not at all. Viewers have access not only to the classic fairy-tale films of Disney, but also to films that move beyond theDisney model, including animated fairy-tale adaptations of the 1930s and 1940s. In the twenty-first century the American fairy-tale film series such as *Once Upon a Time* (ABC, 2011–), *Grimm* (NBC, 2011–), and *Beauty and the Best* (CW, 2012–) indicate that the 're-envisioned' fairy tales will continue to flourish on the small screen and also as DVDs. Once shown on American televisions, these fairy-tale series have spread throughout the world. As a commodity that can be purchased, owned, and privately viewed, the fairy-tale video gives the viewer a degree of freedom over the process of reception that has not been typical or possible with commercial television.

Television and the new technologies associated with it have multiplied the opportunities available for experiencing both classic and alternative fairy tales. Moreover, despite its historical reliance on predictable formulas and the influence of commercial interests, television has participated in the cultural reassessment of the fairy tale and contributed to its renewal by producing fairy tales that are technically, aesthetically, and thematically innovative. The best of these demonstrate the potential that the medium has to help us understand the fairy tale's visual and postmodern possibilities.   DH

Dégh, Linda and Vázsonyi, Andrew, 'Magic for Sale: Märchen and Legend in TV Advertising', *Fabula*, 20 (1979).

Jerrendorf, Marion, *Grimms Märchen in Medien: Aspekte verschiedener*

Erscheinungsformen in Hörfunk, Fernsehen und Theater (1985).

Odber de Baubeta, Patricia Anne, 'Fairy Tale Motifs in Advertising', *Estudos de Literatura Oral*, 3 (1997).

Schmitt, Christoph, *Adaptionen klassischer Märchen im Kinder- und Familienfernsehen: Eine volkskundlich-filmwissenschaftliche Dokumentation und genrespezifische Analyse der in den achtziger Jahren von den westdeutschen Fernsehanstalten gesendeten Märchenadaptionen mit einer Statistik aller Ausstrahlungen seit 1954* (1993).

Zipes, Jack, 'Once Upon a Time beyond Disney: Contemporary Fairy-Tale Films for Children', in *Happily Ever After: Fairy Tales, Children, and the Culture Industry* (1997).

Temple, Shirley (1928–2014) Child star from the 1930s and 1940s whose 50-odd films contain numerous fairy-tale elements. Watched over by her mother (fairy godmother) Gertrude Amelia Temple (*née* Krieger), Shirley began her film career with *The Runt Page* (1931). Subsequently, *New Deal Rhythm* (1933), *Stand Up and Cheer* (1934), *Bright Eyes* (1934), *Wee Willie Winkie* (1937), and other films cast their spells over Depression audiences who watched enchanted as Shirley, usually playing an abandoned child, magically overcame whatever personal and political problems confronted her and her friends. Shirley's films invariably ended with good triumphing over evil, wealth over poverty, marriage over divorce, a booming economy over a depressed economy—classic fairy-tale endings. Unsurprisingly, Shirley Temple described herself as a 'tiny commodity', a 'potential gold mine for Fox' in the fairy tale that is American capitalism. Lone, outspoken critics like Graham Greene, critical of Temple's flirtatious acting, were silenced in the courts.

A successful film career capped by an Oscar in 1935 was followed by a successful TV and political career. She served as narrator for two TV series, 'Shirley Temple Storybook' (1958) and 'Shirley Temple Theatre' (1961), which both included numerous fairy-tale adaptations of the classics, also made into books. In politics she held different elected positions, and in 1987 she was made Honorary Foreign Service Officer. IWA

Black, Shirley Temple, *Child Star* (1988).

Greene, Graham, 'Wee Willie Winkie. Review', in John Russell Taylor (ed.), *Graham Greene on Film: Collected Film Criticism, 1935–1940* (1972).

Tenggren, Gustaf (1896–1970) Swedish artist who emigrated to America in 1922 and had a distinguished career as illustrator and animator. Before he left Sweden, however, he had already established a name for himself with his work for *Bland Tomtar och Troll* (*Among Elves and Trolls*), a Christmas annual for children, and he did drawings for a collection of fairy tales by Hans Christian *Andersen. In America his work found quick recognition, and he provided the illustrations for a number of fairy-tale projects such as *D'Aulnoy's Fairy Tales* (1923), '1925 Fairy Tale Calendar' (Beck Engraving Co.), and *Sven the Wise and Svea the Kind* (1932), as well as some elegant drawings for *Grimms Märchenschatz* (1923) in Germany. Tenggren's illustrations, influenced by Arthur *Rackham and Kay *Nielsen were colourful, florid, and dramatic and always added a new dimension to the tales. In 1936 he went to work for Walt *Disney and designed many of the scenes in *Snow White and the Seven Dwarfs* and *Pinocchio*. After the Second World War, Tenggren abandoned animation and published numerous fairy-tale books such as *Tenggren's Story Book* (1946), *Tenggren's The Giant with the Three Golden Hairs* (1955), *Snow White and Rose Red* (1955), and *Tenggren's Jack and the Beanstalk* (1956), and he also provided drawings for many Little Golden Books, a popular and inexpensive series for children in the United States. But the work of this later period lacked the experimental flair of his early stunning work, for which he is still known today. JZ

Canemaker, John, *Before the Animation Begins: The Art and Lives of Disney Inspirational Sketch Artists* (1996).

Swanson, Mary T., 'From Swedish Fairy Tales to American Fantasy' (Diss., University of Minnesota, 1986).

Tenniel, John (1820–1914) English illustrator and cartoonist for *Punch*. Tenniel is best known for his striking black-and-white illustrations of Lewis *Carroll's *Alice in Wonderland* (1865) and *Through the Looking-Glass* (1872). *Alice in Wonderland* became the most popular children's literary fairy tale of the Victorian period. The working relationship between author and illustrator was strained since Carroll had originally illustrated *Alice's Adventures Under Ground* (1863), the prototype of *Alice in Wonderland*, while Tenniel frequently reused characters and settings from his previous *Punch* drawings. Carroll's respect for Tenniel's artwork is revealed in his recalling of the first edition of *Alice in Wonderland* after Tenniel expressed dissatisfaction with the printing of the illustrations.   JS

> Hancher, Michael, *The Tenniel Illustrations to the 'Alice' Books* (1985).
> Simpson, Roger, *Sir John Tenniel: Aspects of His Work* (1994).

Tennyson, Alfred, Lord (1809–92) English poet, central figure in the Arthurian revival, who drew from classical myth and Celtic legend to write allegorical stories about the ideals and failings of his society. He was particularly influenced by Sir Thomas Malory's *Le Morte d'Arthur* (1485), an important source for his Arthurian idylls. In his first fully Arthurian poem 'The Lady of Shalott' (1833), the lady, whose fairy nature is only referred to in passing, is drawn out of her island-world by the sight of Lancelot on his way to Camelot, and dies. In 1842, Tennyson published three Arthurian poems, 'Morte d'Arthur', 'Sir Galahad', and 'Sir Launcelot and Queen Guinevere', which would later be incorporated into *Idylls of the King* (1859). While Tennyson's poems can be read as socio-political or religious allegories, they are also reflections on art and the artist: in 'Merlin and the Gleam' (1889), Merlin the magician is the figure of the poet ('*I* am Merlin').   AD

Tepper, Sheri S. (1929–) Prolific American writer of speculative and (under pseudonyms) detective fiction. Tepper's characteristic blend of folklore with contemporary environmental and population issues is best seen in her time-travel novel *Beauty* (1991), which uses classic fairy tales like *'Sleeping Beauty', *'Cinderella', *'Snow White', 'Tam Lin', and 'The *Frog King' to structure a parable about the rape of nature in the service of anthropocentric greed. Tepper's emphatic political stance—she advocates abortion in the interest of population control and has been criticized as being anti-sex—earn her both strong supporters and detractors.   NJW

Terayama, Shūji (1935–83) Japanese countercultural poet, playwright, filmmaker, and fiction writer, who often reworked western and Japanese fairy tales into his work. In his 1965 poetry collection *Den'en ni shisu*, a spin on King Midas causes everything a man touches to grow hair. Terayama reworks *'Bluebeard' three times (1961, 1968, 1979), engaging with the entire history of reappropriation of the tale, and merging Bluebeard with Japanese tales such as the 'yamanba' narrative of an old woman sent off to die in the woods. His rendition of *'Red Riding Hood' takes the form of an irreverent mad-lib school examination.   SCR

> Ridgely, Steven, 'Terayama Shūji and Bluebeard', *Marvels & Tales*, 27:2 (2013).
> Sebastian-Jones, Marc, 'Terayama Shūji's *Red Riding Hood*', *Marvels & Tales*, 27:2 (2013).

Tetzner, Lisa (1894–1963) German-born storyteller, collector and editor of folk tales, and author of children's books. After completing her studies in speech communication at the Soziale Frauenschule in Berlin, Tetzner began criss-crossing southern and central Germany in 1918 as a storyteller. Inspired by the ideals of the socialist branch of the German youth movement and with little support, Tetzner tried to reach, help, and enlighten children who had little access to knowledge and information with the one genre that belonged to the people, the fairy tale. After six years of travelling and telling fairy tales, Tetzner reconsidered the impact of what she was doing as well as her motives and opted for less traditional storytelling in a new medium. She returned to Berlin and organized a children's radio programme in 1927.

Two years later, Tetzner collaborated with one of the leading socialist writers and critics, Béla *Balázs, in the production of a fairy-tale play, *Hans Urian geht nach Brot* (*Hans Goes in Search of Bread*, 1927), which became one of the most important proletarian-revolutionary children's plays of the Weimar period. This 'proletarian Nils Holgersson' depicts Hans Urian's fantastic journey around the world on a flying rabbit during which Hans learns about economic conditions and class distinctions. The play is far more revolutionary than its inspirational sources, which include a French novel for children, *Jean sans Pain* (*Jean without Bread*) by Paul Vaillant-Couturier. The desire to enlighten by making untenable social and political conditions transparent became the driving force behind all of Tetzner's writing.

Although Tetzner returned to fairy tales at various times later in life, both writing her own and editing collections, the years following the adaptation of *Hans Urian* into a novel *Hans Urian, oder, Die Geschichte einer Weltreise* (*Hans Urian Sees the World*, 1929), mark a turning-point in her career. From then on, Tetzner moved away from symbolic narration towards a realistic style of writing. *Der Fussball* (*The Soccer Ball*, 1932) is her first social realist story about city kids. It grew out of her contact with working-class children in Berlin who participated in her radio programmes. Both this story and her *magnum opus, Die Kinder aus Nr. 67. Kinder-Odyssee* (*A Childhood Odyssey*, 1933–49), are, as the reference to Homer's epic suggests, the work of a storyteller, not a novelist. This nine-volume work uncompromisingly chronicles the fate of a group of working-class children living in a tenement building in Berlin through 12 years of fascism and war. Most of Tetzner's books were written and published in Swiss exile, where she remained until her death.   EMM

Karrenbrock, Helga, *Märchenkinder—Zeitgenossen. Untersuchungen zur Kinderliteratur der Weimarer Republik* (1995).
Kaulen, Heinrich, and Steinke, Heidi, 'Neue Materialien zu Leben und Werk von Lisa Tetzner (1894–1963). Zum 100. Geburtstag der Jugendbuchautorin', *Der Deutschunterricht*, 3 (1994).
Zipes, Jack (ed.), *Fairy Tales and Fables from Weimar Days* (1989).

Thackeray, William Makepeace (1811–63) English novelist and author of *The Rose and the Ring* (1855). This satirical fairy story, subtitled 'a fireside pantomime for great and small children', was written to amuse his two daughters who were in Rome with him in 1853. The preface describes how they wanted to give a Twelfth Night party, but that no shop in Rome could provide 'the characters—those funny painted pictures of the King, the Queen, the Lover, the Lady, the Dandy, the Captain, and so on, with which our young ones are wont to recreate themselves at this festive time'. Thackeray thereupon drew the characters and wove a story round them. We see King Valoroso and his queen on facing pages—'Here behold the monarch sit | With her majesty opposite'; this running commentary in couplets continues through the book. Valoroso has usurped the throne of his nephew, Prince Giglio, who has been encouraged to lapse into a state of unambitious indolence. At Giglio's christening the gift of Fairy Blackstick—bored with necromancy after two or three thousand years—merely had been that he should have 'a little misfortune'. She had made a similar wish at the christening of Princess Rosalba of Crim Tartary, whose identity is lost when she is a small child, and who becomes maid to Princess Angelica, Valoroso's daughter. The rose and the ring are gifts that Blackstick had once bestowed on godchildren, and have been passed on; they have the power of making wearers seem attractive—even the lumpish Prince Bulbo who comes to woo Angelica.

There are many subsidiary comic characters, among them the hideous Countess Gruffanuff and her husband, porter at Valoroso's palace, who is turned into a door knocker by Blackstick as a punishment for his insolence. The story is labyrinthine in its complexity, and the only moral is a flippant one; Giglio grasps that to be attractive he must have education. He departs for 'Bosforo' (Oxford) where he studies assiduously, then discards his books and goes off to win back his throne. The story finishes with the marriages of Giglio and Rosalba (their respective misfortunes now ended) and of Bulbo and Angelica, Gruffanuff's husband having ceased to be a door knocker just in time to prevent the marriage of the Countess to Giglio, who had once unguardedly proposed to her.   GA

Sorensen, Gail D., 'Thackeray's "The Rose and the Ring": A Novelist's Fairy Tale', *Mythlore*, 15.3 (spring 1989).

Tremper, Ellen, 'Commitment and Escape: The Fairy Tales of Thackeray, Dickens, and Wilde', *The Lion and the Unicorn*, 2.1 (1978).

Thief of Baghdad, The A title which has been used by a cluster of oriental fantasies exploiting the iconography of The *Arabian Nights*—winged horses, omnipotent sorcerers, magic lamps, jinn in bottles, veiled princesses, precious flowers and, above all, flying carpets. Within this context, each production was inflected to catch the mood of the moment.

The first *Thief* was that of Douglas Fairbanks who, in 1924, as producer and star, used Baghdad as a setting for spectacle, morality, and his personal athleticism. The arrogant, flamboyant thief flouts religion and all forms of authority until he sets forbidden eyes on the Princess. Then, pretending to be a prince, he wins her love but is driven to confess the truth to a Holy Man, who sends him on a long, hazardous journey for a magic chest. Only through struggle and penitence will he earn happiness. Finally overcoming all obstacles, he returns on a flying carpet just in time to rescue Baghdad and the Princess from a Mongol invasion.

In 1939, 15 years later, work began on another *Thief*. This was intended by the producer Alexander Korda to show the world that the UK could make films just as colourful and enchanting as those from Hollywood. One of the rivals in Korda's mind was *Snow White*; he boasted that he could do with living actors what Disney had done with drawings. Korda's thief is Abu, a

boy of the Baghdad streets who helps a young king, Ahmad, escape the wicked schemes of Jaffar, the Grand Vizier. In Basra, Ahmad sets forbidden eyes on the Sultan's daughter, and they fall in love, but she has been promised to Jaffar. Through Jaffar's magic Ahmad is blinded, and Abu turned into a dog, until the Princess releases them from the spell by agreeing to marry Jaffar. With the help of a giant jinni, Abu steals the All-Seeing Eye and returns to Baghdad on a flying carpet just as Ahmad is about to be beheaded. Ironically, this film that sought to outdo Hollywood had to move there when the outbreak of war made continued shooting in England impossible. Despite this rupture, the finished film won an Oscar for its achievement in creating Technicolor opulence, magical feats, and the djinni's enormous size.

The start of the 1960s saw a third foray into *Thief* territory; *Il Ladro di Bagdad*, an Italian-French co-production shot in CinemaScope using Tunisian locations, had an American director, Arthur Lubin (who had made the wartime version of *Ali Baba and the Forty Thieves*). The reason for the film's existence was, however, not Lubin but its muscleman star, Steve Reeves. In the early 1950s Reeves got into films through winning the titles 'Mr World' and 'Mr Universe'. Before taking on the role of Karim the thief, he had appeared variously as Hercules, Goliath, and other giant characters. The storyline harks back to Fairbanks in that it gives Karim a series of redemptive tests of character and skill to undergo—hostile trees, burning swamps, sudden floods, a beautiful nymphomaniac—as he searches for the Seven Gates where the blue rose grows which alone will restore the princess to health. Unlike Hercules and Goliath, Karim does not triumph through muscle power alone: thanks to his friendship with a magician, he sometimes uses a vanishing cloak to escape danger, and at the climax is able, by rubbing a magic ring, to summon to his aid an army of acrobats.

This periodic appearance of *Thief* films culminated at the end of the 1970s with a UK–France co-production in 1978, and a

UK-only variant called *Arabian Adventure* a year later. Inspired by the recent world-wide success of special effects movies such as *Superman*, which was sold on the promise that cinema-goers would believe a man could fly, these two films used the same techniques to convince audiences that a carpet could fly.   TAS

Thompson, Alfred (pseudonym of **Thompson E. Jones**, 1831–95) British musical theatre librettist and artist. Thompson studied art at Munich and Paris and was soon one of the most innovative costume and scenic designers of the musical stage, in particular for fantasy burlesques and pantomines. He began writing stage pieces in the 1860s and provided some of the most literate early British music-theatre pieces. Continuing to design, Thompson spent the next 30 years in the London and New York theatre and helped to establish the look and style of the musical entertainment of that era. Many of his scripts and designs celebrated fantasy and famous fairy tales, including *The Lion's Mouth* (London, 1867), *Aladdin II, or An Old Lamp in a New Light* (London, 1870), *Cinderella the Younger* (London, 1871), *Belladonna, or The Little Beauty and the Great Beast* (London, 1878), *Pepita, or The Girl with the Glass Eyes* (New York, 1886), *The Arabian Nights, or Aladdin's Wonderful Lamp* (New York, 1887), and *The Crystal Slipper, or Prince Prettywitz and Little Cinderella* (New York, 1888).   TSH

Thompson, Ruth Plumly (1891–1976) American author of juvenile literature and *Oz* books. L. Frank *Baum's death in 1919 posed a financial problem: who would continue his lucrative *Wizard of Oz* series, so recently recuperated from a First World War sales slump? Thompson was children's editor of the *Philadelphia Public Ledger* when she became the Second Royal Historian of Oz. She carried on the tradition of a new *Oz* book for Christmas for 19 consecutive years, writing five more novels than Baum himself. Her first title (*The Royal Book of Oz*, 1921) was supposedly edited from his notes. This false statement plus the continuation of John

R. *Neill as illustrator eased the transition between authors.

But while the artwork remained the same, Thompson's sequels differed. Her brisk-yet-poetic style full of wordplay was more polished and featured regularized spellings ('Gnome' instead of 'Nome'). She also preferred boys as protagonists. But while she rivalled Baum in creating fanciful places (Bafflesburg, Pumperdink) and colourful characters (Jinnicky the Red Jinn, Kabumpo the Elegant Elephant), her imagination was not as unleashed. Baum's tales were largely original; her enchanted objects and royal weddings recalled *The *Arabian Nights* and European fairy tales, while characters like Captain Salt, Realbad, and the Yellow Knight clearly imitated Long John Silver, Robin Hood, and Don Quixote. Finally, Thompson's references to contemporary culture, while popularizing her titles, rendered them less timeless than Baum's fantasy.

In addition to writing novels, Thompson actively marketed them. She revived characters to increase backlist title sales and wrote promotional playlets. Although the Baum heirs prohibited her from recording Oz stories, her radio contest promoting 'The Enchanted Tree of Oz' (1926–7), for which children submitted their own endings to her unfinished tale, was especially popular. But her shrewdest marketing came in 1939. Foreseeing the impact of the upcoming MGM musical, she negotiated with Walt *Disney Studios about animating Oz, but Baum's widow had already sold the rights. She then capitalized on the film by reprising original characters and scenes for *Ozoplaning with the Wizard of Oz* (1939). Literally offering a bird's eye view of a miniaturized Oz, it seems to presage the books' diminished role in defining Oz in the public imagination.

Thompson passed on the mantle of Royal Historian to the illustrator Neill in 1939. Her plots were repeating; she was straining their juvenile perspective; and she tired of contract disputes about her other fairy tales and (ghost-written) Disney books. She retired to freelance for *Jack and Jill* children's magazine and write fairy-tale scripts for radio and television. Two later Oz novels and a collection of poetry (*Yankee in Oz*, 1972; *The Enchanted Island of Oz*, 1976; *The Curious Citizens of Oz*) were published by the International Wizard of Oz Club.   MLE

Greene, David L., and Martin, Dick, *The Oz Scrapbook* (1977).

Hearne, Michael Patrick, 'Ruth Plumly Thompson', *American Writers for Children* (1983).

Snow, Jack, *Who's Who in Oz* (1954).

Thorpe, Benjamin (1782–1870) British philologist, Anglo-Saxon scholar, and translator. In 1851 his three-volume *Northern Mythology*, which included a selection of Scandinavian literary and folk legends, acquainted the British public with trolls, water sprites, and other Norse supernaturals. In 1853 a companion volume, *Yule-Tide Stories*, helped popularize Scandinavian fairy tales in England. Thorpe retold Northern versions of such popular tales as **'Jack and the Beanstalk' and *'Rumpelstiltskin'*, noting their analogues. His translations of less-known stories like 'The Beautiful Palace East of the Sun and West of the Moon', a Swan Maiden tale, influenced Victorian authors including William *Morris.   CGS

Thousand and One Nights, The See ARABIAN NIGHTS.

'Thumbelina' (or **'Inchelina'**) The diminutive person, only the size of a thumb or of an inch, is a character who commonly appears in fairy tales, for example **'Little Tom Thumb'* (1621) or 'Le Petit Poucet' (1697), but its best-known representation is Hans Christian *Andersen's 'Tommelise' (1836), which relates a tiny young woman's trials and tribulations until she is united with a prince of her own size. The Andersen tale is a coming-of-age story that not only chides society for narrow-mindedness, but also suggests that one may be better off with one's own kind.   NI

Thurber, James (1894–1961) American writer and illustrator; he moved to New York from Ohio in 1933 and became one of the great writers of humour for the *New Yorker*. Known for his irony and wit, Thurber produced the satirical 'The Girl and the Wolf', one of the most remarkable versions of **'Little Red Riding Hood'*, in his unique collection *Fables for our Time* (1940). Here the girl shoots the wolf with a revolver, and the story ends with a moral: 'Little girls are not so easy to fool nowadays as they used to be.' Although most of Thurber's ironic fables and sketches were intended for adults, he also wrote four charming fairy-tale books for young readers: *Many Moons* (1943), *The Great Quillow* (1944), *The White Deer* (1945), and *The Thirteen Clocks* (1950). Of these books, *Many Moons*, in which a fragile princess uses great inner resources to overcome the forces of a castle that threatens to envelop her, is regarded as his best work. Thurber's gloomy view of humankind, however, is more dominant in his other fairy-tale work, where his satire tends to subvert the traditional happy ending of his narratives.   JZ

Holmes, Charles, 'James Thurber and the Art of Fantasy', *Yale Review*, 55 (1965).

Long, Robert, *James Thurber* (1988).

Maharg, Ruth, 'The Modern Fable: James Thurber's Social Criticisms', *Children's Literature Association Quarterly* (1984), 9.

Morsberger, Robert, *James Thurber* (1964).

Tieck, Ludwig (1773–1853) One of the earliest German romantic writers to develop the literary potential of fairy tales. Tieck was born in Berlin, a city with a dynamic literary culture and enhanced opportunities for the middle class. His father, a master ropemaker, who was himself widely read, encouraged his son's literary inclinations and saw to it that he was well educated and poised to rise above his family's social station. From 1782 to 1792 Tieck attended the respected   Friedrich-Werder-Gymnasium, where he developed a close friendship with Wilhelm Heinrich *Wackenroder, another important figure in early German romanticism. During this time Tieck completed diverse literary efforts of his own, including fairy tales, and assisted with the literary projects of his teachers, who recognized his talent.

After studying philology and literature at the universities in Halle, Göttingen, and Erlangen from 1792 to 1794, Tieck embarked on a career as a professional writer. He returned to Berlin, where he remained until 1799, writing moralistic-satiric tales as a hack writer for the Enlightenment publisher Friedrich Nicolai, but also publishing his own innovative fairy tales and fantasy. Throughout the rest of his life, Tieck was able to gain a livelihood as a writer and theatre director in Ziebingen, Dresden, and Berlin.

Tieck worked in many literary genres, including lyrical poetry, novels, novellas, plays, libretti, and adaptations of folk tales, legends, and chapbooks. He also penned critical essays, produced important translations of writers such as Miguel de Cervantes and William *Shakespeare, and edited medieval German texts and the writings of contemporaries such as *Novalis and Heinrich von Kleist. Fairy-tale elements pervade much of Tieck's work, whatever the genre, and are found in his earliest, unpublished literary attempts, as well as in later writings. As early as 1790, at the age of 17, he had written at least two fairy-tale plays in the manner of the Italian writer Carlo *Gozzi: *Das Reh* (*The Deer*) and *König Braddeck* (*King Braddeck*). Nearly half a century later Tieck continued to experiment with the fairy tale in stories like 'Die Vogelscheuche' ('The Scarecrow', 1835), which not only combined novella and fairy tale, but also mixed this romantic hybrid with drama.

Tieck is best known for the fairy-tale novellas and satirical fairy-tale plays that he published in three collections: *Volksmärchen* (*Folktales*, 1797), *Romantische Dichtungen* (*Romantic Works*, 1799–1800), and *Phantasus* (1812–16). The last of these, *Phantasus*, combines selections from the two earlier collections with new works and weaves them into a frame story in which upper middle-class and aristocratic characters read these poetic works to one another in the course of their literary and cultural conversations. The traditional device of the frame story enabled Tieck to emphasize the literary and social contexts in which his stories and plays were produced and consumed. As a professional writer, Tieck was acutely aware that his literary works were commodities, and this self-awareness expresses itself ironically in his writings, which play with readers and their expectations. When he represented his 1797 collection as *Folktales*, 'edited by Peter Leberecht' (a pseudonym), Tieck was toying with his readers' expectations of the genre and ironically underlining the unmistakable literary character of his innovative fairy tales.

Tieck's fairy-tale plays, which sometimes portray their own audiences, exhibit a high degree of literary self-consciousness and playfulness. Plays like *Der gestiefelte Kater* (*Puss-in-Boots*, 1797), *Die verkehrte Welt* (*The Topsy-Turvy World*, 1799), and *Prinz Zerbino* (1799) not only satirize and parody literary conventions of the Enlightenment, but repeatedly break the dramatic illusion in order to question the distinctions artists and spectators make between fantasy and reality. Literary and socio-political satire also characterize Tieck's other fairy-tale plays, which include *Der Blaubart* (*Bluebeard*, 1797), *Rotkäppchen* (*Little Red Riding Hood*, 1800), *Däumling* (*Thumbling*, 1812), and *Fortunat* (1816).

Tieck's fairy-tale novellas challenge perceptions and question conventional truths by disrupting the reader's expectations of the fairy tale itself. In tales like 'Der blonde Eckbert' ('Blond Eckbert', 1797), 'Der Runenberg' ('Rune Mountain', 1804), and 'Die Elfen' ('The Elves', 1812), reality and fantasy do not blend seamlessly, as in conventional fairy tales. Instead, reality and fantasy are juxtaposed, and when they do merge, the results are disorienting and disastrous. Whereas the stereotypical fairy tale leads its hero towards social and psychological integration, Tieck's tales generally depict alienated characters who experience psychological disintegration. In 'Blond Eckbert', for instance, the title character seeks to overcome his solitary life by confiding his innermost secrets to others; but introspection and confession only reveal a more horrible truth, which plunges Eckbert into utter insanity. In 'Rune Mountain' the main character Christian escapes from the ordered life that oppresses him by seeking higher truths in nature and the supernatural; however, in the end the reader is uncertain whether Christian has been liberated by a higher consciousness or suffers from insane delusions. Tales of this kind, which explore unresolved ambiguities and the dark side of the romantic imagination, distinguish Tieck's stories not only from the didactic moral tales of the Enlightenment, but also from the utopian tales of romantic writers like Novalis.

Neither moralist nor prophet, Tieck was a professional writer who sought to burst his readers' illusions even as he sought to sell them new ones. By incorporating this paradox into his work, he created a literary fairy tale that embodied the aesthetic, social, and existential contradictions of his age. With irony, playfulness, and profound ambiguity he created the romantic prototype of the modern fairy tale. DH

Birrell, Gordon, *The Boundless Present: Space and Time in the Literary Fairy Tales of Novalis and Tieck* (1979).

Haase, Donald P., 'Ludwig Tieck', in E. F. Bleiler (ed.), *Supernatural Fiction Writers: Fantasy and Horror*, i (1985).

Jäger, Hans-Wolf, 'Trägt Rotkäppchen eine Jakobinermütze? Über mutmassliche Konnotate bei Tieck und Grimm', in Joachim Bard (ed.), *Beiträge zur Praxis* (Literatursoziologie, ii, 1974).

Lillyman, William J., *Reality's Dark Dream: The Narrative Fiction of Ludwig Tieck* (1979).

Thalmann, Marianne, 'The Tieck Fairy Tale', in *The Romantic Fairy Tale: Seeds of Surrealism* (1964).

Tolkien, J. R. R. (John Ronald Reuel Tolkien, 1892–1973) British author and scholar, best known for his works of fantasy, *The Hobbit* and *The Lord of the Rings*. Though his first three years were spent in South Africa, Tolkien and his younger brother Hilary grew up in an English country village and, after 1900, in Birmingham, where he attended King Edward's School. There he discovered a love of languages—Old English, Gothic, Welsh, Finnish—and began to invent his own. His widowed mother was disowned by her family after her conversion to Catholicism, and when she died in 1904 she named as her two sons' guardian a friendly priest who lodged them in a boarding house. At 16 Tolkien met and fell in love with Edith Bratt, whom he married eight years later. After obtaining a degree in English language and literature from Oxford, he served in the First World War as a signals officer. While he was in the trenches of Flanders, he created a mythology and world based on Elvish languages that he had invented to help keep him sane. After the war, he went on to teach at the University of Leeds and then at Oxford, where he remained until his retirement, achieving an admirable reputation as a scholar in Anglo-Saxon and medieval literature. Among his important works were a definitive edition of *Sir Gawain and the Green Knight* (1925) and his essay '*Beowulf*: The Monsters and the Critics' (1936). In private, he worked on The Silmarillion, a mythological epic of his imagined Middle-Earth, and told stories to his four children. One of the tales became *The Hobbit* (1937). Urged by his publisher to produce a sequel, Tolkien began what soon developed into something darker and far more complex, *The Lord of the Rings*. The coming of the Second World War nearly halted his slow progress, and only the encouragement of his friend C. S. *Lewis and his son Christopher enabled him to complete the three-volume work, published in 1954–5. The 1965 paperback publication of 'The Trilogy' (as early enthusiasts named it) transformed it into a best-seller, particularly on college campuses. Tolkien was still at work on The Silmarillion when he died; it was published and edited by Christopher Tolkien in 1977.

As a child, Tolkien loved George *MacDonald's 'Curdie' books and the fairy-tale collections of Andrew *Lang. Although Bilbo Baggins of *The Hobbit* is not the usual fairy-tale protagonist—not a handsome youngest son, but a plump, middle-aged hobbit of Middle-Earth—he finds himself on a classic quest journey with a group of dwarfs who hope to recover their ancestral treasure from the dragon of the Lonely Mountain. His first adventure, an encounter with three hungry trolls, is closely modelled on those Scandinavian folk tales in which a troll's attention is distracted till the rising sun turns him into stone. His second—in the underground realm of the goblins—recalls Curdie's exploits underground in *The Princess and the Goblin* (1871). The ring of Invisibility that Bilbo finds there seems at first no more than the usual handy magical device. As the story progresses, however, it becomes more original, more serious in tone, and more akin to saga and heroic legend than to folk tale. The expected fairy-tale outcome, in which Bilbo would somehow slay the dragon and win the treasure, is deliberately subverted. A minor character kills the dragon; the unguarded treasure brings dwarfs, elves, and men to the brink of war; and Bilbo's greatest heroic feat is not one of violence but of renunciation, in which he risks his life to make peace. He wins no princess and only a modest share of treasure; his greatest reward is the new self he has realized and his rich store of memories.

The Lord of the Rings amplifies and darkens the pattern of *The Hobbit*. Again, a hobbit sets forth on a quest with his companions, surviving many perilous adventures to reach a lonely mountain. In this fairy-tale novel for adults, however, an act of renunciation becomes the goal. Bilbo's ring has been revealed as a deadly Ring of Power, which its master Sauron is seeking. He intends to enslave all of Middle-Earth with it, and Bilbo's nephew Frodo must reach the mountain where it was forged in order to destroy it forever. Tolkien's work is equally remarkable for the depth of its moral vision and the quality of its imaginary world, whose complexity, detail, and consistency create for the willing reader the illusion of a real yet enchanted universe.

Both the cultural and the literary influence of *Lord of the Rings* have been considerable. Adult fantasy, all but extinct before its startling success, is today a flourishing mainstay of the publishing industry. And although much post-Tolkien fantasy has been weakly imitative, some of today's most original writers—including Diana Wynne *Jones and Ursula K. *Le Guin—have acknowledged Tolkien as a source of inspiration. In *Strategies of Fantasy*, Brian Attebery identifies *The Lord of the Rings* as our 'mental template' for fantasy, suggesting that works we now generally recognize as fantasy share its salient characteristics: violation of natural law, comic structure (that of the traditional fairy tale), and sense of wonder. In the late 1960s, the alternative reality of Middle-Earth endeared Tolkien to the counter-culture, while the ease with which that reality lends itself to role-playing led to the creation of games like 'Dungeons and Dragons' and its successors, as well as the pioneering text-based computer game 'Adventure'.

Tolkien is important not only as a practitioner but as a theorist of fantasy. Two of his short tales, 'Leaf by Niggle' (in *Tree and Leaf*, 1964) and *Smith of Wootton Major* (1967) deal symbolically with the nature of fantasy and the artist who creates it. His influential 1939 essay 'On Fairy-Stories' expresses analytically what 'Leaf by Niggle' says in story. Tolkien argues that the fairy tale is not inherently 'for children' but for adults as well. He defends the making of imaginary worlds as divinely sanctioned 'sub-creation', and suggests that the special significance of the fairy tale lies in its distinctive qualities of Fantasy, Escape, Recovery, and Consolation. For Tolkien, the 'eucatastrophe', in which the story turns suddenly from sorrow to joy, is the defining moment of the fairy tale.   SR

Attebery, Brian, *Strategies of Fantasy* (1992).
Carpenter, Humphrey, *Tolkien: A Biography* (1977).
Drout, Michael (ed.), *J. R. R. Tolkien Encyclopedia: Scholarship and Critical Assessment* (2006).
Lobdell, Jared (ed.), *A Tolkien Compass* (1975).
Shippey, T. A., *The Road to Middle-Earth* (1983).
Shippey, T. A., *J. R. R. Tolkien: Author of the Century* (2000).

Tolstoy, Aleksei (1882/3–1945) Russian novelist. He wrote *The Golden Key, or The Adventures of Burattino* (1935), the Russian version of *Pinocchio*, far more famous in Russia than the original. Instead of the individual dilemma of Pinocchio, striving to become a real boy, Tolstoy focuses on the collective achievements of a group of puppets, revolting against the tyrannical puppeteer and becoming their own masters. The adventure and struggle are highlighted, while the philosophical and existential aspects of *Collodi's novel are deleted. Burattino has become one of the most popular characters of Russian children's literature, almost a national hero.   MN

Tolstoy, Lev (1828–1910) Russian writer, most famous for his novels *War and Peace* and *Anna Karenina*, but also the author of many fairy tales for children. Tolstoy was an ardent educationalist and used the fairy-tale form for didactic and educational purposes. In the 1860s and 1870s he opened several rural schools and published a number of school primers, which mostly contain retellings of folk and fairy tales from all over the world: fables, animal tales, magical tales, and some local aetiological tales. These collections were addressed to peasant children and are very simple in structure and style. When using well-known plots, such as *'Little Tom Thumb', Tolstoy often followed Russian chapbooks rather than *Perrault, and he always described Russian peasant settings in detail. However, he also included in his collections several oriental and Arabian fairy tales, retaining and accentuating their exotic settings. The source of many of his fairy tales are to be found in the collections of the famous Russian folklorists *Afanasyev and Khudyakov. Some of the more complicated and original fairy tales, involving criticism of social injustice, such as 'The Tale of Ivan the Fool' (1885), were banned because of their disrespectful portrayal of Tsars, the state, and the clergy.

Tolstoy's most popular fairy tale, 'The Three Bears' (1872), is a version of 'Goldilocks', which also appears as a subtext in the novel *Anna Karenina*.   MN

'Tom Thumb' *See* 'LITTLE TOM THUMB'.

Topelius, Zacharias (1818–98) Finno-Swedish writer, the creator of Swedish and Finno-Swedish children's literature and especially fairy tale. He was professor of history and later Chancellor of Helsinki University. He also wrote poetry, drama, and historical novels. His *Läsning för barn* (*Reading Matter for Children*, 8 vols., 1865–96) contains a variety of magical tales, moral tales, animal tales, and retellings of traditional tales. Everyday settings and events are intertwined in them with romantic and fantastic motifs to suit the educational purposes of the time. His best-known fairy tales, such as 'Sampo Lappelill' ('Sampo the Little Lapp Boy'), 'Knut spelevink' ('Knut the Musician'), or 'Kyrktuppen' ('The Church Weathercock'), are clearly influenced by Hans Christian *Andersen.   MN

Tournier, Michel (1924–) French author of mythical, multi-layered narratives for adults and children. He was the son of Germanicists, and his family was deeply affected by the Second World War. He experienced at first hand the rise of Nazism in Germany, the adulation by some Frenchmen of their conquerers, the appropriation of his home as Nazi headquarters, and the round-up of fellow villagers for concentration camps. He would later record these reactions and interview prisoners of war in *Le Roi des Aulnes* (translated as both *The Erl King* and *The Ogre*, 1970). He studied philosophy, initially in Paris. After defending his Sorbonne thesis on Plato in 1946, he studied German philosophy at the University of Tübingen and returned in 1950 to take the *agrégation* (the highly competitive examination leading to secondary- and university teaching positions). Ironically, it is because he failed this exam that he eventually turned to literature. He drifted about post-war Paris for a few years, attended ethnology lectures by Lévi-Strauss, translated the novels of Erich Maria Remarque, and edited texts at a Paris publishing house. He then became a radio announcer for Europe Numéro Un (which he would later write about in 'Tristan Vox', 1978), and from 1960–5 hosted a television series called 'La Chambre noire' ('The Black Box'). Photography remains Tournier's passion: he co-founded an international photographic society and has written numerous texts to accompany other photographers' work. The photographic image is also a recurrent theme in his short stories and novels like 'Les Suaires de Véronique' ('Veronica's Shrouds', 1978) and *La Goutte d'or* (*The Golden Droplet*, 1985).

It was not until the age of 43, however, that Tournier began his career as a writer. His first novel won the French Academy's Grand Prix du Roman for *Vendredi ou Les Limbes du Pacifique* (*Friday or The Other Island*, 1967), a metaphysical reworking of *Robinson Crusoe* by way of Freud, Sartre, and Lévi-Strauss. Three years later, by the first-ever unanimous vote, he won the Prix Goncourt for *The Erl King*, his mythic treatment of Nazism. He is a member of the Académie Goncourt and winner of the Prix Goethe, whose other major works include *Les Météores* (*Gemini*, 1975), an intellectual autobiography entitled *Le Vent Paraclet* (*The Wind Spirit*, 1977), and fictionalized accounts inspired by history such as *Gilles et Jeanne* (1983), about Gilles de Rais and Joan of Arc; *Gaspard, Melchior et Balthazar* (*The Four Wise Men*, 1980), which draws from Bible stories; and *Eléazar ou La Source et le buisson* (*Eléazar or The Spring and the Bush*, 1996), a metaphysical interpretation of Moses. He has published travel books about Canada, Madagascar, and Weimar, and written numerous essays on photography (*Des Clefs et des serrures* (*About Keys and Locks*) also translated as *Waterline*, 1979), reading (*Le Vol du vampire* (*Flight of the Vampire*, 1981)), and art criticism (*Le Tabor et le Sinai*, 1988). Tournier also has several short-story collections for adults and for children including *Le Coq de bruyère* (*The Fetishist*, 1978), *Le Médianoche amoureux* (*The Midnight Love Feast*, 1985), and *Sept Contes* (*Seven Tales*, 1991).

A multifaceted and prolific author, Tournier borrows his ideas from folklore, fairy tales, literary masterpieces, and the Bible in a process he terms *bricolage*. He then rewrites these cultural mythologies to reinterpret chapters from Genesis or voyages of initiation. These sources are especially important when addressing juvenile readers, for he uses mythology and familiar texts as

a bridge to bring metaphysics to children's literature. Tournier's reworking of his first novel is a case in point. Feeling that one should write concisely and clearly enough for a 10- or 12-year-old to understand, he distilled his metaphysical *Friday* as *Vendredi ou la vie sauvage* (*Friday and Robinson: Life on Esperanza Island*, 1971). Not only has it become the second most popular children's book after *Le Petit Prince* (*The Little Prince*) (*see* SAINT-EXUPÉRY, ANTOINE DE), but Tournier prefers it to his original text, itself a reworking of Defoe's mythical hero.

In addition to retooling his own novel (a kind of self-plagiarism), Tournier recycles his short stories for a wider, dual readership of children and adults. His favourite tale, 'Pierrot ou les secrets de la nuit' ('Pierrot or the Secrets of the Night', 1978), has appeared in several of his anthologies and presents the *commedia dell'arte* characters Harlequin and Pierrot as embodiments of diametrically opposed aesthetics, Platonism and postmodernism, through their courtship of Columbine. Tournier also excerpts intercalated stories from novels and issues them separately and/or in collections. This is the case of 'Barbedor' ('Goldenbeard, or The Problem of Succession'), an *Arabian Nights*-inspired story of an heiress, ageing king who magically becomes his own successor, which originally appeared as a tale-within-a-tale in *The Four Wise Men* and was subsequently reissued for children in a separate, illustrated edition as well as in the collection *Seven Tales*.

Other 'oriental' fairy tales include 'Barberousse' ('Redbeard') and 'La Reine blonde' ('The Blonde Queen') from *The Golden Droplet*, while two republished stories of European influence are particularly important. Swedish folklore colours 'Le Nain rouge' ('The Red Dwarf'), a disturbing tale about an oversexed, malevolent dwarf. While this story is clearly for adults, 'La Fugue du petit Poucet' ('Tom Thumb Runs Away') appeals to both children and their parents. It is a subversive update of *Perrault's 'Le Petit Poucet' (*'Little Tom Thumb') in which the persecuted ogre, a vegetarian hippy/Christ figure trying to save the forests from urbanization, gives a young boy his magical Seven League Boots to escape spiritual suffocation by his father. Like his best stories, it is written in a brief, clear, and naïve style that has been compared to that of La Fontaine, *Kipling, and Saint-Exupéry. Metatextual and multi-layered, this rewritten fairy tale of social criticism is a prime example of why Tournier is one of the most popular and widely read contemporary novelists today.   MLE

Beckett, Sandra, *Des grands romanciers écrivent pour les enfants* (1997).

Bouloumié, Arlette, *Michel Tournier. Le roman mythologique* (1988).

Petit, Susan, *Michel Tournier's Metaphysical Fictions* (1991).

Redfern, Walter, *Michel Tournier. Le Coq de bruyère* (1996).

Roberts, Martin, *Michel Tournier*. Bricolage *and Cultural Mythology* (1994).

Travers, Pamela Lyndon (1906–96) Australian writer and essayist of Irish and Scottish descent, best known for her *Mary Poppins* (1934), which *Disney made into a movie in 1964, starring Julie Andrews as Mary Poppins and Dick Van Dyke as her friend Bert. Her 1934 book about an eccentric nanny with magical powers was followed by a series of others, including *Mary Poppins Comes Back* (1935), *Mary Poppins Opens the Door* (1943), and *Mary Poppins in the Park* (1952). In 1975 Travers published *About the Sleeping Beauty*, a collection of five versions of the tale (by the *Grimms, Charles *Perrault, Giambattista *Basile, Jeremiah *Curtin, and F. Bradley-Birt) along with her own retelling. Travers has written many essays on folklore and myth which have appeared regularly in the review *Parabola* and have been republished, along with some of her own tales and retellings, in *What the Bee Knows: Reflections on Myth, Symbol and Story* (1989).   AD

Grilli, Giorgia, *Myth, Symbol and Meaning in Mary Poppins: The Governess as Provocateur* (2007).

Trnka, Jiří (1912–69) Czech painter and illustrator, also active in animated film and puppet theatre. He illustrated fairy-tale collections by Wilhelm *Hauff (1941), the Brothers *Grimm (1942), Hans Christian *Andersen (1955), *The *Arabian Nights* (1957), and several volumes of Czech folk tales, such as the *Legends of Old Bohemia* (1960). Among his internationally well-known works are illustrations for *Peter and the Wolf* (1965). His original fairy tales, self-illustrated, include *Through the Magic Gate* (1962). Trnka won the Andersen Medal for illustrations in 1968.   MN

Tucker, Charlotte Maria (1821–93) English writer whose books were published under the acronym A.L.O.E. (A Lady of England). An evangelical missionary, Tucker published numerous popular didactic books that had great success in Britain and the United States. Many of her tales were allegorical in nature, such as *The Giant Killer; or, The Battle which All Must Fight* (1855), in which impatient, greedy, and proud children must abandon their bad traits to overcome the giant. Another interesting allegory is *The Crown of Success; or, Four Heads to Furnish* (1863), in which Mr Learning, who drinks ink and eats paper for breakfast, provides some children the means to furnish the Villa of the Head and also magic purses of time to spend in the Town of Education. In such other books as *Wings and Stings: A Tale for the Young, Fairy Know-a-Bit* (1865) and *Fairy Frisket; or, Peeps at Insect Life* (1874) she included themes dealing with natural history.   JZ

Giberne, Agnes, *A Lady of England: The Life and Letters of Charlotte Maria Tucker* (1895).

Turgeon, Carolyn (1971–) American author of fantasy fiction such as *Godmother: The Secret Cinderella Story* (2009), *Mermaid: A Twist On the Classic Tale* (2011), and *The Fairest of Them All* (2013), three novels which adapt *'Cinderella', *'The Little Mermaid' (Hans Christian *Andersen's fairy tale), and *'Rapunzel'. She is also editor of the quarterly fairy-tale themed *Faerie Magazine*. Turgeon provides reimagined narratological perspectives, as in *Fairest*, which relocates Rapunzel as *Snow White's stepmother, or *Godmother*, a redemption story of a banished fairy. The Swan Maiden fairy-tale motif is also presented in Turgeon's *The Next Full Moon* (2012). KMJ

Tutuola, Amos (1920–1997) Nigerian novelist and writer of short stories who wrote in English and incorporated many motifs from Toruba folklore and traditions. Tutuola's style is crisp and vibrant, and he used folklore and traditional structure in new ways to reveal problems of identity among Nigerians. Famous for his very first novel, *The Palm-Wine Drinkard* (1952), he went on to publish important folk-tale collections such as *Yoruba Folktales* (1986) and *The Village Witch Doctor and Other Stories* (1990). JZ

Collins, Harold, *Amos Tutuola* (1969).
Lindfors, Bernth, *Early West African Writers: Amos Tutuola, Cyprian Ekwensi and Ayi Kwei Armah* (2010).

Twain, Mark (pseudonym of **Samuel Langhorne Clemens**, 1835–1910) American writer and humorist. He incorporated a variety of motifs from folklore and fairy tales in his works from the very outset of his career. In such stories as 'The Celebrated Jumping Frog of Calaveras County' (1865) he developed the traditional tall tale into a unique art form. Such stories as 'L'Arbre Fée de Bourlemont' (1895), 'Two Little Tales' (1901), and 'The Five Boons of Life' (1902) were based on narratives from the European fairy-tale tradition. Many of his stories and novels reflect his strong interest in the *Grimms' fairy tales, and the posthumous '1002nd Arabian Night' (1967) was part of a larger project of rewriting The *Arabian Nights* that he never completed. JZ

Stahl, J. D., *Mark Twain, Culture and Gender: Envisioning America through Europe* (1994).
West, Victor Royce, *Folklore in the Works of Mark Twain* (1930).
Wohnham, Henry B., *Mark Twain and the Art of the Tall Tale* (1993).

Ubbelohde, Otto (1867–1922) Ubbelohde illustrated a three-volume edition of *Grimms' fairy tales (1907–9) with simply and strongly executed designs. His illustrations, which recalled early German woodcuts and expressed his abiding love for the landscape of central Hesse where he spent his adult life, were reprinted in vast numbers in schoolbook editions in the late 1930s and early 1940s.

Ubbelohde studied graphics and painting in Munich and subsequently spent 1894–5 at the north German artists' settlement Worpswede. His fairy-tale *œuvre* also includes 56 drawings for *Deutsches Märchenland* (*German Storyland*), a 'Kalender' for 1921–2; a special edition of *'Iron Hans'; and an oil painting, *The Fairytale of the Goose Girl*.   RBB

'Ugly Duckling, The' With 'Den grimme Ælling' ('The Ugly Duckling', 1837), Hans Christian *Andersen wistfully provided an autobiography in narrative form. The duckling is persecuted by all in the hierarchical duck yard, escapes, perseveres, and eventually realizes that he is not ugly, but a beautiful swan. The tale concludes with the marvellous knowledge that it hardly matters where you are born if you have the right talents. The tale and its message have gained proverbial authority, although Andersen slyly suggests that the swan has become a captive of bourgeois society.   NI

Zipes, Jack, *Fairy Tales and the Art of Subversion* (1983).

Undine The earliest literary representations of the Undine fairy tale are Friedrich de la Motte *Fouqué's *Undine. Eine Erzählung* (1811) and E. T. A. *Hoffmann's opera *Undine. Zauberoper in drei Akten* (1812–14). *Tchaikovsky wrote and destroyed an opera on the theme (1869). In the 20th century reworkings include Jean *Giraudoux's *Ondine* (1938), Hans Werner Henze's ballet *Undine* (1956), and Ingeborg Bachmann's 'Undine geht' (1961).

The Undine plot involves a water sprite who surfaces to marry a human being to gain a soul, which elemental spirits do not have. Her marriage with the knight Huldbrand ends badly on account of Huldbrand's indiscretion in marrying his ex-girlfriend after Undine has returned to the water, on the one hand, and the intercession of Undine's cranky water sprite uncle Kühleborn, who tells her she must kill her husband as a consequence, on the other.

The Kühleborn character remains enigmatic because of the motive behind his mean rules. In Fouqué's version, he seems concerned that his niece will be betrayed in love; in Hoffmann's version, an implication of vengeance exists because Undine had been an important figure in the water sprite world and had been stolen, although her parents sent her earthward.

Undine tales are based on traditional mermaid stories, but especially Paracelsus' treatise on nymphs. The tales emphasize the taboo of boundary violation between the elemental realms of earth, air, fire, and water, with water being a privileged element. In Undine's 20th-century transformations, the privilege of water comes to represent art, an interpretation already implicit in Hoffmann's gorgeous descriptions of the watery world.   WC

Fassbind-Eigenheer, Ruth, *Undine oder die nasse Grenze zwischen mir und mir* (1994).

Ungerer, Tomi (pseudonym of **Jean Thomas**, 1931–) Alsatian French illustrator, author-illustrator, political cartoonist, and

Ubbelohde, Otto The wild man in the Grimms' tale '*Iron Hans' takes the young prince with him into the woods in *Kinder- und Hausmärchen gesammelt durch die Brüder Grimm* (1927), illustrated by Otto Ubbelohde.

Ungerer, Tomi 'They fell in love, married, led an elegant life, and had a lot of children. And, so it would seem, they lived happily ever after.' But in this final illustration of *Zeralda's Ogre*, written and illustrated by Tomi Ungerer, one of the ogre's children holds a knife and fork discreetly behind his back as he views his new sibling. Copyright © 1970 Diogenes Verlag AG Zurich, Switzerland.

commercial artist. Born in Strasbourg, Ungerer emigrated to the United States in 1957, moved to Canada 20 years later, and eventually settled in Ireland with his wife and three children. His children's books—over 80—have been written and published in several languages. Since the 1970s, they have been labelled 'controversial' and 'subversive' for the biting satire, earthy sexuality, or streak of sadism that lurks beneath the seemingly innocuous surface of a colourful illustration or a simple story. In his picture book *Moon Man* (1967), for example, the Moon Man lands on earth, innocently hoping to socialize; instead, he is mobbed by scientists, television crews, thrill-seekers, and policemen, and dragged off to gaol as a dangerous 'invader'. Fortunately, as he wanes, he grows thin enough to slip between the bars and escape. While this fable satirizes contemporary society, in other stories Ungerer uses the fairy-tale form to undermine traditional values. *A Storybook from Tomi Ungerer* (1974) includes Ungerer's own version of **'Little Red Riding Hood'*, no longer a warning to young girls, but a hint that outworn sexual taboos are meaningless in today's world. An elegantly dressed wolf overcomes Red Riding Hood's suspicions, takes her to his castle, and marries her, and they live happily ever after. The grandmother (an authority figure from an older generation) is a nasty-tempered old woman, shrivelling away as the story ends. In *Zeralda's Ogre* (1967), possibly Ungerer's best-known original fairy tale, a little girl tames an ogre by cooking him such delicious gourmet meals that he loses his appetite for children; in the end, he marries her, and they raise a family together. While the text seems to suggest demurely that a nurturing woman with fine domestic skills can civilize a man into domesticity, the illustrations tell a somewhat different story. The staring eyes of the helpless animals and birds hung up in Zeralda's kitchen remind us that she, too, is a practised butcher, who feels no qualms about slaughtering what she serves for dinner. And in the final illustration, one of Zeralda's children admires the new baby—with a sharp knife and fork concealed behind his back. A story that seems to celebrate the triumph of civilization over barbarism also intimates that the murderous ogre survives in all of us.   SR

Ursu, Anne (no dates available) American author who has primarily written fairy tales and fantasy for young readers. Her award-winning fairy-tale novel *Bread Crumbs* (2011) is based on Hans Christian *Andersen's 'The Snow Queen' and is set in contemporary Minneapolis, where a young boy named Jack leaves his best friend Hazel and disappears into a nearby forest with a mysterious woman made of ice. Then Hazel takes a perilous journey into the woods to rescue Jack that is also a journey of self-discovery. This theme is also developed in Ursu's second fairy-tale novel, *The Real Boy* (2013), which deals with a young boy named Oscar who works as an apprentice for a powerful wizard on an island in an immense sea. When strange events begin happening in the nearby forest and children become sick in the city, Oscar is compelled to come out of himself and is bent on discovering the destructive cause that even magic cannot prevent.   JZ

Uttley, Alison (1884–1976) British author of fairy tales for children, notably animal tales, continuing the tradition of Beatrix Potter. Her best-known characters include Little Grey Rabbit, Tim Rabbit, Little Brown Mouse, Little Red Fox, and Sam Pig. A selection of her best animal tales was published in *Magic in My Pocket* (1957). She also wrote a variety of original fairy tales and retold

traditional ones, always focusing on the unexpected appearance of magic in everyday countryside surroundings. Uttley also wrote a play, *The Washerwoman's Child* (1946), based on the life of Hans Christian *Andersen and involving seven of his fairy tales. In these as well, the focus is on the everyday rather than typical fairy-tale features.

Alison Uttley's major contribution to the genre is *A Traveller in Time* (1939), a novel exploiting the motif of time shift, and well ahead of the tradition in its narrative structure. For one thing, it involves a first-person narrator, which is unusual in fairy tales since it demands a stronger identification with the character. Unlike traditional fairy tales, the novel is centred on the protagonist's feelings and sensations, allowing the author to go much deeper into the psyche of the character, to investigate her inmost thoughts, and to register the minimal reactions of her senses. It also shows how the encounter with the supernatural changes the protagonist's life and affects her identity in a negative manner, making her unable to accept herself in 'real' life.

The novel involves a traditional magical object as a means of transportation into another time. However, the reader's attention is not immediately drawn to it: it takes a keen eye to recognize that the little manikin Penelope has for a mascot is possibly the 'key' to the magic door. Besides, Penelope's entrance into the past is anticipated, since from early childhood she has been credited with second sight. Witchcraft is a power permeating the story. With her knowledge of the future, especially the tragic fate of Mary Queen of Scots, Penelope is accused of being an evil witch. A jealous rival and a real witch, daughter of an astrologer, almost kills her. All this stands in sharp contrast to Penelope's ordinary life in her own time.

Unlike many characters in time-shift novels, Penelope does not realize right away that she has arrived in a different time. She comes and goes, in a dreamlike fashion, and she can never be sure when it will happen next. Nor is she quite sure that she will be able to come back to her own time. The story acquires a deeper psychological meaning and might be explained in terms of visions as much as pure magic. Although the novel strays from traditional fairy-tale patterns, it has some characters reminiscent of the fairy tale such as Jude, the dumb kitchen boy, a typical chthonic figure with supernatural powers and senses, and Dame Cecily, the fairy godmother.

The end of the novel is deeply tragic. The usual supposition in fairy tales is that the protagonists will become morally better, wiser, and stronger through their trials. In this novel, a complete disintegration of character is depicted. Thus the foremost characteristic of a fairy tale, the happy ending, is definitely rejected.   MN

Aers, Lesley, 'The Treatment of Time in Four Children's Books', *Children's Literature in Education* (1970).
Nikolajeva, Maria, 'Fantasy: The Evolution of a Pattern', in Rhonda Bunbury (ed.), *Fantasy and Feminism* (1993).
Nodelman, Perry, 'Interpretation and the Apparent Sameness of Children's Literature', *Studies in the Literary Imagination*, 18 (1985).

Valente, Catherynne M. (1979–) American novelist, poet, and essayist, who incorporates folklore and mythology into her experimental works. Her two novels, *The Orphan's Tales: In the Night Garden* (2006) and *The Orphan's Tales: In the Cities of Coin and Spice* (2007), based on *The *Arabian Nights*, assemble extraordinary, intertwined tales about hunchbacked ferrymen, giants, voracious gem eaters, conniving hedgehogs, harpies, djinns, and dangerous thieves told by an orphan girl to a young prince in a garden. The stories are never-ending and mysterious, intended to spark the reader's own storytelling. In another unusual experiment, *The Girl Who Circumnavigated Fairyland in a Ship of her Own Making* (2011), which began as a crowdfunded middle-grade online novel in 2006, Valente depicts the adventures of a 12-year-old girl named September, who is similar to the young protagonists in *Alice in Wonderland* and Dorothy in *The Wizard of Oz*, except here the girl is from Omaha, Nebraska and is whisked away by a fast-talking gentleman called the Green Wind to the world of Fairyland, where she has to retrieve a witch's spoon from the fickle Marquess. This work is part of Valente's *Fairyland* series, which includes a prequel, *The Girl Who Ruled Fairyland—For a Little While* (2011), *The Girl Who Fell Beneath Fairyland and Led the Revels There* (2012), and *The Girl Who Soared Over Fairyland and Cut the Moon in Two* (2013). In keeping with her innovative and feminist approach to fairy tales, Valente has also demonstrated how a tale such as 'Snow White' can be used not only to comment on the disintegration of family life in America but also to critique the barbarity of American imperialism and its devastating effects in the 19th century. Her unique novel, *Six-Gun-Snow White* (2013), is narrated by Native Americans in a conversational, unlettered English, first by Snow White and then by an anonymous storyteller familiar with the girl's history. The language is blunt, ungrammatical, and filled with metaphorical allusions to Indian folklore. It is the language of otherness told by a persecuted young girl and then by an unknown narrator who clearly sympathizes with the fate of the girl, representative of thousands of Native Americans in the 19th and 20th centuries—and in this case, the focus is on the tragic fate of many Native American women. Valente has also published a book of interesting poems, *A Guide to Folktales in Fragile Dialects* (2008). JZ

Valenzuela, Luisa (1938–) Of Argentinian origin, Valenzuela is one of the most important writers in contemporary South American literature. She has produced a good number of novels, a few plays, and several short stories. Throughout her literary career, she has been preoccupied by the way dominant groups use discourse to oppress other people; likewise, her works often deal with sexual politics, making explicit the dual opposition of domination/submission that presides over many male–female relationships. All of this is especially obvious in her revisions of classic fairy tales which she included in a collection of stories called *Simetrías* (*Symmetries*, 1993) in a section entitled 'Cuentos de Hades' ('Tales of Hades') which contains six feminist fairy tales, all of which revise one or several famous stories, such as *'Little Red Riding Hood', 'The *Princess and the Pea', *'Sleeping Beauty', 'The *Frog King', *'Cinderella', *'Snow White', and *'Bluebeard'. The tale of 'Sleeping

Beauty' is particularly important to Valenzuela's creative imagination, considering the fact that it is revised twice, both in 'No se detiene el progreso' ('Progress Cannot be Stopped', 1993) and in 'Príncipe II' ('Prince II'), one of the sections of '4 Príncipes 4' ('4 Princes 4', 1993). The dominant feature of the '4 Princes 4' is the presence of a Prince Charming who rejects his role as rescuer and refuses to make use of his talent for giving spell-breaking kisses, since the passion he has for a beauty that remains forever sleeping would vanish the moment she awoke to her own desire.   CFR

Valeri, Diego (1887-1976) Italian lyric poet, writer, literary critic, and fine translator of French and German poetry. He captured the beauty of his beloved Venice in *Guida sentimentale di Venezia* (*Sentimental Guide to Venice*, 1942) and other works. Valeri was by vocation and by moral choice a poet of the good life, evident in his many collections ranging from *Le gaie tristezze* (*The Merry Sorrows*, 1913) to *Metamorfosi dell'angelo* (*The Transfiguration of the Angel*, 1957) and *La domenica col poeta* (*The Sunday with the Poet*, 1973). It also pervades his tales, particularly those published in *Campanellino* (1928), such as 'Il Fraticello Re' ('The Friar King') in which the beauty of nature and of human feelings does not allow the tragic to prevail, and love and innocence naturally triumph over mischief and betrayal.   MNP

Vande Velde, Vivian (1951-) American writer of fantasy for young adults. Beginning with *Once Upon a Test* (1984), a collection of three innovative fairy tales that break with standard depictions of princesses and princes, Vande Velde has written a series of humorous books geared to upset audience expectations. In *A Hidden Magic* (1985) a plain princess named Jennifer frees a conceited, handsome prince from a witch's spell. *A Well-Timed Enchantment* (1991) concerns a young girl and her cat who retrieve an old watch from the past. *Dragon's Bait* (1992) depicts a courageous girl who denies allegations of witchcraft and becomes the friend of a dragon that is supposed to

devour her. In *Tales from the Brothers Grimm and the Sisters Weird* (1996), she parodies 13 popular fairy tales and gives them unusual twists. For instance, after growing into a beautiful swan, the ugly duckling pecks all his tormentors to death. The elves lock the shoemaker and his wife in the basement of their home, take all their money, and run off to Central America, where they operate a pirate radio station. Though shocking, the tales are told in a light comic vein aimed at exposing social contradictions in such a manner that young adults can easily grasp the targets of criticism.   JZ

Vess, Charles (1951-) American illustrator and fantasy artist who has collaborated with some of the most notable fantasy and fairy-tale writers in North America, such as Emma Bull, Charles de Lint, Neil *Gaiman, Sharyn McCrumb, Jeff Smith, and Jane *Yolen. His major collaboration has been with Gaiman, and he has illustrated Gaiman's story 'The Land of Summer's Twilight' (1989), the fairy-tale novel, *Stardust* (1999), and the children's book *Blueberry Girl* (2009). Vess has also illustrated a series of anthologies edited by Terri *Windling and Ellen Datlow: *The Green Man: Tales from the Mythic Forest* (2002), *The Faery Reel: Tales from the Twilight Realm* (2004), and *The Coyote Road: Trickster Tales* (2007).   JZ

Victorian fairy painting In his final speech of *The Tempest*, Prospero recognizes the necessity for a friendly collusion between the audience and the performer in order that the illusion of fantasy prevails. Victorian fairy painters and illustrators depended upon a similar supportive relationship as they conjured up 'realms of faerie' for appreciative spectators. Their enthusiastic admirers included such diverse luminaries as Queen Victoria, Charles Dodgson (Lewis *Carroll), William Makepeace *Thackeray, Charles *Dickens, John *Ruskin, and Samuel Carter Hall. Fairy paintings appeared regularly in Royal Academy exhibitions throughout the 19th century and well into the 20th. Most of the artists from the early Victorian period took their subjects from the plays of

*Shakespeare, most notably *A Midsummer Night's Dream* and *The Tempest*, and the poetry of Milton and *Spenser. They usually added imaginative details to these works culled from folklore and fairy tales. An even larger audience for fairy images emerged with the expanding readership of illustrated books and magazines after mid-century.

Artists chose to paint fairy pictures for a variety of reasons. Some artists, like Daniel Maclise, Richard *Dadd, and Joseph Noël *Paton, chose fairy painting as one way to establish their professional careers and to solicit critical and public recognition. Other artists, such as John Anster Fitzgerald, John Simmons, Robert Huskisson, and John Atkinson Grimshaw, developed a popular following for their small fantasy works, which mixed fairy scenes with eroticism and dream imagery. The Pre-Raphaelite artists John Everett Millais, William Bell Scott, and Arthur *Hughes found an interest in fairy subject-matter that engaged them with varied success. Of the three, Hughes went on to make a name for himself as a fantasy illustrator.

Not all artists chose an academic career as the best route to public approbation. George *Cruikshank and Richard 'Dicky' *Doyle, for example, were the successful founders of a century-long dynasty of Victorian fairy illustration. Cruikshank's art acted as a link between the satirical broadsides of the Regency period and the moral bromides of the early Victorian era. Doyle helped initiate the Victorian revolution in popular media with his contributions to the satirical journal *Punch* and his illustrations to Charles Dickens's Christmas novels. By the 1870s, Doyle had become one of the most prominent fairy illustrators in a field that included his brother Charles Altamont Doyle, Arthur Hughes, Kate *Greenaway, and Eleanor Vere *Boyle. At the end of the century, Arthur *Rackham, Edmund *Dulac, John Dickson Batten, Henry Justice Ford, Robert Anning Bell, Jessie M. King, and the *Robinson brothers (Charles, William Heath, and Thomas Heath) developed the fairy vocabulary into a variety of sophisticated illustrative styles, both in colour and in black and white.

All of these artists contributed to the popularity of fairy imagery through their illustrations in novels, fairy-tale collections, folklore studies, engraved folios, and popular journals.

Fairy painting would seem to be a quintessentially Victorian product, yet its roots lie firmly within late 18th-century British art. Henry *Fuseli recognized the potential for fairy painting to both entertain and edify the British public. Fuseli, in his efforts to establish a new kind of poetic history painting, established the basic vocabulary of the genre: the quotation of high art and literature, the addition of folkloric themes, and the establishment of a central narrative scene surrounded by collaborative vignettes. In his works for Alderman John Boydell's Shakespeare Gallery, *Titania and Bottom* (*c.*1780-90) and *Titania's Awakening* (1793-4), he set the standards for a new kind of literary history painting. His influence would be felt later in both Victorian fairy painting and illustration, especially in his handling of multiple vignettes that comment upon the central action.

William Blake (1757-1827) also incorporated fairy imagery and lore into his idiosyncratic cosmology. Unlike Fuseli, he had no interest in the grand scale of history painting, preferring to work with the media of engraving and watercolour. He saw fairies as nature elementals. In *Oberon, Titania, and Puck with Fairies Dancing* (*c.*1785), the artist conceives of fairies as nature worshippers, miniature druidic celebrants of the corporeal earth. Blake depicts the king and queen of the fairies presiding over a free-spirited dance, a 'fairy ring'. He differs from Fuseli's approach to the fairy painting by concentrating solely on the diminutive participants and giving the fairies wings, which add to the airy feeling of the dance. Where Fuseli had set the tone for literary history painting, Blake provided the model for an imaginative use of scale and schemata of body language for future artists to use when dealing with fairy subjects. At the same time, Blake served as a spiritual godfather to artists searching for visual metaphors for poetic inspiration in fantasy art.

Surprisingly, the romantic era saw little important work in fairy painting. Artists like Henry Singleton (1766–1839), Henry Howard (1769–1847), Frank Howard (1805–66), and Joshua Cristall (1767–1847) carried on the tradition in small-scale works. These works, however, did little but sustain the prevailing types established by Blake and Fuseli of diminutive figures closely associated with the world of flora and fauna. A more productive expansion of fairy lore came out of the writings of such folklorists as Sir Walter Scott (1771–1832), Nathan Drake (1766–1836), Thomas Crofton *Croker, and Thomas *Keightley. Most important, an English translation of Jacob and Wilhelm *Grimm's *Kinder- und Hausmärchen (Children's and Household Tales) appeared in 1823. The publication of these various collections of ballads, plays, folklore, and fairy tales throughout the Victorian era would offer alternative literary sources for fairy painters and illustrators to those sources associated with the Shakespearian tradition.

Francis Danby (1793–1861), an Irish artist, and David Scott (1806–49), a Scot, represent two notable exceptions to the general lack of inventiveness in fairy painting during the romantic era. Danby painted two watercolour versions of *Scene from a Midsummer Night's Dream* (1832) during a period of self-imposed exile in Switzerland. The works have a Blakean simplicity made evocative through the addition of a moonlit landscape as a setting and the imaginative use of scale and vantage point. Scott, in contrast, grafted the theatricality of Fuseli onto the poetic expressivity of Blake and imbued the mixture with his own peculiar metaphysical temperament. He drives the pictorial narrative of his fairy paintings *Ariel and Caliban* (1837) and *Puck Fleeing the Dawn* (1837) with deliberately asymmetrical compositions, an innovative use of body language and expression, and a robustly applied paint surface. Neither Danby's nor Scott's fairy paintings would have much of an immediate impact upon the Royal Academy and the London art scene, however. Danby, despite the popularity of such fantasy landscape paintings as *The Enchanted Island* (1825) and *The Wood-Nymph's Hymn to the Rising Sun* (1845) suffered from a covert ostracization within the academic hierarchy, while Scott, despite a legendary reputation among younger Scottish artists, led an isolated existence cut short by his death at a relatively young age.

The work of the Irish artist Daniel Maclise (1806–70) represents a more viable link between the Academy and fairy painting, as well as the shift from romantic to Victorian art. He recognized early in his career the possibilities of fairy imagery; his first published drawings appeared, etched by W. H. Brooke, in Thomas Crofton Croker's *Fairy Legends and Traditions in the South of Ireland* (1826). The young artist entered the Royal Academy in 1828. By the beginning of the 1830s, he had turned his attention to unique interpretations of historical genre painting, including fairy scenes, for example *The Disenchantment of Bottom* (1832). Another source of influence on Maclise's art came from the German *Märchen* painters Moritz von Schwind and Ludwig Schnorr von Carolsfeld. This Germanic style can be seen in Maclise's early painting *Faun and the Fairies*, which also served as a wood-engraved illustration to Edward Bulwer-Lytton's *Pilgrims on the Rhine* (1834). Maclise returned to German-derived 'fairy' subject-matter in his *Scene from *Undine* (1843), based upon a story by Friedrich de la Motte *Fouqué. This painting was purchased by Queen Victoria as a birthday present for her husband Albert, the Prince Consort, signalling the royal support of certain kinds of fantasy painting and the affinity some of the British populace felt for German culture at this time.

Victorian fairy painting experienced its heyday during the 1840s. Its popularity arose partly out of the desire for new kinds of art by a growing middle-class audience and partly because of the surreptitious restrictions gradually imposed on other painting genres in the Royal Academy. Fairy painting became a surrogate for certain subject-matter, motifs, and themes unavailable or unacceptable in more élite categories of the academic hierarchy of painting. This genre crossed boundaries between the nude figure study, pastoral landscape, erotic mythological scenes, sentimental narrative, and literary history painting. Its success grew concurrently out of a confusion engendered by a crisis of identity about the nature of history painting within the Royal Academy itself. For the artist, critic, and art lover, this change emerged from the demands of a burgeoning middle-class consumer culture for genre, landscape, and portrait painting, as well as a developing popular taste for a new kind of narrative painting. The cultural sense of an established artistic tradition, always shaky in the British arts, fell prey to the developing values of the middle class as they infiltrated in greater numbers the ranks of patronage, the academic organization, the art publication industry, and the critical press. At this critical juncture in early Victorian art history, fairy painters scored their greatest successes.

Both Richard Dadd and Joseph Noel Paton used fairy paintings as a way of garnering critical and popular attention in the 1840s. Dadd began to experience a gradual success with such works as *Titania Sleeping* (*c.*1841) and *Come unto these Yellow Sands* (1842). His descent into madness, culminating in the murder of his father, led to his incarceration in Bethlem Hospital and his removal from consideration (except as a curiosity) as a member of Victorian art circles. Noel Paton made a satisfying artistic debut with two fairy paintings, *The Reconciliation of Oberon and Titania* (1847) and *The Quarrel of Oberon and Titania* (1849). Planned as possible decorations for the Westminster Hall competitions, these pendant works led to the young artist's highly successful career as a painter of historical, allegorical, and religious scenes.

Even such established artists as William Etty (1787–1849), Joseph William Mallard Turner (1775–1851), and Edwin Landseer (1803–73) briefly explored fairy subject-matter in the 1840s, taking advantage of the genre's popularity. Etty's *The Fairy of the Fountain* (1845) is a fairy painting in name only, while Turner's *Queen Mab's Cave* (1846) uses fairy subject-matter as a peripheral element in what is essentially a landscape and colour study. Landseer, the youngest of the three, had already established his reputation as the best of the Victorian animal painters. His *Scene from 'A Midsummer Night's Dream'* (1849) was privately commissioned for Isambard Kingdom Brunel's dining-room, which the famous engineer had planned to decorate with a Shakespearian gallery.

Early Victorian fairy painters relied not only upon the approval but also the recognition by their audience of their subject-matter. The citation of fairy scenes in Shakespeare's plays brought a special kind of response, because the Victorian audience brought along certain expectations, derived from both their theatre experiences and their readings of Shakespeare, about what a fairy might look like or do. With the advent of Pre-Raphaelitism, the problem of investing fantastic subject-matter with some kind of verisimilitude takes on a new imperative.

The formation of the Pre-Raphaelite Brotherhood grew out of a dissatisfaction on the part of Dante Gabriel *Rossetti, William Holman Hunt (1827–1910), and John Everett Millais (1829–96) with current academic practice and the perceived sterility of subject-matter in contemporary Victorian art. The Brotherhood found some direction in their search for acceptable modern subjects in the technique of realism they found in their study of early Italian and Northern European painting before Raphael and in John Ruskin's first volume of *Modern Painters* (1843). At the same time, these young artists, despite their disaffection with the Royal Academy, felt a sympathy with the work of certain older artists working in the 1840s, including Ford Madox Brown, Maclise, and Paton, who anticipated the Brotherhood's interest in revitalizing history painting through complex narrative schemes and an accurate use of historical details.

One of Millais's early Pre-Raphaelite paintings, *Ferdinand Lured by Ariel* (1849), represents his adoption of the new naturalistic style and, concomitantly, testifies to the popularity of fairy painting at the end of the

1840s. Commissioned by the dealer William Wethered, this work evolved from two earlier versions by Millais on the same subject: a pen-and-ink drawing (1848) and a small oil sketch (1849–50). A dramatic change occurs in the final painting, which contains the highly saturated colours and the meticulously observed details of the nascent Pre-Raphaelite style. Millais's desire to depict the surface detail of every form accurately leads to a flat cut-out effect that emphasizes individual areas and creates a separation of one part from another. This effect can be seen most clearly in the awkward relationship of Ferdinand's head, modelled by F. G. Stephens, and his body, taken from Camille Bonnard's *Costumes Historiques*. Wethered refused to purchase the finished painting, either because of the unusual naturalism of the piece or because he was disappointed with the grotesquely rendered sprites. Millais never painted another fairy subject.

Dante Gabriel Rossetti, the most romantic of the Pre-Raphaelites, interpreted fairy themes in a wholly different way. He contributed an illustration to William Allingham's poetry collection *The Music-Master* (1855), for the poem 'The Maids of Elfin-Mere'. The poem describes the encounter of a parson's son with the world of the supernatural in the form of three sisters, who appear magically every night to sing to the lad and then, at the stroke of the 'Eleventh Hour', disappear. His attraction proves so keen that he tries to keep them past their time on earth, unleashing a gruesome fate on the female trio. Rossetti concentrates on the eerie relationship between the crooning women and the spellbound man, and takes his image of the fairy from the medieval tradition of the fey sorceress, the *femme fatale* who enraptures men. He would continue this interest throughout his career in a series of sexually charged portraits of beatific, predatory, or victimized women. The popularity of Rossetti's imagery would sustain a wholly different kind of fantasy art in the symbolism and Art Nouveau of the 1890s.

William Bell Scott (1811–90) stays closer to the romantic tradition of the small cabinet picture in *Cockcrow* (1856), based upon Thomas Parnell's 18th-century poem 'A Fairy Tale, in the ancient English style'. Scotts pays homage to the work of his older brother David, who had established in the 1830s a pictorial imagery of a private visionary experience associated with fairy phenomena. The younger Scott grafts the brightly hued Pre-Raphaelite style onto this more traditional visual conception of fairy behaviour. In melding fairy mythology to poetic vision, he chose a path more in tune with the direction of fairy painting after 1855.

This more intimate view of fairy life can also be found in the work of Frederick Goodall (1822–1904) and Robert Huskisson (1820–61). Goodall's *Fairy Struck* (c.1846) depicts the placid confrontation of two fairies with a mouse. The artist uses the transparency of watercolours to richly colourful effect, as the sunlight drenches the fairies' bower in a shimmering light. A more erotic mood inhabits Huskisson's *The Midsummer Night's Fairies* (c.1847), which shows Oberon watching a sleeping Titania as belligerent fairies war with fauna in the foreground. The frame makes reference to the human protagonists in the play; the figures of Bottom, Hermia, and Lysander slumber on a ledge beneath the fairy scene. Both artists examine the minutiae of fairy existence, providing the spectator with the experience of eavesdropping on the daily life of these tiny beings.

This voyeuristic element reappears in various guises in the work of John Anster Fitzgerald (1819–1906), John Simmons (1823–76), Thomas Heatherley (exhib. 1858–87), and John Atkinson Grimshaw (1836–93). Fitzgerald created perhaps the most interesting variations on fairy themes with his small, brilliantly coloured oil paintings. For example, his series of works on the conflict between the fairy populace and Cock Robin mingles humanoid fairies and imaginative Boschian grotesques with carefully rendered birds, flowers, and insects. Fitzgerald's fairies, dressed in elaborate finery, possess a childlike bemusement as they move with tremulous bravado through a lush, exotic floral world. Simmons, Heatherley, and Grimshaw present a more forthright eroticism in their depictions of the sylvan creatures. Their paintings usually focus on a single nude female figure, framed by a natural setting and occasionally surrounded by the fairy court. In some of these works, the inclusion of a toadstool adds a phallic detail to the erotic subtext. These works have a dreamy cast to them as the fairies go about their business, unmindful of their human observers.

Interest in fairy subject-matter did not die with the end of the Victorian era. Fairy paintings and illustrations appeared regularly in British exhibitions, magazines, and books well into the 20th century. Artists such as Arthur Rackham and Edmund Dulac revitalized the illustrative tradition with their conceptions of fairies as either fantastic grotesqueries or ethereal beauties. John Dixon Batten (1860–1932) and Henry Justice Ford (1860–1941) illustrated important fairy-tale collections like those of Andrew *Lang, carrying on the tradition of Pre-Raphaelitism and the Aesthetic Movement. Fairies still proved popular in early 20th-century children's book illustrations in the work of Florence Mary Anderson (*fl.* 1914–30), Ida Rentoul *Outhwaite, and Jessie M. King (1876–1949). The post-Second World War era has also witnessed a growing revival of interest in fairy imagery. A painting by the British Pop artist Peter Blake, *Titania* (1978), for example, updates the canon with a depiction of the fairy queen as a barely pubescent young woman; the work makes an explicit association of women with nature and natural processes through the decoration of her breasts and genitalia with flowers, stems, and grass stalks. RAS

Adlard, John, *The Sports of Cruelty: Fairies, Folk-Songs, Charms, and Other Country Matters in the Works of William Blake* (1972).

Briggs, Katherine, *A Dictionary of Fairies* (1976).

Butlin, Martin, *The Paintings and Drawings of William Blake* (2 vols., 1981).

Friedman, Winifred H., *Boydell's Shakespeare Gallery* (1976).

Johnson, Diana L., *Fantastic Illustration and Design in Britain, 1850–1930* (1979).

Landow, George P., 'There Began to Be a Great Talking about the Fine Arts', in Josef L. Altholz

(ed.), *The Mind and Art of Victorian England* (1976).

Maas, Jeremy, *Victorian Painters* (1969).

Maas, Jeremy *et al.*, *Victorian Fairy Paintings* (1997).

Ormond, Richard, *Daniel Maclise, 1806–1870* (1972).

Packer, Alison, Beddoe, Stella, and Jarrett, Lianne, *Fairies in Legend and the Arts* (1980).

Phillpots, Beatrice, *Fairy Paintings* (1978).

Roberts, Helene E., 'Exhibition and Review: The Periodical Press and the Victorian Exhibition System', in Richard Schindler, 'Art to Enchant: A Critical Study of Early Victorian Fairy Painting and Illustration' (Diss., Brown University, 1988).

Shattock, Joanne, and Wolff, Michael (eds.), *The Victorian Periodical Press: Samplings and Soundings* (1982).

Tomory, Peter, *The Life and Art of Henry Fuseli* (1972).

Wood, Christopher, *Fairies in Victorian Art* (2000).

Vidal, Beatriz Martín (1973–) Spanish surrealist illustrator, painter, and author, best known for *Little Red* (2014), a collection of illustrations featuring *'Little Red Riding Hood' with a hood made of feathers. Children are central to much of Vidal's work; she also illustrated *Hansel y Gretel* (*Hansel and Gretel*, 2014) as well as *Miaka* (2014), a Russian fairy tale about a young girl named Anya and her pet bird.   MF

Villardefrancos, Marisa (1915–1975) Spanish writer. Her sister, Gloria Villardefrancos, often collaborated with her in the creation of her works, which include fairy tales, legends, biographies, religious books, novels, screenplays, and plays for children. They all are influenced by her religiosity and her pedagogical intention. *¡Erase que se era!* (*Once Upon a Time!*, 1947) is her most important collection of fairy tales. The stories gathered in this work are written in both prose and verse, among them 'El beso' ('The Kiss'), 'El príncipe Miedo' ('Prince Fear'), 'El enano del bosque' ('The Dwarf in the Woods'), and 'Noche de Reyes' ('The Magi's Night'). Villardefrancos's plays for children are also greatly influenced by the fairy-tale genre. Some of her most famous plays are *La princesita fea* (*The Ugly Little*

Princess, 1949), *El príncipe que no tenía corazón* (*The Prince without a Heart*, 1949), and *La princesa de nieve* (*The Princess of Snow*, 1951).   CFR

Villeneuve, Gabrielle-Suzanne Barbot de (1685–1755) French writer whose 'La Belle et la bête' (**Beauty and the Beast') was the basis for Mme *Leprince de Beaumont's famous version. Unhappily married to a military officer, Villeneuve was left impoverished after his death and attempted to earn extra money through her writings, specifically historical and sentimental novels. She eventually became acquainted with Crébillon fils, another writer of fairy tales (among other things), and, from all accounts, cohabited with him. Although contemporaries were quick to dismiss her as the mere 'governess' and mistress of her more illustrious partner, Villeneuve was in fact his intellectual companion and continued to write fiction on her own.

Her version of 'Beauty and the Beast' appeared in *La Jeune Amériquaine et les contes marins* (*The Young American Girl and the Sea Tales*, 1740). This frame narrative recounts the voyage of a young girl returning to Santo Domingo, where her parents are plantation owners, after finishing her studies in France. During the trip, the girl's chambermaid is joined by everyone on board in telling stories. This volume contains two fairy tales—'Les Naïades' and 'Beauty and the Beast'— but it is the latter that was to be Villeneuve's claim to fame. Later, Villeneuve wrote *Les Belles solitaires* (*Solitary Beauties*, 1745), in which assembled friends tell the fairy tales

Villeneuve, Gabrielle-Suzanne Barbot de The beast reveals his heart to the merchant's daughter in Mme de Villeneuve's *'Beauty and the Beast', illustrated by Jules Pellcoq in *Les Contes des fées offerts a Bébé* (*c.*1900).

'Papa Joly', 'Mirliton ou la prison volontaire' ('Mirliton or the Voluntary Prison'), and 'Histoire du roi Santon' ('Story of King Santon').

Villeneuve's best-known tale, 'Beauty and the Beast', is considerably longer and more complex than Leprince de Beaumont's adaptation for English schoolgirls learning French which appeared in *Le Magasin des enfants* (*The Young Misses' Magazine*) in 1757. In addition to the basic plot retained by Leprince de Beaumont, Villeneuve provides the Beast's story (his enchantment by a fairy whose love he had rebuffed) as well as the narrative of Belle's true identity (she is a princess and not the daughter of the merchant who raised her). Belle's story is crucial to the dénouement when it is revealed that the Beast may marry only a woman of royal blood. For a good part of the narrative—and unlike the vast majority of French fairy tales at the time—Belle is portrayed as a non-noble but none the less virtuous heroine. In the end, though, her virtue is revealed to be the innate consequence of her aristocratic birth, and she may marry the Beast-turned-Prince. Considered as a whole, then, Villeneuve's tale displays a somewhat ambiguous stance towards social class, witnessed especially in the favourable treatment of Belle's adoptive father (a merchant).

Villeneuve's version of the tale also differs from Leprince de Beaumont's in its eroticism and its insistence on the Beast's monstrosity. Villeneuve makes explicit the transgressive sexual union at the heart of this tale type. Not only does the Beast repeatedly ask Belle to *sleep* with him (in Leprince de Beaumont's version he asks her to *marry* him), but Belle has pleasurable dreams of being courted by a handsome prince. The transgressiveness of these descriptions is intensified by details of the Beast's frightening appearance and his equally repulsive stupidity. But at the end of the tale, this transgression is resolved when Belle discovers that the Beast is none other than the prince in her dreams.

Overall, one of Villeneuve's most important contributions is her representation of women. In her novels and fairy tales alike she pays particular attention to women's

plight in marriage, their financial constraints, and ultimately their difficult quest for happiness.   LCS

Hearne, Betsy, *Beauty and the Beast: Visions and Revisions of an Old Tale* (1989).

Vogeler, Heinrich (1872–1942) German painter, architect, illustrator, and writer, who was one of the pioneers of *Jugendstil* at the turn of the century. Influenced by Walter *Crane and William *Morris, Vogeler produced books that had a total unity; he designed the typeface, illustrations, and book covers of his works, and he favoured intricate and florid etchings that ornamented the entire page and heightened particular scenes of a story. Most of his fairy-tale illustration work was accomplished between 1900 and 1911. Among his most notable illustrations of this period were those done for Hugo von *Hofmannsthal, *Der Kaiser und die Hexe* (*The Emperor and the Witch*, 1900), Jacob and Wilhelm *Grimm, *Märchen* (*Fairy Tales*, 1900), Clemens *Brentano and Ludwig *Tieck, *Romantische Märchen* (*Romantic Fairy Tales*, 1902), Oscar *Wilde, *The Ghost of Canterville and Five Other Stories* (1905), and Jacob and Wilhelm Grimm, *Kinder- und Hausmärchen* (*Children's and Household Tales*, 1907). During the First World War Vogeler volunteered for military service as a common soldier; disappointed and outraged by the deceit and hypocrisy of the German government, he joined the revolutionary movement in the 1920s to transform the country into a democratic if not socialist state. Consequently, his art became political, and he was strongly influenced by Dadaism and futurism. He also became involved in architectural projects for communal living and eventually emigrated to the Soviet Union in 1931. His last important fairy-tale illustrations were completed for the radical writer Hermynia *Zur Mühlen's books, *Es war einmal...und es wird sein* (*Once Upon a Time...and the Time Will Come*, 1930) and *Schmiede der Zukunft* (*Smiths of the Future*, 1933).   JZ

Petzet, H. W., *Von Worpswede nach Moskau. Heinrich Vogeler. Ein Künstler zwischen den Zeiten* (1972).

Vogeler, Heinrich The witch in *'Hansel and Gretel' contemplates her next step in this 1895 illustration by Heinrich Vogeler.

Voisenon, Claude-Henri de Fuzée, abbé de (1708–75) French writer, especially known for his plays, who also wrote libertine novels and fairy tales. The parody and light-hearted erotic allegory in his *Tant mieux pour elle* (*So Much the Better for Her*, 1745), *Zulmis et Zelmaide* (1745), and *Le Sultan Mispouf et la princesse Grisemine* (*Prince Mispouf and Princess Grayface*, 1746) are typical of many fairy tales written in 18th-century Parisian salons.　　　LCS

Volkmann, Richard von (pseudonym of **Richard Leander**, 1830–89) A German doctor, he was popular for his poems and stories but only his fairy tales have stood the test of time. These he wrote for his children while serving as a surgeon during the siege of Paris in the Franco-Prussian War: *Träumereien an französischen Kaminen* (*Dreams by a French Fireside*, 1871). Using motifs and themes from both the romantic literary fairy tale and folk tales, the stories evoke an idyll of domesticity. A great success, they had 48 German editions in 40 years and were translated into English in 1886.　　　KS

Volkov, Aleksandr (1891–1977) Russian writer, best known for his series of fairy-tale novels for children. The first of these, *The Wizard of the Emerald City* (1939), is a free adaptation of Frank *Baum's *The *Wizard of Oz*. In Volkov's version, the focus of the story is shifted towards collective rather than individual achievements, and friendship and obedience are presented as main virtues. In order to accentuate this, several new dramatic side episodes are added; otherwise the story follows very closely that of Baum. The five sequels, following the great success of the first book, have nothing to do with Baum: *Urfin Jus and his Wooden Soldiers*

(1963), *The Seven Underground Kings* (1967), *The Fiery God of the Marrans* (1971), *The Yellow Fog* (1974), and *The Mystery of the Deserted Castle* (published posthumously, 1982). The plot of each involves new threats to the Magic Land, as the Land of Oz is called, whereupon first Ellie, the counterpart of Dorothy, and then her little sister Annie, are summoned to assist in the struggle. The three characters of Baum's novel, the Scarecrow, the Tin Woodman, and the Cowardly Lion, are central in all these sequels. The enormous popularity of Volkov must be ascribed to the isolation of Soviet children's literature when the rich variety of Western literary fairy tale was practically unknown to Soviet readers, and Volkov's tales were apprehended as utterly original. If Baum's stories have been regarded as American national myth, Volkov's reflect the communist ideology, not least the views on literature as educational and socializing tool.　　　MN

Mitrokhina, Xenia, 'The Land of Oz in the Land of the Soviets', *Children's Literature Association Quarterly* 21.4 (1996–7).

Voltaire (pseudonym of **François Marie Arouet**, 1694–1778) French author, political polemicist, and Enlightenment philosopher. In his fairy tale 'Le Taureau blanc' ('The White Bull', 1774), Voltaire freely mixes reality and the marvellous in an ironic critique of Old Testament stories. Built around the literal interpretation of Nebuchadnezzar's metamorphosis into a white bull, the tale features humanized talking animals and a princess who reads Locke. True to the Enlightenment belief in rational enquiry, Voltaire specifically targets the Garden of Eden myth and denounces a God that would forbid knowledge to humanity.　　　AZ

Wackenroder, Wilhelm Heinrich
(1773–98) One of the most important writers
of the early romantic movement in Germany. He studied law at Erlangen and Göttingen and was a close friend of Ludwig
Tieck. His early works on Italian Renaissance
painters indicate that he would have played
an important role in German romanticism if
he had not died at an early age. As it is, he
wrote two significant romantic works: *Her-
zensergiessungen eines kunstliebenden Klos-
terbruders* (*Confessions from the Heart of an
Art-Loving Friar*, 1797) and *Phantasien über
die Kunst für Freunde der Kunst* (*Fantasies
on Art for Friends of Art*, published posthumously in 1799), which included 'Ein wunderbares morgendländisches Märchen von
einem nackten Heiligen' ('A Wondrous
Oriental Tale of a Naked Saint'). The protagonist of this tale is a misunderstood genius
who rejects the pettiness of everyday life.
Only music can save him, and he abandons
earth for a more divine artistic life. This
theme was central to the German romantic
fairy tales of the 19th century and was also
picked up by Hermann Hesse at the beginning of the 20th century.   JZ

Alewyn, Richard, 'Wackenroders Anteil',
Germanic Review, 19 (1944).
Frey, Marianne, *Der Künstler und sein Werk bei
W. H. Wackenroder und E. T. A. Hoffmann* (1970).
Schubert, Mary Hurst, *Wilhelm Heinrich
Wackenroder's Confessions and Fantasies* (1971).
Thornton, Karin, 'Wackenroder's Objective
Romanticism', *Germanic Review*, 37 (1962).
Zipes, Jack, 'W. H. Wackenroder: In Defense of
his Romanticism', *Germanic Review*, 44 (1969).

Waddell, Martin (1941–) Prolific British
author for children and young adults who
also writes under the pseudonym Catherine
Sefton. Adept at many different genres, Waddell's books for young children are often
slapstick, while his books for young adults
are either mysteries or novels that deal with
social problems in Northern Ireland. His
Little Dracula series, written between 1986
and 1992, recounts the comic adventures of
a fantastic dracula and his family and employs numerous fairy-tale motifs. His most
significant fairy-tale work, however, is *The
Tough Princess* (1986) illustrated by Patrick
Benson. This delightful feminist story depicts a young feisty princess, who rebels
against her greedy, manipulative parents
and takes a journey to determine her own
destiny. Along the way, she wakes a sleeping
prince with a kiss and bikes off with him into
an unknown future.   JZ

Waechter, Friedrich Karl (1937–2005)
German cartoonist and author of satirical
essays for adults and picture books for children. Waechter had made a name for himself by working for the German satirical
weeklies *pardon*, *Konkret*, and *Twen* before
he turned to children's books. While working at *pardon* in the 1960s he co-founded
the New Frankfurt School, a group of talented comic writers and cartoonists—Robert
Gernhardts, F. W. Bernstein, Bernd Eilert,
Eckhard Henscheid, and Hans Traxler—
who often parodied fairy tales. The name of
the group was intended to mock the serious
school of critical thinking called the Frankfurt School and led by Theodor Adorno and
Max Horkheimer. In contrast, their work was
serious, subversive nonsense. The turning-
point in Waechter's career was his parodistic
retelling of Heinrich Hoffmann's famous *Der
Struwwelpeter*. Waechter had originally intended it for an adult audience, but because
of its subject-matter the *Anti-Struwwelpeter*

(1970) was readily adopted as a children's book by parents who, in the wake of the 1968 cultural revolution, appreciated the book's subversiveness. The upside-down world that can be found in *Anti-Struwwelpeter* and other parodies by Waechter such as *Der Frosch und das Mädchen* (The Frog and the Girl, 2000) is not just playful entertainment, reaffirming existing power structures, but instead an attack on moral taboos and the old social and political order. Waechter's *Tischlein deck dich* (1972) is such an ideologically charged revision of the Brothers' Grimm fairy tale 'The Table, the Ass, and the Stick', in which the stick, the symbol of oppression and violence, is banned forever. In addition to parodies, Waechter also wrote original experimental tales for children. In *Die Kronenklauer* (*The Crown Thieves*, 1972), which Waechter wrote together with Bernd Eilert, the authors not only create exemplary children who are imaginative, active, and stand up for their rights, they apply the lesson to the reading process itself by inviting readers to look behind the scenes and participate in the storytelling process itself. EMM

Wild, Reiner, *Geschichte der deutschen Kinder- und Jugendliteratur* (1990).

Wagner, Richard (1813–83) German opera composer and music theorist who wrote the texts of his musical dramas and who remains as highly controversial as he has been extremely influential. He studied music in Leipzig and held brief appointments at theatres in Würzburg, Magdeburg, and Riga in the 1830s while writing and composing several early operas. It was with one of these, *Rienzi* (1840), in the style of grand opera of the 1830s, that he achieved his first notable stage success and appointment in 1843 as court *Kapellmeister* in Dresden. His fame rests, though, on the operas that followed: *Der fliegende Holländer* (*The Flying Dutchman*, 1841); *Tannhäuser* (1845); *Lohengrin* (1847); the tetralogy *Der Ring des Nibelungen* (*The Ring of the Nibelung*), comprising *Das Rheingold* (*The Rhinegold*, 1854), *Die Walküre* (*The Valkyrie*, 1856), *Siegfried* (1870), and *Götterdämmerung* (*The Twilight of the Gods*, 1874); *Tristan und Isolde* (1859);

Die Meistersinger von Nürnberg (*The Master-singers of Nuremberg*, 1867); and *Parsifal* (1882)—all of which continue to be performed regularly. With the exception of *Die Meistersinger*, these operas that followed *Rienzi* drew heavily on myth, legend, folk beliefs, and medieval epic. Even *Die Meister-singer* prominently employs the biblical story of the Fall and Christian imagery and folk traditions, notably that surrounding St John's Eve. Wagner's very first opera, *Die Feen* (*The Fairies*, 1833), was based on a fairy-tale play by Carlo *Gozzi; and fairy-tale motifs are evident in several of the later operas, particularly the borrowing of the motif of the youth who yearns to experience goose flesh (the fourth story in the *Grimms' *Kinder- und Hausmärchen*) for Siegfried and, less obviously, the motif of a sister's magically transformed brother—as found in a number of Grimm tales, notably 'Die zwölf Brüder' ('The Twelve Brothers'), 'Brü-derchen und Schwesterchen' ('Little Brother and Little Sister'), and 'Die sechs Schwäne' ('The Six Swans')—in *Lohengrin*. The legends of the Flying Dutchman, who is cursed with sailing the seas until he finds salvation through love, and of Tannhäuser's sojourn with the love goddess Venus—legends well-known in Wagner's day as popularized by the poet Heinrich Heine—formed the basis for those two operas. The Wagner operas from *Der fliegende Holländer* to *Parsifal* invariably include such elements of magic, marvel, or miracle, employing it to provide a transcendent or metaphysical dimension to the action and its psychological motivation. His *Musikdramen* (music dramas) represent both a culmination of German romantic opera and a development beyond it towards realism and modernism. JMM

Cooke, Deryck, *I Saw the World End: A Study of Wagner's 'Ring'* (1979).

Donington, Robert, *Wagner's 'Ring' and its Symbols: The Music and the Myth* (1963, repr. 1974).

McCreless, Patrick, *Wagner's Siegfried: Its Drama, History, and Music* (1982).

McGlathery, James M., *Wagner's Operas and Desire* (1998).

Rank, Otto, *Die Lohengrinsage: Ein Beitrag zu ihrer Motivgestaltung und Deutung* (1911).

Walcott, Derek (1930–) Caribbean poet, playwright, visual artist, and author. He was awarded the Queen's Gold Medal for Poetry in 1988, the Nobel Prize for literature in 1992, and the T.S. Elliot Prize in 2001. He is best known for his Homeric epic poem *Omeros* (1990). Much of Walcott's writing provides postcolonial reflections on folk tales of the West Indies through allegory and symbolism. Notable examples include the plays *Dream on Monkey Mountain* (1967), *The Sea at Dauphin* (1954), and *Ti-Jean and His Brothers* (1958), a fable about a family living on the edge of a magical forest haunted by spirits.   MF

Walker, Barbara G. (1930–) American author of feminist books such as *The Women's Encyclopedia of Myths and Secrets* (1983), *The Crone* (1985), and *The Woman's Dictionary of Symbols and Sacred Objects* (1988). In 1996 she published *Feminist Fairy Tales*, a collection of 28 stories with didactic morals. She retells many of the classical tales such as **'Little Red Riding Hood'*, **'Jack and the Beanstalk'*, **'Beauty and the Beast'*, and **'Aladdin'* with new titles. Thus, **'Cinderella'* becomes 'Cinder-Helle', who is born to a priestess of the Goddess of the Underworld. After the mother-spirit enables her to witness the death of goddess worship, she revives the temples of the goddess. Most of Walker's tales are contrived and contain overtly didactic messages that smack of New Age ideology.   JZ

Walker, Wendy (1951–) American writer. Her book *The Sea-Rabbit, or, The Artist of Life* (1988) is a collection of six tales based on the **Grimms'* **Kinder- und Hausmärchen* (*Children's and Household Tales*) along with two new stories about Samson and Delilah and the woman who lived in a shoe, and a parable about the cathedral of Notre Dame. Walker seeks to alter our customary notions about the classical fairy-tale tradition by fleshing out the lives of the original characters, probing their psyches, and altering narrative perspectives. In the title tale of the book, *The Sea Rabbit*, based on the Grimms' 'The Little Hamster from the Water', she presents an unlikely protagonist who refuses to accept the role of hero, for he is not particularly enamoured of the cruel and haughty princess, who takes pleasure in cutting off the heads of her suitors. In another work, *Stories out of Omarie* (1995), Walker revises tales based on the *Lais* of *Marie de France from a feminist perspective that celebrates the powers of women as storytellers.   JZ

Walser, Robert (1878–1956) Well-known Swiss writer. In his fairy-tale dramolettes 'Aschenbrödel' (*'Cinderella', 1901) and 'Schneewittchen' (*'Snow White', 1901), he treated the *Grimm fairy-tale tradition with irony. Metareflections about these dramolettes are integrated in his prose story 'Dornröschen' (*'Sleeping Beauty', 1916). In such stories as 'Märchen' ('Fairy Tale', 1910) and 'Das Ende der Welt' ('The End of the World', 1917) his satire tends to subvert the traditional happy endings of fairy tales.   BKM

Hübner, Andrea, 'Ei, welcher Unsinn liegt im Sinn?' *Robert Walsers Umgang mit Märchen und Trivialliteratur* (1995).

Walsh, Jill Paton (1937–) English novelist who is highly regarded for her historical fiction for young adults. However, Walsh is a versatile writer who has also explored different genres related to the fairy tale. For instance, *A Chance Child* (1978) is a time-travel novel that sends an unloved young boy, locked in a closet, into the past where he learns all about the abuse and exploitation of working-class children in the 19th century. *The Green Book* (1981) is a science-fiction work that recounts the trials and tribulations of a group of families who leave earth as it is about to disintegrate. Another science-fiction novel, *Torch* (1987), is about children in a post-nuclear world, and the torch they carry symbolizes the values of friendship, honesty, and sincerity that they must maintain if the torch is to keep burning in their new society. In her work for adults, Walsh has made use of folk tales, myths, and history in one collection of stories, *Five Tides* (1986), that recall folk tales, legends, and history about people who live along the coast during the time of Cromwell. Her most important fairy-tale work for young adults is *Birdy and the Ghosties* (1989), which is about the ferryman's daughter Birdy, who learns from a mysterious old woman that she has second sight, and this power enables her to reap great benefits. JZ

Walton, Jo (1964–) Welsh-Canadian science fiction and fantasy writer and poet whose novels have won the World Fantasy Award, the Prometheus Award, and the Hugo Award. While she has not produced works that could strictly speaking be called fairy tales, she has written a number of novels such as *The King's Peace* (2000), *The King's Name* (2001), and *The Prize in the Game* (2002) that contain fairy-tale motifs and are steeped in Celtic folklore. In *Among Others* (2011), which won the Nebula Award for best novel, a young girl, Morwenna Phelps, lives in Wales and spends a good deal of her time reading science fiction stories while being persecuted by her witchlike, somewhat mad mother. So she flees to her estranged father in England, where she learns how to use magic and her knowledge of books to overcome her mother in a fierce battle. As in some of her other novels and poems, Walton displays a great talent for mixing medieval folklore, science fiction, and fairy tales to produce unusual fantasy works. JZ

Warner, Marina (1946–) British writer and critic. She has investigated how myths rule our perceptions in several important studies such as *Alone of All Her Sex: The Myth and Cult of the Virgin Mary* (1976), *Monuments and Maidens: The Allegory of the Female Form* (1985), *Managing Monsters: Six Myths of Our Time* (1994), and *No Go the Bogeyman: Scaring, Lulling and Making Mock* (1998). Warner incorporates a feminist perspective in all her endeavours, and her most notable work in the field of the fairy tale is *From the Beast to the Blonde: On Fairy Tales and their Tellers* (1995), a social history which seeks to recuperate the role that women have played in both the oral tradition of the folk tale and the literary one of the fairy tale. Warner has also edited *Wonder Tales: Six Stories of Enchantment* (1994), a collection of 17th-century French fairy tales. Her novel *Indigo* (1992) and her unique stories in *The Mermaids in the Basement* (1993) contain fairy-tale elements that revise conventional motifs and reflect her concern in restoring creative power to women as strong protagonists and authors of their own lives. In *Phantasmagoria* (2006) Warner studied how the spirit has been embodied or represented over several centuries in diverse art forms from waxworks to the cinema, and in *Charmed States and the Arabian Nights* (2011), she provides thorough and astute analyses of fifteen significant fairy tales and demonstrates why and how the *Nights* as an international compendium of stories has had such a significant impact on art and literature throughout the world. JZ

Warner, Sylvia Townsend (1893–1978) English novelist, short-story writer, and biographer. Her first novel, *Lolly Willowes* (1926), was the story of a spinster who moves to the depths of the country and becomes a witch; it was a best-seller. In 1940 she published *The Cat's Cradle Book*, which purports to be a collection of old stories told by cats to their kittens. According to the narrator of the frame story, all our fairy tales originated with cats. That is why their mood is not heated and sentimental, but 'cool . . . objective—and catlike'.

The tone of the Cat's Cradle tales is one of calm, detached amusement. Two of the best are riffs on the future adventures of the characters in *'Puss-in-Boots' and *'Bluebeard' or their descendants. In 'Bluebeard's Daughter', for instance, blue-haired Djamileh and her husband are consumed with curiosity about the locked room in the castle, which fortunately turns out to be empty.

In the last year of her life, when she was 84, Sylvia Townsend Warner published her last and most remarkable book, *Kingdoms of Elfin* (1977). It is a brilliantly written and original fantasy in the form of a series of linked stories. They take off from traditional reports of the appearance and behaviour of the fairies in European folklore and Shakespearian drama. Thus the fairies are slightly smaller than humans but much longer-lived; they can fly and, unless they choose, are usually invisible to mortals. They sing and dance with great skill, enjoy parties and feasts, and live in large groups underground. The way to their world is through the small green hills known in Britain as fairy mounds. As in the folk tales, from time to time the fairies kidnap a human baby, substituting a changeling; they may also take adult captives.

According to Warner, fairies have no souls: they are beautiful and charming, but also cool, rational, and detached. They cannot weep or hate, and their love affairs tend to be brief. In most Elfin societies there are only aristocrats and servants: politically, this suggests Europe in the late Middle Ages, except that the fairy kingdoms are always ruled by queens.

The kingdoms of Elfin are located in several European countries and in Persia, and a satirical intention is visible in the way in which the inhabitants of each kingdom share the characteristics of the local humans. The North German fairies, for example, enjoy metaphysical argument and the Austrians, rich, heavy cooking; the French Elfin court is elaborate, with much emphasis on proper dress and manners, while the Norwegian kingdom is simpler and cruder, and includes witches and trolls.

Kingdoms of Elfin is witty, subtle, and often enchanting; yet there is an undertone of sadness in these stories. Though most of the aristocratic fairies live in idle, frivolous luxury, they are not always happy; their affections are fleeting, and their great dread is boredom. Perhaps, Warner seems to be suggesting, there is something to be said for a short human life of work and struggle and strong emotions.   AL

Crossley, Robert, 'A Long Day's Dying: The Elves of J. R. R. Tolkien and Sylvia Townsend Warner', in Carl B. Yoke and Donald M. Hassler (eds.), *Death and the Serpent: Immortality in Science Fiction and Fantasy* (1985).

Weber, Carl Maria Friedrich Ernst von (1786–1826) German composer and pianist. Appointed director of the Opera at Prague in 1813 and at Dresden in 1816, Weber was at the height of his career when he composed the highly popular *Der Freischütz* (1821). Its plot derives from the common folklore motif of the man who sells the devil his soul; Weber's huntsman protagonist bargains for magic bullets, so that he can win a contest of marksmanship, and with it the hand of the woman he loves. She succeeds in redeeming him with her pure-hearted love, however, and the two lovers are happily united. The high point of the opera is the casting of the magic bullets at midnight in the 'Wolf's Glen', a scene of supernatural horror, expressed musically through imaginative orchestration and unusual harmonies. Weber's serious use of supernatural elements, combined with the wild natural setting, the struggle between forces of good and evil, the theme of redemption, and the source of the story in medieval legend, made *Der Freischütz* the work which defined and established German romantic opera. His last opera, *Oberon, or The Elf King's Oath* (1826), has even closer ties to the world of fantasy and fairy tale. The English libretto, by James Robinson *Planché, is based on *Oberon*, a heroic poem by Christoph Martin *Wieland, and weaves elements from *Shakespeare's *Midsummer Night's Dream*, the Near East of The *Arabian Nights*, and the legendary court of Charlemagne into a far from cohesive whole.   SR

Weldon, Fay (1931–) CBE, FRSL English feminist who in her fiction explores women's experiences trapped in oppressive patriarchal structures and situations, often via traditional and literary fairy-tale references. For example, Ruth, heroine of *Life and Loves of a She-Devil* (1983), compares her cosmetic surgery to the mermaid's transformation in Hans Christian *Andersen's 'The *Little Mermaid'. Weldon's novel *Little Sisters* (1977; US title, *Words of Advice*) parallels 'The Robber Bridegroom' tale type; ingénue/survivor Elsa encounters the rejected wife/old woman

Gemma, who helps Elsa learn the truth about the exploiting men she encounters.　　PG

Walker, Nancy A. 'Witch Weldon: Fay Weldon's Use of the Fairy Tale Tradition', in Regina Barreca (ed.), *Fay Weldon's Wicked Fictions* (1994).

Wells, H. G. (Herbert George Wells, 1866–1946) British novelist and social critic, regarded as one of the pioneers of science fiction. His most famous works in this genre are *The Time Machine* (1895), *The Invisible Man* (1897), and *The War of the Worlds* (1897). He also published numerous stories of the supernatural such as 'The Man who Could Work Miracles' and fairy tales such as 'The Magic Shop' and 'Mr Skelmersdale in Fairyland' in *Twelve Stories and a Dream* (1903). One of his novels, *The Sea Lady* (1902), involves a mermaid who appears to a family on the English coast and influences their lives.　　JZ

Wenz-Viëtor, Else (1882–1973) The most famous German illustrator of picture books for children during the 1920s and 1930s. She produced more than 100 books during a career that lasted until the early 1960s and provided illustrations for works written by popular authors such as Adolf Holst, Sophie Reinheimer, and Max Dingler. She also wrote her own texts. Wenz-Viëtor's early illustrations with anthropomorphized animals and plants were influenced by the *Jugendstil* movement, but later she drew all creatures and flowers in a more natural style. Among her best fairy-tale books are: *Das Schlaraffenland* (*The Land of Milk and Honey*, 1923), *Märchen-Ostern* (*An Easter Fairy Tale*, 1927), and *Das grosse Märchenbuch* (*The Great Fairy Tale Book*, 1957). In addition, she drew illustrations for the classic authors Jacob and Wilhelm *Grimm, Wilhelm *Hauff, Ludwig *Bechstein, and Hans Christian *Andersen with bright colours and cute characters that emphasized the cheerful and humorous aspects of the tales.　　JZ

Werenskiold, Erik (1855–1938) Norwegian illustrator and painter who was greatly influenced by French impressionism. In 1881 he collaborated with Theodor Kittelsen to provide the ink drawings for the first illustrated edition of Peter Christen *Asbjørnsen and Jørgen Moe's *Norwegian Folktales*.　　JZ

Whistler, Rex (Reginald John Whistler, 1905–44) British painter, illustrator, and stage designer. Whistler's illustrations for Walter *de la Mare's *The Lord Fish and Other Tales* (1933), *Andersen's *Fairy Tales and Legends* (1935), and *Gulliver's Travels* (1935) are particularly noteworthy. His *Gulliver*, with maps and pictures in exquisitely detailed pen and ink, is considered one of the great illustrated books of the century. Whistler's first important commission was a series of highly imaginative murals for the Tate Gallery Refreshment Room. *The Expedition in Pursuit of Rare Meats* (1927) depicts a hunting party embarking from an 18th-century palace on horseback, chariot, and bicycle. Journeying through mountains and forests, they encounter mythical beasts, cross a broken bridge haunted by mermaids, and return home bearing caviar, lobsters, scented tea, and other delicacies. The romantic realism of Whistler's style—deliberately reminiscent of rococo painting—and his subtle and witty sense of fantasy were typical of his work. The 18m (58-foot) mural he completed in the late 1930s for the dining room of Plas Newydd—a *trompe-l'œil* panorama of an imaginary Italian city by the sea—has been described as the finest 20th-century example of decorative painting created for a country house; an adjacent room is now a Whistler museum. Whistler had begun to reveal exceptional talent as a stage designer for plays, ballets, and operas when he was killed in action in the Second World War.　　SR

Whistler, Laurence, and Fuller, R., *The Work of Rex Whistler* (1960).

White, T. H. (Terence Hanbury White, 1906–64) English author of novels based on Arthurian legend. The earliest, *The Sword in the Stone* (1938), was published with his own illustrations. Set in a mock medieval England, it is a fantastic and light-hearted account of the education of young Arthur (the

Wart). He is brought up with Kay, his foster-father's son, under the tutelage of Merlyn. Merlyn's lessons include much magic, and in the forest outside there are witches and outlaws. The book ends when the Wart, to-tally unaware of the significance of the act, pulls the sword from the stone and to his dismay becomes king. The original text of the book was altered so that it could be fitted into the four-part novel, *The Once and Future King* (1958). This shows Arthur as king; the romance of Lancelot and Guinevere is a prominent theme.

Mistress Masham's Repose (1947) is a fan-tasy about a colony of Lilliputians, descend-ed from a few brought back to England by the captain of Gulliver's ship. They live on an island in a lake belonging to a ducal man-sion, where 10-year-old Maria, the last sur-vivor of the family who owned the place, chances upon them. Though she at first an-tagonizes them by her attempts to interfere in their lives, they become her friends, and through their resourcefulness and courage she is rescued from the fate the villainous governess and the vicar plan for her, and for the Lilliputians themselves.   GA

Wiechert, Ernst (pseudonym of **Ernst Barany Bjell**, 1887–1950) German teacher and author. His popular novels urged the virtues of simplicity, humility, and ideal love. Despite a three-month internment in the concentration camp Buchenwald for his openly expressed criticism of the Nazi re-gime, he is a controversial figure whose sta-tus as a dissident has been questioned because of his enduring popularity and suc-cess as a published author under the Nazis. Nevertheless, all his work bears testimony to his defiant defence of his beliefs, including the immensely successful *Das einfache Leben* (*The Simple Life*, 1939), which advo-cated living a good life as an answer to the sickness of the age, a guiding light for hu-mankind lost in the gloom of despair. His critical writing survived, buried in his gar-den, to be published after the war: *Die Jer-ominkinder* (*The Earth is Our Heritage*, vol. i, 1945, vol. ii, 1947) and *Der Totenwald* (*The Forest of the Dead*, 1945), a mainly

autobiographical record written expressly as a literary chronicle of Buchenwald and a memorial to the dead. Disenchanted with post-war developments in Germany and the hostile attitude towards his attempts to promote an honest coming-to-terms with the Nazi past, he emigrated in 1948 to Switz-erland, where he died in 1950.

Wiechert saw himself as a poet in the romantic sense, a seer and a translator of the inner world, with a mission to write in defence of the poor and the oppressed and to uphold the morals of his homeland. In works such as *Die Majorin* (*The Baroness*, 1934), and *Der weisse Büffel* (*The White Buf-falo*, 1937) he develops the central idea of the intrinsic worth of the natural man, the simple life, and the possession of a pure heart. *Missa sine nomine* (1950), his last and hugely successful novel, acknow-ledges the presence of evil but suggests that it can be overcome by love and altruistic service to others. All of Wiechert's extensive output contains elements of transposed autobiography, but essentially his is a mys-tical vision which concentrates on the inner suffering of his heroes rather than their actions, and ultimately fails to analyse contemporary society.

In 1944, concerned about the effect of the war on the young, Wiechert wrote 40 fairy tales with the express aim of 'making children's hearts glow again'. Published in the two-volume *Märchen* (1946) and in vol. viii of *Sämtliche Werke* (*Complete Works*, 1957), they are, like all his writing, intense-ly polarized didactic parables about the fight of good versus evil, where good is identified with nature, simplicity, love, and a desire to help, while evil is personi-fied by the city, mass civilization, greed, power, and self-interest. Although there are influences of the Brothers *Grimm— 'Die arme Magd' ('The Poor Maid'), for example, is a version of 'Aschenputtel' (*'Cinderella')—Wiechert's stories are un-like folk tales in their contemplative and reflexive mood, concentrating on the in-ward quest of the hero to resist the temp-tations of ambition and wealth and retain a simple and pure heart.   KS

Boag, Hugh-Alexander, *Ernst Wiechert: The Prose Works in Relation to his Life and Times* (1987).

Venzin, Renate-Pia, *Ernst Wiecherts Märchen. Ein Beitrag zum Kunstmärchen der Gegenwart* (1954).

Wieland, Christoph Martin (1733–1813)

German writer and poet, closely associated with the rise of Weimar culture. He studied theology in a monastery near Magdeburg, but his interest in writing drew him to work with the renowned Swiss critic Johann Jakob Bodmer in Zurich between 1752 and 1754. Thereafter he gained recognition for his poetry, novels, and tales, and by 1772, when he settled in Weimar, he was considered the foremost writer in Germany. Strongly influenced by the French fairy-tale vogue of the 18th century, Wieland published an important collection of tales entitled *Dschinnistan* (1786–9), which included adaptations from the French *Cabinet des fées* (*see* MAYER, CHARLES-JOSEPH DE) as well as three original tales, 'Der Stein der Weisen' ('The Philosopher's Stone'), 'Timander und Melissa', and 'Der Druide oder die Salamanderin und die Bildsäule' ('The Druid or the Salamander and the Painted Pillar'). Typical of all these tales is the triumph of rationalism over mysticism. Among his other works that incorporated fairy-tale motifs are *Der Sieg der Natur über die Schwärmerei oder die Abenteuer des Don Sylvio von Rosalva* (*The Victory of Nature over Fanaticism or the Adventures of Don Sylvio von Rosalva*, 1764), *Der goldene Spiegel* (*The Golden Mirror*, 1772), and *Oberon* (1780). In addition, he wrote 'Pervonte' (1778–9), a remarkable verse rendition of *Basile's 'Peruonto', which concerns a poor simpleton whose heart is so good that he is blessed by the fairies and thus rises in society.   JZ

Bauer, Roger, '"The Fairy Way of Writing": Von Shakespeare zu Wieland und Tieck', in Roger Bauer, Michael de Graat, and Jürgen Werheimer (eds.), *Das Shakespeare-Bild in Europa zwischen Aufklärung und Romantik* (1988).

Lim, Jeong-Taeg, *Don Sylvio und Anselmus: Untersuchungen zur Gestaltung des Wunderbaren bei C. M. Wieland und E. T. A. Hoffmann* (1988).

Nobis, Helmut, *Phantasie und Moralität: Das Wunderbare in Wielands, 'Dschinnistan' und der 'Geschichte des Prinzen Biribinker'* (1976).

Stickney-Bailey, Susan, 'Tieck's Märchen and the Enlightenment: The Influence of Wieland and Musäus' (Diss., University of Massachusetts-Amherst, 1986).

Wilde, Oscar (1854–1900)

Dublin-born poet, playwright and aesthete. The child of two parents who had both contributed to the collection of Celtic folklore, he was the author of two important collections of literary fairy tales. Oscar's father, Sir William Wilde, had retold tales of the Irish Sidhe in *Irish Popular Superstitions* (1852), while his mother, the patriotic poet Lady Jane Wilde or 'Speranza', had used materials collected by her husband and herself to write what *Yeats considered one of the most important books on the Celtic fairy faith, *Ancient Legends, Mystic Charms, and Superstitions of Ireland* (1887). She also wrote on *Ancient Cures, Charms and Usages* in 1890.

Wilde's two volumes of fairy tales, *The Happy Prince* (1888) and *A House of Pomegranates* (1891) were written, according to a letter of 1888, 'partly for children and partly for those who have kept the childlike faculties of wonder and joy'. Their creation may have been prompted by his wife, Constance Lloyd, who published two volumes of children's fantasies in 1889 and 1892; by Wilde's desire for tales to tell his own two young sons; by his mother's publications of collected folklore; and perhaps by Yeats's *Fairy and Folk Tales of the Irish Peasantry* (1889), a collection that Wilde admired and favourably reviewed. Wilde's first volume, illustrated by Walter *Crane and Jacomb Hood and containing five tales, 'The Happy Prince', 'The Nightingale and the Rose', 'The Selfish Giant', 'The Devoted Friend', and 'The Remarkable Rocket', was a great success; most critics still consider 'The Happy Prince' and 'The Selfish Giant', the finest of the fairy tales. Four more stories, 'The Young King', 'The Birthday of the Infanta', 'The Fisherman and his Soul', and 'The

Star-Child', were collected as *A House of Pomegranates*, this time in an elegant volume designed and decorated by Charles Ricketts and Charles Shannon in 1891.

Wilde's literary fairy tales are influenced by the Brothers *Grimm and especially by Hans Christian *Andersen, whose moralized and sentimentalized versions of Scandinavian folk tales are sometimes amplified and sometimes subverted by him. 'The Nightingale and the Rose' is a tough-minded comment on Andersen's 'The Nightingale'; 'The Devoted Friend' an inversion of 'Great Claus and Little Claus'; and 'The Fisherman and his Soul', a reversal of and complex comment on 'The *Little Mermaid'. Vyvyan Holland, Wilde's son, reminded readers that his father spent much time in his childhood in Connemara, and Irish materials also contribute to Wilde's tales. For example, 'The Young King' and 'The Star-Child' may be read as accounts of changelings, while tales of undines and fishermen are particularly popular in Ireland, though common in all Indo-European lore.

What makes Wilde's tales uniquely compelling is the elegance of their language combined with the strangeness of their content. Stylistically, they are perfectly articulated studies in artifice and surface, sometimes biblical in tone ('The Star-Child'), sometimes filled with sensuous and mannered description ('The Birthday of the Infanta' and 'The Fisherman and his Soul'), most often prose-poems in feeling. Yet this artificial, highly decorated prose is used to convey parables of egoism and altruism, of Christian self-sacrifice as in 'The Happy Prince,' 'The Selfish Giant', and 'The Young King'; or of the Christlike artist, as in 'The Nightingale'; or to produce cautionary tales of selfishness and narcissism as in 'The Devoted Friend' and 'The Remarkable Rocket'. The protest against social injustice and inequality, the sympathy with the poor and oppressed which was to figure in Wilde's *Soul of Man under Socialism* (1891), are directly or indirectly expressed in 'The Happy Prince', 'The Devoted Friend', and 'The Selfish Giant', and later in 'The Young King' and 'The Birthday of the Infanta', while Wilde's anti-puritanism and anti-conventionalism are reflected in 'The Nightingale and the Rose' and 'The Fisherman and his Soul'. The artist as martyr and saint figures in several tales, most notably in 'The Nightingale', and the impossibility or failure of romantic love is explored in that tale as well as in 'The Birthday of the Infanta' and 'The Fisherman and his Soul'.

Wilde's fairy tales are also notable for their unhappy or unresolved endings; some are simply sad, others ironic, many are deeply cynical. *A House of Pomegranates* is even more sombre than *The Happy Prince*; three of its four tales conclude with the demise of the sympathetic protagonists as the Dwarf, Star-Child, Fisherman, and Mermaid die. None of the tales has a conventional happy ending.

Wilde's tales are less designed as works for children than as attempts to mirror late Victorian life in a form remote from reality and to embody the problems of the era in an ideal mode. Moreover, the creation of a fairy world enables Wilde to deal symbolically with social taboos and to reveal his repressed feelings and desires. The tales have been read in different ways at various times. Recently they have been viewed as studies in homoerotic relations (see the Prince and the Sparrow in 'The Happy Prince') or as explorations of the author's masochistic and sadistic impulses—see, for example, the self-inflicted torments of the Giant and the Star-Child or the notable cruelty of the Princess in 'The Birthday of the Infanta'—and even as totally ironic in intention. Nevertheless, they remain memorable and haunting additions to the genre of the literary fairy tale.   CGS

Ellmann, Richard, *Oscar Wilde* (1987).

Pine, Richard, *The Thief of Reason: Oscar Wilde* (1995).

Snider, Clifton, 'Eros and Logos in Some Fairy Tales by Oscar Wilde', *Victorian Newsletter*, 84 (fall 1993).

Tremper, Ellen, 'Commitment and Escape: The Fairy Tales of Thackeray, Dickens, and Wilde', *The Lion and the Unicorn* (1978).

Zipes, Jack, 'Oscar Wilde's Tales of Illumination', in *When Dreams Came True: Classical Tales and Their Tradition* (2nd edn., 2007).

Wilde, Oscar The swallow, who is the prince's dear friend, arrives to comfort him in Oscar Wilde's *The Happy Prince and Other Tales* (1888), illustrated by Walter *Crane. The Bodleian Library, University of Oxford (Opie AA 2725).

Wilde's fairy tales, film adaptations

Three of Oscar Wilde's fairy tales have been filmed in their own right, one of them twice; and one of the three is positioned in a biographical film as a commentary on parts of Wilde's life.

The Selfish Giant (Canada/USA, 1972) was the first of a trio to reach the screen in adaptations, co-produced by the Reader's Digest Association, which strive, within the parameters of a 25-minute animation, to be faithful to Wilde's text. A narrator tells the story of a lovely garden where children play until the owner, a giant, comes home from a seven-year absence. He immediately drives the children away, puts up 'Keep Out' signs, and barricades himself in. The result of this selfishness is that Spring and Summer never come to the garden: instead there is always Snow and Frost. Eventually, the children creep back through a hole in the wall; then

the birds and flowers and sun return. The giant, realizing how selfish he has been, knocks down the wall and welcomes the children back. Many years later, one child he especially loves turns out to be an emissary from Christ. The giant dies, and is taken to Paradise.

The Reader's Digest version of Wilde's best-known story, *The Happy Prince* (1974), gives voices to the two main characters, as well as to a narrator. It concerns a bejewelled and gilded statue, the Prince, who is befriended by a Swallow on his way south for the winter. Seeing ugliness and misery all around, the Prince persuades the Swallow to peck out his jewels and peel off his gold leaf to distribute to the destitute people of the town. Thus delayed, the Swallow misses his chance to go with the other birds to Egypt; later, though there is still time to go, he chooses to stay with the Prince, till in the depths of winter he dies of cold. The Prince, who now looks shabby, is pulled down. God summons an angel to bring the two friends to Paradise.

The same story has also been adapted (UK, 1996) as a mini-opera performed by animated models, with the Swallow sung by Jimmy Somerville and the Prince by William Dazely. The requirements of the form and medium result in bits of Wilde's text being selected and expanded, while others are rejected. A dramatist freezing in a garret is identified as Wilde himself, dreaming of a first-night success if he ever gets warm enough to finish his play; a little starving match-girl imagines vast quantities of food dancing before her eyes. At the end, when the Swallow is dead, a modern reference is slipped in: self-important local officials disparage him as a foreign bird, an immigrant that lives by scrounging.

The last Reader's Digest adaptation was *The Remarkable Rocket* (1975), narrated by David Niven. In it a group of fireworks is conversing while waiting to be let off as part of the celebrations at a royal wedding. The rocket, very self-important, does most of the talking; then, because he is so sensitive, weeps at the thought of the royal couple losing their son—not even conceived yet— and in the process makes himself damp. As a result, the other fireworks give a good account of themselves when the moment comes, but the remarkable rocket is discarded as useless. Essentially, this plot is a device to allow Wilde, as storyteller, to make epigrammatic criticisms of certain types of character.

Comments on his own character are implied in the biopic *Wilde* (UK, 1997) by the incorporation of portions of the text of 'The Selfish Giant', sometimes as voiceover, sometimes integrated into the screen action. The idea is that aspects of Wilde's life are reflected in the story. When he has just admitted and released his homosexuality, and consequently is neglecting his family, he sees himself as selfish, like the giant; at the same time, like the children in the story, he faces prosecution if caught trespassing. Later, while his wife is reading a passage

about the beauty of the giant's garden, he is seen walking in just such a place with Lord Alfred Douglas. Back home, telling his children how the giant was 'really very sorry for what he had done', Wilde is wistful. Finally, in Reading gaol, after he has been sentenced to two years' hard labour, Wilde once again sees himself as the giant, who 'grew very old and feeble' and 'could not play about any more'.   TAS

Williams, Jay (1914–78) American writer. Although he published nearly 70 books for children, as well as many adult novels and mysteries, Jay Williams is best known today for his Danny Dunn juvenile science-fiction series (begun with Raymond Abrashkin, who died after the fifth volume appeared). Though some of the plot motifs in these popular books can be traced back to folk-tale sources (invisibility, a monster who lives in a swamp, etc.), the emphasis is on scientific invention and comedy.

Williams was also one of the first and best of the authors who responded to the feminist movement of the late 1960s and early 1970s by writing a new kind of fairy tale. Though his stories are traditional in their choice of episode and motif, they also overturn nearly all the conventions of the genre to illustrate new ideas about women.

Williams's famously funny and very influential picture book *The Practical Princess* (1969) reworked both *'Rapunzel' and *'Sleeping Beauty'. Its heroine, Princess Bedelia, has been promised to a dragon, but instead of waiting for a prince to rescue her, she explodes the monster by arranging for a straw figure filled with gunpowder to be dressed in her court robes and thrown into its open mouth. Later, when she is imprisoned in a tower, she wakes up a prince who is lying there in an enchanted sleep, and then escapes by climbing down his long curly beard.

Williams's other best-known genre-dissolving fairy tale, *Petronella* (1973), declares its intention in the first paragraph: 'In the kingdom of Skyclear Mountain, three princes were always born ... the youngest prince always rescued a princess, brought her home, and in time ruled over the kingdom. That was the way it had always been . . . Until now.' This time the youngest child is a red-headed princess called Petronella. She won't stay home and wait for suitors, but insists on going out into the world with her brothers. As a result of her kindness to an old man, she finds a handsome prince in the garden of an enchanter. The prince is lazy, selfish, and somewhat stupid, but since he is the only prince around, Petronella continues to act out the standard plot. She manages to fulfil three difficult tasks: calming and taming ferocious dogs, horses, and hawks; then she and the prince flee, pursued by the enchanter. Finally, to her amazement, she discovers that the enchanter is glad to be rid of the lazy prince, who came for a visit and just wouldn't leave. The enchanter isn't chasing the prince; he is chasing Petronella, with whom he has fallen in love. Recognizing her true destiny, Petronella agrees to marry him, and the lazy prince has to walk home alone.

Though there are now many stories like these in print, when *The Practical Princess* and *Petronella* first appeared, they caused a minor sensation, and as a result both readers and writers now approach fairy tales in new and interesting ways. AL

Willingham, Bill (1956–) American comic-book author, illustrator, and colourist, acclaimed for creating the award-winning fairy-tale comic-book series *Fables* (2002–). Featuring exiled fairy-tale characters known as Fables, the series follows their adventures living in a New York City neighbourhood called Fabletown. Exemplary volumes include *Legends in Exile* (2003), in which Sheriff Bigby Wolf investigates the murder of Rose Red, known from 'The Two Girls, the Bear, and the Dwarf'; *Storybook Love* (2004), in which *Bluebeard enchants both Snow White and Sheriff Bigby Wolf, and Goldilocks is hired to assassinate them; and *Arabian Nights (and Days)* (2006), which features Sinbad leading a troupe to negotiate peace with the enemy of all Fables. Willingham also published an annotated companion, *Fables Encyclopedia*

(2013), and, additionally, has created spin-off projects, such as the series *Jack of Fables* (2006–11) and *Fairest* (2012–), and the novel *Peter and Max* (2009). KMJ

Willow (film: USA, 1988) The counterpart of *Star Wars* (1977). Premissed on magic rather than technology, *Willow* is a quest-story born from the research George Lucas did into folklore and mythology while writing his space trilogy. Among its numerous sources of inspiration are *Tolkien, *The *Wizard of Oz*, the Bible, and *A Midsummer Night's Dream*. Willow Ufgood, a would-be magician, rescues a birthmarked baby from a river and sets off to find Raziel, the good witch who alone can, through the baby, end the reign of the evil queen Bavmorda. Sometimes helped by Madmartigan, a mercenary who comes to see the point of being compassionate rather than selfish, Willow progresses towards an understanding of true magic. TAS

Windling, Terri American editor, artist, writer, and essayist, who has made major contributions to the fields of fantasy literature and fairy tales. She has promoted the works of some of the best fantasy and fairy-tale writers (Jane *Yolen, Charles *De Lint, Tanith *Lee, Pamela Dean) in series at Ace and Tor Books, and she has co-edited with Ellen Datlow important anthologies of fantasy and horror tales. Her fairy-tale novels include *The Changeling* (1995), *The Wood Wife* (1996), *The Raven Queen* (1999), *A Midsummer Night's Faery Tale* (1999), *The Winter Child* (2001), and *The Faeries of Spring Cottage* (2003). In addition, she edited *The Armless Maiden*, a collection of realistic stories and fairy tales about child abuse. In 1987 she founded the Endicott Studio, a non-profit organization dedicated to literary, visual, and performance arts inspired by *myth, *folklore, and *fairy tales. Her own artworks have been exhibited in America and Europe. JZ

Winterson, Jeanette (1959–) British journalist and novelist who employs fairy-tale motifs in many of her works. After studying English literature at St. Catherine's College, Oxford, she moved to London and published her first novel, *Oranges Are Not the Only Fruit* (1985), in which she parodies numerous fairy tales from a strong feminist perspective. In *Sexing the Cherry* (1989), Winterson adapts the Brothers *Grimm's 'The Twelve Dancing Princesses' with a radical lesbian-feminist agenda. Her novel begins where the Grimms' tale ends: it traces the individual fates of the princesses and reveals that 'happily ever after' and conventional gender expectations can never be fulfilling. There are also fairy-tale motifs in such recent works as *The King of Capri* (2003), a picture book for children; *The Battle of the Sun* (2009), an unusual historical fantasy that has traces of 'The Sorcerer's Apprentice' and King Arthur and Knights of the Roundtable; and *The Lion, The Unicorn and Me: The Donkey's Christmas Story* (2009), a retelling of the nativity tale.   JZ

Doan, Laura, 'Jeanette Winterson's Sexing the Postmodern', in *The Lesbian Postmodern* (1994).

Makinen, Merja, *The Novels Jeanette Winterson: A Reader's Guide* (2005).

Makinen, Merja, Theorizing Fairy-Tale Fiction, Reading Jeanette Winterson', in Stephen Benson (ed.), *Contemporary Fiction and the Fairy Tale* (2008).

Rusk, Lauren, 'The Refusal of Otherness: Winterson's *Oranges Are Not the Only Fruit*', in *The Life Writing of Otherness* (2002).

Wizard of Oz, The (1900) Widely considered the most popular American fairy tale, *The Wizard of Oz* is the first in a series of 14 Oz books by L. Frank *Baum. Hard hit by the brutal economic depression of 1890, this actor, journalist, and window decorator established himself as an author of children's books with *Father Goose: His Book* (1899). From rewritten nursery rhymes, Baum turned to the wonder tales of *Andersen and the *Grimms. Writing during the vogue of utopian novels, he wanted a 'modernized fairy tale' that would omit both romance and nightmare-causing violence yet still provide an entertaining morality for children. He also modernized the talking beasts

of folklore into sentient machines like the Tin Woodman: in this way, he could introduce turn-of-the-century industrialization into a fairyland where no one is injured (wicked witches notwithstanding). First illustrated by W. W. *Denslow, *The Wonderful Wizard of Oz* (as it was first entitled) was a runaway bestseller of the first half of the century, although it received scant literary acclaim. Indeed, the entire Oz series, consisting of 14 novels published between 1900 and 1920, was essentially blacklisted during the McCarthy era by librarians who dismissed it as subversive popular culture of poor literary quality. Nor was the 1939 MGM musical a critical success, losing $1 million in its initial run. Filmed during the Depression when America needed escapist fare, it only began its rise to cult status in 1956, with its first annual televised showing. The public has since re-evaluated both the film and book, which boasts 10 million copies in 22 languages.

This is the story of Dorothy Gale (played by Judy Garland). Ignored by foster-parents on a bleak farm in Kansas, she is transported by a cyclone to the utopia of Oz. Dorothy, however, wants to return home, and sets out to find the Wizard for help. On her quest, she encounters a Scarecrow, Tin Woodman, and Cowardly Lion seeking a brain, a heart, and courage. The Wizard refuses to help unless they kill the Wicked Witch of the West. Dorothy accidentally does this, but Oz cannot keep his promise because he is not really a wizard. He does, however, bestow the physical attributes of the intelligence, compassion, and valour that the trio have demonstrated all along. In the end, it is Dorothy who takes herself home: she has learned that her silver shoes (ruby slippers in the film) have always held the power to fulfil her dreams.

Dorothy's journey to Oz and back is therefore a child's quest of self-discovery, a rite of passage in which she overcomes challenges by learning to use her talents. This individual and societal maturation is neatly underscored in Victor Fleming's Oscar-winning film, whose host of screenwriters tightened Baum's storyline. They eliminated sub-plots and introduced new characters to the

"You ought to be ashamed of yourself!"

The Wizard of Oz 'You ought to be ashamed of yourself!' Dorothy scolds the Cowardly Lion in the first edition of L. Frank *Baum's *The Wizard of Oz* (1900), illustrated by W. W. *Denslow.

prologue (Miss Gulch, Professor Marvel, the trio of farmhands) that are 'ozzified' into the Wicked Witch (Margaret Hamilton), Wizard (Frank Morgan), Scarecrow (Ray Bolger), Tin Woodman (Jack Haley), and Cowardly Lion (Bert Lahr). The film also unifies Dorothy's narrative point of view with songs like 'Over the Rainbow' (by Harold Arlen and E. Y. Harburg), and faithfully exploits the metaphor of grey Kansas vs. Technicolor Oz. The endings of book and film, however, diverge: where Baum's Oz is real, Hollywood's is a dream.

Dreams and the collective unconscious figure in the film's psychoanalytical interpretations. Jungians stress Dorothy's quest for self in which she is aided by personified characters (Scarecrow, Cowardly Lion, etc.). Freudians address ineffectual parent figures and posit a 'family romance' that replaces them with good witches and wizards. They cite numerous images of castration (Oz's floating head, the Tin Woodman's mutilation), note the phallic imagery of the cyclone and witch's broomstick, and find that Dorothy comes to sexual maturity when she appropriates the broomstick and gives it to Oz. Sexuality is further underscored by the colour red (for menstruation) of the film's ruby slippers.

Critics analysing the book, however, equate Dorothy's *silver* shoes with the silver standard of 1890s Populist debates. William Jennings Bryan, farmers, and public-wary presidents are represented by the Cowardly Lion, Scarecrow, and Wizard. Midwestern politics are further allegorized in the Tin Woodman's dehumanization from flesh to tin—a metaphorical industrialization that is vanquished by the Jeffersonian agrarianism of Kansas, geographic and symbolic centre of the United States. This model presents Kansas as a secular Garden of Eden, but Oz-as-Utopia is championed in socio-political commentary of the later Oz books. Feminists cite the numerous emasculated males and analyse the suffragette-type leaders of *The Land of Oz*. Others find in the illness-free *Emerald City of Oz* a (socialist) paradise where poverty and money need not exist because happy workers share their wealth

and talents. Solidarity and pacifism rule Oz, where a giant Love Magnet imbues all who enter with selflessness. In short, Oz is what a disenchanted America is not.

Baum would probably be amused by all these interpretations, for he stressed that he wrote only for children, at their behest. Today, his utopian tale continues to inspire with its hopeful message of individual growth and social reform. In fact, there are more than 100 sequels, parodies, and pastiches of Oz, with notable reinventions from black Broadway musicals (*The Wiz*, 1975) to parallel worlds (*A Barnstormer in Oz*, 1982) to metaphors about Aids (*Was*, 1992). Indeed, the recent auction of Dorothy's ruby slippers for $165,000 attests to Oz's continuing mythic relation to the American collective unconscious.   MLE

Hearn, Michael Patrick, *The Annotated Wizard of Oz* (1973).

Littlefield, Henry, 'The Wizard of Oz: Parable on Populism', in Hennig Cohen (ed.), *American Culture* (1968).

Rahn, Suzanne, *The Wizard of Oz: Shaping an Imaginary World* (1998).

Vidal, Gore, 'The Wizard of the "Wizard"', and 'On Rereading the Oz Books', *New York Review of Books* (September 1977 and October 1977).

Zipes, Jack, 'Oz as American Myth', in *Fairy Tale as Myth/Myth as Fairy Tale* (1994).

Zipes, Jack, 'L. Frank Baum and the Utopian Spirit of Oz', in *When Dreams Came True: Classical Fairy Tales and Their Tradition* (2nd edn., 2007).

Wizard of Oz, The (film: USA, 1939) The most celebrated fairy-tale film ever made, and the most memorable version of the story. Initially a box-office failure, it has over the decades been given repeated, well-received television screenings and thereby achieved iconic status. In public discussion it is taken for granted that absolutely everyone knows Dorothy (played by Judy Garland), the Scarecrow, the Tin Woodman, and the Cowardly Lion. Fragments of the film's dialogue—such as 'Toto, I have a feeling that we're not in Kansas anymore', 'Are you a good witch or a bad witch?', 'Follow the yellow brick road', 'Leaving so soon, my pretty?' and 'I'll get you, and your little dog too!'—have become part of conversational currency. On the Internet the film, plus L. Frank *Baum's original 1900 book, have together spawned over 30 different websites dedicated to Oz clubs, quizzes, festivals, and facsimile Dorothy dresses.

Before this MGM adaptation, there were various short silent Oz films, some produced by Baum himself. The major silent version, made in the 1920s (USA, 1925), is known today mainly for the fact that Oliver Hardy, before he teamed up with Stan Laurel, took the part of the Tin Woodman, but in its day it was conceived and marketed as a vehicle for the acrobatic blank-faced clown Larry Semon, who played the Scarecrow and also directed. Owing rather little to Baum's plot, it starts in a Ruritanian kind of Oz where Prime Minister Kruel, having secretly deposited the baby Princess Dorothy of Oz on a Kansas farm 18 years previously, schemes to seize the throne for himself. Agents sent to Kansas to get rid of the evidence that would support her royal claim are thwarted by the Scarecrow, who is devoted to Dorothy. When a cyclone transports Dorothy and the Scarecrow to Oz, the Tin Woodman joins the party, Dorothy meets Prince Kynde, and the Scarecrow has an encounter with a den of angry lions. By means of a series of comic stunts, the Scarecrow confounds all Kruel's machinations, then generously renounces his love for Dorothy, who marries Prince Kynde and assumes her rightful place on the throne of Oz.

The MGM film follows Baum's plotline more closely than Semon had done, but changes it significantly in tone. Baum, rejecting the 'blood-curdling incident' and 'fearsome moral' associated particularly with the *Grimms' stories, wrote that his intention was to leave out the 'heartaches and nightmares' of fairy tales, while retaining their 'wonderment and joy'. The MGM version could have stuck with Baum and merely delivered singable songs, joyful jokes, merry Munchkins, and Technicolor choreography, but it does not do that. If it had, it would probably be no more remembered today than Semon's film is, even though the film's durability has much to do with

the outstanding musical score by Harold Arlen and E. Y. 'Yip' Harburg. Instead it gives full, fearsome force to the Wicked Witch of the West, and allows her callous minions, the Winged Monkeys, none of the extenuation that the book offers. In this way it is closer to Grimm and to *Disney's *Snow White than it is to Baum. In the UK both *Snow White* and *The Wizard of Oz* were given an 'A' certificate at the time of first release, the force of which was that children on their own could not be admitted to a cinema when either of these films was being screened.

The Witch's nightmare-causing powers are further strengthened by giving her a counterpart—Miss Gulch—in Kansas. This idea of validating a dream or fantasy by having some of the actors play two characters, one in each world, is common to a range of films (e.g. *The Five Thousand Fingers of Doctor T*), the convention being that, when the child wakes up, he or she is holding something tangible from the dream world which proves that it is as real as home. In addition, a film-child returning from another world usually has some newly acquired self-confidence or skill which makes it possible to solve the problem which first created the need for escape. In *The Wizard of Oz* neither of these things happens. Dorothy does not produce the ruby slippers to prove—even to herself—that Oz really is 'a place, not a dream'; and, more disturbingly for a perceptive child in an audience, she does not bring with her from Oz anything that will help her solve the problem of Miss Gulch. Whether or not this was the makers' intention, part of the film's 'heartache' comes from the fact that, though the Wicked Witch has been disposed of, Miss Gulch is still alive; and the legal warrant condemning Toto to death, which was what caused Dorothy to wish to fly away over the rainbow, is still in force when she comes back.

The film's status in the popular imagination has led to a sequel, *Return to Oz*, numerous television parodies, and a parallel black version set in 1970s New York. This was *The Wiz* (USA, 1978), which derived from a successful Broadway musical (*see*

WIZARD OF OZ, THE (STAGE VERSIONS)). Though the credits acknowledge Baum, the storyline is actually based on the MGM film, and indeed presumes audience knowledge of it. For nearly everything in it (except the death warrant on Toto's head), *The Wiz* finds a New York equivalent. Dorothy, an unadventurous 24-year-old Harlem schoolteacher, chases Toto when he runs off in the snow, and hits a tornado which blows them through an electrical sign advertising a product called 'Oz'. Upon landing, Dorothy kills witch Evermean, who had turned the Munchkins into graffiti; on her death they gratefully unpeel themselves from walls. *En route* for the Emerald City Dorothy finds a brainless scarecrow trying to protect a small patch of sunflowers against derisive crows; a heartless tinman buried under fairground junk at Coney Island; and a cowardly lion lurking inside the stone monuments of the New York Public Library. On Poppy Street, a neon-lit alley populated by cocaine pushers, Dorothy and the lion succumb to the drugged atmosphere, but are revived by the tinman's tears of grief. At other points in the story the Wicked Witch of the West, Evillene, is presented as a sweat shop owner; her Flying Monkeys as a squad of motorcyclists; and Oz himself as a failed politician and a complete fraud. Climactically, Dorothy's three friends are comforted by being told that they have already displayed plenty of brains, heart, and courage: 'Believe in Yourself', sing Dorothy and Glinda, before the magic slippers take Dorothy back home to Harlem.

Among other fantasies that testify to the position of *The Wizard of Oz* as a standard reference point is *Zardoz* (UK, 1973). Set in 2293, it depicts the masses as worshipping a giant flying godhead named Zardoz. Gradually Zed, one of his Exterminators (reminiscent of the Winged Monkeys), realizes that the god whom he serves does not really exist at all, but is merely a man-made invention named by a joker who was also a cinephile. The film thus assumes that adult audiences in the 1970s were able to unravel the meanings packed into the name Zardoz, and at the same time prophesies that when *The Wizard*

of Oz is over 350 years old, and industrial society has collapsed, there will still be some who use it as mythology. By contrast, *Rainbow* (UK/Canada, 1995), set in 1990s New Jersey, invokes Dorothy and Toto rather than the Wizard. With the help of a computer, four children and a dog find the end of a rainbow and are carried along by it till it drops them in Kansas. One has taken nuggets of gold from the rainbow, thereby upsetting its balance; as a result the temperature rises drastically, colour fades from everything, society begins to break down. With all plants about to be destroyed by the disappearance of green, the children manage to restore gold to the rainbow. The moral the film illustrates is that ecology begins at home: like Dorothy, we don't need to look further than our own back yard.   TAS

Harmetz, Aljean, *The Making of the Wizard of Oz* (1978).
Rushdie, Salman, *The Wizard of Oz* (1992).
Zipes, Jack, *The Enchanted Screen: The Unknown History of Fairy-Tale Films* (2011).

Wizard of Oz, The (stage versions) A stage show, adapted by L. Frank *Baum from his own story for children, was premièred at the Majestic Theater, New York, in 1903 and ran for 293 performances. Much of the musical score was by A. Baldwin *Sloane and Paul Tietjens, with lyrics by L. Frank Baum. Nevertheless, a collection of other composers and lyricists are known to have collaborated on the work.

One more version of Baum's story, *The Wiz*, appeared in 1975, opening at New York's Majestic Theater. This was an all-black production with a book by William F. Brown updated to suit contemporary audiences. With a rock score by Charlie Smalls, it was extremely successful, attaining a run of 1,672 performances and a film version in 1978. *The Wiz* reached London in 1984.   TH

Swartz, Mark Evan, *Before the Rainbow: L. Frank Baum's* The Wonderful Wizard of Oz *on Stage and Screen to 1939* (2003).

Wolf, Friedrich (pseudonym of **Johannes Laicus**, 1817–55) German scholar, writer, and publisher. Influenced by Jacob and

Wilhelm *Grimm's theories of the folk tale's authenticity, he collected traditional oral tales and published them with a scholarly commentary. His three volumes of folk tales are aimed at an adult readership: *Niederländische Sagen* (*Dutch Legends*, 1843), *Deutsche Märchen und Sagen* (*German Popular Tales and Legends*, 1845), *Deutsche Hausmärchen* (*German Household Tales*, 1851).   KS

Wolff, Albert (1884–1970) Prominent French conductor who, at various stages in his long career, was associated with the Opéra-Comique, eventually serving as its director-general in 1945–6. Study at the Paris Conservatoire was followed by work in cabaret, later combined with the post of organist at the church of St Thomas Aquinas. In his mid-20s he joined the staff of the Opéra-Comique, making his conducting debut in 1911. From 1919 to 1920 he conducted the French repertoire at New York's Metropolitan Opera where, in 1919, he premièred his own opera *L'Oiseau bleu* (*The *Blue Bird*) based on Maurice *Maeterlinck's play.   TH

Woodward, Alice B. (1862–1951) English illustrator whose medium was pen and ink. It is quite likely that she was influenced by Charles *Robinson, a decorative book illustrator noted for his personal application of Art Nouveau and particularly for his black-and-white illustrations of Robert Louis *Stevenson's *A Child's Garden of Verse* (1896). Both were illustrators of the Dent Banbury Cross series. Woodward's black-and-white drawings for *Banbury Cross and Other Nursery Rhymes* (1895), Edith Hall's *Adventures in Toyland* (1897), and Evelyn *Sharp's *Round the World to Nymphland* (1902) are reflective of the Art Nouveau style of the time. The cover illustration for Sheila E. Braine's *Princess of Hearts* also bears Art Nouveau motifs, flowers, and embellishments, and, as was characteristic of publishers' bindings after 1832, the design incorporated gold and colour. In 1895 Woodward was included among the best of black-and-white artists of the day to illustrate a series of articles in the London *Daily Chronicle* intended to support the progressive cause. Illustratively the series was a success; not so politically. Two years later, Woodward illustrated Walter Jerrold's *Bon-Mots of the Nineteenth Century*, good words of wit. As the title-page suggests, the drawings have been done 'Grotesquesly' by Alice B. Woodward; grotesque in the comic sense, yet lyrical and animated and characteristically Art Nouveau in the curving free lines and solid black areas relieved by white.   SS

Wrede, Patricia C. (1953–) American writer of fantasy novels for children and adults. Wrede brings European folklore motifs (enchanted harps, magical rings, dragons, elves, etc.) into the six books of *The Lyra Series* (1982–), the four books of *The Enchanted Forest Series* (1985–); and short stories such as 'Cruel Sisters' (1996), based on Scottish balladry. *Snow White and Rose Red* (1989) is a gentle, romantic retelling of the tale set in Elizabethan England, concerning the plight of two sisters in a woodland cottage at the edge of Faerie.   TW

Wynne-Jones, Tim (1948–) Canadian short-story writer. A multi-talented creator, Wynne-Jones has crafted radio plays, the lyrics for a science-fiction musical, the book and libretto for an opera, and popular songs. He made his children's book debut as a picture-book writer, when he began chronicling the adventures of Zoom, a cat who followed his seafaring uncle. His short stories, including those published in *The Book of Changes* and *Some of the Kinder Planets*, have won numerous awards; they are distinguished by plotlines pared to essentials, emotional truth, and quirky, contemporary, characters. Although reflecting everyday problems such as bullies, hockey-playing, and making money, the stories often include fantastical elements, corkscrew logic, and an off-centre point of view. His version of 'The Goose Girl', published in Datlow and Windling's *Black Thorn, White Rose*, focuses on the story from the viewpoint of the prince. He finds himself fatally drawn to the voluptuous servant girl, the false bride and impostor, rather than the true princess. Departing from the *Grimms'* version, in which the false bride forces the princess to switch places, Wynne-Jones shows the two girls changing places for a lark, the princess herself being quite young and ill-prepared, sexually, to become anyone's wife. As the tale comes to its grisly end, for this particular prince life with a true princess proves to be not such a happily-ever-after reality.   AS

Ellis, Sarah, 'News from the North', *Horn Book Magazine*, 71 (1995).

Yanagi, Miwa (1967–) A Japanese photographer and video artist whose female-focused work serves as non-documentary-style social criticism. Her carefully constructed black-and-white stills in 'Fairy Tales' (2003–6) use young girls, some disguised as crones in wigs, makeup, and latex masks, while their uncovered youthful arms and legs offer an uncanny mix. They enact scenes depicting well-known folk tales such as *'Little Red Riding Hood', literary fairy tales by Hans Christian *Andersen and Gabriel García, as well as the less familiar traditional 'Frau Trude', 'Little Brother and Little Sister', and 'The White Dove', and the Japanese 'Hitotsuya'. Most staged in a domestic environment, these dream/nightmare visions trouble stereotypical binary, disjunctive relations between fairy-tale women.   PG

Mayako, Murai. 'The Princess, the Witch, and the Fireside: Yanagi Miwa's Uncanny Restaging of Fairy Tales', *Marvels & Tales*, 27.2 (2013).

Yeats, William Butler (1865–1939) Irish poet, dramatist, prose writer and anthologist. He was born in Dublin and spent part of his childhood and adolescence there, the remainder being divided between London and the west of Ireland, particularly County Sligo, where his mother's family, the Pollexfens, lived. It was in Sligo, a part of the country especially rich in local legend and folklore, that he was first attracted to the world of Irish traditional story. This interest, while it remained with him throughout his life and writings, was to be of major importance in his earliest work, which began to be published from 1885 onwards. The success of this early work, added to his involvement in the foundation of the Abbey Theatre, soon ensured for Yeats a role as principal figure of the Irish literary revival. This movement had as one of its main goals the restoration of Ireland's cultural heritage, a restoration which involved a rediscovery of its ancient Gaelic sagas and a recognition of the strength and colour of its folklore. While in many of its manifestations this vibrant indigenous folklore exerted a powerful influence on Yeats, he was initially drawn most of all to its fairy-world dimension.

Numerous references to this other-world domain are to be found in the poems from his first collections, starting with *The Wanderings of Oisin and other Poems* (1889). One of the 'other poems' in this collection, 'The Stolen Child', set the note of wistful longing which came to be associated with much of his writing on fairy themes; such work, in his own phrase, constituted the cry of the heart against necessity. It was, however, in his role as anthologist that Yeats brought his fascination with the Irish supernatural to a wider audience.

His first compilation, *Fairy and Folk Tales of the Irish Peasantry* (1888) comprises some 60 items, drawn from a wide diversity of oral and written sources, frequently re-tailored to suit Yeats's own purpose in providing evidence of his country's rich imaginative store of story. It is an element of that purpose that Yeats's thematic arrangement and classification of his material is so methodical. The basic division is into those stories which feature the 'trooping' fairies and stories which feature those described as 'solitary'. The 'troopers' are, in the main, benevolent, while those in the latter group are more inclined to be the agents of mischief and harm: this category includes the leprechaun, the pooka, and the witch. Many of the most striking of these stories, such as 'The Priest's Supper', 'The Legend of Knockgrafton',

'Master and Man', and 'The Giant's Stairs', originated in Thomas Crofton *Croker's seminal three-volume collection *Fairy Legends and Traditions of the South of Ireland* (1825–8), the source most often used by Yeats. 'The Confessions of Tom Bourke', another story originating in Croker, appeared in both Yeats's *Fairy and Folk Tales* and in his *Representative Irish Tales* (1891), as did an anonymous story entitled 'The Jackdaw'. (Otherwise, *Representative Irish Tales* is an anthology, published originally in two volumes of 19th-century Irish fiction, by authors such as Carleton, Lover, and Griffin.)

Irish Fairy Tales, Yeats's second compilation of traditional material, appeared in 1892. A prefatory note expressed the hope that this volume and its *Fairy and Folk Tales* predecessor would comprise 'a fairly representative collection of Irish folk tales', a phrase which, in Yeats's interpretation, stood in both books for an eclectic mixture of content, even managing to encompass poems by himself and others which dealt with fairy lore. In *Irish Fairy Tales* the 14 stories are grouped into four sections, which feature land and water fairies, evil spirits, cats, kings, and warriors. Croker is drawn on for three of these—'The Young Piper', 'Teigue of the Lee', and 'The Lady of Gollerus'—but perhaps the most impressive is 'The Man who Never Knew Fear', a previously unpublished story specially translated for Yeats by Douglas Hyde from Irish. The introductions and notes which Yeats provided for both of these volumes are important not only for giving insights into the methodology and rationale behind Yeats's selections, but also for evincing his sense of commitment to the task in hand and his gratitude to the individual storytellers at whose feet he had sat and listened. These storytellers' unquestioning belief in the existence of the creatures who populated their stories led Yeats to share a vision of a land where, contrary to what might have happened elsewhere, the fairies were still extant.

It is very much the same attitude which underpins Yeats's *The Celtic Twilight*, first published in 1893 and reissued and enlarged in 1902. Here he assembled anecdotes and stories which he himself had collected, principally in County Galway and often with the help of Lady Augusta Gregory, interspersing the narratives with his own ruminations and commentaries. The tone may be light and conversational, but it does not detract from the eloquence of many of the tales or from their universal application. One of the most enduring of these achievements is the story 'Dreams that Have No Moral', described by Yeats himself as 'one of those rambling moralless tales, which are the delight of the poor and the hard-driven, wherever life is left in its natural simplicity'. The most personal of the anecdotes is to be found in 'Regina, Regina Pigmeorum, Veni', where Yeats recounts a meeting on 'a far western sandy shore' with a fairy troop, presided over by a queen whose departing words are a recommendation to the humans not to 'seek to know too much about us'. (The incident which gave rise to this retelling was first described in a letter written in October 1892 to Richard Le Gallienne.)   RD

Deane, Seamus, *Strange Country* (1997).

Foster, John Wilson, *Fictions of the Irish Literary Revival* (1987).

Kelly, John and Domville, Eric (eds.), *The Collected Letters of W. B. Yeats, i. 1865–1895* (1986).

Kiberd, Declan, *Inventing Ireland* (1995).

Thuente, Mary Helen, *W. B. Yeats and Irish Folklore* (1980).

'Yellow Dwarf, The' A tale in d'*Aulnoy's *Contes nouveaux ou les fées à la mode* (*New Tales, or Fairies in Fashion*, 1698) that incorporates many folkloric motifs, including a princess indifferent to love, a pact with a demon-like figure, a quest to free a captive lover, as well as a (relatively rare) tragic ending. Although aspects of this tale resemble an episode of *Spenser's *Faerie Queene* (1590–6), d'Aulnoy seems to have created the basic plot on her own, and not from oral or literary traditions. This story was particularly popular in 19th-century England, where it was the subject of chapbooks and saw numerous performances as a pantomime.   LCS

Yep, Laurence (1948–) Versatile Asian American author for young adults and children. Yep's experience as a third-generation Chinese American growing up in a Black neighbourhood of San Francisco and commuting to a Chinatown bilingual school shaped the cultural open-mindedness and the attentiveness to outsiders which characterize his works. Yep's recurring theme is acculturation, and dragons are the magic or creative embodiment of the fear and wonder that such a challenge entails.

While *Sweetwater* (1973) takes up the encounter with the alien in a science-fiction context, later works (*Dragon of the Lost Sea*, 1982, *Dragon Steel*, 1985, and *Dragon Cauldron*, 1991) recount Princess Shimmer's quest for a lost home by mixing fantasy and Chinese mythology. The award-winning *Dragonwings* (1976) approaches the questions of Chinese American identity more specifically and also represents the first of Yep's efforts to write a 'child's version of history', a more intimate and concrete history, as he states in the essay 'Green Chord'. Later historical novels include *Child of the Owl* (1977), set in the Chinatown of Yep's youth; *The Serpent's Children* (1984), recounting a rebellion in 19th-century China; and *The Star Fisher* (1991), which retells his mother's childhood experiences in 1927 West Virginia. Directed specifically at teens, *American Dragons: Twenty-Five Asian American Voices* (1995) extends Yep's pursuit of a historical tradition to literature; the collection includes poems, short stories, and essays about diverse Asian American expressions of the longing for home.

Yep's first powerful retelling of folk tales, *The Rainbow People* (1989), gathers 20 stories told by Chinese American immigrants in the 1930s. While in most cases the setting is mythic China, the tales help us envision the 'strategies for living' of the men in Chinatown. A second collection of 17 tales, *Tongues of Jade*, followed in 1991, and a third, *Tree of Dreams: Ten Tales from the Garden of Night* in 1995. Among his other retold folk tales are witty and imaginative picture books for younger children such as *The Man who Tricked a Ghost* (1993), *Butterfly Boy* (1993), *The Shell Woman and the King: A Chinese Folktale* (1993), *Tiger Woman* (1996), *The*

Khan's Daughter: A Mongolian Folktale (1997), and *The Dragon Prince: A Chinese Beauty and the Beast Tale* (1997). By privileging trickster stories, Yep breaks away from the stereotype of Chinese passivity. CB

Yolen, Jane (1939–) American poet, playwright, and writer and editor of children's books, fantasy, and science fiction, who is one of the most prolific and experimental writers of fairy tales on the contemporary scene. After graduating from Smith College in 1960 and working for different publishing houses, Yolen turned to full-time professional writing in 1965. Her first book was a delightful comical fairy tale for children, *The Witch who Wasn't* (1964), and since this first publication she has gone on to publish well over 300 titles, including such important non-fiction books as *Touch Magic: Fantasy, Faerie, and Folktale in the Literature of Childhood* (1981) and *The Perfect Wizard* (2004), a biography of Hans Christian *Andersen, and produced film scripts and cassettes based on her work. She has also written fairy-tale books with her son, Adam Stemple, *Pay the Piper: A Rock and Roll Fairy Tale* (2005), her daughter Heidi Stemple, *Pretty Princess Pig* (2011), and three with Robert Harris, *Queen's Own Fool* (2002), *Girl in a Cage* (2002), and *Prince Across the Water* (2004).

One of Yolen's main goals has been to recapture the flavour and spirit of the oral tradition in her literary fairy tales. She writes with grace and painstaking care to create tales that evoke the atmosphere of long ago and other worlds, and she prefers to use metaphors and symbols in unusual combinations that produce new associations. Although she has adapted numerous folk tales and classic fairy tales, her best work can be seen in the fairy tales she herself has created in such books as *The Girl who Loved the Wind* (1972), *The Girl who Cried Flowers and Other Tales* (1976), *The Moon Ribbon and Other Tales* (1976), *The Lady and the Merman* (1977), *The Hundredth Dove and Other Tales* (1977), *Dream Weaver* (1979), *Sleeping Ugly* (1981), *Tales of Wonder* (1983), *Dragonfield and Other Stories* (1985), *The Faery Flag* (1989), *The Dragon's*

Boy (1990), *The Girl in the Golden Bower* (1995), and *Child of Faerie* (1996).

Given her comprehensive knowledge of folk and fairy tales throughout the world—she has edited an important collection of tales entitled *Favorite Folktales from Around the World* (1986) and co-edited another significant anthology with her daughter Heidi, *Mirror, Mirror: Forty Folktales for Mothers and Daughters to Share* (2000)—Yolen has subtly altered many popular tales to undermine and provoke audience expectations in tales that appeal both to adults and young readers. Such stories as 'Moon Ribbon', 'Brother Hart', 'The Thirteenth Fey', 'Happy Dens, or A Day in the Old Wolves Home' and 'The Undine' contain startling metaphors and unusual plots that place traditional tales and their meaning in question. For instance, in **'Undine'* Yolen emphasizes the notion of male betrayal and female autonomy in an implicit critique of Hans Christian **Andersen's 'The *Little Mermaid'. Here the mermaid leaves the prince, who beckoned her, to return to her sisters in the sea. In 'The Thirteenth Fey' Yolen recalls the story of **'Sleeping Beauty' through a first-person narrative of the youngest daughter of a family of fairies and produces a philosophical critique of decadent monarchy in the name of democracy. Though not a writer with a strong ideological bent, Yolen has been influenced by the feminist movement, and one of her major achievements has been to subvert the male discourse that has dominated the fairy tale as genre so that the repressed concerns of women are addressed, and the predictable happy endings that signify male hegemony and closure are exploded or placed into question. Thus, in 'The White Seal Maid' and 'The Lady and the Merman', she has her female protagonists seek refuge in their origins, the sea, which represents for Yolen the essence of restlessness, change, tenderness, and humanity.

Two of her fantasy books, *The Devil's Arithmetic* (1998) and *Briar Rose* (1992), have the Holocaust as their theme. The latter makes use of 'Sleeping Beauty' as the granddaughter of a Holocaust victim tries to make sense out of her grandmother's strange retelling of 'Sleeping Beauty' and discovers how her grandmother had been gassed and revived to survive the Nazi destruction of the Jews.

Yolen has also collaborated with numerous authors to write fairy-tale novels and books such as *Queen's Own Fool* (2000, with Robert J. Harris), *Prince Across the Water* (2004, with Robert J. Harris), *Pay the Piper: A Rock and Roll Fairy Tale* (2005, with Adam Stemple), *The Last Dragon* (2011, graphic novel adapted from the short story 'Dragonfield' [1985] and illustrated by Rebecca Guay), and *Grumbles from the Forest: Fairy-Tale Voices with a Twist* (2013, with Rebecca Kai Dotlich).

In some of her other works, Yolen has sought to revise the myths of Merlin and Arthur, and in her science fiction/fantasy novels and stories she often experiments with shifting narrative voices and perspectives as well as with time slips. From 1990 to 1996 she developed her own imprint at Harcourt Brace to publish fairy-tale novels and works of fantasy by other authors and continued this series at TAR Books. Not only has Yolen made highly original contributions to develop the fairy-tale genre, but she has also encouraged and supported younger writers to produce innovative work in the field.   JZ

Hanlon, Tina, '"To Sleep, Perchance to Dream": Sleeping Beauties and Wide-Awake Plain Janes in the Stories of Jane Yolen', *Children's Literature* (1998).
Weil, Ellen R., 'The Door to Lilith's Cave: Memory and Imagination in Jane Yolen's Holocaust Novels', *Journal of the Fantastic in the Arts*, 5 (1983).

Zelinsky, Paul O. (1953–) Prizewinning American illustrator of *Grimms' Tales. His *Hansel and Gretel* (1984, Caldecott Medal of Honor, text by Rika Lesser), *Rumpelstiltskin* (1986), and *Rapunzel* (1997, Caldecott Gold Medal) incorporate an awareness of historical change into both text and illustration. (There are explanatory notes following each tale.) As in the early Grimm version, his enraged Rumpelstiltskin simply flies out of the window at the end, leaving behind a joyous miller's daughter saved by her faithful servant woman. With similar historicity, his Rapunzel grows to maturity in a 17th-century tower that reflects the tale's (late) 17th-century origins. Zelinsky has also illustrated the delightful fairy-tale poetry books, *Awful Ogre's Awful Day* (2001) and *Awful Ogre Running Wild* (2008).   RBB

Zemach, Margot (1931–89) American author and illustrator of more than 60 children's books including folklore, rhymes, and songs. One of her first adaptations of a folk tale, *The Three Sillies* (1963), provided a hint of the future humour, deft line, and flat colour that can be found in most of her works. Zemach made hundreds of studies in preparation for each book, including *Nail Soup: A Swedish Tale Retold* (1964), *Salt: A Russian Tale* (1965), and *Too Much Noise: An Italian Tale* (1967). In less than a decade beginning in 1967, she illustrated four books by Isaac Bashevis *Singer, *Mazel and Shlimazel*, *When Shliemiel went to Warsaw and Other Stories*, *Alone in the Wild Forest*, and *Naftali the Storyteller and his*

Horse, Sus, and Other Stories. In 1994 she was awarded the Caldecott Prize for *Duffy and the Devil: A Cornish Tale.*   KNH

Zeman, Karel (1910–89) Czech animator, filmmaker, and director, who is one of the great pioneers of fantasy and fairy-tale animated films in Czechoslovakia. Notable among his highly experimental adaptations of classical works are: *Vynález Zkázy* (*The Fabulous World of Jules Verne*, 1958), *Baron Prášil* (*The Fabulous Baron Munchausen*, 1961), and *Pohádky Tisíce a Jedné Noci* (*Adventures of Sinbad the Sailor*, 1974). Two of his most provocative fairy-tale films, *Král Lávra* (*King Lavra*, 1948) and *Krabat* (also known as *The Sorcerer's Apprentice*, 1977), were produced during two different time periods with different styles, but each commenting on political conditions of tyranny with defiant hope to change those conditions. It is not by chance that Zeman chose to animate a satirical poem, 'King Lavra,' written by Karel Havlíček Borovský (1821–56), a teacher and journalist who was exiled from Bohemia at one point because of his political stance and dedication to the liberal national cause of the Czechs. Zeman's adaptation follows the broad outlines of Borovský's work while making it even more satirical. The narrative concerns a king with donkey ears; because he is ashamed of them he grows his hair very long to conceal them. However, since he needs a haircut every now and then, he orders a barber to come to his palace to cut his hair. Since the barber must inevitably discover the donkey ears, the king always has him beheaded to make sure his subjects will not know about the donkey ears. After his executioner has chopped off nine heads, King Lavra orders a young barber to give him a haircut. Fortunately, the barber is working on the executioner's hair when the king's order is sent. The barber quickly ties up the executioner, and after he goes to the king and gives him the haircut, the king cannot have him executed. So, he makes the barber swear that he will never tell a soul about the donkey ears. The barber agrees and is given a medal. However, the young man is haunted by the truth and tells the secret to some green twines growing in a field and eventually exposes the king.

Resistance and hope are the key themes in *Krabat*, which Zeman made several years after the Russians put down the cultural revolution in the Prague Spring of 1968.

Based in part on the German writer Otfried *Preussler's 1971 novel, *Krabat*, the film has deep roots in European folk tradition. This tale type recounts in diverse ways how a father apprentices his son to a duplicitous magician. The son learns all the magic tricks of the magician and manages to gain his release from his service before he has completed the apprenticeship. In a series of events, the magician tries to recapture the apprentice, and they have several transformation battles. Eventually, the apprentice wins by turning himself into a fox and biting off a rooster's head, which is actually the magician's head. In the end, the apprentice marries a princess. Zeman does not trivialize the folklore tradition the way these and other films do. He uses both folklore and Preussler's novel to form his own 'contemporary' version of the tale type to comment on war, poverty, and tyranny.

In his film, Krabat, the protagonist, is a 14-year-old orphan wandering about Saxony in late medieval Europe. War is everywhere, and Krabat, a vagabond, begs and looks for food and shelter and winds up in the hands of the evil sorcerer. In some respects, this film is similar to *King Lavra*: the narrative pits a young man against a tyrant. However, *Krabat* is first of all a longer film made with cell and cut-out animation, and is a much more profound analysis of the deadly consequences of forced labor in the service of a dreadful, powerful tyrant, not a jackass king.   JZ

Zingerle, Ignaz Vinzenz (1825–92) and **Zingerle, Joseph** (1831–91) German folklorists. Ignaz was a literary historian and poet, and Joseph was a priest and professor of theology. Together they collected folk tales and legends in southern Germany and Austria. Their most important collections were *Kinder- und Hausmärchen aus Tirol* (*Children and Household Tales from Tyrol*, 1852) and *Kinder- und Hausmärchen aus Süddeutschland* (*Children and Household Tales from Southern Germany*, 1852). Their emphasis was on the mythological aspects of folk and fairy tales.   JZ

Zur Mühlen, Hermynia (1883–1951) Austrian translator and author of novels, mysteries, and proletarian fairy tales for children. Born a member of the Austro-Hungarian nobility, Zur Mühlen led a privileged life in her youth, travelling widely in Europe, Africa, and the Near East. Despite her conservative upbringing, she developed an interest in the social and political questions of her day fostered by close contacts with Russian émigrés in Geneva (1903). She spent the First World War in Switzerland, studied Marxist theory, and in 1919 moved to Frankfurt am Main and joined the Communist Party. In 1933 she emigrated to Vienna and fled from there via Prague to England in 1938.

Zur Mühlen was prolific as a translator and writer. She translated approximately 150 novels from American and British English, French, and Russian, and wrote several novels and radio plays. Zur Mühlen is one of the best-known writers of proletarian fairy tales from the Weimar period. Her collections include *Das Schloss der Wahrheit* (*The Castle of Truth*, 1924), *Es war einmal . . . und es wird sein* (*Once Upon a Time . . . and it Will Be*, 1930), and *Schmiede der Zukunft* (*Smiths of the Future*, 1933). These emancipatory tales, designed to socialize working-class children to embrace socialism, had a twofold task. They were to illuminate complex social and economic conditions and processes so that children could understand them and relate to them, and they were to present models of a better world. Given their intent, these parables, allegories, and tales are quite didactic, yet the stories were told with such force that they could hold the attention of their intended audience.

In 'Die Brillen' ('The Glasses'), published in the collection *Ali der Teppichweber* (*Ali, the Carpet Weaver*, 1923), a young hero succeeds in pulling off his glasses, glasses that present a false and distorted image of the world and that everyone is obliged to wear. Now seeing the world as it really is, the hero convinces others to do the same and starts a revolution against the forces of oppression and exploitation. The most beloved of Zur Mühlen's tales for young children is *Was Peterchens Freunde erzählen* (*What Little Peter's Friends Tell*, 1920). In this tale, everyday objects, including a piece of coal, matches, a bottle, and a bedcover, come alive to tell Little Peter about the conditions under which they were produced. During the 1920s, Zur Mühlen's fairy tales appeared in communist children's magazines before they appeared in book form, many published by the Malik Verlag. Her work was rediscovered in West Germany in the early 1970s, influencing the anti-authoritarian German children's literature of that decade.   EMM

Altner, Manfred, *Hermynia zur Mühlen: Eine Biographie* (1997).
Karrenbrock, Helga, *Märchenkinder— Zeitgenossen. Untersuchungen zur Kinderliteratur der Weimarer Republik* (1995).
Wallace, Ailsa, *Hermynia Zur Mühlen: The Guises of Socialist Fiction* (2009).
Zipes, Jack (ed.), *Fairy Tales and Fables from Weimar Days* (1989).

Zwerger, Lisbeth (1954–) Austrian illustrator who has achieved international fame with her fine ink-and-wash drawings for classic fairy tales. Among her notable picturebooks are: E. T. A. *Hoffmann, *The Strange Child* (1977), Jacob and Wilhelm *Grimm, **Hansel and Gretel* (1979), Hans Christian *Andersen, *The Swineherd* (1982), Jacob and Wilhelm Grimm, **Little Red Riding Hood* (1983), Oscar *Wilde, *The Selfish Child* (1984), Hans Christian Andersen, *The Nightingale* (1991), Wilhelm *Hauff, *Dwarf Nose* (1993), Clemens *Brentano, *The Legend of Rosepetal* (1995), L. Frank *Baum, *The *Wizard of Oz* (1996), Lewis *Carroll, **Alice in Wonderland*, Hans Christian Andersen, *The *Little Mermaid* (2004), and Jacob and Wilhlem Grimm, *The *Bremen Town Musicians* (2006). Influenced initially by Arthur *Rackham, Zwerger has developed her own inimitable style using pencil-and-ink and watercolour. Her illustrations have a delicate ethereal quality to them and are distinguished by their gentle lines and white space. Though Zwerger has focused mainly on the classical tradition of fairy tales, her illustrations are often interpretations of the well-known stories that she presents in a new light with subtle changes and suggestive commentaries.   JZ

Zwerger, Lisbeth, and Koppe, Susanne, *The Art of Lisbeth Zwerger* (1994).

Bibliography

FAIRY-TALE STUDIES

Aarne, Antti, *The Types of the Folktale: A Classification and Bibliography* (1910; enl., with Stith Thompson, 1928; (2nd rev. edn., 1961).

Adams, D. J., 'The "Contes de fées" of Madame d'Aulnoy: Reputation and Reevaluation', *Bulletin of the John Rylands University Library of Manchester*, 76.3 (autumn 1994).

Adler, Sara Maria, *Calvino: The Writer as Fablemaker* (1979).

Albrecht, Luitgard, *Der magische Idealismus in Novalis' Märchentheorie und Märchendichtung* (1948).

Alderson, Brian, 'Tracts, Rewards and Fairies: The Victorian Contribution to Children's Literature', in Asa Briggs (ed.), *Essays in the History of Publishing* (1977).

Alderson, Brian, *Ezra Jack Keats: Artist and Picture-Book Maker* (1994).

Ali, Muhsin Jassim, *Scheherazade in England: A Study of Nineteenth-Century English Criticism of the* Arabian Nights (1981).

Allan, Robin, '50 Years of Snow White', *Journal of Popular Film and Television*, 15.4 (winter 1988).

Allan, Robin, *Walt Disney and Europe: European Influences on the Animated Feature Films of Walt Disney* (1999).

Alleau, René, 'Les Voiles féeriques de la voie', *Cahiers du Sud*, 324 (1954).

Andersen, Jens, *Hans Christian Andersen: A New Life* (2005).

Anderson, Graham, *Fairytale in the Ancient World* (2000).

Anderson, Graham, *Greek and Roman Folklore: A Handbook* (2006).

Anderson, Graham, *Folktale as a Source of Graeco-Roman Fiction* (2007).

Apel, Friedmar, *Die Zaubergärten der Phantasie. Zur Theorie und Geschichte des Kunstmärchens* (1978).

Apel, Friedmar, 'Die bezauberte Vernunft', in Friedmar Apel and Norbert Miller (eds.), *Das Kabinett der Feen des 17. und 18. Jahrhunderts* (1984).

Apo, Satu, *The Narrative World of Finnish Fairy Tales: Structure, Agency and Evaluation in Southwest Finnish Folktales* (1995).

Apter-Cragnolino, Aida, 'El cuento de hadas y la Bildungsroman: modelo subversión en "La bella durmiente" de Rosario Ferre', *Chasqui*, 20.2 (1991).

Arendt, Dieter, 'Dümmlinge, Däumlinge und Diebe im Märchen—oder: "drei Söhne, davon hiess der jüngste der Dümmling" (KHM 64)', *Diskussion Deutsch*, 91 (October 1986).

Ariès, Philippe, 'At the Point of Origin', *Yale French Studies*, 43 (1969).

Ashliman, D. L., *Folk and Fairy Tales: A Handbook* (2004).

Attebery, Brian, *The Fantasy Tradition in American Literature* (1980).

Aurouet, Carole (ed.), *Contes et légendes à l'écran* (2005).

Avery, Gillian, *Childhood's Pattern: A Study of the Heroes and Heroines of Children's Fiction, 1770–1950* (1975).

Avery, Gillian, 'The Quest for Fairyland', *Quarterly Journal of the Library of Congress*, 38.4 (fall 1981).

Avery, Gillian, 'The Cult of Peter Pan', *Word & Image: A Journal of Verbal/Visual Enquiry*, 2.2 (April–June 1986).

Avery, Gillian, 'Fantasy and Nonsense', in Arthur Pollard (ed.), *New History of Literature*, vi. *The Victorians* (1987).

Avery, Gillian, 'George MacDonald and the Victorian Fairy Tale', in William Raeper (ed.), *The Gold Thread: Essays on George MacDonald* (1990).

Avery, Gillian, and **Briggs, Julia** (eds.), *Children and their Books: A Celebration of the Work of Iona and Peter Opie* (1989).

Avery, Gillian, and **Bull, Angela**, *Nineteenth-Century Children: Heroes and Heroines in English Children's Stories 1780–1900* (1965).

Baader, Renate, *Dames de Lettres: Autorinnen des preziösen, hocharistokratischen und 'modernen' Salons (1646–1698): Mlle de Scudéry—Mlle de Montpensier—Mme d'Aulnoy* (1986).

Bacchilega, Cristina, 'Notes on the Politics of Gender in European Fairy Tales', in Steven Curry and Cristina Bacchilega (eds.), *Imagination: A Bridge to Magic Realms in the Humanities* (1988).

Bacchilega, Cristina, 'Folk and Literary Narrative in a Postmodern Context: The Case of the Märchen', *Fabula*, 29 (1989).

Bacchilega, Cristina, 'The Fruit of the Womb: Creative Uses of a Naturalizing Tradition in Folktales', in Simon Bronner (ed.), *Creativity and Tradition in Folklore* (1992).

Bacchilega, Cristina, *Postmodern Fairy Tales: Gender and Narrative Strategies* (1997).

Bacchilega, Cristina, *Fairy Tales Transformed? Twenty-First Century Adaptations & the Politics of Wonder* (2013).

Bacon, Martha, 'Puppet's Progress: Pinocchio', in Virginia Havilland (ed.), *Children and Literature: Views and Reviews* (1973).

Baker, Ronald L., 'Xenophobia in "Beauty and the Beast" and Other Animal/Monster-Groom Tales', *Midwestern Folklore*, 15.2 (fall 1989).

Bang, Ilse, *Die Entwicklung der deutschen Märchenillustration* (1944).

Barberi Squarotti, Giorgio, 'Problemi di technica narrativa cinquecentesca', *Sigma*, 2 (1965).

Barchilon, Jacques, 'Uses of the Fairy Tale in the Eighteenth Century', *Studies on Voltaire and the Eighteenth Century*, 24 (1963).

Barchilon, Jacques, 'L'Ironie et l'humour dans les "Contes" de Perrault', *Studi francesi*, 32 (1967).

Barchilon, Jacques, *Le Conte merveilleux français de 1690 à 1790* (1975).

Barchilon, Jacques, 'Vers l'inconscient de "La Belle au bois dormant"', *Cermeil*, 2 (February 1986).

Barchilon, Jacques, and **Flinders, Peter**, *Charles Perrault* (1981).

Barzilai, Shuli, 'Reading "Snow White": The Mother's Story', *Signs*, 15.3 (spring 1990).

Barzilai, Shuli, *Tales of Bluebeard and his Wives from Late Antiquity to Postmodern Times* (2009).

Bastian, Ulrike, *Die 'Kinder- und Hausmärchen' der Brüder Grimm in der literaturpä- dagogischen Diskussion des 19. und 20. Jahrhunderts* (1981).

Bausinger, Hermann, '"Historisierende" Tendenzen im deutschen Märchen seit der Romantik. Requisitenverschiebung und Requisitenerstarrung', *Wirkendes Wort*, 10 (1960).

Bausinger, Hermann, 'Möglichkeiten des Märchens in der Gegenwart', in Hugo Kuhn and Kurt Schier (eds.), *Märchen, Mythos, Dichtung. Festschrift für Friedrich von der Leyen* (1963).

Bausinger, Hermann, *Märchen, Phantasie und Wirklichkeit* (1987).

Bausinger, Hermann, 'Concerning the Content and Meaning of Fairy Tales', *Germanic Review*, 42 (spring 1987).

Bausinger, Hermann, *Folk Culture in a World of Technology* (1990).

Becker, Marie Luise, *Die Liebe im deutschen Märchen* (1901).

Beckett, Sandra, *Red Riding Hood for all Ages: A Fairy-Tale Icon in Cross-Cultural Context* (2008).

Beckwith, Osmond, 'The Oddness of Oz', *Children's Literature*, 5 (1976).

Beilharz, R., 'Ondine dans l'œuvre de Giraudoux et de La Motte Fouqué', *Zeitschrift für Französische Sprache und Literatur*, 80 (1970).

Beit, Hedwig von, *Gegensatz und Erneuerung im Märchen* (2nd edn., *Symbolik des Märchens*, 2, 1957).

Beit, Hedwig von, *Das Märchen: Sein Ort in der geistigen Entwicklung* (1965).

Bell, Elizabeth, Haas, Lynda, and **Sells, Laura** (eds.), *From Mouse to Mermaid: The Politics of Film, Gender, and Culture* (1995).

Bellemin-Noel, Jean, *Les Contes et leurs fantasmes* (1983).

Belmont, Nicole, 'Poucet: conception orale, naissance anale: une lecture psychanaly- tique du conte type 700', *Estudos de Literatura Oral*, 1 (spring 1995).

Bémol, Maurice, 'Henri Pourrat et "Le Trésor des contes"', *Annales Universitatis Saraviensis*, 10 (1961).

Ben-Amos, Dan, 'Introduction: The European Fairy-Tale Tradition between Orality and Literacy,' *Journal of American Folklore*, 123 (2010).

Ben-Amos, Dan, 'Straparola: The Revolution That Was Not', *Journal of American Folklore*, 123 (2010).

Bendazzi, Giannalberto, *Cartoons: One Hundred Years of Cinema Animation* (1994).

Bendix, Regina, and **Hasan-Rokem, Galit**, *A Companion to Folklore* (2012).

Benítez-Rojo, Antonio, 'Eréndira o la Bella durmiente de García Márquez', *Cuadernos Hispanoamericanos*, 448 (1987).

Benson, Stephen, *Cycles of Influence: Fiction, Folktale, Theory* (2003).

Benson, Stephen (ed.), *Contemporary Fiction and the Fairy Tale* (2008).

Benz, Richard, *Märchendichtung der Romantiker* (1908).

Berendsohn, Walter A., *Grundformen volkstümlicher Erzählkunst in den* Kinder- und Hausmärchen *der Brüder Grimm* (2nd rev. edn., 1968).

Berendsohn, Walter A., *Phantasie und Wirklichkeit in den Märchen und Geschichten Hans Christian Andersens* (1973).

Berlioz, Jacques, Brémond, Claude, and **Velay-Vallentin, Catherine** (eds.), *Formes médiévales du conte merveilleux* (1989).

Bernard, Véronique, *Fées et princes charmants* (1996).

Bettelheim, Bruno, *The Uses of Enchantment: The Meaning and Importance of Fairy Tales* (1976).

Bettelheim, Bruno, 'A Return to the Land of Fairies', *New York Times*, 12 July 1987, section 2.

Bewley, Marius, 'The Land of Oz: America's Great Good Place', *Masks and Mirrors* (1970).

Biaggioni, Rodolfo, *Pinocchio: cent'anni d'Avventure illustrate: bibliografia delle edizioni illustrate italiane di C. Collodi*, Le Avventure di Pinocchio *1881/83–1983* (1984).

Birkhäuser-Oeri, Sibylle, *Die Mutter im Märchen: Deutung der Problematik des Mütterlichen und des Mutterkomplexes am Beispiel bekannter Märchen*, ed. Marie-Louise von Franz (1983).

Blackwell, Jeannine, 'Fractured Fairy Tales: German Women Authors and the Grimm Tradition', *Germanic Review*, 62.4 (fall 1987).

Blackwell, Jeannine, 'Laying the Rod to Rest: Narrative Strategies in Gisela and Bettina von Arnim's Fairy Tale Novel *Gritta*', *Marvels & Tales*, 11 (1997).

Blamires, David, 'The Early Reception of the Grimms' *Kinder- und Hausmärchen* in England', *Bulletin of the John Rylands University Library of Manchester*, 71.3 (1989).

Blamires, David, 'From Madame d'Aulnoy to Mother Bunch: Popularity and the Fairy Tale', in Julia Briggs, Dennis Butts, and M. O. Grenby (eds.), *Popular Children's Literature in Britain* (2008).

Bluhm, Lothar, *Grimm-Philologie: Beiträge zur Märchenforschung und Wissenschaftsgeschichte* (1995).

Bly, Robert, *Iron John: A Book about Men* (1990).

Bly, Robert, *The Sibling Society* (1996).

Böhm-Korff, Regina, *Deutung und Bedeutung von 'Hänsel und Gretel': Eine Fallstudie* (1991).

Böklen, Ernst, *Schneewittchenstudien* (2 vols., 1910–15).

Bolte, Johannes, and **Mackensen, Lutz**, *Handwörterbuch des deutschen Märchens* (1931).

Bolte, Johannes, and **Polvka, George**, *Anmerkungen zu den* Kinder- und Hausmärchen *der Brüder Grimm* (5 vols., 1913–32; 1963).

Book, Fredrik, *Hans Christian Andersen* (1962).

Borghese, Lucia, 'Antonio Gramsci und die Grimmschen Märchen', in Ludwig Denecke (ed.), *Brüder Grimm Gedenken*, iii (1981).

Bosmajian, Hamida, 'Memory and Desire in the Landscapes of Sendak's *Dear Mili*', *The Lion and the Unicorn*, 19.2 (December 1995).

Bottigheimer, Ruth B., 'Tale Spinners: Submerged Voices in Grimms' Fairy Tales', *New German Critique*, 27 (1982).

Bottigheimer, Ruth B. (ed.), *Fairy Tales and Society: Illusion, Allusion, and Paradigm* (1986).

Bottigheimer, Ruth B., *Grimms' Bad Girls and Bold Boys: The Moral and Social Vision of the Tales* (1987).

Bottigheimer, Ruth B., 'Fairy Tales, Folk Narrative Research and History', *Social History*, 14.3 (1989).

Bottigheimer, Ruth B., 'Cupid and Psyche vs. Beauty and the Beast: The Milesian and the Modern', *Merveilles et Contes*, 3.1 (May 1989).

Bottigheimer, Ruth B., *Fairy Tales: A New History* (2011).

Bottigheimer, Ruth B. (ed.), *Fairy Tales Framed: Early Forwords, Afterwords, and Critical Words* (2012).

Bottigheimer, Ruth B., '"Beauty and the Beast": Marriage and Money—Motif and Motivation', *Midwestern Folklore*, 15.2 (fall 1989).

Bottigheimer, Ruth B., *Fairy Tales: A New History* (2011).

Bottigheimer, Ruth B. (ed.), *Fairy Tales Framed: Early Forewords, Afterwords, and Critical Words* (2013).

Bourke, Angela, 'The Virtual Reality of Irish Fairy Legend', *Eire-Ireland*, 31 (spring/ summer 1996).

Brackert, Helmut (ed.), *Und wenn sie nicht gestorben sind: Perspektiven auf das Märchen* (1980).

Brednich, Rolf Wilhelm (ed.), *Enzyklopädie des Märchens* (20 vols., 1977–2015).

Bredsdorff, Elias, *Hans Christian Andersen* (1975).

Brémond, Claude, 'Les bons récompensés et les méchants punis: morphologie du conte merveilleux français', in Claude Chabrol (ed.), *Sémiotique narrative et textuelle* (1973).

Brémond, Claude, 'Le méccano du conte', *Magazine Littéraire*, 150 (July/August 1979).

Brewer, Derek, 'The Interpretation of Fairy Tales: Implications for Literature, History and Anthropology', in *British Studies Distinguished Lecture* (1992).

Bricout, Bernadette, *Le savoir et la saveur: Henri Pourrat et Le trésor des contes* (1991).

Briggs, Katherine M., *The Anatomy of Puck: An Examination of Fairy Beliefs among Shakespeare's Contemporaries and Successors* (1959).

Briggs, Katherine M., 'The Influence of the Brothers Grimm in England', in Ludwig Denecke and Ina-Maria Greverus (eds.), *Brüder Grimm Gedenken*, Vol. 1 (1963).

Briggs, Katherine M., *The Fairies in English Tradition and Literature* (1967).

Briggs, Katherine M., 'The Folklore of Charles Dickens', *Journal of the Folklore Institute*, 7 (1970).

Briggs, Katherine M., *A Dictionary of British Folk-Tales in the English Language* (1970–1).

Briggs, Katherine M., *A Dictionary of Fairies* (1976).

Briggs, Katherine M., *The Vanishing People: A Study of Traditional Fairy Beliefs* (1978).

Bringsvaerd, Tor Age, *Phantoms and Fairies from Norwegian Folklore* (1979).

Broggini, Barbara, *'Lo cunto de li cunti' von Giambattista Basile: Ein Ständepoet in Streit mit der Plebs, Fortuna und der höfischen Korruption* (1990).

Broome, F. Hal, 'Dreams, Fairy Tales, and the Curing of Adela Cathcart', *North Wind*, 13 (1994).

Brown, Carolyn S., *The Tall Tale in American Folklore and Literature* (1987).

Brown, Nicola, *Fairies in Nineteenth-century Art and Literature* (2001).

Bryant, Sylvia, 'Re-Constructing Oedipus Through "Beauty and the Beast"', *Criticism*, 31.4 (fall 1989).

Bühler, Charlotte, and **Bilz, Josefine**, *Das Märchen und die Phantasie des Kindes* (1977).

Bülow, Werner von, *Märchendeutungen durch Runen. Die Geheimsprache der deutschen Märchen* (1925).

Bürger, Christa, 'Die soziale Funktion volkstümlicher Erzählformen—Sage und Märchen', in Heinz Ide (ed.), *Projekt Deutschunterricht* 1 (1971).

Bürger, Christa, *Tradition und Subjektivität* (1980).

Burns, Lee, 'Red Riding Hood', *Children's Literature*, 1 (1972).

Butor, Michel, 'La Balance des fées', *Cahiers du Sud*, 324 (1954).

Butor, Michel, 'On Fairy Tales', in Vernon W. Gras (ed.), *European Literary Theory and Practice* (1973).

Caillois, Roger, *Au cœur du fantastique* (1965).

Calabrese, Stefano, *Gli arabeschi della fiaba dal Basile ai romantici* (1984).

Calabrese, Stefano, *Fiaba* (1997).

Calvino, Italo, *Sulla fiaba* (1988).

Camarena, Julio, and **Chevalier, Maxime**, *Catálogo tipológico del cuento folklórico español: cuentos maravillosos* (1995).

Cambi, Franco, *Collodi, De Amicis, Rodari: tre immagini d'infanzia* (1985).

Cambon, Glauco, 'Pinocchio and the Problem of Children's Literature', *Children's Literature*, 2 (1973).

Campbell, Joseph, 'Folkloristic Commentary', *Grimm's Fairy Tales* (1956).

Campbell, Joseph, *The Hero with a Thousand Faces* (1956).

Campbell, Joseph, *The Flight of the Gander: Explorations in the Mythological Dimensions of Fairy Tales, Legends, and Symbols* (1969).

Canemaker, John (ed.), *Storytelling in Animation: The Art of the Animated Image* (1988).

Canepa, Nancy L., 'From Court to Forest: The Literary Itineraries of Giambattista Basile', *Italica*, 71.3 (fall 1994).

Canepa, Nancy L. (ed.), *Out of the Woods: The Origins of the Literary Fairy Tale in Italy and France* (1997).

Canepa, Nancy L., *From Court to Forest: Giambattista Basile's 'Lo cunto de li cunti' and the Birth of the Literary Fairy Tale* (1999).

Canton, Katia, *The Fairy Tale Revisited: A Survey of the Evolution of the Tales, from Classical Literary Interpretations to Innovative Contemporary Dance-Theater Productions* (1994).

Caracciolo, Peter L. (ed.), *The Arabian Nights in English Literature: Studies in the Reception of* The Thousand and One Nights *into British Culture* (1988).

Carden, Patricia, 'Fairy Tale, Myth, and Literature: Russian Structuralist Approaches', in Joseph P. Strelka (ed.), *Literary Criticism and Myth* (1980).

Cardigos, Isabel, *In and Out of Enchantment: Blood Symbolism and Gender in Portuguese Fairytales* (1996).

Carpenter, Humphrey, *Secret Gardens: The Golden Age of Children's Literature* (1985).

Carrouges, Michel, 'L'Initiation féerique', *Cahiers du Sud*, 324 (1954).

Castex, Pierre Georges, *Le Conte fantastique en France de Nodier à Maupassant* (1951).

Charrière, G., 'Du social au sacré dans les contes de Perrault', *Revue des histoires des religions*, 197.2 (1980).

Chartier, Roger (ed.), *Les Usages de l'imprimé* (1987).

Chebel, Malek, *La Féminisation du monde: essai sur les Mille et une nuits* (1996).

Cherek, Janina, 'Religious Themes in Polish Magic Fairy Tales', trans. Malgorzata Wiertlewska, *Ethnologia Polona*, 12 (1986).

Chinen, Allan B., *In the Ever After: Fairy Tales and the Second Half of Life* (1989).

Chinen, Allan B., *Once Upon a Midlife: Classical Stories and Mythic Tales to Illuminate the Middle Years* (1992).

Chinen, Allan B., *Waking the World: Classic Tales of Women and the Heroic Feminine* (1996).

Christopher, Joe R., 'C. S. Lewis on Walt Disney's Snow White and the Seven Dwarfs', *Lamp-Post of the Southern California C. S. Lewis Society*, 18.4 (December 1994).

Clancy, Patricia, 'A French Writer and Educator in England: Mme Le Prince de Beaumont', *Studies on Voltaire and the Eighteenth Century*, 201 (1982).

Clausen-Stolzenberg, Maren, *Märchen und mittelalterliche Literaturtradition* (1995).

Clodd, Edward, *Tim Tit Tot: An Essay of Savage Philosophy* (1898).

Cocchiara, Giuseppe, *The History of Folklore in Europe* (1981).

Cohen, Betsy, *The Snow White Syndrome: All about Envy* (1986).

Collier, Mary Jeffrey, 'The Psychological Appeal in the Cinderella Theme', *American Imago*, 18 (1961).

Cook, Elizabeth, *The Ordinary and the Fabulous* (1969).

Cooks, Leda M., Orbe, Mark P., and **Bruess, Carol S.**, 'The Fairy Tale Theme in Popular Culture: A Semiotic Analysis of Pretty Woman', *Women's Studies in Communication*, 16.2 (fall 1993).

Cooper, J. C., *Fairy Tales: Allegories of the Inner Life* (1983).

Coren, Michael, *The Man Who Created Narnia: The Story of C. S. Lewis* (1994).

Cox, Marian Emily Roalfe, *Cinderella: Three Hundred and Forty-Five Variants of Cinderella, Catskin, and Cap o'Rushes, Abstracted and Tabulated with a Discussion of Mediaeval Analogues, and Notes*, intro. Andrew Lang (1893; 1967).

Crafton, Donald, *Before Mickey: The Animated Film 1898–1928* (1982).

Crago, Hugo, 'What are Fairy Tales?', *Signal*, 100 (September 2003).

Cro, Stelio, 'Collodi: When Children's Literature Becomes Adult', *Merveilles et Contes*, 7.1 (May 1993).

Croce, Benedetto, 'Giambattista Basile e l'elaborazione artistica delle fiabe popolari', intro. to Giambattista Basile, *Il pentamerone* (1891).

Cromer, Sylvie, '"Le Sauvage" Histoire Sublime et allégorique de Madame de Murat', *Merveilles et Contes*, 1.1 (May 1987).

Culhane, John, '"Snow White" at 50: Undimmed Magic', *New York Times*, 12 July 1987, section 2.

Cumings, Edith K., 'The Literary Development of the Romantic Fairy Tale in France' (Diss., Bryn Mawr College, 1934).

Cummins, June, 'Romancing the Plot: The Real Beast of Disney's *Beauty and the Beast*', *Children's Literature Association Quarterly*, 20.1 (spring 1995).

Cutolo, Raffaele, *Into the Woods of Wicked Wonderland: Musicals Revise Fairy Tales* (2014).

Dal, Erik, 'Hans Christian Andersen's Tales and America', *Scandinavian Studies*, 40 (1968).

D'Angeli, Concetta, 'L'ideologia "moderata" di Carlo Lorenzini, detto Collodi', *Rassegna della Letteratura Italiana*, 86.1-2 (Jan.–Aug. 1982).

Darnton, Robert, *The Great Cat Massacre and Other Episodes in French Cultural History* (1984).

Darton, F. J., *Children's Books in England* (1960).

Davenport, Tom, 'Some Personal Notes on Adapting Folk-Fairy Tales to Film', *Children's Literature*, 9 (1981).

David, Alfred, and **Mary Elizabeth**, 'A Literary Approach to the Brothers Grimm', *Journal of the Folklore Institute*, 1 (1964).

Davidson, Hilda Ellis, and **Chaudhri, Anna** (eds.), *A Companion to the Fairy Tale* (2003).

Davies, Bronwyn, *Frogs and Snails and Feminist Tales: Preschool Children and Gender* (1989).

Davies, Mererid Puw, '"In Blaubarts Schatten": Murder, "Märchen" and Memory', *German Life and Letters*, 50.4 (October 1997).

Davies, Mererid Puw, *The Tale of Bluebeard in German Literature: From the Eighteenth Century to the Present* (2001).

Defrance, Anne, and **Perrin, Jean-François** (eds.), *Le conte en ses paroles: La figuration de l'oralité dans le conte merveilleux du Classicisme aux Lumières* (2007).

Dégh, Linda, *Folktales and Society: Storytelling in a Hungarian Peasant Community* (1969).

Dégh, Linda, 'Grimm's Household Tales and its Place in the Household: The Social Relevance of a Controversial Classic', *Western Folklore*, 38 (1979).

Dégh, Linda, 'What Did the Grimm Brothers Give to and Take from the Folk?', in James McGlathery (ed.), *The Brothers Grimm and Folktale* (1988).

Dégh, Linda, *American Folklore and the Mass Media* (1994).

Degraff, Amy Vanderlyn, *The Tower and the Well: A Psychological Interpretation of the Fairy Tales of Madame d'Aulnoy* (1984).

Deguise, Alix, 'Mme Le Prince de Beaumont: conteuse ou moraliste?', in Roland Bonnel and Catherine Rubinger (eds.), *Femmes savantes et femmes d'esprit: Women Intellectuals of the French Eighteenth Century* (1994).

Dejean, Joan, *Ancients against Moderns: Culture Wars and the Making of a Fin de Siècle* (1997).

Delaporte, P. Victor, *Du merveilleux dans la littérature française sous le règne de Louis XIV* (1891; 1968).

Delarue, Paul, 'Les Contes merveilleux de Perrault et la tradition populaire', *Bulletin Folklorique d'Île-de-France*, 12 (1951).

Delarue, Paul, and **Tenèze, Marie-Louise**, *Le Conte populaire français. Un catalogue raisonné des versions de France et des pays de langue française et d'outre-mer* (1997; orig. 4 vols., 1957–85).

Demnati, Faouzia, *Le Merveilleux et le realisme et leurs implications sociales et culturelles dans les 'Piacevoli notti' de Giovan Francesco Straparola* (1989).

Démoris, René, 'Du littéraire au littéral dans "Peau d'âne" de Perrault', *Revue des Sciences Humaines*, 166 (1977).

Denecke, Ludwig (ed.), *Brüder Grimm Gedenken*, i (1963); ii (1975); iii (1981); iv (1984); v (1985); vi (1986); vii (1987).

Denecke, Ludwig, *Jacob Grimm und sein Bruder Wilhelm* (1971).

Diederichs, Ulf, *Who's Who im Märchen* (1995).

Dielmann, Karl, 'Märchenillustrationen von Ludwig Emil Grimm', *Hanauer Geschichtsblätter*, 18 (1962).

Dika, Vera, 'Cinema—a Feminist Fairy Tale', *Art in America*, 75 (April 1987).

Di Scanno, Teresa, *Les Contes de fées à l'époque classique (1680–1715)* (1975).

Doderer, Klaus (ed.), *Über Märchen für Kinder von heute* (1983).

Doderer, Klaus, 'Märchen für Kinder: Kontroverse Ansichten', in Ottilie Dinges, Monika Born, and Jürgen Janning (eds.), *Märchen in Erziehung und Unterricht* (1986).

Doerner, Mark Frederick, 'The Influence of the "Kunstmärchen" on German Romantic Opera, 1814–1825' (Diss., University of California, Los Angeles, 1990).

Dolle-Weinkauff, Bernd, 'Märchen und Erziehung. Versuch einer historischen Skizze zur didaktischen Verwendung Grimmscher Märchen', in Helmut Brackert (ed.), *Und wenn sie nicht gestorben sind . . . Perspektiven auf das Märchen* (1980).

Dolle-Weinkauff, Bernd, *Das Märchen in der proletarisch-revolutionären Kinder- und Jugendliteratur der Weimarer Republik 1918–1933* (1984).

Dollerup, Cay, 'Translation as a Creative Force in Literature: The Birth of the Bourgeois Fairy Tale', *The Modern Language Review*, 90.1 (1995).

Dollerup, Cay, *The Grimm Tales from Pan-Germanic Narratives to Shared International Fairytales* (1999).

Dombrowski, Sabine, *Elternfiguren im Märchen: Orientierungshilfen im Alltag* (1994).

Dorson, Richard, *Folklore and Fakelore* (1976).

Duffy, Maureen, *The Erotic World of Faery* (1972).

Duggan, Anne, *Salonnières, Furies, and Fairies: The Politics of Gender and Cultural Change in Absolutist France* (2005).

Duggan, Anne, *Enchantments: Gender, Sexuality, and Class in the Fairy-Tale Cinema of Jacques Demy* (2013).

Duggan, Maryse Madeleine Elisabeth, 'Les Contes de Mlle de Lubert: les textualités du ludique' (Diss., University of British Columbia, 1996).

Dumont, Jean Louis, *Marcel Aymé et le merveilleux* (1970).

Dundes, Alan (ed.), *The Study of Folklore* (1965).

Dundes, Alan, *Cinderella: A Folklore Casebook* (1982).

Dundes, Alan (ed.), *Sacred Narrative: Readings in the Theory of Myth* (1984).

Dundes, Alan, 'The Psychoanalytic Study of Folklore', *Annals of Scholarship*, 3 (1985).

Dundes, Alan, 'The Psychoanalytic Study of the Grimms' Tales with Special Reference to "The Maiden without Hands" (AT 706)', *Germanic Review*, 42 (spring 1987).

Dundes, Alan (ed.), *Little Red Riding Hood: A Casebook* (1989).

Dworkin, Andrea, *Women Hating* (1974).

Eliot, Marc, *Walt Disney: Hollywood's Dark Prince* (1993).

Ellis, John, *One Fairy Story Too Many: The Brothers Grimm and their Tales* (1983).

Engen, Rodney K., *Walter Crane as a Book Illustrator* (1975).

Engen, Rodney K., *Laurence Houseman* (1983).

Escarpit, Denise, *Histoire d'un conte: le chat botté en France et en Angleterre* (2 vols., 1985).

Eschbach, Walter, *Märchen der Wirklichkeit* (1924).

Eschenbach, Ursula, *Hänsel und Gretel: das geheime Wissen der Kinder* (1986).

Espinosa, Aurelio, *The Folklore of Spain in the American Southwest: Traditional Spanish Folk Literature in Northern New Mexico and Southern Colorado*, ed. J. Manuel Espinosa (1985).

Estés, Clarissa Pinkola, *Women who Run with the Wolves: Myths and Stories of the Wild Woman Archetype* (1993).

Estés, Clarissa Pinkola, *The Dangerous Old Woman: Myths and Stories of the Wise Old Woman Archetype* (1996).

Ewers, Hans-Heino, 'Das Kunstmärchen—eine moderne Erzählgattung', in Hans-Heino Ewers (ed.), *Zauberei im Herbste: Deutsche Kunstmärchen von Wieland bis Hofmannsthal* (1987).

Ewers, Hans-Heino, 'Nachwort', in Hans-Heino Ewers (ed.), *Kinder-Märchen von Contessa, Fouqué und E. T. A. Hoffmann* (1987).

Eykmann, Christoph, 'Das Märchen im Expressionismus', in *Denk- und Stilformen des Expressionismus* (1974).

Falassi, Alessandro, *Folklore by the Fireside: Text and Context of the Tuscan Veglia* (1980).

Farrell, Michele L., 'Celebration and Repression of Feminine Desire in Mme d'Aulnoy's Fairy Tale: "La Chatte Blanche"', *Esprit Créateur*, 29.3 (1989).

Fassbind-Eigenheer, Ruth, *Undine, oder, Die nasse Grenze zwischen mir und mir: Ursprung und literarische Bearbeitungen eines Wasserfrauenmythos: von Paracelsus über Friedrich de la Motte Fouqué zu Ingeborg Bachmann* (1994).

Favat, André F., *Child and Tale: The Origins of Interest* (1977).

Fehling, Detlev, *Amor und Psyche: Die Schöpfung des Apuleius und ihre Einwirkung auf das Märchen* (1977).

Filstrup, Jane Merrill, 'Thirst for Enchanted Views in Ruskin's *The King of the Golden Mountain*', *Children's Literature*, 8 (1980).

Fine, Gary Alan, and **Ford, Julie**, 'Magic Settings: The Reflection of Middle-Class Life in "Beauty and the Beast"', *Midwestern Folklore*, 15.2 (fall 1989).

Fink, Gonthier-Louis, 'Les avatars de Rumpelstilzchen. La Vie d'un conte populaire', in Ernst Kracht (ed.), *Deutsch–Französisches Gespräch im Lichte der Märchen* (1964).

Fink, Gonthier-Louis, *Naissance et apogée du conte merveilleux en Allemagne 1740–1800* (1966).

Fischer, Maria, *Es war einmal—es ist noch. Das deutsche Märchen in seinen charakterlichen und sittlichen Werten* (1944).

Flahault, François, *L'Interpretation des contes* (1988).

Fourtane, Nicole, 'Dos versiones peruanas de "Juan el Oso"', *Revista de Dialectología y Tradiciones Populares*, 47 (1990).

Fox, Jennifer, 'The Creator Gods: Romantic Nationalism and the Engenderment of Women in Folklore', *Journal of American Folklore*, 100 (1987).

Franci, Giovanna, and **Zago, Ester**, *La bella addormentata. Genesi e metamorfosi di una fiaba* (1984).

Franson, J. Karl, 'From Vanity Fair to Emerald City: Baum's Debt to Bunyan', *Children's Literature*, 23 (1995).

Franz, Marie-Louise von, *An Introduction to the Interpretation of Fairy Tales* (1970).

Franz, Marie-Louise von, *Problems of the Feminine in Fairytales* (1972).

Franz, Marie-Louise von, *Shadow and Evil in Fairy Tales* (1974).

Franz, Marie-Louise von, *Archetypal Patterns in Fairy Tales* (1997).

Freudenberg, Rudolf, 'Erzähltechnik und "Märchenton"', in Wilhelm Solms (ed.), *Das selbstverständliche Wunder. Beiträge germanistischer Märchenforschung* (1986).

Freudmann, Felix R., 'Realism and Magic in Perrault's Fairy Tales', *Esprit Créateur*, 3 (1963).

Frey, Marianne, *Der Künstler und sein Werk bei W. H. Wackenroder und E. T. A. Hoffmann. Vergleichende Studien zur romantischen Kunstanschauung* (1970).

Frigessi, Delia (ed.), *Inchiesta sulle fate: Italo Calvino e la fiaba*, intro. Cesare Segre, illus. Raffaello Fiumana (1988).

Fromm, Erich, *The Forgotten Language* (1957).

Früh, Sigrid, and **Wehse, Rainer** (eds.), *Die Frau im Märchen* (1985).

Fumaroli, Marc, 'Les Enchantements de l'éloquence: "Les Fées" de Charles Perrault ou De la littérature', in Marc Fumaroli (ed.), *Le Statut de la littérature: mélanges offertes à Paul Bénichou* (1982).

Galef, David, 'A Sense of Magic: Reality and Illusion in Cocteau's Beauty and the Beast', *Literature/Film Quarterly*, 12.2 (1984).

Gamerschlag, Kurt, 'Tom Thumb und König Arthur, oder: Der Däumling als Masstab der Welt: Beobachtungen zu dreihundertfünfzig Jahren gemeinsamer Geschichte', *Anglia: Zeitschrift für Englische Philologie*, 101.3-4 (1983).

Gannon, Susan R., 'A Note on Collodi and Lucian', *Children's Literature*, 8 (1980).

Gannon, Susan R., '*Pinocchio*: The First Hundred Years', *Children's Literature Association Quarterly*, 6 (winter 1981/2).

Gardes, Roger, 'Le *Conte des yeux rouges* et *Gaspard des Montagnes* d'Henri Pourrat', in François Marotin (ed.), *Frontières du conte* (1982).

Gatto, Giuseppe, *La fiaba di tradizione orale* (2006).

Gatto Trocchi, Cecilia, *La fiaba italiana: ipotesi di ricerca in magia semiotica* (1972).

Gehrts, Heino, and **Lademann-Priemer, Gabriele** (eds.), *Schamanentum und Zaubermärchen* (1986).

Gentz, Regina, *Das erzählerische Werk Oscar Wildes* (1995).

Gerstner, Hermann, 'Deutsche Künstler illustrieren Märchenbücher', *Imprimatur*, 4 (1963/4).

Gerstner, Hermann, *Brüder Grimm in Selbstzeugnissen und Bilddokumenten* (1973).

Getto, Giovanni, 'Il barocco e la fiaba di Giambattista Basile', in Alessandro S. Crissafulli (ed.), *Linguistic and Literary Studies in Honor of Helmut A. Hatzfeld* (1964).

Gilman, Richard, 'Barthelme's Fairy Tale', in Richard F. Patterson (ed.), *Critical Essays on Donald Barthelme* (1992).

Gilman, Tod S., '"Aunt Em: Hate You! Hate Kansas! Taking the Dog. Dorothy": Conscious and Unconscious Desire in The Wizard of Oz', *Children's Literature Association Quarterly*, 20.4 (winter 1995-6).

Ginschel, Gunhild, *Der junge Jacob Grimm* (1967).

Girou-Swiderski, Marie-Laure, 'La Belle ou la bête? Mme de Villeneuve, la méconnue', in Roland Bonnel and Catherine Rubinger (eds.), *Femmes savantes et femmes d'esprit: Women Intellectuals of the French Eighteenth Century* (1994).

Godwin, J., Cawthorne, C. G., and **Rada, R. T.**, 'Cinderella Syndrome: Children who Simulate Neglect', *American Journal of Psychiatry*, 137 (1980).

Goldberg, Christine, 'Antti Aarne's Tales with Magic Objects', *The Old Traditional Way of Life: Essays in Honor of Warren E. Roberts* (1989).

Goldberg, Christine, *Turandot's Three Sisters* (1993).

Goldberg, Christine, 'The Donkey Skin Folktale Cycle (AT 501B)', *Journal of American Folklore*, 110 (Winter 1997).

Goldberg, Christine, *The Tale of the Three Oranges* (1997).

Goldman, Paul, *Victorian Illustrated Books: The Heyday of Wood-Engraving* (1994).

Gordon, Andrew, 'E.T. as Fairy Tale', *Science-Fiction Studies*, 10.3 (November 1983).

Gordon, Pierre, 'Mélusine', *Cahiers du Sud*, 324 (1954).

Gordon, Susan, 'The Powers of the Handless Maiden', in Joan Radner (ed.), *Feminist Messages: Coding in Women's Folk Culture* (1993).

Gose, Elliott B., *The World of the Irish Wonder Tale: An Introduction to the Study of Fairy Tales* (1985).

Göttner-Abendroth, Heide, *Die Göttin und ihr Heros: Die matriarchalen Religionen in Mythos, Märchen und Dichtung* (1980).

Grätz, Manfred, *Das Märchen in der deutschen Aufklärung. Vom Feenmärchen zum Volksmärchen* (1988).

Gray, William, *Fantasy, Myth and the Measure of Truth: Tales of Pullman, Lewis, Tolkien, MacDonald and Hoffmann* (2010).

Green, Roger Lancelyn, *Andrew Lang* (1946).

Green, Roger Lancelyn, *Teller of Tales* (rev. edn., 1946).

Green, Roger Lancelyn, *J. M. Barrie* (1960).

Green, Roger Lancelyn, *Lewis Carroll* (1960).

Greenhill, Deborah, 'Thorn Hedges and Rose Bushes: Meaning in "The Sleeping Beauty"', *Folklore and Mythology Studies*, 2 (1978).

Greenhill, Pauline, and **Matrix, Sidney Eve** (eds.), *Fairy Tale Film and Cinematic Folklore: Fantastic Voyages, Monstrous Dreams, and Wonderful Visions* (2010).

Greenhill, Pauline, and **Turner, Kay** (eds.), *Transgressive Tales: Queering the Grimms* (2012).

Greenhill, Pauline, and **Rudy, Jill Terry**, *Channeling Wonder: Fairy Tales on Television* (2014).

Grenby, M. O., 'Tame Fairies Make Good Teachers: The Popularity of Early British Fairy Tales', *The Lion and the Unicorn*, 30 (2006).

Gribble, Lyubomira Parpulobova, 'The Life of Peter and Fevroniia: Transformations and Interpretations in Modern Russian Literature and Music', *Russian Review*, 52.2 (April 1993).

Griswold, Jerome J., 'Sacrifice and Mercy in Wilde's "The Happy Prince"', *Children's Literature*, 3 (1974).

Griswold, Jerome J., *The Meanings of 'Beauty and the Beast': A Handbook* (2004).

Griswold, Jerome J., *Audacious Kids: Coming of Age in America's Classic Children's Books* (1992).

Grønbech, Bo, *Hans Christian Andersen* (1980).

Grotzfeld, Heinz and **Sophia**, *Die Erzählungen aus 'Tausendeinernacht'* (1984).

Guaragnella, Pasquale, 'Sventura e maschere di eros nella società di corte: la fiaba della "bella dormiente" fra Basile e Perrault', in Paolo Bari Carile (intro.), *Eros in Francia nel Seicento* (1987).

Guidi, Augusto, *Collodi e Andersen* (1970).

Haase, Donald, 'Ludwig Tieck', in Everett Franklin Bleiler (ed.), *Supernatural Fiction Writers: Fantasy and Horror*, i. *Apuleius to May Sinclair* (1985).

Haase, Donald, 'Gold into Straw: Fairy Tale Movies for Children and the Culture Industry', *The Lion and the Unicorn*, 12.2 (December 1988).

Haase, Donald, 'Is Seeing Believing? Proverbs and the Film Adaptation of a Fairy Tale', *Proverbium: Yearbook of International Proverb Scholarship*, 7 (1990).

Haase, Donald, 'The Politics of the Exile Fairy Tale', in Sigrid Bauschinger and Susan L. Cocalis (eds.), *Wider den Faschismus: Exilliteratur als Geschichte* (1993).

Haase, Donald (ed.), *The Reception of Grimms' Fairy Tales: Responses, Reactions, Revisions* (1993).

Haase, Donald, 'German Fairy Tales and America's Culture Wars: From Grimms' Kinder- und Hausmärchen to William Bennett's Book of Virtues', *German Politics and Society*, 13.3 (fall 1995).

Haase, Donald, 'The *Arabian Nights*, Visual Culture, and Early German Cinema', *Fabula*, 45.3/4 (2004).

Haase, Donald (ed.), *Fairy Tales and Feminism: New Approaches* (2004).

Haase, Donald, 'Hypertextual Gutenberg: The Textual and Hypertextual Life of Folktales and Fairy Tales in English-Language Popular Print Editions', *Fabula* 47 (2006).

Haase, Donald (ed.), *The Greenwood Encyclopedia of Folktales and Fairy Tales* (3 vols., 2008).

Haase, Donald, 'Decolonizing Fairy-Tale Studies', *Marvels & Tales*, 24.1 (2010).

Hadjadj, Dany, 'Du "relève de folklore" au conte populaire: avec Henri Pourrat, promenade aux fontaines du dire', in François Marotin (ed.), *Frontières du conte* (1982).

Haffner, Hans Jokum Horn, *Asbjørnsen og Moe's norske folkeeventyr: en bibliografisk undersokelse* (1942).

Hagen, Rolf, 'Perraults Märchen und die Brüder Grimm', *Zeitschrift für deutsche Philologie*, 74 (1955).

Hains, Maryellen, 'Beauty and the Beast: 20th Century Romance?', *Merveilles et Contes*, 3.1 (May 1989).

Hamann, Hermann, *Die literarischen Vorlagen der 'Kinder- und Hausmärchen' und ihre Bearbeitung durch die Brüder Grimm* (1906).

Hamman, A.-G., *L'épopée du livre: la transmission des textes anciens, du scribe à l'imprimerie* (1985).

Haney, Jack V., *An Introduction to the Russian Folktale* (1999).

Hanks, Carole and **D. T.**, 'Perrault's "Little Red Riding Hood": Victim of the Revisers', *Children's Literature*, 7 (1978).

Hanlon, Tina L., '"To Sleep, Perchance to Dream": Sleeping Beauties and Wide-Awake Plain Janes in the Stories of Jane Yolen', *Children's Literature*, 26 (1998).

Hannon, Patricia. 'Antithesis and Ideology in Perrault's "Riquet à la houppe"', *Cahiers du Dix-septième*, 4.2 (fall 1990).

Hannon, Patricia, 'Representations of Resistance: Rereading Simone de Beauvoir's *Le Deuxième Sexe* in the Weave of Seventeenth-Century Women's Fairy Tales', *Simone de Beauvoir Studies*, 10 (1993).

Hannon, Patricia, *Fabulous Identities: Women's Fairy Tales in Seventeenth-Century France* (1998).

Hansen, Miriam, 'Of Mice and Ducks: Benjamin and Adorno on Disney', *South Atlantic Quarterly*, 92.1 (winter 1993).

Hansen, William, *Ariadne's Thread: A Guide to International Tales Found in Classical Literature* (2002).

Harf-Lancner, Laurence, *Les Fées au Moyen Âge: Morgane et Mélusine. La Naissance des fées* (1984).

Harmetz, Aljean, *The Making of the Wizard of Oz* (1978).

Harries, Elizabeth W., 'Simulating Oralities: French Fairy Tales of the 1690s', *College Literature*, 23 (June 1996).

Harries, Elizabeth W., *Twice Upon a Time: Women Writers and the History of the Fairy Tale* (2001).

Harris, Jason, *Folklore and the Fantastic in Nineteenth-Century British Fiction*, (2008).

Hassauer, Friederike, *Die Philosophie der Fabeltiere* (1986).

Hearn, Michael Patrick, '(Special W. W. Denslow (First Illustrator of Oz) Issue)', *Baum Bugle: A Journal of Oz*, 16.2 (1972).

Hearn, Michael Patrick (ed.), *The Annotated Wizard of Oz* (1973).

Hearne, Betsy Gould, *Beauty and the Beast: Visions and Revisions of an Old Tale* (1989).

Hearne, Betsy Gould, 'A Story Internalized: 1900–1950', *Merveilles et Contes*, 3.1 (May 1989).

Heidmann, Ute, and **Adam, Jean-Michel**, *Textualité et intertextualité des contes: Perrault, Apulée, La Fontaine* (2010).

Hennig, Dieter, and **Lauer, Bernhard** (eds.), *Die Brüder Grimm. Dokumente ihres Lebens und Wirkens* (1985).

Hennig, John, 'The Brothers Grimm and T. C. Croker', *Modern Language Review*, 41 (1946).

Hermansson, Casie, *Bluebeard: A Reader's Guide to the English Tradition* (2009).

Hervig, Henriette, 'Mann und Frau in Goethes Märchen Die neue Melusine: Text, Kontext und Intertextualität', *Colloquium Helveticum: Cahiers Suisses de Littérature Comparée/Schweizer Hefte für Allgemeine und Vergleichende Literaturwissenschaft*, 17 (1993).

Hetmann, Frederik, 'Die mündlichen Quellen der Grimms oder die Rolle der Geschichtenerzähler in den *Kinder- und Hausmärchen*', *Germanic Review*, 42 (spring 1987).

Heuscher, Julius E., *A Psychiatric Study of Myths and Fairy Tales: Their Origin, Meaning and Usefulness* (1963).

Hewett-Thayer, Harvey Waterman, *Hoffmann: Author of the Tales* (1948).

Heyden, Franz, *Volksmärchen und Volksmärchen-Erzähler. Zur literarischen Gestaltung des deutschen Volksmärchens* (1922).

Hildebrandt, Irma, *Es waren ihrer Fünf. Die Brüder Grimm und ihre Familie* (1984).

Hilgar, Marie-France (ed.), *Actes de Las Vegas: Théorie dramatique, Théophile de Viau, Les Contes de fées* (1991).

Hixon, Martha Pittman, 'Awakenings and Transformations: Re-visioning the Tales of Sleeping Beauty, Snow White, The Frog Prince, and Tam Lin' (Diss., University of Southwestern Louisiana, 1997).

Hoffmann, Kathryn, 'Of Innocents and Hags: The Status of the Female in the Seventeenth-Century Fairy Tale', *Cahiers du Dix-septième*, 4.2 (1997).

Hoggard, Lynn, 'Writing with the Ink of Light: Jean Cocteau's Beauty and the Beast', in Wendell Aycock and Michael Schoenecke (eds.), *Film and Literature: A Comparative Approach to Adaptation* (1988).

Holbek, Bengt, *Interpretation of Fairy Tales: Danish Folklore in a European Perspective* (1987).

Holliss, Richard, and **Sibley, Brian**, *Walt Disney's Snow White and the Seven Dwarfs and the Making of the Classic Film* (1987).

Honeyman, Susan, *Consuming Agency in Fairy Tales, Childlore, and Folkliterature* (2010).

Hood, Gwyneth, 'Husbands and Gods as Shadowbrutes: "Beauty and the Beast" from Apuleius to C. S. Lewis', *Mythlore*, 15.2 (winter 1988).

Horn, Katalin, *Der aktive und der passive Märchenheld* (1983).

Hovannisian, Richard G., and **Sabagh, Georges** (eds.), *'The Thousand and One Nights' in Arabic Literature and Society* (1997).

Hruschka, John, 'Anne Sexton and Anima Transformations: Transformations as a Critique of the Psychology of Love in Grimm's Fairy Tales', *Mythlore*, 20.1 (winter 1994).

Hudde, Hinrich, 'Diderot als Märchenparodist: L'Oiseau blanc, conte bleu', in Titus Heydenreich (ed.), *Denis Diderot: Zeit, Werk, Wirkung: Zehn Beiträge* (1984).

Hult, Marte Hyam, *Framing a National Narrative: The Legend Collections of Peter Christian Asbjørnsen* (2003).

Hyde, H. Montgomery, *Oscar Wilde* (1976).

Irmen, Hans-Josef, *Hänsel und Gretel: Studien und Dokumente zu Engelbert Humperdincks Märchenoper* (1989).

Irwin, Robert, *The Arabian Nights: A Companion* (1994).

Jacobs, Joseph, 'Cinderella in Britain', *Folklore*, 4 (1893).

Jacoby, Mario, Kast, Verena, and **Reidel, Ingrid**, *Witches, Ogres, and the Devil's Daughter: Encounters with Evil in Fairy Tales* (1992).

Jackson, Rosemary, *Fantasy: The Literature of Subversion* (1981).

Jacques, Georges (ed.), *Recherches sur le conte merveilleux: recueil d'études* (1981).

Jaffé, Aniela, *Bilder und Symbole aus E. T. A. Hoffmanns 'Der goldene Topf'* (2nd rev. edn., 1978).

Jäger, Hans-Wolf, 'Trägt Rotkäppchen eine Jakobinermütze?: Über mutmassliche Konnotate bei Tieck und Grimm', in Joachim Bard (ed.), *Beiträge zur Praxis* (Literatursoziologie, ii, 1974).

Jalkotzy, Alois, *Märchen und Gegenwart* (1930).

Janning, Jürgen, and **Gehrts, Heino** (eds.), *Die Welt im Märchen* (1984).

Janning, Jürgen, and **Gobyn, Luc**, *Liebe und Eros im Märchen* (1988).

Janning, Jürgen, Gehrts, Heino, and **Ossowski, Herbert** (eds.), *Vom Menschenbild im Märchen* (1980).

Jarvis, Shawn, 'Spare the Rod and Spoil the Child? Bettina's *Das Leben der Hochgräfin Gritta von Rattenzuhausbeiuns*', *Women in German Yearbook*, 3 (1986).

Jarvis, Shawn, 'The Vanished Woman of Great Influence: Benedikte Naubert's Legacy and German Women's Fairy Tales', in *In the Shadow of Olympus: German Women Writers around 1800* (1992).

Jasmin, Nadine, *Naissance du Conte Féminin. Mots et Merveilles: Les Contes de fées de Madame d'Aulnoy (1690–1698)* (2002).

Jean, Georges, *Le Pouvoir des contes* (1981).

Jeggle, Utz, Korff, Gottfried, Scharfe, Martin, and **Warneken, Bernd Jürgen** (eds.), *Volkskultur in der Moderne: Probleme und Perspektiven empirischer Kulturforschung* (1986).

Johns, Andrea, *Baba Yaga: The Ambiguous Mother and Witch of the Russian Folktale* (2004).

Johnson-Feelings, Dianne, *Presenting Laurence Yep*, Twayne's United States Authors Series, Young Adult Authors, 656 (1995).

Jolles, André, *Einfache Formen* (1930).

Jones, Christine, and **Schacker, Jennifer** (eds.), *Marvelous Transformations: An Anthology of Fairy Tales and Contemporary Critical Perspectives* (2012).

Jones, Jo Elwyn, and **Gladstone, J. Francis**, *The Red King's Dream or Lewis Carroll in Wonderland* (1995).

Jones, Steven Swann, *The New Comparative Method: Structural and Symbolic Analysis of the Allomotifs of 'Snow White'* (1990).

Jones, Steven Swann, *The Fairy Tale: The Magic Mirror of Imagination* (1995).

Jones-Day, Shirley, 'A Woman Writer's Dilemma: Mme de Gomez and the Early Eighteenth-Century Novel', in Roland Bonnel and Catherine Rubinger (eds.), *Femmes savantes et femmes d'esprit: Women Intellectuals of the French Eighteenth Century* (1994).

Joosen, Vanessa, *Critical and Creative Perspectives on Fairy Tales: An Intertextual Dialogue between Fairy-Tale Scholarship and Postmodern Readings* (2011).

Joosen, Vanessa, and **Lathey, Grillian** (eds.), *Grimms' Tales Around the Globe: The Dynamics of Their International Recepiton* (2014).

Jullian, Philippe, *Oscar Wilde* (1969).

Jung, C. G., *Psyche and Symbol* (1958).

Jungblut, Gertrud, 'Märchen der Brüder Grimm—feministisch gelesen', *Diskussion Deutsch*, 91 (October 1986).

Kabani, Rana, *Europe's Myths of Orient* (1986).

Kabani, Rana, 'The Arabian Nights as an Orientalist Text', in Ulrich Marzolph and Richard Van Keeuwen (eds.), *The Arabian Nights Encyclopedia* (2004).

Kaiser, Erich, '"Ent-Grimm-te" Märchen', *Westermanns Pädagogische Beiträge*, 8 (1975).

Kaiser, Mary, 'Fairy Tale as Sexual Allegory: Intertextuality in Angela Carter's *The Bloody Chamber*', *Review of Contemporary Fiction*, 14.3 (fall 1994).

Kamenetsky, Christa, 'Folklore as a Political Tool in Nazi Germany', *Journal of American Folkore*, 85 (1972).

Kamenetsky, Christa, 'Folktale and Ideology in the Third Reich', *Journal of American Folklore*, 90 (1977).

Kamenetsky, Christa, *The Brothers Grimm and their Critics: Folktales and the Quest for Meaning* (1992).

Karlinger, Felix, 'Schneeweisschen und Rosenrot in Sardinien. Zur Übernahme eines Buchmärchens in die volkstümliche Erzähltradition', in Ludwig Denecke (ed.), *Brüder Grimm Gedenken*, i. (1963).

Karlinger, Felix (ed.), *Wege der Märchenforschung* (1973).

Karlinger, Felix, *Grundzüge einer Geschichte des Märchens im deutschen Sprachraum* (1983).

Karrenbrock, Helga, *Märchenkinder—Zeitgenossen: Untersuchungen zur Kinderliteratur der Weimarer Republik* (1995).

Kast, Verena, *Fairy Tales for the Psyche: Ali Baba and the Forty Thieves and the Myth of Sisyphus* (1996).

Kast, Verena, *The Mermaid in the Pond: An Erotic Fairy Tale for Adults* (1997).

Keightley, Thomas, *The Fairy Mythology Illustrative of the Romance and Superstition of Various Countries* (2 vols., 1833).

Kérchy, Anna (ed.), *Postmodern Reinterpretations of Fairy Tales: How Applying New Methods Generates New Beginnings* (2011).

Kiefer, Emma Emily, *Albert Wesselski and Recent Folktale Theories* (1947).

Klone, Ursula, *Die Aufnahme des Märchens in der italienischen Kunstprosa von Straparola bis Basile* (1961).

Klotz, Volker, 'Wie Wilde seine Märchen über Andersen hinwegerzählt', in Gregor Laschen and Manfred Schlösser (eds.), *Der zerstückte Traum: Für Erich Arendt zum 75. Geburtstag* (1978).

Klotz, Volker, 'Dahergelaufene und Davongekommene: Ironisierte Abenteuerer in Märchen von Musäus, Wieland und Goethe', *Euphorion: Zeitschrift für Literaturgeschichte*, 79.3–4 (1985).

Klotz, Volker, *Das europäische Kunstmärchen* (1985).

Knoepflmacher, U. C., 'The Balancing of the Child and Adult: An Approach to Victorian Fantasies for Children', *Nineteenth-Century Fiction*, 37 (March 1983).

Knoepflmacher, U. C., 'Introduction', *A Christmas Carol by Charles Dickens and Other Victorian Fairy Tales by John Ruskin, W. M. Thackeray, George MacDonald, and Jean Ingelow* (1983).

Knoepflmacher, U. C., 'Resisting Growth through Fairy Tale in Ruskin's *King of the Golden River*', *Children's Literature*, 13 (1985).

Knoepflmacher, U. C., *Ventures into Childland: Victorians, Fairy Tales, and Femininity* (1998).

Knoepflmacher, U. C., 'The Hansel and Gretel Syndrome: Survivorship Fantasies and Parental Desertion', *Children's Literature*, 33 (2005).

Kolbenschlag, Maria, *Kiss Sleeping Beauty Good-bye* (1979).

Kondratiev, Alexei, 'Tales Newly Told', *Mythlore*, 13. 2 (winter 1986).

Kosack, Wolfgang, 'Der Gattungsbegriff "Volkserzählung"', *Fabula*, 12 (1971).

Koszinowski, Ingrid, and **Leuschner, Vera** (eds.), *Ludwig Emil Grimm 1790–1863. Maler, Zeichner, Radierer* (1985).

Kotzin, Michael C., 'The Fairy Tale in England, 1800–1870', *Journal of Popular Culture*, 4 (summer 1970).

Kotzin, Michael C., *Dickens and the Fairy Tale* (1972).

Koven, Mikel, *Film, Folklore, and Urban Legends* (2008).

Kravchenko, Maria, *The World of the Russian Fairy Tale* (1987).

Kready, Laura F., *A Study of Fairy Tales* (1916).

Krohn, Kaarle, *Antti Aarne* (1926).

Kümmerling-Meibauer, Bettina, *Die Kunstmärchen von Hofmannsthal, Musil und Döblin* (1991).

Kunzfeld, Alois, *Vom Märchenerzählen und Märchenillustrieren* (1926).

Kürthy, Tamas, *Dornröschens zweites Erwachen. Die Wirklichkeit in Mythen und Märchen* (1985).

Kuttner, Michael, *Psychedelische Handlungselemente in den Märchen der Brüder Grimm* (1995).

Lafforgue, Pierre, *Petit Poucet deviendra grand: le travail du conte* (1995).

Laiblin, Wilhelm (ed.), *Märchenforschung und Tiefenpsychologie* (1969).

Lane, Marcia, *Picturing the Rose: A Way of Looking at Fairy Tales* (1993).

Langley, Noel, Ryerson, Florence, and **Woolf, Edgar Allan**, *The Wizard of Oz: The Screenplay*, ed. Michael Patrick Hearn (1989).

Langstaff, Eleanor De Selms, *Andrew Lang* (1978).

Lappas, Catherine, 'Rewriting Fairy Tales: Transformation as Feminist Practice in the Nineteenth and Twentieth Centuries' (Diss., St Louis University, 1995).

Larivaille, Paul, *Perspectives et limites d'une analyse morphologique du conte: pour une révision du schéma de Propp* (1979).

Larry, Charles E., 'The Art of Tradition: Nancy Ekholm Burkert's Illustrations for "Snow White and the Seven Dwarfs"', *Journal of Children's Literature*, 21.2 (fall 1995).

Laruccia, Victor, 'Little Red Riding Hood's Metacommentary: Paradoxical Injunction, Semiotics and Behavior', *Modern Language Notes*, 90 (1975).

Laski, Marghanita, *Mrs. Ewing, Mrs. Molesworth, and Mrs. Hodgson Burnett* (1950).

Latham, Minor White, *The Elizabethan Fairies: The Fairies of Folklore and the Fairies of Shakespeare* (1930).

Lau, Kimberly J., 'Structure, Society, and Symbolism: Toward a Holistic Interpretation of Fairy Tales', *Western Folklore*, 55.3 (summer 1996).

Lecouteux, Claude, 'Zwerge und Verwandte', *Euphorion: Zeitschrift für Literaturgeschichte*, 75.3 (1981).

Lederer, Wolfgang, *The Kiss of the Snow Queen: Hans Christian Andersen and Man's Redemption by Woman* (1986).

Ledermann, Wilhelm, *Das Märchen in Schule und Haus* (1921).

Lee, Abigail E., 'La paradigmática historia de Caperucita y el lobo feroz: Juan Goytisolo's Use of "Little Red Riding Hood" in *Reivindicación del conde don Julián*', *Bulletin of Hispanic Studies*, 65 (1988).

Lefevre, Andre, *Mitología de los cuentos de Perrault* (1986).

Lehnert, Nicole, *Brave Prinzessin oder freie Hexe?: Zum bürgerlichen Frauenbild in den Grimmschen Märchen* (1996).

Lewis, Philip, *Seeing through the Mother Goose Tales: Visual Turns in the Writings of Charles Perrault* (1996).

Leyen, Friedrich von der, *Das Märchen* (1917).

Leyen, Friedrich von der, *Das deutsche Märchen und die Brüder Grimm* (1964).

Lieberman, Marcia, 'Some Day My Prince Will Come: Female Acculturation through the Fairy Tale', *College English*, 34 (1972).

Lieberman, Marcia, 'The Feminist in Fairy Tales—Two Books from the Jung Institute, Zurich', *Children's Literature*, 2 (1973).

Liebs, Elke, *Kindheit und Tod: Der Rattenfänger-Mythos als Beitrag zu einer Kulturgeschichte der Kindheit* (1986).

Lindahl, Carl, McNamara, John, and **Lindow, John** (eds.), *Medieval Folklore: An Encyclopedia of Myths, Legends, Tales, Beliefs, and Customs*, 2 vols. (2000).

Liptay, Fabienne, *WunderWelten. Märchen im Film* (2004).

Littlefield, Henry M., 'The Wizard of Oz: Parable on Populism', in Hennig Cohen (ed.), *American Culture* (1968).

Lochhead, Marion, *The Renaissance of Wonder in Children's Literature* (1977).

Lods, Jeanne, *Le Roman de Perceforest* (1951).

Loeffler-Delachaux, Marguerite, *Le Symbolisme des contes de fées* (1949).

Loeffler-Delachaux, Marguerite, *Los Hermanos Grimm Conferencias* (1986).

Loskoutoff, Yvan, *La Sainte et la fée: dévotion à l'Enfant Jésus et mode des contes merveilleux à la fin du règne de Louis XIV* (1987).

Lundell, Torborg, *Fairy Tale Mothers* (1990).

Lurie, Alison, 'Fairy Tale Liberation', *New York Review of Books*, 17 December 1970.

Lurie, Alison, 'Witches and Fairies: Fitzgerald to Updike', *New York Review of Books*, 2 December 1971.

Lurie, Alison, 'Ford Madox Ford's Fairy Tales', *Children's Literature*, 8 (1979).

Lüthi, Max, *Die Gabe im Märchen und in der Sage* (1943).

Lüthi, Max, *Das europäische Volksmärchen* (2nd rev. edn., 1960).

Lüthi, Max, *Märchen* (1962).

Lüthi, Max, *Volksmärchen und Volkssage* (2nd rev. edn., 1966).

Lüthi, Max, 'Familie und Natur im Märchen', *Volksliteratur und Hochliteratur* (1970).

Lüthi, Max, *Once Upon a Time: On the Nature of Fairy Tales* (1970).

Lüthi, Max, 'Rumpelstilzchen', *Antaios*, 12 (1971).

Lüthi, Max, *Das Volksmärchen als Dichtung* (1975).

Lüthi, Max, *The European Folktale: Form and Nature* (1982).

Lüthi, Max, *The Fairy Tale as Art Form and Portrait of Man* (1985).

Lyons, Heather, 'Some Second Thoughts on Sexism in Fairy Tales', in Elizabeth Grugeon and Peter Walden (eds.), *Literature and Learning* (1978).

McAra, Catriona, and **Calvin, David** (eds.), *Anti-Tales: The Uses of Disenchantment* (2011).

MacDonald, Ruth, 'The Tale Retold: Feminist Fairy Tales', *Children's Literature Association Quarterly*, 7 (summer 1982).

McGillis, Roderick, 'Lame Old Bachelor, Lonely Old Maid: Harriet Childe Pemberton's "All My Doing; or Red Riding Hood Over Again"', in Maria Nikolajeva (ed.), *Aspects and Issues in the History of Children's Literature* (1995).

McGlathery, James M. (ed.), *The Brothers Grimm and Folktale* (1988).

McGlathery, James M., *Fairy Tale Romance: The Grimms, Basile, and Perrault* (1991).

McGlathery, James M., *Grimms' Fairy Tales: A History of Criticism on a Popular Classic* (1993).

McGlathery, James M., *E. T. A. Hoffmann* (1997).

Macnicol, John, 'Pornography, Fairy Tales, and Feminism: Angela Carter's "The Bloody Chamber"', in *Forbidden History: The State, Society, and the Regulation of Sexuality in Modern Europe: Essays from the Journal of the History of Sexuality* (1992).

Macpherson, Jay, *'Beauty and the Beast' and Some Relatives* (1974).

McQuade, Brett T., 'Peter Pan: Disney's Adaptation of J. M. Barrie's Original Work', *Mythlore*, 20.1 (winter 1994).

Maitlin, Leonard, *The Disney Films* (updated edn., 1984).

Malarte, Claire-Lise, 'Les Contes de Perrault, œuvre "moderne"', in Louise Godard de Donville (ed.), *D'un siècle à l'autre: anciens et modernes* (1987).

Malarte, Claire-Lise, *Perrault à travers la critique depuis 1960* (1989).

Mallet, Carl-Heinz, *Kennen Sie Kinder?* (1980).

Mallet, Carl-Heinz, *Das Einhorn bin ich* (1982).

Mallet, Carl-Heinz, *Kopf ab! Gewalt im Märchen* (1985).

Manlove, C. N., *Modern Fantasy: Five Studies* (1975).

Manna, Anthony L., 'The Americanization of the Brothers Grimm, or Tom Davenport's Film Adaptations of German Folktales', *Children's Literature Quarterly*, 13 (fall 1988).

Marchese, Giuseppe, *Collodi poeta dell'infanzia* (1963).

Marin, Louis, '"Puss-in-Boots": Power of Signs—Signs of Power', *Diacritics*, 7 (summer 1977).

Marin, Louis, *La Parole mangée et autres essais théologico-politiques* (1986).

Marsh, Jan, 'Christina Rossetti's Vocation: The Importance of *Goblin Market*', *Victorian Poetry*, 32.3–4 (autumn–winter 1994).

Marshall, Cynthia, Essays on C. S. Lewis and George MacDonald: Truth, Fiction, and the Power of the Imagination, *Studies in British Literature*, 11 (1991).

Marshall, Howard Wright, '"Tom Tit Tot": A Comparative Essay on Aarne-Thompson Type 500—The Name of the Helper', *Folklore*, 84 (1973).

Martin, Robert K., 'Oscar Wilde and the Fairy Tale: "The Happy Prince" as Self-Dramatization', *Studies in Short Fiction*, 16 (1979).

Martineau, Jane (ed.), *Victorian Fairy Painting* (1997).

Martus, Steffen, *Die Brüder Grimm: Eine Biographie* (2009).

Marzolph, Ulrich, and **Leeuwen, Richard Van** (eds.), *The Arabian Nights Encyclopedia* (2004).

May, Georges, *Les Mille et une nuits d'Antoine Galland* (1986).

May, Jill P., 'Jane Yolen's Literary Fairy Tales: Legends, Folktales, and Myths Remade', *Journal of Children's Literature*, 21.1 (spring 1995).

Mayer, Hans, 'Vergebliche Renaissance: Das "Märchen" bei Goethe und Gerhart Hauptmann', *Von Lessing bis Thomas Mann* (1959).

Mayer, Mathias, *Kunstmärchen* (1997).

Mazenauer, Beat, and **Perrig, Severin**, *Wie Dornröschen seine Unschuld gewann: Archäologie der Märchen* (1995).

Mazon, Jeanne Roche, *En marge de l'Oiseau bleu* (1930).

Mazzacurati, Giancarlo, 'Sui materiali in opera nelle *Piacevoli notti* di Giovan Francesco Straparola', and 'La narrativa di Giovan Francesco Straparola: sociologia e structura del personaggio fiabesco', in *Società e strutture narrative dal Trecento al Cinquecento* (1971).

Meletinsky, Eleasar, 'Die Ehe im Zaubermärchen', *Acta Ethnographica Academiae Scientiarum Hungaricae*, 19 (1970).

Meletinsky, Eleasar, 'Marriage: Its Function and Position in the Structure of Folktales', in P. Maranda (ed.), *Soviet Structural Folkloristics* (1974).

Mendelson, Michael, 'Forever Acting Alone: The Absence of Female Collaboration in *Grimms' Fairy Tales*', *Children's Literature in Education*, 28 (September 1997).

Menninghaus, Winfried, *Lob des Unsinns: Über Kant, Tieck und Blaubart* (1995).

Merritt, Russell, and **Kaufman, J. B.**, *Walt in Wonderland: The Silent Films of Walt Disney* (1993).

Metcalf, Eva-Maria, *Astrid Lindgren*, Twayne World Authors Series, 851 (1995).

Metzger, Michael M., and **Mommsen, Katharina** (eds.), *Fairy Tales as Ways of Knowing: Essays on Märchen in Psychology, Society, and Literature* (1981).

Meyer, Rudolf, *Die Weisheit der deutschen Märchen* (1935).

Michaelis-Jena, Ruth, *The Brothers Grimm* (1970).

Michaelis-Jena, Ruth, 'Edgar and John Edward Taylor, die ersten englischen Übersetzer der *Kinder- und Hausmärchen*', in Ludwig Denecke (ed.), *Brüder Grimm Gedenken* (1975).

Mieder, Wolfgang, 'Survival Forms of "Little Red Riding Hood" in Modern Society', *International Folklore Review: Folklore Studies from Overseas*, 2 (1982).

Mieder, Wolfgang, *'Findet, so werdet ihr suchen!' Die Brüder Grimm und das Sprichwort* (1986).

Mieder, Wolfgang, 'Sprichwörtliche Schwundstufen des Märchens. Zum 200. Geburtstag der Brüder Grimm', *Proverbium*, 3 (1986).

Mieder, Wolfgang, 'Wilhelm Grimm's Proverbial Additions in the Fairy Tales', *Proverbium*, 3 (1986).

Mieder, Wolfgang, 'Grimm Variations: From Fairy Tales to Modern Anti-Fairy Tales', *Germanic Review*, 42 (spring 1987).

Mieder, Wolfgang, *Tradition and Innovation in Folk Literature* (1987).

Mieder, Wolfgang, *Der Rattenfänger von Hameln: Die Sage in Literatur, Medien und Karikaturen* (2002).

Mieder, Wolfgang, *Hänsel und Gretel: Das Märchen in Kunst, Musik, Literatur, Medien und Karikaturen* (2007).

Mikkelsen, Nina, 'Richard Chase's Jack Tales: A Trickster in the New World', in Perry Nodelman (ed.), *Touchstones: Reflections on the Best in Children's Literature: Fairy Tales, Fables, Myths, Legends, and Poetry* (1987).

Miller, Cynthia A., 'The Poet in the Poem: A Phenomenological Analysis of Anne Sexton's "Briar Rose (Sleeping Beauty)"', in Anna-Teresa Tymieniecka (ed.), *The Existential Coordinates of the Human Condition: Poetic—Epic—Tragic: The Literary Genre* (1984).

Miller, Elisabeth, *Das Bild der Frau im Märchen. Analysen und erzieherische Betrachtungen* (1986).

Miller, Patricia, 'The Importance of Being Earnest: The Fairy Tale in Nineteenth-Century England', *Children's Literature Association Quarterly*, 7 (summer 1982).

Mitchell, Jane Tucker, *A Thematic Analysis of Mme d'Aulnoy's Contes de fées* (1978).

Mitrokhina, Xenia, 'The Land of Oz in the Land of Soviets', *Children's Literature Quarterly*, 21 (winter 1996–7).

Mittler, Sylvia, 'Le Jeune Henri Pourrat: de Barrès et Bergson à l'âme rustique', *Travaux de Linguistique et de Littérature*, 15 (1977).

Moen, Kristian, *Film and Fairy Tales: The Birth of Modern Fantasy* (2013).

Mommsen, Katharina (ed.), *Goethes Märchendichtungen: 'Der neue Paris', 'Die neue Melusine', 'Das Märchen'* (1984).

Montresor, Jaye Berman, 'Sanitization and its Discontents: Refuse and Refusal in Donald Barthelme's Snow White', *Studies in American Humor*, 7 (1989).

Moore, Robert, 'From Rags to Witches: Stereotypes, Distortions and Antihumanism in Fairy Tales', *Interracial Books for Children*, 6 (1975).

Morace, Robert A., 'Donald Barthelme's Snow White: The Novel, the Critics, and the Culture', in Richard F. Patterson (ed.), *Critical Essays on Donald Barthelme* (1992).

Moreno-Turer, Fernando, 'Jueguemos en el bosque mientras el lobo no está (a la Caperucita Roja)', *Coloquio Internacional: Lo lúdico y lo fantástico en la obra de Cortázar* (1986).

Morgan, Jeanne, *Perrault's Morals for Moderns* (1985).

Moriconi, Martine, 'Et Disney créa . . . Blanche-Neige', *Studio Magazine*, 90 (September 1994).

Morris-Keitel, Helen G., 'The Audience Should Be King: Bettina Bretanovon Arnim's "Tale of the Lucky Purse"', *Marvels & Tales*, 11 (1997).

Morrisey, Thomas J., and **Wunderlich, Richard**, 'Death and Rebirth in *Pinocchio*', *Children's Literature*, 11 (1983).

Moser, Dietz-Rüdiger, 'Theorie- und Methodenprobleme der Märchenforschung', *Ethnologia Bavarica*, 10 (1981).

Moser, Dietz-Rüdiger, 'Keine unendliche Geschichte. Die Grimm'schen Märchen— eine Treppe in die Vergangenheit', *Journal für Geschichte*, 3 (May/June 1984).

Moser, Hugo, 'Volks- und Kunstdichtung in der Auffassung der Romantiker', *Rheinisches Jahrbuch für Volkskunde*, 4 (1953).

Moser, Hugo, *'Lustige Gesellschaft': Schwank und Witz des 17. und 18. Jahrhunderts in kultur- und sozialgeschichtlichen Kontext* (1984).

Mosley, Leonard, *Disney's World* (1985).

Moss, Anita, 'Mothers, Monsters, and Morals in Victorian Fairy Tales', *The Lion and the Unicorn*, 12.2 (December 1988).

Motte-Gillet, Anne, 'Giovan Francesco Straparola: "Les Facétieuses Nuits"', in A. Motte-Gillet (ed.), *Conteurs italiens de la Renaissance* (1993).

Mourey, Lilyane, *Introduction aux contes de Grimm et de Perrault* (1978).

Mowshowitz, Harriet H., 'Gilles de Rais and the Bluebeard Legend in France', *Michigan Academician: Papers of the Michigan Academy of Science, Arts, and Letters*, 6 (1973).

Mowshowitz, Harriet H., '"Voir est un acte dangereux": An Analysis of Perrault's "La Barbe bleue"', *Proceedings of the Pacific Northwest Conference on Foreign Languages*, 30.1–2 (1979).

Müller, Elisabeth, *Das Bild der Frau im Märchen. Analysen und erzieherische Betrachtungen* (1986).

Naithani, Sadhana, *In Quest of Indian Folktales: Pandit Ram Gharib Chaube and William Crooke* (2006).

Nathanson, Paul, *Over the Rainbow: The Wizard of Oz as a Secular Myth of America* (1991).

Nelson, Claudia, 'Fantasies de Siècle: Sex and Sexuality in the Late-Victorian Fairy Tale', in Nikki Lee Manos and Meri-Jane Rochelson (eds.), *Transforming Genres: New Approaches to British Fiction of the 1890s* (1994).

Nielsen, Erling, *Hans Christian Andersen in Selbstzeugnissen und Bilddokumenten* (1958).

Nikolajeva, Maria, 'The Maker of Modern Fairy Tales', *Merveilles et Contes*, 1.1 (May 1987).

Nikolajeva, Maria, 'Fairy Tales in Society's Service', *Marvels & Tales*, 16 (2002).

Nikolajeva, Maria, 'Fairy Tale and Fantasy: From Archaic to Postmodern', *Marvels & Tales*, 17 (2003).

Nilsson, Nils Ake, 'The Tale of Olaf the Towheaded: An Unpublished Text by Elena Guro', *Scando-Slavica*, 35 (1989).

Nissen, Walter, *Die Brüder Grimm und ihre Märchen* (1984).

Nitschke, August, *Soziale Ordnungen im Spiegel der Märchen* (2 vols., 1976–7).

Nitschke, August, 'Aschenputtel aus der Sicht der historischen Verhaltensforschung', in Helmut Brackert (ed.), *Und wenn sie nicht gestorben sind . . . Perspektiven auf das Märchen* (1980).

Nobis, Helmut, *Phantasie und Moralität: Das Wunderbare in Wielands 'Dschinnistan' und der 'Geschichte des Prinzen Biribinker'* (1976).

Nolte, Reinhard, *Analyse der freien Märchenproduktion* (1931).

Nurse, Paul McMichael, *Eastern Dreams: How the Arabian Nights Came to the World* (2010).

Nye, Russell B., 'The Wizardess of Oz—And Who She Is', *Children's Literature*, 2 (1973).

Obenauer, Karl Justus, *Das Märchen: Dichtung und Deutung* (1959).

Oberfeld, Charlotte, and **Bimmer, Andreas C.** (eds.), *Hessen—Märchenland der Brüder Grimm* (1984).

Oerella, Nicolas J., 'An Essay on Pinocchio', in *The Adventures of Pinocchio: Story of a Puppet* (1986).

Oleksiw, Susan, 'The Fairy Tale and Crime Fiction', *Clues*, 17.1 (spring–summer 1996).

Ong, Walter, *Orality and Literacy* (1982).

Orenstein, Catherine, *Little Red Riding Hood Uncloaked: Sex, Morality, and the Evolution of a Fairy Tale* (2002).

Orenstein, Peggy, *Cinderella Ate My Daughter: Dispatches from the Front Lines of the New Girlie-Girl Culture* (2011).

Paetow, Karl, *Märchen und Sagen um Fraue Holle und Rübezahl—Sagen und Legenden* (1986).

Palacio, Jean de, *Les Perversions du merveilleux: Ma mère l'Oye au tournant du siècle* (1993).

Pallant, Chris, *Demystifying Disney: A History of Disney Feature Animation* (2013).

Pallottino, Paola, 'Beauty's Beast', *Merveilles et Contes*, 3.1 (May 1989).

Pallottino, Paola, 'Alle radici dell'iconografia dell fiaba: Note sulle prime illustrazioni dei *Contes*', *Merveilles et Contes*, 5.2 (December 1991).

Palmer, Melvin D., 'Madame d'Aulnoy in England', *Comparative Literature*, 27 (1975).

Palmer, Nancy and **Melvin**, 'English Editions of French *Contes de fées* attributed to Mme d'Aulnoy', *Studies in Bibliography*, 27 (1974).

Paradiz, Valerie, *Clever Maids: The Secret History of the Grimm Fairy Tales* (2005).

Parent, Monique, 'Langue littéraire et langue populaire dans les "contes" d'Henri Pourrat', in *La Littérature narrative d'imagination. Des genres littéraire aux techniques d'expression* (1961).

Partington, Paul B., *Fairy Tales and Folk Tales on Stamps* (1970).

Patri, Aimé, 'Doctrine secrète des ogres', *Cahiers du Sud*, 324 (1954).

Patten, Robert L., 'George Cruikshank's Grimm Humor', in Joachim Möller (ed.), *Imagination on a Long Rein: English Literature Illustrated* (1988).

Paulin, Roger, 'Fairy Stories for Very Sophisticated Children: Ludwig Tieck's *Phantasus*', *Bulletin of the John Rylands Library University of Manchester*, 76.3 (autumn 1994).

Pauly, Rebecca M., 'Beauty and the Beast: From Fable to Film', *Literature/Film Quarterly*, 17.2 (1989).

Payr, Bernhard, *Theophile Gautier und E. T. A. Hoffmann, ein Beitrag zur Geistesgeschichte der europäischen Romantik* (1932).

Peppard, Murray B., *Paths through the Forest: A Biography of the Brothers Grimm* (1971).

Perkins, Richard, 'A Giant and Some Dwarves: Nietzsche's Unpublished Märchen on the Exception and the Rule', *Marvels & Tales*, 11 (1997).

Perol, Lucette, 'Quand un récit s'intitule "Ceci n'est pas un conte" (Diderot)', in François Marotin (ed.), *Frontières du conte* (1982).

Perrot, Jean, 'Charles Perrault and Jean-Jacques Rousseau to the Rescue of French Research: Literary Symbolism, "The Purloined Letter" of Research', *The Lion and the Unicorn*, 19.1 (June 1995).

Perrot, Jean (ed.), *Tricentenaire Charles Perrault: Les grands contes du XVIIe Siècle et leur fortune littéraire* (1998).

Petrie, Duncan (ed.), *Cinema and the Realms of Enchantment: Lectures, Seminars, and Essays* (1993).

Petrini, Mario, *La Fiaba di magia nella letteratura italiana* (1983).

Petzold, Dieter, *Das englische Kunstmärchen im neunzehnten Jahrhundert* (1981).

Petzold, Dieter, 'Maturation and Education in George MacDonald's Fairy Tales', *North Wind*, 12 (1993).

Petzold, Dieter, 'Beasts and Monsters in MacDonald's Fantasy Stories', *North Wind*, 14 (1995).

Phillips, John, *Nathalie Sarraute: Metaphor, Fairy-Tale and the Feminine of the Text* (1994).

Piarotas, Mireille, *Des contes et des femmes: le vrai visage de Margot* (1996).

Piffault, Olivier (ed.), *Il était une fois . . . les contes de fées* (2001).

Pitts, Mary Ellen, 'Fairy Stories, Textuality, and Evolutionary Psychology: An Interactive Model for Science and the Humanities', *Journal of Evolutionary Psychology*, 14.1–2 (March 1993).

Pizer, John, 'The Disenchantment of Snow White: Robert Walser, Donald Barthelme and the Modern/Postmodern Anti-Fairy Tale', *Canadian Review of Comparative Literature/Revue Canadienne de Littérature Comparée*, 17.3–4 (September–December 1990).

Pletscher, Theodor, *Die Märchen Charles Perraults: Eine Literarturhistorische und literaturvergleichende Studie* (1906).

Popkin, Michael, 'Cocteau's Beauty and the Beast: The Poet as Monster', *Literature/Film Quarterly*, 10.2 (1982).

Pourrat, Claire, 'Inventaires du Trésor. Les 1009 contes de Pourrat et le millier d'images qui les accompagnent', in Henri Pourrat, *Le Bestiaire* (1986).

Pozzi, Victoria Smith, 'Straparola's *Le piacevoli notti*: Narrative Technique and Ideology' (Diss., University of California-Los Angeles, 1981).

Prickett, Stephen, *Victorian Fantasy* (1979).

Profeti, Maria Grazia, 'La bella dormida: Repertorio e codice', *Quaderni di Lingue e Letterature*, 7 (1982).

Propp, Vladimir, 'Les Transformations des Contes Fantastiques', in Tzvetan Todorov (ed.), *Théorie de la littérature* (1965).

Propp, Vladimir, *Morphology of the Folktale* (1968).

Propp, Vladimir, *Theory and History of Folklore* (1984).

Propp, Vladimir, *Die historischen Wurzeln des Zaubermärchens* (1987).

Propp, Vladimir, *The Russian Folktale*, ed. and trans. Sibelan Forrester (2012).

Psaar, Werner, and **Klein, Manfred**, *Wer hat Angst vor der bösen Geiss? Zur Märchendidaktik und Märchenrezeption* (1976).

Quintus, J. A., 'The Moral Prerogative in Oscar Wilde: A Look at the Tales', *Virginia Quarterly Review*, 53 (1977).

Radner, Joann N., and **Lanser, Susan S.**, 'The Feminist Voice: Strategies of Coding in Folklore and Literature', *Journal of American Folklore*, 100 (1987).

Raeper, William (ed. and intro.), *The Gold Thread: Essays on George MacDonald* (1990).

Rak, Michele, 'Storia breve del racconto fiabesco', in Michele Rak (ed.), *Fiabe campagne* (1996).

Rak, Michele, *Logica della fiaba: Fate, orchi, gioco, corte, fortuna, viaggio capriccio, metamorphosi, corpo* (2005).

Rak, Michele, *Da Cenerentola a Cappuccetto rosso: breve storia illustrata della fiaba barocca* (2007).

Ranke, Kurt, 'Der Einfluss der Grimmischen "Kinder- und Hausmärchen" auf das volkstümliche deutsche Erzählgut', in Sigurd Erixon (ed.), *Papers of the International Congress of Western Ethnology* (1951).

Ranke, Kurt, 'Betrachtungen zum Wesen und Funktion des Märchens', *Studium Generale*, 11 (1958).

Rankin, Walter, *Grimm Pictures: Fairy Tale Archetypes in Eight Horror and Suspense Films* (2007).

Ransom, Amy J., *The Feminine as Fantastic in the Conte Fantastique: Visions of the Other* (1995).

Rebel, Hermann, 'Why Not "Old Marie"...or Someone Very Much Like Her? A Reassessment of the Question about the Grimms' Contributors from a Social Historical Perspective', *Social History*, 13 (January 1988).

Reilly, Edward R., 'Rimsky-Korsakov's "The Golden Cockerel": a Very Modern Fairy Tale', *Musical Newsletter*, 6.1 (winter 1976).

Reis, Richard H., *George MacDonald* (1972).

Richter, Dieter, *Schlaraffenland. Geschichte einer populären Phantasie* (1984).

Richter, Dieter, *Das fremde Kind: Zur Entstehung des bürgerlichen Zeitalters* (1987).

Richter, Dieter, and **Merkel, Johannes**, *Märchen, Phantasie und soziales Lernen* (1974).

Ringelmann, Arno, *Henri Pourrat. Ein Beitrag zur Kenntnis der 'littéraire terrienne'* (1936).

Riordan, James, 'Russian Fairy Tales and Their Collectors', in Hilda Ellis Davidson and Anna Chaudhri (eds.), *A Companion to the Fairy Tale* (2003).

Robert, Marthe, 'Un modèle romanesque: le conte de Grimm', *Preuves*, 185 (1966).

Robert, Raymonde, *Le Conte de fées littéraire en France de la fin du XVIIe à la fin du XVIIIe siècle* (1982).

Robert, Raymonde, 'L'Infantalisation du conte merveilleux au XVIIe siècle', *Littératures classiques*, 14 (January 1991).

Robinson, William Andrew, 'The End of Happily Ever After: Variations on the Cinderella Theme in Musicals, 1960–1987' (Diss., Bowling Green State University, 1991).

Roche-Mazon, Jeanne, *Autour des contes des fées* (1968).

Rodari, Gianni, *The Grammar of Fantasy: An Introduction to the Art of Inventing Stories*, trans. and intro. Jack Zipes (1996).

Röhrich, Lutz, *Gebärden—Metapher—Parodie* (1967).

Röhrich, Lutz, *Märchen und Wirklichkeit* (1974).

Röhrich, Lutz, *Sagen und Märchen. Erzählforschung heute* (1976).

Röhrich, Lutz, 'Der Froschkönig', in Wilhelm Solms (ed.), *Das selbstverständliche Wunder: Beiträge germanistischer Märchenforschung* (1986).

Röhrich, Lutz, *Wage es den Frosch zu küssen! Das Grimmsche Märchen Nummer Eins in seinen Wandlungen* (1987).

Röhrich, Lutz, *Folktales and Reality* (1991).

Rölleke, Heinz (ed.), *Die älteste Märchensammlung der Brüder Grimm* (1975).

Rölleke, Heinz (ed.), *Märchen aus dem Nachlass der Brüder Grimm* (3rd rev. edn., 1983).

Rölleke, Heinz, 'Texte, die beinahe "Grimms Märchen" geworden wären', *Zeitschrift für deutsche Philologie*, 102 (1983).

Rölleke, Heinz, *Die Märchen der Brüder Grimm* (1985).

Rölleke, Heinz, *'Wo das Wünschen noch geholfen hat.' Gesammelte Aufsätze zu den 'Kinder- und Hausmärchen' der Brüder Grimm* (1985).

Rölleke, Heinz, 'Die "Kinder- und Hausmärchen" der Brüder Grimm in neuer Sicht', *Diskussion Deutsch*, 91 (October 1986).

Rölleke, Heinz, 'Neue Erkenntnisse zum Beiträgerkreis der Grimmschen Märchen', in Lutz Röhrich and Erika Lindi (eds.), *Volksdichtung zwischen Mündlichkeit und Schriftlichkeit* (1989).

Rölleke, Heinz, *Die Märchen der Brüder Grimm: Quellen und Studien* (2000).

Rölleke, Heinz, *Die Märchen der Brüder Grimm: Eine Einführung* (2004).

Rölleke, Heinz (ed.), *Es war einmal . . . Die wahren Märchen der Brüder Grimm und wer sie ihnen erzählte*, illus. Albert Schindehütte (2011).

Romain, Alfred, 'Zur Gestalt des Grimmschen Dornröschenmärchens', *Zeitschrift für Volkskunde*, 42 (1933).

Rooth, Anna Birgitta, *The Cinderella Cycle* (1951).

Rose, Jacqueline, *The Case of Peter Pan, or the Impossibility of Children's Fiction* (1984).

Rosenberg, Bruce, *Folklore and Literature: Rival Siblings* (1991).

Rosenthal, Melinda M., 'Burton's Literary Uroburos: The Arabian Nights as Self-Reflexive Narrative', *Pacific Coast Philology*, 25.1–2 (November 1990).

Rothstein, Eric, 'In Brobdingnag: Captain Gulliver, Dr. Derham, and Master Tom Thumb', *Études Anglaises: Grande-Bretagne, États-Unis*, 37.2 (April–June 1984).

Rowe, Karen E., *Feminism and Fairy Tales* (1978).

Rowe, Karen E., 'Feminism and Fairy Tales', *Women's Studies*, 6 (1979).

Rowe, Karen E., '"Fairy-born and human-bred": Jane Eyre's Education in Romance', in Elizabeth Abel, Marianne Hirsch, and Elizabeth Langland (eds.), *The Voyage In: Fictions of Female Development* (1983).

Rowe, Karen E., 'To Spin a Yarn: The Female Voice in Folklore and Fairy Tale', in Ruth B. Bottigheimer (ed.), *Fairy Tales and Society: Illusion, Allusion, and Paradigm* (1986).

Ruck, Carl A.P., **Staples, Blaise**, **Daniel, González Celdrán, José Alfredo**, and **Hoffman, Mark Alwin**, *The Hidden World: Survival of Pagan Shamanic Themes in European Fairytales* (2007).

Ruf, Theodor, *Die Schöne aus dem Glassarg: Schneewittchens märchenhaftes und wirkliches Leben* (1995).

Rumpf, Marianne, *Ursprung und Entstehung von Warn- und Schreckmärchen* (1955).

Rumpf, Marianne, 'Spinnerinnen und Spinnen: Märchendeutung aus kulturhistorischer Sicht', in Sigrid Früh and Rainer Wehse (eds.), *Die Frau im Märchen* (1985).

Rushdie, Salman, *The Wizard of Oz* (1992).

Sahr, Michael, '"Stell Dir vor, dass Rotkäppchen Blaukäppchen heisst!" Über den unterrichtlichen Umgang mit Märchen herkömmlicher und neuer Art', *Diskussion Deutsch*, 91 (October 1986).

Saintyves, P., *Les Contes de Perrault et les récits parallèles* (1923).

Sale, Roger, *Fairy Tales and After: From Snow White to E. B. White* (1978).

Sammond, Nicholas, 'Tale As Old As Time: A Fairy Tale for Commodities', *theory@buffalo* (fall 1996).

Sandford, Beryl, 'Cinderella', *Psychoanalytic Forum*, 2 (1967).

Sandner, David, *The Fantastic Sublime: Romanticism and Transcendence in Nineteenth-Century Children's Literature* (1996).

Santucci, Luigi, *Das Kind, sein Mythos und sein Märchen* (1964).

Saupé, Yvette, *Les Contes de Perrault et la mythologie: Rapprochements et influences* (1997).

Saxon, Wolfgang, 'Jack Sendak, 71, a Writer of Surrealist Books for Children', *New York Times*, 4 February 1995.

Schacker, Jennifer, *National Dreams: The Remaking of Fairy Tales in Nineteenth-Century England* (2003).

Schauf, Susanne, *Die verlorene Allmacht der Feen: Untersuchungen zum französischen Kunstmärchen des 19. Jahrhunderts* (1986).

Schectman, Jacqueline, *The Stepmother in Fairy Tales: Bereavement and the Feminine Shadow* (1993).

Schenda, Rudolf, *Volk ohne Buch* (1970).

Schenda, Rudolf, *Die Leserstoffe der Kleinen Leute* (1976).

Schenda, Rudolf, 'Folkloristik und Sozialgeschichte', in Rolf Kloepfer and Gisela Janetke-Dillner (eds.), *Erzählung und Erzählforschung im 20. Jahrhundert* (1981).

Schenda, Rudolf, 'Alphabetisierung und Literarisierung in Westeuropa im 18. und 19. Jahrhundert', in Ernst Hinrichs and Günter Wiegelmann (eds.), *Sozialer und kultureller Wandel der ländlichen Welt des 18. Jahrhunderts* (1982).

Schenda, Rudolf, 'Mären von deutschen Sagen. Bemerkungen zur Produktion "Volkserzählungen" zwischen 1850 und 1870', *Geschichte und Gesellschaft*, 9 (1983).

Schenda, Rudolf, 'Volkserzählung und nationale Identität: Deutsche Sagen im Vormärz', *Fabula*, 25 (1984).

Schenda, Rudolf, 'Volkserzählung und Sozialgeschichte', *Il Confronto Lettario*, 1.2 (1984).

Schenda, Rudolf, 'Der Bilderhändler und seine Kunden im Mitteleuropa des 19. Jahrhunderts', *Ethnologia Europaea*, 14 (1984).

Schenda, Rudolf, 'Jacob und Wilhelm Grimm: Deutsche Sagen Nr. 103, 298, 337, 340, 350, 357 und 514', *Schweizerisches Archiv für Volkskunde*, 81 (1985).

Schenda, Rudolf, 'Orale und literarische Kommunikationsformen im Bereich von Analphabeten und Gebildeten im 17. Jahrhundert', in Wolfgang Brückner, Peter Blickle, and Dieter Breuer (eds.), *Literatur und Volk im 17. Jahrhundert. Probleme populärer Kultur in Deutschland* (1985).

Schenda, Rudolf, *Folklore e Letteratura Popolare: Italia—Germania—Francia* (1986).

Schenda, Rudolf, 'Telling Tales—Spreading Tales: Change in the Communicative Forms of a Popular Genre', in Ruth B. Bottigheimer (ed.), *Fairy Tales and Society: Illusion, Allusion, and Paradigm* (1986).

Schenda, Rudolf, 'Vorlesen: Zwischen Analphabetentum und Bücherwissen', *Bertelsmann Briefe*, 119 (1986).

Schenda, Rudolf, *Von Mund zu Ohr: Bausteine zu einer Kulturgeschichte volkstümlichen Erzählens in Europa* (1993).

Schenkel, Elmar, 'Antigravity: Matter and the Imagination in George MacDonald and Early Science Fiction', *North Wind*, 14 (1995).

Scherf, Walter, 'Family Conflicts and Emancipation in Fairy Tales', *Children's Literature*, 3 (1974).

Scherf, Walter, *Lexikon der Zaubermärchen* (1982).

Scherf, Walter, 'Das Märchenpublikum. Die Erwartung der Zuhörer und Leser und die Antwort des Erzählers', *Diskussion Deutsch*, 91 (October 1986).

Scherf, Walter, *Das Märchen Lexikon* (2 vols., 1995).

Schickel, Richard, *The Disney Version: The Life, Times, Art, and Commerce of Walt Disney* (1968; rev. edn., 1985).

Schmidt, Kurt, *Das Märchen* (1940).

Schödel, Siegfried (ed.), *Märchenanalysen* (1977).

Schöll, Friedrich, *Gott-Natur in Mythos und Märchen* (1986).

Schoof, Wilhelm, *Zur Entstehungsgeschichte der Grimmschen Märchen* (1959).

Schott, Georg, *Weissagung und Erfüllung im Deutschen Volksmärchen* (1925).

Schumann, Thomas B., 'Französische Quellen zu den Grimmschen "Kinder- und Hausmärchen"', *Philobiblon*, 21 (1977).

Schwartz, Emanuel K., 'A Psychoanalytic Study of the Fairy Tale', *Journal of American Psychotherapy*, 10 (1956).

Scott, Carole, 'Magical Dress: Clothing and Transformation in Folk Tales', *Children's Literature Quarterly*, 21 (winter 1996–7).

Sehmsdorf, Henning, 'Folktale and Allegory: Peter W. Cappelen's Briar Rose, the Sleeping Beauty (1968)', *Proceedings of the Pacific Northwest Conference on Foreign Languages*, 30.1–2 (1979).

Seifert, Lewis C., 'Disguising the Storyteller's "Voice": Perrault's Recuperation of the Fairy Tale', *Cincinnati Romance Review*, 8 (1989).

Seifert, Lewis C., 'Female Empowerment and its Limits: The Conteuses' Active Heroines', *Cahiers du Dix-septième*, 4.2 (fall 1990).

Seifert, Lewis C., 'Marie-Catherine le Jumel de Barneville, Comtesse d'Aulnoy', in Eva Martin Sartori and Dorothy Wynne Zimmerman (eds.), *French Women Writers: A Bio-Bibliographical Source Book* (1991).

Seifert, Lewis C., 'Tales of Difference: Infantilization and the Recuperation of Class and Gender in 17th-Century Contes de fées', in Marie-France Hilgar (ed.), *Actes de Las Vegas: Théorie dramatique, Théophile de Viau, Les Contes de fées* (1991).

Seifert, Lewis C., 'Les Fées Modernes: Women, Fairy Tales, and the Literary Field in Late Seventeenth-Century France', in Elizabeth C. Goldsmith and Dena Goodman (eds.), *Going Public: Women and Publishing in Early Modern France* (1995).

Seifert, Lewis C., *Fairy Tales, Sexuality, and Gender in France, 1690–1715: Nostalgic Utopias* (1996).

Seitz, Gabriele, *Die Brüder Grimm. Leben—Werk—Zeit* (1984).

Sellers, Susan, *Myth and Fairy Tale in Contemporary Women's Fiction* (2001).

Sellner, Timothy F., 'Jungian Psychology and the Romantic Fairy Tale: A New Look at Tieck's "Der blonde Eckbert"', *Germanic Review*, 55 (1980).

Semrau, Eberhard, 'Die Illustrationen zu Grimms Märchen im 19. Jahrhundert', *Zeitschrift für die Buchillustration*, 14 (1977).

Semrau, Eberhard, 'Die Illustrationen zu Grimms Märchen. Zweite Folge: Zwischen 1900 und 1945', *Zeitschrift für die Buchillustration*, 14 (1977).

Sennewald, Jens, *Das Buch, das wir sind: Zur Poetik der 'Kinder- und Hausmärchen', gesammelt durch die Brüder Grimm* (2004).

Sheets, Robin Ann, 'Pornography, Fairy Tales, and Feminism: Angela Carter's "The Bloody Chamber"', *Journal of the History of Sexuality*, 1.4 (April 1991).

Shell, Marc, 'Beauty and the Beast', *Bestia*, 1 (May 1989).

Sherman, Sharon, and **Koven, Mikel** (eds.), *Folklore/Cinema: Popular Film as Vernacular Culture* (2007).

Short, Sue, *Fairy Tale and Film: Old Tales with a New Spin* (2015).

Siegmund, Wolfdietrich (ed.), *Antiker Mythos in unseren Märchen* (1984).

Sielaff, Erich, 'Zum deutschen Volksmärchen', *Der Bibliothekar*, 12 (1952).

Sielaff, Erich, 'Bemerkungen zur kritischen Aneignung der deutschen Volksmärchen', *Wissenschaftliche Zeitschrift der Universität Rostock*, 2 (1952/3).

Sigler, Carolyn (ed.), *Alternative Alices: Visions and Revisions of Lewis Carroll's Alice Books* (1997).

Silver, Carole, 'When Rumpelstiltskin Ruled: Victorian Fairy Tales', *Victorian Literature and Culture*, 22 (1994).

Silver, Carole, *Strange and Secret Peoples: Fairies and the Victorian Consciousness* (1998).

Simpson, Robin Smith, 'Fairy-Tale Representations of Social Realities: Madame d'Aulnoy's *Contes de fées* (1697-98)' (Diss., Duke University, 1996).

Sircar, Sanjay, 'E. Nesbit's "The Magician's Heart": New Comedy and the Burlesque Kunstmärchen', *Marvels & Tales*, 9.1 (May 1995) and 9.2 (December 1995).

Smith, Barbara Herrnstein, 'Narrative Versions, Narrative Theories', *Critical Inquiry*, 7 (1980).

Smith, Karen Patricia, *The Fabulous Realm: A Literary-Historical Approach to British Fantasy, 1780-1990* (1994).

Smith, Kevin Paul, *The Postmodern Fairytale: Folkloric Intertexts in Contemporary Fiction* (2007).

Smol, Anna, 'The "Savage" and the "Civilized": Andrew Lang's Representation of the Child and the Translation of Folklore', *Children's Literature Quarterly*, 21 (winter 1996-7).

Solheim, Svale, 'Die Brüder Grimm und Asbjörnsen und Moe', *Wissenschaftliche Zeitschrift der Ernst-Moritz-Arndt-Universität Greifswald*, 13 (1964).

Solms, Wilhelm (ed.), *Das selbstverständliche Wunder. Beiträge germanistischer Märchenforschung* (1986).

Solms, Wilhelm, and **Hofius, Annegret**, 'Der wunderbare Weg zum Glück. Vorschlag für die Behandlung der "Kinder- und Hausmärchen" der Brüder Grimm im Deutschunterricht', *Diskussion Deutsch*, 91 (October 1986).

Soriano, Marc, *Les Contes de Perrault. Culture savante et traditions populaires* (1968).

Soriano, Marc, 'Le Petit Chaperon rouge', *Nouvelle Revue Française*, 16 (1968).

Soriano, Marc, 'From Tales of Warning to Formulettes: The Oral Tradition in French Children's Literature', *Yale French Studies*, 43 (1969).

Soriano, Marc, *Le Dossier Charles Perrault* (1972).

Soriano, Marc, *Guide de littérature pour la jeunesse* (1975).

Spiess, Karl von, *Das deutsche Volksmärchen* (1917).

Spiess, Karl von, and **Mudrak, Edmund**, *Deutsche Märchen—Deutsche Welt* (2nd edn., 1939).

Spink, Reginald, *Hans Christian Andersen and his World* (1972).

Spörk, Ingrid, *Studien zu ausgewählten Märchen der Brüder Grimm. Frauenproblematik—Struktur—Rollentheorie—Psychoanalyse—Überlieferung—Rezeption* (1985).

Stanwood, Paul G., 'Fantasy and Fairy Tale in Twentieth Century Opera', *Mosaic*, 10.2 (1977).

Steig, Reinhold, *Achim von Arnim und Jacob und Wilhelm Grimm* (1904).

Stein, Murray, and **Corbett, Lionel** (eds.), *Psyche's Stories: Modern Jungian Interpretations of Fairy Tales* (3 vols., 1991).

Steiner, Rudolf, *Märchendichtungen im Lichte der Geistesforschung. Märchendeutungen* (1969).

Steinlein, Rüdiger, *Die domestizierte Phantasie. Studien zur Kinderliteratur, Kinderlektüre und Literaturpädogik des 18. und 19. Jahrhunderts* (1987).

Steinlein, Rüdiger, 'Märchen als poetische Erziehungsform: Zum kinderliterarischen Status der Grimmschen "Kinder- und Hausmarchen"', *Zeitschrift für Germanistik*, 5.2 (1995).

Stephens, John, and **McCallum, Robin**, *Retelling Stories, Framing Culture: Traditional Story and Metanarratives in Children's Literature* (1998).

Stewart, Susan, *Nonsense: Aspects of Intertextuality in Folklore and Literature* (1978).

Stewart, Susan, *On Longing: Narratives of the Miniature, the Gigantic, the Souvenir, the Collection* (1984).

Stiasny, Kurt, *Was Hauffs Märchen erzählen: Original und Deutung* (1995).

Stirling, Monica, *The Wild Swan: The Life and Times of Hans Christian Andersen* (1965).

Stone, Harry, 'Dickens, Cruikshank, and Fairy Tales', *Princeton University Library Chronicle*, 35.1–2 (1973).

Stone, Harry, *Dickens and the Invisible World: Fairy Tales, Fantasy, and Novel-Making* (1979).

Stone, Harry, 'Oliver Twist and Fairy Tales', *Dickens Studies Newsletter*, 10 (1979).

Stone, Kay, 'Things Walt Disney Never Told Us', in Claire R. Farrer (ed.), *Women and Folklore* (1975).

Stone, Kay, 'Misuse of Enchantment', in Rosan Jordan and Susan Kalcik (eds.), *Women's Folklore/Women's Culture* (1985).

Stone, Kay, *Burning Brightly: New Light on Old Tales Told Today* (1998).

Storer, Mary Elizabeth, *Un épisode littéraire de la fin du XVIIe siècle: la mode des contes de fées (1685–1700)* (1928).

Storer, Mary Elizabeth, *Contes de fées du Grand Siècle* (1934).

Stork, Jochen (ed.), *Das Märchen—ein Märchen? Psychoanalytische Betrachtungen zu Wesen, Deutung und Wirkung der Märchen* (1987).

Street, Douglas, 'Pinocchio—From Picaro to Pipsqueak', in Douglas Street (ed.), *Children's Novels and the Movies* (1983).

Stumpfe, Ortrud, *Die Symbolsprache der Märchen* (1992).

Sullivan, Paula, 'Fairy Tale Elements in Jane Eyre', *Journal of Popular Culture*, 12 (1978).

Summerfield, Geoffrey, *Fantasy and Reason: Children's Literature in the Eighteenth Century* (1984).

Sumpter, Caroline, 'Fairy Tale and Folklore in the Nineteenth Century', *Literature Compass*, 6.3 (2009).

Sumpter, Caroline, *The Victorian Press and the Fairy Tale* (2009).

Sundland, Egil, *Det var en gang—et menneske: tolkninger av Asbjørnsen og Moes undereventyr som allegorier på menneskelig innsikt og erkjennelse* (1995).

Sutton, Martin, '"Little Red Riding-Hood" Revised and Rationalized: The First English Translation of the Grimms' "Rotkäppchen" (KHM 26)', *Bulletin of the John Rylands Library, University of Manchester*, 76.3 (autumn 1994).

Sutton, Martin, *The Sin-Complex: A Critical Study of English Versions of the Grimms'* Kinder- und Hausmärchen *in the Nineteenth Century* (1996).

Svensson, Conny, 'Carlo Collodi och romanen om Pinocchio', *Kulturtidskriften HORISONT*, 37. 5 (1990).

Swales, Martin, 'Narrative Sleight-of-Hand: Some Notes on Two German Romantic Tales', *New German Studies*, 6 (1978).

Swann, Marjorie, 'The Politics of Fairylore in Early Modern English Literature', *Renaissance Quarterly*, 53.2 (2000).

Swartz, Mark Evan, *Before the Rainbow: L. Frank Baum's* The Wonderful Wizard of Oz *on Stage and Screen to 1939* (2000).

Taggart, James M., *Enchanted Maidens: Gender Relations in Spanish Folktales of Courtship and Marriage* (1990).

Taggart, James M., *The Bear and His Sons: Masculinity in Spanish and Mexican Folktales* (1997).

Talairach-Vielmas, Laurence, *Moulding the Female Body in Victorian Fairy Tales and Sensation Novels* (2007).

Talbot, Norman, 'Where Do Elves Go To? Tolkien and a Fantasy Tradition', *Mythlore*, 21 (winter 1996).

Tatar, Maria M., 'From Nags to Witches: Stepmothers in the Grimms' Fairy Tales', in Joseph H. Smith and William Kerrigan (eds.), *Opening Texts: Psychoanalysis and the Culture of the Child* (1985).

Tatar, Maria M., 'Tests, Tasks, and Trials in the Grimms' Fairy Tales', *Children's Literature*, 13 (1985).

Tatar, Maria M., 'Born Yesterday: Heroes in the Grimms' Fairy Tales', in Ruth B. Bottigheimer (ed.), *Fairy Tales and Society: Illusion, Allusion, and Paradigm* (1986).

Tatar, Maria M., *The Hard Facts of the Grimms' Fairy Tales* (1987).

Tatar, Maria M., *Off with Their Heads! Fairy Tales and the Culture of Childhood* (1992).

Tatar, Maria M., 'Is Anybody Out There Listening? Fairy Tales and the Voice of the Child', in Elizabeth Goodenough, Mark A. Heberle, and Naomi Sokoloff (eds. and intro.), *Infant Tongues: The Voice of the Child in Literature* (1994).

Tatar, Maria M., *Secrets beyond the Door: The Story of Bluebeard and his Wives* (2004).

Tatar, Maria M. (ed.), *The Cambridge Companion to Fairy Tales* (2015).

Taylor, Peter, and **Rebel, Hermann**, 'Hessian Peasant Women, their Families, and the Draft: A Social-Historical Interpretation of Four Tales from the Grimm Collection', *Journal of Family History*, 6 (winter 1981).

Teahan, James. T., 'Introduction', *The Pinocchio of C. Collodi* (1985).

Teahan, James. T., 'C. Collodi, 1826–1890', in Jane M. Bingham (ed.), *Writers for Children: Critical Studies of Major Authors since the Seventeenth Century* (1988).

Temmer, Mark J., 'Henri Pourrat's "Trésor des Contes"', *French Review*, 38 (October 1964).

Tenèze, Marie Louise (ed.), *Approches de nos traditions orales* (1970).

Tenèze, Marie Louise, *Les contes merveilleux français: Recherche de leurs organisations narratives* (2004).

Teverson, Andrew, *Fairy Tale* (2013).

Thalmann, Marianne, *The Romantic Fairy Tale: Seeds of Surrealism* (1964).

Thelander, Dorothy R., 'Mother Goose and her Goslings: The France of Louis XIV seen through the Fairy Tale', *Journal of Modern History*, 54 (September 1982).

Thomas, Bob, *Disney's Art of Animation: From Mickey Mouse to Beauty and the Beast* (1991).

Thomas, Joyce, *Inside the Wolf's Belly: Aspects of the Fairy Tale* (1989).

Thompson, Stith, *Motif Index of Folk Literature* (6 vols., 1932–6; 1955).

Thompson, Stith, *The Folktale* (1946).

Thwaite, Mary F., *From Primer to Pleasure in Reading: An Introduction to the History of Children's Books in England from the Invention of Printing to 1914* (1972).

Tiffin, Jessica, *Marvelous Geometry: Narrative and Metafiction in Modern Fairy Tale* (2009).

Tismar, Jens, *Kunstmärchen* (1977).

Tismar, Jens, *Das deutsche Kunstmärchen des zwanzigsten Jahrhunderts* (1981).

Todorov, Tzvetan, *The Fantastic: A Structural Approach to a Literary Genre*, trans. Richard Howard (1973).

Tonnelat, Ernest, *Les Contes des frères Grimm: Études sur la composition et le style du recueil des 'Kinder- und Hausmärchen'* (1912).

Treglown, Jeremy, *Roald Dahl: A Biography* (1995).

Tremper, Ellen, 'Commitment and Escape: The Fairy Tales of Thackeray, Dickens, and Wilde', *The Lion and the Unicorn*, 2.1 (1978).

Troll, Max, *Der Märchenunterricht* (2nd edn., 1928).

Tucker, Holly, *Pregnant Fictions: Childbirth and the Fairy Tale in Early-Modern France* (2003).

Uther, Hans-Jörg, *The Types of International Folktales: A Classification and Bibliography* (3 vols., 2004).

Uther, Hans-Jörg, *Handbuch zu den 'Kinder- und Hausmärchen' der Brüder Grimm: Entstehung—Wirkung—Interpretation* (2008).

Vaz da Silva, Francisco, *Metamorphosis: The Dynamics of Symbolism in European Fairy Tales* (2002).

Velay-Vallantin, Catherine, 'Le Miroir des contes. Perrault dans les Bibliothèques bleues', in Roger Chartier (ed.), *Les Usages de l'imprimé* (1987).

Velay-Vallantin, Catherine, *La fille en garçon* (1992).

Velay-Vallantin, Catherine, *L'Histoire des contes* (1994).

Velay-Vallantin, Catherine, 'From "Little Red Riding Hood' to the "Beast of Gévaudan": The Tale in the Long Term Continuum', in Francesca Canadé Sautman, Diana Conchado, and Giuseppe Carlo Di Scipio (eds.), *Telling Tales: Medieval Narratives and the Folk Tradition* (1998).

Velten, Harry, 'The Influence of Charles Perrault's *Contes de ma Mère l'Oie* on German Folklore', *Germanic Review*, 5 (1930).

Verdi, Laura, *Il regno incantato: il contesto sociale e culturale della fiaba in Europa* (1980).

Verdier, Gabrielle, 'Les Contes de fées', in Marie-France Hilgar (ed.), *Actes de Las Vegas: Théorie dramatique, Théophile de Viau, Les Contes de fées* (1991).

Verdier, Gabrielle, 'Gracieuse vs. Grognon, or How to Tell The Good Guys from the Bad in the Literary Fairy Tale', *Cahiers du Dix-septième*, 4.2 (1997).

Verdier, Yvonne, 'Grand-mères, si vous saviez: le Petit Chaperon rouge dans la tradition orale', *Cahiers de Littérature Orale*, 4 (1978).

Verweyen, Annemarie, 'Jubiläumsausgaben zu den Märchen der Brüder Grimm. "Wenig Bücher sind mit solcher Lust entstanden . . . "', *Börsenblatt*, 27 August 1985, 77.

Veszy-Wagner, Lilla, 'Little Red Riding Hood on the Couch', *Psychoanalytic Forum*, 1 (1966).

Vidal, Gore, 'The Wizard of the "Wizard"', *New York Review of Books*, 29 September 1977, 24.

Vidal, Gore, 'On Rereading the Oz Books', *New York Review of Books*, 13 October 1977, 24.

Viergutz, Rudolf F., *Von der Weisheit unserer Märchen* (1942).

Vigneron, Fleur, 'Les *Contes* de Perrault: une affaire d'équilibre', *Merveilles et Contes*, 9.2 (December 1995).

Von der Leyen, Friedrich, *Das deutsche Märchen* (1917; 1930).

Vries, Jan de, 'Dornröschen', *Fabula*, 2 (1959).

Waelti-Walters, Jennifer, 'On Princesses: Fairy Tales, Sex Roles and Loss of Self', *International Journal of Women's Studies*, 2 (March–April 1979).

Waelti-Walters, Jennifer, *Fairy Tales and the Female Imagination* (1982).

Wahlgren, Erik, *A List of the Themes in Asbjørnsen–Moe: Norske folke-eventyr* (1936).

Walker, Barbara G., *The Woman's Encyclopedia of Myths and Secrets* (1985).

Warner, Marina, *Cinema and the Realms of Enchantment: Lectures, Sermons, and Essays* (1993).

Warner, Marina, *From the Beast to the Blonde: On Fairytales and their Tellers* (1994).

Warner, Marina, *Six Myths of Our Time: Little Angels, Little Monsters, Beautiful Beasts, and More* (1995).

Warner, Marina, *No Go the Bogeyman: Scaring, Lulling and Making Mock* (1998).

Warner, Marina, *Fantastic Metamorphoses, Other Worlds* (2002).

Warner, Marina, *Phantasmagoria* (2006).

Warner, Marina, *Stranger Magic: Charmed States & The Arabian Nights* (2011).

Warner, Marina, *Once Upon a Time: A Short History of Fairy Tale* (2014).

Watson, Jeanie, *Risking Enchantment: Coleridge's Symbolic World of Faery* (1990).

Watts, Steven, *The Magic Kingdom: Walt Disney and the American Way of Life* (1997).

Weber, Eugen, 'Fairies and Hard Facts: The Reality of Folktales', *Journal of the History of Ideas*, 42 (1981).

Weber, Ludwig Felix, *Märchen und Schwank: Eine stilkritische Studie zur Volksdichtung* (1904).

Wegehaupt, Heinz, *Die Märchen der Brüder Grimm* (1984).

Wehse, Rainer (ed.), *Märchenerzähler—Erzählgemeinschaft* (1983).

Weinrebe, Helge M. A., *Märchen—Bilder—Wirkungen. Zur Wirkung und Rezeptionsgeschichte von illustrierten Märchen der Brüder Grimm nach 1945* (1987).

Welch, Marcelle Maistre, 'Les Jeux de l'écriture dans les *Contes de fées* de Mme d'Aulnoy', *Romanische Forschungen*, 101.1 (1989).

Wenk, Walter, *Das Volksmärchen als Bildungsgut* (1929).

Wesselski, Albert, *Versuch einer Theorie des Märchens* (1931).

Wesselski, Albert, *Deutsche Märchen vor Grimm* (1938).

Wesselski, Albert, *Märchen des Mittelalters* (1942).

Wetzel, Hermann Hubert, *Märchen in den französischen Novellensammlungen der Renaissance* (1974).

Whalley, June, 'The Cinderella Story 1724–1919', *Signal* (May 1972).

Whitley, David, *The Idea of Nature in Disney Animation: From Snow White to Wall-e*, 2nd Ed. (2012).

Willis, Susan, 'Fantasia: Walt Disney's Los Angeles Suite', *Diacritics*, 17.2 (summer 1987).

Wilson, Sharon Rose, *Margaret Atwood's Fairy-Tale Sexual Politics* (1993).

Wisser, Wilhelm, *Das Märchen im Volksmund* (1927).

Wittmann, Reinhard (ed.), *Buchmarkt und Lektüre im 18. und 19. Jahrhundert. Beiträge zum literarischen Leben 1750–1880* (1982).

Woeller, Waltraut, *Der soziale Gehalt und die soziale Funktion der deutschen Volksmärchen* (1955).

Woeller, Waltraut, 'Die Bedeutung der Brüder Grimm für die Märchen- und Sagenforschung', *Wissenschaftliche Zeitschrift der Humboldt-Universität zu Berlin*, 14 (1965).

Wojcik-Andrews, Ian, *Children's Films: History, Ideology, Pedagogy, Theory* (2000).

Wolff, Robert Lee, *The Golden Key: A Study of the Major Fiction of George MacDonald* (1961).

Wolfzettel, Friedrich, 'Fee, Feenland', *Enzyklopädie des Märchens*, iv (1984).

Wolfzettel, Friedrich, 'La Lutte contre les mères: quelques exemples d'une valorisation émancipatrice du conte de fées au dix-huitième siècle', in Michel Zink and Xavier Ravier (eds.), *Réception et identification du conte depuis le moyen âge* (1987).

Wollenweber, Bernd, 'Märchen und Sprichwort', ed. Heinz Ide, *Projektunterricht* 1 (1974).

Wood, Naomi, 'The Ugly Duckling's Legacy: Adulteration, Contemporary Fantasy, and the Dark', *Marvels & Tales*, 20.2 (2006).

Woodcock, George, *The Paradox of Oscar Wilde* (1950).

Woods, William F., 'Sleeping Beauty and the Art of Reading Fairy Tales', *CEA Critic*, 40.2 (1978).

Wührl, Paul-Wolfgang, *Das deutsche Kunstmärchen* (1984).

Wunderlich, Richard, '*Pinocchio* before 1920: The Popular and the Pedagogical Traditions', *Italian Quarterly*, 23 (spring 1982).

Wunderlich, Richard, *The Pinocchio Catalogue* (1988).

Wunderlich, Richard, 'De-Radicalizing *Pinocchio*', in Joe Sanders (ed.), *Functions of the Fantastic* (1995).

Wunderlich, Richard, and **Morrisey, Thomas J.**, 'The Desecration of *Pinocchio* in the United States', *Horn Book Magazine*, 58 (April 1982).

Wunderlich, Richard, and **Morrisey, Thomas J.**, *Pinocchio Goes Postmodern: Perils of a Puppet in the United States* (2002).

Yearsley, Macleod, *The Folklore of Fairy-Tale* (1924).

Yolen, Jane, 'America's Cinderella', *Children's Literature in Education*, 8 (1977).

Yolen, Jane, *Touch Magic: Fantasy, Faerie and Folklore in the Literature of Childhood* (1981).

Zago, Esther, 'Some Medieval Versions of Sleeping Beauty: Variations on a Theme', *Studi Francesi*, 69 (1979).

Zago, Esther, 'Giambattista Basile: Il suo pubblico e il suo metodo', *Selecta*, 2 (1981).

Zago, Esther, 'La Belle au bois dormant: sens et structure', *Cermeil*, 2 (February 1986).

Zago, Esther, 'Carlo Collodi as Translator: From Fairy Tale to Folk Tale', *The Lion and the Unicorn*, 12 (1988).

Zarucchi, Jeanne Morgan, *Perrault's Morals for Moderns* (1985).

Ziegler, Matthes, *Die Frau im Märchen* (1937).

Ziolkowski, Jan, "A Fairy Tale Before Fairy Tales: Egbert of Liège's 'De puellis a lupellis seruata' and the Medieval Background of 'Little Red Riding Hood,'" *Speculum* (1992).

Ziolkowski, Jan, 'Old Wives' Tales: Classicism and Anticlassicism from Apuleius to Chaucer', *Journal of Medieval Latin*, 12 (2002).

Ziolkowski, Jan, *Fairy Tales from Before Fairy Tales: The Medieval Latin Past of Wonderful Lies* (2006).

Zipes, Jack, *Breaking the Magic Spell: Radical Theories of Folk and Fairy Tales* (1979).

Zipes, Jack, 'Grimms in Farbe, Bild, und Ton: Der deutsche Märchenfilm für Kinder im Zeitalter der Kulturindustrie', in Wolfgang Schneider (ed.), *Aufbruch zum neuen bundesdeutschen Kinderfilm* (1982).

Zipes, Jack, *Fairy Tales and the Art of Subversion: The Classical Genre for Children and the Process of Civilization* (1983).

Zipes, Jack, *The Trials and Tribulations of Little Red Riding Hood: Versions of the Tale in Socio-Cultural Context* (1983; 2nd rev. edn., 1993).

Zipes, Jack, 'Mountains out of Mole Hills, a Fairy Tale', *Children's Literature*, 13 (1985).

Zipes, Jack, 'The Enchanted Forest of the Brothers Grimm: New Modes of Approaching the Grimms' Fairy Tales', *Germanic Review*, 42 (spring 1987).

Zipes, Jack, *The Brothers Grimm: From Enchanted Forests to the Modern World* (1988).

Zipes, Jack, *Fairy Tale as Myth/Myth as Fairy Tale* (1994).

Zipes, Jack, *Happily Ever After: Fairy Tales, Children, and the Culture Industry* (1997).

Zipes, Jack, 'Crossing Boundaries with Wise Girls: Angela Carter's Fairy Tales for Children', *Marvels & Tales*, 12 (1998).

Zipes, Jack, *When Dreams Came True: Classical Fairy Tales and their Tradition* (1999).

Zipes, Jack, *Hans Christian Andersen: The Misunderstood Storyteller* (2005).

Zipes, Jack, *Why Fairy Tales Stick: The Evolution and Relevance of a Genre* (2006).

Zipes, Jack, *Relentless Progress: The Reconfiguration of Children's Literature, Fairy Tales, and Storytelling* (2008).

Zipes, Jack, *The Enchanted Screen: The Unknown History of the Fairy-Tale Film* (2011).

Zipes, Jack, *The Irresistible Fairy Tale: The Cultural and Social Evolution of a Genre* (2012).

Zips, Jack, *Grimm Legacies: The Magic Power of the Grimm's Folk and Fairy Tales* (2015).

Zorzi, Rosella Mamoli, 'The Use of Indian and Western Tales in Suniti Namjoshi', in Guiseppe Bellini, Claudio Gorelier, and Sergio Zoppi (eds.), *Saggi e Ricerche sulle Culture Extraeuropee* (1987).

CLASSIC COLLECTIONS

Afanasyev, Aleksandr, *Russian Fairy Tales*, trans. Norbert Guterman (1943).

Andersen, Hans Christian, *Wonderful Stories for Children*, trans. Mary Botham Howitt (1st English edn., 1846).

Andersen, Hans Christian, *Danish Fairy Legends and Tales*, trans. Caroline Peachey (2nd edn., enl. with a memoir of the author, 1852).

Andersen, Hans Christian, *The Complete Fairy Tales and Stories*, trans. Erik Christian Haugaard (1974).

Andersen, Hans Christian, *Eighty Fairy Tales* (1976).

Andersen, Hans Christian, *The Stories of Hans Christian Andersen*, trans. Diana Crone Frank and Jeffrey Frank (2003).

Apuleius, Lucius, *The Golden Ass*, ed. and trans. Jack Lindsay (1962).

Apuleius, Lucius, *The Golden Ass*, ed. and trans. P. G. Walsh (1995).

Apuleius, Lucius, *The Tale of Cupid and Psyche*, ed. and trans. Joel C. Relihan (2009).

Aulnoy, Marie-Catherine Le Jumel de Barneville, Baronne d', *Les Contes de fées* (1st edn., 1697-8).

Aulnoy, Marie-Catherine Le Jumel de Barneville, Baronne d', *Contes nouveaux, ou Les Fées à la mode* (1698).

Aulnoy, Marie-Catherine Le Jumel de Barneville, Baronne d', *Suite des Contes nouveaux, ou Les Fées à la mode* (1698).

Aulnoy, Marie-Catherine Le Jumel de Barneville, Baronne d', *The Fairy Tales of Madame d'Aulnoy*, trans. Annie Macdonell, intro. Anne Thackeray Ritchie (1895).

Aulnoy, Marie-Catherine Le Jumel de Barneville, Baronne d', *The White Cat, and Other Old French Fairy Tales*, ed. Rachel Field, illus. Elizabeth MacKinstry (1967).

Barrie, J. M., *Peter Pan or The Boy Who Would Not Grow Up*, intro. Andrew Birkin and illustr. Paula Rego (1992).

Basile, Giambattista, *Lo cunto de li cunti, ovvero, Lo trattenemiento de peccerille: Le muse napolitane e le lettere*, ed. Mario Petrini (1976).

Basile, Giambattista, *The Pentamerone*, trans. Richard Burton (2 vols., 1893).

Basile, Giambattista, *The Pentamerone of Giambattista Basile*, trans. and ed. N. M. Penzer (1932).

Basile, Giambattista, *Lo cunto de li cunti*, ed. Michele Rak (1986).

Basile, Giambattista, *Il racconto dei racconti*, ed. Alessandra Burani and Ruggero Guarini, trans. Ruggero Guarini (1994).

Basile, Giambattista, *The Tale of Tales, or Entertainment for Little Ones*, intro. and trans. Nancy Canepa, illustr. Carmelo Lettere (2007).

Calvino, Italo (ed.), *Fiabe* (1970).

Calvino, Italo (ed.), *Italian Folktales*, trans. George Martin (1980).

Colum, Padraic (intro.), *The Complete Grimm's Fairy Tales*, commentary by Joseph Campbell, illus. Josef Scharl (1944).

Crane, Lucy (trans.), *Household Stories from the Collection of the Brothers Grimm*, illus. Walter Crane (1882).

Deulin, Charles, *Les Contes de ma Mère l'Oye avant Perrault* (1879).

Gonzenbach, Laura, *Sicilianische Märchen* (2 vols., 1870).

Gonzenbach, Laura, *Angiola: The Lost Sicilian Folk and Fairy Tales of Laura Gonzenbach*, ed. and trans. Jack Zipes (2006).

Grimm, Jacob, and **Grimm, Wilhelm**, *Kinder- und Hausmärchen. Gesammelt durch die Brüder Grimm* (2 vols., 1812, 1815).

Grimm, Jacob, and **Grimm, Wilhelm**, *Kinder- und Hausmärchen. Gesammelt durch die Brüder Grimm* (7th rev. and exp. edn., 1857).

Grimm, Jacob, and **Grimm, Wilhelm**, *German Popular Stories, Translated from the Kinder und Haus Märchen*, trans. Edgar Taylor (2 vols., 1823–26).

Grimm, Jacob, and **Grimm, Wilhelm**, *Gammer Grethel; or German Fairy Tales, and Popular Stories, From the Collection of MM. Grimm*, ed. Edgar Taylor (1839).

Grimm, Jacob, and **Grimm, Wilhelm**, *German Popular Stories*, intro. John Ruskin, illustr. George Cruikshank (1869).

Grimm, Jacob, and **Grimm, Wilhelm**, *Household Stories from the Collection of the Brothers Grimm*, trans. Lucy Crane (1882).

Grimm, Jacob, and **Grimm, Wilhelm**, *Grimm's Household Tales*, ed. and trans. Margaret Hunt, intro. Andrew Lang (2 vols., 1884).

Grimm, Jacob, and **Grimm, Wilhelm**, *The Grimms' German Folktales*, trans. Francis Magoun and Alexander Krappe (1960).

Grimm, Jacob, and **Grimm, Wilhelm**, *The Complete Grimm's Fairy Tales*, trans. Margaret Hunt (1972).

Grimm, Jacob, and **Grimm, Wilhelm**, *Grimms' Tales for Young and Old: The Complete Stories*, trans. Ralph Manheim (1977).

Grimm, Jacob, and **Grimm, Wilhelm**, *The Complete Fairy Tales of the Brothers Grimm*, ed. and trans. Jack Zipes (1987).

Grimm, Jacob, and **Grimm Wilhelm**, *The Original Folk and Fairy Tales of the Brothers Grimm: The Complete First Edition*, ed. and trans. Jack Zipes (2014).

Haney, Jack (ed. and trans.), *Russian Wondertales: I. Tales of Heroes and Villains* (2001).

Haney, Jack (ed. and trans.), *Russian Wondertales: II. Tales of Magic and the Supernatural* (2001).

Lang, Andrew (ed. and trans.), *Perrault's Popular Tales* (1888).

Mayer, Charles-Joseph (ed.), *Le Cabinet des fées; ou Collection choisie des contes de fées, et autres contes merveilleux* (41 vols., 1785).

Mayer, Charles-Joseph, *Nouveau Cabinet des fées*, ed. Jacques Barchilon (18 vols., 1978). Partial reprint of *Le Cabinet des fées*, ed. Charles-Joseph Mayer.

Perrault, Charles, *Griseldis, nouvelle. Avec le conte de Peau d'Ane, et celui des Souhaits ridicules* (1694).

Perrault, Charles, *Histoires ou contes du temps passé* (1697).

Perrault, Charles, *Perrault's Complete Fairy Tales*, illus. W. Heath Robinson (1961).

Perrault, Charles, *Contes de Perrault*, ed. Gilbert Rouger (1967).

Perrault, Charles, *Contes*, ed. Marc Soriano (1989).

Perrault, Charles, *Contes*, ed. Catherine Magnien (1990).

Perrault, Charles, *Contes de ma Mère l'Oye*, ed. Hélène Tronc (2006).

Pitrè, Giuseppe (ed.), *Novelle popolari toscane* (1941).

Pitrè, Giuseppe, *Fiabe, novelle e racconti* (1875).

Pitrè, Giuseppe, *The Collected Sicilian Folk and Fairy Tales of Giuseppe Pitrè*, ed. and trans. Jack Zipes and Joseph Russo (2 vols., 2008).

Ralstone, W. R. W. (ed.), *Russian Folk Tales* (1873).

Seifert, Lewis, and **Stanton, Donna** (eds.), *Enchanted Eloquence: Fairy Tales by Seventeenth-Century Women Writers* (2010).

Straparola, Giovan Francesco, *Straparola, Le piacevoli notti* (2 vols., 1550, 1553).

Straparola, Giovan Francesco, *The Facetious Nights of Straparola*, trans. William G. Waters, illustr. Jules Garnier and E. R. Hughes (4 vols., 1894).

Straparola, Giovan Francesco, *Le piacevoli notti*, ed. Bartolomeo Rossetti (1966).

Straparola, Giovan Francesco, *Le piacevoli notti*, ed. Pastore Stocchi (1979).

Straparola, Giovan Francesco, *Le piacevoli notti*, ed. Donato Pirovano (2 vols., 2000).

Straparola, Giovan Francesco, *The Pleasant Nights*, ed. Donald Beecher (2 vols., 2012).

OTHER COLLECTIONS

Abrahams, Roger D. (ed.), *Afro-American Folktales* (1985).

Afanasiev, Aleksandr Nikolaevich, *Russian Fairy Tales*, trans. Natalie Duddington (1855–63; 1945).

Andreas, Evelyn (ed.), *The Big Treasury Book of Fairy Tales*, illus. Art Seiden (1954).

Arbuthnot, May Hill (ed.), *Time for Fairy Tales* (1952).

Arbuthnot, May Hill, and **Taylor, Mark** (eds.), *Time for Old Magic* (1970).

Árnason, Jon, *Islandic Legends*, trans. G. Powell and E. Magnusson (1864).

Asbjørnsen, Peter Christen, and **Moe, Jørgen** (eds.), *Norwegian Folktales* (1960).

Asbjørnsen, Peter Christen, and **Moe, Jørgen** (eds.), *East of the Sun and West of the Moon* (1963).

Asbjørnsen, Peter Christen, and **Moe, Jørgen** (eds.), *Tales of the Fjeld*, trans. G. W. Dasent, illus. Moyr Smith (1970).

Ashley, Michael (ed.), *The Mammoth Book of Fairy Tales* (1997).

Auerbach, Nina, and **Knoepflmacher, U. C.** (eds.), *Forbidden Journeys: Fairy Tales and Fantasies by Victorian Women Writers* (1992).

Baker, Augusta, *The Talking Tree: Fairy Tales from Fifteen Lands*, illus. Johannes Troyer (1955).

Baker, Augusta (comp.), *The Golden Lynx and Other Tales*, illus. Johannes Troyer (1960).

Balina, Marina, Goscilo, Helena, and **Lipovetsky, Mark** (eds.), *Politicizing Magic: An Anthology of Russian and Soviet Fairy Tales* (2005).

Barbeau, Marius, *The Golden Phoenix and Other French Canadian Fairy Tales*, retold by Michael Hornyansky (1958).

Barchers, Suzanne I. (ed.), *Wise Women: Folk and Fairy Tales from Around the World* (1990).

Baum, L. Frank, *The Wonderful World of Oz: The Wizard of Oz, The Emerald City of Oz, Glinda of Oz*, ed. Jack Zipes (1998).

Beaumont, Jeanne Marie, and **Carlson, Claudia** (eds.), *The Poets Grimm: 20th Century Poems from Grimm Fairy Tales* (2003).

Berger, Terry, *Black Fairy Tales*, illus. David Omar White (1969).

Berry, Jack (trans.), *West African Folk Tales*, ed. Richard Spears (1991).

Bhatta, Somadeva, *The Katha sarit sagara; or Ocean of the Streams of Story*, trans. C. H. Tawney (1968).

Bierhorst, John (ed.), *The Red Swan: Myths and Tales of the American Indians* (1976).

Binchy, Maeve (ed.), *Ride on Rapunzel: Fairytales for Feminists* (1992).

Bloom, Harold (ed.), *Classic Fantasy Writers* (1994).

Booss, Claire, *Scandinavian Folk and Fairy Tales: Tales from Norway, Sweden, Denmark, Finland, Iceland* (1984).

Botkin, B. A. (ed.), *A Treasury of American Folklore* (1944).

Botkin, B. A. (ed.), *A Treasury of New England Folklore: Stories, Ballads and Traditions of the Yankee People* (1947).

Brackert, Helmut (ed.), *Das grosse deutsche Märchenbuch* (1979).

Briggs, Katherine, (ed.), *Nine Lives: The Folklore of Cats* (1980).

Briggs, Katherine, and **Tongue, Ruth L.** (eds.), *Folktales of England* (1965).

Brockett, Eleanor, *Turkish Fairy Tales* (1963).

Brockett, Eleanor, *Burmese and Thai Fairy Tales,* illus. Harry and Ilse Toothill (1967).

Brockett, Eleanor, *Persian Fairy Tales* (1968).

Brody, Ed, Goldspinner, Jay, Green, Katie, Leventhal, Rona, and **Porcino, John** (eds.), *Spinning Tales, Weaving Hope: Stories of Peace, Justice and the Environment* (1992).

Bruchac, Joseph, *Native American Stories* (1991).

Burg, Marie, *Tales from Czechoslovakia* (1965).

Bushnaq, Inea (ed.), *Arab Folktales* (1986).

Campbell, John Francis (trans.), *Popular Tales of the West Highlands, Orally Collected* (1860; 1969).

Carey, Martha Ward (ed. and trans.), *Fairy Legends of the French Provinces* (1903).

Carlson, Ruth Kearney (ed.), *Folklore and Folktales Around the World* (1972).

Carter, Angela (ed.), *Sleeping Beauty and Other Favourite Fairy Tales* (1984).

Carter, Angela (ed.), *The Old Wives' Fairy Tale Book,* illus. Corinna Sargood (1990).

Carter, Angela (ed.), *Strange Things Sometimes Still Happen: Fairy Tales from Around the World* (1992).

Cashorali, Peter, *Gay Fairy and Folk Tales: Traditional Stories Retold for Gay Men* (1997).

Chase, Richard (ed.), *The Jack Tales* (1943).

Chase, Richard (ed.), *Grandfather Tales* (1948).

Chase, Richard (ed.), *American Folk Tales and Songs* (1956).

Chodzko, Aleksander Borejiko, *Fairy Tales of the Slav Peasants and Herdsmen from the French of Aleksander Chodzko,* trans. and illus. Emily J. Harding (1896; 1972).

Christiansen, Reidar Thoralf (ed.), *Folktales of Norway* (1964).

Claffey, Anne, Kavanaugh, Linda, and **Russell, Sue** (eds.), *Rapunzel's Revenge: Fairytales for Feminists* (1985).

Clarkson, Attelia, and **Cross, Gilbert B.** (eds.), *World Folktales: A Scribner Resource Collection* (1980).

Coffin, Tristram Potter, and **Cohen, Hennig** (eds.), *Folklore from the Working Folk of America* (1974).

Cole, Joanna (comp. and ed.), *The Best Loved Folktales of the World,* illus. Jill Karla Schwarz (1982).

Colum, Padraic (ed.), *Legends of Hawaii* (1937).

Cott, Jonathan (ed.), *Beyond the Looking Glass: Extraordinary Works of Fairy Tale and Fantasy* (1973).

Courlander, Harold (ed.), *A Treasury of Afro-American Folklore: The Oral Literature, Traditions, Recollections, Legends, Tales, Songs, Religious Beliefs, Customs, Sayings, and Humor of Peoples of African Descent in the Americas* (1976).

Crane, Thomas Frederick, *Italian Popular Tales* (1889).

Creeden, Sharon, *Fair is Fair: World Folktales of Justice* (1997).

Crossley-Holland, Kevin (ed.), *The Norse Myths* (1980).

Crossley-Holland, Kevin (ed.), *The Faber Book of Northern Folk-Tales*, illus. Alan Howard (1983).

Crossley-Holland, Kevin (ed.), *British Folktales* (1987).

Cruikshank, George, *The Cruikshank Fairy-Book: Four Famous Stories: Puss in Boots, Jack and the Bean-Stalk, Hop-O'-My Thumb, and Cinderella* (1910).

Curtin, Jeremiah, *Fairy Tales of Eastern Europe*, illus. George Hood (1949).

Curtin, Jeremiah, *Tales of Fairies of the Ghost World, Collected from Oral Tradition in South-Western Munster* (1971).

Darrell, Margery (comp.), *Once Upon a Time: The Fairy Tale World of Arthur Rackham* (1972).

Datlow, Ellen, and **Windling, Terri** (eds.), *Black Thorn, White Rose* (1993).

Datlow, Ellen, and **Windling, Terri** (eds.), *Snow White, Blood Red* (1994).

Datlow, Ellen, and **Windling, Terri** (eds.), *Ruby Slippers, Golden Tears* (1995).

Datlow, Ellen, and **Windling, Terri** (eds.), *Silver Birch, Blood Moon* (1999).

Datlow, Ellen, and **Windling, Terri** (eds.), *Black Heart, Ivory Bones* (2000).

David, Alfred, and **Meek, Mary Elizabeth** (comp.), *The Twelve Dancing Princesses and Other Fairy Tales* (1964).

Dawkins, R. M. (comp. and trans.), *Modern Greek Folktales* (1953).

Decaro, Frank, *The Folktale Cat* (1997).

Dégh, Linda (ed.), *Folktales of Hungary* (1965).

Delarue, Paul (comp.), *French Fairy Tales*, illus. Warren Chappell (1968).

Del Rey, Lester, and **Kessler, Risa** (eds.), *Once Upon a Time: A Treasury of Modern Fairy Tales*, illus. Michael Pangrazio (1991).

Doherty, Berlie (ed.), *Tales of Wonder and Magic*, illus. Juan Wijngaard (1st US edn., 1998).

Dorson, Richard M. (ed.), *Folktales Told Around the World* (1975).

Douglas, Sir George Brisbane, *Scottish Fairy and Folk Tales* (1977).

Eberhard, Wolfram (ed.), *Folktales of China* (1965).

Eberhard, Wolfram (ed.), *Chinese Fairy Tales and Folk Tales* (1978).

El-Fasi, Mohammed (comp. and trans.), *Contes fasis* (1988).

El-Shamy, Hasan M. (ed.), *Folktales of Egypt* (1979).

Erdoes, Richard, and **Ortiz, Alfonso** (eds.), *American Indian Myths and Legends* (1984).

Ewers, Hans-Heino (ed.), *Zauberei im Herbste. Deutsche Kunstmärchen von Wieland bis Hofmannsthal* (1987).

Fairbairns, Zoe (ed.), *Cinderella on the Ball* (1991).

Field, Rachel (ed.), *American Folk and Fairy Tales* (1929).

Fillmore, Parker, *The Laughing Prince: A Book of Jugoslav Fairy Tales and Folk Tales*, illus. Jay van Everen (1921).

Forest, Heather, *Wisdom Tales from Around the World* (1997).

Forrester, Sibelan (trans. and intro.), *Baba Yaga: The Wild Witch of the East in Russian Fairy Tales*, ed. Sibelan Forrester, Helena Goscilo, and Martin Skoro (2013).

Fortier, Alcée, *Louisiana Folktales* (1895).

Foss, Michael (ed.), *Folk Tales of the British Isles*, illus. Ken Kiff (1977).

Friedlander, Gerald, *Jewish Fairy Tales* (1997).

Gebert, Helga, *Alte Märchen der Brüder Grimm* (1985).

Gelberg, Hans-Joachim (ed.), *Neues vom Rumpelstilzchen und andere Hausmärchen von 43 Autoren* (1976).

Glassie, Henry (ed.), *Irish Folk Tales* (1985).

Griffis, William Elliott, *Swiss Fairy Tales* (1920).

Grundtvig, Svend, *Danish Fairy Tales*, ed. and trans. Gustav Hein (1914).

Harrison, Michael, and **Stuart-Clark, Christopher** (eds.), *The Oxford Treasury of Children's Stories* (1994).

Hart, Carole, Pogrebin, Letty Cottin, Rodgers, Mary, and **Thomas, Marlo** (eds.), *Free to Be . . . You and Me* (1974).

Hartland, Edwin-Sidney, *English Fairy and Folk Tales* (1890; 1968).

Hartwell, David G. (ed.), *Masterpieces of Fantasy and Enchantment* (1988).

Hatch, Mary Cottam, *Thirteen Danish Tales*, illus. Edgun (1947).

Haverty, P. M. (comp.), *Legends and Fairy Tales of Ireland* (1872).

Haviland, Virginia (ed.), *Favorite Fairy Tales Told in England* (1959).

Haviland, Virginia (ed.), *Favorite Fairy Tales Told in Ireland* (1961).

Haviland, Virginia (ed.), *Favorite Fairy Tales Told in Norway* (1961).

Haviland, Virginia (ed.), *Favorite Fairy Tales Told in Russia* (1961).

Haviland, Virginia (ed.), *Favorite Fairy Tales Told in Poland* (1963).

Haviland, Virginia (ed.), *Favorite Fairy Tales Told in Scotland* (1963).

Haviland, Virginia (ed.), *Favorite Fairy Tales Told in Spain* (1963).

Haviland, Virginia (ed.), *Favorite Fairy Tales Told in Italy* (1965).

Haviland, Virginia (ed.), *Favorite Fairy Tales Told in Czechoslovakia* (1966).

Haviland, Virginia (ed.), *Favorite Fairy Tales Told in Sweden* (1966).

Haviland, Virginia (ed.), *Favorite Fairy Tales Told in Japan* (1967).

Haviland, Virginia, *Selected Tales and Sketches* (1970).

Haviland, Virginia (ed.), *Favorite Fairy Tales Told in Denmark* (1971).

Haviland, Virginia (ed.), *The Fairy Tale Treasury*, illus. Raymond Briggs (1972).

Haviland, Virginia (ed.), *Favorite Fairy Tales Told in India* (1973).

Hawthorne, Nathaniel, *A Wonder Book*, illus. S. van Abbe (1852; 1961).

Hawthorne, Nathaniel, *Tanglewood Tales*, illus. S. van Abbe (1853; 1962).

Hearn, Lafcadio, *Japanese Fairy Tales*, illus. Sonia Roelter (1948).

Hearn, Michael Patrick (ed.), *The Wizard of Oz* (1983).

Hearn, Michael Patrick, *The Victorian Fairy Tale Book* (1988).

Hearne, Betsy (ed.), *Beauties and Beasts*, illus. Joanne Caroselli (1993).

Herda, Helmut, *Fairy Tales from Many Lands* (1956).

Heriz, Patrick de, *Fairy Tales with a Twist* (1946).

Iwaya, Sueo, *Japanese Fairy Tales* (1938).

Jacobs, A. J., *Fractured Fairy Tales* (1997).

Jacobs, Joseph (ed.), *Celtic Fairy Tales* (1892).

Jacobs, Joseph (ed.), *English Fairy Tales* (1892).

Jacobs, Joseph (ed.), *Indian Fairy Tales* (1892).

Jacobs, Joseph (ed.), *More English Folk and Fairy Tales* (1894).

James, Hartwell (ed.), *The Jeweled Sea: A Book of Chinese Fairy Tales*, illus. John R. Neill (1906).

Jones, Diana Wynne (ed.), *Fantasy Stories*, illus. Robin Lawrie (1994).

Jones, Gwyn, *Scandinavian Legends and Folk-tales*, illus. Joan Kiddell-Monroe (1956).

Jung, Jochen (ed.), *Bilderbogengeschichten—Märchen, Sagen, Abenteuer* (1974).

Kaplan, Irma, *Swedish Fairy Tales, Retold in English by Irma Kaplan*, illus. Carol Calder (1957).

Lang, Andrew (ed.), *The Blue Fairy Book*, illus. Ben Kutcher (1889; 1948).

Lang, Andrew (ed.), *The Red Fairy Tale Book*, illus. Marc Simont (1890; 1948).

Lang, Andrew (ed.), *The Green Fairy Tale Book*, illus. Dorothy Lake Gregory (1892; 1948).

Lang, Andrew (ed.), *The Yellow Fairy Tale Book*, illus. Janice Holland (1894; 1948).

Lang, Andrew (ed.), *The Pink Fairy Book* (1897).

Lang, Andrew (comp. and ed.), *Arabian Nights*, illus. Vera Bock (1898; 1951).

Lang, Andrew (ed.), *The Grey Fairy Book* (1900).

Lang, Andrew (ed.), *The Violet Fairy Tale Book*, illus. Dorothy Lake Gregory (1901; 1962).

Lang, Andrew (ed.), *The Crimson Fairy Tale Book*, illus. Ben Kutcher (1903; 1962).

Lang, Andrew (ed.), *The Brown Fairy Book* (1904).

Lang, Andrew (ed.), *The Orange Fairy Tale Book*, illus. Christine Price (1906; 1949).

Lang, Andrew (ed.), *The Olive Fairy Tale Book*, illus. Anne Vaughan (1907; 1949).

Lang, Andrew (ed.), *The Book of Princes and Princesses* (1908).

Lang, Andrew (ed.), *The Lilac Fairy Tale Book*, illus. H. J. Ford (1910; 1968).

Lang, Andrew (ed.), *The Rose Fairy Tale Book*, illus. Vera Bock (1961).

Lang, Andrew (ed.), *Fifty Favorite Fairy Tales Chosen from the Color Fairy Books of Andrew Lang*, illus. Margery Gill (1964).

Lieberman, Syd, *Joseph the Tailor and Other Jewish Tales* (1997).

Lottridge, Celia Barker (ed.), *A Children's Treasury of American Stories & Poems* (1995).

Lowings, John (ed.), *At the Edge of the World: Magical Stories of Ireland* (1998).

Lurie, Alison (ed.), *Clever Gretchen and Other Forgotten Folktales* (1980).

Lurie, Alison (ed.), *The Oxford Book of Modern Fairy Tales* (1993).

MacDonald, Margaret Read (ed.), *Peace Tales: World Folktales to Talk About* (1992).

MacDonald, Margaret Read (ed.), *Tom Thumb*, illus. Joanne Caroselli (1993).

MacKaye, Percy, *Tall Tales of the Kentucky Mountains* (1926).

Mackenzie, Donald Alexander, *Scottish Fairy Tales* (1997).

McKinley, Robin (ed.), *Imaginary Lands* (1986).

MacLeod, Ann, *English Fairy Tales*, illus. Ota Janecek (1968).

MacManus, Seumas, *Donegal Fairy Stories* (1900).

Macmillan, Cyrus, *Canadian Fairy Tales* (1922).

Macmillan, Cyrus, *Mad & Bad Fairies* (3rd edn., 1990).

Manlove, C. N. [Colin Nicholas], *Christian Fantasy: From 1200 to the Present* (1992).

Manning-Sanders, Ruth, *The Glass Man and the Golden Bird: Hungarian Folk and Fairy Tales*, illus. Victor G. Ambrus (1968).

Manning-Sanders, Ruth, *Peter and the Piskies: Cornish Folk and Fairy Tales*, illus. Raymond Briggs (1968).

Manning-Sanders, Ruth, *Jonnikan and the Flying Basket: French Folk and Fairy Tales*, illus. Victor G. Ambrus (1969).

Manning-Sanders, Ruth, *The Book of Kings and Queens* (1977).

Massignon, Geneviève (ed.), *Folktales of France* (1968).

Megas, Georgios A. (ed.), *Folktales of Greece* (1970).

Mehdevi, Anne [Sinclair], *Persian Folk and Fairy Tales*, illus. Paul E. Kennedy (1965).

Mieder, Wolfgang (ed.), *Grimms Märchen—modern* (1979).

Mieder, Wolfgang (ed.), *Disenchantments: An Anthology of Modern Fairy Tale Poetry* (1985).

Mieder, Wolfgang (ed.), *Grimmige Märchen* (1987).

Minard, Rosemary (ed.), *Womenfolk and Fairy Tales* (1975).

Neal, Philip, *Illustrated Book of Fairy Tales*, illus. Nilesh Mistry (1998).

Noy, Dov (ed.), *Folktales of Israel* (1963).

Nyblom, Helena Augusta, *The Witch of the Woods: Fairy Tales from Sweden*, illus. Nils Christian Hald (1968).

O'Donnell, James E. (ed.), *Japanese Folk Tales*, illus. Kasumi Nagao (1958).

O'Faolain, Eileen, *Irish Sagas and Folk-Tales*, illus. Joan Kiddell-Monroe (1954).

Olenius, Elna, *Great Swedish Fairy Tales*, illus. John Bauer (1973).

Opie, Iona and **Peter** (eds.), *The Classic Fairy Tales* (1974).

O'Sullivan, Sean (ed.), *Folktales of Ireland* (1966).

O'Sullivan, Sean, *Over the Rainbow: Tales of Fantasy and Imagination* (1983).

Ozaki, Yei Theodora (comp.), *Japanese Fairy Book* (1967).

Painter, William (trans.), *The Palace of Pleasure: Elizabethan Versions of Italian and French Novels from Boccaccio, Bandello, Cinthio, Straparola, Queen Margaret of Navarre, and Others* (1890; 1966).

Paredes, Americo (ed.), *Folktales of Mexico* (1970).

Phelps, Ethel Johnston (ed.), *Tatterhood and Other Tales* (1978).

Phelps, Ethel Johnston (ed.), *The Maid of the North: Feminist Folk Tales from Around the World (1981).*

Philip, Neil (ed.), *The Cinderella Story* (1988).

Philip, Neil, *Fairy Tales of Eastern Europe* (1991).

Philip, Neil (ed.), *The Penguin Book of Scottish Folktales* (1991).

Philip, Neil (ed.), *The Penguin Book of English Folktales* (1992).

Pickard, Barbara Leonie, *French Legends, Tales and Fairy Tales*, illus. Joan Kiddell-Monroe (1953).

Pino-Saavedra, Yolanda (ed.), *Folktales of Chile* (1968).

Pogrebin, Letty (ed.), *Stories for Free Children* (1982).

Polevoi, Petr Nikolaevich, *Russian Fairy Tales*, ed. and trans. R. Nisbet Bain, illus. Noel L. Nisbet (1927).

Rackham, Arthur (comp.), *Arthur Rackham Fairy Book: A Book of Old Favorites with New Illustrations* (1930).

Rackham, Arthur (comp. and illus.), *Fairy Tales from Many Lands* (1974).

Ragan, Kathleen (ed.), *Fearless Girls, Wise Women & Beloved Sisters: Heroines in Folktales from Around the World* (1998).

Ramanujan, A. K. (ed.), *Folktales from India* (1991).

Randolf, Vance (ed.), *The Devil's Pretty Daughter and Other Ozark Folk Tales* (1955).

Ranke, Kurt (ed.), *Folktales of Germany* (1966).

Ransome, Arthur, *Old Peter's Russian Tales*, illus. Dmitri Mitrokhim (1969).

Reed, Alexander Wyclif, *Fairy Tales from the Pacific Islands*, illus. Stewart Irwin (1969).

Reeves, James, *English Fables and Fairy Stories*, illus. Joan Kiddell-Monroe (1955).

Reneaux, J. J., *Cajun Fairy Tales* (1997).

Riordan, James (comp. and trans.), *The Sun Maiden and the Crescent Moon: Siberian Folk Tales* (1991).

Robert, Raymonde (ed.), *Il était une fois les fées: contes du XVIIe et XVIIIe siècles* (1984).

Robert, Raymonde (ed.), *Contes parodiques et licencieux du 18e siècle* (1987).

Roberts, Moss (ed.), *Chinese Fairy Tales and Fantasies* (1979).

Rodriguez Almodovar, Antonio (ed.), *Los cuentos maravillosos españoles* (1982).

Rodriguez Almodovar, Antonio (ed.), *Cuentos maravillosos: cuentos populares andaluces y cuentos maravillosos españoles* (1986).

Romskaug, Brenda (comp.), *Norwegian Fairy Tales*, illus. Ivar Pettersen (1961).

Rottensteiner, Franz (ed.), *The Slaying of the Dragon: Modern Tales of the Playful Imagination* (1984).

Russell, William F. (ed.), *More Classics to Read Aloud to your Children* (1986).

Schramm, Peninnah, *Jewish Stories One Generation Tells Another* (1987).

Schwartz, Howard, *Elijah's Violin and Other Jewish Fairy Tales*, illus. Linda Heller (1985).

Sébillot, Paul, *Contes populaires de la Haute-Bretagne* (1882).

Seki, Keigo (ed.), *Folktales of Japan* (1963).

Sherman, Josepha, *Trickster Tales: Forty Folk Stories from Around the World* (1997).

Sierra, Judy (ed.), *Cinderella* (1992).

Stephens, James, *Irish Fairy Tales*, illus. Arthur Rackham (1920).

Stephens, John Richard (ed.), *The King of the Cats and Other Feline Fairy Tales* (1993).

Strickland, Agnes, *Tales from English History: For Children* (1868).

Tatar, Maria (ed.), *The Classic Fairy Tales* (1999).

Tezel, Naki, *Fairy Tales from Turkey*, illus. Olga Lehmann (1951).

Thompson, Stith, *One Hundred Favorite Folktales*, illus. Franz Altschuler (1968).

Thorpe, Benjamin (comp.), *Tales on the North Wind, Old Fairy Tales Retold by Benjamin Thorpe and Thomas Keightley* (1956).

Tong, Diane (ed.), *Gypsy Folktales* (1989).

Topelius, Zacharias, *Läsning för Barn* (1883).

Turnbull, E. Lucia, *Fairy Tales of India*, illus. Hazel Cook (1960).

Tyler, Royall (ed.), *Japanese Fairy Tales* (1987).

Uchida, Yoshiko, *The Dancing Kettle and Other Japanese Folk Tales*, illus. Richard C. Jones (1949).

Vande Velde, Vivian, *Tales from the Brothers Grimm and the Sisters Weird* (1997).

Walker, Barbara G., *Feminist Fairy Tales* (1st edn., 1996).

Warner, Marina (ed.), *Wonder Tales* (1994).

Weinreich, Beatrice (ed.), *Yiddish Folk Tales* (1989).

Whitney, Thomas P. (trans.), *In a Certain Kingdom: Twelve Russian Fairy Tales*, illus. Dieter Lange (1972).

Williams-Ellis, Amabel, *More British Fairy Tales* (1960).

Williamson, Duncan, *Fireside Tales of the Traveller Children* (1983).

Williamson, Duncan, *The Broonie, Silkies and Fairies* (1985).

Wilson, Barbara Ker, *Fairy Tales of Germany*, illus. Gertrude Mittelmann (1959).

Wilson, Barbara Ker, *Fairy Tales of Ireland*, illus. G. W. Muller (1959).

Wilson, Barbara Ker, *Fairy Tales of France*, illus. William McLaren (1960).

Wilson, Barbara Ker, *Fairy Tales of India*, illus. Rene Mackensie (1960).

Wilson, Barbara Ker, *Fairy Tales of Persia*, illus. G. W. Muller (1961).

Wolkstein, Diane, *The Magic Orange Tree and Other Haitian Folktales* (1980).

Wyatt, Isabel, *The Golden Stag and Other Folk Tales from India*, illus. Anne Marie Jauss (1962).

Yeats, William Butler, *Fairy and Folk Tales of Ireland* (1892; 1973).

Yolen, Jane (ed.), *Favorite Folktales from Around the World* (1986).

Young, Richard Alan, and **Dockrey, Judy** (eds.), *African-American Folktales for Young Readers* (1993).

Zheleznova, Irina L'vovna (trans.), *Folk Tales of Russian Lands* (1969).

Zipes, Jack (ed.), *Don't Bet on the Prince: Contemporary Feminist Fairy Tales in North America and England* (1986).

Zipes, Jack (ed.), *Victorian Fairy Tales* (1987).

Zipes, Jack (ed.), *Beauties, Beasts, and Enchantment: French Classical Fairy Tales* (1989).

Zipes, Jack (ed.), *Fairy Tales and Fables from Weimar Days* (1989).

Zipes, Jack (ed.), *Spells of Enchantment: The Wondrous Fairy Tales of Western Culture* (1991).

Zipes, Jack (ed.), *The Trials and Tribulations of Little Red Riding Hood* (2nd edn., 1993).

Zipes, Jack (ed.), *The Outspoken Princess and the Gentle Knight* (1994).

Zipes, Jack (ed.), *The Great Fairy Tale Tradition: From Straparola and Basile to the Brothers Grimm* (2001).

Zipes, Jack (ed.), *The Golden Age of Folk and Fairy Tales: From the Brothers Grimm to Andrew Lang* (2013).

SPECIALIST JOURNALS

Africa: Journal of the International African Institute/Revue de l'Institut Africain International

Appalachian Journal: A Regional Studies Review

Baum Bugle: A Journal of Oz

Bealoideas: The Journal of the Folklore of Ireland Society

Bestia: Yearbook of the Beast Fable Society

Bulletin Folklorique d'Île de France

Cabinet des Fées: A Fairy Tale Journal

Children's Literature: Annual of the Modern Language Association Division on Children's Literature and the Children's Literature Association

Cultural Analysis: An Interdisciplinary Forum on Folklore and Popular Culture

Fabula: Zeitschrift für Erzählforschung

Féeries

Folklore: An Electronic Journal of Folklore

Folklore Forum

Folklorica: Journal of the Slavic and East European Folkloric Association

Jarhrbuch der Brüder Grimm-Gesellschaft

Journal of American Folklore

Journal of Folklore Research

Journal of the Fantastic in the Arts

Journal of the Folklore Institute (London)

Marvels & Tales: Journal of Fairy-Tale Studies

Oral Tradition: An Interdisciplinary Academic Journal

Storytelling, Self, Society: An Interdisciplinary Journal of Storytelling Societies

Western Folklore

Zeitschrift für Volkskunde

HELPFUL WEBSITES

American Folklore Society

Center for Studies in Oral Tradition (University of Missouri)

The Cinderella Bibliography

Department of European Ethnology/Wossidlo Archiev (University of Rostock)

Deutsche Gesellschaft für Volkskunde

The Endicott Studi: An Interdisciplinary Organization Dedicated to the Creation and Support of Mythic Art

Enzyklopädie des Märchens

Europäische Märchengesellschaft

Folklinks: Folk and Fairy Tale Sites (D. L. Ashliman)

Folklore and Mythology: Electronic Texts

The Folklore Society (London)

Folklore Studies Association of Canada

The Hans Christian Andersen Center

Il était une fois . . . Les contes de fées (Bibliothèque nationale de France)

International Society for Folk Narrative Research

Museum of the Brothers Bridge

Once Upon a Blog (Gypsy Thornton)

Society for Storytelling

SurLaLune Fairy Tales (Heidi Anne Heiner)

Western States Folklore Society